TRAVEL FREELY

RCS PARIS B 389 191 982 · Photos : GEC ALSTHOM · Desjardins · SNCF/CAV Cambon

An urban public transport system enables a conurbation to develop harmoniously.
Today, the users desire rapid vehicles which are comfortable,
non polluting and efficient, replying to their needs
of leisure or professional travel.
Trams, metros, single and double deck powercar trainsets, all our equipment
is designed to bring the best solution to urban and suburban transport problems.

What is UITP ?

The International Union of Public Transport

is the worldwide association of urban and regional passenger transport operators, their authorities and their suppliers.

It seeks to promote a better understanding of the potential of public transport, and it provides information and analysis about the sector including infrastructure, rolling stock, organisation and management.
These services are available both to its members and to others with a professional interest in transport mobility.

Objectives

UITP aims to :
• **Study all aspects** of public transport and mobility, in order to promote the development of more efficient and attractive public transport services, and gain the maximum benefit of technological advance ;
• **Representing the interests** of its members through its dealings with international authorities ;
• **Promote public transport** by canvassing decision-makers and the media and seeking to develop a climate of opinion in its favour.

Challenges

Challenges for public transport include :
• **To respond effectively** to urban congestion. Public transport represents a credible response, offering city dwellers better living conditions.
• **To fulfil its potential contribution** to reducing air pollution and to improving the health of citizens and quality of urban life.
• **Finding the best forms** of organisation and finance. This includes private capital involvement and contributions from the economic interests which benefit from public transport.
These topics are international in their nature, and require the sharing of experience and inter-company co-operation.

Structure

The UITP represents **more than seventeen hundred members in some 80 countries**. Its members include bus, tramway, light rail and metropolitan rail operators as well as many national railway systems, authorities in charge of transport provision and national public transport associations, research institutes, rail, bus and service suppliers.
A **General Assembly** of members is held every two years, and this ratifies the election of the Management Committee. This **Management Committee** elects the President of UITP for two years (on a mandate that can be renewed for a further two years) and eight Vice-Presidents, ratifies the appointment of members of the International Technical Commissions and working parties and oversees UITP's overall policy.
The **UITP General Secretariat** takes care of the implementation and monitoring of decisions taken by the Management Committee and commissions, prepares the groundwork and keeps members in touch with its activities and with developments in the field.

To achieve its objectives, the UITP has some **20 Commissions and committees** addressing different modes of public transport (from bus and metro to waterborne transport) as well as "horizontal" issues ranging from human resources to transport economics and organisation.
Every two years it organises a **World Congress and Exhibition**. It also organises special meetings and conferences on a wide variety of subjects, and it collates information from the world over and presents and distributes it to meet the needs of its members. It organises networks and projects involving its members (joint testing of new marketing methods).
The UITP is financed by the subscriptions from its members and the sales of its publications and services.

Events

Examples of Congresses and Conferences :
• World Biennial **Congresses and Exhibitions** : Paris 1995, Stuttgart 1997, Toronto 1999, London 2001
• **Regional Conferences** : Kuala Lumpur 1994, Konstanz 1996, Hong Kong 1998
• **Specialised Conferences** : Passenger Information, Göteborg 1996 ; Light Rail, San Jose, California 1996, Regional transport, Palermo, 30.9.97, Safe public transport, 10-11.11.97, Berlin, Towards a single smartcard, 12-15.2.98, Bologna.
More than 50 technical meetings each year world-wide.

International links

UITP maintains close relationships with other international and intergovernmental organisations :

• **UNO** • **World Bank**
• **European Union** (UITP has a special section, its EuroTeam, dedicated to relations with the EU and informing members of EU developments)
• Networking with the international **transport associations** (UIC, CER, UNIFE, World Road Association, IRU, etc) and other specialised organisations.

Publications

UITP Statistical Handbook (last version 1986, new version in June 1997), **Public Transport International**, **UITP Express**, **Euro Express**, Congress and Conference reports, Special studies, etc. Ask us for the updated list of UITP Publications.

Documentation

Documentation Centre • **Biblio Data Base** (16,000 entries, special bibliographies on request) • **Library** (20,000 books and 250 magazines) • Loans and photocopies of documents available to members.

The UITP is a non-profit making company registered under Belgian law

UITP

International Union (Association) of Public Transport
Avenue de l'Uruguay 19, B-1000 Brussels • Tel. ***+32 2 673 61 00***
Fax ***+32 2 660 10 72*** *• E-Mail : administration@uitp.com • For events-related messages : Direct Tel line :* ***+32 2 673 61 05*** *• E-Mail : events@uitp.com*

Jane's

URBAN TRANSPORT SYSTEMS

Edited by Chris Bushell
Contributing Editor Tony Pattison
Cartography by Roger Carvell

Sixteenth Edition
1997-98

Join us on the Internet via WWW http://www.janes.com/janes.html

Jane's can also be accessed by FTP, GOPHER and EMAIL on thomson.com which is the on-line portal for the products, services and resources available from Thomson Publishing. This Internet kiosk gives users immediate access to more than 34 Thomson publishers and over 20,000 information resources. Through thomson.com, Internet users can search catalogues, examine a subject-specific resource centre, purchase products and subscribe to electronic discussion lists.

WWW: http://www.thomson.com GOPHER: gopher://gopher.thomson.com
FTP: ftp.thomson.com email: findit@kiosk.thomson.com

Jane's products are also available on CD-ROM and other forms of electronic delivery. Please contact us for further details.

ISBN 0 7106 1562 0
"Jane's" is a registered trade mark

In the USA and its dependencies
Jane's Information Group Inc, 1340 Braddock Place, Suite 300, Alexandria, VA 22314-1651, USA

British Library Cataloguing-in-Publication Data.
A catalogue record for this book is available from the British Library.

Printed and bound in Great Britain by Butler and Tanner Limited, Frome and London

Contents

ADMINISTRATION

Publishing Director: Robert Hutchinson

Publisher: Janine Boxall

Managing Editor: Mary Webb

Yearbook Database Manager: Ruth Simmance

Editorial Services Manager: Sulann Staniford

Copy Editor: Diana Barrick

OFFICES

Jane's Information Group Limited, Sentinel House,
163 Brighton Road, Coulsdon, Surrey CR5 2NH, UK

Tel: +44 181 700 3700
Telex: 916907 Janes G
Fax: +44 181 700 3788
email: yearbook@janes.co.uk

SALES OFFICES

Send enquiries to International Product Sales Manager:
Tony Kingham (Europe, RFAS, Africa, Middle East)
Jo Moon (Scandinavia, Far East, UK)
Jane's Information Group Limited, UK address as above

Tel Enquiries: +44 181 700 3759
Fax Enquiries: +44 181 763 1006
Fax Orders: +44 181 763 1005

Send USA enquiries to:
Joe McHale, Senior Vice-President Product Sales,
Jane's Information Group Inc, 1340 Braddock Place, Suite 300,
Alexandria, Virginia 22314-1651, USA

Tel: +1 703 683 3700
Telex: 6819193
Fax: +1 703 836 0029

ADVERTISEMENT SALES OFFICES

Advertisement Sales Manager, Transport Division:
Catherine Sneath, Jane's Information Group, Sentinel House,
163 Brighton Road, Coulsdon, Surrey CR5 2NH

Tel: +44 181 700 3853
Fax: +44 181 700 3859
email: jag@janes.co.uk

Australia: Brendan Gullifer, Havre & Gullifer (Pty) Ltd, Level 7,
82 Collins Street, Melbourne 3000

Tel: +61 3 9650 1100
Fax: +61 3 9650 6611
email: 100017.2676@compuserve.com

Benelux: Claire Porter, Jane's Information Group (see UK)

Brazil: L Bilyk, Brazmedia International S/C Ltda, Alameda Gabriel
Monterio da Silva, 366 CEP, 01442-900 São Paulo

Tel: +55 11 853 4133
Telex: 32836 BMED BR
Fax: +55 11 852 6485

France: Patrice Février, Jane's Information Group – France,
BP 418, 35 avenue MacMahon, F-75824 Paris Cedex 17

Tel: +33 (0) 1 45 72 33 11
Fax: +33 (0) 1 45 72 17 95
email: patrice.fevrier@wanadoo.fr

Germany and Austria: Claire Porter, Jane's Information Group
(see UK)

Hong Kong: Jeremy Miller, Major Media Ltd, Room 1402, 14F
Capitol Centre, 5-19 Jardine's Bazaar, Causeway Bay

Tel: +852 890 3110
Fax: +852 576 3397

Israel: Oreet Ben-Yaacov, Oreet International Media, 15 Kinneret
Street, IL-51201 Bene-Berak

Tel: +972 3 570 6527
Fax: +972 3 570 6526
email: oreetimc@netvision.net.il

Italy and Switzerland: Ediconsult Internazionale Srl, Piazza Fontane
Marose 3, I-16123 Genoa

Tel: +39 10 583684
Fax: +39 10 566578

Japan: Intermart/EAC Inc, 1-7 Akasaka 9-chome, Minato-Ku,
Tokyo 107

Tel: +81 3 5474 7835
Fax: +81 3 5474 7837

Korea, South: Young Seoh Chinn, JES Media International, 6th Floor
Donghye Building, 47-16 Myungil-Dong, Kangdong-Gu, Seoul
134-070

Tel: +82 2 481 3411
Fax: +82 2 481 3414

Rest of World: Claire Porter (see UK)

Russian Federation and Associated States (CIS)(RFAS):
Claire Porter (see UK)

Scandinavia: Gillian Thompson, The Falsten Partnership,
11 Chardmore Road, Stamford Hill, London N16 6JA, UK

Tel: +44 181 806 2301
Fax: +44 181 806 8137

Singapore, Indonesia, Malaysia, Philippines, Taiwan and Thailand:
Hoo Siew Sai, Major Media Singapore Pte Ltd, #06-00 Resource
Building, 52 Chin Swee Road, Singapore 169875

Tel: +65 738 0122
Fax: +65 738 2108
email: majmedia@singnet.com.sg

South Africa: Catherine Sneath, Janes Information Group,
Sentinel House, 163 Brighton Road, Coulsdon, Surrey CR5 2NH

Tel: +44 181 700 3853
Fax: +44 181 700 3859
email: jag@janes.co.uk

Spain: Jesus Moran Iglesias, Varex SL, Modesto Lafuente 4,
E-28010 Madrid

Tel: +34 1 448 7622
Fax: +34 1 446 0198

UK: Claire Porter, Jane's Information Group, Sentinel House,
163 Brighton Road, Coulsdon, Surrey CR5 2NH

Tel: +44 181 700 3741
Fax: +44 181 700 3744
email: claire.porter@janes.co.uk

USA
Advertising Production Manager/USA & Canada – Maureen Nute
Jane's Information Group Inc, 1340 Braddock Place, Suite 300,
Alexandria, Virginia 22314

Tel: +1 703 683 3700
Fax: +1 703 836 0029
email: nute@janes.com

USA and Canada
Kimberley Hanson, Global Media Services Inc, 299 Herndon Parkway,
Suite 308, Herndon, Virginia 22070

Tel: +1 703 318 5054
Fax: +1 703 318 9728
email: kim@globlmedia.com

Kristin Schulze
Global Media Services Inc, 5370 East Bay Drive, Suite 104,
Clearwater, Florida 34624 USA

Tel: +1 813 524 7741
Fax: +1 813 524 7562
email: kristin@globlmedia.com

Administration: UK/Rest of World: Fay Lenham
USA and Canada: Maureen Nute

quality - experience - technology

LRV Type T68
Manchester Metrolink

EMU for Milan
underground line 3
ATM Milano

100% Low floor LRV
ATM Torino

Alphabetical list of advertisers

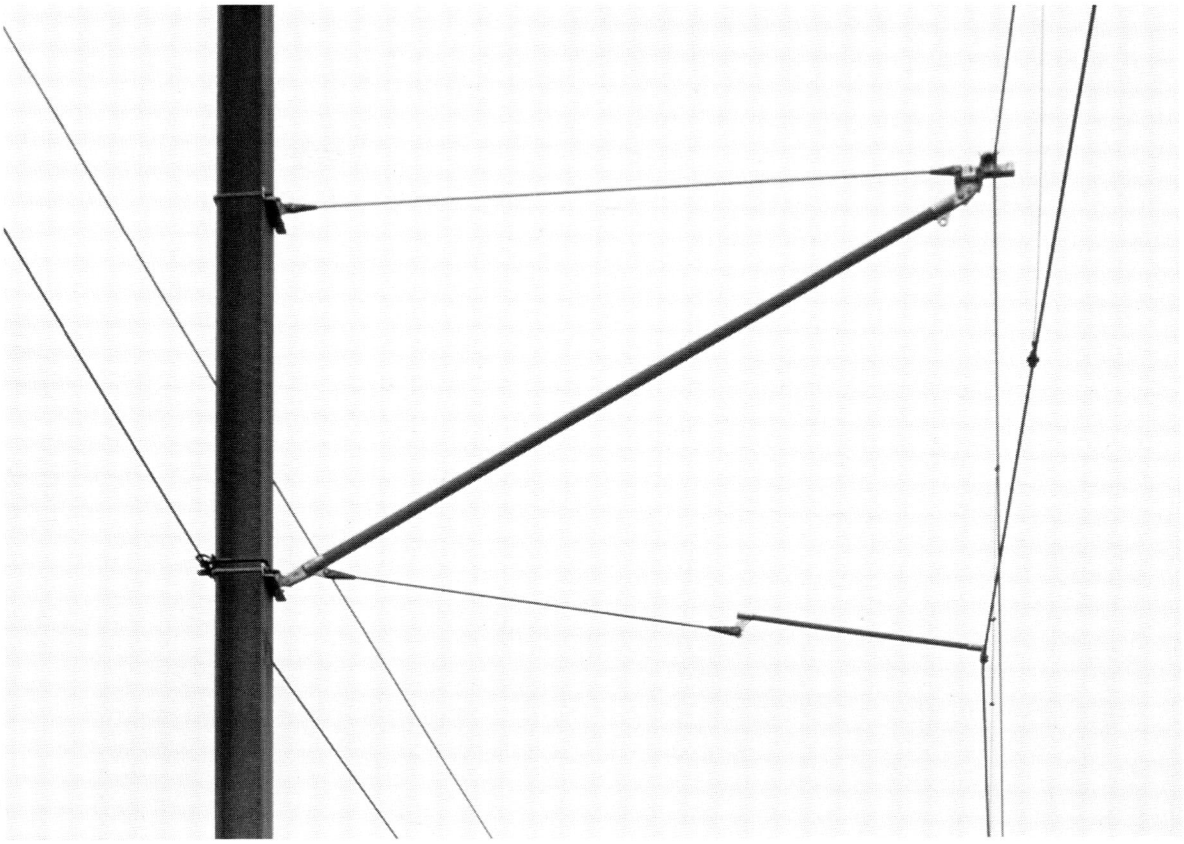

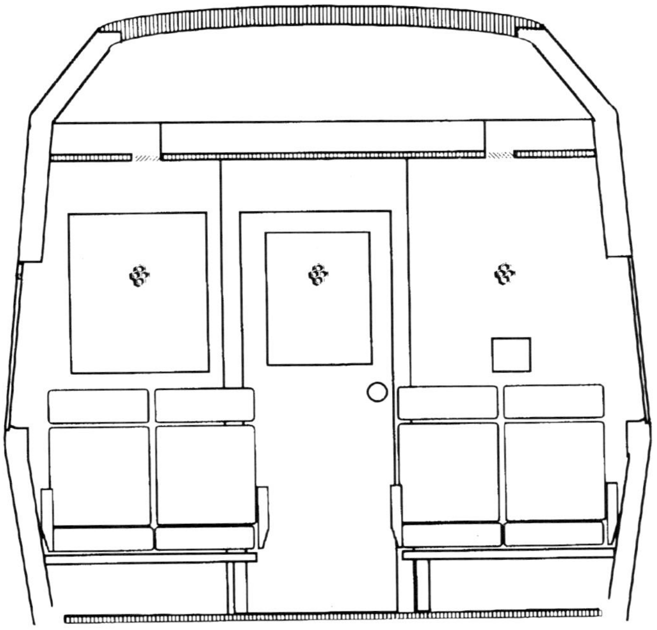

How to use this book

The book is divided into three main sections — Systems, Manufacturers and Consultants.

The Systems section is an alphabetically arranged listing of cities, describing the characteristics of their various modes of public transport. After a brief résumé of the range of services offered and the organisational basis on which they are provided, there are entries for the principal transport authorities, operators and modes. The range of information varies. Bus and trolleybus systems, metros and light rail/tramways generally have detailed tabular data on their physical and operating characteristics, fare structures, provision of facilities for elderly and disabled people, signalling and control systems, integration with other modes of transport, and farebox recovery rates. Commuter railways, ferries, paratransit and other operations are covered in a less detailed format which nevertheless aims to show their main characteristics. The political background to public transport provision is often covered, as are current and future plans for investment.

Traffic statistics (passenger journeys/boardings, vehicle-km) are shown for all operations wherever possible. There has been much confusion over use of the terms 'linked' and 'unlinked' journeys, and we have banished them. Instead the term 'boardings' is used wherever we have a clear indication that unlinked trips are involved; 'journeys' continues to refer to linked trips (one or more boardings on one or more modes).

Dates given with the traffic statistics indicate the financial year to which they apply, generally the most recent (1995 or 1995/96 for the current book). While some other data may have been culled from that year's annual report (for example, the fleet lists) most information will generally be more up-to-date.

Fleet lists are also shown for all modes wherever possible, and may include class designation, builder and manufacturer of principal components (for example, bus chassis and bodywork), year of build and/or delivery, when rebuilt or refurbished, and the numbers in service. For rail vehicles, the letters M and T indicate powered (motor) and unpowered (trailer) cars.

The Manufacturers section lists equipment builders and suppliers to the urban transport industry under eleven main headings, several of which cover both road and rail equipment. The aim is to list product ranges, new developments and recent contracts. Similarly, the final section details the capabilities and recent activities of Consultants.

To help users of this title evaluate the published data, Jane's Information Group has divided entries into three categories:-

● ***VERIFIED*** The editor has received confirmation that the entry is correct.

● ***UPDATED*** During the verification process, significant changes to content have been made to reflect the latest position known to Jane's at the time of publication.

● ***NEW ENTRY*** Information on new equipment and/or systems appearing for the first time in the title.

Where there is no 'Entry Tag' the editor has made a detailed examination of the entry's content and checked its relevancy and accuracy for publication in the new edition to the best of his ability.

Since 1995 all new pictures have been dated with the year of publication. New pictures this year are dated 1997.

We hope these measures increase the value of this title to our thousands of customers worldwide. If you have any comments or suggestions for further enhancements, the Publisher would be pleased to receive them.

This publication is also available in CD-ROM format

Foreword

'Is your journey really necessary?' the famous British wartime poster asked, at a time when fuel was scarce and public transport hard-pressed. Perhaps it could serve again, slightly modified, as an exhortation to would-be motorists as we approach the 21st century. For one thing at least is clear about the early years of the new millennium — traffic is set to rise inexorably as the number of cars on the world's roads grows from 500 million today to maybe 1 billion by 2030. In the European Union alone, traffic is forecast to double in the next twenty years, a rate of growth faster than that recorded in the period since 1970. It seems unlikely that substantial increases can be avoided either in the US or in those vast countries — Russia, India, China — where it is only a matter of time before mass car ownership becomes an issue serious enough to rival other environmental problems.

Not all these journeys will be urban ones, of course, but it is in towns and cities that congestion bears most heavily on the quality of life, bringing with it noise, pollution, insecurity and frustration. EU Transport Commissioner Neil Kinnock has forecast 'massively expensive and noxious paralysis on a continental scale' if new measures are not taken to develop fully integrated public transport networks. If rising car ownership is inevitable, it should at least be possible to curtail the growth in car usage — indeed it must if Commissioner Kinnock's chilling prediction is not to become reality.

The International Union of Public Transport (UITP) believes that urban areas must be replanned to meet the needs of their citizens rather than, as so often, the requirements of the motor car. Reducing space allocated to traffic and parking encourages more intensive use of public transport and non-motorised alternatives like cycling. But the challenge for transport operators will be to further refine their services to make them more attractive to a public accustomed to the privacy and comfort of a private car. There must be better information, safer waiting areas, more frequent services, easy boarding, seamless journeys; and where journeys cannot be seamless, interchange has to be made as smooth as possible. Attainment of such standards will not be a magic solution to tomorrow's urban congestion, rather another stage in the relentless development of services to meet the needs of customers who may at any time decide that the vehicle parked outside is more convenient after all.

Into the driverless era

So what further contribution can public transport make to a world threatened by traffic chaos? Virtual commuting is with us, but it will not totally replace the real thing, and rail's dominant position in mass transit will have to be complemented by measures to raise the poor perception of buses as a quality means of transport. Clearly there is still great scope for technology to be harnessed in aid of moving large numbers of people speedily and safely. After cautious progress with driverless trains over the past thirty years, the 21st century will surely be the era of the automated metro, and of the people mover too. Developments in microprocessor technology have removed the last barriers to widespread adoption of automation, and if the experience of the twenty-or-so existing driverless systems is any guide, public opinion seems unfazed by the concept. Just as well, for driverless trains offer what is probably the nearest that conventional rail rapid transit can hope to achieve in matching the flexibility of private transport.

With headways as low as 60 seconds and no crewing costs, very significant improvements in service quality are attainable on automated metros. Because no staff are required, trains can run very frequently and extra trains can be added to the timetable speedily to cope with sudden surges in demand, for example the early finish of an event due to bad weather. And, like the guards dispensed with at an earlier stage of metro development, drivers are today much better deployed in a public relations role on the platforms and roving the trains, where they can offer a reassuring presence to those more concerned about the possibility of being mugged than riding a driverless train. With no crewing costs to constrain the schedule planners, round-the-clock operation becomes a marketing opportunity limited only by the demands of infrastructure maintenance. Such benefits have been identified by the UITP as contributing substantially to the standing of public transport when a choice has to be made between taking the car or leaving it at home.

Matra's VAL, pioneered in Lille, has led the way in the driverless stakes, along with SkyTrain in Vancouver. Both have managed to transform the perception of public transport in cities formerly dependent on buses, but none of the systems so far installed approaches the high level of usage common on older heavy metros like those of Tokyo, Paris and New York. This should change with the opening in July 1998 of the Météor metro line between Tolbiac and Madeleine in Paris, which will carry RATP's first driverless trains. Intended originally to help relieve the heavy traffic on RER Line A by providing a new dedicated northeast-southwest metro route, the 7.5 km line will now be assimilated into the urban metro network and thus has ATC designed to cope with both driverless and conventional manually driven trains. Operating in an environment quite different from the brand-new networks in smaller cities like Lille and Toulouse, Météor will provide a fully operational testbed for RATP's projected conversion of all 13 metro lines to driverless operation.

Driverless metros are opening soon in Ankara and Kuala Lumpur, and planned in half-a-dozen other cities. Berlin aims to follow Paris with progressive conversion of existing routes to driverless operation in the early years of the next century, while London's Victoria line may be fully automated by 2003. With staff costs making up so large a proportion of public transport expenditure, automation will create new opportunities for metros to handle ever larger volumes of traffic.

Messages from South America

These solutions to the movement of large numbers of people will not suit urban areas with lower population and traffic densities, nor will they be appropriate for the rapidly growing cities of developing countries hard-pressed for cash to fund costly metro-building. Quito's trolleybus route, opened in 1996, is an interesting hybrid. Rubber tyres beat steel on this occasion because of fears that vibration from trams would damage ancient buildings in the centre of Ecuador's capital. With its enclosed 'stations' and priority at intersections, the route is virtually a rubber-tyred light rail system. It links interchanges north and south of the city, where conventional diesel buses feed in passengers from the suburbs. Within weeks of opening, around 150,000 daily journeys were being recorded.

Another one-off, Curitiba's trunk route bus operation, has figured more than once in these columns, but the example bears repetition as a brilliant marriage of bus and metro concepts. The 'Integrated Transport Network' was developed in conjunction with carefully planned expansion of the city along five main axes. At a fraction of the cost even of light rail infrastructure, the city has created a high-capacity transport system so attractive that more than 75 per cent of commuters now take the bus rather than their cars. In twenty years, daily patronage has grown from 25,000 to nearly a million, with the busiest corridor handling 250,000 journeys a day in double-articulated buses carrying 270.

There is a strong message here for cities which have despaired of raising the image of their bus services. Clearly it is possible to woo commuters from their cars without paying the high price of constructing metro or light rail infrastructure, though segregation or priority is essential if buses are not to be bogged down in congested streets. 'Smart' bus routes are now starting to appear in a number of cities, demonstrating just what can be achieved when easy-access low-floor vehicles are combined with stylish bus stops, good information and bright liveries. But whether such measures can ever be sufficiently attractive to make a real impact on traffic congestion is debatable; much evidence exists to show that they cannot.

Birmingham blues

Birmingham, in Britain's West Midlands, will be hoping that Curitiba's experience is not unique. Europe's largest city without a metro, Birmingham is typical of many conurbations struggling to cope with the effects of severe traffic congestion. As a major car-manufacturing centre and the hub of Britain's road network, this is a motor city to rival Detroit. A decade ago, when it seemed possible that government might support widespread construction of light rail networks, Birmingham planned the 200 km area-wide Midland Metro as the basis of a 21st century public transport strategy. Now that dream has been shattered, the city effectively having abandoned its powers to build more than a few extensions to the 20 km Line 1 that opens next year. In the unfavourable political circumstances surrounding public transport projects in the UK, Lines 2 and 3 were deemed unfundable, though parts of both lines may survive as add-on extensions to core Line 1. In addition, the very long lead time before any benefits of light rail become available — ten years from first plans to opening in the case of Line 1 — left Birmingham with few options available to help tackle today's chaotic traffic and damaging phenomena such as out-of-town shopping.

So in February 1997 the first 'Showcase' bus route was launched, bringing together many of the elements mentioned above in a scheme designed to demonstrate whether bus travel can be made appealing enough to achieve the results commonly associated with light rail. The formula has been tried piecemeal elsewhere in Britain, but Birmingham plans a network of 15 such routes over the next five years in a strategy which aims to raise public transport journeys from 25 to 30 per cent of the total by 2005. This is optimistic. The handful of Showcase routes, a tiny proportion of the total in this conurbation of 2.6 million, will have to be very good indeed at winning and keeping new passengers to stand comparison with sparkling new trams and the successful cross-city suburban rail routes. But it is a serious test, and its outcome could determine the direction of British urban transport strategy for years ahead.

Clean diesels

Birmingham's Showcase buses will be diesel-powered, and with stringent Euro-3 regulations and clean fuel it seems certain that emissions from the next generation of diesel engines will be low enough to be environmentally acceptable in general transport use for the foreseeable future. Diesel engines retain their advantage over CNG of better fuel efficiency and lower cost, though both CNG and electric power will play a role in sensitive areas where an 'ultra-green' image is required. Diesel-electric hybrids have the advantage of eliminating the fixed link between engine and wheels, thereby allowing innovative interior designs. Traditionally limited by high cost, development of cheaper transmissions could make the hybrid a better option.

Low-floor models are seen as essential in projecting an image of easy access and modernity that will help buses match the standards of the latest trams, and the long-awaited EU Bus & Coach Directive on bus design is expected to co-ordinate European attitudes. Finding space to accommodate wheels, engines, transmission and auxiliaries in an affordable low-floor package remains a challenge for the designers, while medium- and high-floor vehicles will still be in demand for cities with poor quality roads.

But if the city bus of the immediate future retains diesel power, we must not forget that 300-or-so electric bus (trolleybus) networks continue to do sterling work worldwide. For many smaller cities, trolleybuses are the ideal compromise — quieter and smoother than diesel or petrol buses, good hill climbers, and with some of the appeal of trams but easier on infrastructure costs. They also offer an impression of what cities might be like if all buses were electrically powered.

Acknowledgements

As ever, we owe a huge debt of gratitude to the many operators, manufacturers and suppliers who have provided information in response to our requests, as well as to those friends and colleagues who have contributed data and photographs gathered on their worldwide travels. For this edition, we have been fortunate to receive much new information on city transport systems in Russia and other countries of the former USSR, enabling us to improve coverage in some important areas.

Tony Pattison has compiled the manufacturers' sections with his usual attention to detail, assisted by Buses Worldwide Association, Patric Cunnane, Eric Gibbins, Norman Griffiths, and Doug Jack *(Transport Resources International)*. Regional contributors to the cities section are David Haydock (France), Wilhelm Pflug (Germany), K K Gupta (India), Andy Phipps (Japan), Barry Cross (Spain, Portugal and Brazil), Andrew Jarosz (UK and elsewhere), and David Warner, Julian Wolinsky and Van Wilkins (USA). Steve Morgan once again provided much valuable information on world trolleybus developments, while many others, preferring to remain anonymous, contributed notes on individual cities.

Photo credits are due to John Bamforth, Steve Bidwell, Leroy Demery, Ken Fletcher, C Gray, Norman and Su Griffiths, K K Gupta, David Haydock, Chris Jackson, Andrew Jarosz, Bill Luke, Steve Morgan, Itsuhiro Mori, Brian Morrison, Peter Newman, Aare Olander, Andy Phipps, Ales Pokorny, Anthony Robins, D Trevor Rowe, Marilyn Schwarz, Marcel Vleugels, Van Wilkins, Gordon Wiseman, Julian Wolinsky and anon. Roger Carvell drew and amended the maps.

Chris Bushell — London, April 1997

New entries in this edition

Cities
Bamako
Chelyabinsk
Donetsk
Kazan
Perm
Ufa

Rail Vehicles and Traction Equipment
Bombardier-Concarril, Mexico

Rail and Bus Components and Subassemblies
Air Vehicles, UK
Atlas International, UK
Bharat, India
Bostrom, USA
British Furtex Fabrics, UK
Chapman Seating, UK
Disc-Lock Europe, UK
Dorbyl, South Africa
E G & G Rotron, USA
Electric Fan Engineering, USA
Energy Controls, Australia
European Friction Industries, UK
Freudenberg, Germany
Fuchs, UK
GEC Plessey Semiconductors, UK
The Halo Company, UK
Hepworth Rail, UK
IBG Monforts, Germany
Johnson Matthey, USA
Klübner, Germany
Lab Craft, UK
LPA Industries, UK
MZT Hepos, Macedonia
Parizzi, Italy
POLI, Italy
Proximeter, UK
Ricon, USA
Robert Wagner, Germany
Rose Bearings, UK
Sguinzi Pietro, Italy
Socar, Italy
Stewart & Stevenson, USA
Texstar, USA

Electrification
Clough Smith, UK
Electro Wire, USA
RMC, UK
Spie Enertrans, France

New Technology/Innovative Transit Systems
ANT, Netherlands
Futrex, USA
M-VI Monorail System, Canada
Raytheon, USA

Buses — Chassis, Integrals and Bodies
AAI, USA
BMC Sanayi, Turkey
Buscraft, UK
Ewo, Ireland
Ford (Brasil), Brazil
Kowex, Germany
Q-Bus, Netherlands

Trolleybus Traction Equipment
Mitsubishi, Japan

Road Vehicle Chassis Components
Ballard, Canada

Signalling, Communications & Traffic Control Equipment
Aesys, Italy
Andrew, USA
Casco Signal, P R China
Cegelec AEG, UK
Data Display, Ireland
Fahel, Switzerland
Fokker Space, Netherlands
Globe, USA
Howells, UK
Italtel Telesis, Italy
KE, Japan
Loronix, USA
MDO, France
Oval Window Audio, USA
Poletech, UK
Quantum Sky, USA
RSL, UK
Sécheron, France
Telecom Sud, Italy
Trion, Germany
Wardrop, Canada

Revenue Collection
Agent, USA
BZA, USA
Globe, USA
Höft & Wessel, Germany
Italtel Telesis, Italy
Mobile Data Processing, Italy
Scan Coin, UK
Steria, France
Time 24, UK
Wardrop, Canada

Vehicle Maintenance Equipment and Services
Adtranz, Germany
Containment Corporation, USA
INME, Spain
Proceco, Canada
REW, UK
Technorizon, UK
Wilcomatic, UK

Track Components and Maintenance Equipment
Abloy, UK
Aqua, UK
CAN Geotechnical, UK
Cembre, Italy
First Engineering, UK
Gamble, UK
GrantRail, UK
Jafco, UK
John Kelly (Lasers), UK
KLDLABS, USA
Ortec, Germany
Partner Jonsered, UK
Percevaut, France
Relayfast, UK
Scotland TRC, UK
Semperit, Austria
Spie Batignolles, France
Tensol Rail, Switzerland
Tiefenbach, Germany
WALO, Switzerland

Consultancy and Contracting Services
BAeSEMA, UK
Bovis, UK
BR Business Systems, UK
Carr Agnabrell, UK
Electrowatt Engineering Asia, Thailand
ICB, Germany
Laser Rail, UK
Metro Consulting, UK
RailData, UK
The Railway Consultancy, UK
Railway Technology Strategy Centre, UK
Southdowns Environmental Consultants, UK
Stratec, Belgium
Transcorp, UK
Transport Resources International, UK
TTK, Germany
Vectra, UK

Entries deleted from this edition

Rail Vehicles and Traction Equipment
Cobrasma, Brazil

Rail and Bus Components and Subassemblies
Collins Mobile-Tech, USA
Firth, UK
John Gilbert, New Zealand
Lydney, UK
Matersa, Brazil
MDO, France
Sessa Pasquale, Italy
Siemens Transportation Systems, USA
SPEFEKA, Germany
Stone McColl, Australia
Tickford Rail, UK
TMC, Italy
WECO, Germany

Electrification
Cossonay, Switzerland
Nederland Haarlem, Netherlands
Poletech, UK

New Technology/Innovative Transit Systems
Magnetbahn, Germany

Buses — Chassis, Integrals and Bodies
Acme, Barbados
Adtranz, Germany
Africa Body, South Africa
American Ikarus, USA
Asquith, UK
Atlas, UK
Autokaroserija, Serbia
Avtomontaža, Slovenia
Barbi, Italy
Biamax, Greece
Burem, Nigeria
Bus de Cuernavaca, Mexico
Chardon, France
Coach & Equipment, USA
Comil, Argentina
Constables, UK
Coriasco, Italy
Cubucec, P R China
Deansgate, UK
Devon, UK
Dubigeon, South Africa
Enacma, Angola
Fairfax Industries, New Zealand
Federated Motor Industries, Nigeria
Flxible, USA
Gabonese, Gabon
Gago, Venezuela
General Motors, Egypt
Girardin, Canada
Hanyang, P R China
IBC, UK
IMM, Tunisia
KMC, Cyprus
Lenco, Zambia
Leventis, Nigeria
Manila Motor Works, Philippines
Mednet, USA
Newnham, Australia
Norinco, P R China
PEW, Malawi
Rahali, Morocco
Ramses, Egypt
Renault VI, Spain
SAFAR, Cote d'Ivoire
Samcor, South Africa
Scania, Argentina
Sicca, Italy
Sichler, Germany
SIDAF, Cote d'Ivoire
Sonacome, Algeria
Soon Chow, Singapore
SORIAC, Morocco
Stewart & Stevenson, USA
SuperBus, USA
TAM, Slovenia
TBP, UK
Thomas Chile, Chile
Toluca, Mexico
WBK, UK
Willowvale, Zimbabwe
Zambesi, Zimbabwe

Road Vehicle Chassis Components
Deutz, Germany
Valmet, Finland

Signalling, Communications and Traffic Control Equipment
ANT, Germany
Atlas Elektronik, Germany
Betea, Belgium
Brose, Germany
EFACEC, Portugal
EKE, Finland
IVV, Germany
Krone, Germany
Stone McColl, Australia
VTS, Sweden

Revenue Collection Equipment
AEM Megras, France
FD, Germany
Makomat, Germany
Siemens Nederland, Netherlands

Vehicle Maintenance Equipment and Services
ARI-hetra, USA
Autoglym, UK
ECS, UK
Fleetwash, USA
SBD, UK

Track Components and Maintenance Equipment
Bethlehem Steel, USA
Nikex, Hungary
Omni, USA
Schörling, Germany
Technorail, Switzerland

Consultancy and Contracting Services
Acer Consultants Ltd, UK
Alcatel SESA, Spain
Associate Designers, Spain
Best Impressions, UK
Cobrabell, UK
Cole, Sherman & Associates, Canada
Dar-al-Handasah Consultants, UK
Ebasco Infrastructure, USA
Ernst & Young, USA
Foster Engineering Inc, USA
GA/Partners, USA
Geonik Engineering Research Group, Republic of Korea
Giprokommundortrans Institute, Russia
Gruen Associates, USA
Harland Bartholomew & Associates, USA
Hoff & Overgaard A/S, Denmark
JMP Consultants Ltd, UK
Kampsax International A/S, Denmark
Kellogg Corporation, USA
Light Rail Transit Consultants GmbH, Germany
OTE, Italy
Rendel Palmer & Tritton Limited, UK
Rhein-Consult GmbH, Germany
SNV Studiengesellschaft Verkehr mbH, Germany
Sverdrup Corporation, USA
Transcet SA, France
Transit & Tunnel Consultants Inc, USA
VTS Systems AB, Sweden
Xyzyx Information Corporation, USA

Glossary

ABS	Anti-lock Braking System
AFC	Automated Fare Collection
AGT	Automated Guided Transit
ATC	Automatic Train Control
ATO	Automatic Train Operation
ATP	Automatic Train Protection
ATS	Automatic Train Supervision
AVO	Automatic Vehicle Operation
AVP	Automatic Vehicle Protection
AVS	Automatic Vehicle Supervision
BOT	Build, Operate and Transfer
CAG	Computer-Aided Gear changing
CCTV	Closed Circuit Television
CKD	Completely Knocked Down
CMS	Control and Management/Monitoring System
CNG	Compressed Natural Gas
CTC	Centralised Traffic Control
demu	diesel-electric multiple-unit
dmu	diesel multiple-unit
DPTAC	Disabled Persons Transport Advisory Committee (accessible buses)
DTC	Direct Train Control
EGS	Easy Gear Shift
E&M	Engineering & Maintenance
emu	electric multiple-unit
Euro-1, Euro-2, Euro-3	European Exhaust Emission Standards
GLT	Guided Light Transit
GRP	Glass-Reinforced Plastic
GTO	Gate Turn-Off
GVW	Gross Vehicle Weight
HOV	High-Occupancy Vehicle
HVAC	Heating, Ventilation and Air Conditioning
ICMU	Interference Current Monitoring Unit
IGBT	Insulated Gate Bipolar Transistor
LHD	Left-Hand Drive
LNG	Liquefied Natural Gas
LPG	Liquefied Petroleum Gas
LRT	Light Rapid Transit
LRV	Light Rail Vehicle
M	Motor
MSS	Maintenance Support System
PRT	Personal Rapid Transit
PTE	Passenger Transport Executive
RER	Réseau Express Régional
RHD	Right-Hand Drive
SLF	Super Low Floor
T	Trailer
TGV	Train à Grande Vitesse
TPT	Train Positioning and Tracking
ULF	Ultra Low Floor
ULT	Ultra Light Transit
VVVF	Variable Voltage Variable Frequency

URBAN TRANSPORT SYSTEMS

Statistical data in this section has been collected in co-operation with the International Union of Public Transport (UITP)

*** Metro in operation † Metro under construction or in design**

WORLD URBAN TRAM AND LIGHT RAIL SYSTEMS

(excluding museum, rural and purely interurban lines)

350 light rail and tramway systems are operating in cities and towns worldwide, some serving urban areas too small to be covered in the following pages. Below is a comprehensive list of all urban LRT and tramway systems. We are indebted to *Light Rail & Modern Tramway* and the Light Rail Transit Association for compilation of this list.

* indicates a system built new since 1978
† indicates a system extending or extended (includes tunnels) recently
§ indicates operations suspended
(T) indicates a heritage tramway operated primarily for tourist purposes

Systems in italics are steel-wheeled, automated, fully segregated lines.

ARGENTINA
Buenos Aires*†

ARMENIA
Yerevan

AUSTRALIA
Adelaide
Bendigo (T)
Melbourne†

AUSTRIA
Gmunden
Graz†
Innsbruck
Linz†
Wien†

AZERBAIJAN
Baku
Sumgait

BELARUS
Minsk
Mosyr*
Novopolotsk*
Vitebsk

BELGIUM
Antwerpen†
Bruxelles†
Charleroi†
Gent†
Oostende†

BOSNIA
Sarajevo

BRAZIL
Campinas*§
Campos do Jordão
Rio de Janeiro*

BULGARIA
Sofia†

CANADA
Calgary*
Edmonton*
Toronto†
Vancouver

CHINA
Anshan
Changchun
Dalian

CROATIA
Osijek
Zagreb†

CZECH REPUBLIC
Brno†
Liberec
Most
Olomouc
Ostrava
Plzen
Praha†

EGYPT
Alexandria
Cairo
Heliopolis†
Helwan*†

ESTONIA
Tallinn

FINLAND
Helsinki†

FRANCE
Grenoble*†
Lille
Marseille
Nantes*†
Paris*†
Rouen*
St Etienne†
Strasbourg*†

GEORGIA
Tbilisi

GERMANY
Augsburg†
Bad Schandau (T)
Berlin†
Bielefeld†
Bochum-Gelsenkirchen†
Bonn†
Brandenburg
Braunschweig†
Bremen†
Chemnitz†
Cottbus
Darmstadt†
Dessau
Dortmund†
Dresden†
Düsseldorf†
Duisburg†
Erfurt†
Essen†
Frankfurt/Main†
Frankfurt/Oder
Freiburg/Breisgau†
Gera
Görlitz
Gotha
Halberstadt†
Halle†
Hannover†
Heidelberg†
Jena†
Karlsruhe†
Kassel†
Köln†
Krefeld†
Leipzig†
Ludwigshafen
Magdeburg†
Mainz†
Mannheim†
Mülheim/Ruhr
München†
Naumburg§
Nordhausen
Nürnberg†
Oberhausen*
Plauen
Potsdam†
Rostock†
Schöneiche
Schwerin
Strausberg
Stuttgart†
Ulm†
Woltersdorf
Würzburg†
Zwickau

HONG KONG
Hong Kong
Tuen Mun*†

HUNGARY
Budapest†
Debrecen
Miskolc
Szeged

INDIA
Calcutta

ITALY
Genova*†
Milano†
Napoli†
Roma†
Torino†
Trieste

JAPAN
Enoshima
Fukui
Gifu
Hakodate
Hiroshima
Kagoshima
Kitakyushu
Kochi
Kumamoto
Kyoto
Matsuyama
Nagasaki
Okayama
Osaka
Sapporo
Takaoka
Tokyo
Toyama
Toyohashi

KAZAKHSTAN
Almaty
Karaganda
Pavlodar
Temirtau
Ust-Kamenogorsk

KOREA, DEMOCRATIC PEOPLE'S REPUBLIC
Pyongyang*
Kumsusan*

LATVIA
Daugavpils
Liepaya
Riga

MALAYSIA
*Kuala Lumpur**

MEXICO
Guadalajara*†
Mexico City†
Monterrey*†

NETHERLANDS
Amsterdam†
Den Haag†
Rotterdam†
Utrecht*

NEW ZEALAND
Christchurch (T*)

NORWAY
Oslo†
Trondheim†

PARAGUAY
Asunción§

PHILIPPINES
Manila*†

POLAND
Bydgoszcz
Czestochowa
Elblag
Gdansk
Gorzow
Grundziadz
Katowice
Krakow
Lódź
Poznan†
Szczecin
Torun
Warszawa†
Wrocław

PORTUGAL
Lisboa
Porto (T)

ROMANIA
Arad
Botoşani*

Braila
Braşov*
Bucureşti
Cluj*
Constanta*
Craiova*
Galati
Iasi
Oradea
Ploiesti*
Reşiţa*
Sibiu
Timişoara

RUSSIA
Achinsk
Angarsk
Arkhangelsk
Astrakhan
Barnaul
Biysk
Chelyabinsk
Cherepovets
Dzerzhinsk
Grozniy§
Irkutsk
Ivanovo
Izhevsk
Kaliningrad
Karpinsk
Kazan
Kemerovo
Kharbarovsk
Kolomna
Komsomolsk-na-Amure
Krasnoarmeisk*
Krasnodar
Krasnoturinsk
Krasnoyarsk
Kursk
Lipetsk
Magnitogorsk
Moskva
Nizhnikamsk
Nizhni Novgorod
Nizhniy-Tagil
Noginsk
Novocherkassk
Novokuznetsk
Novosibirsk
Novotroitsk
Omsk
Orel
Orsk
Osinniki
Perm
Prokopyevsk
Pyatigorsk†
Rostov-na-Donu
Ryazan
Salavat
Samara
Saratov
Shakhty
Shushenskoye
Simbirsk
Smolensk
Stary Oskol*
St Petersburg
Taganrog
Tomsk
Tula
Tver
Ufa
Ulan-Ude
Usolye-Sibirskoye
Ust-Ilimsk*
Ust-Katav
Ustinov
Vladikavkaz
Vladivostok
Volchansk
Volgograd
Volzhskiy
Voronezh
Yaroslavl
Yekaterinburg
Zlatoust

SLOVAKIA
Bratislava†
Kosice
Trencianska-Tepla

SOUTH AFRICA
Kimberley*(T)

SPAIN
Barcelona (T)
La Coruna*(T)
Soller
Valencia*†

SWEDEN
Göteborg†
Norrköping
Stockholm (also T*)†

SWITZERLAND
Basel
Bern
Bex
Genève†
Lausanne*
Neuchâtel
Zürich†

TUNISIA
Tunis*†

TURKEY
*Ankara**
Istanbul* (also T*) †
Konya*†

UKRAINE
Avdiyivka
Dniprodzerzhinsk
Dnipropetrovsk
Donetsk
Druzhkivka
Horlivka
Kharkiv
Konotop
Kostyatinivka
Kramatorsk
Kriviy Rih
Kyiv†
Lvhansk
Lviv
Makiyivka
Mariupol
Molochne
Nikolayiv
Odesa
Stakhanov
Vinnitsya
Yenakiyeve
Yevpatoriya
Zaporizhzhya
Zhitomir

UNITED KINGDOM
Birkenhead*(T)
Blackpool
Douglas (T)
*London**†
Manchester*†
Newcastle upon Tyne*†
Sheffield*

UNITED STATES
Baltimore*†
Boston
Buffalo*†
Cleveland†
Dallas*†
Denver*†
*Detroit** (also T)
Fort Worth
Galveston*(T)
Los Angeles*†
Memphis*†(T)
Newark
New Orleans† (also T*)
Philadelphia
Pittsburgh†
Portland*†
Sacramento*†
San Diego*†
San Francisco†
San Jose*†
Seattle*(T)
St Louis*†
Tucson (T)

UZBEKISTAN
Tashkent

YUGOSLAVIA
Beograd

SYSTEMS UNDER CONSTRUCTION

AUSTRALIA
Sydney

BRAZIL
Salvador

GERMANY
Saarbrücken

IRAN
Mashhad

NORWAY
Bergen (T)

PAKISTAN
Karachi

SPAIN
Vitoria

TURKEY
Adana
Bursa
Izmir

UNITED KINGDOM
Birmingham
Croydon

UNITED STATES
Jersey City
Salt Lake City
San Juan

SYSTEMS PLANNED

AUSTRIA
Klagenfurt (T)

CANADA
Vancouver
Victoria (T)

CHINA
Shenyang

COLOMBIA
Cali

DENMARK
København

DOMINICAN REPUBLIC
Santo Domingo

FRANCE
Bordeaux
Clermont Ferrand
Montpellier
Mulhouse
Nice
Orleans
Valenciennes

GERMANY
Aachen
Erlangen
Hagen
Heilbronn

INDIA
Bangalore

INDONESIA
Bandung

IRELAND
Dublin

ISRAEL
Jerusalem
Tel Aviv

ITALY
Bari
Bergamo
Bologna
Firenze (T)
Livorno
Padova
Palermo
Savona

LUXEMBOURG
Luxembourg

NETHERLANDS
Gouda-Leiden
Groningen

NEW ZEALAND
Auckland
Wellington

NORWAY
Bergen

PAKISTAN
Lahore

PORTUGAL
Porto

SPAIN
Barcelona
Malaga
Sevilla

UNITED KINGDOM
Ashford (ULR — ultra light rail)
Bristol
Cardiff
Edinburgh
Glasgow
Leeds
Liverpool
Llandudno (ULR)
Maidstone-Medway
Nottingham
Portsmouth
Weymouth (ULR)

UNITED STATES
Camden
Colorado Springs
Minneapolis
New York
Seattle
Tampa (T)

WORLD URBAN TROLLEYBUS SYSTEMS

Around 300 trolleybus systems are operating in cities and towns worldwide, some serving urban areas too small to be covered in the following pages. Below is a comprehensive list of all urban trolleybus systems known to be operating. We are indebted to *Trolleybus Magazine* and the Trolleybus Museum Company upon whose records we have drawn in the compilation.

*** SYSTEM CURRENTLY NOT OPERATING**
† SYSTEM CURRENTLY OPERATING EXPERIMENTALLY

ARGENTINA
Cordobá
Mendoza
Rosario

ARMENIA
Gümri
Yerevan

AUSTRIA
Innsbruck
Kapfenberg
Linz
Salzburg

AZERBAIJAN
Baku
Gyandzha
Mingechaur
Nakhichevan
Sumgait

BELARUS
Bobruisk
Brest-Litovsk
Gomel
Grodno
Minsk
Mogilev
Vitebsk

BELGIUM
Gent

BOSNIA
Sarajevo

BRAZIL
Araraquara
Recife
Riberão Preto
Santos
São Paulo (2 systems)

BULGARIA
Burgas
Dobrich
Gabrovo
Kazanluk
Khaskovo
Pazardzhik
Pernik
Pleven
Plovdiv
Ruse
Sliven
Sofia
Stara Zagora
Varna
Veliko Turnovo
Vratsa

CANADA
Edmonton
Vancouver

CHILE
Valparaíso

CHINA, PEOPLE'S REPUBLIC
Anshan
Beijing
Benxi
Changchun
Chengdu
Chongqing
Dalian
Fuzhou
Guangzhou
Hangzhou
Harbin
Jilin
Jinan
Lanzhou
Luoyang
Nanchang
Nanjing
Nanning
Qingdao
Qiqihar
Shanghai
Shenyang
Taiyuan
Tianjin
Wuhan (2 systems)
Xi'an
Zhengzhou

CZECH REPUBLIC
Brno
České Budějovice
Chomutov
Hrádec Králové
Jihlava
Mariánské Lázně
Opava
Ostrava
Pardubice
Plzeň
Teplice
Ústí nad Labem
Zlín

DENMARK
København

ECUADOR
Quito

ESTONIA
Tallinn

FRANCE
Grenoble
Limoges
Lyon
Marseille
Nancy
St Etienne

GEORGIA
Batumi
Chiatura
Gori
Kutaisi
Ozurgeti
Rustavi
Samtredia
Sukhumi
Tbilisi

GERMANY
Eberswalde
Essen*
Esslingen
Solingen

GREECE
Athens

HUNGARY
Budapest
Debrecen
Szeged

IRAN
Tehran

ITALY
Ancona
Bologna
Cagliari
Chieti*
Cremona
Milano
Modena
Napoli
Parma
Rimini
San Remo

KAZAKHSTAN
Akmola
Aqtöbe
Almaty
Karaganda
Kustanai
Petropavlovsk
Shymkent
Zhambyl

KIRGIZIA
Bishek
Naryn
Osh

KOREA, DEMOCRATIC PEOPLE'S REPUBLIC
Chongjin
Hamhung
Kimchek
Nampo
Pyongyang
Sinuiju
Wonsan

LATVIA
Riga

LITHUANIA
Kaunas
Vilnius

MEXICO
Guadalajara
Mexico City

MOLDOVA
Balţi
Bender
Chişinău
Tiraspol

MONGOLIA
Ulan Bataar

NEPAL
Kathmandu

NETHERLANDS
Arnhem

NEW ZEALAND
Wellington

NORWAY
Bergen

POLAND
Gdynia
Lublin
Słupsk
Tychy

PORTUGAL
Coimbra
Porto

ROMANIA
Baia Mare
Brăila
Braşov
Bucureşti
Cluj
Constanţa
Galaţi
Iaşi
Mediaş
Sibiu
Slatina
Suceava
Targovişte
Timişoara
Vaslui

RUSSIA
Abakan
Almetyevsk
Archangelsk
Armavir
Astrakhan
Balakovo
Barnaul
Belgorod
Berezniki
Blagoveshchensk
Bratsk
Bryansk
Cheboksary
Chelyabinsk
Cherkessk
Chita
Dzerzhinsk
Engels
Grozniy*
Irkutsk
Ivanovo
Izhevsk
Kaliningrad
Kaluga
Kamensk-Uralskiy
Kazan
Kemerovo
Khabarovsk
Kirov
Kostroma
Kovrov
Krasnodar
Krasnoyarsk
Kurgan
Kursk
Leninsk-Kuznetskiy
Lipetsk

Maikop
Makhachkala
Miass
Moskva
Murmansk
Nalchik
Nizhni Novgorod
Novgorod
Novocheboksarsk
Novokuybyshevsk
Novokuznetsk
Novorossiysk
Novosibirsk
Omsk
Orel
Orenburg
Penza
Perm
Petrozavodsk
Rostov-na-Donu
Rubtsovsk
Ryazan
Rybinsk
Samara
Saransk
Saratov
Shakhty
Smolensk
Stavropol
Sterlitamak
St Petersburg
Taganrog
Tambov
Tolyatti
Tomsk
Tula
Tver
Tyumen
Ufa
Ulyanovsk
Vladikavkaz
Vladimir
Vladivostok
Volgodonsk
Volgograd
Vologda
Voronezh
Yaraslavl
Yekaterinburg
Yoshkar-Ola

SLOVAKIA
Banská Bystrica
Bratislava
Košice
Prešov
Žilina

SWITZERLAND
Basel
Bern
Biel
La Chaux-de-Fonds
Fribourg
Genève
Lausanne
Lugano
Luzern
Montreux-Vevey
Neuchâtel
Schaffhausen
St Gallen
Winterthur
Zürich

TAJIKISTAN
Dushanbe
Khudzhand

TURKMENISTAN
Ashgabat

UKRAINE
Antratsit
Artyemivsk
Bila Tserkov
Cherkasy
Chernigiv
Chernivtsi
Dnipropetrovsk
Dobropilya
Donetsk
Dzerzhinsk
Horlivka
Ivano-Frankivsk
Kharkiv
Khartsyzsk
Kherson
Khmelnitsky
Kirovograd
Kramatorsk
Krasnodon
Kremenchuk
Kriviy Rih
Kyiv
Lisichansk
Lugansk
Lutsk
Lviv
Makiyivka
Mariupol
Mikolayiv
Odesa
Poltava
Rivne
Sevastopol
Severodonetsk
Simferopol
Slavyansk
Stakhanov
Sumy
Ternopol
Vinnitsya
Vuglegirsk
Yalta
Zaporizhzhya
Zhitomir

UNITED STATES
Boston
Dayton
Philadelphia
San Francisco
Seattle

UZBEKISTAN
Almalyk
Andijon
Bukhoro
Fargona
Namangan
Nukus
Samarkand
Tashkent

YUGOSLAVIA
Beograd

SYSTEMS UNDER CONSTRUCTION (*) OR ACTIVE DEVELOPMENT

BULGARIA
Blagoevgrad*
Dimitrovgrad*
Gorna Oryakhovitsa*
Lovech
Shumen*
Vidin*
Yambol*

GEORGIA
Tskhaltubo
Zestafoni

ITALY
Genova*
Lido di Ostia

KAZAKHSTAN
Semipalatinsk

ROMANIA
Piatra-Neamţ*
Sfintu Gheorghe
Tirgu Jiu*

RUSSIA
Elektrostal
Khimki*
Nizhni Tagil*
Podolsk
Pskov
Serpukhov
Verkhnaya Pishma
Volzhski*
Zagorsk

SLOVAKIA
Nitra
Trencin

UKRAINE
Melitopol

UNITED STATES
New York
Oakland

AACHEN

Population: 253,000, region served 555,000
Public transport: Bus services provided by publicly owned transport and electricity company. Fares and services co-ordinated with DB rail services on two lines, regional bus services of Busverkehr Rheinland (BVR), an associated company of German Railway (DB) and other operators within the framework of Aachener Verkehrs Verbund (AVV). Also joint cross-border services run in conjunction with Belgian and Dutch operators

AVV

Aachener Verkehrsverbund GmbH (AVV)
Neuköllner Str 1, 52002 Aachen, Germany
Telephone: +49 241 968970 Fax: +49 241 96897 20
General Manager: H J Sistenich

Current situation: Regional transit authority co-ordinates the services of six operators: ASEAG, BVR, Kreiswerke Heinsberg, Dürener Kreisbahn, Taeter Aachen and Deutsche Bahn (DB). DB rail services were integrated into AVV in 1996.

Passenger journeys: (1991) 76.5 million
(1992) 79.5 million
(1994) 82.6 million

ASEAG

Aachener Strassenbahn und Energieversorgungs AG
PO Box 150, 52002 Aachen
Telephone: +49 241 16880 Fax: +49 241 1688 236
Directors: Karlheinz Wontorra
Dr Joachim Duttenhofer
Operating Manager: Hans-Peter Appel
Administration Manager: Uwe Peifer
Commercial Manager: Klaus Reinartz
Staff: 842 (transport division)

Current situation: Night service known as ASA (ASEAG Sammel Auto) using hired taxis operates half-hourly along certain routes from 00.30-03.45, serving 76 city stops;

Duewag's RegioSprinter on DKB local service
1996

operates on 45 min prebooking by telephone; fares are double those in daytime.

Bus

Passenger journeys: (1993) 54.9 million
(1994) 56 million
(1995) 56.1 million
Vehicle-km: (1993) 18.1 million
(1994) 18.1 million
(1995) 17.8 million

Number of routes: 51
Route length: (One way) 990 km
On priority right-of-way: 12 km
Fleet: 273 vehicles, plus 62 hired

Mercedes O305 (1982/85)	42
MAN SL200 (1979/85)	66
Mercedes O405 (1988)	12
MAN SL202 (1987/89)	31
Mercedes O405N low-floor (1991/92)	12
MAN NL202 low-floor (1991/93)	27
Mercedes O305G articulated (1983/84)	13
Mercedes O405G articulated (1987/88)	6
MAN SG242 articulated (1986/88/92)	47
Van Hool A508 midibus (1990)	10
MAN NG272 articulated (1993)	7

In peak service: 260
On order: 62

Most intensive service: 7 min
One-person operation: All routes
Fare collection: Prepurchase or payment to driver
Fare structure: Stages, single and multitickets, weekly and transferable monthly passes; day tickets
Fares collected on board: 26% (74% hold passes)
Fare evasion control: Roving inspectors
Arrangements for elderly/disabled: Free travel for disabled, reimbursed by Federal government
Operational control: All buses radio-equipped
Average peak-hour speed: 20.5 km/h
Operating costs financed by: Fares 77%, subsidy/grants 23%
Subsidy from: National 80% and state 20% governments
New vehicles financed by: Depreciation and subsidy

DKB

Dürener Kreisbahn GmbH
Kölner Landstrasse 271, 52351 Düren
Telephone: +49 2421 39010 Fax: +49 2421 390188
Manager, Bus: Rolf Schorer
Manager, Rail: Reinhold Alfter
Staff: 232

Passenger journeys: (1993) 9.9 million
(1994) 10 million
(1995) 10.3 million

Current situation: County council owned regional bus operator providing urban and rural services in and around Düren (30 routes, 108 buses). In 1993 the company took over DB train services from Düren to Heimbach (30 km) and Jülich (16 km). A frequent service is provided by 26 lightweight three-section articulated diesel railcars built by Duewag. The two rail routes carry about 3.7 million passengers a year.

BVR

Busverkehr Rheinland GmbH, Verkaufsbüro Aachen
Zollamtstrasse 3, 52064 Aachen
Telephone: +49 241 433336

Current situation: Bus company owned by DB provides suburban and rural services within the AVV region and beyond.

DB

Deutsche Bahn AG, Geschäftsbereich Nahverkehr
Regionalbereich Rheinland
Konrad-Adenauer-Ufer 3, 50668 Köln
Telephone: +49 221 141421 Fax: +49 221 141 2442

Type of operation: Suburban heavy rail

Passenger journeys: (1995) 5.4 million

Current situation: Stopping trains run on lines from Aachen to Düren (and onwards to Köln) and Geilenkirchen (and onwards to Mönchengladbach), at least hourly with extra trains at peak periods. There is no fixed interval service. Electric locomotive-hauled trains with double-deck coaches are used.

ASEAG service in central Aachen
1995

UPDATED

AARHUS

Population: 279,000
Public transport: Bus services provided by municipal undertaking; limited local train service

Aarhus sporveje

Aarhus sporveje
Bryggervej 35, 8240 Risskov, Denmark
Telephone: +45 89 44 55 00 Fax: +45 89 44 55 44
Chair: Olaf P Christensen
General Manager: Leif Marcussen
Staff: 973

Developments: A three-year experiment started in 1995 giving holders of season tickets free transfer between buses and trains in the region.

Bus

Passenger journeys: (1993) 44.8 million
(1994) 45.8 million
(1995) 45.5 million
Vehicle-km: (1993) 14.7 million
(1994) 14.9 million
(1995) 15.1 million

Number of routes: 40, plus 10 on Friday and Saturday nights only
Route length: (One way) 835 km
Fleet: 228 vehicles

Leyland-DAB (1981-89)	121
DAB-Silkeborg (1988-95	88
Volvo B10M (1994-95)	19

In peak service: 205
On order: 6 Volvo/Säffle, 4 Volvo/Aabenraa and 10 DAB

Most intensive service: 10 min
One-person operation: All routes
Fare collection: Self-service with Autelca B-20 ticket vending machines, Almex M canceller, all on board
Fare structure: Zonal, with single and multitickets and season cards; free transfer to local trains

Fares collected on board: 12.1% (63.7% of passengers use passes, 24.2% multitickets)
Fare evasion control: 28 inspectors
Operational control: Mobile radio
Arrangements for elderly/disabled: Price reduction on season cards financed under social law
Average distance between stops: 500 m
Average peak-hour speed: In mixed traffic, 28.3 km/h
Bus priority: 3.1 km bus lanes
Operating costs financed by: Fares 64%, other commercial sources 1%, subsidy/grants 35%
Subsidy from: Local council taxation
New vehicles financed by: Operating budget

UPDATED

Volvo B10M on Aarhus Route 9
1997

ABERDEEN

Population: 209,000 (240,000 including environs)
Public transport: Bus services provided mainly by private companies; commuter rail service

Grampian Transport

Grampian Regional Transport Ltd
395 King Street, Aberdeen AB9 1SP, Scotland
Telephone: +44 1224 637047 Fax: +44 1224 639185
Chief Executive: Moir Lockhead
Managing Director: Mike Mitchell
Staff: 584

Current situation: Formerly the Regional Council's transport undertaking, the company was sold to its workforce in 1989. Subsidiary companies are Mairs Coaches of Dyce and Kirkpatrick of Deeside. GRT Bus Group, the parent company, merged with Badgerline in 1995 to form FirstBus, the UK's largest bus operator.
Developments: Bus priority measures are being promoted following allocation of capital grants. Park-and-ride 'City Quick' service has been introduced on the King Street/Eilan Road corridor, while 'Gold Service' buses have been allocated to the busiest corridors. Hail-and-ride operates after 20.00 on some routes.

Bus

Passenger journeys: (1991/92) 28.8 million
(1992/93) 27.2 million
(1993/94) 26 million
Vehicle-km: (1991/92) 11.4 million
(1992/93) 10.9 million
(1993/94) 11 million

Number of routes: 18
Route length: 170 km
On priority right-of-way: 800 m
Fleet: 202 vehicles, plus Mairs (3 buses, 33 coaches) and Kirkpatrick (11 coaches)

Leyland Olympian double-deck	30
Leyland Atlantean double-deck	111
Daimler CVG6	1
Coaches	14
MCW Metrorider	3
Mercedes minibus	15
Mercedes O405 single-deck	24
Mercedes O405G articulated	1
Renault S56 minibus	3

In peak service: 160

Most intensive service: 5 min
One-person operation: All routes
Fare collection: Pay-as-you-enter; electronic Wayfarer ticket issue and data collection equipment; stored value magnetic pass card
Fare structure: Stage; weekly/monthly/3-monthly passes
Fares collected on board: 76%
Fare evasion control: Inspectors
Operational control: Route inspectors, mobile radio
Arrangements for elderly/disabled: Low maximum fare
Average distance between stops: 180 m
Average peak-hour speed: In mixed traffic, 16.5 km/h
Subsidy from: Local council, for non-commercial routes put out to tender, plus concessionary fare reimbursement

Bluebird's Route 59 (front) and Grampian's 'City Quick' park-and-ride service on Rosemount viaduct
1996

Bluebird

Bluebird Buses Ltd
Bus Station, Guild Street, Aberdeen AB11 6GR
Telephone: +44 1224 591381 Fax: +44 1224 584202
Managing Director: Neil Renilson
General Manager: Ian Mackintosh
Operations Director: Robert Andrew
Finance Director: Norman Strachan
Engineering Director: Bill Devlin

Current situation: Formerly part of the state-owned Scottish Bus Group, the company was purchased in 1991 by Stagecoach. It operates the majority of commuter services into the city and routes throughout Grampian, Highland and Tayside regions.

Fleet: 366 buses

Single-deck	58
Double-deck	122
Coaches	117
Minibuses	69

ScotRail

ScotRail Railways Ltd
Caledonian Chambers, 87 Union Street, Glasgow G1 3TA
Telephone: +44 141 332 9811 Fax: +44 141 335 3125

Current situation: Diesel commuter services provided from Dyce (10 km north, about hourly) and Portlethen (13 km south, limited).

UPDATED

ABIDJAN

Population: 3 million
Public transport: Bus and lagoon boat services in the metropolitan area and inner suburbs provided under concession from government by 'mixed economy' company part owned by vehicle manufacturer and responsible to Ministry. Private 'Gbaka' minibuses serve suburbs and outer areas. Light rail line proposed in lieu of abandoned metro project

SOTRA

Société des Transports Abidjanais (SOTRA)
BP 2009, Abidjan 01, Côte d'Ivoire
Telephone: +225 252942 Fax: +225 259721
Director General: Reine Yeboue-Kouame
Staff: 6,100

Passenger journeys: (1989) 398 million
Vehicle-km: (1989) 64.4 million

Current situation: A 40 per cent stake in SOTRA is held by the French manufacturer Renault, with the remaining 60 per cent held by the Côte d'Ivoire government. An initial exclusive 15-year public transport franchise has been renewed for five-year periods. At the end of the 1980s, SOTRA was catering for about 75 per cent of demand, with the remainder carried by Gbakas.

As well as conventional bus operations extending to 803 km and a ferry service, a minibus service caters for passengers with bulky and heavy parcels. Operated with a fleet of Renault SG2 20-capacity buses with roof racks, the 'Taxi-Bagages' service runs on demand on 14 routes covering 208 km, charging a flat fare and carrying about 1.6 million passengers annually, mainly to and from the city's markets. The 160 Saviem SM8 and SG4 buses in the fleet are mostly used to provide school services. For further background see *JUTS 1991*.

Fleet: 1,203 buses, mainly Renault S105

Boat

Current situation: 19 modern vessels ply three routes on the Abidjan Lagoon totalling 8.1 km; they carry about 8 million passengers annually.

Minibus

Current situation: Most services to the outer suburbs are provided by private minibuses and shared taxis known as Gbakas with 14-22 seats, operating on set routes but with no defined stops. Smaller minibuses and Saviem SG2 minibuses with a luggage capacity similar to the 'Taxi-Bagages' vehicles of SOTRA are widely used. Many services run in the peak periods only.

The SOTRA and Gbaka networks are generally widely separated, but there is some overlapping particularly in the Abobo and Yopougon corridors.

UPDATED

Central bus station in Abidjan

ACCRA

Population: 2 million

Public transport: All services provided by private operators using 'tro-tro' midi and minibuses and shared taxis, plus wooden body trucks (mammy-wagons)

Minibus

Current situation: Following cessation of full-size bus operations by the Omnibus Services Authority, all public transport is provided by tro-tro midibuses and minibuses, shared taxis and mammy-wagons. Generally fixed routes are operated, and vehicles leave their terminals only when full.

There are some 12,000 tro-tros, carrying more than 50 per cent of the city's trips. Vehicle types include Volkswagen Kombis, Toyota Coaster and Willowbrook. Significant numbers of passengers also use taxis, of which there are thought to be more than 30,000.

Services are regulated by the Ghana Private Road Transport Union, which also sets fare levels.

Toyota minibus bearing religious exhortation on Liberation Road, Accra ***1996***

ADDIS ABABA

Population: 1.9 million

Public transport: Bus services operated by public transport division of government-controlled Public Transport Corporation, operating both urban and intercity services. Shared taxi use is extensive and peak-only midibuses operate

Toyota car-based 'Matatu' shared taxis in central Addis Ababa ***1996***

General Ethiopian Transport

National Road Transport Corporation
Addis Ababa City Bus Services
PO Box 5780, Addis Ababa, Ethiopia
Telephone: +251 1 153117 Fax: +251 1 150744
General Manager: Abdu Jemal
Operations Manager: Zelalem G Michael

Current situation: The city bus system operates under a number of constraints, including vehicle shortages, poor terminal and garage facilities, lack of an operations control system and a proliferation of short and duplicated routes running over very poor roads. Lack of capital hampers provision of spare parts and new vehicles.

As part of a transport study financed by the World Bank, recommendations have been made regarding the organisation and management of the Corporation, including operating methods, vehicle acquisition policy, maintenance arrangements and data processing systems. Implementation is proceeding slowly, along with route rationalisation.

Bus

Passenger journeys: (1990/91) 119.4 million
Vehicle-km: (1990/91) 9.3 million

Number of routes: 40
Route length: (One way) 150 km
Fleet: Approx 200 buses, all single-deck standard length, comprising 160 Mercedes OF1621/Jonckheere, plus about 25 Volvo B7F with Italian Borsani bodies and a few

Fiat 331A/Borsani. A small batch of 15 Mercedes was reported as having arrived in early 1995

Most intensive service: 5 min
Fare structure: Flat, higher for suburban journeys
Fare collection: Conductors on board in fixed location
Average peak-hour speed: 14.4 km/h
Operating costs financed by: Fares 88%, subsidy/grants 12%
Subsidy from: Government; PTC is exempted from government duties and taxes on fuel, spare parts, vehicles and workshop equipment and tools

Shared taxi

Current situation: A fleet of around 4,000 private taxis, minibuses and pick-ups provides services on a 609 km system of 99 routes, 20 of them short routes covering 64 km. They operate wholly commercially with 145 million passengers carried in 1990/91.

Midibus

Current situation: A fleet of 46 privately owned 21-44 seat midibuses operates during peak hours over 28 routes totalling 191 km. On average, only some 20 buses were operational, and carried 1.5 million passengers in 1990/91. They operate wholly commercially.

Jonckheere-bodied Mercedes OF1621 of GET ***1996***

ADELAIDE

Population: 1.1 million
Public transport: Bus (including guided busway service), tram and suburban rail services administered by Passenger Transport Board and operated by state government authority, with competitive tendering started in 1995. A few private bus operators serve mainly country and outer-suburban areas

Passenger Transport Board

Passenger Transport Board
GPO Box 1998, Adelaide, South Australia 5001, Australia
Telephone: +61 8 8218 2459 Fax: +61 8 8218 2467
Chair: Michael Wilson
Chief Executive Officer: Adrian Gargett

Current situation: The Passenger Transport Board (PTB) was formed under the 1994 Passenger Transport Act and is responsible for administration and regulation of passenger transport throughout South Australia, including taxis, hire cars, charter bus operators and both country and metropolitan bus, train and tram services. The PTB is charged with the responsibility for overall integration of public transport in terms of services and ticketing. The PTB may not operate services itself.

The act requires that all regular intra-state passenger transport services be operated under contract to the PTB, subject to a limit of five years and a maximum fleet of 100 vehicles. It also guaranteed the existing operator TransAdelaide (the former State Transport Authority) the right to operate at least 50 per cent of bus, tram and trains services until March 1997. The first round of competitive tendering for Adelaide metropolitan services started in March 1995.

TransAdelaide

TransAdelaide
GPO Box 2351, Adelaide, South Australia 5001
Telephone: +61 8 8218 2200 Fax: +61 8 8211 7614
General Manager, Kevin Benger
Group Manager, Support Services: Dale Larkin
Group Manager, Corporate & Business Development: Carolyn Barlow
Group Manager, Finance & Information: Roger Seaman
Group Manager, Technical Services: George Erdos
Group Manager, Human Resources: Sue Filby
Staff: 2,203

Passenger journeys: (All modes)
(1993/94) 48.7 million
(1994/95) 45.5 million
(1995/96) 43.7 million

Current situation: Formerly the State Transport Authority, TransAdelaide operates bus, tram and rail services under contract to or service agreement with the PTB, which funds services and controls the integrated ticketing system.

Since 1995, private operators have tendered in competition with TransAdelaide for contracts to operate public transport services.

Adelaide's guided busway ***1997***

Bus

Staff: 1,417

Passenger journeys: (1993/94) 38.3 million
(1994/95) 36 million
(1995/96) 34.4 million
Vehicle-km: (1993/94) 39 million
(1995/96) 37.7 million

Number of routes: 175
Route length: (One way) 1,082 km
Fleet: 617 vehicles

Volvo B59 (1977)	153
Volvo B58 standard (1980)	35
Volvo B58 articulated (1980)	35
Volvo B10M standard (1981)	15
Volvo B10M articulated (1981)	5
MAN SL200 (1982)	100
MAN SL200 CNG-powered (1984)	10
Mercedes O305 (1984)	41
Mercedes O305G articulated (1985)	51
MAN SG280H articulated (1986)	18
MAN HOCL SL midibus (1990)	3
MAN HOCL 11.190 midibus (1993)	20
MAN SL202 (1992)	25
MAN NL202 ultra-low-floor (1993)	4
MAN SL202 CNG-powered (1993)	100
MAN HOCL Volgren midibus (1994)	1
Mercedes LO812 (1993)	2

In peak service: 617

Most intensive service: 2 min
One-person operation: All routes
Fare collection: Pay-as-you-enter with passenger-operated ticket validating machines; prepurchase multitrip and day tickets
Fare structure: Zonal; prepurchased multitrip, and cash fare tickets
Fares collected on board: 20%
Fare evasion control: Field supervisors
Integration with other modes: Fare system integrated with train and tram; 11 bus/rail interchanges
Operational control: Field supervisors/mobile phone
Arrangements for elderly/disabled: Concessionary fare; low-floor buses with wheelchair ramps being introduced, access ramps also available on trains; wheelchair access taxi cab scheme operated by the taxi industry
Average distance between stops: 300 m
Average peak-hour speed: In mixed traffic, 19 km/h
New vehicles financed from: Capital loan funds

Developments: The PTB is contracting out bus services on an area-by-area basis, and TransAdelaide won the majority of routes tendered in 1995 and 1996. Some 50 per cent of the network remained uncontracted at the end of 1996.

Guided bus

Current situation: The guided bus O-Bahn system provides high-speed (100 km/h) service on the 12 km corridor from Modbury in the northeastern suburbs to Gilberton just outside Adelaide's central business district. See *JUTS 1988* for history and description.

Fleet: 92 Mercedes buses (standard and articulated); buses are equipped with lateral guidewheels for busway operation, but are also suitable for operation on ordinary roads

Tramway

Staff: 155

Type of operation: Conventional tramway

Passenger journeys: (1993/94) 1.6 million
(1994/95) 1.5 million
(1995/96) 1.5 million
Car-km: (Annual) 0.7 million

Route length: 10.8 km (10 km on own right-of-way)
Number of lines: 1
Number of stops: 21
Track: 40 kg/m rail, timber sleepers on ballast
Electrification: 600 V DC, overhead

Service: Peak 7-17 min, off-peak 20-30 min
First/last car: 05.32/23.50
Fare structure: Zonal
Fare evasion control: Field supervisors

Rolling stock: 21 cars

Pengelley Class H (1929)	M20
Class H restaurant tram (1990)	M1

Developments: Passenger information systems are being upgraded to improve facilities for tourists.

Suburban railway

Staff: 656

Type of operation: Suburban heavy rail

Passenger journeys: (1993/94) 8.7 million
(1994/95) 8.4 million
(1995/96) 8.3 million

Current situation: Services provided on six routes totalling 120 km (1,600 mm gauge) with 105 stations, every 20 min peak, 30 min off-peak. Zonal fare structure with all but five stations unstaffed.

Developments: The 70-strong Transit Police Squad was transferred to the South Australian Police in 1994. Passenger Service Attendants now travel on all trains to assist with ticketing, timetable and general information enquiries.

Following conversion of the Adelaide—Melbourne line to 1,435 mm gauge, one 1,600 mm gauge track remains between Adelaide and Belair for TransAdelaide suburban service.

Rolling stock: 106 diesel railcars

300 class (1985)	M4
400 class (1989)	M2
Comeng 2000 class (1980)	M12
Comeng 2100 class (1980)	T18
Comeng/Clyde 3000 class (1988/92/95)	M26
Comeng/Clyde/ABB 3000/3100 class (1988/92/95)	M40

In peak service: 88

Developments: The last of the 300/400 class diesel-hydraulic cars are being phased out during 1997. Programme of station shelter replacement in progress.

UPDATED

AHMEDABAD

Population: 3.3 million
Public transport: Bus services provided by municipally owned undertaking

AMTS

Ahmedabad Municipal Transport Service
Transport House, PO Box 142, outside Jamalpur Gate, Ahmedabad 380022, Gujarat, India
Telephone: +91 79 352911 Fax: +91 79 395648
Transport Manager: V P Shah
Staff: 6,413

Developments: RITES has carried out feasibility studies for a mass rapid transit system extending to 58.5 km. In 1996 Western Railway introduced dmu services between Ahmedabad and Mehsana/Abu Road.

Bus

Passenger journeys: (1993/94) 239.2 million
(1994/95) 228.3 million
(1995/96) 250.2 million
Vehicle-km: (1993/94) 45.1 million
(1994/95) 43.8 million
(1995/96) 43.8 million

Number of routes: 180
Route length: 2,219 km
Fleet: 708 vehicles

Ashok-Leyland single-deck	708

In peak service: 589
Average age of fleet: 15.1 years

Latest Ashok-Leyland Special Viking of AMTS

Most intensive service: 10 min
Fare collection: Conductor
Fare structure: Stage
Fare evasion control: Random inspection with penalty
Average peak-hour speed: 18.3 km/h

Operating costs financed by: Fares 96%, other commercial sources 1%, grants from municipal corporation 3%

UPDATED

ALBANY

Population: City 102,000, service area 769,000
Public transport: Fixed-route bus and paratransit services provided by governmental transit authority in 6,300 km² area including Albany, Schenectady, Rensselaer and Saratoga counties. The authority is governed by a nine-member board of directors. Four private operators run complementary routes within the service area

CDTA

Capital District Transportation Authority (CDTA)
110 Watervliet Avenue, Albany, NY 12206, USA
Telephone: +1 518 482 1125
Chair: Thomas H Clements
Executive Director: Dennis J Fitzgerald
Director of Transportation: Charles Cohen
Director of Information: Carmino N Basile
Staff: 507

CDTA Crown-Ikarus articulated and Orion buses

Current situation: CDTA was created in 1970 and began operations in 1971 when it assumed responsibility for routes of the Albany-Nassau Bus Co. In 1972 CDTA took over operations of four additional bus companies operating in the four-county service area. Five other counties (Green, Colombia, Montgomery, Fulton and Schoharie) may join the transit district by vote of the county legislature.

CDTA operates local, express and special rural service routes between shopping and government centres. Paratransit service began in 1982 under the name STAR (Special Transit Available by Request). Operated seven days a week, STAR provides kerbside service to persons unable to ride regular fixed-route buses.

Developments: ShuttleBug midibus service introduced in June 1996 links residential areas with suburban office developments. Operating on a 20 min frequency at peak hours, the shuttle serves individual office locations rather than conventional roadside stops.

Bus

Passenger journeys: (1992) 12.5 million
(1993) 10.8 million
(1994) 11.6 million
Vehicle-km: (1991) 10.3 million
(1992) 10.1 million

Number of routes: 60
Route length: 1,070 km
Fleet: 231 vehicles

Orion (1984/89)	192
Orion II (1991/92)	12
Ikarus 286 articulated	6
Orion (1996)	16
Minibuses	5

In peak service: 216

Most intensive service: 5-15 min
One-person operation: All routes
Fare collection: Pay-as-you-enter with GFI electronic fareboxes
Fare structure: Zonal, with additional charges for some longer journeys; free transfers; reduced fare tokens and monthly passes; Express bus, STAR and rural service fares higher
Operational control: Route inspectors with radio cars, buses radio-equipped
Arrangements for elderly/disabled: Half fares (also for unemployed); STAR on-demand service (see above) carried 99,000 passengers in 1994; 28 fixed-route buses have wheelchair lifts
Integration with other modes: 3 CDTA-operated park-and-ride lots have Express bus service to downtown Albany; further 15 lots in shopping malls and other privately owned areas; free transfer to buses of Upstate Transit
Average distance between stops: 154 m
Average peak-hour speed: 19 km/h
Operating costs financed by: Fares 29%, other commercial sources 1%, subsidy/grants 62%
Subsidy from: Mortgage/sales tax 41%, state and FTA grants 59%
New vehicles financed by: FTA and state grants

Other operators

Current situation: Services into Albany from surrounding districts are also operated by Adirondack Trailways (70 buses), Hendrick Hudson Bus Lines and Yankee Trails (48 buses).
Developments: Free transfers introduced 1994 between CDTA and Upstate Transit services.

UPDATED

ALEXANDRIA

Population: 3.5 million
Public transport: Bus, light rail and tram services provided by Transport Authority responsible to Governor of Alexandria; suburban rail service run by state railway (ER); metro proposed

Alexandria Passenger Transport

Alexandria Passenger Transport Authority
2 Aflatone Street, Chatby, PO Box 466, 21111 Alexandria, Egypt
Telephone: +20 3 596 1810/597 5223
Chair: M S E Abd El-moneim
Staff: 8,829 (all modes)

Current situation: Two distinct tramway systems are operated — a network of street-running conventional lines in the west and south of the city and six light rail routes running into a terminus at Ramleh Square from the east.

Passenger journeys: (All modes)
(1986/87) 417.2 million
(1988/89) 396.5 million
(1989/90) 390 million

Operating costs financed by: (All modes)
Fares 66%, other commercial sources 7%, subsidy/grants 27%
Subsidy from: Government

Bus

General Managers
Smouha garage area: Eng Mostafa A Haridy
Sidi-Bishr garage area: Eng Ahmed Abd El-Khalek
New Agamy garage area: Eng Nabil Ibrahim Mikhaiel
Staff: 2,678

Passenger journeys: (1986/87) 161.4 million
(1988/89) 137.5 million
(1989/90) 140 million
Vehicle-km: (1985/86) 27 million
(1988/89) 33 million
(1989/90) 40 million

Number of routes: 93
Route length: 1,557 km
Fleet: 483 vehicles

Saviem/Renault S105	129
Volvo-Saracakis	43
Nasr 411	131
Mercedes (Otomarsan) minibus	20
GM Egypt minibus NPR 59SLJ	160

New vehicles required each year: 75-100

One-person operation: On some minibus routes
Fare collection: Mostly conductors (seated)
Fare structure: Flat, with first and second class
Fare evasion control: Roving inspectors
Average peak-hour speed: 19 km/h
New vehicles financed by: State investments

City Tramway

General Manager: Eng Medhat Hafiz

Type of operation: Conventional tramway

Passenger journeys: (1985/86) 132 million
(1986/87) 137 million
(1989/90) 127 million
Car-km: (1985/86) 5.5 million
(1989/90) 6 million

Route length: 32 km
Number of lines: 16
Gauge: 1,435 mm
Electrification: 600 V DC, overhead

Rolling stock: 159 cars

Duewag articulated (1966 ex-Copenhagen)	M99
Kinki/Toshiba	M15 T15
Ganz-Mávag/Duewag (1986)	M15 T15

Light rail (Ramleh lines)

General Manager: Eng Abdel-Moneim Abdel-Ghani

Type of operation: Light rail, mostly on segregated right-of-way

Passenger journeys: (1985/86) 111 million
(1986/87) 118 million
(1989/90) 123 million
Car-km: 3.5 million (annual)

Route length: 16 km
Number of lines: 6
Gauge: 1,435 mm
Electrification: 600 V DC, overhead

Rolling stock: 48 three-car sets

Kinki Sharyo/Toshiba (1976)	108
Kinki Sharyo (1991)	18
Kinki Sharyo double-deck (1994)	M6
SEMAF (1995)	M12

Developments: Modernisation of track and catenary has been completed, along with installation of electronic signalling. New depot and workshops planned.

It is planned to upgrade the Ramleh lines to urban metro standards.

Egyptian National Railways

Egyptian National Railways
Station Building, Ramses Square, Cairo
Telephone: +20 2 751000 Fax: +20 2 574000

Type of operation: Suburban heavy rail

Current situation: Frequent commuter services are operated to Abou Kir, east of Alexandria, and some commuter use made of other main lines. Services on the Abou Kir line run at 15 min intervals. The five-year plan from 1987 envisaged electrification and further improvements, though little progress has been made. Plans for incorporating this line into the proposed metro have been dropped.

Minibus/shared taxi

Current situation: Extensive minibus/shared taxi system operates carrying some 20% of public transport demand in up to 12-seaters (mostly Japanese-built) operating on fixed routes. A further substantial part of the traffic is carried by a fleet of about 100 full-sized buses operated by individual employers.

Metro (proposed)

Current situation: An east-west metro line is proposed, running from Abou Kir via the city centre to El-Aamreya (55 km). French consultancy Systra was awarded a contract for consultancy services for the whole line, and for design and pre-contract documentation of the 22 km first phase (Abou Kir to Misr).

The planning and construction authority for the line is the National Authority for Tunnels (see Cairo entry).

UPDATED

ALGER

Population: 2.5 million
Public transport: Bus services mostly provided by municipal undertaking serving the city, suburbs and coastal area and which is also responsible for two public elevators and a funicular. Suburban railway operated by Algerian National Railways (SNTF); metro under construction. Further funiculars and cable cars planned. Taxi sharing extensive. Much company-sponsored transport provided privately

RSTA

Regie Syndicale des Transports Algérois (RSTA)
21 rue Alfred De Musset, PO Box 460, 21 Alger, Algeria
Telephone: + 213 2 663375
Staff: 4,000

Bus

Passenger journeys: (Annual) 200 million
Vehicle-km: Approx 48 million (annual)

Number of routes: 55
Route length: 470 km
Fleet: 772 vehicles

Articulated	57
Minibuses	65
Van Hool midibus	150
Van Hool citybus	500

One-person operation: None
Fare collection: Pass or payment to conductor
Fare structure: Stages, with singles, 10-journey carnets, daily, weekly, monthly and annual passes; reductions for large families, students and handicapped
Fares collected on board: 86%

Operational control: Route inspectors/mobile radio
Arrangements for elderly/disabled: Fare reductions; other plans under study
Operating costs financed by: Fares 100%

Funicular

Current situation: One funicular carries about 6.3 million passengers annually. A further seven funiculars and cable cars are planned.

SNTF

Société Nationale des Transports Ferroviaires
21-23 Boulevard Mohamed V, Alger
Telephone: +213 2 711510 Fax: +213 2 619693

Type of operation: Suburban heavy rail

Current situation: Service provided on routes from Alger Maritime to Blida (50 km) and Thenia (54 km) using 228 diesel-hauled push-pull cars.
Developments: The metro (see below) will take over provision of suburban passenger service from SNTF, whose trains will terminate at interchanges at the two southern metro terminals.

Metro

Under construction
Entreprise du Metro d'Alger
13 chemin de Wilaya, No 4 Kouba, Alger
Telephone: +213 2 586768 Fax: +213 2 689705
Director General: H Bellil

Current situation: Construction in progress on initial section of Line 1 (12.5 km, 16 stations) of the long-planned metro; 1,435 mm gauge, electrified 750 V DC third-rail, fleet of 120 cars required. From Oued Koriche in the city centre, a 9 km underground section with 10 stations extends to Hamma where the line will come to the surface and take over existing SNTF tracks to Hai el Badr and a depot at Bachdjarah.

Two other lines are proposed, linking Grande Poste with Bab Exxour (21 km, 18 stations) and Hussein-Bey with Birkhadem (10 km, 6 stations).
Developments: Progress has been slow since local contractors took over work from foreign companies. In June 1994 the project was declared to be of national priority, and consultations were taking place on possible involvement once again of foreign contractors. A request was expected to be made to the European Union at the end of 1994 to provide funding to complete the initial section.

Assuming construction is expedited by overseas contractors, opening would be in three stages — Hai el Badr to Grande Poste in 2000, Grande Poste to Place des Martyrs in 2004, and throughout to Oued Koriche in 2004.

ALMATY

Population: 1.7 million
Public transport: Bus and trolleybus/tramway services run by separate municipal authorities; metro construction suspended.

New Manas SL232 in Almaty ***1997***

Almaty Kalasyinyin Koligi

Almaty Kalasyinyin Koligi
Ul Auezova 64, 480008 Almaty, Kazakhstan
Telephone: +7 3272 420318

Developments: Under a master plan for transport improvements up to 1995, a 20 per cent increase in the electric vehicle fleet size was planned, along with construction of an additional 13 km of tramway and 31 km of trolleybus routes. But this has not taken place, at least as far as the tramway network is concerned, which has been reduced from nine to three routes since 1990. Trolleybus Route 6 extension opened late 1996.

At the end of 1996, rehabilitation of the tramway was announced following an agreement with Skoda Plzen.

Fare structure: Flat (for all modes)
Fare collection: Roving conductor sells one-journey ticket; prepurchase monthly pass

Bus

Passenger journeys: (1989) 441.3 million
Vehicle-km: (1989) 118.6 million

Number of routes: 122
Route length: 2,181 km
Fleet: 1,977 buses, including Ikarus 260/280 (some ex-Berlin), Manas SL232, Mercedes Türk O325, Otoyal M24 midibus, Mercedes O305 (ex-Berlin) and others
In peak service: 1,010
On order: Balance of 443 Turkish-built Manas (MAN) being delivered

Trolleybus

Staff: 1,820

Passenger journeys: (1989) 98.1 million
Vehicle-km: (1989) 18 million

Number of routes: 15
Route length: 426 km
Fleet: 233 trolleybuses
In peak service: 210

Tramway

Staff: 835

Type of operation: Conventional tramway

Passenger journeys: (1989) 47 million
Car-km: (1989) 8.2 million

Number of routes: 3

Rolling stock: 110 cars
Riga RV2-6
Riga RVZ-6M2
KTM-5M

Metro

Under construction

Current situation: Construction started in 1984 of the initial 8.9 km section of Line 1 (12.9 km) of a proposed three-line metro which will extend to some 40 km by 2010. Line 1 runs from Oktyabrskaya in the north through the city centre to a large housing development in the west. The initial section from Oktyabrskaya to Auesova has eight stations and was scheduled to open in 1997; construction is reported as having ceased.

Later Line 1 will be extended to serve Almaty main line station. Line 2 will run east-west, while Line 3 will follow a north-south alignment linking principal industrial districts with the city centre.

UPDATED

AMSTERDAM

Population: 724,000
Public transport: Bus, metro, ferry, light rail and tram services operated by municipal transport department under national operating and financial framework. Suburban rail services provided by Netherlands Railways (NS) and buses by regional bus undertakings

GVB

Gemeentevervoerbedrijf Amsterdam (GVB)
Prins Hendrikkade 108-114, PO Box 2131, 1000 CC Amsterdam, Netherlands
Telephone: +31 20 551 4911 Fax: +31 20 551 4250
General Manager: A Testa
Deputy General Manager: J Tjon A Ten
Manager, Metro/Light Rail: H Bourquin
Manager, Tramway: A M van Hulst
Manager, Bus: Mrs J van Kranendonk
Staff: 3,905

Passenger journeys: (1992) 253 million
(1993) 253.6 million
(1994) 250 million

Operating costs financed by: Fares 24.9%, other commercial sources 4.9%, subsidy/grants 70.2%
Subsidy from: City council, drawing a government contribution based on the number of journeys, and city council (ferries only)

Current situation: Since the early 1970s the Ministry of Transport has undertaken to cover deficits in return for control over fares, ticketing and service quality, and development of overall municipal plans for traffic and transport and rolling five-year plans for public transport.
Developments: GVBA's poor financial situation and other problems led the government to seek an independent assessment of the organisation. A report published in June 1996 highlighted poor management practices and overstaffing. A new general manager was appointed to implement the report's recommendations, which include reducing staff by 600.

Bus

Passenger journeys: (1992) 58.5 million
(1993) 58.3 million
(1994) 56.7 million
Vehicle-km: (1993) 21.2 million

Berkhof articulated bus at Sloterdijk NS interchange

Number of routes: 49 (including 12 peak only and 11 night)
Route length: (One way) 395 km
On priority right-of-way: 34.6 km
Fleet: 275 vehicles

Standard buses	170
Articulated buses	85
Minibuses	10
Coaches	10

Most intensive service: 3 min
One-person operation: All routes
Fare collection: Prepurchase or payment to driver for strip tickets and day tickets, checked by driver. Onboard cancelling machines removed due to evasion problems, with all tickets now stamped by driver or shown
Fare structure: Zonal. Prepurchase weekly, monthly and annual passes, multiday tickets and national Strippenkaart scheme tickets, last also available on board and valid for transfers; 1 h ride-at-will ticket; services operate all night with higher flat fare.

Under the Strippenkaart system, the Netherlands is split into zones of 4.5 km each. National prepurchase season tickets, weekly, monthly and annual, can be bought for one zone or more and used on all buses, metro, tramways and urban railways of all companies in the zone(s) paid for. Single rides can be made with the national Strippenkaart, prepurchased in 15 and 45 strips, or from drivers in 2, 3 and 8 strips, cancelling one strip for each zone, plus one 'boarding fee'
Fare evasion control: Bus driver and roving inspectors; spot fines. Despite this, evasion is estimated to be extensive, with at least 9% of passengers travelling without a ticket and a further 6% over-riding, and as a result supervision by drivers has been stepped up with withdrawal of on-bus cancelling machines and reintroduction of conductors on some tram routes
Operational control: Centralised control through centre linked to buses by mobile radio and with CCTV installed at a number of key points for observation; all buses equipped with VETAG
Average distance between stops: 495 m (intended maximum 5 min walking distance)
Bus priority: 34.6 km of reserved bus lanes and traffic light priority
Average peak-hour speed: 16.5 km/h
Integration with other modes: Interchanges at main stations; fully integrated fares and ticket system

Metro/light rail (sneltram)

Type of operation: Full metro and hybrid metro/light rail (sneltram)

Passenger journeys: (1992) 48.9 million
(1993) 49 million
(1994) 49.7 million

Route length: 40 km
in tunnel: 3.5 km
elevated: 24 km
Number of lines: 3
Number of stations: 40
in tunnel: 5
elevated: 9
Gauge: 1,435 mm
Track: 49 kg/m S 49 rail, wood sleepers on ballast
Tunnel: Mainly concrete caisson
Electrification: 750 V DC, third rail/600 V DC, overhead

Service: Peak 3¾-7½ min, off-peak 5-15 min
First/last train: 05.38/00.22
Fare structure: Nationwide zonal system
Revenue control: Ticket and cancelling machines in all entrances, roving inspectors
One-person operation: All trains up to 3 coupled sets
Central control: All operations monitored from central control room; CCTV on all platforms

Rolling stock: 44 two-car sets, 62 dual-voltage LRVs

Linke-Hofmann-Busch M1 (1973)	M8
Linke-Hofmann-Busch M2 (1976/77)	M66
Linke-Hofmann-Busch M3 (1980)	M14
BN dual-voltage Amstelveen line (1990)	M13
BN dual-voltage (1994)	M12
CAF dual-voltage (1996)	M37

Current situation: Light rail line from Zuid-WTC to Amstelveen (Winkelcentrum) and Middenhoven opened 1990 (see below). The route is electrified at 600 V DC overhead, and is operated by cars with both third rail and overhead current collection to allow through running from the metro. Part of the route, between Amstelveen and Zuid-WTC (5 km), is also used by tram Route 5 (see below).
Developments: A second metro/sneltram opens in June 1997, linking Isolatorweg/Sloterdijk and Zuid-WTC. This forms a ring line round the east, south and west sides of the city. A further stage, now under construction, will see the ring extended from Sloterdijk to Centraal station, with a later extension (the IJ line) proposed to run along the banks of the IJ to the future Nieuw Oost residential area. This is scheduled to open in 2002.

A north-south line is also planned to run from the northern suburbs to Centraal and Zuid-WTC, with a later extension to Schiphol airport proposed. Government funding for this line, which is to be in bored tunnel, was approved in mid-1994 and construction is expected to start in 1997.

Extension of the Amstelveen line to Westwijk is a step nearer to construction after approval of government funding amounting to G36 million in 1996.

New-design tramway stop with real-time passenger information ***1995***

Tramway

Staff: 1,564

Type of operation: Conventional tramway

Passenger journeys: (1992) 145.6 million
(1993) 146.3 million
(1994) 143.6 million

Route length: 138 km
reserved track: 66 km
Number of routes: 17
Number of stops: 564
Gauge: 1,435 mm
Track: Ri60 60 kg/m rail, timber sleepers on concrete or ballast
Electrification: 600 V DC, overhead

Service: Peak 5-9 min, off-peak 6-12 min, evening 10-15 min, weekends 5-15 min
First/last car: 05.45/00.15
Fare structure: As bus and metro; nationwide zonal system
Revenue control: Cancelling machines, roving inspectors, conductors
One-person operation: On 12 lines, conductors on lines 4, 6, 7, 10 and 13
Centralised control: Mobile radio contact between drivers and control room; automatic vehicle location and control on all lines, with countdown to departure information in cabs and real-time punctuality data displayed at stops. VETAG/VECOM detection system for traffic light priority, points control and vehicle identification

Rolling stock: 250 tramcars

Bijnes (1957/58/59/61/62)	M59
Werkspoor (1964/66/67/68)	M71
LHB (1974/75/79/80/81)	M75
BN (1989/90/91)	M45

Developments: Line 2 extended in 1994 to new residential areas in the western suburbs; further extension

Route 5 cars pass on the section also served by the Amstelveen sneltram route ***1997***

planned. Other proposed routes under consideration are to the old docklands area in east Amsterdam and to the University/Hospital area in the south. The initial stage of the sneltram ring route on the south and west opens in June 1997. Circular tram Route 8 inaugurated March 1997. Construction of new depot at Diemen started early 1995 for 1997 completion.

Ferry

Current situation: Frequent service operated by nine vessels on three cross-IJ routes over 1.4 km; one route runs 24 h service. Subsidies are provided by the city council.

NS

Netherlands Railways
PO Box 2025, 3500 HA Utrecht
Telephone: +31 30 235 9111 Fax: +31 30 233 2458

Type of operation: Suburban heavy rail

Current situation: Suburban and interurban services, electrified at 1.5 kV DC, radiate from Amsterdam Centraal station on several routes and carry heavy traffic. Nine stations within city boundaries served by 3 to 31 trains hourly, with more at peak times.

Because of the dense pattern of NS operations, differentiation of 'suburban' services is hard; no distinction is made by NS, nor separate traffic figures kept. Stations within city boundaries are included in the Strippenkaart system, and are used as alternatives to bus and trams, particularly for interchange with other NS services. There is also much longer distance commuting.

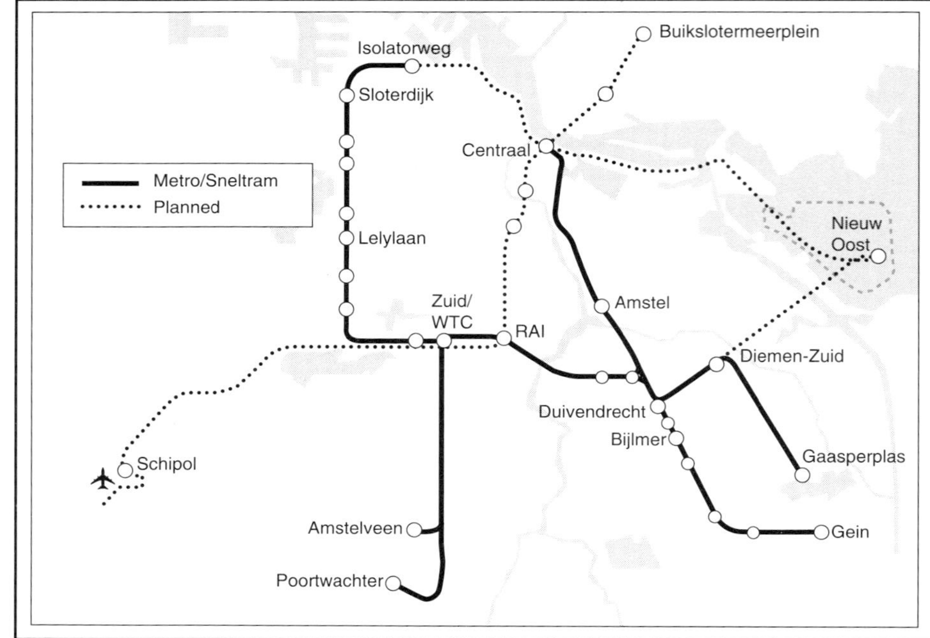

Amsterdam's metro and sneltram

Developments: Two extra tracks between Sloterdijk and Centraal are now in service, while an extra platform at Amsterdam Centraal is being built for 1998 completion. The Amsterdam—Hoofddorp portion of the Amsterdam—Schiphol—Leiden line will gain two extra tracks by 2001, while Schiphol station will have three new tracks, the first of which opened in 1994. Several other capacity schemes are planned for the period 2000 to 2005.

ANCHORAGE

Population: 250,000
Public transport: Fixed-route bus services and paratransit provided by municipal agency

Anchorage Transit System

Anchorage Transit System, Municipality of Anchorage
PO Box 196650, 3560 East Tudor Road, Anchorage, AK 99519-6650, USA
Telephone: +1 907 343 8402 Fax: +1 907 563 2206
Director of Transit: Bob Kniefel
Operating Manager: Gary Taylor
Staff: 136

Current situation: The Anchorage Transit System is known as People Mover.

Bus

Passenger boardings: (1991) 3.2 million
(1992) 3 million
(1994) 3 million
Vehicle-km: (1991) 3.5 million
(1992) 3.5 million
(1994) 3.2 million

Number of routes: 18
Route length: (One way) 616 km
Fleet: 81 buses

Flyer D901 (1981/83)	30
GMC T6H 5307N (1984)	21
Chrysler Maxivan (1994)	12
New Flyer D40 low-floor (1995)	18

In peak service: 39
Average age of fleet: 10.4 years

Flyer D901 heads for Downtown on People Mover Route 45 ***1997***

Most intensive service: 30 min
One-person operation: All routes
Fare collection: Payment to farebox
Fare structure: Flat; 10 cent transfer; prepurchase tokens and monthly passes
Fare evasion control: Driver supervision
Operational control: Shift supervisors
Arrangements for elderly/disabled: Services provided to ADA standards; 75% discount on regular fares
Integration with other modes: Rideshare programme promotes carpools by providing matchlists with employer's help; funding from Federal Highway Administration grant; 837 pools, with 1,730 members; six park-and-ride lots served by Express buses to downtown
Operating costs financed by: Fares 17%, other commercial sources 3%, subsidy/grants 18%, tax levy 62%
Subsidy from: FTA and state grants, Municipal property tax
New vehicles financed by: FTA and state grants

UPDATED

ANKARA

Population: 2.6 million
Public transport: Municipally owned authority operates bus and light metro services. Suburban rail services operated by State Railway. Also private operation of 'Minibus-Dolmus' services and conventional buses. Metro under construction

EGO

General Directorate of Electricity, Gas & Bus Management

Elektrik, Gaz ve Otobüs Işletmesi Genel Müdürlüğü (EGO)
PO Box 294, Toros Sok No 20, Maltepe-Ankara, Turkey
Telephone: +90 312 231 7180 Fax: +90 312 231 8109
General Director: Omar Vebhi Hatipoğlu
Staff: 4,389

Current situation: EGO accounts for about 26 per cent of daily motorised trips. There is substantial overcrowding, and considerable passenger waits are experienced, especially in peak hours. There has been pressure to maintain low fares despite high demand, but fares were increased three times in 1994 due to the high rate of inflation. Some areas of low demand are now served by the midibuses acquired in 1991.

A further 252 Ikarus buses were added to the fleet in 1992 and a further 100 conventional buses are being supplied by BMC Beldesan, fitted with equipment for easy access by disabled people.

Bus

Passenger journeys: (1992) 283 million
(1993) 294 million
(1994) 282 million

Vehicle-km: (1992) 72 million
(1993) 72.5 million
(1994) 78.7 million

Number of routes: 345 (regular 304, express 41)
Route length: (One way) 4,050 km
Fleet: 1,559 buses

Mercedes O302	190
MAN standard	452
MAN articulated	50
Ikarus 280 articulated	401
Ikarus 260 standard	396
BMC Beldesan	50
Isuzu midibus (1991)	20

In peak service: 921
New vehicles required each year: 285

Most intensive service: 4 min
One-person operation: All routes
Fare collection: Prepurchase tickets/monthly passes with ticket box on vehicles
Fare structure: Flat; prepurchase full fare tickets, reduced-rate student tickets, monthly passes, transfer card
Fares collected on board: None; all hold monthly passes (11%), student monthly passes (5%), single tickets (33%), student tickets (32%), reduced rate passes (14%), other methods (5%)
Fare evasion control: By driver; 10 × standard fare surcharge
Operational control: At terminal and dispatching points and by route inspectors
Average peak-hour speed: In mixed traffic, 12-15 km/h; express services, 20-25 km/h
Operating costs financed by: Fares 72%, other commercial sources 12%, subsidy/grants 16%
Subsidy from: Municipality of Greater Ankara
New vehicles financed by: Municipality

Light metro

Type of operation: Light metro, opened 1995

Route length: 8.6 km
Number of lines: 1
Number of stations: 11
Gauge: 1,435 mm
Electrification: 750 V DC third rail

Rolling stock: 33 cars
Breda/Siemens (1994/95) M33

Current situation: This light metro, built as part of the metro project (see below), opened at the end of December 1995. It runs on fully segregated (mostly underground) alignment along the main east-west highway linking Dikimevi with Bohçeliever and the ASOT bus terminal. There are 11 stations, that at Kizilay in the city centre providing interchange with the metro.

Four other lines totalling 13.4 km are proposed.

Metro

Under construction

Current situation: Studies initiated under the Ankara Master Plan in 1986 produced a scheme for a metro and light rail system. The 1994 revision envisages a 130 km network comprising metro (44.5 km), light rail (22 km) and suburban rail (63.5 km), to be in full operation by 2015.

The initial 14.6 km route with 12 stations now under construction will link Kizilay in the city centre with new residential areas at Batikent in the west, running along the congested Atatürk Boulevard. The line will be fully segregated and capable of handling 31,500 passengers/h in each direction on opening, rising to 63,000/h in later stages.

Negotiations for a design, construction and operation agreement with the Canadian/Turkish consortium Bombardier/UTDC/Lavalin/Gama/Güris were concluded and construction started in 1991. Power supply equipment is being supplied by Alcatel Alsthom's Cegelec Projects division. A fleet of 108 cars is being delivered by Bombardier; opening is scheduled for November 1997.

TCDD

Türkiye Cumhuriyeti Devlet Demiryollari
Işletmesi Genel Müdürlüğü
06330 Gar, Ankara
Telephone: +90 312 309 0515 Fax: +90 312 312 3215

Natural gas-powered MAN bus of EGO at Kizilay **1995**

Dolmus bus station at Ulus in Ankara

One of Özel Halk's MAN double-decks on Ataturk Boulevard **1996**

Ankara's light metro cars **1995**

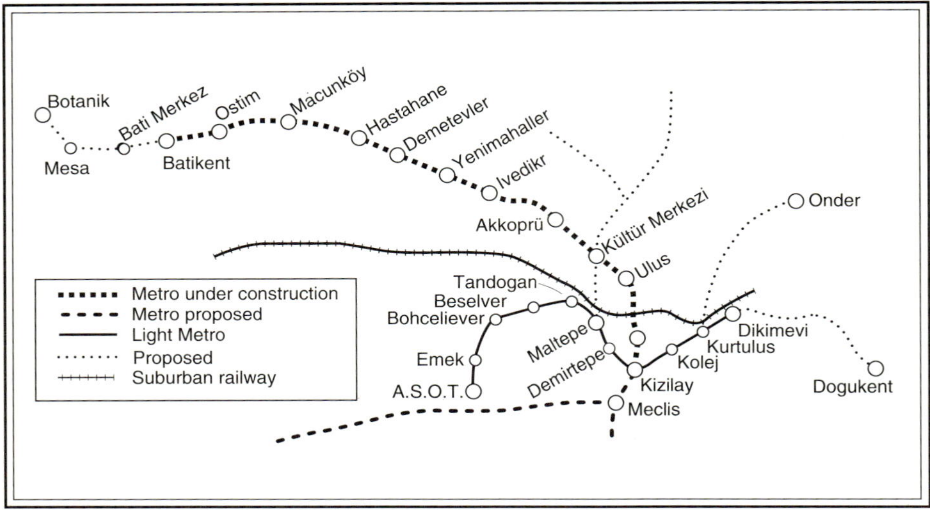

Ankara's metro and light metro projects

Manager, Suburban: Feridun Akyüz

Suburban railway

Type of operation: Suburban heavy rail

Passenger journeys: (1993) 19.2 million
(1994) 13.8 million
(1995) 15.2 million

Current situation: Suburban operations extend over a 37 km route from Sincan through central Ankara to Kayas with 28 stations, electrified 25 kV 50 Hz. Flat-fare system.
Developments: Track-quadrupling between Ankara and Sincan was completed in 1994, with resignalling and other works to raise capacity finished in late 1996. Feasibility studies have been carried out for introduction of double-deck trains in Ankara and Istanbul, and 11 six-car sets are expected to be ordered by 1997.

Rolling stock: 26 emu trains

Private buses

Passenger journeys: (1992) 51 million
(1993) 53 million
(1994) 54.2 million

Current situation: 18 private bus routes operate with some 200 conventional vehicles, accounting for about 5 per cent of daily motorised trips. Their numbers and routes are regulated by the city's transport co-ordination body UKOME. Many other local operators also run services into Ankara from the surrounding area.

An additional 3,500 private buses are contracted by government institutions and some private firms for staff transport to work. Their numbers have increased substantially recently, and they now account for 18 per cent of daily motorised trips.

Developments: A group of new express bus routes was introduced in 1995 between Ataturk Bulvari, close to the city centre, and outlying suburbs, using MAN three-axle double-decks and run by private operator Ankara Özel Halk Otobusleri.

Minibus/shared taxi

Current situation: Over 2,200 Dolmus vehicles are operated by private owners providing services on 35 fixed routes mainly in outer suburbs, with numbers and routes subject to restriction by UKOME. Vehicles are 14-16 seaters, mainly Deutz chassis with Otokar bodies. They account for about 25 per cent of daily motorised trips.

Some 7,000 taxis operate, sometimes on a shared basis, accounting for about 5 per cent of daily trips, compared with 18 per cent by private cars.

UPDATED

ANSHAN

Population: 1.4 million, municipal area 3.3 million
Public transport: Municipal bus, trolleybus and tram services, also electrified passenger railway operated by the Anshan Steel Co. No detailed reports have been received for some time but it is assumed that the municipal organisation remains that of an umbrella undertaking, Anshan Public Transport Corp, with two operating subsidiaries — Anshan City Bus Company (bus only) and Anshan City Electric Traction Company (trolleybus and tram) — sharing responsibility for service provision with the City Planning Bureau. It is likely that some paratransit has been introduced, and there may also be competing or complementary bus services of other operators

Articulated trolleybus operation

Anshan City Bus

Anshan City Bus Company
Anshan, Liaoning Province, People's Republic of China

Current situation: A network of numbered services with its hub at the main railway station covers the city centre and various suburbs to the northeast, south and west, the entire northern quarter of the city being occupied by the steel plant. Many routes continue to more distant suburbs.

Bus

Number of routes: 24 (5 cross-city, 17 radial, 2 peripheral)
Fleet: Approx 300 buses, many articulated, mostly supplied by local builders
Fare collection: Cash payment to seated conductors, monthly passes
Fare structure: Stage
Integration with other modes: Central bus station located close to the main rail station, which is also served by trolleybus and tram routes and the electric railway, but there is no purpose-built interchange. Most radial and cross-city journeys can be made without change of mode or even vehicle, although two peripheral bus routes feed the tramway at its Taipingcun terminus. Monthly all-mode and trolleybus/tram passes available

Dalian-built tramcars in Anshan

Anshan City Electric Traction

Anshan City Electric Traction Company
Anshan

Current situation: The trolleybus network, consisting of two cross-city routes with a long common section linking northeast, southeast and northwest suburbs and a rectangular route in the southwest quarter, has remained static since the mid-1980s, although fleet modernisation has taken place. The single tram route, which links northeastern and southern suburbs with the city centre and the eastern periphery of the steel plant, has not changed for many years, and the 13 trams built at Dalian around 1984 have not been followed by any more new cars. Trams dating from the late 1950s remain the mainstay of the fleet.

Trolleybus

Number of routes: 3
Route length: 25 km
Fleet: Over 100 articulated trolleybuses, recent deliveries are Shenyang SY561

Service: Every few minutes early morning to mid-evening
Fare collection: Cash payment to seated conductors, monthly passes
Fare structure: Stage

Tramway
Type of operation: Conventional tramway

Route length: 12.9 km
Number of routes: 1
Number of stops: 19
Gauge: 1,435 mm
Track: Railway type on side reservation and in centre of street
Electrification: 600 V DC, overhead

Service: Every few minutes, early morning to evening; extra cars run to cater for steel plant shift workers
Fare collection: Payment to roving conductors, monthly passes
Fare structure: Two flat-fare zones

Rolling stock: Approx 70 Dalian-built four-axle motored cars

Anshan Steel Co
Current situation: A public passenger service is operated over about 30 km of essentially industrial trackage with 22 stations. A circle line is electrified at 1.5 kV DC and a short branch line is diesel-worked. Irregular service to suit shift patterns at the steelworks. Industrial locomotives haul main line coaches.

ANTWERPEN
Population: 529,000
Public transport: Bus and tramway/pre-metro services operated by publicly owned regional undertaking. An independent company operates five routes under contract. Suburban rail services operated by state railway

De Lijn (VVM)
Vlaamse Vervoermaatschappij (VVM)
Grotehondstraat 58, 2018 Antwerpen, Belgium
Telephone: +32 3 218 1411 Fax: +32 3 218 1500
Managing Director: L De Kesel
Operating Manager: D Swerts
Staff: 1,710

Passenger journeys: (All modes, Antwerpen urban area)
(1993) 57 million
(1994) 57 million
(1995) 55 million

Operating costs financed by: (All modes) fares 38.5%, other commercial sources 2.7%, government subsidy/grants 58.8%

Current situation: In 1991, control of urban and regional public transport in the Vlaanderen region passed to VVM, known as De Lijn, which took over the former urban and national (SNCV) networks in the area. VVM is also responsible for all operations of the former National Bus Company (NMBV/SNCV) in Flemish-speaking regions. De Lijn Antwerpen's bus operation extends to 45 routes operated by a fleet of 426 vehicles, while a further 31 routes are contracted to private operators. Details below refer to Antwerpen urban operations only.
Developments: Following opening of the latest section of pre-metro (underground tramway) in April 1996 (see below), plans for more tunnelling are in doubt and some completed sections may not now be opened.

Route 12 car loading at Centraal station ***1995***

Bus
Passenger journeys: (1993) 22 million
(1994) 20 million
(1995) 18 million

Vehicle-km: (1993) 6.9 million
(1994) 7 million
(1995) 7.1 million

Number of routes: 22
Route length: One-way 228 km, of which 109 km under contract (see below)
On priority right-of-way: 3.2 km
Fleet: 110 buses, plus 29 Mercedes on services under contract (see below)

Jonckheere-Mercedes O305 'TransCity' (1986)	80
Van Hool A300	30

In peak service: 82
New vehicles required each year: 11

Most intensive service: 10 min
One-person operation: All routes
Fare collection: Prepurchase multiride tickets, single-ride tickets only from driver; Prodata magnetic ticketing system
Fare structure: Flat 1-h tariff with free transfers, with 36% discount for prepurchase of 8-ride multiride tickets (part of national scheme) and variety of day/period passes and tourist cards
Fares collected on board: (Bus and tram) single tickets 13%, multiride 39%, passes 26%, pupil season tickets 22%
Fare evasion control: Drivers and inspectors
Integration with other modes: Integration of services with tramway and regional bus lines
Operational control: Route inspectors/mobile radio; new radio system to be installed
Bus priority: 4 bus lanes totalling 3.2 km
Average distance between stops: 441 m, with some exceptions up to 1.4 km
Average peak-hour speed: In mixed traffic, less than 12 km/h
Operating costs financed by: Fares 28.5%, other commercial sources 2.1%, subsidy 69.43%
New vehicles financed by: Loans

Route 2 car emerging from the Scheldt tunnel in Linkeroever ***1997***

Bus (contracted)
Current situation: Five contracted routes totalling 109 km are operated with 29 buses by the De Polder company which is paid a per-km fee. A standard livery is used.

Tramway/Pre-metro
Rolling Stock Manager: M Verdonck
Fixed Installations Manager: A Wittemans

Type of operation: Pre-metro, light rail, conventional tramway

Passenger journeys: (1993) 35 million
(1994) 37 million
(1995) 37 million
Car-km: (1993) 7.6 million
(1994) 7.3 million
(1995) 7.3 million

Route length: Pre-metro 7.6 km; tramway/light rail 101 km
in tunnel: 7.6 km (pre-metro)
on private right-of-way: 48.9 km light rail (in city 16.9 km, in suburbs 32 km)
Number of lines: Pre-metro 2, conventional 8
Number of stations: Pre-metro 6
Gauge: 1,000 mm
Track: 61.7 kg/m grooved or 50 kg/m flat-bottomed (vignole) rail, timber sleepers on ballast; 530 m section on concrete sleepers with resilient pads
Max gradient: 6%
Minimum curve radius: 18 m, new track 25 m
Tunnel: Bored double-track and cut-and-cover; new work shield tunnelling, single-track; stations built by roof pipe-jacking
Electrification: 600 V DC, overhead

Service: Peak 4-6 min, off-peak 15 min
First/last car: 0430/0100
Fare structure: Flat (see above)
Revenue control: Prepurchase of tickets encouraged by discount; cancelling machines on board
Integration with other modes: As bus
Operating costs financed by: Fares 42.5%, other commercial sources 3.7%, government subsidy 53.8%
One-person operation: All tram lines

Rolling stock: 166 cars

BN PCC (1960/61)	M39
BN PCC (1962)	M22
BN PCC (1966)	M40
BN PCC (1969/70)	M25
BN PCC (1974/75)	M40
Works cars	M8 T12

In peak service: 124

Developments: Further 8.1 km of pre-metro completed and awaiting track-laying as funds become available; eventual total will be 15.6 km with 21 or 22 stations (but see above). Further sections will open depending on design considerations and availability of finance. Preparatory studies made for further tramway extensions, based on studies completed in 1991.

Modernisation started 1989 of 105 PCC tramcars, which are being equipped with chopper control to improve operating characteristics for pre-metro routes.

Tram Route 3 has been upgraded to light rail standards, and extended to Linkeroever; futher extension from Astridplein to Sportpaleis opened April 1996, and extension to Zwijndrecht now approved. New depot under construction at Punt aan de Lijn.

SNCB

Belgian National Railways (SNCB/NMBS), North-East District
Koningin Astridplein 27, 2018 Antwerpen
Telephone: +32 3 204 2111 Fax: +32 3 204 2900

Type of operation: Suburban heavy rail

Current situation: Local services run about hourly on five routes out of Antwerpen Centraal, electrified 3 kV DC.

UPDATED

ASHGABAT

Population: 500,000
Public transport: Bus and trolleybus services provided by municipal operators

Trolleybus

Current situation: Seven routes have been identified, but many streets are equipped with wires, but have no service. There is a fleet of about 30 Uritsky ZIU9s, plus a few Dniepropetrovsk PMZ, 10 ZIU10s and 3 LAZ 52522.

Bus

Current situation: Standard buses, mostly Ikarus 260/262/280 plus some LAZ 697R, are supplemented by a fleet of Iranian-bodied TAM midibuses. The latter also run fixed routes, some of which are shared with buses.

There are also two fleets of minibuses, Iranian-built on Iveco or Irankhodro chassis.

UPDATED

Irankhodro Mercedes-type minibuses at Azadi
1997

ASUNCIÓN

Population: 460,000
Public transport: Bus and minibus services provided by private individual operators and groups. Government-operated tramway

Bus/Minibus

Services under supervision of:
Seccion Transporte Publico
Direccion de Transporte Municipalidad
Oliva 579, Asunción, Paraguay
Telephone: +595 21 47719

Current situation: Extensive private bus operation largely employs 35-40 seat midibuses.

Passenger journeys: Bus 85 million, minibus 95 million (annual)
Vehicle-km: Bus 17 million, minibus 29 million (annual)

Number of routes: 37; bus 25, minibus 12
Route length: Bus 340 km, minibus 220 km
Fleet: About 1,000 vehicles (650 minibuses) including substantial numbers of Volvo 375 and some Henschel buses. Most popular mini/midibuses are Mercedes-Benz 608 derivatives and Austins
Fare collection: Mobile conductors
Fare structure: 2 zonal rates (city centre and elsewhere)

ATE

Administración de Transporte Electrico

Tramway

Type of operation: Conventional tramway

Buses of independent operators in Asunción ***1997***

Passenger journeys: 1.6 million (annual)

Current situation: A 5 km route remains, re-equipped with former Bruxelles cars. A 1983 consultants' study recommended retention and modernisation of the network. Infrastructure remains intact on two other routes, but rolling stock shortages prevent operation of a second route.

Developments: Service was suspended in 1994, though the line is not officially closed. Only one car is reported as being in working order.

Rolling stock: 5 cars

BN 9000 (ex-Bruxelles)	M5

ATHENS

Population: 3.6 million

Public transport: Three independent state-owned companies, ETHEL, ILPAP and ISAP, operate buses, trolleybuses and suburban rail services respectively. A fourth, OASA, is responsible for overall planning of public transport, and for the financial support of the three operating companies; metro under construction

OASA

Urban Transport Organisation of Athens
15 Metsovou Street, 10682 Athens, Greece
Telephone: +30 1 823 6566 Fax: +30 1 821 2219
Director, Planning & Development: P Kontogianis

Operating costs financed by: Fares 39%, other commercial sources 18%, government subsidy 43%

Current situation: OASA was established in 1993 as successor to the similar body OAS. It is responsible for transport planning throughout the city, for financial support of the three operating companies, and for marketing and promotion. OASA's subsidiary ETHEL was created in 1994 to operate all bus services.

Developments: Since abolition of the morning peak-hour fare-free experiment on the bus networks, a uniform fares structure now covers all buses and operators, with a greatly reduced number of free passes. Tickets and passes are sold only in kiosks and all vehicles are now equipped with cancelling machines.

In 1995, private cars were banned from the ancient city centre during daytime, reducing vehicle movements by some 70,000 daily.

ETHEL

Urban Transport Corporation (ETHEL SA)
166 Ionias Ave, Kato Patisia, 11144 Athens
Telephone: +30 1 223 5901
Fax: +30 1 223 6324/201 7447
President: Tsoufis Ioannis
Staff: 8,796

Current situation: Set up in 1994, ETHEL replaced the bankrupt former operator EAS and eight private companies. It runs all the city's bus services, except the ISAP feeder routes.

Bus

Passenger boardings: (1995) 469.3 million
Vehicle-km: (1995) 106.7 million

Number of routes: 326
Route length: (One way) 4,143 km
Fleet: 1,842 vehicles

Chavdar B-13-20 (Balkancar, Bulgaria)	300
Magirus-Deutz M230E 120	300
Ikarus 260	1,047
Volvo B10M articulated	100
Leyland Olympian double-deck	20
Van Hool 507 minibus	33
Others	42

In peak service: 1,644

Most intensive service: 5 min
One-person operation: 100%
Fare collection: Cancelling machines

Five-car set of ISAP 1994 stock built by Hellenic Shipyards ***1995***

Fare structure: Flat; monthly passes
Fare evasion control: Roving inspectors
Average peak-hour speed: 12 km/h
Operational control: 300 bus controllers; computer monitoring planned
Operating costs financed by: Fares 27%, government subsidy/grants 50%, other sources 23%

Developments: A pilot project has seen particulate trap oxidisers fitted to 125 buses, and all buses were to be so equipped over a three-year period to 1995.

Purchases of 250 new buses a year started in 1991 to eliminate over-age vehicles from the fleet. Procurement of 614 buses by leasing was agreed in 1994.

It is planned to increase the number of depots from six to seven. A low-capacity body workshop, where over 400 vehicles have been rebuilt since 1984, is to be expanded into a general overhaul shop able to turn out two fully overhauled buses per day.

ILPAP

Athens-Piraeus Area Electric Buses (ILPAP)
Kirkis & Achaias Street, New Philadelphia, 14342 Athens
Telephone: +30 1 218 3300/3301 Fax: +30 1 253 3030
General Manager: K Kokkoris
Staff: 2,055

Current situation: ILPAP operates the largest trolleybus fleet in western Europe. Environmental advantages favour trolleybuses; accordingly most of the routes serve the central business district.

Developments: Several route extensions and alterations were made in 1995, including prolongment of Route 1 to Moscháto station on the ISAP railway. Three new routes are under construction in the Petralona, Nikea and Halandri areas. A new fleet of 200 trolleybuses is planned.

Trolleybus

Passenger journeys: (1992) 95 million
(1993) 80 million
(1995) 95 million
Vehicle-km: (1992) 11.3 million
(1993) 10.4 million
(1995) 11 million

Number of routes: 18
Route length: 148 km
Fleet: 357 trolleybuses

Uritsky ZIU9 (1977-83)	176
Uritsky ZIU9B1 (1984-85)	80
Uritsky ZIU683B	1
Uritsky ZIU9Bur	100

In peak service: 212

Most intensive service: 5 min
One-person operation: 100%
Fare collection: Prepurchase ticket or monthly pass; cancelling machines on board
Fare structure: Flat; monthly passes
Fare evasion control: Random inspection
Operational control: Route inspectors; mobile radio
Average peak-hour speed: 11 km/h
Operating costs financed by: Fares 28%, other commercial sources 24%, government subsidy/grants 48%
New vehicles financed by: Loans, barter deals

Route 9 trolleybus Petralona-bound on Veikou Street ***1997***

ISAP

Athens-Piraeus Electric Railways Co Ltd
Ilektriki Sidirodromi Athinon-Pireos AE (ISAP)
67 Athinas Street, 10552 Athens
Telephone: +30 1 324 9102 Fax: +30 1 322 3935
General Manager: Panagiotis Lampos
Operating Manager: C Xigakis

Operating costs financed by: Fares 40.5%, other commercial sources 12%, subsidy/grants 47.5%

Current situation: ISAP operates the Athens-Piraeus Electric Railway linking Kifissia in the north with Athens and Piraeus, which is to become Line 1 of the metro (see below). It also runs a small complementary bus network.

Developments: Several projects are under way as the railway prepares for its new role as Line 1 of the metro. A deviation between Faliro and Piraeus will bring the line to a new underground terminal at the port. It is planned to equip the route with the LZB automatic train protection system to raise train frequency above the current 3½ min headway. Older rolling stock will be phased out in favour of the newer metro-style cars on order for Lines 2 and 3 (see below).

Suburban rail

Staff: 1,269

Type of operation: Suburban rapid transit

Passenger boardings: (1993) 82.7 million
(1994) 84.3 million
(1995) 86.8 million

Route length: 25.8 km
in tunnel: 3 km
Number of lines: 1
Number of stations: 23
in tunnel: 3
Gauge: 1,435 mm
Track: Timber sleepers on ballast
Max gradient: 4%
Minimum curve radius: 160 m
Tunnel: Cut-and-cover
Electrification: 750 V DC, third rail

Service: Peak 3½ min
First/last train: 05.00/01.00
Fare collection: Ticket cancelling machines at entry
Fare structure: Metro, zonal; bus, flat with monthly passes

Rolling stock: 227 cars

Wooden-bodied cars (1904)	M3 T3
MAN/Siemens (1958)	M16 T16
MAN/Siemens (1968)	M9 T9
MAN/Siemens/LEW (1983)	M44 T29
LEW G3 (1984)	M48
MAN/Siemens/Hellenic (1994/95)	M30 T20

In peak service: 140

Bus

Staff: 286

Passenger boardings: (1993) 20.7 million
(1994) 19 million
(1995) 18.3 million

Current situation: Seven routes are operated, extending to 67 route-km, with a fleet of 63 buses.

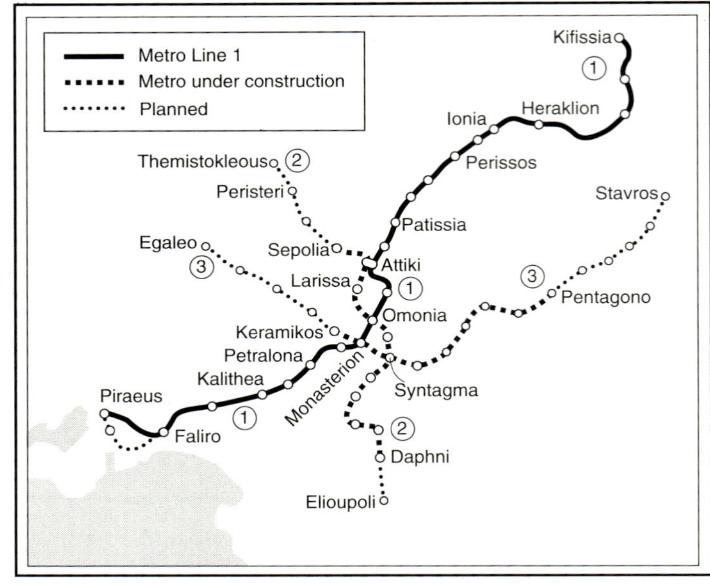

Athens-Piraeus Railway (Metro Line 1) and lines under construction

Attiko Metro

Attiko Metro AE
191-193 Messogion Avenue, 11525 Athens
Telephone: +30 1 679 2399 Fax: +30 1 672 6126
Chief Executive Officer: Theodore G Weigle Jr
Projects Department Manager: William G Leunig
Chief of Construction: Gerry Morneau
Chief of Public Relations: Yiannis P Dokos

Current situation: Construction started 1992 on Lines 2 and 3 of a three-line network (Line 1 being the existing Athens-Piraeus Railway). Line 2 will link Sepolia with Daphni (9.2 km), while Line 3 will run from Keramikos to Pentagono (8.4 km); 1,435 mm gauge, electrified 750 V DC third rail; total 21 stations.

Attiko Metro is a private company set up in 1992 to own and manage the metro. Design and construction is in the hands of a 26-member consortium known as Olympic Metro and headed by Siemens, Interinfra, GEC Alsthom, AEG and MAN with local partners; Bechtel International is the consultant. Consortium members are also building 56 three-car trains required for start of services in 1999. Initially, the lines will be signalled for manual operation at 2½ min headways, reducing to 1½ min when ATO is installed later. Ridership of 450,000 daily is expected in the first phase of operation.

Ten extensions totalling 44.3 km were assessed in planning studies completed in 1993, and four – including a deviation of Line 1 between Faliro and Piraeus – have been approved by the government for construction before the end of the century. These total 13.2 km with 12 stations.

Also now proposed is a circular city-centre light rail distributor, with a possible branch to the coast at Faliro and routes thence along the coast west to Kastella on Line 1 and southeast to the airport and Vouliagmeni.

UPDATED

ATLANTA

Population: 1.2 million
Public transport: Bus and metro services provided in Fulton and De Kalb counties and city of Atlanta by Transit Authority governed by 17-member representative board. Bus services in adjacent Cobb County link with metro; commuter rail proposed

MARTA

Metropolitan Atlanta Rapid Transit Authority (MARTA)
2424 Piedmont Avenue, Atlanta, GA 30324, USA
Telephone: +1 404 848 5000 Fax: +1 404 848 5320
General Manager: Richard J Simonetta
Deputy General Manager: D L Brown
Assistant General Manager, Bus: D Huber
Assistant General Manager, Rail: T Williams
Assistant General Manager, Transit System Development: Carolyn Wylder
Staff: 4,235

Passenger boardings: (1994) 142.7 million
(1995) 143.7 million
(1996) 144.8 million

Indian Creek terminal on the East line

Current situation: MARTA, created in 1965, became an operating agency in 1972 when it purchased the privately owned Atlanta Transit System following the approval in 1971 of a 1 per cent sales tax in Fulton and De Kalb counties and the city of Atlanta, to apply until 2012 (later extended to 2032). The tax was rejected in Clayton and Gwinnett counties, and Cobb County declined to join altogether. The referendum mandated acquisition of ATS and provision of improved bus services, as well as construction of a 100 km metro network. No more than 50 per cent of the annual tax yield may be used to subsidise operating costs. Revenue bonds have been raised against the future tax yield to cover capital costs.

In 1989 an agreement was reached with Cobb County for through ticketing and interchange with metro services.

As each metro line opens MARTA has integrated bus and rail, with bus routes diverted to feed rail lines. The result has been a significant reduction in bus traffic in the central business district. Long-term plans approved 1986 for metro expansion outside the current service district based on interest expressed by both public and private sectors in surrounding communities. This would add a further 28 km to the network under a 10-year development programme, dependent upon federal funding.

Developments: Activity during 1996 was mainly directed towards preparations for the Olympic Games in July, when 24-hour service was run over a 17-day period. The metro bore the brunt of the additional traffic of some 800,000 passengers daily instead of the usual 475,000. A Federal grant of $15 million was made towards the cost of hiring-in 1,485 buses from undertakings all over the USA. A total of 17.8 million journeys was made during the 17-day event.

AVL is being installed on buses, along with bus-stop announcement and passenger counting system. A fleet of 200 CNG-powered buses will be in service by 2000.

Operating costs financed by: Fares 35%, other commercial sources 7%, subsidy/grants 5%, sales tax 53%
Subsidy from: FTA
New vehicles financed by: FTA grants (80%) with local matching funds

Bus

Passenger boardings: (1994) 72.9 million
(1995) 73.3 million
(1996) 72.4 million
Vehicle-km: (1996) 29.8 million

MARTA buses on special events service

Number of routes: 156
Route length: 2,526 km
Fleet: 704 vehicles

Flxible Metro (1986/87/88)	272
New Flyer (1990)	160
New Flyer 35 ft (1990/92)	103
New Flyer low-floor (1994)	51
New Flyer low-floor CNG (1996)	118

In peak service: 586

Most intensive service: 6 min
One-person operation: All routes
Fare collection: GFI registering fareboxes
Fare structure: Flat, with free transfer within service area and to metro; transfer charge on 3 routes into Clayton and Gwinnett counties. Isolated higher fares outside regular service area. Weekly and monthly passes; tokens
Fare evasion control: Driver surveillance, electronic fareboxes
Operational control: Route inspectors/mobile radio; all buses radio-equipped; AVL on 250 buses
Arrangements for elderly/disabled: E-Bus is special door-to-door service for elderly; L-Van for disabled; half fare on regular routes at all times; wheelchair lift-equipped vans and conventional buses with kneeling capability used on request; 82% of buses wheelchair accessible
Integration with other modes: Unified bus/metro fare system with free transfers. All bus routes feed at least one metro station; 9 park-and-ride lots with 2,386 spaces
Average distance between stops: 152 m
Average peak-hour speed: Mixed traffic, 15.3 km/h

Metro

Type of operation: Full metro, first line opened 1979

Passenger boardings: (1994) 69.8 million
(1995) 70.4 million
(1996) 72.4 million
Car-km: (1996) 59.4 million

Route length: 62.9 km
Number of lines: 3
Number of stations: 36
Gauge: 1,435 mm
Track: 52.1 kg/m 119RE continuously welded rail on concrete sleepers; elastomer springing under track in residential areas to reduce vibration; screens on surface and elevated sections to reduce noise

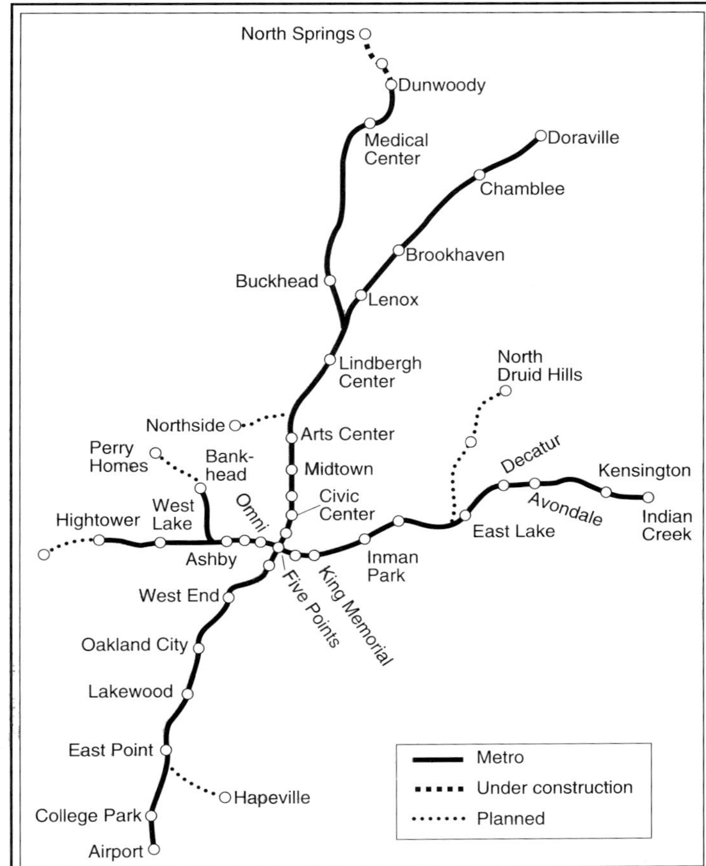

Atlanta metro

Max gradient: 3%
Minimum curve radius: 230 m
Electrification: 750 V DC, third rail

Service: 8 min
First/last train: 04.30/01.00
Fare structure: As bus
Revenue control: Automatic turnstiles accept coins, tokens, magnetic transfer tickets, smartcards and weekly and monthly passes; CCTV at all stations, which are unstaffed
Integration with other modes: Bus feeder services to all stations; 24 park-and-ride stations with 20,000 spaces
Arrangements for elderly/disabled: All stations wheelchair accessible
Signalling: ATP, ATO and automatic line supervision

Rolling stock: 240 cars

Franco-Belge 77A (1978/79)	M120
Hitachi/Itoh 82 (1985/86)	M120

In peak service: 160

Developments: A 9 km North line branch to Buckhead, Medical Center and Dunwoody opened in June 1996; 3.2 km extension to North Springs under construction for late 2000 opening. A further 28 cars are to be ordered.

New plans drafted under the MARTA 2000 programme by the Atlanta Regional Commission in 1989 envisage further metro routes to serve the northern suburbs, plus some 70 km of automated light metro, an exclusive busway and possible commuter rail service. The initial light rail route could be a proposed orbital link between metro stations Lindbergh Center and East Lake.

Cobb Community Transit

Cobb Community Transit
100 Cherokee Street, Suite 150, Marietta, GA 30090-9612
Telephone: +1 770 528 1610 Fax: +1 770 528 1611
Transit Division Manager: Don Griffith
General Manager: Eric Estell
Staff: 111

Passenger journeys: (1993) 2.7 million
(1994) 2.9 million
(1995) 2.8 million

Current situation: Set up in 1989 to provide service in outer Atlanta suburbs in Cobb County; managed by ATE Management & Service. Three express and one local route run to MARTA's Arts Center station, with through ticketing. Total 14 routes; 53 buses. Contracted vanpool service carried 117,000 passengers in 1994.
Developments: Four new routes inaugurated September 1996 in previously unserved areas.

Commuter rail (proposed)

Current situation: The Georgia Rail Passenger Authority has identified six routes over which commuter rail service could be revived and held public hearings on the project during 1995. Routes selected are from Athens, Bremen, Senoia, Gainesville, Madison and Canton to Atlanta.

UPDATED

AUCKLAND

Population: City 355,000, urban area 1 million
Public transport: A mix of commercial and non-commercial bus, train and ferry services is registered with the Regional Council, which also contracts and funds non-commercial services

Auckland Regional Council (ARC)

Auckland Regional Council
Private Bag 68912, Newton, Auckland 1032, New Zealand
Telephone: +64 9 379 4420 Fax: +64 9 366 2148
Transport Group Manager: Barry Mein

Current situation: Deregulation of public transport services was implemented in 1991. ARC is responsible for registration of commercial public transport services and for contracting and funding of non-commercial services. It also funds concessionary fares on all services.
Developments: A 1 km rail extension into the city centre, where a new underground bus/rail interchange would be built in conjunction with a commercial development, looks certain to go ahead. Expressions of interest have been sought for a development of a light rail system (see below), while on the North Shore a bus/HOV lane is planned alongside the Northern Motorway. A restructuring of the city's bus network was being implemented in March 1997.

Arrangements for elderly/disabled: The Total Mobility scheme provides half-price taxi fares for those who cannot use scheduled services; ARC also funds installation of wheelchair hoists in taxivans

Bus

Passenger boardings: (1995) 31.1 million

Operating costs financed by: Fares 46.4%, property taxes and central government funding 53.6%

Current situation: Services are provided by 12 operators, the largest of which, Yellow Bus, is the former Council-owned undertaking now run by a separate semi-public trust. The UK-based operator Stagecoach has a growing presence, running large numbers of buses in South Auckland and soon to take over cross-town and major radial routes in the Auckland isthmus. The other operators are: Birkenhead Transport, BJC Enterprises, Commercial Buses, Devonport Buses, Eastern taxis, Hanham's Buses, Howick & Eastern Buses, Ritchies, Taxi North Shore and Whenuapai Bus Travel. Their combined fleets total 815 vehicles and they employ some 1,300 staff.

Developments: Bus patronage grew by 8 per cent in 1995, mostly in off-peak and weekend journeys. Virtually all buses now have electronic ticket machines capable of handling smartcards as a first step in development of an integrated ticketing system.

Operators, local councils and ARC are planning and implementing a large number of bus priority schemes, including one in the congested Great North Road corridor. A City Loop distributor service inaugurated in early 1997 runs low-floor buses in a distinctive livery.

MAN of Yellow Bus at Takapuna Transport Centre, North Shore **1997**

Suburban rail

Operated under contract by Tranz Metro Auckland
PO Box 37540, Auckland
Telephone: +64 9 270 5140
Manager: Ray Siddalls

Type of operation: Suburban heavy rail

Passenger journeys: (1993) 1.3 million
(1994) 1.6 million
(1995) 2 million

Current situation: Suburban trains operated by Tranz Metro on a 10-year contract run over three routes totalling 79 km with 38 stations. Service at peak hours 15-30 min, 30-60 min off-peak, with limited evening but no Sunday trains. Zonal fare structure; fares cover 36 per cent of operating costs.

Developments: Increased patronage following the 1993 service revamp has led to capacity problems, especially on Waitakere line trains. Platform lengthening and completion of double-tracking are being examined, as opening of the city-centre extension will stimulate further traffic growth.

All trains are being fitted with automatic doors, which should help reduce journey times.

Rolling stock: 19 two-car dmus

Passengers board a Cityrail train at Homai **1997**

Ferry

Passenger journeys: (1994) 2.2 million
(1995) 1.6 million

Current situation: Six ferry services operate in Waitemata Harbour and the Hauraki Gulf, linking central Auckland with Bayswater (started February 1997), Devonport, Stanley Bay, Northcote/Birkenhead, Gulf Harbour and Waiheke Island, mainly for recreational purposes.

Light rail (proposed)

Current situation: Proposals have been put forward by a private sector group, New Zealand LRT Ltd, for a 4 km city-centre route linking with the existing Papakura and Waitakere suburban rail routes. A fleet of 30 cars is envisaged.

The Regional Land Transport Committee sought bids in late 1996 for an urban rail network, which could take the form of light rail or other variants. A short-list of five companies was expected to be asked to tender for a scheme in early 1997.

UPDATED

AUGSBURG

Population: 256,000, region 662,000

Public transport: Bus and tramway services provided by municipal authority. German Railway (DB) provides commuter services. Suburban bus services provided by regional bus company and independent operators. Regional transit authority (AVV) integrates urban and suburban services

AVV

Augsburger Verkehrsverbund GmbH
PO Box 101120, 86001 Augsburg, Germany
Telephone: +49 821 157007 Fax: +49 821 33372
Managing Director: Helmut Hofmann

Passenger journeys: (1995) 17.4 million

Current situation: AVV, the regional transit authority, was created in 1985 by the city of Augsburg and surrounding counties to co-ordinate public transport in the region. The scheme includes six rail lines radiating from Augsburg and 97 regional bus routes operated by 19 companies with a route length of 2,349 km. Full integration of these was completed in 1992. Creation of 2,500 park-and-ride spaces and 780 cycle racks is planned at 20 stations.

Urban services in Augsburg (see below) were fully integrated into AVV during 1995.

Operating costs financed by: Fares 56.7%, other commercial sources 7.8%, local authority subsidies 35.5%

VGA

Stadtwerke Augsburg-Verkehrsbetriebe (VGA)
Hoher Weg 1, 86152 Augsburg
Telephone: +49 821 324 2565 Fax: +49 821 324 2589
General Manager: Dr Werner Pusinelli
Operating Manager: Dipl-Ing P Lessing
Staff: 878

Passenger journeys: (1993) 50.7 million
(1994) 50.2 million
(1995) 50.8 million

Operating costs financed by: Fares 49.7%, other sources 50.3%

Subsidy from: City

Current situation: A big effort has been made to make services more attractive following adoption of a new policy by the city authorities. Frequency on bus and tram routes has been improved, and there are plans for more reserved rights-of-way for both buses and trams. Four suburban routes are served by shared taxis, operating to fixed schedule but on request by phone or radio-call from driver of connecting tram or bus.

Bus
Vehicle-km: (1993) 7.1 million
(1994) 7 million
(1995) 7.1 million

Number of routes: 25
Route length: (One way) 198 km
On priority right-of-way: 2 km
Fleet: 136 vehicles, plus 5 hired

MAN SL200 (1980/85)	9
MAN SG240H articulated (1981/86)	55
MAN SG242 articulated (1987/89)	22
MAN NL202 low-floor (1991)	20
MAN NG272 low-floor (1991)	22
MAN NG232 low-floor articulated (1996)	8

In peak service: 116
On order: 10 MAN NG232 buses

Most intensive service: 10 min
One-person operation: All routes
Fare collection: Payment to driver or prepurchase with validation/cancellation machines on board
Fare structure: Zonal, multitickets, day and period passes, annual subscription
Fares collected on board: 6% (58% hold passes)
Fare evasion control: Random inspection with penalty (DM60)
Operational control: Mobile radio
Arrangements for elderly/disabled: Free travel for disabled, reimbursed by government

Developments: Eight CNG-powered low-floor articulated buses entered service in 1996, and another 10 are on order. VGA operates its own CNG filling station, which is also available to other users.

Tramway
Type of operation: Conventional tramway

Car-km: (1992) 2.6 million
(1994) 2.8 million
(1995) 2.7 million

Route length: 26.7 km
Number of routes: 4
Gauge: 1,000 mm
Electrification: 600 V DC, overhead

Service: All day 5 min
Fare structure: Zonal, as bus

Rolling stock: 89 cars

MAN GT5 (1956/68)	M12
MAN GT8 (1976)	M12
Duewag/MAN M8C (1985)	M12
Esslingen GT4 (1965)	M22 T20
AEG GT6MNF low-floor (1995)	M11

In peak service: 44
On order: 10 double-articulated low-floor cars similar to those of Bremen, plus 1 four-section GT8M

Developments: A new line entirely on private right-of-way (7.5 km) from Hbf to Inninger Strasse to serve the university and Haunstetten opened in April 1996. An extension to Stadtgrenze Königsbrunn is to be built, starting in 1999.

DB
Deutsche Bahn AG, Geschäftsbereich Nahverkehr
Regionalbereich Süd-Bayern
Richelstrasse 3, 80634 München
Telephone: +49 89 128 3330 Fax: +49 89 1223 1931

Ex-Stuttgart GT4 (left) on Augsburg's Karolinenstrasse ***1996***

MAN NG202 low-floor on Route 36 at Moritzplatz ***1996***

Current situation: Commuter services are operated on six lines totalling 160 km, integrated in AVV (see above). Frequencies are irregular. Ordinary railway stock, both electric and diesel, is used.

RBA
Regionalbus Augsburg GmbH
Leonhardsberg 1, 86150 Augsburg
Telephone: +49 821 502150 Fax: +49 821 5021 588
Managing Directors: Walter Jägle
Ralph André
Staff: 418

Passenger journeys: (1992) 31 million
(1993) 30.5 million
(1994) 30.5 million
Vehicle-km: (1992) 23 million
(1993) 22.5 million
(1994) 22 million

Current situation: Formerly owned by DB, this regional bus company was sold to a group of private bus operators in 1992. There are 156 local and regional routes operated, extending well beyond the AVV area, totalling 5,688 km, with a fleet of 156 buses, plus 393 hired.

STWG
Stadtwerke Gersthofen
Augsburger Strasse 1A, 86368 Gersthofen
Telephone: +49 821 2491 480
Operating Manager: Hans Baumer

Current situation: Local authority operator runs a service between Gersthofen and Augsburg, and other local services, with a fleet of 24 buses.

UPDATED

AUSTIN
Population: 536,000
Public transport: Bus services in city and surrounding suburban areas provided by public authority through undertaking managed under contract, other services operated by private company; light rail proposed

Capital Metro
Capital Metropolitan Transportation Authority
2910 East 5th Street, Austin, TX 78702, USA
Telephone: +1 512 389 7400 Fax: +1 512 389 1283
General Manager: Justin T Augustine
Assistant General Manager, Operations: Lawson Albritton
Staff: 800

Current situation: Capital Metro was established in 1985 as a public authority for transport in Austin and seven of its suburbs, replacing the former Austin Transit System. The authority aimed to reduce traffic congestion, improve air quality and enhance regional economic development by increasing service provision.

Service includes park-and-ride routes, local routes, a downtown replica trolley service, vanpools, carpool-matching, door-to-door paratransit for mobility-impaired people, and rural feeder routes. Some services are operated for Capital Metro by the Greater Austin Transportation Co.

A free-fares experiment in 1990 more than doubled ridership. Reimposition of fares at a low level in 1991 was successful in retaining much of this new business.

Plans for 330 km of busways were considered by the city in 1986, and in 1987 some right-of-way was

Gillig Phantom bus of Capital Metro in downtown Austin

purchased from Southern Pacific for future transit use. Light rail is under consideration for a core route from the city centre to Palmer Lane. HOV lanes are also proposed on several corridors.

In 1988, Capital Metro acquired a shuttle service operated for the University of Texas, currently comprising 12 routes. In 1990 three Express park-and-ride routes were contracted out to Laidlaw Transit for five years, at a cost saving of some 20 per cent. Also introduced was TeleRide, a demand-responsive van service of local circulators and feeders to fixed-route buses. Capital Metro resumed control in 1991 of demand-responsive services formerly contracted to Harlen Cab Co.

Developments: A 0.25 per cent sales tax has been agreed by voters. It will finance public transport improvements, including the proposed light rail system.

The experimental bike-and-ride service inaugurated in 1993 was extended in 1996 when racks were installed on 200 buses and bike lockers provided at several park-and-ride sites.

Bus
Staff: 717

Passenger boardings: (1991) 26 million
(1993) 25.6 million
(1994) 26.3 million
Vehicle-km: (1991) 22.7 million

Number of routes: 63
Route length: 884 km
Fleet: 300 vehicles

Gillig Phantom (1985/86/89)	230
TMC RTS (1993)	30
TVI/SVMC trolley replicas (1985/86)	20
Various vans/minibuses	20

Pollution control project has 10 buses equipped with a device to improve combustion efficiency, and 2 trolley replicas are propane-powered
In peak service: 291
On order: 30 CNG-powered buses
Most intensive service: 4-6 min
Fare structure: Flat fare reimposed 1991 after fare-free experiment, higher fare on Express routes, free transfer; 20-ticket books; monthly passes
Fare collection: Exact fare to farebox or prepurchase ticket
Integration with other modes: 11 park-and-ride lots served by a network of commuter Express bus routes, with 'Guaranteed Ride Home' taxi service available up to four times a year for $5 subscription; 51 vanpools
Arrangements for elderly/disabled: Demand-responsive service operated with 55 vans and 24 sedans, carried 373,000 passengers in 1994. Fixed-route fleet is 98% lift-equipped
Operating costs financed by: Fares 12%, other sources 6%, subsidy/grants 1%, sales tax 81%
Subsidy from: FTA and state of Texas

Light rail (proposed)
Current situation: Along with other options, a 22.5 km light rail line with 18 stations has been examined for the corridor north from the city centre to Palmer Lane and the University of Texas. Public consultations were completed in 1993.

In February 1995, Capitol Metro's board proposed a 38 km starter line and authorised fast-track planning of the initial 22.5 km portion. This forms part of a long-term plan to build a network of some 80 km by 2020.

UPDATED

BAKU
Population: 1.7 million
Public transport: Bus and trolleybus/tramway and funicular services operated by separate municipal authorities. Metro run by Ministry of Communications accounts for 25 per cent of journeys, with buses taking 50 per cent. Suburban rail services

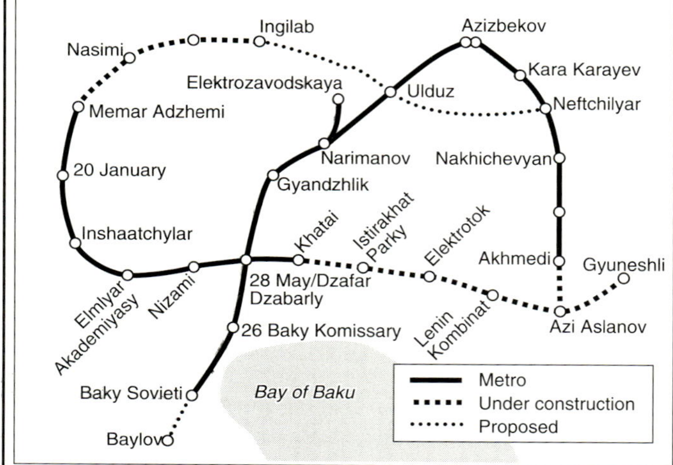

Baku metro

Upravlenie Passajirskogo Transporta
Upravlenie Passajirskogo Transporta
Baku, Azerbaijan

Bus
Route length: 1,512 km
Fleet: 605 vehicles, including some articulated

One-person operation: All routes
Fare collection: Conductors
Fare structure: Flat
Average peak-hour speed: 18 km/h

Tramvaino-Trolleibusnoe Upravlenie
Tramvaino-Trolleibusnoe Upravlenie
Rosa Luxembourg Str 27, 370010 Baku
Tel: +994 12 935005

Trolleybus
Passenger journeys:

Route length: 175 km
Fleet: 340 vehicles

Škoda 9Tr	
Škoda 14Tr	230
ZIU9	

One-person operation: All routes
Fare collection: Conductors
Fare structure: Flat
Average peak-hour speed: 17 km/h

Tramway
Type of operation: Conventional tramway

Route length: 76.6 km
Gauge: 1,524 mm
Fare structure: Flat
Fare collection: Conductors
One-person operation: All routes

Rolling stock: 90 cars

RVZ6	M40
KTM5	M50

Developments: Trams were eliminated from the city centre after opening of the metro, but their use as feeders continues and further extensions are planned into areas where traffic density would not support a metro line.

Baku Metro
Bakinski Metropolitan
Azizbekov prospekt 33A, 370602 Baku
Telephone: +994 12 982500
Chief Executive: N V M Rza
Chief Engineer: M E Enver
Staff: 2,400

Type of operation: Full metro, first line opened 1967

Passenger journeys: (1991) 160 million

Route length: 29 km
Number of lines: 2
Number of stations: 18
Gauge: 1,524 mm
Max gradient: 4%
Minimum curve radius: 300 m
Tunnel: Baku chamber method developed to counter poor geological conditions; stations mostly cut-and-cover
Electrification: 825 V DC, third rail

Service: 2 min
First/last train: 06.00/01.00
Fare structure: Flat; monthly fare card
Fare collection: Automatic barriers
Signalling: Automatic train stop; radio-telephone communication between trains and central control

Rolling stock: 167 cars

E/Ex	M48
Ex3 (1975)	M76
Others	M43

Developments: Extensions are under construction totalling 4.1 km with three stations, and a further 10.2 km with six stations is in design. An eventual network of 52 km with 34 stations is envisaged.

Following the disastrous fire of late 1995, in which 286 people were killed, immediate efforts were made to tackle the backlog of infrastructure maintenance, though progress was hampered by shortage of finance.

UPDATED

BALTIMORE

Population: 750,000

Public transport: Bus, metro and light rail services operated by Mass Transit Administration, an agency of the Maryland Department of Transportation. Commuter services operated for MDoT under contract

Maryland MTA

Maryland Mass Transit Administration
6 Saint Paul Street, Baltimore, MD 21202-1614, USA
Telephone: +1 410 767 3943 Fax: +1 410 333 3279
Administrator:
Deputy General Manager: James Buckley
Director of Transit Operations: Ronald Freeland
Staff: 1,660

Passenger boardings: (All modes)
(1990/91) 105.6 million
(1993) 92.4 million
(1994) 93.4 million

Operating costs financed by: Fares 42.2%, other commercial sources 1.4%, subsidy/grants 51.4%
Subsidy from: Consolidated Transportation Trust Fund

Current situation: MTA's service area has a population of some 2 million. The metro and light rail lines are fully integrated with the bus system, having the same flat fare. Integration has enhanced use of public transport, following a period of declining ridership on the bus system.

MTA operates regular, Express Flyer and Metro Connection circulator routes. Flyer routes originate at park-and-ride lots and operate via expressways direct to downtown Baltimore. Metro Connection is a feeder bus service to Owings Mills, Old Court and Milford Mill metro stations from surrounding areas. In the Washington DC area, MTA contracts with private carriers to operate nine commuter bus routes.

Developments: The MTA is required under a state law of 1982 to recover 50 per cent of its operating costs from fares. To achieve this goal in 1996, while avoiding the drop in ridership that usually accompanies a fares rise, the system of five zones and transfers was eliminated in favour of a new flat fare slightly higher than the former base rate. Instead of transfers, a new $3 all-day pass was introduced. As a result, bus ridership remained stable, metro travel (formerly four zones) rose by about 8 per cent, and light rail by 4 per cent. Fares for long-distance commuter buses, not part of the former zonal system, were also raised to meet the 50 per cent requirement.

Bus

Staff: 1,330 drivers

Passenger boardings: (1993) 74.5 million
(1994) 74.4 million
Vehicle-km: (1990/91) 37.8 million
(1994)

Number of routes: 61
Route length: 2,200 km
Fleet: 805 vehicles

Flxible Metro 40 ft (1983/95)	735
Flxible Metro 30 ft (1984/87)	20
Neoplan AN440 (1986)	10
Grumman 870 (1982)	26
Flxible (1993) (CNG-powered)	4
American Ikarus 436 articulated (1994)	10

In peak service: 678 am, 614 pm
On order: A further 20 North American Bus Industries articulated for 1997 delivery; purchase of more articulateds planned, and 50 40 ft buses per year likely to be ordered through to 2000

Most intensive service: 3-5 min
One-person operation: All routes
Fare collection: Farebox beside driver
Fare structure: Flat; express bus services premiums; transfer by day pass which covers all modes
Arrangements for elderly/disabled: 290 buses lift-equipped, all routes accessible on Sundays; Mobility Bus service operated by 20 lift-equipped vans operates on demand to routes otherwise unserved; demand-response services carried 254,000 passengers in 1994
Average distance between stops: 1 city block
Average peak-hour speed: 20.8 km
Integration between modes: Bus/metro/light rail transfer tickets; 12 routes feed metro stations

Christmas shoppers crowd an MTA Flxible in downtown Baltimore **1997**

Metro ridership is up 8 per cent since introduction of a flat fare **1997**

Ice hockey enthusiasts take an LRV direct to the game **1997**

New vehicles financed by: FTA grant 70%, state funds 30%

Metro

Staff: 314

Type of operation: Full metro, first line opened 1983

Passenger boardings: (1992) 12.8 million
(1993) 10.6 million
(1994) 10.5 million

some Series 1000 rolling stock, and upgrading of stations, maintenance and security. An additional Pta29.7 million has been allocated to infrastructure spending, principally for completing metro Line 2, but also for upgrading substations and transformers, introducing ATP/ATO, and improving depots, communications, escalators, stations and tunnels.

Under the agreement, TMB is required to cover 58 per cent of operating costs from commercial income by 1997, with concomitant savings in costs and productivity, the former having been cut by 50 per cent over the last 15 years while the latter has doubled.

Under study is a link between the city centre, Montjuic Park, the Zona Franca industrial area and the Trade Fair grounds. Modes under study include a monorail.

Passenger journeys: (1993) 462.8 million
(1994) 455.7 million
(1995) 465.3 million

Bus

Staff: 2,583
Operating company: Transports de Barcelona SA
Network Director, Bus: José M Satorres

Passenger journeys: (1993) 197.7 million
(1994) 201.8 million
(1995) 202.5 million
Vehicle-km: (1993) 35.5 million
(1994) 35.3 million
(1995) 26 million

Number of routes: 78
Route length: (One way) 649.2 km
On priority right-of-way: 65.2 km
Fleet: 826 vehicles

Pegaso 6038 (1980/83)	209
Pegaso 6420	179
Pegaso 6035A articulated	15
Mercedes O405	127
Mercedes O405G articulated	118
Mercedes low-floor	79
MAN NL202 low-floor	85
Midibuses	14

In peak service: 715
Average age of fleet: 6.9 years
On order: 56 buses from Mercedes (40 rigid, 16 articulated) and 52 from MAN (40 rigid and 12 articulated); also an unspecified number of City buses from Iveco/Pegaso

Most intensive service: 4-6 min
One-person operation: 100%
Fare collection: By driver or prepurchase with cancelling machines on board
Fare structure: Flat; common bus/metro multiride tickets and passes
Fare evasion control: Inspectors
Fares collected on board: 12.5%
Integration with other modes: Combined bus/metro/FGC tickets; bus multiride tickets also valid on metro; monthly passes also valid on RENFE trains in urban zone
Operational control: Route inspectors; automatic vehicle monitoring on 158 vehicles operating 10 routes
Arrangements for elderly/disabled: Reduced rate or free travel for over-65s according to pension level; 164 low-floor buses in service
Average distance between stops: 350 m
Average peak-hour speed: Bus lanes 12.8 km/h; mixed traffic: urban 11.3 km/h, interurban 15.5 km/h
Operating costs financed by: Fares 58%, other commercial sources 2.6%, subsidy/grants 39.4%
Subsidy from: Local, central and regional government
New vehicles financed by: Credit and leasing

Developments: Magnetic ticketing system being introduced. Automatic vehicle monitoring is being extended to 300 vehicles. Electronic screens display news inside some buses, while others are equipped to show videos

Type 112 emu on the Catalunya y Sarria line **1995**

Metro

Operating company: Ferrocarril Metropolità de Barcelona SA, SPM
Network Director, Metro: Agustin del Castillo
Staff: 2,460

Type of operation: Full metro, first line opened 1924

Passenger journeys: (1993) 265.1 million
(1994) 253.9 million
(1995) 262.8 million

Car-km: (1993) 53.6 million
(1994) 52.7 million
(1995) 52.9 million

Route length: 75.9 km
in tunnel: 74.8 km
Number of lines: 5
Number of stations: 106
in tunnel: 104
Gauge: Line 1, 1,674 mm; others, 1,435 mm
Track: 54 kg/m UIC 54 rail; new lines, sleepers on concrete; other lines, sleepers on ballast
Electrification: Line 1, 1.5 kV DC, steel third rail; others, 1.2 kV DC; Line 5, catenary; Line 2, rigid catenary; Lines 3 and 4, aluminium third rail

Service: Peak 3½ min, off-peak 4½ min
First/last train: 05.00/23.00/01.00 (Friday/Saturday)
Fare structure: Flat; multijourney tickets and passes
Revenue collection: AFC
Operating costs financed by: Fares 81%, commercial and other sources 4.8%, local, regional and central government subsidy 14.2%; other special costs, such as pensions and investment, financed by additional subsidy
Integration with other modes: Combined metro/bus tickets; combined metro/FGC tickets; monthly passes also valid on RENFE trains in urban zone
Arrangements for elderly/disabled: Reduced rate or free travel for over 65s according to pension levels; Line 2 fully accessible by street to platform lifts
Automatic control: ATP on Line 4, ATO/ATP on Line 2; automatic traffic regulation

Rolling stock: 488 cars

MTM/Macosa 1000 1 (1970/76)	M100
MTM/Macosa 1000 2 (1974/79)	M108
MTM/Macosa R1300 1 (1982/83)	T25
CAF R1400 2 (1984/86)	T27
CAF/MTM/Macosa 3000 (1986/88)	M72 T18
CAF/MTM/Macosa 4000 (1987)	M96 T24
CAF 2000 (1992)	M12 T6

Developments: The 3.4 km central section of Line 2, from Sagrada Família to Universitat, with six stations, opened in September 1995, followed by a one-station 0.8 km extension to Parallel in December. The 3.9 km Sagrada Família–La Pau section, with five stations, is under construction for mid-1997 opening. It is intended to transfer the existing La Pau–Pep Ventura section of Line 4 to Line 2.

The regional government is against the proposed Montjuic extension on cost grounds, but supports plans for extension of Line 2 to the Zona Franca industrial zone, and for a branch to serve Ciutat Meridiana. EMT is keen to see an extension from Pep Ventura to a new multimodal station in Badalona.

Medium-term plans are for a six-line metro network extending to 124.5 km with 158 stations, with extensions to Lines 3, 4 and 5 a priority. A major modernisation programme is in progress, including stations, fixed installations and depots.

Low-floor Neoplan of private operator Transports Ciutat Comptal which runs the airport shuttle **1996**

Tramway

Type of operation: Conventional tramway

Current situation: 2.8 km on-street residual tramway (Tramvia Blau), renovated in 1991, links the Av Tibidabo station of FGC with funicular to Tibidabo amusement park. It carries about 0.3 million passenger annually. Fleet of seven cars.
Developments: The line has been under threat of closure for financial reasons, despite recent renewal of track and overhead.

Funicular/cable lift

Current situation: The 750 m Funicular de Montjuic, was rebuilt in 1992 with capacity of 8,000 passengers/h. The 800 m sightseeing Teleferico de Montjuic, rising 99 m, links with the funicular and carries some 0.4 million passengers a year. Both operate summer only, and at weekends and public holidays.

FGC

Ferrocarrils de la Generalitat de Catalunya
Pau Casals 24, 08021 Barcelona
Telephone: +34 3 201 4683 Fax: +34 3 201 1144
President: Enric Roig
Vice President: Ernest Serra
Operating Director: Josep L Arqués
Commercial Director: Josep L Suarez
Staff: 1,325

Type of operation: Suburban/regional rail

Passenger journeys: (1993) 43.4 million
(1994) 42.5 million
(1995) 42.6 million

Operating costs financed by: Fares 54%, other commercial sources 5%, subsidy/grants 41%
Subsidy from: National government 55%, regional 45%

Current situation: FGC operates two groups of lines providing suburban and regional services, totalling 143 route-km with 66 stations. The Catalunya & Sarria line comprises several routes feeding into a 7 km city-centre tunnel section which provides metro-style service. These lines run northwards from metro interchanges at Plaça de Catalunya terminus and Provença, with two main extensions to Terrassa and Sabadell, totalling 45 km, 1,435 mm gauge; electrification was upgraded from 1.2 to 1.5 kV DC overhead in 1995.

The Catalans metre-gauge line runs west from Plaça de Espanya, extending to 98 km, with suburban service as far as Martorell (30 km) and regional services to Manresa (electrified 1.5 kV DC) and the branch to Igualada (diesel-worked).

The state and Catalan regional governments provide subsidy, with fares (54 per cent) and other commercial sources bringing in the remainder. Flat fare on urban sections, graduated elsewhere; multijourney tickets and passes available.
Developments: Under the 1996/98 modernisation programme, all lines are being upgraded to carry heavier traffic. On the Catalunya & Sarria line, platforms were lengthened and double track extended in 1995. New workshop facilities have been completed at Rubí, where the station has been relocated underground.

A fleet of 16 four-car emus entering service in 1996/97 will be used to provide a regular-interval timetable throughout the day to Sabadell and Terrassa, which will be served by five trains/h instead of three.

Track-doubling of the underground section of the Catalans line between Plaça Espanya and Ildefons Cerdà is expected to be completed in 1997, along with the surface section between Moli Nou and Martorell. At the same time, renovation of interlockings has been carried out and most level crossings eliminated in the suburban area.

Twenty three-car emus are on order to replace 15 life-expired trains and to provide service over the Martorell—Igualda branch, which is to be electrified. Plans have been put forward for construction of a branch from Sant Boi to the satellite towns of Gavà, Castelldefels and Cornellà, although EMT favours a light rail line along the main Cornellà road, which would also link with the proposed Baix Llobregat light rail scheme.

Rolling stock: 198 cars

SIG (1945/50)	M2 T4
FC Catalunya (1952/75)	M36 T14
Euskalduna (1966/68)	M10 T5
Naval (1966/68)	M12
FC Catalans (1966/68)	T8
MTM/Macosa/Alsthom (1981/95)	M50 T37
CAF/ABB/Meinfesa (1995/96)	M15 T5

In peak service: 139
On order: Total of 104 cars for suburban and regional services

RENFE

Spanish National Railways
Avenida Ciudad de Barcelona 8, 28007 Madrid
Telephone: +34 1 606 6401 Fax: +34 1 527 6504
Managing Director, Suburban Service: Eduard Albors
Staff: 1,084 (Barcelona area only)

Type of operation: Suburban heavy rail

Passenger journeys: (1993) 70.6 million
(1994) 75.2 million
(1995) 79.2 million

Current situation: A metro-style service is operated on three cross-city routes, with trains every 6-7 minutes during peak periods: Maçanet Massanes—Sant Vicenç de Calders, Maçanet Massanes—Hospitalet/El Prat airport, and Manresa—San Vicenç de Calders. Also less frequent service between Vic and Hospitalet. Four lines totalling 451 km with 112 stations, 1,668 mm gauge, electrified 3 kV DC; zonal fares with multijourney tickets and passes.
Developments: The rapid growth in patronage has continued, with journeys up 18 per cent in 1995 over 1992 figures. Investment during 1995 amounted to Pta3.4 billion, bringing the total invested in station upgrading and new rolling stock since 1991 to Pta61 billion. Outer-suburban services are to be worked by 10 Class 470 emus refurbished to match the standards of the newer Class 446/7 units; a further 63 Class 440s will need to be replaced by the end of the century.

Rolling stock: 180 emu trains

Class 440	M53 T106
Class 470	M18 T36
Class 447	M178 T89
Class 450 bi-level	M24 T36
Class 451 bi-level	M12 T24

Light rail (planned)

Current situation: Further development of the light rail line planned for the Baix Llobregat area is stalled awaiting government funds. Five international consortia have proposed seven possible routes, varying from 10.2 to 17.4 km. When built, the intention is to extend the line along Avinguda Diagonal to the coast.

In the meantime, the city council has decided to build a 600 m demonstration line along the Diagonal to test light rail technology.

A second project has emerged for a line from Plaça de Espanya along Gran Via to Plaça Cerdà running through the Zona Franca, with branches to Montjuic (replacing the proposed extension of metro Line 2) and Pedrova.

UPDATED

BASEL

Population: City 198,000, area of tariff agreement 560,000
Public transport: Bus, trolleybus and tramway services operated by undertaking managed by board elected by city council. Also local railways/tramways extending into the suburbs and into Baselland canton operated by separate undertaking. Tarifverbund Nordwestschweiz sets uniform fares structure for all modes

TNW

Tarifverbund Nordwestschweiz
Address as BLT below

Current situation: TNW, which is operated as a subsidiary of Baselland Transport, organises and administers the uniform fares structure for trams, buses, post buses and SBB trains in the greater Basel area, comprising six cantons with a total population of 560,000. It also co-ordinates marketing, promotional and advertising activities.

BVB

Basler Verkehrs-Betriebe (BVB)
Claragraben 55, 4005 Basel, Switzerland
Telephone: +41 61 267 8181 Fax: +41 61 267 9048
Chair: M Feldges
General Manager: U Hanselmann
Operating Manager: H Ifflander
Staff: 1,096

Gas-powered bus of BVB in Basel city centre ***1997***

Passenger journeys: (All modes)
(1991) 130 million
(1992) 129 million
(1993) 153 million

Fare collection: Ticket machines at all stops; no onboard sales
Fare structure: Zonal; day tickets; reduced-price monthly or annual Umwelt-Abonnement (U-Abo) 'environmental subscription' seasons for motorists signing declaration to use public transport wherever possible, valid on BVB, BLT, SBB trains, and French and German border buses
Fare evasion control: Penalty
Operating costs financed by: Fares 62.6%, other commercial sources 14.5%, subsidy/grants 22.9%
Subsidy from: Canton and city

Current situation: Patronage has grown by some 29 per cent since introduction in 1983 of BVB's 'environmental' season ticket scheme, subsidised by all local authorities in the region, and congestion on tram routes in particular has led to examination of various capacity improvements (see below).

Developments: Rigorous cost-cutting whilst maintaining service standards helped reduce the deficit from roundly SWFr50 million in 1992 to SWFr39 million in 1993. But BVB ran into further financial difficulties in 1995/96, when the deficit reached SwFr48 million. Causes of the deficit include a reduction in the number of single tickets sold, reduced tariff income from TNW, and loss of income due to the popularity of BLT's tram routes in the city centre.

BVB has adopted a new marketing strategy *Bürgernah, Verfügbar, Bequem* (popular, accessible, comfortable).

Bus and trolleybus

Passenger journeys: (1993) 33.3 million
Vehicle-km: (1993) Bus 2.3 million, trolleybus 1.3 million

Number of routes: Bus 9, trolleybus 3
Route length: Bus 55.2 km, trolleybus 13.5 km
Fleet: 56 buses

Standard	35
Articulated	21

Fleet: 28 trolleybuses

FBW/Hess articulated (1975)	10
Mercedes articulated (1982/83)	2
Neoplan low-floor articulated prototype (1992)	1
Neoplan low-floor articulated (1995)	11
Others	4

Trolleybus electrification: 600 V DC

Most intensive service: 10 min
One-person operation: All routes
Integration with other modes: Full integration with tramway service
Average distance between stops: 400 m
Average peak-hour speed: 20 km/h
Subsidy from: City of Basel

Developments: 12 CNG-powered low-floor buses delivered late 1995.

Tramway

Type of operation: Conventional tramway

Passenger journeys: (1993) 120 million
(1994) 121 million
Car-km: (1993) 15.5 million

Route length: 61 km
Number of lines: 9
Gauge: 1,000 mm
Electrification: 600 V DC, overhead

Service: Peak 6 min, day 8 min, evenings 12 min
First/last car: 05.30/00.30
Fare structure: Zonal
Revenue control: Automatic ticket machines
Integration with other modes: Fully integrated with bus and trolleybus and BLT services, and bus services into Germany
One-person operation: All routes

Rolling stock: 338 cars, including 30 Be 4/6 owned by BLT but working on BLT (see below)

SWP Be 4/4 (1948/68)	M45
Duewag Be 4/6 (1967/73)	M58
Schindler Be 4/4 (1986/87)	M26
Schindler Be 4/6	M57
Trailers (various builders)	T113
Others	39

On order: 28 low-floor centre sections from Schindler to augment the 1990/91 fleet of Be 4/6 articulated cars. Trials with a prototype will start in January 1998, and deliveries will run through to May 1999.

Developments: Completion of the reconstructed Wettstein bridge has allowed rerouting of Route 15 to provide better service between Klein-Basel north of the Rhein and the southeastern suburbs. Line 15 is also being extended through the Claragraben (where trams last ran 90 years ago) to reach industrial and shopping areas in the north of the city. Extensive works are planned to permit through running of BLT routes 10 and 11 to the main SBB station, for 1999 completion.

BLT's Route 11 has poached BVB passengers on city-centre journeys ***1997***

Citroën Jumper on BVB's 1A minibus shuttle linking Messeplatz and Brombacherstrasse ***1997***

BLT

Baselland Transport AG
Grenzweg 1, 4104 Oberwil
Telephone: +41 61 401 3388 Fax: +41 61 401 3568
Managing Director: A Büttiker
Financial Director: R Stöckli
Operating Manager: R Zolin
Staff: 150

Type of operation: Upgraded tramway

Passenger journeys: (1989) 28.2 million
(1990) 29 million
(1991) 29.5 million

Current situation: Formerly independent suburban tramways and a local light railway were merged in 1974 to form BLT, which was also given a remit to integrate bus services in the suburbs. The light rail route 17 (the former Birsigthalbahn) was converted to tramway operation in 1984. All four routes use BVB tracks to reach central Basel, and 10 and 11 will be extended to the SBB station in 1999.

Tramway

Current situation: The two original tramways are Route 11 to Aesch and Route 14 to Pratteln (worked by BVB cars). A third, Route 10 serving Dornach, was extended in 1986 from its former terminus at Heuwaage into the city centre over BVB tracks and linked with Route 17 to Rodersdorf. This route passes through French territory and terminates in Solothurn canton; at 25.6 km it is the longest tram route in Switzerland. Total network 57 km of 1,000 mm gauge, electrified 600 V DC.

Developments: Track doubling between Binningen Schloss and Oberdorf is in progress.

Rolling stock: 81 tramcars, of which 30 owned by BVB

Schindler Be 4/6 (1971/72)	M8
Schindler Be 4/6 (1975/76)	M7
Schindler Be 4/6 (1978/81)	M47
Schindler Be 4/8 (1980/87/88/89)	M19

Bus

Current situation: BLT operates six routes itself and contracts operation of eight local bus services in the area around Basel, some of which feed the rail services. Total network 107 km with fleet of 18 vehicles.

People mover (proposed)

Current situation: A 12 km people mover ring route has been proposed by consultants as a means of relieving BVB's congested inner-city tram routes. Various automated systems are under consideration.

Regional metro (proposed)

Current situation: Plans have been examined for S-Bahn operation over several routes radiating from Basel, including lines into France and Germany.

UPDATED

BEIJING

Population: City 7 million, region 10.5 million
Public transport: Bus, trolleybus and metro services operated by municipal agencies; extensive paratransit. Limited commuter service provided by Chinese Railways plays only a minor role in the city's transport; light rail planned

Public Transport Corporation

Beijing Public Transport Corporation
44 Nanlishi Lu, Beijing, People's Republic of China
Telephone: +86 1 895331/895236

Current situation: Subsidiary companies run distinct bus and trolleybus systems and the metro, as well as manufacturing over 1,000 buses and trolleybuses per year for Beijing and other cities.

Over five million bicycles and 300,000 cars make surface public transport severely congested. Average peak-hour speed is about 15 km/h. Computerised traffic control systems are in use, but rising traffic volume may be expected to offset any improvements.

Development of the metro continues to make only slow progress, but an extension is due to open in 1996. Two separate suburban light rail schemes are projected.

Beijing BD562 trolleybus of recent design **1997**

Beijing City Bus

Beijing City Bus Company

Current situation: Bus services are operated throughout the metropolitan area. There is said to be a structure of area subsidiaries, but how this functions is not apparent. About 1,000 articulated buses of Type BK670 and about 500 similar but shorter buses of Type BK663 have entered service since the late 1970s, and these rather dated models continue to be delivered with only minor design changes. The rigid fleet used on less busy routes has been modernised and double-decks are in service on some trunk routes.

Bus

Passenger journeys: 2,000 million (annual)

Number of routes: Inner city 60; suburban and satellite towns 81; night routes 4
Fleet: Approx 3,000 vehicles, including 2,000 articulated, mainly Beijing types BK670 and BK663, and some Jiling double-decks

Fare collection: Payment to seated conductor, most passengers have monthly passes
Fare structure: Stage
Integration with other modes: There is little structured intermodal integration. Completion of metro Line 2 significantly improved journey times for passengers on certain routes, but interchange facilities between surface transport and metro are very poor, with few escalators and no purpose-built links for transferring passengers

Line 1 metro train

Beijing City Trolleybus

Beijing City Trolleybus Company

Current situation: The trolleybus network is currently fairly static in size and the new all-articulated fleet delivered during the 1980s is about 10 per cent smaller than the original part-rigid, part-articulated fleet it replaced. Severe overcrowding still occurs and it is not clear whether the reduction in fleet size is deliberate or caused by the need to supply trolleybuses to other undertakings to replace worn-out vehicles. The system also suffers from severe traffic congestion which has worsened substantially in recent years.

Trolleybus services are augmented by bus routes separate from those of City Bus and recent expansion of the Trolleybus Company's network has been by introduction of more bus routes rather than new trolleybus routes. Two routes, 103 and 104, are worked by both buses and trolleybuses.

Minibuses await passengers at Pingguo Yuan metro terminus

Bus

Number of routes: 16 (2 shared with trolleybuses)
Fleet: Approx 500 Beijing buses, over 75% of which articulated, deliveries since 1982 being of type Beijing BK663. A few new Jinghua rigid buses have entered service recently

Fare collection: Payment to seated conductor, monthly passes
Fare structure: Stage

Trolleybus

Passenger journeys: 600 million (annual)

Number of routes: 13
Route length: 80 km
Fleet: Around 500 BD562 articulated

Fare collection/structure: As bus

Beijing Metro

Beijing Metro Corporation (BMRTC)
2 Beiheyan Road, Xicheng, 100044 Beijing
Telephone: +86 1 802 4566
General Manager: Feng Shuangsheng
Chief Engineer: Yao Jingdi
Staff: 10,000 including 1,600 engineers and technicians

1995; further orders are expected as replacements for the entire fleet.

Tramway

Staff: 2,466

Type of operation: Conventional tramway

Passenger journeys: (1993) 152.2 million
(1994) 154.1 million
(1995) 146.2 million
Car-km: (1993) 37.2 million
(1994) 35 million
(1995) 35.1 million

Route length: 178 km
Number of lines: 27 (4 night)
Number of stops: 359
Gauge: 1,435 mm
Electrification: 600 V DC, overhead

Service: Peak 5 min; 24 h service

Rolling stock: 762 cars

ČKD Tatra KT4D (1980/87)	M211
ČKD Tatra KTD4 (1980/87) modernised	M272
ČKD Tatra T6A2 (1988/90) modernised	M118 T58
Gotha B4 (1962/63)	T15
AEG GT6N low-floor (1994/95)	M60

In peak service: 609
On order: A further 60 Adtranz GT6N

Current situation: After merger of the two public transport operations, expansion of the tramway network into the western part of the city was proposed. The first such route, a 2.7 km extension of Route 23 along Osloer Strasse to Louise Schroeder Platz, was opened in 1995, and is being further extended 2.8 km along Seestrasse to Klinikum Rudolf Virchow for 1997 opening. Work also continues on the Prenzlauer Tor–Alexanderplatz–Hackescher Markt route, for opening in 1998/99.

Private finance is being sought to fund construction of a 4.8 km line partly in tunnel from Alexanderplatz to Magdeburger Platz, on which work is expected to start in 1998. This will be a high-capacity route extending into the former western sector, and it is proposed that the tunnel under Leipziger Str will be used later for proposed metro Line 3.

Additionally, 45 km of extensions were proposed for construction in the longer term at a cost of DM600 million, including links to new and reopened metro and S-Bahn stations in the city centre.

Total modernisation of the existing network is in progress, including renewal of track and overhead, and depot and power supply modernisation. Refurbishment of 447 Tatra tramcars (M388 T59) has been completed, while a new fleet of low-floor cars has been delivered. An option for another 60 GT6N cars has been exercised, and a further 165 cars will be required to complete the fleet proposed for the end of the century. It is proposed to run GT6N cars in pairs, necessitating lengthening of tram stops.

Ferry

Passenger journeys: (1995) 0.3 million

Current situation: Six vessels ply six routes with a total length of 6.8 km, only one of which operates all year round.

S8 train at Bornholmer Strasse **1997**

Berlin's new low-floor tram **1997**

Trams in central Potsdam **1997**

S-Bahn Berlin

S-Bahn Berlin GmbH
Invalidenstrasse 130-131, 10115 Berlin
Telephone: +49 30 297 19801 Fax: +49 30 297 19805
Chairman: Dr Axel Nawrocki
Directors: Günter Ruppert (Technical)
Ernst-Otto Constantin
Staff: 4,660

Type of operation: S-Bahn

Passenger journeys: (1995) 245 million

Current situation: This subsidiary of DB took over operation of the S-Bahn network at the beginning of 1995. Service is provided on 13 routes totalling 292 km with 146 stations; 1,435 mm gauge, electrified 800 V DC third rail; fares fully integrated with other modes. Peak-hour frequency on the busiest section is 2 min, with trains running every 3 min between Hauptbahnhof and Alexanderplatz. Off-peak services run every 5-10 min; trains run from about 04.00 to 01.00; 20 min service to Schönefeld airport.

Developments: The northern S-Bahn ring line between Westend and Jungfernheide was scheduled to reopen in June 1997 along with two other sections, and service between Westkreuz and Spandau is due to resume in 1999. By 2002, all lines which were in operation in 1961 will have been reopened. October 1996 saw reopening of the original S-Bahn tracks between Zoo and Hbf after complete reconstruction.

A standard emu has been designed for the merged S-Bahn network. This is the Series 481, based on the Series 480 stock; first-class accommodation is being reintroduced as these trains enter service. An order for 500 two-car sets has been placed with Adtranz for delivery through to 2004 to replace life-expired stock built between 1927 and 1941.

Some trains now offer a mobile catering service.

Rolling stock: 1,486 cars

Class 476 (1927/32, modernised 1979/89)	M210 T210
Class 477 (1938/41, modernised 1974/82)	M204 T204
Waggon Union/AEG Class 480 (1986/90-94)	M168
LEW/AEG Class 485 (1987/92)	M166 T166
DWA/Adtranz Class 481 (1996)	M158

DB

Deutsche Bahn AG, Geschäftsbereich Nahverkehr
Regionalbereich Berlin-Brandenburg
Ruschestrasse 59, 10365 Berlin
Telephone: +49 30 237 23620 Fax: +49 30 297 24177
Managers: Karl-Heinz Friedrich
Hans Leister

Type of operation: Regional rail

Passenger journeys: (1995) 16,800 daily

Current situation: To complement the S-Bahn network, DB operates 18 regional routes, mostly electrified at 15 kV 16 ⅔ Hz. Services are fully integrated with the joint VBB tariff.
Developments: Work has started on construction of a 3.2 km north-south tunnel beneath the city centre for long-distance and regional traffic.

Suburban tramways

Schöneicher-Rüdersdorfer Strassenbahn GmbH
Dorfstrasse 15, 15566 Schöneiche
Telephone: +49 30 649 5393 Fax: +49 30 649 8984
Operating Manager: Dipl-Ing F K Kietzke

Passenger journeys: (1993) 1.4 million
(1994) 1.3 million
(1995) 1.2 million

Current situation: Metre-gauge tramway providing S-Bahn feeder service over the Rüdersdorf—Schöneiche—Friedrichshagen route (14.5 km).

Woltersdorfer Strassenbahn GmbH
Karl-Langowski-Strasse, 14789 Woltersdorf
Telephone: +49 3362 5215

Passenger journeys: (1993) 1.2 million
(1994) 1.2 million
(1995) 1 million

Current situation: Standard-gauge tramway providing S-Bahn feeder service over Woltersdorf—Rahnsdorf route (5.6 km).

ViP

Verkehrsbetriebe Potsdam GmbH (ViP)
PO Box 601454, 14414 Potsdam
Telephone: +49 331 3750 Fax: +49 331 291706
Operating Manager: Georg Dukiewicz

Passenger journeys: (1993) 29.4 million
(1994) 28.4 million
(1995) 35 million

Current situation: Potsdam is a neighbouring city to the south of Berlin, with a population of 149,000. Bus and tramway services are provided by the municipal authority. Connections and through ticketing with BVG.
Developments: The trolleybus route was converted to diesel bus operation in 1995. Short tramway extension under construction for 1997 opening, between Robert Baberske Strasse and Kirchsteigfeld (1.5 km). A new fleet of 48 Combino LRVs is on order from Siemens for delivery between 1998 and 2000.

Poor patronage of evening tram services was causing concern in mid-1996, leading to consideration of their withdrawal. In a network restructuring implemented in June 1996, tram Route 91 was withdrawn and Route 98 extended to Robert Baberske Strasse.

Havelbus Mercedes awaits passengers in Potsdam ***1997***

Bus

Vehicle-km: (1993) 3 million
(1994) 2.9 million
(1995) 3.3 million

Number of routes: 8
Route length: 125 km
Fleet: 48 buses
Mercedes O405N 48

Tramway

Vehicle-km: (1993) 4.6 million
(1994) 4.5 million
(1995) 4.7 million

Number of routes: 7
Route length: 24.3 km
Gauge: 1,435 mm

Fleet: 100 cars
ČKD Tatra KT4D articulated M100

Havelbus

Havelbus Verkehrsgesellschaft mbH
Johannsenstrasse 12-17, 14482 Potsdam
Telephone: +49 331 749 1300 Fax: +49 331 75161
General Manager: Hans-Joachim Knop

Passenger journeys: (1993) 18.9 million
(1994) 19.2 million
(1995) 19 million

Current situation: Regional bus company formed in 1992 by Potsdam and Nauen county councils to take over the regional bus services previously operated by ViP (see above). Several routes extend into the outskirts of Berlin, where they link with BVG services.

Bus

Vehicle-km: (1993) 10.6 million
(1994) 10.9 million
(1995) 11.2 million

Number of routes: 48
Route length: 1,449 km
Fleet: 199 buses, plus 35 hired

Ikarus	88
Mercedes	55
MAN	49
Others	7

Telebus

Berliner Zentralausschuss für soziale Aufgaben eV
Telebus Fahrdienst für Behinderte in Berlin
Joachimstaler Str 15-17, 10719 Berlin
Telephone: +49 30 880030

Current situation: A fleet of wheelchair-accessible minibuses is available on demand-responsive service to those unable to use ordinary public transport. Services are operated by contractors.

UPDATED

BERN

Population: City 131,000, metropolitan area 189,000
Public transport: Bus, trolleybus and tramway services operated by undertaking responsible to city council. Separate regional company operates light rail and bus services. Swiss Federal Railway (SBB), Bern-Lötschberg-Simplon Railway (BLS) and the PTT postal coaches organisation provide suburban services; S-Bahn network planned

SVB

Städtische Verkehrsbetriebe Bern (SVB)
Eigerplatz 3, PO Box 3000, Bern 14, Switzerland
Telephone: +41 31 321 8888 Fax: +41 31 321 8866
General Manager: H-R Kamber
Staff: 710

Passenger journeys: (All modes)
(1993) 121.7 million
(1994) 127.7 million
(1995) 120.4 million

Low-floor MAN bus of SVB ***1995***

Fare collection: Self-service with Autelca ticket issuing and validating equipment
Fare structure: Zonal, with ticket books and weekly, monthly and annual passes
Fare evasion control: Roving inspectors; penalty fare
Operating costs financed by: (All modes) Fares 62%, other commercial sources 11%, compensation 10%, subsidy/grants 17%
Subsidy from: City of Bern

Bus and trolleybus

Passenger journeys: (1993) Bus 33.5 million, trolleybus 42.1 million
(1994) Bus 28.6 million, trolleybus 44.3 million
(1995) Bus 28.9 million, trolleybus 43.1 million
Vehicle-km: (1993) Bus 3.8 million, trolleybus 2.2 million
(1994) Bus 3.5 million, trolleybus 2.2 million
(1995) Bus 3.5 million, trolleybus 2.1 million

Number of routes: Bus 12, trolleybus 5
Route length: (One way) bus 46 km, trolleybus 21.6 km
On priority right-of-way: Bus 1.3 km
Number of stops: 129
Fleet: 103 buses

Mercedes	2
FBW	22
Volvo	32
Volvo articulated	10
MAN low-floor articulated	37

In peak service: 78 buses, 36 trolleybuses
Fleet: 44 trolleybuses, all articulated
Trolleybus electrification: 600 V DC

Most intensive service: 15 min
One-person operation: All routes
Operational control: Route inspectors
Average distance between stops: 390 m
Average peak-hour speed: 17 km/h
New vehicles financed by: Canton of Bern

Tramway

Type of operation: Conventional tramway

Passenger journeys: (1993) 46.6 million
(1994) 48.8 million
(1995) 48.4 million
Car-km: (1993) 2.4 million
(1994) 2.5 million
(1995) 2.5 million

Route length: 17.2 km
reserved track: 1.7 km
Number of lines: 3
Number of stops: 52
Gauge: 1,000 mm
Max gradient: 6%
Minimum curve radius: 15.5 m
Track: 60 kg/m Ri60 rail
Electrification: 600 V DC, overhead

Service: Peak 5 min, off-peak 6-12 min
First/last car: 05.40/23.45
Integration with other modes: Fully integrated with regional transport systems
One-person operation: All routes

Rolling stock: 63 cars

SWS/MFO Be 4/4 (1947/61)	M14
FFA/SIG/SWS B4 (1951/61)	T21
SWS/BBC Be 8/8 (1973)	M16
Vevey Be 4/8 low-floor (1989/90)	M12

In peak service: 29 motor cars

Developments: It is proposed to convert trolleybus routes 13 and 14 to tramway operation – SBB station to Bimpliz and Gäbelbach. Three extensions are proposed – of Route 3 from Weissenbühl to Morillongut, and of Route 9 from Wabern to Kleinwabern.

Interurban tram of RBS (left) and Vevey low-floor of SVB at Helvetiaplatz **1995**

NAW midibus of RBS on suburban Route A at Egghölzli **1995**

RBS

Regionalverkehr Bern-Solothurn (RBS)
Bahnhofhochhaus, PO Box 119, 3048 Worblaufen
Telephone: +41 31 925 5555 Fax: +41 31 925 5566
General Manager: P Scheidegger

Current situation: Two light railways, which had been under common management since 1965, were merged in 1984. The undertaking also operates 12 bus routes.

Light railway

Type of operation: Suburban light rail

Passenger journeys: (1991) 18.2 million
(1993) 17.6 million
(1994) 17.7 million

Route length: 56 km
Number of routes: 5
Number of stations: 43
Gauge: 1,000 mm
Electrification: 1.25 kV DC (52 km), 600 V DC (11 km), overhead

Service: Peak 15-30 min, off-peak 15-60 min
Fare structure: Zonal
Integration with other modes: Part fare integration with SVB, full integration with other Swiss railways
Fare evasion control: Roving inspectors, penalty fare
Signalling: ATC; all trains single-manned

Rolling stock: 10 railcars, 32 emu sets, 9 articulated trainsets, 18 driving and 3 non-driving trailers

Developments: Extension of the Gümligen line to Bern city centre on SVB tram routes 3 and 5. Further double-tracking planned, and purchase of additional emus to increase capacity.

Bus

Passenger journeys: (1991) 4.2 million

Current situation: Buses provide feeder services on 12 routes totalling 62 km serving a number of rail stations. Fleet of 68 buses, midibuses and rail service vehicles.

S-Bahn (planned)

Current situation: Reorganisation and upgrading of existing local rail services is to be undertaken to create a four-line S-Bahn network serving 118 stations. Two cross-city routes were expected to be in operation by mid-1996, with two more following in 1997 and 1998. The aim is to build on the 50 per cent increase in local rail journeys since 1987. There will be strong emphasis on park-and-ride facilities and good interchange with SVB and RBS services.

UPDATED

BIELEFELD

Population: 325,000
Public transport: Bus and tramway services provided by municipal authority; urban and regional transport co-ordinated by the regional authority VOW

VOW

Verkehrsgemeinschaft Ostwestfalen-Lippe (VOW)
PO Box 102692, 33526 Bielefeld, Germany
Telephone: +49 521 514017 Fax: +49 521 514141

Current situation: VOW co-ordinates urban services of Stadtwerke Bielefeld with suburban and regional bus services provided by BVO and several independent operators.

Stadtwerke Bielefeld

Stadtwerke Bielefeld GmbH
PO Box 102692, 33526 Bielefeld
Telephone: +49 521 514017 Fax: +49 521 514141
Technical Manager: Dr Martin Proske
Operating Manager: Dipl-Ing Manfred Weber
Commercial Manager: Wolfgang Brinkmann
Staff: 601

Passenger journeys: (All modes)
(1993) 31.1 million
(1994) 31.9 million
(1995) 32.3 million

Operating costs financed by: Fares 69.6%, other commercial sources 0.8%, subsidy/grants 24.2%, tax levy 5.4%

Bus

Passenger journeys: (1995) 13.7 million
Vehicle-km: (1993) 4.9 million
(1994) 4.8 million
(1995) 5.4 million

Number of routes: 32
Route length: 468 km
Fleet: 69 buses, plus 29 contracted out

Neoplan low-floor articulated	14
MAN low-floor articulated	7
MAN articulated	4
Neoplan standard	6
MAN standard/low-floor	15
Mercedes standard/low-floor	8
Others	15

In peak service: 64
On order: 22

Most intesive service: 10 min
One-person operation: All routes
Fare collection: Payment to driver

Jahnplatz station on Bielefeld's Stadtbahn Line 1

Arrangements for elderly/disabled: Free travel for disabled, reimbursed by government

Current situation: Shared taxi/dial-a-ride service runs in place of certain bus routes at off-peak periods, at supplementary fare.

Tramway/Light rail

Type of operation: Conventional tramway upgraded to Stadtbahn, with tunnel section in central area

Passenger journeys: (1995) 18.6 million
Car-km: (1993) 2.8 million
(1994) 2.8 million
(1995) 3.5 million

Route length: 26.1 km
in tunnel: 4.5 km
Number of routes: 6
Number of stops: 54
in tunnel: 5
Gauge: 1,000 mm
Track: S41 rail on sleepers in ballast
Electrification: 750 V DC, overhead

Service: Peak 10 min, night 30 min
First/last car: 04.30/01.00
Fare structure: Zonal
Fare collection: Prepurchase from self-service machines or agencies

Control: Siemens ZUB 100 from central control room
Surveillance: CCTV on each platform

Rolling stock: 64 cars

Duewag M8C	M44
Duewag Stadtbahn M8D (1994/95)	M20

In peak service: 59
On order: 8 cars

Developments: Line 3 extension to Stieghorst (2.5 km) opened in September 1996. Line 4 to University proposed for 1999 opening. Further 16 cars and 5 trailers required for 1998/99 delivery.

Patronage on the light rail lines has increased by up to 95 per cent since 1990 and two-car sets now run on all routes. New cars have only one driving cab.

BVO

Busverkehr Ostwestfalen GmbH (BVO)
PO Box 100824, 33508 Bielefeld
Telephone: +49 521 520700 Fax: +49 521 520 7070
Managing Directors: Heinz Georg Planz
Herbert Husser

Current situation: Railway-associated bus company providing suburban and regional bus services.

Fleet: 38 (Bielefeld services only)

UPDATED

BILBAO

Population: City 500,000, conurbation 1 million
Public transport: Most bus services provided by urban transport company, while separate company operates metro. Suburban rail lines operated by local government-controlled authority (Euskotren), and state railways RENFE (broad-gauge) and FEVE (narrow-gauge)

CTB

Consorcio de Transportes de Bizkaia
Calle Alameda Recaldé 18, 48009 Bilbao, Spain
Telephone: +34 4 424 0604 Fax: +34 4 423 1088

Current situation: In 1975 the Bizkaia regional government founded the Bizkaia Transport Consortium to supervise construction of the metro in Bilbao and oversee transport infrastructure planning generally. With metro Line 1 opened in November 1995, it is expected that the organisation will become a unitary authority for overall control of public transport in Bizkaia.

Although details are not yet finalised, it seems likely that CTB will co-ordinate the activities of RENFE and FEVE (owned by the national government), ET/FE (Basque government), and TC's Bizkaiabus and Bilbobus networks (owned by CTB), and will be responsible for creating an integrated public transport network, elimination of competition between modes, and introduction of a unified tariff structure.

Low-floor Van Hool of Bilbobus ***1996***

TC

Transportes Collectivos SA (TC)
Francisco Macía 4, 48014 Deusto Bilbao, Spain
Tel: +34 4 475 8200 Fax: +34 4 475 0355

Current situation: TC operates the Bilbobus (urban) and Bizkaiabus (suburban) bus networks.

Bus

Passenger journeys: (1993) 52.9 million
(1994) 51 million
(1995) 51.7 million

Number of routes: 37 urban, 25 suburban
Fleet: 209 vehicles

Urban fleet	117
Suburban fleet	92

Euskotren

Eusko Trenbideak – Ferrocarriles Vascos
Atxuri 6, 48006 Bilbao
Telephone: +34 4 433 9500 Fax: +34 4 433 6009
President: C Garcia
Director General: Oscar Gómez Barbero
Staff: 760

Type of operation: Suburban rail

Passenger journeys: (1993) 24.4 million
(1994) 23.3 million
(1995) 31.6 million

Current situation: Bilbao local services out of Atxuri (to Lemoa), San Nikolás (to Bolueta) and Calzadas (to Lutxana and Lezama) terminals form the rump of a 1,000 mm gauge network, electrified 1.5 kV DC overhead, following transfer of the San Nikolás—Plentzia line to the urban metro company in November 1995. Also operates eight regional bus routes in Bizkaia, which carried 4.4 million passengers in 1994.

Developments: From a new interchange station with the metro at Bolueta, it is proposed to abandon the San Nikolás terminus in central Bilbao, instead rerouteing trains through a 1.5 km tunnel (opening in 1997) to connect with services from Calzadas to Lezama. A new shuttle service will be introduced linking Calzadas with a new station at Bidarte.

In 1995, a 1.1 km extension opened from La Cruz to the centre of Lezama, with a possible 3.4 km further extension to Larrabetzu, dependent upon population growth. A new station has opened at Derio, replacing two existing sites, and another is planned at Elotxelerri. The depot and workshops at Lutxana are to be modernised.

Management of the Lutxana—Sondika branch is also to pass to the metro authority.

A prototype CNG-powered bus entered service in March 1995.

Rolling stock: 21 emu sets

Metro Bilbao

Elcana 3, 48001 Bilbao
Telephone: +34 4 425 4000 Fax: +34 4 425 4039
Managing Director: Josu Sagastagoitia
Operating Manager: J M Ortega
Staff: 442

Type of operation: Full metro, opened 1995

Route length: 26.5 km
Number of lines: 1
Number of station: 23
Gauge: 1,000 mm
Electrification: 1.5 kV DC, overhead

Service interval: Peak 5 min
First/last train: 06.00/23.00
Fare structure: Zonal; multijourney tickets and passes
Integration with other modes: Planned as part of future integrated transport authority in Bizkaia

Opening day on the Bilbao metro ***1996***

Signalling: Manual operation prior to commissioning of ATO/ATP

Rolling stock: 96 cars

CAF/ABB (1995)	M48 T48

Current situation: Bilbao's first metro line, linking Plentzia and Casco Viejo, was opened in 1995 following transfer of the 20.5 km Plentzia line from ET/FV. This has been linked to a new 5 km city-centre tunnel to create metro Line 1.

Developments: The remaining 4.5 km underground portion of Line 1, between Casco Viejo and Bolueta, with three stations, was due to open in late 1996. At the latter station, a new interchange will provide easy connections to and from ET/FE services to Lemoa, Bermeo and San Sebastián.

Construction of Line 2, running 9.5 km from Lutxana to Santurzi with 9 stations, started in 1996 following approval of a Pta 28.5 billion grant from the Bizkaia government. A further 10 four-car trains will be required for opening in 2000. Plans for a complementary light rail network have been abandoned.

FEVE

Ferrocarriles de Via Estrecha – Spanish Narrow Gauge Railways
General Rodrigo 6, 28003 Madrid
Telephone: +34 1 533 7000 Fax: +34 1 533 7994

Passenger journeys: (1993) 1.5 million
(1994) 1.7 million
(1995) 1.8 million

Current situation: An hourly/half-hourly suburban service operates between Bilbao Concordia and Balmaseda (32 km, 18 stations).

Developments: Electric trains (1.5 kV) started running in 1996 following delays due to infrastructure problems at Iraurogi, junction of the line to Santander. Services are worked by surplus emus from Gijón. Transfer of the line to Euskotren is a possibility once electrification is complete.

RENFE

Spanish National Railways
Avendia Ciudad de Barcelona 8, 28007 Madrid
Telephone: +34 1 606 6401 Fax: +34 1 315 0384
Managing Director, Suburban: Angel Ibañez
Staff: 310 (Bilbao area only)

Passenger journeys: (1993) 23.8 million
(1994) 24.2 million
(1995) 23.5 million

Current situation: RENFE operates 1,668 mm gauge suburban trains from La Naja station (adjacent to the main line terminus at Norte) to Santurzi and San Julian de Musques. Bilbao is RENFE's third busiest suburban network. Total 67 km, 1,668 mm gauge, on three routes with 39 stations; electrified 3 kV DC.

Developments: Patronage fell by 3.4 per cent in 1992 to 72,000 daily, and saw a further 1 per cent decline in 1993. To combat this, train frequencies have been improved to between 3 and 10 trains/h. Voltage on the La Naja route was stepped up from 1.5 to 3 kV in 1991, permitting deployment of 13 Class 446 emus converted for high-platform operation. Restricted platform lengths prevent these trains from being operated in multiple.

The La Naja—Santurzi service will be replaced by Line 2 of the metro, and the remaining service to Musques rerouted over a freight line into Norte station, which itself is to be replaced by the new joint station with FEVE (see above).

Rolling stock: 22 three-car emus

Class 446	M44 T22

UPDATED

BIRMINGHAM (UK)

Population: City 1 million, West Midlands conurbation 2.6 million

Public transport: Bus services operated by a major private company and over 50 other independent companies. As well as running commercial services, some operators are contracted for provision of supported services by Passenger Transport Executive (Centro), which also contracts for provision of local rail services. West Midlands area covers surrounding urban areas of Coventry, Wolverhampton, Walsall, Dudley, Solihull, West Bromwich. Light rail under construction

Travel West Midlands

Travel West Midlands Ltd
1 Sovereign Court, 8 Graham Street, Birmingham B1 3JR, England
Telephone: +44 121 200 7327 Fax: +44 121 233 1217
Group Executive Chairman: Phil White
Staff: 4,500

Current situation: Travel West Midlands was created from the bus operating interests of the PTE and was sold by the Passenger Transport Authority to its workforce in 1991. Acquired by the long-distance coach operator National Express in 1995, it remains the dominant bus operator in the area.

Developments: A number of marketing developments have been implemented in a bid to retain traffic, including major-route brandings on some corridors and maintenance of Smiths 'Your Bus' as a low-cost competitive unit. A showcase corridor was introduced in February 1997 on Route 33 to Kingstanding in partnership with Birmingham City Council and Centro. Low-floor buses, special stops and real-time information are provided.

A new marketing image, Travel West Midlands, is being introduced on 300 low-floor buses now entering service, 14 of which are powered by CNG.

In November 1996, TWM joined the Altram consortium which is building the Midland Metro (see below); it will operate the line on opening in 1998.

Bus

Passenger journeys: (1992/93) 332 million
(1993/94) 318.3 million
(1995/96) 328 million
Vehicle-km: (1992/93) 106 million
(1993/94) 104.2 million
(1995/96) 105 million

Number of routes: 500
Route length: 7,524 km
On priority right-of-way: 7 km
Fleet: 1,870 vehicles

Leyland Fleetline double-deck	144
Daimler double-deck	1
MCW Metrobus double-deck	1,096
Scania double-deck	40
Dennis single-deck	13
Volvo single-deck	79
Leyland National single-deck	72
Leyland Lynx single-deck	256
Leyland Tiger single-deck	8
DAF single-deck	21
Coaches	20
Minibuses	120

In peak service: 1,544
On order: 300

Most intensive service: 2-3 min
One-person operation: All services
Fare collection: Autofare farebox with Wayfarer driver-operated ticket-issuing machine
Fare structure: Graduated stage fares with maximum off-peak fare; prepurchase travelcards for varying areas and time periods, including annual and off-peak only; direct-debit Clubcard
Fares collected on board: 45%; travelcards advance sales 26%; concessionary travel passes 29%
Fare evasion control: Spot checks by revenue control inspectors
Operational control: Route inspectors/mobile radio
Arrangements for elderly/disabled: Passes for free bus travel, at all times, issued by Metropolitan District Councils to all blind persons and, at discretion, to disabled persons. Councils pay WMT to accept these for travel on bus and local rail services outside peak periods and up to 23.29 daily. Passes for free off-peak bus travel issued to the elderly by PTE (Centro)
Average distance between stops: 300 m
Integration with other modes: Travelcard system available on all WMT bus services; combined Centrocard for bus and local services also available; interchanges at a number of rail stations
Operating costs financed by: Fares 97%, tendered service support 3%

Midland Red West

Midland Red West Ltd
Heron Lodge, London Road, Worcester WR5 2EW
Telephone: +44 1905 359393 Fax: +44 1905 351104
Managing Director: Ken Mills

Current situation: This former NBC subsidiary was purchased by its management in 1987 and is now owned by FirstBus.

Commercial minibus and full-size vehicle services have been developed after initial success with West Midland tendered services.

Fleet: 311 buses

Single-deck	134
Dual-purpose	2
Coaches	21
Minibuses	154

Birmingham Omnibus

Birmingham Passenger Transport Services Ltd
Hallbridge Way, Cross Quays Business Park, Tipton Road, Tividale B69 3HY
Telephone: +44 121 555 5522 Fax: +44 121 620 4999
Managing Director: Geoff Howle
Staff: 145

Current situation: Established in 1984, the company has grown quickly by introducing competitive and subsidised routes throughout the city. Acquired Sealandair of West Bromwich in 1994 and thus became the largest independent operator in the area.

Bus

Passenger journeys: (1993/94) 5.2 million

Number of routes: 16
Fleet: 88 vehicles

Leyland single-deck	68
DAF SB220 single-deck	3
Coaches	17

MCW Metrobus of WM at Colmore Circus

1997

Plaxton-bodied Dennis Dart of Midland Red West at Digbeth

1997

Leyland National of BCC loading in central Birmingham **1997**

Merry Hill

Merry Hill Minibus Ltd
100 Dudley Road East, Oldbury B69 3HG
Telephone: +44 1384 573711
General Manager: D J Venables

Current situation: Minibuses are developing routes into the Merry Hill shopping centre at Brierley Hill from various parts of the West Midlands; 12 routes operated by 48 minibuses.

Chase

Chase Coaches Ltd
No Name Road, Chasetown WS7 8FS
Telephone: +44 1543 686937 Fax: +44 1543 686432
Managing Director: G Dodd

Current situation: Operates both local and long-distance routes into north Birmingham; total 25 commercial and tendered routes operated by 66 buses and 10 coaches.

Other operators

Current situation: Among those providing commercial services are Banga Travel of Wolverhampton, Caves of Solihull, City Buses of Hockley, Claribel of Tile Cross, Falcon Travel of Smethwick, Frontline of Tamworth, Flights of Handsworth, Green Bus of Great Wyrley, Lionspeed of West Bromwich, Little Red Bus of Smethwick, Ludlows Travel of Halesowen, Metropolitan of Darlaston, Midland Choice of Willenhall, Midland Red North of Cannock, Midland Red South of Rugby, North Birmingham Busways, Pete's Travel of West Bromwich Great Barr, Sandwell Travel, Serveverse of Tamworth, West Midlands Road Car and Zak's of Great Barr.

Centro

West Midlands Passenger Transport Executive
16 Summer Lane, Birmingham B19 3SD
Telephone: +44 121 200 2787 Fax: +44 121 214 7010
Director General: Rob Donald
Passenger Services Director: Liz Gilliard
Finance Director: Phil Severs
Staff: 197

Passenger journeys: (By operators in Centro's concessionary fares scheme)
(1993/94) 366 million
(1994/95) 370.9 million
(1995/96) 370.5 million

Current situation: West Midlands PTE, which operates as Centro, is responsible for contracting socially necessary bus services and specifying and supporting the local rail network. It is also promoting a light rail system for the area, known as Midland Metro (see below). It has responsibility for those with mobility handicaps and finances West Midlands Special Needs Transport Ltd, a registered charity which operates 'Ring and Ride' services for the elderly and disabled. It also operates concessionary fare schemes for children and pensioners who are entitled to free bus and train travel outside peak hours. Commercial ticketing schemes are also managed on behalf of all bus operators and local rail. Centro is responsible for 11 bus stations and over 3,000 on-street shelters, as well as providing an information service.

Centro's policies and funding come from the Passenger Transport Authority, a body of 27 representatives from the seven district councils which make up the West Midlands metropolitan area. The PTA submits a levy on the councils for funds necessary for it to carry out its work.

Developments: A 20-year strategy for public transport improvements was published in 1993, detailing investment totalling £2.5 billion. The principal features are: completion of the entire 200 km Midland Metro scheme by 2010; creation and electrification of two new cross-city suburban railways, and provision of improved services on existing lines; construction of six new bus stations and 23 new rail stations with an additional 10,000 park-and-ride spaces; creation of 150 km of bus lanes; and major investment in new trains and buses. Amongst other aims for a dramatic improvement in the region's public transport, the strategy suggestions included a fresh look at the way bus service deregulation is operating, closer liaison between planning and transport authorities, and an examination of road pricing.

Contracted bus services

Current situation: Some 410 contracts are let for services which no operator will run commercially; these are worth about £3.1 million. Of these contracts, 45 per cent are operated by Travel West Midlands, 37 per cent by Midland Red West, and the remainder by other operators. Subsidised services are 6.5 per cent of the total network, amounting to about 8.3 million km per year.

Contracted rail services

Operated for Centro by Central Trains Limited
10 Holliday Street, Birmingham B1 1TG
Telephone: +44 121 643 4444 Fax: +44 121 644 4461
Managing Director: Mark Causebrook

Type of operation: Suburban heavy rail

Passenger journeys: (1993/94) 22.8 million
(1994/95) 19.7 million
(1995/96) 20.6 million

Current situation: Services operated with Centro support on eight routes with 71 stations totalling 166 km. Five routes are electrified at 25 kV 50 Hz and three are diesel-worked.

Developments: Birmingham's third cross-city route, the Jewellery line, opened in 1995, linking Snow Hill with Smethwick and allowing operation of new through services from Stourbridge to Solihull and Shirley, avoiding the congested New Street station in the city centre.

Electrification of the Redditch—Lichfield cross-city route (49 km) was completed in 1993, but its operation was blighted by poor performance of the much-delayed new-generation Class 323 emu trains, and the older trains that provided cover for them.

Poor train reliability has now been largely overcome, and the Jewellery line is providing the designed relief to New Street station. Spurred by a rewards and penalties scheme, the operator Central Trains has improved performance markedly.

Rolling stock: 61 dmu and 85 emu cars

The two-level Galton Bridge interchange on the Jewellery line ***1996***

Light rail

Under construction

Current situation: Construction started in late 1995 on the initial phase of the Midland Metro project, a light rail system linking Birmingham with other major towns in the conurbation. Parliament has approved three lines totalling 80 km, including the initial route between Birmingham and Wolverhampton, using former railway alignment and with a 2 km on-street section in Wolverhampton town centre. Total cost will be £145 million.

In 1993 the Altram consortium, comprising Ansaldo Trasporti and civil engineering firm John Laing, was appointed to build Line 1 (20.4 km, 23 stops). The contract, for a 23-year concession to design, build, operate and maintain Line 1, was signed in 1995, and marked the start of the three-year construction period and 20-year operating agreement. Travel West Midlands joined the consortium in late 1996, and will operate the system on completion in 1998.

Centro had been granted parliamentary powers for several other routes. Line 2 runs 27.5 km in tunnel beneath Birmingham's city centre then on the surface to serve Castle Vale, Chelmsley Wood, the National Exhibition Centre and airport. Line 3 runs from Wolverhampton to Brierley Hill via Walsall and Dudley (32.5 km). However, in March 1997 Centro allowed its compulsory purchase powers to lapse for Line 2 and most of Line 3. Only the Wednesbury—Brierley Hill section of Line 3 remains intact, and this may be built as a Line 1 extension along with one or two other short sections.

Powers have also been obtained for a loop around Wolverhampton town centre and for a tunnel extension in Birmingham city centre.

UPDATED

BIRMINGHAM (USA)

Population: 750,000

Public transport: Fixed-route and specialised bus services provided under contract by Transit Authority, controlled by a Board of Directors. Several proposals for light rail lines under study by the Regional Planning Commission

MAX

Birmingham-Jefferson County Transit Authority
PO Box 10212, 3105 Eighth Avenue North, Birmingham, AL 35202-0212, USA
Telephone: +1 205 322 7701 Fax: +1 205 521 0120
General Manager: Phil Gary
Operations Manager: Ray J Taylor
Staff: 311

Current situation: BJCTA is the principal transit operator, using the name Metro Area Express (MAX). The authority includes seven member municipalities and the unincorporated areas of Jefferson County. BJCTA took over the operations of the private Birmingham Transit Company in 1973.

In 1982 the Alabama state legislature approved a Levelised Beer Tax which guaranteed the authority a minimum $2 million per year in local funding. Subsequently, the hours of service and patronage have steadily increased. Routes have been reorganised for more efficient scheduling, bringing additional services without an increase in the workforce.

Maxpool co-ordinates and arranges carpools through a free computerised matching system. Private employer support is encouraged for the vanpool programme by purchase of a 7-15 seat van which is then maintained by MAX. Maxpool is also responsible for operation of park-and-ride lots throughout the service area.

Trolley replicas operate two city-centre off-peak shuttle routes knows as DART (Downtown Area Rapid Transit).

Bus

Passenger journeys: (1991/92) 6.4 million
(1992/93) 6 million

Vehicle-km: (1991/92) 7.5 million
(1992/93) 7.8 million

Number of routes: 40
Route length: 2,703 km
Fleet: 143 vehicles

GMC RTS (1979)	19
Flxible 870 (1981)	37
Gillig Phantom (1987)	47
Boyertown trolley replicas (1990)	6
Flxible Metro (1997)	12
Blue Bird CS (1995)	22

Average age of fleet: 11.5 years
In peak service: 76

Most intensive service: 10 min on DART routes; no late evening service

One-person operation: All routes
Fare collection: Exact fare, registering farebox on board; Maxpass 7-day and monthly tickets
Fare structure: Flat, supplement for transfer
Operational control: Route inspectors/mobile radio
Arrangements for elderly/disabled: Accessible buses and door-to-door operation known as VIP Service; hours of operation extended in 1993 to match those of fixed-route service
Integration with other modes: Maxpool encourages ride-sharing; extensive park-and-ride
Operating costs financed by: Fares 30.6%, FTA subsidy/grants 22.5%, state and local funds 44.9% (Ad valorem and beer tax)
New vehicles financed by: 80% FTA, 20% local funding

Light rail (planned)

Current situation: The planning process started in 1992 for a proposed light rail link in the corridor connecting the city centre with the Birmingham Medical Centre and University of Alabama. Monorail link to the airport also discussed.

UPDATED

Route 42 bus in downtown Birmingham

BLANTYRE

Population: 1 million
Public transport: Bus services provided by company part-owned by the government, also responsible for services in other parts of Malawi. Large number of private minibuses

Stagecoach Malaŵi

Stagecoach Malaŵi Limited
PO Box 176, Blantyre, Malawi
Telephone: +265 671388 Fax: +265 670038
Managing Director: C M Tyler

Current situation: In 1989 United Transport (Malaŵi) became 51 per cent owned by Stagecoach Holdings Ltd of Perth, UK, 34 per cent by the Malawi government (14 per cent directly and 20 per cent through Admarc, a parastatal organisation), and 15 per cent by an employee trust. This followed purchase by Stagecoach of the share formerly held by United Transport International. The change in company name took place in 1990. The company operates urban services in Blantyre, and intercity and country services throughout Malawi.
Developments: Rapidly increasing urbanisation of Blantyre has increased the total public transport market, but most growth has been absorbed by informal transit such as Matolas (pick-ups and government vehicles) and minibuses. With little regulation of these operations, legal services have been badly hit.

ERF Trailblazers at Blantyre Market ***1997***

Bus

Blantyre urban operations only
Staff: 450

Passenger journeys: (1993/94) 24 million
(1994/95) 21.3 million
(1995/96) 20.4 million
Vehicle-km: (1993/94) 5 million
(1994/95) 4.5 million
(1995/96) 4.3 million

Number of routes: 19
Route length: 360 km
Fleet: 66 buses

Leyland Victory Mk1	6
Leyland Victory Mk2	31
ERF (1993/94)	29

In peak service: 48

One-person operation: 4 buses
Fare collection: Floating conductors with Setright or Almex ticket equipment; two conductors on busy routes; prepurchase at certain central area stops.
Fare structure: Per kilometre; graduated fares outside city
Operating costs financed by: Fares 98%, other commercial sources (advertising) 2%

Minibus

Current situation: Around 300 privately owned minibuses provide competing services. Most are poorly maintained, many are unlicensed and untaxed.

UPDATED

BOCHUM-GELSENKIRCHEN

Population: 699,000, area served 975,000
Public transport: Bus and tramway/light rail services in Bochum, Gelsenkirchen and adjoining cities provided by public corporation within framework of Verkehrsverbund Rhein-Ruhr (VRR) (qv). Underground sections of tramway in both Bochum and Gelsenkirchen; standard-gauge Stadtbahn line U35 links Bochum and Herne. Area also served by DB S-Bahn

Bogestra

Bochum-Gelsenkirchener Strassenbahnen AG
Universitätsstrasse 58, 44789 Bochum, Germany
Telephone: + 49 234 3030 Fax: +49 234 303 2300
Directors: Dipl-Ing Gerd Liedtke
Gisbert Schlotzhauer
Dr Burkhard Rüberg

MAN NL202 low-floor bus at Bochum Hbf

paved reserved track usable also by buses where possible.

In 1993 tickets and passes changed to the magnetic strip system, with new cancelling machines installed on all buses and trams, and at the entrances to metro and pre-metro stations.

Passenger journeys: (All modes)
(1992) 205.6 million
(1993) 207 million
(1994) 210 million

Operating costs financed by: (All modes) fares 33%, other commercial sources 5%, subsidy/grants 62%
Subsidy from: Regional government

Bus

Staff: 1,193

Passenger journeys: (1992) 52.4 million
(1993) 56.7 million
(1994) 62 million
Vehicle-km: (1992) 20.8 million
(1993) 21 million
(1994) 27.7 million

Number of routes: 47
Route length: 203 km
Fleet: 537 vehicles

Van Hool-Fiat 409AU9 (1972/73/74)	39
Van Hool-Daf AU115X (1975)	15
Volvo B59-1 (SBMA)/Jonckheere (1975-76)	60
Volvo B59-2 (SBMA)/Jonckheere (1976-77)	70
Van Hool-MAN A120 (1978-79)	73
Van Hool-MAN AG280 articulated (1984-85)	25
Van Hool A500 (1991/92)	180
Van Hool A300 (1992-94)	60
Citroën-C35/Durisotti minibuses (1985/89/91)	12
Renault Master T35D/VD Casteele minibuses (1985)	3

In peak service: 425

Most intensive service: 5 min
One-person operation: All routes
Fare collection: Prepurchase multitickets or passes with validation and cancelling machines on board or payment to driver; over 90% hold passes or multijourney cards
Fare structure: Flat, discount for ticketcards, passes. Free transfers within 60 min
Fare evasion control: Roving inspectors
Operational control: Central control of all modes has radio contact with bus fleet and traffic management monitoring facilities; sophisticated real-time monitoring of all surface vehicles
Arrangements for elderly/disabled: Special minibus service provided; 15 vehicles lift-equipped
Average peak-hour speed: 19.5 km/h
Integration with other modes: MTB annual or monthly season tickets valid on all STIB services and former SNCV and SNCB lines within Bruxelles area

Current situation: Buses are now mainly intended to act as feeders to the metro and tramway system.

Tramway/pre-metro

Drivers: 690

Type of operation: Conventional tramway with 2 pre-metro city-centre tunnels

Passenger journeys: (1992) 60.3 million
(1993) 62.6 million
(1994) 63.5 million
Car-km: (1992) 11.4 million
(1993) 11.4 million
(1994) 11.8 million

Route length: 199.2 km
in tunnel: 12.1 km
reserved track: 62.7 km
Number of routes: 15, including 3 pre-metro
Number of stations: Pre-metro 17 (4 joint with metro)
Gauge: 1,435 mm
Electrification: 600 V DC, overhead

Service: Peak 3 min in city centre, off-peak 4 or 5 cars per hour on most routes
First/last car: 0500/0034
Fare structure: As bus
Fare collection: As bus

Low-floor Van Hool A300 on Route 80 at Merode **1995**

Tram 2000 at Montgomery **1995**

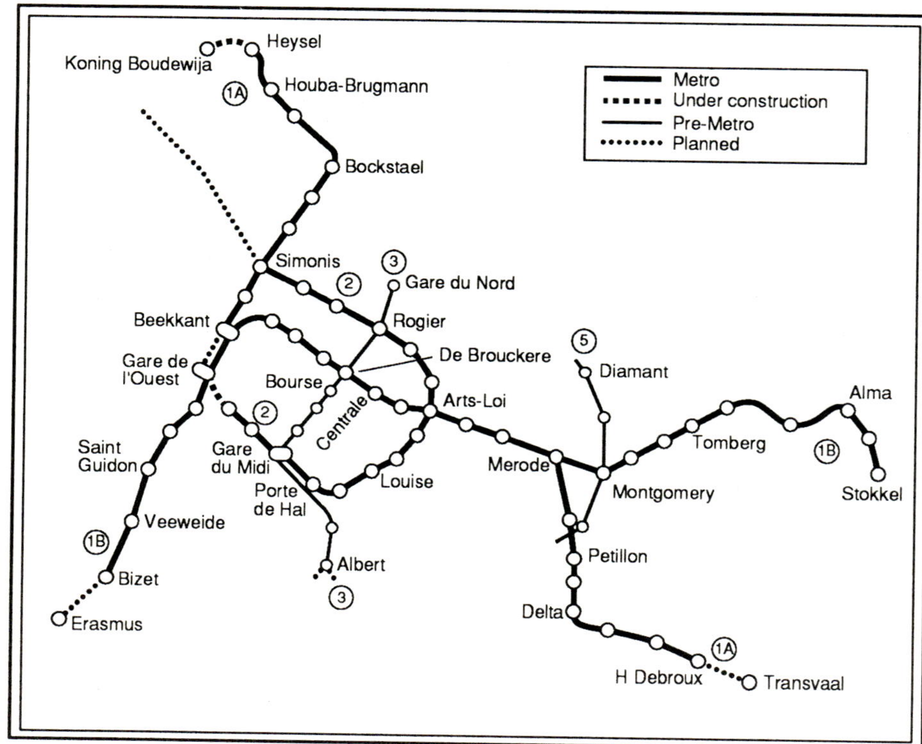

Bruxelles metro and pre-metro

One-person operation: All cars
Automatic control: All light rail and pre-metro cars to be equipped with 'Greenwave' equipment for priority traffic light control

Rolling stock: 330 cars

BN PCC 7000 four-axle (1952/56/57/70)	M91
BN 7700 six-axle articulated (1971-73)	M127
BN 7900 eight-axle articulated (1977)	M61
GEC Alsthom/BN Tram 2000 (1994/95)	M51

In peak service: 224

Current situation: Extensive track renewal in progress, with some routes temporarily replaced by buses. Plans for further segregation of on-street routes, and conversion of routes operating through the Line 3 pre-metro tunnel to

Metro Line 1B trains ***1997***

light rail standards. Lines 18 and 55 extended in 1993, when Line 3 was extended to Albert.

Metro

Drivers: 172

Type of operation: Full metro, first line opened 1976

Passenger journeys: (1992) 93 million
(1993) 87.8 million
(1994)

Route length: 40.5 km
Number of lines: 3
Number of stations: 51
Gauge: 1,435 mm
Electrification: 900 V DC, third rail

Service: Peak 6 min, off-peak 10-20 min
First/last train: 05.15/00.35
Fare structure: Flat

Rolling stock: 192 cars, in 3- and 5-car sets

BN Series 100 (1975/76)	M90
BN Series 200 (1980/81)	M70
BN (1991/92)	M32

In peak service: 151 cars

Current situation: A 60 km metro was planned, based on diversion of existing tramways into tunnel in a 'pre-metro' stage. Construction difficulties and political problems slowed development, but 1985 saw completion of metro Line 1, on which dedicated trains first ran in 1976. In 1988 an extension to Stokkel was opened, along with conversion of the 12 km pre-metro Line 2 (the Inner Circle) to heavy metro operation; six new stations were opened at the same time. Two sections of pre-metro continue to carry tram services in the city centre (see above).

Extension of Line 1A to Roi Baudoin (Amandiers) under construction for early 1999 opening, for which a further 17 cars will be ordered.

TEC/De Lijn

TEC Brabant
Rue de la Loi 89, 1040 Bruxelles
Telephone: +32 2 287 2911 Fax: +32 2 230 0704
De Lijn, Vlaams-Brabant Region
Rue Bara 105-107, 1070 Bruxelles
Telephone: +32 2 526 2811 Fax: +32 2 526 2816

Current situation: Separate organisations are responsible for urban and regional operations in the two language-based areas of the country — Vlaamse Vervoermaatschappij (VVM) operating in Flemish-speaking areas as De Lijn, and Société Regionale Wallonne du Transport Public (SRWT) in French-speaking areas as TEC. These substantial bus operations in and around Bruxelles reflect the former tramway system serving outer areas now swallowed up in the metropolitan area. Services are closely integrated with those of STIB-MIVB.

SNCB

Belgian National Railways (SNCB/NMBS), Central District
Avenue Fonsnylaan 47B, 1060 Bruxelles
Telephone: +32 2 224 5111 Fax: +32 2 224 5337

Type of operation: Suburban and interurban heavy rail

Current situation: Suburban and longer-distance interurban services run at least hourly on 10 routes radiating from Bruxelles. Most trains run through from Nord to Midi or vice versa, providing frequent cross-city link through Centrale station. Also 20-min service to the National airport. Electrified 3 kV DC.

UPDATED

BUCUREŞTI

Population: 2.3 million
Public transport: Bus, trolleybus and tramway services provided by state shareholding company responsible to municipal council, with similar company operating the metro; other bus and minibus services run by private-sector organisations

RATB

Regia Autonomă de Transport Bucureşti (RATB)
1 Bd Dinicu Golescu, Sector 1, 77111 Bucureşti, Romania
Telephone: +40 1 614 7130 Fax: +40 1 311 0595
General Manager: Constantin Popescu
Technical Manager: Constantin Donea
Operating Manager: Mitică Ghită
Staff: 4,027

Passenger journeys: (All modes)
(1993) 682 million
(1994) 629 million
(1995) 575 million

Operating costs financed by: (All modes) Fares 29.8%, government subsidy 70.2%

Current situation: RATB was created in 1991 as successor to the former operator ITB. It is a state-owned autonomous enterprise responsible for bus, tramway and trolleybus operations.

Since 1990 new routes have been introduced every year, and additions to the fleet have helped reduce overcrowding.

Developments: A further 3.5 km of tramway was rebuilt during 1996, and 19 km of new trolleybus wiring completed. Some 60 new buses were delivered and 20 trolleybuses ordered. RATB's works rehabilitated 27 tramcars in conjunction with Faur, as well as converting four Saurer buses to trolleybuses.

Bus and trolleybus

Staff: Bus 2,289, trolleybus 562

DAF SB220 of RATB ***1997***

Passenger journeys: (1993) Bus 289 million, trolleybus 111 million
(1994) Bus 275.7 million, trolleybus 88.3 million
(1995) Bus 252 million, trolleybus 77.8 million
Vehicle-km: (1993) Bus 54.8 million, trolleybus 11.5 million
(1994) Bus 61.2 million, trolleybus 11.7 million
(1995) Bus 66.4 million, trolleybus 11.8 million

Number of routes: Bus 113, trolleybus 16
Route length: (One way) bus 2,400 km, trolleybus 246 km
Fleet: 1,268 buses

DAC 117UD	41
DAC 112UD	799
Ikarus (YU) IK4	5
Ikarus 260	177
Saviem SC109 (ex-Paris)	70
DAF SB220 (1994/95)	171
Rocar UL70	5

Fleet: 265 trolleybuses

Rocar/DAC 312E	1
DAC 117E articulated	132
DAC 217E articulated	38
DAC 117EA articulated	69
DAC 317ED articulated	1
DAC 212ECS	4
Saurer conversion from diesel	20

In peak service: Bus 913, trolleybus 207

Most intensive service: Bus 3-40 min, trolleybus 7-30 min
Fare structure: Flat; express routes at higher fare;

prepurchase 2-journey, multitickets, monthly passes for whole system or one or two lines
Fare collection: Tickets purchased from approved vendors, cancelling machines on board
Fare evasion control: Inspectors
Fares collected on board: None
Arrangements for elderly/disabled: Reduced fare for elderly, disabled free
Operational control: Route inspectors, mobile radio and CCTV; 11 routes equipped with AVM
Average distance between stops: Bus 528 m, trolleybus 484 m
Average peak-hour speed: Bus 17.2 km/h, trolleybus 13.3 km/h

Tramway

Staff: 1,141

Type of operation: Conventional tramway

Passenger journeys: (1993) 281.9 million
(1994) 264.9 million
(1995) 244.4 million
Car-km: (1993) 27.4 million
(1994) 29.6 million
(1995) 31.5 million

Route length: 395 km
Number of lines: 41
Gauge: 1,435 mm
Track: Rail in prefabricated concrete panels on straight sections, in cobbles or tarmac on curves
Electrification: 750 V DC, overhead

Service: 2-25 min
First/last car: 0420/0015
Fare structure/collection: As bus
One-person operation: All routes

Rolling stock: 786 cars, including many unserviceable

Electroputere EP 4-axle (1954 on)	M157 T77
ITB Works V3A 8-axle (1973 on)	M321
ČKD Tatra T4R 4-axle (1971 on)	M130
ITB Works V2A 6-axle (1982)	M49
Rathgeber M4 (1957, ex-München)	M14 T18
Duewag 4-axle (ex-Frankfurt)	M10 T10

In peak service: 461

Metro

Regia Autonomă de Exploatare a Metroului Bucureşti
38 Bdul Dinicu Golescu, Sectol 1, 79917 Bucureşti
Telephone: +40 1 638 7515 Fax: +40 1 312 5149
General Manager: Radu Farmus
Operations Director: Petre Anghel
Technical Director: Iustin Suteu
Staff: 6,565

Type of operation: Full metro, first line opened 1979

Passenger journeys: (1992) 256.7 million
(1994) 211 million
(1995) 170 million

Route length: 59.2 km
Number of lines: 3
Number of stations: 40
Track: UIC 49/60 rail on timber sleepers; twin-block concrete sleepers in tunnel
Minimum curve radius: 150 m
Tunnel: Open-cut rectangular box section or separate bores for each track
Electrification: 750 V DC, third rail

Service: 4-10 min
Fare structure: Flat; 2- and 10-trip tickets, daily/monthly passes
Fare collection: Magnetic tickets
Integration with other modes: Poor; tickets are not interchangeable and stations have no indication that interchange to surface transport is possible
Operating costs financed by: Fares 26.5%, other commercial sources 0.5%, state subsidy 73%
Signalling: Automatic block with cab signalling

Rolling stock: 502 cars in two-car sets, of which 318 cars in working order

Current situation: Extension from Gara de Nord to Laromet (6.4 km, six stations) under construction.

Minibuses of private operators at Bucur Obor – Iveco of Maxi-Taxi Allegro (left) and Rocar TV of Expres Dally ***1995***

Electroputere tram on Route 46 at Bucur Obor ***1996***

Universitatii metro station ***1996***

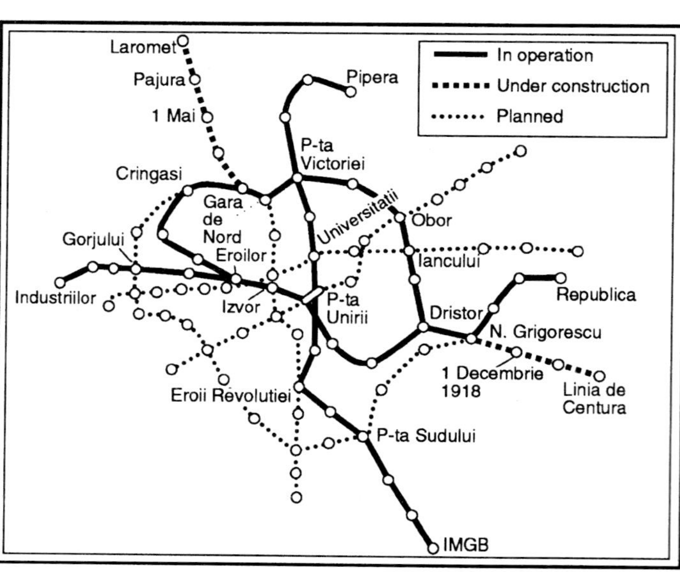

Bucureşti metro

Maxi-Taxi Allegro

SC Maxi-Taxi Allegro SA
Str Chitila Triaj 4, Sector 6 Cartier Giulesti, 77829 Bucureşti
Telephone: +40 1 618 5430
General Manager: Mihai Dumitrache

Minibus

Passenger journeys: (1991) 7.2 million

Current situation: RATB's minibus operations are now run by a private company. About 140 vehicles, mainly Rocar TV and Iveco Daily 40.10, ply over 12 routes.

Expres Dally

Expres Dally

Current situation: This independent operator started services in 1993 with two routes.

UPDATED

Mezes terminus with outer-suburban buses interchanging with tram Route 45
1996

BUDAPEST

Population: 2.1 million
Public transport: Bus, trolleybus, tramway, rack railway, suburban railways and metro operated by former municipal undertaking; river ferries; suburban bus services also provided by Volán No 20 and commuter rail services by Hungarian State Railways (MÀV)

BKV

Budapest Transport Limited (BKV)
Akácfa utca 15, 1980 Budapest VII, Hungary
Telephone: +36 1 122 2860 Fax: +36 1 121 5257
Director General: Botond Aba
Director, Buses: Károly Klér
Director, Tramway & Trolleybus: István Drégeli
Director, Metro: Dr Tamás Szabó
Staff: 19,632

Déak Tér metro station

Passenger boardings: (All modes)
(1993) 1,470 million
(1994) 1,530 million
(1995) 1,520 million

Operating costs financed by: Fares 31.6%, price supplement 23.5%, other commercial sources 7.9%, municipal grants 29.8%, state grants 7.2%
Subsidy from: National government 30.3%, local government 69.7%

Current situation: BKV, which had been transformed from a state company to municipal ownership, became a limited company at the beginning of 1996. It operates the city's bus, trolleybus, tram, metro, rack and suburban railways. Its ferry operations were sold in 1996.
Developments: In a further stage of its bus replacement programme, in 1996 BKV commissioned a further 80 environmentally friendly buses, along with 60 midibuses and eight trolleybuses. Installation of automatic vehicle monitoring continues, and 232 buses were refurbished to higher environmental standards.

Stage II of the reconstruction of tram tracks in the Grand Boulevard has continued, and reconstruction of the metro Millennium line and the city section of tram Line 2 was completed.

Tatra T5 on express Route 1 at Nepstadion terminus ***1995***

The fleet of Ganz articulated trams is being refurbished to extend their life by 15 years in a programme which includes installation of an energy-saving driving system and improved comfort standards for drivers and passengers. Metro stock is to be upgraded too; the original Soviet-built fleet of 195 cars dating from 1969 will be refurbished at a rate of 20 cars per year starting in 1997.

Reconstruction of a further 47 km of tram track is to go ahead with the aid of World Bank funds. Work will be concentrated mainly on the northern and southern sections of Nagykörút boulevard. The World Bank has also financed purchase of modern track construction and maintenance equipment, and the metro rolling stock depot is to have a spray painting booth that meets current European environmental standards.

Bus and trolleybus

Passenger journeys: (1993) Bus 682 million, trolleybus 87 million
(1994) Bus 730 million, trolleybus 85 million
(1995) Bus 749.4 million, trolleybus 82.5 million
Vehicle-km: (1993) Bus 109 million, trolleybus 8.3 million
(1994) Bus 105 million, trolleybus 8.5 million
(1995) Bus 98 million, trolleybus 8.2 million

Number of routes: Bus 152, trolleybus 14
Route length: Bus 1,166 km, trolleybus 68.7 km
Fleet: 1,506 buses

Ikarus IK260	655
Ikarus IK280 articulated	419
Ikarus 435 articulated	168
Ikarus 415	174
Ikarus 405 low-floor minibus	90
Sightseeing buses	24

Average age of fleet: 5.5 years
Fleet: 192 trolleybuses

Uritsky ZIU9	97
Ikarus articulated	95

Average age of fleet: 10 years
In peak service: Bus 1,251, trolleybus 140

Ikarus 280T on Route 75 at Dozsa Gyutca **1995**

Ikarus 405 low-floor minibus at Buda Castle **1997**

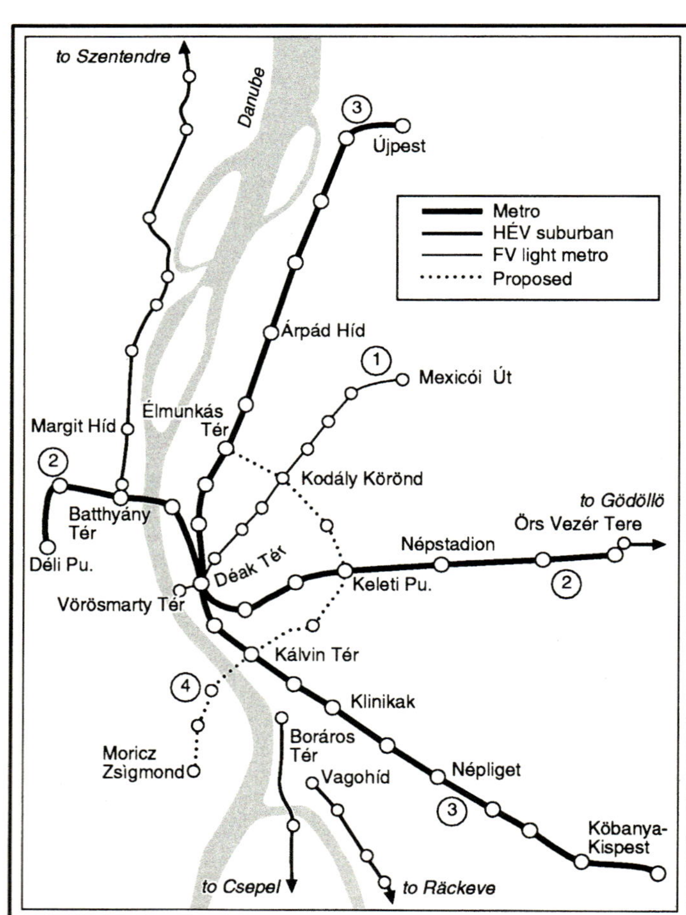

Budapest metro and HEV routes

Most intensive service: Bus 2-12 min peak, 4-30 min off-peak; trolleybus 1.8-7.3 min peak, 3-12 min off-peak
One-person operation: All routes
Average distance between stops: Bus 440 m; trolleybus 340 m
Fare structure: Flat
Fare evasion control: Random inspection
Operational control: Route inspectors/mobile radio with computerised monitoring under development
Average peak-hour speed: Bus 21.1 km/h, trolleybus 12.7 km/h, express bus 29 km/h
New vehicles financed by: Own development fund

Metro

Type of operation: Full metro, including one small-profile line opened in 1896

Passenger journeys: (1993) 280 million
(1994) 289 million
(1995) 271 million
Car-km: (1993) 34.9 million
(1994) 33.4 million
(1995) 32.4 million

Route length: 30.8 km
Number of lines: 3 (including small-profile Millennium Line 1)
Number of stations: 41
Gauge: 1,435 mm
Max gradient: 4%
Minimum curve radius: 300 m
Tunnel: Bored single-track
Electrification: 750 V DC, third rail; Millennium Line, 600 V DC

Service: Peak 2-3 min, off-peak 4-9 min
First/last train: 04.30/23.10
Fare structure: Flat, prepurchase; day, weekly and monthly tickets issued for other modes also valid on metro
Revenue control: Cancellers at inwards gates
Signalling: CTC; ATC with driver-only operation installed on Line 3
Surveillance: CCTV on platforms and escalators

Rolling stock: 387 cars formed as five-car sets, plus 23 cars for Millennium Line

Mytischy EV1/EV3 (1969)	M195
Mytischy 81-714/81-717 (1971)	M176
Ganz-Mávag (1985)	M6
Others	M10
Ganz Art-71 (Millennium Line 1973)	M21
Ganz Art (Millennium Line 1987)	M2

In peak service: 293

Current situation: Millennium Line opened 1896, named to celebrate 1,000 years of the Hungarian State; first new metro line opened 1970. Work completed 1996 on reconstruction of the Millennium Line 1 to improve the infrastructure and raise capacity by rebuilding stations.
Developments: Construction of the 17 km Line 4, part of which was to have opened for the 1996 World Expo, was postponed on cost grounds, but new feasibility studies were made in 1996 in preparation for an application for international funding of the project.

Light rail/Tramway

Type of operation: Light rail and conventional tramway

Passenger journeys: (1993) 348.6 million
(1994) 356 million
(1995) 350 million
Car-km: (1993) 44.6 million
(1994) 43 million
(1995) 40.7 million

Route length: 209.3 km (unduplicated)
Number of lines: 28
Number of stops: 663
Gauge: 1,435 mm
Track: Vignole 48.5 kg/m, Phoenix 59 kg/m rail. About 75 km to light rail standards
Electrification: 600 V DC, overhead

Service: Peak 2-12 min, off-peak 10-30 min
First/last car: 04.00/23.45
Fare structure: Flat; day, weekly and monthly tramway season tickets valid on suburban railway, metro and trolleybuses, but not on buses, rack railway or river buses

Integration with other modes: Full integration, with buses acting as feeders for light rail and metro services
One-person operation: All routes

Rolling stock: 909 cars

Ganz-Mávag UV (1956)	M366 T72
Ganz-Mávag 8 articulated (1967)	M151
ČKD Tatra T5C5	M320

In peak service: 631

Current situation: Many routes already have lengthy sections of reserved track, and conversion to light rail standards is in progress elsewhere. Circular LRT route planned for the eastern suburbs. Route 1 extension to Vajda Peter ut under construction.

Ganz Ansaldo is undertaking rehabilitation of a batch of 30 veteran tramcars in the project financed by the World Bank (see above).

Rack railway/Chair lift/Funicular

Current situation: The Varosmajor—Szechenyihegy rack line, 3.7 km, 1,435 mm gauge, is electrified at 1.5 kV DC. It carried 2.3 million passengers in 1993. There is also a chair lift linking Janoshegy and Zugliget (1 km), and the Buda Castle funicular.

Rolling stock: 7 two-car sets
SGP (1973) M7 T7

Suburban railway (HEV)

Type of operation: Suburban rail

Passenger journeys: (1993) 71 million
(1994) 70.5 million
(1995) 67 million

Current situation: Ten routes are served from four main lines, total 176 km with 137 stations, 1,435 mm gauge, electrified 1.1 kV DC. Trains run every 5-15 min at peak times, 10-60 min off-peak, all one-man operated. Flat fare within city boundaries, zonal elsewhere. The HEV lines are owned jointly by the municipalities of Budapest and the districts served.
Developments: HEV fits poorly into the new structure of BKV, with neither municipalities nor the state anxious to fund essential modernisation of the infrastructure and rolling stock. A new joint stock holding company has been proposed, comprising municipalities and state government.

Rolling stock: 318 emu cars M212 T106

River ferries

Current situation: A fleet of 17 vessels operate a 20-min service on four routes (one summer only), carrying 204,000 passengers in 1995.
Developments: Ferries are now operated by a separate company.

MÀV

Hungarian State Railways (MÀV)
Népköztarsaság utja 75, 1940 Budapest VI
Telephone: +36 1 122 0660 Fax: +36 1 142 8596

Type of operation: Suburban heavy rail

Current situation: Irregular services operated over several routes.

UPDATED

BUENOS AIRES

Population: City 2.9 million, conurbation 11 million
Public transport: Bus services provided by route associations of independent 'colectivo' mini and midibus owners and operators under general direction of national transport authority. Municipally owned metro with light rail extensions, and state-owned suburban railways, all run by private operators on a concessionary basis

Comision Nacional de Transporte Automotor

Comision Nacional de Transporte Automotor
Buenos Aires

Current situation: A new national transport authority was established in 1995 after plans for a Greater Buenos Aires transport authority were shelved. CNTA is controlled by three bodies — the National Transport Department (on account of the city's capital status), the Province of Buenos Aires (controlling routes which cross the city boundary), and suburban municipalities (controlling their own local networks). CNTA is not responsible for railways or the metro.
Developments: A master plan for traffic improvements envisages a network of elevated highways built over existing railway alignments.

Mercedes OA101 of operator Guido at Plaza Constitucion ***1996***

Private bus/Minibus

Current situation: 'Colectivo' minibuses (more properly described as medium-sized), operating scheduled services, account for 80 per cent of all public transport trips and 54 per cent of total trips, amounting to some 7 million journeys daily in 1995.

Participants in the Empresas (route associations) can own more than one vehicle, but many are single vehicle operators and a third are owner-drivers. CNTA oversees fares and minimum frequencies for individual routes, governs the formation of new Empresas, and adjudicates tendering for new routes. In 1995 there were 104 operators, 24 fewer than in 1992. Services are provided on a wholly commercial basis, though fuel prices are subsidised. On some routes, higher-quality vehicles operate, offering seats to all passengers at a higher fare. Vehicles are powered increasingly by CNG rather than petrol.
Developments: Conductors were reintroduced on some routes in 1994 after the transport ministry banned driver-sales of tickets in an attempt to accelerate automation of fare collection. Fareboxes are now installed throughout the fleet, though some buses have a magnetic card reader to alleviate problems with cash shortages and the slow throughput of the fareboxes.

Increasing competition from taxis, illegal and paratransit minibuses and owner-operated old coaches has eroded patronage of scheduled services, which fell by 15 per cent in 1994. Much business has also been lost to the suburban railways (see below), whose services were much improved following privatisation. In addition, traffic congestion, increased car ownership and recession have combined to cut sales of the popular *Diferencial* ticket by 50 per cent, thus putting operators under considerable financial pressure. A claim for a 100 per cent fare rise was made in 1995, along with a request for improved traffic control and restraint of illegal competing services. The fares rise was also seen as essential to finance the mandatory replacement of some 3,800 vehicles aged 10 years or more, scheduled for the end of 1995.

Despite operators' requests for traffic control measures, experiments with bus lanes have met with only partial success due to the reluctance of some operators to use them, and they may be discontinued.

Mercedes LO1114, the traditional Buenos Aires vehicle, now being replaced by more modern types ***1996***

Fleet: 11,000, mainly Mercedes LO1114, OC1214, OF1315,OF1214, OH1314, OH1318, OHL1316, OH1418, OH1420 and old O170 types, plus a few El Detalle OA101, Arbus (one), Zanello (four) and Scania K112 demonstrator

Subte

Subterraneos de Buenos Aires (Subte)
Operated by Metrovías SA
Av Federico Lacroze No 1481 piso 5°, Buenos Aires 1427
Telephone: +54 1 313 8512
President: Sergio Claudio Cirigliano
General Manager: Roberto Macías

Current situation: Subte comprises the metro network and light rail Line E2.

Developments: Privatisation was achieved in 1994, with a 20-year concession awarded to the Metrovías consortium, which also won its bid to take over the Urquiza suburban railways (see below). The combined concession for the metro and Urquiza lines attract a subsidy of US$30 million a year. The group is also permitted to operate feeder bus routes.

Metrovías is required to spend US$175 million during the first five years on projects and rolling stock purchases proposed in the 10-year plan investment programme agreed before privatisation to recoup years of neglect of rolling stock and infrastructure. Work on rehabilitating the system started immediately, and the first months of Metrovias operation saw increased train frequency on several lines, an improvement in car availability, and introduction of 300 security guards to police stations and crack down on fare evasion. AFC is being introduced quickly as a means of combating ticketless travellers. A track-to-train communications system is being installed, and resignalling of Lines B, C, D and E is planned.

Poor availability of the 65-year-old trains on Line B was overcome by introduction in 1995 of 100 cars second-hand from Tokyo, and further cars may come from Berlin.

Two major capital projects were inherited. A US$70 million loan from Italy was agreed in 1991 for complete rebuilding of Line A's power supply, overhead, track and signalling. The second scheme under way is further extension of Line D from Ministro Caranza to Monroe (3.6 km), of which the first 1 km section to Colegiales opened in 1993. Trains should be running to Monroe in 1998.

Attention has again turned to new construction in a bid to ease the city's chronic transport problems. A further extension of Line D is proposed to a bus/rail interchange planned at Vicente López, along with the long-planned extension of Line A. New circumferential Line H (9km) is being assessed by consultants Systra; bids for its construction could be sought in 1997.

It is hoped to order a new fleet of 90 cars to replace the aged Line A trains. A US$200 million loan was being discussed at the end of 1996. A further batch of 18 cars is being acquired second-hand from Tokyo.

Lines B, C, D and E are being resignalled and equipped with ATC by GEC Alsthom Transport.

Metro

Staff: 3,400

Type of operation: Full metro, first line opened 1913

Passenger journeys: (1993) 143 million
(1994) 171.2 million (including Urquiza suburban)
(1995) 217.6 million (including Urquiza suburban)

Route length: 36.5 km
Number of lines: 5
Number of stations: 63 (all in tunnel)
Gauge: 1,435 mm
Track: 44 kg/m or 45.5 kg/m rail on timber sleepers on stone ballast; concrete sleepers on new sections
Tunnel: All double-track; Line A, cut-and-cover; others bored
Electrification: Line A, 1.1 kV DC, overhead; Line B, 550 V DC, third rail; Lines C, D and E, 1.5 kV DC, overhead

Service: Peak 3-6 min, off-peak 10-12 min
Fare structure: Flat, with free transfer
Fare collection: Manual; token to turnstile
Operating costs financed by: Fares 67%, other commercial sources 5%, subsidy/grants 28%

Rolling stock: 467 cars

La Brugeoise, Line A (1913/24, 12 rebuilt 1987)	M105
Siemens/O&K, Lines C, D, E	
(1934)	M29 T28
(1941)	M9 T9
(1944)	M14
Baseler, Lines C, D, E (1954)	T13
Fab Militares/Siemens, Line B (1978)	M20
Nat Movil y Const/GEE, Lines C, D, E (1964)	M30
Fab Militares, Lines C, D, E (1964)	T30
Fab Militares/GE, Line B (1965)	M20
Materfer/Fab Militares/Siemens Lines C, D, E (1980)	M30 T30
Ex-Tokyo Line B	M100

On order: 90 cars for Line A from Fiat/Siemens; some cars being refurbished by Morrison Knudsen

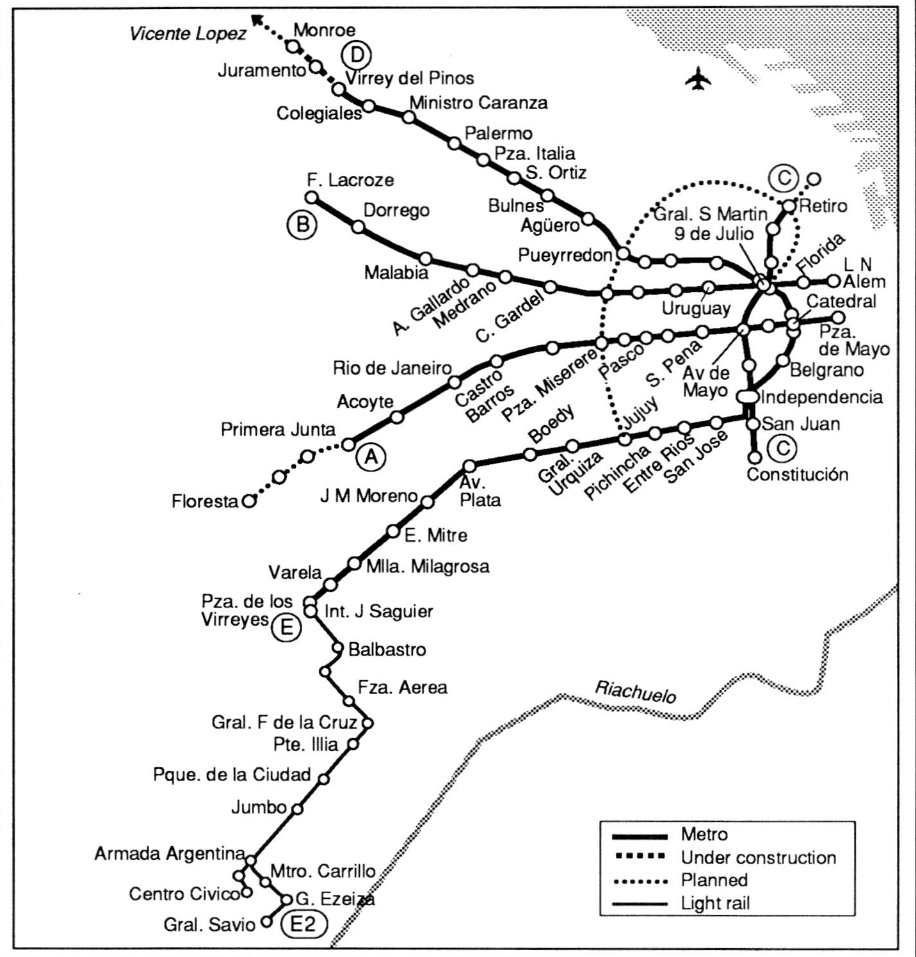

Buenos Aires metro

LRV at Supermercado Jumbo on line E2 ***1997***

Light rail

Passenger journeys: (1991) 2.8 million

Current situation: The 7.4 km light rail line from Line E at Plaza de los Virreyes to Gen Savio opened in 1987; electrified 750 V DC; 13 stations. Further construction in progress to create a loop at the line's outer end. Plans exist for Line E1 to link Plaza de los Virreyes with the national airport.

Rolling stock: 17 cars
Fab Militares/Siemens LRV (1988) M17

Suburban railways

Passenger journeys: (1993) 270 million
(1994) 337 million (includes Subte metro)
(1995) 543 million (includes Subte metro)

Current situation: All Argentine Railways (FA) suburban services were taken over by a holding company, Femesa, in 1991 prior to the offer of operating concessions to the private sector. All services are now in the hands of contractors. These are:

Metrovias, awarded the 20-year joint concession for the Urquiza lines (26 km) and the metro (see above).

Trenes de Buenos Aires, awarded a 10-year concessions for the Mitre (181 km) and Sarmiento (167 km) lines.

Trenes Metropolitanos SA, awarded 10-year concessions for the Roca (235 km), Belgrano South (52 km) and San Martin (55 km) lines.
Ferrovias, awarded a 10-year concession for the Belgrano North line (62 km).

Suburban services operate out of six terminals on 1,000, 1,435 and 1,676 mm gauges, totalling 822 km with 276 stations. Five routes totalling 169 km out of Once and Retiro terminals are electrified at 600 and 800 V DC third rail, while the General Roca lines out of Plaza Constitucion to Glew and Ezeiza (40 km) are electrified at 25 kV 50 Hz with 52 three-car emus.

Developments: Much of the network is badly rundown and the concessionaires have concentrated on patching up the worst deficiencies, such as poorly maintained track, ancient signalling and lack of train control equipment, and even such basic requirements as train lighting. Many timetables were adjusted and services reduced to improve reliability. Some concessionaires inherited cars only a little less ancient than the 70-year-old stock on the metro. Though refurbishment is in progress as a stop-gap measure, modernising these cars would be totally uneconomic, and second-hand vehicles were sought from a number of sources, including Japan.

Within a year, these measures began to pay off, and the number of passengers carried in 1995 was almost double the 1993 figure.

Tren de la Costa

Tren de la Costa SA
Marcelo T de Alvear 684, Buenos Aires 1395
President: E Gonzalez del Solar

Type of operation: Light rail, opened 1994

Passenger journeys: (1995) 2.9 million

Current situation: This 15 km light rail line built on the formation of an abandoned railway links Maipú and Delta in the northern suburbs. It is electrified at 1.5 kV DC overhead. The line serves a number of new commercial developments.

Rolling stock: 9 cars
CAF (1994) M9

UPDATED

BUFFALO

Population: City 328,000, service area 0.9 million
Public transport: Bus and light rail services provided through operating subsidiary of Niagara Frontier Transportation Authority (NFTA), a New York State public benefit corporation created in 1967 and governed by Board of Commissioners

Metro

Niagara Frontier Transit Metro System Inc
181 Ellicott Street, PO Box 5008, Buffalo, NY 14205, USA
Telephone: +1 716 855 7631 Fax: +1 716 855 6679
NFTA Chair: Robert D Gioia
General Manager, NFT Metro: Anthony J Schill
Assistant General Manager: Karen Rae
Staff: 1,183

Current situation: NFT Metro was created in 1973 as a wholly owned subsidiary of NFTA to provide bus services in Erie and Niagara counties after acquisition of six independent companies. It is the major area operator.

The light rail line runs along Main Street in a traffic-free area at the heart of the city's central business district, and service is fare-free over this section. The line is unusual as it runs on the surface in the city centre and in tunnel elsewhere.

In 1990 NFTA obtained a dedicated source of revenue to fund its operating deficit. This consists of a percentage of a sales tax and a mortgage transfer tax. Nevertheless, NFTA remains short of its full requirement for capital expenditure.

Developments: Phased implementation of a paratransit network started in 1993. Expanded park-and-ride facilities and six new transit centres are being developed. Also carried out in 1994/95 was a major restructuring of the bus route network and timetable. Five CNG-powered buses are in service to evaluate use of alternative fuels.

A further restructuring of the network is likely to follow from studies started in late 1996. The existing fixed-route system may be replaced by a network of hubs linked by express bus and rail services, with local connecting routes operated by minibuses, vans or other appropriate vehicles, possibly on a demand-response basis.

Orion city bus of Metro ***1997***

Operating costs financed by: Fares 34%, other commercial sources 2%, subsidy/grants 64%
Subsidy from: FTA 15%, state (general revenues and petrol tax) 30%, and local (general revenues, sales and mortgage transfer tax) 55%

Bus

Passenger boardings: (1993) 22.4 million
(1994) 22.1 million

Vehicle-km: (1991/92) 14.8 million
(1992/93) 14.8 million
(1993/94) 15.3 million

Number of routes: 72
Route length: 2,121 km
Fleet: 423 buses

GMC T84604 (1978/83)	81
Orion (1985/91)	137
TMC TC40102A (1992)	17
Orion CNG-powered (1993)	5
New Flyer D40 (1993)	75
Ikarus USA 416.07 (1995)	67
Novabus TC40102A (1996)	41

Average age of fleet: 7.5 years
In peak service: 295

Most intensive service: 5 min
One-person operation: All routes
Fare collection: Registering farebox
Fare structure: 4 zones
Arrangements for elderly/disabled: 86% of buses wheelchair-accessible; reduced fares

Metro LRV at Church station on Buffalo's Main Street

GM bus in downtown Buffalo

Average distance between stops: 488 m
Integration between modes: Bus services integrated with light rail; rail fare same as city bus with free transfer; 6 park-and-ride sites

Light rail
Staff: 174

Type of operation: Light rail, initial route opened 1985

Passenger boardings: (1991/92) 8.5 million
(1992/93) 8.2 million
(1993/94) 8.2 million
Car-km: (1992/93) 1.7 million
(1993/94) 1.4 million

Route length: 10 km
in tunnel: 7.7 km
Number of routes: 1
Number of stations: 14
in tunnel: 8
Gauge: 1,435 mm
Electrification: 650 V DC, overhead

Service: Peak 5 min, off-peak 10-15-20 min

Integration with other modes: Full integration with bus system
Revenue control: Fare-free on city-centre surface section; AFC, no barriers on underground portion
Arrangements for elderly/disabled: Ramps and snow-melting equipment on surface section; lifts to underground platforms
Signalling: Centrally controlled cab signalling

Rolling stock: 39 cars

Tokyu Car LRV (1984/85)	M27
St Louis Car PCC (in store) (1946/49)	M12

In peak service: 23

Developments: Interim use of refurbished PCC cars was planned on the proposed Tonawanda extension, and 12 cars were bought from Cleveland in 1992. Lack of funding has delayed construction, which may not now take place before the end of the century. Three other extension proposals are included in the region's long-range transit development plan.

UPDATED

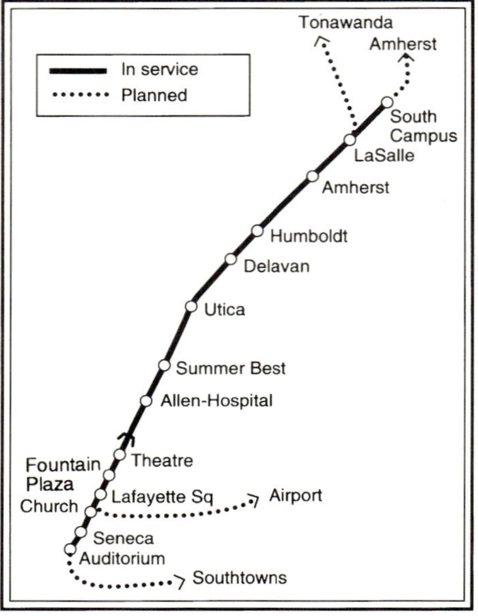

Buffalo's light rail line

BULAWAYO
Population: 550,000
Public transport: Bus services operated by company jointly owned by the government and United Transport, with fixed-route shared 'emergency taxis'

ZUPCO
Zimbabwe Passenger Company Ltd
Southern Division
Khami Road, PO Box 1779, Bulawayo, Zimbabwe
Telephone: +263 9 67291
General Manager, Southern Division: J Matsena
Staff: 1,819

Current situation: See Harare entry for details of ZUPCO. The company's Southern Division operates urban services in Bulawayo and three other towns, as well as a rural network. The figures below refer to the entire operation, except where noted.
Developments: Minibuses have been introduced to supplement full-size vehicle operations.

Future transport options for the city have been examined as part of a consultant's study of the four main urban areas in Zimbabwe.

Buses at Bulawayo bus station

Bus
Passenger journeys: (1992) 45 million
(1993) 50 million
Vehicle-km: (1992) 23 million
(1992) 28 million

Number of routes: Urban 75
Fleet: 430 vehicles
DAF/AVM 615/815
Scania
Toyota/Mazda minibuses
In peak service: 171 (urban only)

Most intensive service: 6 min
One-person operation: All services
Fare collection: By driver, plus sales to queues at major terminals from ticket agency booths
Fare structure: Graduated
Operational control: Inspectors
Operating costs financed by: Fares 100%

Shared taxi
Current situation: 'Emergency taxis' were legalised by government in 1982. They are a form of paratransit shared taxi, with vehicles seating no more than seven passengers, supposed to operate on fixed routes at a maximum fare determined by the municipality. Recent growth of pirate taxis, with minibuses seating more than 20, has gone unchecked despite the breach of the franchise agreement terms.

CAIRO
Population: 8.3 million, conurbation 16 million
Public transport: Bus services provided by government-owned transport authority, which also operates tramway network in Cairo, light rail line to Helwan, and cross-Nile ferries, and by second locally administered bus company. Separate tramway serves Heliopolis, taken over by the Cairo Transport Authority in 1993. Other extensive fixed-route shared-taxi/minibus services by private operators, and minibuses run by the El Rayan Bus Company. Suburban rail and metro operated by state railway

Cairo Transport Authority
Cairo Transport Authority
Madenat Nasr, PO Box 254, Cairo, Egypt
Telephone: +20 2 830533
Staff: 21,200 (all modes)

Current situation: CTA is responsible for a substantial bus operation, the tram networks in Cairo city and Heliopolis (absorbed in 1993), light rail line to Helwan and 12 cross-Nile ferry routes. Problems of previous underinvestment have, to a considerable extent, been remedied by acquisition of new trams and buses, but major operational difficulties are still posed by traffic congestion badly disrupting services, including those tramways not on reserved routes.

Bus
Passenger journeys: 1,000 million (annual)
Vehicle-km: 140 million (annual)

Number of routes: 220
Route length: 1,450 km
Fleet: 3,070 vehicles

Nasr/Iveco	1,700
Iveco	340
Mercedes O302	330
Mercedes minibus	500
Iveco minibus	200

One-person operation: None
Fare collection system: Payment to conductor
Fare structure: City area, flat; elsewhere, distance-related
Fare evasion control: Roving inspectors

Tramway (Cairo city lines)
Type of operation: Conventional tramway

Route length: 54 km
Number of lines: 9
Gauge: 1,000 mm

Fare structure: Flat; monthly seasons
Fare evasion control: Roving inspectors
Fare collection: Coin to conductor

Rolling stock: 441 cars, Kinki cars are wide-bodied for operation on reserved track; plus about 280 cars of the Heliopolis network.

Nasr buses of CTA in Tahrir Square

ČKD Tatra K2
Kinki
Semaf
Trailers T35

Developments: Infrastructure improvements, including provision of some extensions on reserved track, and re-equipment of the rolling stock fleet, have helped to overcome the effects of a long period of underinvestment, but chaotic traffic conditions and poor trackwork still hamper operations on city-centre streets. Such sections will probably close when the urban metro lines are completed (see below). CTA took over operation of the Heliopolis tramway network in 1993. There has been some rationalisation of routes and fleets.

Tramway (Helwan line)

Current situation: 16 km route opened 1981 links Helwan with El Tibbeen, with branch (8 km) to May 15 City (opened 1984). It runs mostly on reserved track and is operated by Kinki Sharyo or Semaf wide-bodied cars.

Ferry

Current situation: A fleet of cross-Nile ferries is operated. Small launches are used on one main route (2 km) between the central business area and the old city.

Greater Cairo Bus

Greater Cairo Bus Company
Cairo
Telephone: +20 2 828656

Current situation: Operates services in part of Cairo in close co-operation with the CTA. A fleet of over 300 locally built Nasr buses is operated.

Heliopolis Company

Heliopolis Housing & Development Company
Heliopolis, Cairo

Egyptian National Railways

Egyptian National Railways
PO Box 466, Ramses Square, 11794 Cairo
Telephone: +20 2 574 2968 Fax: +20 2 574 2950
General Manager, Metro: Mohamed Maher Moustafa

Type of operation: Suburban heavy rail, regional and urban metro

Current situation: ER operates the regional metro Line 1, the urban metro Line 2 and three conventional suburban routes (diesel-operated). Frequent cross-city service provided between El Marg, Cairo (Mubarak) and Helwan (42 km, 33 stations, electrified 1.5 kV DC). This upgraded suburban line is known as Line 1 of the metro. The initial phase of Line 2, the first urban metro route, was opened in October 1996 and extended in 1997.

Kinki Sharyo twinset in Cairo

Rolling stock: 100 three-car emu sets, diesel-hauled trains

Metro

Type of operation: Full metro, opened 1996

Route length: 8 km
in tunnel: 5.6 km
elevated: 1.5 km
Number of lines: 1
Number of stations: 11
Gauge: 1,435 mm
Electrification: 750 V DC, third rail

Service: Peak 2 min

Rolling stock: 15 six-car trains
Mitsubishi (1994/95) M45 T45

Current situation: The first section of urban metro Line 2, the 8 km from Shubra-el-Kheima to an interchange with Line 1 at Mubarak (Ramses Square), opened in October 1996. The National Authority for Tunnels (see below) is the planning and construction authority, whilst the metro has been built by the French Alcatel-Alsthom group with Interinfra managing construction. A further 2.9 km is under construction beneath the city centre from Mubarak to Sadat (Tahrir Square), scheduled for opening in October 1997.

Phase II of Line 2, on which construction started in October 1995, is an 8.6 km extension to Cairo university and an interchange with ER's Upper Egypt line at El Giza. Some 4 km is in bored tunnel beneath the Nile; there will be seven stations. Completion is expected in 2000/2001.

Proposed is Line 3 (10.8 km) linking Imbaba with Salah Salem to the west of Cairo, providing a third cross-city connection. No detailed studies for the rote have yet been made.

National Authority for Tunnels

PO Box 466, 11794 Cairo
Telephone: +20 2 574 2968/2969 Fax: +20 2 574 2950
Chairman: M E Abdel Salam

Current situation: This is the planning, design and construction authority for metros.

El Rayan Bus

El Rayan Bus Company
Cairo

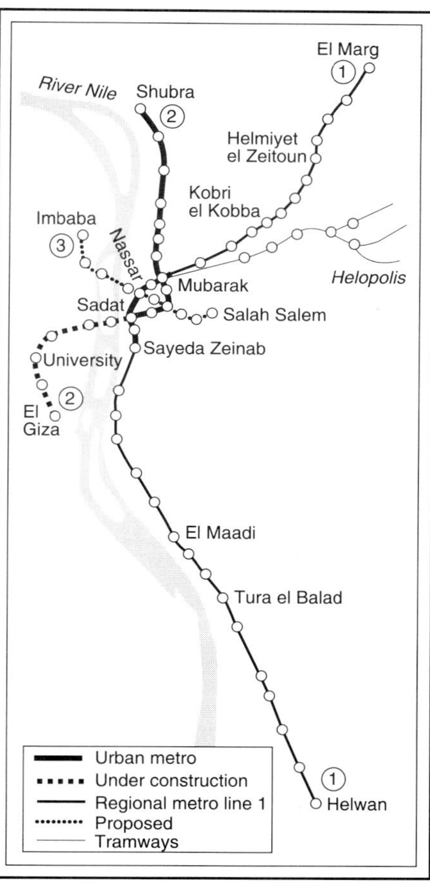

Cairo's metro and regional line

Nasr 811 bus of Greater Cairo Bus Company

Developments: El Rayan was given a licence by the city administration in 1985 for operation of a fleet of 600 Mercedes minibuses, the first officially authorised private bus services in Cairo since 1961.

Minibus/shared taxi

Current situation: Fixed-route jitney operations by shared taxi minibuses were permitted in the late 1970s, joining extensive illegal taxi sharing. Vehicles, licensed as taxis, normally wait until they have a full load before leaving their terminals and new passengers can only join at mid-route when passengers begin to be dropped off.

The most popular vehicles were originally locally assembled Ramses minibuses, but imported Japanese Nissan, Toyota and Mazda minibuses are now widely used. Most new vehicles are said to be owned by entrepreneurs outside the bus and taxi industry who lease vehicles to drivers for 25 per cent of their fare collections. About 20 per cent of vehicles are owner-driven. Fares are three to four times normal bus levels, but demand is high.

UPDATED

CALCUTTA

Population: Conurbation 10 million
Public transport: Bus services provided in part by state-owned undertaking and also by substantial groupings of private bus and minibus owner-operators. State-owned tramway. Suburban rail and metro services provided by Indian Railways

CSTC

Calcutta State Transport Corporation (CSTC)
45 Ganesh Chandra Avenue, Calcutta 700013, India
Telephone: +91 33 271212
Managing Director: S K De
Staff: 11,413

Current situation: CSTC services suffer from severe overcrowding and road capacity is constrained by parked vehicles and heavy pedestrian use. Fare evasion is also widespread. Several long-planned works to augment capacity have yet to be completed due to scarcity of funds.
Developments: Modernisation programmes, including phased introduction of computerisation and installation of automatic vehicle washing machines, are being implemented.

Purchase of 500 buses is planned. During 1993/94, 168 new buses were added to the fleet, and a further 162 were commissioned in 1994/95, enabling CSTC to improve vehicle utilisation. Measures are also being taken to raise the vehicle:staff ratio.

Measures such as optimal fleet utilisation to reduce fuel consumption, fare evasion controls and better scheduling have helped CSTC improve performance.

Bus

Passenger journeys: (1993/94) 290.7 million
(1994/95) 277.5 million
(1995/96) 282.9 million
Vehicle-km: (1993/94) 66.5 million
(1994/95) 59.9 million
(1995/96) 61.5 million

Number of routes: 244
Route length: 23,817 km
Fleet: 1,207 vehicles

Ashok-Leyland single-deck	400
Ashok-Leyland semi-articulated double-deck	40
Tata single-deck	767

Average age of fleet: 4 years

Most intensive service: 5 min
Fare collection: Payment to one or two conductors
Fare structure: Stage
Fare evasion control: Roving inspectors, penalty
Average peak-hour speed: 8 km/h
Operating costs financed by: Fares 43.9%, other commercial sources 1.6%, state government subsidy 54.5%

Calcutta Tramways

Calcutta Tramways Co Ltd
12 R N Mukherjee Road, Calcutta 700001
Telephone: +91 33 248 2681/6856
Chairman & Managing Director: D K Chakraberty
Chief Operating Manager: K Bhattacharya
Staff: 7,567

Type of operation: Conventional tramway

Passenger journeys: (1991/92) 185 million
(1992/93) 119.4 million
(1993/94) 124.5 million
Vehicle-km: (1991/92) 10.4 million
(1992/93) 6.2 million
(1993/94) 7.4 million

Current situation: Tram operations are severely affected by traffic congestion, as a result of which in 1990 the West Bengal government confirmed a long-term policy of abandonment. In an attempt to reduce losses and improve reliability, in 1992 CTC started operating buses in parallel with some tram routes; fleet of 165 buses.
Developments: Despite some recent closures and plans for more, the threat of total closure has receded.

Tramway

Number of routes: 30
Route length: 67 km
Number of lines: 29
Number of stops: 447
Gauge: 1,435 mm

Service: Peak 3 min
First/last car: 04.15/24.00
Fare structure: Graduated
Operating costs financed by: Fares 21%, other commercial sources 1%, state government subsidy 35.6%

Rolling stock: 374 cars

Articulated	M147
Streamlined	M227

In peak service: 225

Tata bus of Calcutta Tramways

Double-deck bus of CSTC at Chowringhee

Shyambazar metro station

1996

Metro

Metro Railway, Metro Rail Bhavan
33/1 Chowringhee Road, Calcutta 700071
Telephone: +91 33 291053 Fax: +91 33 294581
General Manager: S K Gupta

Type of operation: Full metro, opened 1984

Passenger journeys: (1992/93) 50,300 daily
(1993/94) 70,000 daily
(1995/96) 128,000 daily

Route length: 16.5 km
elevated: 1.6 km
Number of lines: 1
Number of stations: 17
Gauge: 1,676 mm
Track: UIC 60 kg/m rail; ballastless track with reinforced concrete bed
Max gradient: 2%
Minimum curve radius: 300 m
Electrification: 750 V DC, third rail

Service: Peak 13 min
First/last train: Weekdays 07.20/21.20, Sunday 15.00/21.00
Fare structure: 4 zones; reduced price carnets
Fare evasion control: AFC with magnetically encoded tickets and microprocessor-controlled entry/exit gates
Integration with other modes: None
Signalling: Colourlights
Surveillance: CCTV
One-person operation: None; all cars suitable

Rolling stock: 144 cars

ICF A	M108
ICF B	T36

Current situation: Public service between Esplanade and Bhowanipur inaugurated 1984 and extended to Tollyganj 1986. Dum Dum–Belgachia opened 1985 and operated in isolation. Remaining 6.5 km central section with six stations opened in stages in 1994/95.

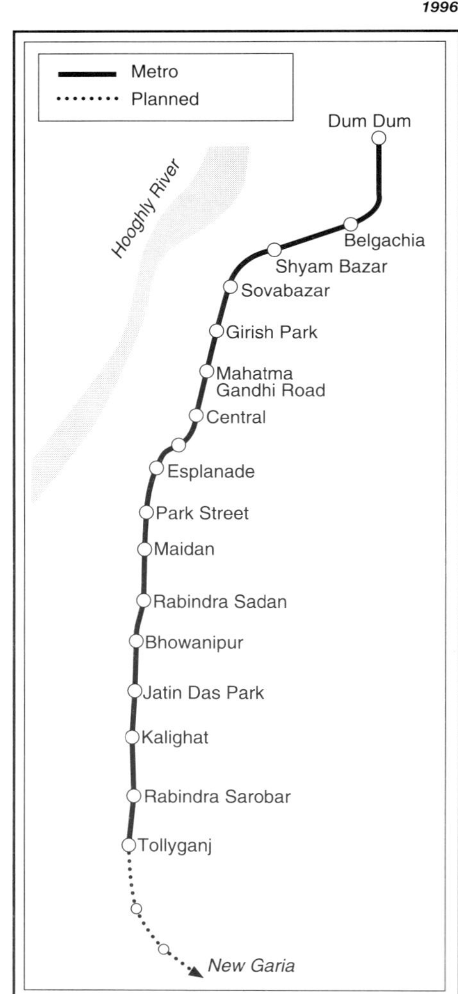

Calcutta's metro

Developments: A final location survey for the planned extension from Tollyganj to New Garia was completed in 1996. In addition, a technical/economic survey for a northern extension to Barrachpur is in progress.

Eastern Railway

Eastern Railway
17 Netaji Subhas Road, Calcutta 700001
Telephone: +91 33 220 6811
General Manager: A P Murugesan
Chief Operations Manager: A K Mita
Chief Public Relations Officer: G S Bannerjee

Type of operation: Suburban heavy rail

Passenger journeys: (1992/93) 387 million
(1993/94) 393 million
(1995/96) 410 million

Rolling stock: 347 motor cars and 752 trailers, now mostly formed in 10-car sets

Inauguration of local emu services between Asansol and Barddhaman, Eastern Railway, July 1994
1995

South Eastern Railway

South Eastern Railway
Garden Reach, Calcutta 700043
Telephone: +91 33 479 1523
General Manager: S Ramanathan
Chief Operating Manager: S Misra

Type of operation: Suburban heavy rail

Passenger journeys: (1992/93) 53 million
(1993/94) 54.4 million
(1994/95) 57.1 million

Rolling stock: 85 motor cars and 183 trailers

Current situation: Two major terminals serve the city — Sealdah and Howrah — to the east and west of the central business district. Sealdah is served by ER trains and Howrah by both ER and SER services; together they handle about 900 daily suburban trains. At peak times, emus are overcrowded heavily in excess of crush loads. Most routes are electrified at 25 kV, 1,676 mm gauge.

Developments: Work continues on several projects to improve capacity, including provision of colourlight signalling and reversible working on the third line between Howrah and Bandel, and survey of the proposed Habra-Bongaon doubling.

Most emus were increased from 9 to 10 cars in 1993, when diesel multiple-units were introduced on non-electrified lines. In 1995/96, ER introduced a further four pairs of dmus and three emus, while SER brought in a further three pairs of each.

A 47.5 km electrified extension of the Lakshmikantapur line is under construction to Namkhana; an initial 10 km section is already in operation. Other works include augmentation of facilities at Howrah, such as provision of double-discharge on three platforms, an additional platform at Sealdah, new berthing sidings at Shalimar, and signalling improvements.

On the SER, construction of a new terminal at Shalimar is in progress to ease congestion at Howrah. Trains will reach Shalimar by a link from SER's main suburban route at Santragachi, some 7 km from Howrah.

Survey work is in progress for extension of the Circular Railway Phase II between Princepghat and Majerhat (5.5 km).

Private bus/Minibus

Current situation: Private bus operations account for about half of the public transport trips and two-thirds of bus trips in the city — around 1,000 million journeys annually. Route associations, generally one for each route, have developed. Owners retain control over operations and retain fares but the associations govern relationships between members and set operating standards. Private bus crews are paid a percentage of the fares, which keeps fare evasion below the high levels suffered by CSTC, and are allotted to individual vehicles, improving maintenance responsibility.

The state regional transport authority allocates licences for private buses and minibuses, as well as taxis.

Fleet: Over 2,200; full-size buses are all Tata, whilst the minibuses comprise Tata, Toyota and Hindustan

UPDATED

CALGARY

Population: 767,000
Public transport: Bus services and light rail system operated by municipal department

Calgary Transit

City of Calgary Transportation Department
928-32 Avenue Connector NE, PO Box 2100, Postal Station M, Calgary, Alberta T2P 2M5, Canada
Telephone: +1 403 277 9711 Fax: +1 403 230 1155
General Manager: R H Irwin
Assistant Controller: Beng Koay
Superintendent of Operations: J Pawson
Staff: 1,645

Passenger journeys: (All modes) (1993) 53.3 million
(1994) 53.9 million
(1995) 56.3 million

Operating costs financed by: Fares 46.7%, other commercial sources 0.5%, provincial grants 2.3%, municipal support (tax levy) 50.3%

Developments: There was a significant increase in ridership in 1995, mostly attributable to the improvement in the economic climate and job prospects. Increases recorded after September 1995 resulted from higher pass rebates offered to high school students by the Board of Education. The trend continued into 1996.

CT added 41 low-floor buses to the fleet, bringing the total of accessible vehicles to 91. Accessible service is now provided on 23 routes. Community Shuttle service using 20-seat minibuses continues to expand, both as new routes to developing suburban areas and as replacement for full-size buses on routes that fail to attract a minimum of 20 passengers/h.

C-train at 7th Avenue Transit Mall

The three-year review of transport policies — the Go Plan project — was completed in 1995. It made many recommendations for policies that will favour an increasing role for public transport over the next 30 years.

Bus

Passenger journeys: (1993) 32 million
(1994) 32.9 million
(1995) 33.8 million
Vehicle-km: (1993) 28.6 million
(1994) 29.7 million
(1995) 31.5 million

Number of routes: 121 including community shuttle
Route length: (One way) 2,510 km
On priority right-of-way: 2 km shared with light rail
Fleet: 564 vehicles

GM Canada 'New Look' (1973-82)	261
Flyer (1979/82)	28
New Flyer (1992)	10
Flyer low-floor (1993/95)	90
Orion (1980/82)	47
Orion II accessible	1
MCI (1991/92)	107
Community shuttle minibuses	20

In peak service: 473

Most intensive service: 3 min
One-person operation: All routes
Fare collection: Exact fare to farebox, prepurchase tickets, monthly passes, transfers
Fare structure: Flat
Fares collected on board: 27% (cash)
Fare evasion control: By driver and inspectors

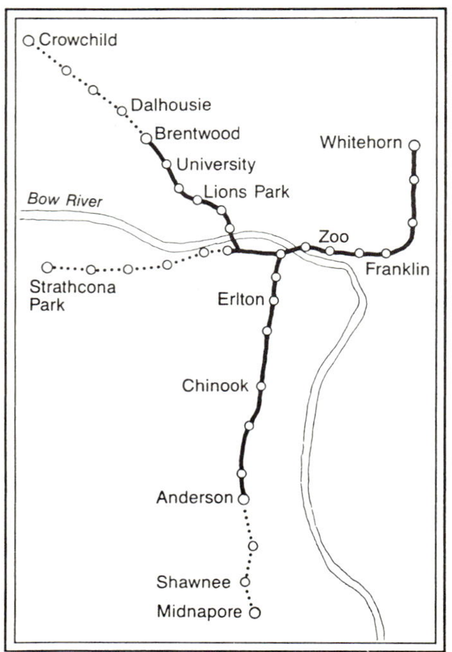

Calgary light rail

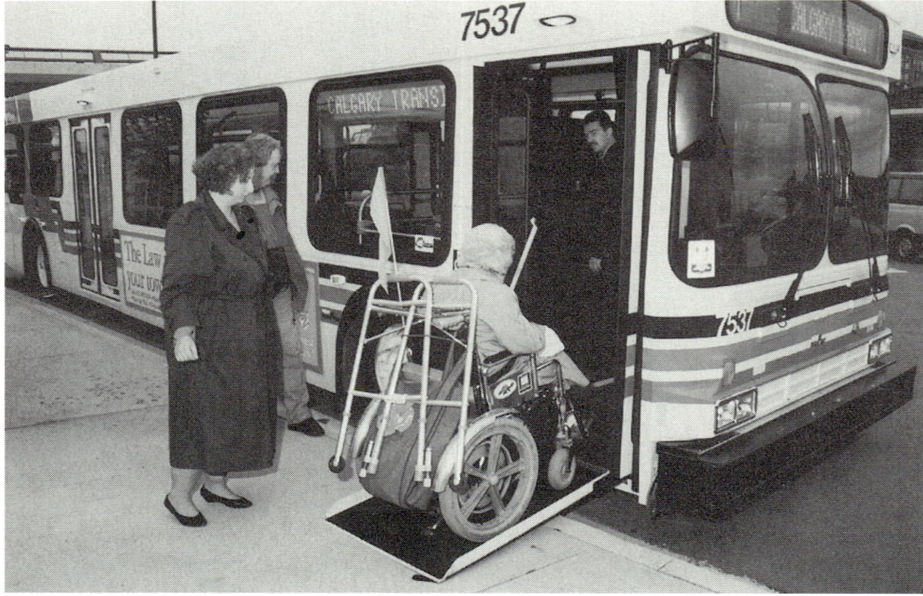

Orion low-floor buses provide accessible service on 11 routes ***1995***

Integration with other modes: Bus and light rail routes integrated; feeder and main line buses serve stations; park-and-ride (250 spaces on bus routes, 6,967 at stations)
Operational control: Field inspectors/radio control
Arrangements for elderly/disabled: Low-floor accessible service on 23 routes; reduced rate annual pass for seniors depending on income
Average distance between stops: 300 m
Average peak-hour speed: 24 km/h
New vehicles financed by: Debentures/Provincial cost-sharing programmes

Light rail

Type of operation: Light rail, initial route opened 1981

Passenger journeys: (1993) 21.3 million
(1994) 21 million
(1995) 22.5 million
Train-km: (1993) 3.1 million
(1994) 3.1 million
(1995) 2.9 million

Route length: 29.3 km
in tunnel: 2 km
Number of routes: 2, operated as 1
Number of stations: 31
Gauge: 1,435 mm
Track: 60 kg/m Ri-60 girder rail on ballasted concrete sleepers, and 50 kg/m ARA 100T welded rail on concrete slab
Electrification: 600 V DC, overhead

Service: Peak 3-5 min, off-peak 10-15 min
First/last car: 05.01/01.19
Fare structure: Flat, as bus; free fare zone on 2 km downtown section of 7th Avenue
Fare collection: Self-service ticket dispensers and prepaid ticket cancellers on platforms; monthly passes; transfer from bus
Integration with other modes: Feeder buses at most stations; park-and-ride (6,767 spaces)
Fare evasion control: Roving inspectors
One-person operation: 100%
Signalling: Automatic block with interlockings at all junctions and terminals; auto-switching and station signs controlled by onboard VETAG in transit mall; all train movements monitored at radio control centre

Rolling stock: 85 cars

Siemens-Duewag U2 (1981)	M27
Siemens-Duewag U2 (1983/85)	M56
Siemens-Duewag U2 AC propulsion	M2

In peak service: 72

Developments: West line alignment approved 1988 and protected for construction once population reaches 1.25 million. Next construction should be the 3.5 km extension to Crowchild. Purchase of 25 low-floor cars planned. Two stations made fully accessible in 1996.

Commuter rail (proposed)

Current situation: A commuter service is planned over existing tracks to link the southern suburbs with Anderson station on the light rail line.
Developments: Siemens' RegioSprinter diesel railcar ran a four-month demonstration service over a 5 km section of track in 1996.

UPDATED

CANBERRA

Population: 300,000
Public transport: Bus services provided by Australian Capital Territory government through a division of the Department of Urban Services, with some independent operations

ACTION

Australian Capital Territory Internal Omnibus Network (ACTION)
Level 3, National Mutual Building, PO Box 235, Civic Square, ACT 2608, Australia
Telephone: +61 6 207 8000 Fax: +61 6 207 8080
Chief Executive: John Flutter
Staff: 826

Current situation: Public transport is based on an integrated feeder-express system which reflects the distinctive urban design of Canberra – a series of discrete 'towns' with major concentrations of government, business, retail and recreational activity in each town centre. Bus interchanges in the four town centres (City, Woden, Belconnen and Tuggeranong) are linked by a 29 km inter-town express route. Local services link suburban areas to their local town centre interchange, or to the two adjoining interchanges. During peak periods this network is supplemented by express services providing direct links between outer suburbs and the city centre.
Developments: New labour agreements negotiated with trades unions, aimed at reducing operating costs and improving efficiency, paved the way for major network revisions implemented in 1994, 1995 and 1996.

Installation of automated ticketing was completed in late 1995.

Two new routes inaugurated October 1995 serving new suburbs of Belconnen and Gungahlin, and an extension to Gungahlin town centre is scheduled to start in 1998.

Bus

Passenger boardings: (1993/94) 23.8 million
(1994/95) 24 million
(1995/96) 24 million

Vehicle-km: (1993/94) 21 million
(1994/95) 20.9 million
(1995/96) 20.9 million

Number of routes: 103
Route length: 1,985 km
Fleet: 386 vehicles

Mercedes O305 (1982-85)	57

Circular Route 307 in Canberra city centre ***1997***

Mack Renault PR100-1/2 (1980)	1
Mack Renault PR100-2 (1987-92)	258
Mack Renault PR100-3 (1994/95)	34
Mack Renault PR180-2 articulated (1987/93)	33
Mitsubishi tram replica	3

In peak service: 354

Most intensive service: 4-7 min, intertown express
One-person operation: All routes
Fare collection: Cash to driver, or prepurchase magnetic tickets
Fare structure: Flat fare on boarding for cash payers; prepurchase 10 single-ride, daily, weekly, monthly and quarterly magnetic tickets
Fares collected on board: 22%
Operational control: Route and ticket inspectors; two-way radio; movements monitored through all interchanges
Arrangements for elderly/disabled: Concession fares with reimbursement provided by ACT government. New buses built to low-floor design with carefully placed handrails for ease of entry and exit; bell push-buttons placed low down; raised bay numerals at interchanges assist blind people; reserved bus seating identified by upholstery colour; first fully accessible bus entered service 1995
Average distance between stops: 300 m
Average peak-hour speed: Local feeder buses 30 km/h, express 35 km/h
Bus priority: All interchanges are bus-only areas; 13.7 km of bus-only lanes on arterial roads; priority sections of road immediately before some intersections; additional bus-only lanes being planned
Operating costs financed by: Fares 24%, other commercial sources 18%, subsidy/grants 58%
Subsidy from: ACT government to cover pensioners' travel 4.2%, school bus services 13.2% and to finance operating deficit 82.6%
New vehicles financed by: Grant and loan funding

Other operators
Current situation: Suburban bus services are operated into central Canberra by Deane's from Queanbeyan in the southeast (three routes) and by Transborder from Yass in the north.

UPDATED

CAPE TOWN
Population: 3.1 million
Public transport: Scheduled bus services throughout metropolitan area provided by privately owned group. Extensive suburban services. Substantial numbers of 'Kombi-taxi' minibus services, many of which are illegal. Transport policy is co-ordinated under a Metropolitan Transport Advisory Board

Golden Arrow
Golden Arrow Bus Services (Pty) Ltd
PO Box 1795, Cape Town 8000, South Africa
Telephone: +27 21 541361 Fax: +27 21 548818
Chair: N S Cronjé
General Manager: H J Grebe
Staff: 1,800

Current situation: Golden Arrow was set up in 1992 when the management of the former City Tramways gained control of the operation from Tollgate Holdings. Strongest demand is in areas where rapid urbanisation has led to settlement of large numbers of lower income group residents. These have been identified as core markets, and improved service frequencies have been introduced. Steady growth has been recorded in this traffic, despite a general decline in patronage.

Unregulated taxi operations, continuing uncertainty about government subsidy policy and high inflation continue to affect bus operations. Although operating conditions have improved since 1993, there is still an urgent need for a proper public transport planning strategy to implement better control and optimise road space. New provincial and metropolitan transport structures are being developed and should be in place during 1996/97.
Developments: New concepts of franchising services and small business units are being developed with a view to increasing community and worker involvement in the company's activities. This process is likely to be accelerated with implementation of new transport policies.

Bus
Passenger boardings: (1992/93) 50 million
(1993/94) 42 million
(1994/95) 36.7 million
Vehicle-km: (1992/93) 42 million
(1993/94) 34 million
(1994/95) 35 million

Number of routes: 900
Route length: 16 km (average)
Fleet: 691 vehicles

Leyland Victory J double-deck	155
Leyland Victory J single-deck	424
ERF Trailblazer	86
Mercedes 1624	13
Others	13

In peak service: 589

Most intensive service: 5-10 min
One-person operation: All routes
Fare collection: Setright for cash fares collected on board; 10-ride clipcards issued by Wayfarer machines
Fare structure: Zonal, discount clipcard
Fare evasion control: Random inspectors
Operational control: Multichannel selective calling two-way radio with 150 field staff under centralised operations control centre with computerised database
Integration with other modes: Complex network of routes interlinking at suburban rail stations
Average distance between stops: 750 m
Operating costs financed by: Fares 94%, other commercial sources 6%
Subsidy from: Recoverable discount system on clipcards, operated in collaboration with government administered fund
New vehicles financed by: Own resources

Leyland Victory J of Golden Arrow

Metro Rail
South African Rail Commuter Corporation Ltd
Western Cape Metropolitan Area
Private Bag X2, Sunninghill, Johannesburg 2157
Telephone: +27 11 804 2900 Fax: +27 11 804 3852

Type of operation: Suburban heavy rail

Passenger journeys: (1990/91) 162.9 million
(1991/92) 154.3 million
(1992/93) 144.1 million

Current situation: Frequent suburban service on 12 routes in the Western Cape area, serving 102 stations on the Cape Peninsula, total 305 km, 1,065 mm gauge, electrified 3 kV DC. Up to 35 trains per hour in the peak, off-peak services every 30 min. Fares cover 38 per cent of operating costs.
Developments: Two routes totalling 15 km — the Blue Downs line and the Khayelitsha extension — are proposed in Metro Rail's 10-year capital development programme. Automatic ticket-issuing machines installed at 236 locations in 1994/95.

Rolling stock: 1,055 emu cars

Union Carriage & Wagon (1957 on)	M289 T714
Siemens (1984)	M4 T4
Hitachi (1984)	M6 T6
Hitachi-Dorbyl (1987/88)	M16 T16

Shared taxis
Current situation: There has been major growth in the numbers of 'Kombi-taxis' to around 2,000, mostly Volkswagen minibuses operating variable routes and schedules outside the normal bus licensing system. Their growth has had a major effect on the patronage of licensed bus operators. The Kombis were legalised under a government transport policy review in 1987, though some still operate illegally.

CARACAS
Population: 3.5 million
Public transport: Bus services mostly provided by private operators; 'Por Puestos' minibus services provided by about 80 associations, plus unlicensed pirates. Jeep transport provided by about 50 associations in the poor areas on steep mountain slopes surrounding the city where only four-wheel drive vehicles can operate. Metro; commuter railway planned

Private bus operators
Passenger journeys: (1995) 90.2 million

Number of routes: 15
Fleet: Approx 350

Current situation: There are about 50 operators; most have poor premises and inadequate maintenance facilities resulting in lack of roadworthy vehicles and operational unreliability. Attempts are made to impose minimum standards of maintenance in the light of accidents, but prosecution has been limited as a general clampdown would provoke a public transport crisis. Few operators can afford new vehicles and closures occur when fleets reach the end of their useful life.

Caracas Metro

Compania Anonima Metro de Caracas
Apartado 61036, Caracas 1060, Venezeula
Telephone: +58 2 208 2111 Fax: +58 3 331908
President: J Gonzalez Lander
Staff: 4,869

Current situation: As well as running the metro, the authority operates a network of feeder bus routes. Under a five-year investment programme for the period through to 1997, Line 3 is to be opened throughout, Line 1 capacity augmented by 43 new cars, and the bus fleet is to be increased by some 200 to 413.

Metro

Type of operation: Full metro, initial route opened 1983

Passenger journeys: (1992) 325 million
(1994) 271 million
(1995) 289 million

Route length: 42.5 km
Number of lines: 3
Number of stations: 40
Gauge: 1,435 mm
Track: 54 kg/m continuously welded rail, on Stedef twin-block sleepers laid on concrete (tunnels) or ballast (surface)
Tunnel: Cut-and-cover and bored
Electrification: 750 V DC, third rail

Service: Peak 1½ min
Fare structure: Zonal; magnetically encoded 10-trip tickets
Revenue control: Entrance and exit turnstiles, ticket-issuing machines
Signalling: Full ATC
Operating costs financed by: Fares 58%, other commercial sources 5.8%, subsidy/grants 36.2%

Rolling stock: 456 cars

CIMT Type A (cab)	M110
CIMT Type B	M268
GEC Alsthom Type C (cab) (1995)	M34
GEC Alsthom Type D (1995)	M22
GEC Alsthom Type R (1995)	T22

In peak service: 345
On order: 28 cars from GEC Alsthom

Current situation: Line 3 from Plaza Venezuela to La Rinconada (12.1 km, 10 stations) under construction, of which the 5.6 km section to El Valle opened in 1994. Line 2 extension from Capuchinos to Plaza Venezuela also under construction, to relieve the busiest central section of Line 1.

A suburban extension (9.5 km) of Line 2 from Las Adjuntas to Los Teques is planned, along with a light rail route in the southeast suburbs.

Bus

Staff: 1,018 (included above)

Passenger journeys: (1991) 26.5 million
(1994) 30.2 million
(1995) 34 million

Current situation: MetroBus feeder buses were introduced in 1987 on a single route and the network has expanded each year. In 1996 there were 25 routes extending to 502 km. Fares cover 29.3 per cent of operating costs.

Fleet: 274 buses

Leyland National Mk1	22
Renault PR100-2	99
Pegaso 6424	99
Renault Unicar Fanabus	54

In peak service: 160

Minibus

Current situation: Most vehicles are now 15 to 24 seaters. With additional (legal) standing capacity for 10 to 15 passengers, they compete directly with conventional buses and have grown at their expense, particularly in the light of bus operational shortcomings.

Fares charged are graduated and generally the same as buses, though with higher levels at evenings and weekends. Authorised operations are grouped into associations covering a number of routes, often in competition, with an estimated fleet of at least 15,000, including pirates outside the associations to which the authorities turn a blind eye. Fleet sizes of the associations vary from 10 to about 100 vehicles.

Commuter rail (planned)

Current situation: The long-planned high-speed commuter link through the 43 km corridor between Caracas and Tuy Medio came a step closer to realisation in 1996 when the government signed an agreement for its construction with the Contuy consortium of Venezuelan, Japanese and Italian companies. Work should start during 1997 for opening in 2001.

Reo/Superior bus of Caracas private operator

MetroBus feeder service

Plaza Sucre station on Line 1

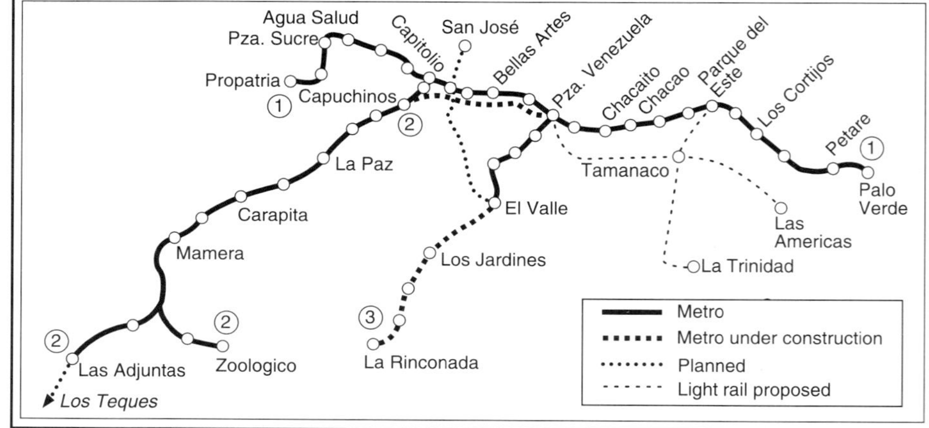

Caracas metro

UPDATED

CARDIFF

Population: 300,000
Public transport: Bus services provided by local authority-owned company, with some suburban operations by others; local rail services; light rail proposed

Bws Caerdydd/Cardiff Bus

Cardiff City Transport Services Ltd
Leckwith Depot, Sloper Road, Cardiff CF1 8AF, Wales
Telephone: +44 1222 787700 Fax: +44 1222 787742
Managing Director: Frank Yates
Staff: 780

Current situation: CCTS was established as a private company in 1986. Its sole shareholder is Cardiff City Council. Fleet composition has been changed from mainly double-deck to a mix of double-deck, single-deck and midibuses.

Bus

Passenger journeys: (1993/94) 30.4 million
(1994/95) 29.6 million
(1995/96) 29.2 million
Vehicle-km: (1993/94) 15.8 million
(1994/95) 15.9 million
(1995/96) 16.3 million

Number of routes: 171
Route length: 430 km
On priority right-of-way: 3.5 km
Fleet: 297 vehicles

Leyland Olympian double-deck	36
Bristol/VRT double-deck	44
Volvo Ailsa double-deck	48
Scania double-deck	10
Leyland Lynx single-deck	41
Scania single-deck	21
Dennis Dart single-deck	7
Optare Metrorider midibus	74
MCW midibus	16

Most intensive service: 3 min (2-3 min on sections with more than one service)
One-person operation: All routes
Fare collection: Driver-operated ticket issue by Wayfarer 2 electronic machine; Multiride all-route ticket (weekly, monthly etc) sold at sales offices in Cardiff city centre and Barry; all-route 'Capital' daily ticket for visitors sold on buses
Fare structure: Zonal; reduced off-peak fares 09.15-15.45 weekdays
Operational control: Route inspectors; all vehicles have mobile radio contact with central control
Arrangements for elderly/disabled: Free travel for over-75s; other seniors and disabled have half fare financed by Cardiff County Council concessionary fares scheme; 150 vehicles have DPTAC features and 7 have kneeling facility
Average peak-hour speed: 17 km/h
Bus priority: Bus lanes used to assist on all services in short sections in city centre; recently introduced lanes have distinctive green finish
Subsidy from: County Council for specific services secured by tender

Alexander-bodied Scania on Barry Island service

Other operators

Current situation: CCTS's main competitor Cardiff Bluebird ceased operating in 1996. South Wales Transport, Brewers Motor Services, Rhondda Buses, Stagecoach Red & White, Newport Transport, Bebbs, Shamrock and Islwyn Borough Transport operate into the city from outlying areas.

Cardiff Railway

Cardiff Railway Co Ltd
Brunel House, Fitzalan Road, Cardiff CF2 1SA
Telephone: +44 1222 499811 Fax: ext 2290
Director: Tom Clift
Staff: 245

Type of operation: Local rail

Passenger journeys: (1991) 8.4 million
(1993) 20,000 daily journeys
(1994) 5.5 million

Current situation: Diesel suburban services run at 15-60 min intervals on seven routes (137 km, 67 stations); fares cover operating costs, but not all infrastructure costs. Operations are franchised to Prism Rail for a seven-and-a-half year period.
Developments: Resignalling of the busy section between Cardiff (Radyr) and Pontypridd was scheduled for completion in early 1997, reducing headway to 5 min. Under its franchise agreement, Prism will run several through trains daily to Pontypridd from its adjacent South Wales & West operation, and will rehabilitate both trains and stations.

Rolling stock: 30 two-car dmus

Light rail (proposed)

Cardiff Bay Development Corporation

Current situation: Various schemes have been discussed for linking the redeveloping Cardiff Bay area with the city centre and the rail lines running into the valleys. A study commissioned by Cardiff Bay Development Corporation, South and Mid Glamorgan county councils and the then BR Regional Railways was published in 1994. This recommended an initial light rail route on the alignment of the existing rail line from the Bay, along Bute Road to Central and Queen Street stations, where there would be interchange with valleys rail services. Some on-street running would be involved. The second phase would see the system extended to Coryton, Radyr, Caerphilly and possibly Pontypridd, sharing existing lines with valleys trains.

The first phase would be complemented by improvements to the valleys rail service, but later these trains might be replaced by dual-mode vehicles able to run through to the electrified light rail network.

For corridors to the east of the development area, a guided busway is proposed along the route of the existing main line railway, diverging at Newport Road to serve St Mellons and Pentwyn. Other bus priority measures, parking controls and additional park-and-ride facilities are also recommended.

The proposals have been accepted as the basis of future public transport strategy for the region.

Four routes to the bay were studied in 1996; a choice was expected to be made at the end of 1996.

UPDATED

CASABLANCA

Population: 3 million
Public transport: Main bus services operated by city council undertaking responsible to Ministry of Interior, supplemented by a number of private companies; light rail under consideration

RATC

Régie Autonome de Transports en Commun de Casablanca (RATC)
PO Box 5076, Maàrif, Casablanca, Morocco
Telephone: + 212 2 252002 Fax: +212 2 252007
Staff: 3,000

Current situation: RATC was established in 1964 to replace private bus services. For history see *JUTS 1988*.

Government policy has been to encourage development of private bus operations to help cope with the substantial passenger demand, including a large student population which accounts for some 20 per cent of traffic. RATC's operations have been slimmed in consequence.

Bus

Passenger journeys: (1989) 185.5 million
Vehicle-km: (1989) 22.4 million

Number of routes: 91
Route length: (One way) 826 km
Fleet: 463 vehicles

Volvo B58/B10M	300
DAF	145
Berliet PM100	10
Volvo articulated	8

In peak service: 364

Most intensive service: 20-30 min
One-person operation: None
Fare collection: Payment to conductor or prepurchase monthly pass with self-validation for students
Fare structure: Stages; monthly student passes or single tickets

Fares collected on board: 90% (remainder hold student passes)
Operational control: Route inspectors/mobile radio
Average peak-hour speed: 10 km/h
Operating costs financed by: Fares 89.3%, student passes 5.4%, other commercial sources 5.3%.
New vehicles financed by: Government sponsored loans

Private bus

Current situation: Capacity and financial problems of RATC encouraged development of small private bus companies with the aim of enhancing service provision without subsidy. Four companies began operation in 1986 and in 1988 a further eight new private companies began operating on 42 new routes. Private operators carry about 100 million passengers a year.

Light rail (planned)

Current situation: Studies have been made by Japanese consultants for a proposed rapid transit system, probably based on light rail technology. Priority route would be a single cross-city line which would be elevated. The studies are being supported by the Japanese Agency for International Co-operation.

CHANGCHUN

Population: 2 million
Public transport: A single municipal company operates bus, minibus, trolleybus and tram services; light rail planned

CCGJ

Changchun City Public Transport Co (CCGJ)
49 Da Jing Road, Changchun, Jilin Province, People's Republic of China
Telephone:+86 431 862735 Fax: +86 431 823548
General Manager: Wang Xian-min
Deputy General Manager: Zhang Yun Xi
Staff: 11,000

Passenger journeys: (All modes)
(1990) 350 million
(1991) 330 million

Current situation: CCGJ was set up in 1987 following merger of the former bus and trolleybus operating companies. As well as regular bus, trolleybus and tram services in the city and suburbs, CCGJ runs a minibus fleet, taxis, tourist buses, a hotel and a hospital, and several other businesses. Since formation, extensive minibus operations have been introduced, the trolleybus fleet has been modernised, and one of the three remaining tram routes closed.

Bus, trolleybus and tram services continue to operate at fares which, although about 100 per cent higher than in the mid-1980s, have not been increased in line with inflation. Minibuses run over the same routes at premium fares which may be 400 per cent higher. All vehicles carry conductors, those in buses and trolleybuses being seated.

All old trolleybuses have been replaced, but there has been no expansion of the system for several years. Trolleybuses were not introduced over the recently abandoned tram Route 53, although this may happen in the future.

The tramway, already reduced to two suburban routes, saw further contraction in April 1996 when Route 52 was closed. Though light rail proposals have been mooted several times in the past decade, there is no evidence of any progress and complete abandonment now seems likely.

Route 54 tram at Hepingdalu terminus

SY561 trolleybuses in early morning service on Route 61

Bus/minibus

Number of routes: 33
Route length: 185 km
Fleet: Approx 400 buses (mostly articulated), mainly from the Nanchang and Shanghai factories, and about 300 minibuses, some by Siping

Trolleybus

Number of routes: 4
Route length: 36 km
Fleet: Approx 160 trolleybuses, mainly Shanghai SK561G and SK561GF, with some Shengyang SY561

Tramway

Type of operation: Conventional tramway

Number of routes: 1
Route length: 12 km
Gauge: 1,435 mm gauge

Rolling stock: 40 four-axle cars

Light rail (planned)

Current situation: A 13 km line is proposed, with 13 stops.

CHARLEROI

Population: City region 450,000
Public transport: Bus and tramway/light rail services provided by regional publicly owned undertaking. Suburban rail services by state railway (SNCB)

TEC Charleroi

Société de Transport en Commun Charleroi
Place des Tramways 9, 6000 Charleroi, Belgium
Telephone: +32 71 234111 Fax: +32 71 234209
Director General: Gilbert Delva
Staff: 886

Passenger journeys: (1991) 22.8 million
(1992) 21.9 million
(1993)

Current situation: TEC was created in 1991 under the reorganisation of local transport that saw control pass to the new regional body Société Regional Wallonne du Transport. TEC replaced the former operators STIC and SNCV and brought public transport in Charleroi under single management. It serves a total of 20 communes covering an area of some 1,100 km². Four longer-distance bus routes are run by private operators.

Part of the former network of interurban tramways in Charleroi and the surrounding area is being converted into a light rail system. Services feed into an 8 km city-centre line, mostly elevated, which may eventually form a loop. The initial section was opened in 1976, though subsequent progress has been intermittent. Two further sections totalling 5.5 km with seven stations opened in 1992, and another portion opened in 1996.

The works, which include new tunnel and elevated sections constructed at vast cost in semi-rural surroundings, represent a major over-provision of facilities and there are design faults such as remote

Van Hool A300 transit bus of TEC at Charleroi Sud station ***1996***

stations. Some completed sections have never been brought into service, others have had trains withdrawn because traffic figures have been disappointing. Most of the rural tramway routes which ran into the TEC Hainaut area have been closed down.

Bus

Number of routes: 52
Route length: 560 km
Fleet: 221 vehicles

Fiat-Van Hool	18
MAN-Van Hool	60
Eagle	12
Others	131

One-person operation: All routes
Fare collection: Payment to driver or prepurchase
Fare structure: Zonal; ticket cards; various passes; free transfers; national system of common zonally valid multijourney strip tickets
Fares collected on board: 19.1%
Fare evasion control: Inspectors; penalty
Operational control: Route inspectors/mobile radio
Arrangements for elderly/disabled: Passes at reduced rates
Average distance between stops: 700 m
Average peak-hour speed: In mixed traffic, 15 km/h
Operating costs financed by: Fares 28.4%, other commercial sources 3.06%, subsidy/grants 68%
Subsidy from: Central government
New vehicles financed by: Loan

Tramway/Light rail

Type of operation: Conventional tramway/light rail

Passenger journeys: (1993) 3 million

Route length: 16 km (new construction), total 36.5 km
Number of stations: 18
Gauge: 1,000 mm
Track: 50 kg/m rail on 'Angleur' tie-plates inclined 1/20; 20/40 ballast
Electrification: 600 V DC, overhead

Service: Peak 5 min, off-peak 30 min
First/last car: 05.00/20.00
Fare structure: Zonal
Fare collection: Prepurchase tickets, or cash to driver
Fare evasion control: Roving inspectors, spot fines
Integration with other services: Bus feeders at many stations
Operating costs financed by: Fares 15.3%, subsidy/grants 84.7%

Rolling stock: 31 articulated cars serviceable out of fleet of 51

BN/ACEC (1980)	M31

Developments: A further section to Janson and Parc opened in August 1996, when two new routes were introduced.

SNCB

Belgian National Railways (SNCB/NMBS), South-West District
Quai de la Gare du Sud 1, 6000 Charleroi
Telephone: +32 71 602111 Fax: +32 71 602391

Type of operation: Suburban heavy rail

Current situation: Services operate about hourly on seven routes out of Charleroi Sud station, electrified 3 kV DC.

UPDATED

Route 90 LRV outside Charleroi Sud station

CHARLOTTE

Population: Metropolitan area 1.2 million
Public transport: Bus services provided by the City of Charlotte under contract

Charlotte Transit

Transit Management of Charlotte
901 N Davidson, Charlotte, NC 28206, USA
Telephone: +1 704 336 2420 Fax: +1 704 336 4058
General Manager: Robert D Lorah
Assistant Manager: Bob Williams
Marketing Director: Margaret Swenson
Staff: 340
Managed by ATE Management & Services Co

Current situation: CT was established in 1976. It provides local and express bus service within the Charlotte city limits. A no-fare zone operates in the main shopping area during off-peak hours. Express bus passengers, mainly commuters whose services run only in peak times, have 'Guaranteed Ride Home' facility for urgent journeys between the peaks.
Developments: Two new cross-town routes and one route extension inaugurated 1994. Central interchange opened 1995. Two new express routes introduced 1996.

Bus

Passenger journeys: (1992) 12 million
(1994) 12 million
(1995) 12.3 million
Vehicle-km: (1992) 7.8 million
(1995) 8.2 million

Number of routes: 41
Route length:
Fleet: 152 vehicles

Flxible ADB (1982)	42
Flxible (1991)	40
MAN (1987)	40
RTS TMC (1990)	10
MAN articulated (1978 ex-Atlanta, rehabilitated)	10
GMC RTC (1979)	10

In peak service: 122

Most intensive service: 10 min
One-person operation: All routes
Fare collection: Farebox, no change given
Fare structure: Flat, surcharge for express routes; free transfers; weekly and monthly passes
Arrangements for elderly/disabled: Reduced off-peak fares; most buses have kneeling capability; wheelchair lifts on 50 buses; demand-responsive service for those who cannot use fixed-route bus/mobile radio
Arrangements for elderly/disabled: Passes at reduced rates
Average distance between stops: 700 m
Average peak-hour speed: In mixed traffic, 15 km/h
Operating costs financed by: Fares 28.4%, other commercial sources 3.06%, subsidy/grants 68%

UPDATED

CHELYABINSK

Population: 1.1 million
Public transport: Bus and trolleybus/tramway services provided by separate municipal undertakings; metro under construction

Bus

Number of routes: 73
Fleet: Ikarus 260/260, LIAZ 677 and Hyundai
Fare collection: Prepurchase, cancellers on board

Tramvaino-Trolleibusnoe Upravlenie

Tramvaino-Trolleibusnoe Upravlenie
Ul Truda 66, 454000 Chelyabinsk, Russia
Telephone: +7 3512 337752

Current situation: This is one of the best Russian tramway systems in terms of maintenance standards and reliability. Metro construction started in 1992 and has progressed erratically; there is no likelihood of opening before 2000.

Trolleybus

Number of routes: 22
Fleet: About 400 vehicles, ZIU9 and ZIU10

Tramway

Passenger journeys: (1989) 185 million

Number of routes: 16
Track length: 155 km
Rolling stock: About 370 cars

KTM5 (1982-92)	M320
KTM8 (1990-96)	M50

NEW ENTRY

ZIU10 articulated trolleybus crossing the central square ***1997***

KTM8 car at Pobedy prospect
1997

CHEMNITZ

Population: 266,000, area served 271,000
Public transport: Bus and tramway services provided by municipal company account for 95% of all public transport journeys; some suburban services of state railway (DB) and regional bus company Autobus Sachsen

CVAG

Chemnitzer Verkehrs AG (CVAG)
PO Box 114, 09001 Chemnitz, Germany
Telephone: +49 371 23700 Fax: +49 371 2370 600
Technical Director: Dipl-Ing-Ök Gert Gottschalk
Commercial Director: Dipl-Volkswirt Werner Jumpertz
Managers: Ilka Caspary
Reinhart Seidel
Staff: 1,012

Passenger journeys: (1993) 52.4 million
(1994) 51.7 million
(1995) 56.7 million

Current situation: CVAG serves an area of 130 km². The bus system is more extensive than in many eastern German cities as the former 925 mm gauge tram network was replaced largely by buses rather than total conversion to 1,435 mm gauge. Conversion was completed in 1988.
Developments: Bus routes are being replanned as feeders to an extended tram network, including new light rail routes into surrounding areas, some of which may take over existing DB routes. Tram service now replaced by buses at times of low demand.

Bus

Staff: 599

Passenger journeys: (1995) 32.7 million

Tatra T3D trams at C-Zentrum

Vehicle-km: (1993) 8.7 million
(1994) 7.8 million
(1995) 8.7 million

Number of routes: 29
Route length: 211 km
On priority right-of-way: 1.2 km
Fleet: 173 vehicles, plus 17 hired

Ikarus 280 articulated	40
Mercedes O405N low-floor	73
Neoplan N4014/2 low-floor	10
MAN NG272 low-floor articulated	31
Mercedes O405GN low-floor articulated	11
Neoplan N4032 Megashuttle double-deck	5
Others	3

In peak service: 154

Most intensive service: 4 min
One-person operation: All routes
Fare structure: Time-based; monthly passes
Fare collection: Prepurchase only, no onboard sales; on-board validation; 70% hold passes or multi-ride tickets
Fare evasion control: Roving inspectors
Arrangements for elderly/disabled: Free or reduced rates for disabled, reimbursed by government

Neoplan Megashuttle of CVAG ***1995***

Average distance between stops: 664 m
Average speed: 20.9 km/h
Operating costs financed by: Fares 32%, other commercial sources 5.1%, subsidy/grants 62.9%
Subsidy from: City of Chemnitz 100%

Developments: A bus-only lane was introduced on Theaterstrasse in 1995, saving up to 8 min on peak-hour journeys.

Tramway

Staff: 410

Type of operation: Conventional tramway

Passenger journeys: (1995) 24 million
Car-km: (1993) 6.6 million
(1994) 6 million
(1995) 6.2 million

Number of routes: 4
Route length: 22.1 km
reserved track: 20.5 km
Gauge: 1,435 mm
Electrification: 600 V DC, overhead

Service: Peak 4 min
Average distance between stops: 470 m
Average speed: 18.2 km/h
Operating costs financed by: Fares 30.5%, other commercial sources 9.2%, subsidy/grants 60.3%

Rolling stock: 181 cars

ČKD Tatra T3D/B3D 4-axle (1968/78)	M94 T36
ČKD Tatra T3D-M/B3D-M modernised	M36 T14
ABB Variobahn 6NGT 6-axle articulated (1993)	M1

In peak service: 158
On order: 23 Variobahn low-floor cars from Adtranz Germany, with an option for a further 30.

Developments: A 4.5 km extension from Falkeplatz to Stolberger Strasse was expected to open in late 1996; other extensions planned including some over DB tracks using diesel generator power.

Autobus Sachsen

Autobus Sachsen GmbH
Strasse de Nationen 33, 09111 Chemnitz
Telephone: +49 371 461380 Fax: +49 371 415391
General Manager: Rolf Kuhfahl

Passenger journeys: (1993) 9.9 million
(1995) 9.5 million
Vehicle-km: (1993) 7.7 million
(1995) 7.9 million

Current situation: Local government-owned bus company providing regional services in the area around Chemnitz with a fleet of 161 buses plus 7 hired.

UPDATED

CHENGDU

Population: 3 million
Public transport: A trolleybus system serves parts of the central area and is augmented by bus services covering the rest of the city. Paratransit exists in the form of large numbers of minibuses. Chinese Railways operates a suburban service of five trains daily on the line from Chengdu main station to Jiwuduan, with journey time of 15-17 min. Metro and light rail planned

Chengdu City Transport

Chengdu City Transport
Chengdu, Sichuan Province, People's Republic of China

Current situation: Having remained unchanged for many years, the trolleybus system was reduced from five to three routes in 1993 or 1994. The remaining old trolleybuses are thought to have been replaced by new vehicles.

CD644 articulated bus in suburban street

Bus

Number of routes: About 50
Fleet: Approx 500, including some 200 articulated
Fare collection: Stage fares paid to seated conductor; monthly passes

Trolleybus

Number of routes: 3
Fleet: Approx 100 Shanghai and Chengdu articulated
Fare collection: As bus

Metro and light rail (planned)

Current situation: Plans for a 20 km three-line metro were announced in 1993. These envisaged a 5 km north-south line from Chengdu to Chengdu South station, a 6 km east-west line from Wuguiqiao to the Emei Film Studios, and a 9 km orbital line beneath the main boulevard encircling the city centre. Private finance was to be sought in Hong Kong to augment the public funds to be allocated.

This scheme seems to have foundered, as a new proposal for a 12 km metro line and 189 km of light rail routes was announced in 1994. A design-build-operate contract was expected to be awarded to a Canadian company, with a possible opening date of 1997 suggested.

CHIBA

Population: 800,000
Public transport: Situated 40 km to the east of central Tokyo, Chiba has seen recent large-scale commercial and residential development and a rapid increase in population, many of whom commute to Tokyo. JR and private rail services; monorail operated by third-sector company; privately operated bus services

Keisei Dentetsu

Keisei Electric Railway
10-3 Oshiage, 1-chome, Sumida-ku, Tokyo 131, Japan
Telephone: +81 3 3621 2231

Interurban rail

Managing Director: H Hosokawa
Staff: 2,169

Passenger journeys: (1991/92) 276 million
(1992/93) 279 million
(1993/94) 281 million
Car-km: (1992/93) 76 million
(1993/94) 76 million

Current situation: Operates from Ueno station in Tokyo to Chiba-Chuo (42.6 km) with nine stations in Chiba city. A reciprocal through service is operated with Chiba Kyuko Dentetsu (see below).

Rolling stock: 496 emu cars

Various builders	M442 T54

Bus

Managing Director: K Sato
Staff: 2,200

Passenger journeys: (Tokyo conurbation, including Chiba)
(1991/92) 138.8 million
(1992/93) 135.3 million
(1993/94) 136.5 million

Current situation: Keisei's bus division runs 980 buses, of which about 730 are operated on routes in Chiba city and prefecture, including feeder services to monorail stations.

JR East

East Japan Railway Company
Higashi Nihon Ryokaku Tetsudo
1-6-5 Marunouchi, Chiyoda-ku, Tokyo 100
Telephone: +81 3 3215 9649 Fax: +81 3 3213 5291

The 596 Budd/Transit America cars built between 1981 and 1987 are to be refurbished and converted for one-person operation.

Metra

NE Illinois Regional Commuter Railroad Corp (Metra)
547 West Jackson Boulevard, Chicago, IL 60661
Telephone: +1 312 322 6900
Chair: Jeffrey R Ladd
Executive Director: Philip A Pagano
Deputy Executive Director: G Richard Tidwell
Chief Operations Officer: Vaughn L Stoner
Director of Passenger Services: Mary M Hughes
Director of Media Relations: Chris Knapton
Staff: 2,300

Type of operation: Suburban heavy rail

Passenger journeys: (1992) 72.8 million
(1993) 72.6 million
(1994) 73.1 million

Current situation: NIRC was formed in 1982 as a subsidiary of the Illinois Regional Transportation Authority to operate the commuter lines of the former Rock Island Railroad (79 route-km) and later those of the Milwaukee Road (135 km), which had been purchased and leased respectively by the RTA. NIRC also had purchase of service agreements for other commuter services provided by the Illinois Central (125 km), Burlington Northern (59 km), Chicago & North Western (249 km), Norfolk Southern (39 km) and Chicago, South Shore & South Bend (between Chicago and the Illinois/Indiana border, now the South Shore line) railroads.

In 1984 the Commuter Rail Service Board took over, adopting the service name Metra. Today Metra owns and operates (through NIRC) the former Rock Island, Milwaukee, IC (Metra Electric) and Norfolk Southern (taken over in 1993) lines. Trains on other lines operate under purchase of service agreements. Metra is responsible for setting fare and service levels, and provides for capital improvements, planning and marketing for all lines.

Operations extend to 775 route-km of 1,435 mm gauge on 11 routes and two branches serving 244 stations, of which 66 km electrified at 1.5 kV DC overhead. Other routes worked by diesel push-pull trainsets. Trains run every 5-20 min at peak times, and every 1, 1½ or 2 h off-peak; limited service evenings and weekends. Zonal fare structure, with monthly tickets giving an opportunity to purchase monthly bus pass (Link-up Passport) at a reduced rate. Fares account for 55 per cent of operating costs.

In addition the South Shore line has 117 km of 1,435 mm gauge route electrified at 1.5 kV DC overhead and operates interurban service from Chicago to Gary, Michigan City and South Bend in Indiana. This route is subsidised 22 per cent by Metra and 78 per cent by the Northern Illinois Commuter Transportation District, which purchased the line in 1991. It carried 3.2 million passengers in 1994, and was undergoing a programme of station refurbishment in 1996.

Southbound Howard/Dan Ryan train at Belmont ***1996***

Rolling stock: 130 diesel locomotives, 684 coaches, 206 emu cars

Budd/Pullman/St Louis Car (1950/84)	T516
Budd cab cars (1970s)	T168
MLW/St Louis Car emu (1970/74)	M129
Bombardier emu (1975/79)	M36
Nippon Sharyo emu for South Shore (1982/83)	M41
Sumitomo emu for South Shore (1992)	M7 T10
Morrison Knudsen cab cars (1994/95)	

On order: 173 cab cars with full wheelchair accessibility being delivered by Morrison Knudsen, which is also rehabilitating 140 existing emu cars

Developments: Major investment in suburban rail and bus networks is proposed under the Future Agenda for Suburban Transportation (FAST), developed by Metra with bus operator Pace (see below), based on the Rail Alternatives Study of 1989. This aimed to identify ways in which Metra might cater for suburb-to-suburb journeys, which are the fastest growing category of travel in the region. As well as eight proposed extensions to the existing rail network, two priorities were selected from a number of non-radial routes assessed – the Wisconsin Central (former Soo Line) and Elgin, Joliet & Eastern (outer circumferential) corridors.

The Wisconsin Central route, a 67 km extension to Antioch with 11 stations, opened in August 1996. Daily patronage of some 5,200 is expected.

Other elements of the strategy include grade separation to eliminate many of the region's level crossings, track-doubling, provision of new park-and-ride stations, and closer co-operation with Pace, whose buses would feed many more stations. It is also aimed to improve journey times for the increasing number of longer-distance commuters.

Pace

550 West Algonquin Road, Arlington Heights, IL 60005
Telephone: +1 708 364 8130 Fax: +1 708 439 8116
Chair: Florence Boone
Executive Director: Joseph DiJohn
Deputy Executive Director, Operations: Melinda Metzger
Staff: 1,320

Passenger journeys: (1993) 38.3 million
(1994) 38.6 million
(1995) 37.2 million

Current situation: Pace was established in 1984 to assume operational responsibility for the three existing RTA-controlled suburban bus divisions and other operations, together covering the 5,500 km², 4.5 million population, six-county suburban region of Chicago.

Pace provides funding for 233 bus routes serving 235 communities. It owns and operates nine suburban carriers, subsidises three municipal carriers and contracts with 12 private operators, primarily running express routes serving suburban employment centres and feeders to 132 CTA metro and Metra rail stations. A uniform fare structure exists for most Pace services.

Some 82.8 per cent of passengers are carried by Pace-owned operations, 7.9 per cent by private contract carriers, 2.8 per cent by municipal services, 4.4 per cent by paratransit and 2.1 per cent by vanpools.

Paratransit services to all parts of the area (excluding that covered by CTA) have seen increasing patronage. They are operated mainly by dial-a-ride shared taxi, fixed route deviation types of service on 60 routes. There are also four 'mobility limited' routes. There are 56 local operators and six private contractors; Pace-owned lift-equipped vehicles are used. All satellite cities have fully accessible service.

Developments: Several capital projects are under way in the Comprehensive Operating Plan, including provision of more transit centres and park-and-ride sites. A transit vehicle management system is to be installed, with passenger counting and automatic vehicle location facilities as well as traffic signal pre-emption.

The VIP vanpool programme continues to expand, with over 200 vehicles, despite the reduced emphasis now placed on the Employee Commute Options programme.

Fleet: 991 vehicles

Chance RT50	8
Orion I (1987 on)	454
Ikarus USA (1992)	71
Novabus Classic (1995)	22
Chance RT52 (1995)	18
Gillig Phantom (1988)	20
Orion II (1987)	5
Goshen buses/vans	84
Champion	70
Braun vans	24
National/Eldorado	215

Average age: 5.4 years
In peak service: 581 buses, including contractors' vehicles

Arrangements for elderly/disabled: Paratransit operations serve 224 municipalities
Fare structure: Flat with 10 cent transfers, or monthly pass; premium fares on express/commuter routes; paratransit fares vary
Operating costs financed by: Fares 36.3%, subsidy/grants 63.7%
Subsidy from: RTA provides support drawn from sales tax, federal operating assistance and state subsidy via the public transportation fund

UPDATED

CHIŞINĂU

Population: 676,000
Public transport: Extensive trolleybus network and smaller feeder bus system operated by separate undertakings controlled by Ministry of Transport. These are supplemented by small buses known as 'marshroutniy taxis'

City Trolleybus Company

Chişinău City Trolleybus Company
Chişinău, Moldova

Trolleybuses at the Alba Lulia terminus

Current situation: The trolleybus network forms the basis of the city's public transport and services are extremely crowded.

Trolleybus

Number of routes: 20 regular, plus 3 at shift-change hours only
Fleet: Approx 450 trolleybuses, Uritsky ZIU9 and some ZIU10
Fare structure: Flat
Fare collection: Single tickets purchased from driver or from kiosks, cancelling machines on board; calendar monthly and semi-monthly passes
Fare evasion control: Roving inspectors

City Bus Company

Chişinău City Bus Company

Current situation: Buses play a smaller, mainly feeder role. The fleet is mostly Ikarus 260/280; fare structure is the same as for trolleybuses, but with single tickets 50 per cent higher.

UPDATED

CHONGQING

Population: 3 million, metropolitan area 14 million
Public transport: The city centre occupies a hilly peninsula at the confluence of the Yangzi and Jialing rivers. Suburbs fan out from the neck of land west of the centre and are also located north of the Jialing and west of the Yangzi. Each river is crossed by only one road bridge. Public transport is of particular importance because the hilly terrain is considered unsuitable for cycling, though the topography is ideal for trolleybus operation and Chongqing adopted this mode in 1955. An extensive network of bus services complements the trolleybuses. Rail plays little part in local transport; though a direct line exists between the centre and the outer trolleybus terminal at Shapingba, a 7 km tunnel restricts operation of suburban services to two trains morning and afternoon between Chongqing and Chongqing West. A few local trains also run between Chongqing and Chongqing South (7 km); light rail proposed

Two-axle and articulated trolleybuses in Chongqing

Chongqing City Transport

Chongqing City Transport Department
Chongqing, Sichuan Province, People's Republic of China

Current situation: A tree-shaped network of overlapping trolleybus routes runs from the river confluence up the spine of the peninsula to three suburban terminals, one route crossing the Jialing bridge. The busiest part of the system has sections of duplicated overhead to increase capacity. There is also an intersuburban route. In 1989 the network had remained unchanged for many years apart from an alteration near the central junction to conform to a one-way traffic scheme.

Chongqing CQ662 articulated bus at suburban terminal

Bus

Passenger journeys: (1985/86) 568 million
Vehicle-km: (1985/86) 54 million

Number of routes: 50
Route length: 500 km
Fleet: Approx 800 buses, including many articulated, all Chongqing including types CQ643, CQ650 (two-axle), CQ662, CQ663 and CQ670 (articulated)
Fare collection: Stage fares paid to seated conductor; monthly passes

Trolleybus

Passenger journeys: (1985/86) 57 million
Vehicle-km: (1985/86) 5.4 million

Number of routes: 5
Route length: 30 km
Fleet: Approx 150 Chongqing trolleybuses, including about 130 articulated; current type is CQ563 articulated
Fare collection: As bus

Other modes

Current situation: There is an aerial cableway across each river but ferries remain the principal cross-river links away from the two bridges. Three funiculars provide short-distance transport at difficult locations.

CINCINNATI

Population: 364,000, city region 867,000
Public transport: Bus services in city and environs provided by operating arm of Southwest Ohio Regional Transit Authority, governed by representative Board of Trustees. Services also run into the city from Covington and Newport across the Ohio river in Kentucky, operated by similar undertaking

Metro

Southwest Ohio Regional Transit Authority (SORTA)
1014 Vine Street, Cincinnati, OH 45202-1122, USA
Telephone: +1 513 621 9450 Fax: +1 513 621 5291
President, SORTA Board of Trustees: Eleanor Hicks
General Manager: Paul C Jablonski
Assistant General Manager, Operations: Michael L Brown
Assistant General Manager, Administration: Barry E Frank
Manager, Marketing & Communications: Rita Potts
Staff: 918

Current situation: Metro, SORTA's bus operating subsidiary was established in 1973 when voters approved a tax increase to fund purchase of the Cincinnati Transit bus system. It serves a total population of 867,000; 34 per cent of riders live outside the city of Cincinnati in other parts of Hamilton and Clermont counties, and are served by 18 per cent of vehicle-km operated.
Developments: Informal proposals exist for light rail in two corridors where moribund rail routes could be utilised. Purchase of rail rights-of-way was authorised in 1992, and in 1994 the city bought a share in the 25.6 km former Conrail freight line running northeast to Evendale.

A five-year plan approved in 1992 envisaged purchase of 131 buses through to 1997, along with replacement of the radio communications system and purchase of three bus-wash machines. In the event, a contract for up to 250 buses was signed with Gillig in 1995, with the first vehicles in the initial batch of 117 delivered at the end of 1995.

Construction of four new park-and-ride lots per year is also planned.

Two new commuter routes inaugurated March 1995 from northern suburbs previously unserved; three additional park-and-ride sites established.

Bus

Passenger journeys: (1993) 26 million
(1994) 22.8 million
(1995) 23.7 million
Vehicle-km: (1993) 19.8 million
(1994) 19.5 million
(1995) 19.8 million

Number of routes: 45
Route length: (One way) 1,993 km
Fleet: 378 vehicles

Flxible Corp (1980)	64
Neoplan (1989)	100
Neoplan (1990)	64
Champion minibus (1991)	33
Gillig Phantom (1995/96)	117

On order: 117 Gillig delivered 1995/96, with an option for a further 133

Most intensive service: 4 min
One-person operation: All routes

Fare collection: Cash or token to registering GFI farebox with vault, or magnetic passes
Fare structure: Flat, city; zonal, suburbs; prepurchase tickets, monthly passes; 10 cent transfers, 40 cent to TANK services; peak surcharge on both local and express services; flat weekend fare
Fare evasion control: None
Arrangements for elderly/disabled: Access service with 33 lift-equipped minibuses operated under contract by Mayflower; carried 215,000 passengers in 1995. Elderly and disabled eligible for reduced fares on conventional services
Average distance between stops: 161 m
Average peak-hour speed: 20.5 km/h
Integration with other modes: 13 suburban park-and-ride sites; 4 are dedicated for Metro riders while others are provided as community service by local municipalities or property owners
Operating costs financed by: Fares 33.8%, other commercial sources 0.4%, subsidy/grants 15.5%, tax levy (0.3% payroll tax for transit) 50.3%

Cincinnati Flxible bus in Fountain Square ***1996***

TANK

Transit Authority of Northern Kentucky
3375 Madison Pike, Fort Wright, KY 41017
Telephone: +1 606 341 8265 Fax: +1 606 331 1526
General Manager: Mark Doherty
Operations Manager: Robert Mason
Staff: 195

Current situation: As well as serving the cities of Covington and Newport, TANK runs several routes across the Ohio river to downtown Cincinnati.
Developments: Express service to Cincinnati/Northern Kentucky airport started 1995, making public transport available to passengers and airport workers for the first time, though it is the latter group that benefits from the irregular timetable. New routes inaugurated to four suburbs in August 1995.

Fleet: 120 buses

AMG (1975)	1
MCI Classic (1981)	10
Gillig Phantom (1983/88/92/95)	66
Startrans (1990/94)	10
Flxible Metro (1992/93)	33

UPDATED

CLEVELAND

Population: City 505,000, service area 1.6 million
Public transport: Bus, metro and light rail services provided for Cleveland, 65 towns in Cuyahoga County and some small outside areas by Regional Transit Authority under the control of representative Board of Trustees. Paratransit system, Community Responsive Transit, provided for elderly/disabled. Part of this, and some bus services, operated under contract to RTA

Greater Cleveland RTA

Greater Cleveland Regional Transit Authority
615 Superior Avenue W, Cleveland, OH 44113, USA
Telephone: +1 216 566 5100 Fax: +1 216 781 4043
Web: http://little.nhlink.net/~rta
President, Board of Trustees: George F Dixon III
General Manager: Ronald J Tober
Deputy General Manager: R L Barnes
Assistant General Managers
Operations: Leilia M Bailey
Marketing & Development: RoseMary Covington
Human Resources: Mary Jo LaPorte
Finance & Administration: Loretta Baks
Engineering & Construction: Charles Stanford
Materials: Maynard Z Walters
Staff: 2,700

LRV on Waterfront line ***1997***

Passenger boardings: (All modes)
(1993) 60 million
(1994) 60.2 million
(1995) 58.3 million

Operating costs financed by: (All modes) fares 24%, other commercial sources 3%, subsidy/grants 72%
Subsidy from: Dedicated sales tax 64%, state and federal operating assistance 8%

Current situation: The long-term decline in bus ridership has continued, while rail patronage has shown significant increases even before opening of the Waterfront light rail line in July 1996. New pricing policies are being introduced to stimulate new ridership.
Developments: An alternatives analysis published in 1990 examined possible metro/light rail system extensions and bus service improvements. These proposals were refined into an $800 million 25-year development plan – the RTA's first long-term plan – known as Transit 2010; this was adopted by the RTA board in 1993. Some current upgrading schemes have been incorporated into Transit 2010.

The main provisions of the plan affect the bus services used by some 88 per cent of RTA riders. A major restructuring of the network will cater for changed travel patterns, especially suburb-to-suburb and reverse flow commuting. Community circulator routes have been implemented as feeders both to local activity nodes such as shopping centres and hospitals, and interchanges with main bus and rail routes. Timed transfer will be offered at all hubs where two or more services intersect.

Many new park-and-ride lots are planned, including major sites on the I-77 and I-90 highway corridors. Dedicated express buses with full accessibility are to serve these routes in commuting hours. The first of 14 dedicated Flyer routes started in 1994, serving the park-and-rides at Strongsville and newly opened Euclid. Five coaches with high-back seats, luggage racks and reading lights were purchased to run the initial service. Another site at Westlake opened in late 1995.

Rail plans centred on the long-proposed Dual Hub corridor scheme under which the Red line metro would be relocated to a new alignment along Euclid Avenue between Tower City and University Circle. After much controversy and reversal of an earlier decision to shelve the project, it was cancelled once again in late 1995. A busway along Euclid Avenue is planned instead.

At the metro's southern end a 4 km extension was planned to serve the developing suburb of Berea, close to Hopkins International airport, but this is now not to go ahead. A similar short extension is proposed for the light rail Blue line from its current terminus at Warrensville to Highland Hills, where a 0.3 million m^2 commercial development is under way. Preliminary studies are being made of both extensions, while a third route – the Waterfront line – opened in 1996.

Later stages of Transit 2010 would see commuter service provided on obsolete rail rights-of-way. The Northeast Ohio Areawide Coordinating Agency has made feasibility studies of commuter rail service over five routes radiating from Cleveland, of which the most promising is

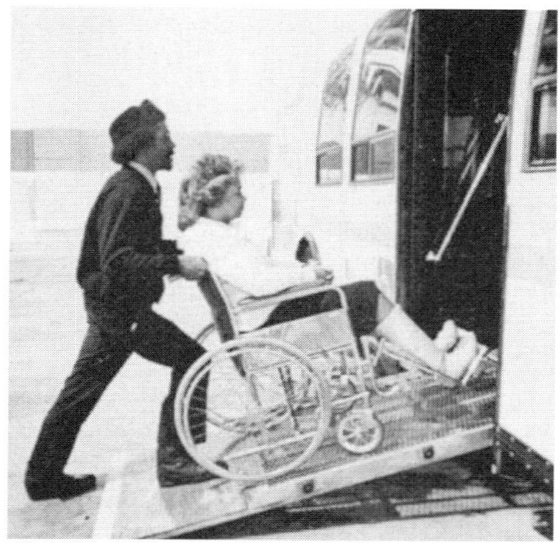

RTA's Community Responsive Transit fleet is equipped to take passengers in wheelchairs

CNG-powered downtown loop bus meets radial service at Tower City interchange

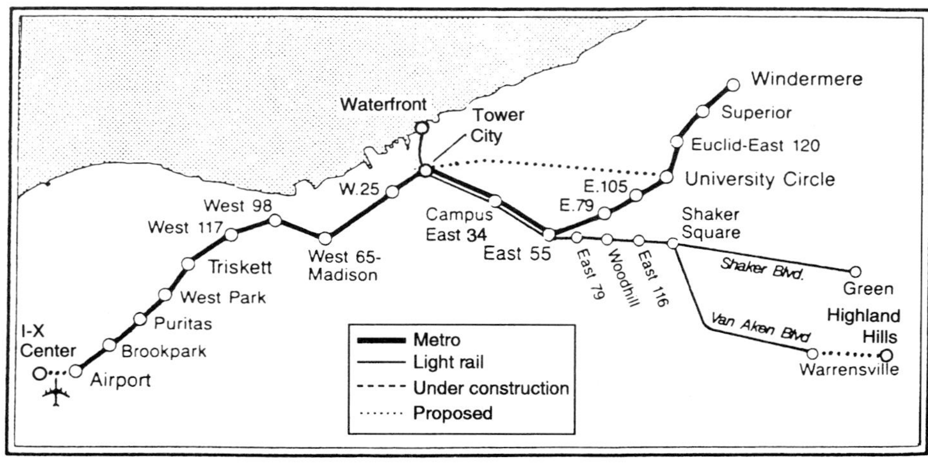

Cleveland metro and light rail

the 100 km Cleveland—Akron—Canton corridor, where disused freight trackage is being purchased by local authorities. The first section, 56 km to Akron, might open in 1997 as a limited-duration demonstrator.

Central to all the proposals is further development of the Tower City transport hub, where expanded rail facilities are to be provided.

Bus

Passenger journeys: (1992) 47.9 million
(1994) 50.6 million
(1995) 48.6 million
Vehicle-km: (1992) 35.3 million
(1994) 32.8 million
(1995) 36.3 million

Number of routes: 102
Route length: 2,404 km (includes contracted services)
Fleet: 785 vehicles, of which 55 inactive

GMC T8H-203 (1979)	78
GMC RTS-4 (1982)	77
Flxible Metro (1984)	57
Flxible Metro (1985)	105
Flxible Metro (1988)	77
Flxible Metro CNG-powered (1990/91/92/94)	294
Flxible Metro suburban (1994/95)	20
TMC RTS-6 (1989)	77

In peak service: 636

Most intensive service: 5 min
One-person operation: All services except light rail
Fare collection: Farebox adjacent to driver
Fare structure: Flat fare for each local and express (premium), with two free transfers; reduced flat fare on downtown circulators; weekly and monthly passes
Fares collected on board: 75%
Integration with other modes: Total; extensive park-and-ride facilities with 8,500 spaces; more planned
Operational control: Route inspectors (stationary and mobile)/mobile radio
Arrangements for elderly/disabled: Fleet of paratransit vehicles operated (plus some contracted), including 73 wheelchair-accessible on Community Responsive Transit service; discount fares on conventional services
Average peak-hour speed: In mixed traffic, 18.5 km/h
New vehicles financed by: FTA grants 80%, state 10%, sales tax revenue, bond anticipation notes, and/or permanent improvement bonds 10%

Contracted bus

Maple Heights Transit System
5501 Dunham Road (Rear Building), Maple Heights, OH 44137
Telephone: +1 216 662 6075 Fax: +1 216 662 2880
Director of Transit: E Fairfax

North Olmsted Municipal Bus Line
5200 Dover Center, North Olmsted, OH 44070
Telephone: +1 216 777 2662 Fax: +1 216 777 5774
General Manager: Kenneth Mues

Passenger journeys: (1994) Maple Heights 0.6 million, North Olmsted 1.2 million
(1995) Maple Heights 0.6 million, North Olmsted 1.1 million

Current situation: Some 62 buses are operated by these two companies under contract to the RTA, in addition to 18 paratransit vehicles hired as part of the Community Responsive Transit fleet. Fixed-route services extend to 312 km.

Metro

Type of operation: Full metro (Red line), initial route opened 1955

Passenger journeys: (1993) 4.1 million
(1994) 4.5 million
(1995) 4.7 million
Car-km: (1994) 1.9 million
(1995) 1.6 million

Route length: 30.7 km
in tunnel: 0.8 km
on surface: 29.8 km
Number of lines: 1
Number of stations: 18
in tunnel: 2
Gauge: 1,435 mm
Track: 45 kg/m ARA-A continuously welded rail; sleepers on ballast
Tunnel: Cut-and-cover, or within structure
Electrification: 600 V DC, overhead

Service: Peak 6 min, off-peak 12 min
First/last train: 03.45/00.55
Fare structure: Flat, with free transfer to and from express bus lines; monthly and weekly passes
Revenue control: One-way turnstiles
Integration with other modes: 8,500 park-and-ride places at metro and light rail stations
One-person operation: Of one-car trains
Signalling: GRS three-aspect lights with automatic stop; cab signalling

Rolling stock: 60 cars

Tokyu Car (1985/86)	M60

In peak service: 38

Light rail

Type of operation: Light rail, first line opened 1920

Passenger journeys: (1993) 2.7 million
(1994) 2.9 million
(1995) 3.1 million
Car-km: (1992) 1.8 million
(1994) 1.6 million
(1995) 1.7 million

Route length: 21.5 km
Number of lines: 2
Number of stops: 29
Electrification: 600 V DC, overhead

Service: Peak 4 min, off-peak 10 min
First/last car: 04.05/00.11

Rolling stock: 48 cars

Breda LRV (1983)	M48

In peak service: 28

UPDATED

COIMBATORE

Population: 1.1 million
Public transport: Bus services provided by transport corporation controlled by state government

CTC

Cheran Transport Corporation Ltd
PO Box 7015, 37 Mettupalayan Road, Coimbatore 641043, India
Telephone: +91 422 431521
Managing Director: R C Jeyaraj
Staff: 7,940

Current situation: CTC provides bus services in Coimbatore town and neighbouring districts. Figures below refer to the total regional operation.

Bus

Passenger journeys: (1993/94) 623.5 million
(1994/95) 588.7 million
(1995/96) 612.4 million
Vehicle-km: (1993/94) 166.3 million
(1994/95) 153.3 million
(1995/96) 157.1 million

Fleet: 1,143 vehicles
Operating costs financed by: Fares 114.4%, other commercial sources 4.9%

COLOMBO

Population: 587,000

Public transport: Bus services in Greater Colombo provided by subsidiaries of Government Central Transport Board, and by independent firms operating private buses and minibuses under control and supervision of the Department of Private Omnibus Transport. Also suburban rail services provided by state railway. Government attempting to co-ordinate public and privately operated bus services but civil unrest has encouraged minibuses

Sri Lanka Central Transport Board

200 Kirula Road, PO Box 1435, Colombo 5
Telephone: +94 1 81121

Current situation: Following the 1990 decentralisation, bus services have been provided by a number of small companies based on the former north and south regional transport boards' garages. In addition, some 4,000 buses are run by private operators.

Developments: Decentralisation has not achieved the desired results, as many of the companies created were too small to be viable. Now it is proposed to merge them into a single city-wide undertaking, Colombo Metropolitan Transport (CMT), which would have a fleet of 1,080 buses. The CTB will resume its former responsibilities for running workshops and handling purchasing, to which will be added staff training.

A further attempt is to be made to regulate private operators either by forcing them to merge into larger undertakings, or redefining their role as contractors to CMT. They will be supervised by the city council.

Bus

(Figures for city area operations unless stated)

Number of routes: 283 (designated)
Route length: (One way) 8,892 km (including duplication)
Fleet: Total 3,129 vehicles, including Ashok Leyland, Leyland, Tata, Isuzu and ex-London Routemasters. Operational fleet about 2,400 vehicles

Most intensive service: Less than 1 min
One-person operation: None
Fare collection: Conductor on board
Fare structure: Stage; monthly seasons, annual passes
Fares collected on board: 76.2%
Fare evasion control: Random inspectors. Penalty collected
Integration with other modes: Bus services to most rail stations in Colombo
Operational control: Route inspectors
Average distance between stops: 300-350 m
Average peak-hour speed: In mixed traffic, 20 km/h
Operating costs financed by: Fares 81.2%, subsidy/grants 11.3%
Subsidy from: Government
New vehicles financed by: International Development Authority and government loans

Current situation: A major fleet modernisation and engineering improvement programme has been taking place with the aid of the World Bank and consultants.

Developments: Reintroduction of trolleybuses has been suggested.

A new generation of bus designed for local conditions, the low-floor ColomboRider, will enter service during 1997. The vehicles are the result of co-operation between UK builder Optare and local insurance company Ceylinco (see Bus manufacturers section).

Sri Lanka Railways

Sri Lanka Railways
PO Box 355, Colombo 10
Telephone: +94 1 21281 Fax: +94 1 446490

Type of operation: Suburban heavy rail

Passenger journeys: (1990) 33 million
(1991) 37 million

Current situation: Diesel services provided on three lines out of Colombo Fort station to Veyangonda, Kalutara South, and Negombo, totalling 138 km with 31 stations. Feasibility studies have been made of electrification, and the scheme received government approval in 1989, but 20 diesel power cars and 60 trailers were delivered in 1991 as a stop-gap measure to upgrade existing fleet of diesel locomotives, coaches and dmus.

Rolling stock: 51 four-car dmu sets

Private bus/minibus

Current situation: Private bus and minibus services were introduced in 1978/79 to complement services operated by the state sector. After a slow start the private bus industry developed very rapidly and now operates over 4,000 vehicles in the Greater Colombo area, and double that number in the rest of the country. About 90 per cent are in the 15-35 capacity range, most Japanese-built.

The government has made various attempts to co-ordinate services operated by the transport boards and the private sector to eliminate wasteful competition and streamline the services offered to the public.

Impetus has been given to the minibuses by recent civil unrest, with informal co-operation with SLCTB allowing the minibuses to use CTB bus stations.

COLUMBUS

Population: 634,000, metropolitan area 1.3 million

Public transport: Bus services provided for 961,400 residents of Franklin County in central Ohio by Regional Transit Authority under control of representative Board of Trustees. Service area includes small portions of Delaware, Fairfield, Licking and Pickaway counties whose boundaries adjoin Franklin County

COTA

Central Ohio Transit Authority (COTA)
1600 McKinley Avenue, Columbus, OH 43222, USA
Telephone: +1 614 275 5800 Fax: +1 614 275 5933
General Manager: Glenna L Watson
Assistant General Manager, Marketing & Communication: Raymond C Miller
Staff: 739

Current situation: COTA operates three types of regular routes: Locals, which make all stops and travel through or terminate downtown; Expresses, which make few or limited stops and start or terminate downtown; and Crosstowns, which operate between two non-downtown points. See earlier editions for history.

Developments: Operating improvements have been made, including an ambitious increase in transit provision along High Street, traditionally the spine of COTA's network.

There are now 188 lift-equipped buses in service; all crosstown routes are now accessible.

Having adopted a schedule of service improvements for the period through to 1999 under the Short Range Transit Plan published in 1995, COTA approved a resolution to double the size of the bus network by 2005. A further 0.25 per cent sales tax was sought from voters in November 1995.

Lack of funding precluded progress with an earlier plan to develop a 17.8 km light rail line running northwards from the city centre.

Bus

Passenger boardings: (1991) 17 million
(1992) 18 million
(1994) 17.1 million
Vehicle-km: (1991) 15.4 million
(1992) 15.2 million
(1994) 15.2 million

Flxible bus of COTA

Number of routes: 59
Route length: (One way) 1,645 km
Fleet: 310 vehicles

Grumman/Flxible Metro (1984/91/93)	243
GMC (1987)	67

Plus 32 Flxible 870 (1982) in reserve to provide additional services at times of fuel shortage, when ridership can increase by 20% at short notice
In peak service: 252

Most intensive service: 4 min
One-person operation: All routes
Fare collection: Cash to electronic counting farebox with dollar bill facility
Fare structure: Flat, no change, or prepurchase tickets; monthly passes for Local and Express routes; 10 cent transfers, 35 cent premium for Express services
Fare evasion control: Driver monitors payment
Operational control: Two-way radio
Arrangements for elderly/disabled: Reduced fares; 32 fixed routes accessible to wheelchairs. Project Mainstream provides transport for those who cannot use fixed-route services — Subscription riders make the same journey at least once a week, whilst Reservation riders request trips as required. Since 1987, Project Mainstream operations have been contracted to DAVE Transportation Services. SCOT (Senior Citizens on the Town) provides group demand-responsive service for the elderly during mid-day and evening hours. Demand-responsive services carried 92,000 people in 1994
Integration with other modes: Some 22 park-and-ride lots have a total of 1,989 spaces, and there are two parking loops with 12 spaces each. Development of five additional lots planned, mostly around the I-270 orbital highway; guaranteed ride home scheme reimburses participants 90% of fare of four taxi rides per year at times when regular buses do not run
Average peak-hour speed: 22.1 km/h
Bus priority: Peak-hour priority lane in central business district
Operating costs financed by: Fares 24.7%, other commercial sources 1.2%, subsidy/grants 18.7%, tax levy 55.4%
Subsidy from: FTA 12%, state 10.4%, local 75%, other 2.6%
New vehicles financed by: FTA and local grants

CÓRDOBA

Population: 1.2 million
Public transport: Bus and trolleybus services provided by private companies and route co-operatives supervised by municipal transport department

Direccion del Transporte Publico

Palacio 6 de Julio, Córdoba, Argentina
Director of Transport: Lic Gustavo Reartos

Current situation: This authority supervises all public transport in Córdoba, which is provided by private operators. An exception has been the trolleybus network, which has variously been in private and municipal hands. Public transport co-operatives were merged by the municipal authorities in 1970 into 13 route associations. Excessive competition between members led in 1980 to reorganisation of services by route-corridor, which were then put out to tender.

Bus

Current situation: There are 50 routes concentrated along nine corridors, plus three radial and 12 other routes. Mergers and takeovers have reduced the number of operators to six, employing some 3,400. These are: Dr Belgrano, Ciudad de Córdoba, El Coniferal, Union 12 de Octubre, America and Konfort.
Developments: An air conditioned express network of 12 midibus routes has been set up, run in part by new operator Konfort and using Mercedes LO709 and Toyota Coaster vehicles.

A new fare collection system is planned to replace the existing clipcard/token arrangements.

Passenger journeys: (1994) 200 million
Vehicle-km: (1994) 80 million

Number of routes: 65
Route length: 2,123 km
Fleet: 1,025 vehicles, mainly Mercedes midibuses but with some Brazilian-bodied Mercedes buses and an increasing number of El Detalle OA101s; there are also some Fiat-Iveco AU130s and re-engined Zanellos, both built locally; the Express network is operated by Mercedes LO710/OF1215 and Toyota Coasters

Fare collection: Prepurchase ticket or token to driver
Fare structure: Flat, with transfer permitted to two orbital routes
Average peak-hour speed: 16 km/h

Trolleybus

Current situation: Construction of a 60 km network started in 1987, but was curtailed by financial difficulties; five short routes are now operating.
Developments: Operations have been hampered by difficulties, with the municipality taking over from the three private companies that have so far attempted to run the system. A new private operator was expected to be chosen at the beginning of 1997.

Trolleybus in Córdoba's new livery and with municipal logo ***1996***

San Miguel-bodied Diferencial of Ciudad de Córdoba ***1996***

Electrical equipment from 31 ex-Montevideo vehicles was acquired for renovation in 1993.

Passenger journeys: (1994) 13 million
Vehicle-km: (1994) 2.5 million

Fleet: 44 trolleybuses	
ZIU 682 (1989/93)	32
ZIU 683 (1990/92)	12

CURITIBA

Population: 1.6 million
Public transport: Integrated bus services provided by 10 independent companies contracted by city authority, which is responsible for provision of system of busways and terminals and setting of fares and service levels

URBS S/A

Urbanização de Curitiba S/A
Empresa Gerenciadora do Transporte Coletivo, Prefeitura Municipal de Curitiba
PO Box 17017, Av Presidente Affonso Camargo 330, CP 80060-090, Curitiba, Paraná, Brazil
Telephone: +55 41 322 4846 Fax: +55 41 232 9475
President: Carlos Eduardo Ceneviva

Current situation: The highly integrated service network is operated by 10 private companies, each allocated a share in the different types of express, conventional, feeder, intersuburb, neighbourhood, executive and the new direct routes.

Volvo Padron on 'conventional' Route 285 ***1997***

The contract with public transport companies, extended for 10 years in 1981, was later declared null and void. Operating companies are no longer franchise holders and operate under contract on the authority of the governor, in accordance with regulations which ensure that they meet quality standards set by URBS, a municipal company established as the only franchise holder. Failure to comply with URBS requirements may result in permission to operate a particular line being withdrawn.

The arrangement has overcome artificial area boundaries inhibiting planning of the transport system and prohibiting one company from picking up passengers while crossing the 'territory' of another, and creating an operating monopoly.

Remuneration of operating companies is made on the basis of km actually covered — journeys not made and timetables cancelled are not paid for, potentially resulting in fines.

Income from the system has become public; the daily takings of each bus are deposited in a local authority account with Banestado, managed by URBS. A balance sheet is published each month so that the receipts of the system can be clearly monitored.

Operating companies:
Auto Viação Marechal Ltda
Transporte Coletivo Glória Ltda
Auto Viação Nossa Senhora da Luz Ltda
Empresa Cristo Rei Ltda
Auto Viação Nossa Senhora do Carmo Ltda
Auto Viação Redentor Ltda
Auto Viação Agua Verde Ltda
Auto Viação Curitiba
Auto Viação Mercês
Leblon Transporte de Passageiros Ltda (operating a feeder route from the suburb of Fazenda Rio Grande)
Total staff: 8,425

Bus (contracted)

Passenger journeys: (1991) 323 million
(1992) 320 million
Vehicle-km: (1991) 90 million
(1992) 98 million

Number of routes: Total 277, including 114 conventional, 13 express, 90 feeder, 12 very fast (Ligeirinho)
Route length: 1,217 km, including express routes (reserved corridors) 53.7 km, feeders 294 km, intersuburb 176 km, very fast 200 km
Fleet: 1,206 vehicles, including Mercedes, Fiat, Scania and Volvo (Padron and articulated), also Volvo bi-articulated

Conventional/intersuburb/feeder routes	863
Express routes	71
Very fast	135
Express articulated	108
Express bi-articulated	29

Fare structure: Flat; set by city. Double for executive midibus services and lower for city centre and neighbourhood routes
Fare collection: By driver or prepurchase from roadside ticket machines on main routes
Fares collected on board: 60%
Operational control: Route inspectors
Arrangements for elderly/disabled: Free travel for over-65s/blind persons
Bus priority: 56 km of busways and bus lanes under city pro-public transport policy (see below), and priority at junctions by bus actuations or area traffic control
Operating costs financed by: Fares 100%
New vehicles financed by: Municipality, with fares recovery element

Volvo double-articulated leaving a 'tube station' ***1997***

Current situation: An extensive system of reserved busways and bus lanes has been implemented by the city authority under an integrated land use/transport policy favouring public transport dating from 1974 (see *JUTS 1991* for details). Introduced between 1974 and 1981, the 'Integrated Transport Network' expanded the length of express bus exclusive lanes, and patronage rose from 25,000 per day to 997,000 per day by 1993.

The north-south corridor of 26.2 km is operated by a fleet of 168 standard and articulated buses, and caters for 250,000 passengers a day with peak-hour flows of 14,000 passengers/direction. Volvo/Marcopolo bi-articulated buses were introduced in 1995 to cope with increased demand. This corridor serves 56 'stations' and seven terminals. Operation is in the hands of three companies — Glória, Redentor and Cidade Sorriso — all members of the Golin group.

The Boqueirão corridor of 12.4 km has a fleet of 33 bi-articulated buses catering for 146,000 passengers a day and 14,116 in the peak hour, the East 12.2 km corridor has 44 vehicles carrying 6,525 in the peak hour and the West corridor is served by 17 vehicles carrying 46,000 passengers a day.

Developments: Rapid growth of patronage was addressed by the Ligeirinho (very fast) system introduced on two corridors in 1991, and later extended. These routes are served by high-capacity luxury buses running on limited-stop schedules, providing an additional level of service and comfort within the existing network. They serve 'tube stations', which are stylish cylindrical glass shelters with a ticket machine at the single turnstile access and same-level entry to the buses from two side turnstiles. Stations have since been upgraded to allow the bi-articulateds to open three or more doors at once, so reducing dwell time from 23 to 19 sec.

The buses have no steps; instead extending platforms reach out to bridge the gap with the station platform. Loading is about four times faster than at conventional stops. Several new routes and extensions are planned, with a further north-south corridor converted in 1995 (see below).

In a further step to reduce overcrowding, 1992 saw introduction of bi-articulated buses to raise capacity from 160 to 270 passengers.

Onboard computers are being fitted throughout the fleet to control passenger flow and monitor adherence to the timetable.

URBS is now proposing implementation of its integrated system to neighbouring cities, to help solve their problems of traffic congestion and stagnation of public transport.

Trolleybus (planned)

Planning authority: The Research & Urban Planning Institute of Curitiba (IPPUC)
Rua Bom Jesus 669, CEP 8000 Curitiba
Telephone: +55 41 352 1414 Fax: +55 41 252 6679
President: Cassio Taniguchi

Current situation: Detailed plans have been prepared by IPPUC, responsible for the municipality's planning, for the introduction of trolleybus operations on a 59 km network, based on the current dedicated radial express bus corridors with central area distribution. Designed to enhance capacity and achieve energy savings, the four corridors at present cater for some 50 per cent of the city's passengers.

The plans envisaged a phased conversion programme beginning with the most congested north-south corridor, with 87 articulated trolleybuses carrying about 235,000 passengers a day. No progress has been reported, and it now appears that the plans have been shelved in favour of further extensions of the Ligeirinho network.

UPDATED

DAKAR

Population: 1.8 million
Public transport: Bus services provided by mixed public-private company, established by government and vehicle manufacturer, and route associations of independent operators in suburban area. Ferry service to offshore island. Suburban rail service

SOTRAC

Société de Transports en Commun du Cap Vert (SOTRAC)
BP 4036, Route de Ouakam Km 4, Dakar, Senegal
Telephone: +221 231443 Fax: +221 233329
Director General: Babacar Diop
Director of Operations: Ibou Diouf
Staff: 2,560

Current situation: Established in 1971 as a joint company between the government (which now owns 67 per cent) and French vehicle builder Renault (holding 24 per cent); private sector involvement accounts for 9 per cent.

The operation has struggled to cope with an expanding population in a widely spread urban area split between industrial and commercial centres around the port and Plateau, and a number of dormitory towns up to 20 km from the city centre. Growth of competition from private services has reduced SOTRAC's share to about one-third, with competitors creaming off traffic from the most profitable routes. It is required to carry schoolchildren and soldiers at reduced rates, such traffic amounting to some 10 per cent of the total. Other problems include high absenteeism, poor vehicle availability and corruption.

A period of losses was followed by introduction of state subsidies. A system of three-year 'contract-plans' setting

The Saviem SG2 is the most common vehicle of Dakar's independent operators

out agreement between SOTRAC and the state came into operation in 1981. This was intended to put finances on a firmer footing and allowed purchase of 50 new buses. In place of subsidy an agreed state contribution is made in advance, with the state also fixing fares levels (unchanged for political reasons, except from flat to zonal, since 1980). But SOTRAC has been so badly run that it has not been able to meet its obligations despite some CFAFr4.4 billion in annual grants and tax exemptions. Some 80 million passengers a year were being carried at the beginning of the 1990s with a fleet of mainly Saviem S105 buses.

One-person operation: None
Fare collection: Monthly pass, prepurchase multitickets or payment to conductor
Fare structure: Stages; prepurchase passes and carnets
Fare evasion control: None
Fares collected on board: 56%
Operational control: Route inspectors/mobile radio
Operating costs financed by: Fares 94%, subsidy/grants 6%
Subsidy from: Government

SOTRAC Saviem S105 in Dakar

New vehicles financed by: Internal resources 20%, credit 80%

Minibus

Current situation: Between 2,000 and 3,000 minibuses and other small vehicles are operated by private firms in competition with SOTRAC. These are the so-called 'cars rapides'; they are not licensed to operate in the Plateau (city centre area), and this restriction is generally respected as most development since 1980 has taken place in the suburbs.

There are no formal unions or co-operatives, but some 85 per cent of operators are loosely affiliated to religious brotherhoods. Only 12 operators own more than 10 minibuses, the largest having a fleet of 100.

Vehicles are Renault SG2 with 25 seats and Mercedes 407D with 32 seats, all operated with driver and conductor. Standees are not permitted. Fares are nominally the same as SOTRAC's, but widespread malpractice means that many journeys cost twice as much as by conventional services.

Unregulated 'cars rapides', originally permitted only to operate interurban and long-distance services, now also ply in the urban area particularly at times of low demand for their regular services. Some hold two licences, one legally obtained for interurban operations, the other fraudulently entitling them to ply in the Plateau.

Between 3,000 and 4,000 taxis operate, carrying up to five passengers.

In Pikine, a satellite town with a population of 600,000 and no surfaced roads, all public transport is by shared taxi. These are still referred to as 'Clandos' (clandestine), although they have been recognised officially for several years.

Ferry

Current situation: The Dakar port authority operates a passenger ferry to the island of Gorée 11 times daily. Journey time is 25 min.

RCFS

Regie des Chemins de Fer du Senegal
PO Box 175, Cité Ballabey, Thies, Senegal
Telephone: +221 511013 Fax: +221 511393

Current situation: Diesel-hauled suburban trains marketed as *Le Petit Train Bleu* run to Tiaroye (13 km), Rufisque and Bargny about hourly, carrying 20,000 passengers daily.

UPDATED

DALIAN

Population: 1.5 million, municipal area 4.5 million
Public transport: Bus, trolleybus and tram services operated by single authority; limited local rail service; paratransit operations

Dalian City Transport Company

Dalian City Transport Company
Dalian, Liaoning Province, People's Republic of China
Staff: 9,300

Current situation: Tramway modernisation was begun in 1983 with construction of 10 new four-axle trams in the undertaking's own manufacturing plant. A series of six-axle articulated cars followed.

Plans to build a modern light rail line over the former tram route which was replaced by trolleybuses in 1977, or alternatively to upgrade an existing route, have been considered several times. In 1991 the project came to the fore again, with consultants studying a scheme to upgrade one line to light rail.

Bus

Passenger journeys: Approx 1 million daily

Number of routes: 18
Route length: 140 km
Fleet: Approx 500 buses (approx 300 articulated) including Dalian DL643 (two-axle), DL663, DL663A, DL670, DL670A (articulated), Wafangdian WK642

Fare collection: Payment to seated conductor, monthly passes available for all modes
Fare structure: Flat
Integration with other modes: Convenient interchange between modes at nodal points. Monthly passes

Trolleybus

Passenger journeys: Over 500,000 daily

Dalian DL661 articulated trolleybuses at central terminus

Dalian tram

Number of routes: 2
Route length: 14.5 km
Number of stops: 23
Fleet: Approx 150 trolleybuses (all articulated), mainly Dalian DL661 and Shenyang SY561

Fare collection: Payment to seated conductor, monthly passes
Fare structure: Flat
Most intensive service: Every few minutes
Integration with other modes: Convenient interchange between modes at nodal points. Monthly passes

Tramway
Type of operation: Conventional tramway

Passenger journeys: Over 600,000 daily

Route length: 14.7 km
Number of routes: 3
Number of stops: 29
Gauge: 1,435 mm
Track: Railway type on side reservation and in centre of street
Electrification: Overhead

Service: 1 min
First/last car: 04.10/00.08
Fare collection: Payment to seated conductor, monthly passes
Fare structure: Flat
Integration with other modes: Convenient interchange between modes at nodal points. Monthly passes available for all modes

Rolling stock: About 100 motored cars including up to 21 articulated, all built locally

---

DALLAS
Population: 1 million, metropolitan area 1.9 million
Public transport: Fixed-route bus, paratransit van, light and commuter rail services, and HOV lanes provided by regional transit authority controlled by representative board. Suburban bus and some paratransit services provided under contract; short heritage tramway

DART
Dallas Area Rapid Transit
1401 Pacific Avenue, Dallas, TX 75266, USA
Telephone: +1 214 749 3278 Fax: +1 214 749 3653
Chair: Billy J Ratcliff
President & Executive Director: Roger Snoble
Vice President, Operations: Frank Jennings
Senior Vice President, Project Management, Light Rail: Thomas Larkin
Vice President, Commuter Rail: Lonnie Blaydes
Vice President, Paratransit: Doug Douglas
Vice President, Maintenance: Michael Hubbell
Vice President, Marketing & Communications: Sue Bauman
Vice President, Human Resources: Ben Gomez
Chief Financial Officer: Christopher Poinsatte
Staff: 2,071

Current situation: DART was created in 1983 following passage of a referendum to fund a regional transit agency through a 1 per cent sales tax. The DART service area covers more than 1,110 km^2 and 13 cities. The 15-member board of directors is appointed by the member city councils, with representation based on population.

In 1984 DART took over operation of the Dallas Transit System and began expanding bus and paratransit service to all member cities, including non-stop express service between suburban transit centres and central Dallas. The first light rail route opened in June 1996, followed by commuter rail service to the suburban city of Irving in December 1996.

HOV lanes have been developed in a joint project between DART and the Texas DoT; they are reserved for DART buses and vehicles carrying two or more passengers. The first, opened in 1991, extends for 16 km on I-30 and is configured for contraflow traffic. It is used by about 19,000 commuters daily, travelling at twice the average speed of vehicles in the general purpose lanes.

Lanes were opened in September 1996 on the I-35 Stemmons Freeway, running with-flow and extending to 9.6 km northbound and 11 km southbound. They are located on the inside median and are separated from general traffic by a 0.9 m wide barrier. Both lanes are open 24 hours a day; an interchange by-pass lane operates during weekday peak hours.

A third project, for 10.4 km of with-flow lanes on I-635, was scheduled for December 1996 completion.

DART's transit system plan, updated in 1996, envisages a light rail network extending to 84.5 km, plus 59.6 km of commuter rail and 158 km of HOV lanes.

Developments: With opening of the light rail line in June 1996, some 25 per cent of bus routes were rerouted to connect at stations. New east and west transfer stations were opened at each end of the central business district. A fleet of 433 CNG-powered buses is planned.

Bus
Passenger journeys: (1993/94) 44.7 million
(1994/95) 44.2 million
(1995/96) 45.5 million
Vehicle-km: (1991) 51.3 million
(1995/96) 50 million

Number of routes: 103
Route length: 3,919 km
On priority right-of-way: 13.6 km

Passengers change from rail to bus at Westmoreland **1997**

Dallas light rail

Fleet: 1,066 vehicles

Flxible 870 (1980/81)	55
GMC T80204 (1983/84)	128
Neoplan AN440 (1985/86)	443
Neoplan AN460 articulated (1986)	30
Flxible Metro CNG-powered (1990)	2
TMC/MCI coaches (1991)	162
New Goshen vans (1991)	45
Lewis vans (1991)	120
Others	81

In peak service: 565
On order: 25 buses

Most intensive service: 5 min
One-person operation: All routes
Fare collection: Data-collecting electronic registering fareboxes accepting coins and dollar bills
Fare structure: Two flat fares based on local and express service, lower fare in city-centre and on Ozone Action days; free transfer between bus and rail; 1-day, 3-day and monthly passes; 11-ride bonus ticket pack
Fares collected on board: 60%
Operational control: Route inspectors/mobile radio; satellite navigational system tracks all vehicles
Arrangements for elderly/disabled: Demand-responsive lift-equipped van service, carried 876,600 passengers in 1994; reduced fares on regular services
Average peak-hour speed: 29 km/h
Bus priority: HOV lanes on three major roads; plans for lanes on a further six roads
Integration with other modes: Park-and-ride facilities on suburban express routes being expanded; local bus networks feed light and commuter rail stations
Operating costs financed by: Fares 16.6%, other commercial sources 0.9%, sales tax 81.2%, FTA grants 1.3%
New vehicles financed by: FTA 80%, city of Dallas 20%

Light rail
Type of operation: Light rail, first line opened 1996

Passenger boardings: (1996, first few weeks of operation) 19,000 daily

Route length: 32 km
in tunnel: 5.6 km
Number of lines: 2
Number of stations: 21
Gauge: 1,435 mm
Electrification: 750 V DC, overhead

Service: Peak 5-10 min, off-peak 20-30 min
First/last car: 05.30-00.10
Fare structure: As bus
Fare collection: Ticket machines at stations
Fare evasion control: Spot checks by inspectors; uniformed and plain clothes transit police
Arrangements for elderly/disabled: Stations and cars are wheelchair accessible

Rolling stock: 40 cars
Kinki Sharyo (1995) M40

Current situation: DART's initial light rail route opened in three stages between June 1996 and May 1997, linking Fair Oaks Park (Park Lane) in the north with central Dallas and branching in the south to serve West Oak Cliff (Red line) and South Oak Cliff (Blue line). One further station, City Place on the underground section running beneath the North central expressway, will not open until 1998.

Two extensions are planned for opening in 2002/03, north to Richardson and Plano, and northeast to Garland. It is intended that the network will extend to 85 km by 2010, with some routes built with 'intermediate capacity' — that is single track with passing loops. Ultimate fleet size is put at 125 cars.

Commuter rail
Current situation: The first stage of the city's Trinity Express commuter rail network, the 16 km from Union station to South Irving opened in December 1996. Fifteen return journeys are operated in weekday peak periods over former Rock Island tracks now owned by the cities of Dallas and Fort Worth; 1,500 daily trips are expected. Operation is contracted to Herzog Transit Services Inc.
Developments: The service will be extended to Fort Worth in 1999, and a branch to Dallas/Fort Worth international airport will open in 2005.

Rolling stock: 13 diesel railcars
Budd (ex-VIA Rail Canada) M13

McKinney Avenue Transit Authority
Current situation: MATA, an association of volunteers, operates a 2 km tramway in the McKinney Avenue tourist area. The route is being extended at each end.

UPDATED

DAR ES SALAAM
Population: 1.9 million
Public transport: Bus services operated by undertaking 51 per cent owned by city council and 49 per cent by government National Transport Corporation. Extensive private Dala Dala minibus services; suburban rail services proposed

UDA
Shirika la Usafiri Dar es Salaam Limited (UDA)
Bandari Street, New Port Area, PO Box 872, Dar es Salaam, Tanzania
Telephone: +255 51 25011/2/3
General Manager: P N M Kushoka
Staff: 441

Current situation: The ageing fleet and consequent maintenance problems continue to affect the number of vehicles available, with only 72 in service daily on average in 1995, against some 650 buses required to provide an adequate service. There has been a considerable reduction in the number of routes since 1989, and a further 13 were withdrawn in 1994.

UDA Mercedes bus

Bus
Passenger journeys: (1989) 44.9 million
(1993) 14.5 million
(1994) 14.1 million
Vehicle-km: (1989) 4.8 million
(1993) 3.8 million
(1994) 3.5 million

Number of routes: 20
Route length: 276 km
Fleet: 72 vehicles
Leyland DAF 56
Ikarus 281 articulated 1
Daimler Benz 1617 5
Tata LPO 1313 5
Ashok Leyland 5
In peak service: 54

Fare collection: Payment to conductor
Fare structure: Flat; monthly tickets
Fares collected on board: 99%
Operational control: Route inspectors/mobile radio
Average peak-hour speed: 12.6 km/h
Operating costs financed by: Fares 82%, other commercial sources 18%

Private bus/minibus
Current situation: 3,000 private buses — mostly midibuses known as Dala Dala — are licensed by the government. Fares for private buses match those charged by UDA. With the decline in UDA operations, Dala Dalas now handle most journeys.

Suburban rail (proposed)
Current situation: Tanzanian Railways Corp has studied schemes for commuter service on three existing freight routes which are well placed to serve new residential developments.

UPDATED

DAYTON
Population: City 182,000, region 589,000
Public transport: Bus and trolleybus services operated by Regional Transit Authority, controlled by representative board of trustees

Miami Valley RTA
Miami Valley Regional Transit Authority
PO Box 1301, 600 Longworth Street, Dayton, OH 45401, USA
Telephone: +1 937 226 1333 Fax: +1 937 443 3121
President: James R Payne
Executive Director: Dr Minnie Fells Johnson
Director of Administrative Services: Judith Pepper
Director of Marketing & Planning: Carla Lakatos
Director of Operations: John Pappas
Chief Engineer: Steve Park
Chief Transportation Officer: John W Brown
Chief Maintenance Officer: Jim Fourcade
Staff: 675

Current situation: RTA serves the Montgomery County area, with total population of 573,000.
Developments: RTA is pressing ahead with rebuilding the trolleybus network to restore it to its former position at the heart of the city's transit system (see *JUTS 1992* for background). A contract was awarded at the end of 1994 for a new fleet of trolleybuses, with three prototypes delivered in early 1996 and the balance during 1997/98. There is an option to purchase up to 30 additional vehicles. The trolleybuses are based on Skoda's 14Tr

model and will be supplied by Electric Transit Inc, a joint venture between Skoda and the AAI Corp of Baltimore, a defence industry contractor. A total of eight extensions is planned for opening in two phases by 2000, partly to bring trolleybuses into the new regional hubs (see below).

Some of the existing trolleybuses have been refurbished, and two purchased second-hand from Edmonton. Two Kaman/Novabus duobuses are also on order for service beyond the wires.

RTA is reorganising its bus services on a multihub system, to be based on a major hub planned for 1998 opening in downtown Dayton. Buildings and land have been acquired so that construction can start in 1997. The aim is to make better use of existing resources whilst providing new suburb-to-suburb journey opportunities for commuters.

Bus and trolleybus

Passenger boardings: (1993) Bus 9.3 million, trolleybus 2.4 million
(1994) Bus 9.4 million, trolleybus 2.7 million
(1995) Bus 11.4 million, trolleybus 3 million
Vehicle-km: (1993) Bus 13.4 million, trolleybus 1.7 million
(1994) Bus 13.4 million, trolleybus 1.9 million
(1995) Bus 12.1 million, trolleybus 1.8 million

Number of routes: Bus 29, trolleybus 7
Route length: (One way) Bus 1,564 km; trolleybus 166 km

Fleet: 261 vehicles	
GMC (1981)	30
GMC T80 204 (1982)	21
Flxible Metro (1985)	58
TMC RTS T80 (1989/91)	60
Gillig Spirit (1990)	15
Flxible Metro (1992)	20
Ford Supreme van (1992)	2
Chance VS24 (1992)	4
Dodge minivan (1995/96)	43
Goshen coach (1995)	8
Fleet: 40 trolleybuses	
Flyer E800 (1976/77)	35
GM/BBC (1981/82, ex-Edmonton)	2
ETI/Skoda prototypes (1995/96)	3

RTA's prototype trolleybus from ETI/Skoda **1997**

In peak service: 167 buses, 32 trolleybuses
On order: 57 trolleybuses from ETI (see above)

Most intensive service: 10 min
One-person operation: All routes
Fare collection: Exact fare or token to farebox; magnetic strip passes and onboard electronic readers
Fare structure: Flat; free 1-h transfers and 'stop-and-shop' facility; prepurchase tokens, weekly, monthly passes
Fares collected on board: 34%
Operational control: Route inspectors/mobile radio
Arrangements for elderly/disabled: Lift-equipped vehicles on all routes; paratransit service operates door-to-door facility; reduced rate passes; TDD information and reservation service. Demand-responsive services carried 120,000 passengers in 1995
Average peak-hour speed: Bus 23 km/h, trolleybus 17 km/h
Operating costs financed by: Fares 15.4%, other commercial sources 9.2%, subsidy/grants 12.5%, tax levy 62.9%
Subsidy from: State operating assistance 44.5%; FTA operating assistance 55.5%
New vehicles financed by: FTA and local matching funds

UPDATED

DELHI

Population: Conurbation 8.4 million
Public transport: Bus services provided by the Delhi government's Transport Corporation, and other private bus and minibus services granted permits by State Transport Authority. Limited suburban rail services by Northern Railway. Metro, rapid transit and surface rail systems planned

Delhi Transport Corporation

Delhi Transport Corporation
Indraprastha Estate, New Delhi 110002, India
Telephone: +91 11 331 5085 Telex: 066039
Managing Director: G S Cheema
Deputy Manager, Public Relations: S K Bhatti
Staff: 31,063

Current situation: DTC handles extremely large passenger volumes and experiences severe overcrowding, though private bus and minibus service now account for a major proportion of total demand. Substantial deficits have been incurred mainly because of uneconomic fare levels, concession and free passes to various categories of passenger, surplus staff and increased operating costs. Losses amounted to over Rs2.9 billion in 1994/95.
Developments: In August 1996, control of DTC was transferred from the Union government to the Delhi local government, and loans and interest amounting to Rs21.2 billion were written off. The Delhi government has started to restructure DTC, with money advanced for repair of defective vehicles and purchase of new buses. DTC is also trying to earn more funds from commercial developments at its 33 bus terminals.

Bus

Passenger journeys: (1993/94) 890 million
(1994/95) 636 million
(1995/96) 578 million
Vehicle-km: (1993/94) 268 million
(1994/95) 212 million
(1995/96) 169.7 million

DTC and private buses at Connaught Place **1995**

Number of routes: 870

Fleet: 3,206, of which 1,250 in service	
Ashok Leyland single-deck	2,517
Tata	665
Ashok Leyland double-deck	15
Others	9

Average age of fleet: 6.1 years

Most intensive service: 5-10 min
One-person operation: None
Fare collection: Payment to conductors; passes
Fare structure: Distance-related; various passes
Fare evasion control: Checking staff, field officers and mobile courts
Integration with other modes: Some bus routes feed electric rail service
Average distance between stops: 500 m
Operating costs financed by: Fares 61.1%, other commercial sources 3.3%, loans from central government 28.6%
New vehicles financed by: Interest-bearing loans from central government

Private bus/minibus

Current situation: Heavy pressure on the public transport system has encouraged the growth of private bus and minibus services, which now account for a substantial part of the traffic.

There are about 2,350 'Red and Blue Line' private buses in service with a fare structure similar to DTC's, 580 'Suvidha' buses operated in place of those formerly hired-in by DTC, and 815 minibuses and old-permit buses. In addition, 'White Line' service introduced on 20 longer-distance routes in 1992 is operated by about 90 buses.
Developments: Despite their success, private operators have failed to provide reliable and safe services due to rash driving and the poor condition of many vehicles.

Northern Railway emu at Shivaji Bridge

Northern Railway

Northern Railway
Baroda House, New Delhi 110001
Telephone: +91 11 338 7227
General Manager: Shanti Narain

Type of operation: Suburban heavy rail

Current situation: Limited emu services provided on ring railway (35 km, 23 stations), between Delhi and Aligarh (122 km) and on two other routes totalling 96 km with 23 stations.

Developments: With completion of electrification, emu service was introduced between Delhi and Panipat (89 km) in February 1995. NR also increased the number of cars from 9 to 10 or 12 on some trains. Additional emu trains were introduced on the Delhi-Palwal and Delhi-Gaziabad routes.

Metro (planned)

Delhi Metro Rail Corporation

Developments: A 1991 feasibility study by RITES recommended a 184.5 km network of rapid transit routes, including 27 km of metro and 30 km elevated, with 67.5 km to be in operation by 2001 and the remainder by 2011. Outline approval for a mass rapid transit system broadly based on this study was given in 1994, and in September 1996 the government approved the 'Modified Phase I'.

As now planned, the metro will comprise two lines interseccting at ISBT in the city centre — north-south from Delhi University to Central Secretariat (11 km, underground), east-west from Nangloi to Shahdara (25 km, surface), plus a branch from the latter line running northeast from Subzimandi to Holambi Kalan (19.3 km, elevated). Electrification would be at 750 V DC third rail.

The Delhi Metro Rail Corporation has been formed to build and operate the system, which is expected to be open throughout by 2006. At current prices the network will cost Rs48.6 billion, 60 per cent of which is to be loaned by the Overseas Economic Co-operation Fund of Japan, with most of the remainder coming from the Indian and Delhi governments. Construction is expected to start during 1997, and Line 1 should open in 2002. When fully operational, the network is expected to carry 3 million passengers daily.

UPDATED

DEN HAAG

Population: 445,000
Public transport: Bus and tramway services (including interurban route to Delft) provided by company owned by the city, with additional suburban bus services operated by regional bus undertakings. Suburban rail services provided by Netherlands Railways (NS)

HTM

NV Gemengd Bedrijf Haagsche Tramweg-Maatschappij (HTM)
Postbus 28503, Dynamostraat 10, 2502 KM Den Haag, Netherlands
Telephone: +31 70 384 8484 Fax: +31 70 384 8729
Director General: G A Kaper
Staff: 1,851

Current situation: HTM is constituted as a private company, but all shares are owned by the city. From the start of 1996, the regional authority Stadsgewest Haagland became the overall co-ordinating body for public transport. It receives subsidy funding from the national government and transfers to HTM such subsidy as it is entitled to. Services extend beyond the city boundary to serve a total population of some 565,000, and there is close integration of routes and fares with regional bus services. The national standard tariff 'Strippenkaart' multiticket system applies (see Amsterdam for details).

Developments: The tramway Route 17 extension to Rijswijk Steenvoorde has been approved, and construction was expected to start in early 1997 for opening at the beginning of 1999. Two other routes are planned to serve the new residential areas of Ypenburg and Wateringse veld, while a tramway tunnel at Hollands Spoor NS station opened in July 1996. Construction of a tunnel under Grote Marktstaat, the city's main shopping street, started in March 1996 as part of a major project to revitalise the city centre.

The new tram tunnel at Hollands Spoor station opened in July 1996 ***1997***

HTM is also participating in the RandstadRail project. In co-operation with RET Rotterdam, the rural operator ZWN and Netherlands Railways, a plan has been drawn up to convert main line rail operations on the Zoetermeer and Hofplein lines to light rail, and at the same time extend the lines into the city centres of Den Haag and Rotterdam. The intention is to help ease traffic congestion in the southern Randstad area. The plan awaits government approval.

A number of unemployed people assist HTM roving inspectors and other staff by providing passengers with information; they also help improve security. They are paid by the city authorities under a national employment programme.

Because of changes in the method of calculation, 1995 operating statistics are not comparable with those of earlier years.

Passenger boardings: (1995) 114.9 million

Operating costs financed by: Fares 27.9%, other commercial sources 3.3%, subsidy/grants 68.8%
Subsidy from: Government

Bus

Passenger boardings: (1995) 38.7 million
Vehicle-km: (1995) 9 million

Number of routes: 14
Route length: 149.2 km
On priority right-of-way: 9.7%
Fleet: 185 vehicles

DAF 201 (1980/83)	39
DAF 201 CSA2 (1984/88)	76
Neoplan N4016 low-floor (1990/91)	70
Mercedes low-floor	

In peak service: 153

Service: Peak 5-15 min, evening 15 min
One-person operation: All routes
Fare collection: Prepurchase pass or ticketcard with card validation on board by driver; or payment to driver
Fare structure: Zonal; prepurchase passes and national Strippenkaart multitickets valid on all modes, Strippenkaart also available from driver
Fare evasion control: Check by driver on boarding; roving inspectors
Bus priority: Philips VETAG/VECOM, also used for point setting and passenger information on tramway
Integration with other modes: Services co-ordinated with those of neighbouring regional bus operators;

Staff seconded to HTM under the national employment programme are briefed by an inspector ***1997***

Strippenkaart gives nationwide standard tram, bus and metro fares
Average speed: 19.8 km/h

Tramway
Type of operation: Conventional tramway

Passenger boardings: (1995) 76.2 million
Car-km: (1995) 8.3 million

Route length: 128.1 km
reserved track: 81.8%
Number of lines: 10

Gauge: 1,435 mm
Electrification: 600 V DC, overhead

Service: Peak 5-10 min, evening 15-20 min
Fare structure: As bus
Fare collection: Pass, prepurchase ticket card or payment to driver; boarding at other doors with cancelling machines
Fare evasion control: Roving inspectors
Tram priority: As bus
One-person operation: All routes

Rolling stock: 147 cars, plus 10 PCC cars in store

PCC 1100 (1957/58)	M1
PCC 1300 (1971/72)	M9
BN GTL8-1 double-articulated (1981/84)	M100
BN GTL8-2 double-articulated (1992/93)	M47

In peak service: 110

NS
Netherlands Railways
P O Box 2025, 3500 HA Utrecht
Telephone: +31 30 235 9111 Fax: +31 30 233 2458

Type of operation: Suburban heavy rail

Current situation: Services provided on five routes into Centraal station. There are seven stations within the city boundaries, served by 5 to 20 trains per hour, more at peak times.
Developments: An additional platform has been built at Centraal station, along with two four-tracking projects to raise capacity. Other major capacity schemes are planned for the late 1990s and through to 2010.

UPDATED

DENVER
Population: City 491,000, metropolitan area 2.1 million
Public transport: Bus and light rail services for 3,700 km² six-county area provided by Regional Transportation District, set up in 1969 by a State Act and operational from 1973 with the acquisition of six local bus systems, and governed by 15-member directly elected board

RTD
Regional Transportation District (RTD)
1600 Blake Street, Denver, CO 80202, USA
Telephone: +1 303 628 9000 Fax: +1 303 299 2217
Board Chair: Ben Klein
General Manager: Clarence Marsella
Staff: 2,078

Current situation: The 8.5 km light rail line, marketed as 'TheRide', opened in 1994, is one of several projects designed to improve the city's public transport. At the same time, 29 bus routes were diverted to act as feeders, eliminating more than 500 movements through the downtown area daily. But the light rail proved so popular that 10 bus routes into the city centre had to be reinstated to ease pressure on the LRVs. A further six cars entered service in 1996, allowing two-car operation at peak times.

Also opened in 1994 and extended in 1995 was the North Corridor high-occupancy vehicle (HOV) lane, a two-lane segregated route running for some 11 km in the median of the I-25 highway north of the city centre. It provides with-flow fast route for buses and car/vanpools. Two park-and-ride sites have been expanded as part of the scheme, to provide a total of 2,140 spaces.

A state directive that 20 per cent of services be contracted out has been complied with, and by late 1996 a total of 76 routes or parts of routes were in the hands of contractors Laidlaw Transit, ATC/Vancom and Mayflower Contract Services.

The EcoPass scheme was introduced in 1992, promoted by RTD and the Denver Regional Council of Governments. Companies agree to purchase the pass for all employees, at a price ranging from $25 to $185 per employee depending on the location and size of the company. By mid-1996, some 1,150 companies with over 32,000 employees had joined the scheme.

Bus
Passenger boardings: (1991) 56.7 million
(1993) 61.3 million
(1995) 62.9 million

Neoplan AN340 on RTD SkyRide service at Denver international airport ***1997***

Vehicle-km: (1991) 48.4 million
(1995) 56.9 million

Number of routes: 162
Route length: (One way) 3,800 km
Fleet: 825 vehicles, including 170 operated by contractors

RTA fleet	
Neoplan AN 440 Transliner city bus (1986/87)	272
TMC (1989)	5
Flxible (1992)	45
Gillig (1994)	85
MCI/GMC/Neoplan intercity coaches	122
MAN articulated (1983)	89
Stewart & Stevenson small (1991)	10
MCR/Vetter shuttlebuses (1982/85) (of which 6 battery-electric)	26
Neoplan shuttle (1994)	1
Contractors' fleet	
Gillig Transit (1992)	20
Gillig Transit (1994)	136
Metrotrans 22 ft (1994)	14

In peak service: 683

Most intensive service: 1½ min
One-person operation: All routes
Fare structure: Flat for each type of service; half fares on local services off-peak
Fare collection: Exact fare or prepurchase tokens/tickets to farebox; monthly pass; discounted 10-trip coupons for local, express and regional service; EcoPass available for employer-purchase
Integration with other modes: 14 RTD-owned park-and-ride sites, 20 transit centres and transfer stations, 37 leased and 4 jointly owned park-and-ride sites
Bus priority: Total 16.7 km in four sections, one operates 24 h
Operational control: 8 service monitors and 25 street supervisors; mobile radio on all buses; automatic vehicle locator (AVL)
Arrangements for elderly/disabled: 94% of buses have wheelchair lifts; all off-peak services operated by lift-

equipped buses. Discounted off-peak fares and monthly passes; door-to-door subscription and demand-response service for disabled, SeniorRide programme to events and Senior Shopper services for elderly
Operating costs financed by: Fares 19.9%, other commercial sources 6%, subsidy/grants 4.6%, tax levy 69.5%
New vehicles financed by: FTA grants and sales/use tax

Light rail

Type of operation: Light rail, opened 1994

Passenger boardings: (1995) 4 million

Route length: 8.5 km
Number of lines: 1
Number of stations: 14
Gauge: 1,435 mm
Track: Concrete sleepers set in concrete on-street, in ballast elsewhere
Electrification: 750 V DC, overhead

Service: Peak 5 min, off-peak 10 min, evening and weekend 15 min
First/last car: 04.00/01.00
Fare structure: Peak and off-peak fares
Fare collection: Vending machines at each stop; proof-of-payment
Fare evasion control: Roving inspectors
Arrangements for elderly/disabled: Ramps at all stations; retractable platforms at cab end of each car
Signalling: Automatic block outside city centre

Rolling stock: 17 cars

Siemens-Duewag SD-100 (1993/94)	M11
Siemens-Duewag SD-100 (1996)	M6

Current situation: Initial 8.5 km central corridor route linking a park-and-ride site at 30th & Downing with park-and-ride at I-25 & Broadway opened 1994 and immediately exceeded patronage targets for the first months of operation. So heavy was the pressure on the rolling stock that RTD immediately ordered a further six cars.

Denver's LRV at 10th & Colfax (Auraria) ***1997***

A southern extension along South Santa Fe Drive to West Mineral Avenue (13.4 km, 5 stations) was approved in 1994 and received Federal funding in March 1996; construction is expected to start during 1997. This line will utilise part of the consolidated main line corridor, where the existing BN/Santa Fe freight routes have been grade-separated in a joint Colorado DoT/RTD project. West Mineral Avenue and South Santa Fe Drive is the location of a major park-and-ride terminal currently served by buses. A further 14 cars will be required.

Three other routes are under consideration for rapid transit. A light rail line or bus/HOV route is being studied for the southeast corridor along I-25 from I-25/Broadway to Lincoln Avenue in the south, and from I-25 along I-225 to the east. In the east corridor, from Denver to the new Denver international airport, three rapid transit alternatives are being evaluated – commuter rail, light rail and bus/HOV lanes. While in the west corridor to the Federal Center (11.5 km), the technologies under consideration are light rail, bus/HOV and trolleybus. The regional process to select the most appropriate technology was scheduled for early 1997 completion.

Commuter rail (proposed)

Current situation: Six routes have been studied by the Colorado DoT for possible commuter/interurban rail service, four of which would serve Denver. All involve substantial portions of existing rail right-of-way. Of lines to Colorado Springs, Boulder and Fort Collins via Boulder or Greeley, the latter (136 km) was seen as the most promising on account of its ability to attract an estimated 700,000 passengers a year.

UPDATED

DETROIT

Population: 1.2 million, 4.5 million city region
Public transport: Fixed-route and paratransit services in Detroit metropolitan area (city and six surrounding counties) provided by two operating authorities supervised by a Regional Transit Co-ordinating Council. Operations include a 2 km tourist tramway and a central area people mover

SMART

Suburban Mobility Authority for Regional Transportation
660 Woodward Avenue, Detroit, MI 48226, USA
Telephone: +1 313 223 2100 Fax: +1 313 223 2390
General Manager: Richard Kaufman
Assistant General Manager: Paul Majka
Staff: 881

Current situation: In 1989 the reconfigured seven-member Southeast Michigan Transit Authority changed the authority's name to SMART. SMART no longer acts as grant recipient agency for D-DOT (the City of Detroit Department of Transportation), but receives grants from the Regional Transit Co-ordinating Council on an equal basis with D-DOT. The board comprises two members each from Wayne, Oakland and Macomb counties and one representing Livingston, St Clair and Monroe counties.

SMART operates fixed-route and paratransit (Connector) services in Wayne, Oakland and Macomb counties, independently of those provided in the city centre and some suburbs by D-DOT. Also operates in Monroe, Livingston and St Clair counties through purchase-of-service agreements, and in areas of Mt Clemens, Harper Woods, Redford Township and the Nankin Transit Commission.
Developments: Merger with D-DOT had been canvassed as a means of stemming SMART's losses, but this did not come about. In 1995, voters approved a 0.3 per cent property tax increase to enable SMART to maintain operations in the medium term. There has been an attempt at rationalisation of routes also served by D-DOT, but co-operation was short-lived.

Detroit DOT articulated bus

Bus

Passenger journeys: (1993) 9.4 million
(1994) 10.2 million
Vehicle-km:

Number of routes: 56
Route length: (One way) 2,582 km
Fleet: 401 vehicles

GMC RTS (1991)	65
Gillig Phantom (1992/93)	49
TMC RTS (1993/94/95)	124
Goshen van (1989)	18
Chance Challenger (1993/94/95)	145

In peak service: 202 buses

Most intensive service: 15 min
One-person operation: All routes
Arrangements for elderly/disabled: Extensive Connector paratransit services carried 950,000 passengers in 1994
Operating costs financed by: Fares 21%, other commercial sources 0.5%, subsidy/grants 78.5%
Subsidy from: State 77%, FTA 23%

D-DOT

Department of Transportation, City of Detroit
1301 East Warren Avenue, Detroit, MI 48207-1099
Telephone: +1 313 935 4910 Fax: +1 313 833 5523

Detroit's Downtown People Mover ***1995***

Director: Albert A Martin
Deputy Director, Administration: Sandra B Parker
Director of Operations: Elliot C Jones
Staff: 2,056

Current situation: D-DOT was created in 1974 to take over all Detroit municipal transport-related functions. It is the major bus carrier in Michigan, serving the city of Detroit and 25 suburban communities, and carries about 83 per cent of the area's bus passengers.

Bus

Passenger journeys: (1993) 41.8 million
(1994) 40 million
Vehicle-km:

Number of routes: 56
Route length: 1,196 km

Fleet: 487 vehicles

GMC (1980)	56
GML TC40102N (1986)	99
MCI Classic (1989)	85
Neoplan AN460 articulated (1989)	14
New Flyer D40 (1993)	121
Novabus RTS T80 (1995/96)	112

In peak service:

Most intensive service: 30 min
Fare collection: Coin to farebox
Fare structure: Flat, with some reduced fare zones; monthly passes, reduced rate carnets; small charge for transfers
Average peak-hour speed: 21.3 km/h
Arrangements for elderly/disabled: All routes wheelchair accessible; reduced fare for eligible passengers, free for elderly and blind

Integration with other modes: Transfers available to SMART services
Operating costs financed by: Fares 25%, subsidy/grants 75%
Subsidy from: FTA 13 per cent, state petrol tax 47%, local 40%

Tramway

Current situation: 2 km tourist tramway runs in downtown area using nine historic cars.

DTC

Detroit Transportation Corp
150 Michigan Avenue, Detroit, MI 48226
Telephone: +1 313 224 2160 Fax: +1 313 224 2134
Chair: Angela Brown
Staff: 100

Type of operation: Automated people mover, opened 1987

Passenger journeys: (1992) 2.5 million
(1993) 3.4 million

Current situation: Linear motor-powered automated people mover loop (4.6 km, 13 stations), serving the central area loop (journey time 14 min) with capacity for 5,000 per hour (flat fare, monthly passes), was originally intended as a distributor for the planned LRT system.

In 1993 fares covered 13 per cent of operating costs.

Rolling stock: 12 cars

Light rail (planned)

Current situation: A 24 km light rail line in the busy Woodward Avenue corridor was approved by the Michigan State Legislature in 1980, but funding was not forthcoming. An alternatives analysis and preliminary engineering studies were completed at the end of 1995 for a 5.3 km start-up line extending along Woodward Avenue from Downtown to the New Center business complex.

UPDATED

DHAKA

Population: 1.5 million
Public transport: Bus services provided by national road transport corporation and about 10,000 independent 'autorickshaw' three-wheeler taxis; suburban rail; metro proposals studied

Buses, cycle rickshaws and autorickshaw taxis in Dhaka

BRTC

Bangladesh Road Transport Corp (BRTC)
Paribahan Bhaban, 21 D I T Avenue, Dhaka, Bangladesh
Telephone: +880 2 235051
Staff: 3,500

Bus

Passenger journeys: 170 million (annual)
Vehicle-km: 54.2 million (annual)

Route length: 1,200 km
Fleet: 576 vehicles, including Nissan, Isuzu, Ashok-Leyland double-deck

One-person operation: None
Fare collection: Payment on board
Fare structure: Stages
Average peak-hour speed: 15.6 km/h

Bangladesh Railway

Bangladesh Railway
Headquarters Building, Chittagong
Telephone: +880 2 500120 Telex: 66200

Type of operation: Suburban heavy rail

Current situation: Frequent local diesel trains run between Dhaka and Naryanganj (12 km), metre-gauge.

DNIPROPETROVSK

Population: 1.2 million
Public transport: Bus and trolleybus/tramway services provided by separate municipal undertakings. Metro under construction

Upravlenie Automobil'novo Transporta

Upravlenie Automobil'novo Transporta
Dnipropetrovsk, Ukraine

Bus

Number of routes: 35
Route length: 330 km
Fleet: 125 vehicles, Ikarus and Liaz 677

Fare collection: Conductors
Average speed: 19 km/h

Dniprogorelektrotrans

Dniprogorelektrotrans
Prospekt K Marksa 119A, 320038 Dnipropetrovsk
Telephone: +380 562 426524

Trolleybus

Number of routes: 17
Route length: 131 km
Fleet: 320 vehicles

ZIU9	281
ZIU10	14
YuMZ-T1	25

Uritsky ZIU9 passes the statue of Lenin

T3 on tram Route 1 in the city centre

One-person operation: All routes
Fare collection: Conductors
Fare evasion control: Roving inspectors check tickets as passengers exit
Average speed: 19 km/h

Tramway

Type of operation: Conventional tramway

Route length: 153 km
Number of lines: 16
Number of stops: 338
Gauge: 1,524 mm

Fare collection: As trolleybus
One-person operation: All routes

Rolling stock: About 400 cars

ČKD Tatra T3	M270
KTM5	M110
KTM8	M17

Current situation: Routes in the city centre, which had been closed during metro construction work, were reopened in 1996.

Metro

Current situation: Line 1 extends to 11.2 km from Oktyabrskaya in the east to Kommunarovskaya in the west, of which the 7.8 km from Kommunarovskaya to Vokzalnaya (main station) was opened in December 1995. The remaining section with three stations is under construction. Line 2 would run north-south.

UPDATED

DONETSK

Population: 1.1 million
Public transport: Bus and trolleybus/tramway services provided by separate municipal undertakings; metro under construction

Bus

Number of routes: 66
Fleet: Mainly Ikarus 260/ 280, LIAZ 677, and LAZ 695

Fare collection: Prepurchase, cancellers on board, or cash to conductor

Tramvaino-Trolleibusnoe Upravlenie

Tramvaino-Trolleibusnoe Upravlenie
Donetskaya ul 39, 340086 Donetsk, Ukraine
Telephone: +380 622 934629

Tatra T3 cars at Donetsk main station ***1997***

Current situation: Donetsk has suffered from the problems of its chief industry — coal — and since independence has experienced shortages of funding and technical expertise, and considerable unemployment. Operation of trams and trolleybuses is erratic, being plagued by spare parts and electricity supply problems. No new tramcars have been delivered since 1988.

The trolleybus network has expanded from 16 to 18 routes since 1993, and Route 7 runs to the neighbouring town of Makeyevka but does not connect with the system there.

Fare collection: Prepurchase, cancellers on board; monthly ticket valid on trolleybus and tram

Trolleybus

Number of routes: 18
Fleet: About 320 vehicles; some ZIU9s run in double traction mode

ZIU9	About 290
ZIU10	19
YuMZ-T1	10
LAZ 52523	1

Tramway

Passenger journeys: (1994) 57.6 million

Number of routes: 13
Track length: 131 km
Rolling stock: About 220 cars

ČKD Tatra T3 (1967-87)	M220

NEW ENTRY

DORTMUND

Population: 602,000, area served 687,000
Public transport: Bus and tramway services provided by municipal company, also responsible for other public utilities, operating as part of Rhein-Ruhr Verkehrsverbund, co-ordinating fares and services with regional rail (S-Bahn). Experimental people mover

Dortmunder Stadtwerke

Dortmunder Stadtwerke AG
PO Box, 44127 Dortmund, Germany
Telephone: +49 231 95500 Fax: +49 231 955 3300
Directors: Harald Heinze
Karl-Heinz Faust

Transport Division: Dr Erhard Schrameyer
Technical/Transport Manager: Udo Griebsch
Operating Manager: Dipl-Ing Ernst Helmich
Administration Manager: Gerhard Pitt
Personnel: Joachim Basista
Staff: 1,711

Passenger journeys: (All modes)
(1993) 107.5 million
(1994) 109.1 million
(1995) 107.1 million

Fare structure: Zonal; as Rhein-Ruhr (qv), plus various special fares

Operating costs financed by: Fares 30%, other commercial sources 5.3%, subsidy/grants 24.4% including cross-subsidy from gas and water supply, remainder as deficit
Source of subsidy: Region 91.7%, local 8.3%

Current situation: DSW is to take over operation of DB's Dortmund-Lüdenscheid line in May 1998, having been awarded a five-year contract.

Bus

Passenger journeys: (1995) 45.9 million
Vehicle-km: (1993) 11.2 million
(1994) 11.6 million
(1995) 9.6 million

Number of routes: 44
Route length: (One way) 642 km
Fleet: 145 vehicles, plus 52 hired

MAN SL200 standard (1983/85)	33
MAN SG240H articulated (1981/83)	2
MAN SG242H articulated (1987/88)	33
MAN NG272 low-floor articulated (1989/93)	41
MAN NL202 low-floor (1991/93)	36

In peak service: 130
On order: 10 buses

Most intensive service: 10 min
One-person operation: All routes
Fare collection: Prepurchase pass or multitickets with validation and cancelling machines; payment to driver
Fare evasion control: Roving inspectors
Integration with other modes: At passenger's request, bus and tram drivers may summon a taxi to any stop
Average speed: 22 km/h
Operating costs financed by: Fares 32.2%, other commercial sources 5.6%, subsidy/grants 27.2%, remainder as deficit

Tramway/Light rail

Type of operation: Conventional tramway; 5 routes upgraded under the Rhein-Ruhr Stadtbahn project with city-centre tunnels

Passenger journeys: (1995) 61.2 million
Vehicle-km: (1993) 8.2 million
(1994) 7.7 million
(1995) 7 million

Route length: 75.5 km (tramway 45 km, light rail 30 km)
reserved track: 50.6 km
in tunnel: 13.7 km
Number of routes: 9 (5 tram, 4 light rail)
Number of stops: 215
Gauge: 1,435 mm
Electrification: 600 V DC, overhead

Rolling stock: 120 cars

Duewag N8C articulated (1978/80/82)	M52
Duewag GT8 (1974)	M14
Duewag B80C 6-axle articulated (1986/94)	M54

In peak service: 102
On order: 10 three-section B80 cars from Duewag for 1998 delivery

Current situation: 12.8 km of new reserved track in operation with 20 stations, comprising Line 80 from Hacheney through city centre, and other short sections. Work completed 1992 on the initial northern section of Line 90, 10.3 km, to be followed by the two southern branches totalling 5.2 km, the first section (0.7 km) of which was opened in 1995. Line 95 and other extensions still in planning stage. Surface route movements are accelerated by induction of traffic lights at intersections.

Under the Rhein-Ruhr Stadtbahn plan, which comprises four stages through to 2000, 10 branches of the tramway network are being linked by three cross-city tunnels to create a light rail system of 41 km, with 59 stations, of which 20 km will be in tunnel. The remainder will be upgraded tramway, though much of the present system is already at or close to Stadtbahn standards (see under Rhein-Ruhr).

Van Hool articulated bus of Dortmunder Stadtwerke **1995**

H-Bahn now provides a public service  **1997**

Type B80 LRV emerging from the tunnel at Bergmannstrasse on Line 90, serving Route U42

DB

Deutsche Bahn AG

Type of operation: Regional metro (S-Bahn)

Current situation: A 9 km extension of Rhein-Ruhr Line S1 from Bochum-Langengreer serves Dortmund Hbf with a 20-min service. Route S4 links Lütgendortmund with Unna and Herne via Dortmund-Stadthaus, and in 1994 S5 was opened from Dortmund to Witten and Hagen with trains every 30 min (see Rhein-Ruhr entry). Other local services operate on five routes out of Dortmund Hbf.

Separate tracks are under construction for S4 between Dortmund and Herne, including a 1.4 km tunnel section.

H-Bahn

H-Bahn Gesellschaft Dortmund mbH
Joseph-von-Fraunhofer Strasse 25, 44227 Dortmund
Telephone: +49 231 75755 Fax: +49 231 759246
Director: Dipl-Ing Wolfgang Schönfeldt
Operations Manager: Dipl-Ing Wolfgang Schlotmann
Staff: 7

Type of operation: People mover (H-Bahn – now known as Sipem, Siemens People Mover)

Passenger journeys: (1993) 0.7 million
(1994) 1 million
(1995) 1.2 million

Operating costs financed by: Fares 33%, other commercial sources 1%, subsidy/grants 66%
Subsidy from: City 40% (through DS), state 60%

Current situation: Suspended-car people mover links the two campuses of Dortmund University. Three cars with top speed of 50 km/h provide capacity of up to 4,000 passengers/h.
Developments: The line has been extended at both ends to a total length of 1.8 km, linking a residential area at one end with an S-Bahn station at the other and thus the system is now of use to the general public.

In 1996, H-Bahn became a wholly owned subsidiary of Dortmunder Stadtwerke, and it has been agreed to keep the line in operation at least until 2020.

Extensions are planned to Barop (2.6 km) and to the technology park (1.2 km), for which feasibility studies were made at the end of 1996.

UPDATED

DRESDEN

Population: 473,000, area served 573,000
Public transport: Central area served almost wholly by tramways operated by municipal company which also operates bus services in suburbs, ferries across the River Elbe and two funiculars. Suburban rail services run by German Railway (DB)

DVB

Dresdner Verkehrsbetriebe AG
PO Box 10 09 15, 01076 Dresden, Germany
Telephone: +49 351 8570 Fax: +49 351 807 1010
Directors:
Personnel: Hans-Juergen Credé
Technical: Frank Müller-Eberstein
Commercial: Reiner Zieschank
Personnel Manager: Klaus Baumgart
Infrastructure Manager: Leonhard Hanusch
Rail Vehicle Maintenance Manager: Ulrich Jakob
Staff: 2,498

Passenger journeys: (All modes)
(1993) 135.6 million
(1994) 137.2 million
(1995) 139.4 million

Developments: Reorganisation of DVB as a joint stock company was completed in 1993, but financial difficulties have continued and there has been a big reduction in staff numbers. The dramatic decline in patronage (down by over 120 million between 1990 and 1992) has been reversed.

Only two bus routes penetrate the city centre, trams being the backbone of the transport system. Large-scale modernisation of the network is continuing; no line closures are planned.

Operating costs covered by: Fares 29%, other sources 12%, subsidy/grants 59%
Subsidy from: Local sources 98%, other 2%

Bus

Staff: 595

Passenger journeys: (1993) 36.9 million
(1994) 37.5 million
(1995) 39.1 million
Vehicle-km: (1993) 12.5 million
(1994) 12 million
(1995) 11.8 million

Number of routes: 26
Route length: 195 km
Fleet: 146 buses, plus 42 hired

Ikarus 280 articulated (pre-1990)	56
Daimler-Benz O405 (1990)	10
Daimler-Benz O405N (1990/3)	34
Daimler-Benz O405GN articulated (1992/94)	19
MAN NG272 articulated (1993/94)	27

In peak service: 118, plus 42 hired

Most intensive service: 10 min
One-person operation: All routes
Fare collection: Single tickets from kiosks, machines or driver, with cancelling machines on board; over 80% use passes

Daimler-Benz O405N low-floor of DVB

DWA/Siemens NGT6DD low-floor tram ***1997***

Fare structure: Changed to distance-related in 1995; short distance ticket, daily/weekly/monthly/annual passes
Fare evasion control: Roving inspectors; penalty fare
Average speed: 21.9 km/h
Average distance between stops: 556 m
Integration with other modes: Weekly/monthly passes good for travel on DVB, S-Bahn and urban buses in Freital
Operating costs finannced by: Fares 34%, other commercial sources 16%, subsidy/grants 50%

Current situation: Ikarus buses are being phased out; all future purchases will be Mercedes and MAN low-floor types. Private contractors run several routes to reduce costs.

Tramway

Staff: 1,854

Type of operation: Conventional tramway

Passenger journeys: (1993) 98.5 million
(1994) 99.5 million
(1995) 99.6 million
Car-km: (1993) 33.3 million
(1994) 31.7 million
(1995) 30.1 million

Route length: 129.6 km
Number of lines: 16, plus 7 all night
Number of stops: 249
Gauge: 1,450 mm
Electrification: 600 V DC, overhead
Operating costs financed by: Fares 27%, other commercial sources 12%, subsidy/grants 61%

Rolling stock: 560 cars

ČKD Tatra T4D/B4D 4-axle (1968/79)	M172 T104
(1971/84) modernised	M213 T65
ČKD Tatra T6A2/B6A2	M4 T2
DWA/Siemens NGT6DD low-floor (1995)	

In peak service: 429
On order: 40 low-floor cars from DWA/Siemens, delivery started late 1995; plus option for a further 43

Developments: It is planned to accelerate services by introducing priority at traffic lights and separation of trams from road traffic by lane markings, initially on Route 2 between Prohlis and Gorbitz as a demonstration project. Tracklaying and civil engineering activities are gradually being contracted to private companies to reduce costs.

A new depot at Gorbitz was commissioned in April 1996, accommodating 240 Tatra cars or 120 LRVs.

Funicular/monorail

Current situation: A funicular links the suburb of Loschwitz on the right bank of the Elbe with the hillside residential areas of Weisser Hirsch, 94 m higher. It is 547 m long, of metre gauge, and has a maximum gradient of 28 per cent.

A 274 m suspended monorail links Loschwitz with Oberloschwitz. Out of use from 1984 to 1991, this technical monument has now been fully restored. It also

Renault bus of RVD in Freital ***1995***

works on the funicular principle and climbs 84 m with a maximum gradient of 40 per cent.

Ferry

Current situation: DVB operates four passenger ferries and the Kleinzschachwitz—Pillnitz vehicular ferry across the River Elbe. A new ferry capable of carrying eight cars replaced the 33-year-old vessel in 1994.

RVD

Regionalverkehrs-GmbH Dresden (RVD)
PO Box 120168, 01002 Dresden
Telephone: +49 351 495 5012 Fax: +49 351 495 4033
Directors: Dieter Unger
Gisela Mühle
Staff: 318

Passenger journeys: (1993) 13.2 million
(1994) 13.4 million
(1995) 13.2 million
Vehicle-km: (1993) 8.2 million
(1994) 10.1 million
(1995) 9.7 million

Current situation: Regional services are operated from Dresden to surrounding towns with a fleet of 98 Mercedes, MAN, Setra and Renault buses plus 86 on hire, on 72 routes extending to 1,800 km, from depots in Dresden, Dippoldiswalde, Freital and Radeberg. A five-route urban network in Freital was introduced in 1992.

DB

Deutsche Bahn AG, Geschäftsbereich Nahverkehr
Regionalbereich Sachsen
Amonstrasse 8, 01069 Dresden
Telephone: +49 351 3356 Fax: +49 351 461 5547
Managers: Klaus-Dieter Martini
Lianne Schöneich

The Standseilbahn funicular, 100 years old in 1995 ***1996***

Type of operation: Suburban heavy rail and narrow-gauge local railways

Current situation: Services at S-Bahn zonal fares are provided on five routes serving 52 stations in an area bounded by Meissen, Arnsdorf, Pirna and Tharandt, 18 of them within the Dresden municipality. The level of service does not meet the standards of the true S-Bahn concept, the nearest approach being on the 14 km Dresden—Tharandt section where a half-hourly interval service runs. A frequent service is advertised over the 4 km Dresden Hbf—Dresden Mitte—Dresden Neustadt axis, but this elevated route offers no advantage for short-distance riders over the parallel tram service at street level. High-capacity double-deck rolling stock is used, hauled by diesel or electric locomotives.

The steam-worked 750 mm gauge line from Radebeul Ost to Radeburg also carries suburban traffic, much of it transferring to the Dresden—Weinböhla tram route, while the first station along the similar line from Freital-Hainsberg is included in the S-Bahn zone.

UPDATED

DUBLIN

Population: 1.1 million
Public transport: Bus and suburban rail services operated by autonomous divisions of state transport undertaking responsible to Department of Transport, Energy and Communications; light rail proposed

Bus Atha Cliath

Dublin Bus/Bus Atha Cliath
59 Upper O'Connell Street, Dublin 1, Ireland
Telephone: +353 1 872 0000 Fax: +353 1 873 1195
Chief Executive: Liam Walsh (Acting)
Staff: 2,950

Current situation: Legislation was implemented in 1987 splitting the state-owned transport company CIE into separate autonomous operations for rail, Dublin city buses and provincial and rural bus services, with CIE itself remaining only as a holding company, with responsibility for overall financial control.

With patronage at record levels, buses now account for some 25 per cent of peak-hour journeys.

Developments: A major study into the city's transport needs for the early years of the next century, the Dublin Transportation Initiative (DTI), was published in 1994. Its major elements are construction of a core light rail network, extension of the DART suburban rail network (see below) and development of a Quality Bus Corridor network. An integrated ticketing system to cover all modes is being studied, and park-and-ride is to be expanded.

A Dublin Transportation Office was set up in 1996 to oversee implementation of the DTI strategy. Five of the 11 City Swift Quality Bus Corridors have already been implemented and there are now eight City Imp high-frequency minibus routes in operation. In addition, express services for commuters are provided under the Cityspeed branding.

DASH smartcard for paying bus fares, car park fees, public telephone and bridge tolls was tried out during 1994.

Bus

Passenger journeys: (1993) 180 million
(1994) 185 million
(1995) 182 million

Mercedes 709D on City Imp service 123 ***1995***

Vehicle-km: (1993) 44.7 million
(1994) 47.3 million
(1995) 51.1 million

Number of routes: 139
Route length: (One way) 845 km
On priority right-of-way: 105 sections totalling 26.2 km
Fleet: 906 vehicles

GAC Ireland double-deck	221
Volvo Olympian/Alexander double-deck	325
GAC Ireland single-deck	125
Mercedes minibus	115
DAF Bus/Plaxton single-deck	40
DAF Bus/Alexander single-deck	70
Volvo/Alexander single-deck	10

Average age of fleet: 8 years

Most intensive service: 4-8 min
One-person operation: 97.5%
Fare structure: Stage. Range of daily, weekly, monthly and annual commuter tickets; 10-journey tickets for the different stages are also available; arrangements for bus-rail through ticketing on feeder services to DART trains
Fare collection: Wayfarer electronic ticket machines and magnetic card validators on all vehicles. Almex and TIM hand-held machines used by conductors
Fares collected on board: 66%
Fare evasion control: Random inspectors
Integration with other modes: Plans for city-centre transport interchange, with terminus for local and long-distance buses; feeder buses to DART
Operational control: System-wide computerised online real-time automatic vehicle monitoring
Arrangements for elderly/disabled: Free travel at all times for blind and disabled people attending workshops etc; off-peak for the elderly (paid for by relevant government departments); wheelchair-accessible route 300 introduced 1996
Average peak-hour speed: In mixed traffic, 20 km/h; in bus lanes, 30 km/h
Bus priority: Substantial system of bus lanes — 105 sections extending to 26.2 km; the majority operate during peak hours only, but 20 bus lanes operate 07.00-19.00
Operating costs financed by: Fares and other commercial sources 95.6%, subsidy/grants 4.4%

Subsidy from: Central government subvention
New vehicles financed by: Repayable government loans

Developments: A project is in progress to convert all peak-hour lanes to 12 h operation. Under the DTI strategy, a substantial increase in the number of bus lanes and other priority measures is planned for 1997/98.

DART

Iarnrod Eireann (Irish Rail)
Connolly Station, Dublin 1
Telephone: +353 1 636 3333 Fax: +353 1 836 4760
Chief Executive: David Waters
Manager, Suburban Rail: Michael Murphy
Media & Public Relations Manager: Cyril Ferris
Staff: 206

Type of operation: Suburban heavy rail

Passenger journeys: (All Dublin suburban)
(1993) 18.2 million
(1994) 18 million
(1995) 18.8 million

Current situation: Frequent suburban service (minimum 15-min off-peak) operated over single route Howth—Dublin—Bray (37 km) known as DART, 25 stations, 1,600 mm gauge, electrified at 1.5 kV DC overhead. Also diesel service between Dublin and Maynooth (26 km, eight stations), and on other lines outside the DART area to Malahide, Drogheda, Dundalk, Arklow and Kildare (Arrow service), total 201 km.

Fares cover 67 per cent of DART's operating costs, the remainder coming from government grants. Stations are manned, but with ticket-controlled turnstiles.

Developments: Extension of DART electric service from Bray to Greystones (7.5 km) in progress, and a northern extension from Howth Junction to Malahide (8.7 km) has been authorised. Both should be completed in 1999.

DAF SB220 on City Swift service ***1997***

New stations open in 1997 at Fairview (June) and Barrow Street (December). A further 27 diesel railcars are on order for outer-suburban services and another 10 DART emu cars will be required.

The government's plans for public transport improvements through to 1999, published in 1994, envisage construction of a core light rail network (see below), extension and improved frequency on DART services, upgrading of the Maynooth suburban operation, introduction of integrated ticketing, and development of park-and-ride facilities.

Rolling stock: 40 two-car emu sets, 24 diesel-hauled push-pull coaches, 17 dmu cars

Linke-Hofmann-Busch emu (1983/84)	M40 T40
Tokyu Car dmu (1994)	M17

Light rail (proposed)

Developments: European Union funding is being sought for construction of a three-line light rail network. In Phase I (20 km, 32 stations), to be completed by 2000, lines will link the city centre with Tallaght and Dundrum, the latter route using the alignment of the Harcourt Street suburban railway closed in 1959. The third line would run to Ballymun. In a later phase, routes would be built to Finglas and Dublin airport. A fleet of 30 cars would be required for operation of the first phase.

UPDATED

DUISBURG

Population: 535,000, population served 604,000
Public transport: Bus and tramway services provided by municipally owned company operating as part of Rhein-Ruhr Verkehrsverbund, co-ordinating fares and services. DB S-Bahn services wholly integrated with urban services

Duisburger Verkehrsgesellschaft

Duisburger Verkehrsgesellschaft AG
PO Box 100452, 47004 Duisburg, Germany
Telephone: +49 203 6040 Fax: +49 203 604 4440
Directors: Uwe Steckert (Chair)
Dr Edmund Baer
Helmut Heckner
Wolfgang Linke
Staff: 1,364

Passenger journeys: (All modes)
(1993) 52.5 million
(1994) 50.3 million
(1995) 49.9 million

Operating costs financed by: Fares 47%, other commercial sources 7%, subsidy/grants 46%
Subsidy from: Duisburger Versorgungs- und Verkehrsgesellschaft mbH, city of Duisburg 90% and state Nordrhein-Westfalen (public grants) 10%

Bus

Staff: 830

Vehicle-km: (1993) 11.4 million
(1994) 10.8 million
(1995) 10 million

Number of routes: 27
Route length: (One way) 284.3 km
Fleet: 194 vehicles, plus 43 hired

Mercedes O305 (1977/84)	67
Mercedes O405 (1985/93)	117
Van Hool AG300 articulated (1995)	10

Most intensive service: 10-20 min
One-person operation: All routes

Duisburg LRV on Route 901 in Mülheim

Fare collection: Payment to driver or prepurchase pass or multitickets with validation and cancelling machines
Fare structure: Zonal; as Rhein-Ruhr (qv)
Fare evasion control: Roving inspectors with penalty
Operational control: Route inspectors/mobile radio
Arrangements for elderly/disabled: 1 minibus operating on demand; free travel for disabled, reimbursed by government
Average speed: 22 km/h

Tramway/Light rail

Type of operation: Light rail/upgraded tramway (Stadtbahn), conventional tramway

Car-km: (1993) 4.3 million
(1994) 4.6 million
(1995) 4.4 million

Route length: Tramway 41.5 km, Stadtbahn 17.1 km
in tunnel: 6 km
Number of routes: 4

Number of stations/stops: 163
in tunnel: 5
Max gradient: 4%
Minimum curve radius: 183 m
Gauge: 1,435 mm
Electrification: 600 V DC, overhead

Service: Peak 10 min, off-peak 30 min
First/last car: 04.00/24.00
One-person operation: All cars
Fare evasion control: Roving inspectors

Rolling stock: 64 cars

Duewag 8-axle articulated (1966, rebuilt 1968)	M1
Duewag B80C Stadtbahn 6-axle articulated (1983/85)	M18
Duewag GT8NC 8-axle articulated (1986/93)	M45

Current situation: Portions of existing tram network being upgraded as part of the Rhein-Ruhr Stadtbahn (qv); 6 km city-centre tunnel (partially completed long ago) with five stations opened in 1992, with northwards extension to Meiderich under construction.

Stadtbahn in Duisburg will eventually extend to a 31 km north-south line and a 9.5 km east-west line. Former tram Route D, now upgraded to LRT standards, runs to Düsseldorf and is jointly operated (see under Rhein-Ruhr). Long-loop continuous inductive ATC to be installed.

DB

Deutsche Bahn AG, Geschäftsbereich Nahverkehr
Regionalbereich Rhein-Ruhr
Am Hauptbahnhof 3, 45127 Essen
Telephone: +49 201 182 3330 Fax: +49 201 182 4475
Regional Manager: Christian Plattenteich

Type of operation: Regional metro (S-Bahn)

Current situation: Duisburg is served by Line S1 (Dortmund–Duisburg–Düsseldorf) of the Rhein-Ruhr (qv) S-Bahn, and other suburban and regional services of DB.

UPDATED

DURBAN

Population: City 746,000, conurbation 3 million
Public transport: Bus services provided by municipal undertaking, large private commuter service operator (PUTCO), and some 350 other operators running buses and minibuses and legal and illegal combi-taxis. Suburban rail services

DTMB

Durban Transport
PO Box 1746, 102 Alice Street, Durban 4000, South Africa
Telephone: +27 31 309 4126 Fax: +27 31 309 5108
Executive Director: Jenny Gray
Staff: 1,373

Current situation: Operates two distinct services, the Aqualine serving Durban and surrounding area, and a city-centre midibus network known as the Mynah. It also provides dedicated services for schoolchildren, and charter operations. Its tours operation was privatised in 1993. Strong competition is provided by the large number of private bus operators, licensed and unlicensed 'kombis' (minibuses).
Developments: In 1994 the former Green and Blue line services were consolidated into a single network, called Aqualine. Its launch coincided with a major marketing campaign to increase patronage following the losses suffered in 1993/94 due to political disturbances.

Fleet renewal began in 1995 following trials with six buses from three chassis builders and three body manufacturers.

Bus

Passenger journeys: (1991/92) 46 million
(1992/93) 44.7 million
(1993/94) 41.1 million
Vehicle-km: (1991/92) 34.7 million
(1992/93) 34.6 million
(1993/94) 34.1 million

Number of routes: 601
Route length: (One way) 12,343 km
Fleet: 681 vehicles

MAN A51	303
Mercedes 1317	223
Leyland Victory	140
ERF Trailblazer	13
Dennis	2

In peak service: 608

One-person operation: 100%
Fare collection: Cash via driver with Setright ticket machine; prepurchase coupons cancelled on board; Mynah, no cash sales; automatic cancellers on all vehicles
Fare structure: Stage; flat for Mynah service
Fare evasion control: Inspectors
Integration with other modes: Services co-ordinated with rail
Arrangements for elderly/disabled: concessionary fares
Average peak-hour speed: 30 km/h
Operating costs financed by: Fares 46.8%, other commercial sources 4.4%, subsidy/grants 48.8%
Subsidy from: Government and city council (rates and general services fund)

Metro Rail

South African Rail Commuter Corporation Ltd
Durban Metropolitan Area

MAN A51 of Durban Transport ***1995***

Leyland Victory of PUTCO near Durban rail station

Private Bag X2, Sunninghill, Johannesburg 2157
Telephone: +27 11 804 2900 Fax: +27 11 804 3852

Type of operation: Suburban heavy rail

Passenger journeys: (1990/91) 73 million
(1991/92) 73.1 million
(1992/93) 70.5 million

Current situation: Frequent suburban services in the Natal metropolitan area on eight routes totalling 273 km, 1,067 mm gauge, electrified 3 kV DC; up to 22 trains per hour at peak times, every 30 min off-peak. Fares cover 22.8 per cent of operating costs.
Developments: 3 km Inanda extension proposed under Metro Rail's 10-year capital investment programme.

Rolling stock: 825 emu cars
Union Carriage 5M2A (1957 on) M227 T598

PUTCO

Current situation: See Johannesburg entry for general description of PUTCO. The company's Durban operation carries commuters on medium and long-distance journeys (20-35 km); some 80 per cent of routes are peak-only.

Private bus/minibus

Current situation: There are extensive and growing operations by private minibuses known locally as 'kombi-taxis', licensed as taxis but operating illegally as shared-taxis and accused of poaching passengers from conventional bus routes, as well as over 100 other private bus operations mostly running from suburban areas, including Kwa Zulu bus service and around 80 small Indian operators.

DÜSSELDORF

Population: 572,000, area served 1.2 million
Public transport: Bus, tramway, light rail and leisure ferry services provided in city and surrounding area by municipal company and suburban rail services by DB, both operating as part of Rhein-Ruhr Verkehrsverbund (VRR), co-ordinating fares and services. See also Rhein-Ruhr entry

Rheinische Bahngesellschaft

Rheinische Bahngesellschaft AG
PO Box 104263, 40033 Düsseldorf (Oberkassel), Germany
Telephone: +49 211 58201 Fax: +49 211 582 1966
Directors: Dipl-Ing Georg Püttner (Chair)
Personnel: Walther Holshoff
Commercial: Gert Blumenthal
Infrastructure Manager: Frank Dix
Workshops & Technical Manager: Helmut Döpfer
Operations Manager: Volkmar Pfaff
Personnel Manager: Ulrich Reisenhauer
Purchasing Manager: Michael Becker
Staff: 3,733

Passenger journeys: (All modes)
(1993) 191 million
(1994) 195 million
(1995) 196 million

Bus

Vehicle-km: (1993) 24.8 million
(1994) 24.5 million
(1995) 24.7 million

Number of routes: 71
Route length: 1,025 km
Fleet: 400 vehicles, plus 49 hired

Mercedes O305/O405 standard	126
Mercedes O405N low-floor	21
Mercedes O305G/O405G articulated	61
MAN SL200/202 standard	60
MAN NL202 low-floor	39
MAN SG242 articulated	35
MAN NG272 low-floor articulated	17
Neoplan N4016NF low-floor	6
Mercedes O405GN low-floor articulated	14
Others	21

In peak service: 352

Most intensive service: 10 min
One-person operation: All routes
Fare collection: Prepurchase tickets or pass with validation and cancelling machines; payment to driver
Fare structure: Zonal; prepurchase multiride tickets, weekly and monthly passes, Jobticket (see below)
Fares collected on board: 16%
Fare evasion control: Roving inspectors
Arrangements for elderly/disabled: Free travel for disabled, reimbursed by government

Trams and buses at Jan Wilhelm Platz ***1996***

Operational control: Route inspectors/mobile radio
Average peak-hour speed: 19 km/h

Tramway/Light rail

Type of operation: Stadtbahn and conventional tramway

Car-km: (1993) Tram 12.2 million, LRT 8.6 million
(1994) Tram 11.9 million, LRT 9.3 million
(1995) Tram 12 million, LRT 9.4 million

Route length: Tramway 82.2 km, LRT 64.1 km (in tunnel 6 km)
Number of lines: 17 (LRT 3, tram 14)

Current situation: Plans envisage a 4-line LRT network of some 68 km, of which 15 km will be in tunnel. Under the Rhein-Rhur Stadtbahn scheme, the existing tramway is being upgraded and transformed. Tunnels now extend to 6 km and are used by five routes, including the interurbans to Neuss, Krefeld and Duisburg. At Hbf there is interchange with the S-Bahn. Restaurant facilities are available on the interurban services to Krefeld and Duisburg.
Developments: Construction of east-west light rail line from Grafenberg to Bilk (7.4 km), with a tunnel in the city centre, approved in 1991 for opening in 1994/96, will not now be ready before 2000. Conversion of two DB routes to Stadtbahn operation proposed (see below).

A total of 43 companies with 47,000 employees make use of the Jobticket, a bulk purchase scheme for public transport passes for all employees.

Rolling stock: 351 cars

Duewag 4-axle (1955/66)	T73
Duewag GT6 6-axle articulated (1956/61)	M42
Duewag GT8 8-axle articulated (1958/69) some ex-GT6	M65
Duewag GT8S 8-axle articulated (1974/75)	M29
Duewag GT8SU 8-axle articulated (1973/75)	M38
Duewag B80D 6-axle articulated Stadtbahn (1981/93)	M104

On order: 118 low-floor cars from Duewag, plus 15 low-floor trailers for delivery starting in late 1997 and options for a further 44

Ferry

Current situation: Four boats operate leisure services on the Rhein.

DB

Deutsche Bahn AG

Type of operation: Regional metro (S-Bahn)

Current situation: Düsseldorf is served by 4 lines of the Rhein-Ruhr S-Bahn (see under Rhein-Ruhr), and by other (non-S-Bahn) suburban services of DB.
Developments: Negotiations are under way for transfer of the Kaarst–Neuss and Düsseldorf–Gerresheim–Mettmann lines to local authority control. A through service from Kaarst to Mettmann is envisaged using lightweight low-floor diesel railcars running over DB tracks on the central section.

Operation is to be contracted out to Deutsche Eisenbahn Gesellschaft (DEG) and service is expected to start in May 1998.

Regional bus

Current situation: Regional bus services provided by Busverkehr Rehinland (BUR), an associated company of DB. For full details see under Rhein-Ruhr entry.

UPDATED

EDINBURGH

Population: City 421,000, Lothian Region 724,000
Public transport: Most bus services provided by company owned by local council, with some by private operators. Local rail services

Lothian Region Transport

Lothian Region Transport plc
1-4 Shrub Place, Edinburgh EH7 4PA, Scotland
Telephone: +44 131 554 4494 Fax: +44 131 225 6276
Chairman: Alexander Kitson
Managing Director: Charles Evans
Commercial Manager: Ronald House
Finance Director: George B Kirk
Staff: 1,812

Current situation: Following abolition of Lothian Regional Council in April 1996, LRT is owned by the new district council – City of Edinburgh. The company operates commercial services and submits competitive tenders for any contracted operations. A comprehensive city route network is supplemented by routes extending into surrounding towns.

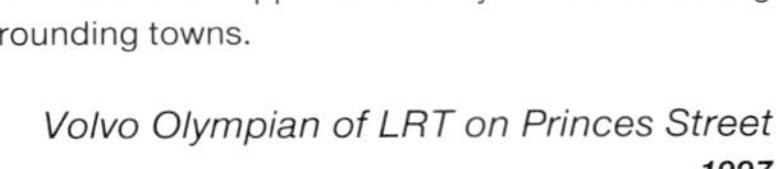

Volvo Olympian of LRT on Princes Street ***1997***

SMT Mercedes Citybus on Fauldhouse service ***1997***

Developments: Service expansion continues beyond the city limits. Recent expansion saw introduction of more limited-stop services to suburbs, and an upgrading of the Airport Express service.

The Edinburgh Greenways bus priority scheme, proposed in 1994 and awaiting government approval, would add 32 km of busway on three corridors into the city from the west. In addition, priority will extend to Princes Street and Leith Walk in the city centre, and will form an integral part of the central traffic management plan.

Edinburgh District Council had produced a proposal for a busway between the city centre and the airport. The City of Edinburgh Rapid Transit scheme (CERT) envisages a segregated busway carrying four services which would attract some 30,000 passengers a day. The £30 million project would require private finance and a dedicated fleet of 39 vehicles. Approval is expected to be granted in 1997. In addition, six park-and-ride schemes have been suggested to help relieve traffic congestion, and one site at Hermiston has been purchased.

Bus

Passenger journeys: (1991/92) 98.7 million
(1992/93) 97.8 million
(1995/96) 90.3 million
Vehicle-km: (1991/92) 32.2 million
(1992/93) 32.1 million
(1995/96) 21.2 million

Number of routes: 78
Route length: 1,370 km
On priority right-of-way: 10 km
Fleet: 556 vehicles

Leyland/Volvo double-deck	461
Leyland/Dennis single-deck	51
Open-top double-deck	26
Coaches	18

In peak service: 424
New vehicles required each year: 34 double-deck

Most intensive service: 6 min (2-3 min on combined routes)
One-person operation: All routes
Fare collection: Wayfarer electronic machines with farebox on board; passes and season tickets
Fare structure: Stage; 4-week, 1-week and annual 'Rida Cards'; flat fare on all-night buses
Fares collected on board: 54%
Fare evasion control: Inspectors
Operational control: Patrol inspectors in vans/mobile radio
Average peak-hour speed: In mixed traffic, 15.6 km/h
Operating costs financed by: Fares 93%, other commercial sources 7%
Subsidy from: Company operates fully commercially with specific support from council's rate fund for any contracted services won by tender

SMT

Eastern Scottish Omnibuses Ltd
2 Westfield Avenue, Edinburgh EH11 2QH
Telephone: +44 131 313 1515 Fax: +44 131 313 1555
Chief Executive: Moir Lockhead
Staff: 979

Bus (Operations in Lothian area only)
Passenger journeys: (1991) 38 million
(1992) 36.8 million
(1993) 36.4 million
Vehicle-km: (1991) 26.6 million
(1992) 26.4 million
(1993) 26.4 million

Fleet: 335 buses

Single-deck	86
Double-deck	143
Coaches	31
Minibuses	75

Current situation: The company was purchased from the Scottish Bus Group in 1990 by its workforce and became a subsidiary of FirstBus in 1995. It operates a substantial proportion of the bus services in the Lothian area, including Edinburgh. There is a network of services to surrounding towns including commuter express workings. Within Edinburgh high-frequency minibus routes operate between residential areas and the centre under the City Sprinter brand name, although competitive operations have been cut back.

Management has been merged with the FirstBus subsidiary Lowland Scottish.

Other operators

Current situation: Guide Friday of Stratford on Avon has established a base in the city and has challenged LRT on sightseeing services and the Airport Express route. Stagecoach Fife works some services from towns across the Forth bridge.

ScotRail

ScotRail Railways Ltd
Caledonian Chambers, 87 Union Street, Glasgow G1 3TA
Telephone: +44 141 332 9811 Fax: +44 141 335 3125

Type of operation: Local rail

Current situation: Hourly/half-hourly diesel services provided on several routes, plus electric trains to North Berwick (36 km).
Developments: Despite earlier rejection of similar proposals, Lothian Regional Council funded a study into reopening the Edinburgh south suburban loop line to passenger services.

In 1994 the Fife Regional Council approved expenditure of £8.8 million to fund an improved service on the Fife Circle route north of Edinburgh, together with construction of three new stations. ScotRail commissioned consultants to evaluate both proposals.

Light rail/Busway (planned)

Planning authority: City of Edinburgh Council
12 St Giles Street, Edinburgh EH1 1PT
Telephone: +44 131 469 3415 Fax: +44 131 469 3417
Leader, Metro Development Group: David Scotney

Current situation: While earlier studies had identified a long-term requirement for north-south and east-west light rapid transit lines across the city, the current view is that light rail is not feasible on cost and other grounds. Nevertheless, it remains a long-term aim for the region. In 1996 a line linking the city centre with Leith and Newhaven was being canvassed by a private company, the Edinburgh Tram Company.

Instead, a 10 km guided busway is proposed between the airport and West Approach Road (see above).

UPDATED

EDMONTON

Population: 637,000
Public transport: Bus, trolleybus and light rail services operated by municipal undertaking with two small suburban bus systems

Edmonton Transit

Edmonton Transit
PO Box 2610, Edmonton, Alberta T5J 3R5, Canada
Telephone: +1 403 496 5740 Fax: +1 403 496 4244
Manager of Transit: Wayne Mandryk
Director, Light Rail: L J McLachlan
Director, Bus: J Sirovyak
Director, Marketing & Planning: Wayne Ramsbottom
Director, Plant & Equipment: Dave Geake
Staff: 1,778

Current situation: A new city transport department was established in 1984 with its General Manager reported to by four divisions including Edmonton Transit. Bus services have been reshaped to feed the light rail line, but the route is poorly placed in relation to several of the area's major traffic generators.

On-demand Dial-a-Bus network called Service Plus provides night, Sunday and holiday service to several suburbs, operating regular services to defined pick-up points on request. 'Stop Request' system operates, under which buses will stop for passengers to alight at any safe location on the regular route after 21.00.

In operation
Planned
Northgate
Clareview
Belvedere
Coliseum
Stadium
Churchill
Central
Bay
Corona
Grandin
West Edmonton
University
Health Sciences
North Saskatchewan River
Southgate

Edmonton's light rail system

Developments: Trolleybus operation has been blighted by high costs and inefficiency, and the system's future had been in doubt. But in 1994 it was decided to spend C$6.7 million on a four-year programme to upgrade the infrastructure.

Following a six-month trial of CNG in joint test programme with Calgary Transit, a pilot scheme started in 1994 using a fully accessible 24-passenger CNG-powered bus.

Provincial grants for public transit operations ceased in 1994 for cities of more than 500,000 people, except for disabled service, leading to some budget cuts. Service provision was reduced by about 4,000 hours during 1994, fares were raised and vacant staff positions went unfilled. Revisions introduced in 1995 brought major changes to West Edmonton services, with five new routes and others altered or curtailed. Subsequently, ETS has developed a new service strategy comprising Base and Community networks, due to be implemented in June 1997.

Passenger journeys: (All modes)
(1993) 39.2 million
(1994) 38.1 milion
(1995) 37.1 million

Operating costs financed by: Fares 43%, other commercial sources 5.5%, tax levy 51.5%
Subsidy from: Disabled transport grants from Province of Alberta

Bus and trolleybus

Vehicle-km: (1993) 29.5 million
(1994) 29.3 million
(1995) 29.4 million

Number of routes: Bus 116, trolleybus 6
Route length: Bus 2,593 km, trolleybus 200 km
Fleet: 597 buses

GMC	510
Flyer	18
New Flyer low-floor (1993/94)	59
Community buses	10

Fleet: 98 trolleybuses, of which 36 surplus

GMC-Brown Boveri (1981/82)	98

In peak service: 595 vehicles

Most intensive service: 7-8 min
One-person operation: All routes
Fare collection: Exact fare payment to farebox; prepurchase multitickets or monthly pass
Fare structure: Flat; monthly passes, 10-journey discount multitickets, free 90 min transfers; ET tickets and passes valid on suburban operators' buses within city limits
Arrangements for elderly/disabled: Discount annual senior passes. Door-to-door Disabled Adult Transportation System (DATS) operated with special vehicles; 59 scheduled service buses on 22 routes have low floor, kneeling capability, hydraulic ramp and two wheelchair positions
Integration with other modes: Common fare for buses and LRT, free transfers apply; free central area rides on LRT 09.00-15.00; cycle racks tried out on one route during 1995

Light rail

Type of operation: Light rail, initial route opened 1978

Car-km: (1993) 2 million
(1994) 2.5 million
(1995) 2.5 million

Route length: 13.7 km
Number of lines: 1
Number of stations: 10
Gauge: 1,435 mm
Tunnel: Cut-and-cover and bored
Electrification: 600 V DC, overhead

Southbound LRV on the University extension

Trolleybus on Route 42 at 105th Street Bridge ***1996***

Service: 5 min
First/last car: 05.30/01.31
Integration with other modes: Common fare systems on bus and LRT; Jasper Avenue section in city centre fare free 09.00-15.00 weekdays and 09.00-18.00 Saturdays; cycles carried off-peak; minibus feeder to Clareview station

Rolling stock: 37 articulated cars

Duewag/Siemens (1978)	M14
Duewag/Siemens (1979)	M3
Duewag/Siemens (1982)	M20

Two three-phase AC motored cars on trial as part of joint test programme of Alberta province, Edmonton and Siemens AG
In peak service: 27 cars

Current situation: Proposed extensions put on indefinite hold in 1993, but next section likely to be built is the short extension to Health Sciences.

Other operators

Current situation: Operators in the adjacent localities of St Albert and Sherwood Park run services through to downtown Edmonton, and issue passes valid on ET services. These are St Albert Transit (29 vehicles) and Strathcona County Public Transit (31 vehicles).

UPDATED

ESSEN

Population: 618,000, area served 659,000
Public transport: Bus, Stadtbahn, tramway and guided bus/dual-mode services operated by municipal company and suburban rail and bus services by DB, both operating as part of Rhein-Ruhr Verkehrsverbund (qv) co-ordinating fares and services. Tramway sections being upgraded as part of Rhein-Ruhr Stadtbahn. See also under Rhein-Ruhr

EVAG

Essener Verkehrs-AG
Zweigertstrasse 34, 45115 Essen, Germany
Telephone: +49 201 8260 Fax: +49 201 826 1000
Directors: Hermann Derks
Johannes Werner Schmidt
Falkobert Obst
Operations Manager: Ulrich Deinhardt
Workshops Manager: Hans Ahlbrecht
Personnel Manager: Wolfgang Daub
Planning & Construction Manager: Hans-Joachim Maass
Staff: 2,192

Passenger journeys: (All modes)
(1993) 113.6 million
(1994) 115 million
(1995) 106 million

Metrofor

Autarquia de Regiao Metropolitana de Fortaleza
Rua Jose Laurenco, Aldeota, Fortaleza 60000
Staff: 439

Type of operation: Suburban heavy rail

Passenger journeys: (1994) 35,000 daily
(1995) 7.6 million

Current situation: Two separate metre-gauge routes (43 km, 17 stations) have been upgraded and resignalled to form the first stage of a commuter railway. Fares cover 18% of operatibg costs.

Developments: With Metrofor (CBTU) taking full control of the suburban services, train frequency has been increased to half-hourly. Modernisation of locomotives and coaches started in 1994 and continued through 1996. A programme of station modernisation and improvement is also in progress.

A US$260 million loan from Japan's Eximbank, which has been frozen since 1992, was to finance electrification of the 23 km southern line and construction of a 3.5 km elevated link between the two lines. With cross-city service established, some 420,000 daily journeys are expected.

Fortaleza suburban train at João Felipe terminal

Rolling stock: 6 diesel locomotives, 45 coaches

UPDATED

FORT WORTH

Population: 475,000
Public transport: Bus services managed under contract for Regional Transit Authority. Privately operated light rail line

The T

Fort Worth Transportation Authority
PO Box 1477, 2304 Pine Street, Fort Worth, TX 76101, USA
Telephone: +1 817 871 6221 Fax: +1 817 871 6217
Managed by McDonald Transit Associates Inc
Chair: Walker C Friedman
General Manager: John P Bartosiewicz
Assistant General Manager: Anthony V Johnson
Manager of Transportation: David Harris
Manager of Development: Nancy Amos
Staff: 377

Current situation: In 1983 responsibility for the former City Transit Service of Fort Worth (Citran) passed to a new Regional Transportation Authority, created by a vote which also authorised the raising of dedicated funds from a ¼ per cent sales tax; this was increased to ½ per cent in 1989. Lake Worth, Richland Hills and Blue Mound joined the RTA area in 1992. The RTA makes an annual payment to the cities' funds for improvements to streets served by bus routes.

A gradual expansion of services has taken place over the past few years. Central area services are fares-free. A ride-sharing programme operates vanpools. In 1992 The T inaugurated a programme for conversion of all buses to CNG power by 1998.

Developments: A new five-year plan approved in 1996 emphasised the importance of the planned Railtran commuter rail service between Fort Worth and Dallas, a project jointly managed by the two cities. See Dallas entry for details.

Other aspects of the plan cover fleet renewal and expansion, provision of increased express service and expansion of vanpooling.

Bus

Passenger boardings: (1992) 4.3 million
(1993) 4.7 million
(1995) 6 million
Vehicle-km: (1992) 9.5 million
(1993) 10.4 million
(1995) 9.8 million

Number of routes: 37
Route length: 570 km

Flxible Metro bus of The T

Fleet: 184 vehicles

Flxible Metro (1986)	35
Flxible Metro (1987)	33
Flxible Metro (1990)	7
Flxible Metro (1991)	9
Flxible Metro (1992)	32
Flxible Metro (1995)	13
MCI coach (1984)	3
MCI coach (1990)	2
Vans/minibuses (disabled service)	33
Champion Route (1994)	12
Eldorado Route (1996)	5

In peak service: 116

Most intensive service: 15 min
One-person operation: All services
Fare collection: Registering farebox on vehicle, tokens or passes
Fare structure: Exact flat fare; monthly passes, tokens; free transfers; free central area travel
Fare evasion control: Driver supervision
Operational control: Route inspectors/mobile radio
Arrangements for elderly/disabled: On-demand minibus service with 32 vehicles carried 269,000 passengers in 1995
Average peak-hour speed: 13 km/h
Bus priority: Peak-hour bus lanes on some inner radial routes
Integration with other modes: 21 park-and-ride sites, 13 served by special express routes; ride-sharing/vanpools promoted; special service to airport with vans
Operating costs financed by: Fares and other commercial sources 14.8%, FTA subsidy/grants 16%, state and local sales tax 69.3%
New vehicles financed by: FTA 80%, 20% FWTA funds (sales tax)

Tandy

Tandy Center Subway
100 One Tandy Center, Fort Worth, TX 76102
Telephone: +1 817 336 5248 Fax: +1 817 338 2388
General Manager: Jim Lincecum
Vice President, Operations: Jim Giese

Type of operation: Light rail

Passenger journeys: (Annual) 1.5 million

Current situation: Tandy Corp operates a 1.6 km light rail line, partly underground, to link its downtown headquarters building and department store with a 3,000-vehicle parking lot. Free service is provided.

Rolling stock: 8 cars
PCC (rebuilt 1977/78) M8

UPDATED

FRANKFURT AM MAIN

Population: 654,000; metropolitan area 2.6 million
Public transport: Bus, tramway and metro services provided by municipal authority operating as part of Rhein-Main Verkehrsverbund (RMV) co-ordinating fares and services with regional bus and rail services provided by DB and a local railway

RMV

Rhein-Main Verkehrsverbund GmbH (RMV)
Am Kreishaus 1-5, 65719 Hofheim, Germany
Telephone: +49 6192 201515 Fax: +49 6192 201623
Director: Volker Sparmann
Deputy Director: Uwe Stindt
Corporate Manager: Herbert Jack
Traffic Planning Manager: Gerhard Staneck
Marketing Manager: Hansjörg Rörich

Passenger boardings: (All modes, FVV figures)
(1993) 244.5 million
(1994) 223.5 million
(1995)

Current situation: RMV is the new regional transit authority set up in 1994; it became operational in 1995 as successor to Frankfurter Verkehrsverbund (FVV). It is the largest regional transit authority in Germany, covering an area of 14,000 km² with a population of 4.9 million. Extending from Marburg in the north to Erbach in the south and from Limburg in the west to Fulda in the east, the area includes the cities of Darmstadt, Frankfurt, Offenbach and Wiesbaden, seven other cities and 15 rural counties.

RMV is mainly aimed at regional transit, while purely local services will be the responsibility of cities and counties. Tickets are interavailable. An integrated fixed-interval timetable is planned, with S-Bahn trains running every 15 min at peak periods and 30 min off-peak, and regional trains every 30 or 60 min.

While FVV was an association of transport operators, RMV is formed by local authorities and will buy-in services from existing operators. RMV embraces 50 rail routes and 250 bus routes, served by 4,000 buses run by 132 operators. There are 350 ticket sales outlets.

In 1993, there were 3.9 million daily journeys made in the RMV area and modal split was 14 per cent by public transport, 23 per cent walking/cycling and 63 per cent by private transport. By the year 2000 is it expected that daily journeys will total 4.2 million, and RMV hopes to raise public transport's share to 25 per cent.

Fare structure: Zonal; single tickets (reduced fares during off-peak hours), passes (weekly/monthly), day tickets. Short-distance tickets and other special offers; all ordinary passes transferable; no ticket sales on board rail vehicles (S-Bahn, metro, tram), but vending machines at every station/stop; free transfers
Operating costs financed by: Fares 45.5%, other commercial sources 1.2%, subsidy/grants 52.9%

Stadtwerke Frankfurt

Stadtwerke Frankfurt am Main GmbH
60276 Frankfurt am Main
Telephone: +49 69 2130 Fax: +49 69 213 22740
Directors: Hermann Dieter Oehm
Manfred Ott
Deputy Director: Jürgen Wann
Operations Manager: Udo Salamon
Technical Manager: Christian Lambrecht
Planning & Construction Manager: Klaus Gierse
Staff: 3,035 (all modes)

Passenger journeys: (All modes)
(1993) 161.6 million
(1994) 154.9 million
(1995) 151.8 million

Operating costs financed by: Fares 44.9%, subsidy/grants 55.1%
Subsidy from: City budget

Current situation: Most central area services are provided by metro, tram or S-Bahn with buses acting as feeders and serving suburban areas. Surface tramways were due to be eliminated from the city centre, leaving the metro as the only means of cross-city-centre transport, but in 1989 the newly elected city council resisted and there was strong public pressure to retain the trams.

U6 train at Konstablerwache **1997**

Although overall journeys rose, there was a decline in city-centre trips of 10 per cent, and it was felt that eliminating trams would accelerate the decline. One cross-city-centre tram route was retained; a 0.7 km city-centre link is now under construction for 1997 opening.
Developments: Cleaning of buses and tramcars has been contracted out to a private company, bringing savings of DM3.5 million annually.

Arrangements for elderly/disabled: 1 tram and 7 urban bus routes served by lift-equipped low-floor vehicles; installation of lifts at metro stations envisaged

Bus

Staff: 609

Vehicle-km: (1993) 13.4 million
(1994) 13.7 million
(1995) 12.6 million

Number of routes: 47
Route length: 368 km
On priority right-of-way: 15.5 km; extension planned
Fleet: 193 vehicles, plus 73 hired; including 32 articulated and 81 low-floor, all Mercedes and Neoplan
In peak service: 224

Most intensive service: 10 min
One-person operation: All routes
Fare structure: Zonal (see RMV)
Fare evasion control: Roving inspectors; penalty fare
Average speed: 18-20 km/h

Developments: Introduction of bus priority lanes under study. Passengers may leave buses other than at designated stops after 20.00, except in the central area. Rail feeder minibuses in northern suburbs run by independent operator under contract.

Contracting out of 25 per cent of routes is planned; operating costs are expected to be reduced by one-third. The workshops at Rebstock have been reorganised and now also undertake work for outside customers.

Metro

Staff: 694 (including tramway)

Type of operation: Full metro, initial route opened 1968

Car-km: (1993) 15.8 million
(1994) 15.6 million
(1995) 15.1 million

Route length: 56.1 km
Number of lines: 7
Number of stations: 82
Gauge: 1,435 mm
Tunnel: Box section
Electrification: 600 V DC, overhead

Service: Peak 2 min
Fare structure: Zonal (see RMV)
Integration with other modes: Common tariff structure throughout RMV area

Rolling stock: 372 cars (including tramway)

Duewag U2 (1968/85)	M101
Duewag U3 (1980)	M34
Dueway U4 (1996)	M21
Duewag Pt (1972/77)	M100
Duewag/Siemens U4/U2000 (1995)	M18
Crede K (1954)	M4
Duewag 4-axle (1956/66)	T40
Fuchs 2-axle (1954)	T6
Duewag O (1969)	M8
Duewag R (1993/94/96)	M40

Type Pt cars (see above) also used on tram routes

Current situation: Line U4 from Hauptbahnhof via Messegelände to Bockenheimer Warte (1.7 km), and the U6 extension from Zoo to Ostbahnhof (0.6 km), are both under construction for 1999 opening. Further extension from Südbahnhof to Sachsenhausen Warte is at the planning stage, and in total 11 km of extensions were approved in October 1996.
Developments: Experiments with fully automated driverless operations are planned for 1998. Funding for the project will be provided by the Federal Ministry for Research & Technology (BMFT).

Tramway

Car-km: (1993) 9.2 million
(1994) 8.7 million
(1995) 8.3 million

Route length: 63.1 km
Number of routes: 8

Developments: Three extensions into the suburbs are being evaluated following the 1989 change in policy towards tramways, and a programme of short-term

Duewag Type R low-floor trams on truncated Route 16 at Südbahnhof **1997**

improvements is under way. Construction of 2.3 km from Bockenheim to Rebstock has been approved by the city council amongst 10 km of extensions, but citizens have protested against cutting-down of trees along the route and the supervisory authorities have refused to permit single-track operation.

Route 16 to Offenbach was closed beyond the Frankfurt city boundary in June 1996, following opening of the S-Bahn extension to Offenbach (see below).

New Ost depot for 150 cars is planned for 1998 opening, replacing three central area facilities.

DB

Deutsche Bahn AG, Geschäftsbereich Nahverkehr
Regionalbereich Rhein-Main
Friedrich-Ebert-Anlage 35, 60327 Frankfurt am Main
Telephone: +49 69 265 4191   Fax: +49 69 265 4035
Manager: Jochen Schiebeler

Regional metro

Type of operation: Regional metro (S-Bahn)

Passenger journeys: (1993) 101 million
(1994) 92 million
(1995) S-Bahn 98 million, other RMV routes 55 million

Current situation: S-Bahn services are operated over seven routes on the north bank of River Main converging at Hbf and continuing in tunnel via Konstablerwache in the central business district and under the River Main to Mühlberg and Südbahnhof (4.3 km), with two routes running through to Stresemannallee. Outer termini at Wiesbaden, Offenbach Ost, Niedernhausen, Bad Soden, Kronberg, Friedrichsdorf, Friedberg, Hanau and Mainz; latter route also serving the airport. Total S-bahn routes 288 km, 1,435 mm gauge, electrified 15 kV 16 ⅔ Hz. In addition, DB operates over 46 other routes within the RMV area, totalling about 1,200 km.

Upgrading of line to Darmstadt (south) in progress for May 1997 extension of S-Bahn service. Similar work on branches to Dietzenbach and Rödermark is at the planning stage. Planned construction of separate S-Bahn tracks on the Frankfurt—Bad Vilbel section has been shelved. Construction has started on an S-Bahn station at the fairground (Messe).

A private station has been built at Niedernhausen to serve the venue of the musical 'Sunset Boulevard'. Combined travel and entrance tickets are available, and it is hoped that one-third of the 1,500 audience at each performance will use public transport.

Rolling stock: 118 ET420 emus (S-Bahn)

VU

Verkehrsgesellschaft Untermain GmbH (VU)
Mainzer Landstrasse 189, 60327 Frankfurt
Telephone: +49 69 758 0950
Directors: Dr Siegfried Freihube
Manfred Bohr
Staff: 316

Current situation: Railway associated regional bus company operating services within the RMV area with a fleet of 113 Mercedes buses, plus 394 hired. Statistics for 1992 relate only to operations in the former FVV area.

Buses of VU on Frankfurt Süd-Darmstadt regional service **1997**

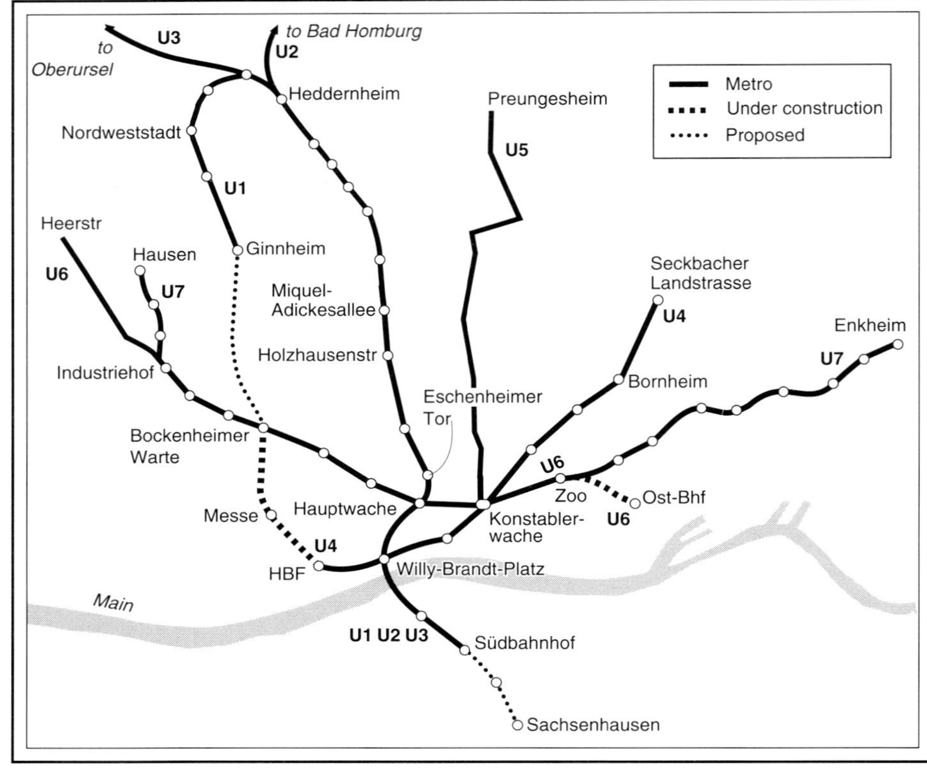

Frankfurt metro

Bus

Passenger journeys: (1992) 11.4 million
(1994) 22.3 million
(1995) 20.5 million
Vehicle-km: (1992) 6.9 million
(1994) 33.6 million
(1995) 24.3 million

FKE

Frankfurt-Königsteiner Eisenbahn AG
Bahnstrasse 13, 61462 Konigstein
Telephone: +49 6174 29010   Fax: +49 6174 290115
Director: P Berking
Staff: 148

Passenger journeys: (Both modes)
(1993) 5.1 million
(1994) 5.1 million

Current situation: Local railway operating diesel railcars between Frankfurt-Höchst and Königstein (25 km), the Höchst—Bad Soden line (part of S3 taken over from DB in 1992), total 46 km, and local bus feeder services in the Frankfurt-Höchst/Kelkheim/Hofheim/Königstein area. Company owned by state of Hessen via Hessische Landesbahn holding. Connects with S-Bahn at Höchst, but during peak hours some trains continue over main line tracks to Frankfurt Hbf.
Developments: FKE assumed responsibility for operation of the Taunusbahn in 1993.

Bus

Vehicle-km: (1993) 4 million
(1994) 5.4 million
(1995) 5.1 million

Number of routes: 21
Route length: 366 km
Fleet: 34 buses, plus 94 hired

Mercedes O307 (1983/87)	13
Mercedes O303 (1987)	1
Mercedes O408 (1991/94)	16
Mercedes O405 (1995)	4

Local railway

Car-km: (1993) 1.1 million
(1994) 1.5 million
(1995) 1.6 million

Rolling stock: 21 diesel railcars

OVB

Offenbacher Verkehrsbetriebe GmbH
Heberstrasse 14, 63065 Offenbach
Telephone: +49 69 800580   Fax: +49 69 80058 190
Director: Claus Steinberg
Staff: 276

Current situation: Municipally owned company provides bus service in the city and county of Offenbach.

Bus

Passenger journeys: (1995) 12.1 million
Vehicle-km: (1995) 3.4 million

Number of routes: 12
Route length: 188 km
Fleet: 63 buses, plus 10 on hire

ESWE

Stadtwerke Wiesbaden AG Verkehrsbetriebe (ESWE)
Kirchgasse 2, 65184 Wiesbaden, Germany
Telephone: +49 611 7800   Fax: +49 611 780 2339
Chair: Dr Gerhard Heunemann
Directors: Klaus Kopp
Diether Sammet
Operations Manager: Uwe Cramer
Staff: 750

Bus

Passenger journeys: (1993) 56.6 million
(1994) 57 million
(1995) 54.9 million
Vehicle-km: (1993) 12.8 million
(1994) 11.5 million
(1995) 10.6 million

Number of routes: 23
Route length: (One way) 534 km
On priority right-of-way: 13.5 km
Fleet: 200 vehicles, plus 28 hired

Mercedes O405 (1986/89)	83
Mercedes O405G articulated (1988/92)	44
Mercedes O405N low-floor (1990/94)	49
MAN NL202 low-floor (1993)	23
Others	1

In peak service: 194

Most intensive service: 5 min
One-person operation: All routes
Fare structure: As RMV
Fares collected onboard: 13.9%
Operational control: Route inspectors/mobile radio. Computer-based bus control system RBL with infra-red beacons along routes activated by onboard equipment; activation of traffic signals for bus priority
Arrangements for elderly/disabled: Disabled travel free, partly funded by government; new buses have wheelchair ramp at centre door
Integration with other modes: Cross-river routes to Mainz operated jointly with Stadtwerke Mainz. Transfer facilities between Wiesbaden and Mainz networks. Season tickets for DB trains and buses or on buses of three other operators also valid on ESWE network with subsidy from state government and local authorities
Average peak-hour speed: 20.7 km/h
Operating costs financed by: Fares 41.6%, other commercial sources 27.5%, subsidy/grants 30.9%
Subsidy from: In part by cross-subsidy from other municipal enterprises which are part of the company (electricity, gas, water etc) and in part from city and state

HEAG

HEAG Verkehrs-GmbH
Jägertorstrasse 207, 64289 Darmstadt
Telephone: +49 6151 7090 Fax: +49 6151 709 4105
Directors: Horst Blechschmidt
Siegfried Bittner
Staff: 495

Passenger journeys: (1995) 29.9 million

Current situation: Municipally owned company provides bus and tramway services in Darmstadt and the surrounding area.

Bus
Vehicle-km: (1995) 4.9 million

Route length: 227 km
Fleet: 65 buses, plus 22 on hire

Tramway
Car-km: 4.3 million

Route length: 36.2 km
Rolling stock: 73 cars M43 T30

UPDATED

FUKUOKA
Population: 1.3 million
Public transport: Bus services provided by private company also operating two separate commuter railways. Metro operated by municipal undertaking; suburban rail services provided by Japan Railways (JR); ferry services across Hakata Bay

Nishi Nippon Tetsudo 'Nishitetsu'
Nishi Nippon Railway
1-11-17 Tenjin, Chuo-ku, Fukuoka-shi 810, Japan
Telephone: +81 92 761 6631 Fax: +81 92 722 1405
President: G Kimoto

Current situation: Operates the local bus network, a 75 km interurban/commuter railway and a separate 21 km suburban railway. A 5 km tramway is operated in Kitakyushu.

Nishi Nippon is the largest bus operator in Japan. Bus operations generate about 55 per cent of income and include urban networks in Fukuoka, Kitakyushu, Kurume and Omuta as well as rural, interurban, express and sightseeing services. Of note is the network of frequent motorway express services linking Fukuoka, Fukuoka airport, Kitakyushu and other towns in northern Kyushu.

Associated companies include Nishi Nippon Shatai, bus body manufacturers, and Fukuoka Nishitetsu Taxi Company.

Bus
(Fukuoka operations)
Passenger journeys: Approx 150 million (annual)

Number of routes: 122 including 7 express routes and an airport service
Fleet: Total 3,020 buses and 472 coaches. Approx 1,000 buses committed to Fukuoka local operations; types include Nishi Nippon Shatai-bodied Nissan Diesel, Hino, Isuzu and Mitsubishi

Fare structure: Flat fare zone covering central and inner Fukuoka with stage fares beyond. Some routes entirely flat fare. Prepurchase coupon tickets, season tickets, one-day city bus tickets (valid in flat fare zone)
Fare collection: Payment to farebox by driver on alighting, or prepurchase
One-person operation: All routes

Suburban railway
Staff: 916 (including tramway)

Type of operation: Suburban/interurban railway

Passenger journeys: (Whole network, including Kitakyushu tramway)
(1990/91) 156 million
(1991/92) 159 million
(1992/93) 155 million
Car-km: (1992/93) 11 million (including Kitakyushu tramway)

Rolling stock: 355 emu cars

1,435 mm gauge	M201 T119
1,067 mm gauge	M23 T12

Series 1000 metro train ***1996***

Current situation: Nishi Nippon operates a 116 km rail network including the 75 km Fukuoka—Omuta main line with branches, 1,435 mm gauge, electrified 1.5 kV DC, and the 21 km 1,067 mm gauge Miyajidake line from Kaizuka in the eastern suburbs of Fukuoka to Tsuyazaki. Interchange with metro Line 2 at Kaizuka.

Fukuoka-shi Kotsu Kyoku
Fukuoka Municipal Transportation Bureau
2-5-31 Daimyo, Chuo-ku, Fukuoka 810
Superintendent, Transportation: Masato Watanabe
Telephone: +81 92 714 3211 Fax: +81 92 721 0754

Metro
Type of operation: Full metro, initial route opened 1981

Passenger journeys: (1990) 249,000 daily
(1992) 96 million
(1994) 111 million

Route length: 17.8 km (trains also operate over 44.8 km of JR tracks)
in tunnel: 16.7 km
Number of lines: 2
Number of stations: 19 (trains also serve 16 JR Chikuhi line stations)
Gauge: 1,067 mm
Electrification: 1.5 kV DC, overhead

Service: Peak 3-6 min, mid-day 4-8 min; Line 1 trains operate through to JR Chikuhi line destinations every 15-30 min
First/last train: 05.30/23.50
Fare structure: 4-section distance-related scale; monthly passes; prepaid 'F-Card' introduced 1995
Fare collection: Full AFC
Arrangements for elderly/disabled: Free travel for over 70s and severely disabled
One-person operation: All trains
Signalling: Full ATO, ATC
Operating costs financed by: Fares 38.8%, other commercial sources 3.2%, subsidy/grants 30.6%

Rolling stock: 132 cars formed into six-car sets
Kinki Sharyo, Toshiba, Hitachi and Mitsubishi

Series 1000	M72 T36
Series 2000	M16 T8

On order: One six-car set

Current situation: Line 1 connects with JR Chikuhi line at Meinohama and a through service is operated between Fukuoka-kuko and Nishi-karatsu (57.9 km) using metro and JR rolling stock. Interchange between Line 2 and Nishitetsu Miyajidake line at Kaizuka.
Developments: A 3.3 km two-station extension of Line 1 from Hakata to Fukuoka-kuko (airport) opened in 1993. Proposed Line 3 between Tenjin in central Fukuoka and Hashimoto in the western suburbs (12.7 km, 16 stations) is due to open in 2006.

The 1,435 mm gauge small-profile line will be operated by six-car linear-motor powered trains. An extension from Tenjin to Hakada Waterfront and a branch from Watanabe-dori to Hakata JR station, totalling 4 km, are also planned but not yet authorised for construction.

Fukuoka City Ferries
Fukuoka City Ferries
13-6, Chikko-honmachi, Hakata-ku, Fukuoka
Telephone: +81 92 291 1085

Mitsubishi Fuso of Nishitetsu at Hakata bus terminal on Fukuoka city service

Current situation: Fukuoka municipality operates passenger ferry services across Hakata Bay.

JR Kyushu

Kyushu Railway Company
Kyushu Ryokaku Tetsudo
1-1 Chuogai, Hakata Eki, Hakata-ku, Fukuoka 812
Telephone: +81 92 474 2501 Fax: +81 92 473 4805
Chair: T Yamashita
President: Y Ishii

Type of operation: Suburban/interurban heavy rail

Passenger journeys: (Fukuoka city only) (1990/91) 51.4 million

Current situation: JR Kyushu operates frequent 'Town Shuttle' between Fukuoka, Kokura and Moji with some trains running through from Kurume, Omuta and Kumamoto. Diesel services run to Nogata (41 km), with some trains continuing to Kurosaki in Kitakyushu. Also diesel railcar service on the 25 km Kashii line in Fukuoka's eastern suburbs. A fleet of six-car Series 103 emus operates the through service between the Chikuhi line and Line 1 of the metro.
Developments: Work has started on upgrading 11.1 km of the Chikuhi line from single to double track, including elevation of a 1.8 km section, to provide greater capacity for growing commuter traffic from new dormitory suburbs to the west of the city. JR Kyushu, Fukuoka city and central government are all contributing towards the cost of the project, which is due for completion in 1999.

JR West

West Japan Railway Company
Nishi Nihon Ryokaku Tetsudo
4-24, Shibata 2-chome, Kita-ku, Osaka 530
Telephone: +81 6 375 8981 Fax: +81 6 375 8919
Chair: T Tsunoda
President: M Ide

Type of operation: Suburban/interurban heavy rail

Passenger journeys: (1994/95) 1.6 million

Current situation: JR West operates a unique local passenger service using shinkansen trains running on the 8.5 km 1,435 mm gauge line between the Sanyo shinkansen terminus at Hakata and the shinkansen depot at Hakata Minami; runs about hourly with no intermediate stops.

UPDATED

FUSHUN

Population: 1.2 million, municipal area 2.1 million
Public transport: Two distinct public transport systems: extensive network of municipal bus services and frequent electric train service on the tracks of the Fushun Mining Administration; developing paratransit services

Fushun City Bus

Fushun City Bus Company
Fushun, Liaoning Province, People's Republic of China

Current situation: No recent report has been received but it is assumed that the extent of the bus system remains largely unchanged. Paratransit almost certainly exists in Fushun as in other Chinese cities, but it is not known whether operations are in the hands of Fushun City Bus or other agencies.

Commuter train on the Mining Administration Railway

Bus

Number of routes: Approx 30
Fleet: Approx 400 buses, including many articulated supplied by Shenyang and other factories in northeast China
Fare collection: Payment to seated conductors, monthly passes

Fushun Mining Administration Railway

Type of operation: Conventional heavy rail

Current situation: Operates a public passenger service on 2 routes (25 stations) over more than 30 km of its 600 km of standard-gauge railway. This operation is the only true urban/suburban electric railway using multiple-unit rolling stock in China, apart from the metros at Beijing, Shanghai and Tianjin. Electrified 1.5 kV DC overhead, with trains every 20-60 min.

Rolling stock: Approx 20 trains comprising 5 to 7 cars, including some articulated. Trains are mostly emu sets, but there are a few sets of coaches hauled by industrial-type electric locomotives.

GDANSK

Population: Gdansk 480,000, Sopot 50,000
Public transport: Bus, tramway and seasonal ferry services provided by local authority agency; suburban rail services

PKM

Przedsiebiorstwo Komunikacji Miejskie
ul Jaskowa Dolina 48, 80952 Gdansk-Wrzeszcz, Poland
Telephone: +48 58 410021
Director: Seweryn Gorski
Staff: 3,200

Passenger journeys: (All modes) (1989) 280 million

Operating costs financed by: Fares 25%, subsidy/grants 75%
Subsidy from: Local budget

Current situation: The former public transport operator WPK which served the three cities of Gdansk, Gdynia and Sopot was split into three undertakings in 1989, PKM becoming responsible for operations in Gdansk and Sopot.

Bus

Passenger journeys: (1989) 150 million
Vehicle-km: (1989) 15.3 million

Number of routes: 53
Route length: (One way) 618 km
Fleet: 322 vehicles

Ikarus 280 articulated	172
Ikarus 260	59
Jelcz M11	74
Jelcz PR110	2
Mercedes O405N low-floor	15

105N tramcar on PKM's Route 15

Most intensive service: 10 min
Fare collection: Prepurchase tickets with validation/cancellation machines on board
Fare structure: Flat

Tramway
Type of operation: Conventional tramway

Passenger journeys: (1989) 130 million
Vehicle-km: (1989) 12.5 million

Number of lines: 8
Route length: 50 km
Number of stops: 368

Rolling stock: 265 cars

Chorzów 105N	M114
Chorzów 105NA	M151

PKP
Polish State Railways (PKP)
ul Chalubinskiego 4, 00928 Warszawa
Telephone: +48 22 620 4512 Fax: +48 22 621 2705

Type of operation: Suburban heavy rail

Passenger journeys: 120 million (annual)

Current situation: At least five trains per hour run in the electrified Gdansk—Gdynia urban corridor (27 km), some extended to Wejherowo (44 km). Also Gdansk to Tczew (32 km) about hourly, Gdansk to Gdansk Nowy Port two or three trains per hour, and from Gdynia southwards to Koscierzyna every 2 h.

PKP suburban train on the Gdansk—Gdynia route

GENÈVE
Population: 399,000
Public transport: Bus, trolleybus and tramway services operated by municipal authority. Swiss Federal Railways services on local lines; also French National Railways local route to Genève Eaux-Vives. Lake steamers providing mostly tourist services

TPG
Transports Publics Genevois (TPG)
Route de la Chapelle 1, PO Box 950, 1212 Grand-Lancy 1, Switzerland
Telephone: +41 22 308 3311 Fax: +41 22 308 3400
President: Jean-Pierre Etter
General Manager: Christoph Stucki
Staff: 1,286

Passenger boardings: (All modes)
(1993) 102.9 million
(1994) 101.3 million
(1995) 101.2 million

Operating costs financed by: (All modes)
Fares 39%, other commercial sources 8%, subsidy/grants 53%
Subsidy from: Canton, plus 2% from government for country routes

Current situation: The authority has been successful in raising patronage despite high car ownership. An increase in the number of articulated vehicles has helped cope with peak capacity problems. Several tramway/light rail extensions have been considered, including a route to Annemasse in France, and an automated light metro is proposed.

Bus and trolleybus
Passenger boardings: (1993) Bus 55.1 million, trolleybus 30.1 million
(1994) Bus 54.2 million, trolleybus 29.8 million
(1995) Bus 51.1 million, trolleybus 30 million

Vehicle-km: (1993) Bus 10.1 million, trolleybus 3.3 million
(1994) Bus 10 million, trolleybus 3.3 million
(1995) Bus 9.8 million, trolleybus 3.3 million

Number of routes: Bus 42, trolleybus 4
Route length: Bus 299 km, trolleybus 29 km
Fleet: 221 buses

Standard	56
FBW articulated	31
Volvo B10M articulated	25
Mercedes O405	40
Mercedes O405G articulated	48
Mercedes O405GN articulated	21

Fleet: 73 trolleybuses

Saurer/Hess/BBC-Sécheron articulated (1982/83)	24
FBW	16
NAW/Hess/BBC-SE (1988)	20
NAW/Hess/Siemens	13

Trolleybus electrification: 600 V DC

In peak service: 190 buses, 56 trolleybuses

Most intensive service: 5 min
One-person operation: All routes
Fare collection: Self-service, from machines at stops; no fares payable on board
Fare structure: Flat for 1 h transfer tickets and 3-stop only tickets; multitickets of both types; monthly and annual passes, monthly passes also valid on all public transport in Canton of Genève; passes to be introduced to include journeys on SNCF route (see below)
Fares collected on board: None
Fare evasion control: Roving inspectors
Average distance between stops: 300 m
Average peak-hour speed: In mixed traffic, 15-20 km/h

Tramway
Type of operation: Conventional tramway

Buses, trams and trolleybuses of TPG at Cornavin station

Passenger boardings: (1993) 17.7 million
(1994) 17.3 million
(1995) 20.1 million
Car-km: (1993) 2.1 million
(1994) 2.1 million
(1995) 2.2 million

Route length: 9.6 km
Number of lines: 3
Number of stops: 57
Gauge: 1,000 mm
Electrification: 600 V DC, overhead

Service: Peak 5 min, off-peak 10 min
First/last car: 05.30/00.30
Fare structure: As bus
One-person operation: All trams

Rolling stock: 46 cars
Vevey/Duewag B4/6 M46
In peak service: 40

Developments: New tram Route 16 linking Moillesulaz and Cornavin SBB station was partially opened in September 1996 and will be completed in late 1997. Extension of the existing Line 13 from Bachet de Pesay to a new park-and-ride terminal at Les Palettes (2.8 km, 3 stops) under construction for June 1997 opening.

Futher construction is proposed to serve two other major park-and-ride sites, in the north at Sécheron (Place des Nations) and at Etoile in the south, for opening by 2005.

Light metro (proposed)

Current situation: The 8.5 km tram line originally proposed to serve the airport and Meyrin is now planned as a light metro eventually linking the two areas of France that surround the city. Running from Meyrin to the airport and Cornavin SBB station, the line would then continue to Annemasse (16 km, 30 stations). Phase I, between Annemasse and central Genève, could open in 1999, with the remainder in 2004.

In 1995 the willingness of the French authorities to collaborate with the city of Genève was established; operation of the metro will be in the hands of a mixed-economy company with minority French participation. Still to be decided are the method of financing the project and new customs formalities to ease border crossings.

SBB-CFF

Swiss Federal Railways, Lausanne Division
PO Box 345, 1001 Lausanne
Telephone: +41 21 342 2201 Fax: +41 21 342 2797
Divisional Manager: Philippe Gauderon

Type of operation: Suburban heavy rail

Current situation: Local trains run hourly (half-hourly at peak times) to La Plaine, Nyon and Lausanne, frequently to Genève airport.

Developments: In the first stage of a reorganisation of the city's transport, in 1994 a half-hourly service of LRVs was introduced on the La Plaine line. Feeder buses replaced through services from the suburbs to the city centre. A fleet of five LRVs based on the TSOL Lausanne design was supplied by Vevey/ABB.

This line and the route to Nyon have been branded as Rhône Express Régional (RER).

TPG's local circulator Route W meets RER railcar at Satigny on the La Plaine line ***1997***

SNCF

French National Railways

Type of operation: Local railway

Current situation: The electrified line from Annemasse extends across the Swiss border to serve Genève at Eaux-Vives in the southeast of the city. Trains run about hourly.

MG

Mouettes Genevoises
8 quai de Mont Blanc, Genève
Telephone: +41 22 332 2944

Current situation: Operates two regular ferry routes across Lac Leman, plus leisure services. Multijourney tickets available, fares integrated with TPG.

CGN

Compagnie Générale de Navigation sur le Lac Léman
PO Box 116, 1000 Lausanne 6
Tel: +41 21 617 0666 Fax: +41 21 617 0465

Current situation: Operates steamers and motor boats on Lac Leman, linking 41 ports on the Swiss and French shores (see Lausanne entry).

UPDATED

GENOVA

Population: 654,000
Public transport: Urban and suburban bus networks operated by municipal undertaking also responsible for regional services, 9 elevators, 2 funiculars and 1 rack railway, and a light rail route

AMT

Azienda Mobilita e Trasporti
Via L Montaldo 2, CP 1756, 16137 Genova, Italy
Telephone: +39 10 59971 Fax: +39 10 599 7400
President: Aldo Cavagnetto
Chief Officer: Dott Ing Domenico Mastropasqua
Staff: 3,266

Current situation: Distinct urban and suburban/regional route networks are operated, the latter in conjunction with other local undertakings. There are 60 suburban routes served by 145 buses; they carried 3.2 million passengers in 1995.

Initial section of light rail opened 1990. Construction of a 17 km three-route trolleybus network started 1994, and a fleet of 20 vehicles is being supplied by Breda/Ansaldo. Operation of the 7 km route between S Benigros and Foce will start during 1997.

City-centre circular route 'CompraBus' serving mainly pedestrian streets runs weekdays 09.30-13.00 and 16.30-20.00.

Developments: 1996 brought a change of name and legal status for AMT, which now has greater autonomy and more responsibility for its financial performance. AMT now has a contract with the Comune (city council) for provision of service.

There was a drop of 6.5 per cent in ridership during 1996, brought about by changes in the regulations governing issue and use of social passes. A new airport route, the Volabus (10.2 km), was introduced in 1996, as was a 29 km city circular route.

A bus-only reservation will open on the Corso Europa in 1997. Also in 1997 an experimental vehicle location system comes into operation; 400 buses are to be equipped within three years.

Metro
Funiculars
Proposed
Rivarolo
V.Brin
Granarolo
Righi
to Gavette
Marassi
Principe
S Anna
Darsena
Corvetto
Dinegro
Montano
De Ferrari
Brignole
S.Giorgio
Sarzano
Foce
to Sturla

Genova light rail

Bus (urban operations only)
Passenger journeys: (1994) 181.2 million
(1995) 169.4 million
Vehicle-km: (1994) 30 million
(1995) 32.1 million

Route length: 780 km

Dual-mode Altrobus at Piazza Fontane Maose ***1995***

Number of routes: 121
Fleet: 826 vehicles

Fiat 418 (1972/82)	207
Fiat 421 (1975)	68
Fiat 470 (1979/84)	75
Fiat 409 (1973/75)	29
Fiat 3471 (1985/88)	40
Fiat 471 (1985/88)	50
Menarini 201 (1984/88)	43
Inbus 150 (1991/92)	26
Inbus U210 (1984/88)	55
Others	233

In peak service: 643
Average age of fleet: 13.6 years
On order: 16 low-floor articulated, 32 low-floor standard, 13 low-floor midi and 35 partial low-floor standard

Most intensive service: 3-10 min
One-person operation: All routes
Fare collection: Automatic issuing machines or roadside points of sale
Fare structure: 90 min period tickets, passes; suburban, zonal, passes
Fare evasion control: Inspectors
Fares collected on board: Urban less than 1%, suburban 18%
Average distance between stops: 250 m
Average peak-hour speed: 12.4 km/h
Operating costs financed by: Fares and other commercial sources 32.9%, subsidy/grants 67.7%
Subsidy from: City, region and province; balance as deficit

Elevators

Current situation: Nine public lifts are operated to serve areas built on steeply sloping hillsides.

Funiculars/rack railway

Current situation: Two funiculars (Righi — 1.4 km and Sant'Anna — 358 m) and a 1.1 km rack tramway from Principe to Granarolo are operated; two cars serve each route. In 1990, proposals to upgrade the rack line were accepted by the municipality, but lack of funds prevented their implementation. Now the work is to be undertaken in a four-year programme.

Light rail

Type of operation: Light rail, opened 1990

Passenger journeys: (1991) 3.5 million
(1993) 3.4 million
(1994) 5.2 million
(1995) 2.9 million (partial closure)

Route length: 2.9 km
Number of routes: 1
Number of stations: 3
Gauge: 1,435 mm
Electrification: 750 V DC, overhead

Service interval: 10 min
First/last car: 06.30/21.12

Rolling stock: 6 cars
Ansaldo (1989) M6
On order: 12 cars

Current situation: Initial section between Brin and Principe in operation of light rail line under construction utilising an existing tunnel and right-of-way of former tramway system. Extension from Dinegro to Principe opened 1992 and further section to San Giorgio under construction. Funding is now available for construction of a further 3.5 km with five stations.

Further extension from Brignole to Gavette proposed, possibly with on-street running.

FS

Italian Railways (FS), Genova Division

Type of operation: Suburban heavy rail

Current situation: Services run on several cross-city routes with major flows concentrated on the coastal route from Voltri in the west to Nervi/Borgio F in the east, where train frequency is often 10 min. Less busy routes to Acqui terme and Ronco Scrivia have half-hourly service. There are 19 stations within the urban area.

In 1993, a new mostly underground alignment was introduced linking Sampierdarena in the east with Brignole in the west, making it possible to segregate suburban services on the congested central section between Porta Principe and Brignole, where trains run every 5 to 7 min. A new underground suburban station at Porta Principe links with buses and metro as well as FS long-distance trains. Brignole is a major bus interchange.

FS has standardised tariffs on regional services in Liguria, with the same fare charged on routes regardless of mode. An integrated timetable covers all operators, and unnecessary duplication of services eliminated. An hourly ticket gives free transfer to ATM bus and metro services for incoming commuters. In addition, there are new monthly passes valid on both trains and buses throughout the region.

FGC

Ferrovie Genova-Casella
Via Alla Stazione per Casella 15, 16122 Genova
Telephone: +39 10 839 3285 Fax: +39 10 839 1433
General Manager: G Bertoldi

Current situation: An hourly service is provided from Genova Piazza Manin to Casella (25 km, 19 stations). Operated mostly by second-hand emus, FGC has three rebuilt cars plus a further three two-car sets delivered in 1996. Two more two-car sets were on order from Adtranz in early 1997.

Rolling stock: 9 emu cars

UPDATED

LRV at Dinegro ***1995***

Operating costs financed by: Fares 78.6%, other commercial sources 2%, subsidy from PTA 19.4%

Rolling stock: 41 cars

Metro-Cammell (1979)	M33
Hunslet TPL (1992)	T8

in peak service: 36

Developments: Complete resignalling was commissioned in late 1996, involving a change from AC relay detection to fixed audio-frequency jointless track circuits, with depot interlocking converted from relay operation to vital processor. The new control centre combines signalling and traction control functions with communications, station functions and alarms, drainage pumping indications and train describers.

Dial-a-Bus

Telephone: +44 141 333 3252 Fax: +44 141 332 2595
Manager: J B Duncan

Current situation: Door-to-door wheelchair-accessible bus service provided throughout SPT's area, serving about 200,000 mobility impaired people; 7 operators provide 28 services using 36 vehicles; they carried 304,600 passengers in 1995/96.

Suburban rail

Operated by ScotRail Railways Ltd
Caledonian Chambers, 87 Union Street, Glasgow G1 3TA
Telephone: +44 141 332 9811 Fax: +44 141 335 4365

Type of operation: Suburban heavy rail

Passenger journeys: (1993/94) 37.6 million
(1994/95) 36.1 million
(1995/96) 36.9 million

Current situation: Electric and some diesel services operate on 14 routes on the north and south sides of the Clyde, and two cross-city lines — routes/services total 486 km, mostly electrified at 25 kV AC (346 km), with 177 stations.

Developments: In May 1996, a new hourly service was introduced between Cumbernauld and Motherwell, adding 3.7 km to the network. In October an improved service started between Kilmarnock, Ayr and Girvan, and Sunday trains were reintroduced on the East Kilbride line. Also, a new morning service was started from Garelochhead to Glasgow (52 km) at commuting time, a journey not previously possible by rail. The area of SPT's support has thus been extended to Girvan and Garelochhead.

Future plans include reopening of the Hamilton—Larkhall line and a reopened north-south cross-city route (the Tron line). The feasibility of a link to Glasgow airport is also being investigated.

Rolling stock: 104 three-car emus, 31 two-car dmus

UPDATED

GÖTEBORG

Population: 434,000

Public transport: Bus and tramway/light rail and ferry services to the southern archipelago and in the port managed by city planning authority Stadstrafiken Göteborg, for which the main contractor for bus and light rail service is Göteborgs Spårvägar, with bus services also contracted to a second operator Linjebuss Trafik AB, a private company, and one express route to Buss i Väst AB/Leja Touring. Styrsöbolaget is the ferry contractor. Regional buses of several operators, and commuter rail services (operated by Swedish State Railways) are managed by the regional authority Göteborgsregionens Lokaltrafik AB (GLAB)

Volvo CNG-powered low-floor bus at the refurbished Drottningtorget terminal ***1996***

Stadstrafiken

Stadstrafiken
PO Box 2403, 40316 Göteborg, Sweden
Telephone: +46 31 613700 Fax: +46 31 711 4513
General Manager: Magnus Arnström
Director of Development: Ragnar Domstad

Current situation: The public transport authority Stadstrafiken was formed at the beginning of 1991, when a new organisation for transport planning came into force. It is a department of the traffic and transit authority Trafikkontoret, another department of which is responsible for light rail infrastructure as well as roads.

Stadstrafiken is responsible for network planning, service standards, finance and fares policy, and acts as purchaser of service in the new competitive situation. The former public authority Göteborgs Spårvägar (GS) became a city-owned shareholding company in 1989 and is the main operator.

Developments: Starting in 1993 competition is allowed in public transport, and five groups of bus routes in the western part of the city — 30 per cent of the network, amounting to 4.3 million vehicle-km — were put out to tender in 1992. GS won some 55 per cent of the vehicle-km and private operator Linjebuss Trafik the remainder. Tendering produced much lower prices for identical service levels, while bringing newer buses with higher comfort standards and better emission values. Contracts are for 4½ years from January 1993. Subsequently, a few individual routes have been contracted out; the remainder are being put out to tender during 1996/98.

GS has contracts for the remaining bus services at a market price, and tram/light rail are now operated by GS at a lower price than before.

GS operates 24 natural-gas-powered buses, five of them low-floor. Favourable parking fees are granted for electric cars, and an environmental zone was introduced in the city centre in July 1996 where only low-emission vehicles will be permitted. Because their emission standards are already tough, city buses will have no problem in accessing the environmental zone.

A major revision to the tramway network was implemented in 1993, in part to take account of declining population in areas served by the trams. A new route was added, others changed and some service intervals increased, designed to reduce operating costs without reducing service standards as a whole. Further adjustments were made in 1994. Due to growth in demand, some express tram services have been introduced from the boat terminal at Saltholmen to the main hospital at Sahlgrenska, and a new line opened from the southern suburbs to Eketrägatan.

In the year to February 1997, a demand-response service for elderly and disabled people was tested in part of northern Göteborg. Called Flexline, it is a mix of regular and special transport provision.

Passenger journeys: (Bus and tram/light rail)
(1993) 80 million
(1994) 85 million
(1995)

Fare structure: Within the city, there is a flat fare, but the fare system is integrated with the regional fare structure valid in Göteborg and the 12 other municipalities administered by GLAB; magnetic tickets and monthly passes

Fare collection: Validators for magnetic ticket; tickets and monthly passes (valid 30 days from validation) are both magnetic; drivers sell tickets for single journeys, and magnetic tickets; prepurchase at reduced rate; stored-value cards cheaper if bought at kiosks

Fares collected on board: Less than 20%

Fare evasion control: Roving inspectors; spot penalty

Operating costs financed by: Fares 56%, city council subsidy 44%

Arrangements for elderly/disabled: Responsibility of a separate organisation; fare structure decided by Trafikkontoret. A fleet of 80 vehicles is run by 28 operators, along with 275 contract taxis. They carried 6,500-7,000 passengers a day in 1994 from an entitled group of 27,000; a computer-based system Planet is used to arrange ride-sharing. A special 'Service Line' with low-floor buses operates on a regular route in areas where many senior citizens live, connecting with day centres and main hospitals. This route is operated by GS as part of the regular bus system and regular passes are valid.

Most intensive service: 10 min

Bus priority: Traffic management system for central Göteborg divides the area into five sections to which access for private traffic is only possible for internal movement, thereby preventing through traffic, though buses and trams can move freely

GS

Göteborgs Spårvägar AB (GS)
PO Box 424, 40126 Göteborg
Telephone: +46 31 809000 Fax: +46 31 159011
General Manager: Thomas Torkelsson
Staff: 1,840 (including part-time)

Current situation: Following its 1989 conversion into a shareholding company, GS was given three years to prepare for competition. It underwent rationalisation and staff cuts, and was able to reduce its operating costs substantially. In the first round of competitive tendering, GS won over half of the vehicle-km on offer, with the price for operating west Göteborg bus services coming in at only 55 per cent of the 1989 figure. GS is the main contractor to Stadstrafiken and also operates a regional bus line for GL.

Bus

Number of routes: 70
Route length: 1,060 km
Fleet: 171 buses

Scania CN112 (1985/87)	29
Scania CN113	24
Volvo B10M 55	65
Volvo B10M optimised natural gas (1993)	19
Ontario II (1989)	6
Volvo B10BLE optimised natural gas (1994)	5
Volvo B10MA (1993)	18
Volvo B10M60 (1982/83)	5

In peak service: 156

Light rail/tramway

Type of operation: Light rail/tramway

Car-km: (1992) 13.7 million
(1993) 13.1 million
(1994) 12.9 million

Route length: 117.6 km
reserved track: 90%
Number of lines: 9, plus one peak-hours only
Gauge: 1,435 mm
Max gradient: 6%
Minimum curve radius: 17 m
Electrification: 750 V DC, overhead
Service: Peak 10 min, off-peak 12-20 min

Rolling stock: 205 cars

Hägglunds M29 (1969/72)	M58
ASEA/ASJ M28 (1965/67)	M67
ASEA/ABB M21 articulated (1984/91)	M80

Styrsöbolaget's new ferry *1996*

Styrsöbolaget

Styrsöbolaget
PO Box 5085, 42605 Västra Frölunda
Telephone: +46 31 696400 Fax: +46 31 694285
General Manager: Ove Boström
Operations Manager: Gunner Söderberg
Staff: 51

Ferry

Passenger journeys: (1991) 2.1 million
(1994) 2.5 million
(1995) 2.7 million

Current situation: Ferry services across the River Göta between Lindholmen and Rosenlund and from Saltholmen to the southern archipelago operated under contract to Stadstrafiken by the city-owned shareholding company Styrsöbolaget with nine vessels; four routes total 43 km. All ferries are integrated into the fares system, and there is no transfer fee. Fares cover 33 per cent of operating costs

Developments: Demand for ferry service has increased over the past few years, due to opening of a new college at Lindholmen and housing development on the northern bank of the Göta.

Linjebuss

Linjebuss Sverige AB
Toltorpsgatan 137, 43141 Mölndal
Telephone: +46 31 870190 Fax: +46 31 270483
Manager: Jonas Rydberg

Current situation: In 1993 this private operator took over eight routes totalling 94 km in the western part of the city. Also operates 18 minibuses on services for disabled people.

Bus

Vehicle-km: (1996) 2.1 million

Fleet: 29 buses

Scania N113 (1993)	13
Volvo B10B (1993)	7
Volvo B10M (1993/94/95)	7
Scania C113 (1990)	2

SJ

Swedish State Railways (SJ)
PO Box 1522, 40158 Göteborg
Telephone: +46 31 104100 Fax: +46 31 104103
Area Manager: L-A Antonsson

Type of operation: Suburban heavy rail

Current situation: Services operated on several routes under contract, electrified 15 kV 16⅔ Hz.

UPDATED

GRAZ

Population: 238,000
Public transport: Bus, tramway and funicular services operated by municipal undertaking, part of public utility trading company responsible also for gas, electricity and water services

Grazer Stadtwerke

Grazer Stadtwerke AG, Verkehrsbetriebe
Steyrergasse 114, 8010 Graz, Austria
Telephone: +43 316 887 Fax: +43 316 887788
Chair: Dr Alfred Edler
Directors: Mag Heinzl
Dr Ott
Manager of Verkehrsbetriebe: Prok Dr Scholz
Staff: 700 (transport 402)

Passenger journeys: (All modes)
(1993) 86.8 million
(1994) 94.9 million
(1995) 98.1 million

Fare collection: Ticket purchase on buses, from shops or machines at main stations; validating equipment on board
Fare structure: Zonal, flat within zones; prepurchase 10-zone and zonal 24-h, weekly and monthly passes, annual tickets
Fares collected on board: 6.6%

Trams outside Graz Hbf *1995*

Operating costs financed by: Fares 90%, other commercial sources (cross-subsidy) 6%, subsidy 4%
Subsidy from: Government and city

Developments: In 1994 a total of 41 operators in the greater Graz area joined in formation of the Verkehrsverbund Grossraum Graz tariff region, extending a uniform zonal fare structure to a population of some 700,000. Finance comes from the national government (33.4%), the Province of Steiermark (42.4%) and the city of Graz (24.2%).

Bus

Staff: 241 (operating)

Passenger journeys: (1993) 34.4 million
(1994) 40.7 million
(1995) 42 million
Vehicle-km: (1993) 8.8 million
(1994) 8.8 million
(1995) 8.7 million

Number of routes: 30
Number of stops: 275
Route length: (One way) 179.9 km
On priority right-of-way: 9.5 km
Fleet: 127 vehicles

MAN, Steyr, Büssing standard	65
Neoplan standard	20
MAN/Gräf & Stift/Neoplan articulated	38
Steyr Citybus	4

In peak service: 107

Most intensive service: 6 min
One-person operation: All routes
Fare evasion control: Inspectors
Operational control: Route inspectors/mobile radio with computerised online monitoring
Arrangements for elderly/disabled: Reduced rate

monthly and annual passes for unrestricted travel on weekdays after 08.15 and at weekends
Average distance between stops: 347 m
Average peak-hour speed: 20.1 km/h

Tramway
Staff: 161

Type of operation: Conventional tramway

Passenger journeys: (1993) 51.1 million
(1994) 54.2 million
(1995) 56.1 million
Car-km: (1993) 8.3 million
(1994) 8.5 million
(1995) 8.5 million

Route length: 48.9 km
Number of lines: 7
Number of stops: 76
Gauge: 1,435 mm
Track: 66 kg/m Ri60 rail on concrete

Electrification: 600 V DC, overhead

Service: Peak 5 min, off-peak 15 min
First/last car: 04.30/00.30
One-person operation: All cars
Average distance between stops: 357 m
Average peak-hour speed: 15.3 km/h

Rolling stock: 67 cars

Duewag 550 (1958)	M5
SGP 260 (1963)	M18
Lohner Wien 260 (1963)	M5
Duewag 520 (1971)	M17
SGP 500 (1978)	M10
SGP 600 (1986)	M12

In peak service: 56
On order: 10 low-floor cars

Developments: Line 6 extension of 1.9 km planned at St-Peter in the southeast of the city for 1998 opening, also other proposals. New workshops under development. Major reconstruction of the city-centre junction at Jakominiplatz completed late 1996.

Funicular
Current situation: The Schlossbergbahn Funicular, which was 100 years old in 1994, carries 0.4 million passengers annually.

Light rail (proposed)
Current situation: A regional light rail network has been proposed for the greater Graz area, sharing existing OBB and local railway alignments.

UPDATED

Neoplan N4014 low-floor bus

GRENOBLE
Population: City 150,000, area served 370,000
Public transport: Bus and trolleybus services mostly provided under contract concession by company formed by 23 local authorities in city region with 10 per cent provided by arrangement by second company (VFD), owned by Département. Light rail network; limited local service provided by state railway

TAG
Société d'Economie Mixte des Transports de l'Agglomération Grenobloise (Semitag)
PO Box 258, 38044 Grenoble Cedex, France
Telephone: +33 4 76 20 66 11 Fax: +33 4 76 20 66 99
Chairman: M Descours
Director General: François-Xavier Perin
Staff: 830

Passenger journeys: (All modes)
(1993) 50.1 million
(1994) 50.1 million
(1995) 47.3 million

Current situation: Semitag (marketed as TAG) operates as a 'mixed economy' company responsible to the Syndicat Mixte des Transports en Commun (SMTC) representing 23 local authorities in the city region. The network is 94 per cent operated by Semitag directly, with the remainder provided under contract by VFD. Figures below include both operations.

The light rail network has been an unqualified success and now carries 110,000 passengers daily. It has become the model for many recent light rail projects worldwide. Two core routes have replaced the city's busiest bus routes, around which other bus lines have been replanned as feeders. Light rail now accounts for 45 per cent of all public transport trips. Many city-centre streets traversed by the trams have been pedestrianised, and several new car parks have been built at the fringes of the central area. Removal of street traffic has also permitted restoration of the historic city-centre area.

The poor 1995 results were mainly due to the effects of a strike in December.

Grenoble's low-floor tramcar

Bus and trolleybus
Passenger journeys: (1993) 27.5 million
(1994) 27.4 million
(1995) 26.1 million
Vehicle-km: (1993) 9.5 million
(1994) 9.9 million
(1995) 9.7 million

Number of routes: Bus 18 (of which 4 operated by VFD), trolleybus 2
Route length: (One way) bus 185 km, trolleybus 30 km
On priority right-of-way: 12 km
Fleet: 211 buses

Heuliez GX107	34
Berliet/Renault PR100	56
Renault R312	16
Heuliez 0305 articulated	11
Heuliez GX187 articulated	48
Renault PR180 articulated	12
Renault Master minibus	8
Gruau MG36 minibus	14
Breda minibus	6
Heuliez GX317	6

Average age of fleet: 8 years
Fleet: 33 trolleybuses

Renault ER100	33

Trolleybus electrification: 620 V DC
In peak service: 155 buses, 35 trolleybuses
On order: 22 Renault Agora low-floor articulated buses

Most intensive service: 2 min
One-person operation: All services
Fare collection: Prepurchase carnets or daily/weekly/monthly passes, or payment to driver; validation on board buses or at tram stops
Fare structure: Flat; single ticket gives free transfer within 1 h; carnets/passes
Fares collected on board: 19%

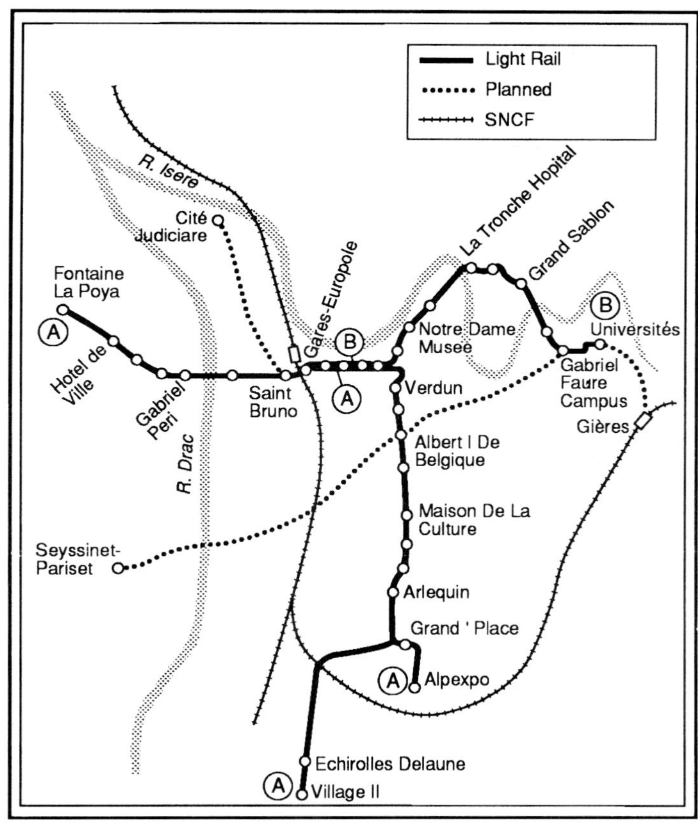

Grenoble light rail

Fare evasion control: Inspectors
Operational control: Route inspectors/mobile radio
Arrangements for elderly/disabled: 8 minibuses operate services for disabled; free or reduced-rate travel for over-60s and invalids
Average distance between stops: 300 m
Bus priority: On-vehicle traffic-light control by Philips VETAG; plus SAE central control and reporting system
Operating costs financed by: Fares 36.6%, other commercial sources 0.9%, subsidy/grants 62.5%, tax levy 1.75%
Subsidy from: Consortium of local authorities owning Semitag, and through 1.75% payroll tax on employers (versement transport)

New vehicles financed by: Versement transport

Developments: Fr200 million has been spent during the period 1992/97 to improve bus routes — new buses, creation of priority rights-of-way and modernisation of street furniture.

Accessibility is also being improved, with an experimental kneeling low-floor bus on trial since 1995.

Light rail
Type of operation: Light rail, initial route opened 1987

Passenger journeys: (1993) 22.6 million
(1994) 22.6 million
(1995) 21.2 million
Car-km: (1993) 1.6 million
(1994) 1.6 million
(1995) 1.6 million

Route length: 18 km
Number of lines: 2
Number of stops: 37
Gauge: 1,435 mm
Track: 55 kg/m Type 35G grooved rail on twin-block sleepers with elastic fastenings, resting on rubber pads and mounted in concrete slab
Electrification: 750 V DC, overhead

Service: Peak 2 min, off-peak 6-10 min
First/last car: 04.51/24.00
Fare structure: As bus
Integration with other modes: 3 major city-centre interchanges; bus routes replanned as feeders; park-and-ride at 3 stops; full access for wheelchairs

Rolling stock: 53 six-axle low-floor articulated cars
Alsthom-Francorail (1986/87) M20
Alsthom-Francorail (1989) M18
GEC Alsthom (1996) M15
In peak service: 36

Current situation: Line A was extended 3.4 km southwest from Grand' Place to Echirolles Delaune, opening in two sections in 1995 and March 1996. The 1996 extension was accompanied by commissioning of a further 15 cars, this time with asynchronous motors.

Line A is being further extended 0.5 km from Echirolles to Village II, a dense housing development, for late 1997 completion. Extension of Line B to Cité Judiciaire and Gières is under study.

In the longer term it is planned to refurbish the city's principal boulevards to incorporate an east-west Line C from Seyssinet-Pariset to Universités.

SNCF
French National Railways, Chambéry Region

Type of operation: Suburban heavy rail

Current situation: Limited service on routes to Lyon, Valence, Chambery and Veynes.

UPDATED

GUADALAJARA
Population: 4 million
Public transport: Trolleybus and some bus services operated by state authority. Light rail service; most bus services provided by independent operators who are mostly members of a co-operative

Sistecozome
Sistema de Transporte Colectivo de la Zona Metropolitana (Sistecozome)
Antiguo Central Camionera, Guadalajara, Mexico
Telephone: +52 3 619 0820 Fax: +52 3 650 0485
Director General: Javier Ramírez Acuña
Operating Manager:
Staff: 458

Current situation: Sistecozome is a public corporation formed in 1974. It also supervises a network of Colectivos on 41 routes. Sistecozome owns all vehicles and leases them to individual drivers. Originally intended as a trolleybus feeder service, the Colectivos now form a network in their own right, running into the central area in competition with buses. This is said to be the only profitable activity of Sistecozome. The fleet comprises 760 Volkswagen 9-seaters. Of the five trolleybus routes, one (Route 300) is out of service due to road construction work.

Trains at the Line 2 terminus at Juárez ***1996***

Developments: New trolleybus Route 600, which opened in February 1995, is one of two north-south routes almost completed in 1988 but then postponed because there was no finance available for sufficient vehicles to run these high-density routes. The new state administration that took office in 1989 had no interest in the project, but nearly all the infrastructure was left in place and the substations were maintained. Work on Route 600 resumed in October 1994 with the intention of opening before the city and state elections to be held on 12 February 1995, and thereby helping the incumbent party.

Infrastructure of the second route (700) remains largely intact, and nearly all the material to complete it is still in store, but there are no funds to finish the job or purchase vehicles. Furthermore, the metropolitan area has since grown beyond the planned termini, so further wiring would be necessary before the route could fulfil its proper role. There also remains the problem of restricting competition from the many private motor bus operators on the corridor.

The city's first articulated vehicles entered service in

Refurbished 1982 MASA trolleybus on new Route 600, Calzada Independencia ***1996***

late 1994, and all 18 were in service on opening of Route 600. Sistecozome's parallel bus Route 60 continues to operate.

Bus and trolleybus

Passenger journeys: 60 million (annual)
Vehicle-km: 10 million (annual) (320 km per vehicle per day)

Number of routes: Bus 8, trolleybus 5
Route length: 105 km
On priority right-of-way: 5 km
Fleet: Approx 145 trolleybuses

MASA-Toshiba (1982/85)	97
Marmon-Herrington (1951/52) in store	approx 30
MASA/Toshiba articulated (1985/87 ex-Mexico City)	18

Fleet: Approx 225 buses

Most intensive service: 5 min
Fare collection system: Payment to driver
Fare evasion control: Roving inspectors
Average distance between stops: 300 m
Average peak-hour speed: 18 km/h
Operating costs financed by: Fares 75%, other commercial sources 5%, subsidy/grants 20%
Subsidy from: Government
New vehicles financed by: State and federal governments

Siteur

Sistema de Tren Eléctrico Urbano (Siteur)
Calz del Federalisimo Sur 217, 44100 Guadalajara
Telephone: +52 3 613 1826 Fax: +52 3 613 4517
Director General: Juan Sánchez Aldana Ramírez
Director, Technical: Victor M Monraz Ponce
Director, Operations: Arturo Herrera Ramírez
Director, Rolling Stock & Engineering: José M Romo Perez
Director, Public Relations: Sandra Carballo Flores
Staff: 652

Light rail

Type of operation: Light rail, first line opened 1989

Passenger journeys: (1993) 21.7 million
(1994) 30.8 million
(1995) 34 million

Route length: 24 km
in tunnel: 15.1 km
Number of lines: 2
Number of stations: 29
Gauge: 1,435 mm
Track: 115RE 52 kg/m rail on concrete sleepers
Electrification: 750 V DC, overhead

Service: Peak 5 min, off-peak 10 min
First/last car: 06.00/23.00
Fare structure: Stage; transfer fee payable between Lines 1 and 2
Fare collection: Coin or token to turnstile
Integration with other modes: Bus feeders to each terminal
Operating costs financed by: Fares 100%

Rolling stock: 48 cars

Concarril/Melmex TLG88 (1989)	M16
Bombardier/Siemens TEG90 (1993/94)	M32

In peak service: 40 cars

Developments: Initial 8.5 km section of east-west Line 2 opened 1994, linking Benito Juarez and Tetlan. This line (including the proposed 4.3 km western extension to Minerva, if built) is entirely underground except for a large new maintenance depot just beyond Tetlán terminus. Three additional lines are planned for opening by 2010.

Private bus

Current situation: There are two major operators – Alianza, an owners' co-operative, and Servicios y Transport, a franchised private company with 99 per cent of shares now held by the state of Jalisco.

Alianza, formed in 1957, has 730 licence-holders who between them own 1,642 buses; the maximum number of buses that can be owned by any licence-holder is five. Operations are divided into seven sectors of 10-15 routes each. Alianza oversees operations with a small staff; all maintenance is contracted out. New vehicles are financed from a renewals fund supplied by 20 per cent of daily fares receipts.

Servicios y Transport runs a fleet of about 900 vehicles.

Passenger journeys: 500 million (annual)
Vehicle-km: 130 million (annual)

Number of routes: 140
Route length: 1,351 km

One-person operation: All routes
Fare collection: Payment to driver, or prepurchase
Fare structure: Flat, depending on route
Average speed: 15 km/h

UPDATED

Guadalajara light rail

GUANGZHOU

Population: 3.3 million, municipal area 8 million
Public transport: Bus, trolleybus and ferry services provided by municipal enterprises with two separate bus companies, a trolleybus company, ferry company, minibus and taxi company. Extensive minibus and taxi paratransit services. Metro under construction, light rail planned

Guangzhou Public Utilities

Guangzhou Public Utilities Bureau
Guangzhou, Guangdong Province, People's Republic of China
Director: Liang Zhu Ze
Staff: 30,000 (transport)

Current situation: The organisation is responsible for the planning and management of Guangzhou's public transport, water supply, gas and other public utilities.

Subsidiaries include the No 1, No 2 and No 3 Bus Companies, trolleybus company, passenger ship company, Guangzhou taxi company, Baiyun taxi and

Old two-axle trolleybus near the Zhongshan Lu terminus

minibus company and other enterprises. At last report some 1,100 million passengers were carried annually.

Manufacturing subsidiaries assemble and overhaul buses.

Guangzhou No 1 , No 2 and No 3 Bus Companies

Current situation: The distinction between the No 1 and No 2 Bus Companies is unclear, but the former is understood to operate predominantly city services, while the latter's services are more suburban in nature. No 3 Bus Company was created in 1995 by splitting No 1. A fourth company, Guangzhon Kwoon Chung, has been created in a joint venture between No 2 and Kwoon Chung Motors of Hong Kong. Ordinary and express services are operated throughout the city and suburbs, long-distance routes link the city with counties in Guangdong Province, and tourist services are also provided. Locally built buses are still powered by petrol engines, but diesel-engined vehicles have been obtained second-hand from Hong Kong, Singapore, Berlin and Pittsburgh.

Bus

Passenger journeys: (1986) City buses 790 million

Number of routes: 269 (42 ordinary city, 61 express city, 31 suburban and 135 long-distance)
Fleet: Approx 1,800 buses, including many articulated, most supplied by Guangzhou factory; some Daimler Fleetline, Dennis Dominator and Leyland Atlantean double-deck ex-Hong Kong and Singapore, including examples third-hand from London and Derby, plus some Chinese-built

Fare collection: Payment to seated conductors, monthly passes
Fare structure: City, flat; express, suburban and long-distance, stage

Guangzhou Trolleybus

Guangzhou Trolleybus Company

Current situation: The trolleybus plays a relatively minor role in Guangzhou's city transport. Lines are located in the central area, especially on principal east-west and north-south arteries.

Trolleybus

Passenger journeys: (1986) 96.2 million

Number of routes: 5
Route length: 45 km
Fleet: Over 100 trolleybuses, mainly Shanghai SK516G articulated (built in the 1980s) and Guangzhou GZ660 (1975-80); both rigid and articulated vehicles of new unidentified types have also been reported

Paratransit minibus plies for hire in central Guangzhou

Buses at Guangzhou's central bus station

Fare collection: Payment to seated conductors, monthly passes
Fare structure: Flat
Integration with other modes: Monthly pass valid on both bus and trolleybus

Guangzhou City Ferry

Guangzhou Passenger Ship Company

Current situation: The company is mainly responsible for ferry services across the Pearl River, but also serves tourist needs.

Passenger journeys: (1986) 107.9 million
Fleet: 58 vessels

Guangzhou City Taxi & Minibus

Baiyun Minibus & Taxi Company

Minibus

Current situation: Ten paratransit routes were introduced around 1983 with minibuses built in China, bought new from Japan and second-hand from Hong Kong. The operation is thought to have expanded substantially since.

Taxi

Current situation: A fleet of over 6,500 taxis carried 68.7 million passengers in 1986.

Metro

Under construction
Guangzhou Subway Company
204 Huan Shi Road, Guangzhou 510010
Telephone: +86 20 667 3276 Fax: +86 20 667 8232
Project Manager: Jin Feng
Deputy Chief Engineer: Ning Zi Rong

Current situation: The Guangzhou Subway Company was incorporated in 1992 to oversee construction of Line 1 of the city's metro, which began in early 1994 after a bidding process complicated by political difficulties. A German consortium headed by Siemens and AEG is providing the rolling stock, power supply equipment and other items, while Balfour Beatty Power Construction of the UK will provide the catenary.

Line 1 will be an 18.5 km east-west route from the East station of Chinese Railways to the Guangzhou Iron & Steel Works at Huang-sha, running mostly underground and with a crossing of the Pearl river between Huang-sha and Fang-cun. There will be 16 stations. Opening of the initial 5 km with five stations is now scheduled for late 1997, the remainder in the following year.

A contract for the 20 six-car trains, power supply equipment, signalling and telecommunications was awarded in 1994. Delivery of the rolling stock started in early 1997.

A second line was also included in the feasibility study completed in 1988, and build-operate-transfer bids for this were called in 1994. Line 2 will run 26 km roughly north-south from Xinshi, north of the main railway station, to the university, requiring a second crossing of the Pearl river. It will have 22 stations, an interchange with Line 1 at Hai Zhu Square, and a depot at the north end.

Line 3 will be a 5.2 km link between the university end of Line 2 and the eastern end of Line 1, where a new sports centre is planned. A 7.8 km extension would run along the river bank to Xinshou.

Light rail (proposed)

Current situation: Several schemes have been proposed for light rail feeders to the metro. In 1994 the agency which is funding the metro unveiled a plan for a 26 km line with 18 stations along the north bank of the Pearl river between the eastern end of metro Line 1 and a new development zone at Xiagang.

Previously the city was reported to be studying conversion of a 5 km underground air-raid shelter into a tram subway, which was estimated to require two years to complete.

A third scheme, originally promoted by the Foshan Communications Development Corp, would see construction of an 18 km line from Foshan to connect with the western end of metro Line 1 near the steelworks. It is thought that responsibility for this project has passed to the same agency which is promoting the waterfront line, which may have been given a higher priority.

HABANA

Population: 2 million
Public transport: Bus and minibus services operated by government authority with extensive shared taxi system; ferry and suburban railways

Empresa Omnibus Urbano Habana

Empresa Omnibus Urbano Habana
San José Belascuain, Habana, Cuba

Bus/Minibus

Passenger journeys: 100 million (annual)

Number of routes: 200
Route length: 2,410 km
Fleet: Some 3,000 vehicles including 400 Ikarus articulated; other types include Girón XII (used on suburban routes), Girón XIII (Ikarus 260), Girón XIV (Ikarus 255), Hino RC, Girón VI midibuses

Fare collection: Payment to driver
Fare structure: Flat
Average peak-hour speed: 18 km/h

Current situation: The majority of vehicles are Girón models, built by the local Habana factory assembling kits supplied by Ikarus, though the Ikarus 280 articulated buses appear to be supplied complete. About half the Ikarus fleet was reported out of use in 1992 due to shortage of spares, and in 1993 a fleet of 110 buses ex-Rotterdam was delivered under a barter deal to eliminate the Ikarus fleet entirely. Some vehicles second-hand from Spanish cities are also in service.

Buses on Habana urban services ***1996***

Huge 'Tren Bus' tractor-hauled vehicles came into service in the early 1990s, capable of carrying up to 350.

The long-distance interurban National bus fleet employs mostly Hino RC buses though a few MCW-bodied Leyland Olympics of 1963 vintage remain. Public institutions and collectives operate their own Girón V and Soviet-built PAZ 672/699 midibuses.

Developments: Fuel shortages due to the country's poor economic situation have put many routes out of action, while lack of spare parts has led to a big reduction in the number of Girón buses fit for service.

Shared taxis

Current situation: Shared taxi 'colectivo' services are operated with 1950s American sedans.

Ferry

Current situation: Two ferry services operate across Habana Bay providing links within the city between the main quayside and Casablanca and Regla. The standard city flat fare is charged. The Casablanca service provides a link into the main central business district from trains terminating at Casablanca station.

FdeIC

Cuban National Railways (FdelC)
Estación Central, Egido y Arsenal, Habana
Telephone: +53 7 621530 Fax: +53 7 338628

Type of operation: Suburban heavy rail

Current situation: Frequent services provided over 90 km Habana (Casablanca)—Matanzas line (the 'Hershey'), electrified 1.2 kV DC. Also diesel services from Tulipan station to San Antonio (35 km, six stations) and Central station to ExpoCuba (20 km, six stations), Los Palos (81 km, 15 stations, peak hours only), and other routes.

Modernisation of the electrification system and cars (both dating from the 1920s) of the Hershey interurban has long been planned. Track doubling Habana—Guanajay—Artemisa completed 1992. New service to Guanabo proposed.

Rolling stock: 15 electric cars, locomotive-hauled coaches

Brill (1928)	M15

Hershey Brill railcar at Casablanca

HAKODATE

Population: 350,000

Public transport: Bus and tramway services operated by municipal undertaking. Privately operated buses serve Hakodate and surrounding areas

Hakodate-shi Kotsu Kyoku

Hakodate City Transport Bureau
4-13 Shinome-cho, Hakodate-shi, Hokkaido 040, Japan
Telephone: +81 138 26 0131

Bus

Staff: 108

Passenger journeys: (1994) 10.1 million
Vehicle-km: (1994) 3.4 million

Number of routes: 31
Route length: 95 km
Fleet: 107 vehicles, including Hino and Mitsubishi
In peak service: 92

One-person operation: All routes
Fare collection: Farebox
Fare structure: Stage; prepurchase cards, 1- and 2-day tickets, 1- and 3-month seasons, 1- and 3-month off-peak discount seasons ('Shopper's Season Ticket'), all valid for bus and tram
Operational control: Bus location system

Alna Koki car 3001 on Hakodate Route 2 ***1996***

Tramway

Staff: 101

Type of operation: Conventional tramway

Passenger journeys: (1994) 8.3 million
Car-km: 1.1 million

Route length: 11 km
Number of routes: 2
Number of stops: 26
Gauge: 1,372 mm
Electrification: 600 V DC, overhead

Service: Peak 10 min, off-peak 10-20 min

First/last car: 06.30/22.00
Fare collection: Farebox
Fare structure: As bus
One-person operation: All cars

Rolling stock: 36 cars

Nippon Sharyo Type 500 (1948-50)	M4
Nippon Sharyo Type 1000 (ex-Tokyo, 1955)	M3
Niigata Type 710 (1959-61)	M10
Niigata Type 800 (1962-66)	M6
Niigata Type 8000 (1962, rebodied 1990-94)	M6
Alna Koki Type 2000 (1993/94)	M2
Alna Koki Type 3000 (1993/94/96)	M4
Historical car (1993)	M1

In peak service: 23 cars

Hakodate Bus

Hakodate Bus
10-1 Takamuri-cho, Hakodate-shi, Hokkaido 040
Telephone: +81 138 51 3960

Bus

Passenger journeys: (Annual) 16 million

Fleet: 204 buses, 13 coaches

Current situation: Hakodate Bus is a subsidiary of the Tokyu Corporation, which has extensive bus and rail interests in the Tokyo area.

UPDATED

HALIFAX

Population: 300,000
Public transport: Bus and ferry services provided by undertaking under control of municipal authority

Metro Transit

Transportation Services Division, Regional Operations
200 Ilsley Avenue, Dartmouth B3B 1V1, Canada
Telephone: +1 902 490 6614 Fax: +1 902 490 6688
Director: Brian T Smith
Manager, Transit Operations: Brian R Taylor
Manager, Traffic & Planning: Kenny Silver
Manager, Transit Maintenance: Paul A Beauchamp
Supervisor, Marketing & Public Relations: Lori Patterson
Staff: 425

Current situation: The former Metropolitan Transit Commission, established in 1981 to bring together separate Halifax and Dartmouth transit undertakings, was absorbed in 1986 by its parent body, the Metropolitan Authority. In April 1996, Metro Transit became part of the Halifax Regional Municipality under the amalgamation of four municipal units as a single regional authority. The bus and ferry service is now part of a larger Regional Operations Department, which also covers municipal engineering and public works.
Developments: Metro Transit is completing a C$2 million upgrade of its GoTime automatic vehicle location system. In June 1996, a private rural transport operation was absorbed, becoming a Community Transit service. In September, the 15-vehicle Access-A-Bus operation was also transferred from a private contractor to Metro Transit following a public tendering process.

Bus

Passenger journeys: (1992/93) 16.6 million
(1993/94) 16.2 million
(1994/95) 13 million
Vehicle-km: (1992/93) 9.1 million
(1993/94) 9.2 million
(1994/95) 8.8 million

Number of routes: 43
Route length: (One way) 645 km
Fleet: 175 vehicles

MCI Classic/Novabus (1993/94/95)	96
GM New Look	54
Articulated	14
Scania CN112 (1984)	7
Orion (1990)	4

In peak service: 143

Most intensive service: 7-8 min
Fare collection: Prepurchase or exact fare to farebox
Fare structure: Flat; prepurchase adult, senior and children's tickets; monthly passes
Fares collected on board: 66%

MCI 'Classic' articulated bus of Metro Transit

Dartmouth—Halifax ferry in Metro Transit livery ***1995***

Integration with other modes: Free transfer to ferry; routes serve carpool areas and 11 park-and-ride lots
Operational control: Route inspectors/mobile radio AVL
Arrangements for elderly/disabled: 15 lift-equipped vehicles known as Access-A-Bus, plus hired taxis; 3,200 registered users made 75,000 trips in 1994, with a further 33,000 transported by taxi; funded 35% by province, 65% by municipalities
Average peak-hour speed: 19.5 km/h
Operating costs financed by: Fares 66%, other commercial sources 2.6%, subsidy/grants 32.4%
New vehicles financed by: Province 50%, Halifax Regional Municipality 50%

Ferry

Current situation: Services between Dartmouth and Halifax are provided every 15 min on a route which is the oldest such salt water operation in North America.

UPDATED

HALLE

Population: 227,000, area served 352,000
Public transport: Tramway and bus services provided by municipal company. State railway runs regional metro (S-Bahn) and two regional bus companies provide suburban services

MDV

Mitteldeutscher Verkehrsverbund (MDV)

Current situation: This is the regional transit authority planned for the Halle/Leipzig region. For details see Leipzig entry.

HAVAG

Hallesche Verkehrs AG (HAVAG)
PO Box 200658, 06007 Halle, Germany
Telephone: +49 345 568550 Fax: +49 345 5685 440
Technical Director: Dr-Ing Werner Colditz
Commercial Director: François Girard
Technical & Maintenance Manager: Gerd Blumenau
Permanent Way Manager: Peter Thomas
Staff: 1,313

Passenger journeys: (1993) 69.8 million
(1994) 70.6 million
(1995) 68.3 million

Tatra three-car set in Halle city centre

Operating costs financed by: Fares 26.8%, other commercial sources 10.5%, subsidy/grants 62.7%
Subsidy from: Regional government 31%, local government 69%

Current situation: HAVAG provides tramway and feeder bus services in the Halle/Merseburg area, serving a total population of 352,000. Bus services in Halle-Neustadt were taken over from Omnibusbetrieb Saalekreis GmbH when the latter town was incorporated into Halle in 1991. A regional transit authority, Verkehrs- und Tarifgemeinschaft, co-ordinates the services of HAVAG, the S-Bahn and regional bus companies Omnibusbetrieb Saalekreis GmbH and Regiobus Merseburg GmbH.

Bus

Vehicle-km: (1993) 5.9 million
(1994) 6 million
(1995) 6.4 million

Number of routes: 23
Route length: (One way) 210 km
On private right-of-way: 3.6 km
Fleet: 84 vehicles, plus 23 hired

Ikarus 260 (1988/89)	7
Ikarus 280 articulated (1988/90)	4
Mercedes O405N low-floor (1991)	21
Neoplan N4014 low-floor (1991)	10
MAN NL202 low-floor (1992)	19
Mercedes O405G articulated (1992/94)	7
Others	16

In peak service: 79

Most intensive service: 10 min
One-person operation: All routes
Fare collection: Fare to driver or prepurchase; 57% of passengers use passes; 14 sales outlets plus vending machines
Fare structure: Flat, single and multijourney tickets, short-distance ticket valid 10 min; off-peak/daily/monthly passes; annual subscription
Integration with other modes: Joint fare scheme with HAVAG and DB S-Bahn
Arrangements for elderly/disabled: Reduced fares for disabled
Average distance between stops: 610 m

Developments: A 3.6 km private right-of-way was inaugurated in 1993 on the Neustadt—Hallorenring route, and is used by 50 buses/h/direction in the morning peak.

Five CNG-powered buses joined the fleet in 1996; their range is 250 km.

Tramway

Type of operation: Conventional tramway

Car-km: (1993) 16.4 million
(1994) 16 million
(1995) 16 million

Number of routes: 13
Route length: 76.7 km
Average distance between stops: 696 m
Gauge: 1,000 mm
Electrification: 600 V DC, overhead
Service: Peak 10 min

Rolling stock: 373 cars

Esslingen GT4 4-axle articulated (ex-Stuttgart/Freiburg 1959/64)	M13
ČKD Tatra ZT4D 4-axle (1969, rebuilt 1983/84)	M2
ČKD Tatra T4D/B4D 4-axle (1971/86)	M184 T43
ČKD Tatra T4D/B4D 4-axle (1971/86, modified 1992/94)	M78 T41
Duewag MGT6D 6-axle low-floor (1992/94)	M12

In peak service: 326
On order: 31 Duewag low-floor, plus option for 96 for delivery through to 2004

Developments: Extensions planned to Halle-Nord and Halle-Neustadt, plus two short links between existing routes. Studies have been made of plans to deliver goods to businesses in the historic central area by tram. Though technically feasible, this would be more expensive than using road vehicles, as at present.

Construction of a new depot at Rosengarten is in progress.

DB

Deutsche Bahn AG, Geschäftsbereich Nahverkehr
Regionalbereich Sachsen-Anhalt/Leipzig
Ernst-Kamieth-Strasse 2, 06112 Halle
Telephone: +49 345 215 3331 Fax: +49 345 841 5378
S-Bahn Manager: Thomas Hoffmann

S-Bahn

Type of operation: Regional metro (S-Bahn)

Passenger journeys: (1991) 3.1 million
(1992) 4.5 million
(1993) 5.1 million

Current situation: The S-Bahn runs 22.8 km over a U-shaped loop from Halle-Trotha in the northeast via Halle Hbf and Halle-Neustadt to Halle-Dölau in the northwest. Most intensive service is every 20 min, provided by seven push-pull sets of double-deck cars hauled by electric locomotives.
Developments: Introduction of park-and-ride is planned at the Trotha and Dölau terminals, which are to be linked by the year 2000 to provide a full circular service. The connection would serve a new housing development.

Construction work has started to link services with those of the Leipzig S-Bahn.

UPDATED

HAMBURG

Population: 1.7 million, area served 2.3 million
Public transport: All public transport in Hamburg and the adjoining metropolitan area is co-ordinated by a public transit authority, Hamburger Verkehrsverbund (HVV). Bus and metro services are provided by city transport company, ferry services by city shipping company, urban and regional rail (S-Bahn) by DB, other regional services by three bus companies and a local railway (AKN), and park-and-ride facilities by a separate company, all government-owned

HVV

Hamburger Verkehrsverbund (HVV)
Steinstrasse 12, 20095 Hamburg, Germany
Telephone: +49 40 30230 Fax: +49 40 3023 112
Directors: Dr-Ing Martin Runkel
Dipl-Ing Peter J Westphal
Transport & Infrastructure Manager: Bernd Rust
Commercial Manager: Jörg Mampe
Purchasing Manager: Hans-Heinz Kirchhoff

Passenger journeys: (All modes)
(1993) 470 million
(1994) 476 million
(1995) 481 million

Fare collection: Single tickets (payment to driver or from vending machine), day tickets, weekly or monthly passes, annual subscription, bulk sales of passes to employers at reduced rates; Card+Ride introduced 1994; onboard sales (bus only) 19%. As an experiment, 50 HHA ticket machines have been adapted to accept payment by a smartcard which also serves as a telephone card
Fare structure: Zonal, transfers free, premium for express bus or first class on S-Bahn; reduced price passes for off-peak travel
Fare evasion control: Random inspection; penalty
Arrangements for elderly/disabled: Reduced rate passes for disabled, paid by government
Operating costs financed by: Fares 52%, contractual grants 7%, subsidy 41%

Current situation: HVV, which was formerly a co-ordinating body of transport operators in the conurbation, was restructured in 1996. It is now controlled by the city of Hamburg (85 per cent), the *Land* of Schleswig-Holstein (2 per cent) and four rural counties. Some functions of the former organisation have been ceded to transport operators.

HVV has established a zonal ticket system allowing free intermodal transfer and integrated services with an overall passenger information system. Park-and-ride sites total 84 with 14,590 spaces, and developers wishing to provide inner city parking are required to pay for construction of an equal number of parking places at a suburban park-and-ride station.

More than 88 per cent of passengers hold monthly, daily or weekly passes; the remainder buy single tickets.

All fare receipts are pooled, and in 1994 were allocated in these proportions:

Hamburger Hochbahn	55.1%
DB	29.9%
VHH	9.5%
AKN	1.8%
PVG	1.2%
KVG	0.8%
HADAG	0.8%

Developments: Feasibility studies were made of possible reintroduction of trams, and in 1994 the city council approved plans for a four-line network extending to 35.3 km. The project was cancelled on financial grounds in June 1996, when the city council also vetoed plans for extending the S-Bahn network.

Hamburger Hochbahn

Hamburger Hochbahn Aktiengesellschaft (HHA)
PO Box 102720, 20019 Hamburg

DT2 and DT4 metro trains on the Hamburg waterfront

Telephone: +49 40 32880 Fax: +49 40 326406
Board of Directors: Dipl Econ Günter Elste
Dipl-Ing Holger Albert
Dr Ulf Lange
Operating Manager, Bus: Dipl-Ing Herbert Hussmann
Operating Manager, Metro: Dipl-Ing Ulrich Sieg
Staff: 5,404

Passenger journeys: (All modes)
(1993) 393 million
(1994) 398 million
(1995) 402 million

Operating costs covered by: (All modes) Fares 51%, other commercial sources 10%, subsidy/grants 35%
Subsidy from: State and city

Current situation: HHA provides services both direct and through nine subsidiary companies and affiliated divisions. These include the shipping lines HADAG (see below) and ATG Alster-Touristik, the bus undertaking PVG, central bus station, the cleaning company TEREG, a bus company, a staff accommodation service, and a security company. HHA also operates the vehicle research and development company FFG and has a consulting subsidiary Hamburg-Consult.

Arrangements for elderly/disabled: All future bus purchases will be of low-floor types with wheelchair ramp; 70% of the fleet is currently accessible. Lifts have been installed at 25 metro stations; guidelines being installed in platform floors for visually impaired and blind people

Bus
Staff: 2,139

Passenger journeys: (1993) 218.8 million
(1994) 221.8 million
(1995) 224.1 million
Vehicle-km: (1993) 54.6 million
(1994) 55.9 million
(1995) 53.2 million

Number of routes: 123
Route length: (One way) 760 km
On priority right-of-way: 21 km
Average distance between stops: 576 m ordinary, 691 m express
Fleet: 602 vehicles, plus 258 hired or leased

Mercedes O405 standard (1984/86)	131
Mercedes O405G articulated (1987)	50
Mercedes O405N low-floor (1991/94)	345
Mercedes O405GN low-floor articulated (1992)	75
Others	1

In peak service: 518

Most intensive service: 3-5 min
One-person operation: All routes
Fares collected on board: 26%
Operational control: 2-way radio links to 6 control centres; computerised vehicle location system in use on 75 express and 160 feeder buses
Integration with other modes: Tickets interchangeable between all modes; single ticket covers any journey by any combination of modes. Computerised passenger information system provides personalised optimal travel details. Many stations have bus feeders, with other main corridors served by express buses to the city centre; park-and-ride encouraged. At Dehnhaide metro/bus interchange signals warn bus drivers of late running of metro trains so they may wait for transferring passengers; more such installations under construction
Average speed: 20.3 km/h ordinary, 22.3 km/h express
New vehicles financed by: Leasing

Developments: A bus acceleration programme was completed in 1993 over 15.7 km of route, embracing measures such as provision of bus lanes and priority at 48 intersections. A second stage is proposed, covering 47 km of route. A batch of 90 buses has been equipped to influence traffic lights.

A fleet of 245 rigid and 75 articulated buses has been leased from Mercedes-Benz Charter-Way rather than purchased. Maintenance is the responsibility of the lessor. A further 82 buses are on order in 1996/97. From 1997, all new vehicles will be equipped with electronic ticket printers.

HHA Mercedes O405G articulated city bus

Air conditioned Mercedes O405N2, PVG Pinneberg's first low-floor bus ***1997***

Metro
Staff: 1,224 (operational)

Type of operation: Full metro, first line opened 1912

Passenger journeys: (1993) 174.1 million
(1994) 176.4 million
(1995) 178.2 million
Car-km: (1993) 56.9 million
(1994) 58.6 million
(1995) 58.4 million

Route length: 100 km
in tunnel: 41.5 km
elevated: 37.4 km
Number of lines: 3
Number of stations: 89
Gauge: 1,435 mm
Track: 49 kg/m S49 rail, sleepers on ballast
Max gradient: 5%
Minimum curve radius: 70 m
Tunnel: Bored single-track, concrete caisson, bored double-track
Electrification: 750 V DC, third rail

Service: Peak 2-5 min, off-peak 5-10 min
First/last train: 04.05/01.16
Surveillance: CCTV on most platforms

Rolling stock: 955 cars

Linke-Hofmann-Busch DT2 (1962/66)	M332
Linke-Hofmann-Busch DT3 (1968/71)	M375
Linke-Hofmann-Busch DT4 (1989/95)	M204
Works cars	44

In peak service: 621
On order: 20 DT4 four-car sets being delivered during 1996/97

Developments: Conversion of the AKN line between Garstedt and Norderstedt Mitte (3.8 km, 3 stations) to metro standards was completed in September 1996.

Station staff are to be eliminated by 2000, when new technology will permit 'self dispatch' of trains by drivers.

Ferry
Operated by ATG Alster-Touristik GmbH

Current situation: 17 ships operate one short crossing of the Alster plus tourist cruises.

HADAG
HADAG Seetouristik und Fährdienst AG
St Pauli Fischmarkt 28, 20359 Hamburg
Telephone: +49 40 311 7070
Director: Jens Wrage

Ferry
Staff: 113

Passenger journeys: (1990) 2 million
(1991) 2.1 million
(1994) 2.2 million

Current situation: This subsidiary of HHA operates 14 vessels on seven routes in the harbour and on the River Elbe. It has a 50 per cent shareholding in Elbe-City-Jet (see below).

DB
Deutsche Bahn AG, Geschäftsbereich Nahverkehr
Regionalbereich Hamburg
Museumsstrasse 39, 22756 Hamburg
Telephone: +49 40 3918 3030 Fax: +49 40 184326
Manager, S-Bahn: Dipl-Volksw E Erber
Operations Manager: Dipl-Ing G Stock
Technical Manager: Dipl-Ing R Gladigau
Commercial Manager: Dipl Volksw P Herschel

Current situation: S-Bahn services consist of two distinct systems, the S-Bahn proper, segregated from main line operations, and conventional suburban trains running on main line tracks but integrated in the HVV regional transit scheme.

S-Bahn
Type of operation: Urban heavy rail

Passenger journeys: (1990) 136.4 million
(1991) 141.1 million
(1994) 148.9 million

Current situation: The network comprises six routes with 58 stations extending to 110 km, 1,435 mm gauge, electrified at 1.2 kV DC third rail. Trains run every five minutes in the peak, 10-20 minutes off-peak, with service 04.00-24.00. Most stations are unstaffed, and all trains are driver-only operated. Fares cover about 50 per cent of operating costs.
Developments: Upgrading of stations and signalling installations on the Wedel–Poppenbüttel line planned, along with a computer-based system to guarantee connections for the 50 per cent of passengers who transfer to or from other modes. Long-term plans envisage extension of third-rail S-Bahn routes beyond present terminals to Buxtehude and Elmshorn (at present served by regional rail, see below), and a route from Ohlsdorf to Fuhlsbüttel airport, though these were vetoed by HVV in 1996. New rolling stock to replace Series 471

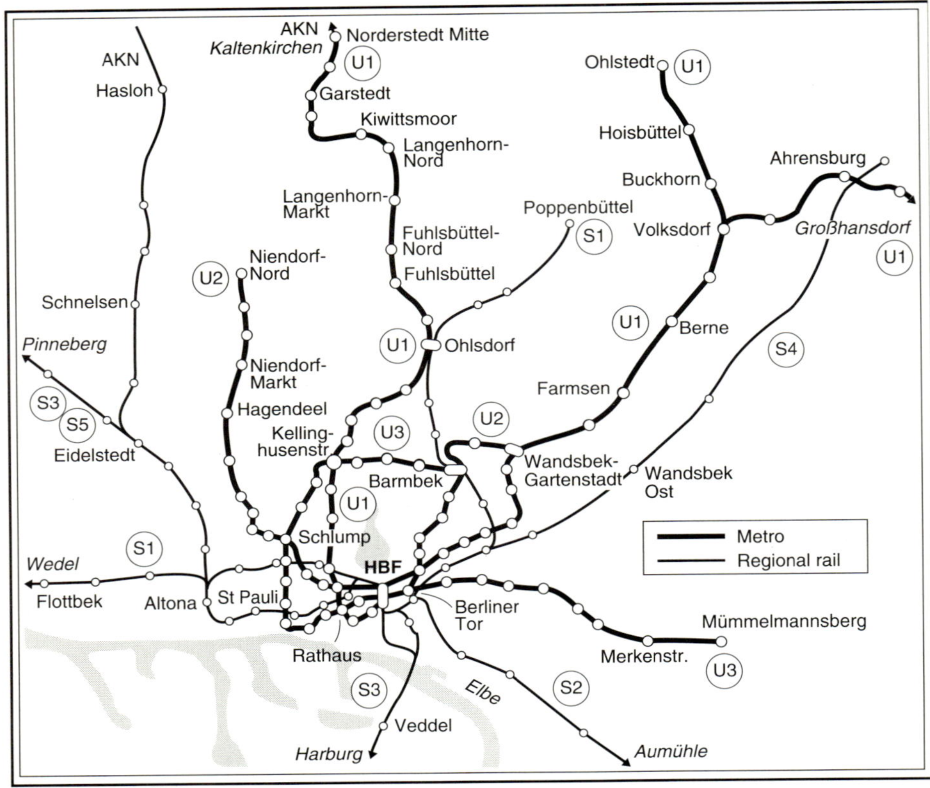

Hamburg's metro and S-Bahn

and 470 emus is on order. Linke-Hofmann-Busch and Adtranz are supplying 103 three-car ET474 series emus, the first of which were due to enter service in mid-1997.

It is planned to transfer operation of the S-Bahn to a DB subsidiary company, as in Berlin.

Rolling stock: 168 three-car emus

Series 471/871 (1939/58)	M122 T61
Series 470/870 (1959/70)	M90 T45
LHB/MBB Series 472/473 (1974/84)	M186

On order: 103 three-car emus for delivery between 1997 and 2000

Regional rail
Type of operation: Suburban heavy rail

Passenger journeys: (1990) 10.4 million
(1991) 10.8 million
(1994) 11.4 million

Current situation: Outer suburban services provided over 38 route-km to 12 stations.

Rolling stock: 47 coaches, push-pull trains propelled by main line AC electric or diesel locomotives

AKN
Altona-Kaltenkirchen-Neumünster Railway
PO Box 106322, 20019 Hamburg
Telephone: +49 40 733341 Fax: +49 40 733 34288
Board of Directors:
Götz Dietsche
Dipl-Ing Holger Albert
Staff: 335

Type of operation: Local rail

Passenger journeys: (1993) 6.8 million
(1994) 6.1 million
(1995) 6.6 million

Current situation: Provides suburban services over three routes run in connection with metro and S-Bahn lines, totalling 52 km with 30 stations.

Rolling stock: 44 diesel railcars

VHH
Verkehrsbetriebe Hamburg-Holstein AG
Curslacker Neuer Deich 37, 21029 Hamburg
Telephone: +49 40 725 6070 Fax: +49 40 725 60722
Board of Directors:
Dipl-Volksw Josef Hoffstadt
Dipl-Ing Holger Albert
Staff: 1,135

Bus
Passenger journeys: (1993) 38.4 million
(1994) 38.6 million
(1995) 38.2 million
Vehicle-km: (1993) 17.8 million
(1994) 17.1 million
(1995) 15.6 million

Number of routes: 66
Route length: 708 km
Fleet: 282 buses, plus 40 hired

Current situation: Under the same management as HHA, VHH provides regional bus services under the auspices of HVV. Some routes also operated outside the HVV area (not included in statistics above).

PVG
Pinneberger Verkehrsgesellschaft mbH
PO Box 1326, 22860 Schenefeld
Telephone: +49 40 839940 Fax: +49 40 83994 280/281
Director: Ralf-Dieter Pemöller
Staff: 520

Bus
Passenger journeys: (1993) 6.3 million
(1994) 5.8 million
(1995) 5.9 million
Vehicle-km: (1993) 2 million
(1994) 1.6 million
(1995) 1.6 million

Number of routes: 7 (in HVV area)
Route length: 81 km
Fleet: 183 buses

Current situation: PVG, a subsidiary of HHA, provides local bus services in the Pinneberg region (both within and outside the HVV area), and in the western part of Hamburg under contract to HHA. Statistics above apply only to operations directly for HVV, but more than 80 per cent of all kilometrage is provided on HHA contracted services.

KVG
Kraftverkehr GmbH
PO Box 1525, 21655 Stade
Telephone: +49 4131 60610 Fax: +49 4131 606124
Directors: Heinz-Dieter Pohl
Reinhard Stüttgen

Bus
Passenger journeys: (1994) 2.5 million
Vehicle-km: (1994) 1.4 million

Fleet: 30 buses

Current situation: Regional bus company, formerly associated with DB. The company, which was taken over by local government in 1996, provides rural and urban transit in area south of River Elbe from Cuxhaven in north to Luneburg in south. Only 10 out of a total of 197 routes are integrated in HVV. Statistics apply only to operations within the HVV area.

Elbe-City-Jet
SAL Schiffahrtskontor/Altes Land GmbH & Co
Bürgerei 29, 21720 Steinkirchen
Telephone: +49 4142 81810 Fax: +49 4142 3511
Managing Director: Hans Heinrich

Current situation: This joint venture between HHA's ferry subsidiary HADAG and operator SAL was formed to run a commuter ferry route on the River Elbe between Hamburg and Stade, which was inaugurated in July 1996 using two jet catamarans. Claimed to offer a much faster journey than road or rail, the service did not immediately attract substantial patronage. In October 1996, there were only some 150 regular passengers of the estimated 16,000 daily commuters between the two cities.

P+R
P+R Betriebsgesellschaft mbH
Steinstrasse 20, 20095 Hamburg
Telephone: +49 40 3288 2553 Fax: +49 40 3288 2874
Managing Directors: Dr-Ing Armin Wirsching
Dipl-Ing Axel von Knobloch

Current situation: At 85 stations in the Hamburg area some 16,000 park-and-ride spaces are available. Expansion in 1998 will raise this figure to 18,500. Cycle lockers were introduced at some locations in 1996.

P+R, a management company for park-and-ride, operates sites at 17 stations with some 6,000 spaces. It became a full member of HVV in 1990. It is controlled by the City of Hamburg commercial holding, with the German Automobile Club (ADAC) having a 5 per cent shareholding.

UPDATED

HAMILTON

Population: 400,000
Public transport: Bus services provided by publicly owned company operating as a division of Regional Transportation Department

Hamilton's first low-floor bus entered service in late 1996 ***1997***

Hamilton Street Railway

The Hamilton Street Railway Company
330 Wentworth Street North, Hamilton, Ontario L8L 5W2, Canada
Telephone: +1 905 528 4200 Fax: +1 905 528 5410
Chair, Transportation Services: Terry Anderson
Commissioner of Transportation: Dale Turvey
Director of Operations: Don Hull
Staff: 721

Current situation: HSR is publicly owned by the Regional Municipality of Hamilton-Wentworth. The undertaking, along with Mississauga Transit and OC Transpo, Ottawa, participated in the government of Ontario's programme for evaluation of computer applications in transport operations. HSR took the lead role in the Transit Information, Communications & Control Systems (TICCS) project, now superseded by AVLC (Automatic Vehicle Location & Control) which provides automatic location and both voice and digital communication for all vehicles. This was commissioned in 1990. 'Bus Check' next bus arrival time telephone enquiry system operates system-wide.

Developments: Following a decision to retain trolleybuses after consultants recommended abandonment, the network closed in 1992 for rebuilding. However, it was subsequently decided that closure should be made permanent.

Low-floor buses were introduced at the end of 1996.

Bus

Passenger boardings: (1993) 27.8 million
(1994) 26.7 million
(1995) 26.3 million

Number of routes: 31
Route length: 300 km (one way)

Fleet: 214 buses

GM Canada	75
Flyer (1979)	20
GMC articulated (1982)	12
MCI Canada (1987/88)	29
GMC natural gas-converted	8
Orion (1989)	15
Orion CNG-powered (1991/92)	30
New Flyer low-floor (1996)	25

In peak service: 175

Most intensive service: 4-6 min
One-person operation: All routes
Fare collection: Exact fare to electronic farebox or prepurchase
Fare structure: Flat; free transfer to next available bus; monthly passes, student semester passes
Fare evasion control: By driver
Operational control: Mobile radio on all vehicles, with automatic passenger counting as part of AVLC project (see above); emergency button access to control room
Arrangements for elderly/disabled: 25 low-floor buses on regular service; special service provided by another regional department; 45 buses have kneeling capability; accessible taxi service. 'Easier Access' programme designed to improve access to public transport for elderly and disabled people
Average peak-hour speed: 21 km/h
Operating costs financed by: Fares 40.5%, other commercial sources 5.3%, subsidy/grants 54.2%
Subsidy from: Region of Hamilton and Ontario government
New vehicles financed by: 75% government of Ontario, 25% Regional Municipality

UPDATED

HANGZHOU

Population: 1.4 million
Public transport: Bus and trolleybus services provided by municipal agency; extensive paratransit services by private operators; light rail planned

Hangzhou Public Transport

Hangzhou Public Transport Company
195 Kaixuan Road, Hangzhou, Zhejiang Province, People's Republic of China
Telephone: +86 571 604 9800 Fax: +86 571 604 9101
Chief Engineer: Jin Ling

Current situation: A city-wide bus network is operated using two-axle and articulated buses, supplemented by four trolleybus routes. Ex-Hong Kong double-deckers run on one scenic route. One trolleybus route, though complete and shown on maps, seems not to have been opened.

Developments: Three light rail routes are planned, totalling 37.7 km.

Bus

Staff: 6,500

Vehicle-km: (1994) 35.6 million

Number of routes: 63
Route length: 869 km
Fleet: 738 vehicles, including 240 articulated. All Hangzhou except for 100 Chang Jiang CJ6922CH recently delivered and a few Daimler double-deck from Hong Kong

Fare collection: Stage fares paid to seated conductor; monthly passes

Articulated trolleybus in Hangzhou

Trolleybus
Staff: 2,000

Vehicle-km: (1994) 7.3 million

Number of routes: 4
Route length: 40.1 km
Fleet: 142 Hangzhou 561 articulated, also about 40 buses for suspended trolleybus route (Hangzhou 661 and 641 articulated)

Fare collection: Stage fares paid to seated conductor; monthly passes
Integration with other modes: Suburban trolleybus terminals are interchange points for bus services to outer suburbs

Hangzhou central bus station
1996

HANNOVER

Population: 528,000, Greater Hannover 1.1 million
Public transport: Tramway/light rail and bus services provided by municipally controlled company, and regional rail services by DB, both operating as part of Grossraum-Verkehr Hannover transport association

GVH

Grossraum-Verkehr Hannover
Arnswaldtstrasse 19, 30159 Hannover, Germany
Telephone: +49 511 366 1325 Fax: +49 511 366 1452
President: Valentin Schmidt

Passenger journeys: (1993) 174 million
(1994) 174 million
(1996) 175 million

Current situation: After HVV Hamburg, GVH is the second oldest regional transit authority in Germany, having been established in 1970.

Suburban rail services of DB still use main line tracks, but upgrading to S-Bahn status is envisaged for 1997. Tickets allow free transfer between Üstra services as well as to regional bus and DB rail services. Üstra carries about 77 per cent of all passengers in Grossraum area. Regional bus services are provided by Busverkehr und Service Grossraum Hannover (B.U.S.), formed in 1992 by Regionalverkehr Hannover GmbH (a regional bus company), Steinhuder Meer Bahn GmbH, Wunstorf (local government owned), and a private company Verkehrsbetriebe Bachstein GmbH, Burgdorf. Dial-a-bus service (Ruf-Bus) and dial-a-taxi operated in several communities by StMB, RVH and VB, mainly during weekends and evening hours.

Kommunalverband Grossraum Hannover, a political entity uniting the city and county of Hannover, is a partner in GVH. In 1995, public transport accounted for 40 per cent of all motorised trips in the GVH area.

Fare structure: Zonal, multiple-ride tickets at reduced fare, daily/monthly passes, annual subscription, free intermodal transfers, first class available on DB trains, special fares (including 50% discount offer to employers who buy annual subscriptions for all their staff); 79% of passengers use passes, which are transferable

Operating costs financed by: Fares 50%, other commercial sources 16%, subsidy/grants 34% (excluding DB operations)

Üstra

Üstra Hannoversche Verkehrsbetriebe AG
PO Box 2540, 30025 Hannover
Telephone: +49 511 16681 Fax: +49 511 1668 666
Chair/Executive Director: Dr Heinrich Ganseforth
Technical and Operations Director: Dipl-Ing Bernd Kosiek
Personnel Director: Günter Limbach
Light Rail Manager: Rainer Schülmann

Tram stop at Steintor, designed as part of a project financed by the state lottery ***1997***

Personnel Manager: Günter Ernst
Staff: 2,403

Passenger journeys: (All modes)
(1993) 138.5 million
(1994) 140 million
(1995) 140.2 million

Operating costs financed by: Fares 65%, subsidy/grants 35%
Subsidy from: Kommunalverband Grossraum Hannover (regional authority formed by city and county) for operating costs; federal and state grants for new investment

Current situation: Operations serve approximately 750,000 people. Conversion of tramways to form a light rail system with city-centre sections entirely in tunnel completed in 1992. Seasonal lake ferry leisure operation on Maschsee with three small vessels.

Bus

Passenger journeys: (1993) 34.4 million
(1994) 29.2 million
(1995) 29.2 million
Vehicle-km: (1993) 13.6 million
(1994) 13.3 million
(1995) 13.4 million

Number of routes: 34
Route length: 433 km
Average route length: 12.7 km
Fleet: 196 vehicles plus 30 hired

MAN SL202 standard (1985/86)	30
Mercedes O405 standard (1985/87)	14
Mercedes O305G articulated (1983/86)	59
MAN NL202 low-floor (1992/94)	67
Mercedes O405N low-floor (1994)	5
Mercedes O405N low-floor CNG-powered (1994)	10
MAN A15NL low-floor CNG-powered (1994)	5
Others	6

In peak service: 175

Most intensive service: 3 min
One-person operation: All routes
Fare collection: Fare to driver or prepurchase tickets/passes with validation and cancelling machines on board; some roadside vending machines
Fares collected on board: 9%
Fare evasion control: Roving inspectors; spot fine
Operational control: Operation supervisors/mobile voice radio on all vehicles. BON computerised operating control system with centralised online monitoring in operation for all buses and LRT vehicles (see earlier *JUTS* editions). All fleet to be included, providing permanent voice and datalink
Average peak-hour speed: 24 km/h
Bus priority: Bus lanes and vehicle-activated traffic signals by inductive loop and computer-controlled system
New vehicles financed by: Internal resources and subsidies
Operating costs financed by: Fares 42%, subsidy/grants 58%

Developments: 15 CNG-powered buses (10 Mercedes, 5 MAN) entered service in 1994; their fuel capacity of 800

MAN bus on B.U.S. Route 600 in Grossburgwedel ***1996***

litres gives an operating range of 300 km compared to 700 km for a diesel bus. A new fuelling station allows full refuelling of a bus within 10 min.

Light rail

Type of operation: Light rail with city-centre underground sections

Passenger journeys: (1993) 104 million
(1994) 110.8 million
(1995) 111 million
Car-km: (1993) 19.1 million
(1994) 20 million
(1995) 20.8 million

Route length: 103.4 km
in tunnel: 17 km
reserved track: 61 km
Number of lines: 11
Number of stops: 172
Gauge: 1,435 mm
Electrification: 600 V DC, overhead

Service: Peak 2 min
Fare collection: Prepurchase only, vending machines at all LRT stations
Fare evasion control: As bus
One-person operation: All routes
Centralised control: Priority at traffic lights; BON system (see above)
Operating costs financed by: Fares 76%, subsidy/grants 24%

Rolling stock: 260 cars

Duewag Stadtbahn Series 1 (1974/78)	M100
LHB Stadtbahn Series 2 (1979/83)	M90
LHB Stadtbahn Series 3 (1985)	M15
LHB Stadtbahn Series 4 (1988/89)	M25
LHB Stadtbahn Series 5 (1991)	M20
LHB Stadtbahn Series 6 (1992)	M10
Works cars	15

In peak service: 237
On order: 144 LRVs from Linke-Hofmann-Busch/Siemens for delivery 1997/99

Current situation: Conversion of conventional tramways to light rail operation started in 1976 when the first tunnel sections were opened, and is now practically complete. A 5.5 km extension to Garbsen opened in September 1996. Extension of Route A to Wettbergen planned for 1999 opening, along with further extension of Route D to provide a second link to the fairground in time for Expo 2000.

DB

Deutsche Bahn AG, Geschäftsbereich Nahverkehr
Regionalbereich Niedersachsen
Joachimstrasse 8, 30159 Hannover
Telephone: +49 511 286 3330 Fax: +49 511 128 4439
Manager, Local Railways: Peter Schatte

Type of operation: Suburban heavy rail

Passenger journeys: (1990) 23 million
(1994) 21 million

Current situation: Suburban rail services operated over 233 km on 11 routes in association with GVH. Ordinary rolling stock rebuilt to 'City-Bahn' standards and main line tracks are used. Double-deck stock introduced 1995.
Developments: Upgrading is in progress of the east-west Lehrte–Hannover Hbf–Wunstorf line (38 km) to S-Bahn standards with separate tracks. Dedicated tracks will be available between Seelze and Hbf in late 1997, enabling start-up of S-Bahn service before the end of the year. Construction of an extension to the airport started in 1995. A total of five routes and 226 km should be operated to S-Bahn standards by 2000. A fleet of 40 four-car emus of Series 424 is on order for delivery from 1998 onwards.

Bus meets train at suburban Wennigsen ***1996***

B.U.S.

Busverkehr und Service in Grossraum Hannover GmbH
Georgstrasse 54, 30159 Hannover
Telephone: +49 511 368880 Fax: +49 511 368 8899
Directors: Dieter Behrendt
Wolfgang Stack

Passenger journeys: (1993) 18.1 million
(1994) 19.7 million
(1995) 19.5 million
Vehicle-km: (1993) 19.1 million
(1994) 18.8 million
(1995) 19.2 million

Current situation: Company founded by RVH, VB and StMB (see below) to co-ordinate bus services of the partners in the Greater Hannover area. All route licences held by partners have been transferred to the new company. Vehicles and staff will remain with the partners, who continue to run services under the direction of B.U.S. There are 82 routes extending to 1,960 km operated with a fleet of 294 buses provided by the partners.

RVH

Regionalverkehr Hannover GmbH
PO Box 4909, 30049 Hannover
Telephone: +49 511 338000 Fax: +49 511 312508
Managing Directors: Hans-Peter Mahn
Ulrich Rau
Staff: 161

Current situation: This regional bus company passed from DB to local authority control in 1996. It provides suburban and rural services within GVH area and beyond. Also runs R-Bus service at Neustadt. Services within the GVH area now provided as a partner in B.U.S., and statistics are included in the B.U.S. figures (see above).

VB

Verkehrsbetriebe Bachstein GmbH
Zweigniederlassung Burgdorf, Ostlandring 1, 31303 Burgdorf
Telephone: +49 5136 80910 Fax: +49 5136 809140
Operations Manager: Udo Beran
Staff: 79

Passenger journeys: (1994) 4 million
(1995) 3.5 million

Current situation: This private company runs local bus services in Burgdorf area as a partner in B.U.S. (see above); fleet of 34 buses, plus 10 hired.

StMB

Steinhuder Meer Bahn GmbH
Hindenburgstrasse 45, 31515 Wunstorf
Telephone: +49 5031 1750 Fax: +49 5031 17575
Managing Director: Wolfgang Stack
Staff: 63

Passenger journeys: (1994) 2.3 million
(1995) 2.2 million

Current situation: Local government-owned operator providing services in the Wunstorf area as a partner in B.U.S. (see above); fleet of 34 buses, plus 10 on hire. Most R-Bus services have reverted to fixed-route operation, but some stops off the normal route continue to be served on request.

UPDATED

HANOI

Population: 2.6 million
Public transport: Bus services provided by public authorities; metro planned

Hanoi Bus Company

Cong Ty Xe Dien Ha Noi
Hanoi, Vietnam

Bus

Current situation: City bus services are provided by a fleet of Karosa vehicles including both elderly SM models and recent B731 buses, supplemented by vehicles obtained second-hand from French cities. More basic front-engined Radinh buses and other similar vehicles operate suburban and long-distance routes, with Soviet-built PAZ minibuses operating for public institutions and collectives.

Developments: In 1993 a joint venture company was set up between the Hanoi Bus Company and Singapore Bus Service (SBS), under which SBS will operate all bus services in the city and suburbs.

Traffic congestion has been exacerbated by a 1996 ban on daytime rail movements over the line through the city centre, which was intended to ease traffic problems caused by delays at the many pedestrian and road crossings.

Ex-Lyon Saviem in Hanoi **1997**

Metro (proposed)

Current situation: Feasibility studies for a core metro route were made in 1994, though in 1995 the city authorities were reported to be considering various rail-based options. ITF Intertraffic, a Daimler-Benz subsidiary, was contracted to produce a master plan for developing a rail network for the city.

An alternative scheme could see Vietnam Railways' main route through the city doubled and relocated on elevated structures to eliminate the many level crossings.

UPDATED

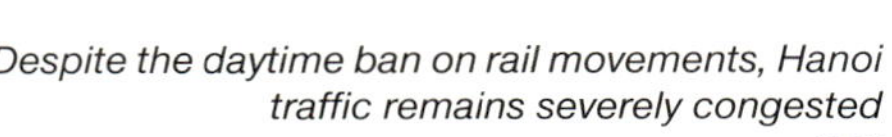

Despite the daytime ban on rail movements, Hanoi traffic remains severely congested **1997**

HARARE

Population: 1 million, including Chitungwiza
Public transport: Bus services provided by company jointly owned by the government and United Transport, management of which is subcontracted to UT. Limited independent operations include 'emergency taxis', shared-taxi and taxi paratransit

ZUPCO

Zimbabwe Passenger Company Ltd
Harare Division
109 Belvedere Road, PO Box 3298, Harare, Zimbabwe
Telephone: +263 4 750750 Fax: +263 4 794850
General Manager, Harare Division: G Chifamba
Staff: 2,930

Current situation: ZUPCO remains 51 per cent owned by the government of Zimbabwe and 49 per cent by the United Transport Group (see *JUTS 1991* for history). The company operates bus services in Harare, Bulawayo (qv) and six urban areas under a 10-year franchise agreement with the Ministry of Local Government, Rural & Urban Development, which expires in 1999. It also operates an extensive network of long-distance routes. Fares require government approval but are determined by market forces. There is a management agreement between ZUPCO and United Transport.

The Harare Division operates conventional bus services within a franchise area extending 30 km from Harare, and a small number of rural services up to 100 km distant.

AVM buses of ZUPCO at South Street, Harare

Substantial population growth in Harare has led to studies of possible trolleybus, light rail and commuter rail services.

Bus

Passenger journeys: (1991) 161 million
(1992) 148 million
(1993) 141 million

Vehicle-km: (1991) 63 million
(1992) 61 million
(1993) 83 million

Number of routes: 62
Fleet: 825 vehicles
DAF/AVM 625/825
MAN articulated

ERF
Scania
Toyota/Mazda minibuses 111
In peak service: 696

Most intensive service: 10 min
One-person operation: All urban routes
Fare collection: By driver, plus sales to queues at major termini from ticket agency booths
Fare structure: Graduated
Operational control: Inspectors
Operating costs financed by: Fares 100%

Developments: Infrastructure improvements including additional depots and city-centre operating facilities. Minibuses have been introduced to supplement full-size vehicle operations.

Shared taxi

Current situation: 'Emergency taxis' were legalised in 1982. They are a form of paratransit shared taxi, with vehicles seating not more than seven passengers, supposed to operate on fixed routes at maximum fares determined by the municipality. There has been rapid growth of pirate taxis using minibuses seating more than 20, to which the authorities have not responded.

Suburban railway (planned)

Current situation: As a result of the urban transport study carried out in 1985/86, engineering design of an electrified suburban network has been undertaken. Building on the National Railways of Zimbabwe electrified main line westwards out of Harare, and by energising other lines, three new routes would serve the growing suburbs of Chitungwiza in the south and Glenview in the west. Upgrading and electrification of existing lines would see suburban trains running from Mufakose and Dzivarasekwa through central Harare to Msaka and Mabvuku.

Prequalification bids were sought by the government in mid-1995 for construction of the initial 22 km route to Chitungwiza on build-own-operate-transfer terms. The line's five stations would be served by a fleet of 11 eight-car emus.

HARBIN

Population: 4 million
Public transport: Bus, minibus and trolleybus services provided by at least two operators. Before the economic reforms of the late 1980s, the Harbin City Bus Company operated bus services and the Harbin City Electric Traction Company ran trams and trolleybuses. By 1992 at least two overlapping bus networks and premium-fare minibuses duplicating bus and trolleybus services were in operation. The relationship of these operations to the long-established services is unclear but it is assumed that all services remain centrally planned

Articulated trolleybus, with Ikarus bus following and Longjiang bus passing

Harbin City Bus

Harbin City Bus Company
Harbin, Heilongjiang Province, People's Republic of China

Current situation: Little official information is available and the extent of operations is difficult to determine. In 1992 there were 20 urban routes numbered 1 to 20 and an overlapping network of at least 15 routes numbered in the range 51 to 67. There are also suburban routes with other numbers. Buses of Harbin City Bus run on all three groups of services, but certain routes, notably 66, are worked by buses which do not appear to belong to the same fleet as most of the city buses.

Bus

Number of routes: At least 35
Fleet: About 700, of which some 500 articulated, mainly Harbin HB645 (2-axle) and Harbin HB665 (articulated); some older vehicles still in service
Fare collection: Payment to seated conductors, monthly passes

Harbin City Electric Traction

Harbin City Electric Traction Company

Current situation: The trolleybus system has been expanded and modernised during the past decade. A bus service introduced over the former tramway route has been replaced by a new trolleybus service. Almost all trolleybuses are 11 years old or less; about 200 new Beijing trolleybuses have been delivered since 1984.

Trolleybus

Number of routes: 10
Route length: Approx 60 km
Fleet: 300, almost all articulated
Beijing BD562 articulated At least 190
Shanghai SK561/SK561G articulated (1985) At least 30
Shenyang SY561 articulated (1982) At least 40

Fare collection: Payment to seated conductors, monthly passes

Minibus

Current situation: Minibuses charging premium fares duplicate certain bus and trolleybus services. The organisation and extent of operations is not known, but at least 60-70 minibuses are believed to cover trolleybus routes 101 and 103 alone.

Light rail (planned)

Current situation: A 14.5 km line is proposed.

HARTFORD

Population: 664,000
Public transport: Bus services provided by publicly owned state-wide transit company managed under contract. Separate Transit District regulates private bus operators and is instrumental in operation of separate dial-a-ride, suburban and commuter express services; light rail planned

MCI bus of CT Transit in Hartford

Greater Hartford Transit District

Greater Hartford Transit District
1 Union Place, Hartford, CT 06103, USA
Telephone: +1 860 247 5329 Fax: +1 860 247 5329
Chair: Paul A Earhardt
Executive Director: Arthur L Handman
Service Development Manager: Tyler Polhemus

Passenger boardings: (1993) 0.9 million
(1994) 0.7 million

Current situation: The Transit District is a federally funded quasi-governmental organisation comprising 15 towns including Hartford. It is responsible for co-ordinating and planning transport facilities in its area, and is the regulating agency for taxis and privately operated bus services. It owns and operates the multimodal Union station transit centre, where suburban and long-distance buses connect with rail services. It has acquired 22 buses for operation by five private companies on state-supported commuter express routes, provides demand-responsive service for the elderly and handicapped (120 vehicles carrying about 450,000 passengers annually), and the 'Scooter' downtown Hartford distribution service. There is a total fleet of some 130 paratransit vehicles, about half of which are lift-equipped, and 25 buses for suburban services.
Developments: In its planning role, the District has supported studies of possible fixed-guideway transit linking Bradley international airport with downtown Hartford (the Griffin line, 24 km) and in the East Hartford—Manchester—South Windsor corridor. In 1990 the Griffin corridor was selected as the most promising route for either light rail or a busway, and in July 1995 the light rail alternative was selected by the Capitol Region Council of Governments. This planning body will now work with the Transit District to produce a detailed funding proposal.

The initial route will be run 15 km north from Hartford's Union station to Griffin Center Office Park in Bloomfield, with later extensions south to downtown and north to the airport.

CT Transit

Connecticut Transit
PO Box 66, 100 Leibert Road, Hartford, CT 06141-0066
Telephone: +1 860 522 8101 Fax: +1 860 247 1810
General Manager: David Lee
Assistant General Managers
Maintenance: Stephen Warren
Planning & Marketing: Ginny Schneider
Administration: John Capell
Staff: 798 (503 drivers)

Current situation: Connecticut DoT acquired Connecticut Transit in 1976. The undertaking is now managed under contract by HNS Management, a wholly owned subsidiary of Ryder/ATE. There are three systems based in Hartford, New Haven and Stamford, with a total fleet of 375 buses and 74 routes. The total operation carried 22 million passengers in 1995, of which 7 million in New Haven and 2.3 million in Stamford.

Bus

Hartford Division, address as above
Staff: 480

Passenger journeys: (1993) 13.9 million
(1994) 13.4 million
(1995) 12.9 million
Vehicle-km: (1993) 10.9 million
(1994) 10.7 million
(1995) 10.9 million

Number of routes: 42
Route length: 1,456 km
Fleet: 228 buses

MCI Classic (1990)	88
MCI Classic (1992)	33
New Flyer (1993)	40
New Flyer (1994)	53
Novabus Classic (1996)	14

In peak service: 184
Average age of fleet: 4 years

Most intensive service: 5 min

Fare structure: Local, four zones; commuter, three zones at higher fares; tokens; monthly passes
Fare collection: Exact fare or magnetic pass to electronic farebox which also issues transfers
Arrangements for elderly/disabled: Most buses have wheelchair lifts; reduced-rate 10-ride ticket
Integration with other modes: Park-and-ride lots throughout the service areas; bus/rail Uniticket with Metro-North Railroad
Operating costs financed by: (For whole system) fares 35%, subsidy/grants 65%

UPDATED

Hartford's downtown 'Scooter' service

HELSINKI

Population: 525,000
Public transport: Bus, metro and tramway services operated by city transport undertaking, under overall policy of City Council. Five private bus companies and one other municipally owned provide services under contract. Ferry services to the Suomenlinna islands run by SLL, jointly owned by the city and state; privately operated waterbuses run summer only. Suburban services provided by State Railways (VR) and bus companies operate between Helsinki and neighbouring municipalities under contract with the Metropolitan Area Council

HKL/HST

Helsingin kaupungin liikennelaitos (HKL)/Helsingfors stads trafikverk (HST)
PO Box 314, Toinen linja 7, 00530 Helsinki, Finland
Telephone: +358 9 4721 Fax: +358 9 472 3701
Email:http://www.hel.fi/hkl/eindex.html
Managing Director: Martti Lund
Manager, Bus: Tapio Hölttä
Information Manager: Eeva Mustonen
Staff: 2,028

Volvo-Wiima articulated in Helsinki city centre

Passenger boardings: (All modes)
(1993) 186.8 million
(1994) 191.9 million
(1995) 194.6 million

Operating costs financed by: (All modes) fares 39.8%, other commercial sources 4.9%, subsidy/grants 55.3%
Subsidy from: Municipal taxes

Fare structure: Flat; free transfers; multitrip tickets; 30-day passes; annual passes for persons resident in Helsinki, Espoo, Vantaa and Kauniainen only; regional tickets
Fares collected on board: 14% of total revenue
Fare evasion control: 49 roving inspectors for bus, tram and metro; spot fine

Current situation: There is a common flat fare system on all modes operating within the city, including the contracted bus and rail services, and the ferry, with revenue pooling through HKL or the Metropolitan Area Council, and payment to operators according to their contribution.

Developments: Public transport journeys started to grow again in 1993, a trend which has been sustained and which has led to several developments. The city council approved a programme of public transport improvements, and more funds were allocated to traffic management measures to reduce journey times.

Thanks to the impending introduction of competition amongst contract service providers, HKL was able to reduce its costs for bus, tram and metro service by some 3.5 per cent in 1995/96. Preparations for competition, to be implemented after the current contract period ends in 1997, included changes in HKL's organisation to take account of the new situation.

The bus and tram fleets are being renewed with low-floor vehicles, and metro and suburban rolling stock augmented. There will also be new emphasis on improving the quality of the passenger environment and information. A new smartcard system is being implemented in 1996/98.

HKL's status changed slightly in 1993, when it became a statutory public transport board, with the bus operation now accounted for separately. Late in 1993 HKL put forward a development programme for consideration by the city government. Several tramway extensions are planned for the years through to 2005, including some 14 km of new track and 20 new low-floor cars for delivery by 1998. The metro extension to Vuosaari is under construction for 1998 opening.

Bus (HKL)

Staff: 975

Passenger boardings: (1993) 69.1 million
(1994) 70.8 million
(1995) 70.7 million
Vehicle-km: (1993) 18.4 million
(1994) 18.3 million
(1995) 18.8 million

Number of routes: 52 (43 regular, 9 peak-only)
Route length: 443 km
Fleet: 361 buses

Volvo B10M (1986/87/88/89/90/91)	201
Volvo B10BLE low-floor	12
Volvo-Wiima articulated	80
Volvo-Wiima articulated low-floor	2
Scania N112CL60 (1988)	25
Scania N113CLB low-floor	11
Scania L113TLL low-floor	4
MAN LPG-powered (1991)	1
Mercedes O405 N2 low-floor	4

In peak service: 303

Most intensive service: 5 min; about 20 sec on route with several lines
One-person operation: All routes
Fare collection: Prepurchase or single tickets from driver with Almex-M self-service cancellers
Average distance between stops: 400 m
Average peak-hour speed: 24 km/h
Bus priority: 42 km of bus lanes
Integration with other modes: Full integration of fares and services
Operational control: Mobile radio on all vehicles; central control room and radio patrol cars
New vehicles financed by: Municipal grant

Contract bus services (SLH/STA)

SLH (private companies in joint fares arrangement) and STA (Suomen Turistauto Oy)
Operated under contract to HKL
Staff: 690

Passenger boardings: (1993) STA 17.4 million, SLH 16.1 million
(1994) STA 16.9 million, SLH 16.4 million
(1995) STA 16.4 million, SLH 16 million
Vehicle-km: (1993) STA 6.4 million, SLH 8.4 million
(1994) STA 6.5 million, SLH 8.3 million
(1995) STA 6.4 million, SLH 8.3 million

Number of routes: 29 (STA 10 regular, 4 peak only; SLH 11 regular, 4 peak only)
Route length: STA 189 km; SLH 246 km
Fleet: 277 vehicles
In peak service: 226

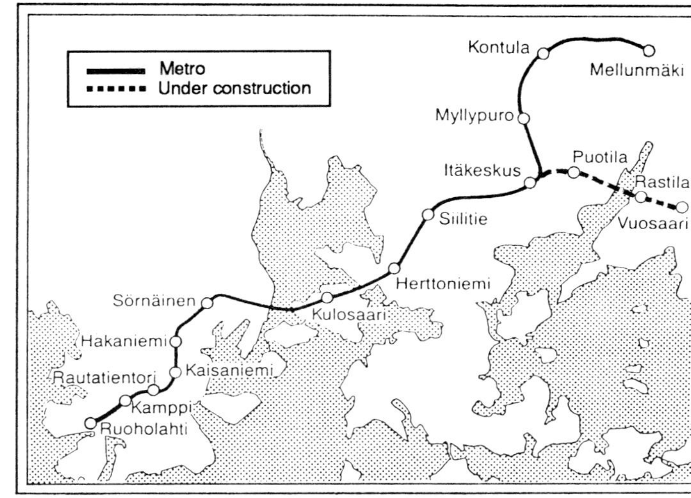

Helsinki metro

Metro

Type of operation: Full metro, initial route opened 1982

Passenger boardings: (1993) 35.8 million
(1994) 37.1 million
(1995) 38.8 million
Car-km: (1993) 8.3 million
(1994) 8.7 million
(1995) 8.6 million

Route length: 16.9 km
in tunnel: 4 km
Number of stations: 13
in tunnel: 6
Gauge: 1,524 mm
Max gradient: 3.5%
Minimum curve radius: 300 m
Electrification: 750 V DC, third rail

Service: 3-10 min
First/last train: 05.25/23.18

Rolling stock: 42 two-car sets
Valmet Oy/Strömberg Oy M84
In peak service: 16 trains

Current situation: The line is the first of a planned network agreed by the city council in 1969. Extension to Ruoholahti (1.2 km) opened 1993, and new city-centre station at Kaisaniemi opened 1995. A 4 km branch from Itäkeskus to Vuosaari with three stations is under construction for opening in 1999.

VR suburban train at Malmi ***1997***

Raised platforms have been introduced at tram stops to facilitate boarding ***1996***

Tramway

Type of operation: Conventional tramway

Passenger boardings: (1993) 47.9 million
(1994) 49.6 million
(1995) 51.6 million
Car-km: (1993) 5.1 million
(1994) 5.1 million
(1995) 5.2 million

Route length: 75 km
reserved track: 53 km
Number of lines: 12
Max gradient: 8%
Minimum curve radius: 15 m
Electrification: 600 V DC, overhead

Service: Peak 5 min
First/last car: 05.30/01.30
One-person operation: All routes

Rolling stock: 105 cars

Karia/Valmet 4-axle (1959)	M23
Valmet 6-axle articulated (1973/75)	M40
Valmet 6-axle articulated (1983/87)	M42

In peak service: 86
On order: 20 low-floor cars on order from Adtranz and Rautaruukki Oy for delivery in 1998

VR

VR Ltd
S-Train Unit, Helsinki
PO Box 488, 00101 Helsinki
Telephone: + 358 9 7071 Fax: +358 9 707 2895
Route Manager: Kari Pekka Rosenholm

Type of operation: Suburban heavy rail

Passenger journeys: (1993) 33.4 million
(1994) 33.1 million
(1995) 33.2 million

Current situation: VR operates suburban trains on three routes out of Helsinki, to Karjaa, Vantaankoski and Riihimäki, totalling 173 km, 54 stations, electrified 25 kV 50 Hz. Minimum one or two trains per hour (four trains peak hours, every 5 min between Helsinki and Tikkurila); zonal fares.

In the Helsinki metropolitan area, VR has an agreement with the Helsinki Metropolitan Area Council (YTV) regarding provision of suburban service, under which tickets issued by the participating municipalities are valid on VR trains. Outside the metropolitan area only VR's zonal tickets are valid. The traffic figures above apply to the whole Helsinki suburban operation.

Developments: A new agreement has been concluded between VR and the Helsinki Metropolitan Area Council, allowing for continuation of services on the present scale and planning for future expansion. Running through to the end of 1999, the agreement will remain in force thereafter unless new provisions are required to encourage competing services.

VR is refurbishing suburban trains at a rate to ensure that half the services currently purchased by the council will be operated by refurbished units by 1999. Starting in 1996, the council pays VR a special fee linked to the number of refurbished trains in operation. VR has ordered 10 two-car emus from Fiat for introduction in 1998.

August 1996 saw completion of the fourth track between Helsinki and Tikkurila, allowing one pair to be dedicated to suburban trains. Under traffic plans for Helsinki in the period through to 2020, additional tracks are proposed from Helsinki to Leppävaara and later Espoo Centre, as well as from Tikkurila to Kerava.

The new agreement will also allow implementation of the LILI programme of co-ordination with other operators, designed to improve feeder services at many stations. The unified ticketing system is being extended, and smartcards are to be introduced in 1998. The ultimate aim is to for electronic ticketing to cover the whole metropolitan area.

Rolling stock: 100 two-car emus, 57 coaches, 6 electric locomotives

Valmet Oy Sm1 (1968)	M50 T50
Valmet Oy Sm2 (1975)	M50 T50
Coaches VR Pasila works (1982)	T57

On order: 10 two-car emus from Fiat

Ferry

Current situation: 10 routes operate both short inner-harbour crossings and longer routes to off-islands. One ferry operates all year round.

UPDATED

HIROSHIMA

Population: 1 million, metropolitan area 1.1 million

Public transport: Bus, light rail and tramway services provided by private company. Three other main private bus operators. Commuter rail services run by JR West. Astram automated guideway

Hiroshima Dentetsu 'Hiroden'

Hiroshima Electric Railway Company
2-9-29 Higashi Senda-machi, Naka-ku, Hiroshima 730, Japan
Telephone: +81 82 241 1191 Fax: +81 82 241 8561
President: Masaji Ishimatsu
General Manager: O Okutsubo
Staff: 2,387

Current situation: Hiroden is responsible for a substantial proportion of the Hiroshima area public transport. Tramways serve the inner city; a through service is operated across the city centre over tramway tracks to the main railway station from Hiroden's Miyajima light rail line. Bus services are provided by Hiroden and five other companies.

Other commercial activities, including the New Hiroden Hotel, retail stores and housing development, assist the public transport operation to remain generally subsidy-free apart from support to maintain bus services to outlying areas. Bus services account for 63.8 per cent of income, trams and light rail 25.2 per cent, and other activities 11 per cent.

Bus

Staff: 1,579

Passenger journeys: (1990/91) 67.4 million, city routes 32 million

Vehicle-km: (1990/91) 38.3 million, city routes 9.4 million

Number of routes: 439, including 14 city routes

Route length: 2,506 km (city routes 100 km)

On priority right-of-way: 128.3 km

Fleet: 771 buses and coaches, of which 237 buses used on city routes

Most intensive service: 2-3 min

One-person operation: All routes

Fare collection: Payment to farebox by driver on alighting, or prepurchase

Fare structure: Stage; 1-, 3- and 6-month passes; prepurchase coupons and stored fare 'Bus Card' valid for all six bus operators

Fare evasion control: Penalty payment

Integration with other modes: Bus operations fully integrated with light rail and Astram

Average distance between stops: 300-400 m

Average peak-hour speed: In mixed traffic, 12-13 km/h; in bus lanes, 20 km/h

Operational control: Computerised bus location and passenger information system on city routes

Bus priority: Bus lanes. Onboard traffic light control to give priority as bus approaches. A 'Centre Line Transfer System' was introduced on National Road Route 54, which connects the northwest area with the city centre, with one bus every 30 s in peak hours and one every 2 min at other times. One lane of a four-lane 5.7 km section of road is exclusively available to buses in peak hours.

Operating costs financed by: Fares 97%, other commercial sources 2%, subsidy/grants 1%

Subsidy from: Cross subsidy from commercial developments and associated profitable activities

New vehicles financed by: Internal funds

Current situation: Operations include a network of numbered city routes and a large number of unnumbered outer suburban and rural routes mainly serving the western half of Hiroshima Prefecture.

Hiroden Hino on city Route 12 ***1995***

Hiroshima's Astram ***1996***

Light rail

Staff: (Light rail and tramway) 571

Type of operation: Light rail transit

Passenger journeys: (1990/91) 18.1 million

Route length: 16.1 km

Number of lines: 1

Number of stops: 18

Gauge: 1,435 mm

Electrification: 600 V DC, overhead

Service: Peak 5 min, off-peak 15 min

First/last train: 05.50/23.00

Hiroden Class 3900 stock on the Miyajima line ***1996***

One-person operation: None
Fare structure: Graduated; day tickets (city tramway and light rail); monthly and 3-monthly passes
Fare collection: Payment to farebox on alighting; at Hiroshima station pavement conductors collect fares with mobile fareboxes
Operating costs financed by: (Light rail and tramway) fares 93.9%, other commercial sources 4.2%, subsidies 1.9%

Rolling stock: 33 articulated trams, 4 two-car sets and a single car; fleet includes 2 Duewag cars ex-Dortmund

Tramway
Type of operation: Conventional tramway

Passenger journeys: (1990/91) 43.9 million
Car-km: (1990/91) 4.8 million

Route length: 18.8 km
Number of lines: 7
Number of stops: 60
Gauge: 1,435 mm
Electrification: 600 V DC, overhead

Service: Peak 5-10 min; off-peak 5-11½ min
First/last tram: 06.00/22.33
Fare structure: Flat; day tickets (city tramway only and city tramway/light rail)
Fare collection: Coin to farebox
One-person operation: Off-peak, all routes; in peak hours some cars have conductors with extra farebox

Rolling stock: 94 bogie cars and 3 two-axle historical cars used on city routes; includes many second-hand cars from other Japanese systems

Umebachi Sharyo (1929)	M1
Kinami Sharyo (1940/42)	M7
Fuji Car (1950)	M5
Naniwa Koki (1953/55/57/58)	M29
Kobe Municipal Transport (1954)	M3
Kawasaki Rolling Stock (1956/60)	M7
Kisha Seizo Kaisha (1958)	M2
Osaka Sharyo Kogyo (1957/59/60)	M17
Alna Koki (1982/83/85/87/89/90/92)	M23
Osaka Sharyo (1984) (historical car)	M1
Class 150 (1987) (historical car)	M1
Class 200 ex-Hannover	M1

Current situation: The city tramway system is the only Japanese tramway with a centralised control system. The location of cars is shown on an indicator board in the control centre and instructions to drivers are given by means of light signals at some stops. At some stops passenger information about the route of the next car is shown by light signals.

Hiroshima Kosoku Kotsu
Hiroshima Rapid Transit
2-12-1, Choraku-ji, Asa minami-ku, Hiroshima-shi 731-01
Telephone: +81 82 830 3111 Fax: +81 82 830 3114
Staff: 262

Type of operation: Rubber-tyred guideway system Astram

Passenger boardings: (1994/95, 9 months) 9.8 million
Car-km: (1994/95, 9 months) 5.7 million

Hiroden car 805 at Hiroshima station ***1997***

Route length: 18.4 km
Number of lines: 1
Number of stations: 21
Track: Elevated with side guidance
Electrification: 750 V DC

Service: 3-20 min
First/last train: 06.00/23.50
One-person operation: All trains
Fare structure: Graduated distance-related; commuter and student passes; bus/Astram transfer tickets; stored fare 'Astram Card'
Fare collection: AFC

Rolling stock: 22 six-car trains
Niigata/Mitsubishi (1994) M132
In peak service: 114 cars

Current situation: This third sector line opened in 1994 linking central Hiroshima and the Asian Games stadium in the northern suburbs. Feeder bus routes link residential areas with several Astram stations.

Hiroshima Kotsu 'Hiroko'
Hiroshima Transport Company Limited
14-17 Misasa-machi 3-chome, Nishi-ku, Hiroshima 733
Telephone: +81 82 238 7755
President: Morito Mae
General Manager: Katsuhiko Hiraoka
Staff: 470

Bus
Passenger journeys: (Annual) 26 million

Number of routes: 21
Fleet: 274 vehicles, including Nissan Diesel and Mitsubishi Fuso
Operating costs financed by: Fares 100%
Bus priority: Services use 'Centre Line Transfer System' on National Road Route 54 (see above)

Hiroshima Bus
Hiroshima Bus Co Ltd
13-13 Osuga-cho, Minami-ku, Hiroshima-shi 732
Telephone: +81 82 261 5141
Staff: 603

Bus
Passenger journeys: (Annual) 26.5 million
Vehicle-km: (Annual) 8.4 million

Number of routes: 45, including 10 city routes
Fleet: 202 buses, 43 coaches including Nissan Diesel and Mitsubishi Fuso

Current situation: Hiroshima Bus operates a network of numbered city bus routes.

Geiyo Bus
Geiyo Bus
Showa-machi, Saijo, Higashi Hiroshima-shi 724
Telephone: +81 8242 23121

Bus
Passenger journeys: 15 million (annual)

Fleet: 109 vehicles including Hino

Current situation: This Hiroden subsidiary operates suburban and longer distance routes to the east of Hiroshima.

JR West
West Japan Railway Company
Nishi Nihon Ryokaku Tetsudo
4-24, Shibata 2-chome, Kita-ku, Osaka 530
Telephone: +81 6 375 8981 Fax: +81 6 375 8919
Chair: T Tsunoda
President: M Ide

Type of operation: Suburban/interurban heavy rail

Passenger journeys: (Hiroshima operations only) (1993/94) 56 million

Current situation: Frequent all-stations interurban/

commuter emu services run on the Sanyo main line, Hiroshima—Iwakuni (41 km) with some trains continuing to Ogori (138 km) or Shimonoseki (206 km) and Hiroshima—Shiraichi (41 km) with some continuing to Okayama (162 km). A number of trains start/finish at Hiroshima whilst others run through, for example Iwakuni—Hiroshima—Okayama. Also emu service on Kure line, Hiroshima—Kure—Mihara (96 km), and the Kabe line, Hiroshima—Kabe (17 km). Also dmu service on Geibi line, Hiroshima—Miyoshi (69 km).

UPDATED

HOBART

Population: 180,000

Public transport: Bus services provided by state government business enterprise. Private operators run services to some suburbs

Metro

Metropolitan Transport Trust
PO Box 61, Moonah 7009, Tasmania, Australia
Telephone: +61 03 6233 4232 Fax: +61 03 6272 8108
Chief Executive Officerr: Laurie Hansen
Staff: 467 (Hobart operations 354)

Current situation: The Trust was formed in 1954 to provide public road transport in the metropolitan areas of Hobart, Launceston and Burnie; its business name is Metro. Its Hobart operating area is within a 22 km radius of the general post office. Metro does not operate exclusively within this area, and some private operators are licensed to serve some districts.

In addition to local services, express buses link outer suburbs with the city centre, and midibuses provide a high-frequency service to the university.

Developments: In 1995/96 Metro reduced the number of depots from three to one, releasing land for residential development and reducing operating costs.

Bus (Metro Hobart operations only)
Passenger journeys: (1993/94) 8.7 million
(1994/95) 8.8 million
(1995/96) 8.6 million
Vehicle-km: (1993/94) 8.5 million
(1994/95) 8.8 million
(1995/96) 8.9 million

Number of routes: 114
Route length: (One way) 320 km
Fleet: 161 vehicles

Scania N112/N113 (1990/94)	130
Volvo B58 articulated (1980)	3
Volvo B10M articulated (1985)	19
MAN midibus 10-180 (1990)	9

In peak service: 147
Average age of fleet: 5.5 years

Most intensive service: 10 min
One-person operation: All routes
Fare collection: Payment to driver for single and daily multitrip tickets; prepurchase 10-trip, 10-day and monthly tickets
Fare structure: Sections; 20% discount for prepurchase multitickets; flat fare for children and concession travellers
Fares collected on board: 50%
Fare evasion control: Electronic warning on ticket validator; inspectors
Operational control: Supervisors/mobile radio
Arrangements for elderly/disabled: All buses have kneeling capability, low-floor buses on trial
Average peak-hour speed: 26.5 km/h
Average distance between stops: 400 m
Operating costs financed by: Fares 46%, other commercial sources 10.5%, subsidy/grants 46.9%
Subsidy from: State government consolidated revenue fund
New vehicles financed by: Own resources

Passengers board a Metro service in suburban Hobart ***1997***

Other operators

Current situation: Three private operators are licensed to provide service within Metro's operating area. Tasmanian Redline Coaches runs two routes and TigerLine three. The services together carry about 15,000 passengers weekly. Apart from a few Hobart Coaches peak-hour services, there is no common ticketing with Metro.

UPDATED

HO CHI MINH CITY

Population: 4 million

Public transport: Bus services provided by public authorities, and also widely by employers and other organised groups. Extensive use of shared taxis, 'Xiclos' (pedicabs) and 'Selam' (scooter taxis)

Doan Thanh Mien Cong San

City Bus Administration
Ho Chi Minh City, Vietnam

Bus

Current situation: Bus services in Ho Chi Minh City are provided with a fleet of Hino RC and Karosa B731 buses, plus some Isuzus with Kawasaki bodies second-hand from Japan, IFA, Desoto and LAZ.

Suburban and out-of-town services are run with a varied assortment of older vehicles including Renault and BMC van-derived mini- and midibuses and various types

Selam scooter taxi

Desoto bus operating in Ho Chi Minh City ***1995***

surviving from the US presence in Saigon, including Dodge, Ford and Desoto models. Most have provision for the carriage of roof luggage, including bicycles.

A Dutch operator, VSN International, started running some city routes in 1995.

Shared taxis

Current situation: There is extensive use of shared taxis, 'Xiclos' (pedicabs) and 'Selam' (scooter taxis).

UPDATED

Local suburban paratransit

HOHHOT

Population: 500,000

Public transport: Bus services provided by municipal authority

Hohhot City Bus

Hohhot City Bus Company

Hohhot, Neimongol Province, People's Republic of China

Current situation: A network of routes worked largely by modern buses covers the urban area. Unusually for Chinese cities, few articulated buses are in use, distributed over several routes alongside two-axle vehicles.

Bus

Number of routes: 18

Fleet: Approx 110 buses, including Beijing BK645 and Siping SP642

Beijing BK663 articulated: approx 10

Most intensive service: Approx 10 min

One-person operation: None

Fare collection: Payment to seated conductors, monthly passes

Fare structure: Stage

Siping SP642 bus in Hohhot

HONG KONG

Population: 5.5 million

Public transport: Main bus services provided by four large government-franchised private companies serving Hong Kong Island, Kowloon and the New Territories, including Lantau Island. Private company operates tramway. Government-owned Mass Transit Railway in urban area, and KCR railway to Chinese border; also light rail network serving new town of Tuen Mun. Ferries operated by two main companies and extensive government-licensed 'Public Light Bus' and maxicab operations. 'Residents' Services' coaches licensed to serve outlying residential areas. Funiculars. Total operations cater for about 10 million daily journeys. Overall policies formulated by Secretary for Transport, advised by Transport Advisory Committee. Major operators introducing smartcard ticketing system

All operations, except railways, are under direct supervision of:

Commissioner for Transport

41F Immigration Tower, 7 Gloucester Road, Wan Chai, Hong Kong

Telephone: +852 2829 5258 Fax: +852 2824 0433

Commissioner: Lily Yam Kwan

Deputy Commissioner, Transport Services: Isaac Chow

Kowloon Motor Bus

The Kowloon Motor Bus Co (1933) Ltd

1 Po Lun Street, Lai Chi Kok, Kowloon, Hong Kong

Telephone: +852 2786 8888 Fax: +852 2745 0300

Chair: Woo Pak Chuen

Managing Director: John C C Chan

General Manager: Charles C Y Lui

Staff: 11,778

Current situation: Operations are in Kowloon and the New Territories, and also through the two cross-harbour tunnels. KMB is Hong Kong's largest public transport operator. It was first granted a franchise in 1933, and its current franchise extends to August 1997. Negotiations with the government for extension of the franchise were in progress at the end of 1996.

The gradual population shift from urban Kowloon to housing estates in the New Territories is creating new demands for bus service, and 11 additional routes were introduced in 1995.

Introduction of air conditioned double-deckers has gained general acceptance, and further air conditioned routes are being introduced in line with demands to provide higher quality service. AC buses normally run alternately with conventional buses to give passenger choice.

Developments: In 1993 the government lifted the ban on KMB's buses picking up and setting down within the Transit Service Area in Tuen Mun (see under North West Rail, below).

A KMB subsidiary has been granted a franchise to operate 12 routes at the new airport and Tung Chung new town, the latter starting in mid-1997. Contactless smartcard fare system scheduled to start operation on cross-harbour routes in mid-1997.

The Dennis Dart, introduced in June 1996, is KMB's first low-floor bus with wheelchair ramp ***1997***

Bus

Passenger boardings: (1993) 966 million

(1994) 977 million

(1995) 996 million

Vehicle-km: (1993) 243 million

(1994) 255 million

(1995) 271 million

Number of routes: 359

Route length: (One way) 5,717 km

Fleet: 3,555 vehicles, of which 1,136 air conditioned

Dennis Jubilant double-deck	331
Leyland Victory Mk II double-deck	325
Leyland Olympian double-deck	123
Leyland Olympian 3-axle double-deck	630
Metro-Cammell 3-axle double-deck	254
Metro-Cammell 9.7 m double-deck	86
Dennis Dragon 3-axle double-deck	559
Dennis Dragon 3-axle air conditioned	425
Leyland Olympian 3-axle air conditioned	149
Scania N113 3-axle air conditioned	22
Volvo Olympian 3-axle air conditioned	245
Volvo Olympian 3-axle	30
Dennis Dominator double-deck	40
Mercedes-Benz double-deck	41
Dennis Dart air conditioned	49

Dennis Lance air conditioned	24
Dennis Falcon coach air conditioned	19
Toyota Coaster midibus air conditioned	20
Mitsubishi MK117J air conditioned	183

In peak service: 2,901
New vehicles required each year: Approx 200
On order: 505 ordered in 1995; 370 on order late 1996, all 3-axle double-deck with air conditioning, Volvo or DSV chassis, Walter Alexander bodies

One-person operation: All services
Fare collection: Payment to farebox on board
Fare structure: Sectional and flat; no prepurchase
Fares collected on board: 100%
Fare evasion control: Inspectors
Operational control: Route inspectors/mobile radio
Arrangements for elderly/disabled: Reserved seats, more handholds, coloured and textured stanchions; half fare for over 65s
Average speed: 19.9 km/h
Bus priority: On the congested Lion Rock Tunnel Road, Tuen Mun Highway and Tsing Yi Bridge, and other smaller-scale measures
Integration with other modes: Some through ticketing to KCR and MTR services
Operating costs financed by: Fares 99%, other commercial sources (advertising) 1%
New vehicles financed by: Loans from banks and Export Credit Guarantee

China Motor Bus

China Motor Bus Company Ltd
510 King's Road, North Point, Hong Kong
Telephone: +852 2561 6171 Fax: +852 2811 1432
Managing Director: Ngan Shing-Kwan
Traffic Manager: J A Sykes
Staff: 3,243

Current situation: Operations serve 1.3 million population of Hong Kong Island and Aplei Chau Island, together with cross-harbour services to Kowloon and the New Territories.

Bus

Passenger journeys: (1988/89) 312 million
(1989/90) 283.8 million
(1990/91) 275.9 million
Vehicle-km: (1988/89) 51 million
(1989/90) 50.4 million
(1990/91) 52.3 million

Number of routes: 141 (including 33 cross-harbour)
Route length: (One way) 1,648 km
Fleet: 1,055 vehicles

Ailsa Volvo MkIII	2
Dennis Condor 11 m	28
Dennis Condor 11 m air conditioned	36
Dennis Condor 12 m	48
Dennis Dart air conditioned (1991)	20
Dennis Dominator	7
Dennis Jubilant	30
Guy Arab 6LX double-deck	117
Leyland Fleetline 9 m	166
Leyland Fleetline 10 m	288
Leyland Olympian 11 m air conditioned	5
Leyland Olympian B45	2
Leyland Titan (B15) double-deck	1
Leyland Victory double-deck	167
MCW Metrobus 10 m double-deck	12
MCW Metrobus 11 m double-deck	40
MCW Metrobus 12 m double-deck	84
MCW Metrorider air conditioned single-deck	2

In peak service: 777

Most intensive service: 4 min
One-person operation: 100%
Fare collection: Farebox on board; mobile fareboxes used at peak times on some routes to permit boarding through centre doors
Fare structure: Stage/flat fare; no prepurchase
Fares collected on board: 100%
Fare evasion control: Inspectors
Operational control: Inspectors with mobile radio; route regulators
Arrangements for elderly/disabled: Reserved seats
Average peak-hour speed: 5-20 km/h
Integration with other modes: Many routes are feeders to MTR stations, some terminating in purpose-built interchanges; intensive service from KCR's Hung Hom terminus to Hong Kong Island
Operating costs financed by: Fares 100%

Developments: Various routes introduced or extended to serve new housing developments at Siu Sai Wan and Wah Kwai. In 1992 the government withdrew 26 of CMB's routes (see below), and a further 14 were withdrawn in 1995.

HK Tramways double-deck tram and other operators' buses

MTR train bound for Yau Ma Tei

Mass Transit Railway

Mass Transit Railway Corporation
17/F Chevalier Commercial Centre, 8 Wang Hoi Road, Kowloon Bay
Telephone: +852 2993 2111 Fax: +852 2798 8822
Chairman & Chief Executive: Jack C K So
Operations Director: W R Donald
Project Director, Airport Line: Russell Black
Staff: 7,397

Type of operation: Full metro, initial route opened 1979

Passenger journeys: (1993) 779 million
(1994) 804 million
(1995) 813 million
Car-km: (1993) 81.8 million
(1994) 83.8 million
(1995) 86.4 million

Route length: 43.2 km
in tunnel: 34.4 km
elevated: 8.8 km
Number of lines: 3
Number of stations: 38
Gauge: 1,432 mm
Track: BS 90A 45 kg/m continuously supported FB rail, discretely supported on overhead sections of Tsuen Wan extension; UIC60 60 kg/m continuously supported FB rail in tunnels of Island line and Eastern Harbour crossing, discretely supported on overhead sections
Max gradient: 3%
Minimum curve radius: 300 m
Tunnel: Bored single-track, bored double-track and cut-and-cover
Electrification: 1.5 kV DC, overhead

Service: Peak 112 sec, off-peak 3-10 min
First/last train: 06.00/01.00
Fare structure: Zonal, with single and stored value tickets
Integration with other modes: Common stored value ticket valid for travel also on KCR and some bus routes of KMB and Citybus
Revenue control: AFC at all stations
Operating costs financed by: Fares 91.6%, other commercial sources 8.4%
One-person operation: All trains
Automatic control: All tracks except within depots
Surveillance: CCTV on platforms and concourses

Rolling stock: 759 cars

Metro-Cammell (1979 on)	M470
Metro-Cammell (1984/86)	T152
Metro-Cammell (1988/89)	M38 T11
GEC Alsthom (1994/95)	M88

In peak service: 664

Developments: In 1993 a seven-year investment programme was unveiled, designed to further raise capacity and provide a better environment for both passengers and staff. Signalling on all three lines is being renewed to reduce headways so that 34 trains/h can be run; GEC Alsthom is installing the SACEM system, with completion scheduled for late 1997. In addition, complete refurbishment of the rolling stock fleet is to be carried out in a programme extending to 2001.

Work is in progress on the 34 km line to serve the new airport being built at Chep Lap Kok on Lantau Island and scheduled to open in 1998. The line is on an entirely new route from Central, serving reclaimed areas with stations at Kowloon and Tai Kok Sui before making interchange with the Tsuen Wan line at Lai King. This section will provide relief for the existing line in the Nathan Road corridor. From Lai King the route runs partially on reclaimed land to separate terminals at the airport and Tung Chung.

Two levels of service will operate — the Tung Chung mass transit and Airport Express — with eventual capacity for two mass transit and one airport train running every 4½ min at a speed of 135 km/h. Journey time from Central to the airport and Tung Chung will be 23 min. Initially, the Airport line service will run every 8 min, requiring 11 six-car trains, while a 4 min service on the Tung Chung line, with alternate trains turning back at Tsing Yi, will require 13 trains. The initial rolling stock fleets are being supplied by Adtranz and CAF.

Kowloon-Canton Railway

Kowloon-Canton Railway Corporation
KCR House, 9 Lok King Street, Fo Tan, Sha Tin, New Territories, Hong Kong
Telephone: +852 2688 1333 Fax: +852 2688 0983
Chairman & Chief Executive Officer: Yeung Kai-yin
Director, KCR East Rail: Samuel M H Lai
Director, KCR West Rail: Ian McPherson
Telephone: +852 2864 5777 Fax: +852 2601 5287
Staff: 3,013

Current situation: KCRC, formerly a government department, was vested as a public corporation in 1983. Besides the local (Kowloon—Lo Wu) and long-distance (Hong Kong—Guangzhou) rail services operated by the East Rail division, KCRC runs a light rail network, feeder buses and freight services. It also has property and related commercial interests.

In 1995 KCRC submitted an invited proposal to the government for the design, construction and operation of the West Rail line. This would offer local passenger service between the northwest New Territories and Kowloon, a new long-distance route into China, and a freight link that would help relieve road congestion. The project is being taken forward by the West Rail division.

Disputes with the Chinese authorities over the West Rail project led to a decision in December 1996 to postpone the long-distance element, bringing down the estimated cost from HK$75 billion to HK$50 billion. Construction of the New Territories portion of the route could start in mid-1997 for opening in 2002.

KCR East Rail

Type of operation: Regional metro, opened 1910

Passenger journeys: (1993) 206 million
(1994) 220 million
(1995) 232 million

Route length: 34 km
Number of lines: 1
Number of stations: 13
Gauge: 1,435 mm
Track: UIC 54 kg/m rail on concrete sleepers
Max gradient: 1%
Minimum curve radius: 200 m
Electrification: 25 kV 50 Hz, overhead

Service: Peak 3 min, off-peak 5-6 min
First/last train: 05.35/00.25
Fare structure: Zonal
Revenue collection: Automatic machines and entrance/exit barriers
Integration with other modes: Stored value ticket also valid for travel on MTR
Operating costs financed by:

Rolling stock: 351 cars

Metro-Cammell L	M120
Metro-Cammell S	T60
Metro-Cammell (1987/88)	M75
GEC Alsthom (1989/91)	M96

Developments: GEC Alsthom is resignalling the route and installing cab signalling and ATP. On completion capacity will be raised 25 per cent to 24 trains/h. An HK$1.3 billion redevelopment of the main station at Hung Hom started in 1995.

KCR Light Rail

55-65 Lung Mun Road, Tuen Mun, New Territories, Hong Kong
Telephone: +852 2468 7600 Fax: +852 2455 0030
Director: Jonathan Yu

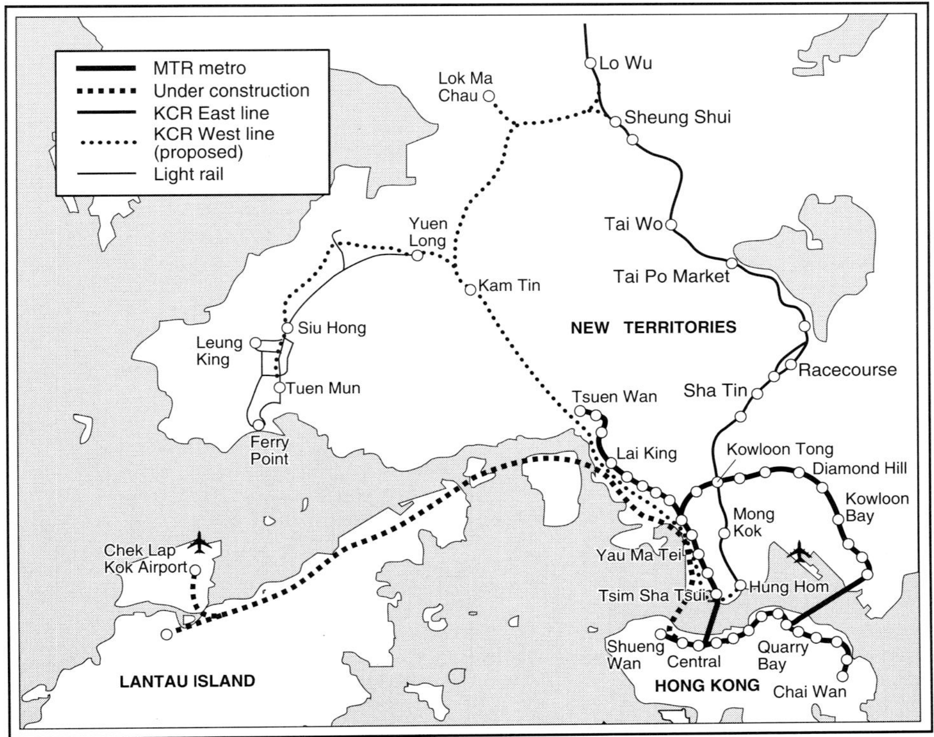

Hong Kong's mass transit system and Kowloon-Canton Railway

Type of operation: Light rail, first line opened 1988

Passenger journeys: (1993) 107 million
(1994) 117 million
(1995) 123 million

Route length: 31.7 km
reserved track: 28 km
Number of lines: 8
Number of stops: 57
Gauge: 1,435 mm
Track: UIC 54 kg/m flat bottom on concrete sleepers, and some grooved rail; 3 km paved track in concrete
Max gradient: 6.1%
Minimum curve radius: 23 m
Electrification: 750 V DC, overhead

Service: Peak 5-10 min, off-peak 10-13 min
First/last car: 05.30/00.39
Fare structure: 5 zones, free transfer to feeder buses
Revenue control: Ticket vending machines on all platforms, inspectors, spot penalty
Integration with other modes: KCR feeder buses

Rolling stock: 99 cars

Comeng (1987/88)	M69
Kawasaki (1992/93)	M20 T10

On order: 20 cars from Australia's Goninan for mid-1997 delivery

Current situation: Ridership and revenue continued to grow in 1995 (by 5.1 per cent and 13.3 per cent respectively) despite a fall in local population growth and relaxation of the requirement that non-KCR buses should not operate in the 'Transit Service Area'. This was set up on opening of the light rail system to protect the line from competition.
Developments: Service improvements are planned for mid-1997 when 20 new cars are commissioned; better platform and ticketing facilities are also promised.

KCR Bus

General Manager: David Hassey

Passenger journeys: (1993) 33 million
(1994) 35 million
(1995) 32 million
Vehicle-km: (1995) 5.8 million

Current situation: Feeder services provided to KCR stations (10 routes), and light rail stops (11 routes). Fleet of 103 buses.
Developments: Eighteen air conditioned buses were purchased in 1995 to replace 20 older double-decks.

Hongkong Tramways

Hongkong Tramways Ltd
A wholly owned subsidiary of Wharf (Holdings) Ltd
Whitty Street Tram Depot, Connaught Road West, Western District, Hong Kong
Telephone: +852 2559 8918 Fax: +852 2858 3697
Operations Manager: Allan Leech
Staff: 675

Type of operation: Conventional tramway, first line opened 1904

Passenger journeys: (1993) 125.2 million
(1994) 123.1 million
(1995) 114.1 million
Car-km: (1993) 6.9 million
(1994) 6.9 million
(1995) 6.8 million

Route length: 23.8 km
Number of routes: 6
Number of stops: 118
Gauge: 1,067 mm
Track: Ri60 grooved 60.5 kg/m rail directly fixed to concrete slab embedded in road surface
Electrification: 500 V DC, overhead

Service: Peak 2-6 min
First/last car: 05.16/00.45
Fare structure: Flat; monthly tickets; tourist tickets (with Star Ferry Co); seniors concessionary fare
Operating costs financed by: Fares 80.2%, advertising 19.5%, private hire 0.3%
One-person operation: All services

Kawasaki LRV at Siu Hong on the Tuen Mun light rail network

Rolling stock: 163 double-deck cars, mainly built by local dockyard and Hongkong Tramway workshops

M-2X (1949 on, rebuilt 1985/90)	M161
Open-top leisure cars	M2

In peak service: 155 cars

Current situation: Future of the system is now assured as patronage has stabilised following an initial 8 per cent loss on opening of the MTR Island line.
Developments: A plan has been prepared for replacing existing timber bodies on tramcars with slightly extended alloy bodies designed for bidirectional running. A new type of rubber suspension is also being fitted to all trams.

Two extensions are proposed to serve new housing developments. A link is planned to the Central and Wanchai reclamation areas which lie parallel with the existing tram route between Central and Causeway Bay. The second line would be an extension of the Kennedy Town service into a new housing estate, park and leisure area planned on reclaimed land at Green Island.

A light rail line is being studied which would run from Central/Admiralty to the Aberdeen area, with a possible link to the existing network.

New railways planned

Current situation: Plans for further construction to ease traffic congestion, relieve current overcrowding on rail and absorb projected travel demand through to the year 2001 were put forward in the second Comprehensive Transport Study (CTS-2) published in 1989. Some 19 rail proposals were assessed, of which only three were recommended for early implementation.

The priority of these links was affected, however, by the need for a rail connection to the new international airport which is to open on Lantau Island in 1997. This 34 km MTR line, linking Hong Kong Island with West Kowloon via a third cross-harbour tunnel, will parallel the MTR on the congested Nathan Road corridor before reaching the airport by way of the new Lantau Bridge.

Further assessment of these and a further 70-or-so schemes linked to housing and industrial developments proposals was made in the Railway Development Study carried out in 1992. Three preferred network options emerged — a relief route for the KCR line to the border with China, a link from this line to Tuen Mun to provide a fast route from the western New Territories to Hong Kong, and a line to serve the eastern New Territories.

An elevated people mover linking Hung Hom with Tsim Sha Tsui was approved in 1991, and a revised plan was put forward in 1992. This is the privately promoted Kowloon Sky Rail scheme.

Hongkong & Yaumati Ferry

Hong Kong Ferry (Holdings) Co Ltd
West Kowloon Reclamation Area Lot No SSP Misc 58, Po Lun Street extension, Lai Chi Kok, Kowloon, Hong Kong
Telephone: +852 2786 9383 Fax: +852 2786 9001
Group General Manager: David C S Ho
Staff: 1,312

Passenger journeys: (1993) 37.2 million
(1994) 38.5 million
(1995) 35.8 million

Operating costs financed by: Fares 100%

Current situation: Operates cross-harbour passenger (six routes) and vehicle (one route) ferries, eight routes to new towns and outlying districts and four excursion routes on a 15-year franchise which ends in 1999. Also operates hoverferry service Hong Kong to China (Whampoa and Shekou) and Macau. Fleet of 84 vessels.
Developments: Stored-value ticketing system installed 1996.

Star Ferry

The 'Star' Ferry Company Limited
16F Ocean Centre, Harbour City, Canton Road, Kowloon, Hong Kong
Telephone: +852 2118 6223 Fax: +852 2311 4395
Operations Manager: Johnny T H Leung
A member of the Wharf Group
Staff: 344

Passenger journeys: (1993) 35.7 million
(1994) 36.1 million
(1995) 35 million

Current situation: Operates three cross-harbour passenger routes from Edinburgh Place to Tsim Sha Tsui and Hung Hom, and Kowloon Point to Wan Chai, totalling 7.1 km, with a fleet of 12 vessels. Fares cover 59 per cent of operating costs.

Licensed ferries

Licensed by: Transport Department

Current situation: Six operators with 31 vessels ply eight minor routes, carrying about 9 million passengers a year. There are also 118 local services 'Kaitos', with 103 operators.

Public Light Bus/Red Minibus and Green Minibus

Current situation: Legalised in 1969, the Public Light Buses were carrying an estimated 25 per cent of all trips within three years. The government then fixed the number of vehicles permitted, and Red and Green Minibus networks now account for about 17 per cent of trips.

PLBs (now known as 'Red Minibuses') concentrate on the main urban corridors and are demand-responsive. There are no fixed routes, stops or fares, though they are prohibited from certain areas and there are some restrictions on pick-up points to avoid congestion.

Green Minibus services have been licensed additionally to act as feeders to major routes (see below).

There are also 2,550 private light buses authorised only to carry groups, and collection of separate fares is not permitted.

Red Minibus

Independent 'Public Light Bus'
Licensed by: Transport Department
Staff: 6,000 drivers

Passenger journeys: (1993) 1 million daily

Number of routes: 120 unscheduled routes including two groups cross-harbour, 30 routes on Hong Kong Island, 47 in Kowloon, 23 Kowloon—New Territories and 18 New Territories internal routes
Fleet: 2,676 minibuses (16-seat)

One-person operation: All services
Fare collection: Driver collected
Fare structure: Stage, not controlled; surcharge generally applied for peak and night services
Operating costs financed by: Fares 100%

Green Minibus

Represented by:
HK Kowloon & NT Public Maxicab Operators General Association Limited
Shop 14 G/F, Kam Po Court, Sai Kung, New Territories
Telephone: +852 792 2948
Supervised by: Transport Department

Passenger journeys: (1993) 0.7 million daily

Current situation: Green Minibuses are scheduled PLB services on specified routes, with fixed timetables and fare scales approved by the Transport Department. In 1993 there were 244 routes — 64 on Hong Kong Island, 56 in Kowloon and 124 in the New Territories, with a total of 1,657 16-seat vehicles. Fares are distance-based.
Developments: The government favours introduction of more of the scheduled and route-controlled Green Minibus operations rather than the unscheduled PLBs. In 1994, 21 new Green Minibus routes were opened for competitive bidding.

New Lantau Bus

New Lantau Bus Co (1973) Ltd
Shop D, Silver Centre Building, Silvermine Bay, Lantau
Telephone: +852 2984 8304
Chair: Brook Bernacchi
Staff: 110

Current situation: New Lantau Bus is Hong Kong's third franchised bus company. It was formed in 1973 by an amalgamation of small companies and franchised in 1979 to serve Lantau Island for nine years, extended to 1993.

Bus

Passenger journeys: (1990) 3.7 million
(1993) 5 million

Number of routes: 7, plus 2 Sunday only
Route length: (One way) 123 km
Fleet: 70 vehicles

Leyland Victory double-deck	4
Commer/Fargo	16
Dodge	11
Isuzu JCR 460	12
Dodge midibus	3
Others	24

One-person operation: All except one route. Route 1 was converted in 1985, but conductors reintroduced following protests, and this is now Hong Kong's only crew-operated service

Citybus

Citybus Ltd
8/F Rediffusion House, 822 Lai Chi Kok Road, Kowloon
Telephone: +852 2745 8888 Fax: +852 2786 5876
Managing Director: Lyndon Rees
Traffic Manager: Dave Lam
Staff: 280

Passenger journeys: (1991) 13 million
(1993) 60 million
Vehicle-km: (1991) 1.7 million
(1993) 11.4 million

Number of routes: 68
Route length: 370 km
Fleet: 209 buses
Dennis Dragon
Volvo/Alexander Olympian (1995) 21

Current situation: In 1991 privately owned Citybus became the fourth franchised bus company following granting of one franchised coach route by the government. Also in 1991, Citybus acquired the exclusive franchise to provide airport coach service between Hong Kong and the new airport at Shenzhen (special economic zone in China). Other activities include private hire, contract business, student and employee transport, in addition to cross-border services to China and local residents' coach services.
Developments: In 1992 Citybus was awarded the 26 routes withdrawn from CMB (see above), and started operations in September 1993 as a separate entity called Network 26 with a fleet of 180 buses. It took over a further 14 ex-CMB routes in 1995.

'Public Light Buses' in Hong Kong

Residential coaches

Current situation: To cater for the peak-hour transport demand of residential areas which do not have adequate access to franchised buses and Green Minibuses, residents' services were introduced in 1982. Controlled under the passenger service licence, the service can only operate according to the route, timetable and stopping places approved. In 1994 there were 53 routes which carried about 66,000 passengers a day. The fleet of licensed non-franchised vehicles totalled 371.

Funicular/cable car

Current situation: The Peak Tramway and Ocean Park Cable Car are almost entirely leisure operations, and carry about 3 million passengers annually.

UPDATED

HONOLULU

Population: 885,000
Public transport: Bus services provided by private non-profit undertaking under contract to public transit authority which co-ordinates bus and paratransit services

PTA

Honolulu Public Transit Authority
Pacific Park Plaza, Suite 275, 711 Kapiolani Boulevard, Honolulu, Hawaii 96813, USA
Telephone: +1 808 527 6890 Fax: +1 808 596 2380
Acting Executive Director: Howard K Takara
Staff: 23

Current situation: In 1992 the PTA assumed responsibility for administration and operation of public transport in the city and county of Honolulu, replacing the bus systems division of the Department of Transportation Services. It contracts operation of bus services (TheBus) to Oahu Transit Services, a non-profit corporation, and the Handi-Van paratransit service to Mayflower Contract Services.
Developments: The PTA is a member of the Hawaii Electric Vehicle Demonstration Project Consortium and is testing two hybrid electric buses.

Bus

Operated under contract by Oahu Transit Services Inc
President: James E Cowen
Staff: 1,350

TMC bus with wheelchair lift and kneeling capability

Passenger boardings: (1993/94) 80.4 million
(1994/95) 80.5 million
(1995/96) 77.9 million
Vehicle-km: (1993/94) 30.4 million
(1994/95) 31.3 million
(1995/96) 30.9 million

Number of routes: 80
Route length: (One way) 2,400 km
Fleet: 525 vehicles

Gillig Phantom (1983/84)	104
Scania CN112 (1985/87)	127
Neoplan (1985)	10
TMC RTS-06 (1991)	35
TMC RTS-08 (1992/93)	95
Gillig (1994/95)	132
Gillig (1996)	22

In peak service: 438
On order: 68 buses will be ordered in 1997

Most intensive service: 4 min
One-person operation: All routes
Fare collection: Exact fare, farebox on bus
Fare structure: Flat or prepaid monthly bus pass; 4-day tourist pass
Fare evasion control: By driver
Arrangements for elderly/disabled: 250 TMC buses have wheelchair lifts; Handi-Van paratransit service contracted to Mayflower Contract Services, 97 vehicles carried 650,000 passengers in 1995/96
Average distance between stops: In high-density areas, 160 m; in rural areas, 305 m
Average peak-hour speed: In mixed traffic, 22.5 km/h; in bus lanes, 32-40 km/h
Operating costs financed by: Fares 30%, subsidy/grants 70%
Subsidy from: City government 93%, FTA 7%
New vehicles financed by: FTA grants and city government

UPDATED

HOUSTON

Population: 1.7 million; service area 2.5 million
Public transport: Bus services provided by Metropolitan Transit Authority of Harris County, controlled by representative board

Metro

Metropolitan Transit Authority of Harris County
PO Box 61429, 1201 Louisiana, Houston, TX 77208-1429, USA
Telephone: +1 713 739 4000 Fax: +1 713 754 9537
Chair: William F Burge III
General Manager: Robert G MacLennan
Deputy General Manager, Transit Operations:
Fred Gilliam
Staff: 3,507

Current situation: Voters in Harris County approved creation of the MTA in 1978, allowing the State to collect a 1 per cent sales tax to partially fund the authority. After the 1983 rejection of a bond issue to finance an initial metro line, voters approved in 1988 a $2.6 billion 13-year programme of public transport improvements known as the Phase 2 Mobility Plan. As a result, by 1995 14 transit centres, 23 park-and-ride sites, over 1,400 bus shelters and 102 km of high-occupancy transitways had been commissioned. Also approved in 1988 was a measure to set aside at least 25 per cent of sales tax revenue for general mobility projects such as road, bridge and pavement construction.

Nine park-and-ride and two local bus routes are operated under contract using Metro-owned buses. Takeover of a bus depot by a private contractor is under discussion.

Developments: In 1992 the board approved the Regional Bus Plan — a $1 billion long-range plan for bus and related capital improvements to be implemented throughout the 3,300 km^2 service area by 2010. Federal funding of $500 million towards the project was granted in 1994. Building on the existing network, the plan includes improvements to speed up bus operations, an increase in the fleet by some 400 buses, increased service to suburban employment centres and expansion of local routes. A sixth bus maintenance depot is being built at Fallbrook, capable of housing 250 vehicles.

The bus fleet is being renewed and expanded to about 1,600 during the plan period; all will be lift-equipped. General mobility plans also call for extension of transitways to some 166 km, to be served by 18 transit centres and 2,100 sheltered stops. All bus routes are to be fully accessible to disabled people by 2000. Vanpooling is being encouraged in areas where bus service is limited, with subsidies offered to employers who participate. The MetroVan scheme started in 1994 attracted 115 companies in its first year of operation, and grew to 100 vans.

Two new park-and-rides were opened in 1996, bringing the total to 24. Hours of HOV lane operation were changed in September 1996 to 05.00-11.00 inbound and 14.00-20.00 outbound. Service-km were raised by 5 per cent in October 1996.

There have been several proposals for rail schemes, including a seven-line commuter network based on existing freight railways promoted by a grouping of private operators. Metro owns 250 km of rail alignment purchased from Southern Pacific, along with some trackage rights. Two routes were assessed for a possible start-up service, but poor ridership projections led to

Metro's 1996 low-floor bus from New Flyer ***1997***

shelving of the project. In late 1996 there were no further plans for rail development.

Bus

Passenger journeys: (1993) 59.6 million
(1994) 59.6 million
(1995) 58.5 million
Vehicle-km: (1993) 83 million
(1994) 84.5 million
(1995) 86.5 million

Number of routes: 122
Route length: 3,628 km

Fleet: 1,365 vehicles

Eagle 10 coaches (1985)	99
GMC RTS-II 04 (1981/83)	288
Neoplan 40 ft (1984)	15
Crown-Ikarus articulated (1985)	34
Flxible (1985)	197
Neoplan 30 ft (1986)	30
Ikarus 40 ft (1990/91/92/93/94)	300
S&S Mercedes (1992)	85
Marcopolo 26 ft (1990)	45
Neoplan articulated (1992/93)	54
Neoplan 45 ft (1993/94)	61
Collins van for MetroLift (1990/92)	86
Goshen minibus for MetroLift (1990)	12
New Flyer low-floor (1996)	30
Others	29

In peak service: 1,064
On order: 122 articulated buses from Neoplan, delivery started 1996; 115 New Flyer low-floor 40 ft for 1996/97; and 128 New Flyer low-floor 29 ft for 1997/98

Most intensive service: 3 min
One-person operation: All routes
Fare collection: Coin, prepurchase ticket or token, weekly or monthly pass
Fare structure: Local and express, flat; commuter, zonal; weekly pass
Average peak-hour speed: 25.6 km/h
Integration with other modes: 22 park-and-ride sites have 25,000 spaces; buses, carpools and vanpools (20.5 million riders in 1995) use the transitways
Arrangements for elderly/disabled: MetroLift demand-responsive service operated under contract caters for about 888,000 trips annually using 98 lift-equipped vans on prebooked journeys, supplemented by subscription taxi service and subsidised on-demand service of commercial taxis; 33 regular routes accessible; reduced fares on regular routes
Bus priority: Barrier-separated transitways on five freeways available to buses, high-occupancy vehicles and carpools; reversible HOV lanes extend to over 100 km
Operating costs financed by: Fares 22.5%, tax levy 77.5%

Busway

Current situation: Transitways are barrier-separated, one-direction single carriageways for use inbound from 05.00-11.00 and outbound from 14.00-21.00. They provide direct links with most park-and-ride lots and are open to all high-occupancy vehicles. Plans envisage a network of more than 166 km by 2010.

UPDATED

HULL

Population: 262,000
Public transport: Most bus services provided by two private companies

Stagecoach (KHCT)

Kingston upon Hull City Transport Ltd
Foster Street, Hull HU8 8BT, England
Telephone: +44 1482 222333 Fax: +44 1482 217623
Managing Director: Malcolm Howitt
Traffic & Marketing Director: Stephen Warnock-Smith
Finance Director: Peter Solomon
Staff: 300

Current situation: Formerly owned by the city council, KHCT was sold to Cleveland Transit of Stockton in 1993, with employees holding 49 per cent of shares. Following the end of a two-year bus war with East Yorkshire in 1994, the company cut back services and reduced the fleet. Both KHCT and its parent company were bought by Stagecoach in 1994.
Developments: KHCT rationalised its core facilities in Hull prior to sale to Cleveland Transit. Co-ordination with East Yorkshire has been developed on city routes, and the two operators have established joint ticketing arrangements. Limited stop express services introduced to Leeds, Sheffield and Grimsby.

Dennis Dominator of KHCT Stagecoach on Bransholme route ***1997***

Bus

Passenger journeys: (1991/92) 18.4 million
(1992/93) 17.7 million
(1995/96) 14.3 million
Vehicle-km: (1991/92) 7.1 million
(1992/93) 7.9 million
(1995/96) 7.5 million

Number of routes: 85
Route length: 416 km
Fleet: 126 vehicles

MCW Metrobus double-deck (1980/81)	15
Dennis Dominator/Alexander double-deck	5
Dennis Dominator/East Lancs double-deck	36
Volvo Olympian/Northern Counties double-deck	3
Dennis Lance single-deck	1
Leyland National single-deck (1984)	1
Scania/East Lancs single-deck (1988)	6
Scania/East Lancs double-deck (1989/90)	16
Volvo B10M/Northern Counties single-deck (1995)	12
Mercedes minibus	14
Coaches	17

In peak service: 100
On order: 5 double-deck and 5 single-deck

Most intensive service: 8 min
One-person operation: All services
Fare collection: Wayfarer equipment with change-giving; magnetic stored-value cards
Fare structure: Coarse stages; daily, weekly, monthly and 11-journey cards
Fares collected on board: 86% (14% of journeys by card holders)
Fare evasion control: Ticket inspectors
Operational control: Inspectors; mobile radios
Arrangements for elderly/disabled: Low flat fare at all times paid for by county council subsidy; 'Handyrider' wheelchair-accessible bus operates on different services each day; new vehicles conform to DPTAC standards
Bus priority: Bus lanes on Beverley road; pedestrianisation in city centre around Queen Victoria Square does not prohibit buses
Operating costs financed by: Fares 84%, other commercial sources 2%, subsidy/grants (for specific services/concessions) 14%
Subsidy from: City and county council grants

East Yorkshire

East Yorkshire Motor Services Ltd
252 Anlaby Road, Hull HU3 2RS
Telephone: +44 1482 27142 Fax: +44 1482 212040
Joint Managing Directors: Peter Shipp
Godfrey Burley
Staff: 680

Current situation: The company was a subsidiary of National Bus until 1987, when it was sold to EYMS Group, a management consortium which has grown into a major holding company. It is the main operator of services outside the city, but has introduced several routes within the city boundary and carries local passengers on its longer distance routes.
Developments: Since 1987 EYMS Group has acquired several operators and has formed East Yorkshire Travel, consolidating its coach operations into this new leisure travel company. In 1992, additional city services were introduced in competition with KHCT, but services were cut back in 1994/95 after the end of a two-year bus war.

Passenger journeys: (1990) 13.3 million
(1991) 13.5 million
Vehicle-km: (1990) 11 million
(1991) 11.6 million

Number of routes: 170
Fleet: 333 vehicles

Bristol VR/ECW double-deck	90
Leyland Atlantean/Park Royal double-deck	7
Leyland Atlantean/MCW double-deck	1
Leyland Olympian/ECW double-deck	18
Leyland Atlantean/Roe double-deck	2
Leyland Atlantean/East Lancs double-deck	2
Leyland Atlantean/ECW double-deck	9
Leyland Atlantean/NC double-deck	8
Leyland Olympian/NC double-deck	35
Leyland Olympian/Alexander double-deck	1
Volvo Olympian/Alexander double-deck	14
Volvo Olympian/NC double-deck	6
AEC Regent/Willowbrook double-deck	1
DAF/Optare double-deck	1
Leyland National single-deck	8
Volvo B6 single-deck	1
Mercedes/Optare single-deck	8
Dennis/Plaxton single-deck	3
Optare Excel low-floor	6
Leyland and Volvo coach	60
MCW Metroliner double-deck coach	1
Ford Transit/Carlyle minibus	10
Mercedes/Reeve Burgess minibus	41

Most intensive service: 7-8 min
One-person operation: Nearly all services
Fare collection: Wayfarer equipment with change given; magnetic stored-value tickets

Other commercial operators

Current situation: Services also provided by North Bank Travel and City Traveller.

UPDATED

Low-floor Optare Excel on East Yorks Service 181 ***1997***

HYDERABAD/ SECUNDERABAD

Population: 4.3 million (with Secunderabad)
Public transport: Bus services provided by State Road Transport Corporation with additional private buses, minibuses and autorickshaws. Suburban services of South Central Railway; light rail planned

Metro Liner luxury coach and standard double-deck of APSRT at Secunderabad bus station ***1995***

APSRT

Andhra Pradesh State Road Transport Corporation
Mushirabad, Hyderabad 500020, India
Telephone: +91 40 761 7571 Fax: +91 40 761 7135
Vice Chairman & Managing Director: K C Misra
Staff: (State-wide total) 121,438

Current situation: Provides services throughout Andhra Pradesh with a fleet of 15,790 buses (including some hired); total of 4,095 million passengers carried in 1994/95. City services account for only about 12 per cent of vehicle-km.

Bus

Hyderabad City Region
Jubilee Bus Station, Secunderabad 500003
Telephone +91 40 518828
Executive Director: M Mallanna
Staff: 13,000

Vehicle-km: (1990/91) 120.3 million
(1993/94) 144.1 million

Number of routes: 723
Route length: (One way) 11,295 km
Fleet: 1,915 vehicles, mostly Ashok Leyland and including double-deck Metro Liner luxury coaches

Most intensive service: 2 min
Fare collection: Payment to conductor or prepurchase pass
Average peak-hour speed: Ordinary services, 17 km/h; express, 26 km/h
Fare evasion control: Random checks, with penalty
Operational control: Route inspectors/radio
Arrangements for elderly/disabled: Free travel for disabled; cost borne by operator
Operating costs financed by: Fares 96.5%, other commercial sources 3.5%
New vehicles financed by: IBDI and other financial institutions

SCR

South Central Railway
Rail Nilayam, Secunderabad 500371
Telephone: +91 40 834234 Fax: +91 40 833 3203

Current situation: Limited suburban services are operated from Medchal and Umdanagar to Secunderabad, and Bolarum to Hyderabad.

Light rail (planned)

Urban Mass Transit Co Ltd (UMTC)

Current situation: In 1993 the government approved plans for light rail in the busiest corridors between the twin cities. UMTC was formed as a consortium by the Indian and Andhra Pradesh governments, financial institutions and private sector companies to design and build the infrastructure.

In 1994 UMTC called for expressions of interest from companies to prequalify for a build-own-operate-transfer or turnkey contract to implement the project. The 18 km initial phase was to be mostly elevated, linking Balanagar and Charminar, with a branch of 6 km to Dilsukhnagar planned as a second phase.

Four companies responded, but they all wanted the state government to contribute at least 25 per cent of the cost. No decision has yet been taken.

UPDATED

expected to start once tunnelling on the initial section is complete.

Turkish Maritime Lines

City Maritime Lines
Türkiye Denizcilik Işletmeleri
Rihtim Caddesi Karaköy, 80120 Istanbul
Telephone: +90 212 151 5000

Current situation: Extensive ferry services across the Bosphorus and the Golden Horn are operated on four routes by ferries of the state-owned company TDI, accounting for some 12 per cent of public transport journeys. Fleet of 76 vessels carry about 110 million passengers annually.

Generally the operation has been kept in surplus by cross-subsidy from profits made on pilotage for cruise liners and by staff reductions and increased fares. Smaller private launches cover short routes, with a 1 per cent share of public transport.

TCDD

Türkiye Cumhuriyeti Devlet Demiryollari Işletmesi
Genel Müdürlüğü, 06330 Gar, Ankara
Telephone: +90 212 309 0515 Fax: +90 212 312 3215

Type of operation: Suburban heavy rail

Passenger journeys: (1993) 90.1 million
(1994) 72.7 million
(1995) 62.1 million

Current situation: TCDD operates suburban services over two routes totalling 72 km with 45 stations, electrified 25 kV 50 Hz, Haydarpaşa to Gebze and Sirkeci to Halkali, carrying about 8 per cent of Istanbul's commuters. Strong bus competition has led to reduced patronage.

Ford Transits are beginning to replace the traditional taxi-based Dolmus **1996**

Developments: Double-deck trains may be introduced here and in Ankara; a fleet of 40 six-car trains is expected to be ordered for both networks in the period 1997-2001.

Plans exist for a 58 km extension of suburban service on the western (Sirkeci) side of the Bosphorus, of which the Halkali—Çerkezköy section is nearing completion.

There is also a proposal to build a third track parallel to the existing routes, dedicated to TCDD main line trains. This would allow provision of a metro-style service in place of the current suburban operation.

Rolling stock: 75 emu trains

Minibus/shared taxi

Current situation: More than 50 per cent of public transport trips are made by the two paratransit modes. The 4,000 minibuses are 14-seaters and 16,000-or-so Dolmus licensed shared taxis normally carry eight or nine. Together they carry about 400 million passengers a year.

Operations vary from fixed route to shared taxi, which may be undertaken by both minibuses and car-derived vehicles. There is considerable additional illegal operation. All modes have grown in step with increasing population and are reputedly very profitable but overcrowded and unregulated, leading to congestion and disputes over fares. The numbers of Dolmus and minibuses were officially frozen in 1963 by the municipality, which is responsible for regulation. They are most dominant in the Asian part of Istanbul.

UPDATED

IZMIR

Population: 2 million
Public transport: Bus services provided by municipal undertaking also responsible for gas and water supply, and other bus operations by new private company. Extensive private minibus and shared taxi 'Dolmus' operation. Cross-harbour ferries and suburban rail services; light rail under construction

ESHOT

Elektrik Su Havagazi Otobüs Troleybüs (ESHOT)
PO Box 167, Basmahane Otobüs Atolyesi, Izmir, Turkey
General Director: Suat Günay
Assistant General Director: Oktay Erdine
Staff: 2,802

Developments: In 1991 the public utility operator ESHOT formed a new private shareholding company, Izulas, to take over about half its bus routes and fleet. In addition, some vehicles are leased out to Izulas. ESHOT ran Turkey's last trolleybus routes, which ceased operation in 1993.

Rapidly expanding population has put pressure on services and the fleet has grown substantially since 1990. Due to non-availability of finance the undertaking developed its own front-engined articulated bus based on MAN components. About 100 Ikarus and Mercedes/Otomarsan buses were delivered in 1992.

Bus

Passenger journeys: (1993) 169.3 million
Vehicle-km: (1993) 48 million

Number of routes: 247
Fleet: 1,063 buses

MAN/Büssing 590	
Mercedes/Otomarsan O302T	40
ESHOT-built articulated	19
Ikarus IKIII (1990)	
BMC Beldesan (1991)	
Ikarus IK161 articulated (1992)	

New vehicles required each year: 35 buses for fleet expansion, plus replacements

Most intensive service: 5 min
One-person operation: All routes

Yugoslav Ikarus IKIII of ESHOT

BMC Belde of Izulas with an elderly Deutz Dolmus behind

Fare collection: Prepurchase tickets
Fare structure: Flat, prepurchase ticket strips of 10; monthly cards
Fares collected on board: None
Operating costs financed by: Single budget covers gas, water and transport operations

Izulas

Izulas Izmir Transport Company
Izmir

Current situation: Established in 1991 solely as a bus operator, Izulas runs about half the city's routes with a fleet initially taken over or leased from ESHOT. Fleet composition is similar to ESHOT's; services do not carry route numbers. Fare structure and collection arrangements are the same as ESHOT, and tickets are interchangeable. Amongst recent fleet acquisitions, in 1993 Izulas purchased 26 DAF DB250 double-decks with Optare bodies.

Minibus/shared taxi

Current situation: Several hundred minibuses and 'Dolmus' shared taxis operate, carrying an estimated 150 million passengers a year. Numbers have officially been limited for 10 years with any increases subject to city approval after consultation with ESHOT. Minibus and Dolmus stops are differentiated from bus stops where the private vehicles are not allowed to pick up passengers.

Buses are estimated to hold about a 70 per cent share of public transport journeys, with the remainder shared between the minibuses, Dolmus, suburban trains and ferries.

Refurbished Fiat railbus on Izmir local service ***1995***

Ferry

Current situation: There is a ferry service from Konak across the bay to residential suburbs at Karşiyaka.

TCDD

Turkish State Railways
TCDD Iştelmesi Genel Müdürlüğü
06330 Gar, Ankara
Telephone: +90 312 309 0515 Fax: +90 312 312 3215

Type of operation: Suburban heavy rail

Passenger journeys: (1993) 9.2 million
(1994) 5.9 million
(1995) 3.6 million

Current situation: Services on four routes operated by diesel railbuses. These are Basmane—Çiğli/Bornava and Alsancak—Adnanmenderes/Buca, totalling 45 km with 24 stations.
Developments: Track-doubling has been completed on three sections. A short branch opened in 1995 from Menemen to Aliağa to form part of a 78 km route Aliağa—Menemen—Basmane—Izmir, scheduled for electrification before the end of the century to provide an integrated system with the light rail network. Feasibility studies for resignalling and electrification were completed in 1996.

Light rail

Under construction

Current situation: Consultants and manufacturers examining a Master Plan for the city's transport proposed a light rail network. Initially planned as a city-centre distributor, the scheme has matured into a two-line network extending to 50 km. The first phase, an 11.5 km section of Line 1, is being built by a consortium of ABB and Yapi Merkezi, with which a contract was signed in 1993. A fleet of 45 LRVs is being supplied by Adtranz for the initial service, which is scheduled to start in early 1998.

Line 1 runs from Üçyol in the south to Bornova in the northeast, with 10 stations. Some 4.5 km in the city centre is in tunnel, and a further 3 km is elevated. The route from Üçyol through the city centre to Halkapina forms the core of the 50 km network.

Extensions are planned to Buca, Narlidere and Çigli.

Substantial ridership is expected; initially three-car trains will provide capacity of 18,000 passengers/h. Later five-car sets will run, raising capacity to 37,000 passengers/h.

UPDATED

JACKSONVILLE

Population: 732,000
Public transport: Bus and people mover services provided by transit authority governed by appointed board

JTA

Jacksonville Transportation Authority
PO Drawer O, 100 N Myrtle Avenue, Jacksonville, FL 32203, USA
Telephone: +1 904 630 3181 Fax: +1 904 630 3166
Chair: Carol S Miner
Executive Director: Miles N Francis Jr
Director of Mass Transit: Michael J Blaylock
Marketing & Media Relations: Charles Dixon
Staff: 464

Current situation: JTA, formed in 1972, provides public transport throughout Duval county. Dedicated funding for transit services was assured from 1989 when a ½ per cent sales tax was instituted. Unlike the former bridge and highway tolls, the sales tax can be used for both road construction and support of public transport, and $5 million was earmarked for bus service improvements through to 1995.

Bus

Passenger boardings: (1993) 9.6 million
(1994) 9.2 million
(1995) 9.1 million

Vehicle-km: (1993) 10.2 million
(1994) 10.2 million
(1995) 10 million

Route length: (One way) 936 km
Fleet: 184 buses

Flxible 870 (1982)	63
Ikarus (1983)	2
Flxible Metro (1986)	30
Boyer trolley replica (1987)	1
Ikarus (1989)	8
Neoplan (1990/91)	37
Flxible Metro (1992/93)	23
Flxible Metro (1995)	20

In peak service: 138

Most intensive service: 7 min
One-person operation: All routes
Integration with other modes: 7 Express Flyer routes serve suburban park-and-ride sites; also park-and-people mover shuttle in downtown
Fare structure: Flat, surcharge for special services; reduced rate multiride pass books; weekly passes
Fare collection: Coin to farebox
Arrangements for elderly/disabled: 63 lift-equipped buses provide fixed-route services; 100 minibuses and other vehicles operate a contracted-out dial-a-ride service; over 60s travel free
Operating costs financed by: Fares and parking revenues 26%

People mover

Passenger journeys: (1993) 492,000
(1994) 409,000
(1995) 401,000

Current situation: A 1 km demonstration line opened 1989, based on VAL technology, was to have formed the nucleus of a 10 km 'Skyway Express' elevated people mover.
Developments: In 1994, Bombardier's UTDC Systems Division was awarded a contract to substitute its UM-III monorail technology on the 1 km route and build 1 km extensions at each end to serve Florida Community College and San Marco, across the St Johns River. When completed in late 1997, nine vehicles will serve six stations. Further extension proposed to form 10 km Skyway Express route.

Suburban rail/light rail (proposed)

Current situation: JTA and Florida DoT collaborated in a 1995 systems planning study to consider options for commuter rail and long-range mass transit services.

Light rail is proposed for four alignments — northwest to Edgewood Avenue, east to Neptune Beach, southeast to The Avenues, and southwest to Kingsley Avenue. An extensive network of park-and-ride lots is also proposed.

JAIPUR

Population: 1.5 million

Public transport: Bus services provided by State Road Transport Corporation; autorickshaws, tempos and minibuses operated by private companies

Matador minibus in Jaipur

Rajasthan State Road Transport

Rajasthan State Road Transport Corporation
PO Box 210, Parivahan Marg, Jaipur 302001, India
Telephone: +91 141 382906 Fax: +91 141 380897
Managing Director: Umesh Kumar
Staff: (State-wide total) 25,904

Current situation: Provides services throughout Rajasthan with a total fleet of 4,828 vehicles in 1995/96.

The present bus service in Jaipur is inadequate for the rapidly growing population, and much of the city's transport is provided by private operators.

Bus

(Jaipur city service only)
Passenger journeys: 30 million (annual)
Vehicle-km: 5 million (annual)

Number of routes: 10
Route length: 250 km
Fleet: 100 buses, including Ashok Leyland and Tata
Fare collection: Floating or seated conductor
Fare structure: Stage

Minibus

Current situation: Private 'Matador' minibuses seating about 20 passengers, three-wheelers seating about 12, and cycle rickshaws provide much of the city's public transport. These are considered wasteful of road space, and congestion on city streets is increasing rapidly.

Light rail (proposed)

Current situation: A draft report on a proposed light rail system for the city was put forward by consultants RITES in 1991, recommending a 50.4 km network to be built in phases. Subsequently the government selected the Central Road Research Institute (CRRI) to carry out studies of suitable rapid transit systems, including a high-speed tramway. CRRI recommended phased construction of light rail routes extending to 58.7 km with 48 stations.

UPDATED

JAKARTA

Population: 8.4 million

Public transport: Two main bus companies, one government-owned, the other private, cater for less than half of public transport provision. The remainder is supplied by two private minibus co-operatives (using vehicles with a maximum of 25 seats), and a large fleet of independent Mikrolet (microbuses with 10-15 seats), supplemented by some short-distance Bemo routes run by vehicles with fewer than 10 seats. There are also some 13,000 Becak trishaws. State railway Perumka provides suburban service, being upgraded to regional metro; metro and light rail planned

Volvo double-decker of PPD in Jakarta city centre

Dllajr Dki Jakarta

Highway Transportation & Traffic Agency of the Jakarta City Government
Jalan Taman Jatibaru 1, Jakarta 10150, Indonesia
Telephone: +62 21 375367

Passenger journeys: (All modes)
(1990) 1,379 million

Current situation: This city government authority is responsible for co-ordination and licensing of all public road transport. It also operates 14 bus terminals and maintains bus shelters. Three of the terminals serve as interchange points between urban and interurban buses, the latter not permitted to penetrate the central area.

Developments: A guided busway runs through the city centre on elevated alignment. Linking Kota in the central business district, the route runs to the Blok M bus terminal in the suburb of Kebayoran Baru.

Mikrolets of various types and operators at a suburban terminal

PPD

PERUM Penangkutan Penumpang Djakarta (PPD)
Jalan Kramat Raya 21, Jakarta Pusat
Telephone: +62 21 342413/345670/340814/356020/347259
President Director: Drs Sudaryono
Director, Operations: Drs Sobri Nawawi
Director, Technical Affairs: Ir Erlan Prasetyo
Staff: 14,000

Current situation: PPD is the successor of the former Dutch-owned transport company Bataviasche Verkeers Mij, and was reorganised as a public corporation in 1984. Out of 14 private city-bus companies established in 1969 and equipped with buses provided through US-Aid, 13 were unable to repay their debts. These were taken over by PPD in 1979 and fully absorbed in 1985.

Route length varies between 11 and 40 km, with some routes extending beyond the city boundary. One air conditioned express route is operated, linking central Jakarta with an upper-class residential area.

Developments: A separate network of schools buses now operates because crews of service buses often refused to admit students (paying reduced fares) during peak hours.

Bus

Passenger journeys: (Annual) 220 million

Number of routes: 112
Route length: 2,200 km
Fleet: About 1,600 vehicles

Volvo Ailsa B55 double-deck	About 200
Mercedes O306/OH408	1,400

One-person operation: None
Fare collection: 2 conductors per vehicle; no tickets issued
Fare structure: Flat; surcharge for express (100%) and air conditioned (300%) services
Fares collected on board: 100%
Arrangements for elderly/disabled: None
Average peak-hour speed: Urban 8 km/h; suburban 17 km/h

Cikini station on the new elevated section of Jakarta's regional metro

Bus priority: Bus lanes along some main routes, not always respected by other vehicles
Integration with other modes: Interchange with interurban buses at 3 terminals
Operating costs financed by: Fares 100%; capital investment provided free by government

Mayasari

PT Mayasari Bhakti
Jalan Raya Bogor, Jakarta
Telephone: +62 21 840 0923/1903

Current situation: This is the only one of the 14 companies established in 1969 and equipped with US-Aid buses to have been able to repay its debt. It thus continues to operate under the ownership of its founder. Its operations amount to about half the extent of those of government-owned PPD.

Bus

Number of routes: 48
Fleet: 825 vehicles, all Mercedes-Benz and Hino single-deck
One-person operation: None
Fare collection: 2 conductors per vehicle, no tickets issued
Fare structure: As PPD
Operating costs financed by: Fares 100%
New vehicles financed by: Own resources

AJA

PT Arimbi Jaya Agung
Jalan Daan Mogot Km 20, Jakarta
President: Anton Priyanto

Current situation: This company applied to run a fleet of 200 buses over 34 routes in Jakarta, Tangerang and Bekasi, but only four routes were granted to operate from Tangerang via freeways to two terminals in Jakarta. These are legally considered as intercity services. A fleet of 34 buses is used, and 24 h service provided.

Minibus

Current situation: Four co-operatives operate minibus services within Jakarta. Metro Mini was founded in 1962 and originally restricted to vehicles of not more than 15 seats, but was reorganised in 1977 and authorised to operate vehicles with up to 25 seats. Kopaja was founded in 1980, and two other co-operatives (Koantas Bima and Kopami Jaya, with a combined fleet of 241 minibuses) came into being more recently.

Number of routes: 111
Fare collection: Conductor
Fare structure: Flat; minibus fares are 20% higher than ordinary city buses
Operating costs financed by: Fares 100%

PT Metro Mini

Jalan Pemuda Kav 721, Jakarta
Telephone: +62 21 489 5287/5585/5649

Fleet: 3,005 vehicles, mainly Mitsubishi, Isuzu and Daihatsu with local bodywork

Kopaja

Koperasi Angkutan Jakarta (Kopaja)
Jalan Warung Buncit III/7, Jakarta Selatan
Telephone: +62 21 799 6745/9048

Fleet: 1,182 vehicles, mainly Mitsubishi, Isuzu and Daihatsu with local bodywork

Mikrolet

Current situation: Two co-operatives operate Mikrolets (vehicles with 10-15 seats) on regular routes, one within the city and the other mainly on suburban routes. Mikrolets do not operate into the central business district. Vehicles are either owned by their drivers or by investors and hired out on a daily basis. The city government specifies a number of types which are eligible for Mikrolet operation, which may then be further restricted by the co-operative. City government also defines a uniform livery and lettering. Membership of the professional organisation (Organda) is compulsory. All operations are expected to cover their costs from fares.

Mikrolet Koperasi

Jalan Petonjo Enclek IV/13, Jakarta Pusat

Number of routes: 48, mainly urban
Fleet: 5,419 vehicles, mainly Toyota Kijang
One-person operation: Most vehicles
Fare collection: By driver
Fare structure: Flat, sectional on some longer routes; fares are 20% higher than on city buses

APK

Angkutan Pinggir Kota, Koperasi Wahana Kalpika
Jalan Raya Bekasi Timur No 202, Jakarta Timur

Number of routes: 70, mainly suburban
Fleet: 3,332 vehicles, mainly Suzuki, Daihatsu and Mitsubishi
Fare collection: By driver or conductor
Fare structure: Flat

Bemo

Current situation: Public service vehicles with fewer than 10 seats are officially referred to as Bemos. These are not licensed by the city government, but by the various districts. They operate on short intra-neighbourhood routes which may change frequently according to demand. There are a total of 1,096 three-wheel scooters with longitudinal seats for six passengers, also known locally as Toyokos. It is estimated that each carry some 35 passengers a day, amounting to around 14 million annual journeys.

Perumka

Perum Keteta Api (Perumka)
Jalan Perintis Kemerdekaan No 1, Bandung, Java Barat
Telephone: +62 22 430039/430054 Fax: +62 22 430062

Type of operation: Suburban heavy rail

Current situation: Services operate over 50 route-km between Jakarta and Bogor with 19 stations, and over a loop line in Jakarta, electrified at 1.5 kV DC. Sporadic diesel-hauled trains operate over several other routes. Together they carry about 20 million passengers a year.

The existing suburban network is being upgraded into a regional metro to serve the Jabotabek planning region, a 6,000 km^2 area covering Jakarta and its satellite towns of Bogor, Tangerang and Bekasi, with a total population of 13.6 million. Of these, 40 per cent use motorised transport every working day, the modal split being 60 per cent for public buses, 25 per cent for private cars and only 2 per cent for rail. By the year 2005, it is planned that the regional metro should achieve a 20-30 per cent share.

Electrification and grade separation of the Western Corridor was completed in 1986. Elevated track on the Central Corridor from Jakarta Gambir station to Manggarai (8.8 km) was opened in 1992, along with an extension to Gondongdia. Grade-separation permits train frequency to be raised from half-hourly to 12 min, but shortage of rolling stock has so far prevented this. Electrification now extends to Bekasi, but there are no electric trains available.

Developments: Electrification and double-tracking of the Tangerang line is in progress, with a planned link to Soekarno-Hatta (Cengkareng) international airport. Project engineering is being carried out by JARTS. Two more construction projects were approved in early 1995, including replacement of further sections of suburban railway on elevated alignment.

Plans for a major multimodal interchange and commercial development on Perumka land at Manggerai were approved in 1995. It would be the first instance of a joint public/private enterprise involving development of railway land.

Rolling stock: 50 two-car emus, plus 25 diesel railcars/coaches
On order: 40 four-car emus being supplied by PT Inka following joint production with BN of Belgium and Holec of the Netherlands of 7 four-car sets; total fleet of 150 emu sets planned

Aeromovel

Coester SA

Type of operation: Demonstration people mover, powered by compressed air

Current situation: A 3.2 km circular track has been built in the Taman Mini-Indonesia theme park as a demonstrator, and is now used for pleasure rides. The three cars serve six stations. It is not part of the public transport network.

Metro/Light rail (planned)

Current situation: Successful bidder to build an 82 km light rail network linking central Jakarta with Tangerang and Bekasi, adjudicated in mid-1995, was a consortium of local companies. Some routes could use the alignments of existing suburban railways (see above).

At the beginning of 1995, the government approved plans for a US$1.4 billion initial metro network, extending to 14.5 km in tunnel with 14 stations. A German/British/Japanese consortium of ABB/AEG, Ferrostaal, Siemens, Taylor Woodrow and Itochu is financing the design stage of the project, and hopes to win the construction contract. Work is expected to start in 1997 for opening in 2000.

JERUSALEM

Population: 250,000, region 608,000

Public transport: Most bus services provided by local members of national transport co-operative society; light rail proposed

EGGED

Israel Transport Co-operative Society Ltd (EGGED)
PO Box 13178, Jerusalem 91131, Israel
Telephone: +972 2 304444

Current situation: The Jerusalem Region is the smallest of EGGED's three divisions, extending from Beit Shemesh to the Jordan Valley. For details of EGGED operations see Tel Aviv entry.

Bus

(Jerusalem Region operations only)
Staff: 1,760

Passenger journeys: Specific figures not available

Fleet: 667 buses
One-person operation: All routes
Fare collection: Manually by driver from ticket board
Fare structure: Flat
Fares collected on board: 100%
Fare evasion control: Inspectors
Average peak-hour speed: In bus lanes, 20 km/h; in mixed traffic, 18.6 km/h
Bus priority: 3.9 km of bus lanes; further 4.8 km planned
Subsidy from: Government

Mercedes-Benz O305 of EGGED in Nablus Road, Jerusalem

Light rail (proposed)

Current situation: The city authorities have considered proposals for a two-line light rail system. In 1994 the ministry of transport and Jerusalem municipal authorities created the Jerusalem Transportation Masterplan agency to take the light rail proposals forward. At the beginning of 1995, US consultant Parsons Brinckerhoff was selected to carry out feasibility studies and examine an alternative guided-bus scheme; PB also advised on short-term bus service improvements.

By mid-1996, proposals had been clarified into a mix of heavy and light rail on five routes totalling 20 km. It was hoped that construction could start in 1998.

UPDATED

JILIN

Population: 1.4 million

Public transport: Single municipal transport operator providing bus, minibus and trolleybus services

Jilin City Transport

Jilin City Transport Company
Jilin, People's Republic of China

Current situation: The backbone of transport is a trolleybus system which has remained static in extent for many years, but which is now worked by a second generation of articulated vehicles, many received since 1985, although it is not clear whether they were new or cascaded from Shanghai. Only about 20 per cent of the fleet consists of trolleybuses, however, and the bus network covers a far larger area of the city. Minibuses at premium fares, thought to have been introduced around 1986, duplicate some bus and trolleybus services.

Jilin's central trolleybus terminus, with Shanghai SK561G vehicles

Bus

Number of routes: Approx 30
Fleet: Approx 300 buses, of which about 130 articulated, mainly Jiangcheng and Siping types
Fare collection: Payment to seated conductors, monthly passes
Fare structure: Stage
Integration with other modes: Number of bus routes act as feeders to trolleybus system; minibuses augment ordinary services

Minibus

Number of routes: At least 4
Fleet: Over 100 Siping SP320N, SOK6650 and SP6651 minibuses
Fare collection: Payment to conductors
Fare structure: Probably flat

Trolleybus

Number of routes: 3
Fleet: Approx 62 trolleybuses, all articulated

Shanghai SK561G	about 57
Shenyang	5

Service interval: Every few minutes
Fare collection: Payment to seated conductors, monthly passes
Fare structure: Stage
Integration with other modes: Bus routes from outer suburbs terminate at two suburban trolleybus termini; premium-fare minibuses augment services

JOHANNESBURG

Population: 1.7 million

Public transport: Bus services provided for part of city by municipal undertaking, with network of suburban commuter routes by private company (PUTCO) and shared 'Kombi-taxis'. Suburban rail services operated by SA Rail Commuter Corp

Johannesburg Transportation

City of Johannesburg Transportation Directorate
Transportation House, Raikes Road, PO Box 1787, Newtown, Johannesburg 2000, South Africa
Telephone: +27 11 339 5716 Fax: +27 11 339 6813
Executive Director: S Verrier
Staff: 1,100

Bus

Passenger journeys: (1991/92) 48.1 million
Vehicle-km: (1991/92) 12.1 million

Number of routes: 73
Route length: (One way) 630 km
Fleet: 405 buses

Leyland Fleetline double-deck	73
Mercedes O305 double-deck	284
Mercedes O305 single-deck	46
AEC Mk V	1
MAN midibus	1

In peak service: 312
On order: 100 vehicles from Busaf were expected in 1996

Most intensive service: 10 min
One-person operation: All services
Fare collection: Monthly tickets and prepurchase coupons with cancellation machines or payment to driver
Fare structure: Zonal (4 and 5 zones); monthly tickets (peak or off-peak); 10-trip coupons
Operational control: Mobile inspectors with radio communication and computerised online monitoring

Mercedes O305 double-deck in Eloff Street

'Metro' train of Rail Commuter Corp at Vereeniging

PUTCO buses at Johannesburg bus station

Arrangements for elderly/disabled: Free off-peak travel for persons over 70, low flat fare for pensioners. Cost of concessions included in city council's compensation for the undertaking's deficit
Average peak-hour speed: 17 km/h
Bus priority: With flow and contraflow bus lanes
Operating costs financed by: Fares 42%, other commercial sources 3%, subsidy/grants 55%
Subsidy from: Johannesburg ratepayers 48%, other local authorities 4%, Central Witwatersrand regional services council 3%
New vehicles financed by: Loans

Metro Rail

South African Rail Commuter Corporation Ltd
Johannesburg Metropolitan Area
Private Bag X2, Sunninghill, Johannesburg 2157
Telephone: +27 11 804 2900 Fax: +27 11 804 3852

Type of operation: Suburban heavy rail

Passenger journeys: (1990/91) 209 million
(1991/92) 172.3 million
(1992/93) 116.4 million

Current situation: Extensive network of 1,065 mm gauge suburban trains on 12 routes serving the whole southern Transvaal (Witwatersrand–Vereeniging area, population 5.5 million), totalling 305 km with 167 stations, electrified at 3 kV DC. Links with northern Transvaal area services (see under Pretoria). Up to 35 trains per hour run at peak times on the busiest sections, while off-peak the normal frequency is hourly. Fares cover 20.3 per cent of operating costs.
Developments: As well as proposals for two new lines totalling 16 km in northern Johannesburg, the Corporation is also planning a route to serve the Baralink commercial and residential development in the south-west of the city. Comprising a loop and branch, the 20 km alignment would be built with private-sector finance.

Rolling stock: 1,757 emu cars, mostly four-car sets

Union Carriage & Wagon	
Steam side door (1932 onwards)	T14
5M2A (1957 onwards)	M521 T1,222

PUTCO

Putco Ltd
PO Box 3, Wendywood 2144

Current situation: PUTCO operates extensive long-distance commuter services. Separate eastern and western networks have a combined fleet of about 1,600 buses, carrying about 90 million passengers a year. The Department of Transport provides a fares subsidy of about one-third.

Shared taxis

Current situation: Since the 1977 Road Transportation Act there has been major growth in the numbers of Kombi-taxis, mostly Volkswagen minibuses operating variable routes and schedules. Originally illegal, the Kombi-taxis are now licensed, though deregulation is planned.

Light rail (proposed)

Current situation: Plans for a light rail system were prepared in 1985, but were superseded by proposals for an extensive metro network in 1987. This plan was rejected on cost grounds. In 1991 the Masstran Consortium of local authorities recommended a seven-line light rail network, and in 1994 go-ahead was given for construction of Line 1 from the city centre to the suburb of Observatory.
Developments: Work had been expected to start in 1995, but the project was reported shelved in early 1995.

Nissan Kombi-taxis in Johannesburg

Other operators

Current situation: Mayflower Contract Services provides service in Johnson County, Kansas, under contract, linking with KCATA routes. Kansas City, Kansas, runs some local routes (The Bus), and one suburban express route is operated by an outlying town, Excelsior Springs, Missouri.

Light rail (planned)

Current situation: The initial phase of a proposed light rail network remains under study, although a draft environmental impact statement published in 1995 recommended alignments on Main Street, Volker Boulevard and Bruce Watkins Drive as a core network. Line 1 (8.3 km) would run from downtown Kansas City along Grand and Main streets to Crown Center/Union station, and extend southwards to the Country Club Plaza. Construction is unlikely to start until after 2000.

Later extensions would serve the international airport and the Truman sports complex. Construction programmes for all lines is dependent on the availability of federal funding.

UPDATED

KAOHSIUNG

Population: 2.2 million
Public Transport: Bus services within city limits provided by city bus administration, with limited picking-up and setting-down rights accorded to private company which is sole provider of service in metropolitan and country areas of Kaohsiung County; metro planned

City Bus

City Bus Company
2 Chien Chun Road, Ling Ya District, Kaohsiung, Taiwan
Telephone: +886 7 749 0515 Fax: +886 7 749 1422
Deputy Operations Manager: Chang-chien Hrong Sheng
Staff: 1,386

Current situation: Kaohsiung has suffered from under-investment in bus capacity, despite a rapidly expanding population. No new buses were acquired from 1982 to 1989, and the impact of the 1979/83 bus replacement programme was diluted by a decision to include over 100 low-capacity minibuses and midibuses which are utilised on an *ad hoc* basis with standard buses on some of the principal trunk routes.

Failure to match supply to demand has caused a substantial shift from public to private transport, principally scooters and motor cycles, as disposable incomes have risen. As a result, KCB caters for only 4.5 per cent of trips in the metropolitan area, compared with 65 per cent by two-wheel transport.

Because of the city's broad streets this did not immediately lead to serious traffic congestion, unlike Taipei, though this has changed as scooter owners switch to cars.

Bus

Passenger journeys: (1994)
Vehicle-km: (1994)

Number of routes:
Fleet: 607 vehicles

Isuzu (1973)	74
Hino (1975)	67
Hino (1989/91)	80
Mercedes (1979/83)	249
Isuzu minibus (1980)	20
Mercedes minibus (1982)	117

In peak service: 350

Fare structure: Flat; 10% discount on 10-trip ticket
Fare collection:
Average peak-hour speed: 15.4 km/h
Operating costs financed by: Fares 75%

Old Mercedes bus on City Route 70

County Bus

County Bus Company
138 Chung Shen Road, Kaohsiung County
Telephone: +886 7 748 0500 Fax: +886 7 748 0551
Operating Manager: Chang Gin-hu
Staff: 839

Bus

Current situation: Operations within the city are restricted by limitations on picking up and setting down. Though County Bus is the sole local operator in the metropolitan area, it caters for only 3 per cent of trips. Graduated fares

Fleet: 362 buses, mostly Isuzu and Fuso

Metro

Under construction
Department of Kaohsiung Mass Rapid Transit
10th Floor, 2 Ssu Wei 3rd Road, Kaohsiung
Telephone: +886 7 331 4396 Fax: +886 7 331 4366
Chief Engineer: Chia-Yang Sun

Current situation: The 1988/89 feasibility study recommended a four-line network of 78 km with 71 stations, and these plans were adopted by the city authorities in 1990. The initial phase comprises the underground Orange line (14.4 km, 14 stations) running east-west through the city centre from Ku Shan to Feng Shan, and the north-south Red line (28.3 km, 23 stations) linking Chiao Tou and Lin Hai, intersecting in the city centre. This route will be partially elevated.

The second phase proposals, comprising the 21.6 km Blue line and 14.4 km Brown line, are now to be the subject of further feasibility studies.

Developments: Government approval of the scheme was granted in 1994, following appointment of US consultants De Leuw Cather and four local firms to manage the planning and design phases. Funding was made available for Lines 1 and 2 in mid-1995, and construction of the first section of the Orange line was expected to start before the end of 1995 for opening in 2003. Work on the Red line will start in 2000, with a target opening date of 2005.

KARACHI

Population: 7 million
Public transport: Bus services provided by state-owned city road transport corporation and private firms operating as association. Additional private minibus owners association provides services on 50 routes, with extensive contract bus services also provided and more than 10,000 scooter rickshaws. Limited suburban rail services; light rail under construction

KTC

Karachi Transport Corporation (KTC)
Civic Centre, Hasan Square, Gulshan-e-Iqbal, Karachi, Pakistan
Telephone: +92 21 424365
Staff: 4,000

Current situation: The Karachi operations of the Sind Road Transport Corp were separated in 1977 to form the Karachi Transport Corp. Originally jointly owned by central government and Sind state, responsibility passed wholly to the state and KTC operations are controlled by a state transport department. A Provincial Road Transport Authority is responsible for issuing route permits to other operators but not the KTC, which has freedom to choose its own routes. Operational and engineering problems affecting KTC, and restrictions on funds for new investment, have resulted in a diminishing operational fleet and deteriorating level of service, which has encouraged development of private bus and minibus services. KTC operates express (blue livery) and ordinary (red) services; its share of total passenger journeys is probably under 10 per cent in total but as much as 50 per cent on some corridors.

All buses must have a separate ladies' compartment; on minibuses the front seats serve this purpose.

There is some laxity by conductors in issuing tickets, and total journeys are estimated unofficially as around 100 million.

Bus

Passenger journeys: (1988) 68.9 million
Vehicle-km: (1988) 32.1 million

Number of routes: 50
Fleet: About 1,000 buses

One-person operation: None
Fare collection: Conductors
Fare structure: Stage (local); flat (express; a few monthly passes)
Fares collected on board: Almost 100%
Fare evasion control: Conductors/inspectors
Average peak-hour speed: 18 km/h
Integration with other modes: Irregular service to airport; 3 routes serve main rail station

Karachi Bus Owners Association

Current situation: Represents the operators of 30 bus

Hino bus of KTC on express working

routes licensed by the Provincial Road Transport Authority. Permits are issued on three classes of route, specifying the maximum age of vehicles to be used. Individual routes usually operated by vehicles of the same type or size.

Bus

Passenger journeys: Approx 200 million (annual)
Vehicle-km: Approx 30 million (annual)

Number of routes: 30
Fleet: Over 1,000 vehicles, mostly Mazda 25-seaters but including Bedford, Dodge and others

One-person operation: None
Fare collection: Conductors
Fare structure: Stage
Fare evasion control: Conductors/inspectors
Average peak-hour speed: 18 km/h

Karachi Minibus Owners Association

Current situation: Represents the operators of more than 3,000 paratransit vehicles.

Minibus/shared taxi

Current situation: Some 50 routes operate with about 3,000 vehicles, including Mazda and Ford Transit with up to 30 seats, and pick-up trucks. Also three-wheeler autorickshaws and horse-drawn Tongas on regular routes in some areas but not penetrating city centre. About 200 million passengers are carried annually.

There are in addition some 40,000 taxis and rickshaws.

Pakistan Railways

Divisional Office, Karachi City
Telephone: +92 21 233359

Passenger journeys: 2.5 million (annual)

Current situation: Operates diesel suburban service on four routes, including a circular route, totalling 98 km with 39 stations, irregular service, graduated fares. Rail plays a very small part, local trains being slower than road transport despite traffic congestion.
Developments: Rehabilitation of the circular route approved 1992 to expand capacity in the hope of relieving traffic congestion.

Light rail

Under construction
National Mass Transit Authority
3059 Cabinet Block, Islamabad
Telephone: +92 51 818454 Fax: +92 51 818225
Director: Dr Soomro

Current situation: World Bank funding was agreed in 1989 for construction of an initial 15 km elevated light rail route between Mereweather Tower and Sohrab Goth. Tenders for construction on a build-operate-transfer basis were called in 1990, but no progress was made with the scheme. Proposed alignments follow in part existing traffic corridors and part of the PR circular railway. A scheme to construct busways for later conversion to light rail has been dropped.
Developments: In 1992, the NMTA was established to administer the rapid transit project and expressions of interest to design, build and operate the two designated routes were sought in mid-1994. It remains the intention to utilise PR's circular line for rapid transit, and bidders were asked to consider this option also.

The proposed network now comprises Line 1 from Mereweather Tower to Sohrab Goth (17 km), intersecting at Empress Market with Line 2 which will link Cantt station with Orangi (10.5 km); total 15 stations. Four other routes are planned, including a line to the airport.

The Canadian company SNC Lavalin received a letter of intent for construction of the project in January 1996, and construction started in March. GEC Alsthom will supply 22 cars.

UPDATED

Typically decorated Mazda 25-seater — the most common type in Karachi

---

KARLSRUHE

Population: 269,000, area served 581,000
Public transport: Bus and light rail/tramway services provided by municipal undertaking also responsible for other public utilities; suburban services provided by AVG interurban railway and DB, sharing tracks on certain routes. Regional transit authority established in 1994

KVV

Karlsruher Verkehrsverbund GmbH (KVV)
Tullastrasse 71, 76131 Karlsruhe, Germany

Current situation: This regional transit authority was set up in 1994 by the cities of Karlsruhe and Baden-Baden and the counties of Karlsruhe, Germersheim and Rastatt, with a total population of about 1 million.

Services are provided by VBK/AVG, DB and RVS (see below), and also by the municipal bus companies of Rastatt and Baden-Baden, SWEG (a regional railway and bus company), and eight other bus operators over a network of 11 rail, seven light rail and six tram lines, and 150 bus routes, carrying about 125 million passengers a year.

VBK

Stadtwerke Karlsruhe Verkehrsbetriebe (VBK)
PO Box 1140, 76001 Karlsruhe
Telephone: +49 721 61070 Fax: +49 721 6107 5009
Operating Director: Dipl-Ing Dieter Ludwig
Commercial Director: Rupert Bruder
Assistant Director: Georg Drechsler
Staff: 909

Passenger journeys: (All modes)
(1993) 80.4 million
(1994) 75.7 million (revised counting method)
(1995) 76.3 million

Operating costs financed by: Fares 35.5%, other commercial sources 22.8%, subsidy/grants 41.7%
Subsidy from: Internal cross-subsidy from overall municipal trading activities

Current situation: Extension of light rail is taking place, and consideration is being given to further new lines. Through running of Stadtbahn services over DB lines inaugurated in 1992.

Bus

Vehicle-km: (1993) 4.9 million
(1994) 4.9 million
(1995) 4.7 million

Number of routes: 28
Route length: 164 km, plus school contract services
Fleet: 86 buses, plus 20 hired

Mercedes O305	12
Mercedes O405	42
Mercedes O405N	15
Mercedes O408	5
Mercedes O310	2
Mercedes L613	2
Neoplan N409	8

New vehicles required each year: 5

One-person operation: All routes
Fare collection: Monthly and annual tickets sold in kiosks; vending machines at bus stops; drivers sell single and 24 h tickets; tickets also sold at post offices
Fare structure: Zonal, 7 zones; monthly tickets or annual subscription, various special offers

New Duewag low-floor tram and connecting bus at Jägerhaus terminus of Route 4 ***1997***

Fare evasion control: Ticket inspection
Integration with other modes: Fully integrated with light rail/tramway and regional bus services
Average distance between stops: 553 m
Average peak-hour speed: In mixed traffic, 25.4 km/h

Light rail/tramway

Type of operation: Light rail/conventional tramway
Car-km: (1993) Tram 4.1 million, LRT 2.5 million
(1994) Tram 4 million, LRT 2.5 million
(1995) Tram 3.6 million, LRT 2.9 million

Route length: 209.1 km, including AVG (see below), of which 59.2 km over DB tracks
Number of lines: 6 tram, plus 7 light rail (AVG)
Number of stops: 210
Gauge: 1,435 mm
Track: Grooved NP 4/40 rail; flat-bottomed S 41/10 rail conventional sleepers on ballast; sleepers on concrete
Max gradient: 6%
Minimum curve radius: 21 m
Electrification: 750 V DC, overhead; 15 kV AC on DB tracks

Service: Peak 5 min (central section on Kaiserstrasse 1 min), off-peak 10 min
First/last car: 02.45/00.36
Fare structure: Zonal
Integration with other modes: Through running to and common fare system with AVG (see below); some through running with DB lines (see below); through ticketing with regional bus services
One-person operation: All routes

Rolling stock: 189 cars (pool includes AVG fleet and 4 DB LRVs)

Duewag A4Z 8-axle articulated (1958/59)	M6
Rastatt A4Z 8-axle articulated (1959)	VBK M1 AVG M7
DWM K4Z 6-axle articulated (1959)	M2
DWM K4 6-axle articulated (1961/64)	M5
DWM K4F 6-axle articulated (1963/64)	M7
DWM K4F 8-axle articulated (1964)	M1
DWM K4 8-axle articulated (1964/69)	M24
Waggon Union K4 8-axle articulated (1972/78)	M16
Waggon Union A4Z 8-axle (1975)	AVG M4
Waggon Union A6Z GT6-80C 6-axle articulated (1983/84)	VBK M4 AVG M16
Duewag A6Z-80C 6-axle articulated (1987)	M10
Duewag D6Z GT8-100C/2SY 8-axle dual-voltage	VBK M21 AVG M11 DB M4
Duewag A6Z GT8-80C 8-axle articulated (1987/91)	VBK M28 AVG M2
Duewag GT6-70D/N 6-axle low-floor articulated (1995/96)	M20

On order: 12 dual-voltage GT8 LRVs from Duewag

Current situation: Network comprises urban tramway now mostly on reserved track, plus the AVG interurban tramway to Herrenalb and Ittersbach, converted from a metre-gauge light railway in 1958/61.

New route to Stutensee (northeast) scheduled to open in 1996, and further extension to Remchingen (southeast) planned. Eventually, the Mörsch and Remchingen lines may be extended over DB tracks to Rastatt and Pforzheim (see below).

Developments: Work is in progress to link the tramway network with DB routes, to allow dual-system LRVs to reach outer suburban destinations. The first route came into operation in 1992 – Route B (30.2 km) linking central Karlsruhe with Bretten-Gölshausen.

From Karlsruhe Hbf, the route runs over existing tramway tracks through the city centre for 6.4 km, then on new-built light rail alignment for 2.8 km before joining existing DB tracks between Durlach and Brötzingen. The service was an immediate success, and at peak times cars run every 20 min. Patronage has more than tripled to 7,500 weekday journeys compared with the former DB trains which carried about 2,000 daily. Stadtwerke Karlsruhe tariffs apply, including journeys on the DB semi-fasts which continue to share the tracks, and bus services in Bretten have been reorganised as feeders.

A similar service is planned for the line to Pforzheim. This will follow the Bretten route to Grötzingen, then run on a new third track alongside the existing DB main line to Söllingen, whence it will share the DB line into Pforzheim. Inauguration is planned for 1996. Extension of the original route to Heilbronn is also envisaged.

Further services are planned to Wörth (across the Rhein in the west) and to Rastatt (in the south), with extensions to Baden-Baden and into the Murgtal area under consideration. A new physical link between the VBK and DB networks is planned at Albtalbahnhof.

Because the city-centre section on Kaiserstrasse is saturated and could not cope with further regional LRT routes, a 3 km underground line was planned to carry the regional routes. The project was rejected in a referendum held in October 1996.

Dual-system LRV on Route B on DB tracks at Bretten

AVG

Albtal-Verkehrs-Gesellschaft mbH
(Address as Stadtwerke Karlsruhe)
Staff: 355

Passenger journeys: (Both modes)
(1993) 27.1 million
(1994) 28.2 million
(1995) 31.2 million

Current situation: Company with same ownership and management as Stadtwerke Karlsruhe, but different legal status and operating to railway rather than tramway regulations. AVG originally operated electric interurban railway from Karlsruhe southwards via Ettlingen to Bad Herrenalb and Ittersbach. This line has now been fully integrated with LRT operations of VBK. The Neureut–Leopoldshafen LRT line, a converted DB freight line, legally a railway, is also owned by AVG.

Since 1994, AVG operates over DB's Karlsruhe–Bruchsal and Bruchsal–Bretten lines, replacing DB trains. More trains are operated than under DB, and the number of passengers has more than doubled. At present only running over DB tracks, these services will eventually be linked with the Karlsruhe tramway network.

AVG also operates small bus network based on Ettlingen, serving as a feeder to the interurban rail line and catering for local needs. The 22 buses ran 1.1 million km in 1994.

Developments: In 1994 AVG acquired the regional railway lines from Bruchsal to Menzingen and Odenheim from SWEG, and started electrification. Electric traction was introduced between Bruchsal and Menzigen in 1996, with the branch to Odenheim following in late 1997.

Fleet: Included in VBK details above

DB

Deutsche Bahn AG, Geschäftsbereich Nahverkehr
Regionalbereich Baden-Rheinpfalz
Lammstrasse 19, 76133 Karlsruhe
Telephone: +49 721 938 3330 Fax: +49 721 134492
Manager, Suburban and Regional Traffic:
Dipl-Ing Horst Emmerich

Current situation: Commuter trains, both electric and diesel-hauled, operate on seven lines radiating from Karlsruhe, but have been replaced in part by AVG's light rail vehicles (see above). On the route to Baden-Baden DB runs its own LRVs, which will also run through to the Karlsruhe tramway network at a later stage.

Tracks are shared with other operations. Karlsruhe Hbf is situated about 2 km from the central business district, which is inconvenient for commuters. This provided the impetus for the scheme to run LRVs over DB tracks (see above).

Developments: DB has acquired four LRVs which are operated in a pool with those of VBK/AVG.

RVS

Regionalverkehr Südwest GmbH
Amalienstrasse 14b, 76133 Karlsruhe
Telephone: +49 721 181610 Fax: +49 721 181660
Directors: Helmut Müller
Manfred B Vogt

Current situation: Suburban and regional bus services operated by RVS, a DB subsidiary. Some routes which previously ran through to Karlsruhe have been cut back to feed the LRT line of VBK at Leopoldshafen.

UPDATED

KATHMANDU

Population: 350,000
Public transport: Bus and trolleybus services provided in populous area including neighbouring cities of Patan and Bhaktapur by public corporation, with additional private buses and minibuses and extensive use of rickshaws, autorickshaws (based on motor scooters) and taxis

Transport Corporation of Nepal

Transport Corporation of Nepal
Baneshwar, Kathmandu, Nepal
Staff: 250

Current situation: Established in 1966 to operate the country's two short railways. In 1974 inaugurated the trolleybus route from Kathmandu to Bhaktapur, a gift from the Chinese Government. Bus operations started at the same time.
Developments: The trolleybus system faced considerable operating difficulties due to power supply shortages and maintenance problems. Chinese technicians had carried out some rehabilitation work, and the system, which was reported to have closed in late 1993, is now operating again with a new fleet of trolleybuses from China's Shenfeng Trolleybus Works.

Bus and trolleybus

Passenger journeys: Bus 10 million, trolleybus 2 million (annual)
Vehicle-km: Bus 1 million, trolleybus 400,000 (annual)

Number of routes: Bus 7, trolleybus 1
Route length: Bus 80 km, trolleybus 11 km
Fleet: Approx 100 buses, all Isuzu
Fleet: At least 30 trolleybuses, including Shanghai SK541 and Shenfeng types

New Kathmandu trolleybus overtakes a conventional vehicle **1997**

Trolleybus electrification: 600 V DC
In peak service: Trolleybus 15

Most intensive service: Off-peak 12 min
One-person operation: None
Fare collection: By seated conductors on board at front of vehicle, or at roadside on boarding or alighting

Fare structure: Stage (4-stage) colour-coded tickets issued by conductors

UPDATED

KATOWICE

Population: 370,000, area served 2 million
Public transport: Bus and trolleybus services operated by agency of each municipality; competing private bus and minibus services; tramway operated by region-wide agency; suburban rail services of Polish State Railways (PKP). The former regional transport undertaking WPK Katowice has been broken up into a single tram operation and an unknown number of separate bus operations each based on one town in the region but with overlapping service areas. Trolleybuses run only in the town of Tychy

PKM Katowice

Przedsięborstwo Komunikacji Miejskie Katowice
ul Mickiewicza 59, 40058 Katowice, Poland
Telephone: +48 32 588071 Fax: +48 32 596946
General Manager: Andrezej Jeremicz
Staff: 1,128

Current situation: Bus services within and radiating from Katowice city have been taken over by PKM from the former regional undertaking WPK. Some minibuses are also operated.

Bus

Vehicle-km: (1995) 16.6 million

Number of routes: 53
Route length: 1,058 km
Fleet: 251 buses

Ikarus 280	112
Ikarus 260	1
Jelcz M121M	2
Jelcz 120MM/1	30
Jelcz M11	105
Jelcz 120 MM	1

Fare structure: Flat; higher fare for longer journeys
Fare collection: Prepurchase tickets, 5-day pass

Scania CR111 of PKM Jaworzno with PKM Katowice Jelcz M11 and Ikarus 280 buses at Katowice station

Trams of PKT on reserved track **1997**

PKT Katowice

Przedsięborstwo Kommunikacji Tramwajow Katowice
Katowice

Current situation: Tram services operated throughout the Upper Silesian conurbation, serving the towns of

Bytom, Chorzow, Dąbrowa Gornicza, Gliwice, Ruda Şlaska and Sosnowiec as well as Katowice.

Tramway

Type of operation: Conventional tramway

Number of lines: 31
Gauge: 1,435 mm
Fare structure: Flat
Fare collection: Prepurchase tickets, 5-day pass
One-person operation: All routes
Fleet: Mainly Konstal 105N 4-axle and 102N 6-axle articulated cars; a few Type N 2-axle cars still used

Other operators

Current situation: Municipal buses of PKM Bytom, PKM Jaworzno, PKM Sosnowiec, PKM Tychy and competing private buses and minibuses all serve the centre of Katowice city as well as providing extensive local services in their respective areas. PKM buses are mainly Ikarus 280 articulated and Jelcz M11 standard, but PKM Jaworzno has Scania CR111 buses second-hand from Sweden and one MAN articulated second-hand from Germany. Private buses are mainly Autosan and Ikarus. Minibuses are mainly Nysa 522, but there are also Mercedes and Volkswagen; premium fares apply on minibus routes.

PKM Tychy has a small fleet of trolleybuses on routes within its own operating area.

PKP

Polish State Railways (PKP)
ul Chalubinskiego 4, 00928 Warszawa
Telephone: +48 22 620 4512 Fax: +48 22 621 2705
Type of operation: Suburban heavy rail

Current situation: An irregular but frequent service is operated over a 71 km route linking Zawiercie, Dąbrowa Gornicza, Sosnowiec, Katowice, Chorzow, Ruda, Zabrze and Gliwice, serving 23 stations. Similar services run on other lines. Class EN57 three-car emus are used.

UPDATED

KAWASAKI

Population: 1.4 million
Public transport: Situated between Tokyo and Yokohama, Kawasaki is served by JR suburban trains linking those two cities and by four private railways. Direct links to the Tokyo metro system are provided by through running from all four private railways. Bus services provided by municipal undertaking, three of the private railways, one other private bus operator and the Yokohama municipal operator (one route only)

Kawasaki-shi Kotsu Kyoku

Kawasaki City Transport Bureau/Kawasaki City Bus
6 Miyamoto-cho, Kawasaki-ku, Kawasaki-shi 210, Kanagawa-ken, Japan
Telephone: +81 44 200 3231 Fax: +81 44 233 8444
General Director: Yasuo Usui
Staff: 899

Current situation: Kawasaki-shi Kotsu Kyoku and private operators' routes are numbered in a common system. Municipal and private operators also share a common flat fare with prepurchase ticket strips valid on all routes within Kawasaki except that operated by Yokohama-shi Kotsu Kyoku.

Bus

Passenger journeys: (1990/91) 58.7 million
(1991/92) 59.1 million
(1992/93) 58.3 million
Vehicle-km: (1990/91) 12.9 million
(1991/92) 13 million
(1992/93) 13 million

Number of routes: 28
Route length: 246 km
On priority right-of-way: 16.8 km
Fleet: 349 vehicles

Isuzu	184
Mitsubishi	165

Fuji-bodied vehicles of Kawasaki City Bus

In peak service: 302
New vehicles required each year: 25

Most intensive service: 1 min
One-person operation: All routes
Fare collection: Payment to farebox by driver or prepurchase ticket strips
Fare structure: Flat; prepurchase ticket strips; monthly and 3-monthly passes
Integration with other modes: Services integrated with JR and other railways
Average distance between stops: 380 m
Operating costs financed by: Fares 83.6%, other commercial sources 3%, subsidy/grants 17%
New vehicles financed by: Public bonds, subsidy and internal funds

Developments: Premium fare late journeys introduced on six 'Midnight Bus' routes.

Series 209 emu on JR East's Keihin-Tohoku line ***1997***

Kawasaki Tsurumi Rinko Bus

Kawasaki Tsurumi Rinko Bus
15-2 Nishin-machi, Kawasaki-ku, Kawasaki-shi 210
Telephone: +81 44 233 6501

Current situation: This private company operates in Kawasaki and Yokohama; 30 of the routes (including five express) serve Kawasaki, some jointly with Kawasaki City Bus.

Bus

Passenger journeys: (1990/91) 53.2 million
(1991/92) 53.6 million
(1992/93) 53 million
Vehicle-km: (1990/91) 11.9 million
(1991/92) 12.2 million
(1992/93) 12.2 million

Number of routes: 36
Route length: 162 km
Fleet: 360 vehicles

JR East

East Japan Railway Company
Higashi Nihon Ryokaku Tetsudo
6-5, Marunouchi 1-chome, Chiyoda-ku, Tokyo 100
Telephone: +81 3 3215 9649 Fax: +81 3 3213 5291
Chair: S Yamanouchi
President: M Matsuda

Type of operation: Inner and outer suburban heavy rail

Current situation: JR services in Kawasaki are operated by JR East's Tokyo Metropolitan Area. Kawasaki is linked to both Tokyo and Yokohama by frequent Keihin-Tohoku line inner suburban E-den trains and by outer suburban services on the Tokaido main line. Outer suburban trains on the Yokosuka line link Shin-Kawasaki with Tokyo and Yokohama.

E-den trains on the 35.5 km Nambu line serve 18 stations in Kawasaki providing a link between central Kawasaki and suburban areas to the northwest. Part of the Nambu line is being rebuilt on an elevated alignment to eliminate level crossings.

E-den service also on 4.1 km branch from Shitte to Hama-Kawasaki and on 7 km Tsurumi line from Tsurumi to Ogimachi.

Keihin Kyuko Dentetsu 'Keikyu'

Keihin Express Electric Railway
20-20 Takanawa 2-chome, Minato-ku, Tokyo 108
Telephone: +81 3 3280 9122 Fax: +81 3 3280 9193
President: I Hiramatsu

Interurban railway

Current situation: Keihin-Kawasaki station on the main line between Tokyo and Yokohama serves central Kawasaki. Through services are operated to central Tokyo via the Toei Asakusa line metro and on to the Keisei Railway. The 4.5 km Daishi branch links Keihin-Kawasaki with Kojima-Shinden (see main entry under Tokyo).

Bus

Current situation: Operates buses in Kawasaki, Yokohama and other parts of Kanagawa Prefecture as well as in Tokyo.

Local service of Tokyu Bus **1997**

Tokyu/Odakyu/Keio Teito

Suburban/interurban railways

Current situation: These railways serve areas to the northwest of central Kawasaki which function largely as outer suburbs of Tokyo. All three railways operate through trains to the Tokyo metro system. The Tokyu Toyoko line from Tokyo to Yokohama serves two stations in Kawasaki (through service to Hibiya line metro) and the Denentoshi line serves six stations (through service to Hanzomon line metro). The Odakyu Odawara line serves seven Kawasaki stations (through service to Chiyoda line metro) with three other stations served by the Tama branch line. Keio Teito has two stations in Kawasaki on the Sagamihara line (through service to Shinjuku line metro). (See main entries for these railways under Tokyo.)

Bus

Current situation: Tokyu Corp has two bus depots in Kawasaki and operates 23 local routes, including one demand-responsive, with some of the 300 buses allocated for Yokohama and Kawasaki operations. Odakyu Bus also operates routes in Kawasaki. Both operators also serve Yokohama and Tokyo.

UPDATED

KAZAN

Population: 1.1 million
Public transport: Bus and trolleybus/tramway services provided by separate municipal undertakings

A dozen ZIU9 trolleybuses wait for custom in central Kazan **1997**

Bus

Number of routes: 40
Fleet: Ikarus 260/280, LIAZ 677, Mercedes-Benz Türk O325
Fare collection: Prepurchase, cancellers on board

Gorelektrotransport

Ul Yershova 1, Kazan 420045, Russia
Telephone: +7 8432 367652

Current situation: In terms of maintenance levels and frequency, this is a medium-scale tramway. No new track has opened so far during the 1990s, but a new 10 km route is under construction in the east of the city.

Trolleybus

Number of routes: 12
Fleet: Approx 270 vehicles, all ZIU9
Fare collection: Prepurchase, cancellers on board

Tramway

Passenger journeys: (1989) 152 million

Number of routes: 18
Track length: 151 km
Fare collection: As trolleybus

Rolling stock: Approx 440 cars

RVZ6 (1976/87)	About M260
KTM5 (1988/92)	M148
KTM8 (1993)	M24
LM93 (1993)	M3

NEW ENTRY

KHARKIV

Population: 1.6 million
Public transport: Bus and trolleybus/tramway services provided by separate municipal undertakings; metro

Upravlenie Automobil'novo Transporta

Upravlenie Automobil'novo Transporta
Kharkiv, Ukraine

Bus

Passenger journeys: 269 million (annual)
Vehicle-km: 41 million (annual)

Route length: 597 km
Fleet: 741 vehicles, including some articulated

One-person operation: All routes
Fare collection: Prepurchase with validation and cancelling machines, or payment to farebox
Fare structure: Flat

Gorelektrotrans

Gorelektrotrans
Ul Molodoy Gvardii 5, Kharkiv 310006
Telephone: +380 57 227 5658

Trolleybus

Passenger journeys: 200 million (annual)
Vehicle-km: 26 million (annual)

Route length: 134 km
Number of routes: 46

Trams await custom at Pivdennyy Vokzal ***1997***

ZIU9 and DAC 217E trolleybuses ***1997***

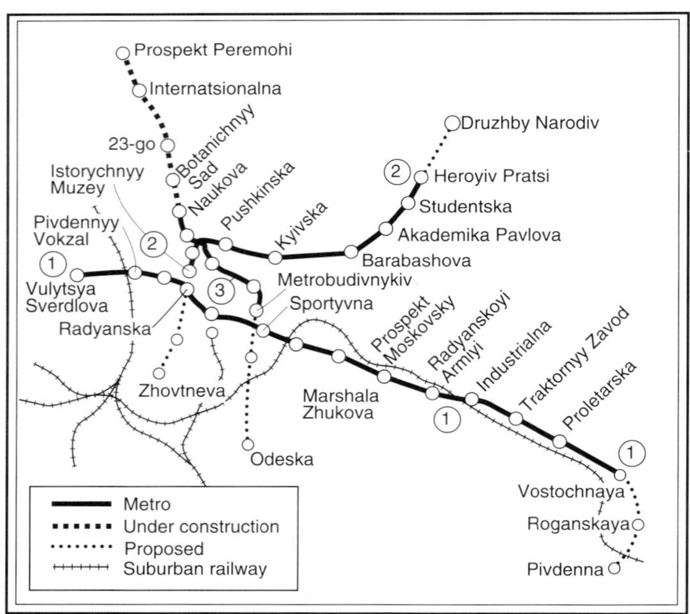

Kharkiv metro

Fleet: 654 vehicles

ZIU9	530
ZIU10	8
DAC 217E (1989/90)	79
Rocar 217E (1995)	27
YuMZ-T1	10

One-person operation: All routes
Fare collection: Prepurchase with onboard validation/cancellation, or payment to farebox
Fare structure: Flat

Tramway

Type of operation: Conventional tramway

Route length: 166 km
Number of lines: 23
Number of stops: 350
Gauge: 1,524 mm

Fare structure: Flat
Fare collection: Prepurchase or coin to farebox; validation and cancelling machines on board
One-person operation: All routes

Rolling stock: 750 cars

T3	M635
KTM5	M60
T3M	M55

Kharkiv Metro

Kharkiv Metropolitena
Ul Engelsa 29, Kharkiv 310012
Chief Executive: Nikolai Yakovlevich Bessonov
Chief Engineer: Leonid Ivanovich Vstavskii

Type of operation: Full metro, initial line opened 1984

Passenger journeys: (1991) 250 million

Route length: 26 km
Number of lines: 3
Number of stations: 27
in tunnel: 23
Gauge: 1,524 mm
Max gradient: 4%
Minimum curve radius: 300 m
Electrification: 750 V DC, third rail

Service: Peak 2½ min, off-peak 6 min
First/last train: 06.00/01.00
Fare structure: Flat, monthly season card
Revenue control: Prepurchase token or magnetic-strip season ticket activate access gates
One-person operation: None
Signalling: Automatic train stop; cab signalling, with automatic speed control; no signals; radio communication between control and trains

Rolling stock: 287 cars in five-car sets

EJ-79	M287

Current situation: Line 1 originally planned as a suburban rail cross-city route, hence the non-standard 750 V DC traction supply.
Developments: The initial section of Line 3 in the city centre was opened in 1995; northwards extension to Peremohi under construction.

UPDATED

KINGSTON

Population: 500,000
Public transport: Bus services provided by 10 franchised operators, each allocated a mixed group of routes. Local rail service reported closed

Private bus

Supervised by:
Public Passenger Transport Board of Control
Ministry of Water & Transport
PO Box 9000, Kingston, Jamaica
Telephone: +1 809 926 9170 Fax: +1 809 926 2835

Current situation: Bus services run by 10 operators were introduced in 1984 under a new franchise system. For details see *JUTS 1988*.
Developments: In 1994 consultant Wilbur Smith & Associates was planning a major reorganisation of bus operations to counter a long-term deterioration in service

Midibuses in Kingston

quality, attributed in part to the multiplicity of operators. In the new Rationalised Bus System, the Kingston metropolitan area will be divided into five franchise areas, with routes, service levels and fares determined by the ministry. Franchises will be awarded for five years.

Fleet: Total of about 1,300 vehicles, of which around 1,200 reported to be operational
Fare collection: Conductors on routes within urban area; no tickets
Fare structure: 2 levels (short and longer urban area journeys)

Ferry

Current situation: An hourly ferry service operates from Jamaica waterfront to Port Royal, near the new airport.

KINSHASA

Population: 4 million
Public transport: Bus services provided by five organised companies and private companies with management arrangements with overseas manufacturers, privately operated 'fula-fula' truck-derived 'auxiliary buses', minibus 'taxibuses' and 'kimalu-malu' pick-up trucks. Extensive shared taxis. Many firms run their own staff transport. Some commuter trains run by national railway

Sotraz

Société des Transports Zairois (Sotraz)
BP 8226, Kinshasa 1, Zaïre
Telephone: +243 12 78445/78211/24503
Staff: 2,800

Current situation: Founded in 1979, Sotraz is 80 per cent owned (directly or indirectly) by the government, and 20 per cent by Renault. From a peak of over 300 vehicles carrying 122 million passengers a year in 1989, poor management control, severe over-staffing and other difficulties saw the fleet reduced to a mere 35 buses in 1991. In addition, lack of a co-ordinating body for public transport meant that fares increases were often rejected by government fiat, and in any case revenues were depressed by the large numbers entitled to free travel.

A new management attacked the spare parts shortage and implemented a planned maintenance system which brought availability up to almost 50 per cent by 1992.

Van Hool/Fiat bus of independent operator Zaibel-tours

SITAZ

Current situation: Established in 1985 as a successor to the former wholly government-owned Société de Transports de Kinshasa, with Portuguese manufacturer UTIC taking a 60 per cent stake. Operations started with 30 UTIC/Leyland buses, plus a batch of 50 DAF TB2105s with UTIC bodywork.

Other operators

Current situation: Amongst other operators are City-Car, Transzam and City-Train. City-Car is a private company established in 1984 with Belgian capital, while Transzam (Société de Transport Zairo-Marocaine) was formed in 1989 with a fleet of 200 Volvo buses assembled in Morocco. City-Train, a government corporation set up in 1989, runs tractor/semi-trailer combinations with DAF prime movers and locally built bodywork on low-loaders.

Onatra

Office National des Transports
BP 98, Kinshasa 1
Telephone: +243 12 24761 Fax: +243 12 24892
Director, Urban Rail: Mbu Kindundu

Current situation: Limited diesel-worked commuter rail service operated over two routes from Kinshasa Est to Ndjili Airport and Lemba, 44 km, 9 stations, 1,067 mm gauge. Extension planned to serve industrial sites at Kintambo, also 5 km branch from Lemba to Kiseno.

Private bus/minibus/shared taxi

Current situation: There are some conventional bus routes operated by private firms. Once predominant, the

Mercedes truck-based 'fula-fula' of Auto Service Zaïre

'fula-fula' buses based on truck chassis with locally built bodies, are giving way to smaller vehicles with 15-25 seats. There are, nevertheless, reported to be substantial numbers of second-hand Volkswagen buses in service. The main independent operator is Auto Service Zaïre.

Fula-fulas are generally used for radial routes into the city of about 12 km length, and are often fed in the outer areas by 'kimalu-malu' smaller pick-up trucks. These are generally tarpaulin-covered Peugeot 504 models with planks for seating up to 15 with another 10 or so more as standees.

Minibuses, officially called taxibuses, provide services over short distances into the central area and are mainly Volkswagen, Toyota Coaster and Mercedes O309 vehicles. A capacity restriction of nine seats is largely ignored and they carry up to 20.

All the paratransit modes are theoretically subject to government regulation but this is largely inoperative, except in the case of fares. A standard flat fare is set for both the private operations and those of the state-owned bus companies.

UPDATED

KITAKYUSHU

Population: 1 million
Public transport: Bus services operated in part of area by municipal undertaking and more extensively by private company, also responsible for tramway, and bus and rail services in other parts of region. Privately owned light rail line; monorail operated by third-sector company; JR suburban/interurban rail; ferry services

Kitakyushu-shi Kotsu Kyoku

Kitakyushu Municipal Transportation Bureau
6-4-41 Nishima, Wakamatsu-ku, Kitakyushu-shi, Fukuoka-ken 808-01, Japan
Telephone: +81 93 791 0031

Current situation: The towns of Moji, Kokura, Tobata, Yahata and Wakamatsu were merged in 1963 to become the city of Kitakyushu, with the municipal bus undertaking in Wakamatsu becoming Kitakyushu-shi Kotsu Kyoku. Although the former Wakamatsu route network has been extended, operations are still concentrated on what is now Wakamatsu Ward in the new city. Nishi Nippon is the predominant operator in the other six wards.

Bus

Passenger journeys: 25 million (annual)
Vehicle-km: 10 million (annual)

Fleet: 143, comprising 132 buses and 11 coaches, including Nissan Diesel, Hino and Mitsubishi with Nishi Nippon Shatai bodies; includes lift-equipped vehicles

Nishi Nippon Tetsudo 'Nishitetsu'

Nishi Nippon Railway
1-11-17 Tenjin, Chuo-ku, Fukuoka-shi 810
Telephone: +81 92 761 6631 Fax: +81 92 722 1405

Current situation: Operates buses and residual tramway service in Kitakyushu as well as bus services in many parts of Fukuoka Prefecture, including the city of Fukuoka (qv). Also operates the Chikuho Electric Railway (see below).

Nishi Nippon is the main bus operator in Kitakyushu with a comprehensive network of routes, except in Wakamatsu which is served by the municipal undertaking. Some local express bus routes are operated as part of the urban network and motorway express services provide direct links from various parts of Kitakyushu to Fukuoka and Fukuoka airport.

Bus

(Kitakyushu operations)
Passenger journeys: 100 million (annual)
Vehicle-km: 30 million (annual)

Number of routes: 113 local routes
Fleet: Approx 700 vehicles, including Hino, Mitsubishi and Isuzu with Nishi Nippon Shatai bodies

Fare structure: Stage; prepurchase coupon tickets, season tickets

Fare collection: Payment to farebox by driver on alighting, or prepurchase
Bus priority: Peak-hour bus lanes, 07.00-09.00 and 17.00-19.00; also a 4 km busway on the roadside alignment of the former reserved track Tobata line tramway which closed in 1985. The busway has 11 stops and is served by 226 return journeys per day including express journeys

Tramway
Type of operation: Conventional tramway

Passenger journeys: (1995) 1.7 million

Route length: 4.9 km
Number of lines: 1
Gauge: 1,435 mm
Electrification: 600 V DC, overhead
Fare structure: Stage; prepurchase coupon tickets, 1- and 3-month seasons

Rolling stock: 14 cars
Kinki Sharyo (1952/53) M9
Kinki Sharyo articulated (1955/58) M5

Developments: The remaining street-running section between Sunatsu and Kurosaki (12.7 km) was closed in 1992, reducing the system to the 4.9 km reserved track portion between Kurosaki and Orio. Management of the line was transferred to the associated Chikuho Electric Railway in 1995.

Chikuho Denki Tetsudo
Chikuho Electric Railway Company
3-14-3 Kurosaki, Yahata Nishi-ku, Kitakyushu-shi 806
Telephone: +81 93 420033
Staff: 100

Current situation: This Nishitetsu subsidiary connects with the remaining section of the Kitakyushu tramway at Kumanishi. Services run Kurosaki–Nogata (16.1 km) using tramway tracks between Kurosaki and Kumanishi (0.7 km).

Light rail
Type of operation: High-speed light rail

Passenger journeys: (1995) 9.8 million
Car-km: (1995) 3.8 million

Route length: 15.4 km
Number of lines: 1
Gauge: 1,435 mm
Electrification: 600 V DC, overhead

Fare structure: Stage; 1- and 3-month seasons
Operating costs financed by: Fares 100%

Rolling stock: 24 articulated tramcars
Hitachi Type 2000 (1963/64) M5
Kyushu Sharyo Type 2000 (1967) M2
Kinki Sharyo Type 2100 (1959/61/64) M8
Alna Koki Type 3000 (1988/89) M9
In peak service: 21

Kitakyushu Kosoku Tetsudo
Kitakyushu Urban Monorail Company
13-1, Kikugaoka 2-chome, Kokura-minami-ku, Kitakyushu-shi 803
Telephone: +81 93 961 0101 Fax: +81 93 961 0555
President: T Morisaki
Managing Director: A Takegami
Staff: 155

Current situation: The Kokura line, opened in 1985, is one of three urban monorail lines planned for Kitakyushu but the only one so far to be authorised and constructed. The line is built partly on the alignment of a former Nishitetsu tramway and links Kokura with a new residential area to the south. The company is half-owned by the Kitakyushu Municipality.

Monorail
Type of operation: Straddle monorail

Passenger journeys: (1990/91) 9.8 million
(1994/95) 11.8 million
(1995/96) 11.4 million

Kitakyushu-shi Kotsu Kyoku buses at Orio station ***1995***

Chikuho line articulated car (right) and Nishitetsu tram at Kurosaki

JR Kyushu Series 811 emu at Kokura, Kitakyushu

Car-km: (1990/91) 0.6 million
(1994/95) 0.6 million

Route length: 8.4 km
Number of lines: 1
Number of stations: 12
Electrification: 1.5 kV DC

Service: Peak 6 min, off-peak 10 min

First/last train: 05.45/23.35
Fare structure: Zonal; commuter and student passes
Operating costs financed by: Fares 88%, other commercial sources 12%
One-person operation: All trains

Rolling stock: 9 four-car trains
Hitachi/Kawasaki (1982/84) M36

JR Kyushu

Kyushu Railway Company
Kyushu Ryokaku Tetsudo
1-1 Chuogai, Hakata Eki, Hakata-ku, Fukuoka 812
Telephone: +81 92 474 2501 Fax: +81 92 493 4805
Chair: T Yamashita
President: Y Ishii

Type of operation: Suburban/interurban heavy rail

Current situation: Frequent local emu service links Moji, Kokura, Tobata and Yahata with Fukuoka. Emus also serve local stations on Nippo main line south from Kokura. Less frequent dmu services from Wakamatsu and Kurosaki to Nogata with some trains continuing to Fukuoka. Dmus also serve local stations south of Kokura on Hitahikosan line.

Ferries

Current situation: Ferries operate across the Kanmon Straits between Moji and Shimonoseki (10 min journey, runs every 10-20 min) and across the inlet between Tobata and Wakamatsu ports (4 min journey, runs every 10-20 min).

UPDATED

KOBE

Population: 1.5 million
Public transport: Bus services provided by municipal undertaking also operating metro. Automated guideway systems; private railways; JR suburban services; funiculars

Kobe-shi Kotsu Kyoku

Kobe Municipal Transportation Bureau
5-1, 6-chome, Kano-cho Chuo-ku, Kobe-shi 650, Japan
Telephone: +81 78 831 8181
General Manager: Kenji Tsubota
Staff: 1,830

Bus

Passenger journeys: (1990/91) 118.7 million
(1991/92) 120.1 million
(1992/93) 121.3 million
Vehicle-km: (1990/91) 21.8 million
(1991/92) 22.4 million
(1992/93) 22.9 million

Number of routes: 71
Route length: 442 km
On priority right-of-way: 98 km
Fleet: 649 vehicles, including Hino, Nissan and Isuzu

One-person operation: All routes
Fare collection: Payment to farebox by driver on alighting, or prepurchase tickets or passes
Fare structure: Flat; prepurchase ticket strips, 1- and 3-monthly passes, 1- and 2-day tickets, combined bus/metro passes
Average speed: 13.5 km/h
Operational control: Computer-controlled 'bus operation improvement system' installed on the Ishiyagawa route
Integration with other modes: Feeder bus routes link residential districts with purpose-built bus/metro interchanges within Seishin New Town

Developments: A computer-controlled bus location system, which relays information about approaching buses and anticipated journey times to bus stop display panels, has been installed.

Metro

Staff: 222

Type of operation: Full metro, first line opened 1977

Mitsubishi-Fuso buses of Kobe-shi Kotsu Kyoku at Myodani bus/metro interchange ***1995***

Passenger journeys: (1990/91) 83.4 million
(1991/92) 90 million
(1992/93) 92.5 million
Car-km: (1990/91) 12.3 million
(1991/92) 13.5 million
(1992/93) 13.6 million

Route length: 22.7 km
in tunnel: 15.5 km
Number of lines: 2 (1 route, referred to as 2 lines)
Number of stations: 16
Gauge: 1,435 mm
Track: 50 kg/m N long-welded rail on concrete sleepers with double elastic fastenings
Max gradient: 2.9%
Minimum curve radius: 300 m
Tunnel: Bored single-track (shield tunnelling method), bored double-track (mountain tunnelling method), and cut-and-cover
Electrification: 1.5 kV DC, overhead

Service: Peak 3-8 min, off-peak 7½-8 min
First/last train: 05.23/23.40

Latest Series 3000 metro train ***1995***

Fare structure: 8-section distance-related scale; 1- and 3-month passes, combined bus/metro passes
Revenue control: Automatic entrance barriers, electronic reading devices at all stations; stored-value AFC
Operating costs financed by: Fares 19.3%, other commercial sources 10.3%, government grants 70.4%
Signalling: Cab signalling, CTC and ATC
Surveillance: CCTV at each station

Rolling stock: 168 cars, operated as six-car sets

Kawasaki 1000	M72 T36
Kawasaki 2000	M16 T8
Kawasaki 3000 (1993/94)	M24 T12

Current situation: The Seishin and Yamate lines operate as a single route linking central Kobe with the large-scale Seishin New Town. Interchange is available with the Portliner at Sannomiya and the Shin-kansen at Shin-Kobe.

The Hokushin Express Electric Railway (see below) is designed for through running to the metro.

Developments: A small profile linear-motor metro, the 8 km Kaigan line, is planned to run from Shin-Kobe to Shin-Nagata via Sannomiya and Wadamisaki, with opening scheduled for 1998.

Hokushin Kyuko Dentetsu

Hokushin Express Electric Railway
27 Kami Aza Ohashi, Shimotani, Yamada-cho, Kita-ku
Kobe-shi 651-12
Telephone: +81 78 581 1070 Fax: +81 78 583 5269
Staff: 74

Type of operation: Suburban railway/metro

Passenger journeys: (1992/93) 8.9 million
(1993/94) 9.1 million
(1994/95) 9.7 million

Current situation: This 7.9 km private sector railway, opened 1988 and jointly owned by Hankyu Electric Railway and Kobe Electric Railway, extends the Kobe metro from Shin-Kobe through a tunnel under the Rokko mountains to Tanigami where there is interchange with Kobe Electric Railway's Sanda line. The line is 1,435 mm gauge with 1.5 kV DC overhead current collection for through running with the metro.

Rolling stock: 5 six-car emus

Kawasaki 7000	M15 T15

Series 3000 stock of Kobe Dentetsu ***1995***

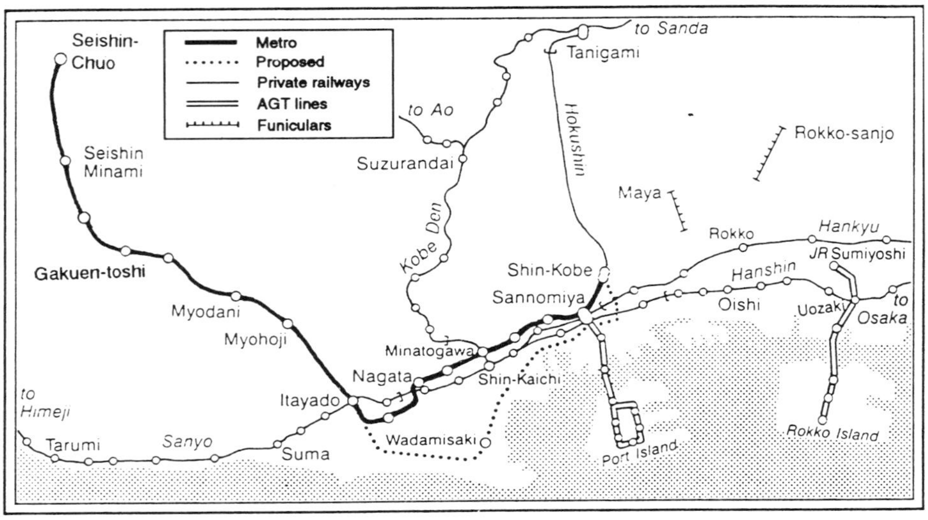

Kobe metro and other transit systems

Hankyu Series 8000 train at Rokko, Kobe ***1996***

Kobe Shin Kotsu Kyoku

Kobe New Transit Company
Minato-jima 6-chome, Chuo-ku, Kobe 650
Telephone: +81 78 302 2500 Fax: +81 78 302 4504
Staff: 181

Type of operation: Rubber-tyred automated transit systems; fully computerised unmanned operation controlled by ATO and ATC — Portliner (opened 1981) and Rokko Liner (opened 1990)

Passenger journeys: (1990/91) Portliner 17.6 million, Rokko Liner 3.8 million
(1991/92) Portliner 18.8 million, Rokko Liner 6 million
(1992/93) Portliner 19.6 million, Rokko Liner 8.3 million
Vehicle-km: (Both services) (1990/91) 4.7 million
(1991/92) 4.8 million
(1992/93) 5.2 million

Current situation: 6.4 km link from Sannomiya station (Kobe) to Port Island was the world's first unmanned metro. The guideway is entirely elevated, and having reached Port Island, 2.9 km from Sannomiya, forms a loop round the island. Flat fare; minimum service 3 min; electrified 600 V DC three-phase; nine stations.

A second medium-capacity transit line, the Rokko Liner, was opened in 1990, linking JR's Sumiyoshi station with Marine Park on Rokko Island, an artificial island constructed in Osaka Bay for industrial and residential development. The 4.5 km elevated line has six stations including interchange with the Hanshin Electric Railway at Uozaki. Flat fare; minimum service 5 min; electrified 600 V DC.

Kobe New Transit is a third-sector company, 55.1% owned by Kobe City Council.

Rolling stock: Portliner 12 six-car trains, Rokko Liner 10 four-car trains

Kawasaki 8000 (Portliner)	M48 T24
Kawasaki 1000 (Rokko Liner)	M20 T20

Kobe Kosoku Tetsudo

Kobe Rapid Railway

Type of operation: Underground railway, opened 1968

Passenger boardings: (1990/91) 144.3 million
(1991/92) 143.3 million
(1992/93) 144.3 million
Car-km: (1990/91) 5.9 million
(1991/92) 6.3 million
(1992/93) 6.3 million

Current situation: The 7.6 km Kobe Rapid Railway does not operate its own trains but provides central area access for the four private interurban railways which serve Kobe. It is 50 per cent owned by Kobe City Council, with the remainder held by the four railways. A 7.2 km east-west line with six intermediate stations links the Sanyo Electric Railway west of Kobe, with the Hanshin and Hankyu railways to the east. Frequent cross-city trains run through from the Sanyo system to the Hanshin/Hankyu lines and vice versa, providing a metro-type service. A 0.4 km section of 1,067 mm gauge underground line brings Kobe Electric Railway trains to an interchange with the 1,435 mm gauge east-west line at Shin-Kaichi.

Kobe Dentetsu

Kobe Electric Railway
1-1, Daikai-dori 1-chome, Hyogo-ku, Kobe 652
Telephone: +81 78 575 2236 Fax: +81 78 577 2467
President: D Nakada

Type of operation: Suburban/interurban railway

Current situation: Operates 69.6 km 1,067 mm gauge system, electrified 1.5 kV with 167 emu cars, on routes to Ao, Arima Spa and Sanda from Shin-Kaichi on the Kobe Rapid Railway. The Hokushin Express Electric Railway, part-owned by Kobe Electric Railway, provides an alternative route to central Kobe from Sanda line destinations via an interchange at Tanigani.

A 5.5 km branch serving a new town development at Kobe-Sanda Garden City was completed in March 1996.

Sanyo Denki Tetsudo

Sanyo Electric Railway
1-1, Oyashiki-dori 3-chome, Nagata-ku, Kobe
Telephone: +81 78 611 2211
President: T Watanabe

Interurban rail

Current situation: Operates 63.3 km 1,435 mm gauge system, electrified 1.5 kV with 199 emu cars on route to Himeji. Trains run via Kobe Rapid Railway to Rokko and Oishi, suburban destinations on the Hankyu and Hanshin railways respectively.

Bus

Passenger journeys: (1990/91) 23.4 million
(1991/92) 23.8 million
(1992/93) 23.9 million
Vehicle-km: (1990/91) 4.4 million
(1991/92) 4.6 million
(1992/93) 4.8 million

Current situation: Also operates fleet of 128 buses and 10 coaches. Services include suburban feeder routes which link with railway stations and the metro; total route length 48.3 km.

JR/Hankyu/Hanshin

Type of operation: Suburban/interurban railways

Current situation: JR, Hankyu and Hanshin operate competing local rail services between Kobe and Osaka. Local and rapid service trains, operated by JR West, cover 130 km between Himeji and Kyoto via Kobe and Osaka with some trains extending further. Journeys on Kobe services amounted to 137 million in 1990/91.

Hankyu and Hanshin services from Osaka operate to Sumaurakoen or Higashi-Suma on the Sanyo Railway via the Kobe Rapid Railway (see main entries under Osaka).

Rokko Maya Tetsudo

Rokko Maya Railway
Kobe

Type of operation: Funicular railways

Current situation: Operates two funiculars which climb Mt Rokko (Rokko Cable, 1.7 km, four cars) and Mt Maya (Maya Cable, 0.9 km, two cars). Both connect at their upper terminals with ropeways operated by a separate company.

UPDATED

KØBENHAVN

Population: 1.7 million

Public transport: All bus services in the metropolitan area are planned and co-ordinated by the public authority Hovedstadsområdets Trafikselskab (HT). The area is also served by local and regional trains of Danish State Railways (DSB) and five local railways. There is free transfer between buses and trains throughout the region. Mini-metro under construction

HT

Hovedstadsområdets Trafikselskab (HT)
Toftegårds Plads, Gammel Køge Landevej 3, 2500 Valby, Denmark
Telephone: +45 36 44 36 36 Fax: +45 36 44 01 19
Staff: HT 280, Bus Division 2,200, private contractors 1,650

Current situation: Development of fully integrated services has been a major feature of HT, which was formed in 1974 and until 1989 was responsible for overall supervision of all public transport in the region. For history and development see *JUTS 1988*.

In 1990 the Greater København Council was abolished and overall control of local rail services passed back to DSB, though fares co-operation continued (see below). HT's operating role is now confined to bus services, planning and co-ordination, and it receives all fare income and pays operating costs of contractors for provision of service.

Deregulation in the København region was approved by parliament in 1989. Based on the present operations of both HT and private contractors, deregulation has taken place in three phases in 1990, 1992 and 1994, when the extent of deregulated services reached 45 per cent. HT's own operating division and the state-owned bus company DSB-busser were forbidden to tender. The tendering process has brought about decreases in contract prices of up to 25 per cent.

Developments: A new public transport bill provides for tenders to be sought for 100 per cent of HT's operations over the next eight years. In this new process HT's bus division, which is currently being converted into an independent limited company, will be allowed to bid on equal terms with private contractors. HT's role will then be confined to inviting tenders, co-ordinating, planning and marketing public transport.

A mini-metro connecting København with the island of Amager is under construction and is scheduled to open in 2000. It is being planned and constructed by an independent company, Ørestadsselskabet (see below), which is also responsible for development of the new urban area Ørestaden in the western part of Amager.

In addition, HT's plans for three light rail lines totalling 22 km to connect central København with surrounding urban districts and suburbs have been adopted by the board. In addition, other strategies for improving public transport provision in the city's busiest corridors are expected in a report due in mid-1997.

Bus

(Figures for HT and contracted operations, unless stated)
Passenger journeys: (1991) 176 million
(1992) 188 million
(1993) 190 million

Number of routes: 251
Route length: (One way) 4,500 km
Fleet: 1,140 buses

HT fleet	
12 m single-deck	557
Articulated	49
Articulated duobus	2
DAB Servicebus	12
Contractors' fleet	
12 m single-deck	506
Articulated	3
Tele-bus vehicles	11

Average age of fleet: HT 10 years, contractors' 6 years
In peak service: 981

Most intensive service: 4-5 min
One-person operation: All services
Fare collection: Preprinted tickets issued by driver with manually operated ticket machine; multijourney tickets sold by bus drivers, at 165 rail ticket offices and by about 70 agents. Multijourney tickets cancelled in buses and at stations, about 2,000 ticket cancellers in use
Fare structure: Zonal; all tickets valid for free transfer between buses and between bus and rail; single, multijourney and season tickets (monthly). Tourist cards including bus and rail travel and admissions to attractions and reduced ferry travel to Sweden
Fares collected on board: 10%; 12% of passengers use single tickets, 41% use multijourney tickets, 47% season tickets
Fare evasion control: On-the-spot penalty payment to inspectors
Operational control: Route inspectors/mobile radio/traffic centre
Arrangements for elderly/disabled: 3-month off-peak season tickets at one-tenth normal adult price; no special finance provided
Operating costs financed by: Fares 52%, other commercial sources 2%, subsidy/grants from HT member counties 46%

Developments: Two Mercedes/AEG duobuses were tried out over a two-year period, but the high capital and running costs led to a decision in mid-1995 not to order a fleet. Further trials have been made with five CNG- and five LPG-powered buses, though the duobuses were expected to be given a further chance to prove themselves.

With the fourth round of tendering, almost 200 new low-floor buses came into service ***1995***

S-Bane train at Valby ***1996***

New-style bus stops are being introduced throughout the HT region *1995*

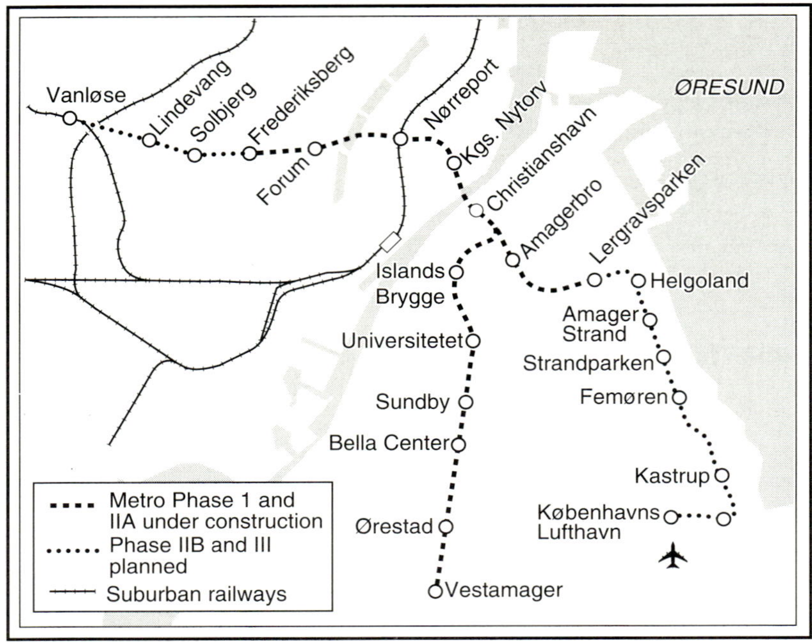

København light metro under construction

Development continues of the network of 'S-line' express bus routes established in 1993 to provide orbital links between S-Bane rail stations. Accounting for 10 per cent of bus-km in 1994, expansion to some 20 per cent is planned.

In 1995 HT starts trials of real-time information provision to customers, along with active traffic signal priority for buses by means of satellite positioning. Two test areas have been chosen — part of the suburban ring road and a heavily-trafficked route in central København.

Bus (contracted)

Current situation: The number of private contractors has dropped since the first round of tendering in 1990, from 19 to only 7 in 1994. HT's bus division has 54 per cent of services, the Swedish-owned firm Linjebus 25.8 per cent, and Unibus 8.1 per cent. The remaining five contractors have between 1.5 and 3 per cent. Typically, contracts are for four years.

Light rail (planned)

Current situation: Three routes are proposed — Hellerup—Glostrup via the city centre, Herlev—Nørrebro—Nørreport, and an orbital route Lyngby—Herlev—Glostrup—Ishøj.

DSB

Danish State Railways (DSB), S-Train
Kalvebod Brygge 34, 1560 København V
Telephone: +45 33 14 04 00 12062
Fax: +45 33 12 21 47
Operations Manager: Erik Maglehøj

Suburban rail (S-Bane)

Passenger journeys: (1992) 95.6 million
(1993) 93.4 million

Operating costs financed by: Fares 77%, other commercial sources 9%, national subsidies 14%

Current situation: Extensive and frequent services operated over network of 170 route-km, with 79 stations, 1,435 mm gauge, electrified 1.65 kV DC overhead. Integrated fares system applies with automatic ticket vending/cancelling machines. Also operates 25 km local railway linking Hillerød and Helsingør; service increased from hourly to half-hourly between Hillerød and Fredensborg in 1994.

Developments: Upgrading is in progress between Ballerup and Frederikssund, including installation of double-track on the Ballerup—Veksø section and construction of two new stations. Completion in 1998 will permit introduction of a 10-min interval service.

A proposal for an outer circle route to link all the radial branches of the S-Bane, by extending the existing line from Hellerup to Vanløse round to Sjaelør, is being redrafted as light rail.

The first two four-car sets of new-generation S-Bane trains on order from Siemens/Linke-Hofmann-Busch were delivered in November 1995. The trains are to a four-section articulated design with single steerable wheelsets. There is an option on 112 sets to replace the existing fleet by 2008. If trials are successful, a further six sets will be delivered by July 1997 prior to start of series production in 1998.

Rolling stock: 582 emu cars (S-Bane), 12 diesel railcars

Scandia/GEC (1967/78)	M275 T275
Scandia/ASEA (1986)	M16 T16
LHB/Siemens protoypes	8
Diesel railcars	M7 T5

Regional rail

DSB Regional, address as above
Telephone: +45 33 14 04 00 14083
Fax: +45 33 93 06 16
Operations Manager: Henrik Nørgaard

Current situation: Other DSB regional, local and suburban services link København with Helsingør (electrified 25 kV, 20-min service), west and southern Zeeland via Roskilde (three routes), and Roskilde—Køge—Næstved.

Local railways

Current situation: Four railways, the Helsingør-Hornbaek-Gilleleje Bane (HHG), the Gribskov and Hillerød-Frederiksvaerk-Hundested Jernbane (GDS/HFHJ), and the Lyngby-Naerum Jernbane (LNJ) provide local services, with some connections to S-Bane services.

Developments: In 1997, HHG and GDS will each receive three two-car sets of Flexliner dmu from the batch of 13 ordered in 1994 by the Association of Danish Private Railways on behalf of members.

Mini-metro

Under construction
Ørestadsselskabet
Grøns Pakhus, Holmens Kanal 7/4, 1060 København K
Telephone: +45 33 11 17 00 Fax: +45 33 11 23 01
Director: Anne-Grethe Foss
Project Manager: Helge Erlandsen

Current situation: A new urban development corporation, Ørestadsselskabet, was set up in 1993 to promote development of the Ørestad area close to København's international airport on Amager island. A key element in the development is a rapid transit link with the city centre, for which construction and equipment contracts were signed in 1996.

The system chosen is an automated mini-metro, with

DAB of Unibus on HT contracted service *1996*

driverless trains running at 90 sec headway in peak hours. It will run on segregated tracks at surface level and elevated, except for the link into the city centre which will be in bored tunnel. Phase I and IIA (16 km, 14 stations) will run from the DSB station at Frederiksberg in an 8 km tunnel to the island, where it will divide to serve the development area in the west, terminating at Vestamager, and existing built-up areas in the east at Lergravsparken. This is planned to be in operation by 2000.

Civil engineering is in the hands of the Comet consortium of Danish, British, French, Italian and Austrian contractors, while track, signalling, power supply and rolling stock (19 low-floor cars) will be supplied by Ansaldo.

In Phase IIB, the line would be extended in the city from Frederiksberg to Vanløse, taking over the S-Bane alignment between the two stations. The third phase would extend the Lergravsparken branch into the international airport. Two interchanges are planned with the Øresund high-speed link to Sweden.

With all three phases completed, the system will extend to 22 km (8 km in tunnel) with 24 stations; it is expected to be carrying some 70 million passengers a year by 2005.

UPDATED

KÖLN

Population: 1 million, area served 1.3 million

Public transport: Bus, tramway and pre-metro services provided by municipal authority, co-ordinated under the Verkehrsverbund Rhein-Sieg (VRS) to provide integrated local transport throughout the region. Tramway being upgraded to Stadtbahn; S-Bahn

VRS

Verkehrsverbund Rhein-Sieg GmbH
Barbarossaplatz 1, 50674 Köln, Germany
Telephone: +49 221 208080 Fax: +49 221 208 0840
Managing Directors: Karl-Heinz Wolf
Horst Krämer

Passenger journeys: (All modes)
(1993) 356 million
(1994) 382 million
(1995) 384 milion

Current situation: Formed in 1987 as the successor to Verkehrsgemeinschaft Rhein-Sieg (VGRS). Covering an area of 3,900 km^2 with a population of 3 million, VRS territory extends from Gummersbach in the east to Düren in the west, from Leverkusen/Monheim in the north to Bonn/Bad Honnef in the south. VRS co-ordinates all public transport services by road and rail within its area, including regional rail services of DB. A uniform tariff scheme with free transfers, irrespective of mode or operator, is applied.

Services are provided by Stadtwerke Bonn (SWB, and its associate SSB) (qv), Kölner Verkehrs Betriebe (KVB), Regionalverkehr Köln (RVK), Kraftverkehr Wupper-Sieg (KWS), Rhein-Sieg Verkehrsgesellschaft (RSVG), Oberbergische Verkehrsgesellschaft (OVAG), Bahnen der Stadt Monheim (BSM), the independent bus operators Verkehrsbetrieb Hüttebräucker at Leichlingen, Kraftverkehr Gebr Wiedenhoff at Solingen and Rhein-Erft Verkehrsgesellschaft (REVG), whose services are operated by RVK under contract, and DB.

One of the first measures taken by VRS was to cut back regional bus routes into Köln at the outer termini of the city's tramways where passengers now have to change. Throughout the VRS area, some 20 per cent of commuters use public transport, rising to 27 per cent in the core cities.

Developments: VRS timetables, comprising 25 million connections, are now available on personal computer disks and via Videotext. Introduction of express bus services planned.

Fare structure: Zonal; single, day and multiride tickets, weekly and monthly passes (non-transferable), transferable monthly passes (not valid before 09.00); free transfer within area, irrespective of mode or operator; 70% of passengers use passes

Operating costs financed by: Fares 42%, other commercial sources 3%, subsidy/grants 55%

KVB

Kölner Verkehrs-Betriebe AG (KVB)
Scheidtweilerstrasse 38, 50933 Köln
Telephone: +49 221 5471 Fax: +49 221 547 3950
Directors: Dipl-Ing K D Bollhöfer (Chair)
Dr Wolfgang Meyer
Wilfred Räpple
Operating Manager: Dipl-Ing Herbert Berg
Infrastructure Manager: Karl-Heinz Dresselhaus
Rolling Stock Manager: Hans Köhler
Personnel Manager: Erwin Fey
Finance Manager: Horst Huchtemann
Staff: 3,323

Passenger journeys: (All modes)
(1993) 186.4 million
(1994) 202.8 million
(1995) 210.2 million

Operating costs financed by: Fares 65%, subsidy/grants 35%

Developments: The Köln–Bonn interurban railway KBE, which also operated its own fleet of 34 buses, was merged with KVB in 1992. In recognition of KVB's contribution to the life of the city, the authorities have approved an annual grant of 25 per cent of tramway track maintenance costs.

Bus

Vehicle-km: (1993) 20.8 million
(1994) 20.5 million
(1995) 20.4 million

Number of routes: 32

Route length: 441 km

Fleet: 224 vehicles, plus 76 hired

Neoplan N416 (1984/86)	28
Neoplan N421/N4021 articulated (1989/92)	15
Mercedes O405N low-floor (1989/91)	54
Neoplan N4014NF low-floor (1992/93	52
MAN NG272 low-floor articulated (1994/95)	65
Volvo Steyr S66F58 (1993)	10

Most intensive service: 10 min

One-person operation: All routes

Fare collection: Vending machines on board or prepurchase multitickets or pass; validation and cancelling machines on board

Fare evasion control: Roving inspectors; DM40 penalty

Operational control: Mobile radio

Average peak-hour speed: 22.5 km/h

Developments: Minibuses introduced 1991, now operating on two local routes.

Tramway/Pre-metro

Type of operation: Tramway and pre-U-Bahn

Car-km: (1993) 24.8 million
(1994) 25.5 million
(1995) 27.3 million

Route length: 138.9 km, of which 77.8 km on segregated right-of-way and 36.2 km in tunnel; plus 49.6 km railway (ex-KBE interurban)

Number of routes: 14

Number of stations: 28 (in tunnel)

Gauge: 1,435 mm

Max gradient: 4%

Minimum curve radius: 60 m

Electrification: 750 V DC, overhead

Service: Peak 4 min, off-peak 20 min

First/last car: 04.20/02.00

Rolling stock: 313 cars

Duewag 8-axle articulated (1963/70)	M102
Duewag B100S 6-axle Stadtbahn (1973/85)	M68
Duewag B80S 6-axle Stadtbahn (1977)	M20
Duewag B80D 6-axle Stadtbahn (1987/96)	M73
Waggon Union B80D 6-axle Stadtbahn (1987/90)	M10
Bombardier K4000 6-axle articulated (1995/96)	M40

On order: Option exercised for a further 40 low-floor Stadtbahn cars from Bombardier Eurorail for 1996/97 delivery

Current situation: Tramways being upgraded under the Rhein-Sieg Stadtbahn project. Route 16 runs to Bonn (Bad Godesberg), and Route 18 to Bonn via Brühl, over former KBE interurban tracks. Extension from Ostheim to Adenauer Siedlung under construction. First section (1.5 km) of full U-Bahn with high-level island platforms and not accessible to tramway rolling stock opened beneath Venloer Str in 1989. Another section (3.4 km), mainly on surface reserved track but with 900 mm platforms, opened in Amsterdamer Str in 1992.

Developments: Upgrading in progress of Ehrenfeld, Bickendorf and Gurtel sections (6.7 km, six stations); Mulheim east-west section (3.9 km, four stations); Heumarkt University section (4.1 km, one station).

All east-west routes in future to be operated with low-floor LRVs. These routes will become a largely separate system and only three stations on the belt line would be shared with the high-platform LRT network. Ultimately, a fleet of some 400 cars is planned for the two systems. A new depot is planned at Ossendorf, as is a computer-based control system for the Brück and Bocklemünd tram routes.

Vandalism has become a serious issue for KVB, and security measures have been increased. Two LRVs were destroyed in an arson attack in 1996.

KVB's new low-floor car from Bombardier ***1996***

Interurban rail

Current situation: The KBE lines, now merged into KVB and SWB Bonn (qv), total 58.5 km with 40 stations, electrified 750 V DC overhead.

DB

Deutsche Bahn AG, Geschäftsbereich Nahverkehr
Regionalbereich Rheinland
Domprobst-Ketzer-Strasse 1-9, 50667 Köln
Telephone: +49 221 141 3330 Fax: +49 221 141 2442
Managers: Hans-Joachim Geupel
Rainer Graichen

Type of operation: S-Bahn and regional rail

Current situation: S-Bahn service is now provided on three cross-city routes from Düsseldorf-Gerresheim to Bergisch Gladbach through Köln Hbf; Rhein-Ruhr S-Bahn (qv) Route S6 Essen via Düsseldorf-Langenfeld to Köln Hansaring, created a second link between the Rhein-Ruhr and Köln (Rhein-Sieg) S-Bahn systems; and Köln—Troisdorf—Siegburg—Aug (Sieg).

City-Bahn regional rail service in operation between Köln and Gummersbach in the east, to Horrem in the west, and to Euskirchen in the southwest. The route to Horrem and onwards to Düren (40 km) is being upgraded to S-Bahn standards, with separate tracks. An S-Bahn line to Köln/Bonn airport is planned.

A total of 14 regional rail lines extending to 503 km is included in the VRS joint tariff scheme.

Rolling stock: Three-car push-pull trains

RVK

Regionalverkehr Köln GmbH
PO Box 140173, 50491 Köln
Telephone: +49 221 16370 Fax: +49 221 1637 239
Directors: Karl-Heinz Klöker
Norbert Pietzka
Staff: 726

Current situation: This regional bus company, formerly controlled by DB, was taken over by eight local government owned transport companies (including KVB and SWB) in 1996. It provides suburban, interurban and rural bus services.

Passenger journeys: (1993) 40.9 million
(1994) 42.7 million
(1995) 42.7 million
Vehicle-km: (1993) 26.6 million
(1994) 26.5 million
(1995) 26.8 million

Route length: 3,905 km, plus contracted services
Fleet: 358 buses, plus 306 contracted out to independent operators
Fare structure: VRS within area; separate km-based tariff beyond

KWS

Kraftverkehr Wupper-Sieg AG
PO Box 300569, 51338 Leverkusen
Telephone: +49 2171 50070 Fax: +49 2171 500749
Director: Gerd Wasser
Staff: 388

Current situation: Local government owned bus operator serving Leverkusen and Bergisch Gladbach and adjoining rural area, population 522,000.
Developments: Following formation of VRS, several routes were cut back to act as rail feeders. KVB bus routes outside Köln city limits have been taken over by KWS in compensation.

Passenger journeys: (1993) 21.1 million
(1994) 21.5 million
(1995) 22 million
Vehicle-km: (1993) 9.6 million
(1994) 9.7 million
(1995) 9.7 million

Route length: 577 km
Fleet: 164 buses, plus 36 on hire
Fare structure: As VRS

UPDATED

KRAKOW

Population: 835,000
Public transport: Bus and tramway services provided by municipal undertaking; suburban rail services by Polish State Railways (PKP); some bus services by Polish State Buses (PKS)

MPK

Miejskie Przedsiębiorstwo Komunikacyjne z o o w Krakówie
ul Brozka 3, 30405 Krakow, Poland
Telephone: +48 12 662022 Fax: +48 12 667513
Director: Julian Pilszczek
Traffic Director: Bogdan Zelazo
Finance Director: Krzysztof Wąsowicz
Staff: 4,576

Passenger journeys: (All modes)
(1992) 394.6 million
(1993) 508 million
(1994) 564 million

Operating costs financed by: Fares 64.5%, subsidy/grants 35.5%
Subsidy from: City budget

Current situation: In 1990 the old MPK operation was divided into six city-owned limited companies — MZRB (construction), MZT (lorries and taxis), MZNA (bus overhaul), MZNT (tram overhaul), MZTSiPT (tramway construction and maintenance), with MPK reconstituted solely as operator of urban passenger services. MZRB and MZNT were liquidated in 1992.

The political situation, the city's financial problems and the transition to a free market economy had a severe effect on the undertaking, with subsidies reduced, costs increased and patronage down. Accordingly, MPK undertook a big marketing exercise to attract new customers. The decline was reversed in 1992, and there has since been substantial growth.

Bus

Vehicle-km: (1992) 37.5 million
(1993) 37.7 million
(1994) 37.7 million

Number of routes: 112
Route length: (One way) 1,472 km
Fleet: 584 vehicles

Ikarus 260	39
Ikarus 280 articulated	189
Jelcz M11	171
Jelcz 120M	130
Scania CR111/112	20

Scania of MPK on ul Basztowa ***1997***

Ex-Nürnberg bogie car on Route 5 at ul Długa ***1997***

Scania CN113LAB (1992/93)	20
Scania Max Ci	11
MAN SG242/SL200	3
Jelcz MN121M	1

In peak service: 446

Most intensive service: 5 min
One-person operation: All services
Fare collection: Prepurchase with validation/cancellation equipment on board, or payment to driver
Fare structure: Urban, flat; suburban, zonal
Fare evasion control: Roving inspectors
Operational control: Traffic regulators and route inspectors; control by mini-computer to be introduced
Arrangements for elderly/disabled: Disabled soldiers, pensioners, students, scholars half fare; over-75s and blind people with escorts, free
Average distance between stops: 690 m
Average peak-hour speed: 18 km/h

New vehicles financed by: Central budget

Tramway

Type of operation: Conventional tramway/light rail

Car-km: (1992) 25.6 million
(1993) 24.6 million
(1994) 24.8 million

Route length: 79.5 km
Number of lines: 28
Gauge: 1,435 mm

Fare structure: As bus
One-person operation: All routes

Rolling stock: 525 cars

Konstal 102N articulated	M95
Konstal 105N	M372
MAN/Siemens T4/B4 ex-Nürnberg	M27 T27
T6	M4

In peak service: 352

PKP

Polish State Railways (PKP)
ul Chalubinskiego 4, 00928 Warszawa
Telephone: +48 22 620 4512 Fax: +48 22 621 2705

Type of operation: Suburban heavy rail

Current situation: Trains run about hourly to Skawina (21 km), and to Wieliczka/Niepolomice. Also irregular services on several other routes.

UPDATED

KREFELD

Population: 246,000, area served 535,000
Public transport: Municipal company provides local bus and tramway services and regional bus services in an area extending to Geldern in the north and the Dutch border in the west. Bus service to Mönchengladbach provided jointly with that town's operator. Interurban LRT line to Düsseldorf operated by Rheinbahn of Düsseldorf (qv). DB operates local trains on four lines plus some regional bus services. All services co-ordinated by Rhein-Ruhr Verkehrsverbund (VRR) (qv)

SWK

Städtische Werke Krefeld AG
PO Box 2760, 47727 Krefeld, Germany
Telephone: +49 2151 980 Fax: +49 2151 982503
Directors: Horst Hannappel (Chair)
Klaus Evertz
Dr Dirk König
Volkmar Kretkowski
Staff: 353 (transport division only)

Passenger journeys: (All modes)
(1993) 35.8 million
(1994) 35.2 million
(1995) 33.7 million

Operating costs financed by: Fares 38%, other commercial sources 7%, subsidy/grants 55%
Subsidy from: City and Nordrhein-Westphalia Land government and other communities served

Current situation: The former municipal transport operator Krefelder Verkehrs AG was merged in 1990 with other public utilities into a single authority, SWK.

Tramway services continue to be improved by double tracking and driver control of traffic signals to give tram priority. Further bus routes have been contracted out and hired buses now account for 25.6 per cent of all bus-km.

MAN SG220 articulated buses at Krefeld Hbf

Metre-gauge tram of SWK (right) with standard-gauge Rheinbahn interurban to Düsseldorf ***1995***

Bus

Vehicle-km: (1993) 7.2 million
(1994) 7.3 million
(1995) 7.4 million

Number of routes: 23
Route length: 519 km
Fleet: 94 vehicles, plus 38 hired

MAN SL200 standard (1985)	6
MAN SG220 articulated (1979/84)	27
MAN SG242H articulated (1988/90)	22
Mercedes O405 (1988)	10
MAN NL202 low-floor (1993/94)	20
Others	9

On order: 16 Van Hool low-floor articulated

Most intensive service: 15 min
One-person operation: All routes
Fare collection: Prepurchase of tickets, passes, with validation/cancelling machines on board, or payment to driver
Fare structure: Zonal; multiride tickets, weekly and monthly passes, reduced off-peak fares
Fare evasion control: Roving inspectors
Average peak-hour speed: 23.1 km/h

Tramway

Type of operation: Conventional tramway

Car-km: (1993) 2.3 million
(1994) 2.4 million
(1995) 2.3 million

Route length: 37.7 km
Number of lines: 4
Gauge: 1,000 mm
Fare structure: As bus

Rolling stock: 40 cars

Duewag 8-axle articulated (1964/76)	M20
Duewag M8C articulated (1980/81)	M20

Current situation: Upgrading in progress, with street sections being replaced by reserved tracks; 0.5 km extension opened 1993. New main workshops completed 1996.

Rhein-Ruhr Stadtbahn Route 76 runs to Düsseldorf (1,435 mm gauge, operated by Rheinbahn, Düsseldorf).

DB

Deutsche Bahn AG, Geschäftsbereich Nahverkehr
Regionalbereich Rheinland
Domprobst-Ketzer-Strasse, 50667 Köln
Telephone: +49 221 141 3330 Fax: +49 221 141 2224

Type of operation: Suburban heavy rail

Current situation: Though not part of the Rhein-Ruhr S-Bahn network, two DB suburban rail routes provide frequent links to the S-Bahn at Duisburg and Düsseldorf. Parallel bus route to Duisburg has been withdrawn at request of VRR. DB subsidiary company also operates some regional bus services.

UPDATED

KUALA LUMPUR

Population: 1.2 million

Public transport: Conventional bus services in metropolitan area provided by eight main area-franchised private companies with many owner-operated route-licensed 'Bas Mini' fixed-route minibuses and metered taxis licensed by government board as well as special school and factory buses. Suburban rail; light rail; mini-metro under construction

STAR LRV in Kuala Lumpur **1997**

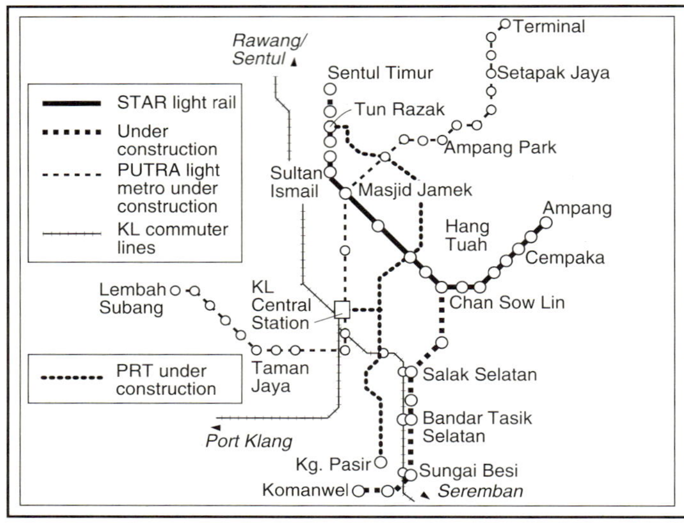

Kuala Lumpur's railways, operating and under construction

Bus (franchised operators)

Regulated by: Road Transport Licensing Board
Ministry of Public Enterprise
Blok A, Komplek Pejabat Damansara, Jalan Dungun, Damansara Heights, 50620 Kuala Lumpur, Malaysia
Telephone: +60 3 254 9044

Current situation: The two main operators are Park May Bhd and Intrakota Consolidated Bhd. Other operators include: Sri Jaya Kenderaan; Toon Fong; Foh Hup; Kuala Lumpur, Klang & Port Swettenham Bus; Selangor Bus; Len Bus; Len Seng; Len Chee. Each main bus operator is franchised to serve a specific sector of the city. Fleets range from 30 to 361 vehicles, with over 1,000 vehicles operated in total. Services run 06.00-24.00 on most routes at intervals varying from 2 min to hourly. There is considerable overlapping of routes.

Minibus (Bas Mini)

Regulated by: Road Transport Licensing Board

Current situation: Conventional services are largely duplicated by minibus routes, which have drawn business from buses and led the conventional operators into Bas Mini operation too. Minibuses were introduced in 1975; each is licensed for a particular route. A flat fare is set.

The largest bus operator, Sri Jaya Kenderaan, runs a fleet of Mercedes O309 minibuses on more lightly used routes.

Developments: The Board started franchising of minibus routes in 1994 as a direct replacement for Bas Mini operations, in an attempt to improve vehicle and passenger standards. The Optare Metrorider has been selected as the fleet vehicle, and is equipped with air conditioning, tinted glazing, wide doors and low entry steps. The minibuses, known as Pekanriders, are imported in knocked-down form for local assembly by Diversified Resources Bhd (DRB), though there will be an increasing proportion of local content. A total of 1,000 is on order for delivery over a five-year period starting in 1996, to replace 800 Bas Mini vehicles.

Eight cross-city routes have been franchised to Intrakota, which is a subsidiary of DRB.

KTM

Malayan Railways (KTM)
PO Box 100001, 50050 Kuala Lumpur
Telephone: +60 3 274 9422 Fax: +60 3 230 3939

Type of operation: Local railway

Passenger journeys: (1996) 25,000 daily

Current situation: Cross-city 'Komuter' suburban service between Seremban, Rawang and Pelabuhan Klang, total 153 km, metre-gauge, electrified 25 kV 50 Hz.

Developments: The immediate success of electric trains, introduced in 1995, led KTM to order two further batches of 22 emus, which were expected to be in service by mid-1997.

Rolling stock: 62 three-car emus

Hunslet TPL/Holec (1993/94)	M18 T36
Mitsubishi/Hyundai (1996)	M22 T44
Union Carriage (1996)	M22 T44

STAR

Sistem Transit Aliran Ringan Sdn Bhd
PO Box 39, 68000 Ampang, Selangor Darul Ehsan
Telephone: +60 3 494 2550 Fax: +60 3 494 2554
Chief Executive Officer: Zainal Abdul Ghani
General Manager, Operations: Guido Vandenbril
Manager, Operations: Peter Gillen
Manager, Engineering: Leong Yee Foong

Type of operation: Light rail, opened 1996

Route length: 12 km

Number of lines: 1
Number of stations: 13
Gauge: 1,435 mm
Electrification: 750 V DC, bottom contact third rail

Service interval: Peak 3 min
First/last car:
Fare structure: Single and stored-value tickets; closed system
Fare collection: Ticket machines and automatic barriers at all stations
Signalling: Block signalling with automatic train stops; radio communication between drivers and control

Optare Metrorider operated by DRB franchisee Intrakota **1995**

Rolling stock: 34 cars

Walkers/AEG (1995)	M34

On order: A further 56 cars for Line 2

Current situation: Phase I from Ampang to Sultan Ismail was opened throughout in November 1996. Most of the route (9.5 km) follows a disused state railway right-of-way with a 2.5 km elevated section in the city centre. The line is fully segregated.

Construction has been undertaken by the Kuala Lumpur Transit Group, a consortium formed by Taylor Woodrow and Adtranz, on a build-own-operate contract. STAR is the operator on a 60-year franchise from the government.

Developments: Construction of two extensions (Phase II) started in August 1996. These run 11.5 km southwest from Chan Sow Lin to Komanwel, to be operational by mid-1998, and 3.2 km northwards from Sultan Ismail to Sentul Timur, scheduled to open in late 1998.

PUTRA

PUTRA Sdn Bhd
Ground Floor, MUI Plaza, Jalan P Ramlee, 50250 Kuala Lumpur
Telephone: +60 3 241 8866 Fax: +60 3 248 3515
Chairman: Zulfikli Mahmood

Mini-metro

Under construction

Current situation: Construction in progress of a 29.2 km automated light metro line, designated LRT System 2 — Phase I, linking western and eastern suburbs across the city centre. This is being built by concessionaire Projek Usahasama Transit Ringan Automatik Sdn Bhd (PUTRA),

Komuter emu of KTM ***1997***

a subsidiary of the investment company Renong. The technology and vehicles, based on Vancouver's SkyTrain system, will be supplied by Canadian companies Bombardier and SNC-Lavalin under contracts worth $C961 million signed in 1994.

PUTRA has a concession from the Malaysian government to build the infrastructure, which comprises a 4.4 km tunnel beneath the city centre, 22 km on viaduct, and the remainder at grade. There will be 24 stations. The Canadian consortium will supply mechanical and electrical equipment, and a fleet of 70 linear-motor powered cars — sufficient to provide initial capacity of 10,000 passengers/h in each direction, though this will rise to 16,000/h in Phase II.

Phase I, scheduled to open in July 1998, runs 13.7 km from Lambah Subang/People's Park in the western suburbs via the university and Taman Jaya to the city centre, where there will be interchange with the STAR light rail line at Banteng. Phase II will extend the line eastwards to Keramat and then north to Wangsa Maju, with the third segment continuing to Gombak (Terminal PUTRA). The entire route should be operating by mid-1999.

People mover

Under construction

Current situation: Construction of a 16 km automated people mover linking the Pekeliling bus terminal at Jalan Tun Razak with Kg Pasir via the central business district was expected to start at the end of 1996. The initial phase from Tun Razak to KTM's Central station is due to open late 1998 and throughout in 1999. There will be 21 stations and a fleet of 14 trains.

UPDATED

KUMAMOTO

Population: 632,000
Public transport: Bus and tram services operated by municipal undertaking with additional bus services provided by private operators, one of which also runs suburban railway. JR suburban/interurban rail

Kumamoto-shi Kotsu Kyoku

Kumamoto City Transportation Bureau
5-1-40 Oe, Kumamoto-shi 862, Japan
Telephone: +81 96 361 5211 Fax: +81 96 363 5955
Staff: Bus 303; tramway 128

Passenger journeys: (All modes)
(1989/90) 28 million
(1991/92) 29.5 million

Operating costs financed by: Fares 65.5%, other commercial sources 15.3%, subsidy/grants 19.2%
Subsidy from: City and regional government

Bus

Passenger journeys: (1989/90) 19.2 million
(1991/92) 19.7 million
Vehicle-km: (1991/92) 6.9 million

Number of routes: 27
Route length: 167.6 km
Fleet: 190 vehicles

Isuzu	50
Hino	45
Nissan Diesel	50
Mitsubishi	45

In peak service: 181
On order: 10 buses

Fare structure: Stage; prepurchase discount strip tickets, 1- and 3-month season tickets, 1-day tickets
Fare collection: Payment to farebox or prepurchase
Operating costs financed by: Fares 69.2%, other commercial sources 8.4%, subsidy/grants 22.4%
Subsidy from: City and regional government
Bus priority: Peak-hour bus lanes, 07.00-09.00 and 17.00-19.00

Kumamoto-shi Kotsu Kyoku bus

Tramway

Passenger journeys: (1993) 10.3 million
(1994) 10.2 million
(1995) 10.2 million
Car-km: (1991/92) 1.6 million

Route length: 12.1 km
Number of routes: 2
Gauge: 1,435 mm
Electrification: 600 V DC, overhead

Service: Peak 4-15 min, off-peak 5-17 min
First/last car: 06.00/23.40
Fare structure: As bus

Alna Koki tramcar on Kumamoto's Route 2

Fare collection: Farebox
One-person operation: Almost all cars
Operating costs financed by: Fares 58.4%, other commercial sources 28.4%, subsidy/grants 13.2%
Subsidy from: City government

Rolling stock: 42 air conditioned cars

Hirose Sharyo (1951)	M1
Shin Kinami Sharyo (1954)	M3
Toyo Koki (1954/55/57/58/60)	M20
Kawasaki articulated (1957) ex-Nishitetsu	M4
Nippon Sharyo (1982)	M2
Alna Koki (1985/86/88/91/93/94)	M12

Developments: Plans for extensions into residential areas and for town-centre underground sections are under consideration.

Kumamoto Denki Tetsudo

Kumamoto Electric Railway
3-7-29 Kurokami, Kumamoto-shi 860
Telephone: +81 96 343 4191

Bus

Current situation: Operates 109 buses on services to the north of Kumamoto.

Suburban railway

Passenger journeys: (Kumamoto city only)
(1990/91) 1 million

Current situation: Operates a 9.7 km suburban rail service from Kumamoto, Fujisakigumae, to Miyoshi, plus a shuttle service on the 3.4 km branch from Kita-Kumamoto to Kami-Kumamoto.
Developments: Two former Tokyo (Toei) Series 6000 metro cars entered service in December 1995, re-formed as a two-car set and converted from 1.5 kV to 600 V DC.

Rolling stock: 12 cars, including second-hand cars from the Tokyu system in Tokyo

Kyushu Sangyo Kotsu

Sanko Bus
3-35 Sakura-machi, Kumamoto-shi 860
Telephone: +81 96 325 1111 Fax: +81 96 322 2730

Bus

Passenger journeys: (1994/95) 20 million

Current situation: Many of the Sanko fleet of more than 600 buses are used on services in the Kumamoto area where a network of 75 urban/suburban routes is operated. Fleet includes lift-equipped vehicles. Services are also provided throughout Kumamoto Prefecture with some express routes serving cities such as Fukuoka and Nagasaki in adjoining prefectures.
Developments: A stored-fare card is planned for introduction from 1997.

JR Kyushu

Kyushu Railway Company
Kyushu Ryokaku Tetsudo
1-1 Chuogai, Hakata Eki, Hakata-ku, Fukuoka 812
Telephone: +81 92 474 2501 Fax: +81 92 473 4805
Chair: T Yamashita
President: Y Ishii

Type of operation: Suburban/interurban heavy rail

Passenger journeys: (Kumamoto city only)
(1990/91) 7.6 million

Current situation: Local emu and occasional dmu services on Kagoshima main line; dmus serve suburban stations on the Hohi main line.

Kumamoto Bus

Kumamoto Bus
11-18 Shinichi-machi, Kumamoto-shi 860
Telephone: +81 963 366 9211

Bus

Current situation: Runs a fleet of some 75 buses on services to the south of Kumamoto.

UPDATED

KUNMING

Population: 3 million
Public transport: Bus services provided by municipal agency, also minibus and microbus paratransit operations. Chinese Railways operates a suburban service of two trains each way daily on the metre-gauge line from Kunming Bei to Wangjiaying (23 km), and on the 1,435 mm gauge lines from Kunming to Zhongyicun (53 km) and Jinmacun (15 km); on the latter route another pair of trains runs between Kunming and Kunming Dong (7 km). Light rail proposed

Kunming City Bus

Kunming City Bus Company
Kunming, Yunnan Province, People's Republic of China

Current situation: Articulated buses predominate in the city centre, with two-axle buses in use on routes with lighter traffic. New buses have been received from factories in Beijing, Guangzhou and elsewhere. Competition exists from paratransit, with probably several hundred minibuses and microbuses in service, but demand is sufficiently high for both modes to co-exist.

Bus

Number of routes: 30
Fleet: Approx 450 vehicles, including many articulated; types include CC641 (two-axle), CC660-3 (articulated), Beijing BK670 articulated, Guangzhou articulated and two-axle, Chongqing CQ643 (two-axle) and CQ662 (articulated) and others
Fare collection: Stage fares paid to seated conductor; monthly passes

Minibus

Current situation: Two levels of service are offered at premium fares above those of city bus services. Many minibuses built all over China to designs based on the Japanese Coaster are in operation, along with a smaller number of microbuses, also based on Japanese designs.

Light rail (proposed)

Current situation: Consultants from VBZ, the operator in Kunming's twin city of Zürich, have recommended a 12 km tram line on the city's busiest corridor, along with improvements to the bus network.

Minibuses in Kunming

KYIV

Population: 2.6 million
Public transport: Bus and trolleybus/tramway services provided by separate undertakings. Metro; funicular operated by city authority; suburban rail services; river ferries

Current situation: With fares substantially reduced in real terms since 1992 because of inflation and widespread route closures instituted to reduce costs, severe overcrowding now affects all modes. In addition, timetabling and operational control seem to have broken down, leading to lengthy intervals in service.

One-person operation: All services
Fare collection: Prepurchase from booths with validation/cancellation on board
Fare structure: Flat, higher for bus; single, monthly and quarterly seasons
Arrangements for elderly/disabled: Free travel

Tatra T3 in advertising livery at Dvorets Sporta

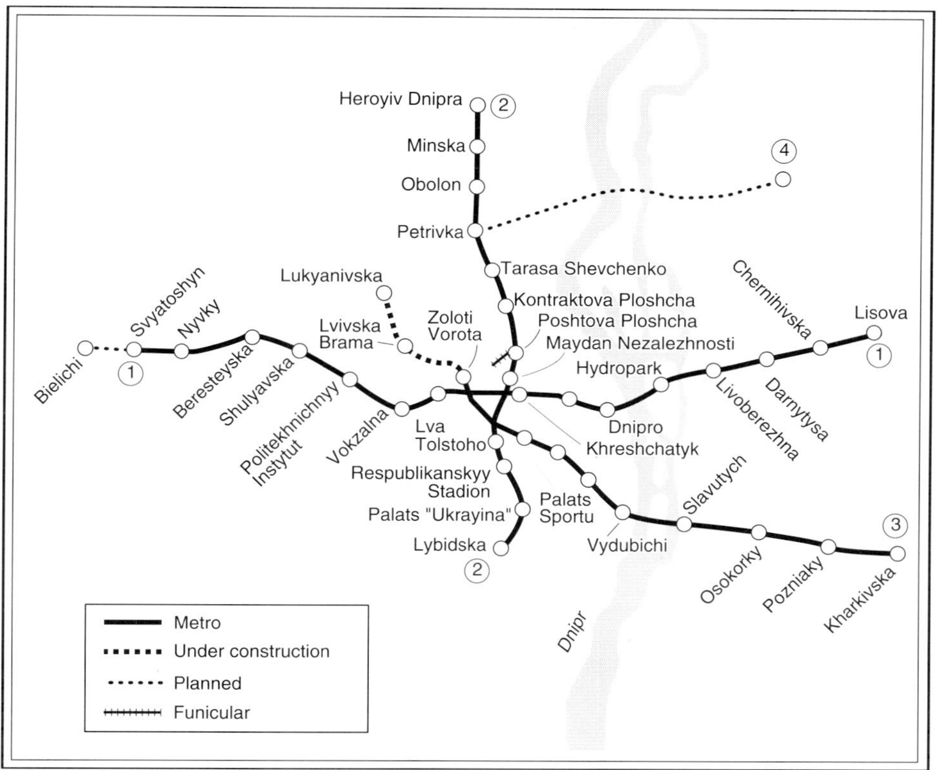

Kyiv metro

Skoda 9Tr at Tolstogo trolleybus terminus **1996**

UZ suburban trains at Passazhirskvv station **1997**

Kyivelektrotrans

Kyivelektrotrans
Nabereshnoje Chusse 2, Kyiv 252201, Ukraine
Telephone: +380 44 291 0470

Current situation: Trolleybus is the principal mode in the city centre. Five cross-city trolleybus routes have closed since 1992, service frequencies have been reduced on economic grounds, and double-coupled operation has ceased. One route has been under construction in the north of the city, but work appears to have ceased.

Shortage of spare parts has led to withdrawal of locally built Kyiv 11 articulated trolleybuses, though the design is now being produced by the Yuzhmash armaments factory at Dnipropetrovsk as types YuMZ, T1 and T2.

Some short sections of tramway have been abandoned as the metro extended in the city centre. Poor track throughout the network makes journeys slow and unreliable. Network includes 9.5 km fully segregated section used by Routes 1/1k and 3 to satellite housing developments southwest of the city, equipped with ATC and operated by three-car sets. Though some cars run through from the urban network, this route is proposed for extension through the city centre to the river bank.

Similar service reductions have been made on the tram network, and further cuts have been caused by lack of spare parts for the 100 per cent Czech-built fleet. Despite these problems, some track relaying has been carried out, and Route 28 was extended northwards from Saborova to new residential areas in late 1994.

New rolling stock is likely to become available in 1995 from Yuzhmash, which is offering Tatra-Yug vehicles, essentially Tatra T6 (T3M) cars built under licence.

Trolleybus

Number of routes: 26

Fleet: 872 vehicles

Skoda 9Tr	200
Skoda 14Tr	330
Skoda 15Tr articulated	32
DAC 217E articulated	257
Kyiv 11u	23
YuMZ T1 articulated	30

Tramway

Staff: 4,197

Type of operation: Conventional tramway/light rail

Number of lines: 26, some with as few as one daily journey
Gauge: 1,524 mm

Rolling stock: About 800 cars

ČKD Tatra T3SU	M700
ČKD Tatra T3M	M95
Tatra-Yug T3M	M2

Kyiv Metro

Kyivskiy Metropoliten
Prospekt Peremogi 35, Kyiv 252055
Telephone: +380 44 226 2727 Fax: +380 44 229 1857
General Manager: N E Balatskiy
Chief Engineer: M I Mitrofanov
Staff: 5,315

Type of operation: Full metro, first line opened 1960

Passenger journeys: (1990) 375 million
(1992) 365 million
(1994) 423 million

Route length: 46.5 km
Number of lines: 3
Number of stations: 37
Gauge: 1,524 mm
Max gradient: 4%
Minimum curve radius: 400 m
Electrification: 825 V DC, third rail

Service: Peak 1 min 35 s, off-peak 6 min
First/last train: 06.00/01.00
Fare structure: Flat, monthly season card
Revenue control: Prepurchase token or magnetic-strip season ticket activate access gates
One-person operation: None
Signalling: Automatic train stop; radio communication between trains and control

Rolling stock: 537 cars

Mytischy D60 (1960/89)	M259
Mytischy E79 81-714/715 (1979)	M248
Others	M30

Developments: Line 3 was extended to Kharkivska in December 1994, while the extension from Zoloti Vorota to Luk'yanivska is under construction.

Bus

Current situation: Buses play only a limited supporting role to the other modes. Operations are in the hands of six local ATPs (Automobil'novo Transporta Pasagirskogo), with a fleet of mainly Ikarus 280 plus some 260 and 263, and LAZ. Fares are 50 per cent higher than tram and trolleybus.

UPDATED

KYOTO

Population: 1.5 million

Public transport: Bus and metro services provided by municipal undertaking. Suburban services by JR, private railways and bus company

Isuzu Cubic of Kyoto-shi Kotsu Kyoku ***1995***

Kyoto-shi Kotsu Kyoku

Kyoto Municipal Transportation Bureau
48 Bojocho, Mibu Nakagyo-ku, Kyoto-shi 604, Japan
Telephone: +81 75 822 9115 Fax: +81 75 822 9240
Chair: T Tanabe
General Manager: S Miura
Staff: 2,814

Passenger journeys: (All modes)
(1991) 245.4 million
(1992) 245.3 million
(1993) 244.3 million

Operating costs financed by: Fares 82.4%, other commercial sources 11.3%, subsidy/grants 6.3%
Subsidy from: City, prefecture and government

Bus

Staff: 2,113

Passenger journeys: (1991) 171.6 million
(1992) 171.5 million
(1993) 170.6 million
Vehicle-km: (1991) 37.1 million
(1992) 39.6 million
(1993) 36.8 million

Number of routes: 89
Route length: 469 km
On priority right-of-way: 94.9 km; 40 bus priority signals; staff patrol during peak hours to prevent illegal parking and ensure observance of lane discipline
Fleet: 928 vehicles, including Isuzu, Mitsubishi, Hino and Nissan, all air conditioned; tram replica buses operate on sightseeing services

One-person operation: All routes

Fare collection: Farebox on vehicle
Fare structure: Flat; coupon tickets, transfer tickets (bus/bus, bus/metro); 1-, 3- and 6-month passes, day passes (bus/metro)
Fares collected on board: 31.8%
Fare evasion control: Driver inspection; penalty
Average distance between stops: 420 m
Average peak-hour speed: In bus lanes, 17 km/h; in mixed traffic, 14 km/h
Operational control: Inspectors; computerised bus location and passenger information systems installed on some routes
Arrangements for elderly/disabled: Fleet includes lift-equipped buses
Operating costs financed by: Fares 85.8%, other commercial sources 8.2%, subsidy/grants 6%

Subsidy from: City and prefecture
New vehicles financed by: Debenture

Developments: Following trials during the 1980s, a computerised total bus operations system is being introduced, comprising bus location, passenger information and data collection.

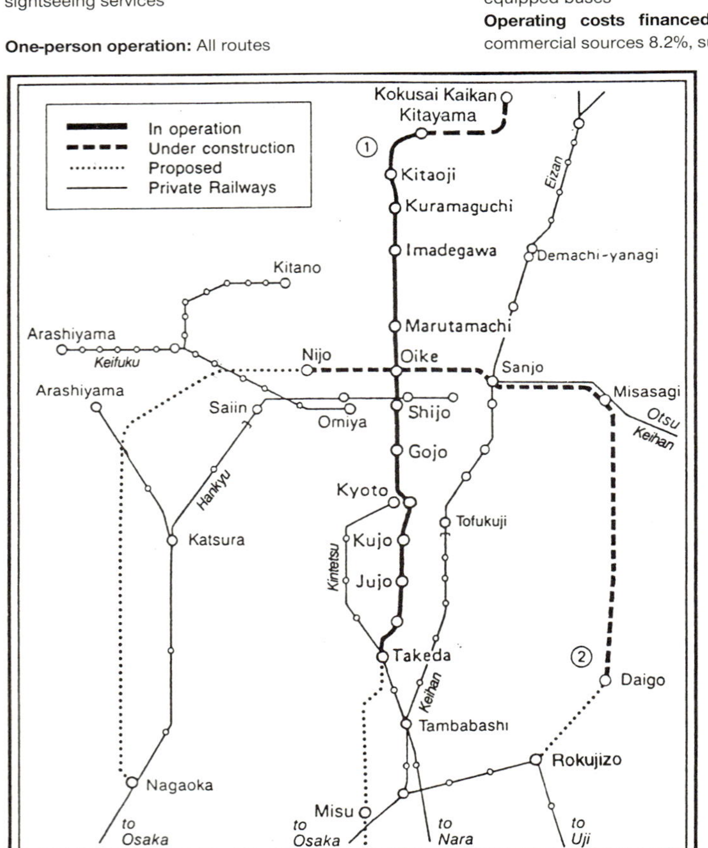

Kyoto metro and connecting lines

Metro

Staff: 713

Type of operation: Full metro, initial route opened 1981

Passenger journeys: (1992) 73.8 million
(1993) 73.7 million
(1994) 74 million
Car-km: (1991) 6.7 million
(1992) 7.3 million
(1993) 7.3 million

Route length 11.1 km
 in tunnel: 10.5 km
Number of lines: 1
Number of stations: 13
 in tunnel: 12
Gauge: 1,435 mm
Track: 60 kg/m rail; sleepers on concrete with resilient pads, partly conventional sleepers on ballast
Max gradient: 3.2%
Minimum curve radius: 260 m
Tunnel: Bored plus some cut-and-cover
Electrification: 1.5 kV DC, overhead

Service: Peak 4-5 min, off-peak 6-7½ min
First/last train: 05.21/23.28

Fare structure: Four-section fare scale; coupon tickets, bus/metro transfer tickets; 1-, 3- and 6-month passes; bus/metro day passes
Revenue control: AFC
Operating costs financed by: Fares 75.4%, other commercial sources 17.7%, subsidy/grants 6.9%
Signalling: CTC and ATC

Rolling stock: 102 cars, in six-car sets

Hitachi/Kinki Sharyo Series 10	M68 T34

Current situation: A through service is operated over Kinki Nippon Railway track from Takeda to Shin Tanabe (16 km) using metro and Kintetsu stock.

A 2.6 km northern extension to Kokusai Kaikan

Kintetsu (right) and Kyoto metro trains on through running services at Takeda **1995**

Keihan Type 600 set and Keihan Bus Route 12 in central Kyoto **1997**

Route 71 service of Kyoto Bus at Kyoto station **1995**

(International hall) is under construction for opening in July 1997, and a southern extension to Rakunan-Shintoshi is planned.

Developments: Kyoto city and a third-sector company, Kyoto Rapid Railway, 51 per cent owned by Kyoto Municipality, 12 per cent by Keihan Electric Railway and 37 per cent by other investors, are building the first 12.7 km section of Kyoto's second metro, the 1,435 mm gauge 1.5 kV DC Tozai line. The line will run east-west through central Kyoto from JR's Nijo station to Daigo via Oike, for interchange with the existing metro line, and Keihan's Sanjo terminus. Between Sanjo and Misasagi the metro will replace the parallel on-street section of Keihan's Otsu line and a through running service will be operated from Shiyakusho-mae to Otsu. Construction began in 1989 with completion planned for November 1997. Extensions are projected at both ends to provide a 30 km line between Nagaoka and Rokujizo.

The first of 14 six-car VVVF inverter-controlled trains for the new line was delivered in May 1996.

Keihan Denki Tetsudo

Keihan Electric Railway
2-27, Shiromi 1-chome, Chuo-ku, Osaka 540
Telephone: +81 6 944 2521 Fax: +81 6 944 2501
Staff: 3,788

Interurban rail

Current situation: Frequent limited-express, express and local trains on Keihan main line compete with Hankyu and JR for Kyoto—Osaka traffic. Direct services run between Yodoyabashi (Osaka) and Demachi-yanagi in north Kyoto (for interchange with the Eizan Railway) via a 5.1 km underground link through central Kyoto. Also Kyoto—Uji local service (see Keihan entry under Osaka).

Light rail

Passenger journeys: (1991) 34 million
(1992) 36.4 million
(1993) 34.7 million
Car-km: (1992) 3.8 million
(1993) 3.8 million

Route length: 25.2 km
Number of lines: 2
Number of stations: 32
Gauge: 1,435 mm
Electrification: 600 V DC, overhead

Fare structure: Zonal; prepurchase coupon tickets, season tickets
One-person operation: None

Rolling stock: 60 cars in two-car sets

Kinki Sharyo Type 80 (1961/70)	M16
Naniwa/Kinki Type 260 (1957/68)	M8
Kinki Sharyo Type 350 (1966)	M6
Keihan Type 600 (rebuilt 1984/88)	M20
Keihan Type 700 (rebuilt 1992/93)	M10

Current situation: Keishin line runs 11.1 km from Sanjo to Hama-Otsu mainly on reserved track but with street running in Kyoto and Otsu. 14.1 km Ishiyama—Sakamoto line runs north-south through Otsu connecting at Hama-Otsu.

Developments: When the Tozai line metro opens in 1997, most of the Kyoto—Otsu service on the section duplicated by the metro will be withdrawn and replaced by a through service.

Keihan Bus

Keihan Bus Company
5 Minami Ishida-cho, Higashi-Kujo, Minami-ku, Kyoto-shi 601
Telephone: +81 75 682 2310 Fax: +81 75 682 2327

Bus

(Entire operations)
Passenger journeys: (1990/91) 79.7 million
(1991/92) 79.6 million
(1992/93) 77.4 million
Vehicle-km: (1990/91) 18.6 million
(1991/92) 18.8 million
(1992/93) 19 million

LAHORE

Population: 3.9 million
Public transport: Bus services in city and surrounding districts provided by provincial government-owned road transport corporation with monopoly on urban routes. Punjab government issues permits for extensive paratransit operations by private buses, horse-drawn 'tongas', autorickshaws and taxis. Suburban trains operated by Pakistan Railways. Light rail plans approved

PRTC

Punjab Road Transport Corporation
Transport House, 11-A Egerton Road, Lahore, Pakistan
Telephone: +92 42 631 6206
Managing Director: Imtiaz Ahmed Sadiq
Staff: 4,702

Current situation: PRTC operates both urban services in Lahore and interurban elsewhere in the Province of Punjab. Lahore services are extensively challenged by paratransit and, with only a small proportion of the fleet required to service demand, PRTC patronage has declined dramatically. About 35 per cent of passengers are students who pay only some 5 per cent of the regular fare, thus contributing further to a substantial operating deficit.
Developments: Considerable progress has been made in reducing staff levels from the 12,000 or so employed countrywide in 1993, when a redundancy payment scheme was instituted. A reorganisation of urban services was carried out in 1994.

Bus

Passenger journeys: (1992/93) 13.4 million
(1993/94) 6.2 million
(1995) 5.5 million
Vehicle-km: (1992/93) 6.3 million
(1993/94) 3.2 million
(1995) 3 million

Number of routes: 12
Route length: (One way) 264 km
Fleet: 707 vehicles, including Fiat, Hino, Isuzu and Volvo B57, of which 95 in roadworthy condition
In peak service: 44

Most intensive service: 10 min
Fare collection: Conductors
Fare structure: Stage; single tickets and monthly passes
Fares collected on board: 95%
Fare evasion control: Checking squads and fines by special traffic magistrates
Operational control: Route inspectors
Arrangements for elderly/disabled: Special free buses financed by government subsidy
Average peak-hour speed: 17 km/h
Operating costs financed by: Fares 6%, subsidy/grants from Punjab government 93%
New vehicles financed by: Government grant

Volvo B57 city bus of PRTC

Urban minibus terminal in Lahore

Private bus/Minibus

Current situation: Privately operated buses and minibuses (Suzuki vans) run, along with horse-drawn 'tongas'; they are subject to Punjab government permits and not officially supposed to ply in the city itself. They nevertheless carry the bulk of the city's traffic.

PR

Pakistan Railways
31 Sheikh Abdul Hamid bin Bades, Lahore
Telephone: +92 42 65450

Type of operation: Suburban heavy rail

Current situation: Services run between Lahore Junction, Jallo and Wagah (39 km) at peak hours, plus irregular services on three other routes.

Light rail (planned)

Current situation: Plans for a light rail system have been studied by the city authorities and consultants, and metro plans were examined by the Punjab government and Lahore Development Authority. In 1992 the government approved construction of Line 1 (14.6 km, 15 stations) of a light rail network, which is to be partly funded by Japan. The 1,435 mm gauge line, linking Chowk Bhaati and Kok Lakhpat, will be largely elevated above the city's busy Ferozepur corridor. A fleet of 105 cars would be required.
Developments: Following completion of pre-feasibility studies funded by the World Bank, bids were to be sought from consortia interested in financing and building the line.

UPDATED

LA PAZ

Population: 1 million
Public transport: Bus services provided by confederation of independent owners and drivers operating minibuses, known as 'micros', formed into 45 route associations and regulated by Servicio Nacional de Transito (a state police department). Suburban and light rail plans

Bus

Regulated by: Servicio Nacional de Transito
Av Mariscal Santa Cruz 1000, La Paz, Bolivia
Telephone: +591 2 379981

Current situation: All bus services are operated by small vehicles known locally as 'microbuses', but including some larger vehicles seating up to 35 and often carrying up to 50 with standees. Each route (designated by letters or numbers) is operated by a 'comite' of owner-drivers or company-operated vehicles. Several owners share each

A Dodge 'microbus' is overtaken by a Japanese minibus

1997

route, though there are some large firms. Longer-distance routes tend to be served by licensed passenger-carrying lorries able to carry up to 200 on perimeter bench seats and standing or sitting on the floor. Maximum loads are indicated on the side of the vehicles, which also carry goods.

Passenger journeys: Approx 140 million (annual)
Vehicle-km: Approx 25 million (annual)

Number of routes: 45
Route length: 380 km
Fleet: Mostly Ford or Dodge short chassis with either US school bus (mostly Blue Bird) or local bodies

Most intensive service: Frequent
One-person operation: 60%
Fare collection: By driver
Fare structure: Flat in central area; fares fixed by Ministry of Transport
Average peak-hour speed: 11 km/h

Light rail (proposed)

Current situation: The National Railways (ENFE) has studied several schemes for a fixed guideway transit system to relieve severe road traffic congestion. Amongst them is upgrading of the freight-only La Paz—Alto tramway (8.3 km) to form a light rail route to the airport, for which design and construction supervision bids were sought in mid-1995.

Another proposed scheme would see electrification of existing ENFE lines around the city.

UPDATED

LAS VEGAS

Population: 260,000, area served 1.1 million
Public transport: Bus services in city and surrounding area of Clark County operated under contract to Regional Transportation Commission; monorail

CAT

Citizens Area Transit (CAT)
3200 West Tompkins, Las Vegas, NV 89103, USA
Telephone: +1 702 262 1000 Fax: +1 702 262 1070
Director, RTC: Kurt Weinrich
General Manager: Steve Thoms
Operations Manager: Sim Wolf
CAT operated under contract by ATC/Vancom Inc
Staff: 450

Current situation: The Regional Transportation Commission of Clark County was set up in 1965 and is governed by an eight-member board. A new public transit operation, CAT, was inaugurated in 1992 to provide co-ordinated fixed-route service in Clark County which has seen rapid population growth. At the same time, privately owned Las Vegas Transit ceased operation of almost all its routes and CAT assumed responsibility for these also. Funding for CAT comes from a ¼ per cent sales tax which was approved by voters in 1990.

Paratransit services are operated by a separate organisation, the Economic Opportunity Board, which carried about 150,000 passengers on its 50 vehicles in 1992.

Developments: New bus maintenance depot under construction in North Las Vegas, with capacity for 250 buses and 150 paratransit vehicles. It is intended that all new buses should be LNG powered.

Agreement of a new 5-year contract with ATC/Vancom at the end of 1996 paves the way for further development of this rapidly growing system. Services have increased substantially to cope with the city's 29 million annual visitors, and new Crosstown Express and Strip Express routes have been introduced.

Bus

Passenger journeys: (1993) 15 million
(1994) 22.2 million
(1995) 26 million
Vehicle-km: (1993) 10.3 million

Number of routes: 21
Fleet: 190 vehicles

New Flyer D40/D40LF (1992/94)	94
GMC/TMC T80204/80206	25
Gillig Phantom (1990)	13
New Flyer low-floor (1995)	40
New Flyer articulated (1991/95/96)	18

Most intensive service: 30 min; three routes operate 24 h to serve the casino area south of downtown
One-person operation: All routes
Fare collection: Coin to farebox
Fare structure: Flat, reduced off-peak; monthly passes
Arrangements for elderly/disabled: All buses lift-equipped
Operating costs financed by: Fares 25%

Monorail

The Monorail Company

Current situation: A 2 km monorail link between the MGM Grand and Bally's Resort hotels was opened in 1995. Designed initially for hotel patrons only, the line could become part of an initial core route to the airport. It caters for about 15,000 daily journeys.

Rolling stock: 2 six-car trains

UPDATED

LAUSANNE

Population: 244,000
Public transport: Bus, trolleybus and light rail services provided by publicly owned undertaking, controlled by representative board. City-owned rack line, known locally as Metro. Rail services by Swiss Federal Railways, local railway and lake steamers

TL

Transports Publics de la Région Lausannoise SA (TL)
PO Box 3960, 1002 Lausanne, Switzerland
Telephone: +41 21 621 0111 Fax: +41 21 312 4030
Chair: M Blanc
General Manager: Jean-Pierre Kallenbach
Staff: 849

Current situation: TL is owned by the canton of Vaud (26 per cent), local communities (67 per cent), the Vaud Cantonal Bank (4 per cent) and private individuals (3 per cent). It operates buses and trolleybuses, owns the vehicles and operates the light rail route built by TSOL (see below), and also embraces the Metro LO rack line. Though separately constituted, the three undertakings are operated under a single administration.

Developments: The trolleybus fleet, which dates from the closure of street tramways in 1964, is to be modernised. The computer-controlled monitoring system SAE has been fitted to 113 trolleybuses, 84 buses and 64 trailers.

Though patronage is stable and farebox recovery has risen, rationalisation of operations is urgently necessary to reduce costs, following enactment of the Federal Transport Law of 1994 which raises the charges falling upon local authorities. In particular the complex historic ownership structures of the city's transport undertakings demands action, and negotiations are in progress to amalgamate them into a single modern management structure.

Bus and trolleybus

Passenger journeys: (1991) 69.3 million
(1992) 72.5 million
(1994) 73.6 million
Vehicle-km: (1991) 11.5 million
(1994) 11.3 million

Number of routes: Bus 21, trolleybus 11
Route length: Bus 120 km, trolleybus 61.7 km
On priority right-of-way: 9.4 km
Fleet: 108 buses

Standard buses	82
MAN SG280H articulated	17
Trailers	9

Fleet: 118 trolleybuses

FBW/BBC	76
NAW/Lauber/BBC-Sécheron	42
Hess trailers	62

Average age of fleet: Buses 12 years; trolleybuses 15 years; trailers 18 years
Trolleybus electrification: 600 V DC

Most intensive service: 6 min
One-person operation: All routes
Fare collection: Prepurchase tickets, passes or carnets; or payment to driver; Autelca and Sadamel prepurchase equipment at stops, Almex (urban) and Prodata (suburban) on board
Fare structure: Zonal system cover suburban and interurban operators and SBB trains; 10-ticket carnets (from shops), monthly passes, 24-h and 3-day tourist tickets
Fare evasion control: Roving inspectors; penalty
Operational control: Route inspectors/mobile radio
Arrangements for elderly/disabled: Reduced rate monthly passes
Average peak-hour speed: 15 km/h
Operating costs financed by: Fares 49.1%
Subsidy from: State and city councils
New vehicles financed by: Loans

Metro Ouest car at UNIL- Dorigny ***1997***

Metro Ouest

Société du Tramway du Sud-Ouest Lausannois SA (TSOL)
Address as TL (above)

Type of operation: Light rail, opened 1991

Passenger journeys: (1992) 7.5 million
(1993) 8.3 million
(1994) 7.2 million
Car-km: (1991) 0.5 million
(1993) 0.9 million
(1994) 0.8 million

Route length: 7.8 km
in tunnel: 0.7 km
Number of routes: 1
Number of stops: 15
Gauge: 1,435 mm
Electrification: 750 V DC, overhead

Service: 10 min, evening 15 min; being reduced to 7½ min
First/last car: 05.23/24.00
Fare structure: As TL, through passes to Metro LO and SBB/CFF services

Rolling stock: 12 cars
Vevey (1990/91) M12
On order: Further 5 cars from Vevey/ABB

Current situation: Runs from the city centre at Flon westwards to the Institute of Technology and the suburb of Renens (SBB/CFF station). Single track route with 12 passing loops mostly at grade and segregated; interchange with SBB trains at Renens and with the LO metro at Flon, to which the LEB local railway is being extended.
Developments: A 7½ min interval service is to be introduced as soon as track doubling of the University section is complete.

Metro LO

Metro Lausanne-Ouchy SA
PO Box 3333, 1002 Lausanne
Telephone: +41 21 621 0380 Fax: +41 21 312 4030
Staff: 73

Type of operation: Rack railway

Passenger journeys: (1992) 7.3 million
(1993) 7.6 million
(1994) 7.2 million

Current situation: 1.8 km former funicular (now rack-operated) with 10 cars links the lakeside at Ouchy with the centre of Lausanne, known locally as the 'Metro'. It was acquired by the municipality in 1985.
Developments: A 4.6 km extension northeast to Croisettes (Epalinges) is planned as a rubber-tyred light metro. The existing line would be converted to provide a through service.

SBB/CFF

Swiss Federal Railways, Lausanne Division
PO Box 345, 1001 Lausanne
Telephone: +41 21 342 2201 Fax: +41 21 342 2797
Divisional Manager: Philippe Gauderon

Type of operation: Suburban heavy rail

Current situation: Hourly or half-hourly services, electrified 15 kV 16⅔ Hz, provided on routes to Genève, Vallorbe, Yverdon, Payerne, Fribourg and Aigle. More frequent service on line to Renens (5 km), connecting with light rail services.

LEB

Lausanne-Echallens-Bercher Railway
Place de la Gare 5, 1040 Echallens
Telephone: +41 21 881 1115 Fax: +41 21 881 5995
Manager: U Gachet
Staff: 54

Type of operation: Local railway

Passenger journeys: (1991) 1.8 million
(1995) 1.7 million

Current situation: Electric trains (1.5 kV DC) run half-hourly from Lausanne-Chauderon to Echallens, extended hourly to Bercher (23 km). 1.1 km tunnel under construction from Chauderon to Flon to link with LO and light rail services. The initial 0.3 km section to a new underground station at Chauderon opened in 1995.

Rolling stock: 10 emu cars, 7 trailers

CGN

Compagnie Générale de Navigation sur le lac Léman
PO Box 116, 1000 Lausanne 6
Telephone: +41 21 617 0666 Fax: +41 21 617 0465

Current situation: Runs boats on Lac Leman, linking Genève, Lausanne and St Gingolph, and from Lausanne to Evian and Thonon, carrying about 1.6 million passengers annually.

UPDATED

LEEDS-BRADFORD

Population: Leeds 714,000, Bradford 464,000, conurbation 2 million
Public transport: Bus services in the West Yorkshire area including Leeds and Bradford and surrounding towns such as Huddersfield and Halifax, are provided by more than 30 operators, the largest of which (with 90 per cent of km) is Yorkshire Rider. Other major operators include Yorkshire Bus Group. The Passenger Transport Executive is responsible for contracting non-commercial bus services by competitive tender, and local rail services

Superbus in guided mode on Scott Hall Road ***1996***

Yorkshire Rider

Yorkshire Rider Ltd
Kirkstall Road, Leeds LS3 1LH, England
Telephone: +44 113 245 1601 Fax: +44 113 242 9721
Divisional Director: Ray O'Toole
Staff: 3,000

Current situation: Yorkshire Rider was established in 1986 from the former PTE bus operations as a separate operating company, wholly owned by West Yorkshire PTA, which sold it to a management/workforce consortium in 1988. Yorkshire Rider was bought by Badgerline in 1994.
Developments: In June 1995, a merger between Badgerline and GRT absorbed Yorkshire Rider into the FirstBus Group. Further reorganisations within the Rider Group split the five operations in Leeds, Halifax, Huddersfield, Bradford and York into five separate trading divisions — Leeds (Leeds CityLink), Bradford (Bradford Traveller), Halifax (CalderLine), Huddersfield (Kingfisher), with York remaining unchanged under the name Rider York.

The first phase of the Leeds guided busway was launched in 1995 on the A61 Scott Hall Road. The guideway extends for 500 m and is operated by 21 special-liveried superbuses. The second phase opened in late 1996, with the third scheduled for 1997. All Scania single-deck buses are equipped with guidewheels on their front axles.

Bus

Passenger journeys: (1992/93) 183 million
(1993/94) 180 million
(1994/95)
Vehicle-km: (1992/93) 65 million
(1993/94) 63 million
(1994/95) 64 million

Number of routes: 170
Most intensive service: 3 min
One-person operation: 100%
Fare collection: By driver with Wayfarer; exact fare to farebox in Bradford, prepaid sales through 300 outlets
Fare structure: Stage, with off-peak maximum fare; weekly, monthly, quarterly and annual 'Metro Cards'; District Rider cards; Day Rover
Fares collected on board: 70% of passengers pay cash
Fare evasion control: Roving staff
Integration with other modes: Prepurchase tickets/passes interavailable between bus and rail
Operational control: Route inspectors/mobile radio; radio communication between drivers and inspectors based at four district control rooms; some vehicles radio-equipped
Arrangements for elderly/disabled: Concessionary fares financed by PTE (half adult fare in peak hours, nominal inter-peak)
Operating costs financed by: Fares 73%, concessionary fares reimbursement 12.5%, contracted services 11.5%, other income 3%
Subsidy from: PTA levy for contracted services

Leeds CityLink

Kirkstall Road, Leeds LS3 1LH
Telephone: +44 113 245 1601 Fax: +44 113 244 0290
Managing Director: Ray O'Toole
Operations Director: David Kaye
Finance Director: Martin Wilson
Engineering Director: Andy Campbell

Fleet: 495 vehicles

Leyland Atlantean double-deck	158
Leyland Olympian double-deck	28
MCW Metrobus double-deck	63
Scania N113 double-deck	42
Dennis Dart single-deck	98
Scania N113 single-deck	55
Scania L113 single-deck	5
Dennis Lance single-deck	33
Mercedes minibus	8
Volvo B10M coach	5

Bradford Traveller

61 Hall Ings, Bradford BD1 5SQ
Telephone: +44 1274 734833 Fax: +44 1274 736768
Managing Director: Steve Graham
Operations Director: Richard Potter
Financial Director: Christina Haigh
Engineering Director: Steve Adkin

Fleet: 204 vehicles

Plaxton-bodied Dennis Lance on CityLink service ***1997***

Mercedes minibus of Bradford Traveller at St George's Hall, Bradford ***1997***

Leyland Atlantean double-deck	66
Leyland Olympian double-deck	100
Volvo Olympian double-deck	10
Leyland Tiger coach	5
Mercedes minibus	23

Yorkshire Bus Group

West Riding Automobile Company Ltd
Yorkshire Woollen District Transport Co Ltd
South Yorkshire Road Transport Ltd
24 Barnsley Road, Wakefield WF1 5JX
Telephone: +44 1924 375521 Fax: +44 1924 300106
Managing Director: Brian Jackson
Engineering Director: Vernon Barfoot
Staff: 1,029

Current situation: The Yorkshire Bus Group operates as three companies, with West Riding and Yorkshire Woollen in the Leeds/Bradford area. There is a network of services to the east of Leeds and to the south and west of the two cities. The company was privatised in 1987, was later sold to Caldaire Holdings, and became part of the Cowie Group in 1996.

Bus

Number of routes: 210
Fleet: 387 vehicles

Leyland Olympian double-deck	90
Leyland National single-deck	39
Leyland Lynx single-deck	131
Volvo B10B single-deck	26
Dennis Lance single-deck	30
Optare Metrorider midibus	51
Dodge minibus	1
Mercedes minibus	14
Scania coaches	5

Most intensive service: 10 min
One-person operation: 100%
Fare structure: As Yorkshire Rider, but Ridercard not available

Black Prince

Black Prince Coaches Ltd
York Cottage, Texas Street, Morley, Leeds LS27 OHG
Telephone: +44 113 252 6033 Fax: +44 113 253 6082
Managing Director: Brian Crowther
Staff: 85

Current situation: The company developed commercial services from Morley to Leeds city centre in 1986, and moved progressively into other areas.

Fleet: 62 vehicles

Volvo-Ailsa double-deck	23
Leyland PD3 double-deck	1
AEC Routemaster double-deck	3
Volvo B10M double-deck	3
Scania double-deck	11
Leyland National single-deck	8
Optare Vecta single-deck	4
Mercedes O405/Optare single-deck	1
Scania single-deck	1
Optare Metrorider minibus	4
Coaches	3

Other commercial operators

Current situation: A number of smaller operators run commercial or tendered services but none is of any considerable size: Miramare, Taylors Coaches, and Bigfoot Buses.

Metro

West Yorkshire Passenger Transport Executive
Wellington House, 40-50 Wellington Street, Leeds LS1 2DE
Telephone: +44 113 251 7272 Fax: +44 113 251 7333
Director General: Kieran Preston

Passenger journeys: (Bus and rail)
(1993/94) 251.4 million
(1994/95) 248.1 million
(1995/96) 246 million

Current situation: Metro is the corporate name adopted by the Passenger Transport Executive, which co-ordinates and promotes public transport throughout West Yorkshire on behalf of the Passenger Transport Authority. Metro's activities include securing subsidised bus services to complement the commercial network, specifying and financing the local rail network, administration of all concessionary travel and prepaid ticketing schemes, provision and maintenance of all bus stops, most shelters and the majority of bus stations, timetable and promotional information, planning new systems, and working with the district councils' planning and highway teams to promote increased use of public transport.

MetroTrain service is now contracted from Regional Railways North East Ltd, with North West Regional Railways Ltd handling the Manchester–Huddersfield–Wakefield service.

Contracted bus services

Current situation: Changes in the market and better appreciation by operators of the commercial basis of their operations cause constant change in the bus network, and Metro is required to secure socially necessary services when commercial operators withdraw. Subsidised services run about 22.5 million km a year, and the average cost per km has fallen due to competition and increased efficiency.

Contracted rail

Operated by Regional Railways North East Ltd
York YO1 1HT
Telephone: +44 1904 653022 Fax: +44 1904 523075
Director: Robert Urie

Passenger journeys: (1993/94) 15.8 million
(1994/95) 16.1 million
(1995/96) 16 million

Current situation: Local rail services operated to Metro's specifications on 15 routes totalling 295 km with 64

Black Prince Optare Vecta overtakes Mercedes mini of Quickstep Travel in Briggate ***1997***

stations, and on the Manchester—Huddersfield—Wakefield route (69 km) supported jointly with Greater Manchester PTE and operated by North West Regional Railways Ltd.

Developments: Patronage held steady during 1995/96, when the full electric service between Leeds, Bradford, Ilkley and Skipton was introduced. But unreliability of the 35-year-old trains dogged the service and Metro continued to explore ways of providing new rolling stock.

Options for future network and service development are being considered in the light of privatisation of the train operating companies in March 1997. The long-planned restoration of service between Bradford and Huddersfield came a step closer in late 1996 following an award of £4 million to Calderdale Council under the Environment Department's Capital Challenge scheme.

Rolling stock: 102 dmu cars, 65 emu cars

Light rail (planned)

Current situation: The Leeds Transport Strategy of 1991 proposed a three-line light rail network, together with two initial routes for guided bus, designed to supplement the existing local rail network focused on Leeds. The aim was to provide a fixed-track service in all major radial routes into the city.

The Leeds Supertram Act, covering Line 1 running 12 km from the city centre to Tingley and Stouton in South Leeds, received Royal Assent in 1993. The Eurotrans consortium, comprising Taylor Woodrow, Morrison Construction, Cristiani & Neilson, Cowie and Vevey, was selected in 1996 as preferred bidder for a design, build, operate and maintain contract for Line 1. Private sector funding is being sought under the government's private finance initiative, and it was hoped that construction could start in early 1997 for 1999 opening.

Parliamentary approval is being sought for Line 2, which would run 18 km from north Leeds through Headingley and the city centre to east Leeds and Seacroft.

Guided bus

Under construction

Current situation: Government grant has been provided to Leeds City Council for the first of two guided bus routes to north and east Leeds. Phase I, running 2 km along the A61 Scott Hall Road, was opened in 1995 and extended in November 1996; construction of the route continues. The second route, along the A64, is being promoted by the city council as a private finance initiative scheme.

UPDATED

LEICESTER

Population: 282,000

Public transport: Most bus services provided by former municipally owned company and local private companies. Local rail service expanding

Citybus

Leicester Citybus Ltd
Abbey Park Road, Leicester LE4 5AH, England
Telephone: +44 116 251 6691 Fax: +44 116 253 8270
Managing Director: Chris Mahoney
Operations Director: Julian Heubeck
Staff: 450

Current situation: On deregulation the city council established its transport undertaking as a separate company. This was offered for sale in 1993 and is now owned by FirstBus. A co-ordinated network has been developed with Midland Fox.

Developments: Double-deck replacement by high-capacity single-decks continued, with delivery of 10 Optare Prismas in 1995 and low-floor buses are on order for 1997.

Bus

Passenger journeys: (1990/91) 25.4 million
(1991/92) 25.6 million
(1992/93) 25.3 million

Vehicle-km: (1990/91) 9.8 million
(1991/92) 10.3 million
(1992/93) 10.5 million

Number of routes: 55
Route length: 800 km
On private right-of-way: 3.6 km
Fleet: 175 vehicles

Leyland Titan PD2 double-deck	1
MCW Metrobus/Alexander double-deck	11
Dennis Dominator/East Lancs double-deck	83
Dennis Falcon/East Lancs single-deck	9
Dennis Falcon/NC single-deck	7
Leyland Tiger/Alexander single-deck	7
Leyland Leopard/Alexander single-deck	1
Mercedes O405/Optare single-deck (1995)	10
LAG/Volvo/Leyland coaches	9
Iveco/Carlyle minibus	12
Renault/Northern Counties minibus	16
Renault/Plaxton minibus	7
Renault/Alexander minibus	2

Most intensive service: 15 min
One-person operation: All services
Fare collection: Driver with Wayfarer equipment
Fare structure: Stage; single, return, weekly and monthly tickets
Operational control: All buses have two-way radio; 12 locations monitored by CCTV
Operating costs financed by: Fares 86%, other commercial sources 12%, tenders 2%
Subsidy from: County Council for pensioners' concession fares and specific contracted routes

Mercedes O405 of Leicester Citybus passes Renault and Iveco minibuses ***1997***

Midland Fox

Midland Fox Ltd
30 Millstone Lane, Leicester LE1 5RN
Telephone: +44 116 262 8156 Fax: +44 116 251 5972
Managing Director: Peter Harvey
Staff: 650

Current situation: 'Fox Cub' minibus services cover Leicester and surrounding towns, while conventional buses run interurban services and a number of longer distance out-of-town routes. The company had reduced its single-deck fleet in favour of increased minibus operation, but new single-deck buses have been introduced, branded as Urban Fox. It is a subsidiary of the Cowie Group.

Developments: Hackney carriage taxi operations introduced in 1994 using 20 FX4 'Foxcabs'.

Bus (Whole company operations)

Passenger journeys: (1992) 27 million
(1993) 27 million
(1994) 26 million

Vehicle-km: (1992) 23 million
(1993) 23 million
(1994) 21 million

Number of routes: 95
Route length: (One way) 1,170 km
Fleet: 316 vehicles

Leyland Fleetline double-deck	10
MCW Metrobus double-deck	21
Leyland Olympian double-deck	48
Scania double-deck	28
Leyland National single-deck	11
Scania single-deck	14
Ford Transit minibus	1
Iveco minibus	67
Mercedes minibus	62
Renault minibus	12
Coaches	42

One-person operation: All services
Fare collection: Payment to driver with Wayfarer ticket machine; magnetic card system to be introduced 1997
Fare structure: Single, day return, season and area tickets
Fares collected on board: 73%
Operational control: VHF radio for inspectors
Operating costs financed by: Fares 87%, other commercial sources 13%

Other operators

Current situation: Hylton & Dawson of Glenfield operates three routes and Kinchbus of Barrow-on-Soar some tendered services. Virgin and TRS operate limited commercial services.

Central Trains

Central Trains Limited
Po Box 4323, Birmingham B1 1TH
Telephone: +44 121 643 4444 Fax: +44 121 654 4461
Managing Director: Mark Causebrook

Type of operation: Local rail

Current situation: Trains run about hourly to local stations on two routes.

Developments: In a £16 million package approved in 1992, restoration of services is planned over a freight line to Coalville and Burton on Trent (the Ivanhoe line—48 km) with eight new stations. Opening of the route has been delayed on account of cost increases attributable to privatisation of the rail network. Provision of finance to implement the scheme was rejected by the Department of Transport in late 1996.

LEIPZIG

Population: 491,000, area served 588,000
Public transport: Central area served almost entirely by tramways operated by municipal company which also runs bus services in the suburbs; regional bus company; suburban rail services by German Railway (DB)

MDV

Mitteldeutscher Verkehrsverbund
Vorbereitungsbüro zur Gründung des Mitteldeutschen Verkehrsverbundes GbR
Naunhofer Strasse 50, 04299 Leipzig, Germany
Telephone: +49 341 862 8716/8717

Current situation: This regional transit authority was expected to start operations in early 1997. It comprises the cities of Halle and Leipzig and four rural counties, covering an area of 2,700 km² with a population of 1.2 million.

LVB

Leipziger Verkehrsbetriebe GmbH (LVB)
PO Box 100910, 04009 Leipzig
Telephone: +49 341 4920 Fax: +49 341 492 1005
Directors: Walter Kietz (Chair, Technical)
Operations: Wolfgang Jähnichen
Commercial: Heinz-Jörg Panzner
Personnel: Wilhelm Georg Hanss
Purchasing Manager: Frank Sporleder
Finance Manager: Dr Brigitte Teltscher
Staff: 2,632

Passenger journeys: (1993) 119.2 million
(1994) 118.5 million
(1995) 119.3 million

Operating costs financed by: Fares 25.2%

Current situation: The former state-owned undertaking passed to Leipzig municipality in 1993; it is now a joint stock company, the shares of which are held entirely by the city and county of Leipzig. Fares were raised to a level closer to those charged in west German cities in 1995. To attract passengers back to public transport after a 25 per cent decline in patronage, some 500 modern shelters have been erected, low-floor buses and trams introduced, and cycles can be carried on trams and buses outside peak hours. Measures have also been taken to improve operating efficiency, including computerised recording of bus fuel consumption and vehicle-km.

Studies into possible modernisation of the city's public transport have been undertaken by LVB, Daimler-Benz and TransTec, the consulting arm of the transport undertaking in Leipzig's west German partner city of Hannover. However, the idea of putting central area tramways underground has been discarded as too expensive and offering only limited benefits.

A cross-border lease agreement for 205 trams was concluded with FBBC Leasing Corporation of New York in April 1996. Worth US$180.5 million, the deal is valid for 30 years.

Bus

Passenger journeys: (1995) 20.2 million
Vehicle-km: (1993) 7.3 million
(1994) 7.1 million
(1995) 7.6 million

Number of routes: 241
Route length: 197 km
Fleet: 133 vehicles, plus 6 hired

Ikarus 260/263 (pre-1991)	18
Ikarus 280 articulated (1986/90)	24
MAN SL202 (1983)	15
MAN SL200 (1992)	10
MAN NL202 (1992)	45
Mercedes O405GN (1992)	20
Neoplan Cityliner N116 coach (1990)	1

In peak service: 109

Most intensive service: 15 min
One-person operation: All routes
Fare collection: Prepurchase single and multiride tickets from kiosks, cancelled on board; day tickets, weekly and monthly passes; 64% of passengers use passes
Fare structure: Time-based — 15 and 60 min
Fare evasion control: Roving inspectors
Integration with other modes: Joint monthly passes for LVB and S-Bahn
Average peak-hour speed: 20.8 km/h

Current situation: Very few buses penetrate the city centre, the lettered routes being mainly suburban and tramway feeders. All Ikarus buses are to be phased out by 2000, being replaced by MAN and Mercedes types.

No basic changes to the bus network are envisaged, but expansion of tangential services in the east of the city is planned. Routes will also be modified to conform to new tramway and S-Bahn service patterns. Some reduction of service on lightly used routes is seen as inevitable and may take the form of smaller vehicles or dial-a-ride systems.

Tramway

Type of operation: Conventional tramway

Passenger journeys: (1995) 98.7 million
Car-km: (1993) 34.2 million
(1994) 31.5 million
(1995) 31.2 million

Route length: 152.6 km
Number of routes: 23
On private right-of-way: 82.5 km
Number of stops: 261
Gauge: 1,458 mm

Rolling stock: 676 cars

ČKD Tatra T4D/B4D (1969/83)	M344 T125
ČKD Tatra T4DM/B4DM (1969/86)	M97 T45
ČKD Tatra T6A2/B6A2 (1988/89)	M28 T14
Siemens/Duewag/ABB/Bautzen NGT8 (1994/95)	M23

Plus 16 historic and many works cars
In peak service: 206 sets
On order: 55 NGT8 low-floor articulated tramcars from a consortium of Siemens, Adtranz, Duewag and Bautzen being delivered through to 1998

Current situation: The system is the second largest in eastern Germany and has half its route-km on private right-of-way. Leipzig's wide gauge caused problems with testing modern trams, though 55 cars are now being delivered at a rate of 20 a year. These resemble cars supplied to Bochum, Halle and Kassel but are only 2.2 m wide and have a number of technical differences. LVB has rebuilt 142 Tatra cars and trailers with assistance from LHB and Adtranz, and a further 100 cars are to be similarly modernised.

Extension to the Neue Messe (new fairgrounds, 2 km) in the north of the city opened in March 1996.

DB

Deutsche Bahn AG, Geschäftsbereich Nahverkehr
Regionalbereich Sachsen-Anhalt/Leipzig
Ernst-Kamieth Strasse 2, 06112 Halle
Telephone: +49 345 842 3331 Fax: +49 345 841 5378
Manager: Thomas Hoffmann

Type of operation: Suburban heavy rail

Current situation: A 20-min interval service is provided on the 23-station U-shaped S-Bahn Route A from Gaschwitz via Stötteritz, Hbf, Leutzsch and Plagwitz to Miltitzer Allee, linking numerous suburbs in the course of a 62-min journey. In peak hours a direct Gaschwitz–Plagwitz service constitutes Route C, while irregular local trains from Hbf to Borsdorf and Wurzen are advertised as Route B. Push-pull sets of high-capacity double-deck coaches are hauled by Class 143 electric locomotives.

The Leipzig rail network cannot easily be adapted to carry a larger share of urban traffic as there are no lines within the inter-suburban loop served by S-Bahn routes A/C apart from a branch to the old Bayerische Bahnhof on the southern edge of the centre. Many routes into the vast Hbf (the largest station in Europe) are circuitous and Hbf itself is on the fringe of the central area rather than the focal point of the city.

Developments: Extension of S-Bahn service to the Leipzig–Halle corridor has been agreed (38 km, 11 intermediate stations). A separate track is to be laid alongside those for main line services. Construction started in 1995.

Ultimetaly, the lines to Bitterfeld, Eilenburg, Grimma, Bad Lausick, Borna/Altenburg and Merseburg via Grünau/Markranstädt are to be included in the S-Bahn network. At present, local services on these lines are irregular and in some cases infrequent.

Construction of a 3 km underground link is planned between Hbf and Bayerische Bahnhof, with four stations.

RVL

Regionalverkehr Leipzig GmbH
Cottaweg, 04177 Leipzig
Telephone: +49 341 474271 Fax: +49 341 470209
Director: Sabine Minet
Manager: Ulrike Chüo
Staff: 191

Current situation: RVL was created in 1992 out of the former state-owned Kraftverkehr Leipzig; its shares are entirely held by the county of Leipzig. It is responsible for establishing an efficient local transport network with integrated fare and information systems in the Leipzig region, and operates 19 suburban and regional bus services from depots in Leipzig and Zwenkau. About 10 per cent of its vehicle-km are run in neighbouring counties.

Passenger journeys: (1993) 5.6 million
(1994) 4.6 million
(1995) 7.2 million
Vehicle-km: (1993) 4.9 million
(1994) 4.6 million
(1995) 4.5 million

Fifty-five of these Duewag NGT8 low-floor cars are joining LVB's fleet **1997**

Fleet: 79 buses

Ikarus 280 articulated (1978/90)	25
Ikarus 260 (1978/90)	11
Ikarus 250/255/256/263 (1976/90)	30
Mercedes O407 (1991)	8
MAN ÜL242 (1991)	5

On order: All Ikarus buses are being replaced

SAX-BUS

Eilenberger Busverkehr GmbH
Postweg 16, 04849 Bad Düben
Telephone: +49 34243 22002 Fax: +49 34243 22118
Managing Director: Beyer
Staff: 57

Passenger journeys: (1995)1.5 million

Current situation: Private company founded in 1993 provides regional bus services in the area northeast of Leipzig with a fleet of 35 buses.
Developments: Route S26 between Leipzig and Bad Düben was taken over from RVL at the beginning of June 1996, with SAX-BUS contracting to operate it without subsidy and increase weekend service.

Auto Webel

Auto Webel GmbH
Hallesche Strasse 70, 04509 Delitzsch
Telephone: +49 34202 52128

Current situation: This family-owned company was reprivatised in 1991. It operates most regional bus services in the county of Delitzsch, north of Leipzig.

UPDATED

LIÈGE

Population: 195,000 (conurbation 500,000, region 997,000)
Public transport: Urban bus services for city and province provided by publicly owned regional undertaking. Suburban rail services by state railway (SNCB)

TEC Liège-Verviers

Société de Transport en Commun Liège-Verviers
rue du Bassin 119, 4030 Liège, Belgium
Telephone: +32 4 361 9111 Fax: +32 4 367 1200
Chair: Hector Magotte
Director General: Freddy Joris
Staff: 1,616

Current situation: TEC was created in 1991 under the reorganisation of local transport that saw control pass to the new regional body Société Regionale Wallonne du Transport. TEC replaced three former operators, STIL, STIV and SNCV; it serves a total population of 991,000 throughout the province of Liège. About 25 per cent of routes are contracted out, mainly in rural areas.

Van Hool A120 of TEC at Guillemins station ***1995***

Developments: Magnetic ticketing introduced 1994. Minibus services for mobility-impaired passengers introduced 1996.

Bus

Passenger journeys: (Total operations, including contracted)
(1993) 81.4 million
(1994) 81.1 million
(1995) 77.5 million
Vehicle-km: (1993) 34.6 million
(1994) 31.4 million
(1995) 31.2 million

Number of routes: 185, of which 51 Liège urban
Route length: (One way) 4,050 km
On priority right-of-way: 16.6 km
Fleet: 545 vehicles (Liège urban), total 1,052

Volvo B59 (1976/77)	6
Van Hool/MAN A120/20/50/051/60 (1978/80/81/82/90)	235
Van Hool/DAF A120/3 (1978/79/80/81)	34
Van Hool/MAN AG280 (1981/84/86)	40
Van Hool/DAF AG280/3 (1986)	11
Van Hool/MAN AG700 (1993)	7
Van Hool/MAN A600 (1991/92)	90
Van Hool/DAF A600 (1991)	18
Van Hool/MAN A500PL (1993)	41
Renault R312 (1994)	62
MAN minibus (1988)	1
Standard	448
Articulated	58
Midibus	1

In peak service: 440 (Liège urban)

Most intensive service: 2 min
One-person operation: All routes
Fare collection: Single tickets, multijourney cards, monthly and annual passes
Fare structure: Stage
Arrangements for elderly/disabled: Trials being made with lift-equipped buses on a city-centre route
Average distance between stops: 378 m
Average peak-hour speed: 24 km/h
Bus priority: Bus lanes total 16.6 km, of which 10.6 km are physically separated
Integration with other modes: Combined road-rail tickets available; several interchanges between rail and interurban bus
Operational control: Radio-telephone enables controller to call drivers individually or in groups; 300 buses at the main Robermont depot are linked to a computer which programs departures into service and checks and maintains battery charging, preheating and fuel levels
Operating costs financed by: Fares 31.2%, other commercial sources (advertising) 4.4%, regional subsidy/grants 64.4%
New vehicles financed by: Loans

SNCB

Belgian National Railways (SNCB/NMBS), South-East District
Place des Guillemins 2/002, 4000 Liège
Telephone: +32 41 520130

Type of operation: Suburban heavy rail

Current situation: Hourly services run on six routes out of Guillemins station.

UPDATED

LILLE/ROUBAIX/ TOURCOING

Population: Conurbation 1.1 million
Public transport: Bus, tram and automated metro services for conurbation of Lille/Roubaix/Tourcoing operated for the Communauté Urbaine de Lille (CUDL), comprising 87 towns, by undertaking managed under contract, with private companies contracted to operate suburban bus routes. Suburban rail services by SNCF

Transpole

Transports en Commun de la Métropole Lilloise
BP 1009, 908 avenue de la République, 59701 Marcq-en-Baroeul, France
Telephone: +33 3 20 81 43 43 Fax: +33 3 20 81 43 14
General Manager: Yves Lancelot
Operations Manager, Bus: Hugues Le Besnerais
Operations & Maintenance Manager, Metro & Tram: Jean Wildemersch
Staff: 1,550

Current situation: Transpole is a private company (part of VIA-GTI) linked by a 'high risk' contract to a 'syndicat mixte' involving the city of Lille and the département du Nord, with overall policy and financial responsibility for the bus, tram and VAL automated metro operations.

Suburban bus services are operated by private firms under contract to Transpole; their operations are fully integrated into the conurbation's fares and ticketing system.
Developments: A further expansion of rail-based transport is under way. Metro Line 1bis was extended to Lille Europe TGV station in 1994 and was further extended to Mons-en-Baroeul in 1995, when it became known as Line 2. Construction is under way of another extension to Roubaix and Tourcoing.

Transpole is to assume responsibility for co-ordination of transport for disabled people within the CUDL area.

Passenger journeys: (All modes)
(1993) 104 million
(1994) 106 million
(1995) 100.5 million

Fare collection: Single tickets from driver on buses and machines on trams and metro stations, free transfer within 1 h; monthly passes or carnets prepurchased and cancelled on board
Fare structure: Urban and suburban tariffs; 10-journey carnets for single journeys; monthly and weekly passes; 'Ticket Plus' offers unlimited travel on all modes including SNCF trains; also cross-frontier tickets to Mouscron, Waasten, Wervik, Komen and Herseaux in Belgium
Fares collected on board: 10.5% on buses, 21.6% from station machines

VAL metro train at CHR Calmette

Breda LRV at Croisé Laroche ***1995***

Fare evasion control: Inspectors
Arrangements for elderly/disabled: Fare reductions for over-65s and unemployed within CUDL area
Operating costs financed by: Fares 60%, concessionary fares compensation 11%, subsidy/grants 28.9%

Bus

Passenger journeys: (1993) 39.2 million
(1994) 38.8 million
(1995) 36.8 million
Vehicle-km: (1993) 12.8 million
(1994) 13.1 million
(1995) 13 million

Number of routes: 33
Route length: (One way) 502 km
Fleet: 311 vehicles

Renault PR100-2	79
CBM TDU11	86
Renault R312	122
Renault PR180 articulated	20
Heuliez 6X317	4

In peak service: 286
Average age of fleet: 8.1 years

Most intensive service: 3 min
One-person operation: All services
Integration with other modes: Integration between buses, trams and metro, with buses as metro feeders; common ticketing
Operational control: Radio-telephone, particularly aimed at ensuring bus-metro co-ordination
Average peak-hour speed: 17.2 km/h
Bus priority: 5.1 km bus lanes/priority right-of-way

Tramway (Le Mongy)

Type of operation: Conventional tramway

Passenger journeys: (1993) 7.6 million
(1994) 10.6 million
(1995} 9.3 million

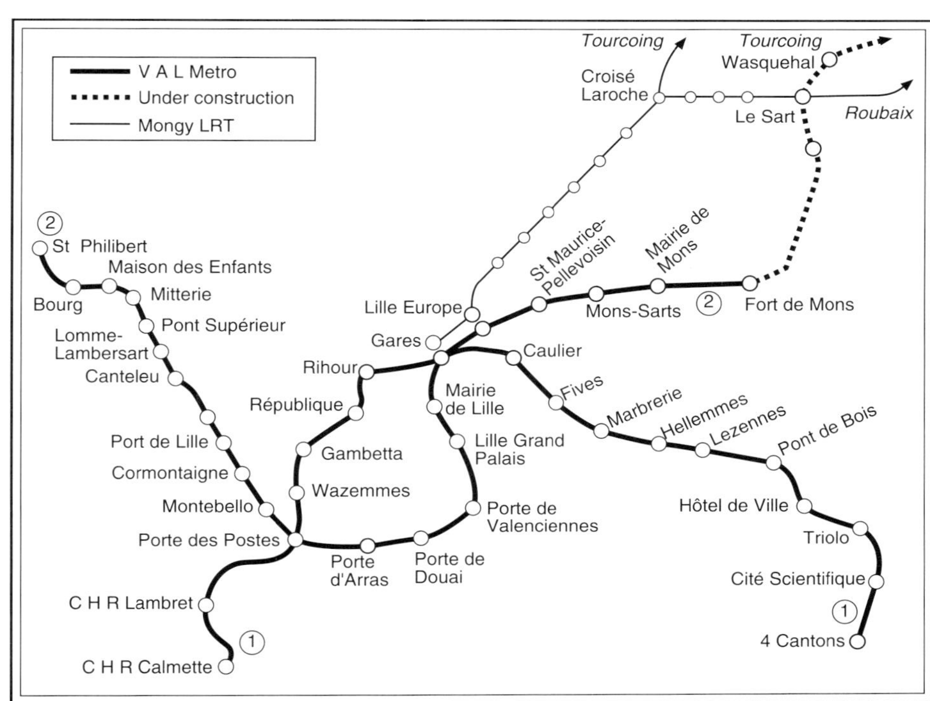

Lille's metro and light rail

Car-km: (1993) 1.9 million
(1994) 1.6 million
(1995) 1.4 million

Route length: 22 km
Number of routes: 2
Number of stations: 36
Gauge: 1,000 mm
Electrification: 750 V DC, overhead

Service: 3-4 min on common route
First/last car: 0515/0130

Rolling stock: 24 cars
Breda LRV (1993/94) M24

Current situation: The tramway known as Le Mongy links central Lille with Roubaix and Tourcoing, running mostly on reserved track from an underground interchange with VAL at Gares. Upgrading was completed in 1994.

Contracted bus

Passenger journeys: (1993) 3.2 million
(1994) 3.3 million
(1995) 3.5 million
Vehicle-km: (1993) 2.3 million
(1994) 2.4 million
(1995) 2.5 million

Number of routes: 37
Route length: (One way) 450 km
Fleet: 105 buses
Integration with other modes: Services and fares integrated with Transpole bus, tram and metro

Current situation: Transpole retains responsibility for planning, network changes, management and information provision, while standard fares and ticket systems apply. In 1995 the contractors were: Cariane, Bolle, Lapage, Phylpo, Accou, Mariot-Gamelin, Dumont, T2C, ID Voyages and Descamps-Duavrant.

Metro (VAL)

Type of operation: Fully automated (unmanned) metro (rubber-tyred), VAL system, opened 1983

Passenger journeys: (1993) 54 million
(1994) 53.3 million
(1995) 50.9 million
Car-km: (1993) 5.8 million
(1994) 6 million
(1995) 6.4 million

Route length: 28.3 km
Number of lines: 2
Number of stations: 39

Gauge: 2,060 mm between H-type guide bars also used for power supply
Track: Precast concrete longitudinal sleepers, with track heating provided by cables embedded in sleepers. Track equipment specific to system's automatic controls includes 170 mm wide strip carrying transmission lines; aluminium plate contacts used for command and control and regulation of traffic; ultrasonic transceiver at the entry and exit to every station
Electrification: 750 V DC, collected by shoes from guide bars

Service: Peak 1 min, off-peak 3-6 min
First/last train: 05.12/00.12
Fare structure: Flat, common tariff for all modes
Fare collection: Automatic ticket machines with touch-screens and accepting credit cards, validating machines at entrance to all platforms
Integration with other modes: At several stations, including connection with Le Mongy tramway at Gares; bus feeders
Control: VAL was Europe's first fully automated driverless metro; in normal operation VAL stations are unmanned too. Surveillance is provided by 444 CCTV cameras linked to 24 TV monitors in the control room. For full description see *JUTS 1987*

Rolling stock: 83 two-car sets

CIMT	M88
Alsthom	M78

Developments: Line 2 (previously 1bis) extension from Gares to Lille Europe TGV station opened in 1994 and was extended to Fort de Mons (Mons-en-Baroeul) in 1995. Further extensions under construction to Tourcoing-Centre for 1999 opening and Tourcoing-Dron planned for late 2000 opening, totalling 16 km with 21 stations.

A new fleet of 60 two-car trains was ordered in 1996, comprising 34 VAL 208 cars sets from Matra and 26 VAL 206 sets from GEC Alsthom.

SNCF

French National Railways, Lille Region
33 avenue Charles Saint-Venant, 59043 Lille
Telephone: +33 3 20 87 31 13

Type of operation: Suburban heavy rail

Current situation: Limited suburban services provided on seven routes, that to Tourcoing (13 km) served about hourly, the rest intermittently, mainly by a fleet of 65 three-car RIB push-pull trains.
Developments: SNCF opened a new station at the regional teaching hospital (CHR) in September 1996. Six four-car double-deck emus entered service at the same time, and a further 20 two-car double-deck sets are on order.

UPDATED

LILONGWE

Population: 300,000
Public transport: Services provided largely by private minibus operators and unlicensed 'matola' shared taxis

Minibus

Current situation: Regular bus services ceased in April 1996 when Stagecoach Malaŵi withdrew from operations in the capital. At the start of the 1990s there had been little paratransit in the city, but more recently Stagecoach had suffered increasing competition from largely uncontrolled minibuses.

Most service is now provided by owner-operated minibuses and matola shared taxis. They are generally unregulated and unlicensed.

UPDATED

LIMA

Population: 3 million, with Callao 6.5 million
Public transport: Bus services operated in Lima and adjacent Callao by independent operators, with additional minibus and midibus services, supervised by government department

Bus

Current situation: Since the end of the 1980s, services have been provided almost entirely by small operators, often owner-drivers or one-route companies. There are networks of conventional, mini and midi buses, which together cater for more than 500 million journeys a year. There has been little attempt at regulation by the official licensing authority Comision Reguladora Tarifas de Transportes (CRTT), but new moves to bring some order into the operating chaos were planned for late 1996. Route-numbering is rudimentary and many buses carry no such identification.

Different flat fares are charged for conventional midi and mini services, with the minibuses commanding the highest charge. Most vehicles of all three types carry conductors, though some full-size buses using the Via Expresa busway are driver-only.

Canada station on the Via Expresa busway **1997**

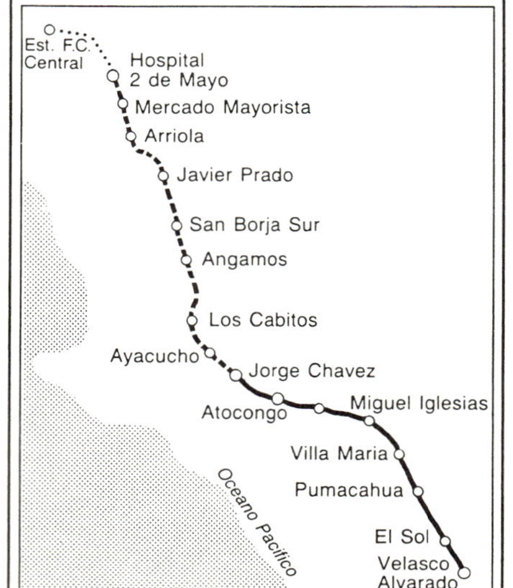

Lima metro

Typical minibuses in Miraflores **1997**

Fleet: A wide variety of vehicles is in use, including Mercedes, Scania, Volvo, second-hand US school buses, Chinese, Japanese and Brazilian, and many with locally built or rebuilt bodies. Midibuses are mainly new or second-hand Toyota Coaster, Asia AM818 or Mitsubishi Rosas, while minibuses are Toyota, Nissan and Kia Asia.

AATE Metro

Autoridad Anónima del Tren Eléctrico (AATE)
Avenida Aviacion 2401, San Borja, Lima
Telephone: +51 14 374037 Fax: +51 14 763323
General Manager: Elba Verastegui

Current situation: Construction started 1989 on the initial section of a 20.8 km north-south metro line linking Hospital 2 de Mayo with Vila el Salvador, being built by the Intermetro consortium of Italian companies. The initial 9.8 km section of Line 1 with eight stations runs from Velasco Alvarado (Vila el Salvador) to Jorge Chavez. The double-track alignment, to 1,435 mm gauge, is electrified at 1.5 kV DC overhead, and will be served initially by a fleet of six-car trains built by Breda.
Developments: Originally scheduled to open in 1992, the 4 km section between Vila el Salvador and San Juan was expected to open in July 1996 despite earlier reports that the project was being abandoned on economic grounds. Trial running has been taking place, but visitors in mid-1996 reported no sign of public service having started.

Rolling stock: 32 cars

Trolleybus (proposed)

Current situation: City officials have consulted with representatives of the public/private trolleybus systems in Santiago and Valparaiso as to the feasibility of running trolleybuses in Lima.

UPDATED

LINZ

Population: 200,000
Public transport: Bus, trolleybus, tramway and rail line operated by municipally owned company also responsible for other public utilities

ESG

Linzer Elektrizitäts-, Fernwärme- und Verkehrsbetriebe AG (ESG)
Museumstrasse 6-8, 4020 Linz, Austria
Telephone: +43 732 78010 Fax: +43 732 7801 3299
General Manager: Dkfm Max Stockinger
Operating Manager: Dipl-Ing Herbert Brandt
Staff: 613

Passenger journeys: (All modes)
(1993) 78.9 million
(1994) 81.1 million
(1995) 82.1 million

Operating costs financed by: Fares 67.2%, internal cross-subsidy 32.8%

Current situation: Profits from the electricity and district heating trading divisions help support the public transport operation.
Developments: An underground light rail line to serve Linz Hbf has been studied, and a 4.8 km Route 1 tramway extension to Ebelsberg is under construction for 2000 opening. It is planned to order 20 low-floor cars for this route.

Three new routes to poorly served areas were started in 1995, feeding tram Route 1.

Volvo/Steyr Citybus, ESG's new low-floor vehicle ***1997***

Bus and trolleybus

Passenger journeys: (1993) Bus 16.3 million, trolleybus 25.4 million
(1994) Bus 16.9 million, trolleybus 26.1 million
(1995) Bus 17.1 million, trolleybus 26.3 million
Vehicle-km: (1993) Bus 3.8 million, trolleybus 1.5 million
(1994) Bus 3.8 million, trolleybus 1.5 million
(1995) Bus 3.9 million, trolleybus 1.4 million

Number of routes: Bus 22, trolleybus 4
Route length: Bus 126.9 km, trolleybus 18.8 km
Fleet: 92 buses

Gräf & Stift GU210 articulated (1974)	4
Gräf & Stift NG272 articulated (1993)	21
Gräf & Stift GSGU280M18 articulated (1981/82)	16
Gräf & Stift 200M18 articulated prototype (1978)	1
Gräf & Stift GSLH240M11 (1981)	1
Gräf & Stift GSLH200M12 (1984/85)	14
Gräf & Stift OSU210/591A (1974)	3
Volvo City III (1995)	5
Steyr SS11 HU200 (1979/84/85/88/89/90)	26
Gräf & Stift 200M11 prototype (1978)	1

Fleet: 24 trolleybuses

Gräf & Stift GSGE150 M18 articulated (1983/84/85)	20
Steyr STS11HU (1988)	4

In peak service: Bus 74, trolleybus 22

Most intensive service: 5 min
One-person operation: All routes
Fare collection: Prepurchase, and automatic machines for ticket issuing and cancellation at all stops
Fare structure: Stage; ticketcards, passes (weekly, monthly and annual)
Fares collected on board: None
Fare evasion control: Random inspection
Operational control: Route inspectors/mobile radio
Average peak-hour speed: Bus 20 km/h, trolleybus 20 km/h, tram 19 km/h
New vehicles financed by: Free financing and credit

Tramway

Type of operation: Conventional tramway

Passenger journeys: (1993) 36.7 million
(1994) 37.7 million
(1995) 38.1 million
Car-km: (annual) 2 million
Route length: 15.3 km
Number of lines: 2
Number of stops: 39
Gauge: 900 mm
Max gradient: 4%
Minimum curve radius: 18 m
Electrification: 600 V DC, overhead

Service: Peak 4-6 min, off-peak 6-15 min
First/last car: 04.01/23.48
Fare collection: Prepurchase and automatic machines for ticket issuing and cancellation at all stops
One-person operation: All vehicles

Rolling stock: 43 cars

Bombardier-Rotax GTW8 (1970/71)	M8
Bombardier-Rotax GTW8 (1970/71 rebuilt 1973/74)	M7
Bombardier-Rotax GTW10 (1977 rebuilt 1979/80)	M12
Bombardier-Rotax GTW10 (1985/86)	M16

In peak service: 35

Local railway (Bergbahn)

Type of operation: Local railway

Current situation: ESG also operates the Bergbahn, a 2.9 km railway with eight stations running from Bergbahnhof at the tramway Line 3 terminal to Pöstlingberg, operating on 600 V DC catenary. It carries about 500,000 passengers a year.

Rolling stock: 14 cars

UPDATED

LISBOA

Population: 610,000, city region 2.5 million
Public transport: Bus and tramway services provided in city area by public company also responsible for three funiculars and a public elevator. Metro operated by separate public undertaking, suburban rail lines by Portuguese Railways (CP), cross-river ferries by CP and Transtejo, and suburban bus services by municipal-owned bus company and private operators. Though fares are integrated, no overall authority directs transport planning for the region, but the Basic Law of Land Transport passed in 1991 allows for creation of such a body. Rail infrastructure planning and construction is undertaken by a quasi-autonomous transport ministry department. Other arrangements apply in the south Tagus conurbation (see separate section below)

Carris

Companhia Carris de Ferro de Lisboa SARL (Carris)
Rua Primeiro de Maio N° 101-103, 1399 Lisboa, Portugal
Telephone: +351 1 363 0266 Fax: +351 1 649399
President: Duarte Amandio
Director of Planning: L A Caetano Trindade
Staff: 5,017

Passenger boardings: (All modes)
(1992) 430 million
(1993) 395 million
(1994) 381 million

Air conditioned Volvo articulated of Carris at Praça dos Restauradores ***1997***

Operating costs financed by: Fares 68.5%, government subsidy 31.5%

Current situation: Carris operates as exclusive concessionnaire for provision of public transport to the framework followed by the previous owners, Lisbon Electric Tramways Ltd, taken into public ownership in 1978. The ageing fleet of buses and trams inherited (some trams dating from 1900-14) poses continuing investment problems. Consideration has been given to the most appropriate form of ownership and control of public transport given the growth of the need for external support and development of the metro. Moves to integrate and co-ordinate the five publicly owned transport operations have been under discussion, and a multimodal pass system extends to part of the suburban area.

Bus

Staff: 4,055

Passenger boardings: (1992) 389 million
(1993) 363 million
(1994) 354 million
Vehicle-km: (1992) 43.8 million
(1993) 43.6 million
(1994) 44.3 million

Number of routes: 93
Route length: (One way) 588 km
On priority right-of-way: 38.4 km
Fleet: 805 vehicles

Volvo B10R	98
Volvo B59	312
Volvo B10M articulated	30
MAN SL200F	86
MAN SL200	112
MAN 10150 HOCL (1990/91)	40
Magirus/Fiat-Iveco 470	100
Daimler Fleetline double-deck	11
Volvo B58 articulated	1
Renault B120 minibus	15

In peak service: 712
Average age of fleet: 13.8 years
On order: 54 Volvo articulated, 40 MAN midibuses and 15 Renault B120 minibuses

Most intensive service: 8-10 min
One-person operation: All routes
Fare collection: Payment to conductor or driver, prepurchase tickets and passes, 10-journey carnets; cancellers at entrance
Fare structure: Flat, city centre; zonal, outside (3 zones); monthly passes; tourist passes for 4 or 7 days
Fares collected on board: 14.3% of revenue; prepurchase 20%, passes 65/7%
Fare evasion control: Roving inspectors
Arrangements for elderly/disabled: 6 lift-equipped minibuses including 4 Renault SG3/Gruau and 2 Guy Victory

ML90 prototype at Picoas metro station ***1997***

Integration with other modes: Passes valid on all services in Lisboa area in different zone combinations; minibus link to airport
Average distance between stops: 394 m
Average peak-hour speed: In mixed traffic, 14.8 km/h
Operating costs financed by: Fares 76.7%, subsidy/grant 23.3%
New vehicles financed by: Loans

Developments: All new buses are air conditioned. Carris would like to replace 200 buses dating from 1975/76, but does not have the necessary finance.

Trials have been made with low-floor buses and future orders of this type will be placed for delivery before the 1998 Lisboa Expo. Buses powered by natural gas have also been tested.

A seven-route articulated-bus network is being implemented on corridors with demand exceeding 1,000 passengers/h. A radio-based traffic management system known as SICRA has been installed in 400 vehicles. It will also be installed on the remaining tram routes. The system will be upgraded to allow tracking of vehicles and monitoring by a central control room at Santo Amaro.

Tramway

Type of operation: Conventional tramway, plus one light rail line

Passenger boardings: (1993) 28 million
(1994) 22.4 million
(1995) 27 million
Car-km: (1993) 3.6 million
(1994) 3.2 million
(1995)

Route length: 72 km
On priority right-of-way: 11.2 km
Number of lines: 7
Number of stops: 135
Gauge: 900 mm
Track: 45% conventional sleepers on ballast, 55% on concrete with resilient pads
Max gradient: 14%
Minimum curve radius: 10 m
Electrification: 580 V DC, overhead

Service: Peak 6-11 min, off-peak 8-18 min
First/last car: (Line 15) 05.05/01.55
Fare structure: Zonal, but flat-fare season tickets across the network account for most journeys
One-person operation: All routes
Operating costs financed by: Fares 24%, subsidy/grants 76%

Rolling stock: 100 cars

CCFL (1931-40)	M42
CCFL (1941-50)	M6
CCFL (1951-60)	M19
CCFL (1960 on)	M23
Siemens (1995)	M10

In peak service: 71

Current situation: In recent years much of the tramway network has been abandoned as hopelessly uneconomic; its turn-of-the-century cars have to be maintained by artisans. A total of 50 heritage cars are to be rebuilt with modern electrical and mechanical equipment, whilst retaining their original exterior appearance. All other cars will be scrapped, sold or sent to the Carris museum.

The seven surviving routes are to be retained, with the five hill routes being developed as a tourist attraction whilst continuing their traditional public transport role in the narrow, steeply graded streets of the old city. Some streets are barely wide enough for a single track, and the section between São Tome and Graca (Route 28) has interlaced track on sharp curves.

Developments: Waterfront Route 15 is being upgraded to near light rail standards, including creation of 4.2 km of reserved track and introduction of 10 three-section articulated cars for which upgraded depot facilities have been provided at Santo Amaro. These are currently operating between Praça Figueira and Belém, although further upgrading work should see operations extended to Algés and eventually to the terminus at Cruz de Quebrada, where a park-and-ride is planned.

Similarly, Route 18, which shares part of its alignment with Route 15, is due to be upgraded to light rail standards and extended once again to Santa Apolónia CP station, although this would necessitate exercising of options for a further 20 LRVs from Siemens.

Should money become available, Carris would like to reopen its lines to the suburb of Benfica, upgrading them to light rail standards. In addition, the northern suburb of Odivelas urgently needs some form of fixed-track transport system, and the government is paying Carris to undertake a feasibility study to determine whether light rail would cater for its needs or if it would be better served by the metro. A 14 km route is also proposed from central Lisboa to the CP suburban station at Póvoa, requiring 20 cars.

Funiculars/elevator

Passenger journeys: (1992) 5.2 million
(1993) 3.9 million
(1994) 4.8 million

Current situation: Carris operates three funicular (cable tram) routes and one vertical public elevator.

ML

Metropolitano de Lisboa EP (ML)
28 Avenida Fontes Pereira de Melo, 1069 Lisboa Codex
Telephone: +351 1 355 8457 Fax: +351 1 357 4908
President: A Santos Machado
Managing Director, Operations: A Pinto Dantas
Fixed Installations: A Cerdeira Baptista
Rolling Stock: P Vazão de Almeida
Staff: 2,026

Lisboa's first new tram for more than 40 years ***1996***

Type of operation: Full metro, opened 1959

Passenger journeys: (1993) 146.7 million
(1994) 136.2 million
(1995) 123.9 million
Car-km: (1994) 10.3 million
(1995) 10.5 million

Route length: 19 km
in tunnel: 17 km
Number of lines: 2
Number of stations: 25
Gauge: 1,435 mm
Track: Vignole (FB) 50 kg/m U50 profile rail on timber sleepers, normally on ballast, with resilient pads; new lines twin-block Stedef sleepers; on concrete at stations
Max gradient: 4%
Minimum curve radius: 150 m (some 100 m)
Tunnel: Cut-and-cover except 1 km bored
Electrification 750 V DC, third rail

Service: Peak 3 min, off-peak 6 min
First/last train: 06.30/01.00
Fare structure: Flat
Fare collection: AFC at all stations, open access
Fare evasion control: Spot checks at stations or on trains
Integration with other modes: Fares integrated with suburban bus, ferry and rail services through monthly zonal passes
Surveillance: CCTV on all platforms
Operating costs financed by: Fares 27%, other commercial sources 11%, government subsidy/grants 62%

Rolling stock: 197 cars, in four-car sets except for two ML90 three-car prototypes

Linke-Hofmann-Busch ML7 (1959)	M20
Linke-Hofmann-Busch ML7 (1964)	M14
Sorefame ML7 (1972)	M32
Sorefame ML7 (1975)	M14
Sorefame ML79 (1984)	M40
Sorefame ML79 (1985/88)	M16
Sorefame ML90 prototype (1992)	M4 T2
Sorefame ML90 (1995/96)	M38 T17

On order: 114 ML95 cars are on order with options for a further 120

Developments: A major expansion programme now under way is transforming the present network into three separate lines and adding a new cross-city route, effectively doubling the size of the network by the end of the century, when annual patronage of 200 million is expected. There will be eight interchanges with CP suburban trains and three with cross-Tagus ferries; park-and-ride facilities are planned at six outlying stations.

In 1995, the existing 19 km single route was split into two wholly separate lines, the 5.3 km Girassol line (formerly Line B) being segregated from the remaining network thanks to inauguration of a second station at Rotunda. An extension to Rato is under construction for 1997 opening.

The Gaivota line (Line A) is being extended 3 km to a new terminus at Pontinha (opens 1997), and Terreiro do Paço, while a Varavela line (Line C) extension to CP's Cascais line station at Cais do Sodré is also under construction.

Further extensions to all three routes are planned. The Gaivota line will be extended to CP's Santa Apolonia terminal, the Girassol from Campo Grande to Alto do Lumiar, and the Caravela from Campo Grande to Telheiras.

Also under construction is the new Oriente line (formerly Line D) from Alameda to Oriente, scheduled to open in 1998 to serve the Expo 98 site. Later, extensions are proposed northwards to Moscavide and westwards across the city centre to Campolide, where there will be interchange with CP suburban trains on the future cross-Tagus line.

A fifth line is under study, linking the southwest riverside suburb of Belem with Oriente, while a proposed line to serve Loures is now to be built as light rail rather than full metro. By the end of the century the network will comprise four lines totalling some 40 km and serving 50 stations.

All existing stations are undergoing refurbishment and lengthening of platforms. By 1998 all stations will be able to handle six-car trains.

Volvo rigid of Transportes Colectivos at Barreiro ***1996***

Lisboa Rail Development Board

Gabinete do Nó Ferroviário de Lisboa
Estaçao do Rossio, 4° piso, 1200 Lisboa
Telephone: +351 1 342 0969/0947
Fax: +351 1 342 3300
President: Dr Braamcamp Sobral

Current situation: GNFL was set up by the Ministry of Public Works, Transport & Communications in 1987 as a quasi-autonomous government department to oversee railway development. Its remit is to modernise infrastructure serving the city, adapt the network to meet current requirements, build new lines where necessary, and to create conditions under which the cross-Tagus rail link can be built. However, its functions were expected to pass in 1997 to a new national infrastructure authority.
Developments: GNFL is working on seven projects: upgrading the ring railway, including the Alcântara branch; modernising the Sintra line; extending suburban service on the western line to Torres Vedras; upgrading the Cascais line; restructuring the northern line to Azambuja to permit introduction of suburban service; building a new main line terminal in Lisboa; implementing the cross-Tagus line, and planning a second such link.

Construction of the cross-Tagus link, which is to be incorporated into the lower deck of the existing road bridge, is costed at Esc78 billion. Initial build-operate-transfer bids from the private sector were rejected on cost grounds, and separate contracts are now to be let for each aspect of the project. So far, contracts have been awarded for the rail link itself and for strengthening of the bridge.

Cross-Tagus rail service is due to start in April 1998, when trains will run through from Azambuja on CP's northern line to Pinhal Novo and Setúbal on the south side via the ring line. Initially, 300 trains a day will use the bridge, rising to 500 daily when patronage will have grown to some 40 million journeys a year.

CP

Caminhos de Ferro Portugueses (CP)
Calcada do Duque 20-1, 1294 Lisboa Codex
Telephone: +351 1 346 3181 Fax: +351 1 347 6524

Suburban rail

Type of operation: Suburban heavy rail

Passenger journeys: (1995) 139 million

Current situation: Suburban services provided by CP on three routes. From Santa Apolónia electric trains (25 kV 50 Hz) run hourly (peak half-hourly) on the northern line to Azambuja (54 km), with a shuttle serving the orbital line between Alcântara and Areeiro (10 km), and an irregular hourly service to Sacavém. Some 15 trains run to destinations further afield. From the Cais do Sodré terminus a frequent service is operated to Estoril and Cascais (26 km), electrified at 1.5 kV DC. Lisboa's most intensive service is on the Sintra line (electrified 25 kV 50 Hz) out of Rossio station, where there is a 16-min service throughout the day, plus a similar inner-suburban service between Terminal Av 5 and Cacém (18 km).

Developments: The Sintra line carries the heaviest traffic of any CP route. It is being completely modernised, with four tracks being provided as far as Cacém for 1998 completion, when the current 13 trains/h will rise to 20. Track and catenary are being upgraded, modern signalling including CTC is being installed, and many level crossings are being eliminated. A new fleet of 42 four-car emus provides all services.

The Cascais line is also being modernised. Track is being rehabilitated, level crossings eliminated, catenary remodelled, new substations built, stations refurbished and platforms lengthened to accommodate 10-car trains, and new interchange facilities introduced. The fleet is being increased from 10 to 13 trains.

On the orbital route, colourlight signalling will permit 15-min frequency, thereby allowing some Cascais line trains to run to Areeiro and so reduce pressure on Cais do Sodré. This route will eventually be used by the cross-Tagus service from Azambuja to Setúbal.

Under a proposed reorganisation, management of suburban routes in Lisboa will be grouped into one or more profit centres better to identify costs, although central government will continue to provide subsidy. The Sintra line will be the first to be granted this level of autonomy, and will market itself under a separate brand name.

Ferry

Current situation: CP's cross-Tagus ferries from Terreiro do Paco pier to Barreiro were transferred in 1993 to a subsidiary, Soflusa. Eight vessels operate between 05.45 and 02.45, providing a 10-min peak service, 30-45 min off-peak.

In addition, Transtejo provides frequent services across the estuary from three points on the north shore to five on the south. Main departure point in Lisboa is Terreiro do Paço with vehicle ferries leaving from Cais do Sodré. Belem, 5 km west of the city, handles departures for downstream destinations.

There are seven routes totalling 37 km, operated by 26 vessels (five carrying vehicles); about 44 million passengers are carried annually.

Lisboa metro

LISBOA - SOUTH TAGUS

Population: 440,000

Public transport: The south bank communities of Almade, Seixal, Barreiro and Moita form the third largest conurbation in Portugal. Ferry services provide a link with Lisboa, while CP operates suburban rail services from its Barreiro station. Bus services are provided by a number of operators, notably Transportes Colectivos and Rodoviário Sul do Tejo. A four-line light rail network is planned

CP

Address as above

Current situation: About hourly (peak half-hourly) service provided from 05.00 to 02.05 between Barreiro, where there is connection with the cross-Tagus ferries, and Setúbal (29 km).

Developments: The cross-Tagus rail link is being built to improve access to central Lisboa. Improvements on the south bank include a new line to the bridge with six stations, an 8,000-space park-and-ride at Penalva, and electrification and upgrading between Pinhal Novo and Setúbal.

Private bus

Current situation: The former state-owned Rodoviário Sul do Tejo, which is now owned by Barraqueiro, provides suburban bus services on the south bank.

Transportes Colectivos do Barreiro

Rua Resistentes Antifascistas, 2830 Barreiro
Telephone: +351 1 207 8354 Fax: +351 1 207 8368
General Manager: Pedro Alberta Correira de Andrade Canário

Staff: 234

Passenger journeys: (1994)
Vehicle-km: (1994)

Number of routes: 14
Route length: 129 km
Fleet: 65 vehicles, plus 12 hired

Current situation: A municipal bus service is provided in Barreiro on the south bank of the Tagus, connected to Lisboa by ferry. Fares cover 88 per cent of operating costs.

Light rail (proposed)

Current situation: With the population of the four south bank municipalities expected to double by 2030, a four-line light rail network has been recommended by a feasibility study. The 41 km would serve 55 stops, linking the four towns and ferry terminals, as well as the university, hospital and local beaches. A 25.8 km core network would be built initially, requiring a fleet of up to 47 cars. Construction is expected to start in 1997 for 1999 opening.

On completion of the cross-Tagus rail link, CP's existing Barreiro—Moita line will no longer be a main route and will be converted to light rail.

UPDATED

Lisboa suburban emu awaits commuters at Cascais ***1997***

LIVERPOOL

Population: City 470,000, Merseyside county area 1.5 million

Public transport: Main bus services provided by employee-owned company, with other services operated by private firms. Passenger Transport Executive, under direction of a joint board of local districts and trading as Merseytravel, has direct responsibility for ferry operation, the Mersey road tunnels, subsidising contracted non-commercial bus services, rail services within Merseyside county area, including central area metro loop line, operated under contract, service promotion, and provision of bus station facilities; rapid transit options being evaluated

MTL

MTL Trust Holdings Ltd
Edge Lane, Liverpool L7 9LL, England
Telephone: +44 151 254 1254 Fax: +44 151 220 0665
Managing Director: Peter Coombes
Commercial Director: Dominic Brady
Engineering Director: Robert Dawson
Financial Director: Colin Fuller
Staff: 2,490

Current situation: Established in 1986 from the former PTE bus operation as a separate company wholly owned by the PTA, the company was sold to its workforce in 1992. It operates a network of commercial services throughout the Merseyside area, plus subsidised services both wholly within Merseyside and running into neighbouring areas of Lancashire and Cheshire.

Developments: The company has expanded with the takeover of Fareway Passenger Services, now absorbed into the main company as a low-cost unit, Blue Triangle of Bootle, Heysham Travel and Liverbus. MTL later bought London Buses' subsidiary London Northern, and subsequently acquired London Suburban Buses and R&I Tours, both based in north London. The company was awarded the franchise to operate the Merseyrail network in late 1996.

Bus

Passenger journeys: (1990/91) 140.6 million
(1991/92) 138 million
(1992/93) 134 million

Vehicle-km: (1990/91) 49.6 million
(1991/92) 48 million
(1992/93) 48 million

Number of routes: 110
Route length: 651 km
Fleet: 1,133 vehicles

Leyland Atlantean double-deck	365
MCW Metrobus double-deck	64
Leyland Olympian double-deck	94
Leyland Titan double-deck	180
Volvo Olympian double-deck	39
Scania double-deck	11
Volvo B10 single-deck	135
Leyland National single-deck	100
DAF/Ikarus single-deck	5
Neoplan N4016 single-deck	12
Scania single-deck	20
Volvo B6 midibus	50
Dennis Dart midibus	5
Leyland coach	12
Optare Metrorider midibus	11
Mercedes midibus	19
Dennis Javelin coach	2
Volvo B10M coach	9

Most intensive service: 5 min
One-person operation: All routes
Fare collection: Prepurchase season tickets/passes, or payment to driver for single tickets
Fare structure: Zonal for season tickets, stage for single fares
Fare evasion control: Inspectors and other measures
Average distance between stops: 400 m
Average peak-hour speed: In mixed traffic, 20 km/h
Operating costs financed by: Fares 87%, other commercial sources 5%, contracted operations/subsidies 8%

North Western

North Western Road Car Co Ltd
73 Ormskirk Road, Aintree, Liverpool L9 5AE
Telephone: +44 151 525 1733 Fax: +44 151 525 9556
Managing Director: Bob Hind
Engineering Director: Gary Raven
Staff: 800

North Western Dennis Dart on CityPlus route **1996**

Current situation: Formed in 1986 by separating off Ribble's Merseyside garages together with a depot in Wigan, it was privatised and sold to Drawlane in 1988. It is now a subsidiary of the Cowie Group. NW is the largest private operator in Liverpool.

Developments: Services, buses and minibuses of British Bus subsidiary Amberline were absorbed in 1993. Liverline is now a subsidiary. Services in Liverpool are now integrated with those of MTL.

New high-quality CityPlus image is being promoted in Liverpool, using new Dennis Dart midibuses which are replacing life-expired double-decks. During 1995 the company took over responsibility for Bee Line and Star Line operations in Manchester.

Bus

Number of routes: 145
Fleet: 422 vehicles

Leyland Atlantean double-deck	38
Leyland Olympian double-deck	38
Bristol VR double-deck	22
Dennis Dominator double-deck	14
Volvo double-deck	14
Scania single-deck	10
Dennis Lance single-deck	10
Dennis Falcon single-deck	8
Dennis Dart single-deck	106
Leyland National single-deck	80
Scania single-deck	6
Leyland coach	10
Mercedes minibus	66

Most intensive service: 5 min
One-person operation: 100%
Fare structure: Single tickets paid on board; Merseyside zonal and day tickets
Operating costs financed by: Commercial services 90%, tendered/subsidised services 10%

Crosville

Crosville Motor Services Ltd
Hobson Street, Burslem ST6 2AQ
Telephone: +44 1782 524444 Fax: +44 1782 524466
Managing Director: Steven Ellis

Current situation: Crosville is an operating subsidiary of PMT of Stoke. It is the second largest operator in the Wirral peninsula, and services are operated into Liverpool, but only via the Mersey tunnels. The company operates about 110 buses from depots at Birkenhead, Ellesmere Port and Chester.

CMT

CMT Buses
Unit D3, Liver Industrial Estate, Long Lane, Aintree L9 7ES
Telephone: +44 151 523 3118 Fax: +44 151 525 0432
Managing Director: Jeff Grant

Ex-London Buses Leyland Titan on Village Bus service **1997**

Neoplan low-floor at Albert Dock on SMART service operated by MTL for Merseytravel **1997**

Merseytravel's new Huyton bus station **1997**

Current situation: Operates seven commercial routes along major corridors, and three subsidised routes in partnership with Merseytravel.

Bus

Number of routes: 10
Fleet: 58 vehicles

Leyland National single-deck	33
Volvo B108/Wright single-decks	6
Dennis Dart midibus	19

Other commercial operators

Current situation: A number of smaller operators run commercial and contracted services in the area. These include RedRider (a subsidiary of PMT of Stoke-on-Trent) in Wirral, Halton Transport, ABC of Southport, Merseyline of Garston, AIA of Birkenhead, Liverpool City Coaches, Aintree Coachlines, Avon Buses of Preston, J & C Minicoaches and Village Bus of Garston.

Merseytravel

Merseyside Passenger Transport Executive
24 Hatton Garden, Liverpool L3 2AN
Telephone: +44 151 227 5181 Fax: +44 151 236 2457
Chief Executive: Roy Swainson

Current situation: Merseytravel funds socially necessary bus services, funds the Merseyrail network, and owns and operates the Mersey ferries and tunnels. It operates Merseylink, a door-to-door bus service for people with mobility difficulties, and funds free travel for elderly and mobility-impaired people. It also provides comprehensive public transport information.

Developments: New bus stations were opened in 1995/96 at St Helens, Huyton and Birkenhead, and the first construction phase of central terminal facilities at Queen Square in Liverpool was completed. New bus stations are planned for Kirkby and Bootle Strand, as well as improvements at Southport. Merseytravel is also planning a rapid transit network (see below).

Working closely with the five district authorities on Merseyside, Merseytravel is introducing highway measures designed to increase the attractiveness of bus travel, including development of high-quality SMART services and bus priority measures on radial corridors in partnership with local operators. A commercial 'SMART Quality' corridor was inaugurated in October 1996 along West Derby Road from Stockbridge Village. Merseytravel provided the infrastructure and MTL the 20 low-floor Scanias which run the service.

Trials are in progress with contactless smartcard ticketing.

Merseyrail

Merseytravel Rail Services
Address as Merseytravel above

Type of operation: Suburban rail linked by full metro loop and link line

Passenger journeys: (1992) 39.1 million
(1993) 31 million
(1995) 29 million

Current situation: Ten services are provided on three groups of lines totalling 141 km, of which 92 km electrified at 750 V DC. Electric services feed into the city-centre loop and cross-city link lines, while the diesel lines terminate at Lime Street station where there is interchange with the other routes. Total 75 stations within the PTA supported network; 1,435 mm gauge; basic 15 min daytime service.

Rail services are operated on behalf of Merseytravel by Merseyrail Electrics Ltd (electric lines) and North West Regional Railways Ltd (diesel lines).

Fully integrated fare structure, with day and period tickets valid on all public transport in the Merseyside area.

Developments: Another two new stations have been approved and two more are at the planning stage. Further electrification of the Wirral line is being studied. Extensive rebuilding and refurbishment are under way to improve passenger facilities, including better personal security and access to stations and trains. Modifications are being made to the rolling stock fleet to provide wheelchair access. Expansion of park-and-ride and bus interchange opportunities also in progress.

In late 1996, the bus operator MTL was awarded the operating franchise for Merseyrail.

Rolling stock: 189 emu cars, also dmus
Class 507 three-car emu (1978/80)
Class 508 three-car emu (1979/80)

Mersey Ferries

Mersey Ferries Ltd
Victoria Place, Seacombe, Wallasey L44 6QY
Telephone: +44 51 639 0609 Fax: +44 51 639 0578
General Manager: Brian Fisher
Staff: 90

Ferry

Passenger journeys: (1993/94) 585,000
(1994/95) 656,000
(1995/96) 710,000

Current situation: Cross-Mersey ferry services are provided between Liverpool Pier Head, Seacombe and Woodside (Birkenhead). Service is split into peak-hour commuter operations and daytime leisure cruises with three vessels. Fares cover 36 per cent of operating costs.

Light rail (proposed)

Liverpool Light Rail Group

Current situation: In 1994, a private sector consortium comprising two bus operators and the electricity generator Powergen, put forward proposals for a 16 m light rail line linking the city centre with the airport.

Line 1 would be built almost exclusively on former tramway alignments abandoned in the 1950s, thus speeding construction. A fleet of 28 low-floor cars would be required.

Rapid transit (proposed)

Merseyside Rapid Transit (MRT)

Current situation: Consultation started in 1996 on three options for an 8.5 km rapid transit corridor from Page Moss to the waterfront. The MRT consortium is headed by Merseytravel, Liverpool City Council and Knowsley Borough Council. The plans form a key element of the long-term Merseyside Integrated Transport Study, which involves five local authorities, the Merseyside Task Force and the Merseyside Development Corporation.

Three traction options are offered as the consortium bids for funds and seeks backers – light rail, GLT (guided light transit) and guided bus. Two other public transport corridors not currently served by the local rail network have been identified as possible routes, serving a population of 220,000.

UPDATED

Merseyrail train at Birkenhead Park **1995**

ŁÓDŹ

Population: City 851,000, province 1.1 million
Public transport: Bus and urban tramway services operated by municipal undertaking, with suburban tram routes operated by separate companies; suburban rail services operated by Polish State Railways (PKP); metro planned

MPK

Miejskie Przedsiębiorstwo Komunikacyjne-Łódź
Społka z o o
ul Tramwajowa 6, 90132 Łódź, Poland
Telephone: +48 42 780033 Fax: +48 42 783407
President: Czesław Rydecki
Staff: 6,680

Current situation: MPK's longer suburban and interurban tram routes were transferred to two new operators in 1994.

Operating costs financed by: Fares 55.5%, subsidy/grants 44.5%
Subsidy from: City budget

Bus

Staff: 1,544

Passenger journeys: (1989) 473.5 million
(1993) 204 million
Vehicle-km: (1989) 66.6 million
(1993) 28.6 million

Number of routes: 58 (plus 8 night-only)
Route length: (One way) 714 km
Fleet: 437 vehicles

Jelcz M11	80
Ikarus 260	115
Ikarus 280 articulated	222
MAN	11
Mercedes	4
120 MM	5

Most intensive service: 5 min
One-person operation: All routes
Fare collection: Prepurchase single tickets, 1-, 7-, 14-day or monthly pass with validation and cancelling machines on board
Fare structure: Flat
Fares collected on board: None
Fare evasion control: Roving inspectors
Operational control: Roving inspectors
Arrangements for elderly/disabled: Disabled servicemen, blind persons and their escorts, and over-75s, free; other retired or pensioners, half fare
Average peak-hour speed: 18.7 km/h

Tramway

Staff: 1,009

Type of operation: Conventional tramway

Passenger journeys: (1989) 452 million
(1993) 183 million
Car-km: (1989) 36.8 million
(1993) 25.1 million

Route length: 113 km
Number of lines: 16
Gauge: 1,000 mm
Max gradient: 2.5%
Minimum curve radius: 21 m
Electrification: 600 V DC, overhead

First/last car: 03.38/23.18
Fare structure/collection: As bus
One-person operation: All cars

Rolling stock: About 300 cars
Konstal 805N

Suburban/interurban tramways

Current situation: In 1994 interurban tramways were taken over by two new companies. Tramway Podmieskie operates two routes with 15 cars, and MKT runs four routes with 40 cars.

Metro (planned)

Current situation: A 54 km two-line metro system has been planned. Line A (28 km) would run northwest to southeast, while Line B would run east-west.

PKP

Polish State Railways (PKP)
ul Chalubinskiego 4, 00-928 Warszawa

Type of operation: Suburban heavy rail

Current situation: Trains run at least half-hourly to Koluszki (27 km), and about hourly to Tomaszow Mazowiecki and Zdunskawola. Also irregular services provided on several other routes.

Pair of Konstal 805N on Route 3 near Fabryczna ***1996***

LONDON

Population: Greater London area 6.3 million
Public transport: Bus and metro services responsibility of London Transport, under overall control of government through nominated board, with bus services run by private companies under contract. Extensive network of suburban rail services run by 10 train operating companies, franchised to the private sector. Light rail system owned by development agency serves Docklands area, operated under franchise. Suburban light rail network under construction in Croydon

London Transport

London Transport (LT)
55 Broadway, London SW1H 0BD, England
Telephone: +44 171 222 5600 Fax: +44 171 222 6016
Chair: Peter Ford
Board Member, Finance: Tony Sheppeck
Board Member & Managing Director, London Underground: Denis Tunnicliffe
Board Member & Managing Director, LT Buses: Clive Hodson
Director of Planning: David Bayliss

Passenger journeys: (Bus and metro)
(1993/94) 1,847 million
(1994/95) 1,923 million
(1995/96) 1,982 million

Current situation: Since coming under the control of central government once again in 1984, LT's remit has been to plan, provide or procure services to meet the present and future public transport needs of London. In 1994/95 LT sold its remaining bus operating companies into the private sector. These companies, together with other private operators, now run London's bus services under contract to LT, which retains direct responsibility for running the metro.

LT works with Railtrack, the franchised suburban rail operators, Docklands Light Railway and the private bus companies to plan and co-ordinate the city's public transport, and to provide integrated ticketing and information services for metro, bus and suburban rail.

Developments: A new strategy for development of London's public transport over the coming 25 years was launched in 1995. It consolidated a number of existing proposals for new railways (see London rail/light rail plans, below), which are costed at some £10 billion and could be funded in part under the government's Private Finance Initiative. Also published in 1996 was a detailed study of nine suburban corridors, on which the introduction of trolleybus, guided bus, tramway or light rail might be considered. A similar study of introducing new modes in central London was made during 1996.

Commuting into London is growing again, but LT remains grossly under-funded with a maintenance and renewal backlog amounting to £1.2 billion. In the government's budget announced in November 1996, funding for LT was cut from £950 million for 1996 to £650 million for 1997, £310 million for 1998 and £150 million for 1999. From these reduced amounts, LT must also fund an over-run of £400 million in the cost of building the Jubilee line metro extension, for which the government refused to pay. All major infrastructure investment projects for London Underground were re-evaluated at the beginning of 1997; many appeared likely to be deferred for at least two or three years.

In February 1997 the government announced plans for privatisation of the metro, with a pledge that the funds raised by the sale would be ploughed back as investment.

Fare structure: Zonal, six concentric zones with the outer three counting as one zone for bus travel; differing standard fares for bus and metro journeys within each zone or combination of zones; off-peak short-distance bus fare; range of all-modes and bus-only passes; 10-trip carnets introduced on metro central zone in 1996

Arrangements for elderly/disabled: Free travel for the elderly at all times except in morning peak is funded by the London boroughs. LT's Unit for Disabled Passengers funds locally administered dial-a-ride minibus services as well as working to improve accessibility of all public transport. Network of lift-equipped Mobility Bus routes, whilst fully accessible low-floor buses have begun to be introduced on conventional routes. Plans are under way for achieving step-free access to a number of metro stations; new infrastructure will be fully accessible

London Transport Buses

London Transport Buses Ltd
172 Buckingham Palace Road, London SW1W 9TN
Telephone: +44 171 222 5600
Chair: Peter Ford
Managing Director: Clive Hodson
Staff: 583

Passenger journeys: (1993/94) 1,112 million
(1994/95) 1,159 million
(1995/96) 1,198 million

Vehicle-km: (1993/94) 311 million
(1994/95) 322 million
(1995/96) 329 million

Operating costs financed by: Fares 85.5%

Current situation: In 1994 this new organisation was created to regulate and control the bus network following sale of London Buses' operating companies (which had owned 5,000 vehicles) to the private sector for some £220 million. It took over all of LT's bus-related activities, and its aim is to procure safe, reliable, attractive and efficient services. Its responsibilities include provision and control of 35 bus stations, 100 bus stands, 17,000 bus stops and (with the Adshel advertising group) 9,000 bus shelters.

Services are now provided under contract by more than 30 private operators (see below), with some 6,500 buses serving 700 routes. For full history of the privatisation process see *JUTS 1994-95*.

Developments: Newly-tendered contracts for some 10 per cent of the network started during 1995/96. Combined with higher fares and tight financial control, these helped reduce the operating deficit by one-third to £42.3 million. Patronage grew by a further 3.4 per cent in 1995/96. Work was in progress on several new bus stations, and 3,000 stops had location names and other information added to them. The Countdown bus information system was extended to further locations during the year, including two groups of routes in west London.

Government funding to the London boroughs for the London Bus Priority Network was increased by some 30 per cent to £8 million for 1995/96 and further priority lanes were commissioned during 1996.

Automatic vehicle location is to be installed on all 6,500 buses operating LT services; SLE is preferred bidder.

Contracted bus

Current situation: The following companies are major contractors to LTB.

LTB's new Stratford bus station in east London

1996

Uxbridge Buses (Centrewest) Dennis/Plaxton Pointer at Uxbridge bus station ***1997***

Centrewest

Centrewest London Buses Ltd
Macmillan House, Paddington Station, London W2 1TY
Telephone: +44 171 706 0877 Fax: +44 171 706 8789
Managing Director: Peter Hendy
Operations Director: R M Muir
Engineering Director: J A Whitworth
Finance Director: John Storey
Staff: 1,400

Current situation: This employee-owned company operates services in west and southeast London from six depots.

Developments: Won an LT contract to operate network of services in Orpington, Kent, taking over staff from Stagecoach Selkent and opening a new depot. In 1996, acquired Beeline and London Buslines; operating under existing trading names, the Berks Bucks Bus Company combines operations based at Bracknell, Slough and Southall.

Centrewest is part of the Tramtrack Croydon consortium which is to build and operate the Croydon Tramlink system (qv).

Fleet: 544 vehicles

AEC Routemaster double-deck	49
MCW Metrobus double-deck	115
Volvo Olympian double-deck	27
Bristol LH single-deck	1
Leyland National single-deck	9
Leyland Lynx single-deck	5
Dennis Dart single-deck	148
Dennis Lance SLF single-deck	14
Dennis Dart SLF single-deck	7
Mercedes minibus	108
Renault minibus	60
LDV minibus	1

Fleet (Berks Bus): 210 vehicles

Leyland Olympian double-deck	38
Bristol VRT double-deck	4
Daimler Fleetline double-deck	2
Leyland National single-deck	12
Leyland Lynx single-deck	8
Scania single-deck	10
Dennis Dart single-deck	40
Dennis Dart SLF single-deck	7
MCW Metrorider midibus	2
Mercedes midibus	30
Renault midibus	33
Scania coach	15
Leyland Tiger coach	3
Volvo coach	6

Leaside

Leaside Bus Company Ltd
16 Watsons Road, Wood Green, London N22 4TZ
Telephone: +44 181 889 0404 Fax: +44 181 889 2177
Managing Director: Stephen Clayton
Staff: 1,700

Current situation: This subsidiary of the Cowie Group operates 31 routes in northeast London from six depots.

Fleet: 544 vehicles

AEC Routemaster double-deck	91
MCW Metrobus double-deck	338
AEC Regent double-deck	1
Leyland Titan double-deck	2
DAF DB250 double-deck	13
Leyland Olympian double-deck	40
Scania low-floor single-deck	14
Dennis Dart single-deck	38
MCW Metrorider minibus	3
DAF/Volvo coach	4

IN peak service: 446

London Central

London Central Bus Co Ltd
1 Warner Road, London SE5 9LU
Telephone: +44 171 738 3666 Fax: +44 171 737 0381
Managing Director: Keith Ludeman
Staff: 1,600

Current situation: This subsidiary of the Go-Ahead Group operates 48 routes in southeast London from four depots.

Fleet: 546 vehicles

AEC Routemaster double-deck	102
Leyland Titan double-deck	261
Leyland Olympian double-deck	15
Leyland Atlantean double-deck	1
Optare Spectra double-deck	24
Volvo Olympian double-deck	57
Dennis Dart single-deck	27
Optare Metrorider minibus	28
Optare Starrider minibus	30
Leyland Tiger coach	1

London General

London General Transport Services Ltd
25 Raleigh Gardens, Mitcham CR4 3NS
Telephone: +44 181 646 1747 Fax: +44 181 640 2317
Managing Director: Keith Ludeman
Staff: 1,900

Current situation: Operates 51 routes in central and south London from six depots.

Developments: This employee-owned company was sold to the Go-Ahead Group in 1996. Some head office functions are being merged with London Central (see above). The Sutton area bus network was gained under

London's traditional Routemaster double-deck on London Central's Route 36 ***1997***

retendering and 100 new buses entered service in late 1996.

Fleet: 734 vehicles

AEC Routemaster double-deck	69
MCW Metrobus double-deck	290
Volvo Citybus double-deck	39
Volvo Olympian double-deck	42
Dennis Dart single-deck	111
Leyland National single-deck	45
Volvo B10B single-deck	13
Volvo B6LE single-deck	1
Dennis Dart SLF single-deck	44
Marshall minibus	14
Mercedes minibus	31
Optare Metrorider minibus	35

In peak service: 516

London United

London United Busways Ltd
Wellington Road, Twickenham TW2 5NX
Telephone: +44 181 977 6665 Fax: +44 181 943 2688
Managing Director: David Humphrey
Staff: 1,450

Current situation: This employee-owned company operates services in southwest London from five depots.
Developments: Has developed high-quality Airlink services to Heathrow airport following purchase of new Volvo Olympians in 1995. Latterly, low-floor Dennis SLFs have replaced wheelchair-accessible vehicles.

Fleet: 580 vehicles

AEC Routemaster double-deck	54
MCW Metrobus double-deck	172
Leyland Olympian double-deck	23
Leyland Titan double-deck	15
Volvo Olympian double-deck	10
Optare Delta single-deck	8
Leyland National single-deck	21
MAN/Optare Vecta single-deck	8
Dennis Dart single-deck	201
Leyland Lynx single-deck	6
Dennis Lance SLF single-deck	10
Dennis Dart SLF single-deck	6
MCW Metrorider minibus	30
Iveco minibus	8
Omni minibus	8

Metroline

Metroline Travel Ltd
118-122 College Road, Harrow HA1 1DB
Telephone: +44 181 861 4080 Fax: +44 181 427 3304
Managing Director: Declan O'Farrell
Staff:

Current situation: This employee-owned company operates services in northwest London from five depots.

Fleet: 474 vehicles

AEC Routemaster double-deck	52
MCW Metrobus double-deck	164
Volvo Olympian double-deck	22
Dennis Dart single-deck	134
Dennis Lance SLF single-deck	14
Dennis Lance	31
MCW Metrorider minibus	1
Optare Starrider minibus	29
Coaches	27

MTL London

MTL London Northern Bus Company
3rd Floor, Hillhouse, 17-19 Highgate Hill, London N19 5NA
Telephone: +44 171 561 6900 Fax: +44 171 561 9220
Managing Director: Bob Dawson
Staff:

Current situation: This company, a subsidiary of Liverpool-based MTL Trust Holdings, operates services in north London from two depots.
Developments: Purchased London Suburban Buses of Edmonton in 1995 and has integrated the two companies' services. Also acquired R&I Tours which has been absorbed into the bus operation, though the coach fleet continues to trade separately.

Fleet: 476 vehicles

AEC Routemaster double-deck	65
MCW Metrobus double-deck	193
Leyland Titan double-deck	17
Scania double-deck	10
Auwaerter double-deck	1
Volvo Olympian double-deck	10
Leyland Olympian double-deck	20
Dennis Dart single-deck	42
Mercedes minibus	34
MCW Metrorider minibus	9
MAN/Optare Vecta single-deck	5
DAF SB220 single-deck	3
MAN single-deck	12
Optare Metrorider minibus	19
Iveco minibus	7
Marshall minibus	1
Coaches	12
Minicoaches	16

South London

South London Transport Ltd
799 London Road, Thornton Heath CR7 6AW
Telephone: +44 181 684 1023 Fax: +44 181 684 1004
Managing Director: Stephen Clayton
Staff: 1,900

Current situation: This subsidiary of the Cowie Group operates services in south London.

Fleet: 434 vehicles

AEC Routemaster double-deck	64
Leyland Titan double-deck	74
Leyland Olympian double-deck	161
MCW Metrobus double-deck	75
Dennis Dart single-deck	25
MCW Metrorider minibus	23
Mercedes minibus	12

Stagecoach East London

East London Bus & Coach Company Ltd
16-20 Clements Road, Ilford IG1 1BA
Telephone: +44 181 553 3420 Fax: +44 181 478 2315
Managing Director: Roger Bowker
Staff: 1,900

Current situation: Operates services in east London from six depots.

Fleet: 604 vehicles

AEC Routemaster double-deck	61
Leyland Titan	312
Scania double-deck	50
Optare Spectra double-deck	1
Optare Delta single-deck	26
Dennis Dart single-deck	77
Scania low-floor single-deck	16
MCW Metrorider minibus	31
Optare Starrider minibus	30

F E Thorpe operates the Stationlink shuttle with low-floor Optare Excels ***1997***

Stagecoach Selkent

South East London & Kent Bus Company Ltd
180 Bromley Road, Catford, London SE6 2XA
Telephone: +44 181 695 0707 Fax: +44 181 695 9232
Chairman: Roger Bowker
Staff:

Current situation: Operates services in south London from four depots.

Fleet: 387 vehicles

AEC Routemaster double-deck	1
Leyland Olympian double-deck	87
Leyland Titan double-deck	128
Volvo Olympian double-deck	50
Dennis Dart single-deck	21
Dennis Lance single-deck	28
Iveco minibus	17
Mercedes minibus	22
MCW Metrorider minibus	2
Optare minibus	31

Capital Citybus

Walthamstow Citybus Ltd
Chequers Lane, Dagenham RM9 6QD
Telephone: +44 181 517 9924 Fax: +44 181 595 3369
Managing Director: Leon Daniels
Staff: 548

Current situation: Formerly owned by Citybus of Hong Kong, the company was sold to its management in 1996. It built up operations through winning franchised LT contracts for both conventional and mobility services. Some commercial work is also undertaken.

Fleet: 249 vehicles

Volvo Olympian double-deck	30
Dennis Dominator double-deck	53
MCW Metrobus double-deck	50
Leyland Olympian double-deck	52
AEC Routemaster double-deck	1
Leyland DAB articulated	2
Volvo B6 single-deck	15
Optare Excel single-deck	4
Leyland National single-deck	13
Dennis Dart single-deck	1
Optare Metrorider single-deck	15
Mercedes single-deck	13

Kentish Bus

Kentish Bus & Coach Co Ltd
Invicta House, Armstrong Road, Maidstone ME15 6TY
Telephone: +44 1622 697000 Fax: +44 1622 697001
Managing Director: John Piper

Current situation: Sold to the Cowie Group in 1996, the company operates an extensive commercial network in northwest Kent, as well as LT contracted services.

Fleet: 347 vehicles

AEC Routemaster double-deck	24
Leyland Atlantean double-deck	25
Leyland Olympian double-deck	74
Volvo B10M double-deck	12
Volvo Olympian double-deck	8
Leyland National single-deck	16
Leyland Lynx single-deck	15
Dennis Dart single-deck	64
Volvo B6 single-deck	12
Scania low-floor single-deck	10
MCW Metrorider minibus	18
Talbot Pullman minibus	21
Optare Metrorider midibus	21
Mercedes minibus	4
Ford Transit minibus	3
Freight Rover minibus	2
Leyland Tiger coach	11
Volvo B10M coach	4
DAF SB3000 coach	3

Grey Green

Grey Green Coaches
53 Stamford Hill, London N16 5TD
Telephone: +44 181 800 8018 Fax: +44 181 700 3900
Managing Director: John Pycroft

Current situation: Formerly a coach operator, Grey Green is a subsidiary of the Cowie Group. Operates extensive bus network in central and east London, including a number of LT contracts, and commuter services from north Kent and Essex.

Fleet: 182 vehicles

Volvo double-deck	55
Leyland Olympian double-deck	15
Scania double-deck	14
MCW Metrobus double-deck	14
Leyland Lynx single-deck	9
Volvo single-deck	20
DAF Ikarus single-deck	6
Dennis Dart single-deck	10
Volvo coach	19
Scania coach	4
DAF coach	16

Suburban bus

Current situation: Bus service in suburban areas around London are provided by six main companies and several smaller operators. Unlike London itself, bus operations in these areas were deregulated in 1986. For history see *JUTS 1989*.

Between them the companies provide an extensive network of local bus services, including many routes feeding stations on the rail network in London's outer suburban centres such as Watford, Croydon, Bromley, Uxbridge, Enfield and Romford, and towns further afield.

London Underground

(address as for LT)
Chair: Peter Ford
Managing Director: Denis Tunnicliffe
Director of Passenger Services: Hugh Sumner
Director of Engineering: David Hornby
Director of Development: David Bailey
Staff: 16,000

Type of operation: Full metro, first line opened 1863

Passenger journeys: (1993/94) 735 million
(1994/95) 764 million
(1995/96) 784 million
Train-km: (1993/94) 52.6 million
(1994/95) 54.8 million
(1995/96) 57.2 million

Route length: 392 km
in tunnel: 171 km
Number of lines: 12
Number of stations: 261 (including 21 managed by Railtrack)
Gauge: 1,435 mm
Track: Running rail, 47 kg/m BH and 54 kg/m FB; conductor rail (open and subsurface), 74 kg/m FB and 53 kg/m FB; conductor rail (tube tunnel), 64 kg/m rectangular; conventional sleepers on ballast (concreted in tube tunnels)
Tunnel: Bored single-track (tube) and cut-and-cover double-track; 5 lines cut-and-cover, remainder bored tunnel
Electrification: 630 V DC, third and fourth rail

Service: Peak in central area, 2 min
Revenue control: Fully automated system with self-service machines at nearly all stations; automatic checking on entry and exit at all central area and some

Central line metro stock at Bank ***1995***

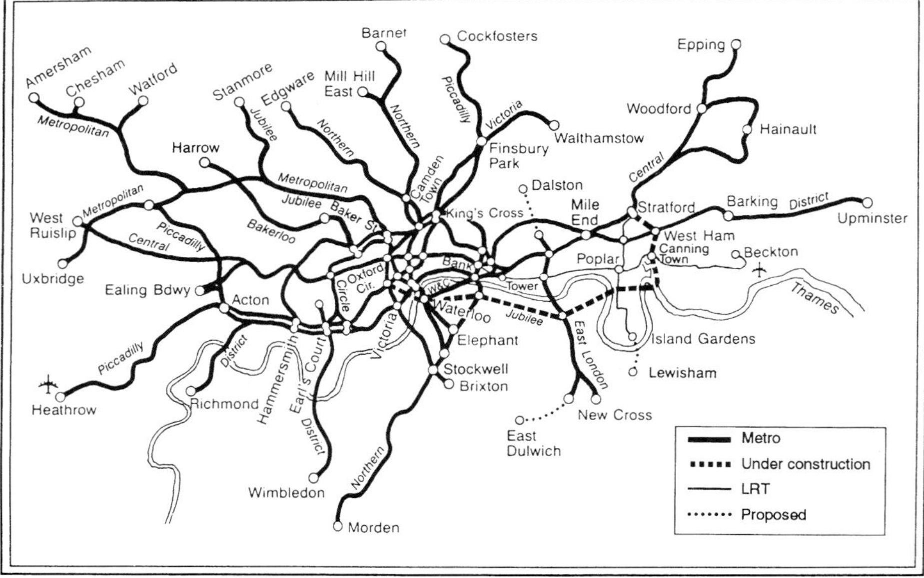

London's metro system and light rail line

suburban stations; random on-train inspection; penalty fare
One-person operation: All lines except Northern; Victoria line has full automatic train control ATO/ATP
Surveillance: CCTV at almost all stations
Operational control: Two-way radio on all lines
Operating costs financed by: Fares 125% (before depreciation and renewals)

Rolling stock: 3,922 cars

Tube stock (small profile)	
Metro-Cammell	
(1959/62) Northern line	M410 T164
(1972) Mk I/II Bakerloo/Northern lines	M238 T175
(1967/72) Victoria line (ATO fitted)	M172 T172
(1973) Piccadilly line	M349 T174
(1983) Jubilee line	M126 T63
ABB Transportation (1992) Central/W&C lines	M700
Surface stock (normal profile)	
Cravens A60/62 Metropolitan/E London lines	M226 T227
Metro-Cammell C69/C77 (1969/77) District/ Circle/Hammersmith lines	M138 T138
D78 (1978) District line	M300 T150

On order: 59 six-car trains being delivered for the Jubilee line and 106 six-car trains for the Northern line from GEC Alsthom

Developments: Construction is in progress of the 16 km extension of the Jubilee line from Green Park to Stratford via London Bridge and the Docklands development area. Part of the funding is being provided by the private sector. The Jubilee line's new rolling stock was expected to enter service in February 1997, but opening of the extension has been delayed until mid-1998.

Modernisation of the Central line, with new trains, signalling and ATO, is nearing completion. Refurbishment of Bakerloo line trains has been completed, and work on the Metropolitan and Piccadilly line fleets is in progress. The first new cars for the Northern line were also expected in service at the beginning of 1997. These are being built on a leasing and maintenance contract arranged under the government's private finance initiative. GEC Alsthom is financing construction of the 106 trains, and will maintain them at Northern line depots, under a 20-year service contract valued at £40 million annually. The Northern is also being equipped with track-to-train CCTV to enable one-person operation.

A substantial backlog of engineering work was being tackled in 1996/97. Reopening of the East London line, closed for complete refurbishment in 1995, is delayed until 1998, while portions of the Northern and Bakerloo lines were closed in 1996 and 1997. Several major station refurbishment and rebuilding projects were also in progress, at Bank, London Bridge, Westminster and Waterloo. Many of these projects were likely to be delayed because of the financial crisis affecting LU at the beginning of 1997 (see above).

Steps were taken to obtain powers to extend the Piccadilly line to the proposed Terminal 5 at Heathrow airport, and to extend the East London line northwards to Dalston. In the 25-year plan announced in 1995, the long-proposed Chelsea—Hackney line reappeared as part of a three-route cross-city regional metro, along with the east-west Crossrail and north-south Thameslink 2000 plans.

Suburban rail

Type of operation: Suburban heavy rail

Passenger journeys: (To and from central London stations)
(1992/93) 401,000 daily
(1993/94) 382,000 daily
(1994/95) 392,000 daily

Current situation: Suburban services run on all routes out of London to a distance of over 100 km, with an extensive network of inner-suburban routes serving east and northeast London, and the area south of the River Thames which is poorly served by metro. Much of the network is electrified – south of the Thames at 660/750 V DC, the remainder mostly at 25 kV 50 Hz. Operations are franchised to 10 private-sector companies. They run over track owned by the privatised infrastructure company Railtrack, with trains owned by the privatised rolling stock leasing companies.

Trains run generally from about 05.00 to 24.00. Off-peak the service interval is 10-30 min, stepped up in the peak hours to every few minutes at some stations. Fares are graduated, though zonal all-modes passes are available within Greater London, along with conventional season tickets. Most stations have self-service ticket machines; inspection is manual.

The area served by the 10 train operating companies created in 1994 extends far beyond the London commuting area, and separate data for London suburban operations is not available. Figures given in the entries below cover the companies' entire operations. An eleventh company, Gatwick Express, runs the dedicated service linking Victoria station in central London with Gatwick airport (43 km).

Developments: South West Trains was the first British Rail train operating company to be franchised, passing to the bus operator Stagecoach in February 1996. Franchises for all 10 railways had been awarded by March 1997.

A major London scheme, Thameslink 2000, is one of the two Railtrack infrastructure projects to be accorded priority by the government. This proposal would raise capacity of the existing Thameslink cross-city line to provide a 5 min service, and comprises construction of a flyover on the approaches to London Bridge station, enlarged stations at Blackfriars and St Pancras, and provison of a connection to the Great Northern suburban lines in the north. Funding for the £650 million scheme was approved in February 1996. Completion is scheduled for 2002.

North London Railways

North London Railways
Melton House, 65-67 Clarendon Road, Watford WD1 1DP
Telephone: +44 1923 207777 Fax: +44 1923 207023
Managing Director: David Watters
Staff: 1,171

Passenger journeys: (1993/94) 32 million
(1995/96) 100,000 daily

Current situation: Operates outer-suburban route running north from London to Milton Keynes and Northampton (electrified 25 kV), along with several local lines in north London (750 V DC third rail, dual 750 V/25 kV, diesel) and one rural route; total eight routes, 278 km, 97 stations. Operation is franchised to the National Express group.

Rolling stock: 26 dmu and 217 emu cars

Class 117/121 dmu (1959/60)	M26
Class 313 AC/DC emu (1976/77)	M46 T23
Class 321 AC emu (1989/90)	M37 T111

WAGN

West Anglia & Great Northern Railway
Hertford House, 1 Cranwood Street, London EC2A 2AA
Telephone: +44 171 928 5151 Fax: +44 171 713 2116
Managing Director: Ken Bird
Staff: 1,750

Passenger journeys: (1993/94) 47 million
(1994/95) 45 million

Current situation: WAGN operates 15 routes serving 104 stations running north from London to Peterborough, Cambridge and King's Lynn, extending to 415 km; mostly electrified at 25 kV DC. Operation is franchised to Prism Rail.

Rolling stock: 509 emu cars

Class 313 AC/DC emu (1976/77)	M86 T43
Class 315 AC emu (1980/81)	M36 T36
Class 317 AC emu (1981/82)	M72 T216
Class 322 AC emu Stansted airport (1990)	M5 T15

Great Eastern

Great Eastern Railway
Hamilton House, 3 Appold Street, London EC2A 2AA
Telephone: +44 171 928 5151 Fax: +44 171 922 4847
Managing Director: Bob Breakwell
Staff: 1,600

Passenger journeys: (1994/95) 28 million

Current situation: Runs extensive suburban services in east London and Essex, electrified 25 kV AC.
Developments: At the end of 1996, the FirstBus group was awarded a seven-year franchise to operate Great Eastern.

Rolling stock: 576 emu cars

Class 312 AC emu (1976/77/78)	M24 T72
Class 315 AC emu (1980/81)	M86 T86
Class 321 AC emu (1989/90)	M77 T231

LTS Rail

LTS Rail Ltd
Central House, Clifftown Road, Southend-on-Sea SS1 1AB
Telephone: +44 1702 357889 Fax: +44 1702 357823
Managing Director:

Passenger journeys: (1993/94) 23 million

Current situation: Running local trains between London, Southend and Shoeburyness, LTS serves 25 stations over 129 route-km, electrified 25 kV AC. It is operated on a seven-year franchise by Prism Rail.
Developments: Resignalling is in progress and a new fleet of 44 four-car trains was ordered from Adtranz in early 1997.

Rolling stock: 336 emu cars

Class 302 AC emu (1958/60)	M28 T84
Class 310/0 AC emu (1965/67)	M35 T105
Class 312 AC emu (1976/78)	M21 T63

Connex South Eastern

Connex Rail Ltd
Friars Bridge Court, 41-45 Blackfriars Road, London SE1 8NZ
Telephone: +44 171 620 5000 Fax: +44 171 620 5550
Managing Director: Richard Fearn
Staff: 4,443

Passenger journeys: (1993/94) 103 million

New Class 365 emu in Connex South Eastern livery ***1997***

Current situation: Runs 17 groups of routes extending to 720 route-km, serving southeast London and Kent; electrified 750 V DC third rail. It is operated on a 15-year franchise by Connex Rail.

Connex was hoping to introduce the long-awaited Class 365 emus on longer distance services in early 1997.

Rolling stock: 1,510 emu cars

Class 365/5 AC/DC emu (1994/95)	M32 T32
Class 411 DC emu (1958/60/63)	M212 T212
Class 421 DC emu (1964/65)	M21 T63
Class 423 DC emu (1967/74)	M66 T198
Class 465/0/1 DC emu (1993/94/95)	M194 T194
Class 465/2 DC emu (1993)	M100 T100
Class 466 DC emu (1993)	M43 T43

Connex South Central

Connex Rail Ltd
Stephenson House, 2 Cherry Orchard Road, Croydon CR9 6JB
Telephone: +44 181 667 2500 Fax: +44 181 667 2555
Managing Director: Geoff Harrison-Mee
Staff: 2,908

Passenger journeys: (1993/94) 83 million
(1995/96) 83 million

Current situation: Routes serve south London, Surrey and Sussex, extending to 687 km on 22 routes, electrified 750 V DC third rail.
Developments: With takeover of the former Network SouthCentral on a seven-year franchise in 1996, Connex launched a revamp of its inner-suburban services under the South London Metro banner, with improved frequencies at many stations and a new livery.

Rolling stock: 41 dmu and 864 emu cars

Class 205 dmu (1956/62)	M9 T18
Class 205/2 dmu (1956/62)	M1 T2
Class 207 dmu (1956/62)	M1 T1
Class 207/2 dmu (1962)	M3 T6
Class 319/0 AC/DC emu (1987/90)	M20 T60
Class 421/3/4/6 DC emu (1964/72)	M78 T234
Class 422 DC emu (1966/72)	M15 T45
Class 422/0 DC emu (1966/72)	M8 T24
Class 423 DC emu (1967/74)	M37 T111
Class 455 DC emu (1982/84)	M46 T138
Class 456 DC emu (1990/91)	M24 T24

In peak service: 705 cars

Thameslink

Thameslink Rail Ltd
Friars Bridge Court, 41-45 Blackfriars Road, London SE1 8NZ
Telephone: +44 171 928 5151 Fax: +44 171 620 5550
Managing Director: Cliff Perry

Passenger journeys: (1993/94) 23 million
(1995/96) 25.6 million

Current situation: Operates the cross-city link from Bedford in the north to Brighton in the south, plus a south London suburban service; electrified 750 V DC/25 kV AC. Operation is franchised to the Govia consortium.

Rolling stock: 264 emu cars

Class 319/0/1 AC/DC emu (1987/88)	M66 T198

South West Trains

South West Trains
Friars Bridge Court, 41-45 Blackfriars Road, London SE1 8NZ
Telephone: +44 171 928 5151 Fax: +44 171 620 5550
Managing Director: Brian Cox

Passenger journeys: (1993/94) 95 million
(1995/96) 90 million

Current situation: Serves the southwest London suburbs, Surrey, Hampshire, Dorset and Devon; extending to 940 route-km with 203 stations; mostly electrified at 750 V DC third rail.
Developments: In February 1996, SWT was franchised for a seven-year period to a consortium headed by the bus operator Stagecoach. In early 1997, SWT found itself short of drivers when a staff reduction programme misfired, and was forced to cancel a large number of services. The company's poor performance in February 1997 caused the Director of Passenger Rail Franchising to impose a penalty of £750,000 and threaten withdrawal of SWT's franchise.

Rolling stock: 66 dmu and 956 emu cars

Class 159 dmu (1992)	M66
Class 412 DC emu (1964/65)	M14 T14
Class 421 DC emu (1970)	M34 T102
Class 423 DC emu (1967/74)	M77 T231
Class 442 DC emu (1988/89)	M24 T96
Class 455/7/8/9 DC emu (1982/84/85)	M91 T273

Thames Trains

Victory Railway Holdings
Venture House, 37-43 Blagrave Street, Reading RG1 1RY
Telephone: +44 1734 575977 Fax: +44 1734 579648
Director: Roger McDonald

Passenger journeys: (1993/94) 21 million

DLR trains at Canary Wharf ***1995***

Current situation: Trains run westwards from London serving the Thames valley, Reading, Newbury, Oxford and Banbury. Thames is operated on a seven-and-a-half year franchise by the Victory Railway Holdings consortium.
Developments: Under its franchise agreement, Victory will increase its Oxford service from hourly to half-hourly in 1998 and run more trains on the Newbury line.

Rolling stock: 168 dmu cars

Class 165/0 dmu (1991/92)	M14
Class 165/0/1 dmu (1992)	M91
Class 166 dmu (1992/93)	M63

Chiltern

The Chiltern Railway Co Ltd/M40 Trains
Western House, 14 Rickfords Hill, Aylesbury HP20 2RX
Telephone: +44 1296 332100 Fax: +44 1296 332126
Director: Adrian Shooter
Staff: 300

Passenger journeys: (1993/94) 5.2 million
(1995/96) 7.5 million

Current situation: Trains run northwest to Aylesbury by two routes, Banbury and Birmingham, extending to 245 km.
Developments: With the takeover by a management buyout team in 1996, Chiltern ordered four three-car trains for its planned fast service between London and Birmingham.

Rolling stock: 79 dmu cars

Class 165/0 dmu (1991/92)	M79

In peak service: 75 cars

Docklands Light Railway

Docklands Light Railway Limited
PO Box 154, London E14 0DX
Telephone: +44 171 363 9500 Fax: +44 171 363 9532
Managing Director: Malcolm Hutchinson
Operations Director: Jim Gates
Staff: 418

Type of operation: Automated light metro, opened 1987

Passenger journeys: (1993/94) 8.3 million
(1994/95) 11.5 million
(1995/96) 14.5 million
Train-km: (1993/94) 1.1 million
(1994/95) 1.5 million
(1995/96) 1.9 million

Route length: 21.7 km
Number of lines: 3
Number of stations: 28
Gauge: 1,435 mm
Track: Running rail, 40 kg/m FB and 56 kg/m FB; conductor rail 3 kg/m shrouded steel/aluminium composite; mixture of concrete sleepers on ballast and concrete slab track
Electrification: 750 V DC shrouded third rail, underside contact

Service: Peak 2 min on city routes
First/last train: 05.30/00.43
Fare structure: As LT zonal system (see above)
Revenue control: Self-service machines at all mostly unstaffed stations with on-train checks
Train control: ATO, ATP and ATS; there are no lineside signals or driving cabs, but each vehicle has emergency driving positions at the car ends. The original signalling and control system has been replaced by Alcatel's Seltrac system to cope with higher train frequencies
Surveillance: CCTV monitoring of unstaffed stations from control centre with video recording of incidents; passenger alarms on platforms
Arrangements for elderly/disabled: Fully accessible to wheelchairs via ramps or lifts

Rolling stock: 70 articulated cars

BN B90 (1990/91)	M23
BN B92 (1992)	M47

Current situation: DLR is owned by the London Docklands Development Corporation. Its trains are

driverless but carry a Train Captain whose job in normal circumstances is to close doors and initiate the start from each station, as well as making ticket checks and assisting passengers.
Developments: Approval was granted in 1993 for a cross-river extension from Island Gardens to Greenwich and Lewisham (4.2 km, seven stations). The project is being financed and built under the government's private finance initiative by a private-sector consortium City Greenwich Lewisham Rail Link. Construction of the extension, which includes a 1.1 km tunnel beneath the River Thames and 800 m elevated, started in late 1996. Opening is scheduled for 2000.

From April 1997, operation and maintenance of DLR was transferred to Docklands Railway Management Ltd on a seven-year franchise.

London rail/light rail plans

Current situation: The effects of recession on patronage and finance, and more recently the moves towards privatisation, have combined to put most recent proposals in abeyance. Apart from the projects outlined below, there are more than a dozen schemes for various guided modes in the suburbs. Amongst them are extensions of metro services along BR suburban tracks, and several light rail schemes.

A 1996 study by London Transport concluded that both CrossRail (see below) and the Chelsea-Hackney metro line were necessary to meet forecast demand levels for the early years of the next century.
CrossRail: This is a joint LU/BR project to connect suburban lines now terminating at Paddington and Marylebone in west London with those at Liverpool Street in the east, with the intention of providing RER-style service. In April 1996 the project was shelved until the beginning of the next century.
Heathrow Express: A 25 kV electrified link to Heathrow airport is under construction for mid-1998 opening. The project, which comprises construction of a 7 km branch from the London—Bristol main line and electrification thence to London's Paddington station, is largely funded by the airports authority BAA. A fleet of 56 cars is on order from Siemens Transportation Systems, comprising 14 four-car trains of Class 332.

BAA has made studies of six other rail links to Heathrow in connection with its bid to build a fifth terminal at the airport and its associated initiative to encourage use of public transport. Included in the plans is possible construction of a main line station adjacent to the airport. BAA has also decided to start a second Express service to St Pancras in 1999.

Croydon Tramlink

TCL Ltd
1st Floor, Macmillan House, Paddington Station, London W2 ITY
Telephone: +44 171 706 0877 Fax: +44 171 706 1300
Chairman: Bob Dorey
Project Director: Ian Kendall

Current situation: Construction of the 28 km Tramlink light rail scheme started in late 1996 following signing of a 99-year concession agreement with the TCL Ltd consortium. Members of the consortium include Bombardier Eurorail, bus operator Centrewest and construction companies Amey and Sir Robert McAlpine.

Promoted jointly by London Transport and Croydon Council, the route links central Croydon with Wimbledon, New Addington, Beckenham Junction and Elmers End. It makes considerable use of existing or disused railways, with about 3 km of on-street in central Croydon; 1,435 mm gauge, electrified 750 V DC. The fleet of 24 cars will be built by Bombardier Eurorail's UK subsidiary Bombardier Prorail.

As well as some disused right-of-way, Tramlink will take over the existing suburban rail route between Croydon and Wimbledon, on which several new stations will be built; there will be a total of 33 stations. Public service is expected to start in late 1999.

There are proposals for several extensions, including a loop to serve the Purley Way shopping area and a line to Sutton.

UPDATED

LOS ANGELES

Population: 3.6 million; 9.2 million in Los Angeles County; 14.5 million in Southern California urbanised area
Public transport: Bus services throughout most of Southern California, light rail and metro, operated by Metropolitan Transportation Authority, also responsible for administration, planning and rail construction. Separate authority operates commuter rail network. Sixteen municipal or sub-regional operators provide services in Los Angeles County, while many of 88 incorporated cities in LA County have contracted local circulator routes. Some bus routes contracted out to private operators. Separate transit authorities operate in Orange, Riverside, San Bernardino and Ventura counties

MTA's Gateway transit centre at Union station, opened in October 1995 ***1996***

MTA

Los Angeles County Metropolitan Transportation Authority
PO Box 194, Los Angeles, CA 90053, USA
Telephone: +1 213 972 6000 Fax: +1 213 244 6013
Chair: Larry Zarian
Chief Executive Officer: Linda Bohlinger
Deputy Chief Executive Officer:
Executive Officers
Planning & Programming: James de la Loza
Operations: Ellen Levine
Construction:
Director of Engineering: Ted Lewis
Director, External Relations: Mark Littmann
Staff: 8,320

Passenger boardings:(All modes)
(1993) 391.3 million
(1994) 396.6 million
(1995) 361.5 million

Current situation: The MTA was created in 1993 by merger of the Southern California Rapid Transit District and Los Angeles County Transportation Commission. MTA's divisions have responsibility for operating the bus and metro/light rail networks (former RTD), for constructing the metro and light rail network (former LACTC Rail Construction Corp), for overall planning of the region's public transport needs (former RTD and LACTC), and for administration of the entire network.

Serving a 5,928 km² area, MTA runs the third largest bus system in the USA, two light rail lines, and the metro.
Developments: A revised 20-year plan was adopted in 1995. This was designed to take account of lower projected revenues than those forecast in the boom years of the late 1980s. At that time, planners had hoped to create an elaborate mass transit network over a 30-year period, but the lingering recession, coupled with cutbacks in California's defence and aerospace industries, forced a re-evaluation of projected sales tax, farebox and bond revenue. In addition, MTA's reserve fund had been depleted to make up for revenue shortfalls.

The plan's $72.4 billion price tag will pay for new buses and improved bus services, construction of more HOV lanes, and promotion of ride-sharing and telecommuting. It also includes three metro extensions and the Pasadena light rail line.

At the same time, MTA adopted a cost-cutting package which would save $443 million over 20 years. Most of the savings come from running fewer metro trains off-peak and reducing train-length during the peak.

Contracting-out of bus services started in 1996, when seven routes were taken over by ATE Management & Service Co for a three-year term. Cost savings are put at $4.5 million a year.

The methanol-powered bus fleet is now being converted to ethanol on account of poor performance and higher fuel and maintenance costs. A further 544 buses were being delivered or on order at the end of 1996.

The need to meet new clean air regulations has fostered the Advanced Technology Transit Bus project (ATTB) (for details see *JUTS 1996-97*), which is being supervised by MTA on behalf of 20 transit undertakings. The first operating prototype was unveiled by prime contractor Northrop Grumman in October 1996, and six will be field tested in several cities during 1998.

In-service testing began in 1993 of a stored-value fare collection system built by GFI to MTA's specifications. Initial trials involving 28 buses of Culver City Municipal Bus Lines (see below) were later extended to 200 Foothill Transit and 55 Montebello vehicles. Customer acceptance has been good, but plans for county-wide adoption were shelved due to lack of funds and opposition amongst MTA officers. There was talk of reviving the plans in 1996.

Work continues on the 31.4 km HOV lanes on the Harbor freeway, scheduled to open in 1997.

MTA Operating Division

General Managers
Southern Region: Ralph Wilson
Northern Region: Jon Hillmer
Western Region: Rick Hittinger (Acting)
Eastern Region: Tony Chavira
Staff: 7,186

Bus

Passenger boardings: (1993) 375.8 million
(1994) 379.7 million
(1995) 335 million
Vehicle-km: (1993) 155.2 million
(1994) 157.3 million
(1995) 139.7 million

existing lines, with the aim of providing rail service for all communities of more than 30,000 population.

Rolling stock: 735 emu cars

Class 440 three-car emu	M32 T64
Class 446 three-car emu	M286 T143
Class 470 three-car emu	M26 T52
Class 451 three-car bi-level emu	M40 T80
Class 442 two-car emu metre-gauge	M6 T6

Private bus

Passenger journeys: (1993) 169.1 million
(1994) 174.7 million
(1995) 191.6 million
Vehicle-km: (1993) 75.5 million
(1994) 78 million
(1995) 89.4 million

Current situation: A total of 41 private operators provide monopoly services, either urban routes in the outer municipalities or interurban within the conurbation. All services are co-ordinated by CRTM.

Main operators are De Blas, Martín, Autocares Urbanos del Sur, Llorente, Interbus and Continental Auto.

Number of routes: 186 suburban, 7 night and 45 urban (in municipalities other than Madrid)
Route length: (One way) 14,436 km
Fleet: 958 vehicles

Pegaso	447
Scania	263
Setra	16
Volvo	209
Others	23

Average age of fleet: 5.6 years

Most intensive service: 3 min
One-person operation: All routes
Fare structure: Zonal or distance-based, according to route; CRTM monthly and annual travelcards integrated with urban and suburban buses, and suburban rail
Fare collection: Driver sells single tickets; prepurchase 10-journey tickets, CRTM travelcards
Bus Priority: 12.5 km exclusive bus and HOV double lanes in northwest corridor, also 4 km bus-only lane
Operating costs financed by: Fares 100%

UPDATED

Rebuilt Class 440/470 emu of RENFE at Vilaverde Baja, south of Atocha ***1996***

MAGDEBURG

Population: 274,000
Public transport: Bus, tramway and ferry services provided by municipal company; S-Bahn operated by DB; regional bus services

MVB

Magdeburger Verkehrsbetriebe AG (MVB)
PO Box 3565, 39010 Magdeburg, Germany
Telephone: +49 391 5480 Fax: +49 391 543 0046
Directors: Wolfgang Madzek
Dr-Ing Herbert Preil
Operations Manager: Hans-Dieter Haake
Staff: 1,079

Passenger journeys: (1993) 91.5 million
(1994) 65 million
(1995) 63.2 million

Operating costs financed by: Fares 48%, subsidy/grants 52%

Developments: A co-operation agreement concluded between MVB, DB and bus operators from four surrounding counties in 1996 envisages introduction of joint timetables and tariffs.

Bus

Passenger journeys: (1995) 13.4 million
Vehicle-km: (1993) 3.1 millon
(1994) 2.9 million
(1995) 3.2 million

Number of routes: 18
Route length: 108 km
Fleet: 63 buses

MAN NM152 midibus	6
MAN NL202 low-floor	8
MAN NG272 low-floor articulated	12
Mercedes O405N low-floor	24
Mercedes O405GN low-floor articulated	13

In peak service: 56

Most intensive service: 8 min
One-person operation: All routes
Fare collection: By driver
Fare structure: Transferable daily, weekly, monthly and annual passes, also valid in certain other cities by mutual agreement
Arrangements for elderly/disabled: Free travel for disabled, reimbursed by government
Average distance between stops: 570 m
Average speed: 21.1 km/h

Tramway

Type of operation: Conventional tramway

Passenger journeys: (1995) 51.4 million
Car-km: (1993) 14.8 million
(1994) 13.7 million
(1995) 13.2 million

Number of routes: 10
Route length: 59 km
Gauge: 1,435 mm
Electrification: 600 V DC, overhead

Service: Peak 10 min
First/last car:
Average distance between stops: 540 m
Average speed: 19.2 km/h

Rolling stock: 303 cars

ČKD Tatra T4D/B4D 4-axle (1968/86)	M120 T57
(modernised 1991/94)	M64 T20
ČKD Tatra T6A2 4-axle (1989)	M7 T3
(modernised 1995)	M4 T3
LHB NGT8D 8-axle low-floor articulated (1994/95)	M25

In peak service: 227
On order: Further 100 low-floor tramcars from Linke-Hofmann-Busch/Waggonbau Dessau/Adtranz, but deliveries were stopped in 1996; M10 and T11 are expected by 2000

Developments: New workshops under construction for 1999 completion. Following cessation of new trancar deliveries (see above), Tatra cars are now programmed to remain in service until 2015.

Ferry

Current situation: Four vessels ply two short cross-Elbe routes and operate excursions, carrying around 100,000 passengers a year.

DB

Deutsche Bahn AG, Geschäftsbereich Nahverkehr
Regionalbereich Sachsen-Anhalt
Ernst-Kamieth Strasse 2, 06112 Halle
Telephone: +49 345 215 3331 Fax: +49 345 215 5378

Current situation: S-Bahn services from Zielitz and Haldensleben feed into a single cross-city route extending to Schönebeck. Four fare zones.

Regional bus

Current situation: Services radiating from the city are provided by several independent and local government operators.

UPDATED

Refurbished Tatra T4D/B4D cars in MVB's new livery

MALAGA

Population: 600,000
Public transport: Local bus and midibus services provided by municipal company, with longer-distance services to neighbouring resorts in the hands of private operators; local rail service; light rail network planned

EMT

Empresa Malaguena de Transportes SAM
Camino de San Rafael s/n, 29006 Malaga, Spain
Telephone: +34 52 235 7271 Fax: +34 52 235 8807
Director General: Rafael Fernandez Barrera
Director of Operations: Manual Fernandez Andrade
Staff: 655

Developments: Introduction of split-shift working by drivers has allowed increased capacity at peak periods and stimulated an additional 1.5 million journeys. Routes which terminate at Muelle de Heredia may be diverted into the city centre, with the aim of increasing their patronage.

EMT would like to start replacement of its oldest vehicles and augment the fleet to meet growing demand, but finance is not available. Difficulties have been experienced with the electronic vehicle management system Siclic which uses satellite tracking; inadequate maintenance was the cause, and remedial action was taken in 1995.

Pegaso 6038 of EMT

Bus

Passenger journeys: (1992) 34.3 million
(1993) 33.4 million
(1994) 34.8 million
Vehicle-km: (1992) 7.5 million
(1993) 7.7 million
(1994) 8.6 million

Number of routes: 37, plus 2 night
Route length: 150 km
Fleet: 182 buses

Pegaso 5023	1
Pegaso 5062	6
Pegaso 5720	3
Pegaso 6038 citybus (1982/83/84/85/86)	107
Linea 90	6
Pegaso 6424	31
Pegaso 5317 midibus	28

Average age of fleet: 8 years

Most intensive service: 10 min
Fare structure: Flat
Fares collected on board: 33.2%; multijourney tickets 47.2%, passes for students and elderly 19.5%
Arrangements for elderly/disabled: Special Route 48 operated for disabled

Operating costs financed by: Fares and other commercial sources 63.5%, municipal subsidy 24.2%, state subsidy 9%

RENFE

Spanish National Railways (RENFE)
Final Avenida Pio XII, Madrid
Telephone: +34 1 606 6401 Fax: +34 1 315 0384
Managing Director, Suburban Operations:
Abelado Carrillo Jiménez
Director, Malaga: Rafael Rodríguez Rebollo
Staff: 122

Type of operation: Local railway

Passenger journeys: (1993) 7.1 million
(1994) 7.3 million
(1995) 7.3 million

Current situation: Electric trains (3 kV DC) run half-hourly from Malaga Centro-Alameda to Fuengirola and Alora, two routes totalling 68 km with 27 stations. A 30-min service runs to the airport on the Fuengirola line, which carries heavy tourist traffic.
Developments: A rolling programme of investment in stations is in progress, including provision of ticket barriers to reduce fraud.

Rolling stock: 8 three-car emus

Intermodal transport plan

Current situation: An intermodal transport plan for the city covering the period 1995-2007 has been approved by the Andalucia regional government. Pta113 billion has been allocated for infrastructure works (90 per cent) and new rolling stock. Upgrading of RENFE's Fuengirola line will involve four-tracking of the Malaga—Los Prados section and selective double-tracking elsewhere, permitting operation of a 15-min service. There will be improved access to the airport, and a new intermodal terminal created at Malaga central station. Pta2.2 billion will be spent on new trains. Integrated ticketing is to be introduced.

The plan also calls for development of a four-line light rail network running on reserved track. Initially, Line 1 will be operated by buses sharing reserved lanes with interurban services. Lines 2, 3 and 4 have been accorded priority. Line 2 will run to the north of the city, where demand is put at 94,500 passengers daily. Line 3 will link the hospital and university in the northwest (40,000 daily), while Line 4 will serve the western suburbs (54,000 daily).

UPDATED

MALMÖ

Population: 234,000
Public transport: Bus services provided by private operator Linjebuss under contract from the regional transport authority, Länstrafiken Malmöhus. Suburban and interurban bus and rail services also operated under contract

Linjebuss

Linjebuss Sverige AB
PO Box 3054, 200 22 Malmö, Sweden
Telephone: +46 40 343000 Fax: +46 40 303223
Managing Director: Ragnar Norbäck
Traffic Manager: Bo Fröjd
Staff: 630

Scania 113 of Linjebuss at the Stock Exchange ***1996***

Current situation: In 1991 the former municipal operator Malmö Lokaltrafik became a limited company in the ownership of the city. In 1993 the contract for operation of city services was put out to tender and awarded to Linjebuss. As a result, Linjebuss purchased ML, and commenced operations at the beginning of 1994. It continues as the operator of bus services under contract from the transport authority Länstrafiken Malmöhus, which acts as purchaser of all public transport.

Five levels of service are provided — a Head network, linking residential areas, local shopping centres and the city centre; an Express network running mainly at commuting times; a Feeder network providing connections into Head and Express services from sparsely populated areas; Service-Bus operated by low-floor minibuses for elderly and slightly disabled passengers, running on special routes that pass close to main entrances of shops and offices to minimise walking distances; and a Special service for major events and festivals.

Bus

Passenger journeys: (1992) 26 million
(1993) 20.3 million
(1994) 20.3 million
Vehicle-km: (1990) 11 million
(1992) 10.5 million
(1994) 10.3 million

Number of routes: 35
Route length: 566 km

Fleet: 195 vehicles

Scania CR112 (1981)	26
Volvo B10R (1983/84)	33
Scania CR112 CNG-powered (1984)	1
Scania N112 (1984/86)	42
Scania CN113 (1988)	7
Scania CN113 CNG-powered (1988)	9
Neoplan N4007 (1989)	5
Mercedes O405G articulated (1990)	10
Scania CN113 (1991)	8
Mercedes O405G articulated (1992)	7
Scania CN113 (1992)	10
Scania CN113AL articulated (1992)	6
Scania CN113AL articulated (1994)	1
Volvo B10BLE CNG-powered (1995)	30

In peak service: 1,719

Most intensive service: 10 min
One-person operation: All routes
Fare collection: Payment to driver, or prepurchase magnetic cards (also sold on board) and monthly passes
Fare structure: Flat; prepurchase cards
Fares collected on board: 45.3% of journeys, 61% of total fares
Fare evasion control: Inspectors
Operational control: Route inspectors/mobile radio
Arrangements for elderly/disabled: 2 seats with folding arms reserved on each bus for disabled passengers. Buses with 100 mm kneeling capability and low split step arrangement. Low-floor minibus Service-Bus network operates route with stops close to entrances, reducing walking distance
Average peak-hour speed: 19.1 km/h
Average distance between stops: 400 m
Integration with other modes: One route connects with ferry services to Denmark
Operating costs financed by: Fares 50%, other commercial sources 6%, subsidy/grants 44%
Subsidy from: Local taxes

SSK

Sydvästra Skaånes Kommunalförbund
PO Box 2500, 200 12 Malmö
Telephone: +46 40 342249
Transport Manager: Lennert Serder

Type of operation: Suburban heavy rail

Passenger journeys: 4 million (annual)

Current situation: SSK contracts operation to Swedish State Railways (SJ) of suburban services over three routes totalling 130 km from Malmö to Höör, Landskrona and Helsingborg, electrified 15 kV 16⅔ Hz. About hourly off-peak, half-hourly Malmö—Lund (17 km). Zonal and monthly travelcards available for half or all system, monthly cards accepted on buses. Fares contribute 47% of income, local subsidy 53%.

Rolling stock: 18 two-car emus
ASEA X10 (1983/85/88) M18 T18

UPDATED

MANCHESTER

Population: City 451,000, county area 2.6 million
Public transport: Bus services in Greater Manchester metropolitan area are provided by 55 private companies operating about 1,000 vehicles, alongside the two GM Buses companies which are now subsidiaries of large UK bus groups. The PTE invites tenders for supply of loss-making and socially desirable bus services which are not provided by commercial operators. Light rail and local rail systems

Greater Manchester

Greater Manchester Buses North
Wallshaw Street, Oldham OL1 3TR
Telephone: +44 161 627 2929 Fax: +44 161 627 5845
Chair: Robbie Duncan
Managing Director: Alan Westwell
Director & General Manager: Rodney Dickinson
Finance Director: Nigel Barrett
Engineering Director: Richard Noble
Staff: 2,500

Current situation: Formed by the break-up of GM Buses in 1994, and was purchased by its staff through an employee share ownership plan. Operates extensive services throughout north Manchester from six depots. The company was acquired by the FirstBus group in 1996.
Developments: Acquired the business and services of Citibus Tours in 1995, and concluded an agreement with MTL to withdraw from services in Liverpool, in return for MTL withdrawal from Manchester. Also took over some services and staff of Bee Line in the east Manchester area. Commenced a programme of fleet renewal which included low-floor purchases at the end of 1995. Over 100 new buses were delivered after the FirstBus take over, including Volvo low-floor single-decks.

GMN Volvo B6 sandwiched by two buses of Bee Line **1995**

Bus

Passenger journeys: (1994/95) 96 million

Number of routes: 500
Fleet: 1,006 vehicles

Leyland Lynx	4
Leyland National single-deck	19
Volvo B10M Citybus single-deck	1
Volvo B6 single-deck	44
Volvo B10B single-deck	60
Dennis Dart single-deck	53
Leyland Atlantean double-deck	311
Daimler Fleetline double-deck	92
MCW Metrobus double-deck	132
Leyland Olympian double-deck	165
Volvo Citybus double-deck	13
Renault/Dodge minibus	35
MCW Metrorider minibus	49
Iveco 59-12 minibus	9
Mercedes minibus	19

Most intensive service: 5 min
One-person operation: 100%
Fare collection: Payment on bus with ticket issue by driver
Fare structure: Stage, multijourney ticket; range of prepurchase weekly passes including add-on to rail season tickets and all modes
Fares collected on board: 73.5%
Fare evasion control: Revenue inspectors charging higher fares
Arrangements for elderly/disabled: On ordinary services low flat fare charged. Semi-fixed route accessible services in the Stockport and south Manchester areas operate under the 'Localine' identity; vehicles designed

Mosley Street Metrolink station **1995**

New Scania N113 on Mayne's Premier Service route to Mossley ***1997***

for passengers with impaired mobility, with wheelchair lifts
Average peak-hour speed: In bus lanes, 24 km/h; in mixed traffic, 18 km/h
Bus priority: 8 km of bus lanes; turning ban lifted at certain traffic lights; bus-only use of several main streets in city and surrounding town centres, generally during shopping hours
Integration with other modes: Co-ordination with supported rail services and light rail at major interchanges, and smaller feeder schemes
Operating costs financed by: Fares 72.8%, concessionary fares support 16%, other commercial sources 12.2%

Stagecoach Manchester

GM Buses South Limited
151 Charles Street, Stockport SK1 3JU
Telephone: +44 161 273 3377 Fax: +44 161 476 3625
Managing Director: Les Warneford
Commercial Director: Ben Colson
Finance Director: A Fuller
Operations Director: M Threapleton
Staff: 1,955

Current situation: GMS was formed when GM Buses was split in 1994, and was purchased by staff through an employee share ownership plan. It operates in south and central Manchester. In 1996 the company was sold to Stagecoach.
Developments: Since the acquisition of GMS by Stagecoach, over 100 new vehicles have entered service. The Charterplan coaching division was sold to the EYMS group of Hull. New fares initiatives introduced in late 1996 included low-fare 'Magic Buses' on the Wilmslow Road corridor, and a general £5 weekly ticket valid on all services.

Bus

Passenger journeys: (1993/94) 79 million
(1995/96) 71.8 million
Vehicle-km: (1993/94) 43.2 million
(1995/96) 35.7 million

Number of routes: 243
Fleet: 690 vehicles

Leyland National single-deck	21
Volvo B6 single-deck	20
Volvo B10M single-deck	40
Leyland Leopard coach	2
Leyland Tiger coach	1
Scania coach	3
Dennis Domino single-deck	5
Leyland Atlantean double-deck	194
MCW Metrobus double-deck	87
Leyland Olympian double-deck	155
Dennis Falcon double-deck	3
Scania double-deck	7
Dennis Dominator double-deck	40
Renault/Dodge minibus	5
MCW Metrorider minibus	49
Mercedes minibus	58

In peak service: 609

Most intensive service: 5 min
One-person operation: 100%
Fare collection: Payment on bus with ticket issue by driver
Fare structure: Stage, multijourney ticket; range of prepurchase weekly passes including add-on to rail season tickets and all modes
Fares collected on board: 73.5%
Fare evasion control: Revenue inspectors charging higher fares
Arrangements for elderly/disabled: On ordinary services low flat fare charged. Semi-fixed route accessible services in the Stockport and south Manchester areas operate under the 'Localine' identity; vehicles designed for passengers with impaired mobility, with wheelchair lifts
Average peak-hour speed: In bus lanes, 24 km/h; in mixed traffic, 18 km/h
Bus priority: 8 km of bus lanes; turning ban lifted at certain traffic lights; bus-only use of several main streets in city and surrounding town centres, generally during shopping hours
Integration with other modes: Co-ordination with supported rail services and light rail at major interchanges, and smaller feeder schemes
Operating costs financed by: Fares 72.8%, concessionary fares support 16%, other commercial sources 12.2%

Bee Line

The Bee Line Buzz Co Ltd
Hulme Hall Road, Manchester M15 4LY
Telephone: +44 161 832 2688 Fax: +44 161 839 5839
Managing Director: Bob Hind
Engineering Director: Gary Raven
Staff: 280

Developments: Extensive rationalisation in 1995 saw the company give up east Manchester services to GMN. Takeover of Heatons of Leigh established a new depot at Leigh, operating as Wigan Bus.

Bus

Fleet: 144 vehicles

Leyland Olympian double-deck	22
Leyland National single-deck	40
Scania single-deck	40
Mercedes midibus	42

Timeline

Timeline Travel Ltd
12 Bold Street, Leigh WN7 1AL
Telephone: +44 1942 680088 Fax: +44 1942 680808
Managing Director: Ian Longworth
Commercial Director: Peter Green
Staff: 235

Current situation: Intensive services operate from three garages in the Manchester area and one in Shropshire. Six low-floor buses operate on services between Bolton and Bury.

Fleet: 130 vehicles

Leyland Tiger single-deck	12
Volvo B10M single-deck	16
Volvo B10L low-floor single-deck	6
Volvo B6 single-deck	12
Leyland Leopard single-deck	15
Leyland Atlantean double-deck	6
Leyland Tiger dual-purpose	3
Dennis Javelin coach	17
Mercedes minibus	40
Talbot minibus	3

Stagecoach Ribble

Stagecoach (North West) Ltd
Frenchwood Avenue, Preston PR1 4LU
Telephone: +44 1772 254754 Fax: +44 1772 258314
Managing Director: Michael Chambers
Staff: 900

Current situation: Services are predominantly in Lancashire, operated from seven depots, and in north Manchester from a depot in Bolton. Articulated coaches are operated from Manchester to Blackpool as part of a network of interurban services introduced in 1995 under the Stagecoach Express branding.

Fleet: 415 vehicles

Double-deck	125
Single-deck	116
Dual-purpose	33
Coach	5
Minibus	136

Mayne

A Mayne & Son Ltd
974 Ashton New Road, Manchester M11 4PD
Telephone: +44 161 223 8111 Fax: +44 161 223 1835
Managing Director: Steven Mayne
Staff: 98

Current situation: This old-established family firm expanded its services in 1986 and now runs routes in Manchester, Tameside, Trafford and parts of Derbyshire.

Bus

Passenger journeys: (1993/94) 3.1 million
Vehicle-km: (1993/94) 3.7 million

Number of routes: 44
Fleet: 56 vehicles

Leyland/Daimler Fleetline double-deck	12
Scania double-deck	12
Leyland Leopard coaches	7
Leyland Tiger coach	6
Scania single-deck	2
Dennis Falcon single-deck	6
Dennis Dart single-deck	4
Bova coach	3
Dennis Javelin coach	4

Finglands

Finglands Coachways Ltd
261 Wilmslow Road, Rusholme, Manchester M14 5JL
Telephone: +44 161 224 3341 Fax: +44 161 257 3154
Managing Director: D Shurden
Staff: 55

Current situation: Acquired in 1992 by the EYMS Group of Hull and has subsequently upgraded its fleet; 33 routes are operated.

Fleet: 66 vehicles

Leyland Atlantean double-deck	18
MCW Metrobus double-deck	5
Volvo Citybus double-deck	1
Volvo Olympian double-deck	10
Volvo B10M single-deck	13
Leyland Leopard single-deck	3

Passenger journeys: (All modes)
(1993) 31.2 million
(1994) 36 million
(1995) 36.7 million

Current situation: Provides tramway and bus services in Heidelberg and to neighbouring communities, serving population of 280,000. Two tourist-oriented funiculars also operated.
Developments: A short link line along Berliner Strasse in 1995, joining the former Route 1 and 4 terminus at Blumenthalstrasse with Route 3 and OEG lines at Hans-Thoma-Platz. It is proposed to double the existing single track between Handschusheim (terminus of routes 1, 3 and 4) and Dossenheim (4 km), allowing extension of HSB services to Dossenheim over OEG track.

Bus
Vehicle-km: (1993) 4.6 million
(1994) 4.8 million
(1995) 5.1 million

Route length: 167 km
Number of routes: 39
Fleet: 99 buses

Tramway
Type of operation: Conventional tramway

Car-km: (1993) 2 million
(1994) 2 million
(1995) 2 million

Route length: 20.7 km
Number of routes: 4
Gauge: 1,000 mm
Integration with other modes: Interurban trains of OEG (see below), providing services to Mannheim and Weinheim, share HSB tracks within Heidelberg.

Rolling stock: 52 cars

Rastatt 8-axle articulated	M32
Duewag M8C 8-axle	M8
Duewag MGT6D 6-axle low-floor (1995/96)	M12

RHB
Rhein-Haardtbahn GmbH
PO Box 211223, 67012 Ludwigshafen
Telephone: +49 621 5051 Fax: +49 621 505609
General Manager: Karl Heinz Ries
Staff: 44

Passenger journeys: (Both modes)
(1993) 1.8 million
(1994) 1.9 million
(1995) 1.7 million

Current situation: RHB, owned by the local authorities of Ludwigshafen am Rhein and Bad Dürkheim, operates 16.3 km of 1,000 mm gauge route, electrified at 750 V DC, linking Mannheim Hbf with Bad Dürkheim, and local bus services at Bad Dürkheim.

Light rail
Car-km: (Annual) 0.4 million

Route length: 16.3 km owned
Rolling stock: 8 cars M6 T2

Bus
Vehicle-km: (Annual) 0.1 million

Fleet: 4 buses

OEG
Oberrheinische Eisenbahn Gesellschaft AG
Käfertalerstrasse 9-11, 68167 Mannheim
Telephone: +49 621 330860 Fax: +49 621 330 8618
Chair: Dr Karl Wimmer
General Manager: Dipl-Ing Eduard Stephan
Staff: 288

Current situation: The publicly owned OEG system operates light rail routes linking Mannheim with Heidelberg, Heddesheim and Weinheim, and an associated bus network.
Developments: See MVG notes above for route changes that took place in 1995.

Bus and tram of HSB connect at Heidelberg's Bismarkplatz ***1996***

Passenger journeys: (Both modes)
(1993) 11.5 million
(1994) 12.7 million
(1995) 13.1 million

Operating costs financed by: Fares 47%, subsidy/grants 53%
Subsidy from: City of Mannheim and other communities served

Bus
Vehicle-km: (1993) 1.5 million
(1994) 1.4 million
(1995) 1.4 million

Number of routes: 10
Route length: (One way) 105 km
Fleet: 24 buses

Mercedes O405	24

Light rail
Type of operation: Interurban light rail

Car-km: (1993) 2.4 million
(1994) 2.3 million
(1995) 2.5 million

Route length: 61 km
On private right-of-way: 84%
Number of lines: 2
Number of stops: 72
Gauge: 1,000 mm
Electrification: 750 V DC, overhead

Service: Peak 5-20 min, off-peak 30-60 min
First/last car: 04.40/01.00

Fare structure: Stage, with single and multiride tickets sold from platform machines

Rolling stock: 48 cars

Rastatt 4-axle (1957/8)	T4
Duewag 8-axle (1966/88)	M35
Duewag Variobahn low-floor	M6
Cycle carriers	T2
Historic tram	M1

Developments: Short extension to Heidelberg Hbf opened 1995; automatic block to be extended to the Edingen—Heidelberg section.

BRN
Busverkehr Rhein-Neckar
PO Box 100564, 68005 Mannheim
Telephone: +49 621 120030 Fax: +49 621 120060
Directors: Irene Heiland
Werner Ott

Passenger journeys: (1993) 26.5 million
(1994) 26.7 million
(1995) 26.9 million
Vehicle-km: (1993) 18.1 million
(1994) 18 million
(1995) 19.1 million

Current situation: Regional bus company, owned by DB, providing suburban and regional services with a fleet of 177 buses plus 214 hired.

UPDATED

OEG interurban at Neuostheim ***1996***

MARSEILLE

Population: 808,000, area served 881,000
Public transport: Bus, trolleybus, tramway and metro services provided by municipal undertaking supervised by the city of Marseille and Bouches du Rhoñe département, with separate metro construction authority. Four bus routes run to adjoining suburbs of Aubagne, La Penne, Allauch and Plan de Cuques. Limited suburban rail services operated by French National Railways (SNCF)

RTM

Régie des Transports de Marseille
PO Box 334, 13271 Marseille Cedex 8, France
Telephone: +33 4 91 10 55 55 Fax: +33 4 91 10 53 09
Director General: Alain Gille
Staff: 2,706

Passenger boardings: (All modes)
(1993) 153.1 million
(1994) 150 million
(1995) 148.2 million

Operating costs financed by: (All modes) Fares 57.1%, other commercial sources 6%, subsidy/grants 36.9%
Subsidy from: City council and Bouches du Rhône département

Metro and feeder buses at Bougainville

Bus and trolleybus

Passenger journeys: (1992) Bus 87 million, trolleybus 6.4 million
(1993) Bus 83.1 million, trolleybus 6 million
(1995) Bus 85.4 million, trolleybus 6.6 million
Vehicle-km: (1992) Bus 21.4 million, trolleybus 0.8 million
(1993) Bus 19.8 million, trolleybus 0.8 million
(1995) Bus 21.6 million, trolleybus 0.8 million

Number of routes: Bus 77, trolleybus 3, including 13 night
Route length: Bus 575 km, trolleybus 19 km
On priority right-of-way: 24.1 km
Fleet: 542 buses

Berliet PR100	168
Heuliez GX113	293
Mercedes O405N	37
Heuliez GX77 narrow-body	27
Van Hool AU138 narrow/short wheelbase	16
Renault R312	1

Fleet: 47 trolleybuses, all Berliet ER100
Average age of fleet: Bus 9.4 years, trolleybus 15.6 years
In peak service: Bus 460, trolleybus 41

Most intensive service: 5 min
One-person operation: All routes
Fare collection: Prepurchase passes and multitickets from agencies of metro station ticket machines with validation and cancelling machines on board, or payment to driver
Fare structure: Flat, weekly/monthly passes and multitickets/carnets including transfers; single tickets do not allow interchange
Fares collected on board: 17%
Fare evasion control: Roving inspectors
Arrangements for elderly/disabled: Reduced fares or free travel for over-65s and invalids
Bus priority: 2 main corridors into city centre from north and south equipped with bus-activated traffic lights; also some bus lanes on busiest route, Line 21
Operational control: Electronic bus monitoring; all buses, trams and metro cars equipped with radio
Average peak-hour speed: Bus 15.5 km/h, trolleybus 10.1 km/h

Developments: The 10 busiest stops of Route 21 are equipped with Alphabus displays, showing next bus waiting times. Five bus/metro interchanges are equipped with Topbus displays giving next bus departure times; a buzzer warns passengers of imminent departure.

In 1996 RTM introduced the Carte Réseau Libertés, a magnetic card which can be used to pay for all modes of public transport, plus car parks, parking meters and tolls. The ticket allows a one-hour journey including transfers and, unusually, a return journey if required. There are three versions: single journey, fixed-value and rechargeable.

Metro

Operated by: RTM
Construction authority: Société du Métro de Marseille (SMM)
44 avenue Alexandre Dumas, 13272 Marseille Cedex 8
Telephone: +33 4 91 23 25 25 Fax: +33 4 91 71 05 87
Director General: Michel Croc

Type of operation: Rubber-tyred full metro, initial route opened 1978

Passenger boardings: (1992) 54.7 million
(1993) 56.1 million
(1994) 53.8 million
Car-km: (1993) 9 million
(1995) 9.1 million

Route length: 19.5 km
Number of lines: 2
Number of stations: 24
Track: 2 steel guideways (2,000 mm gauge) for train's pneumatic tyres; 2 steel guidance rails fixed outside running guideways; 2 conventional rails for running in case of tyre punctures and guiding through sections without guidance rails
Tunnel: Bored or blasted
Electrification: 750 V DC, collected by side shoe from guidance rail

Service: Peak 3 min, off-peak 5-10 min
First/last train: 05.00/21.00
Fare structure: Flat
Integration with other modes: Ticket integration with bus services. Monthly ticket for unlimited travel on metro, tramway, trolleybus and bus; also monthly 'Carte Azur' ticket allowing in addition travel on SNCF trains within RTM area
Fare collection: Automatic ticket machines
Signalling: Cab signalling; continuous speed display to drivers; automatic operation with monitored manual drive
Centralised control: Traffic control station or computer ensures regulation of traffic by modifying inter-station

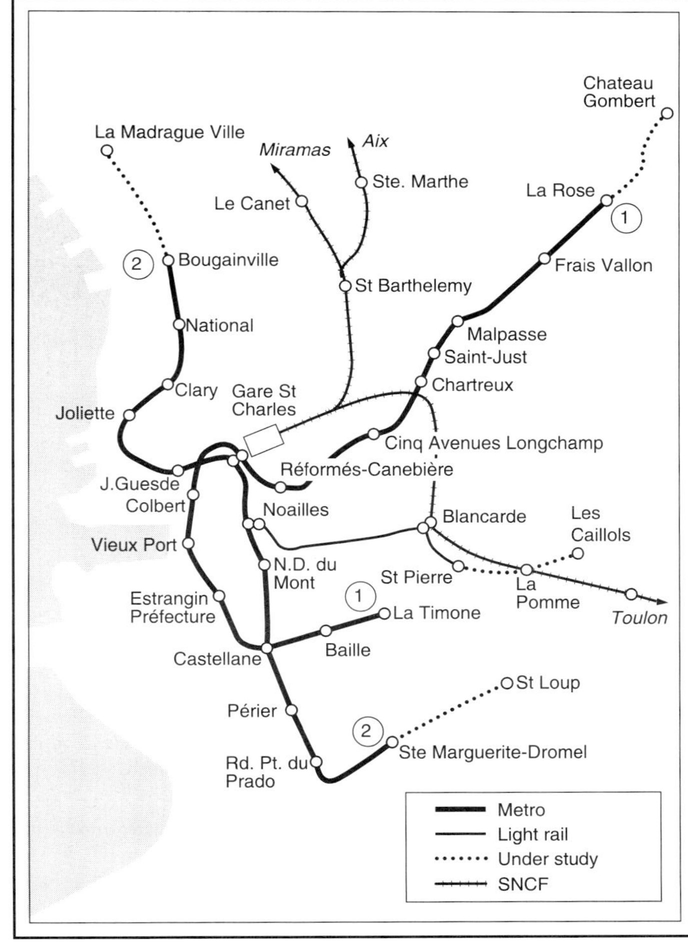

Marseille metro

Refurbished PCC cars at St Pierre ***1996***

speeds and calculating stopping times at stations
Surveillance: CCTV on stations

Rolling stock: 144 cars, in four-car sets

CIMT Series A (1977)	M42 T21
CIMT Series B (1984)	M30 T15
CIMT Series N (1985/86)	M36

In peak service: 116 cars

Current situation: 1.5 km Line 1 extension between Castellane and Hôpital La Timone opened 1992; extensions under study.

Tramway
Type of operation: Conventional tramway

Passenger journeys: (1992) 5.1 million
(1993) 4.9 million
(1995) 4.6 million
Car-km: (1992) 0.6 million
(1993) 0.6 million
(1995) 0.5 million

Current situation: A 3 km tram line (Route 68) with 14 stops links Noailles Line 2 metro station with St Pierre; 3 min peak service.
Developments: A 1994 study proposed four new tram lines and extension of the existing route to Les Caillols.

Rolling stock: 19 cars, operated as 9 two-car sets

PCC	M16
BN (1984)	M3

In peak service: 16 cars

SNCF
French National Railways (SNCF), Marseille Division

Current situation: Limited suburban services are provided on SNCF lines out of Marseille St Charles station. Busiest routes are to Aix-en-Provence (37 km) and Toulon (67 km), each with about 18 return trips daily.

A project has existed for some years to create an RER-style network on the lines to Aix, Aubagne and Marignane airport, near Vitrolles. Plans to double the Aix line have come up against financial and construction problems in an area of dense development and difficult terrain.

UPDATED

MEDELLÍN
Population: 2.5 million
Public transport: Bus and minibus services provided by private companies. Metro

Private bus/minibus
Supervised by:
Ministry of Transport
Calle 26 No 25-50, Piso 3, Apartado Aero 1978, Bogotá DE, Colombia

Passenger boardings: (1993) 2.5 million daily

Current situation: Bus services are operated by private companies and co-operatives on concessions awarded by the Ministry of Transport, initially for a year and then for progressively longer periods after review.

A fleet of more than 4,200 vehicles runs 209 routes.

Medellín metro

Line 1 train at Poblado ***1997***

Metro de Medellín
Empresa de Transporte Masivo del Valle de Aburrá — Metro de Medellín
Calle 44 Nro 46-001, Bello, Antioquia
Telephone: +57 4 526000 Fax: +57 4 524450
General Manager: Alberto Valencia Ramirez

Type of operation: Full metro, opened 1995

Passenger journeys: (1995/96, 10 months) 55 million

Route length: 29 km
elevated: 9 km
Number of lines: 2
Number of stations: 25

Gauge: 1,435 mm
Electrification: 1.5 kV DC, overhead

Service: Peak 5 min, off-peak 10 min
First/last train: 05.00/23.00
Fare structure: Flat; tickets for 1, 2 and 20 trips
Fare collection: Turnstiles

Rolling stock: 126 cars, in three-car sets

MAN/Ateinsa/Siemens	M84 T42

Current situation: Line A opened in November 1995 between Niquía and El Poblado, followed by Line B in February 1996 and the remainder of Line A in September 1996.

Line A totals 23 km with 19 stations, while east-west Line B is 6 km with six stations and interchange with Line A at San Antonio.

UPDATED

MELBOURNE

Population: 2.9 million

Public transport: The Public Transport Corporation operates all heavy rail, light rail, tram and a few bus services in the metropolitan area; extensive private bus operations

PTC

Public Transport Corporation
589 Collins Street, Melbourne 3000, Australia
Telephone: +61 3 9619 1111 Fax: +61 3 9619 2343
Chief Executive: Ian Dobbs
Managing Director, Met Bus: John Wilson
Managing Director, Met Tram: Russell Nathan
Managing Director, Met Trains: Simon Lane
Staff: 10,209 (total PTC)

Passenger boardings: (All modes, excluding private bus)
(1992/93) 228.8 million
(1993/94) 218.5 million
(1994/95) 219.9 million

Current situation: The PTC was formed in 1989 when the Metropolitan Transit (The Met) and State Transport authorities were merged. Melbourne's public transport is operated by three businesses — Met Bus, Met Tram and Met Trains; trams are the principal mode of urban transit. Met Bus was constituted in 1993 to operate the portion that remained following award of 80 per cent of the city network to the National Bus Company, a private sector operator.

Developments: Government reforms of 1993 designed to reduce the huge deficit on public transport operations by $A245 million are being implemented over a three-year period. In 1994/95 recurrent funding was reduced by $A38 million or 10 per cent; government appropriations have been reduced by 35 per cent since 1992, and accumulated savings amount to $A440 million. Revenue from metropolitan operations exceeded target by $A5.7 million in 1994/95.

An all modes automated smartcard ticketing system was introduced throughout the network during 1995. It is being administered by a private consortium; AES Prodata and Fujitsu are installing the system.

Met Tram

Staff: 2,046

Type of operation: Conventional tramway and light rail

Passenger journeys: (1992/93) 100.9 million
(1993/94) 104.1 million
(1994/95) 108.5 million
Vehicle-km: (1990/91) 22.3 million
(1994/95) 21.7 million

Route length: 238 km
Number of routes: 42
Gauge: 1,435 mm
Track: 43 kg/m rail; some tram rail also used, weight 43/50.6 kg/m
Electrification: 600 V DC, overhead

Service: Peak 4-8 min, off-peak 6-12-20 min
First/last car: 05.30/00.30
Fare collection: Roving or seated conductor; driver-only operation of some routes after 20.00 and at weekends
Fare structure: Time-based multimodal system operating within 3 zones; discount for prepurchase
One-person operation: See fare collection
Centralised control: Vehicle monitoring system being extended to whole tram network

Rolling stock: 537 cars

W5/SW5	
SW6	
W6/W7	
Comeng/ASEA Z1/Z2 (1975/79)	M115
Comeng/Duewag/AEG Z3 (1979)	M115
Comeng/Duewag/AEG A1/A2 (1984)	M69
Comeng LRV (1986/88/90/91/93)	M130

In peak service:

Developments: A 2.1 km extension of the Bundoora line to Mill Park was opened in 1995. The free city-centre distributor service, operated by heritage tramcars, carried over 2 million passengers in its first year of operation. Reviews were carried out on all routes to improve customer service.

LRV for Bundoora in central Melbourne

Volvo B59 of The Met in central Melbourne

Mercedes O405 of Quince's, one of Melbourne's many suburban operators

A new tram depot was due to open at the end of 1996, replacing outdated facilities at South Melbourne Kingsway. There is storage space for 97 cars. The Z1 and Z2 tram fleets are to be refurbished at a cost of A$5.7 million.

Met Trains

Staff: 1,951

Type of operation: Suburban heavy rail

Passenger journeys: (1992/93) 105.9 million
(1993/94) 100.9 million
(1994/95) 105.4 million

Current situation: Suburban services operate over a total of 366 km on 15 routes with 197 stations, linked in the city centre by an underground loop line, all electrified at 1.5 kV DC overhead; track gauge is 1,600 mm. Fare structure is as tram.

Developments: In a A$25 million project, the Upfield line is to be resignalled and the track upgraded.

A total of 51 stations have been designated 'Premium' and are staffed at all times when trains are running. They have improved customer service facilities and better security arrangements. All stations are being upgraded, with A$14.2 million allocated to the work for 1996/98.

Rolling stock: 907 emu cars

Comeng Harris-type (1961/71)	
Martin & King Hitachi-type (1972/81)	M234 T117
Comeng Harris-type (rebuilt 1982)	M8 T8
Comeng (1982/89)	M380 T190

Met Bus

Staff: 204

Passenger journeys: (1992/93) 22.1 million
(1993/94) 13.6 million
(1994/95) 6.1 million

Current situation: Created in 1993, Met Bus is the only government-owned bus operator in Victoria. It operates the remainder of the metropolitan network — 9 routes — not taken over by National Bus in 1993; fleet of 99 buses.

Private bus

Passenger journeys: (1992/93) 69.5 million
(1993/94) 74.7 million
(1994/95) 85.8 million

Number of routes: 225
Fleet: 1,023 vehicles
In peak service: 795

Current situation: Some 50 private companies using their own names and liveries operate in suburban areas; integrated multimodal fares system applies. The National Bus Co operates about two-thirds of the former government bus network in Melbourne, from depots at Doncaster and North Fitzroy. It must sell and honour Met tickets, but may offer its own fares in competition.

UPDATED

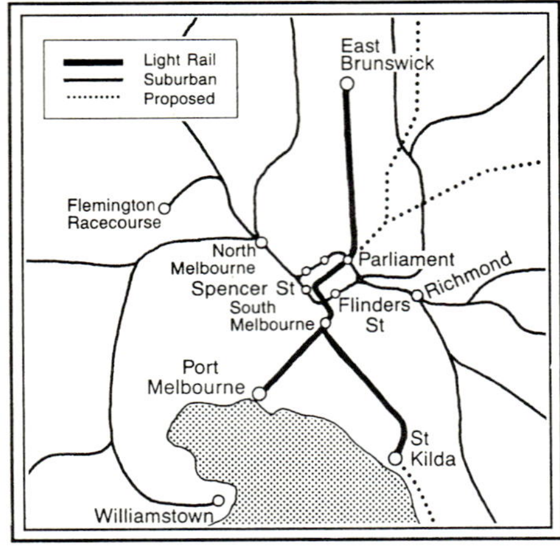

Melbourne's tramways and light rail

MEMPHIS

Population: 702,000
Public transport: Bus services managed under contract for city-owned Transit Authority, governed by representative board; city-centre tramway

MATA

Memphis Area Transit Authority (MATA)
1370 Levee Road, Memphis, TN 38108, USA
Telephone: +1 901 722 7100   Fax: +1 901 722 7123
Chair: Vernon N Grose
Director of Transit: Charlie Dyson
General Manager: William Hudson Jr
Managed and operated by: Mid-South Transportation Management Inc
Staff: 470

Current situation: MATA was established as a publicly owned transit system in 1960, providing fixed-route and demand-responsive service in the Memphis metropolitan area.

Developments: Historic tramway route opened on Main Street in 1993, intended as the nucleus of a future light rail network. Initial ridership exceeded expectations by a substantial margin, and funding was granted in 1994 for an extension.

Studies have been made of proposed commuter rail service in two corridors using existing track to link central Memphis with Colliersville and Cordova.

Air Park Express service inaugurated 1991, providing reverse-flow journey opportunities to outer suburban workplaces in southeast Memphis. Some fixed-route services now deviate on demand to serve less accessible/low-density suburban areas. In 1993 MATA Ltd demand-responsive service was introduced in three areas previously unserved by fixed routes.

Memphis Central station is to be rebuilt as a major interchange between Amtrak trains, local and intercity bus routes and light rail.

Bus

Passenger boardings: (1991/92) 13.2 million
(1992/93) 12.8 million
(1993/94) 12.1 million
Vehicle-km: (1991/92) 11.9 million
(1992/93) 12.9 million
(1993/94)

TMC bus of MATA

Ex-Porto trams at Linden Avenue on the street-running section of MATA's tramway ***1997***

Number of routes: 40
Route length: 1,238 km
Fleet: 223 vehicles

GMC RTS (1979/85/86)	121
MAN articulated (1983/87)	20
TMC (1988/89/94)	41
Chance replica trolleys (1990/91/92)	10
Minibuses (1985/87)	23
Chance RT52 paratransit (1992)	8

In peak service: 154
On order: 13 buses

Most intensive service: 15 min
Fare collection: Exact change to farebox
Fare structure: Flat; higher fare for limited stop peak-hour 'Blazer' routes; 10 cent transfers; passes for 10 rides; monthly passes
Arrangements for elderly/disabled: 28 lift-equipped vans carried 136,000 passengers in 1994; reduced fare on fixed-route services

Integration with other modes: Park-and-ride on many routes
Operating costs financed by: Fares 37%, other commercial sources 5%, subsidy/grants 58%
Subsidy from: FTA 21%, state 17%, city 62%

Tramway

Type of operation: Conventional tramway

Passenger boardings: (1993/94) 0.5 million

Route length: 3 km
Number of routes: 1
Number of stops: 22
Gauge: 1,435 mm
Track: RI59 and 115 lb/yd T rail; sleepers set in concrete
Max gradient: 5%
Minumum curve radius: 8.5 m
Electrification: 600 V DC, overhead

Service: Peak 8 min, off-peak 13 min
First/last car: 06.38/24.00
Fare structure: Flat, reduced rate 'Lunch Fare'
Integration with other modes: Free transfer to bus

Rolling stock: 20 cars, of which 9 serviceable

Brill-type 2-axle ex-Porto	M6
Brill/Brill-type 2-axle ex-Porto in store	M8
Ex-Porto 4-axle (1930) in store	M2
Ex-Melbourne W2 (1926/27)	M3
Gomaco replica (1993)	M1

In peak service: 6 cars

Current situation: Initial 3 km section of tramway along Main Street in the Mid-America Mall redevelopment area opened 1993, designed as a downtown distributor and intended to become the core route of a future light rail network.

Developments: To emphasise the line's role as a

distributor, a 500-vehicle parking garage is to be built near its north terminus at Main and Auction streets. Funding was granted in 1994 but start of construction was delayed and may go ahead in 1997.

Construction of a 4 km loop to and along the riverfront area is in progress for opening in late 1997. This makes use of little-used rail track running north-south and parallel to the existing tramway, with which it will be connected by new east-west links to form a loop. Four ex-Melbourne W2 cars are being restored to operate the new service.

Proposed is a 3.5 km eastern extension to Medical Center. In 1994 a $4 million grant was made available towards the cost of the Medical Center line, but indecision over its routeing and whether it should be built for light rail operation has delayed design work.

UPDATED

MENDOZA

Population: 475,000
Public transport: 'Colectivo' bus and minibus services provided by private operators and groups operating through an association, and supervised by Provincial transport department. Trolleybus services run by Province-owned corporation

Private bus/minibus/shared taxi

Supervised by:
Departmento Provincial de Transportes (DPT)
Mendoza, Argentina

Current situation: The Provincial DPT is in charge of co-ordinating and regulating the colectivo bus operations of the city's 10 main groupings of private operators and co-operatives, each franchised for one or more specific routes. There are about 50 routes, many of which started as branches of the original 10-route core network but are now numbered and operated separately. The principal operators are: El Trapiche, El Plumerillo, Antartida Argentina, Paso de los Andes and TAC.

In 1990 consultants BVC carried out traffic management studies, which were expected to lead to improved operating conditions for buses.

The DPT is also in charge of regulating city and regional taxi services, as well as the Taxi-Flet public-hire freight pick-ups which charge by the hour.

Passenger journeys: Approx 70 million (annual)
Vehicle-km: Approx 20 million (annual)

Number of routes: 40
Route length: 560 km
Fleet: Approx 500 vehicles, including Mercedes LO1114, OF1214, OH1314 and OH1419 types, El Detalle OA101 and Zanello, many bodied by local companies
Fare structure: Urban, flat; suburban, distance-related
Fare collection: Payment to driver

EPTM

Empresa Provincial de Transportes de Mendoza (EPTM)
Calle Peru 2592, Mendoza 5500
Telephone: +54 61 245819

Refurbished ex-Solingen trolleybus on EPTM's Parque route ***1997***

Trolleybus

Passenger journeys: Approx 6.5 million (annual)

Route length: 50 km
Number of routes: 5
Fleet: 95 trolleybuses

Tokyu/Nissan/Toshiba (1962, refurbished 1996)	1
Uritsky ZIU9 (1984)	16
Krupp (ex-Solingen) some stored	78

In peak service: 34

Most intensive service: 5-8 min
One-person operation: 100%
Fare structure: Flat, higher in late evening
Fare collection: Payment to driver

Current situation: A phased expansion of the network has begun but progress has been slowed by shortage of funds. The first two new sections opened in 1986, with a third stage following in 1987. Route 4 to Barrio San Martin opened 1989. Further wiring was under way in 1996 under a scheme approved in 1991 for elimination of diesel buses from the city centre on environmental grounds. This is a new 17 km north-south cross-city route connecting Las Heras with Godoy Cruz, which was expected to open at the beginning of 1997.

One 1962 Toshiba trolleybus was rebuilt with a new rear-end in 1996, but the project was deemed uneconomic and others of the type withdrawn in 1995 will now be scrapped. Ten of the ex-Solingen vehicles have been refurbished for the new north-south line. The operation is expected to remain commercially self-sufficient; privatisation may be undertaken during 1997.

UPDATED

MEXICO CITY

Population: 20 million
Public transport: Bus, trolleybus/tramway and metro services operated for urban area by separate public authorities, under overall control of co-ordinating body. Extensive private 'colectivo' shared taxi operation and privately run suburban bus services

STV

Secretaría de Transportes y Vialidad
Lerma 62, Mexico City DF 06500, Mexico
Telephone: +52 5 207 6815
Director General: Lic Jorge Ramírez de Aguilar

Current situation: STV came into being at the beginning of 1995 as successor to the Coordinacíon General de Transporte. It is responsible for regulation of the city's public transport, and for control of roads, streets and parking. One of its first tasks was to cope with the killing of its chief officer in April 1995, closely followed by the shut-down of Ruta 100 (see below).

Bus services were provided by numerous private firms and paratransit modes until the early 1980s, when urban bus operations were taken over by the government with a legacy of elderly and poorly maintained vehicles. Extensive shared taxi 'colectivo' operations continue, with about 60,000 vehicles, and suburban bus services remain in private hands.

Considerable problems are faced in catering for the massive demands of the world's fastest growing urban

Refurbished Flyer E800 of STE at Villa de Cortés metro station ***1996***

area. A further complication is the pressure created by the high levels of atmospheric pollution. Transport provision, in particular the metro, has been expanded rapidly to handle some 30 million daily journeys in the city region. Government environmental regulations stipulate that the city's 2.8 million cars and commercial vehicles must not be used on one day each week, and taxis and 'colectivo' minibuses must be fitted with catalytic converters.

Amongst many proposals for public transport improvements have been schemes to expand trolleybus and light rail, though the existing trolleybus network has been cut back since 1991. Long-standing plans to create a high-speed regional rail network based on poorly used national railways routes have made little progress.

STP

Servicio de Transporte Provisional

Current situation: STP was hastily organised to restart operations of Ruta 100, the state-owned city bus operator which collapsed in April 1995. After a month or so about three-quarters of Ruta 100's 260 routes had been restored using the same vehicles but with newly employed drivers, and this was still the situation in November 1995. The remaining Ruta 100 vehicles, out of a fleet of some 4,000, have been redeployed elsewhere in the city, some to boost services on secondary routes and others on routes previously served only by jitneys. Most buses retained their Ruta 100 livery and markings.

STP was intended to be a temporary 'umbrella' whilst a new organisation was set up, but STV is believed to prefer an arrangement which splits the operation into several co-operatives.

STE

Servicio de Transportes Eléctricos del Distrito Federal (STE)
Av Municipio Libre 402 Ote, Col San Andrés Tetepilco, Mexico City 09440, DF
Telephone: +52 5 539 6500/6509 Fax: +52 5 539 2649
Director General: Benjamín Hedding Galeana
Director of Operations: Hugo J Nieto de la Torre
Staff: 2,100

Current situation: STE is responsible for operation of trolleybus routes and a light rail line. A major programme of renovation and expansion of the trolleybus network was under way, and in 1990 the system extended to 30 routes. Subsequently there have been several closures, some on account of metro construction, but 5 km Route LL was opened in December 1995 and extended 0.5 km in August 1996. Also, a 1.4 km extension of Route A opened in january 1996.

Current policy is to concentrate operations on the busiest routes as a prelude to possible expansion in the future. A total of 26 of the stored ex-Edmonton trolleybuses have been refurbished and returned to service, and an order was placed in 1996 with Mitsubishi/Melco for supply of a new fleet of 200 AC-powered vehicles.

The tram route has been modernised similarly to light rail standard, and the ancient PCC cars largely replaced by new vehicles.

Trolleybus

Passenger journeys: (1989) 225.2 million
(1991) 120 million
(1993) 99.3 million

Number of routes: 15
Route length: 188 km
Fleet: 457 trolleybuses

MASA/Toshiba (1984/85)	248
MASA/Melco (1988)	45
MASA/Kiepe (1991)	30
Flyer/GE E800 (ex-Edmonton 1974/76)	26
Flyer/GE E800A (ex-Hamilton 1978)	1
Marmon Herrington (rebuilt Moyada 1984/87)	104
Mitsubishi (ex-Kurobe Dam, 1966/71, in store)	6

In peak service: 323
On order: 200 Mitsubishi/Melco, with 50 due for delivery in mid-1997
Trolleybus electrification: 600 V DC

Most intensive service: 2 min
One-person operation: All routes
Fare collection: Payment to driver or sheet of 30 discounted tickets
Fare structure: Flat, no transfers
Fare evasion control: Driver's check

Light rail

Passenger journeys: (1989) 6.8 million
(1991) 5.5 million
(1993) 10.5 million

Route length: 12.7 km
Number of routes: 1
Number of stations: 17
Max gradient: 1%
Minimum curve radius: 30 m
Electrification: 600 V DC, overhead

Service: Peak 4 min, off-peak 6 min
First/last car: 06.00/23.00
Fare structure: Flat, single and two-weekly tickets
Fare collection: As trolleybus

Rolling stock: 16 cars

Concarril/Siemens (1991)	M12
Bombardier/Siemens (1995)	M4

In peak service: 10

Current situation: Links metro Line 2 terminus at Tasqueña with Xochimilco. The short on-street branch to Tlalpan, which reopened in 1990 after closure since 1984, was closed and reopened in 1991, and closed yet again in October 1993 because of poor patronage.
Developments: Three new stations were opened between Tasqueña and Xochimilco in late 1993. 0.7 km extension in the centre of Xochimilco opened in September 1995.

Two extensions were suggested by the new administration which came into office at the beginning of 1995, but were postponed in 1996. One was for reopening of the moribund Tlalpan branch and extending it by some 2 km westward along Avenida San Fernando to Villa Olímpica. The other proposed an entirely new and physically separate light rail line linking Constitucíon de 1917 station on metro Line 8 with Cárcel de Mujeres and Valle de Chalco.

Control system planned to give LRV priority at traffic lights and for protection of road crossings.

Elevated station on metro Line 8, opened 1994 ***1995***

Concarril LRV northbound on the fenced reserved track typical of the northern part of STE's light rail line ***1996***

STC Metro

Sistema de Transporte Colectivo
Organismo Público Decentralizado
Delicias 67, Mexico City 06070 DF
Telephone: +52 5 510 0529 Fax: +52 5 512 3601
Director General: Alfonso Caso Aguilar
Director of Administration: Antonio Garcia Rojas Barbosa
Director of Operations: Miguel Gerardo Requis Bustos
Director of Planning: Andres Figueira Cobian
Staff: 13,118

Type of operation: Full metro, first line opened 1969

Passenger journeys: (1993) 1,421 million
(1994) 1,422 million
(1995) 1,474 million
Car-km: (1993) 279 million
(1994) 291 million
(1995) 308 million

Route length: 178 km
in tunnel: 107.9 km
elevated: 14.3 km
Number of lines: 10
Number of stations: 154
Gauge: 1,436 mm (auxiliary guide rails, except Line A)
Track: Guideway for rubber tyres, security rail (39.6 kg/m); Line A is steel-wheel (57 kg/m rail)
Max gradient: 7%

Minimum curve radius: 105 m
Tunnel: Concrete caisson or bored tunnel with double-track
Electrification: 750 V DC, collected from two lateral guide bars; Line A, overhead

Service: Peak 2-5.8 min
First/last train: 05.00/00.30
Fare structure: Flat; single-trip and sheet of 25 discounted tickets
Revenue control: Separate entrance turnstiles for passes and metro-only tickets; mechanical exit turnstiles
Operating costs financed by: Fares 42.1%, other commercial sources 7.3%, subsidy/grants 50.5%
Integration with other modes: Multimode pass with STE tram and trolleybus
One-person operation: All services
Signalling: Automatic block and interlocking; ATO; 3 control centres

Rolling stock: 2,559 cars

Alsthom MP68 (1969/73)	M352 T176
CNCF NM73A-B-C (1975/79)	M231 T114
CNCF NM79 (1980/83)	M350 T177
Alsthom MP82 (1982/83)	M150 T75
Bombardier NC82 (1982/83)	M120 T60
CNCF NM83A (1984/85)	M184 T91
CNCF NM83B (1986/89)	M150 T74
CNCF MF86 (1990/92)	M80 T40
CAF NE92 (1994/95)	M90 T45

On order: 234 MP68 cars are being refurbished by Bombardier, while with Spain's CAF Bombardier is building 78 steel-wheel cars to raise capacity on Line A

Developments: Construction of east-west Line B (21.8 km, 21 stations) is in progress for mid-1998 opening. This links Cd Azteca in the northeast with Buenavista main line railway station in the city centre. This will be the first rubber-tyred line to extend beyond the Distrito Federal boundary.

Despite the rapid pace of construction, metro development still fails to keep pace with the prodigious growth of the city. STC's master plan envisages expansion to 17 lines with 342 route-km by 2020, when 12 million daily journeys are expected. In the short-term (through to 2003), a further 30.6 km will be built, comprising new Line 12 and extensions to Lines 7 and 8.

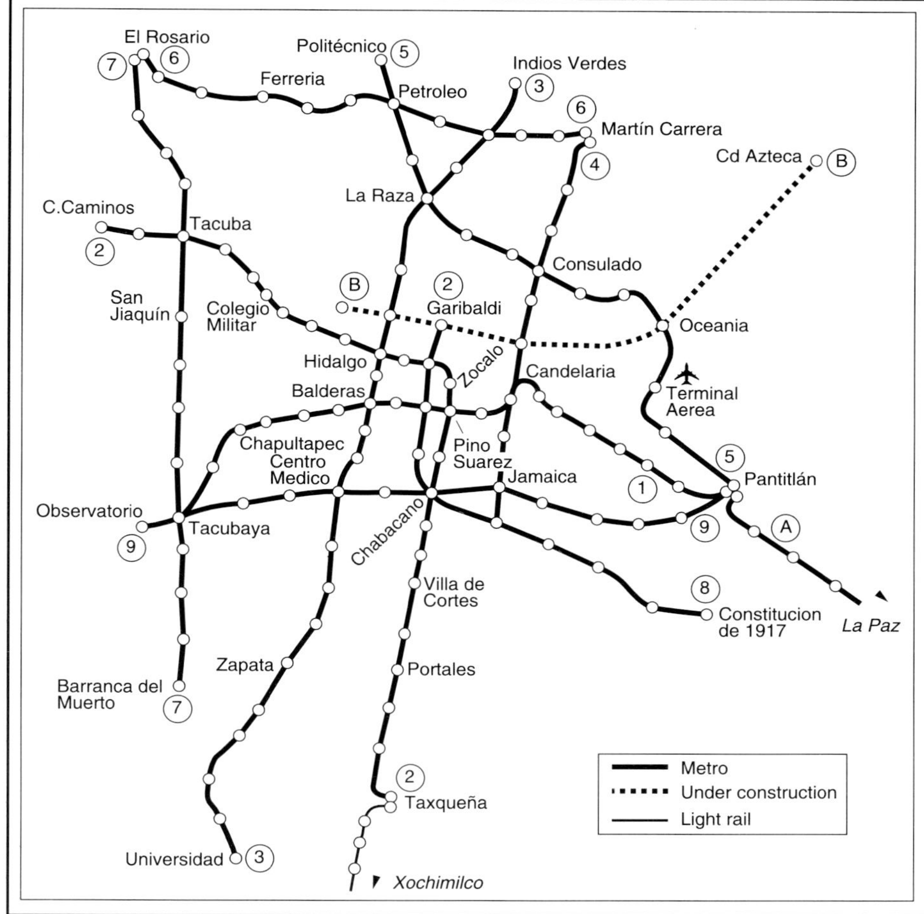

Mexico City's metro

Private buses/minibuses/shared taxis

Passenger journeys: (1991) 8 million daily

Current situation: Licensed private operators run a total of some 65,000 vehicles, including 30,000 vans, 15,000 minibuses and 4,000 'colectivo' minibuses/shared taxis. There are in addition about 60,000 conventional taxis, while a further 28,000 vehicles of various types operate services in outer suburban areas beyond the DF boundary.

Regional rail (planned)

Current situation: The National Railway (NdeM) started construction of its first regional rail route in 1991, between Mexico City and Cuautitlán (70 km). Work was halted almost immediately in the face of protests from environmentalists. This was to be the first of six radial routes planned to provide high-speed commuter service into the city, in part over existing NdeM lines which are under-utilised. There has been little progress since.

In 1992 an agreement between the state government and the federal district (DF) paved the way for concessions to be offered to the private sector for construction of a network of elevated lines linking the city with major satellite towns. Several consortia put forward schemes, and a contract for an initial mainly elevated route between Tlalnepantla and the city centre at Colon (19.7 km, 22 stations) was let at the beginning of 1994 to a consortium of three local companies and Canada's Bombardier. This is known as the Tren Ecologico Metropolitano (Ecotren). A fleet of 93 cars will be required.

There was no progress on this project during 1995, and it is reported that much opposition has arisen to the proposed elevated structures.

UPDATED

MIAMI

Population: 1.9 million
Public transport: Bus, metro, downtown people mover and paratransit services provided by department of county authority, responsible to board of county commissioners; commuter rail service; extensive unlicensed jitney operations

Metro-Dade

Metro-Dade Transit Agency
111 NW 1st Street, Miami, FL 33128, USA
Telephone: +1 305 375 5765 Fax: +1 305 375 4605
Executive Director: Chester E Colby
Staff: 2,396

Current situation: In 1991, voters again rejected a proposed additional 1 cent sales tax dedicated to transit operations and improvements, leading to an immediate reduction in service levels and the number of routes, and forcing a 25 per cent rise in fares. Metro-Dade continues to press for the tax increase, which would be used to fund implementation of the 'Year 2010 Plan' to expand bus service and extend the metro.

Bus

3300 NW 32nd Avenue, Miami Beach, FL 33142
Telephone: +1 305 637 3809
Assistant Director, Bus Operations: Roosevelt Bradley
Staff: 1,841

Passenger boardings: (1992/93) 64.4 million
(1994/95) 63.8 million
(1995/96) 62.2 million
Vehicle-km: (1992/93) 41.9 million
(1994/95) 42.5 million
(1995/96) 41.9 million

Number of routes: 69
Route length: (One way) 1,134 km
Fleet: 743 vehicles, including contracted, of which 677 active

GMC RTS-II (1980)	150
National coach (1985)	1
Flxible (1987/88/90)	308
Flxible alternative fuel (1993)	13
FRD (1985/90)	15
GMC (1982/85/89/90)	13
Oshkosh (1992)	2
Senator	2
Flxible (1993/94)	103
Ikarus (1994/95)	51
Orion	18
Thomas (1990)	1
Inactive fleet	66

In peak service: 517

Most intensive service: 6 min
One-person operation: All routes
Fare collection: Exact fare to farebox or prepurchase pass/token

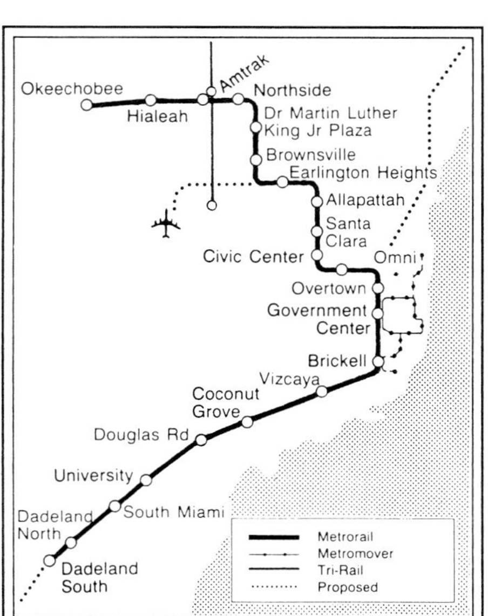

Miami's metro and people mover

Fare structure: Flat; drivers issue 25 cent transfer; monthly passes
Arrangements for elderly/disabled: Special Transportation Services ($2.50 fare) and Medicaid ($1) services

Florida DoT's Tri-Rail commuter train **1995**

carried around 1.5 million passengers in 1995/96; reduced ordinary fares and discount passes on fixed routes to those eligible
Operating costs financed by: Fares 41%, subsidy/grants 59%
Subsidy from: Local government 70%, state government 19%, FTA 11%
New vehicles financed by: FTA grants 80%, state 10%, local 10%

Developments: An 18 km busway scheduled to open in South Dade in March 1997, using former rail right-of-way; later conversion to metro is proposed (see below). Automatic vehicle location and monitoring commissioned 1995/96.

Metro
Operations Director, Rail: Frank Martin
Staff: 430

Type of operation: Full metro, initial section opened 1984

Passenger journeys: (1992/93) 14.8 million
(1994/95) 14.3 million
(1995/96) 14.2 million

Route length: 33 km, mostly elevated
at surface level: 1 km
Number of lines: 1
Number of stations: 21
Gauge: 1,435 mm
Track: Direct fixation fasteners with resilient pads
Electrification: 700 V DC, third rail

Service: Peak 5 min, off-peak 15 min
First/last train: 05.30/24.00
Fare structure: Flat
Fare collection: Exact fare to turnstile; prepurchase pass/token
Arrangements for elderly/disabled: Reduced fare and discount passes
Integration with other modes: Transfers to bus at extra fare, free transfer to people mover; monthly pass; interchange with commuter rail; park-and-ride at some stations
One-person operation: All trains
Automatic control: Partial, with full operator over-ride
Surveillance: CCTV for passenger/train control
Operating costs financed by: Fares 26%, subsidy/grants 74%

Rolling stock: 136 cars
Transit America (Budd) (1983/84) M136
In peak service: 80

Developments: Plans for Line 2 have been abandoned after the poor ridership results of Line 1, but two extensions have been discussed. Funding was agreed in 1993 for studies of a 15.3 km extension along Northwest 27 Avenue to serve several educational and leisure facilities, while a proposed 32 km line (also canvassed as a busway, see above) southwards to Cutler Ridge, Homestead and Florida City is seen as an important means of boosting the economy of an area devasted by the 1992 hurricane. Federal funding is to be sought on this basis.

Meanwhile a 1.8 km extension is in design from Okeechobee to NW 74th Street/826 (Palmetto Expressway) where a 2,000-car parking garage is to be built. This is scheduled to open in November 2000.

People mover
Staff: 124

Passenger journeys: (1992/93) 2.3 million
(1994/95) 3.6 million
(1995/96) 4.3 million

Current situation: Metromover, a downtown people mover opened 1986, extended 1994, links with metro and bus services for central area passenger distribution; 7.1 km, 21 stations. Unmanned cars carrying up to 120 passengers run at 90 sec intervals on mostly elevated guideway using right-of-way integrated into a number of commercial developments. Fares cover 5 per cent of operating costs.

Fleet: 29 cars
In peak service: 19

Tri-Rail
Tri-County Commuter Rail Authority
One River Plaza, 305 S Andrews Avenue, Fort Lauderdale, FL 33301
Telephone: +1 954 728 7245 Fax: +1 954 763 1345
Chair: David Rush
Executive Director: Gilbert M Robert
Director of Operations: W Simmons

Suburban rail
Passenger journeys: (1992) 2.2 million
(1993) 2.9 million
(1994) 2.5 million

Current situation: Commuter trains between Miami, Fort Lauderdale and West Palm Beach (103 km, 15 stations), serving Dade, Broward and Palm Beach counties, inaugurated 1989 over tracks now owned by the state of

Metromover people mover **1996**

Florida. Fare-free Tri-Rail feeder buses serve each station, and transfer to local buses of each county's transit system and the Miami metro is also free. Shuttle buses also link Miami terminal with the city's international airport (3 km).

Trains run hourly at commuting times; all-day service

Flxible bus of MDTA in downtown Miami **1995**

Metro trains at Government Center **1995**

totals 30 trains; all trains and stations wheelchair accessible; zonal fares. Operation is contracted to Herzog Transit Services.
Developments: Main elements in a five-year capital plan to 2000 are double-tracking and upgrading of signalling, station improvements and an increase in park-and-ride spaces from 1,100 to over 7,000. In the south, a 3 km extension is planned to a new Miami airport station, while an 8 km northern extension would extend service to Riviera Beach.

The first 13 km of double-tracking is to be completed in early 1997, but disruption caused by the work has contributed to a decline in ridership of some 2,000 passengers daily.

Rolling stock: 9 diesel locomotives, 21 coaches

UPDATED

MIDDLESBROUGH-TEESSIDE

Population: Teesside urban area 500,000
Public transport: Most bus services in Teesside urban area provided by two operators, both subsidiaries of large UK bus groups. Local rail services; guided busway proposed

Stagecoach Transit

Cleveland Transit Ltd
Church Road, Stockton TS18 2HW, England
Telephone: +44 1642 607124 Fax: +44 1642 617733
Managing Director: Malcolm Howitt
Traffic & Marketing Director: Stephen Warnock-Smith
Finance Director: Peter Solomon
Staff: 415

Current situation: The company was purchased by its employees in 1991 from a consortium of local authorities. It purchased Kingston upon Hull City Transport in 1993, and was itself sold to the Stagecoach Group in 1994.

Responsibility for Hartlepool Transport and Stagecoach Darlington passed to the company in 1995, and both are operated as divisions.
Developments: Service rationalisation between ST and North East Bus was concluded at the end of 1995, including a joint ticketing arrangement, enabling savings in peak vehicle run-out and transfer of operating areas between the companies.

Bus

Passenger journeys: (1992/93) 17.5 million
(1993/94) 17.3 million
(1995/96) 22.5 million
Vehicle-km: (1993/94) 8.3 million
(1995/96) 10.6 million

Number of routes: 84
Route length: (One way) 593 km
Fleet: 151 vehicles

Volvo B10M single-deck	13
Volvo B10 single-deck	12
Volvo B6 single-deck	18
Leyland Lynx single-deck	30
Mercedes midibus	33
Leyland Fleetline double-deck	26
Dennis Dominator double-deck	13
Leyland PD2 open-top double-deck	1
Volvo Olympian double-deck	5

In peak service: 92

Most intensive service: 5 min
One-person operation: 100%
Fare collection: By driver; Wayfarer machine with change-giving
Fare structure: Stage, monthly passes
Fare evasion control: Inspectors
Operational control: Route inspectors; all vehicles with mobile radio
Arrangements for elderly/disabled: Reduced fares financed by council
Average distance between stops: 400 m
Average peak-hour speed: In bus lanes, 22.5 km/h; in mixed traffic, 21 km/h
Subsidy from: Borough councils for tendered routes

Volvo B10M single-deck of CT ***1996***

NEB

North East Bus Ltd
United House, Morton Road, Yarm Road Industrial Estate, Darlington DL1 4PT
Telephone: +44 1325 355415 Fax: +44 1325 283752
Group Managing Director: Michael Widmer
Operations Director: Stephen Burd
Finance Director: Ken Watson
Engineering Manager: Jim O'Kane
Subsidiaries: Tees & District, Newport Road, Middlesbrough
Teesside Motor Services, Boathouse Lane, Stockton
United Automobile Services, Morton Road, Darlington

Current situation: Both Tees & District and Teesside Motor Services operate local and interurban services in the Middlesbrough area. The company was owned by West Midlands Travel, but was sold to the Cowie group in 1996.

Other operators

Current situation: Go-Ahead Northern, United and Hartlepool Transport run services into Teesside. Other independents include Robson and Leven Valley.

Regional Railways North East

Regional Railways North East Ltd

Type of operation: Local railway

Current situation: Local diesel trains run hourly/half-hourly on four routes radiating from Middlesbrough.

Guided bus (proposed)

Current situation: Light rail plans were scrapped in 1993 when Cleveland County Council approved the concept of guided busways and a package of measures to improve frequency of local rail services. A new programme of bus priority over a 'green route' with linked traffic lights and bus-only lanes was introduced in Middlesbrough in 1994.

UPDATED

MILANO

Population: 1.5 million, metropolitan area 4 million
Public transport: Bus, trolleybus, tramway and metro services provided by municipal undertaking now serving neighbouring communities and also operating suburban and interurban services. Suburban rail services operated by national and regionally owned railways, being upgraded to regional metro

ATM

Azienda Trasporti Municipali
Foro Buonaparte 61, 20121 Milano, Italy
Telephone: +39 2 805 5841 Fax: +39 2 86 463795
Director General: Roberto Massetti
Deputy Director General: Italo Quaranta
Director, Personnel: Giuseppe Pinna
Director, Commercial: Pierluigi Silvestri
Director, Logistics: Francesco Lipari
Manager, Surface Routes: Bruno Decio
Manager, Metro & Tram: Ettore Kluzer
Staff: 10,780

Current situation: ATM is responsible for bus, trolleybus, tram and metro services within the Milano city boundaries, and for metro, bus and tram routes in area extending to about 30 km from the city centre. In this suburban region there are three extensions of metro in the northeast, tram routes to Limbiate and Carate, and 45 bus routes.

Since 1985 ATM has staffed parking areas at metro park-and-ride stations, and in 1988 took over control of many city-centre parking meters. Area-wide integrated fares structure implemented in 1991 covering ATM and private operators' services, based on urban and interurban zones.
Developments: Plans to extend metro further into suburbs have been temporarily halted, but tramway upgrading and segregation is continuing. In an attempt to curb traffic congestion, park-and-ride sites are planned with a total of 35,000 spaces.

Passenger boardings: (All modes)
(1992) 979.5 million
(1993) 950.3 million
(1994) 891.9 million

Operating costs financed by: (Bus and trolleybus) Fares 31.9%, other commercial sources 3.3%, subsidy/grants 49.9%, deficit 15%
Subsidy from: National government

Bus and trolleybus

Passenger boardings: (1992) Bus 313.6 million urban, 49 million suburban; trolleybus 56.6 million
(1993) Bus 299.2 million urban, 47.6 million suburban; trolleybus 54.3 million

Fiat/Iveco bus and Peter Witt tram of 1928 on Via Galvani ***1996***

(1994) Bus 266 million urban, 45.5 million suburban; trolleybus 49.7 million
Vehicle-km: (1992) Bus 31.9 million urban, 21.5 million suburban; trolleybus 4.5 million
(1993) Bus 31.9 million urban, 19.9 million suburban; trolleybus 4.7 million
(1994) Bus 31.9 million urban, 20 million suburban; trolleybus 4.6 million

Number of routes: Bus 54 urban, 45 suburban; trolleybus 3
Route length: Bus 371.6 km urban, 633 km suburban; trolleybus 40.3 km
Fleet: 1,537 buses

Standard Fiat 421/418/INBUS 210	831
Fiat 471 Effeuno (1984/88)	266
Fiat 571-12 (1982)	5
Iveco Turbocity (1990)	92
Iveco-Macchi 580 (1989)	51
Bredabus (1991)	71
Menarini NU201/1 (1981)	62
Lancia 718-441 (1973)	2
Lancia 703-08 (1962)	7
Mauri Turbo 5500-5529 (1991)	30
Others	90
Disabled service vehicles	30

Fleet: Approx 155 trolleybuses

Fiat 2472F/Viberti articulated (1958/59)	about 10
Fiat 2470/Socimi (1983)	70
Bredabus 200-232 articulated (1991)	33
Socimi/Macchi articulated (1994/95)	42

Trolleybus electrification: 600 V DC
In peak service: 709 urban, 490 suburban; 114 trolleybuses

Most intensive service: 5 min
One-person operation: All routes
Fare structure: Urban, flat; interurban, zonal; multitickets;* prepurchase tickets and multitickets sold through machines and shops; weekly, monthly and annual passes
Fare collection: Prepurchase with cancellation on board, or passes
Fares collected on board: None
Fare evasion control: Random inspection with penalty
Operational control: Inspectors; computerised monitoring system being evaluated on 1 route
Arrangements for elderly/disabled: Fleet of lift-equipped midibuses
Average distance between stops: Interurban 620 m, urban 305 m
Average peak-hour speed: Bus urban 12.3 km/h, suburban 20.6 km/h; trolleybus 12.3 km/h
Bus priority: Reserved trolleybus lanes provided for part of city circular route (6.9 km) on central reserved alignment originally intended for tramway operation; priority measures to be completed for whole route
New vehicles financed by: Regional grants

Metro

Operated by ATM
Construction authority: Metropolitana Milanese SpA

Type of operation: Full metro, first line opened 1964

Passenger boardings: (1992) 342.6 million
(1993) 343.8 million
(1994) 344.7 million
Car-km: (1992) 49.8 million
(1993) 50.6 million
(1994) 51.8 million

Route length: 68.7 km
in tunnel: 47.4 km
Number of lines: 3
Number of stations: 83
in tunnel: 67
Gauge: 1,435 mm
Track: 50 kg/m UNI rail; ballasted and slab-track
Electrification: Red line: 750 V DC, third-rail collection and fourth-rail return, conversion to 1.5 kV overhead planned. Green and Yellow lines: 1.5 kV DC, overhead

Service: Peak Red line 2-2½ min, off-peak 5 min
First/last train: 05.56/00.20
Fare structure: Flat, integrated with surface transport systems for urban lines; zonal for interurban line
Revenue control: Automatic entry barriers
Automatic control: Wayside and cab signalling, automatic block with automatic train stop, and CTC; ATO, ATP and ATS on Line 3 from new computerised control centre
Surveillance: Remote control of all stations by CCTV with voice/video datalinks

Rolling stock: 714 cars

Marelli Line 1 (1962-89)	M126
Asgen Line 1 (1962-88)	M122 T82
Ansaldo/Breda/OMS Line 2 (1970-87)	M176 T88
Socimi/Fiat/Breda/OMS Line 3 (1989/90)	M80 T40

In peak service: 534 cars

Developments: Following a change of city government in 1993, plans for further major metro schemes have been postponed. But a feasibility study for a proposed light metro Line 4 to Linate airport may go ahead, though no funding has been provided. There would be interchanges with Lines 1, 2 and 3.

The only project currently active is the next stage of Line 3 construction from Zara to Maciachini (0.9 km), on which work should start in 1997 following approval of grants towards the cost in late 1996.

Funding was also approved for the projection of Line 2 from Famagosta to P le Abbiategrasso (1.3 km). A 12.6 km Line 3 extension to the northern suburbs is also proposed.

Tramway

Type of operation: Conventional tramway

Passenger boardings: (1992) 217.7 million
(1993) 205.4 million
(1994) 185.0 million
Car-km: (1992) 22.3 million
(1993) 22.1 million
(1994) 22.4 million

Route length: 158.1 km urban, 40.4 km suburban
Number of lines: 16 urban, 2 suburban
Number of stops: 523 urban, 55 suburban
Gauge: 1,445 mm
Track: 52 kg/m grooved and 50 kg/m standard rail, conventional sleepers on ballast
Max gradient: 5%
Minimum curve radius: 20 m
Electrification: 600 V DC, overhead

Service: Peak 2-5 min, off-peak 5-12 min
First/last car: 05.00/01.30
Fare structure: Flat
Fare evasion control: Travelling inspectors
One-person operation: All routes

Rolling stock: 642 cars

M4X 1500 (1928)	M353
6X 4200 articulated (1955/56/84)	M34
M8X 4800 (1973)	M44
Marelli/Asgen M8X 4900 (1976)	M100
Suburban fleet	M38 T73

In peak service: 427 cars

Current situation: Also operated are two remaining suburban tram lines, totalling 40.4 km.
Developments: Current policy is for modernisation and strengthening of the electrification equipment, along with construction of two extensions and three new light rail lines (see below). Lines 8 and 24 are being extended to the municipal boundary. The light rail schemes are

Socimi/Macchi articulated trolleybus on Route 90/91 ***1996***

FMN emus at Milano's Cadorna station **1995**

Milano metro

Piazza Castello–Parco Nord (7.1 km), Duomo–Porta Lodovica–P le Abbiategrasso (4.2 km), and Lagosta–Zara–Cinisello (8.3 km). Of the 19.6 km total, 14.9 km comprises new or rehabilitated infrastructure. New Route 27 opened in January 1996.

Orders were placed with Adtranz in 1996 for 20 low-floor trams based on the Strasbourg Eurotram design, with options for further batches.

People mover

Current situation: A Poma 2000 people mover is under construction to link Cascina Gobba metro station with San Raffaele (730 m), designed to help overcome severe traffic congestion. The line is being funded by suppliers Poma and Sasib, but will be integrated into ATM's tariff structure. Cars seating 70 will run at 2 min intervals; opening is scheduled for mid-1997.

Light rail

Under construction

Current situation: The Milano Centrale development company is financing construction of a 2.2 km light rail line on reserved track to serve the Biccoca redevelopment scheme in the northeast of the city. The route links the FS Greco Pirelli station with Zara (metro Line 3) and Precotto (Line 1). Construction, which includes 600 m of tunnel, was due to start in January 1997, for opening in 1998. Capacity of 5,000 passengers/h is being provided, and 40,000 daily journeys are expected.

SFR

Servizio Ferroviario Regionale (SFR)

Current situation: From January 1997, all regional and suburban rail services of FS and FNM (see below) in Lombardy will become the responsibility of a joint management organisation SFR. Staff from both railways will be transferred to SFR, which will co-ordinate all services but will not own trains.

The integration process started in 1995 with adoption of joint tariffs, which will be extended to include urban bus and tram services in 1997, and interurban buses in 1999. From January 1996, FS suburban services were nominally transferred to SFR control.

FS

Italian Railways (FS)
Piazza Croce della Rossa, Roma
Telephone: +39 6 84901 Fax: +39 6 883 1108

Type of operation: Suburban heavy rail

Current situation: Services provided on routes into four city terminals, electrified 3 kV DC; 20 min interval service to Malpensa airport. These are being linked by a cross-city railway (see below) to provide better distribution of passengers in the city centre, improve metro interchange, and create a regional metro serving districts between 30 and 60 km from the city centre.

Developments: Quadrupling started in late 1995 of a 22 km section of the Milano–Venezia main line between Pioltello and Treviglio. With the doubling already in progress between Lambrate and Pioltello, scheduled for 1996 opening, this will complete segregation of the new cross-city services from main line trains. Capacity will thus be raised by over 50 per cent. Stations at Lambrate, Rogoredo and Certosa are being rebuilt.

FNM

Ferrovie Nord Milano Esercizio SpA
Piazzale Cadorna 14, 20123 Milano
Telephone: +39 2 85111 Fax: +39 2 851 1551
General Manager: Arnaldo Siena
Operations Manager: Luigi Legnani
Staff: 2,096

Type of operation: Interurban railway

Passenger journeys: (1993) 42.8 million
(1994) 42.4 million
(1995) 41.1 million

Current situation: FNM, largely owned by the Lombardy region, operates 184 km of 1,435 mm gauge route out of Piazza Cadorna terminal to Saronno, Como and Laveno, with branches, electrified at 3 kV DC. A subsidiary operates local bus services. Fares cover 17.7 per cent of operating costs.

Rolling stock: 24 electric locomotives, 86 driving trailers (of which 18 bi-level) and 147 intermediate cars (of which 42 bi-level)

OM/TIBB Class 700 (1928/33)	M22
Class 730/40 (1929/30/32/53/55/57)	M27
Breda Class 750 (1982/94)	M24

Developments: Quadrupling completed of 17 km between Milano and Saronno and a third track commissioned between Bovisa and Seveso (1.9 km). A new connection at Bovisa will give access to the Passante cross-city tunnel (see below), which will carry a service of six trains per hour through to the city centre and so provide relief to the congested approaches to the existing terminal at Cadorna.

Also proposed is a further 15 km of track-doubling beyond Saronno to Busto Arsizio. A 12 km link from the Busto Arsizio–Novara line into Malpensa airport is scheduled to open in 1998. A dedicated 20-min airport service will run from central Milano.

A fleet of electric locomotives from Skoda has been commissioned for use with bi-level coaches on Passante services; FNM's share of the order for bi-level emus (see below) is 12.

Regional metro

Under construction
Construction authority: MM Strutture ed Infrastrutture del Territorio SpA
Via del Vecchio Politecnico 8, 20121 Milano
Telephone: +39 2 77471 Fax: +39 2 780033

Current situation: A 9 km underground line is under construction to bring FNM and FS lines from the north into a new city-centre station at Porta Venezia. This forms the first stage of a cross-city link which would ultimately see the line extended to Porta Vittoria, allowing through running to several FS routes in the east and south. All lines are or will be electrified at 3 kV DC.

The first section, likely to open in 1997, comprises a link from FNM lines at Bovisa, through new stations at Lancetti, P Garibaldi and Repubblica, to P Venezia. All four stations will be major bus and/or metro interchanges. At Lancetti, a link will join from FS lines at Certosa, allowing all suburban trains from the north and west to use the cross-city line.

For the start of services, a joint FS/FNM fleet of 50 four-car double-deck emus is on order from a consortium of Ansaldo, Breda, Firema and Adtranz for delivery starting in March 1997. When the entire route is completed, a further batch of some 120 trains will be needed to operate eight routes and provide a 3 min service through the cross-city tunnel.

UPDATED

Southern New Jersey light rail

Current situation: NJT is also planning two diesel-operated light rail routes in southern New Jersey. Designed to improve access to Philadelphia for areas east of the Delaware river, both routes would run to Camden for interchange with PATH metro trains. The initial route would run 55 km from Trenton (interchange with local and Amtrak trains) through Burlington county to Camden. Prospective participants in bidding for a design-build-operate-maintain contract were sought at the end of 1996.

A second route would run south from Camden to Woodbury and Glassboro (32 km), possibly utilising existing rail rights-of-way.

PATH

Port Authority of New York and New Jersey

Metro

Current situation: Services between New York (33rd Street/Penn station and World Trade Center) and New Jersey (Hoboken, Journal Square and Newark Penn) are operated by PATH. Extension of PATH's metro to Newark airport has been proposed, though an automated transit link is also being canvassed.

The Port Authority also operates the New York bus terminal into which many New Jersey commuter operations run, and the Hoboken—Battery Park ferry (for full details see under New York).

UPDATED

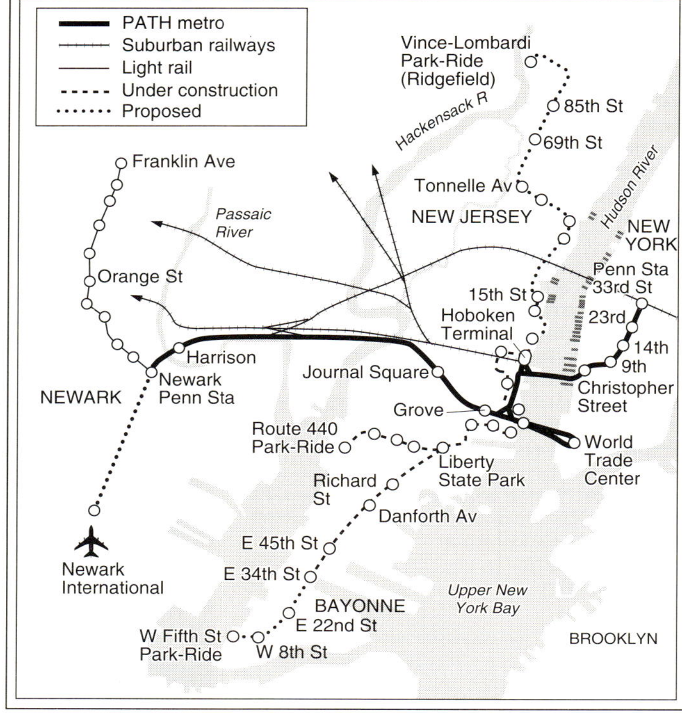

Northern New Jersey metro lines

NEWCASTLE UPON TYNE

Population: Newcastle 281,000, Tyne & Wear metropolitan area 1.1 million

Public transport: Main city services and longer distance routes operated by private companies. Metro and ferry services operated by Passenger Transport Executive (Nexus), which also subsidises one of the three local rail services. The PTE area covers surrounding urban areas of Tyne & Wear (including Gateshead and Sunderland) as well as Newcastle itself.

Network Ticketing, formed jointly by the PTE and most of the commercial bus operators in the area, issues and promotes area-wide inter-operator ticketing schemes

Optare Vecta on Busways' Metro Centre shuttle ***1995***

Stagecoach Busways

Busways Travel Services Ltd
Manors, Newcastle upon Tyne NE1 2EL, England
Telephone: +44 191 232 7371 Fax: +44 191 261 5807
Managing Director: John Conroy
Commercial Director: Peter Nash
Staff: 1,576

Current situation: Established in 1986 as a private company based on the PTE's former bus operations, the company was purchased by its management and employees in 1989. In 1994 Busways was sold to Stagecoach and operates as an autonomous regional company.

Busways trades via a number of separate divisions which had their own identities. In the Newcastle area it trades as Newcastle Busways and Blue Bus Services. In the Sunderland and South Shields areas it trades as Sunderland Busways, South Shields Busways and Economic Bus Services and in the Durham area as Favourite Services, and also runs a coaching division which trades as Armstrong Galley.

Bus

Passenger journeys: (1993/94) 82.5 million
(1994/95) 88.8 milion
(1995/96) 81.2 million

Vehicle-km: (1993/94) 23.1 million
(1994/95) 23.1 million
(1995/96) 22.7 million

Number of routes: 108
Route length: 1,420 km
On priority right-of-way: 4 km
Fleet: 524 vehicles

Leyland Atlantean double-deck	55
Leyland Olympian double-deck	95
Volvo Olympian double-deck	40
Leyland Fleetline double-deck	14
Scania N113DR6 double-deck	10
Leyland Lynx single-deck	27
Scania N113CRB single-deck	38
Dennis Dart single-deck	82
Volvo B10M single-deck	17
Volvo B10B single-deck	2
Dennis Lance single-deck	4
Scania L113CRL single-deck	4
Leyland Leopard single-deck	5
Bristol RESL single-deck	3
Bristol RELL single-deck	7
Leyland Tiger coach	9
Volvo B10M coach	15
DAF SB230 coach	2
Mercedes-Benz 709 minibus	70
Renault S56 minibus	2
Optare Metrorider	16
Iveco 59.12 minibus	7

In peak service: 454

Most intensive service: 6 min
One-person operation: 100%
Fare collection: Almex driver-operated Eurofare machines; prepurchase own-account Faresaver tickets and inter-operator Travelcards
Fare structure: Graduated for first 5 km then zonal. Limited through-ticketing with BR and metro. Some bus to bus through-ticketing within the company. Travelcards for groups of zones and Faresavers for geographic areas
Operational control: Roving inspectors/radio
Integration with other modes: Partial integration with metro
Average peak-hour speed: In mixed traffic, 18.6 km/h
Operating costs financed by: Fares 96%, contract service subsidy 4%
Subsidy from: PTE for contracted services
New vehicles financed by: Leasing or direct purchase

Go-Ahead Group

Go-Ahead Group North East Ltd
117 Queen Street, Gateshead NE8 2UA
Telephone: +44 191 420 5050 Fax: +44 191 420 0225
Managing Director: Paul Matthews
Finance Director: Julie Green
Staff: 2,755

Current situation: Operates services in Tyne & Wear, County Durham and parts of Cleveland, Northumberland and North Yorkshire. Also operates a network of limited-stop, regional and commuter services, local minibus networks, bus and coach hire, coaching holidays and long-distance coach contracts.

The company comprises a number of operating subsidiaries — VFM Buses, Coastline, Go-Ahead Gateshead, Wear Buses, Northern General (including Diamond, Shaws Coaches), and OK Travel (including Armstrongs, Gypsy Queen, Low Fell Coaches).

Developments: A guided busway had been proposed between Newcastle and Sunderland as an alternative to the planned metro extension. Following the decision to extend the metro to Sunderland over existing rail tracks (see below), further studies are to be made of guided bus service to the Washington area.

Vehicle-tracking and real-time information displays introduced in 1996 on one group of routes in the Gateshead area.

Bus

Passenger journeys: (1990/91) 113 million
(1994/95) 86 million
Vehicle-km: (1990/91) 50.7 million
(1994/95) 54 million

Fleet: 885 vehicles

Leyland Atlantean/Olympian, Metrobus, Bristol VRT double-deck	290
Dennis Dart/Lance/Javelin, Volvo B6/B10B/B10M, Leyland Leopard/Lynx/National, DAF, Optare Delta, Scania, Bristol LH single-deck	375
Iveco, Renault, Mercedes, Metrorider minibus	170
Bova, DAF, Dennis, Leyland, Scania, Volvo coach	50

In peak service: 714

One-person operation: All except one low-floor bus route in Wallsend

Fare collection: Payment to driver or prepurchase. Conversion to Wayfarer 3 system with magnetic card reader capability in progress; stored-value magnetic tickets

Operational control: Radio

Integration with other modes: Extensive integration continues with metro

Operating costs financed by: Fares 97.5%, subsidy/grants 2.5%

New vehicles financed by: Internal resources and leasing

Northumbria

Northumbria Motor Services Ltd
6 Portland Terrace, Jesmond, Newcastle upon Tyne NE2 1QQ
Telephone: +44 191 281 1313 Fax: +44 191 281 4634
Managing Director: Stephen Noble
Engineering Director: John Greaves

Current situation: Formed in 1986 when the United Automobile Company was split. Most routes run into Newcastle from outside the city, but a sizeable network has been developed in the northern suburbs and new developing areas. The company became part of the Cowie group in 1996.

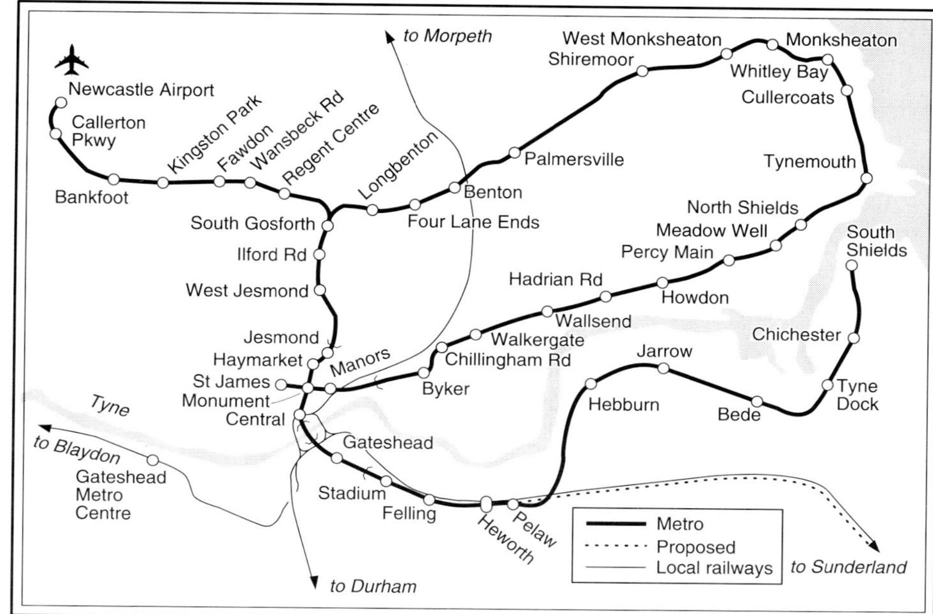

Tyne & Wear metro

Fleet: 386 vehicles

Volvo Olympian/Scania/Leyland Olympian/ Bristol VR double-deck	118
Bristol LH/Leyland National/Scania/ Optare Delta single-deck	94
Mercedes/MCW/Optare/Freight Rover minibus	130
Leyland/Volvo/Bova coach	44

Other operators

Current situation: A large number of smaller companies operate both commercial and secured routes in Newcastle and the surrounding Tyne & Wear County. These include Amberline, Classic Buses, ERB, Kingsley's North Rider, Catch-a-bus, Snaiths, and Wrights.

Nexus

Tyne & Wear Passenger Transport Executive
Cuthbert House, All Saints, Newcastle upon Tyne NE1 2DA
Telephone: +44 191 203 3333 Fax: +44 191 203 3180
Director General: Michael Parker
Head of Operations: Ian Clayton

Current situation: Following the local government changes, a joint board of district council nominees — the Passenger Transport Authority — determines policy within budgets established by the levying district councils, whose total spending is constrained by government limits. The Passenger Transport Executive, which adopted the marketing name Nexus in 1996, carries out these policies and remains directly responsible for metro and ferry services. It is empowered to provide bus services not operated on a commercial basis, and also to provide travel information and support concessionary fares schemes in conjunction with the PTA.

Since deregulation, the former policy of integration between bus and metro has had to be promoted on a commercial basis with additional metro feeder services secured by Nexus. There remains a high level of bus/metro interchange, with 23 per cent of passengers arriving at stations by bus; 22 per cent of passengers use Travelcards.

Although Nexus no longer operates buses, it secures socially necessary services not provided by commercial operators, and is involved in management of some bus stations on behalf of the local authorities which own them. Nexus has also part-funded refurbishment of Eldon Square bus concourse in Newcastle, and was involved in reconstruction of the bus station in the Haymarket area of the city.

Developments: In a draft policy document called Towards 2010 published in July 1996, Nexus put forward a range of improvements that might help stem the drift away from public transport. Since bus deregulation in

Busways' first new double-decks for five years — 40 Volvo Olympians **1996**

Easy Access Bus low-floor demonstration Route 326 **1995**

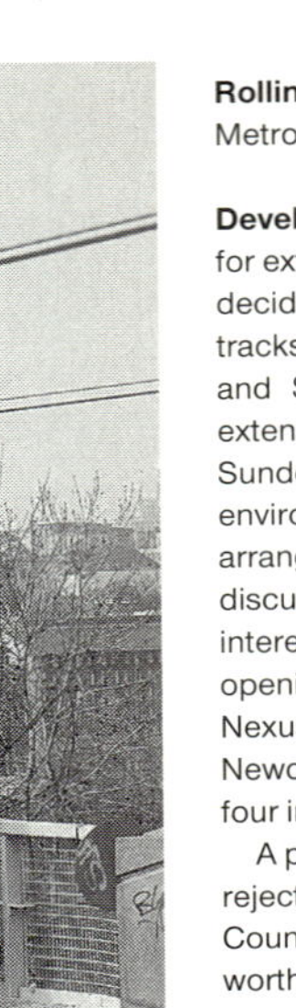

Metro train in new red livery ***1996***

1986, there has been a decline of 27 per cent in public transport patronage in the region. Amongst the suggestions is a network of busways to be run as metro feeders.

In conjunction with local bus operator Coastline, Nexus was awarded Department of Transport funding for a low-floor bus demonstration project. This involves equipping a route in north Tyneside with wheelchair accessible vehicles. The route concerned is already heavily used by elderly and disabled passengers; it offers interchange with the metro, which is itself fully accessible.

Metro

Type of operation: Full metro, first line opened 1980

Passenger journeys: (1993/94) 38.5 million
(1994/95) 37.2 million
(1995/96) 36.5 million

Route length: 59.1 km
in tunnel: 6.4 km
Number of lines: 2
Number of stations: 46

Gauge: 1,435 mm
Track: BS113A rail laid on tied concrete sleepers in tunnels; on concrete and timber sleepers with ballast on surface; PACT slab track on Byker Viaduct
Max gradient: 3.3%
Minimum curve radius: 210 m
Electrification: 1.5 kV DC, overhead

Service: 7/8-10-15 min
First/last train: 05.22/00.14
Fare structure: Zonal
Integration with other modes: High level of integration; county-wide Traveltlcket, plus substantial multimodal single through-ticket network (Metrolink Transfares); through-ticketing to airport from rail stations nationwide
Fare collection: Crouzet automatic ticket vending machines; roving inspectors
Signalling: Two-aspect lineside signals with repeaters; inductive train stop equipment to prevent over-running signals; Philips Vetag vehicle identification system
Operating costs financed by: Fares 84%, grants from central and local government, and European Social Fund 16%

Rolling stock: 90 cars
Metro-Cammell (1979/80) M90

Developments: Various options have been considered for extending the metro to Sunderland, and in 1993 it was decided to adopt a 19 km route involving sharing existing tracks with Regional Railways North East between Pelaw and Sunderland. Beyond Sunderland station a short extension would run over disused rail alignment to Sunderland University and South Hylton. Engineering and environmental studies were made in 1995, and funding arrangements for the £52 million project were being discussed with government, the EU and private sector interests. Construction could start in 1997 for 1998/99 opening. With opening of the extension to Sunderland, Nexus would no longer support the rail service between Newcastle and Sunderland, and it is proposed that the four intermediate stations would be served only by metro.

A proposal for a northern extension to Cramlington was rejected in a study carried out for Northumberland County Council in 1996, but a link to Ashington was deemed worthy of further study.

Ferry

Current situation: Cross-Tyne ferry operations by Nexus between North and South Shields carried about 600,000 passengers in 1995/96. There is half-hourly service (peak 20 min); journey time is 7 min; two vessels.

Regional Railways North East

Regional Railways North East Ltd
York YO1 1HT
Telephone: +44 1904 522354 Fax: +44 1904 523075
Director: Robert Urie

Type of operation: Local railway

Current situation: Diesel service operated on three routes totalling 82 km. Newcastle–Sunderland line (every 15 min) receives Section 20 grant payments from Nexus. Services also run to Gateshead Metro Centre (every 15 min), and to Hexham on the line to Carlisle (about half-hourly), and to Morpeth (irregular).

UPDATED

NEW ORLEANS

Population: City 497,000, city-region 1.2 million
Public transport: Regional Transit Authority controls and operates bus services and tramway. Authority also supervises other bus operations including routes contracted out to private sector. River ferries operated by Bridge Authority

Regional Transit Authority

New Orleans Regional Transit Authority
6700 Plaza Drive, New Orleans, LA 70127, USA
Telephone: +1 504 242 2600 Fax: +1 504 248 3637
General Manager: John F Potts Jr
Assistant General Manager, Operations:
W Lee Burner II
Staff: 1,414

Passenger boardings: (1993) 48.9 million
(1994) 50.7 million
(1995) 70.5 million

Operating costs financed by: Fares 45%, other commercial sources 4%, subsidy/grants 10%, tax levy 41%
Subsidy from: FTA 19.7%, local sales tax 80%

Buses run on the former tramway reservation on Canal Street, while St Charles tramcar uses its on-street loop

Current situation: The RTA, controlled by a board appointed by the City of New Orleans and Jefferson Parish Council, was created in 1979 and took over transit operations in 1983. In 1985 the RTA took over transit operations in the neighbouring city of Kenner. Contracted operations ended in 1989, when a local management team, Transit Management of Southeast Louisiana, took over.

An increase in the sales tax allocated to the RTA from ½ cent to 1 cent was approved in 1985 and is used to fund capital improvements (25 per cent) and operations (75 per cent). The RTA demands that 45 per cent of operating costs be covered from fares.

The tramway plays a modest part in the city's transit. Several proposals exist for modern light rail routes, in particular in the former tram right-of-way in the median of busy Canal Street from the Waterfront to City Park Avenue (6.4 km), to link the airport with downtown (21 km) using mostly existing rail right-of-way, and several extensions. A new fleet of 35 cars would be required (see below).

The 1988-built Riverfront line is being converted to 1,586 mm gauge to standardise the rolling stock fleet.

Bus
Passenger boardings: (1993) 42.9 million
(1994) 44.3 million
(1995) 63.4 million
Vehicle-km: (1995) 20.5 million

Number of routes: 62
Route length: 936 km
On priority right-of-way: 3.5 km
Fleet: 553 vehicles

Blue Bird (1986/87)	36
GMC (1979)	173
MAN 792 (1985/86)	165
Orion V (1990)	13
Boyerville trolley replicas (1989)	8
New Flyer D40 (1994)	73
Orion (1996)	85

In peak service: 420

Most intensive service: 2-3 min
One-person operation: All routes
Fare collection: Cash or token to GFI electronic farebox; monthly or visitor pass
Fare structure: Flat base ordinary and express fares; prepurchase tokens; 10 cent coupon for multitransfers; monthly pass (not valid in Kenner); 1- and 3-day visitor passes
Operational control: Route inspectors; on-bus radio
Integration between modes: Park-and-ride
Arrangements for elderly/disabled: 'The Lift' special door-to-door lift service operated under contract carried 214,000 passengers in 1994; some fixed-route buses lift-equipped; dial-a-ride; reduced fare
Average peak-hour speed: 16.9 km/h

Tramway
Type of operation: Conventional tramway, opened 1835

Passenger boardings: (1993) 5.9 million
(1994) 6.1 million
(1995) 7.1 million
Car-km: (Annual) 1.1 million

Route length: 26 km
Number of lines: 2
Gauge: St Charles line 1,586 mm, Riverfront line 1,435 mm
Electrification: 600 V DC, overhead

Service: Peak 4-5 min, off-peak 7 min; 24-h service on St Charles route
Fare structure: Flat (as bus)
One-person operation: All cars

Rolling stock: 54 cars

Perley Thomas Car Co (1923)	M37
W2 (ex-Melbourne)	M2
PCC (ex-SEPTA Philadelphia)	M12
Others	M3

Current situation: The St Charles route runs along a median strip in St Charles Avenue and is the last remaining US tram line to run pre-PCC cars. It is designated a national monument. A three-year refurbishment was completed in 1990. Unconnected Riverfront route opened 1988 and extended in 1990.
Developments: Refurbishment of 1923-vintage cars was completed in 1995. Further extensions planned (see above).

RTA has bought 12 PCC tramcars from SEPTA Philadelphia. Three are to be rebuilt with Perley Thomas replica bodies and wheelchair access for use on the Riverfront line. In addition, it is seeking interest in providing 35 replica cars based on the Perley Thomas veterans. These would be required for the proposed Canal Street line.

Other operators
Current situation: Services in Jefferson Parish are provided by two operators – Louisiana Transit (east bank), and Westside Transit (west bank). There are 13 routes, five of which run to central New Orleans. Jefferson Parish itself owns the fleet of 29 Flxible buses which operates the east bank service; a further 33 Flxibles serve the west bank.

Mississippi River Bridge Authority
2001 Behrman Avenue, New Orleans, LA 70114

Ferry
Current situation: Operates a single ferry route across the Mississippi river, with three vessels, carrying foot passengers and vehicles.

UPDATED

NEW YORK
Population: 7.3 million, metropolitan area 13.2 million
Public transport: Bus, metro (subway) and two suburban rail networks operated by various subsidiaries of the Metropolitan Transportation Authority including sub-urban bus operations contracted for Nassau County. MTA, also responsible for seven bridges and two tunnels, is governed by a board representing city and suburban communities served. A regional metro (PATH) is operated between New York and New Jersey by the Port Authority. A number of private bus lines provide substantial additional suburban and commuter services from and within New York under City Department of Transportation, and other commuter bus services operate from New Jersey (see also Newark/New Jersey). There are also some private door-to-door minibus pick-up services and express routes to Manhattan. A private bus operation is contracted for the Westchester County area. Ferries operate to Staten Island, New Jersey and Long Island leisure areas

MTA
Metropolitan Transportation Authority (MTA)
347 Madison Avenue, New York, NY 10017, USA
Telephone: +1 212 878 7000
Fax: +1 212 878 7030/7031
Chair: E Virgil Conway
Executive Director: Marc V Shaw
Chief Financial Officer: Stephen V Reitano
Chief Information Officer: Albert Gabbay
Headquarters staff: 441

Passenger journeys: (All modes)
(1993) 1,629 million
(1994) 1,706 million
(1995) 1,711 million

Operating costs covered by: Fares 40.7%, toll income 11.2%, other commercial sources 11.6%, subsidy/grants 22.4%, state and regional tax levy 14.2%

Current situation: Created in 1965 by New York State as the Metropolitan Commuter Transportation Authority, it was initially given responsibility for purchase and rehabilitation of the Long Island Rail Road. In 1968 it was renamed MTA and its powers expanded to include additional agencies. These agencies, renamed in 1994, include the MTA Long Island Rail Road, MTA NYC Transit, MTA Metro-North Railroad, MTA Bridges & Tunnels, MTA Staten Island Railway, MTA Card Company, and MTA Long Island Bus. Some 13.2 million people in 14 counties are served.

Some 5.7 million riders use MTA public transport services each weekday, and 734,000 vehicles use the seven bridges and two tunnels operated by MTA Bridges & Tunnels. Surplus revenue from bridge and tunnel tolls helps support the other MTA operations. Since 1970 the Triborough Bridge & Tunnel Authority (now MTA Bridges & Tunnels) has handed over some $4,100 million to the parent organisation. The surplus generally accounts for 6 per cent of MTA's funds, with fare income, government subsidies and revenues from freight hauling, concessions, rents and investments helping support the costs of MTA operations.
Developments: Recession in the early 1990s caused a reduction in patronage and income from taxes, leading to financial difficulties, but, rather than cutbacks, MTA proposed major investment designed to stimulate ridership by provision of better service. These plans were late confounded by an annual deficit of some $400 million.

In late 1995, the new Chairman E Virgil Conway announced a revised $11.9 billion five-year capital programme, of which the principal feature is expenditure of $1.9 billion on 840 metro cars, $888 million on refurbishment of 70 metro stations, $610 million on new and refurbished emus for Long Island Rail Road, and $282 million emus for Metro-North. In addition, $700 million will buy 2,300 new buses for NYCTA. In April 1996 these plans were further revised and confirmed, together with increased financial support from the city, state and federal governments designed to eliminate MTA's deficit and ensure financial stability through to the end of the century. MTA's costs will be reduced by $3 billion over the 1995-99 period, during which there will be just one fares increase.

Amongst revisions to the plan were provision of funds for infrastructure projects such as extension of the Long Island Rail Road to Grand Central to free capacity at Penn station, and reconstruction of the Franklin Avenue metro shuttle.

Bombardier (right) and Kawasaki prototypes of NYCTA's next generation of metro rolling stock
1996

MTA New York City Transit

New York City Transit Authority (NYCTA)
370 Jay Street, Brooklyn, NY 11201
Telephone: +1 718 330 3000 Fax: +1 718 243 4566
President: Lawrence G Reuter
Executive Vice President: Barbara R Spencer (Acting)
Senior Vice President, Subways: Joseph E Hofmann
Senior Vice President, Buses: Millard L Seay
Staff: 42,632

Passenger journeys: (Bus and metro)
(1993) 1,475 million
(1994) 1,531 million
(1995) 1,559 million

Operating costs financed by: Fares 61%, other commercial sources including tolls 3.4%, subsidy/grants 12.9%, tax levy 25.9%
Subsidy from: Federal, state and local government

Current situation: Almost all surface public transport in the five boroughs of New York City is provided by the TA and its subsidiaries.
Developments: Automatic fare collection is being installed in all buses and metro stations, for completion during 1996. In the MTA capital programme announced in November 1996, NYCTA will place large orders for metro cars and buses (see below).

NYCTA and the Port Authority of NY State are considering conversion to trolleybus operation of bus Route 15, the second most heavily used route in the US.

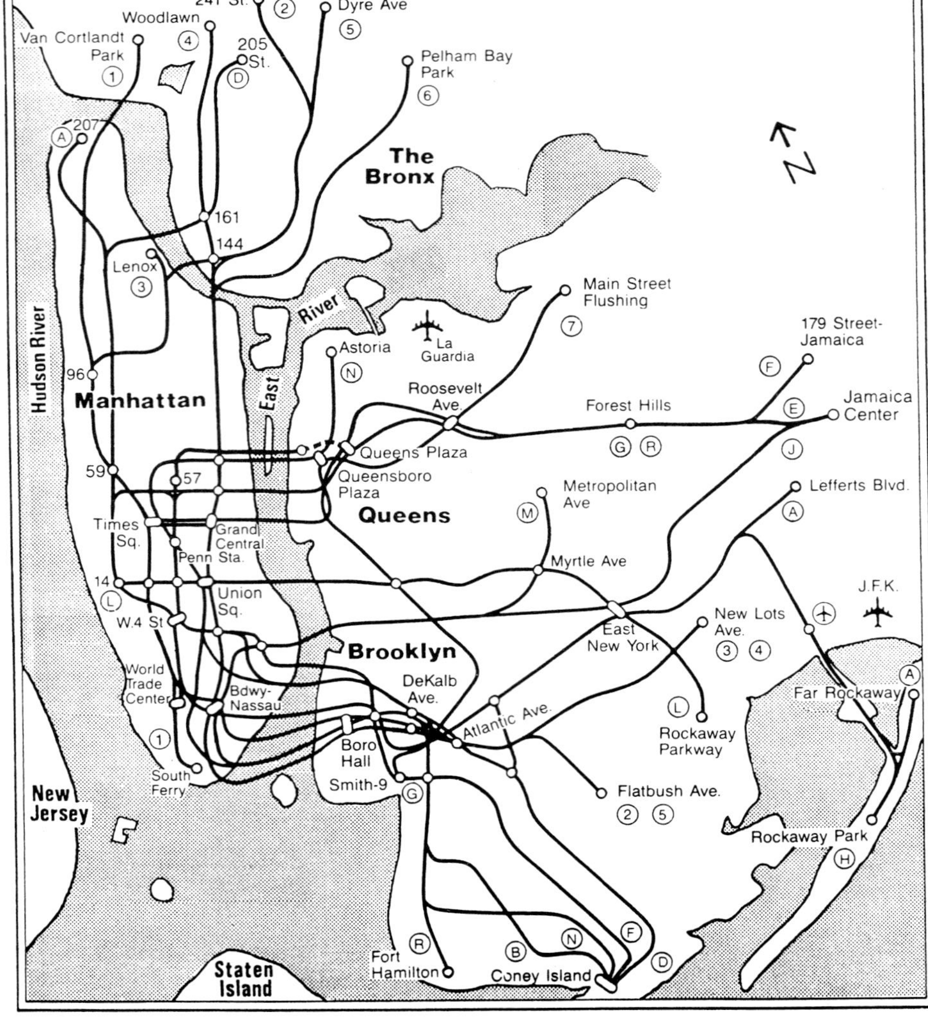

New York's metro

MTA New York City Bus

Staff: 11,486

Passenger journeys: (1993) 445 million
(1994) 451 million
(1995) 460 million
Vehicle-km: (1993) 142 million
(1994) 144 million
(1995) 143 million

Number of routes: 227
Route length: (One way) 2,695 km
Fleet: 3,554 vehicles, all air conditioned

GMC RTS 04 (1981/85)	1,924
GMC RTS 05 (1986)	294
TMC RTS 06 (1987)	294
TMC RTS (1990)	394
TMC RTS (1993)	167
BIA Orion V (1993)	213
TMC RTS 06 (1994)	104
BIA Orion V (1996)	164

In peak service: 3,067
On order: 380 buses, including 50 Orions and options being exercised for a further 200; 60 being remanufactured by Midwest Bus; plus 70 articulated from New Flyer Industries, with an option for 40 more

Most intensive service: 1½ min
One-person operation: All routes
Fare collection: Prepurchase token, electronic fare card (MetroCard) or cash to driver (exact fare); tokens and fare cards sold at metro stations and retail outlets
Fare structure: Flat, higher for express routes; free transfer to Jamaica Buses, Green Bus, Command Bus and Queens Surface services; discounted return trip tickets sold for selected routes feeding metro stations
Operational control: All buses with mobile radio link to central dispatch office
Arrangements for elderly/disabled: A half-fare pass is offered in co-operation with the NY City Department for the Aging, the NY City DoT and MTA; senior citizens' fare concessions financed by reimbursement from the City of New York; bus fleet lift-equipped; Access-A-Ride contracted demand-response service provides door-to-door transport for ADA eligible persons at standard bus fares, carried 0.2 million passengers in 1995

New York Bus Service Manhattan express route contracted by the NY DoT **1997**

Operating costs financed by: Fares 43.7%, other commercial sources 5%, subsidy/grants 18.6%, tax levy 37.3%
Source of subsidy: City and State of New York (including proceeds of gross receipts tax on oil companies), FTA grants, MTA Bridge & Tunnel Authority surplus
New vehicles financed by: Capital programme funds

Developments: All buses were retrofitted to accept the MetroCard electronic fare card in 1995. New bus deliveries totalled 245 in 1995 and 666 in 1996, with a further 1,154 likely to be purchased in the period 1997-2000, and another 90 remanufactured. In addition 500 RTS 04s from the early 1980s are being overhauled to extend their service life until retirement in 2001. Of the new buses, 460 will be articulated vehicles intended for the busiest routes.

NYC Transit is managing an industry/government consortium led by Bus Industries of America (Orion) and General Electric which is developing a prototype low-floor bus with hybrid electric propulsion.

MTA New York City Subway

Staff: 24,969

Type of operation: Full metro, initial route opened 1904

Passenger journeys: (1993) 1,029 million
(1994) 1,080 million
(1995) 1,093 million
Car-km: (1993) 475 million
(1994) 483 million
(1995) 487 million

Route length: 371 km
in tunnel: 221 km
Number of lines: 25
Number of stations: 468
in tunnel: 277
elevated: 153
Gauge: 1,435 mm
Track: Timber sleepers on ballast or embedded in concrete, or concrete with resilient pads

Tunnel: Cut-and-cover, under-river bored tunnel, cast-iron with concrete liners, some concrete horse-shoe
Electrification: 625 V DC, third rail

Service: Peak 2-10 min, off-peak 5-15 min, late night 20 min; 24 h service at most stations
Fare structure: Flat
Fare collection: Automatic turnstiles accessed by token or electronic fare card (MetroCard), sold at stations and retail outlets
Operating costs financed by: Fares 70.6%, other commercial sources 2.6%, FTA, state and local government subsidies 9.7%, tax levy 19.5%
One-person operation: Being tried out on five shuttles (see below)
Signalling: Wayside signals/train control

Rolling stock: 5,801 cars

51 ft 4 in cars	
AC&F R26 (1959/60)	M110
AC&F R28 (1960/61)	M100
St Louis Car R29 (1962)	M236
St Louis Car R33 (1962/63)	M494
St Louis Car R33S (1962/63)	M39
St Louis Car R36 (1963/64)	M424
Kawasaki R62 (1984/85)	M323
Bombardier R62A (1985/87)	M825
Kawasaki R110A test train (1992)	M10
75 ft cars	
St Louis Car R44 (1972/74)	M278
Pullman Standard R46 (1975/77)	M752
Westinghouse-AmRail R68 (1986/88)	M425
Kawasaki R68A (1988/89)	M200
Bombardier R110B test train (67 ft) (1992)	M9
60 ft 6 in cars	
Budd R32 (1964/65)	M594
St Louis Car R38 (1965/67)	M196
St Louis Car R40 (1968/69)	M296
St Louis Car R40M (1968/69)	M98
St Louis Car R42 (1969/70)	M392

In peak service: 4,758

Developments: Substantial rolling stock purchases are envisaged at a cost of $1.9 billion in the MTA capital improvement programme, with a new fleet of 840 advanced-technology cars, designated R142, planned for delivery by 2001. Based on two prototype trains currently on trial, the stock will be powered by AC traction motors with gate turn-off thyristor control. NIAC/Kawasaki built ten 51 ft cars and Bombardier nine 67 ft cars. Most of the new cars will replace ageing equipment, but 100 will be needed for service expansion in 2001 when the Queen's Connector project (see below) is completed.

Three builders submitted bids for the initial order for 740 R142 cars for the IRT lines — Kawasaki, Bombardier and GEC Alsthom — and a contract was to be placed in early 1997. A further 100 cars, designated R143, will be ordered in 1998 for the IND and BMT lines. These cars will be equipped with transmission-based signalling and train control, as will the R142s after commissioning. A further 662 cars will be purchased after 2001.

By late 1996, 124 stations had been renovated, most under the Station Renovation Programme inaugurated in 1994. Plans call for a work on a further 43 stations between 1997 and 2001, plus completion of 34 projects started between 1992 and 1996 but delayed through shortage of funds. In addition, a real-time information system is to be provided at 140 stations.

A major programme of resignalling will start with the L-Carnasie line, where equipment installed prior to World War I will be replaced by transmission-based signalling. Work is under way on a trial installation planned for operation by 2003.

Crime and fare evasion have been brought under control, helped in particular by the automatic revenue collection system being installed to accept the electronic MetroCard. Staff-operated entry gates with card-swipe readers and full-height fencing have been installed at 250 stations, with the remainder scheduled for similar upgrading by mid-1997.

A major investment project from the MTA's 1992-96 development plan is construction of the connection between the 63rd Street tunnel terminal at Queensbridge/21st Street and Queen's Boulevard line. This will bring substantial capacity benefits at a cost of $645 million. Completion is scheduled for 2001.

Trials of driver-only operation started on five shuttle routes in September 1996.

Flxible on crosstown Route M42 **1997**

Morrison Knudsen M-6 emu of Metro-North **1996**

PATH metro train at Newark, NJ

MTA Staten Island Railway

Staten Island Rapid Transit Operating Authority
60 Bay Street, Staten Island, NY 10301
Telephone: +1 718 876 8239 Fax: +1 718 876 8258

Chief Officer: Samuel S Holmes
General Superintendent, Operations: Owen P Swords
General Superintendent, Maintenance: John H McCabe
Staff: 328

Type of operation: Full metro

Passenger journeys: (1993) 5.1 million
(1994) 5.1 million
(1995) 5.1 million

Route length: 23 km
Number of lines: 1
Number of stations: 22
Gauge: 1,435 mm
Track: 50 kg/m ARA-B rail on timber sleepers in rock and/or cinder ballast
Electrification: 600 V DC, third rail

Service: Peak 5 min, off-peak 30-60 min; 24 h service
Fare structure: Flat
Fare collection: Entry/exit collection and/or onboard token sale; MetroCard accepted at some stations
Operating costs financed by: Fares 32.8%, other commercial sources 1.6%, subsidy/grants 54.4%, tax levy 11.2%
One-person operation: None
Signalling: Colour-position-approach light signals; double rail track circuit

Rolling stock: 64 cars

St Louis Car R44 (1974)	M44
St Louis Car R44 rebuilt (1972/74)	M20

In peak service: 36

Current situation: Major track and roadbed upgrading in progress to install 56 kg/m long-welded rail throughout.

MTA Long Island Bus

MTA Long Island Bus
700 Commercial Avenue, Garden City, NY 11530-6434
Telephone: +1 516 542 0100 Fax: +1 516 542 1428
Chair: E Virgil Conway
President: Helena E Williams
Staff: 1,028

Current situation: MTA Long Island Bus, the former Metropolitan Suburban Bus Authority, operates services for an area with about 1 million population throughout Nassau County and parts of western Suffolk County and eastern Queens, serving four metro stations at Flushing, Jamaica and Far Rockaway, New York, and 45 LIRR stations.

A consolidation of 10 formerly private bus companies, MTA Long Island Bus is an agency of the Metropolitan Transportation Authority operating under a lease and operating agreement with Nassau County.

Developments: Unlike other MTA agencies which are directly funded by the MTA, LI Bus receives all of its operating subsidies and capital funding from Nassau County as designated recipient of federal and state funds. As a result, funding is erratic. As a remedy, it is proposed to fully integrate LI Bus into the MTA, with its capital programme funded and administered by the MTA.

In 1995, LI Bus took over the Nassau County paratransit operation, with 22 vehicles. Installation of an automated vehicle location system is under way, based on global positioning. Automatic fare collection equipment is also being installed throughout the fleet.

JFK Flyer service from several southern Nassau and Queens county locations to JFK international airport started in September 1996, with 24 round trips daily.

Bus

Passenger journeys: (1993) 25 million
(1994) 25.5 million
(1995) 25 million
Vehicle-km: (1993) 16.4 million
(1994) 16.6 million
(1995) 16.8 million

Number of routes: 53
Route length: (One way) 1,469 km
Fleet: 318 vehicles

GMC (1968/73)	20
Flxible, various (1970/78/81)	102
Gillig Phantom (1988)	61
Flxible Metro (1984)	34
Orion V (1990/91/92)	88
Orion II	5
Coach & Equipment	8

In peak service: 252
On order: 25 40 ft buses from BIA/Orion

Most intensive service: 8 min
Fare collection: Exact fare or token to farebox; prepurchase ticket
Fare structure: Base fare with 1 zone surcharge; additional charge for transfer; bus/rail through 'Unitickets' with LIRR (see below); 20-trip prepurchase ticket savings book
Fares collected on board: 97%
Operational control: Route dispatchers/radio-based control centre
Arrangements for elderly/disabled: Half-fare at all times; 125 buses lift-equipped, operating 16 routes
Integration with other modes: Routes serve 45 LIRR and 4 metro stations; joint weekly/monthly tickets
Operating costs financed by: Fares 46.4%, other commercial sources 1.1%, subsidy/grants 52.5%
Subsidy from: County of Nassau 45.9%, State of New York 50.7%, FTA 3.4%

MTA Long Island Rail Road

MTA Long Island Rail Road
93-02 Sutphin Boulevard, Jamaica Station, Jamaica, NY 11435
Telephone: +1 718 990 7400 Fax: +1 718 990 8212
President & General Manager: T F Prendergast
Chief Transportation Officer: James Dermody
Staff: 5,987

Type of operation: Suburban heavy rail

Passenger journeys: (1993) 71.6 million
(1994) 73.2 million
(1995) 73.6 million

Current situation: Operates 520 km of route with 11 branches, serving 134 stations, radiating from terminals in Manhattan (Penn station, shared with Amtrak and New Jersey Transit), Brooklyn (Flatbush Avenue) and Queens (Hunterspoint Avenue), 1,435 mm gauge, 220 km electrified at 750 V DC third rail. Zonal ticket system, with some higher price 'Unitickets' valid on local buses; most commuters use monthly tickets. Operating subsidy from MTA accounts for about half of operating costs, the rest comes from fares revenue.

Electric trains provide service on virtually all lines in New York City and Nassau County, and from most major Suffolk County destinations. Remaining services are diesel-hauled (mostly push-pull).

Rolling stock: 934 emu cars, 191 coaches, 73 diesel locomotives

Metropolitan M-1 emu (1968-72)	M760
Metropolitan M-3 emu (1984-86)	M174
Coaches (1950-63)	T181
Mitsubishi/Tokyu Car bi-level (1991)	T10

Developments: Investment in the 1992/96 period was focused on replacement of the diesel loco fleet and general infrastructure renewal. A train of 10 bi-level cars hauled by electro-diesel locomotives went into service in 1993. Following trials, an order was placed in 1994 with Mitsui/Kawasaki Railcar for 114 bi-level cars to replace the ageing diesel-hauled fleet, while 23 diesel and 10 dual-mode locomotives were ordered from GM EMD in 1995.

Under the current MTA capital improvement programme, LIRR will also begin replacement of its oldest emus dating from 1968, with $610 million allocated for purchase of 133 cars and rebuilding of a further 208 from the existing fleet. $243 million will fund track rehabilitation and there will be $172 million for station improvements, including construction of high platforms at many locations.

MTA Metro-North

MTA Metro-North Railroad
347 Madison Avenue, New York, NY 10017
Telephone: +1 212 340 3000 Fax: +1 212 340 4037
President: Donald N Nelson
Vice President, Operations: George Walker
Vice President, Finance & Administration:
Genevieve T Firnhaber
Vice President, Planning & Development: Howard Permut
Vice President, Capital Programs: William M Aston
Staff: 5,598

Type of operation: Suburban heavy rail

Passenger boardings: (1993) 58.9 million
(1994) 61.9 million
(1995) 62.2 million

Current situation: Almost all commuter rail services in New York and Connecticut states formerly operated by Conrail came under the control of Metro-North in 1983. Three main lines — the Hudson, Harlem, and New Haven — run north and east from New York's Grand Central terminal, while the Port Jervis and Pascack Valley lines run from Hoboken in New Jersey, west of the Hudson river; total 429 km, of which 111 km electrified at 11 kV 60 Hz and 133 km at 600 V DC third rail, with 118 stations.

Service on the New Haven line and its three branches is provided under a contract with the Connecticut Department of Transportation, which funds capital improvements within the Connecticut service area. Service west of the Hudson river, in the New York State counties of Orange and Rockland on the Port Jervis (103 km, eight stations) and Pascack Valley (10 km, three stations) lines, is operated by New Jersey Transit (qv) under a contract with MNR.

Developments: The 1992/96 $954 million capital programme continued the emphasis on infrastructure upgrading and replacement of equipment, which account for some two-thirds of the cost. Capacity improvements have included provision of a third track on the Mid-Harlem line and additional cars for east of Hudson services where service provision was raised in 1995. An 8 km extension of the Dover Plains line to Wassaic is in progress for 1997/98 completion.

MNR's share of the new MTA capital improvement programme includes $282 million for 80 emu cars, seven dual-mode locomotives, and 15 push-pull coaches.

Several intermodal improvements are also under way. Parking is being expanded, and feeder buses run under contract by private operators serve major stations on all three main lines. Joint ticketing with suburban bus lines has been extended, and a new monthly MNR/New York City Transit ticket became available in 1995.

In collaboration with NJ Transit and PATH, construction is in progress of the Secaucus transfer, which will provide through running to Penn station from New Jersey lines

PATH's ferry terminal at Battery Park City

which currently terminate at Hoboken. A new Hudson river crossing has also been proposed.

Rolling stock: 725 emu cars, 78 coaches, 39 diesel and 7 dual-mode locomotives

Pullman-Standard ACMU (1962/65)	M61
Budd M-1 (1971/73)	M178
GE M-2 (1973/76)	M242
Budd M-3 (1983/84)	M142
Bombardier Shoreliner (1985/87)	T78
Tokyu Car M-4 (1987)	M54
Morrison Knudsen M-6 (1994/95)	M48
Bombardier (1996)	T34
Others	12

Bureau of Transit Operations

New York City Department of Transportation, Bureau of Transit Operations
Battery Maritime Building, New York, NY 10004-1498
Telephone: +1 212 806 6900 Fax: +1 212 806 6905
Commissioner: Elliot G Sander
Chief Transportation Officer: Janet O Lanphier

Passenger journeys: (All modes)
(1993) 87.1 million

Current situation: The Bureau directly operates the Staten Island ferry, and licenses operation of other ferry routes by private companies. It also contracts operation of local buses, primarily in the borough of Queens, with limited services also in Brooklyn, Manhattan and the Bronx. Express commuter buses link Queens, Brooklyn and the Bronx with Manhattan's business districts. The Bureau's responsibilities for paratransit services were transferred to NYCTA in mid-1993.

Ferry

Passenger journeys: (1990) 22.2 million
(1991) 21.2 million
(1993) 18.3 million

Current situation: The Staten Island ferry links Manhattan and Staten Island with seven double-deck ferries operating a maximum 15 min peak frequency, and hourly all night. Fares cover 12.8 per cent of operating costs.

Contracted bus

Passenger journeys: (1990) 74.8 million
(1991) 73.1 million
(1993) 68.8 million
Vehicle-km: (1993) 45.2 million

Current situation: Bus operations are contracted with seven private companies – Command Bus (140 vehicles), Green Bus Lines (188), Jamaica Buses (96), Liberty Lines Express (109), New York Bus Service (113), Queens Surface (273) and Triboro Coach (208). Buses are owned mainly by the DoT, with a fleet of 79 provided by the contractors themselves.

Number of routes: 91
Route length: (One way) 2,334 km
On priority right-of-way: 57 km
Fleet: 1,131 buses

NYCDoT vehicles	
GMC P8M-4905A (1979)	18
Flxible 870 (1980)	15
GMC RTS-04 (1985)	270
GMC RTS-06 (1986)	131
MCI Classic (1988/89)	350
TMC RTS-06 (1994)	268
Contractors' vehicles	
GMC New Look (1970/72/73/74/75/76)	25
GMC RTS-02 (1979)	26
GM Canada New Look (1979/82)	19
MC RTS-04 (1984)	6
GM Canada Classic	3

In peak service: 898
Average age of fleet: 6.3 years

Most intensive service: 2 min
Fare structure: Flat
Fare collection: Exact fare in coins or tokens to farebox; prepurchase tickets
Operating costs financed by: Fares 45.3%, subsidy/ grants 54.7%

Port Authority of NY & NJ

The Port Authority of New York & New Jersey
1 World Trade Center, Suite 67W, New York, NY 10048
Telephone: +1 212 435 7000 Fax: +1 212 435 4107
Executive Director: George J Marlin
Director & General Manager: Michael DePallo

Current situation: The bi-state Port Authority runs PATH, a metro crossing the Hudson river and linking stations in New York with Hoboken, Journal Square and Newark in New Jersey, and owns and operates two New York bus terminals for commuter services to Manhattan. With private sector partners, PATH in 1989 reinstated ferry service across the Hudson river.

PATH has under way a capital improvement programme costing $1 billion. This includes new and rehabilitated cars, a car maintenance facility opened in 1990, modernisation of electrical power and signal systems, station improvements, continued work on safety improvement, and provision of facilities for the elderly and disabled. The PA has also purchased, from surpluses made on Hudson river bridge and tunnel tolls, buses and bus-related facilities at a cost of $440 million for lease to the two states for use within 120 km of the Authority's bus terminal, which is served by a 4 km exclusive contraflow peak-only busway. Some 3,000 buses have been purchased for use in New York and New Jersey, representing about 50 per cent of the fleets.

Metro (PATH)

Staff: 1,173, including police

Type of operation: Full metro, initial route opened 1908, PATH created 1962

Passenger journeys: (1992) 55.4 million
(1993) 56.5 million
(1994) 59.2 million

Route length: 22.2 km
in tunnel: 11.9 km
Number of lines: 4
Number of stations: 13 (7 in NJ, 6 in NY)
in tunnel: 10
Gauge: 1,435 mm
Track: Conventional sleepers on ballast; some sections on concrete trackbed with resilient pads, with 60 kg/m rail
Max gradient: 4.8%
Minimum curve radius: 27.4 m
Tunnel: Single track, mainly cast-iron or concrete construction
Electrification: 650 V DC, third rail

Service: Frequent, 24 h
Fare structure: Flat; multijourney tickets; through-ticketing with other operators
Revenue control: Exact change, automatic turnstiles
Surveillance: Police monitoring; CCTV; surveillance of turnstiles by CCTV
Operating costs financed by: Fares 35%, other commercial sources 1.6%; deficit financed from revenues of the parent Port Authority, which is self-supporting

Signalling: Block signal system with automatic tripper

Rolling stock: 342 cars

St Louis Car PA1 (1965)	M157
St Louis Car PA2 (1967)	M44
Hawker Siddeley Canada PA3 (1972)	M46
Kawasaki PA4 (1986)	M95

Developments: Work is in progress on a new interchange station at Secaucus in the New Jersey Meadowlands, where PATH and NJT/Amtrak routes cross.

The fleet of 1972-built PA3 cars is to be refurbished with AC traction motors and ATO.

Commuter bus and coach terminal

Current situation: Extensive commuting by bus and coach into New York takes place, much of it across the Hudson river from New Jersey. Nearly 1,600 buses daily use the exclusive bus lane into the PA's terminal in Manhattan. The 4 km bus lane operates in the eastbound direction along the westbound median lane of highway I-495 between the New Jersey Turnpike and the Lincoln Tunnel. Ramps link the tunnel direct to the bus terminal, facilitating commuter bus operations and helping to reduce traffic congestion in Manhattan streets. Interchange is provided with several metro lines.

The terminal handles some 200,000 passengers daily, most of whom are commuters using 40 bus lines providing some 6,700 movements (900 arrivals in the morning peak hour). Flows of up to 26,000 passengers/h have been estimated to pass through Lincoln Tunnel at peak times.

Ferry

Passenger journeys: (1991) 2.1 million
(1993) 2.3 million
(1994) 2.4 million

Current situation: Operation started 1989 of ferry service between floating terminals at Hoboken, NJ, and Battery Park City, lower Manhattan, running every 10 min between 07.00 and 10.00 and 16.00 and 21.00, and every 20 min all day Saturday; journey time 8 min; fleet of three vessels.

The operator, the Arcorp/Hartz group, has a 20-year franchise and must provide service quality sufficient to relieve demand in excess of PATH's rail capacity.

Light rail (planned)

Current situation: Amongst several proposals, that for a 3.5 km light rail line with seven stations along 42nd Street in Manhattan was approved by the New York City Council in May 1994. The promoters, the New York City DoT and the 42nd Street Development Corp, received expressions of interest from 13 groups in 1992. A planning grant of $0.9 million was made by the FTA in 1993 to maintain the project's impetus. A fleet of 17 cars would be required to handle traffic estimated at 9 million passengers annually.

Following scrapping in 1995 of plans for a 32 km automated link from Manhattan to LaGuardia and JFK airports, the PA now plans an automated metro at JFK airport. The 17 km network would act as a distributor linking car parks with six local and international terminals at the airport. Branches would run to the metro station at Howard Beach and to the Long Island Rail Road's Jamaica station. A further line could be built to provide the long-planned link to LaGuardia airport (18 km), but its very high cost of $3.4 billion renders the project improbable.

More than $400 million of the $1 billion estimated cost has already been raised from the $3 Passenger Service Tax that the PA has been levying on air passengers since 1992, and this source will provide a further $300 million. The remainder will come from a bond issue secured against revenue from fares.

UPDATED

NICE

Population: 356,000
Public transport: Bus services operated by franchised undertaking responsible to local concessionaire. Some local rail services run by National Railways (SNCF) and Provence Railway (CP). Light rail proposed

Semiacs Transport

Société d'Economie Mixte Intercommunale pour l'Amélioration de la Circulation et du Stationnement
38 boulevard Raimbaldi, 06000 Nice Cedex 1, France
Telephone: +33 4 92 17 52 53 Fax: +33 4 93 13 08 65
President: Gilbert Stellado

Current situation: In 1992 the city authorities granted the public transport operating concession to Semiacs, the semi-public regional traffic and parking authority. Operations are contracted to ST2N.

ST2N

Société Nouvelle des Transports de l'Agglomération Niçoise
PO Box 1209, 16 avenue Thiers, 06004 Nice Cedex 1
Telephone: +33 4 93 16 52 52 Fax: +33 4 93 88 72 14
President & Director General: Francois Baronnet-Fruges
Director General: Jean-Claude Bermond
Staff: 678

Developments: Operational control and passenger information systems have been developed with the Serel microwave videobus system. Constant monitoring of a vehicle's position is obtained by a central control point and is retransmitted to each stop providing an updated schematic panel illuminated display of progress and approximate waiting times. Over 200 stops are equipped.

ST2N markets and promotes its services under the corporate title 'Sunbus'.

Bus

Passenger journeys: (1993) 36.8 million
(1994) 38 million
(1995) 36.8 million
Vehicle-km: (1993) 8.3 million
(1994) 8.4 million
(1995) 8.2 million

Number of routes: 32
Route length: (One way) 329 km
On priority right-of-way: 24 km
Fleet: 209 buses

Renault SC10	76
Renault PR100	14
Renault R312	52
Renault PR180 articulated	47
Heuliez GX107	4
Heuliez GX187 articulated	1
Van Hool AU138 midibus	5
Gruau MG36 minibus	2
Peugeot Durisotti J9 minibus	8

In peak service: 168

Most intensive service: 8 min
One-person operation: All routes
Fare collection: Single tickets validated on board; carnets; monthly passes; 1-, 5- and 7-day tourist passes
Fare structure: Flat
Operational control: Inspectors/mobile radio; computerised cibus system
Average peak-hour speed: 12 km/h

Renault PR312 in Sunbus promotional livery

Operating costs financed by: Fares 50.3%, other commercial sources 5.5%, subsidy/grants 44.2%
Subsidy from: City

SNCF

French National Railways, Marseille Division

Current situation: Local trains known as Metrozur run about hourly along the coastal route from Cannes through Nice to Ventimiglia (more frequently in summer), and irregularly from Nice-Ville to Breil-sur-Roya (44 km).
Developments: Introduction of double-deck emus planned for the Cannes—Ventimiglia route.

CP

Société Nouvelle des Chemins de Fer de la Provence
PO Box 387, 40 rue Clement Roassal, 06007 Nice
Telephone: +33 4 93 88 34 72 Fax: +33 4 93 16 28 71

Type of operation: Local railway

Current situation: Metre-gauge route runs inland from Nice to Digne (151 km).
Developments: Much of the line was severely damaged by floods in late 1994 and did not reopen throughout until 1996.

Light rail (proposed)

Current situation: Three routes totalling 26 km have been under study as possible rapid transit alignments, and in 1995 the group of local authorities involved decided to press ahead with light rail proposals rather than the VAL automated metro considered earlier. Line 1 (11 km) will run east-west through the city centre to the airport and will have extensive park-and-ride lots at its extremities. Two other lines are planned, one of which might utilise part of the route of the CP railway.

UPDATED

NICOSIA

Population: 170,000
Public transport: Bus services provided for city and suburbs by private company supervised by Ministry of Transport

Leoforeia Leikosias

Leoforeia Leikosias Ltd (Nicosia Bus)
2 Heroes Str, PO Box 3641, Nicosia, Cyprus
Telephone: +357 2 448841 Fax: +357 2 466323
Chair: Stefos Kaloyeros
Operating Manager: Costas Christodoulou
Staff: 103

Current situation: Formed in 1971 with private capital and remains unsubsidised. Activities were begun with very old equipment and small buses (up to 35-seat capacity). Now 90 per cent of the fleet has been renewed and most vehicles can carry up to 90 passengers.

Bus

Passenger journeys: (1993) 3.8 million
(1994) 3.6 million
(1995) 3.4 million
Vehicle-km: (1993) 4 million
(1994) 3.7 million
(1995) 3.8 million

Number of routes: 16
Route length: (One way) 234 km
Fleet: 109 vehicles

Bedford	18
Fiat	48
Mercedes	5
Renault	1
KMC	1
Ford	1
Mercedes/Hino/Isuzu coach	17
MITS/Hino/Asia/Toyota minibus	18

Most intensive service: Peak 10-15 min, off-peak 20-30 min
One-person operation: All routes
Fare collection: Payment to driver/prepurchase
Fare structure: Zonal (2 types of tickets). Monthly passes
Fares collected on board: 70%
Fare evasion control: Spot checks by inspectors; penalty
Operational control: Route inspectors with radio
Average distance between stops: 250 m
Average peak-hour speed: In mixed traffic, 16 km/h
Operating costs financed by: Fares 100%, other commercial sources 4%
New vehicles financed by: Long-term bank loans

UPDATED

Asia minibus of Nicosia Bus ***1997***

NIZHNI NOVGOROD

Population: 1.4 million
Public transport: Bus and trolleybus/tramway services operated by municipal undertakings; metro.

Upravlenie Automobil'novo Transporta

Upravlenie Automobil'novo Transporta
Nizhni Novgorod, Russia

Bus

Passenger journeys: 119 million (annual)

Current situation: Bus, express bus and fixed-route taxibus services are operated.

Fare collection: Prepurchase tickets; day tickets for bus only or combinations of other modes

Fleet: Comprises Ikarus 260/280, LIAZ 677/5256, LAZ 695, MAN and others ex-German cities, and PAZ 3205 taxis

Ex-East German Ikarus 260 at the main railway station terminus of express Route 80 ***1997***

Tramvaino-Trolleibusnoe Ob'yedinenie

Tramvaino-Trolleibusnoe Ob'yedinenie
Yaroslavskaya ul 25, Nizhni Novgorod 603000
Telephone: +7 8312 332315

Trolleybus

Passenger journeys: 175 million (annual)

Current situation: A fleet of about 250 Uritsky ZIU9 trolleybuses is operated over 21 routes extending to some 300 route-km. The system comprises three portions, of which one on the right bank of the Oka river is physically separate.

Tramway

Current situation: There are 15 routes, many on segregated right-of-way, extending to some 183 route-km.

Rolling stock: 382 cars

ČKD Tatra T3	M200
ČKD Tatra T3m	M32
Kirov KTM5	M140
Riga RVZ6	M10

T3 cars cross the Oka river bridge ***1997***

Upravlenie Metropolitena

Type of operation: Full metro, initial route opened 1985

Passenger journeys: 66 million (annual)

Route length: 13 km
Number of lines: 2
Number of stations: 12
Gauge: 1,524 mm
Electrification: 825 V DC, third rail

Service: Peak 2 min, off-peak 6 min
Fare structure: Flat
Fare collection: Token to turnstile

Rolling stock: 50 cars

Mytischy G-1	M50

Current situation: Line 1 opened 1985, linking suburban industrial area with the main railway station; extended 1986. Further 15.1 km Line 2 with nine stations under construction, of which portion with two stations opened 1994.

UPDATED

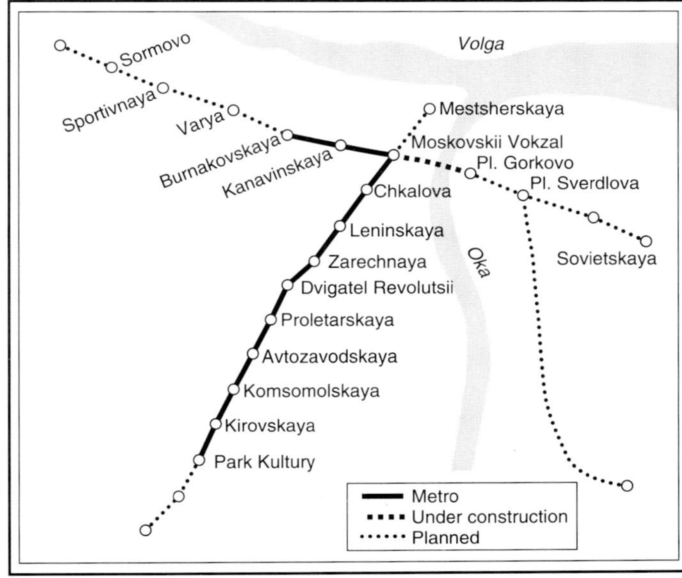

Nizhni Novgorod metro

NORFOLK

Population: City 260,000, area served 1 million
Public transport: Bus and ferry services provided by public authority controlled by representative board; paratransit and vanpool schemes operated; light rail planned

Tidewater Regional Transit

Tidewater Transportation District Commission
PO Box 2096, 1500 Monticello Avenue, Norfolk, VA 23501, USA
Telephone: +1 757 640 6200 Fax: +1 757 640 6303
Chair: John Butt
Executive Director: L A Kimball
Operating Manager: Milton Woodhouse
Staff: 430

Current situation: Established in 1973, TTDC is a regional transportation authority covering Norfolk and four other cities in southeastern Virginia — Portsmouth, Virginia Beach, Suffolk and Chesapeake — with a service area of some 1,600 km². TTDC is responsible for planning, regulation, acquisition, operation or provision of public transport. It does not have taxing authority so relies on annual contributions from the state and cities served.

To provide for the many low-density areas, contracted on-demand services, paratransit and vanpool schemes (called Maxi-Ride) have replaced conventional bus services. Paratransit carried 194,000 passengers in 1994/95.

Vanpooling was launched in 1977 with vehicles leased by TRT to employees. The number of leasings has declined from a peak of 103 vehicles carrying 455,000 passengers in 1981, to 13 carrying 109,000 in 1994/95.

TRT's Elizabeth river ferry

TRT vanpool minibus

TRT also leases vehicles to communities and private-interest groups.

Developments: TRT has implemented the multicentred timed transfer system (known as Direct Transfer) which brings all fixed-route and paratransit services together in a unified network. Services have timed connections with each other on a 30 min (sometimes 60 min) interval basis at a number of transfer centres. All transport services, including taxis, have been encouraged to participate.

Merger of TRT with neighbouring Peninsula Transportation District Commission is under consideration; the two organisations would form a regional transportation authority covering the entire Hampton Roads cities region. The new executive director, Kim Kimball, was appointed on a one-year contract in September 1996 to take the merger forward.

Bus

Passenger boardings: (Including ferry)
(1992/93) 8.5 million
(1993/94) 8.4 million
(1994/95) 8.2 million

Vehicle-km: (1992/93) 9.2 million
(1993/94) 9 million
(1994/95) 9.8 million

Number of routes: 30
Route length: (One way) 472 km
Fleet: 163 vehicles, plus 85 vans on contract operations

Grumman Flxible (1973)	3
GMC/TRS (1980)	15
Flxible Metro (1989/90)	62
Boyertown replica trolley (1983-88	28
BIA 02501 (1992)	6
BIA 05501 (1993/95)	49
Dodge B350 van (contract)	85
Chance replica trams (1996)	15

In peak service: 125

Most intensive service: 15 min
One-person operation: All services
Fare collection: Payment to driver or pass
Fare structure: Flat; free transfer; 10-ticket carnets
Arrangements for elderly/disabled: Fleet of Handi-Ride vans and minibuses, 60 lift-equipped; network of accessible fixed-route services; Handi-Ride services carried 167,000 passengers in 1994/95
Integration with other modes: Carpools, lease of vans to vanpool participants (84,000 trips in 1994/95); park-and-ride
Operating costs financed by: Fares 45%, subsidy/grants 55%
Subsidy from: FTA 17%, state 22%, local 23%

Ferry

Current situation: Service across the Elizabeth river between Norfolk and Portsmouth is aimed at both residents and visitors, but most use is for leisure purposes. The two vessels carry about 0.5 million passengers annually.

Light rail (planned)

Current situation: A 28 km light rail line with 13 stations to link Norfolk and Virginia Beach, utilising the alignment of a disused main line railway, is at the planning stage. Construction is not expected to start before 2000. Also under study is a link to the Norfolk naval base.

UPDATED

NOTTINGHAM

Population: 272,000
Public transport: Most bus services in city and suburbs provided by municipally owned company, with others operated by private firms. Local rail service; light rail proposed

Nottingham Transport

Nottingham City Transport Ltd
Lower Parliament Street, Nottingham NG1 1GG, England
Telephone: +44 115 950 5745 Fax: +44 115 950 4425
Managing Director: John Pope
Engineering Director: John Lowrie
Staff: 1,140

Current situation: The city established its bus undertaking as a separate company in 1986. The fleet of Erewash Valley Services of Ilkeston, acquired in 1988, was integrated in 1990. South Notts of Gotham was acquired and integrated in 1991.

Developments: Dennis Arrow double-decks were introduced on the Forest park-and-ride service in 1996; low-floor Optare Excels being delivered.

Barton Buses Optare Excel on park-and-ride shuttle ***1997***

Bus

Number of routes: 100
Route length: (One way) 284 km
Fleet: 422 vehicles

Leyland Atlantean AN68 double-deck	83
Leyland Lion double-deck	13
Scania double-deck	35
Volvo Citybus double-deck	37
Leyland Olympian double-deck	2
Volvo Olympian double-deck	11
Dennis Arrow double-deck	4
Leyland National single-deck	30
Leyland Lynx single-deck	28
Scania single-deck	16
Volvo B6 single-deck	13
Volvo B10B single-deck	20
Volvo B10M single-deck	5
Optare Excel low-floor single-deck	5
Leyland Atlantean single-deck	1
Volvo coach	1
Leyland Tiger/Royal Tiger/Bova coach	11
Renault midibus	36
Mercedes minibus	47
Optare Metrorider minibus	24

Most intensive service: 2½-5 min
One-person operation: 100%
Fare collection: Autofare (farebox), and Eurofare
Fare structure: Stage; 1-, 2- and 4-week network passes
Fare evasion control: Uniformed inspectors
Operational control: Route inspectors/mobile radio
Arrangements for elderly/disabled: Free travel in city and half rate in county area, financed by rate fund grants
Average distance between stops: 200-250 m
Average peak-hour speed: 15 km/h
Bus priority: City-centre access priority by sections of bus-only road

Barton

Barton Buses
Manvers Street, Nottingham NG2 4PQ
Telephone: +44 115 950 1274

Current situation: Barton operates rural and interurban routes with coaches adapted for local services. In 1989 the company was taken over by the holding company which owns Trent Motor Traction. The fleet profile has been improved by replacement of 20-year-old coaches with new and second-hand buses.

Fleet: 110 buses, 10 coaches

Other operators

Current situation: Three operators run competitive local services, while Trent and East Midland run long-distance services. Camm's (10 buses), Dunn Line (18) and Pathfinder of Newark (20) operate services within the city.

Central Trains

Central Trains Limited
Stanier House, 10 Holliday Street, Birmingham B1 1TH
Telephone: +44 121 643 4215 Fax: +44 121 644 4461
Managing Director: Mark Causebrook

Type of operation: Local railway

Current situation: Services run into Nottingham from stations on lines to Derby (26 km), Grantham (35 km), Newark (28 km) and Mansfield (30 km); diesel-worked, about hourly service.
Developments: Reopening is in progress of the local railway to Worksop. The service to Newstead, inaugurated in 1993, was extended to Mansfield in 1995. The final section through to Worksop is scheduled to open in June 1998.

Light rail (planned)

Greater Nottingham Rapid Transit Ltd
4-8 Regent Street, Nottingham NG1 5BQ
Telephone: +44 115 950 2233 Fax: +44 115 950 0320
Managing Director: Pat Armstrong

Current situation: A light rail route, Nottingham Express Transit (NET), is planned linking the city's Midland station with Hucknall and Cinderhill to the north. The 14 km route would run 4 km on-street from the city centre to Wilkinson Street where it would join the reopened railway to Newstead and Mansfield (see above), over which it is proposed to share track to Hucknall. A short branch runs to Cinderhill and Phoenix Park. There will be 23 stops, five of them with park-and-ride spaces for a total of 3,000 cars.

This is the initial route of a proposed network of six lines extending to 45 km. It is being promoted by GNRT, which is a joint venture between Nottingham City Council, Nottinghamshire County Council, and Nottingham Development Enterprise, representing 13 private sector investors.

Developments: Parliamentary approval for Line 1 was granted in 1994, and the track-sharing proposal has been declared feasible by the Railway Inspectorate, subject to a second-stage assessment of local conditions and detailed design considerations. A fleet of 15 cars will be required, and a design has been sought from potential bidders. In 1995 a private sector consortium consisting of manufacturers AEG/ABB (now Adtranz), civil contractor Tarmac and operators Transdev and Nottingham City Transport joined the promoters to develop the project through to tendering. Subject to availability of government and private sector funding, a concession is expected to be awarded in September 1997 for construction to start in 1998.

Buses of three operators in Market Square — NCT Mercedes mini, Barton Leyland National and Pathfinder Peugeot tri-axle
1997

UPDATED

NOVOSIBIRSK

Population: 1.5 million
Public transport: Bus and trolleybus/tramway services provided by separate municipal undertakings. Metro; suburban rail

Avtotrans

Avtotrans
Novosibirsk, Russia

Bus

Passenger journeys: 90 million (annual)

Route length: 637 km
Fleet: About 400 vehicles, including Ikarus 260/280, LIAZ 677 and LAZ 695

One-person operation: All routes
Fare collection: Cash to conductor
Fare structure: Flat
Average peak-hour speed: 19 km/h

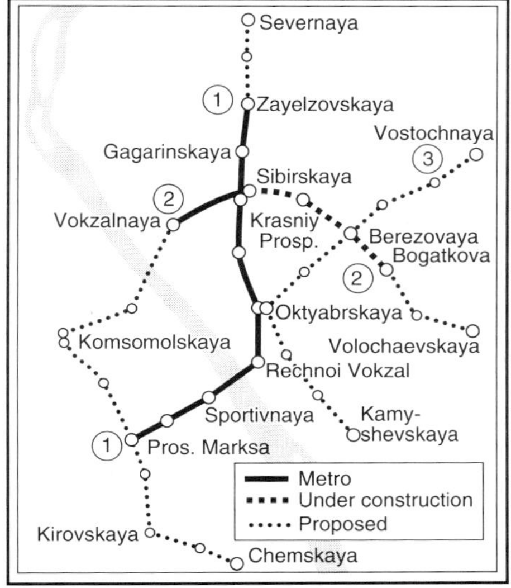

Novosibirsk metro

Urban Electric Transport

Urban Electric Passenger Transport Executive
Lenina ul 59, Novosibirsk 630004
Telephone: +7 3832 220844
General Manager: B Y Ten

Trolleybus

Passenger journeys: (1990) 121.2 million

Number of routes: 30
Route length: 500 km
Fleet: Approx 250 vehicles

Uritsky ZIU9	About 240
ZIU10	8

One-person operation: All routes
Fare collection: As bus
Fare structure: Flat
Average peak-hour speed: 19 km/h

Tramway

Staff: 639

ZIU9 trolleybus at the central market
1997

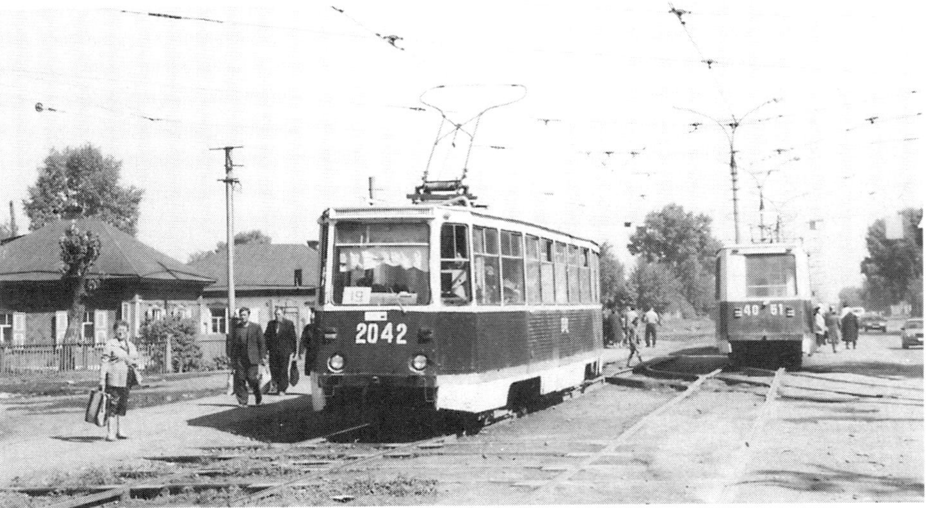

KTM5 cars on Route 19 in the southwestern suburbs ***1997***

Type of operation: Conventional tramway

Passenger journeys: (1990) 119.4 million

Number of routes: 18
Route length: 353.7 km
Electrification: 550 V DC, overhead

Rolling stock: 260 cars

Riga RVZ6	M30
Ust-Katav KTM5	M230

Current situation: Changes took place in 1990 on opening of the metro spur from Sibirskaya to Vokzalnaya (main station), when the network was split into two separate systems. Elimination of all but one route from the city centre has been balanced by new construction in the western suburbs.

Novosibirsk Metropolitan

Novosibirsk Metropolitan Municipal Enterprise
Ul Serebrennikovskaya 34, 630099 Novosibirsk
Telephone: +7 3832 223170
General Manager: V I Demin
First Deputy Director: V A Lokhmatov
Chief Engineer: N P Balakleevskiy
Staff: 1,500

Type of operation: Full metro, initial route opened 1985

Passenger journeys: (1991) 62.4 million
(1992) 82 million
(1993) 90.9 million

Route length: 13 km
Number of lines: 2
Number of stations: 10
Gauge: 1,520 mm
Electrification: 825 V DC, third rail

Service: Peak 3-5 min, off-peak 4-10 min
Fare structure: Flat
Signalling: Full ATC with first Russian application of computers to train control

Rolling stock: 76 cars

Current situation: Initial section of Line 1 opened 1985 along with short section of Line 2 to the main railway station opened 1990. Line 1 extended north from Sibirskaya to Pl Kalinina in 1992.

Planned four-line system totalling 52 km with 36 stations now augmented by proposed orbital Line 5. Construction of Kirov Line 2 (4.2 km with five stations) started 1987.

Suburban rail

Passenger journeys: (1990) 53.9 million

Current situation: Suburban trains operate over several routes extending to some 550 km, electrified 3 kV DC; fleet of 378 emu cars.

UPDATED

NÜRNBERG

Population: 493,000, region 1.7 million
Public transport: Bus, tramway and metro services operated in Nürnberg and on behalf of the municipalities of Erlangen and Fürth by VAG, a subsidiary of municipally owned utilities holding company Städtische Werke Nürnberg GmbH. Regional metro (S-Bahn) services operated by German Railway (DB). All public transport in area around Nürnberg, including local bus services in Schwabach and regional bus services, are co-ordinated by the regional transit authority VGN

VGN

Verkehrsverbund Grossraum Nürnberg GmbH
Rothernburger Strasse 9, 90443 Nürnberg, Germany
Telephone: +49 911 270750 Fax: +49 911 270 7550
Directors: Norbert Mahr
Dr Willi Weisskopf

Passenger journeys: (All modes and operators)
(1993) 163.9 million
(1994) 165.1 million
(1995) 167.1 million

Fare structure: Zonal, free transfer between all modes and operators
Fare collection: Season tickets (62%), multiride tickets (26%), single tickets (10%), others (2%); vending machines at metro stations and all tram stops, sales by driver only on buses
Operating costs financed by: Fares 32%, subsidy/grants 68%
Subsidy from: Federal government 51%, state 11%, local 38%

Current situation: Regional transit authority founded by city of Nürnberg and 14 other local authorities, with the Bavarian state government, to co-ordinate public transport in Nürnberg and the surrounding area. Federal government participation ended in January 1996. Integration of services started 1987. Fare structures have been standardised, allowing free transfer between modes and operators. Schedules have been co-ordinated to reduce travelling time. Revenues are pooled between operators and local authorities provide subsidy. All planning and marketing is undertaken by VGN.

VAG

VAG Verkehrs-Aktiengesellschaft
Am Plärrer 27, 90443 Nürnberg
Telephone: +49 911 2830 Fax: +49 911 283 4641
Chair: Dr Wolfgang Krug
Directors: Dr Friedrich König
Herbert Dombrowsky
Dr Rainer Müller (Manager, Bus)
Manager, Metro & Tram: Ernst Wentzel
Staff: 2,096

Passenger boardings: (All modes, including Fürth and Erlangen)
(1993) 140 million
(1994) 143 million
(1995) 143 million

Current situation: Operations are conducted jointly with those of Stadtwerke Fürth, which operates a fleet of 76 buses, and incorporating local services for the town of Erlangen (traffic figures for both operations included in VAG's totals).

The future of the tramway network appears assured, though the new city council elected in 1996 favours extension of the metro rather than the tramway.

Some of the statistics given below have been restated and so differ from those previously published.

Developments: VAG has formed a joint venture with Würzburg transport operator WVV to operate local rail services which are being divested by DB under its regionalisation programme. Frankenbahn GmbH will initially run four local lines, one of which links Nürnberg with Gräfenberg.

CNG-powered low-floor MAN NL202 kneeling at a street-level stop ***1997***

U-Bahn train at Rathenauplatz **1997**

VAG's new low-floor tram at Plärrer **1997**

Bus

Pssenger journeys: (1995) 39.1 million
Vehicle-km: (1993) 19.5 million
(1994) 20.1 million
(1995) 20 million

Number of routes: 60
Route length: (One way) 599 km
Fleet: 208 vehicles (including Erlangen), plus 85 hired

MAN SL202 (1985/88)	54
MAN NL202 (1990/94)	38
MAN NL222 (1995)	28
Mercedes O405 (1986)	7
Mercedes O405N (1992/94)	12
Mercedes O405G articulated (1987)	5
MAN SG292 articulated (1988)	3
MAN SG272 low-floor articulated	47
Others	14

Most intensive service: 5 min
One-person operation: All routes
Fare collection: Prepurchase at ticket sales offices, kiosks and ticket vending machines or driver-issued by ticket printers
Fare structure: Zonal, common throughout VGN area, with additional short-distance ticket; 75% of sales are passes
Fares collected on board: Bus 8%
Fare evasion control: Surveillance by driver and specialised staff; penalty
Operational control: Mobile radio
Integration with other modes: Some park-and-ride
Average distance between stops: 521 m
Average peak-hour speed: 22.2 km/h
Operating costs financed by: Fares 61%
Subsidy from: Cross-subsidy from other municipal activities (electricity and water supply) and, where necessary, from city
New vehicles financed by: Internal resources

Developments: VAG is testing an 'Economy' bus, of which purchase price is about DM40,000 or 10 per cent lower than that of a standard vehicle.

Metro

Type of operation: Full metro (U-Bahn), initial route opened 1972

Passenger boardings: (1993) 79 million
(1994) 81.8 million
(1995) 88.2 million
Car-km: (1993) 5.6 million
(1994) 6 million
(1995) 6 million

Route length: 24.9 km
in tunnel: 18.4 km
Number of lines: 2
Number of stations: 35
in tunnel: 27
Gauge: 1,432 mm
Track: Track on concrete, without ballast
Max gradient: 4%
Minimum curve radius: 100 m
Tunnel: Cut-and-cover with some bored single-track
Electrification: 750 V DC, third rail

Service: Peak 3⅓ min, off-peak 3⅓-10 min
First/last train: 05.00/01.00
Fare structure: As bus
Operating costs financed by: Fares 95%
Arrangements for elderly/disabled: All metro stations to be retrofitted with lifts
Integration with other modes: Park-and-ride
One-person operation: All trains
Surveillance: CCTV at all stations

Rolling stock: 75 two-car sets

MAN/Siemens DT1 (1970/84)	M63 T63
AEG/Siemens DT2 (1993)	M12 T12
Works cars/locomotives	8

On order: 12 two-car sets

Current situation: Northeastern extension of Line U2 from Schoppershof to Herrnhütte (1.7 km) opened in January 1996. A further extension to the airport (3.3 km) is under construction for opening in 2000.

Also under construction is an extension of Line 1 with five stations in Fürth. A firm decision on construction of proposed Line 3 (Wetzendorf—Plärrer—Zoo, 12.4 km, 18 stations), has yet to be taken but this now looks likely to go ahead.

Tramway

Type of operation: Conventional tramway

Passenger boardings: (1993) 36.3 million
(1994) 36.3 million
(1995) 30.7 million
Car-km: (1993) 7.1 million
(1994) 6.6 million
(1995) 6.4 million

Route length: 39.5 km
On private right-of-way: 19.8 km
Number of lines: 6
Number of stops: 79
Gauge: 1,435 mm
Max gradient: 7%
Minimum curve radius: 18 m

First/last car: 04.30/01.30
Fare structure: As bus
Fare collection: Vending machines only, no onboard sales
One-person operation: All routes
Operating costs financed by: Fares 44%

Rolling stock: 135 cars

MAN/Siemens some TR4X (1957/66)	
MAN/Siemens 300 articulated (1962/66)	M50
MAN/Siemens 360 articulated (1976, rebuilt 1992)	M12
Adtranz/Siemens GT6N 6-axle (1996)	M14

On order: 26 four-section from Adtranz/Siemens for 1998 delivery

Developments: The tramway is to be retained and upgrading to light rail standards is planned. In particular, it is hoped to raise average speed from the present 15 km/h to 18-20 km/h.

A new route from Thon to Kornburg is planned, as is a route to Erlangern, but metro extension is now likely to be given priority. Long-term infrastructure spending is estimated at DM130 million.

Wutzer

Stadtverkehr Wutzer & Co
Schillerplatz, 91126 Schwabach
Telephone: +49 9122 84011
Manager: Dieter Frank

Passenger journeys: (1994) 0.7 million
(1995) 0.8 million
Vehicle-km: (Annual) 0.4 million

Current situation: Independent operator providing local bus services in Schwabach over six routes.

OVF

Omnibusverkehr Franken GmbH
Nelson-Mandela-Platz 18, 90459 Nürnberg
Telephone: +49 911 244010 Fax: +49 911 244 0199
Manager: Adolf Eiber

Passenger journeys: (1992) 6.6 million
(1993) 6.9 million
(1995) 7.2 million
Vehicle-km: (1992) 6.4 million
(1993) 7.8 million
(1995) 9.3 million

Current situation: Regional bus company, owned by DB, providing suburban and rural services.

Other operators

Current situation: Thirty-five independent operators provide bus services as associate members of VGN, carrying about 0.5 million passengers a year for 3.8 million vehicle-km.
Developments: Services in outlying areas are to be improved, especially feeders to rail stations.

DB

Deutsche Bahn AG, Geschäftsbereich Nahverkehr
Regionalbereich Nordbayern
38-40 Sandstrasse, 90443 Nürnberg
Telephone: +49 911 219 3330 Fax: +49 911 219 3287
Manager, S-Bahn: Nikolaus Meyer

Suburban railway

Type of operation: Suburban heavy rail

Passenger boardings: (1993) 20.1 million
(1994) 21.1 million
(1995) 21.4 million

Current situation: DB operates suburban and rural services within the VGN area on two S-Bahn and 15 other routes. Lines radiating from Nürnberg are being upgraded to form an S-Bahn (regional metro) network under a public-transport-orientated Total Traffic Plan limiting highway construction. Stage 1 involves provision of additional tracks and electrification over three routes, from the city centre to Lauf (17 km, inaugurated 1987), Altdorf (24 km, inaugurated 1992), and Roth (26 km) under construction for 1999 completion.

A second stage taking in the line to Erlangen and Forchheim would bring the total to 100 route-km on completion, expected before 2000. A third track is required on the Nürnberg—Fürth corridor to relieve saturation.

Services are operated by three- and five-car push-pull trainsets with Class 243 electric locomotives running at 20 min intervals during peak hours, and every 40 min off-peak.

H-Bahn (proposed)

Current situation: The city authorities have discussed with Siemens possible construction of an H-Bahn (qv) suspended monorail linking Messezentrum U-Bahn station with Moorenbrunn, serving the new fairgrounds and hospital complex.

UPDATED

ODESA

Population: 1.2 million
Public transport: Bus and trolleybus/tramway services provided by separate municipal undertakings with growing private-sector involvement; metro planned

Upravlenie Automobil'novo Transporta

Upravlenie Automobil'novo Transporta
Odesa, Ukraine

Bus

Passenger journeys: (Annual) 170 million
Vehicle-km: 30 million

Number of routes: 65
Route length: 570 km
Fleet: 260 vehicles, including Ikarus 260, 280, LAZ and LIAZ

One-person operation: All routes
Fare collection: None

Developments: Private operators were permitted from 1993 and now account for about 20 per cent bus-km. Routes or groups of routes are franchised to the highest bidder. Most are in the hands of six major private operators, but there are also a large number of entrepreneurs running leased vehicles. Operations are largely unregulated.

No fares are charged on city buses and trams since the operating ratio fell below 10 per cent in 1995 and receipts from fares failed to cover the cost of collection.

ZIU9 trolleybus in central Odesa ***1997***

Tramvaino-Trolleibusnoe Upravlenie

Tramvaino-Trolleibusnoe Upravlenie
Vodoprovodnaya ul 1, Odesa 270046
Telephone: +380 48 222 6088

Trolleybus

Number of routes: 19
Route length: 136 km
Fleet: Approx 320 vehicles

ZIU9	300
YuMZ-T1	21

One-person operation: All routes

Tramway

Type of operation: Conventional tramway

Route length: 259 km
Number of lines: 25
Number of stops: 423
Gauge: 1,524 mm
Electrification: 600 V DC, overhead

Rolling stock: About 450 cars, all T3, many of which are out of use

Metro (planned)

Current situation: Engineering design studies in progress for a 55 km network, of which Line 1 would run 11 km from the city centre to the southwest suburbs and the new Black Sea port being developed at Yuzhny.

UPDATED

OKAYAMA

Population: 590,000
Public transport: City bus services provided by private company which also operates tramway. Additional suburban and longer-distance services provided by six other private companies and JR

Okayama Denki Kido 'Okaden'

Okayama Electric Tramway Company
2-8-22 Tokuyashicho, Okayama-shi 703, Japan
Telephone: +81 862 722101 Fax: +81 862 721288
President: Motoi Matsuda
Staff: 399

Passenger journeys: (Both modes)
(Annual) 22.5 million

Operating costs financed by: Fares 97.4%, other commercial sources 2.6%

Current situation: Okaden is the main bus operator in central Okayama and also runs a tramway.

Standard Okaden bus on city Route 27 in central Okayama ***1995***

Bus

1-14-41 Konancho, Okayama-shi 700
Telephone: +81 862 23 7221
Director: Takuya Miyake
Staff: 238

Number of routes: 65
Route length: (One way) 151.7 km
On priority right-of-way: Bus lanes 7.7 km
Fleet: 138 buses, 43 coaches, including Mitsubishi Fuso

Most intensive service: 5 min
One-person operation: All routes
Fare collection: Control tickets on entry from machine at centre doors, payment on exit to farebox at front door
Fare structure: Flat/stage; 1-, 3- and 6-month passes
Fares collected on board: 76.4%
Operational control: Route inspectors
Arrangements for elderly/disabled: Half fare
Average distance between stops: 400 m

Average peak-hour speed: Bus lanes 18 km/h; mixed traffic 14 km/h

Tramway

2-8-22 Tokuyashicho, Okayama-shi 703
Telephone: +81 862 722101
President: Motoi Matsuda
Directors: Toshio Ishizu, Motoji Yoshinaga
Staff: 70

Type of operation: Conventional tramway

Passenger journeys: (1990/91) 4.4 million

Route length: 4.7 km
Number of lines: 2
Number of stops: 15
Gauge: 1,067 mm
Track: Conventional sleepers on ballast, sleepers on concrete, both types with resilient pads
Electrification: 600 V DC, overhead

Service: Peak 3 min, off-peak 5 min
First/last car: 06.00/21.50
Fare structure: Flat; prepurchase coupon tickets and 1-, 3- or 6-month passes
Fare collection: Farebox or prepurchase
Operating costs financed by: Fares 96.6%, other commercial sources 3.4%
One-person operation: All cars

Rolling stock: 21 cars

Utsunomiya Sharyo (1953) (ex-Nikko)	M4
Alna Koki air conditioned (1980-95)	M17

Alna Koki car No 7401 at Okayama station ***1995***

JR West

West Japan Railway Company
Nishi Nihon Ryokaku Tetsudo
4-24, Shibata 2-chome, Kita-ku, Osaka 530
Telephone: +81 6 375 8981 Fax: +81 6 375 8919
Chair: T Tsunoda
President: M Ide

Suburban/Interurban railway

Passenger journeys: (Okayama operations only)
(1990/91) 31 million
(1993/94) 46 million

Current situation: Operates local emu services Himeji–Okayama and Okayama–Hiroshima, also on routes to Uno, Niimi and Aioi. Dmu services operated on routes to Tsuyama and Kibi.

Bus

Current situation: Local bus services provided by the Chugoku JR Bus Co.

Ryobi Bus Co

Ryobi Bus Co Ltd
7-23 Nishikimachi, Okayama-shi 700
Telephone: +81 862 32 2111 Fax: +81 862 27 1766
Staff: 847

Bus (Whole company operations)

Passenger journeys: (Annual) 16.5 million
Vehicle-km: (Annual) 13 million

Number of routes: 163
Route length: 2,789 km
Fleet: 234 buses and 220 coaches, predominantly Mitsubishi Fuso
In peak service: 214
Operating costs financed by: Fares 98.1%, other commercial sources 1.9%

Current situation: Serves suburban areas of Okayama in the southern part of Okayama Prefecture, as well as regions beyond.

Chutetsu Bus Co

Chutetsu Bus Co Ltd
2-8-50 Nakasange, Okayama-shi 700
Telephone: +81 862 226601

Bus

Current situation: Serves suburban areas of Okayama, in the northern part of Okayama Prefecture, with fleet of 136 buses.

Shimotsui Dentetsu

Shimotsui Electric Railway
3-53 Omoto-ekimae, Okayama-shi 700
Telephone: +81 862 338811

Bus

Current situation: Runs bus services in suburban Okayama covering the southern part of Okayama Prefecture, with 124 buses and 90 coaches.

Uno Bus Co

Uno Bus Co Ltd
2-3-18 Omotecho, Okayama-shi 700
Telephone: +81 862 253111

Bus

Current situation: Serves suburban areas of Okayama, in the eastern part of Okayama Prefecture, with 64 buses.

UPDATED

OKLAHOMA CITY

Population: Metropolitan area 983,000, service area 469,000
Public transport: Bus services provided by independent trust, controlled by transit/parking authority. Light rail plans approved

Bus routes meet at downtown transit centre for timed transfers

METRO Transit

City of Oklahoma City Department of Transit Services
300 SW 7th Street, Oklahoma City, OK 73109, USA
Telephone: +1 405 297 2484 Fax: +1 405 297 2111
Chair, Transit Board: Harold Stansberry
Administrator: Randall J Hume
Staff: 165

Current situation: Bus and paratransit services for Oklahoma City, and the suburban cities of Edmond, Norman and Midwest City are provided by the Central Oklahoma Transportation & Parking Authority (COTPA), under the marketing name METRO Transit. Figures below refer to the METRO operation only. In the suburban city of Norman, the marketing name is CART (Cleveland Area Rapid Transit), operating six local routes and contributing to the Express Commuter service to downtown Oklahoma City. CART also runs a demand-responsive van service for elderly and disabled people.

The city of Edmond contracts with COTPA for Express and local service, while Midwest City contracts for Express service only.

Developments: In February 1994 voters approved a five-year 1 per cent sales tax dedicated to the city's Metropolitan Area Plan (MAP), main element of which is the proposed light rail line (see below).

Under the MAP, the undertaking has lost the use of its city-centre terminal, which has been given over to car parking. In its place a timed-transfer system has been implemented at several downtown nodes.

METRO's operations and maintenance depot has been designated as the location for a new baseball stadium under the MAP, and a new site is being sought.

Bus

Passenger journeys: (1988/89) 3.5 million
(1990/91) 3.6 million
(1993/94) 2.4 million

Vehicle-km: (1988/89) 3.1 million
(1990/91) 4.2 million
(1993/94) 3.5 million

Route length: 1,764 km
Number of routes: 42 (35 local, 4 commuter, 3 subscription)
Fleet: 76 vehicles

RTS II T80604/6 (1981/83/87)	57
Escort RE (1990)	4
Collins 2000 (1992)	9
Lazy N Spart (1991)	1
Dodge (1980)	1
Others	4

In peak service: 52

Most intensive service: Peak 20 min (10 min in Norman)
Fare structure: Flat on local routes, free transfers; express and subscription routes, variable
Fare collection: Exact fare to driver; monthly passes
Arrangements for elderly/disabled: 46 vehicles lift-equipped; reduced fares; on-demand taxi and van service (METRO-Lift) free or at reduced cost, also STEP van service linking certain areas with shopping malls and medical facilities
Integration with other modes: Cycle racks and lockers accommodating 262 cycles; 14 park-and-ride lots; carpool assistance
Operating costs financed by: Fares 12.3%, other commercial sources 0.4%, FTA grants 31.2%, Oklahoma City 43.5%, other cities and agencies 0.8%
New vehicles financed by: FTA 80%, local 20%

Light rail (proposed)
Current situation: Feasibility studies continue for a fixed-guideway system; portions of the necessary right-of-way were purchased by COTPA and the state DoT in 1989 and 1990. Revenue from the 1% sales tax approved in 1994 could fund a 10 km light rail route from Union station to Remington Park, which has been proposed for early opening using diesel traction.

In addition, a state-wide study has evaluated fixed-guideway alternatives for metropolitan areas, and there are proposals for commuter rail service over the BN freight route to Tulsa.

OMAHA
Population: 544,000 (with Council Bluffs)
Public transport: Bus services provided in Omaha, Council Bluffs and environs by operating subsidiary of city transit authority controlled by representative board

MAT
Metro Area Transit
Transit Authority of the City of Omaha
2222 Cuming Street, Omaha, NE 68102, USA
Telephone: +1 402 341 7560 Fax: +1 402 342 0949
Chair: Judy Schweikart
Executive Director: Robert Curttright
Operating Director: Curt Simon
Staff: 290

Current situation: Created in 1972 from two private undertakings, MAT serves Omaha, Bellevue and surrounding communities in Nebraska, along with the city of Council Bluffs, Iowa. MAT is participating in a project with the city of Omaha to provide seven transit stations and a transit information centre on a three-block 16th Street transit mall in central Omaha.

MAT's 16th Street transit mall **1995**

Bus
Passenger journeys: (1993) 5.4 million
(1994) 5.3 million
Vehicle-km:(Annual) 6.5 million

Number of routes: 38 (4 in Council Bluffs)
Route length: 491 km
Fleet: 164 vehicles

Flxible (1973)	20
GMC (1979)	18
Flxible Metro (1986/87/90)	114
Ford Econo van (1985/87)	12

In peak service: 145

Most intensive service: 30 min
One-person operation: All routes
Fare collection: Exact fare; cash or prepurchase tickets
Fare structure: Flat; prepurchase multitickets available in Nebraska; transfers available; higher fares on Iowa operations, where free transfers apply
Fares collected on board: 62%
Operational control: Route inspectors/mobile radio
Arrangements for elderly/disabled: MOBY door-to-door subscription van service; reduced flat fare on conventional services, financed from general operating funds; demand-response services carried 424,000 passengers in 1994
Average peak-hour speed: 20.5 km/h
Operating costs financed by: Fares 30%, other commercial sources 4%, subsidy/grants 65%
Subsidy from: Local tax 69%, FTA 27%, state 4%
New vehicles financed by: FTA 80%, local funds 20%

OMSK
Population: 1.1 million
Public transport: Services provided by 10 municipal undertakings — two tramway, two trolleybus and six bus — with no overall control of transport policy

Upravlenie Automobil'novo Transporta
Upravlenie Automobil'novo Transporta
Omsk, Russia

Bus
Current situation: It is believed that a fleet of 200-250 buses is operated, comprising Ikarus 260/280, LIAZ 677/5256, LAZ 695/52523, and Karosa B731/B741.

Omskelektrotrans
Marx prospekt 45, 644048 Omsk
Telephone: +7 381 241 2570
General Manager: Vladimir Matveev

ZIU9 trolleybus and KTM5 tramcar on routes in the northern suburbs **1997**

Trolleybus
Passenger journeys: (1989) 114 million

Number of routes: 15
Route length: 146.4 km
Fleet: Approx 240 trolleybuses, mostly ZIU9

Tramway
Passenger journeys: (1989) 123 million

Number of routes: 10
Route length: 130 km
Gauge: 1,524 mm
Rolling stock: 190 cars

KTM5	M183
KTM8	M7

Metro
Under construction
Current situation: Construction started mid-1993 of the first 7 km line of a proposed 17 km metro. The line will run from the city centre to industrial and residential development areas on the left bank of the River Irtish.

UPDATED

ORLANDO

Population: City 887,000, Tri-county area 1.3 million
Public transport: Fixed-route bus and demand-responsive services provided by authority governed by nine-member board; extensive private operations

LYNX

Central Florida Regional Transportation Authority
1200 West South Street, Orlando, FL 32805, USA
Telephone: +1 407 841 2279 Fax: +1 407 245 0327
Chair: Daryl McLain
Executive Director: Paul P Skoutelas
Director of Operations: William Schneeman
Staff: 645

Current situation: The former Orange-Seminole-Osceola Transportation Authority was formed by inter-local agreement in 1972 to serve Orange, Seminole and Osceola counties. It adopted the trading name LYNX in 1992, and was merged with the Central Florida RTA in 1994 to create the Central Florida Regional Transportation Authority.

Fixed-route bus service is provided in a 5,418 km² area, with 'Freebee' downtown circulator providing a fares-free link with parking and employment centres. I-Drive is a 5 min frequency downtown shuttle with operating subsidy provided by businesses on International Drive. LYNX runs shuttle services from parking lots to major entertainment areas in downtown Orlando, and also operates van and car pools and a ride-matching service throughout central Florida.

LYNX has no dedicated funding source and is hoping to gain voter approval for a local sales, property or petrol tax.

Developments: LYNX has doubled its weekday ridership since 1992 thanks to innovative services and promotions. This success led to a federal grant of $2 million to begin design and funding strategies for an 83 km light rail network planned for the first decade of the new century.

Purchase of 40 buses is planned to replace older vehicles and augment the fleet, and installation of 100 new bus shelters is under way. Land has been acquired in the city centre for development of an intermodal transit interchange over the next five years. Also completed is a 4.3 km fixed guideway route in the city centre, served by CNG-powered low-floor vehicles branded as LIMMO.

Gillig Phantom picks up at a new-style Lynx Paws (bus stop) ***1997***

Bus
Passenger journeys: (1993) 11.3 million
(1994) 12.4 million
(1995) 14.1 million
Vehicle-km: (1995) 13.6 million

Number of routes: 53
Route length: (One way) 1,152 km
Fleet: 250 vehicles

Flxible (1987)	37
Gillig 40 ft (1994/95/96/97)	92
Gillig Suburban (1996)	7
Neoplan articulated	2
Neoplan USA (1985)	12
Neoplan (1990)	18
Orion II minibus (1993)	12
Orion V 40 ft (1994)	37
Orion V Suburban (1994)	4
Orion V CNG-powered (1994)	6
Gillig 35 ft (1997)	13
Gillig CNG-powered (1997)	10

In peak service: 170

Most intensive service: 5 min
One-person operation: All routes
Fare structure: Flat; multiride ticket books and monthly passes; scholars travel free
Arrangements for elderly/disabled: Demand-responsive door-to-door service for disabled; reduced fare on fixed-route services; seniors travel free
Operating costs financed by: Fares 35.2%, other commercial sources 4.1%, subsidy/grants 60.7%
Subsidy from: Orange County, Seminole County, City of Orlando, Osceola/Kissimmee, City of Altamonte Springs, International Drive Transit District total 63%, state 16%, FTA 21%
New vehicles financed by: Local 10%, state 10%, FTA 80%

Walt Disney World

WED Transportation Services
Telephone: +1 305 824 4457

Current situation: Bus transport is provided within the Disney World complex and from the Buena Vista area of Orlando on 28 routes. Some operate until 02.00; most buses lift-equipped. Two circular monorail routes operate within the complex.

Fleet: 160 buses

GMC RTS III	43
TMC RTS III	115
Ford van	2

UPDATED

OSAKA

Population: 2.6 million
Public transport: Bus, metro and elevated automated guided transport system operated by municipal authority responsible to city council, with additional small profile metro line. Several private commuter and interurban rail lines provide suburban services along with Japan Railways (JR), with through running to the metro from three lines. Rail-based travel is dominant with a 61 per cent share compared with only 3 per cent by bus, 4 per cent by taxi and 32 per cent by private car. Private railways handle about 26 per cent, the municipal metro some 20 per cent and JR lines about 15 per cent. Some privately operated buses. Ferry service on the Yodo river.

Major expansion of the rail network in the Kansai metropolitan region (Osaka, Kyoto, Kobe) has been proposed by the Committee for Investigation of Railway Network Construction, involving 27 new lines totalling 220 km, with a further 110 km of additional tracks alongside existing lines to be built by 2005

Osaka-shi Kotsu Kyoku

Osaka Municipal Transportation Bureau
Kujo Minami-1, Nishi-ku, Osaka 550, Japan
Telephone: +81 6 582 1101 Fax: +81 6 582 7997
General Manager: Harumi Sakai
Staff: 9,958

Passenger journeys: (All modes)
(1990/91) 1,147 million
(1991/92) 1,149 million
(1992/93) 1,148 million

Current situation: The metro carries the vast majority of city travellers, being one of the most intensively used in the world, with 508,000 a day using the busiest station at Umeda.

A 'ride and ride' system operates by division of the city into 18 zones, with public transport reorganised around area transport for each zone, with trunk services interconnecting them and serving the city centre. Local zone bus services connect with rail trunk routes supplemented by high-frequency bus corridors. Some 25 transfer terminal points have been identified for interchange between trunk and local routes.

Bus
Staff: 2,307

Passenger journeys: (1990/91) 120.2 million
(1991/92) 123.1 million
(1992/93) 123.6 million
Vehicle-km: (1990/91) 29.8 million
(1991/92) 30 million
(1992/93) 30.1 million

Number of routes: 107
Route length: (One way) 446 km
On priority right-of-way: 106.2 km
Fleet: 936 vehicles, all air conditioned, including Mitsubishi, Isuzu, Hino and Nissan Diesel types

In peak service: 854
New vehicles required each year: 100

Most intensive service: 3 min
One-person operation: All routes
Fare collection: Payment on alighting to farebox by driver, ticket or pass; fareboxes have cancellation facility for stored-value multiride tickets also valid on metro and New Tram
Fare structure: Flat, with transfer without charge between trunk and local routes; multiride tickets, 1- or 3-monthly passes (student, commuter, all routes), monthly daytime (10.00-16.00) discount passes: day, 1-, 3- and 6-month multimode tickets (bus/metro/New Tram); stored-fare 'Rainbow' cards introduced March 1996 valid on bus/metro/New Tram, and Hankyu/Hanshin/Nose/Kita Osaka rail and bus services
Fare evasion control: None
Operational control: Computerised system (see Developments)
Arrangements for elderly/disabled: Free passes and concessionary fares financed by city welfare bureau; newer buses have wheelchair space; lift-equipped buses on 9 routes
Integration with other modes: All routes integrated with metro; zonal interchange system; unified bus/rail fare scale
Average distance between stops: 423 m
Average speed: In mixed traffic, 12.8 km/h
Bus priority: 75.1 km bus-only lanes; 8.3 km bus-only roads; 22.8 km bus priority lanes; 136 bus priority signals. Staff on duty during rush hours to ensure observance of lane discipline
Operating costs financed by: Fares 59.8%, other commercial sources 21.1%, subsidy/grants 19.1%
Subsidy from: City council
New vehicles financed by: Subsidy from city's general account and prefectural government

Developments: New Urban Bus System concept adopted, involving bus priority measures, computerised operational control and real-time travel information displays at bus stops.

Metro

Staff: 7,535

Type of operation: Full metro, initial route opened 1933

Passenger journeys: (1991/92) 1,003.5 million
(1992/93) 1,001.9 million
(1993/94) 992 million
Car-km: (1990/91) 92.8 million
(1991/92) 92.5 million
(1992/93) 92.6 million

Route length: 105.8 km
in tunnel: 93.3 km
elevated/surface: 12.5 km
Number of lines: 7
Number of stations: 85
in tunnel: 76
Gauge: 1,435 mm
Track: 50 kg/m flat-bottomed
Max gradient: 3.5%
Minimum curve radius: 100 m
Electrification: 750 V DC, third rail; 1.5 kV DC, overhead (Line 6 and 7)

Service: Peak 2 min, off-peak 4-7 min
First/last train: 05.00/24.00
Fare structure: 7-section distance-based fare scale; multiride tickets; 1-, 3- and 6-month commuter and student passes; day, 1-, 3- and 6-month multimode tickets (bus/metro/New Tram); 'Rainbow' stored-fare cars (as bus) replaced 'Town Card'
Fare collection: Ticket machines and automatic barriers at all stations; with introduction of stored-value multiride tickets, almost all tickets are magnetically encoded for use in automatic barriers
Arrangements for elderly/disabled: Cars with wheelchair space introduced 1992
Operating costs financed by: Fares 90.7%, other commercial sources 8.2%; subsidy/grants 1.1%
Subsidy from: National government 11.5% and city 88.5%
Integration with other modes: Free interchange with New Tram (see below) and reduced fare bus/metro transfer tickets and passes; reduced fare single tickets for short distance travel from/to reciprocal running sections of private railways

Osaka-shi Kotsu Kyoku's Route 34 in central Osaka ***1995***

Series 10 metro train bound for Nakamozu on Line 1 ***1995***

Series 70 linear-motor powered train on Line 7

Signalling: ATC, CTC, and automatic block; cab signalling and ATC (Line 7)
Surveillance: CCTV at some stations

Rolling stock: 1,086 cars, Hitachi, Kawasaki, Kinki, Tokyu and Alna Koki; all cars air conditioned

Series 10 Line 1	M150 T82
Series 20 Lines 1/2/3/4/5	M295 T277
Series 30 Lines 2/3	M55 T23
Series 60 Line 6	M30 T10
Series 66 Line 6	M48 T48
Series 70 Line 7	M68

In peak service: 774 cars

Current situation: Reciprocal through running services operate between Line 1 and North Osaka Express Electric Railway, between Line 6 and the Hankyu Senri and Kyoto lines, and between Line 4 and Kintetsu's Higashi–Osaka line. Line 7 is built to a small profile with trains powered by linear motor.
Developments: Line 6 was extended 1.5 km in March 1993 from Dobutsuen-mae to an interchange with the Nankai Railway at Tengachaya. Extension of small profile Line 7 into central Osaka (8.5 km, 11 stations) under construction, and the 5.7 km section between Kyobashi and Shinsaibashi opened in December 1996.

To increase capacity of Line 1, which carries about 1.3 million passengers daily (50 per cent of the metro traffic), nine-car trains were augmented in 1995 by an additional car. A major programme of station renovation has been undertaken to accommodate the longer trains and ease congestion.

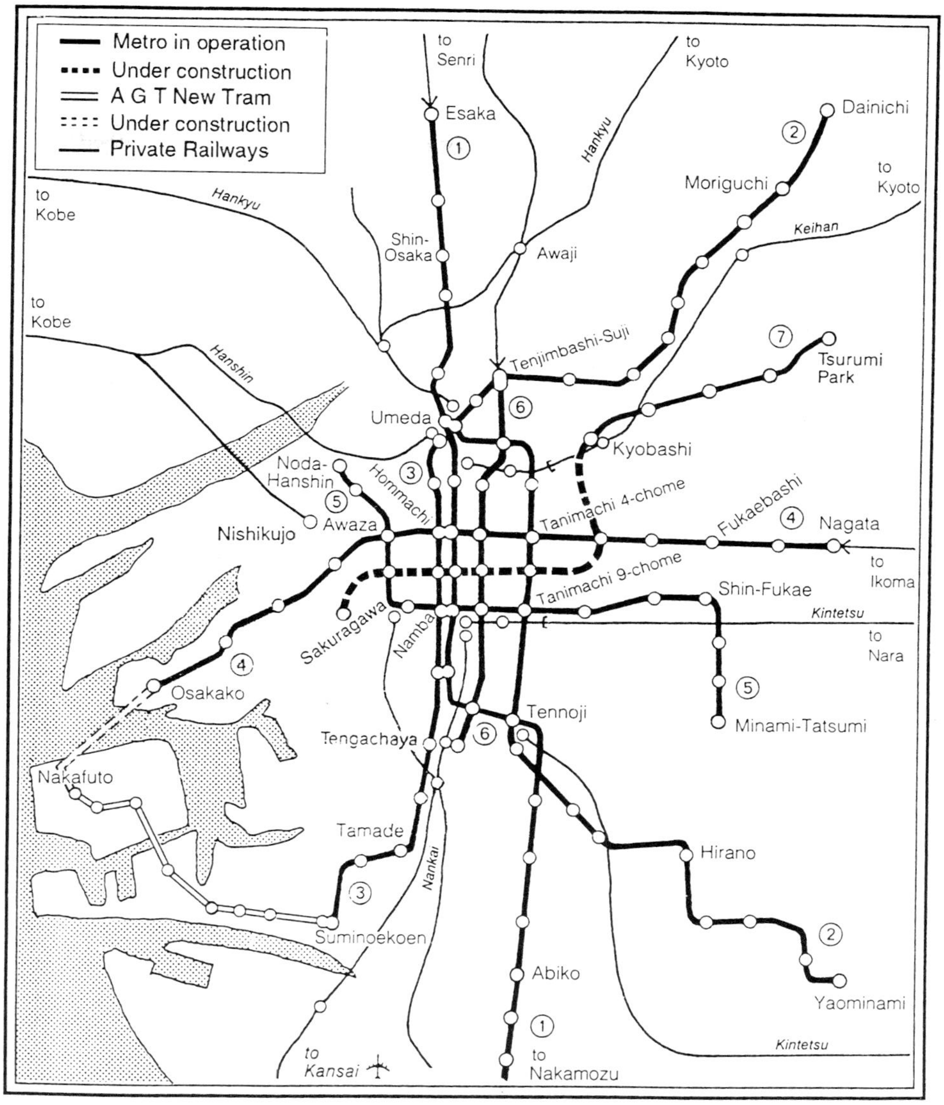

Osaka's urban rail network

ICTS
Staff: 116

Type of operation: Newtram Intermediate Capacity Transit System (ICTS) opened 1981, fully automatic operation, rubber-tyred cars on concrete guideway

Passenger journeys: (1990/91) 21.9 million
(1991/92) 22 million
(1992/93) 22.5 million
Car-km: (1990/91) 3.7 million
(1991/92) 3.8 million
(1992/93) 4 million

Route length: 6.6 km
Number of stations: 8
Electrification: 600 V AC, third rail

Service: Peak 2 min, off-peak 7½ min
First/last train: 05.17/24.00
Fare structure: As metro
Operating costs financed by: Fares 66.9%, other commercial sources 0.2%. subsidy/grants 32.9%
Subsidy from: City 100%
Revenue control: Ticket machines and automatic barriers
Train control: Fully automated operation; no driver, but some trains have an attendant to provide customer information and deal with emergencies

Signalling: Fixed block (continuous transmission and receiving with check-in and check-out system); ATC, CTC
Surveillance: CCTV on all platforms

Rolling stock: 21 four-car trains, air conditioned
Niigata Iron Works Series 100 M84

Current situation: Under the same management as the metro, the elevated Newtram serves new residential and commercial development on land reclaimed from Osaka Bay.

Developments: An extension from Nakafuto to the Osakako terminus of metro Line 4 (3.6 km, four stations), crossing the harbour in tunnel, is under construction for late 1997 opening by the Osaka Port Transport System Co, a third sector venture.

Hankyu Bus suburban services at Senri-chuo bus/rail interchange ***1995***

Hankyu Dentetsu
Hankyu Electric Railway
16-1, Shibata 1-chome, Kita-ku, Osaka 530
Telephone: +81 6 373 5092 Fax: +81 6 373 5670
President: M Sugai
Staff: 5,227

Interurban railway
Passenger journeys: (1991/92) 815 million
(1992/93) 796 million
(1994/95) 758 million
Car-km: (1992/93) 157 million

Current situation: Operates nine lines with 90 stations over 147 km of 1,435 mm gauge route, electrified 1.5 kV DC. Interurban routes run to Kobe, Kitasenri, Kyoto and Takarazuka, through running from Kitasenri and Kyoto line stations to metro Line 6.
Developments: A stored-fare card system was introduced in 1992 and its validity was extended in March 1996 to include all Hanshin, Nose, Kita Osaka and Osaka municipal bus and rail services.

Rolling stock: 1,338 emu cars M749 T589

Bus
Passenger journeys: (Whole conurbation)
(1990/91) 116.9 million
(1991/92) 118.6 million
(1992/93) 115.8 million
Vehicle-km: (1992/93) 28 million

Current situation: Hankyu Bus operates 733 buses on services linked to rail operations, including suburban bus routes in Osaka. A computer-controlled bus terminal/route information system is in operation between Osaka international airport and Hankyu Hotarugaike terminals.

Kita Osaka Kyuko Dentetsu

North Osaka Express Electric Railway
2-4-1, Terauchi, Toyonaka-shi, Osaka 560
Telephone: +81 6 865 0601 Fax: +81 6 866 0254
President: J Konishiike
Staff: 161

Passenger journeys: (1990/91) 66.6 million
(1991/92) 66.8 million
(1992/93) 67.8 million
Car-km: (1990/91) 6 million
(1991/92) 6.1 million
(1992/93) 6.1 million

Number of lines: 1
Route length: 5.9 km
Number of stations: 4
Electrification: 750 V DC, third rail

Rolling stock: 70 emu cars in ten-car sets
8000 series Alna Koki (1986-96) M35 T35

Current situation: This expressway median line extends from Esaka to Senri-Chuo serving residential development north of Osaka (Senri New Town). A reciprocal through running service is operated to Line 1 of the metro; trains were lengthened from nine to 10 cars in 1995 to provide extra capacity on this intensively used line.

The company is part owned by the prefectural government and the Hankyu Electric Railway; operations are on a wholly commercial basis.

Developments: Stored-fare card system introduced March 1996, also valid on the Hanshin, Hankyu, Nose and Osaka municipal bus and rail services.

Hanshin Denki Tetsudo

Hanshin Electric Railway
1-24, Ebie 1-chome, Fukushima-ku, Osaka 553
Telephone: +81 6 457 2123
President: M Tezuka
Staff: 2,322

Interurban railway

Staff: 1,201

Passenger journeys: (1991/92) 249 million
(1992/93) 246 million
(1994/95) 229 million
Car-km: (1992/93) 36.6 million

Current situation: Operates 40.1 km of 1,435 mm gauge route with 42 stations, comprising Osaka–Kobe main line and two branches, electrified 1.5 kV DC. Through services operate to Sumaurakoen on the Sanyo Railway via the underground Kobe Rapid Railway.

Developments: A 1.6 km extension of the Nishi-Osaka line is under construction from Nishi-kujo to Kujo; this is the first stage of a planned link through to the Nankai Railway terminus at Namba.

Stored-fare card system introduced March 1996, also valid on Hankyu, Nose, Kita Osaka and Osaka municipal bus and rail services.

Rolling stock: 314 emu cars M231 T83

Bus

Passenger journeys: (1990/91) 21.7 million
(1991/92) 21.9 million
(1992/93) 24.4 million
Vehicle-km: (1990/91) 7.8 million
(1991/92) 7.8 million
(1992/93) 7.9 million

Current situation: Operates 165 buses on 15 local routes extending to 153 km, consisting of Osaka–Kobe and Osaka–Takarazuka trunk routes, and feeder services to rail stations. Bus lanes and computer-aided bus location system introduced. Also operates sightseeing, long-distance express and airport services.

Keihan Denki Tetsudo

Keihan Electric Railway
2-27, Shiromi 1-chome, Chuo-ku, Osaka 540
Telephone: +81 6 944 2521 Fax: +81 6 944 2501
Chair: H Sumita
President: M Miyashita
Staff: 3,420

Interurban railway

Staff: 2,740

Passenger journeys: (Including Kyoto light rail)
(1991/92) 414 million
(1992/93) 412 million
(1994/95) 401 million
Car-km: (1992/93) 92.4 million

Current situation: Operates 66.3 km of 1,435 mm gauge route, electrified at 1.5 kV DC. Main line, 51.6 km with 42 stations, runs from underground terminal in Osaka (Yodoyabashi station) to Kyoto, with two branches. Frequent service of limited-express, express and local trains on main line. Also operates 25.2 km light rail system in Kyoto and Otsu (see under Kyoto).

Developments: Plans exist for a 2.7 km underground link in central Osaka (Nakanoshima line) to provide a connection with the proposed Naniwa-suji line to Kansai international airport (see JR West entry).

Nankai train bound for Kansai international airport at Hamadera-koen ***1995***

Rolling stock: 651 emu cars, M360 T291, all air conditioned; limited-express trains feature two cars with televisions, with speakers at every seat

Bus

Passenger journeys: (including Kyoto)
(1992/93) 77.4 million
Vehicle-km: (including Kyoto)
(1992/93) 19 million

Current situation: Keihan Bus, a railway subsidiary, operates approx 350 of its 514 buses on services in Osaka Prefecture, including routes in Osaka's northeastern suburbs (see Kyoto entry).

Ferry

Current situation: Osaka Aqua-Bus, a subsidiary of the Keihan Electric Railway, offers a limited peak-hour service with four stops on a 5.1 km section of the Yodo river running through central Osaka.

Kinki Nippon Tetsudo 'Kintetsu'

Kinki Nippon Railway
6-1-55, Uehommachi, Tennoji-ku, Osaka 543
Telephone: +81 6 775 3444 Fax: +81 6 775 3468
President: S Kanamori
Staff: 12,568

Interurban railway

Passenger journeys: (1991/92) 806 million
(1992/93) 802 million
(1994/95) 791 million
Car-km: (1990/91) 301 million
(1992/93) 324 million

Current situation: Operates express and local services over main line of 190 km from Osaka to Nagoya, and over several other routes totalling 595 km on 1,435, 1,067 and 762 mm gauges, electrified at 1.5 kV DC and 750 V DC. A reciprocal through running service operates between the Higashi–Osaka line and Line 4 of the Osaka metro. This is the largest private railway in Japan.

Rolling stock: 2,125 emu cars M1,181 T944

Developments: Plans exist for a future link between Kintetsu's Nara line at Ikoma and its Kyoto line at Takanohara to provide a through service between west Osaka and south Kyoto.

Bus

Passenger journeys: (1990/91) 38 million
(1992/93) 32.3 million

Current situation: 331 buses run on 49 routes related to rail operations in the Osaka region, extending to 3,467 km.

Osaka monorail running alongside the Kinki Expressway ***1996***

JR West Rapid service en route for Kansai international airport ***1995***

JR West

West Japan Railway Company
Nishi Nihon Ryokaku Tetsudo
4-24, Shibata 2-chome, Kita-ku, Osaka 530
Telephone: +81 6 375 8981 Fax: +81 6 375 8919
Chair: T Tsunoda
President: M Ide

Type of operation: Interurban/suburban railway

Passenger journeys: (Osaka operations only)
(1993/94) 320 million

Current situation: JR West's urban network comprises 12 lines (about 600 km) serving Kobe, Osaka and Kyoto. Osaka is the hub of the network, with frequent local and rapid service emus colour-coded according to line of operation on eight routes including the 21.7 km Osaka loop around the central area.

Faster and more frequent services and new rolling stock on urban lines have led to increased passenger-km. Further growth is expected from large development projects such as the new Kansai international airport and Kansai Science City, and from the continuing movement of population to suburban areas.

Developments: The 12.3 km Katafuku line with seven stations opened in March 1997, providing an east-west link through central Osaka connecting two important commuter routes, the Gakkentoshi line serving Kansai Science City, and JR's Takarazuka line. The line was built by Kansai Rapid Railway, a third sector company whose shareholders include JR West, Osaka prefecture and Osaka city.

Kansai international airport, constructed on an artificial island in Osaka Bay, opened in September 1994. JR West operates a rapid service from central Osaka using Series 223 emus and an express service 'Haruka' from Kyoto and Shin-Osaka using purpose-built five-car Series 281 emus. Access to the airport is via a new 11.2 km link from JR's Hanwa line, 6.9 km of which is shared by competing Nankai airport services. Plans exist for through airport services to Kobe and Nara via existing freight connections on to the Sanyo and Kansai lines respectively. From August 1995 a new fleet of Series 223-1000 emus was introduced on rapid services to Kobe and Kyoto.

Plans also exist for a new link through central Osaka, the Naniwa-suji line, to connect Minato-machi and Shiomibashi and provide direct access for JR and Nankai trains from Kansai airport to the central business districts. Connecting links between the Naniwa-suji line and the Hanshin and Hankyu systems are also planned.

Work is in progress for start-up of passenger service on JR's 18.6 km Joto freight line. An outer orbital service will be provided through Osaka's eastern suburbs linking Shin-Osaka, Shigino, Hanaten and Kami. JR West, Osaka prefecture and Osaka city have set up a third sector company to undertake the ¥140 billion project which includes double-tracking, electrification, new stations and new trains. Opening is scheduled for 2005.

Nankai Denki Tetsudo

Nankai Electric Railway
1-60 Namba 5-chome, Chuo-ku, Osaka 542
Telephone: +81 6 644 7121
President: S Yoshimura
Staff: 3,207

Interurban railway

Passenger journeys: (1991/92) 311 million
(1992/93) 305 million
(1994/95) 304 million
Car-km: (1992/93) 79.7 million

Current situation: Operates 163.5 km of 1,067 mm gauge lines of which 149.2 km electrified 1.5 kV DC and 14.3 km at 600 V DC.

Main routes Osaka—Wakayama (Nankai main line) and Osaka—Gokurakubashi (Koya line) served by frequent local and express services. Also through service using Nankai and Semboku cars from Namba to the Semboku Rapid Railway to serve suburban housing.

Rolling stock: 718 emu cars M416 T302

Developments: In 1994 new services were introduced between Nankai's Namba terminal in central Osaka and the newly opened Kansai international airport, a distance of 43 km. The express 'Rapi:t' service, operated by distinctively styled purpose-built Series 50000 units, is supplemented by local services, both of which compete with JR services for airport traffic. Access to the airport is via an 8.8 km branch line from Izumi-Sano, part of which is shared with JR. To further compete with JR, Nankai proposes to lay mixed gauge track along its existing 1,067 mm main line to enable airport services to operate through central Osaka via the 1,435 mm Sakaisuji line metro and on to Kyoto and Nara via the Hankyu, Keihan and Kintetsu systems. A 4 km link between the Nankai and Hanshin terminals in Osaka would also permit through running to Kobe.

Bus

Passenger journeys: (1992/93) 62.6 million

Current situation: Approx 570 vehicles run on routes related to rail services in southern half of Osaka Prefecture.

Semboku Kosoku Tetsudo

Semboku Rapid Railway
Osaka Prefectural Urban Development Company
5-7, Kawaramachi 3-chome, Chuo-ku, Osaka 541
Telephone: +81 6 201 9771 Fax: +81 6 201 9788

Suburban railway

Passenger journeys: (1991/92) 58.1 million
(1992/93) 57.8 million
(1993/94) 58.1 million
Car-km: (1991/92) 6.9 million
(1992/93) 7.3 million
(1993/94) 7.5 million

Current situation: This 12.1 km line (1,067 mm gauge, electrified 1.5 kV DC), constructed and operated by Osaka Prefectural Urban Development Company, serves Semboku New Town (population 160,000) to the south of Osaka. A reciprocal through running service is operated to central Osaka via the Nankai Railway.

Rolling stock: 126 emu cars M69 T57
On order: 10 cars of new Series 7000 stock

Developments: A 2.2 km extension to serve a new residential district at Trivert Izumi opened in April 1995.

Hankai Denki Kido

Hankai Electric Tramway
3-14-72 Shimizuoka, Sumiyoshi-ku, Osaka 558
Telephone: +81 6 671 3080
President: N Hiramatsu
Staff: 261

Current situation: 100 per cent owned by the Nankai Electric Railway, this tramway became a separate operation in 1980. Serves the southern part of Osaka and Sakai City from two terminals in Osaka.

Tramway

Passenger journeys: (1990/91) 15.2 million
(1991/92) 17.2 million
(1992/93) 16.7 million
Car-km: (1992/93) 2.2 million

Number of lines: 2
Number of routes: 3
Route length: 18.7 km
Number of stops: 40
Gauge: 1,435 mm
Electrification: 600 V DC, overhead

Service: 2-15 min
First/last car: 05.16/23.32
Fare collection: Farebox or prepurchase
Fare structure: Stage; transfer tickets available between routes; prepurchase coupon tickets, 1- and 3-month passes
One-person operation: All cars

Rolling stock: 52 cars

Kawasaki Ship Building (1927)	M6
Kawasaki Rolling Stock (1928)	M10
Fuji Nagata Ship Building (ex-Osaka) (1929)	M9
Osaka Iron Works (1930)	M3
Tanaka Sharyo (1930)	M3
Teikoku Sharyo (1957/62/63)	M10
Tokyu Car (1987/93/94/95)	M11

Osaka Kosoku Tetsudo

Osaka Rapid Railway (Osaka Monorail)
5-1-1, Higashi-machi, Shin-Senri, Toyonaka-shi, Osaka-fu 565
Telephone: +81 6 871 8280 Fax: +81 6 871 8284
Staff: 153

Type of operation: Straddle monorail, opened 1990

Passenger journeys: (1991/92) 7.4 million
(1992/93) 7.8 million
(1993/94) 8.4 million
Car-km: (1991/92) 1.4 million
(1992/93) 1.4 million
(1993/94) 3.6 million

Current situation: This orbital monorail line round north-east Osaka links Shibahara and Minami-Ibaraki providing interchange with the North Osaka Express Electric Railway at Senri-chuo, the Hankyu Senri line at Yamada, and the Hankyu Kyoto line at Minami-Ibaraki.

Route length: 10.3 km
Number of lines: 1
Number of stations: 7
Electrification: 1.5 kV DC

Service: 5-12 min
One-person operation: All trains

Fare collection: Full AFC
Signalling: Cab signalling, ATP
Surveillance: CCTV
Operating costs financed by: Fares 100%

Rolling stock: 8 four-car sets
Hitachi/Kawasaki Type 1000 M32
On order: Two four-car sets

Developments: The line was extended 3.6 km from Senri-Chuo to Shibahara in 1994. Three further sections, totalling 13.6 km with 9 stations, are planned for completion by 1998 including 3.1 km between Shibahara and Osaka international airport (opening 1997). The line is designed for eventual operation by six-car trains running at 3 min headways.

Private bus

Current situation: A number of private bus operators, mainly private railway subsidiaries, provides suburban and commuter services, carrying around 170 million passengers a year and catering for about 6 per cent of Osaka's travel demand.

UPDATED

OSLO

Population: 480,000, metropolitan area 800,000
Public transport: Bus, metro, light rail and tramway services operated by authority governed by nominated board (including employee representatives) under overall control of city council, and which also contracts private ferry and bus lines, and provides support for common overall fare structure within city area, extending to local rail journeys on State Railway (NSB). Agreements with Stor Oslo Lokaltrafikk A/S (responsible for public transport within the county surrounding Oslo and services into Oslo) give an integrated fare structure and transfer system for the whole region. Road pricing in force

T2000 dual-system car (right) alongside original Western metro stock at Majorstuen ***1995***

Oslo Sporveier

A/S Oslo Sporveier
Økernveien 9, Postbox 2857-Tøen, 0608 Oslo 6, Norway
Telephone: +47 22 084000 Fax: +47 22 084030
Managing Director: Knut Skuland
Director, Metro Division: Rolf Gillebo
Director, Tramway Division: Rolf Bergstrand
Director, Bus Division: Kjell Knarbakk
Staff: 2,425

Passenger boardings: (All modes, including contracted operations)
(1993) 141 million
(1994) 145 million
(1995) 147 million

Operating costs financed by: Fares 66%, other commercial sources 7%, subsidy/grants and special agreements 27%
Subsidy from: City of Oslo 96% (financed by municipal income and property taxes), special agreements (Akershus/Baerum counties) 4%; concessions to pensioners financed by operator
New vehicles financed by: Loans through Municipality of Oslo

Current situation: OS, popularly named Sporveien, has overall responsibility for public transport provision in the Oslo area through its own direct operations and contracts with two private bus operators, boat services and about 100 km of State Railway lines. For these Sporveien collects all the revenue and pays the contractors a set rate, assuming responsibility for any deficits except those of the State Railway. Contracted services carried about 27 million passengers in 1995.
Developments: Patronage rose again (by 1.5 per cent) in 1995, helped in part by opening of the Vika tram line in August and inauguration of metro service on the Frognerseteren line. Other 1995 service improvements included route-restructuring on the tramway and conversion of more bus routes to low-floor operation.

The objective put forward in 1991 to increase patronage by some 10 per cent by the end of 1995 was not quite reached, the final figure being 8.1 per cent. But the 1991 target of 25 per cent growth by the year 2001 still appears attainable if service improvements continue.

Having fallen to 32 per cent of operating income in 1992, the City of Oslo subsidy rose substantially in 1993. The purpose of the extra funding was to help improve Sporveien's capital reserve. In 1995 the subsidy was back at the 1992 level, while profits totalled NOK50 million, some NOK4 million over budget.

There are now seven suburban 'Service Routes' operated by lift-equipped buses and easily accessible by the elderly and disabled, but open to all passengers at ordinary fares.

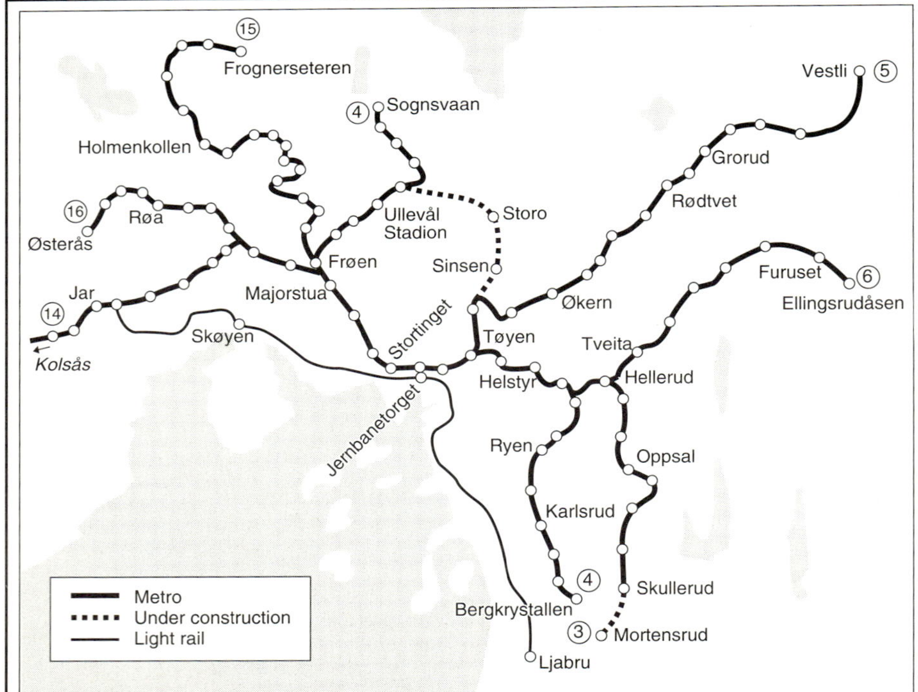

Oslo's metro and light rail

Bus (Direct operations only)
Staff: 652

Passenger journeys: (1993) 31.5 million
(1994) 33 million
(1995) 33 million
Vehicle-km: (1993) 8.8 million
(1994) 9.3 million
(1995) 9.3 million

Number of routes: 17
Route length: (One-way) 757 km
Fleet: 189 buses

One-person operation: All routes
Fare collection: Coupon cards cancelled on board; passes; single tickets available from drivers
Fare structure: Flat, common single ticket permits free transfer within 1 h; 8-ticket Flexicard; 24-h tourist card; 7-day season, monthly and 6-monthly passes
Operational control: Mobile radio; two-way radio on all vehicles
Arrangements for elderly/disabled: Door-to-door service for those with disability lasting more than one year provided by subsidised hiring of taxis or, for carriage of wheelchairs, by private contractor with minibuses, catering for about 1 million journeys in 1995 by 16,500 participants, an increase of 6% on 1994. Approx 90% of trips made by taxi. Unlimited number of trips given for travel to work or medical treatment, and up to 77 rides per year for leisure purposes, at same fares as ordinary public transport. Blind and partially sighted people, and wheelchair users, have unlimited use of door-to-door service. Elderly on municipal pension scheme travel at half fare on regular services. Five special routes with lift-equipped buses run in the suburbs between metro Lines 3 and 6
Average peak-hour speed: 16 km/h
Bus priority: Buses and trams equipped to gain priority at some 120 signal-controlled intersections under plan for general adoption of system

Integration with other modes: Full integration between modes with free transfers (see above)

Developments: Additions to the fleet in 1995 included 12 low-entrance buses from Scania, with a further 13 on order. Nine of these are low-floor Volvo articulated, the remainder low-entry MAN midibuses. All have low-emission diesel engines and the new vehicles comply with Euro 2 standards.

Metro

Type of operation: Full metro, initial route opened 1966; suburban rail upgraded to metro standards

Passenger journeys: (1993) 56 million
(1994) 56.5 million
(1995) 56 million
Car-km: (1993) 14.9 million
(1994) 15.2 million
(1995) 15.5 million

Route length: 98 km
in tunnel: 14.5 km
Number of lines: 5
Number of stations: 114
in tunnel: 13
Gauge: 1,435 mm
Max gradient: 5%
Minimum curve radius: 200 m
Electrification: 750 V DC, third rail; Frognerseteren line 750 V DC overhead, Kolsås line 680 V DC overhead

Service: 15 min all day on branches; peak 1¾ min, off-peak 3¾ min in central area
Fare structure: Flat, with common ticket permitting one free transfer and monthly 'go-as-you-please' season ticket; also 24 h tourist card
Integration with other modes: Full fare integration with all other modes within the city boundaries
Signalling: Cab signalling

Rolling stock: 207 cars

Strømmens Vaerksted	
Single-cab cars	M120
Dual-cab cars	M26
Single-cab cars dual-system	M34
Dual-cab cars dual-system	M15
ABB T2000 dual-system (1994)	M12

Developments: Through cross-city service on all lines was completed in 1995. Through service started in April from the Frognerseteren line (15) to Helsfyr using new T2000 dual-system cars. Line 16 was reopened as full metro in November 1995, while Line 14 was turned over to metro operation using existing cars converted for dual third-rail and overhead current collection.

Extension from Skullerud to Mortensrud under construction for November 1997 opening; it is being built and financed by the State Highway Administration. A preferred alignment along Store Ringvei has been selected for the link between Lines 4 and 5, planned to create a circular route.

Duewag/Strømmens LRV in suburban Oslo

Tramway/light rail

Type of operation: Conventional tramway and light rail Lines 10 and 19

Passenger journeys: (1993) 29 million
(1994) 30 million
(1995) 31.5 million
Car-km: (1993) 3.9 million
(1994) 4.3 million
(1995) 3.9 million

Route length: 128 km
Number of lines: 8
Electrification: 600 V DC, overhead

Service interval: Peak 15 min
One-person operation: All cars

Rolling stock: 93 cars plus 40 LRVs for Lines 10 and 19

MBO (1952/58)	M26
MBO rebuilt (1983)	M11
TBO/G (1952/58)	T36
Strømmens Verksted/Duewag LRV (1979-I)	M25
Strømmens Verkstad/Duewag LRV (1979-II)	M15
M25 ex-Göteborg	M20

On order: 17 cars from Ansaldo Trasporti

Developments: Zoning plans for a tramway extension to the Aker hospital have been approved, and a further extension to Tonsehagen is planned. The 1.6 km Vika tram line in the city centre opened in August 1995, and a route to Blindern/Rikshositalet is at the planning stage.

A new fleet of 17 low-floor air conditioned cars is on order from Italy's Ansaldo, with an option for a further 15. Delivery starts in late 1997.

Ferry

Current situation: Operated under contract by Skibs A/S Bygdøfergene from Rådhusplassen to Bygdø and by Oslo Fergene to islands in the Oslofjord. The four routes (22 km) carry about 0.8 million passengers annually.

NSB

Norges Statsbaner
0048 Oslo
Telephone: +47 2 315 0000 Fax: +47 2 315 3146

Type of operation: Suburban heavy rail

Passenger journeys: (1993) 25 million
(1995) 25.5 million
(1996) 24 million

Current situation: NSB's suburban lines link Oslo Central with Moss, Mysen, Kongsvinger, Jaren, Eidsvoll, Kongsberg and Spikkestad, totalling 568 km, electrified 15 kV 16⅔ Hz. Trains run hourly or half-hourly. Services within the city boundaries extend to about 100 km.
Developments: The line to serve the new airport at Gardemoen is scheduled to open in late 1998. A fleet of 16 three-car trains for airport service is on order from Adtranz Norway. For delivery in 1997/98, they will be capable of 220 km/h. Double-tracking between Ski and Moss completed September 1996.

Rolling stock: 182 emu cars

UPDATED

OSTRAVA

Population: 330,000
Public transport: Bus, trolleybus and tramway services operated by municipal authority

Dopravní podnik Ostrava AS

Dopravní podnik Ostrava AS
Podebradova 2, 70171 Ostrava 1, Czech Republic
Telephone: +42 69 248 8111 Fax: +42 69 236863
Director: František Vaštik
Staff: 2,890

Passenger boardings: (All modes)
(1992) 289 million
(1993) 269 million
(1994) 252 million

Development: In a reorganisation implemented in February 1996 the authority's name and status changed. Trolleybus extensions opened September and December 1995.

Bus, trolleybus and tram await departure at Central station

Trolleybus Route 108 on Hladnovska Str ***1995***

Fare collection: Prepurchase with validation/cancelling machines on board
Fare structure: Flat fare for each route
Fare evasion control: Roving inspectors
Operating costs financed by: Fares 36%, other commercial sources 13%, subsidy/grants 51%

Bus and trolleybus

Passenger journeys: (1992) Bus 128.8 million, trolleybus 17.1 million
(1993) Bus 120.4 million, trolleybus 16.4 million
(1994) Bus 112 million, trolleybus 16 million
Vehicle-km: (1992) Bus 21.3 million, trolleybus 2.8 million
(1993) Bus 20.7 million, trolleybus 2.8 million
(1994) Bus 20.8 million, trolleybus 3.1 million

Number of routes: Bus 44, trolleybus 8
Route length: Bus 582 km, trolleybus 62 km
Fleet: 368 buses

Karosa B731	94
Karosa B732	182
Karosa C734	11
Karosa C735	1
Karosa LC	1
Ikarus 280 twin-set	42
Karosa C744 twin-set	8
Karosa B741 twin-set	29

In peak service: 287
Fleet: 65 trolleybuses, some 14Tr second-hand ex-Potsdam

Skoda 9Tr	15
Skoda 14Tr	39
Skoda 15Tr twin-set	11

In peak service: 54

Most intensive service: 1-2 min
One-person operation: All routes
Average peak-hour speed: In mixed traffic, bus 26.6 km/h, trolleybus 18.5 km/h

Tramway

Type of operation: Conventional tramway

Passenger journeys: (1992) 143 million
(1993) 133 million
(1994) 124 million
Car-km: (1992) 15.9 million
(1993) 15.6 million
(1994) 15.4 million

Route length: 231 km
Number of lines: 18
Number of stops: 91
Gauge: 1,435 mm
Electrification: 600 V DC, overhead

Service: Peak 10 min
First/last car: 24 h service

Rolling stock: 307 cars

ČKD Tatra Tr	M30
ČKD Tatra T3	M221
ČKD Tatra K2	10
ČKD Tatra KT8 articulated	M16
ČKD Tatra T6A5	M30

In peak service: 231

UPDATED

OTTAWA

Population: 635,000
Public transport: Bus services in Ottawa and surrounding urban area are the responsibility of a Regional Transit Commission governed by board of commissioners drawn from Regional Municipal Council

OC Transpo

Ottawa-Carleton Regional Transit Commission
1500 St-Laurent Boulevard, Ottawa K1G 0Z8, Canada
Telephone: +1 613 741 6440 Fax: +1 613 741 7359
Chair: Peter D Clark
General Manager: Ian G Stacey
Director, Transitway Programme: Réjean Chartrand
Staff: 2,149

Current situation: Established in 1972, OC Transpo has exclusive rights to operate within the area of the 719,000 population Regional Municipality of Ottawa-Carleton. The Council of the Regional Municipality appoints the controlling board of the commission from amongst its members. In practice the Regional Council has established a designated Urban Transit Area with some 635,000 inhabitants within which OC Transpo is the sole service provider. Outside this area there is a policy of entering into agreements with municipalities for provision of service or permitting private operations. Less than 1 per cent of OC Transpo km is contracted under this arrangement.

OC Transpo has authority over its own operations, service levels and fares but works within the Regional Council's overall transport policy and to the levels of financial support to be provided from the municipal property tax levy.

Regional policy established in the 1970s determined that the majority of growth in demand should be accommodated by public transport. A key feature is the bus Transitway in three main corridors with 23 'stations' and central area bus priority access. See *JUTS 1990* for background. A further 1.5 km opened in November 1996, completing the initial 31 km project; more extensions are planned.

Patronage has remained stable over the past few years, with some 20 per cent of area motorised trips now made by bus following a policy to expand services, introduce bus priority, deter car use in the central area, and improve ticketing and information systems. Further service improvements, more bus priority and higher productivity are sought in a 10-year long-range plan.

An automated passenger information system is in operation. Telephone information is provided relating to the timetable of services from any bus stop, operated by dialling 560 plus a unique four-digit bus stop number. Electronic displays at main departure points and in shopping centres are also provided. Automatic vehicle

Transitway station at Place d'Orleans ***1995***

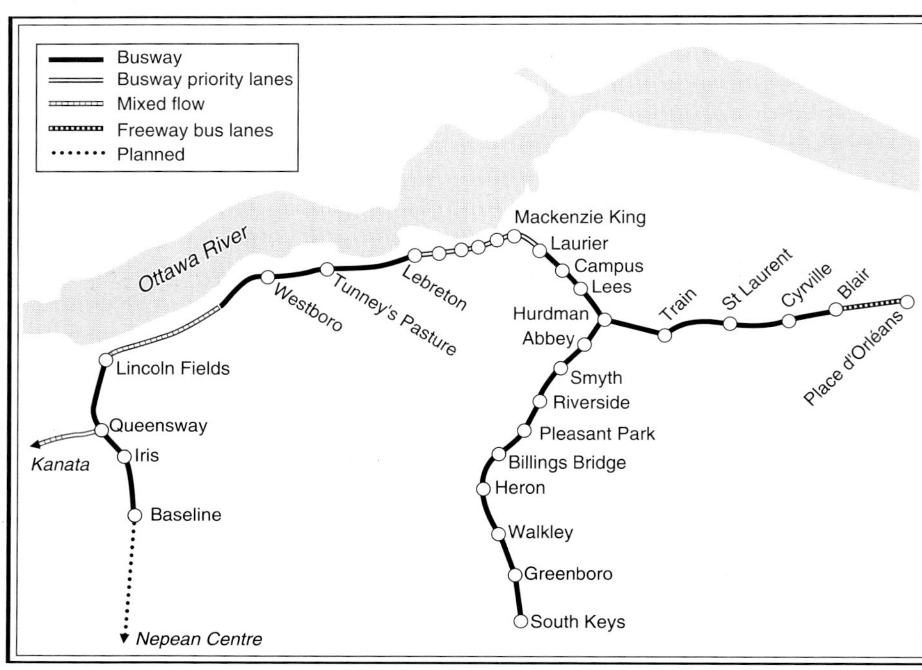

Ottawa's Transitway system

and location operates for all buses, and it is to be integrated with the 560 system to provide real-time information to passengers at each stop.

Bus

Passenger journeys: (1993) 76.1 million
(1994) 73.4 million
(1995) 71.8 million
Vehicle-km: (1993) 50 million
(1994) 49.5 million
(1995) 48.2 million

Number of routes: 155
Route length: (One way) 2,624 km
On priority right-of-way: 29.3 km
Fleet: 794 vehicles

Ikarus articulated (1985/86/87/88)	108
GM/MCI Novabus 40 ft (1989/93)	542
New Flyer 40 ft (1990/92)	87
Orion 40 ft (1991/92)	53
Orion 25 ft	4

In peak service: 702
Average age of fleet: 11.7 years

Most intensive service: 3 min
One-person operation: All routes
Fare collection: Exact fare to Duncan farebox or prepurchase multitickets or monthly passes
Fare structure: Peak and off-peak rates, with premium on express routes during peaks; free transfer; multitickets; monthly passes
Fares collected on board: 26% (62% of passengers use passes, 12% use prepurchase tickets)
Operational control: Central radio control, plus route inspectors/mobile radio, with automatic vehicle monitoring being developed
Arrangements for elderly/disabled: Private company provides contract operation of 141 Para Transpo vehicles (70 lift-equipped minivans, 61 cars and 10 buses designed specifically for transport of groups in wheelchairs), carried 759,000 passengers in 1995. Funded 42.1% by province, 46.5% by municipality, and 8.2% by fares, with 3.2% reserves
Integration with other modes: Four park-and-ride and eight bike-and-ride sites
Average distance between stops: 300 m
Average peak-hour speed: In mixed traffic, 24.5 km/h
Bus priority: 12.5 km of exclusive bus lanes on city streets; 10.6 km bus lane on Provincial highway; exclusive bus transitways (see below)
Operating costs financed by: Fares 49.1%, other commercial sources 1.1%, subsidy/grants 47.3%, reserves 2.5%
Subsidy from: Province 18.2% (by transit levy in Urban Transit area), Municipality (by property taxes) 29.1%
New vehicles financed by: Provincial subsidy 75%, local share from current funds and reserves 25%

Busway (Transitway)

Current situation: The Transitway is fully grade-separated. It penetrates the central area using bus lanes for 2 km on two one-way streets. A study is under way to determine priorities for future extensions.

Ramp access is provided to the Transitway so express routes may operate direct from residential areas if the demand is sufficient for frequent service; otherwise feeder service is provided, with passengers transferring to Transitway services at stations.

The final segment of the Southeast Transitway between Riverside Hospital and Billings Bridge opened in November 1996. Planned extensions would link the Queensway with the Bayshore shopping centre, for which an environmental study report has been approved by the provincial government, while an environmental assessment has been submitted for a southwest extension from Baseline to the growing suburb of Barrhaven/Nepean. A 500-space park-and-ride lot opened in the western suburb of Kanata at the end of 1995.

As an interim measure in the east of the region, a 6 km reserved bus lane was opened in 1992 to provide priority access to the Transitway. A similar 3 km bus lane from Kanata eastbound opened in late 1995. A westbound lane to Kanata was opened in late 1996, while a lane eastbound to Orléans is planned for 1997.

Commuter rail (proposed)

Current situation: Commuter service over two existing CP freight routes has been evaluated and is under review by the regional council.

UPDATED

PALERMO

Population: 900,000
Public transport: Bus services provided by municipal undertaking; suburban railways operated by Italian Railways (FS), being upgraded to regional metro

AMAT

Azienda Municipalizzata Autotrasporti (AMAT)
Via Roccazzo 77 (Passo di Rigano), 90135 Palermo, Sicily, Italy
Telephone: +39 91 404233
President: Dr Leonardo Liggio
Director General: Prof Nunzio Sofia
Staff: 2,000

Bus

Passenger journeys: (Annual) 100 million

Number of routes: 63
Route length: (One way) 800 km
Fleet: Approx 400 vehicles
One-person operation: All routes
Fare structure: Flat; weekly and monthly passes
Fares collected on board: 10%
Operational control: Route inspectors/mobile radio
Arrangements for elderly/disabled: Reduced fares paid for by city subsidy
Average peak-hour speed: 6.2 km/h
Operating costs financed by: Fares 11%, other commercial sources 5%, subsidy/grants 84%
Subsidy from: Region and city council
New vehicles financed by: From annual subsidy

FS

Italian Railways (FS)

Current situation: Services on existing FS lines are being upgraded to regional metro standards under a plan announced in 1988. A short branch to Giacchery was refurbished and electrified in 1990, and a cross-city service is to be provided between the airport and Termini Imerese. The scheme includes several new stations, and construction of a branch to the airport. In a third stage, double-tracking of the existing cross-city tunnel would allow train frequency to be improved.

Developments: Emphasis has shifted away from the regional metro proposals, with regional authorities favouring use of FS alignments as a light metro and the city council preferring light rail. Swiss consultants have recommended a 54 km six-line network which would require 80 to 100 cars.

Palermo was unable to secure funds for mass transit under 1995's Law 11 which provided finance for schemes in other cities, but Lit246 billion is being sought for an automated light metro. In addition, municipal, provincial and regional government is promoting a light rail or metro utilising part of the Palermo—Camporeale narrow-gauge railway, built years ago but never opened. This would link the outskirts of Palermo with Baccadiflaca and Monreale. A full proposal is to be presented to central government for approval in 1997.

UPDATED

PARIS

Population: City 2 million, region 11 million
Public transport: Bus, metro, light rail and a funicular operated by Paris Transport Authority (RATP) under overall control of a board (syndicat) consisting of government and local authority representatives. Syndicat also supervises operation of regional cross-city metro (RER) shared by RATP with French National Railways (SNCF), and SNCF's extensive suburban services. Some suburban bus lines operated by private firms are also integrated under the Syndicat

Syndicat des Transports

Syndicat des Transports Parisiens (STP)
9 avenue de Villars, 75007 Paris, France
Telephone: +33 1 47 53 28 00 Fax: +33 1 47 05 11 05

Current situation: Has overall responsibility for policy and co-ordination of urban and suburban transport provision in the greater Paris area (Ile de France region) with a population of about 11 million in a 12,000 km² area designated as La Région des Transports Parisiens.

Its powers have been strengthened under recent government devolution moves. The body, with representatives of the government and local authorities, brings together the operations of RATP, SNCF and private bus operators, and is responsible for authorising provision of transport, overseeing the level of service and setting fares.

STP is responsible for authorising major projects, and it has administered the very substantial investment in public transport facilities, including RER development, electrification of suburban railways, improved bus fleet, bus lane and shelter provision and information developments.

STP administers a range of contractual arrangements with private bus operators for provision of suburban services. All give the operator a local monopoly but this may be in the form of own risk operation, guaranteed receipts, a contracted price or a management contract.

Developments: Under discussion is the 'Plan Directeur' – a master plan for strategic development in the Ile de France region through to 2015, when some 28 million daily journeys will be made. The emphasis remains strongly on high-quality public transport provision, and in particular on orbital links between suburbs.

RATP

Régie Autonome des Transports Parisiens (RATP)
LAC B 916/54 Quai de la Rapée, 75599 Paris Cedex 12
Telephone: +33 1 44 68 20 20 Fax: +33 1 44 68 31 70
Director General: Jean Paul Bailly
Joint General Managers
Passenger Service: Henri Schwebel
Management, Finance & Development: Robert Sammut
Maintenance, Works & Industrial Policy: Jean Stablo
Social & International Policy: Guy-Noël Payan
Director of Bus Services: Robert Jung
Director of Metro Services: Jacques Rappoport
Director of RER Services: Jean Marc Mocquiaux
Staff: 38,340

Passenger journeys: (All modes including RER)
(1993) 2,398 million
(1994) 2,371 million
(1995) 2,127 million

Operating costs financed by: Fares 42.5%, subsidy/grants 57.5%
Subsidy from: Compensation for 'social fares' reductions, Indemnité Compensatrice, employers ('versement'), national and local government

Current situation: RATP, established in 1949, is controlled by a board composed of representatives of central government, local authorities, staff and transport professionals. Central area public transport is based on a dense Metro network with closely spaced stations. Express Metro (Réseau Express Régional) RER routes traverse the conurbation and serve large areas of the suburbs.

Government policy has been to encourage use of public transport, establishing a dedicated employee tax (the 'versement') for operating support, and legislation introduced in 1982 provided for employers to become liable for paying part of the cost of commuters' season tickets. In 1991 the employer's payroll tax was raised from 2.2 to 2.4 per cent.

Developments: To relieve RER Line A, a new fully automated metro line known as Meteor (Metro Rapide Est-Ouest) is under construction from Tolbiac to Gare de Lyon, Gare du Nord and Madelaine for 1998 opening. In addition, a fifth RER line called Est-Ouest Liaison Express (EOLE) is under construction linking Nord and Est stations to St Lazare. Eventually this will permit through running between SNCF's eastern and western suburban networks.

RATP plans to build a main network of 200 km of exclusive public transport rights-of-way covering one-third of the radial and two-thirds of the orbital bus routes, fully integrated with the existing rail system. The aim is to improve service quality while handling increased traffic without the expense of full metro technology. Plans envisage that buses will use the alignments in the southern part of the city, with possible later conversion to light rail. The first such route, known as Trans-Val-de-Marne (TVM), opened in 1993 between Rungis and St Maur-Créteil. A guided bus system (TVR) is to be tested over 2 km of the route in 1997.

RATP's 1995 results were adversely affected by the effects of terrorist bombs and strikes. The undertaking has made the fight against fraud a priority, as some 10 per cent of revenue is lost in this way.

RATP's first low-floor buses make Route 20 more easily accessible ***1997***

Bus

Staff: 12,230, plus 2,941 maintenance staff

Passenger journeys: (1993) 859 million
(1994) 838 million
(1995) 774 million
Vehicle-km: (1993) 149 million
(1994) 151 million
(1995) 133 million

Number of routes: 241; urban 57, plus one circular route; suburban 184; 10 night routes
Route length: (One way) 2,560 km; urban 530 km, suburban 2,030 km
On priority right-of-way: 304 km in city, 173 km in suburbs

Fleet: 3,988 vehicles

SC10 (all types and dates)	2,049
Renault PR100	89
Renault R312	1,494
Articulated	335
Heuliez GX317 low-floor	21

In peak service: 84%

Most intensive service: 3-4 min
One-person operation: All routes
Fare structure: 7 zones; multiticket books, and weekly, monthly and yearly all-mode passes (Carte Orange), day tickets
Fare collection: Tickets validated by machine on board, passes shown to driver
Fares collected on board: Less than 33%; over 50% of passengers use zonal passes (Carte Orange)
Fare evasion control: Roving inspectors in teams
Operational control: All buses fitted with radio; other methods include centralised despatching by route controllers, now covering 131 routes, initiating terminal departures. A system of computerised monitoring linked to 'next bus' information at stops, known as ALEXIS and introduced on TVM and the tramway, is being tested on routes 26 and 29
Bus priority: 'Ligne Pilote' routes use extensive system of bus lanes; one route also equipped for experimental on-board traffic light control. Now 40% of route-km in central area operate over bus lanes, covering 304 route-km, with further 173.5 route-km in suburbs. Extensive system of reserved busways proposed for suburbs (see above). Further plans for city-centre busways and control of traffic congestion
Integration with other modes: Multitickets valid for use on buses, metro and RER; zonal passes valid on all modes; buses timed to meet trains at certain interchange stations
Average distance between stops: Urban 320 m; suburban 420 m
Average peak-hour speed: Urban 9.9 km/h; suburban 13.9 km/h
New vehicles financed by: Capital budget investments

Developments: Suburban bus services are being restructured area by area in a project called Autrement Bus. A fleet of 21 low-floor air conditioned buses has been introduced on Route 20 and pavements raised at each stop to aid disabled passengers.

Metro

Staff: 9,176, plus maintenance staff (see RER below)

Type of operation: Full metro, first line opened 1900

Passenger journeys: (Including funicular)
(1993) 1,177 million
(1994) 1,170 million
(1995) 1,029 million
Car-km: (1993) 201 million
(1994) 200 million
(1995) 186 million

Route length: 201.5 km
Number of lines: 15, 4 of which operated by rubber-tyred trains
Number of stations: 294
Gauge: 1,435 mm
Electrification: 750 V DC, third rail

Service: 1 min 35 s to 3 min 50 s minimum
Fare structure: Flat
Fare collection: Automatic machines with change-giving facility or carnets of 10 tickets at reduced price, entrance gates at all stations, exit gates at RER stations; roving inspectors
Integration with other modes: Greater Paris area divided into 7 zones. Monthly pass, Carte Orange, for unlimited journeys within valid zones on metro, buses, RER, suburban SNCF lines and coach lines; used by more than 60% of RATP passengers
Signalling: All lines linked to central control and monitoring post (PCC) which receives all data on train movements and locations, issues appropriate

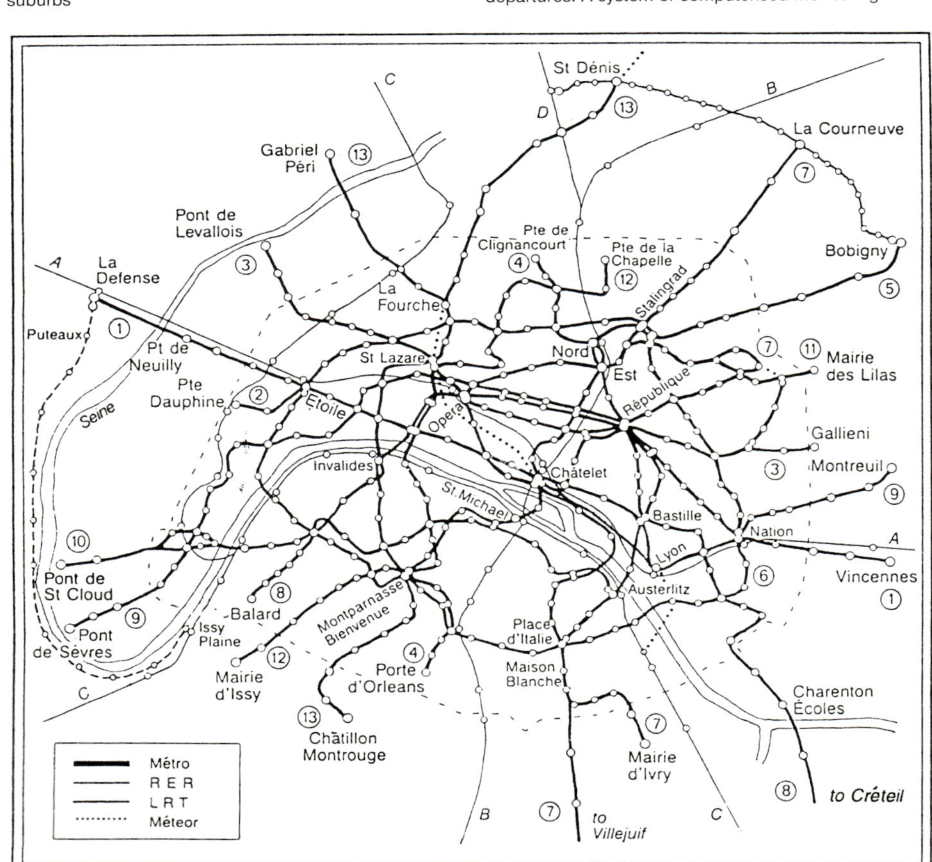

Paris Metro

instructions, and remotely controls all trackside equipment; ATO on all lines

Rolling stock: 3,399 cars

B&L/RNUR/CEM/JS MP55 (1956/57)	M48 T16
CIMT MP59 (1966/67)	M405 T202
CIMT MP73 (1974)	M245
CIMT/B&L MF67 (1967/76)	M904 T581
Franco-Belge/Alsthom MF77 (1978/86)	M708 T270
GEC Alsthom/Bombardier-ANF MF88 (1992)	M10 T5
GEC Alsthom MP89 (1996)	M5

MP cars are rubber-tyred, MF steel-wheeled

On order: The new generation 'Boa' Metro trains started public trials in 1994, when five MF88 prototype trains entered service on Line 7b. They have steerable axles with independent wheels and full-width gangways between cars. GEC Alsthom started deliveries in 1996 of 665 Type MP89 rubber-tyred cars. Two-thirds of this fleet will replace stock on Lines 1 and 11, and by cascade on Line 4, while the rest will be used on the automated Meteor line

Developments: The 7.5 km Meteor line is under construction from Tolbiac-Massina via Bercy and Châtelet to Madeleine. With seven stations, it will connect four RER routes and eight metro lines. Due to open in 1997, Meteor will be worked by a fleet of MP89 rubber-tyred Boa-derived six-car driverless trains. The line may later be extended at its southern end to Nationale. At the northern end, it may be extended to St Lazare and then take over the alignment of the western branch of Line 13.

A short extension of Line 13's eastern branch from St Denis Basilique to St Denis Université is under construction, also for opening in 1997.

RATP envisages that in the long term the entire urban metro network will be converted to driverless operation. This will achieve the twin objectives of reducing operating costs and providing more frequent service. Conversion is only considered economic if introduction is phased to coincide with rolling stock replacement.

Longer-term proposals outlined in the 'Plan Directeur' (see above) include several suburban extensions of existing lines. Under study are Line 1 from La Défense to Nanterre La Folie, Line 8 from Créteil to Créteil Sud, and Line 11 from Mairie des Lilas to Rosny Bois Perrier.

Renault PR180 articulated on the Trans-Val-de-Marne service at Choisy-le-Roi **1995**

MF67 at Austerlitz on Line 5

Regional metro (RER)

Operated jointly by RATP and SNCF (see below)
Staff: 2,890, plus 2,792 maintenance staff shared with metro

Type of operation: Regional express metro

Passenger journeys: (RATP lines)
(1993) 361 million
(1994) 364 million
(1995) 323 million
Car-km: (1993) 84.5 million
(1994) 83.8 million
(1995) 77.7 million
SNCF line figures included in suburban railway total, see below

Route length: 366 km, of which 115 km operated by RATP and 251 km by SNCF
Number of lines: 4 with numerous branches (Lines A and B jointly operated, Lines C and D SNCF only)
Number of stations: 159 (RATP 65, SNCF 94)
Gauge: 1,435 mm
Electrification: 1.5 kV DC and 25 kV 50 Hz, overhead

New M12N double-deck train on RER Line A **1997**

Rolling stock: RATP, 377 Type MS61 cars, 566 MI79/84 cars (see SNCF entry also)

Developments: Substantial through working and SNCF/RATP integration has been achieved under the Interconnexion schemes. The current SNCF project EOLE will become Line E when the initial section opens in mid-1998. See previous editions of *JUTS* for background.

The additional pair of tracks between Châtelet and Gare de Lyon opened in September 1995, allowing the long-awaited projection of Line D services into the southeastern suburbs (see under SNCF below).

Further extensions are planned at the western end of Line A, of Line B to the Ile de France boundary at Dammartin-Juilly-St Mard, and of Line C from Montigny-Beauchamp to Pontoise for 1999 completion.

Funicular

Current situation: The 102 m Funiculaire de Montmartre was built in 1901 as a water balance system and electrified in 1935. It has an incline of 36 per cent. After refurbishment, it reopened in 1991 with new cars offering capacity of 2,000 passengers/h in each direction.

Light rail

Type of operation: Light rail, initial route opened 1992

Passenger journeys: (1993) 15 million
(1994) 17 million
(1995) 15.7 million

Route length: 9.1 km
Number of lines: 1
Number of stops: 21
Gauge: 1,435 mm
Electrification: 750 V DC, overhead

Service: Peak 5 min, off-peak 8 min
First/last car: 05.00/23.59
Fare structure: As bus
Fare collection: Automatic vending machines, onboard validators

Rolling stock: 39 cars

GEC Alsthom (1991/92)	M17
GEC Alsthom (1996)	M22

Current situation: The city's first light rail line links St Denis and Bobigny in the northeast suburbs. Some 6 km is segregated from street traffic and there are 28 bus feeders.
Developments: A second light rail route is under construction. Known as Trans-Val-de-Seine, the 11.3 km line takes over SNCF's last third-rail suburban line from Puteaux to Issy-Plaine, closed in 1993, with a northern extension from Puteaux to La Défense. Construction has been much delayed by a dispute with the local authority at Puteaux, and opening will now take place in late 1997. GEC Alsthom has supplied a further 22 cars.

It is proposed to extend this line over the disused SNCF Petite Ceinture alignment from Issy Plaine to Porte de Versailles and beyond. Construction of the first 2.7 km to Porte de Versailles is likely to start in 1999, while a further 8 km to a new interchange with metro Line 7 and Meteor at Maison Blanche could follow early in the next century.

Plans are also in hand to extend Line 1 from Bobigny to Noisy-le-Sec.

People mover (OrlyVAL)

Passenger journeys: (1993) 1.3 million
(1994) 1.5 million
(1995) 1.6 million

Current situation: A 7.3 km automated people mover with three stations opened in 1991 between Orly airport and Antony station on RER Line B. A 4 min interval service is operated. RATP undertook the project jointly with Matra using VAL technology; the scheme was funded with contributions from Air Inter and a number of banks.
Developments: Traffic did not reach expectations, and the operating company went into liquidation; RATP assumed control of the line in 1993 by way of an operating company RATP VAL Service, of which RATP owns 51 per cent and Matra 49 per cent. Nevertheless, normal ticketing (including Carte Orange) is still not valid. The line receives a FFr10 million annual subsidy from the Ile de France region.

RATP has improved interchange at Orly and Antony, and has increased publicity for the route. As a result, traffic rose by 40 per cent between 1993 and 1994.

A study is under way into diversion of the line to an interchange with RER Line C at Rungis La Fraternelle.

Rolling stock: Eight two-car trains

SNCF

Société Nationale des Chemins de Fer Français
88 rue St Lazare, 75436 Paris Cedex 09
Telephone: +33 1 53 25 73 28 Fax: +33 1 53 25 88 15
General Manager, Ile de France Region: Pierre Ceriser

Trial running on tramway Line T2 ***1997***

Type of operation: Suburban heavy rail

Passenger journeys: (1992) 542 million
(1994) 554 million
(1995)

Route length: Suburban lines, 1,263 km; RER-SNCF lines, 274 km
Number of lines: Suburban, 37; RER-SNCF, 4 (Lines A and B operated jointly with RATP, Lines C and D SNCF only)
Number of stations: 382
Electrification: 25 kV AC, overhead (654 km); 1.5 kV DC, overhead (512 km)

Fare structure: 67% of passengers use the zonal Carte Integrale (annual pass) or Carte Orange (monthly or weekly pass); remainder use graduated-fare tickets (15%), weekly workers' passes or student passes. Zonal system is increasing its share
Integration with other modes: Carte Integrale and Carte Orange valid on SNCF, RATP and private bus services; other combined passes available (including 'Formule 1' — one-day travel on all modes), SNCF-RER/RATP or Metro/RATP
Fare evasion control: Automatic turnstiles, roving inspectors
Operating costs financed by: Fares 43%, employers' tax (versement transport) 40%, other commercial sources 1%, subsidy 16%. Subsidy provided by state (70%) and local authorities (30%)
One-person operation: Totally or partially on RER and suburban lines, except trains out of Paris Est (planned for introduction when EOLE opens)

Rolling stock: 3,505 cars, formed as emus or 6- to 8-car push-pull sets hauled by electric locomotives. Many of both types of train comprise double-deck cars (1,491 total). SNCF is aiming for 100% double-deck operation by 2005
On order: 30 four-car double-deck emus for outer suburban services and 53 five-car double-deck sets for EOLE, plus options for a further 86 sets. This stock is a shared SNCF/RATP design with three doorways per side and all axles motored

Current situation: SNCF operates suburban services from six termini, of which 1,161 km electrified — at 25 kV 50 Hz from Gare de l'Est, Gare du Nord and Gare St Lazare, at 1.5 kV DC from Gare de Lyon, Gare d'Austerlitz and Gare Montparnasse — and 102 km operated by diesel trains. Fare collection is largely automated and is fully compatible with the Metro and RER.

In 1991 SNCF's Paris suburban area was extended to cover the whole Ile de France region, increasing the number of communities served from 532 to 1,281.
Developments: Under the EOLE scheme a 3.6 km double-track link electrified at 25 kV is under construction between new two-track stations at Nord-Est and St Lazare-Condorcet. Access will be through a 1.3 km tunnel from the Gare de l'Est approaches. Services will start in 1998.

A 1.7 km tunnel will then be built from Condorcet to Pont Cardinet, allowing trains from La Défense, Versailles and other western suburbs to run through to Nord-Est. A final stage would see construction of a new station at La Villette.

A fleet of high-capacity double-deck emus is being delivered for these services, comprising 53 five-car trainsets with three doorways per car.

OrlyVAL train near Rungis ***1995***

Dual-voltage double-deck emus on RER Line D at Villiers-le-Bel-Gonesse ***1995***

September 1995 saw completion of two 2.5 km single-track tunnels to form the central section of RER Line D between Châtelet-les-Halles and Gare de Lyon. Through trains now run from Orry-la-Ville-Coye in the north to Melun, Evry, Corbeil-Essonnes and La Ferté-Alais in the southeast, with six trains per hour during the day and 12 at peak times. Opening of this 2.5 km connection has brought relief to the hard-pressed Line A service between Châtelet and Gare de Lyon by creaming off some 10,000 passengers/h in the peaks.

Several track modelling schemes are in hand to raise capacity. Studies are being made of a sixth RER line linking St Lazare with Montparnasse.

The last major diesel-operated outer-suburban line, from Paris Nord to Beauvais, is being electrified.

Private bus

Represented by:
Association Professionnelle des Transporteurs Routiers (APTR)
Telephone: +33 1 49 50 11 97

Current situation: APTR members operate most of the outer suburban bus routes, many acting as feeders to SNCF, RER and Metro stations. Some routes, particularly in new towns, are operated directly under contract to STP, though a range of contract/management arrangements is available, with the standard feature being the provision of a local service monopoly. Fare structure is common with that of RATP, with subsidies provided through the Syndicat and Carte Orange passes accepted.

A fleet of about 1,600 vehicles operates over some 5,700 route-km carrying about 150 million passengers a year.

UPDATED

PERM

Population: 1.1 million
Public transport: Bus and trolleybus/tramway services provided by separate municipal undertakings

Bus

Number of routes: 64
Fleet: Ikarus 260/280, LIAZ 677, plus MAN and others ex-German cities
Fare collection: Prepurchase, cancellers on board

Tramvaino-Trolleibusnoe Upravlenie

Uralskaya ul 108A, 614600 Perm, Russia
Telephone: +7 3422 362466

Trolleybus

Number of routes: 10
Fleet: Approx 100 trolleybuses

Uritsky ZIU9	85
Uritsky ZIU10	8
Jelcz	1
Ex-Arnhem	8

Tramway

Passenger journeys: (1992) 129 million

Number of routes: 11
Route length: 129 km

ZIU9 trolleybus on Perm's Route 5 ***1997***

Rolling stock: 250 cars

KTM5 (1979-92)	M210
KTM8 (1992-96)	M40

NEW ENTRY

PERTH

Population: 1.3 million
Public transport: Bus, suburban rail and ferry services in Perth and Fremantle metropolitan area provided by private and public operators co-ordinated and monitored by an agency of the state Department of Transport

Transperth

Department of Transport, Metropolitan Transport Division
Level 5, 19 Pier Street, Perth, WA 6000, Australia
Telephone: +61 9 325 1633 Fax: +61 9 325 5747
Executive Director, Metropolitan Transport: Greg Martin
Director, Transperth: Brett Inchley

Suburban train at Joondalup ***1995***

Principal Consultant, Transperth: Hugo Wildermuth
Staff: 31

Current situation: Following reforms enacted in 1993, the Department of Transport took over responsibility for co-ordination of Perth's public transport. Competitive tendering started in 1996, and the Department has contracted with one public and three private sector operators to provide bus services, and with a private sector operator for ferry service. The suburban train network continues to be provided by the Western Australian Government Railways (Westrail). Contracts for management of the Transperth infrastructure and the passenger information system have also been let to private sector companies.

The metropolitan area is divided into 14 contract areas, of which nine have been tendered for. In addition to its competitive contracts for operation in three areas, state-owned MetroBus continues to run services on a non-competitive basis in five areas where services have yet to be contracted-out. The other operators are Swan Transit (three contracts), Transport Management Group (one contract), and Australian Transit Enterprises (two contracts).

Bus

Passenger journeys: (1993/94) 37 million
(1994/95) 37 million
(1995/96) 35.8 million
Vehicle-km: (1993/94) 48.7 million
(1994/95) 48.5 million
(1995/96) 47.6 million

Number of routes: 322 (with 5 free central area routes plus 650 school trips daily)
Route length: (Unduplicated) 1,999 km
Priority right-of-way: 3.7 km, plus 7 km with-flow Kwinana Freeway exclusive bus lane

Fleet: 851 vehicles

Cummins 844	2
Mercedes O303	3
Mercedes O305	407
Mercedes O305 CNG-powered	28
Mercedes O405 CNG-powered	15
Mercedes O405	35
Renault PR100-2	248
Renault PR100-3 CNG-powered	1
Scania BR112H	1
MAN SG290H articulated	8
Mercedes O305G articulated	38
Renault PR180-2 articulated	65

In peak service: 775

Most intensive service: 3 min on trunk sections
One-person operation: All routes
Fare collection: Onboard cash purchase, some prepurchase from machines at bus stations; prepurchase 10-trip tickets; validating machines on board
Fare structure: Eight zones and short-distance two-section fare valid 2 h in specified zone, 1-day fare, at full fare and concession; family day (up to 2 adults/5 children) tickets on weekends/holidays; bus and rail fares free within city-centre zone
Fare evasion control: Ticket inspection
Operational control: Two-way radio covers 81% of vehicles
Integration with other modes: Zonal fare structure covers all modes; unlimited transfer between modes within 2 h validity
Average distance between stops: 300 m
Average peak-hour speed: In Kwinana Freeway bus lane 85 km/h; in other bus lanes 40 km/h; in mixed traffic 22 km/h
Bus priority: Several bus lanes around city centre; 7 km peak hours with-flow bus lane in Kwinana Freeway
Operating costs financed by: Fares 28.5%, subsidy/grants 71.5%
New vehicles financed by: Loans from state treasury

Developments: Central Area Transit (CAT) scheme inaugurated August 1996, comprising accessible buses, attractive stops and other facilities, and high-quality information. All new buses are to be accessible.

CAT distributor features DAB easy access buses and smart new shelters ***1997***

Suburban rail

Operated under contract by Westrail
Staff: 255

Type of operation: Suburban heavy rail

Passenger journeys: (1993/94) 16.2 million
(1994/95) 16.7 million
(1995/96) 16.5 million

Operating costs financed by: Fares 18%, subsidy/grants 82%

Current situation: Westrail operates suburban train services under a non-competitive contractual agreement with the Department of Transport.

Services operated on routes to Armadale, Midland, Fremantle and Currambine; total 95 km, 1,067 mm gauge, electrified at 25 kV 50 Hz. Most stations unstaffed; ticket machines installed at all stations; free transit zone in central area, as bus. Trains are driver-only operated, with cab-mounted CCTV. Passenger Service Assistants travel on all trains.
Developments: Both trains and stations are being made accessible to those with disabilities.

Rolling stock: 43 two-car emus

Walkers/ABB AEA (1991/92)	M24
Walkers/ABB AEB (1990/91)	M24
Walkers/ABB AEA (1992/93)	M16
Walkers/ABB AEB (1992/93/94)	M22

Ferry

Operated by Perth Water Transport Pty Ltd
Jetty 1, Barrack Street, Perth 6000
Telephone: +61 9 221 2722 Fax: +61 9 221 2739
Director: Tony Baker

Current situation: Ferry services provided under contract cross the Swan river from Perth to South Perth (1.3 km) with two vessels; carried 0.4 million passengers in 1995/96. Fares cover 59.6 per cent of operating costs.

UPDATED

PHILADELPHIA

Population: City 1.6 million, metropolitan area 4 million
Public transport: Bus, trolleybus, metro, tramway and suburban rail services provided by divisions of transportation authority controlled by representative board appointed by state and local government jurisdictions, and based on acquired undertakings. Additional metro route to Lindenwold, New Jersey, run by Port Authority, with connecting NJ Transit local trains running Philadelphia—Lindenwold—Atlantic City

SEPTA

Southeastern Pennsylvania Transportation Authority (SEPTA)
1234 Market Street, Philadelphia, PA 19107, USA
Telephone: +1 215 580 7070 Fax: +1 215 580 7328
General Manager: John K Leary
Assistant General Managers
Surface Transit: Luther Diggs
Subway-Elevated Transit: Juan Torres
Regional Rail: Michael Burns
Light Rail & Contract Operations: Kim Heinle
Paratransit: George Hague
Staff: 9,130

GM RTS (retrofitted with air conditioning) at 69th Street with light rail cars behind ***1997***

Passenger journeys: (All modes)
(1993/94) 209.1 million
(1994/95) 199.8 million
(1995/96) 197.7 million

Operating costs financed by: (All modes) fares 47%, subsidy/grants 53%
Subsidy from: FTA 2%, state 55% and 5 county governments 43%

Current situation: SEPTA, created in 1964, is the fifth largest transit system in the USA. It consists of a City Transit Division with bus, trolleybus, tramway/light rail and rapid transit/metro lines in the city of Philadelphia, a Suburban Transit Division with tramway/light rail and bus lines in Bucks, Chester, Delaware and Montgomery counties, and a Regional Rail Division serving the five-county area.

SEPTA's financial difficulties had been compounded by lack of a dedicated funding source or local funding provisions. Following a crisis in 1990, a new Public Transportation Assistance Fund was created in 1991, from which SEPTA receives some $135 million a year. Funding comes from a flat $1 tax on new vehicle tyres, a 6 per cent sales tax on magazines, a 3 per cent road vehicle lease tax, a $2 daily rental vehicle tax, and an increase in property tax. In 1994 it was also agreed that the existing imbalance in allocation of state funding between SEPTA and rural areas should be corrected, with $100 million diverted from road to transit spending and a goal of an additional $100 million for the following three years if funding was available. The second $100 million tranche, due in 1995/96, did not materialise.

1992 saw withdrawal of 1947-vintage PCC tramcars and closure of the three City Transit surface routes (15, 23 and 56) they operated. These routes are proposed for rehabilitation along with purchase of a fleet of 70 LRVs, but financial considerations have caused the plan to be delayed. Other service cuts were made to reduce costs, including replacement of metro night service by buses. Some small extensions of wiring are proposed to increase trolleybus use.

Financial difficulties led to a decision in October 1996 to make further service cuts, and some suburban rail services were withdrawn immediately.

City Transit Division

Current situation: SEPTA's City Transit Division is responsible for city bus and trolleybus, metro and tramway operations. The bus figures include services of the Red Arrow and Frontier suburban operations (see below).

Bus and trolleybus

Passenger journeys: (1993/94) Bus 104 million, trolleybus 7 million
(1994/95) Bus 101 million, trolleybus 6.5 million
(1995/96) Bus 104.8 million, trolleybus 6.6 million
Vehicle-km: (1993/94) Bus 66.9 million, trolleybus 1.4 million
(1994/95) Bus 65.6 million, trolleybus 1.6 million
(1995/96) Bus 63.9 million, trolleybus 1.9 million

CNG-powered Orion IIs run the 'Philly Phlash' downtown circulator **1997**

Number of routes: Bus 110, trolleybus 5
Route length: (One way) bus 2,201 km, trolleybus 34 km
Fleet: 1,434 buses (includes suburban fleet)

GM RTS (1980)	292
Neoplan (1982/83/84/85)	600
Volvo articulated (1985)	50
Neoplan (1986/87/89)	492
American Ikarus (1996)	
Orion II	

In peak service: 1,099
On order: 400 Ikarus buses
Fleet: 110 trolleybuses

AM General (1979)	110

In peak service: 51
Trolleybus electrification: 600 V DC

Fare collection: Prepurchase tokens, weekly and monthly passes; coin to registering Duncan fareboxes at entrance
Fare structure: City, flat; suburban, zonal; weekly and monthly passes, tokens; all modes day pass
Fares collected on board: 40%
Fare evasion control: Random checks
Integration with other modes: Integrated fares with metro and light rail with transfer charges and add-on to commuter rail season tickets; connections with rail and major LR interchanges
Arrangements for elderly/disabled: Free off-peak travel financed by state lottery funds. Paratransit services carry about 8,000 passengers daily
New vehicles financed by: FTA grants 80%, state 16.7%, local 3.3%

Developments: The FTA awarded SEPTA a grant of $7.9 million in late 1996 to finance purchase of 105 buses. This brings the total FTA funding for the current bus replacement programme to $21.3 million.

Metro

Market–Frankford subway-elevated line, Broad Street subway and Ridge Avenue spur

Type of operation: Full metro

Passenger journeys: (1993/94) 55.5 million
(1994/95) 51.4 million
(1995/96) 52.5 million

Route length: 41 km
Number of lines: 3
Number of stations: 62
Gauge: Broad Street line 1,435 mm, Market–Frankford line 1,581 mm
Max gradient: 5%
Minimum curve radius: Market–Frankford line 32 m, Broad Street line 49 m
Track: 49.6 kg/m flat bottom rail
Tunnel: Cut-and-cover
Electrification: 625 V DC, third rail; Broad Street line top contact, Market–Frankford line bottom contact

Service: Peak 2-3½ min, off-peak 7½ min
Fare structure: Flat
Fare evasion control: Barrier access to paid area; random checks
Integration with other modes: Transfers to and from bus

Rolling stock: 396 cars

Budd A49/50/51 Market St line (1956-60)	M239
Kawasaki BIV Broad St line (1982)	M125
Adtranz N5/M4 (1994/95/96)	M32

In peak service: 283
On order: 220 cars being delivered by Adtranz for the Market Street line, with an option to buy up to 120 more

Tramway

Type of operation: Conventional tramway routes feeding into city-centre tunnel

Passenger journeys: (1993/94) 14.9 million
(1994/95) 14 million
(1995/96) 11.5 million
Car-km: (1993/94) 4 million
(1994/95) 4.1 million
(1995/96) 5.1 million

Route length: 107 km
in tunnel: 4 km
Number of lines: 5
Number of stations: 8 in tunnel section
Gauge: 1,581 mm
Track: 49.6 kg/m ASCE standard rail
Max gradient: 5%
Minimum curve radius: 22.5 m
Tunnel: Cut-and-cover
Electrification: 600 V DC, overhead

Service: Peak 10 min, off-peak 20 min
Fare structure: Flat
Revenue control: Fare to driver
Integration with other modes: Transfers to and from bus and metro
Signalling: Automatic block on tunnel section

Rolling stock: 112 cars

Kawasaki LRV (1980)	M112

In peak service: 90

Multiple-unit operation on Route 13 **1996**

Suburban Division

Current situation: Serves the western and northern suburbs (former Red Arrow and Frontier divisions), with three light rail lines totalling 45.8 route-km and 38 bus routes. Statistics for the bus network are included in the City Transit figures above.

Light rail

Passenger journeys: (1993/94) 4.8 million
(1994/95) 4.6 million
(1995/96) 3.2 million

Current situation: SEPTA's suburban light rail operation comprises three routes: a 1,435 mm gauge line Route 100 from 69th Street to Norristown (third rail), and tram routes 101 and 102 from 69th Street to Media and Sharon Hill (1,581 mm gauge, overhead), all 600 V DC. Routes 101 and 102 are largely on private right-of-way, while the Norristown line, refurbished in 1990, is more akin to a light metro, having high platforms, third-rail current collection and no grade crossings.

Rolling stock: 55 cars

Kawasaki LRV Routes 101/102 (1982)	M29
ABB N5 LRV Norristown line (1993/94)	M26

In peak service: 33

Regional Rail Line Division

Type of operation: Suburban heavy rail

PATCO train on the Ben Franklin bridge ***1996***

Passenger journeys: (1993/94) 20.9 million
(1994/95) 22.6 million
(1995/96) 22.5 million

Current situation: Network of 13 routes with 174 stations totalling 470 km, electrified at 11 kV AC overhead. Trains run every 10-30 min at peak times, 30-60 min off-peak. Zonal fare structure, with a monthly travel pass allowing free transfers to other SEPTA services.

The system comprises former Reading and Pennsylvania railroad lines connected since 1984 by a city-centre underground link. Lines are grouped into seven cross-city services.

Developments: A new circumferential route known as the Cross-Country Metro has been proposed over 74 km of former rail alignment from Downingtown to Morrisville, designed to facilitate suburb-to-suburb journeys and improve access to existing radial routes into Philadelphia. Consultants were appointed in mid-1996 to examine the feasibility of the proposal. An extension of the existing Wilmington service to Newark, Delaware, is also planned.

Some lines which carry very light traffic are proposed for conversion to light rail as a means of more economical operation.

Service between Downingtown and Parkesburg was withdrawn as an economy measure in late 1996, and four other stations were closed.

Rolling stock: 304 emu cars, 35 push-pull coaches, 7 electric locomotives

Budd Silverliner II (1963)	M53
St Louis Car Silverliner III (1967)	M20
GE Silverliner IV pairs (1974/76)	M184
GE Silver IV singles (1974)	M47
Bombardier push-pull cab (1987)	T10
Bombardier push-pull coach (1987)	T25

In peak service: 279

PATCO

Port Authority Transit Corporation (PATCO)
Lindenwold, NJ 08021
Telephone: +1 609 772 6900 Fax: +1 609 772 6957
President: Paul Drayton
General Manager: R G Schwab
Assistant General Manager, Maintenance & Engineering: E M Hughes
Assistant General Manager, Operations & Planning: J C Gallagher
Staff: 330

Type of operation: Full metro, opened 1969

Passenger boardings: (1993) 11.2 million
(1994) 11.1 million
(1995) 10.9 million
Car-km: (1993) 7.3 million
(1994) 7.3 million
(1995) 7.2 million

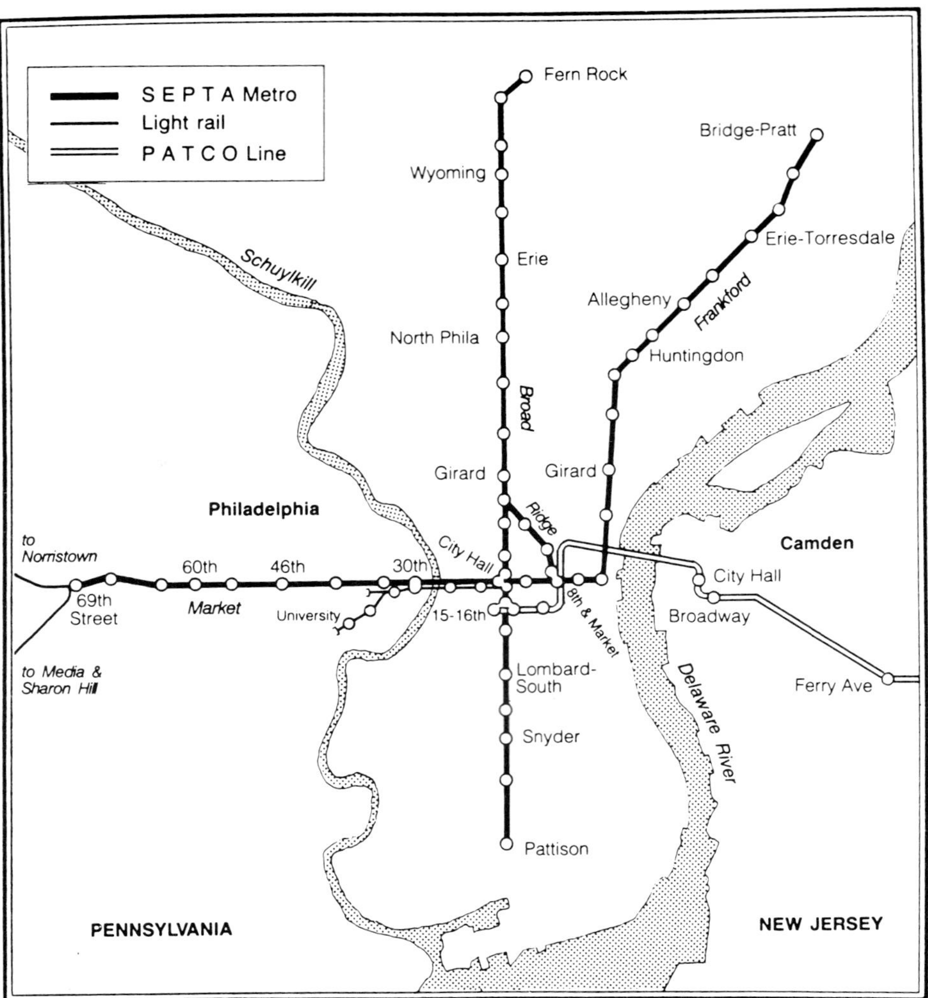

Philadelphia metro and light rail

SEPTA commuter train on the Norristown regional line ***1996***

Route length: 23.3 km
in tunnel: 4.1 km
elevated: 3.7 km
Number of lines: 1
Number of stations: 13
in tunnel: 6
Gauge: 1,435 mm
Track: 66 kg/m continuous welded rail; in tunnel, sleepers encased in concrete; at grade, timber sleepers on ballast; on viaduct, track anchored to concrete deck
Max gradient: 5%
Minimum curve radius: 61 m

Tunnel: Cut-and-cover
Electrification: 685 V DC, third rail

Service: Peak 3-4 min, off-peak 7-12 min; 24 h service
Fare structure: Zonal fares in 5 zones; 2-ride and 10-ride tickets
Revenue control: All stations unstaffed and equipped with change machines, automatic ticket vendors and bi-directional gates
Fare evasion control: CCTV in all fare areas, monitored at control and enforced by PATCO police
Arrangements for elderly/disabled: Reduced fare

Integration with other modes: Intersystem transfer arrangements with New Jersey Transit feeder buses and with SEPTA; also with NJT trains to and from Atlantic City; 7 stations have parking for over 12,000 cars
Operating costs financed by: Fares 56.4%, deficit financed by loans from Delaware River Port Authority
One-person operation: All trains
Signalling: Cab signals, with wayside signals at all interlockings; full automation except doors and PA announcements
Surveillance: In 4 tunnel stations

Rolling stock: 121 cars
Budd (1968-69) single cars M25
Budd (1968) M50
Vickers Canada (1980-81) M46
In peak service: 96

Current situation: PATCO was the first of the new generation of highly automated transit lines in North America. Rebuilt from an existing (1935) line operated by the PTC (SEPTA's predecessor) connecting downtown tunnels in Philadelphia and Camden via the Ben Franklin Bridge, it was extended into the New Jersey suburbs over moribund rail right-of-way. It is owned by the Delaware River Port Authority, which subsidises PATCO from its toll bridge and river port operations.
Developments: Current efforts are being directed towards rehabilitation and improvement of the existing line and rolling stock. Overhaul of the 1968-built Budd cars continues, and several platform and embankment reconstruction projects under way.

Light rail (planned)
Current situation: NJ Transit (see Newark entry) is planning two light rail routes in Camden, Gloucester and Burlington counties to connect with PATCO trains at Camden. The northern route would run 55 km from Camden to Trenton, while a southern line to Woodbury and Glassboro is also proposed.

UPDATED

PHNOM PENH
Population: 600,000
Public transport: Bus services throughout the city provided by government-owned undertakings

Bus
Current situation: A number of operators, believed to be government-owned, provide services in different areas of the city, using fleets of second-hand vehicles from various countries. Amongst them are Soviet LAZ midibuses, Karosa B731 and C734, ex-Nagoya and Osaka Hinos, and ex-Paris Saviems.

Ex-Osaka Hino bus in Phnom Penh

PHOENIX
Population: 1 million
Public transport: Bus services for city and suburban area with total population of 2 million managed by the City of Phoenix Public Transit Department and operated by several contractors. Other smaller local operations are integrated into a common fares and scheduling system; some are funded by the Regional Public Transportation Authority, others by local city authorities

RPTA
Regional Public Transportation Authority
302 North First Avenue, Suite 700, Phoenix, AZ 85003, USA
Telephone: +1 602 262 7242 Fax: +1 602 495 2002
Chair: Jay Tibshraeny
Executive Director: G Kenneth Driggs
Staff: 26

Current situation: Formed in 1986 after voters approved a 0.5 per cent increase in sales tax to 6.5 per cent to finance implementation of a $5,800 million roads and public transport plan for the metropolitan area over the next 20 years. It provides regional planning and some current operations assistance funding. The regional transit authority was allocated $167 million over the period for improvements to regional bus and community transport services.

RPTA developed a 30-year region-wide transit plan known as ValTrans (Valley Transit), proposed for funding by a ½ cent sales tax. This scheme, which included rapid transit proposals, was rejected in 1989 by voters of Maricopa County (where Phoenix is located).
Developments: Starting in 1994, RPTA was to receive funds from Maricopa County's share of state lottery proceeds to fund capacity expansion. But revenues from the lottery were less than anticipated and no transit funding was forthcoming in 1994 or 1995.

In 1994 a further attempt was made to pass a ½ cent sales tax increase to fund a new regional transit improvement plan, but the proposition was defeated.

Light rail is under consideration once again, along with a busway, to serve the East Valley corridor development area. A firm proposal is expected in late 1997.

CNG-powered New Flyer low-floor, new to Valley Metro in 1996 ***1997***

Valley Metro
Phoenix Public Transit Department
302 North First Avenue, Suite 700, Phoenix, AZ 85003
Telephone: +1 602 262 7242 Fax: +1 602 495 2002
Public Transit Director: Neal Manske (Acting)
Staff: 79

Operated under contract by:
Phoenix Transit System
PO Box 4275, Phoenix, AZ 85030
Telephone: +1 602 534 1284
General Manager: T J Ross
Staff: 797

Arnett Transportation Services Inc
129 E Pima, Phoenix, AZ 85004
Telephone: +1 602 253 4191
President: William W Arnett
Staff: 125

Mayflower Contract Services
7710 N 68th Avenue, Glendale, AZ 85303
Telephone: +1 602 842 9606
General Manager: Heidi Killough
Staff: 68

Current situation: The City of Phoenix manages transit services throughout the region for a population of over 2 million, and on behalf of the city (population 1 million), under the marketing name Valley Metro. Some routes are funded by RPTA and the cities of Glendale, Scottsdale and Tempe. Phoenix operations are contracted to three private operators. Phoenix Transit System, a division of ATC/Vancom, operates 25 local and 19 express routes; Mayflower operates 30 city-owned vehicles on eight local routes; and Arnett operates eight city-owned vehicles on the DASH downtown shuttle route, as well as 70 dial-a-ride vehicles.

All Phoenix buses have cycle racks ***1996***

In addition, one express and nine local routes are administered by RPTA and funded by RPTA and the cities of Chandler, Scottsdale, Mesa and Tempe; these are operated by ATE Management & Services. In addition, DAVE Transportation runs seven circulator routes funded by Mesa, and Forsythe & Associates runs three routes funded by Scottsdale. Dial-a-ride services are provided in Chandler, El Mirage, Gilbert, Glendale, Mesa, Peoria, Phoenix, Scottsdale, Surprise, Tempe and the Sun Cities, mostly by private contractors.

Developments: A new city-centre bus station was expected to open in May 1997, replacing existing facilities as part of a land-exchange agreement with a developer. The location will be served by 12 routes, dial-a-ride services and the DASH circulator.

Bus

Passenger boardings: (1993/94) 31.5 million
(1994/95) 34.9 million
(1995/96) 35 million
Vehicle-km: (1993/94) 20.9 million
(1994/95) 21.6 million
(1995/96) 26.9 million

Number of routes: 74
Route length: (One way) 1,437 km
Fleet: 468 buses (regional fleet)

AM General (1975)	46
GMC RTS (1979/81/82)	83
Flxible (1983)	67
MAN (1984/85)	36
Orion I (1987)	10
TMC (1988/89/90)	75
Gillig (1990)	7
Orion II (1990/92)	8
Neoplan (1993)	1
New Flyer (1994)	71
National (1994/95)	29
Bluebird (1996)	6
New Flyer low-floor LNG-powered (1996)	29

In peak service: 390
On order: 113 low-floor LNG-powered buses from North American Bus Industries for delivery starting early 1998

Most intensive service: 5 min
One-person operation: All routes
Fare collection: Duncan recording fareboxes, rebuilt to include magnetic card capability; credit card payment for full fare
Fare structure: Flat, premium for express and dial-a-ride services; tokens and tickets; magnetic-strip tickets and credit card for direct billing of transit service; free transfers
Fares collected on board: 33%
Integration with other modes: All bus and dial-a-ride services have common fare structure; free transfers amongst all operators; park-and-ride; all buses have cycle racks
Operational control: Route inspectors/mobile radio
Arrangements for elderly/disabled: 216 buses lift-equipped on 41 dedicated routes; city-wide dial-a-ride on weekdays; demand-response services carried 567,000 passengers in 1994
Bus priority: HOV lanes on Interstate 10 through city and Red Mountain Freeway; priority bus and carpool entrance ramps at 5 freeway locations; reserved lanes on 2 downtown approach streets
Average distance between stops: 400 m
Average peak-hour speed: Local 22 km/h
Operating costs financed by: Fares 29%, subsidy/grants 62%, tax levy 9%
Subsidy from: FTA, city of Phoenix general revenues, state lottery and funds from RPTA and other cities purchasing service
New vehicles financed by: FTA grants 80%, RPTA and Phoenix general fund revenues 20%

UPDATED

PITTSBURGH

Population: City 370,000, metropolitan area 1.4 million
Public transport: Bus, reserved busway, tramway/light rail and funicular services provided by transport authority serving county area controlled by representative board

Port Authority Transit (PAT)

Port Authority of Allegheny County
Beaver & Island Avenues, Pittsburgh, PA 15233, USA
Telephone: +1 412 237 7000 Fax: +1 412 237 7101
Executive Director: Paul Skoutelas
Director, Transit Operations: Thomas Letky
Staff: 2,951

Passenger boardings: (All modes)
(1992) 79.1 million
(1993) 76.2 million
(1994) 75.4 million

Operating costs financed by: Fares 38.2%, other commercial sources 7.3% subsidy/grants 44%, tax levy 10.5%

Current situation: Pittsburgh's high level of transit usage, its extensive system of exclusive rights-of-way and the survival of its tramway are all due to its extreme topography, located in hilly terrain where the Allegheny and Monongahela rivers join to form the Ohio.

Partial upgrading of the tramway has been carried out, with new alignments and conversion to light rail standards of the 17 km route to South Hills. There are two busways, two contraflow bus lanes, and a high-occupancy vehicle lane.

Developments: Construction started in 1994 on the Airport Busway—Wabash HOV lane, and a 4 km extension of the Martin Luther King Jr East Busway is proposed.

A Pennsylvania Public Transportation Assistance Fund created in 1991 has generated up to $38.2 million a year in dedicated funding for PAT; for details see Philadelphia entry. Despite this, reduced state funding and lower revenues as a result of declining ridership led to an 8 per cent cutback in services in 1993.

Purchase of 170 buses, previously approved by the PAT Board, is to be financed by a bond issue agreed in early 1996.

New American Ikarus (NABI) articulated on the East Busway ***1997***

Bus

Staff: 2,076 (operational)

Passenger boardings: (1992) 67.3 million
(1993) 67.3 million
(1994) 64.7 million
Vehicle-km: (1992) 52.1 million
(1993) 49.9 million
(1994)

Number of routes: 195
Route length: 3,996 km
On priority right-of-way: 18.7 km
Fleet: 1,063 vehicles

Neoplan (1983/86)	294
MCI MC9 (1980/83)	32
MAN SG310 articulated (1983)	29
Ikarus (1991)	25
Flxible (1994)	250
Orion/Bus Industries (1991/92)	263
Novabus Classic (1996)	170

In peak service: 784

Most intensive service: 3 min
One-person operation: All routes
Fare collection: Exact fare to electronic fareboxes; fare collected on entry for in-bound trips, on leaving for out-bound; passes
Fare structure: Zonal (central area plus 5 zones); 10-trip tickets; annual, weekly and monthly passes from 181 outlets
Average speed: 21.6 km/h
Bus priority: 7 km two-lane purpose-built exclusive busway (South Busway) and 11 km Martin Luther King Jr East Busway; both on own right-of-way, with sheltered passenger stations (see below); exclusive right-of-way on two contraflow bus lanes in downtown Pittsburgh and Oakland; also 8 km of HOV lanes on I-279 expressway, used by 7 routes at peak hours
Integration with other modes: Tramway shares portion of South Busway track and connects with Martin Luther King Jr East Busway; park-and-ride extensively developed

Arrangements for elderly/disabled: ACCESS door-to-door service with lift-equipped vehicles provided by 10 contractors carried 2 million passengers in 1994. Senior citizens free on all regular services off-peak, funded by Pennsylvania lottery proceeds
New vehicles financed by: Dedicated funding sources

Busway

Current situation: The South Busway, opened in 1977, carries some 19 bus routes with 470 movements and more than 13,000 riders on an average weekday. Certain portions share a pre-existing tramway alignment and the route is available for emergency police, ambulance or fire service use. The second exclusive busway, Martin Luther King Jr East Busway, from Wilkinsburg to the city centre at Penn Park station, opened in 1983, is 11 km and has six stations for walk-on riders. With buses originating from 12 suburban communities it is served by 27 Express and Flyer routes as well as an end-to-end shuttle. More than 27,000 riders per day are carried. Some 35 park-and-ride facilities with 3,461 spaces are provided on bus and tram routes, including those serving the busway.
Developments: Extension of the East Busway to Swissvale is planned for 1998 completion, with the Airport Busway and Wabash HOV lane also scheduled to open in 1998. The 13 km busway will have eight stations; estimated ridership is 53,000 daily.

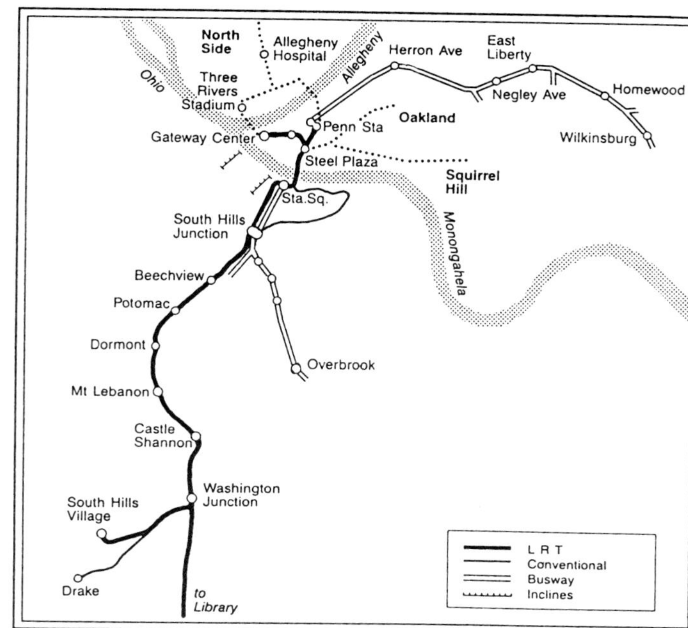

Pittsburgh's light rail and busways

Tramway/Light rail

Staff: 390

Type of operation: Conventional tramway partially reconstructed to light rail standards

Passenger boardings: (1992) 8.8 million
(1993) 8.8 million
(1994) 8.1 million
Car-km: (1992) 3.4 million
(1993) 3.5 million
(1994)

Route length: 17.2 km
in tunnel: 3.9 km
Number of lines: 3
Gauge: 1,588 mm
Track: 57.5 kg/m RE standard rail; ballasted track at grade, ballasted track bridges, open deck bridges, direct fixation subway, direct fixation bridges
Electrification: 650 V DC, overhead

Service: Peak 3 min, off-peak minimum 15 min
Integration with other modes: Connections with local bus routes at 9 stations
Fare collection: Fareboxes on vehicles, peak-hour platform collection at 7 stations

Cars pass on a short section of street running in Beechview ***1997***

Rolling stock: 68 cars

PCC 4000 series (1981/90 to 1949 style)	M13
Siemens-Duewag SD400 LRV (1984/85)	M55

In peak service: 41 cars

Developments: In 1993 the Overbrook line was closed until the long-discussed rebuilding under Stage II of the LRT upgrading had been carried out. Funding for this has now been approved and the scheme was in final design in early 1997; work should start in 1998.

Study continues of the Spine Line project, which would extend the city-centre underground section to Northside and Oakland, the city's university and medical centre district and the third largest generator of transit trips in the state. Together these would form a 9.3 km east-west route.

A further 27 cars are likely to be ordered to provide increased service frequency when a major road reconstruction project gets under way in 1998.

Funicular

Current situation: The 200 m 71 per cent incline Monongahela Incline funicular was reopened in 1983 after rehabilitation which coincided with its integration into the PAT system and the Station Square commercial redevelopment project adjacent to the lower station. Built in 1870 it is the oldest inclined plane in the USA. It carries about 1 million passengers a year.

The neighbouring Duquesne Incline carries around 500,000 passengers a year. It is owned by PAT but operated by a non-profit-making historic society.

UPDATED

PORT ELIZABETH

Population: 1.5 million
Public transport: Bus services across most of metropolitan area provided by subsidiary of industry-owned trust company. Suburban rail services. Shared taxi 'Kombi' minibuses. Transport policy gradually being formalised under a Metropolitan Transport Advisory Board. Light rail plans abandoned, suburban rail extensions proposed

Algoa Bus

Algoa Bus Company (Pty) Ltd
PO Box 225, Port Elizabeth 6000, South Africa
Telephone: +27 41 414241 Fax: +27 41 437437
Managing Director: Gerald Botha
Staff: 619

Current situation: Algoa Bus was formed in 1991 to take over the assets of the former operating company PE Tramways, and was later incorporated as a non-profit utility company.

Bus

Passenger boardings: (1992/93) 15.2 million
(1993/94) 13.2 million
(1994/95) 13.8 million
Vehicle-km: (1992/93) 12.3 million
(1993/94) 12 million
(1994/95) 12.6 million

Number of routes: 60
Route length: 900 km
Fleet: 273 vehicles

Leyland Victory MkII	154
Guy Big J MkI	40
ERF single-deck	56
Mercedes/Busaf Speedliner midibus	10
Others	13

In peak service: 248

Most intensive service: 1 min
Fare collection: Setright ticket machines; mobile ticket offices at major loading points; shops acting as agents for prepurchase multijourney coupons, exchanged for tickets on board
Fare structure: Flat and zonal, discount coupons
Fare evasion control: On-bus inspection
Bus priority: On certain main arterials, extreme left lane demarcated 'no stopping, except buses' in direction of peak flow for duration of peak period. New bus lanes in long-range planning stage by Metropolitan Transport Advisory Board
Average distance between stops: 400 m

Average peak-hour speed: In mixed traffic, 20 km/h
Operating costs financed by: Fares 57%, other commercial sources 5%, subsidy/grants 47%
Subsidy from: National government 91%, regional 9%

Metro Rail

South African Rail Commuter Corporation Ltd
Port Elizabeth Metropolitan Area
Private Bag X2, Sunninghill, Johannesburg 2157
Telephone: +27 11 804 2900 Fax: +27 11 804 3852

Type of operation: Suburban heavy rail

Passenger journeys: (1990/91) 3.4 million
(1991/92) 3.1 million
(1992/93) 2.4 million

Current situation: Operates 10 return weekday journeys between Port Elizabeth and Uitenhage (33 km), serving 11 stations, with a fleet of 51 diesel-hauled cars. Fares cover 19 per cent of operating costs.

Extension to Motherwell proposed using existing trackage plus a new short branch.

Leyland bus on city-centre circle Route O

Minibus/shared taxi

Current situation: There are extensive operations by private minibuses known locally as 'Kombi-taxis', licensed as taxis but operating as shared taxis. They have been responsible for substantial poaching of passengers from conventional bus routes and the suburban railway.

PORTLAND

Population: City 471,000, metropolitan area 1.5 million
Public transport: Bus and light rail services provided by Tri-Met, a public agency responsible to the state and governed by a local volunteer representative board of directors appointed by the state governor. Service area is 1,533 km² covering three Oregon counties and Clark County, Washington, the latter mainly served by a separate transit authority that integrates fares and co-ordinates services with Tri-Met

Tri-Met

Tri-County Metropolitan Transportation District of Oregon
4012 SE 17th Avenue, Portland, OR 97202-3993, USA
Telephone: +1 503 238 4910 Fax: +1 503 239 6469
Board President: Philip Bogue
General Manager: Tom Walsh
Director, Bus Transportation: Clyde Earl
Director, Bus Maintenance: Tony Bryant
Director, Rail Operations: Dan Caufield
Manager, Rail Equipment Maintenance: Richard Rogers
Staff: 2,226

Current situation: Tri-Met was established in 1969 to serve the Portland metropolitan area, replacing private operations. Since 1979 the bus route network has been restructured in accordance with the dual concept of suburban timed-transfer and urban grid; there are now eight timed-transfer centres (for description see *JUTS 1990*). The grid plan was implemented in the city area in 1982, and both it and the suburban timed-transfer trunk-feeder system have led to significant increases in ridership and productivity.

Service hours were increased by 3.7 per cent in 1992, by 3.3 per cent in 1993, 1.5 per cent in 1994, and 1.3 per cent in 1995, notable achievements in a period when many US undertakings have found it necessary to reduce service. The increased service has been rewarded with growing patronage.

Developments: A bond issue to finance construction of a third light rail line was approved in 1994, but rejected by voters in Clark County in 1995. This is the 40 km south-north route linking Clackamas County with downtown Portland and Vancouver, Washington. A shorter first phase for the 18 km Clark County portion was adopted in late 1995, but funding for this was also rejected by voters in November 1996.

Passenger journeys: (Both modes)
(1993/94) 45.4 million
(1994/95) 47.2 million
(1995/96) 49.3 million

Operating costs financed by: Fares 21.1%, subsidy/grants 78.9% (of which local employee payroll and other taxes 90.5%, federal sources 2.7%, state sources (cigarette tax) 1.7%, miscellaneous 5.1%)
New vehicles financed by: FTA grants 80%, with local match from state funds

LRVs at Oregon Convention Center station

Bus

Vehicle-km: (1993/94) 38.5 million
(1994/95) 38.8 million
(1995/96) 39.5 million

Number of routes: 90
Route length: 1,254 km (one way)
Fleet: 642 vehicles

Flxible 35 ft (1972)	47
Crown-Ikarus articulated (1981/82)	86
GMC RTS-II (1982)	75
Flxible Metro 40 ft (1988/89)	138
Gillig Phantom 30 ft (1990/91)	43
Gillig Phantom 40 ft (1990)	63
Gillig 40 ft LNG-powered (1992)	2
Flxible Metro 40 ft (1992)	108
Flxible Metro 30 ft (1992)	10
Flxible Metro 40 ft LNG-powered (1993)	8
Flxible Metro 40 ft (1994)	37
Champion Cutaway minibus (1991/95)	25

In peak service: 517
Average age of fleet: 7.4 years

On order: 65 Gillig Phantom 40 ft and 22 Flyer 40 ft low-floor for 1997/98 delivery

Most intensive service: Peak 5-20 min, off-peak 15-60 min
Fare collection: Cash or discount ticket to farebox, day and monthly passes
Fare structure: Zonal (3 radial zones); 1 h free transfer; free travel in 10 × 20 block city centre 'Fareless Square' area; discount fares for youth, elderly and disabled; 10-ride discount multitickets
Fare evasion control: Driver monitoring and random inspection
Arrangements for elderly/disabled: Door-to-door LIFT van service (146 vans) caters for some 600,000 trips annually; fixed routes 95% accessible; elderly and disabled travel at discounted fare at all times
Bus priority: 18-block city-centre transit mall; two adjacent one-way bus-priority streets offer improved passenger waiting facilities, information kiosks, and TV monitors with real-time information; intersection queue and signal priority at several locations
Integration with other modes: 59 park-and-ride lots; 14 are purpose-built, the rest are shared-use mainly church parking areas. Connections with light rail at 14 stations outside the city centre, including timed-transfer at 2 suburban transit centres on the rail line; carpooling

encouraged and assistance provided; cycles carried on all bus routes using front-mounted racks

Light rail

Type of operation: Light rail, opened 1986

Passenger boardings: (1993/94) 8.1 million
(1994/95) 8.5 million
(1995/96) 8.9 million
Car-km: (1993/94) 1.4 million
(1994/95) 1.4 million
(1995/96) 1.4 million

Route length: 24.2 km
Number of lines: 1
Number of stations: 30 (8 are unidirectional)
Gauge: 1,435 mm
Track: Continuously welded rail on timber sleepers in ballast
Max gradient: 7%
Electrification: 750 V DC, overhead

Service: Peak 5-10 min, off-peak 15 min, 12 min summer Saturdays
First/last car: 04.29/00.33
Fare structure: Zonal, as bus
Fare collection: Honour system with random inspectors. Change-giving ticket vending machines and prepaid ticket cancellers at all stations; monthly passes, free transfer to and from bus
Integration with other modes: Bus connections at 13 stations, including timed transfers at 2 transit centres; 5 park-and-ride lots providing 2,125 spaces, and kiss-and-ride; cycle racks at 7 stations and storage bins at 1 transit centre; up to 6 cycles allowed on two-car train outside peak hours in peak direction
Arrangements for elderly/disabled: 100% accessible with wheelchair lifts at all stations, ordinary lifts at stations where platforms are below street level
Signalling: Automatic block on short single-track sections and 7.2 km Banfield freeway portion; traffic light priority on most other sections; driver-controlled signals in downtown

Rolling stock: 30 cars

Bombardier/BBC/BN (1983/86)	M26
Gomaco Brill replica cars (1991)	M4

In peak service: 22
On order: 46 cars from Siemens-Duewag (see below)

Developments: Construction is in progress of the 28.4 km Westside line, including the 9.8 km Hillsboro extension approved later. The route includes a 4.5 km tunnel and underground station serving Washington Park zoo. Delays in tunnelling mean that the initial phase will not now open throughout until late 1998, a year later than planned, though the Hillsboro extension will open at the same time.

Due in service in 1997 are 46 cars from Siemens-Duewag, of which 29 are required to work the Westside route and the balance to raise capacity. These are low-floor LRVs for pairing with existing cars so that all trains will have a low-floor section, allowing elimination of wheelchair lifts at stations.

Vintage Trolley

Current situation: A fares-free vintage tram service funded by local businesses and other non-Tri-Met sources, inaugurated 1991, shares city-centre tracks, complementing regular services at off-peak times (daily from May to New Year's Day), weekends (March and April) and holidays. Operated under contract by Tri-Met, the service is managed by a non-profit-making body, Vintage Trolley Inc.

In 1994, service was expanded to daily in the summer and autumn months and made fares-free, since when monthly ridership has risen by some ten-fold, making the 'Vintage Trolley' a significant player in transit provision between the city centre and Lloyd District.

Flxible Metro of Tri-Met southbound on the 1994 extension of Portland's city-centre Transit Mall ***1996***

C-Tran

Clark County Public Transportation Benefit Area Authority
PO Box 2529, 2425 NE 65th Avenue, Vancouver, WA 98668-2529
Telephone: +1 360 696 4494 Fax: +1 360 696 1602
Executive Director: Les White
Director of Operations: Thomas G Hartley

Current situation: C-Tran operations began in 1981 after voter endorsement of a plan to develop services for the fast-growing Clark County area with a total population that had grown to 300,000 by 1996, and including the city of Vancouver. Based on a private operation run by Vancouver city since 1969, C-Tran is now a Public Transportation Benefit Area Authority under a representative board. C-Tran and Tri-Met co-operate to provide a regional network for the Portland/Vancouver metropolitan area, including express commuter routes between the towns. Four per cent of km is operated under contract to Tri-Met. Vanpool service inaugurated 1988, carpools in 1995.

Bus

Passenger journeys: (1993) 3.5 million
(1994) 3.8 million
(1995) 4.3 million
Vehicle-km: (1993) 5.9 million
(1994) 5.5 million
(1995) 7 million

Number of routes: 29
Route length: 980 km
Fleet: 139 vehicles

GM RTS-II (1982)	34
Gillig Phantom (1991/95)	60
Diamond minibus (1991)	3
GMC 'New Look' (1981)	10
Champion minibus (1986)	2
Collins Diplomat 25 ft	7
Escort 20 ft	7
El Dorado 25 ft	10
Dodge vans	6

In peak service: 116

Arrangements for elderly/disabled: C-VAN paratransit service with 13 lift-equipped vehicles carried 78,600 passengers in 1992. Contract staff are employed. It covers only 4% of costs from fares
Operating costs financed by: Fares 16.8%, other commercial sources 5.9%, subsidy/grants 77.3%
Subsidy from: A ½% sales tax is dedicated to transit and matched from annual Motor Vehicle Excise tax collected by Washington state and FTA grants

Developments: Under the Washington state Commute Trip Reduction Law of 1992, major employers are required to implement reductions in the number of 1992 car commuting journeys by their employees – 15 per cent by 1995, 25 per cent by 1997 and 35 per cent by 1999. Some expansion of public transport has been implemented to cope with the extra trips generated.

C-Tran is lead agency of eight counties undertaking a preliminary alternatives analysis phase of a high-capacity transit study. Amongst the new services under consideration are express buses, HOV lanes, exclusive busways and light rail.

Bicycles carried on buses starting in 1995, and lockers installed at a number of locations.

UPDATED

PORTO

Population: 380,000, metropolitan area 800,000
Public transport: Bus, trolleybus and tram services operated in Porto and surrounding municipalities of Gaia, Matosinhos, Maia, Valongo and Gondomar by municipal authority controlled by board responsible to central government, and contracting some bus services from private operators. Suburban and commuter bus services provided by 63 private operators and rail services by Portuguese Railways (CP); light rail planned

STCP

Sociedade de Transportes Colectivos do Porto (STCP)
Avenida da Boavista 806, Apartado 1090, 4100 Porto, Portugal
Telephone: +351 2 606 4054 Fax: +351 2 609 1909
President: Eng Carlos Eugénio Pereira de Brito
Traffic Manager:
Eng Albano Augusto Natividade Carneiro
Staff: 2,935

Passenger journeys: (All modes)
(1993) 265 million
(1994) 249 million
(1995) 250 million

Developments: The once extensive tram network has been reduced to one route, 18, which connects Boavista and Carmo. Although also under threat of closure, this route now appears to be secure until STCP is able to launch a tourist tram service using vehicles from the museum fleet on track paralleling the coast. Trolleybuses linger on, also running on borrowed time following a period of closure during 1995/96.

Nevertheless, a 68 km light rail network is being developed by a separate organisation (see below).

Operating costs financed by: Fares 66%, other commercial sources 3%, government grants 8%, remainder as deficit

Bus and trolleybus

Vehicle-km: (1993) 32.8 million
(1994) 30.5 million
(1995) 33.9 million

Number of routes: Bus 65, trolleybus 1
Route length: Bus 416 km

Fleet: 579 buses

Volvo B58	266
Volvo B10R	83
Volvo B10M	20
Volvo B10M articulated	65
Mercedes O405	135
Renault PS150 minibus	10

Average age of fleet: 11.5 years
Fleet: 25 trolleybuses

Caetano-EFACEC two-axle (1983/84)	15
Caetano-EFACEC articulated (1984/85)	10

Most intensive service: 5 min
One-person operation: All routes
Fare collection: To driver or conductor or prepurchase
Fare structure: Zonal; carnets, monthly passes for various groups of services
Fares collected on board: 7%
Fare evasion control: Roving/route inspectors
Integration between modes: Common ticket system with passes also covering private operators and CP
Operational control: Route inspectors with control centre operating private telephone network
Arrangements for elderly/disabled: Reduced rate passes for city or total network now valid at all times
Average peak-hour speed: Bus 16.2 km/h
Bus priority: Some bus access to pedestrianised areas; traffic signal control allows bus priority over Luis I bridge from Vila Nova de Gaia
New vehicles financed by: Government/bank loans

Tramway

Current situation: Only Route 18 remains in operation, extending to 13.9 km and operated by 6 cars.

Bus (contracted operations)

Current situation: Several city routes are operated under contract to STCP by a number of private companies, including Auto Viação Espinho, Valpi, J Espirito Santo & Irmaos and others.

CP

Caminhos de Ferro Portugueses (CP)
Calcada do Duque 20-1, 1294 Lisboa

Type of operation: Suburban heavy rail

Current situation: Commuter services operate into three city-centre terminals. From Sao Bento trains run to Sao Romao (19 km) and Braga (57 km); from Trinidade a frequent diesel service operates to Vilar do Pinheiro (17 km) and Póvoa (30 km), carrying about 6.5 million passengers a year, while hourly trains run to Guimaraes (62 km); lastly, from Sao Bento and Campanha stations there is a combined suburban/regional service to Aveiro (67 km).

Mercedes O405 of STCP at Carma **1996**

Porto Railway Development Board

Gabinete de Nó Ferroviário do Porto
President: José Espinho
Director of Planning & Studies: Duarte Pereira

Current situation: This quango was set up by the Ministry of Transport to undertake all rail infrastructure improvements in the Porto metropolitan area. It is to be merged with the new national rail infrastructure authority being set up in 1997.
Developments: The Porto—Braga line is being double-tracked and electrified to raise line speed to 170 km/h, and so reduce journey times to stimulate a 68 per cent growth in patronage by 1999. Between Trofa and Guimaraes the existing metre-gauge track is being replaced by 1,668 mm gauge; after conversion, trains will be diverted from Trinadade to Sao Bento station in Porto. Campanha station is being replaced, and that at Sao Bento extensively remodelled for its future role as terminus for all services on the Northern and Minho lines.

Private bus

Current situation: Services on 190 suburban and commuter routes are provided by 39 operators, 37 privately owned and two owned by the government. Plans have been considered (see above) for integration of private routes into the STCP network.

Passes are available providing travel on privately operated, CP, and STCP services.

Light rail (planned)

Metro do Porto SA
Av dos Aliados 133, 3°, 4000 Porto
Telephone: +351 2 208 8028/8813
Fax: +351 2 208 8814

Current situation: This limited company was set up in 1993 to implement proposals to build a light rail network. Its share capital is held by Porto Metropolitan Region (80 per cent), Lisboa metro (5 per cent), and CP (15 per cent). A 68.1 km two-line system is planned, based on 49.4 km of route transferred from CP supplemented by 18.7 km new build, of which 7.4 km will be underground and 11.3 km at surface.

North-south Line 1 will run 8 km from Santo Ovídio in Vila Nova de Gaia to Sao Joao hospital, crossing the Duoro river on the upper deck of the existing Luis I road bridge and serving the city centre by means of a 3.2 km tunnel section. East-west Line II will start at CP's Campanha station and run in a 3.7 km tunnel via Sao Bento to Trinidade, where it will take over CP's metre-gauge alignment to the north. At Senhora da Hora the line will branch to serve Póvoa (24.3 km), Matosinhos (4.8 km) and Maia (4.7 km), and perhaps Trofa (22 km). There will be a 0.8 km tunnel beneath the town centre at Maia.

Estimated cost of construction is Esc134 million, all of which has been guaranteed by central government. Seven consortia prequalified to build the network, of which two, led by Adtranz and Siemens, were invited to present detailed proposals in October 1996. No private finance is involved in the project, though the private-sector operating concessionaire will receive a subsidy.

Porto's last tram route limps towards museum status **1996**

UPDATED

PORTO ALEGRE

Population: 1.3 million, metropolitan area 2.7 million
Public transport: Bus and minibus services provided by 26 private operators holding concessions, and fixed-route shared taxi system, supervised by municipal administration which has established busway system. Electrified suburban rail system being developed from existing lines

Volvo articulated bus loading in the city centre; fare turnstiles at each loading point

Secretaria Municipal dos Transportes

Secretaria Municipal dos Transportes (SMT)
Prefeitura Municipal de Porto Alegre
Av Ipiranga 1138, 9000 Porto Alegre, RS, Brazil
Telephone: +55 512 237000
Secretary of Transport: Jarbas Luiz Macedo Haag
Director of Operations: Luiz Mário Magalhães Sá

Current situation: SMT was established in 1976. It has overall responsibility for co-ordination of public transport provided by private operators, highway provision and management, pedestrianisation, road safety and area traffic control. Pursuit of an integrated policy led to establishment of a five-route central area bus system run by a designated private firm and seven corridors segregating buses on radial services from all other traffic in busways.

SMT is also involved in improvement of the bus fleet, and has replaced small 'combi' minibuses by 17-seaters increasing capacity of the shared taxi operation from 45,000 to 90,000 passengers per day. Further integration planned including establishment of a comprehensive service information system.

Bus/Minibus/Shared taxi

Passenger journeys: (Annual) Bus 325 million (5 central area routes, approx 20 million); shared taxi 60 million

Number of routes: Central area 5; general area bus 116, shared taxi 28
On priority right-of-way: 30 km
Fleet: 1,559 buses, mostly Mercedes with some Volvo articulated and including about 150 midibuses
Fleet: 348 shared taxis (17-seaters)
New vehicles required each year: 50 buses

Most intensive service: 3 min
One-person operation: Some
Fare collection: Turnstile at centre of bus, payment to conductor
Fare structure: Flat
Operational control: Traffic police regulate operations, give advice and information and deal with emergencies. Each has a central control point in radio contact. SMT staff supervise grouping the buses, using the reserved lanes, into convoys under the Comonor system to increase lane capacity
Average distance between stops: 150 m
Average peak-hour speed: In mixed traffic, 17 km/h; in bus lanes, 19 km/h

Bus priority: System of seven corridors of bus lanes along central carriageways of roads into city centre reserved exclusively for buses (see below)
Operating costs financed by: Fares 100%

Busway

Current situation: Bus-only lanes in the centre of major roads on seven radial corridors are used by both urban services and those originating outside the city, and some bus flows are in excess of 350 per hour. The Comonor convoy system is used to maximise the capacity of the lanes which are up to 4.9 km long. Buses to/from various destinations are held at lane entry points to travel as a unit halting in unison at each stop, enabling volumes of up to 20,000 passengers/h to be carried at speeds of more than 20 km/h including stops. Buses serve protected 'stations', though passengers generally must cross the outer (general) traffic lanes to reach them. SMT staff assist in this by undertaking traffic control.

Some vehicles are operated with trailers to increase capacity, though articulated buses have been introduced by SMT on one corridor, with an alternative operating system based on a single trunk route using the dedicated bus lane run by express buses serving interchanges, with local feeder bus connections as in Curitiba (qv).

Trensurb

Empresa de Trens Urbanos de Porto Alegre SA
Rua Ernesto Neugebauer 1985, Bairro Dona Teodora, 90250-140 Porto Alegre, RS
Telephone: +55 51 337 3533 Fax: +55 51 337 4204
President: Adeo Dornelles Faraco
Director of Operations: Renato Guimarães
Director of Administration: Daniel Lenna Souto
Superintendent of Development & Expansion: Nelson Lidio Nuñes
Staff: 1,101

Type of operation: Regional metro, opened 1985

Metro
Under construction
Proposed
Aeromovel
Novo Hamburgo
Fenac
Liberdade
Rio dos Sinos
São Leopoldo
Unisinos
Horto
Sapucaia
Luiz Pasteur
Esteio
Petrobas
São Luis
Mathias Velho
Canaos
Fatima
Niterói
Anchieta
Aeroporto
Farrapos
São Pedro
Rodoviáro
Mercado
Rio Guaiba

Porto Alegre metro

Porto Alegre metro train at Sapucaia

Passenger journeys: (1991) 38.6 million
(1993) 33.1 million
(1995) 29.7 million

Route length: 26.7 km
Number of routes: 1
Number of stations: 15
Gauge: 1,600 mm
Track: Conventional ballasted, twin-block concrete sleepers with 57 kg/m welded rail
Electrification: 3 kV DC, overhead

Service: Peak 5 min
First/last train: 05.15/23.20
Fare structure: Flat
Integration with other modes: Transfer to some bus routes at higher charge; 60 bus routes feed Trensurb stations
Operating costs financed by: Fares 25%, other commercial sources 6%, subsidy/grants 69%

Rolling stock: 25 four-car trains
Nippon Sharyo/Hitachi/Kawasaki (1984) M100
In peak service: 14 trains

Current situation: Trensurb was established in 1980 to develop a high-capacity regional metro from the existing RFFSA suburban line north from the city centre to Novo Hamburgo, an important development corridor. The service currently links Mercado and Sapucaia.
Developments: A 6.3 km extension from Sapucaia to São Leopoldo is nearing completion, with the first 3.4 km to Unisinos scheduled to open during 1997. Once open, the two new stations are expected to generate more than 40,000 passengers daily. Adtranz is supplying overhead, power supply and communications equipment for the extension, and will also upgrade the existing CTC system.

Though not part of the state commuter railway operation CBTU, Trensurb is managed directly by the federal government; transfer to local state control has been discussed. This would involve the federal government assuming responsibility for the line's accumulated debt, and for completing construction through to Novo Hamburgo, adding a further 9 km to the route. Bids for studies of this final section were due to be called in early 1997.

A feasibility study was expected to report in February 1997 on a proposal for a 9 km surface-running northeast line in the corridor currently served by buses of Assis Brasil which handle one-way peak-hour flows of 25,000 passengers.

Marcopolo-built bus and trailer combination on Porto Alegre trunk route passing Trensurb airport station

Aeromovel
Coester SA

Type of operation: Demonstration people mover, powered by compressed air

Current situation: Porto Alegre firm Coester developed the Aeromovel system in the 1970s, and a 600 m demonstration track was built in 1979-81 with financial assistance from EBTU; later extended to 1.1 km. The elevated route lies in the median of the Avenida Loureiro da Silva.

UPDATED

PORT OF SPAIN
Population: 400,000
Public transport: Bus services in Port of Spain and other areas of Trinidad operated by state corporation which also operates busway; extensive private shared taxi operations

PTSC
Public Transport Service Corporation (PTSC)
Railway Building, South Quay, PO Box 391, Port of Spain, Trinidad
Telephone: +1 809 623 2341 Email: ptsc@wow.nwt
General Manager: Dr Trevor Townsend
Staff: 250

Current situation: Though PTSC services operate throughout Trinidad and Tobago, its market share has declined substantially due to strong competition from shared taxis.
Developments: Long-standing government subsidies were phased out in 1994, and PTSC implemented a restructuring which reduced costs by cutting staff and services. As a consequence, the 1994 operating deficit of $55 million after subsidy was transformed in 1995 into a $4 milion deficit without subsidy, and the company expected to break even in 1996. At the same time, PTSC's market share rose from about 10 per cent to 14 per cent in June 1996, while its private hire business grew by 100 per cent.

Two new business units have been established to boost income. The Engineering Services Division will provide contract maintenance to private vehicle operators, and the Property Development unit will maximise revenues from PTSC-owned property.

Bus
Number of routes: 19
On priority right-of-way: 24.8 km
Fleet: 100 vehicles

Most intensive service: Priority busway 10-15 min, other heavily used routes 15-30 min
One-person operation: All routes
Fare collection: Prepurchase tickets
Fare structure: Graduated (telescopic)
Fare evasion control: Inspectors
Operational control: Inspectors
Arrangements for elderly/disabled: Pensioners and persons receiving public assistance carried free
Average peak-hour speed: In bus lanes 40 km/h; in mixed traffic 15-20 km/h
Bus priority: 24.8 km busway links Port of Spain with Arima (see below), also used by maxi-taxis to which a controlled number of passes are issued for a fee
Operating costs financed by: Fares 95%, other commercial sources 5%

Busway
Current situation: The Port of Spain to Arima busway is a two-lane 7.3 m wide single carriageway reserved route using former railway trackbed with four major 'stations' and 27 stops. The route is shared with 700 privately owned minibuses (maxi-taxis) and over 600 private cars with special passes.

Shared taxi
Current situation: Shared taxis carry some four times as many passengers as buses, amounting to over 150 million journeys a year. There are about 20,000 sedan taxis and 4,600 12-25 seater minibuses (maxi-taxis). They operate fixed routes and make pick-ups at central points according to the areas served. They also engage in random pick-up/set-down en route in a bid to maximise earnings, causing traffic delays and congestion. This has prompted the Ministry to relocate 'taxi stands' or designated pick-up areas, and to regulate access to many urban streets.

UPDATED

POZNAN
Population: 590,000
Public transport: Bus and tramway services provided by municipal authority, with some contracted bus operations. Suburban rail services by State Railway (PKP)

MPK
Miejskie Przedsiębiorstwo Komunikacyjne (MPK)
ul Glogowska 131, 60244 Poznan, Poland
Telephone: +48 61 699361 Fax: +48 61 663708
Director: Jerzy Babiak
Staff: 3,193

Passenger journeys: (All modes)
(1991) 212.5 million
(1992) 209 million
(1995) 194.5 million

Operating costs financed by: Fares 50.9%, subsidy/grants 49.1%
Subsidy from: Municipal budget

Developments: MPK is installing a computer-based traffic control system using equipment from Germany's ITF Intertraffic. When fully commissioned, the system will provide operational control with radio data links, passenger information, demand-control of buses and tram movements, timetable database, and financial data.

Bus
Passenger journeys: (1991) 99.9 million
(1992) 111 million
(1995) 83.6 million
Vehicle-km: (1991) 20.9 million
(1995)16 million

Number of routes: 45 (plus 11 night routes)
Route length: (One way) 452 km
Fleet: 306 vehicles

Jelcz M11	47
Jelcz/Berliet PR110	4
Ikarus 260	28
Den Oudsten	25
Jelcz M121M low-floor	1
MAN NL202 low-floor	40
Neoplan N4016 low-floor	13
Ikarus 280 articulated	127
Ikarus IK160P articulated	15
Ikarus 435 articulated	1
Neoplan N4020 Megatrans low-floor	5

In peak service: 220
On order: Deliveries were expected at the end of 1996 of 10 MAN NG272 articulated low-floor, 14 Neoplan N4020, 18 Neoplan N4016, and 22 Neoplan N4009 midibuses

One-person operation: All routes
Fare collection: Prepurchase passes or tickets; validation/cancelling machines on board
Fare structure: Flat; prepurchase single tickets, carnets and monthly passes
Fares collected on board: Nil; 56% of passengers hold prepurchase tickets, 44% passes
Fare evasion control: Inspectors
Operational control: Route inspectors
Arrangements for elderly/disabled: Invalids and over-75s travel free, pensioners pay reduced fare; seats allocated for disabled
Average distance between stops: 603 m
Average peak-hour speed: 19.2 km/h
New vehicles financed by: Supplied free of charge by government department

Tramway
Type of operation: Conventional tramway

Passenger journeys: (1991) 112.6 million
(1992) 98 million
(1995) 110.9 million
Car-km: (1991) 17.8 million
(1995) 14 million

Route length: 152 km
Number of lines: 13
Number of stops: 237
Gauge: 1,435 mm
Max gradient: 5.6%
Minimum curve radius: 25 m
Electrification: 600 V DC, overhead

Service: 15 min, evenings 20 min
First/last car: 04.49/22.49
Fare structure: 10, 30, 60 and 90 min tickets with free transfer
Fare collection: Prepurchase single tickets, carnets or day passes; onboard purchase from machines; roving inspectors
One-person operation: All routes

Rolling stock: 322 cars

Konstal 105N	M243
Konstal 102N articulated (1970/72)	M56
HCP Cegielski 105N/2 low-floor articulated	M1
Linke-Hofmann-Busch 1G (1957, ex-Amsterdam)	M17
ČKD Tatra RT6N low-floor articulated (1996)	M5

In peak service: 239
On order: A further 5 Tatra RT6N for August 1997 delivery

Developments: A section of rapid tramway (PST) running from the city centre to the northern suburbs, including 7 km fully segregated, opened in January 1997. Lines 12, 14 and 15 have been diverted to the new alignment, operated by a dedicated fleet of 10 low-floor and 15 standard cars.

A Line 14 extension to Górczyn is planned as rapid tramway, as is new Line 16 from Miloslowo in the east to Górczyn. Both are to be built by the year 2000.

Extensions approved but work halted due to funding difficulties. Through running to the main tram network is to be introduced, using a new fleet of 10 eight-axle cars on order.

Jelcz bus of MPK in central Poznan

Konstal 105N twin-set on central reservation

PKP
Polish State Railways
ul Chalubinskiego 4, 00-918 Warszawa

Type of operation: Suburban heavy rail

Current situation: Services operate irregularly (about every 2 h, more frequently at commuting times) over nine routes into Poznan's main and inner suburban stations.

UPDATED

PRAHA
Population: 1.2 million
Public transport: Bus, tramway and metro services provided by municipally owned corporation, some bus services contracted from private operators. Suburban services by State Railway and private bus operators

Dopravní podnik hlavního města Prahy
Dopravní podnik hlavního města Prahy a s
Bubenská 1, 17026 Praha 7, Czech Republic
Telephone: +42 2 9619 2000 Fax: +42 2 9619 2003
Director General: Milan Houfek
Director, Metro: Jaromir Stejskal
Director, Tramway: Milan Pokorný
Director, Bus: Jiri Machač
Staff: 12,189

Passenger journeys: (1993) 1,385 million
(1994) 1,364 million
(1995) 1,074 million

Current situation: As the metro network has expanded, the role of the tramway has been reduced. Tramway construction was suspended for a time in the 1980s, but resumed in 1988. In 1994 the metro's share of public transport journeys was 39 per cent, while that of the tramway was 31 per cent. Buses provide a supplementary network to the rail-based modes, mainly serving outer areas. Public transport usage though declining, is still high, accounting for 65 per cent of weekday journeys.

Developments: The undertaking became a public company in 1991, with the city of Praha its sole shareholder. Contracting out of bus services has started.

Current fares policy is driven by the need to improve the farebox ratio to between 30 and 50 per cent, but rapidly rising operating costs have absorbed the quite substantial fares increases implemented since 1991.

Fare structure: Flat rate for single tickets valid for 15 (no transfer) and 90 min (with transfer) within Praha inner and outer zones P and 0; 24 h, 3-, 7- and 15-day, monthly, 3-monthly and yearly passes; concessions for children, students, elderly and military
Fare collection: Prepurchase tickets with mechanical validation on buses and trams, electronic validation on metro; most passengers use passes
Fare evasion control: Inspectors on board and in paid station areas
Arrangements for elderly/disabled: Some special bus services
Operating costs financed by: Fares 28%, other sources 2%, subsidy/grants 70%

Bus
Staff: 3,844

Passenger journeys: (1993) 441 million
(1994) 427 million
(1995) 327 million
Vehicle-km: (1993) 62 million
(1994) 63.5 million
(1995) 63.3 million

Number of routes: 214 (10 night routes)
Route length: 1,989 km
Fleet: 1,323 vehicles

Karosa B731/B732/B734/LC735	982
Karosa B741 articulated	104
Ikarus 280 articulated	234
Neoplan	3

In peak service: 978

Most intensive service: Peak 2.4 min
One-person operation: All routes
Average peak-hour speed: 23.3 km/h

Metro
Staff: 4,194

Type of operation: Full metro, initial route opened 1974

Passenger journeys: (1993) 555 million
(1994) 531 million
(1995) 413 million

Route length: 43.6 km
Number of lines: 3
Number of stations: 43
Gauge: 1,435 mm
Tunnel: Cut-and-cover and bored; over the Nusle valley metro tunnel incorporated beneath highway on Nusle bridge, 43 m above ground
Electrification: 750 V DC, bottom-contact third rail

Service: Peak 1 min 50 s
First/last train: 05.00/24.00

Signalling: Automatic block; ATP
Centralised control: Radio communication with trains individually or en masse

Rolling stock: 532 cars in five-car sets

Mytischy Ecs (1973/77)	M28
Mytischy T 81717 cab cars (1978 on)	M202
Mytischy T 81714 non-driving cars	M302

In peak service: 79 trains

Current situation: Eastern extension of Line B under construction to Černý Most (6.4 km, five stations), part of which will open in 1998.

Still at the planning stage is a northern extension of Line C to Ládví (4 km, 3 stations) to serve satellite housing developments, which could open in 2003, and Line D is proposed.

Developments: A fleet of 110 new-generation cars is on order from a consortium of builders comprising ČKD, Adtranz, Siemens and SGP, with delivery starting in 1998.

In 1994 a contract was awarded to Matra Transport for modernisation of Line C with the PA135 automatic train control system. This work will be completed in 1997.

Tramway
Staff: 3,422

Type of operation: Conventional tramway, with new light rail sections

Passenger journeys: (1993) 390 million
(1994) 405 million
(1995) 333 million
Car-km: (1992) 38.8 million
(1994) 41.5 million
(1995) 44 million

Route length: 471 km
Number of lines: 29 (8 night)
Number of stops: 606
Gauge: 1,435 mm
Electrification: 600 V DC, overhead

Service: Peak 4-12 min
First/last car: 04.30/24.00 (day service); night service runs every 40 min with timed transfers at interchanges
One-person operation: All cars

Rolling stock: 967 cars

Tatra T3 standard (1961/76)	M738
Tatra T3M (thyristor control)	M102
Tatra KT8D5 (1990)	M47
Tatra T6A5 (1995)	M80

In peak service: 647
On order: A new fleet of 150 cars is being supplied by ČKD Tatra, with 80 delivered in 1995, 50 in 1996 and 20 in 1997

Developments: After a period of suspension in favour of metro construction, tramway construction resumed in 1988 and two extensions have opened since. In May 1995 a 5.8 km extension with light rail characteristics opened from Braník to Modřany.

Future plans include an extension to the Barrandov housing estate in the southwestern suburbs, while new routes are planned to feed the metro Line C extension in the north.

Funicular
Current situation: The 510 m funicular which climbs Petřín Hill carries 1.1 million passengers annually.

ČD
Česky Dráhy
Na přikopě 33, 11005 Praha 1

Type of operation: Suburban heavy rail

Current situation: Services provided on eight routes, partially electrified, to a distance of about 60 km. Approximately hourly on three routes, irregular services elsewhere.

Developments: Improved service is to be offered on the line to Kladno (37.5 km), which is to be upgraded and electrified by a new private company PRAK. Two branches are proposed for construction, to Ruzyne international airport and Kladno town centre.

UPDATED

Praha's new Tatra T6A5 cars ***1997***

Karosa standard in suburban Praha ***1997***

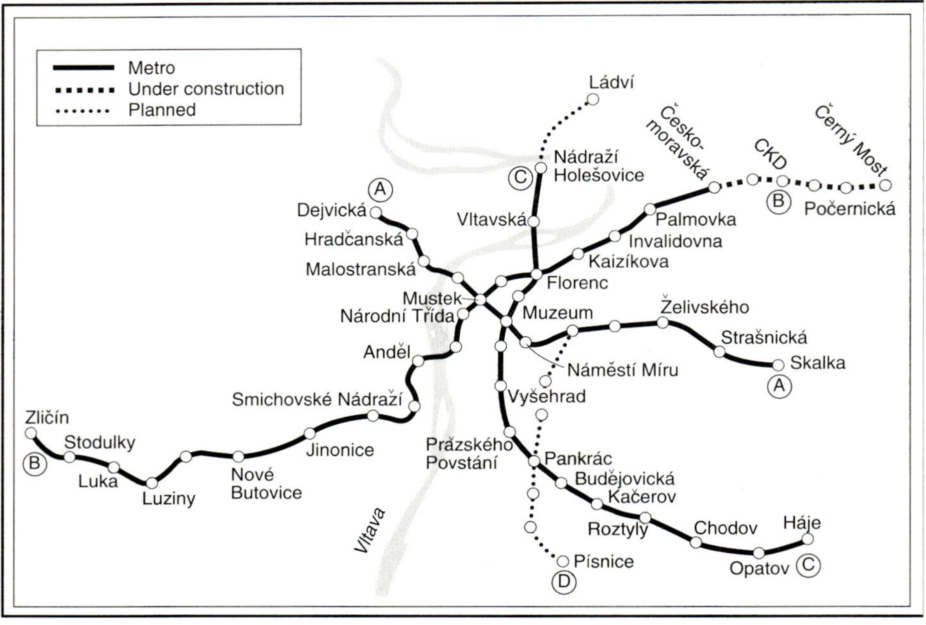

Praha metro

PRETORIA

Population: 1 million
Public transport: City bus services provided by transport department of the city council. Extensive longer-distance commuter bus services operated by private companies and suburban rail services by Rail Commuter Corp

Pretoria City Transport

City Council of Pretoria
Logistic Services Department, Transportation Services
PO Box 890, 1 Schoeman Street, Pretoria 0001, South Africa
Telephone: +27 12 308 0200 Fax: +27 12 308 0213
Executive Director, Logistic Services: C Bosch
Staff: 687

Current situation: Public transport policy is being revised and integration of various operators' services is under consideration to reduce costs and improve service quality.

Bus

Passenger journeys: (1993/94) 17.2 million
(1994/95) 16 million
(1995/96) 13.8 million
Vehicle-km: (1993/94) 12.3 million
(1994/95) 11.5 million
(1995/96) 11.3 million

Number of routes: 241, including school and contract routes
Route length: (One way) timetabled routes 685 km
Fleet: 344 vehicles

MAN City Bus	20
MAN semi-luxury	15
MAN double-deck	20
Mercedes O305 city bus	131
Mercedes O305 semi-luxury coach	50
Mercedes O305 double-deck	108

In peak service: 267
New vehicles required each year: 20

Most intensive service: 5 min
One-person operation: All services
Fare collection: Cash to driver or prepurchase
Fare structure: Stage; multiticket books (coupons); trip tickets valid 1 month for 1, 2, 3 or 4 stages allowing 4 trips per day, 2 on any route within the municipal boundary and 2 within the central area. Monthly tickets allowing 6 trips per day on any routes within the municipal boundary
Fares collected on board: 26.7%; 9.9 million passengers took prepurchase tickets in 1994/95
Fare evasion control: Ticket inspectors
Operational control: Route inspectors
Arrangements for elderly/disabled: Disabled and over-68s free; low-price senior citizens' monthly pass for unlimited off-peak travel
Average peak-hour speed: In bus lanes, 23.5 km/h; in mixed traffic, 20.5 km/h
Bus priority: 7.5 km of bus lanes
Operating costs financed by: Fares 50%, subsidy/grants 50%
Subsidy from: City tax funds
New vehicles financed by: Loans/tax fund

Other operators

Current situation: PUTCO provides mostly longer-distance bus services to bring commuters to work (see Johannesburg entry). Its Pretoria area operations carry more than 50 million passengers annually. A second private operator Northwest Star (formerly BTH) also runs services.

Mercedes O305 in central Pretoria

Metro Rail

South African Rail Commuter Corporation Ltd
Pretoria Metropolitan Area
Private Bag X2, Sunninghill, Johannesburg 2157
Telephone: +27 11 804 2900 Fax: +27 11 804 3852

Type of operation: Suburban heavy rail

Passenger journeys: (1990/91) 69 million
(1991/92) 60.8 million
(1992/93) 61.5 million

Current situation: Suburban rail serving whole of Pretoria (Northern Transvaal area, population 1.5 million); seven routes totalling 146 km with 78 stations, 1,065 mm gauge, electrified 3 kV DC; links with Johannesburg area services. Peak service 10 trains per hour, off-peak every 20 min. Fares cover 30 per cent of operating costs.
Developments: An 18 km extension is proposed in Metro Rail's 10-year capital development programme.

Rolling stock: 589 emu cars

Union Carriage & Wagon	M163 T426

UPDATED

PROVIDENCE

Population: 596,000
Public transport: Bus services in Providence and in 35 of the other 38 towns in the state of Rhode Island provided by public transit authority controlled by representative board; commuter rail link to Boston

RIPTA

Rhode Island Public Transit Authority (RIPTA)
PO Box 2816, 265 Melrose Street, Providence, RI 02907, USA
Telephone: +1 401 781 9450 Fax: +1 401 784 9595
Director of Transit Administration: Edward Scott
Director of Transit Operations: William Dame
General Manager: Beverly A Scott
Staff: 520

Volvo bus in Providence

Current situation: Established in 1966 to take over residual private bus operations. A 10-year development programme expanded services throughout the state.

Bus

Passenger journeys: (1993) 16.4 million
(1994) 17.4 million
Vehicle-km: (1990/91) 12.2 million

Number of routes: 73
Route length: 580 km
Fleet: 242 vehicles

GMC RTS-II (1981)	15
Neoplan AN460 articulated (1984)	5
Volvo B10M (1985)	55
Neoplan AN440 (1988)	64
TMC RTS T80 (1990)	28
TMC RTS T80 (1992)	48
Boyertown trolley replicas (1984)	2
Eldorado Aerotech (1993)	25

In peak service: 196

Most intensive service: 30 min
One-person operation: All routes
Fare collection: Registering fareboxes
Fare structure: Zonal (4 zones); transfers (15-60 min dependent on frequency); 10-ticket books; monthly passes; free downtown loop service
Fares collected on board: 85%
Operational control: Route inspectors; radio
Arrangements for elderly/disabled: 179 buses lift-equipped; free off-peak travel
Bus priority: Buses use 300 m former tram tunnel under College Hill in central Providence
Integration with other modes: 14 park-and-ride sites served by 9 commuter bus routes
Average peak-hour speed: 16 km/h
Operating costs financed by: Fares 27%, subsidy/grants 73%
Subsidy from: FTA 74%, state 26%
New vehicles financed by: Voter-approved bonding and federal grants

---

Suburban rail

Current situation: About 10 Amtrak trains daily link Providence with Boston (69 km), plus commuter-hour services operated by MBTA Boston under auspices of Rhode Island DoT. Because the state cannot subsidise the commuter operation, it has instead purchased two diesel locomotives and five cars for MBTA, which in exchange will operate into Providence for nine years.
Developments: Electrification of the Amtrak route is in progress.

UPDATED

PUNE

Population: 2.6 million
Public transport: Bus services provided by municipal undertaking operating within the urban and suburban area, with some longer-distance routes running into the service area of a second municipal operator serving the twin city of Pimpri-Chinchwad (population 516,000). Extensive taxi and autorickshaw services; interdistrict and state routes operated by the Maharasthra State Road Transport Corporation

Ashok Leyland bus of PMT ***1996***

Pune Municipal Transport

Pune Municipal Transport
Swargate, Pune 411037, India
Telephone: +91 212 440417/441189
General Manager: H L Satpute
Staff: 6,952

Bus

Passenger journeys: (1992/93) 226.2 million
(1993/94) 214.1 million
(1994/95) 225.9 million
Vehicle-km: (1992/93) 52.2 million
(1993/94) 56.9 million
(1994/95) 62 million

Number of routes: 221
Route length: 3,442 km
Fleet: 806 vehicles

Tata	136
Ashok Leyland single-deck	665
Ashok Leyland double-deck	5

Average age of fleet: 7 years
In peak service: 642
On order: 674 buses

Most intensive service: 5 min
One-person operation: None
Fare collection: Conductors
Fare structure: Stage; higher fare for night and express services; monthly passes
Fares collected on board: 92%
Arrangements for elderly/disabled: Concessional fare
Average peak-hour speed: 20 km/h
Operating costs financed by: Fares 95.7%, tax levy 3.6%, subsidy/grants 0.6%

PCMT

Pimpri-Chinchwad Municipal Transport
Nigdi, Pune 411044
Telephone: +91 212 83624
General Manager: S M A Kazi
Transport Manager: N N Bothe
Staff: 2,072

Current situation: Competes with PMT on some busy routes, but is the sole provider in some areas of Pune's twin city Pimpri-Chinchwad. Has introduced high-quality minibus services at premium fares.

Bus

Passenger journeys: (1993/94) 43.2 million
(1994/95) 48 million
(1995/96) 49 million
Vehicle-km: (1993/94) 13.4 million
(1994/95) 15.5 million
(1995/96) 16.8 million

Fleet: 248 vehicles

Ashok Leyland single-deck	152
Ashok Leyland double-deck	30
Tata	57
Others	9

Average age of fleet: 7.6 years

Operating costs financed by: Fares 105.4%, other commercial sources 10.3%

UPDATED

PUSAN

Population: 3.9 million
Public transport: Bus services provided by private companies organised into statutory associations. Urban transit authority operates metro; light rail planned

Private bus

Current situation: Buses carry over 1,000 million passengers a year, accounting for around 45 per cent of public transport, with a further 14 per cent handled by taxis and smaller vehicles. Each bus company typically operates up to five routes. Frequencies and fares (flat, with a premium for seat buses) are set by government agency.

Fleet: About 2,500, including mostly standard locally built 72-capacity and some smaller 'seat buses' providing premium all-seated services

PUTA

Pusan Urban Transit Authority
861-1 Bum Chun-dong, Pusan-Jin-ku 614-021
Telephone: +82 51 463 4206
President: Kim Chang-Gap
Staff: 1,667

Type of operation: Full metro, opened 1985

Passenger journeys: (1991) 181.5 million
(1992) 192 million

Route length: 32.5 km
Number of routes: 1
Number of stations: 30
Gauge: 1,435 mm
Minimum curve radius: 180 m
Electrification: 1.5 kV DC, overhead

Service: Peak 3½ min
Fare structure: 3 zones
Fare collection: Ticket or stored-value pass

Pusan metro train

Hyundai buses in Pusan

Signalling: ATO-equipped, but currently operating in manual mode
Operating costs financed by: Fares 11%

Rolling stock: 216 cars formed into 6 six-car sets
Marubeni/Hyundai (1984/85) M216
On order: 336 cars being built by Hanjin for opening of Line 2 in 1998.

Current situation: Initial 16.1 km section of Line 1 opened 1985, further 5.2 km in 1987, and the remainder a year later.
Developments: Line 1 extension to Shinp'yong (6.4 km) opened June 1994. The 22.4 km Phase I of east-west Line 2 under construction from Hop'o to Somyon was due to open in 1995 but now delayed until 1998. Phase II, from Somyon to Changsan (16.6 km), should open in 1999.

A network of five lines totalling 138 km had been scheduled for completion by 2001, but work on Lines 3, 4 and 5 totalling 67 km is unlikely to start before the end of the century.

Light rail (proposed)

Current situation: A light rail link to Kimhae airport has been proposed.

UPDATED

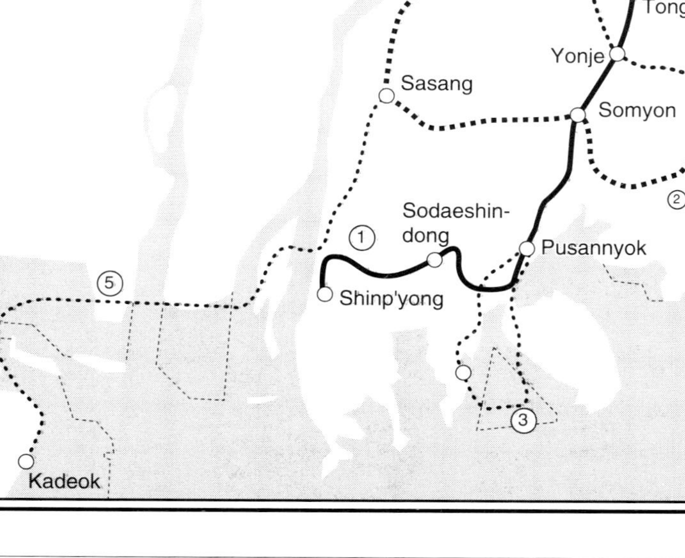

Pusan metro

PYONGYANG

Population: 2.5 million
Public transport: Bus, trolleybus and tram services provided by People's Assembly of city under government supervision. Metro operated by government department

Pyongyang People's Assembly

Pyongyang People's Assembly Transport Committee
Pyongyang, Democratic People's Republic of Korea

Bus and trolleybus

Passenger journeys: Approx 150 million (annual)

Number of routes: 50
Fleet: Approx 500 buses, including Ikarus 260 and 280 articulated; Karosa SM and B731
Fleet: There are about 1,000 locally built trolleybuses, both two-axle and articulated

One-person operation: None
Fare structure: Flat, prepaid tickets deposited in box at rear of vehicle
Fare collection: Conductors

Current situation: The trolleybus operation acts mainly as a feeder to the metro, though there are signs that the system is to be run down as the tramway develops. There are 10 routes.

Yonggwang metro station ***1997***

Tram and trolleybus outside Pyongyang's main station ***1997***

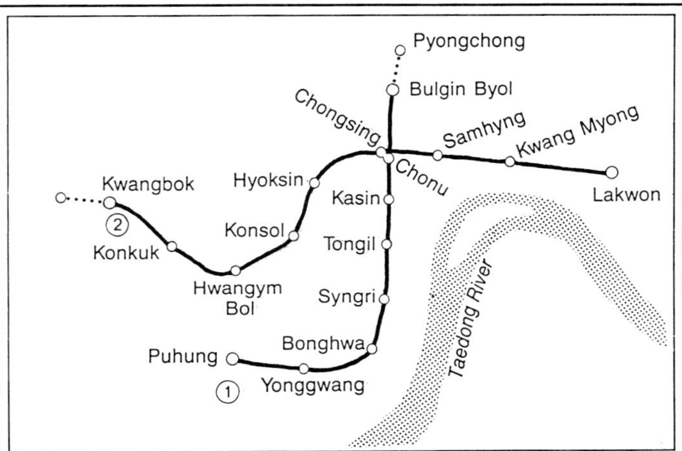

Pyongyang metro

Tramway

Current situation: The first tramway route was opened in 1991 and extended in 1992 and 1994. There are three routes extending to at least 50 km, operated by a fleet of ČKD Tatra and Chinese-built cars. A batch of cars second-hand from Leipzig was due to arrive at the beginning of 1997. An extensive network is planned, including a circular route.

Rolling stock: 234 cars

ČKD Tatra KT8 articulated	M45
ČKD Tatra T6B5	M129
Shenfeng Trolleybus Works KT4 articulated	M60

Pyongyang Metro

City Metro Unit, Railway Section, Transport & Communication Commission

Type of operation: Full metro, initial route opened 1973

Passenger journeys: (1990) 42 million
(1994) 35 million

Route length: 22.5 km
Number of routes: 2
Number of stations: 17
Gauge: 1,435 mm
Track: Concrete trackbed
Tunnel: Bored and blasted to maximum depth of 150 m; mostly single-bore
Electrification: 825 V DC, third rail

Service: Peak 2 min, off-peak 5-7 min
First/last train: 05.00/23.00
Fare structure: Flat
Fare collection: Automatic entry barriers, coin in slot, no tickets; manual surveillance

Signalling: Colourlights; CTC

Rolling stock: 168 cars

Kim Chong The works (1973)	M48
Ex-BVG Berlin	120

Current situation: Line 1 opened 1973, Line 2 in 1978. The two lines are not connected but interchange is provided in the city centre between Chonu station on Line 1 and Chongsing station on Line 2.
Developments: An east-west route through the city centre is planned in connection with a major residential development in the eastern suburbs, but progress has been hampered by shortage of funds.

Pressure on the rolling stock fleet will be eased during 1997 by delivery of 120 cars of 1960s vintage second-hand from the Berlin U-Bahn.

UPDATED

QUEBEC

Population: 480,000
Public transport: Bus services provided by transport commission responsible to urban municipal authority

STCUQ

Société de Transport de la Communauté Urbaine de Québec (STCUQ)
720 rue des Rocailles, Quebec G2J 1A5, Canada
Telephone: +1 418 627 2351 Fax: +1 418 622 8405
President: Claude Larose
General Manager: Rénald Blouin
Director of Operations: André Lapierre
Director of Research & Marketing: Pierre Bouvier
Staff: 1,034

Current situation: STCUQ was created in 1969 and acquired the buses and services of seven companies which had previously served the 400 km² area and 13 municipalities in and around the city.
Developments: Following a major reorganisation in 1992, STCUQ implemented the second phase of its transit development programme in 1995. At the heart of the plan is the Metrobus system of high-frequency limited-stop routes using designated bus lanes, designed to provide metro-like service quality.

MCI Classic on limited-stop Metrobus route ***1995***

Bus

Passenger journeys: (1991) 38.3 million
(1992) 37.2 million
(1993) 37.2 million
Vehicle-km: (1991) 23.5 million
(1992) 21.2 million
(1993) 21.5 million

Number of routes: 85 (including 38 express)
Fleet: 473 vehicles

GM Canada	276
MCI Classic	193
OBI minibus (1994)	4

Most intensive service: 5 min
One-person operation: All services

Fare collection: Payment to driver or prepurchase pass
Fare structure: Flat; exact fare; monthly passes
Bus priority: 30 km peak-hour bus lanes
Average peak-hour speed: 20 km/h
Operating costs financed by: Fares 35%, subsidy/grants 65%
Subsidy from: Province and 13 municipalities

QUITO

Population: 800,000, metropolitan area 1.3 million
Public transport: Bus and minibus services mostly provided by independent operators forming route or area associations and co-operatives, supervised by the municipality. Municipal services also operate some routes; trolleybus route

Municipality of Quito

Municipio de Quito
PO Box 17-17-484, Quito, Ecuador
Telephone: +593 2 513518 Fax: +593 2 460341
Director of Planning: Cesar Arias

Current situation: The municipality is the overall planning and licensing authority for the city's transport services. It also built the trolleybus route opened in 1995 and owns the vehicles. Bus services are being progressively franchised to private operators.
Developments: All bus routes serving the north-south Villa Flora/El Recreo to La Y corridor through the city centre were cut back to the new interchanges built at the northern and southern terminals of the trolleybus line. In total, 110 bus routes were revised in the period from late December 1995 to April 1996, when full trolleybus operation commenced.

Nearly all operations are contracted to private companies, though Empresa Metropolitana del

Ejido northbound 'station' on Quito's trolleybus line ***1997***

Transporte (EMT) runs some of the secondary routes feeding its trolleybus line.

Private bus/Minibus

Passenger journeys: (1995) 1 million daily
Vehicle-km: 55 million (annual)

Number of routes: 50
Route length: 700 km
Fleet: 1,500, including 500 buses and 1,000 minibuses; types include Ford, Dodge, Mercedes, Bedford. Thomas locally built bodywork is widely used

One-person operation: All services
Fare collection: Payment to driver; some vehicles with turnstiles
Fare structure: Flat
Fares collected on board: 100%
Average peak-hour speed: 18 km/h

Trolleybus

Passenger journeys: (1996) 150,000 daily

Current situation: An 11.2 km route constructed on new bus-only lanes throughout opened in 1995/96, along with two other parallel busways which are diesel bus operated. Built by the municipality, the system is being managed initially by the Empresa Metropolitana del Transporte prior to seeking a private-sector concessionaire.

This unique system has been described as a rubber-tyred light rail line; light rail was rejected only on the grounds that vibration might harm historic buildings in the city centre. The route is entirely segregated and forms the city's central trunk route. All bus routes in the north-south corridor have been cut back to act as feeders; 70 routes now run to huge interchanges built at the Villa Flora/El Recreo and La Y trolleybus terminals. Some of the feeders are operated by EMT using Ikarus articulated buses.

All passenger boarding and alighting is at high-platform enclosed 'stations' (20 southbound, 19 northbound), which give stepless access to the vehicles. New traffic signals have been installed at 140 intersections along the route, with detectors beneath the road surface. All fare collection takes place off the vehicles, tickets being issued either on board the feeder buses or from vending machines and sales staff at the stations, which also have security personnel. Access to the 'platforms' is by turnstiles which accept the prepurchased tokens, tickets or stored-fare cards.

Developments: The immediate success of the trolleybuses has led to proposals for extensions at each end of the route, southwards to Chillogallo and northwards to Cotocollao, both about 6 km. They are unlikely to be built within five years.

Fleet: 54 trolleybuses with auxiliary diesel engines
Mercedes/Hispano Carrocera/AEG articulated (1995/96) 54

UPDATED

RAWALPINDI-ISLAMABAD

Population: Rawalpindi 800,000, Islamabad 200,000
Public transport: Bus services in Rawalpindi provided by provincial government-owned Road Transport Corporation, also operating intercity routes and urban services in Lahore and Faisalabad. Between Rawalpindi and Islamabad there are frequent services of private buses known as 'Flying Coaches'. Extensive paratransit operations

PRTC

Punjab Road Transport Corporation
Rawalpindi, Pakistan

Current situation: PRTC operates urban services in Rawalpindi with a fleet of Fiat 331A, Volvo B57 and Isuzu buses, this fleet being distinct from that used on long-distance routes. Older buses have perimeter seating but transverse seats are fitted to newer vehicles. Buses have separate compartments for men and women and carry two conductors.

Other operators

Current situation: Most of the demand in Rawalpindi and the neighbouring new capital city Islamabad is satisfied by 10-seat microbuses based on Suzuki pick-ups, Morris Minor taxis, Vespa autorickshaws and horse-drawn 'tongas'.

Rapid transit (planned)

Current situation: A mass transit network for the twin cities has been proposed by the Capital Area Development Authority, which in 1995 sought bids from parties interested in developing detailed proposals.

Micros touting for business in central Rawalpindi ***1996***

RECIFE

Population: 1.2 million, metropolitan area 2.5 million
Public transport: Bus services provided by private companies, with trolleybus network and some bus routes run by state-owned undertakings. System of reserved route trolleybusways being established; suburban railway

EMTU

Empresa Metropolitana de Transportes Urbanos (EMTU)
Recife, Pernambuco, Brazil
President: Oswaldo Lima Neto

Volvo B58 Marcopolo-bodied 'Padron' city bus in Recife

Current situation: EMTU was created in 1980 to eliminate conflict between public transport operators licensed by the federal, state and municipal authorities. Prior to this date, the municipal bus operator had *de facto* control of concessions to new operators, new routes, timetabling and overall supervision of the network, in spite of this officially being the responsibility of a state government department. EMTU currently supervises a network of 270 bus routes operated by 2,296 vehicles, 2,081 of which belong to 20 private companies. The operators are no longer paid subsidy according to the number of passengers carried; instead they must achieve an agreed set of objectives.

Developments: Oswaldo Lima Neto is President once again, having previously been in charge during 1987/90 when he began upgrading of the rundown bus fleet. His current objectives are to improve customer service, upgrade information systems and raise vehicle availability. Automated ticketing system is also proposed. There is a plan to equip the city with six trunk routes served by a feeder network. Four are in operation (one is the Metrorec regional metro), and finance has been made available for the others.

A traffic management system known as SIMAV was introduced in 1994, with 72 transmitters installed along the city's main corridors giving a 95 per cent real-time location fix on all vehicles. Linked to onboard ticket issuing and validating equipment, it is now possible to know how many passengers are being carried at any time.

Private bus/Minibus

Current situation: Operations of some 33 private companies carry over 500 million passengers annually with a total fleet of about 2,080 buses.

Transportadora Itamarac (TI) is one of the largest operators, with 19 routes carrying 43,000 daily. Its fleet numbers 120 vehicles, mostly Padrons with either Mercedes or Ford chassis; average age 2.6 years.

CTU

Companhia de Transportes Urbanos
Recife
President: Carlos Farache
Staff: 1,604

Current situation: CTU is a mixed-capital company linked to the municipality of Recife. It started operations in the early 1960s and by the mid-1970s was providing four-fifths of the city's public transport. After creation of EMTU, CTU's role was drastically reduced and today it operates only 23 routes. Productivity is low, with 7.9 employees per bus, 57 per cent more than in private companies.

Bus

Number of routes: 20
Fleet: 215 buses

Trolleybus

Current situation: A mid-1970s study led to recommendations for encouragement of public transport journeys into the restricted city centre by integrated trunk services based, in the northwest quarter of the city, on concentrated trolleybus services operating on dedicated lanes of five highway corridors, and in the southwest by buses feeding an upgraded suburban railway.

The operation is complemented by provision of exclusive trolleybus right-of-way on a distribution loop around the central business district, which is only open to trolleybuses, buses, taxis and vehicles requiring access, by control over bridges crossing the water which surrounds the city centre on three sides, thus effectively ensuring public transport priority.

The trolleybusway system involves provision of exclusive lanes on three-lane dual carriageways serving five radial corridors. Trolleybuses are allocated to the outer lanes adjacent to the central reservations of the dual carriageways, separated from the main traffic flow by road markings and served by 'stations' built on the median strip. Access to the stations, provided at about 1 km intervals, is by overbridges or light-controlled crossings. Hourly one-direction passenger flow capacity for the system is intended to be 25,000, with a potential of 40,000 achievable with a guided bus system. Buses may also use the reserved lane system and stations.

A system of bus feeders is provided with free interchange to trolleybuses for journeys to the city centre. There are also connections with private bus services, but these require payment of an additional fare. The trolleybusways incorporate turnround points for short workings and interchange. Eventually 42.5 km of segregated trolleybus route will be operated.

Developments: Route to Olinda and Bultrins (15 km) completed earlier but not opened until late 1994 or early 1995. Further routes are due to open and others are being extended under the trunk route public transport priority scheme.

Plans called for a fleet of 300 trolleybuses to carry 30 per cent of city traffic; 40 vehicles in store were rebuilt for opening of the Olinda/Bultrins route and further rebuilds are planned.

Number of routes: 3
Route length: Approx 28 km
Fleet: 48 trolleybuses
Scania/Marmon-H/Villares (1958/59 rebuilt 1981/84) 48

Metrorec train at Werneck station

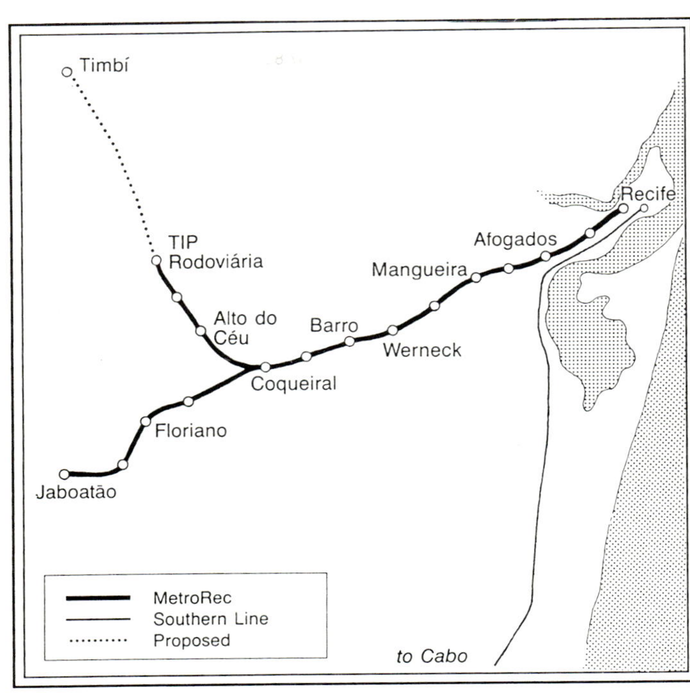

Recife metro

Metrorec

CBTU STU/REC, Companhia Brasileira de Trens Urbanos, Recife Division
Rua José Natario 478, 50780 Recife, Pernambuco
Telephone: +55 81 251 0933 Fax: +55 81 251 4844
President: J Dias Fernandes
Staff: 1,612

Type of operation: Regional metro, first line opened 1985

Passenger journeys: (1993) 33 million
(1994) 36 million
(1995) 37.2 million

Route length: 52.5 km
Number of routes: 2
Number of stations: 27
Gauge: 1,600 mm
Track: Conventional ballasted
Electrification: 3 kV DC, overhead (20.5 km Metrorec line)

Service: Peak 6 min
First/last train: 05.00/23.00
Integration with other modes: 30 bus routes provide feeder services; interchange with suburban rail
Operating costs financed by: Fares 20%, central government subsidy 80%

Rolling stock: 25 four-car emus, 7 diesel locomotives, 36 coaches
CISM/Santa Matilde (1984) M50 T50

Current situation: Initial route from Central station to Werneck extended 1986 to Coqueiral and Rodoviaria-Lacerda, with further extension to Jaboatão opened 1987. This regional metro is being created by laying 1,600 mm gauge track on existing 1,000 mm gauge alignment. Metrorec is the local subsidiary of CBTU, the Brazilian Urban Railways Company.

CBTU has also substantially upgraded the city's remaining 1,000 mm gauge conventional diesel-worked suburban service, the South line linking Cinco Pontas with Pontezinha and Cabo (32 km, 10 stations), and increased services to build patronage with an eye to future electrification, which is under study for the 13.6 km section to Pontezhina. This route carries about 5 million passengers annually (included in figures above).

Developments: The World Bank is to fund half of the US$204 million cost of resignalling and electrifying the Joana Bezerra—Cajueiro Seco section of the South line. In addition to modernising the two existing stations, CBTU would like to build a further 10, as well as quadrupling the track to permit segregation of metro traffic from freight trains. The money will also pay for remodelling of the rest of the line to Cabo, with track-doubling between Pontezinha and Cabo. On the main route, a 4.5 km extension will be built from TIP to Timbi, over which some 60,000 daily journeys are expected. Tenders for this work were sought in 1996.

Ownership of Metrorec is to be transferred eventually from CBTU to EMTU, the Pernambuco state-owned urban bus authority (see above), but the state government is unhappy about the system's monthly deficit of US$2 million and is seeking to raise farebox recovery to 85 per cent.

UPDATED

RENNES

Population: City 205,000, conurbation 331,000
Public transport: Bus services provided by franchised operator under control of a semi-public company representing 33 towns; VAL automated metro under construction

Semtcar

Société d'Economie Mixte des Transports Collectifs de l'Agglomération Rennaise (Semtcar)
16 rue du Puits Mauger, 35069 Rennes cedex, France
Telephone: +33 2 99 85 89 30 Fax: +33 2 99 65 11 51
President: Jean Normand
Director General: Jean-François Blache
Staff: 30

Current situation: Formed of representatives of the Rennes District (33 towns) and private shareholders (District 55 per cent, Transdev 44 per cent), Semtcar is responsible for public transport policy and construction of the metro. Operations are franchised to STUR under the commercial name STAR (Service de Transport de l'Agglomération Rennaise). Suburban routes (30 per cent of vehicle-km) are operated by 10 private companies.

STUR

Société des Transportes Urbains Rennais (STUR/STAR)
Rue J M Huchet, PO Box 198, 35004 Rennes cedex
Telephone: +33 2 99 36 24 12 Fax: +33 2 99 38 37 82
Director General: François Xavier Gelin
Operating Manager: Bruno Loy
Project Manager, Metro: Roland Clavel
Staff: 701

Current situation: STUR, which is a subsidiary of VIA-GTI, holds the franchise for operation of bus services within the Rennes conurbation, branded as STAR, under the control of Semtcar.

Bus

Passenger journeys: (1992) 36.8 million
(1993) 37.3 million
(1995) 34.5 million
Vehicle-km: (1992) 9.4 million
(1993) 10 million
(1995)

Number of routes: 16 urban, 4 peak-only, 23 suburban, 9 Sunday, 4 evening (after 21.00)
Route length: 459 km
On priority right-of-way: 18.8 km
Fleet: 251 vehicles, plus 80 hired for suburban services

Renault SC10	50
Renault R312	57
MAN SB220 articulated	52
Renault PR180	59
Heuliez GX187	13
Van Hool low-floor (1995)	20

In peak service: 198
Average age of fleet: 9.2 years

Buses of STAR in central Rennes

Most intensive service: Peak 4 min, off-peak 7 min
One-person operation: All routes
Fare structure: Flat, reduced rate carnets of 10 tickets or 6 return journeys; single tickets valid 1 h; weekly and monthly passes; Carte Hermine STAR/SNCF season ticket
Fare collection: Tickets sold by approved vendors and drivers; cancellers on board
Fares collected on board: 22%
Fare evasion control: Inspectors
Average peak-hour speed: Urban 14 km/h, suburban 24 km/h
Arrangements for elderly/disabled: Special services operated by STH with 14 minibuses; free travel for invalids
Operating costs financed by: Fares 38%, subsidy/grants 62%
Subsidy from: District
New vehicles financed by: District

Developments: In 1995 peak-hour Route B was replaced by all-day Route 30 linking northern suburbs without passing through the city centre. Two other services were rerouted. In 1996, 20 Van Hool low-floor buses were introduced. Over the coming five years, vehicle-km will be increased by 0.7 million.

Metro

Under construction

Current situation: Construction is expected to start in 1997 on the 8.6 km Line 1 of a VAL automated metro with 15 stations. It will run from the University and the Villejean hospital district in the northwest via the city centre to the Le Blosne residential area in the southeast. Opening is scheduled for 2001, when 77,000 daily passengers are expected.

After cancellation in 1993 through lack of funding, the project finally got under way after the May 1995 municipal elections, when a slightly revised plan was approved by a substantial majority. Finding the money for metro construction has been a problem for this city of only 331,000 inhabitants, but the cost of tunnelling is justified by the extent of city-centre pedestrian areas and the narrow streets.

Line 2 is planned to run northeast from the city centre, but proposed Line 3, an east-west route paralleling the River Vilaine, has been rejected on account of poor traffic predictions.

SNCF

French National Railways, Rennes Region
22 Boulevard de Beaumont, 35040 Rennes
Telephone: +33 2 99 29 11 10

Current situation: Limited suburban services operate on five routes. There are proposals for construction of several new halts in the conurbation as future interchanges with the metro.

UPDATED

REYKJAVIK

Population: 101,000, capital region 155,000
Public transport: Bus services provided by municipal company

SVR

Straetisvagnar Reykjavíkur (SVR)
Borgartún 35, 105 Reykjavik, Iceland
Telephone: +354 581 2533 Fax: +354 581 4626
Managing Director: Lilia Olafsdottir
Staff: 190

Current situation: As well as the urban services of SVR, six communities in the capital region operate their own transport undertaking Almenningsvagnar (AV), which contracts with private operators to run bus services within and between the communities and to central Reykjavik.
Developments: In 1993 municipally owned SVR became a limited liability company with all shares held initially by local authorities prior to privatisation. However, after local elections in 1994, this decision was reversed and the company was restored to municipal ownership.

In 1995 there was a further reorganisation designed to put increased emphasis on improved service, marketing and development.

Latest Volvo B10M on Laugavegur, Reykjavik's main shopping street

Bus
Passenger journeys: (1992) 7.1 million
(1993) 7.1 million
(1994) 7.1 million
Vehicle-km: (1992) 4.5 million
(1993) 4.5 million
(1994) 4.7 million

Number of routes: 20
Route length: (One way) 397 km
Fleet: 72 buses

Volvo B58 museum model (1968)	1
Volvo B59 (1975)	1
Volvo B10M (1981/83/84/85)	30
Volvo B10M Mk3 (1989/90/91/92/93)	18
Volvo B10M Mk4	2
Scania CN112 (1986/87/88)	20

In peak service: 60

Most intensive service: 07.00-19.00 weekdays 20 min, evenings and weekends 30 min
One-person operation: All services
Fare structure: Exact flat fare, payment to farebox; free transfers; prepurchase multitickets; transferable 30-day pass
Fares collected on board: 51%
Arrangements for elderly/disabled: Half fares charged, financed jointly by SVR and city social services department
Operating costs financed by: Fares 62.7%, other commercial sources 2.4%, city council subsidy/grants 34.9%
New vehicles financed by: City council

RHEIN-RUHR

Population: 7.4 million
Public transport: The Rhein-Ruhr conurbation, covering an area of roughly 5,100 km² between Düsseldorf and Dortmund, also encompasses the major centres of Duisburg, Mülheim, Essen, Bochum, Krefeld and Wuppertal and many smaller towns. Bus, express bus, tram, Stadtbahn (light rail) and S-Bahn (regional metro) services, provided by various local authority undertakings and German Railway (DB), are co-ordinated at a regional level by VRR. For local transport in main towns see individual entries

VRR

Verkehrsverbund Rhein-Ruhr GmbH
PO Box 10 30 52, 45801 Gelsenkirchen, Germany
Telephone: +49 209 15840 Fax: +49 209 23967
Directors: Wolfgang Teubner
Dieter Lippert
Divisional Manager, Technical: Jürgen Handke
Divisional Manager, Economics: Gerhard Schmier
Staff: 172 (Planning and administration)

Current situation: VRR is responsible for co-ordinating public transport for the region. Its remit extends to marketing, planning, integration of services and operation of a common tariff system and public relations. A limited liability company, VRR was reorganised in 1990, when the Stadtbahn-Gesellschaft Rhein-Ruhr was merged into VRR. Sole shareholder of VRR is now the Zweckverband Verkehrsverbund Rhein-Ruhr, a political body representing 24 local authorities. The following municipal transport undertakings, previously also shareholders, have signed co-operation agreements with VRR:
Bochum-Gelsenkirchener Strassenbahnen AG (qv)
Dortmunder Stadtwerke AG (qv)
Duisburger Versorgungs- und Verkehrsgesellschaft mbH (qv)
Verkehrsgesellschaft Ennepe-Ruhr mbH
Essener Versorgungs- und Verkehrsgesellschaft mbH (qv)
Hagener Versorgungs- und Verkehrsgesellschaft mbH
Strassenbahn Herne-Castrop-Rauxel GmbH (HCR)
Krefelder Versorgungs-, Verkehrs- und Entsorgungs GmbH (qv)
Monheimer Versorgungs- und Verkehrs GmbH
Stadt Mülheim an der Ruhr Verkehrsbetriebe
Stadt Neuss Verkehrsbetriebe
Stadtwerke Oberhausen AG
Stadtwerke Remscheid GmbH
Rheinische Bahngesellschaft AG, Düsseldorf (qv)
Stadt Solingen Verkehrsbetriebe
Vestische Strassenbahnen GmbH (for Recklinghausen) (see below)
Stadtwerke Viersen GmbH
Wuppertaler Stadtwerke AG (qv)
In addition, the federal-owned transport undertakings (Deutsche Bahn and Busverkehr Rheinland GmbH) and Niederrheinische Verkehrsbetriebe (NIAG) have signed special co-operation agreements with VRR corresponding to their exceptional status in the new organisation.

Allocation of fares revenue also changed, and is now based on demand rather than offer of transport facilities. Previously all fares revenue went to VRR for allocation amongst its members on a vehicle-km basis. This encouraged to some extent operation of unnecessary services. Now each operator will retain the fares collected, and a compensation scheme is envisaged to account for passengers transferring between operators. DB has been guaranteed a lump-sum payment. Infrastructure will be paid for partly by the state of Nordrhein-Westfalen.

MAN low-floor articulated of HCR, one of the smaller municipal operators in VRR, at Herne ***1997***

Essen Hbf, interchange between S-Bahn, Stadtbahn and bus services

Within the VRR area, the undertakings provide service on a total of 709 routes extending to 11,700 route-km. An integrated interurban light rail (Stadtbahn) network is under construction (see below), designed to complement the expanding S-Bahn. There is also an extensive network of DB local and suburban rail routes, some of which are to form part of a new express S-Bahn network.

A new service concept has been implemented by VRR with a revised hierarchy of services:
Regional Express Railway — hourly limited stop trains for intercity travel within the region, replacing semi-fast trains accessible to VRR ticket-holders but running on an irregular basis.
Regional metro (S-Bahn).
City Railway (CityBahn) — to supplement S-Bahn services, but to a generally lower standard and on tracks shared with freight trains.
LRT (Stadtbahn) — accelerated tramway and accelerated bus services to be promoted jointly as 'CityExpress' for fast suburb-to-city-centre travel, with common livery adopted.
Regional Express Bus (StädteSchnellBus) — see below.
Urban services — by local tram and bus.
Night Express — late night services at weekends.

Park-and-ride is provided at about 250 stations with 15,000 spaces. This is insufficient and it has been

Rhein-Ruhr Line U18 linking Mülheim and Essen

estimated that another 20-30,000 spaces are needed. Sites with more than 3,000 spaces are planned at some stations.

Bike-and-ride is also being promoted, and lockable bicycle boxes installed at some S-Bahn stations have met with great success. Also, as an experiment, some operators have started to carry bicycles during off-peak periods.

Express bus services, marketed as 'StädteSchnellBus', are being introduced on routes where local bus service is insufficient to meet demand, but which do not warrant a rail service. Only limited stops are served and an average speed of 40 km/h is scheduled. More comfortable vehicles equipped to coach standards are used.

Developments: All university students are compelled to buy a VRR pass.

Passenger journeys: (All modes)
(1993) 1,064.4 million
(1994) 1,081 million
(1995) 1,076 million

Fare collection: Single tickets (15% of journeys), multiride cards (15%), daily, weekly, monthly, off-peak and annual passes (70% of all passes)
Fare structure: Zonal with short-distance ticket, free intermodal transfers
Operating costs financed by: Fares 36%, other commercial sources 3%, subsidy/grants 61%
Subsidy from: Local governments (municipal operators only), federal government (DB only), state Nordrhein-Westfalen

Bus

(Aggregate of local operations)
Vehicle-km: (1993) 183 million
(1994) 182.6 million
(1995) 184.9 million

Number of routes: 610
Route length: 7,564 km

Trolleybus (Solingen and Essen)

Vehicle-km: (1993) 2.9 million
(1994) 3.7 million
(1995) 3.7 million

Number of routes: 4
Route length: 47.7 km

Developments: Closure of the Solingen trolleybus system is planned on financial grounds; operations in Essen were suspended in 1995.

Tramway

Type of operation: Conventional tramway

Vehicle-km: (1993) 34.2 million
(1994) 35.8 million
(1995) 30.5 million

Number of routes: 44
Route length: 395 km
Gauge: 1,435 mm and 1,000 mm, partly in tunnel/segregated track

U-Bahn, Stadtbahn and connecting tramway routes in the Rhein-Ruhr conurbation

Developments: A new tramway (8.4 km) was opened in June 1996 in Oberhausen. This is virtually an extension of the Mülheim network; though Oberhausen owns its own tramcars, all maintenance is being carried out by Mülheim.

LRT (Stadtbahn)

Type of operation: Light rail (Stadtbahn), first line opened 1977 (Essen/Mülheim, Düsseldorf, Dortmund, Bochum, Duisburg)

Vehicle-km: (1993) 7.2 million
(1994) 8.8 million
(1995) 9.2 million

Number of routes: 12
Route length: 138 km
in tunnel: 61 km
Number of stations: 113, plus 111 on feeder lines
in tunnel: 76
Max gradient: 4% (metro)
Minimum curve radius: 300 m (metro)
Gauge: 1,435 mm
Electrification: 750 V DC, overhead

Arrangements for elderly/disabled: All stations to be equipped or retrofitted with lifts

Rolling stock: See under individual city entries

Current situation: Stadtbahn-Gesellschaft Rhein-Ruhr was formed in 1969 by the cities of Bochum, Dortmund, Düsseldorf, Duisburg, Essen, Gelsenkirchen, Hattingen, Herne, Mülheim, Oberhausen, Recklinghausen, and Witten. Its remit was to establish guidelines for the construction and operation of a Stadtbahn (interurban light rail) system in the Rhein-Ruhr conurbation. It was merged with VRR in 1990. Actual planning and construction is the responsibility of individual cities. See earlier editions for background to the project.

There are four LRT networks, three of which will ultimately be linked, though a standard-gauge link between Essen and Bochum will not be realised in the foreseeable future.

Section A: Düsseldorf, Neuss, Krefeld and Duisburg, extensions planned to Dinslaken and link with Essen network at Mülheim; worked by Rheinbahn, Düsseldorf jointly with Duisburger Verkehrgesellschaft.

Section B: Essen/Mülheim, link with Bochum network ultimately planned at Gelsenkirchen; worked by Essener Verkehrsgesellschaft jointly with Betriebe der Stadt Mülheim.

Section C/D: Gelsenkirchen, Herne, Bochum, and Witten, extension planned to Hattingen worked by Bochum-Gelsenkirchener Strassenbahn. Some tunnel sections temporarily used by metre-gauge tramways.

Section E: Dortmund, extension planned to Castrop-Rauxel; worked by Dortmunder Stadtwerke.

Some 35 km is under construction, and by 2000 there should be 120 km of Stadtbahn and 62 km of converted tramways in operation. Future Stadtbahn routes will be built mainly on surface alignment.

This entry gives a general impression of the Stadtbahn. See entries under Bochum, Dortmund, Duisburg, Düsseldorf and Essen for individual progress in these cities.

Suspended monorail (see Wuppertal entry)

LRT Type B car of Essener Verkehrs AG in tunnel station

DB

Deutsche Bahn AG, Geschäftsbereich Nahverkehr
Regionalbereich Rhein-Ruhr
Bismarckplatz 1, 45128 Essen
Telephone: +49 201 182 3330 Fax: +49 201 182 4475
Manager, S-Bahn: Christian Plattenteich
Responsible for northern part of the network

Deutsche Bahn AG, Geschäftsberiech Nahverkehr
Regionalbereich Rheinland
Konrad-Adenauer-Ufer 3, 50668 Köln
Telephone: +49 221 141421 Fax: +49 221 141 4224
Manager, S-Bahn: Hans-Joachim Geupel
Responsible for southern part of the network

Type of operation: Regional metro (S-Bahn) and other suburban services

Current situation: S-Bahn (segregated tracks) and other suburban services provided over networks of 336 and 1,104 km respectively, electrified at 15 kV 16⅔ Hz. S-Bahn comprises seven routes with 116 stations; 30 suburban rail routes. Fare structure is as VRR, with supplement for first class travel; services co-ordinated with other modes.

Network of lines links Unna, Dortmund, Bochum, Essen, Mülheim, Duisburg, Düsseldorf, Neuss, Mönchengladbach, Wuppertal and Hagen, with branches.

Developments: Further upgrading of S2 from Dortmund to Duisburg via Herne and Oberhausen in progress. North-south S9 from Haltern via Essen to Wuppertal, and S5 from Dortmund to Witten via Hagen, are at the planning stage. Separate tracks are to be built between Düsseldorf and Duisburg to segregate S-Bahn services. Minibar catering service is provided by contractors on some trains.

VRR and Dortmunder Stadtwerke have commissioned studies into whether S-Bahn service on some routes might be provided more economically by operators other than DB.

Rolling stock: S-Bahn services operated by push-pull trainsets of between three and five cars; conventional stock used elsewhere

VESTISCHE

Vestische Strassenbahnen GmbH
Westerholter Str 550, 45701 Herten
Telephone: +49 2366 1860 Fax: +49 2366 186444
Managers: Georg Aigner
Ulrich Rogat
Staff: 1,112

Push-pull trains on Line S2 at Dortmund-Westerfilde

Bus

Passenger journeys: (1993) 52.7 million
(1994) 54.1 million
(1995) 54.1 million
Vehicle-km: (1993) 21.3 million
(1994) 20.4 million
(1995) 20.1 million

Route length: 1,465 km
Fleet: 244 vehicles, plus 82 hired

Current situation: Local authority-owned bus company providing service in Recklinghausen and Bottrop and the densely populated area between and around these cities. Neoplan N4012 Metroliner carbon-fibre buses used in the Gladbeck area.

Both the Neoplan 15 m Megatrans and the N4014DE diesel-electric bus with hub motors have been evaluated.

BVR

Busverkehr Rheinland GmbH
Worringer Str 34-42, 40211 Düsseldorf
Telephone: +49 211 169900 Fax: +49 211 169 9066
Managing Directors: Dipl-Ing Jürgen Asmuth
Norbert Schomaker

Passenger journeys: (1994) 38.7 million
(1995) 40.3 million
Vehicle-km: (1994) 28.2 million
(1995) 27.8 million

Fleet: 156 buses, plus 517 hired

Current situation: Regional bus company associated with DB, providing suburban and regional bus services on some 60 routes within VRR area and others beyond. Figures above apply to all BVR operations.

UPDATED

RIGA

Population: 826,000
Public transport: Bus and tramway/trolleybus services provided by separate companies under control of municipal authority; suburban rail services by State Railway; metro construction suspended

City Council of Riga

City Council of Riga
Valdemara iela 3, 1539 Riga, Latvia

Current situation: Public transport in Riga, formerly co-ordinated by the ministry of transport, is now the responsibility of the city council, which has direct control of the trolleybus and tramway system. Bus operations are in the hands of two companies, Imanta and Talava.

The trolleybus network has expanded in the past decade, in particular to routes across two new bridges over the Daugava river.

Fare structure: Flat
Fare collection: On board or prepurchase single tickets or monthly passes (all modes), with validating/cancelling machines on board

Bus

Operated by:
Imanta, Kleistu iela 29, 1067 Riga

Talava, Vestienas iela 35, 1039 Riga

Ex-København Volvo still in HT livery on Route 16

1997

Passenger boardings: (1993) 109.8 million
(1994) 108 million
(1995) 105.8 million
Vehicle-km: (1994) 18 million

Number of routes: 37
Route length: 504 km
Fleet: 333 vehicles

Ikarus 280 articulated	207
Ikarus 260/263	81
Volvo ex-København	27
MAN	10
Scania CR111 ex-Uppsala	7
DAF	1

In peak service: 207

Operating costs financed by: Fares 53.5%, other commercial sources 1.7%, subsidy/grants 31.8%, deficit 13%

Taxi/shared taxi/minibus

Staff: 1,190

Passenger journeys: (1991) 13 million
(1992) 3.8 million
(1993) 2.6 million

Current situation: Shared taxis operate on seven urban and four suburban routes totalling 360 km; over 4,000 ordinary taxis also ply for hire.

Fleet: 850 vehicles, including 50 AF2203 Latvia microbuses

TTP

Tramway & Trolleybus Board
Brivibas iela 191, 1012 Riga

Trolleybus

Passenger journeys: (1993) 112 million
(1994) 110.6 million
(1995) 98.7 million
Vehicle-km: (Annual) 17 million

Number of routes: 24
Route length: 180 km
Fleet: 350 trolleybuses, some 9Tr run in multiple

Skoda 9Tr	100
Skoda 14Tr	226
Skoda 15Tr articulated	24

In peak service: 271

Operating costs financed by: Fares 68.2%, other commercial sources 1.7%, subsidy/grants 20.7%, deficit 7.3%

Tatra T3s and Skoda double traction trolleybus on Brivibas iela ***1997***

Tramway

Type of operation: Conventional tramway

Passenger journeys: (1993) 90 million
(1994) 88.1 million
(1995) 79.7 million
Vehicle-km: (Annual) 15 million

Route length: 123 km
Number of routes: 8
Gauge: 1,524 mm
Electrification: 600 V DC, collection by trolley pole

Rolling stock: 271 cars

ČKD Tatra T3 (1975/87)	M209
ČKD Tatra T3M (1988/90)	M62

In peak service: 171

Latvian Railway (LDZ)

Latvijas dzelzcels
Gogola iela 3, 1003 Riga
Telephone: +371 2 234440 Fax: +371 2 820231

Type of operations: Suburban heavy rail

Passenger journeys: (1991) 75 million
(1992) 70 million
(1993) 50 million

Current situation: Suburban services are operated over six routes totalling 710 km, electrified 3 kV DC, fleet of 57 emus.

Metro (planned)

Current situation: Approval granted 1982 for construction of a 19.9 km line with 16 stations linking the city centre with housing and industrial areas on the opposite bank of the Daugava river; 1,524 mm gauge, electrified 825 V DC. Construction started 1986 on the initial section of Line 1, with eight stations, but was suspended in 1990 pending re-examination of the 1975 plans for tramway expansion. This reflected loss of metro expertise and rolling stock supply following independence.

UPDATED

RIO DE JANEIRO

Population: 5.8 million, metropolitan area (including Niterói and 13 other cities) 10.2 million
Public transport: Bus services (and also residual tramway) provided in part by state-controlled public company and in part by more than 60 independent operators and co-operatives, which provide all services in adjoining city of Niterói and also operate a number of premium express services across conurbation. Metro run by separate company; ferries across Guanabara Bay; suburban railways controlled by regional authority; extensive illegal bus and van services

Refurbished Series 1000 emu in new Flumitrens livery ***1996***

CTC-RJ

Companhia de Transportes Colectivos do Estado do Rio de Janeiro
Rua Bérgamo, 320 ZC 15 Rio de Janeiro, Brazil
Telephone: +55 21 281 9922
President: Luiz Armando de Matos

Bus

Current situation: Rio's municipally owned bus operation, which had been reduced to a mere 27 routes, was being prepared for privatisation in 1996 by a new President. But the company's chronic financial state seemed destined to force complete closure at the end of 1996. The fleet is mothballed awaiting disposal, with 177 gas-powered buses and 50 articulated to be sold. The remaining diesel buses cannot be used again in Rio because of a prohibition of vehicles over seven years old.

Tramway

Type of operation: Conventional tramway

Passenger journeys: Approx 3 million (annual)

Current situation: Two tram routes totalling 8.2 km survive to serve the hilly suburb of Santa Teresa, operated with vintage rolling stock, partly as a tourist attraction. The Carioca tramway has survived due to its unique central area access across a broad valley on a single track atop an arched stone aqueduct. Trams run half-hourly from 06.00 to 23.30; fares revenue covers only the cost of the electricity required to run the service.

Developments: With the likely closure of CTC, the tramway is to be taken over by either the Rio municipality or a co-operative of former CTC workers.

Rolling stock: 17 cars

St Louis Car/General Electric (1909)	M17

Cia do Metropolitano

Companhia do Metropolitano do Rio de Janeiro
Av NS de Copacabana 493, CEP 22020-000 Rio de Janeiro
Telephone: +55 21 255 9292 Fax: +55 21 235 4546
President: Alvaro José Martins Santos
Director of Operations: Luiz de Lucca e Silva
Staff: 2,700

Type of operation: Full metro and light rail, first line opened 1979

Passenger journeys: (1992) 87 million
(1993) 86.8 million
(1995) 85 million

Route length: Metro (Line 1) 11.6 km, all in tunnel; light rail/pre-metro (Line 2) 13.9 km
Number of lines: 2
Number of stations: 24
Gauge: 1,600 mm
Max gradient: 4%
Minimum curve radius: 500 m
Tunnel: Mainly cut-and-cover; various techniques, including diaphragm walls up to 1.2 m thick, used to prevent soil subsidence and property damage due to high water table
Electrification: 750 V DC, third rail

Service: 3 min 45 s Line 1, 5 min Line 2; Sunday service operates only on special occasions
First/last train: 06.00/23.00
Fare structure: Flat, with combined bus/rail and rail/ferry ticket for some journeys
Revenue control: Automatic fare collection
Integration with other modes: Suburban rail, ferries, and some bus
Automatic control: Automatic pilot system

Rolling stock: 146 metro and 30 LRVs, of which 76 metro and 12 LRVs in serviceable condition

Mafersa A cab cars	M46
Cobrasma B	M100
Cobrasma/BN LRV	M30

On order: Six trains; a further 44 existing cars being refurbished

Current situation: Development of Rio's metro has not met with the success recorded in São Paulo. Funding problems and lack of commitment on the part of city and state government led to difficulties in getting the first sections into operation. Only part of the metro and pre-metro car fleets had been delivered when the money was cut, so services are limited by shortages, and by the problems caused in 1988 when the city was declared bankrupt.

In a reversal of the state government's previous stance, a plan was approved in 1987 for a 4 km extension from Botafago through the Copacabana area to General Osório, and for rehabilitation and completion of the truncated Line 2. A further 22 metro cars were supplied, but deliveries were stopped during a further financial crisis in 1990.

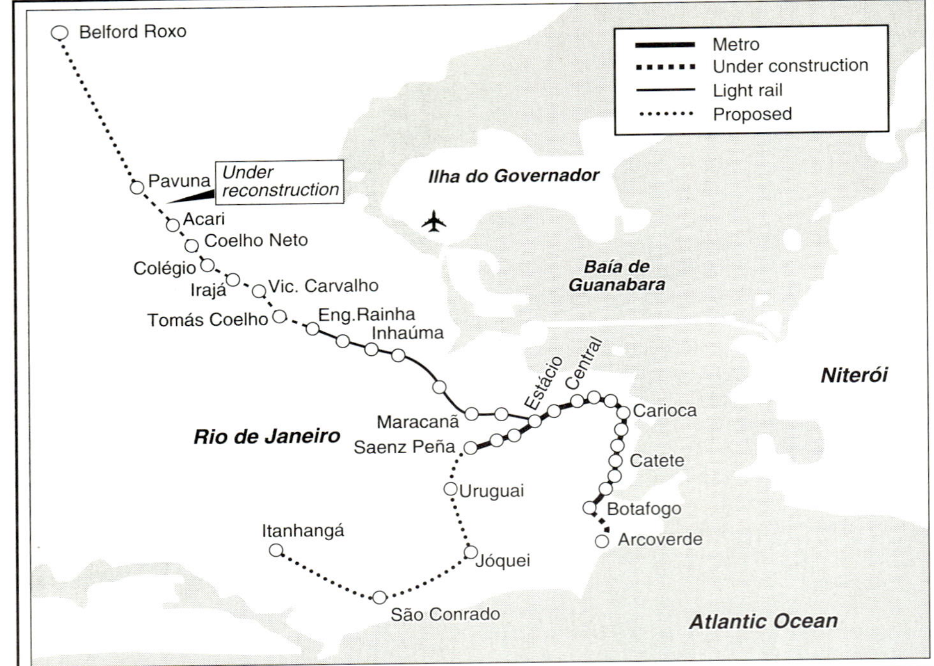

Rio de Janeiro metro

Volvo-Ciferal bus at bus-metro interchange at São Cristovão station

Line 1 is in operation from Botafago to Saenz Peña, while Line 2 from Estácio to Inhaúma (reopened from Maria da Gracia in 1987) is worked by pre-metro cars powered from a third rail following dismantling of the overhead current collection system. The extension to Pavuna, closed in 1985, has suffered from vandalism and looting of equipment, but the section from Inhaúma to Engenho da Rainha was reopened as light rail in 1990.

Developments: The municipality has decided not to assume managerial control of the metro; although it has shown a willingness to provide operating funds, it has not so far done so. The metro authority continues to seek further loans from the World Bank, but Brazil's national development bank BNDES agreed funding of R$171 million to enable construction to continue. Work on Line 1, paralysed for more than six years, started again in 1995 on the Botofago–Arcoverde section, along with construction of a new turnback facility at Saenz Peña. The extension to Arcoverde is scheduled to open in October 1997. Still under discussion is a 12 km extension of this line from Saenz Peña to Itanhangá.

Line 2 construction also recommenced in 1995 between Engenho da Rainha and Pavuna, now due to open in June 1998, although more ambitious suggestions have been proposed for an eventual extension to Belford Roxo where there would be connections with Flumitrens suburban services. These two extensions will add 12 km to the network and are expected to boost patronage from the current 400,000 daily to around 1 million. On completion, operational changes are planned for Line 2, with a heavy metro service between Estácio and Irajá and light rail vehicles running thence to Pavuna; 6.5 min headways would apply on both sections.

Rio de Janeiro's state government is seeking US$1.6 billion to finance an intermodal public transport project in the metropolitan region; half of the money would come from the World Bank and the balance from the state. Some $400 million would go to the metro, with a further $100 million earmarked for the proposed Niterói–São Gonçalo light rail line.

The state government wants to put maintenance and operation of the metro out to tender on a 20-year concession. Assets would remain with the state, which would also fund expansion.

CTC-RJ feeder bus service linking metro with Copacabana

Flumitrens

Companhia Fluminense de Trens Urbanos
Edificio da Estacão Dom Pedro II, Praca Cristiano Ottoni, s/no Centro, Rio de Janeiro, CEP 20221-250
Telephone: +55 21 233 8594 Fax: +55 21 253 3089
President: Marcus Poggi
Staff: 7,000

Type of operation: Suburban heavy rail

Passenger journeys: (1992) 160 million
(1993) 132 million
(1994) 111 million

Current situation: Flumitrens operates frequent suburban services (peak hours every 7-15 min) over some 264 km of route on 1,600 mm gauge (171 km, of which

163 km electrified 3 kV DC overhead) and 1,000 mm gauge (92 km), operated as eight routes with 127 stations. Fares cover 16 per cent of operating expenditure (1995).

Developments: Under plans for decentralisation of the national urban rail operator CBTU, Rio's suburban railways came under the control of a new regional (state) company at the end of 1994. Funding shortages had brought Rio's suburban railways to near-collapse; the accumulated debt has been retained by the federal government, but all assets passed to Flumitrens. Staff numbers have been substantially reduced as a prelude to privatisation.

The decentralisation project includes an investment component to complete the modernisation programme begun more than a decade ago, but which had made little progress, and a further element to fund implementation of a modernised management strategy. An agreement with the World Bank was signed in 1994, under which a US$272 million investment programme was approved, and a further scheme valued at US$372.5 million was being negotiated with BIRD in 1995. This forms part of a state programme of transport improvements for the Rio metropolitan area, involving both public and private operators. Amongst other aims, this master plan would increase private sector participation in urban transport provision, encourage integration, and develop new funding policies.

Rolling stock upgrading continues, with 73 cars being refurbished under a World Bank loan and a further 46 funded by BNDES. A further 15 emu trains are on order, also funded by the World Bank.

Rolling stock: 243 emu sets, normally operated as six- or eight-car trains; 86 loco-hauled coaches, 61 diesel locomotives

Metro-Vick S-200 (1957)	M90 T180
GE S-400 (1964)	M90 T180
Nippon Sharyo S-500 (1977)	M60 T60
Mafersa S-700 (1980)	M60 T60
Santa Matilde S-800 (1980)	M120 T120
Cobrasma S-900 (1980)	M120 T120

In peak service: 58 emu sets, 6 diesel-hauled trains

Private bus

Licensed and supervised by:
Superintêndencia Municipal de Transportes Urbanos (SMTU)
Secretary: Márcio Queiroz

Current situation: A major part of the city's services is provided by 33 independent bus operators under licences issued by the municipality for the operation of defined services at set fares levels, though the level of supervision is low. Services include all-seated premium express commuter links with air conditioned coaches aimed particularly at private car commuters, and microbuses. SMTU also licenses the city's 20,000 legal taxis.

Developments: In March 1996, Rio municipality issued tenders for operation of 12 new bus routes, the first time this has been done for 22 years. This implies acquisition of 150 new buses, with concessions being awarded to the companies promising most investment (in terminals and signalling), as well as the most modern and comfortable buses. The new routes are needed because the existing network is saturated. SMTU no longer requires operators to have a minimum fleet of 120 buses.

Bus

Passenger journeys: (1991) 1,870 million
Vehicle-km: (1991) 557.5 million

Number of routes: 450
Route length: 18,433 km

PT-20 hydrofoil Flecha de Niteroi *operated by Transtur*

Fleet: 6,205 buses, of which 5,864 are standard Mercedes or Volvo chassis with Padron bodies, and the remainder microbuses and air conditioned seat-only coaches
In peak service: 5,770

Fare collection: Payment to conductor seated at turnstile near rear entrance
Fare structure: Flat in city
Average peak-hour speed: 9 km/h
Operating costs financed by: Fares 100%; Vale Transporte tickets subsidised by employers up to 6% of wage levels

Other bus operators

Current situation: In addition to the licensed operations described above, there are estimated to be some 2,000 buses and 5,000 vans which operate illegally. Unlicensed paratransit vans originally provided late-evening shuttle services from the city centre to the suburbs, but they now run regular commuter services to the north and west of the city, and also to Niterói. Vehicles range from Kombis to imported 14-seater Topics with air conditioning, music and reclining seats. Some operators offer free drinks and sweets.

Some vans shadow regular bus routes, calling at the same stops and poaching passengers, while others demand references from prospective passengers to avoid police surveillance. SMTU's tiny staff cannot keep pace with the spread of illegal operations, and in any case attempts to close them down have led to violent confrontations between passengers and the authorities. Surveys by the illegal operators apparently show that 85 per cent of their passengers are car owners attracted by the fast and comfortable services, even though fares are higher than on regular routes.

Many of the illegal buses are run by co-operatives, with better-paid drivers and lower fares than licensed vehicles. It is estimated that 10 to 15 pirate buses begin operating every day.

CONERJ

Companhia de Navigação do Estado do Rio de Janeiro
Praça 15 de Novembro 21, Rio de Janeiro, CEP 20010-010
Telephone: +55 21 231 0398
President: J Washington Lobo
Staff: 930

Ferry

Passenger journeys: (1991) 33 million

Current situation: CONERJ is the Rio de Janeiro government-owned ferry operator, providing services between Rio and Niterói, Paquetá Island and Governador Island across Guanabara Bay, plus Mangaratiba–Grande Island and Grande Island–Angra dos Reis; total five routes. On the Niterói route (5 km) a fleet of 2,000-passenger vessels provides departures every 7 min during peak hours, 15-30 min off-peak.

On the longer routes to Paquetá Island (18.8 km) and Governador Island (11.5 km) there are eight journeys daily taking about 1 h 40 min, using vessels of 1,000-passenger capacity.

Total fleet of 18 vessels; fares cover about one-third of costs with Rio state funding the difference.

Transtur

Aerobarcos do Brasil, Transportes Maritimos e Turismo
Praça Iaia Garcia 03, Ribeira, Rio de Janeiro 21930-040
Telephone: +55 21 396 3567/594 Fax: +55 21 396 3965
Director of Administration: Hamilton Amarante Carvalho
Staff: 207

Ferry

Passenger journeys: (1994) 5.2 million

Current situation: Operates between Rio and Niterói, every 10 min from 06.15 to 20.15, and between Rio and Paquetá Island every 2 h weekdays and hourly at weekends and holidays. Fares cover 100 per cent of costs.

Developments: In 1996, six air conditioned catamarans were purchased from Singapore, replacing hydrofoils on many journeys and cutting the Rio–Niterói journey time from 30 to 10 min.

Light rail (planned)

Current situation: Attempts to build a 25 km light rail line in the western suburbs were abandoned in 1995. Despite extending the concession period from 10 to 30 years, no private sector companies entered compliant bids of sufficient standing. The project is now being taken forward by the municipality as a busway, or possibly a trolleybusway.

Monorail

Current situation: An Intamin straddle monorail (1.9 km, 3 stations) opened in May 1996 serving the Barra shopping retail development in the west of the city. Two 10-car trains provide capacity of 7,000 passengers/day. Extensions have been proposed to serve the Barra residential district and, later, to the Alvorada bus terminal.

UPDATED

RIYADH

Population: 700,000
Public transport: Bus services provided on a concession basis by SAPTCO, a semi-government company sponsored by the Ministry of Communications, also serving other Saudi cities and providing interurban network for total population of 9 million. Also privately owned shared taxis, limousines and minibuses

SAPTCO

Saudi Public Transport Company (SAPTCO)
PO Box 10667, Riyadh 11443, Saudi Arabia
Telephone: +966 1 454 5000 Telex: 402414/200987
Director General: Dr Saad A Al-Ghamdi
Marketing Manager: Kalid A Al-Jarallah
Staff: 2,418 (company total)

Current situation: Formed in 1979, SAPTCO developed rapidly into a fully fledged bus operation. Apart from operations in Riyadh, eight other cities are served by both urban and intercity services. In addition, every year SAPTCO is called upon to provide special services for the large numbers of pilgrims travelling during the Hajj period. See *JUTS 1988* for history of SAPTCO.

Bus (Riyadh city operations)
Passenger journeys: (1988/89) 8.1 million
(1990/91) 7.2 million

Number of routes: 21
Fleet: 1,195 for urban services, of which 413 used in Riyadh city

Neoplan 442/2 double-deck	129
Neoplan 414 single-deck	720
Neoplan N421 articulated	2
Isuzu minibus	28
Leyland	1
Toyota Coaster 25-seat	21
Toyota Coaster 29-seat	110
Mitsubishi Coaster 27-seat	84
Mercedes 91 (1992)	100

SAPTCO buses in Riyadh

One-person operation: All services
Fare collection: Exact fare to farebox
Fare structure: Flat; prepurchase ticket books at discount
Fares collected on board: 70%
Fare evasion control: Spot checks and observation
Operational control: Route inspectors and mobile bus regulators
Arrangements for elderly/disabled: Half fare
Operating costs financed by: Fares 50%, charter and contract work 10%, government subsidy/grants 40%
New vehicles financed by: Government grant

ROCHESTER

Population: 690,000
Public transport: Bus services provided in Rochester and surrounding areas by operating agency of regional transport authority controlled by representative board

Regional Transit Service

Rochester-Genesee Regional Transportation Authority
PO Box 90629, 1372 E Main Street, Rochester, NY 14609, USA
Telephone: +1 716 654 0200 Fax: +1 716 654 0293
Chairman: Andrew F Caverly
Chief Executive Officer: Donald J Riley
Director of Special Services: Robert Finke
Director of Urban Service: Ellen Cicero
Staff: 500

Current situation: As well as a fixed-route urban network in Rochester and surrounding areas of Monroe County, supplemented by peak-hour express routes, RTS operates rural bus services in Livingston County (LATS), the city of Batavia (B-Line) in Genesee County, Wayne County (WATS) and Wyoming County (WYTS) — all operated by small buses, some on dial-a-bus basis. It also operates Lift Line Inc, a fully accessible paratransit service. Figures below cover all operations; rural services carried some 350,000 passengers in 1994/95.

Developments: New Express Flyer services were introduced in 1994, serving park-and-ride in the eastern and western suburbs. Fixed-route and dial-a-bus schedules were improved in Wyoming and Genesee counties, and a campus shuttle service inaugurated at the University of Rochester supported by an 80 per cent subsidy from the university.

The undertaking's only dedicated funding source, a Mortgage Recording Tax, declined in 1994/95 after two windfall years, and it was necessary to draw on reserves to avoid a deficit. New sources of dedicated funding are being sought.

The New York State DoT awarded a grant of $0.4 million to finance improved co-ordination of transport services for disabled people in Monroe County.

Bus
Passenger boardings: (1991/92) 15 million
(1993/94) 13.2 million
(1994/95) 14.2 million

RTS bus in downtown Rochester

Vehicle-km: (1991/92) 9.4 million
(1993/94) 9.1 million
(1994/95) 12.6 million

Number of routes: 31
Route length: (One way) 960 km
Fleet: 337 vehicles

GMC RTS (1982/83)	75
Flxible Metro (1986)	17
Gillig Phantom (1988/91)	33
MAN SG310 articulated (1984)	10
Orion V (1990/93)	48
Orion V CNG-powered (1992)	5
Thomas/BIA/other midi/minibus	80
NovaBus Classic (1995/96}	69

In peak service: 244

Most intensive service: 15 min
Fare structure: Flat; prepurchase 10-ride tickets and monthly pass; transfers 10 cents; free service 11.00-14.00 in downtown Rochester
Fare collection: Coin to farebox
Arrangements for elderly/disabled: 100 lift-equipped buses; Lift Line is demand-responsive accessible service provided throughout RTS area using 21 low-floor buses, carried 132,000 passengers in 1994/95.
Integration with other modes: Peak-hour express buses serve 31 suburban park-and-ride sites; Park-and-Ride Plus express routes provide suburb-to-suburb commuter service
Operating costs financed by: Fares 39%, subsidy/grants 45%, other commercial sources 6%, tax levy 10%
Subsidy from: FTA, state and county funds

UPDATED

ROMA

Population: 2.8 million
Public transport: Bus and tramway services provided by municipal undertaking. Metro, suburban railway and suburban bus services operated by separate authority. Other suburban rail services by State Railway (FS)

ATAC

Azienda Tranvie e Autobus del Comune di Roma (ATAC)
Via Volturno 65, 00185 Roma, Italy
Telephone: +39 6 46951 Fax: +39 6 4695 2087
President: Lucciano Niccolai
General Manager: Domenico Mazzamurro
Operating Manager: Ottavio Mirabelli
Staff: 12,691

Passenger journeys: (All modes)
(1991) 817 million
(1992) 811 million
(1994) 821 million

Operating costs financed by: Fares 23%, other commercial sources 2.5%, subsidy/grants 74.5%

Current situation: ATAC is responsible for bus and tramway services. Creation of new connections and extension of existing routes has been an objective, but increases in fares to improve on the very low farebox recovery rate led to significant passenger losses. Some recovery has been evident since 1991, with growth in bus traffic particularly strong.

A new city government elected in 1993 had as one of its principal aims a dramatic improvement in public transport provision, and several new tram routes in the historic city centre and extensions have been proposed. There are to be more interchanges and park-and-ride, designed to encourage more drivers to leave their cars at home.

Developments: A new transport authority is planned for the region. It will comprise Roma municipality (51 per cent), Lazio region (30 per cent) and FS (20 per cent), and will take responsibility for all modes including FS trains, though assets would be retained by members. The debts of ATAC and Cotral would pass to the municipality.

Merger of the two undertakings has been proposed, but apparently is not now to go ahead. Nevertheless, an integrated management structure has been established. This has seen staffing levels cut by 17.5 per cent, with more redundancies planned. Nevertheless, the deficits for 1995 and 1996, at Lit65 billion for each year, were much higher than budget.

An all-modes integrated tariff system known as Metrebus was introduced throughout the Lazio region in 1994, covering some 378 municipalities and believed to be the largest scheme of its type in Europe. ATAC, Cotral and FS bus and train services are involved in the system, which is based on zones. A 5 per cent increase in patronage was recorded in the first few months; the ultimate goal is to raise public transport's market share by 25 per cent by the end of the century.

ATAC tram and buses at the Route 19 terminus close to the Vatican **1996**

Former metro stock now operates on Cotral's Lido line **1996**

Bus

Passenger journeys: (1991) 696 million
(1992) 740 million
(1994) 749.3 million
Vehicle-km: (1991) 120 million
(1992) 121.4 million
(1994) 120.4 million

Number of routes: 235 (27 night routes)
Route length: (One way) 2,042 km
On priority right-of-way: 66 km
Fleet: 2,452 vehicles

Fiat 306EX	10
Fiat 418AL	549
Fiat 421A	60
Pollicino TH16	4
Pollicino 35P/A	20
Fiat 470	183
Menarini 201/1-2	96
Inbus/U210	670
Fiat Effeuno	512
Fiat 480	200
Bredabus 2001	96
Fiat Microbus	40
Fiat Micro Electric	8
Fiat 242	4

In peak service: 77% of fleet

Most intensive service: 2 min
One-person operation: 99%
Fare collection: Prepurchase from machines; cancelling machines on board
Fare structure: Flat; prepurchase multitickets; weekly and monthly passes; ticket with 90 min time limit; combined ATAC/Acotral/FS passes
Fares collected on board: 71% of passengers hold passes; onboard ticket sales confined to 3 daytime routes and all night services
Fare evasion control: Inspectors
Integration with other modes: Connections with two metro lines; flat fare and passes for all modes
Operational control: Route inspectors; mobile radio with computerised online monitoring
Arrangements for elderly/disabled: Experimental operation of 4 lift-equipped minibuses
Average distance between stops: 250-350 m
Average peak-hour speed: In bus lanes, 16-18 km/h; in mixed traffic, 13.8 km/h

Developments: Route 119 city-centre tourist shuttle inaugurated September 1996 using electric minibuses, following an earlier experiment with such vehicles which was not successful. Automated dot-matrix destination displays are being adopted. Mobile radio installed on 400 vehicles.

Finance is being sought for purchase of 240 high-capacity 18 m buses and 50 urban midibuses.

Tramway

Type of operation: Conventional tramway

Passenger journeys: (1992) 71 million
(1994) 71.6 million
(1995) 72 million
Car-km: (1992) 4.7 million
(1994) 4.9 million

Route length: 60 km
Number of lines: 7
Gauge: 1,445 mm
Max gradient: 7.4%
Minimum curve radius: 18 m
Track: Conventional sleepers on ballast
Electrification: 600 V DC, overhead

Service: Peak 3 min, off-peak 14 min
First/last car: 05.00/24.00
Fare structure: Flat
One-person operation: On most cars
Centralised control: Radio-telephone

Rolling stock: 118 cars

Stanga	M58
PCC	M22
MRS	M8
Socimi Type T8000 (1990/92)	M30

On order: 28 double-articulated low-floor cars from Fiat to operate the Casaletto-Torre Argentina line

One-person operation: All routes   Uritsky ZIU9   Approx 250   ČKD Tatra T3m   M40

extension opens in June 1998. Funding comes from the federal Congestion Mitigation & Air Quality Improvement Programme, state rail bonds and local sales tax revenue.

Completion of the Mather Field extension will be followed by a start on constructing the 5 km to Sunrise Boulevard. A further 38 cars are required for the four extensions.

Other operators

Current situation: Contracted 'Yolobus' services are provided on eight routes in Yolo County into central Sacramento from Davis and West Sacramento by Yolo County Transit Authority (27 buses). Unitrans (40 buses) operates in Davis only. These two operators together carry some 2 million passengers annually.

Other local door-to-door services are provided in Roseville, Folsom, Marysville/Yuba City and El Dorado County.

Commuter rail (proposed)

Current situation: A suburban rail service is proposed to link Folsom with the future Mather Field light rail station. Folsom city council is to fund rehabilitation of the 16 km Southern Pacific line between the two locations, and will purchase or lease five diesel railcars.

UPDATED

SALT LAKE CITY

Population: 726,000, area served 1.3 million

Public transport: Bus services provided by regional transit authority for city and surrounding areas of Salt Lake, Utah, Davis, Weber and Tooele counties. Light rail under construction

UTA

Utah Transit Authority
3600 South 700 West, PO Box 30810, Salt Lake City, UT 84130-0810, USA
Telephone: +1 801 262 5626   Fax: +1 801 287 4614
President: Steven Randall
General Manager: John C Pingree
Staff: 1,050

Current situation: UTA started operations in Salt Lake County in 1970, and operations in Davis and Weber counties were annexed by voter approval in 1973. All private transit operations in the three-county area were incorporated into UTA in 1975.

In 1974, voters in Salt Lake and Weber counties approved a ¼ per cent sales tax to fund public transport, and Davis County followed suit a year later. In 1985, UTA expanded service into the Provo and Orem city areas of Utah County. In 1989, four cities in northern Utah County agreed to join the transit district and impose the ¼ per cent tax. The following year, elections brought one more Utah County city, plus Tooele and Grantsville in Tooele County, into the district. Operations were extended to the cities of Alpine, Cedar Hills and Highland in 1994, and to Mapleton, Payson, Salem, Spanish Fork and Sundance in 1995.

Of 133 regular routes, 78 run in the Salt Lake area, 33 in Ogden, and 15 serve Utah and Tooele counties. There is a summer-only downtown circulator in Salt Lake City operated by replica trolleys. During the winter months, UTA operates seven busy routes to four nearby skiing areas.

Developments: In 1992, Salt Lake County voters rejected imposition of a further ¼ per cent sales tax to fund the local share of a transit expansion programme. Three-quarters of the money raised would have been used to finance a greatly expanded bus system and an initial 24 km light rail line. Despite the election result, preliminary engineering work on the expansion programme continued, and construction of the light rail route was expected to start in early 1997 (see below) following final approval by the UTA board in July 1996.

Heavily discounted passes introduced for large employers and the University of Utah have proved successful in reducing parking demands and costs, as well as increasing ridership.

After community-wide consultation, a comprehensive transit plan has been developed for the coming 20 years. Planned improvements include expansion of Flextrans service, and extension of service to developing suburban communities.

Bus

Passenger journeys: (1992) 22.6 million
(1993) 22.8 million
(1994) 23.3 million

GM Classic of UTA on downtown service

Vehicle-km: (1992) 29.9 million
(1993) 31.2 million
(1994) 32.5 million

Number of routes: 153
Fleet: 446 vehicles, plus 48 inactive

GMC Classic (1983/84)	77
Gillig Phantom (1984/87)	89
Orion II (1988/89)	52
MCI TAC40102N (1990)	66
Orion I (1991)	9
Orion V (1992/93)	128
Chance replica trolleys (1984/85)	8
Ford vans (paratransit)	15
Classic (1991)	2

In peak service: 377, plus 33 for ski service

Most intensive service: 10 min
One-person operation: All routes
Fare collection: Manual drop fareboxes; tokens
Fare structure: Flat, free in Salt Lake city-centre and state capitol zone; Express, worker and ski bus services have higher fare; discount passes for large employers, university students, faculty and staff
Fares collected on board: 50%
Fare evasion control: Periodic observation of operators by outside security firm
Integration with other modes: Park-and-ride service to local ski resorts; Utah LIFT regional ride-sharing programme encourages car- and vanpools, 77 operating in 1994; 43 park-and-ride lots used for ride-sharing, with several also served by buses
Operational control: Route supervisors/mobile radio
Arrangements for elderly/disabled: Reduced fares; accessible fixed-route service offered on several main corridors in Salt Lake City; over 300 buses lift-equipped; Flextrans demand-responsive and accessible fixed-route service with low flat fare; separate demand-responsive service in other counties; customer services for persons with disabilities, eg Braille timetables; all fixed routes to be fully accessible by 1998
Operating costs financed by: Fares 16.5%, other commercial sources 4.8%, FTA subsidy 6.2%, sales tax 72.5%

Light rail

Under construction

Current situation: Construction was expected to start in early 1997 on a light rail line linking the centre of Salt Lake City with Sandy City (24 km, 17 stations) utilising Union Pacific rail right-of-way. This would form the initial stage of a corridor route linking Ogden, Salt Lake City and Provo.

The FTA had originally accorded the scheme low priority on account of its undue reliance (75 per cent) on traffic mitigation funds likely to be provided for reconstruction of highway I-15. But this situation changed in 1995 following selection of Salt Lake City to host the 2002 Winter Olympics. Federal funding amounting to $241 million was approved in August 1995, and will be supplemented by $70 million raised locally. A fleet of 23 cars is on order from Siemens Transportation. The line is expected to open in late 1998.

The line will take over a single-track UP route purchased by UTA in 1993, and over which freight trains are run by a short line operator. The route will be doubled for its new role as a passenger carrier, but freight trains will still run during night hours.

UPDATED

SALVADOR

Population: 2.3 million

Public transport: Bus services provided by one public undertaking and 18 franchised private groups supervised by municipal organisation. Suburban rail services operated by Brazilian Urban Railways Company (CBTU). Ferry service. Funiculars and public elevator. Mass transit proposed

STP

Superintendência de Transporte Público
Avenida Tancredo Neves 2.681, 41820-021 Salvador, Bahia, Brazil
Telephone: +55 71 231 9645   Fax: +55 71 231 7180
Superintendent: José Ivan Dantas Pugliese
Staff: 535

Current situation: Organising provision of bus services is the responsibility of STP, set up in 1992 as successor to the former SETRAM organisation. STP co-ordinates and supervises the services of 18 private and one publicly owned bus operator (for which SMTU is the holding company) working under franchises issued by the municipality (see below for list of private operators and

their fleets). It also operates the major Lapa and Pirajá bus stations and plans bus priority and promotional measures. STP oversees planning of bus services, sets fares levels and supervises the franchisees.
Developments: Studies are taking place into possible introduction of a high-capacity mass transit system over a 25 km corridor, probably on existing surface rights-of-way. The technology has yet to be chosen.

Passenger journeys: (All operators)
(1993) 498 million
(1994) 498.4 million
(1995) 533.5 million
Vehicle-km: (1993) 181 million
(1994) 184 million
(1995) 212 million

Number of routes: 424 (including 9 executive, 6 semi-express and 15 night)
Route length: 15,919 km (roads covered 1,475 km)
Fleet: 2,569 buses
In peak service: 2,078
Operating costs financed by: Fares 100%

Buses of several franchised operators

Private bus

Current situation: There are 18 franchised companies: Axé Transportes (138 buses), Bahia (158), Boa Viagem (266), Campo Grande (92), Farol da Barra (192), Itapoan Transportes Triunfo (166), Joevanza (71), Lapa (128), Liberdade (76), Ondina (197), Rio Vermelho (140), São Pedro (172), Sul America (182), Transol (110), Verdemar (115), União (157), Visa (42), and Vitral (87).

Fleet: 2,489 buses including Mercedes types LPO1113, OF1113, OH1313, OH1517, O364 and Volvo Padron

Transur

Empresa de Transportes Urbanos de Salvador (Transur)
Rodovia BR-324 Km 85, Pirajá, Salvador, Bahia CEP 40000
Executive Director: Marcus Flores Carneiro

Current situation: Transur provides publicly owned bus and funicular services. The bus operation is now much reduced.

Bus

Passenger journeys: (1990) 35 million
(1994) 12.7 million

Funiculars

Current situation: The Plano Inclinado Liberdade–Calçada carries some 350,000 passengers a month. There is also a second funicular, the Gonçalves.

Elevator

Current situation: The Elevador Lacerda provides a lift service of four cars between the upper and lower town areas, used by about 1.2 million passengers a month.

Ferry

Current situation: Harbour ferries operated by the Cia de Navegação Bahiana carry some 2,500 daily commuters.

CBTU

Companhia Brasileira de Trens Urbanos (CBTU)
Largo de Calçada 1, 40410-360 Salvador, Bahia
Staff: 221

Type of operation: Suburban heavy rail

Passenger journeys: (1991) 4.6 million
(1995) 1.5 million

Current situation: CBTU operates a 13.7 km 3 kV DC electrified line with nine stations; four emus run a 20 min interval peak-hour service. Fares cover 4.5 per cent of operating costs. Plans for further electrification and upgrading of 69 route-km to form a regional metro have been delayed by the country's poor economic conditions.
Developments: Transfer of this system to Bahia state control is under discussion. A group of local businesses has put forward a proposal to rehabilitate the line and operate a service over a further 24 km of RFFSA route, with the aim of carrying 22,000 passengers daily. The idea is to replace the 2,000 daily bus movements carrying workers to the Camaçari petrochemical and Aratu industrial complexes.

An initial approach to the Brazilian Development Bank was rejected, but a new proposal involving a 30-year operating concession and a US$65 million loan is being considered. A fleet of 20 coaches and 10 RFFSA diesel locomotives would be refurbished, and 71 bilevel cars purchased. A protocol has been signed between the project manager Enefer, civil engineering contractor Mendes Junior and the rolling stock builder Cobrasma.

Two projects have emerged. The first would add 8 km to the existing line, from Calsçada to Paripe, at cost of US$110 million. The second envisages a 12 km extension with 14 stations from Retiro to Cajazeiras. Half of the US$172 million cost of this proposal would come from the private sector, which would also furnish the operator; the remainder would come from the state. Traffic projections for the two schemes are respectively 133,000 and 243,000 passengers daily.

Under the planned decentralisation of CBTU, these services are likely to pass to regional control.

UPDATED

SAMARA

Population: 1.3 million
Public transport: Bus and trolleybus/tramway services provided by separate municipal undertakings; metro

Upravlenie Automobil'novo Transporta

Upravlenie Automobil'novo Transporta
Samara, Russia

Bus

Passenger journeys: Approx 26 million (annual)

Number of routes: 56
Route length: 216 km
Fleet: 145 vehicles

Tramvaino-Trolleibusnoe Upravlenie

Tramvaino-Trolleibusnoe Upravlenie
Kommunisticheskaya ul 8, Samara 443030
Telephone: +7 8462 321203

Trolleybus

Passenger journeys: Approx 55 million (annual)

Double-coupled ZIU9 trolleybuses at Samara main station (Voksal) ***1996***

Number of routes: 19
Route length: 125 km
Fleet: Approx 250 vehicles
ZIU9
ZIU10

Tramway

Type of operation: Conventional tramway

Passenger journeys: Approx 127 million (annual)

Route length: 171 km
Number of routes: 24
Gauge: 1,524 mm

Rolling stock: 450 cars
ČKD Tatra T3SU
ČKD Tatra T3M (1993) M48

Samara Metro

Samara Metropolitena

Type of operation: Full metro, first line opened 1987

Route length: 12.5 km
Number of lines: 1
Number of stations: 7
Gauge: 1,524 mm
Electrification: 825 V DC, third rail

Three-car set of Tatra T3s in the city centre ***1997***

Current situation: Extension under construction to complete 17 km Line 1.
Developments: Two further lines planned, totalling 36 km. Line 2 will run from the main station to the northeast of the city, with Line 3 (Samara line) branching at the Lenin Works station and running to a proposed new housing estate on the River Samara.

UPDATED

SAN ANTONIO

Population: 1 million, metropolitan area 1.4 million
Public transport: Bus services provided by metropolitan transit authority, controlled by representative board

VIA

VIA Metropolitan Transit Authority
800 West Myrtle Street, PO Box 12489, San Antonio, TX 78212, USA
Telephone: +1 210 227 5371 Fax: +1 210 227 0584
Chair: Revd Richard E Tankerson
General Manager: John M Milam
Staff: 1,688, including part-time

Current situation: Created in 1978, VIA is a political subdivision of the state of Texas with a board of trustees appointed by the city, Bexar County, and 20 other incorporated cities in the county.

Voters approved a ½ cent sales tax to support VIA in 1977. The income from this helps reduce the effect of declining federal operating aid. An additional ½ cent sales tax was approved in 1989 to fund construction of the Alamodome sports facility which also included an underground bus station. On expiry of the additional tax in 1994, VIA sold the Alamodome to the city of San Antonio, but continues to maintain and operate the transit centre.

Developments: Following introduction of electronic fareboxes in 1994, allowing more accurate ridership counting and improved route-planning, a major restructuring of the fares system was implemented in October 1995. Zones were eliminated in favour of flat fares with an express supplement. VIAtrans patrons now travel free on fixed-route services.

VIAtrans paratransit vehicles now operate on propane, in the first phase of the undertaking's commitment to an alternative fuel policy. Catalytic converter silencers are being installed on rebuilt engines in compliance with Environmental Protection Agency regulations.

A major review of all routes and services was undertaken during 1996, and proposed route additions were scheduled for January 1997.

New passenger facilities are under construction at two park-and-ride sites, and a further new site was commissioned in conjunction with the Texas DoT. VIA is also taking part in a regional commuter rail feasibility study.

Bus

Passenger journeys: (1993/94) 46.4 million
(1994/95) 43.8 million
(1995/96) 43.3 million
Vehicle-km: (1993/94) 32.8 million
(1994/95) 33.8 million
(1995/96) 33.7 million

Number of routes: 96
Route length: (One way) 2,728 km
On priority right-of-way: (Contraflow) 820 m
Fleet: 522 vehicles

GMC/TMC RTS II (1977/78/80/84/88/92)	463
Chance VS-24 replica streetcar (1987/90)	26
Chance minibus	33

In peak service: 420

Most intensive service: 3-5 min
One-person operation: All routes
Fare collection: Cash to farebox or prepurchase multitickets or monthly passes
Fare structure: Flat, double-fare for express service; monthly passes and employer-purchase pass scheme
Integration with other modes: 8 park-and-ride terminals in outlying areas offer free parking; local bus service available at intercity bus terminals
Arrangements for elderly/disabled: VIAtrans service carried 983,800 passengers in 1995/96; 128 out of 156 vehicles lift-equipped
Average distance between stops: 200 m
Operational control: Two-way radios on all buses with automatic vehicle monitoring
Average peak-hour speed: 23.2 km/h
Operating costs financed by: Fares 26%, other commercial sources 4%, FTA grant 1%, local ½ cent sales tax 69%
New vehicles financed by: FTA grants 80%, local funds and revenue 20%

UPDATED

San Antonio GMC RTS-II
1995

SAN DIEGO

Population: City 1 million, metropolitan area 2.3 million
Public transport: Bus and light rail services provided by operating subsidiaries of Metropolitan Transit Development Board in southern part of San Diego County, and bus services and commuter rail by North County Transit District in the north. MTDB also contracts DART network of taxi feeders and co-ordinates other taxi and jitney services. Ferry service by private operator

MTDB

San Diego Metropolitan Transit Development Board
1255 Imperial Avenue, Suite 1000, San Diego, CA 92101, USA
Telephone: +1 619 231 1466 Fax: +1 619 234 3407
Chair: Leon Williams
General Manager: Thomas F Larwin
Director of Planning & Operations: William Lieberman

Current situation: MTDB was created in 1975 to develop a rail transit system for the San Diego metropolitan area. Member agencies comprise the city and county of San Diego, and the cities of Chula Vista, El Cajon, Imperial Beach, La Mesa, Lemon Grove, Coronado, Poway, Santee and National City. MTDB's jurisdiction covers a 1,400 km² area and a population of 1.7 million.

Operation of the light rail network is delegated to a public corporation, San Diego Trolley Inc. Separate private and public bus operators provide local, urban and express bus service throughout the region. Operators include private contractors and these public operators: County Transit System, National City Transit, Chula Vista Transit and San Diego Transit. The bus and light rail transit operations are promoted as the MTS (Metropolitan Transit System).

Planning and engineering for further expansion of the light rail network, which is planned to total 138 km by the year 2010, was curtailed after the failure of tax Proposition 156 in 1992. Approval for a further transport bond was rejected in 1994. Nevertheless such a network remains the aim of MTDB, although some of the proposed alignments would not necessarily be built as light rail.

MTDB's two operating subsidiaries have separate boards of directors, administrative and operating staffs. MTDB approves each operator's annual budget, and handles planning and certain marketing and public information functions. In addition, MTDB co-ordinates taxi and jitney services in San Diego and other suburban cities.

Various options are under consideration to raise the amount of dedicated funding available towards operating costs, including an increase in sales tax or vehicle registration fees, and a payment for single-occupant usage of HOV lanes.

Passenger journeys: (All modes)
(1991/92) 59 million
(1992/93) 60.8 million
(1993/94) 51 million

South line train on C Street in downtown San Diego

Operating costs financed by: Fares 50%, subsidy/grants 50%
Subsidy from: Local Transportation Development Act funds, State Transit Assistance and FTA grants

San Diego Transit

San Diego Transit Corporation
100 Sixteenth Street, PO Box 2511, San Diego, CA 92112
Telephone: +1 619 238 0100 Fax: +1 619 696 8159
Chair: Donna Alm
President & General Manager: Ron Yagura
Vice President, Human Resources: Frank Shipman
Vice President, Finance & Administration: Cliff Telfer
Vice President, Operations: Richard A Murphy
Manager, Public Relations: Carmen Sandoval
Staff: 961

Developments: Further expansion of CNG-powered fleet planned, with 29 buses on order.

Bus

Passenger boardings: (1992/93) 33.9 million
(1993/94) 32.9 million
(1994/95) 32.7 million
Vehicle-km: (1992/93) 21.6 million
(1993/94) 21.2 million
(1994/95) 21.8 million

Route length: (One way) 913 km
Number of routes: 33
Fleet: 285 vehicles

GM Canada New Look (1981)	22
Gillig Phantom (1983/90/91)	155
Ikarus USA 416 (1989)	25
New Flyer D60 articulated (1993)	50
New Flyer CNG-powered (1994/95)	33

In peak service: 226

Most intensive service: 5 min
One-person operation: All routes
Fare collection: GFI dollar bill accepting farebox
Fare structure: Flat; zonal for express routes; free transfers; month and half-month passes; multiride tickets
Fare evasion control: Driver supervision
Arrangements for elderly/disabled: 295 buses wheelchair lift-equipped; demand-response services carried 265,000 passengers in 1994
Average distance between stops: 2-3 blocks
Average peak-hour speed: 24.6 km/h
Integration with other modes: Timed interchange and co-operative transfer arrangements with light rail system and some other bus operators, and through booking on taxi dial-a-ride feeder services (see below)
Operating costs financed by: Fares 42.7%, other commercial sources 5.5%, subsidy/grants 51.8%
Subsidy from: FTA 16%; state, local and other sources 84%
New vehicles financed by: FTA grants 80%, local funds 20%

Dial-a-ride taxi feeders

Current situation: 'DART' network of taxis provide, under contract, feeder service to San Diego Transit bus routes in Mid-City, Mira Mesa, Paradise Hills, Rancho Bernardo and Scripps Ranch. They operate as fixed-route feeders in peak hours and as local community dial-a-ride at other times.

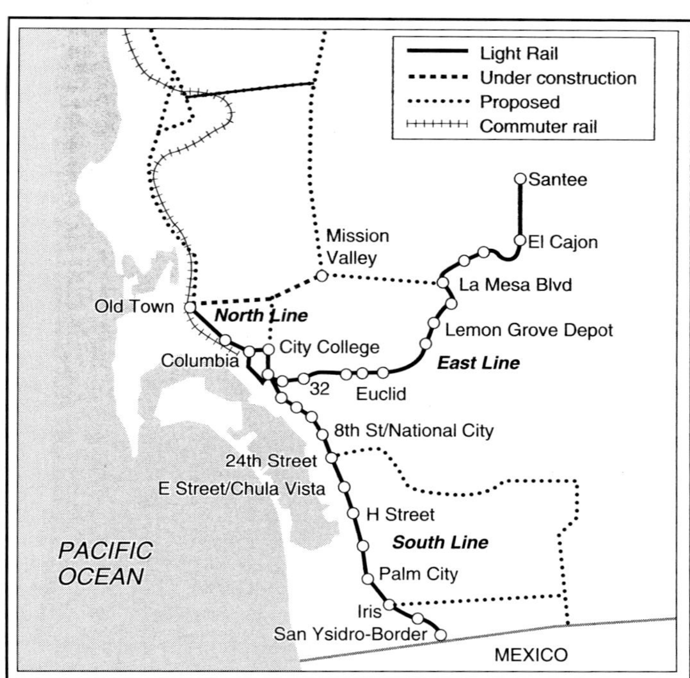

San Diego light rail

San Diego Trolley

San Diego Trolley Inc
Address as MTDB above
Telephone: +1 619 595 4949 Fax: +1 619 238 4182
Chair: Harry Mathis
President: Langley C Powell
Staff: 283

Light rail

Type of operation: Light rail, initial route opened 1981

Passenger journeys: (1994) 15.6 million
(1995) 16.7 million
(1996) 18.7 million
Car-km: (Annual) 6.8 million

Route length: 65.6 km
Number of lines: 2
Number of stations: 38
Gauge: 1,435 mm
Electrification: 600 V DC, overhead

Service: Day 10 min, evenings 30 min
First/last car: 04.26/01.02
Fare structure: Floating zone, two-week/monthly and multiride passes

Buses of NCTD at Oceanside transit centre

Revenue collection: Vending machines at all stations; spot checks
Integration with other modes: Monthly pass valid on buses; free and upgrade transfers to bus; bus connection from San Ysidro to downtown Tijuana (see Tijuana entry)
Operating costs financed by: Fares 67%, subsidy/grants 33%

Rolling stock: 123 cars

Siemens/Duewag U2 (1980/89)	M71
Siemens/Duewag SD100 (1995/96)	M52

In peak service: 64

Current situation: North line extension to Old Town (5.1 km, three stations) opened June 1996. Mission Valley line from Old Town to Jack Murphy Stadium (9.7 km, seven stations) under construction for December 1997 opening. Two further extensions are in design – a 10.4 km link from Mission Valley to the East line at La Mesa, accorded top priority and scheduled to open after 2000, and a line from Old Town northwards (maximum 13 km).

NCTD

North County Transportation District
311 South Tremont Street, Oceanside, CA 92054
Telephone: +1 619 967 2828 Fax: +1 619 967 0941
Executive Director: Richard L Fifer
Operating Manager: Robert A Durant
Staff: 550

Passenger boardings: (1993) 10.8 million
(1994) 10.8 million

Current situation: Established in 1976, NCTD operates fixed-route bus services in northern San Diego County, including routes into downtown San Diego.

It also operates the Coaster (Coast Express Rail) commuter rail service inaugurated 1995 over the Amtrak route between Oceanside and San Diego, for which NCTD purchased the right-of-way from Santa Fe. Coaster tickets are valid on NCTD buses, and San Diego buses and light rail.

At the planning stage is a 45 km light rail line linking Oceanside and Escondido, again using Santa Fe right-of-way. This could open earlier and at lower cost using diesel railcars.

Bus

Fleet: 165 vehicles

Flxible ADB	142
GMC RTS	8
Vans	15

Commuter rail

Passenger journeys: (1995) 2,100 daily

Current situation: Five return trips, including one reverse-flow, are operated between Oceanside and San Diego (70 km, nine stations). Operation is contracted to Amtrak.

Rolling stock: 5 diesel locomotives, 16 double-deck push-pull coaches

UPDATED

SAN FRANCISCO BAY AREA

Population: City 724,000, conurbation 6 million
Public transport: The San Francisco Bay region embraces nine counties – Alameda, Contra Costa, Marin, Napa, San Francisco, San Mateo, Santa Clara, Solano and Sonoma, and nearly 100 cities and towns. There are eight primary public transport systems and 17 other local operators providing service. In addition there are numerous special services for elderly and disabled people. Planning, performance monitoring and administration of certain funds is the responsibility of the Metropolitan Transportation Commission.

The following text is arranged on a county-by-county basis

Muni's new Breda LRVs entered service at the end of 1996 ***1997***

MTC

Metropolitan Transportation Commission
101 Eighth Street, Oakland, CA 94607-4700, USA
Telephone: +1 510 464 7700 Fax: +1 510 464 7848
Executive Director: Larry Dahms

Passenger journeys: (1991/92) 471.6 million
(1992/93) 470.7 million
(1993/94) 458.6 million

Current situation: The MTC was created in 1970 to provide transport planning for the nine-county region. It has been assigned responsibility for administering several sources of transit funding, including monies from the Transportation Development Act and FTA. In addition, the Commission has become responsible for overseeing the efficiency and effectiveness of transit operators in the region. MTC monitors their budgets, conducts performance audits, and sets capital investment priorities for both public transport and highways in the Bay Area.

MTC's role has expanded beyond planning, programming and monitoring to include technical assistance, providing staff to the Regional Transit Connection clearing house which markets transit passes and tickets through Bay Area employers. MTC addresses the problems of growth, traffic congestion and air pollution. Guidelines produced by MTC are helping counties to prepare state-mandated congestion management programmes that evaluate the impact of new land development on the transport network.

MTC is co-ordinating development of the TransLink stored-fare ticket intended as an area-wide all-modes pass. It has also inaugurated a commuter journey subsidy programme in which employers buy vouchers for their staff to use in part payment for transit passes.

The MTC is given policy direction by a 19-member panel, 14 of whom are appointed directly by local elected officials. Two members represent regional agencies – the Association of Bay Area Governments and the Bay Conservation & Development Commission. In addition, three non-voting members have been appointed to represent federal and state transport agencies and the federal housing department.

Developments: In 1994 MTC approved a 20-year $74 billion spending plan, aimed principally at maintaining and refurbishing the region's existing road and rail infrastructure. Projects approved include rehabilitation of BART's original 34 stations and its fleet of Rohr cars; new LRVs for Muni; extension of CalTrain to a city-centre terminal in San Francisco; the Tasman light rail line in San Jose; and a region-wide ticketing system.

SAN FRANCISCO

Public transport: Bus, trolleybus, cable car and tramway/light rail services provided for city area by municipal undertaking; regional metro service by Bay Area Rapid Transit District (BART) within and between San Francisco, San Mateo, Alameda and Contra Costa counties. Suburban rail service links San Jose and San Francisco serving Santa Clara and San Mateo counties. Ferry and bus services offered on several cross-bay routes by various operators

Muni

San Francisco Municipal Railway (Muni)
949 Presidio Avenue, San Francisco, CA 94115, USA
Telephone: +1 415 923 6212 Fax: +1 415 923 6218
Director of Public Transportation: Emilio R Cruz
Staff: 3,441

Passenger boardings: (All modes)
(1993/94) 219.9 million
(1994/95) 216 million
(1995/96)

Current situation: Muni is under direct city control, responsible to the San Francisco Public Transportation Commission established in 1994, which has replaced the Public Utilities Commission as governing body. It operates bus, trolleybus and cable car services, the Muni Metro tramway/light rail network, and the F-Market historic tramway.
Developments: As part of the ½ per cent sales tax proposals for transport capital projects approved by voters in 1989, studies have been made for provision of fixed guideway transit in the Bayshore, Geary and Chinatown/North Beach corridors. Light rail has been chosen for 3rd Street on the Bayshore corridor, and studies of major investment for the Geary corridor will be made if finance becomes available.

In 1995 regular tram service returned to the section of Market Street between the Transbay Terminal and Castro Street, after a lapse of 15 years. The resurrected route, F-Market, operates with 17 rebuilt PCC cars plus the historic fleet. It replaces the 8-Market trolleybus line; patronage is reported to have exceeded the most optimistic projections.

Operating costs financed by: Fares 32.6%, other commercial sources 1.1%, subsidy/grants 66.3%
Subsidy from: City General Fund 12.7%, city parking revenues 27.4%, other city revenue transfers 4.3%, federal/state/regional revenues 19.6%, state and local paratransit revenues 2.3%

Bus and trolleybus

Staff: Bus 1,269, trolleybus 736

Passenger journeys: (1993/94) Bus 94 million, trolleybus 78.8 million
(1994/95) Bus 90.6 million, trolleybus 79.3 million
Vehicle-km: (1992/93) Bus 20.8 million, trolleybus 11.3 million
(1993/94) Bus 20.4 million, trolleybus 11.4 million

Number of routes: Bus 54, trolleybus 17
Route length: Bus 625 km, trolleybus 158 km
Fleet: 455 buses, plus 45 in reserve

New Flyer (1980) (reserve)	45
Flyer D902 (1984)	180
New Flyer (1988/89)	106
MAN SA310 articulated (1984)	100
Orion (1990)	45
New Flyer articulated (1991)	24

Fleet: 364 trolleybuses

Flyer E800 (1975/77)	302
Flyer E700A (1972/73) (in store)	2
New Flyer articulated (1992/94)	60

In peak service: Bus 356, trolleybus 257
Trolleybus electrification: 600 V DC

New Flyer trolleybus on Muni's Route 31-Balboa ***1997***

One-person operation: All routes
Fare collection: Coin or note to farebox on board. Prepurchase monthly passes sold by over 200 vendors
Fare structure: Flat, monthly passes. Free 1½ h transfers valid for two uses in any direction

Developments: The 31-Balboa route was converted to full trolleybus operation in 1994. Wiring of Route 71-Noriega was to follow, for opening in 1997, but work has been suspended due to shortage of funds.

Purchase is planned of 30 articulated trolleybuses and 213 two-axle trolleybuses, with options of a further 15 of the former and 32 of the latter. An order was placed with Škoda in April 1997.

Tramway/Light rail ('Metro')

Staff: 627

Type of operation: Conventional tramway upgraded to light rail standards, 10 km city-centre tunnel with high-platform stations

Passenger journeys: (1992/93) 39.3 million
(1993/94) 37.6 million
(1994/95) 37.2 million
Car-km: (1991/92) 6.5 million
(1992/93) 6.2 million
(1993/94) 5.1 million

Route length: 42 km
Number of lines: 6
Gauge: 1,435 mm
Electrification: 600 V DC, overhead

Service: 6-10 min
First/last car: 05.00/00.30
Fare structure: Flat, monthly passes, Muni 'Passport'
Fare collection: In tunnel section, fares collected in stations with barrier access to platforms; on surface sections, coin or note to farebox, also two proof-of-payment surface stations
Signalling: Seltrac moving block in Market Street tunnel

Rolling stock: 157 cars

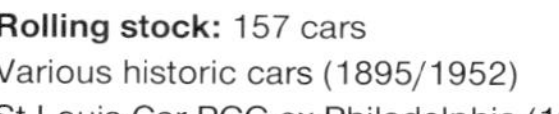

Various historic cars (1895/1952)	M13
St Louis Car PCC ex-Philadelphia (1948)	M14
St Louis Car PCC double-ended (1948, rebuilt 1994)	M3
Boeing-Vertol SLRV 1200 (1978/80)	M94
Boeing-Vertol SLRV 1252 (1982)	M1
Boeing-Vertol SLRV 1300 (1983/84)	M28
Breda (1996)	M4

In peak service: 90 Boeing cars, 8 others

On order: 77 LRVs being delivered from Breda

Developments: After some delay, the first new Breda cars entered public service in December 1996. Muni hopes to have replaced all of the troubled Boeing fleet in 1999. The original order for 50 cars was increased to 77 in September 1996, and a further 59 may be ordered.

December 1996 also saw opening of the 600 m turnback facility at Embarcadero, designed to ease operation of the terminus and so increase capacity of the Market Street tunnel from 20 to 30 trains/h. A further extension, opening in early 1998, will bring the Market Street tunnel to a new surface terminus at 6th & Berry, close to the CalTrain suburban rail terminal.

Cable cars

Staff: 272

Type of operation: Cable-and-grip tramway, opened 1873

Current situation: Three-route, 1,067 mm gauge network totalling 8.5 km carries about 8.8 million passengers annually.

Rolling stock: 40 cars

Powell single-end	M28
California double-end	M12

TMC bus of Golden Gate Transit at Larkspur ferry terminal

Golden Gate Transit

Golden Gate Bridge, Highway & Transportation District
Box 9000, Presidio Station, San Francisco, CA 94129-0601
Telephone: +1 415 921 5858 Fax: +1 415 923 2367
President, Board of Directors: Robert McDonnell
General Manager: Carney J Campion
Staff: 865

Passenger journeys: (All modes)
(1993/94) 10.4 million
(1994/95) 10.1 million
(1995/96) 8.9 million

Current situation: The Golden Gate Bridge, Highway & Transportation District provides services for a population of 1.4 million in San Francisco, Marin and Sonoma counties, through Bus, Ferry and Bridge operating divisions. A 19-member board of directors is appointed by six constituent counties.

Surplus bridge tolls are used to subsidise services between San Francisco and North Bay counties, but the Bridge District is prohibited from using any toll revenues to subsidise local routes within Marin County (see below). Commuter carpools of three or more people are encouraged with toll-free passage of the Golden Gate Bridge.

Developments: District and local bodies now own a total of 247 km of abandoned rail right-of-way in Marin County for future transport development. These are the 23 km Larkspur line and the Northwestern Pacific Railroad corridor running north and east from Novato to Willits and Napa Junction. In 1995 the District joined with Marin County and the North Coast Rail Authority to form an agency that would take the rail project forward.

Bus

Bus Transit Division, 1011 Andersen Drive, San Rafael, CA 94901-5381
Telephone: +1 415 457 3110 Fax: +1 415 257 4411
Web: http://goldengate.org
Bus Division Manager: Wayne T Diggs
Staff: 500

Passenger journeys: (1993/94) 9 million
(1994/95) 8.9 million
(1995/96) 7.5 million
Vehicle-km: (1993/94) 13.2 million
(1994/95) 14.5 million
(1995/96) 15.5 million

Number of routes: 62
Route length: (One way) 988 km
Fleet: 265 vehicles

GMC RTS T80 (1982/83)	67
TMC RTS T80 (1989/91)	143
MCI (1987)	10
Gillig Phantom (1986)	4
Flxible Metro (1994)	41

In peak service: 224
On order: 30 buses from MCI

Most intensive service: 5 min
One-person operation: All routes
Fare collection: GFI farebox on bus
Fare structure: Zonal
Fare evasion control: Zone identification checks by driver
Integration with other modes: Buses integrated with Golden Gate ferry services; buses serve BART/Muni stations; 25 park-and-ride lots with 3,823 spaces
Average distance between stops: 400m
Average peak-hour speed: 32-40 km/h; on freeways, up to 88 km/h
Arrangements for elderly/disabled: All buses wheelchair-accessible
Bus priority: 6 km bus/carpool with-flow lane in peak periods; 3 km bus/carpool lane
Operating costs financed by: Fares 32%, other commercial sources (bridge tolls) 49%, subsidy/grants 19%
Subsidy from: State and local Transportation Development Act funds
New vehicles financed by: FTA grants 80%, local 20%

Current situation: Basic services operate all day every day, with express Commute service operated in the peak direction only, and some local bus routes run under contract in Marin County. Private operators under contract operate 13 subscription-type 'Club Buses' during commuting periods to serve markets not catered for by scheduled buses.

BART commuters head for downtown San Francisco **1995**

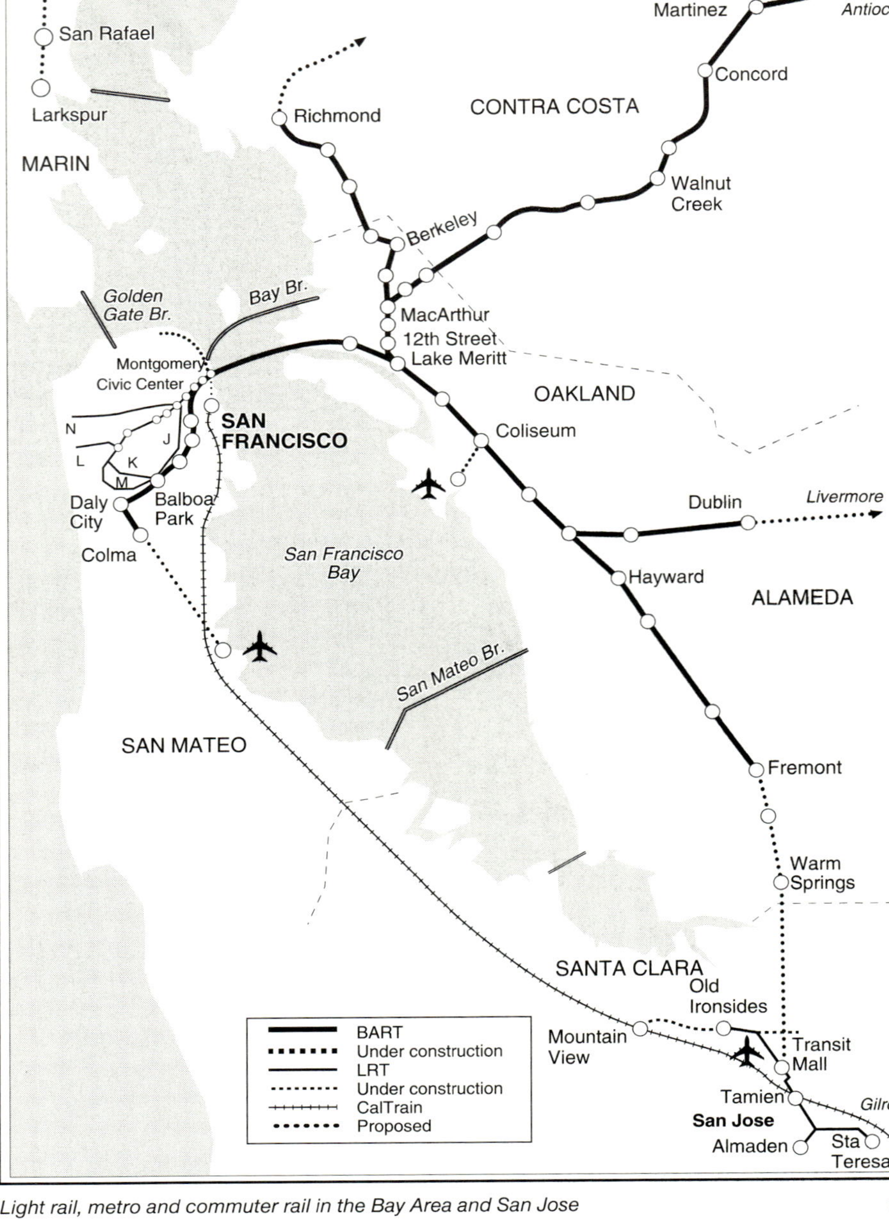

Light rail, metro and commuter rail in the Bay Area and San Jose **1996**

Ferry

Ferry Transit Division
101 East Sir Francis Drake Blvd, Larkspur, CA 94939-1899
Telephone: +1 415 925 5570 Fax: +1 415 925 5510
Manager: Eric A Robinson
Staff: 83, plus 2 part-time

Passenger journeys: (1993/94) 1.4 million
(1995/96) 1.4 million

Current situation: Operates three vessels on its 45-min service between San Francisco and Larkspur, and one for the 30-min journey between San Francisco and Sausalito; total route 27 km. Free connecting shuttle buses operate during commuter period.

Developments: To accommodate growing patronage on the Larkspur route, a new fast ferry is to enter service in 1997/98, when the journey time from Larkspur will be cut from 45 to 30 min. A new landing is under construction at Sausalito.

BART

Bay Area Rapid Transit District (BART)
PO Box 12688, 800 Madison Street, Oakland, CA 94604-2688
Telephone: +1 510 464 6000 Fax: +1 510 464 7103
President: Dan Richard
General Manager: Thomas E Margro
Deputy General Manager: Dorothy W Dugger
General Manager, Operations: James T Gallagher
Staff: 2,400

Type of operation: Full metro, first line opened 1972

Passenger journeys: (1993/94) 74 million
(1994/95) 72 million
(1995/96) 73 million
Car-km: (1992/93) 67.6 million
(1993/94) 69.2 million
(1995/96)

Route length: 135 km
in tunnel: 31 km
elevated: 37 km
Number of lines: 4
Number of stations: 37
Gauge: 1,676 mm
Track: Concrete sleepers on resilient pads
Max gradient: 4%
Minimum curve radius: 120 m
Tunnel: Transbay tube: twin-section submerged caisson of steel and concrete designed for high resistance to seismic disturbances
Electrification: 1 kV DC, third rail

Service: Peak 4-15 min, off-peak 5-15-20 min
First/last train: 04.02/00.02
Fare structure: Graduated; BART-Plus passes include unlimited travel on other modes
Integration with other modes: Feeder buses co-ordinated with other Bay Area public transport operators through the Regional Transit Association. Feeder bus services on 12 routes contracted to Laidlaw Transit serve outlying areas of future BART extensions
Operating costs financed by: Fares 42.3%, other commercial sources 15.3%, subsidy/grants 42.4% (sales tax, property tax and state funds)
Revenue collection: IBM change and ticket vending machines and gates at stations, Cubic equipment at

Embarcadero station. Entry gate records time, date and station and returns ticket. Exit gate computes required fare, accepts exact-fare ticket, instructs if additional payment is needed, or deducts proper amount from multiride ticket. Credit-card-size tickets, magnetically encoded with up to $32 of fares
One-person operation: All trains

Rolling stock: 679 cars

Rohr A cab (1970-72)	M176
Rohr B (1970-72)	M273
Alsthom C (1988/90)	M150
Amerail C2 (1994/95)	M80

Developments: The first fares increase for nine years was implemented in April 1995, with the estimated $100 million in additional revenue going towards fleet and station rehabilitation, and introduction of a new paratransit network. The 15 per cent increase in 1995 was to be followed by rises of 13 per cent in April 1996 and 11.4 per cent in April 1997.

BART's first extension since the original network was completed in 1972 opened in December 1995. This is the initial portion to North Concord/Martinez of the 12.5 km extension to Pittsburg, the remainder of which opened in December 1996. The 2.3 km Colma extension opened in February 1996, and the 20.6 km from Bay Fair to Dublin/Pleasanton is due to open during 1997.

A financing agreement signed in 1994, and approval of Federal funding in March 1996, could lead to a 1997 start on the airport line (12.9 km, four stations), which will be an extension of the spur to Colma. Location of the airport station, which had been subject to months of dispute, was settled 1995, allowing detailed design of the route to go ahead. Legal arrangements have also been made permitting work to go ahead in San Mateo County, which is not a member of BART.

Work has yet to start on the 8.7 km extension from Fremont to Warm Springs, where construction has been delayed due to environmental problems. Neither line is likely to open until after 2000.

Future projects include further extensions from Pittsburg to Antioch, from Dublin to Livermore (18 km), and from Warm Springs to connect with an extension from the San Jose LRT system. A line across the Golden Gate Bridge into Marin County has also been mooted.

In mid-1994 BART approved raising of $200 million over six years to refurbish stations and rolling stock in a $1 billion programme. The original fleet of 439 cars is being refurbished by Adtranz over a seven-year period, 34 stations are being upgraded, and the entire track renewed. The fare collection and communciations systems will also be replaced.

In July 1997 BART was expected to take over management of the 'Capitols' regional trains, formerly sponsored by the California DoT. A new Capitol Corridors joint powers board controls the trains, which link San Jose with Oakland and Sacramento. BART plans to increase service from four to six trains daily.

Red & White Fleet

Red & White Fleet
Harbor Carriers, Inc, Pier 41, San Francisco, CA 94133
Telephone: +1 415 546 2856
Marketing Manager: Terry Koenig

Ferry

Current situation: This privately owned operation has recently introduced improved ferry service using a high-speed catamaran on its routes San Francisco—Tiburon and San Francisco—Sausalito.

SAN MATEO

Public transport: Main bus operations by SamTrans, which also administers the CalTrain rail service operated under contract, supplemented by bus, metro and light rail services of Muni, BART, Santa Clara County Transportation Authority and Dumbarton Express

SamTrans

San Mateo County Transit District (SamTrans)
1250 San Carlos Avenue, PO Box 3006, San Carlos, CA 94070-1306
Telephone: +1 415 508 6200 Fax: +1 415 508 6443
Chair: Jerrold D Buck
General Manager: Gerald T Haugh

Neoplan articulated bus of SamTrans

Director of Transit: John Ficarra
Staff: 642

Current situation: SamTrans special transit district serves San Mateo County, including the southern suburban areas of San Francisco and neighbouring areas, with a population in excess of 600,000. The corridor service between Palo Alto and San Francisco city centre is operated under contract by Grosvenor Lines Inc, and the 'Redi-Wheels' door-to-door service for the disabled is also run under contract with vehicles supplied by SamTrans. One other fixed route and one paratransit service are contracted out.

In 1982, a ½ per cent sales tax was implemented, the proceeds being used to underwrite the SamTrans operating budget, capital projects and as a consistent source of working capital. The BART station at Colma (see above) was funded under a special agreement necessary because San Mateo was not at that time a member of the BART district. This changed in 1992, when San Mateo citizens voted to join BART, and also endorsed the BART extension to San Francisco airport. Service to Colma started in February 1996.

In 1991 SamTrans purchased from Southern Pacific the right-of-way of the CalTrain service linking San Francisco and San Jose, under a joint agreement between the counties of San Mateo, San Francisco and Santa Clara. This Joint Powers Board appointed SamTrans to administer the rail operation, which was taken over in 1992 (see below).

Bus

Passenger boardings: (1991/92) 19.6 million
(1992/93) 19.2 million
(1994/95) 19.5 million
Vehicle-km: (1991/92) 17.2 million
(1992/93) 15.6 million
(1994/95) 16 million

Number of routes: 85
Route length: (One-way) 879 km
Fleet: 362 vehicles

Gillig (1983/84)	72
Volvo articulated (1985)	15
Neoplan articulated (1985)	15
Gillig (1990)	38
New Flyer articulated (1990)	40
Gillig (1993)	137
Eldorado for Redi-Wheels (1991)	10
Champion for Redi-Wheels (1993)	18
Plymouth vans for Redi-Wheels (1994/95)	15

In peak service: 251

Most intensive service: Peak 5 min
One-person operation: All routes
Fare collection: Prepurchase monthly pass or exact fare to farebox; other Bay Area operators' passes valid as fare credits
Fare structure: Flat; distance-based express supplement
Fares collected on board: 85.7%
Fare evasion control: Driver supervision
Operational control: Route inspectors/mobile radio, with route checks
Arrangements for elderly/disabled: Door-to-door Redi-Wheels service, operated under contract by Mayflower with 28 vehicles provided by SamTrans, carried 159,000 passengers in 1994; reduced fare cards; lift-equipped buses on 14 fixed routes
Integration with other modes: Services and passes integrated with other operators including BART, CalTrain, Santa Clara Transit, and Muni
Operating costs financed by: Fares 26.1%, other commercial sources 2%, subsidy/grants 53.4% (state law requires that fares must cover at least 24.3% of costs), sales tax 18.5%
New vehicles financed by: Local matching of FTA grants

CalTrain

Peninsula Corridor Joint Powers Board (JPB)
Address as SamTrans above
Executive Director: Gerald T Haugh
Director of Rail: Jerome Kirzner
Staff: 335

Type of operation: Suburban heavy rail

Passenger journeys: (1993/94) 6.9 million
(1994/95) 7 million
(1995/96) 7.4 million

Operating costs financed by: Fares 29.6%, other commercial sources 7.2%, subsidy/grants 63.2%

Current situation: Commuter service known as CalTrain provided over 123 km route with 34 stations from Gilroy

CalTrain commuter service awaits departure from San Francisco

Other operators

Current situation: Buses of Stanford Marguerite Shuttle provide a free 10-min service linking Palo Alto CalTrain station with the campus of Stanford University and other local destinations.

The San Joaquin Regional Rail Authority plans to introduce commuter rail service in 1997 over a 137 km route from Stockton to San Jose.

CONTRA COSTA

Public transport: As well as the following local operators, the county is served by routes of AC Transit, BART and BART Express

County Connection

Central Contra Costa Transit Authority
2477 Arnold Industrial Way, Concord, CA 94520
Telephone: +1 510 676 1976 Fax: +1 510 687 7306
General Manager: Robert C Patrick Jr
Staff: 300

Passenger boardings: (1991/92) 4.2 million
(1992/93) 4.1 million
(1993/94) 4.1 million

Current situation: Established in 1980, CCCTA took over existing operations in Walnut Creek and Concord and has subsequently expanded throughout Contra Costa. Many connections with other operators, and there is through-ticketing (TransLink) to BART trains using the first on-board microprocessor ticket system in the USA.

There is a free shuttle between BART's Walnut Creek station and downtown, while County LINK provides door-to-door service for elderly and disabled people.

Bus

Number of routes: 28
Route length: 787 km
Fleet: 112 buses

Gillig Phantom (1981-89)	98
Flyer D901 (1981)	14

In peak service: 98

Most intensive service: 10 min
Fare structure: Flat
Fare collection: Cash to driver
Operational control: Radio; inspectors
Operating costs financed by: Fares 16.5%, various subsidies/grants 83.5%

Other operators

Current situation: Local services and connections to BART Express buses and/or BART stations provided by Western Contra Costa County Transit (Westcat, 24 buses), Traveler's Transit and Eastern Contra Costa Transit Authority (Tri-Delta Transit, 32 vehicles).

MARIN

Public transport: As well as the following local operators, the county is served by extensive bus and ferry routes of Golden Gate Transit (see under San Francisco)

Local operators

Current situation: Principal bus services provided by Golden Gate Transit, and Red & White ferry link to San Francisco (see above). Marin-Oakland Commute provides peak-hour service from Novato to Oakland.

NAPA

Public transport: Bus services provided by local operators

Napa Valley Transit/VINE

Napa County Transit
1151 Pearl Street, Napa, CA 94559
Telephone: +1 707 255 7631 Fax: +1 707 257 9522
General Manager: Celinda Dahlgren
Staff: 33 contracted

Passenger boardings: (1991/92) 0.7 million
(1993/94) 0.7 million
(1995/96) 0.8 million

Current situation: Operator of Valley Intracity Neighborhood Express (VINE) in Napa expanded service in 1991 to other areas; total nine routes; fleet of 18 buses. Timed connections with Vallejo Transit Bartlink to El Cerrito del Norte station and Vallejo Ferry. Fares cover 25.6% of operating costs.

SOLANO

Public transport: Bus services provided by local operators

Vallejo Transit

Vallejo Transit/Vallejo Ferry
555 Santa Clara Street, Vallejo, CA 94590
Telephone: +1 707 648 4315 Fax: +1 707 648 4691
General Manager: Pamela J Belchamber
Staff: 90

Bus

Passenger journeys: (1993/94) 2.3 million
(1994/95) 2.3 million
(1995/96) 2.5 million

Current situation: Operates 11 routes on a 30 min frequency with timed connections at two transit centres and with ferries (see below). Hourly Bartlink runs from El Cerrito del Norte station to Richmond, Crockett, Vallejo, Solano College and Fairfield. Fleet of 49 buses; fares cover 44 per cent of operating costs.

Ferry

Current situation: Operates between Vallejo and San Francisco ferry terminal with one vessel, carrying about 220,000 passengers annually.
Developments: Two fast ferries commissioned in April 1997, when service was expanded.

Other operators

Current situation: Benicia Transit, Fairfield-Suisun Transit (Fairfield Flyer, 26 vehicles) and Vacaville Transit (City Coach) provide fixed-route and some demand-responsive services in their local areas, some under contract. Benicia and Fairfield Flyer also link with BART stations and/or BART express buses.

SONOMA

Public transport: Bus services provided by local operators

CityBus

Santa Rosa Transit
PO Box 1678, Santa Rosa, CA 95402
Telephone: +1 707 543 3325 Fax: +1 707 543 3326
Director: Robert E Dunlavey
Staff: 48

Passenger journeys: (1991/92) 1.6 million
(1992/93) 1.6 million
(1993/94) 1.6 million

Current situation: Runs fixed-route service in the city of Santa Rosa with timed transfers; 12 routes; 25 buses. Connections with Sonoma County Transit and Golden Gate Transit, which offer part-payment of CityBus fare.

Sonoma County Transit

Sonoma County Transit
355 West Robles Avenue, Santa Rosa, CA 95407
Telephone: +1 707 585 7516 Fax: +1 707 585 7713
General Manager: David Knight
Staff: 85

Passenger journeys: (1993/94) 1.2 million
(1994/95) 1.2 million
(1995/96) 1.3 million

Current situation: Provides county-wide service from Santa Rosa to nine incorporated cities and many small towns; 21 routes; 51 buses, 7 minibuses/vans. Operated under contract by ATC/Vancom. Services co-ordinated with Golden Gate Transit routes to San Francisco and other local operators. Fares cover 22 per cent of operating costs.

Other operators

Current situation: Local services operated by Cloverdale Transit, Healdsburg Transit, Mendocino Transit Authority and Petaluma Transit.

UPDATED

SAN JUAN

Population: Metropolitan area 1 million
Public transport: Bus services provided by private company under contract from the Department of Transportation; feeder, express and shuttle services operated by state bus authority, with private shared taxi 'publico' minibuses and Metrobus services; metro under construction

Metropolitan Bus Authority

Metropolitan Bus Authority
PO Box 5349, Hato Rey, Puerto Rico 00919
Telephone: +1 809 767 7979 Fax: +1 809 751 0527
General Manager: Hector Rivera
Operations Manager: Cesar Cintron
Staff: 981

Current situation: To accommodate US federal requirements for a reduction in operating subsidies, the Puerto Rico DoT had examined the possibility of replacing some publicly owned services with 'publico' minibuses (see below). In addition, in 1991 it decided to contract out operation of its core bus route under a restructuring of the network into a trunk and feeder system with express services between major centres. Route 1 is now operated by City Bus. MBA's role is relegated to providing feeder express and shuttle services.

Bus

Passenger journeys: (1993) 18.7 million
(1994) 18.2 million
Vehicle-km: (1992) 5.3 million

Number of routes: 41
Route length: 1,169 km
On priority right-of-way: 27.4 km exclusive bus lane
Fleet: 248 vehicles

GMC (1980)	33
GMC (1983)	81
Flxible (1987)	19
Flxible (1988)	70
Flxible (1991)	12
MAN articulated	12
Ford 350	15
Wayne paratransit (1990)	6

In peak service: 158

One-person operation: All routes
Fare collection: Exact fare to farebox on entry
Fare structure: Flat; premium for travel on air conditioned vehicles
Fares collected on board: 100%
Arrangements for elderly/disabled: 138 buses wheelchair lift-equipped; paratransit services carried 32,000 passengers in 1994
Average peak-hour speed: 16 km/h
Operating costs financed by: Fares 14%, subsidy/grants 86%
Subsidy from: State 74%, US FTA 26%

Private bus

Current situation: Privately owned bus companies are authorised to operate in specific sectors within the metropolitan area. 'Publico' shared-taxi minibus (mostly

Trial methanol-powered bus

Acuaexpreso ferry at Hato Rey terminal

vans) carry about 11,000 passengers daily, while the Metrobus network using contraflow bus lanes caters for some 20,000 journeys.

Acuaexpreso

Puerto Rico Ports Authority
PO Box 362829, San Juan, Puerto Rico 00936-2829
Telephone: +1 787 729 8649 Fax: +1 787 724 6644
Executive Director: Herman Sulsona
Staff: 117

Ferry

Passenger journeys: (1995/96) 1.1 million

Current situation: Operates nine vessels on two routes across San Juan Bay. Bus connections operated in Hato Rey. Fares cover 10 per cent of operating costs, cross-subsidised from other port activities; about 2 million passengers carried annually.

Developments: A service is planned from Cataño and Old San Juan to a new intermodal terminal at Hato Rey, utilising the recently dredged Martin Peña canal. Together with purchase of new vessesl, the project will cost $62.7 million.

Metro

Under construction
Department of Transportation & Public Works
PO Box 41269, Minillas Station, Puerto Rico 00940-1269
Telephone: +1 787 729 1538 Fax: +1 787 727 5456
Secretary of Transportation: Dr Carlos I Pesquera
Deputy Executive Director: Carlos A Colón

Current situation: After earlier plans failed to materialise, construction of the Tren Urbano automated metro scheme started in September 1996. The 17.2 km route with 14 stations will link Bayamon with Rio Piedras and Santurce, with a second phase projected to serve the airport. Some 60 per cent of the alignment will be elevated. Federal funding was agreed in March 1996.

A consortium led by Siemens and including amongst others Parsons Brinckerhoff was awarded a turnkey contract for construction of Phase I, which is scheduled to open in 2001. Siemens also has a contract to maintain the system for its first five years of operation, with an option for a further five years.

Projected ridership of 115,000 daily will be handled by a fleet of 32 two-car trainsets with AC traction motors collecting power from a third rail at 750 V DC. Automatic train control will be microprocessor-based, with transmission-based signalling for train detection and control.

Extensions are planned to the government centre in Minillas, Carolina, Old San Juan and the airport.

UPDATED

SANTA ANA/ORANGE COUNTY

Population: City 200,000, County urban area 2.3 million
Public transport: Bus services in Santa Ana and 28 other cities in Orange County, including Anaheim, Garden Grove and Irvine, provided by County Transit Authority controlled by representative board, in co-operation with other public agencies and some employers with own operations. Demand-responsive dial-a-ride minibus scheme with operation contracted serves local neighbourhoods. Commuter rail

OCTD buses at the Fullerton transit centre

OCTA

Orange County Transportation Authority
Po Box 14184, Orange, CA 92613-1584, USA
Telephone: +1 714 560 6282 Fax: +1 714 560 5795
Chair: William G Steiner
Chief Executive Officer: Stan Oftelie
Director of Operations: David Armijo
Director of Planning & Development: Lisa Mills
Director of Finance & Administration: James Kenan
Staff: 1,500 (includes dial-a-ride)

Current situation: The former Orange County Transit District (fixed-route operator), the Transportation Commission, the Consolidated Transportation Service Agency (provider of demand-responsive service) and other transit-related agencies were merged in 1991 to form the OCTA, with an 11-member governing board.

Suburban and interurban services are operated, as well as city routes and a demand-responsive (dial-a-ride) scheme. A ride-sharing brokerage is promoted for car- and vanpools by the Commute Management Services department, and overall services are co-ordinated under co-operative agreements with MTA Los Angeles, Long Beach Transit and other local transit agencies.

Developments: After the December 1994 declaration of bankruptcy by Orange County, all public spending was halted and OCTA rushed through emergency plans to keep transit services running. During 1995, OCTA fought off proposals to give up a portion of the ½ cent sales tax that sets aside $340 million annually to fund future rail transit development. Eventually, a $15 million annual budget reduction was agreed. This led to a service restructuring implemented in October, which eliminated some 5 per cent of vehicle-km. Full-size buses on six low-demand routes were replaced by eight new community 'Runabout' lines operated by small propane-powered vehicles. Some of the service cuts were later reinstated under OCTA's bus system improvement project.

Development of a rapid transit system has long been proposed and a ½ cent tax was approved by voters in 1990. This will raise $775 million for a 20-year development programme based on the Countrywide Rail Study published in 1991. See *JUTS 1991* and *JUTS 1994/95* for history and background to these projects, whose immediate prospects have not been improved by OCTA's bankruptcy.

Staged development continues of barrier-separated bus/carpool median transitways on freeway rights-of-way as busways which could ultimately be connected to the core rail system. Two transitway projects totalling 31 km received outline approval in 1988, and construction started in 1991. These are designed to serve the many rapidly growing employment centres located throughout central Orange County and will be directly connected to them via exclusive access/egress ramps.

Construction of the Costa Mesa—St Diego HOV lane was expected to start in 1997.

Bus

Passenger journeys: (1991/92) 44 million
(1993) 42 million
(1994) 41.1 million

Number of routes: 73
Route length: 2,878 km
Fleet: 493 vehicles

GMC T8H (1980)	124
Gillig Phantom (1983/88/89)	241
New Flyer (1991)	53
Superbus	12
New Flyer D40LF low-floor (1995)	50
Others	13

On order: 38 CNG-powered low-floor buses from ElDorado; refurbishment completed of 75 Gillig Phantoms

One-person operation: All routes
Fare collection: Payment to driver or pass
Fare structure: Flat; 5 cent transfers; prepurchase 40-ticket books and monthly passes
Arrangements for elderly/disabled: Dial-a-Ride scheme (zonal fares) also serves needs of elderly and disabled (see below), uses vans with wheelchair lifts; all full-size buses lift-equipped; reduced fare peak travel
Integration between modes: Ride-sharing/carpooling promoted; 33 park-and-ride/ride-sharing sites; many inter-connection agreements with neighbouring operators; 17 operators use Santa Ana downtown transit terminal
Operating costs financed by: Fares 27%, other commercial sources 7%, subsidy/grants 59%, tax levy 6%
Subsidy from: Local transportation fund (from sales tax) 91.6%, FTA 8.2%, state 0.2%

Truck-based Superbus on Freeway Express service from Fullerton to downtown Los Angeles

Minibus/Dial-a-Ride (contracted)

Staff: 130

Passenger journeys: (1990/91) 1.3 million

Fleet: 172 vans and minibuses, all propane-powered

Current situation: County-wide Dial-a-Ride service, using District-owned vehicles operated by private companies under contract, is provided for short trips within 30 zones covering local communities. The operations, on-demand with no fixed stops, provide both a facility for local trips within the zones (at a flat fare), and transfers to main conventional routes and to adjacent Dial-a-Rides.

In addition, Dial-a-Ride vans provide express and local commuter service to major work centres over routes which will be upgraded to full-size buses as ridership develops. These routes have been developed in response to Transportation Management Associations — a joint promotion between OCTA and employers to provide tailor-made alternatives to private car commuting.

Commuter rail

Current situation: The single commuting-hour train to Los Angeles, which was sponsored by OCTA and introduced in 1990, was replaced in 1994 by Metrolink service of six trains between Oceanside, Santa Ana and LA (see Los Angeles Metrolink entry). At Oceanside the trains connect with those to San Diego run by the North County Transit District (see San Diego entry).

UPDATED

SANTIAGO DE CHILE

Population: 4.3 million
Public transport: Bus, minibus ('Liebre') and fixed-route shared taxi services provided by numerous private operators under deregulated regime, now modified to include a tendering process and partially relicensed. Government-owned metro

Private bus/Minibus

Supervised by: Ministry of Transport
Amunategui 139, Santiago de Chile, Chile
Telephone: +56 2 672 6503 Fax: +56 2 699 5138

Current situation: Following the decontrol of fares and services between 1973 and 1980, there was an expansion in the extent and frequency of bus service provision, but generally higher fares were charged. See *JUTS 1988* for history.

Widespread complaints of high fares, corruption and poor safety standards, plus an urgent need to curb the city's appalling traffic congestion and high level of vehicle-emissions, led to changes in the system. Lack of regulation caused many obsolete (and polluting) buses to continue in service, and after protracted negotiations in 1991 the government was able to 'buy out' vehicles built before 1974 from their mainly small operators. This action eliminated about 2,600 buses, micros and Liebres (30-seaters), though some were sold for service in rural areas.

Traffic congestion and pollution control requirements have also led to re-establishment of a form of regulation. The method selected does not constitute tendering as there are no charges or licences. Operators now bid for exclusive access to certain streets over a period of three to five years. Winners are selected according to several criteria: large, purpose-built buses are favoured — truck conversions and minibuses are disqualified; those with automatic fare collection take preference, otherwise conductors are favoured over driver-only operation, as is a lower than standard fare; uniforms are required to be worn; and operators must provide better terminals for their services.

Many city-centre streets are now less congested, fares are lower, and the public image of bus services has improved. The number of buses plying in the city has been cut by about half to 8,200. Of these vehicles, 7,047 were regulated by the ministry in 1996, operating 256 routes; they carry about 1,500 million passengers a year.

Private buses in Santiago

Easing of competition has also allowed the metro to play a bigger role in relieving traffic congestion.

Shared taxi

Current situation: At deregulation taxis were freed from quantity control and shared taxis permitted, leading to substantial introduction of taxis operating on fixed routes on main corridors with diversions to serve immediate environs. An association of some taxi drivers emerged to regulate fares, but others remained subject to individual bargaining. There are some 40,000 taxis operating in Santiago, which approximates to 1 per 100 inhabitants, an extremely high figure.

Fixed-route taxi fares are now related to bus fare levels, averaging about five times greater, and the services operate from recognised termini in the city centre. They account for about 6 per cent of passenger trips in the city.

Metro de Santiago

Metro de Santiago
Av Libertador B O'Higgins 1414, Santiago de Chile
Telephone: +56 2 671 3119 Fax: +56 2 699 2475
President: Daniel Fernández K
General Manager: Pedro Villar I
Operating Manager: Jorge Inostroza S
Staff: 1,344

Type of operation: Full metro, rubber-tyred system, opened 1975

Passenger journeys: (1993) 164.2 million
(1994) 167 million
(1995) 166.5 million

Route length: 37.6 km
in tunnel: 24.9 km
Number of lines: 3
Number of stations: 47
in tunnel: 30
Gauge: 1,435 mm
Track: Concrete surface with 40 kg/m guide rail for rubber-tyred operation
Max gradient: 4.8%
Minimum curve radius: 205 m
Tunnel: Cut-and-cover
Electrification: 750 V DC, collected from 2 lateral guide rails

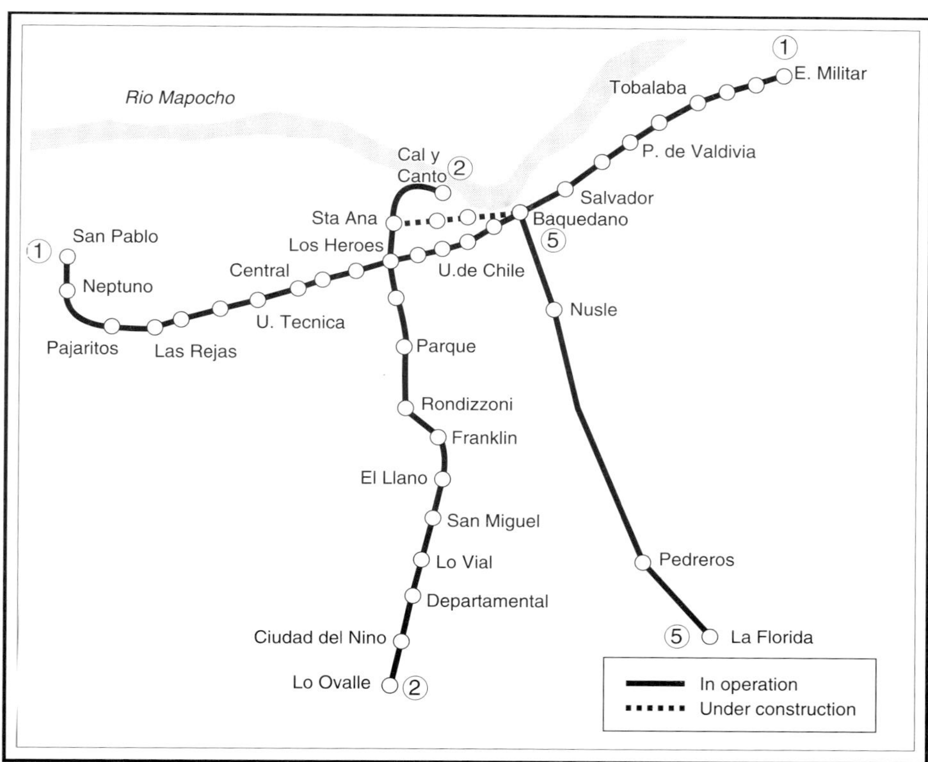

Santiago de Chile metro

Service: Peak 2 min 55 s, off-peak 3 min 40 s - 8 min
First/last train: 06.30/22.30
Fare structure: Differential fares (high, medium and low) on each line according to day and time, non-working days rate medium fare; ticket buys 1 or 2 journeys, or attracts discount, according to time of day; stored-fare pass; through fares to suburban rail and some taxi-route feeders; scholars travel free
Revenue control: Magnetic ticket control at all stations; stored fare tickets
Integration with other modes: Feeder buses on 20 routes run to 5 stations
One-person operation: All trains; full ATC
Signalling: Centralised control system
Operating costs financed by: Fares 90.3%, other commercial sources 9.7%

Rolling stock: 322 cars

Alsthom-Atlantique (1975-80)	
M	M100
N	M45
P/R	T100
Concarril NS88 (1990)	M5
GEC Alsthom (1996)	M72

In peak service: 62 trains
On order: A further 42 cars from GEC Alsthom

Developments: The metro had faced unusual problems as the only state-owned public transport in Santiago. For more than a decade, bus services were entirely deregulated and the stiff competition stifled growth of metro patronage. In an attempt to win business back from the private carriers, a network of metro feeder buses was started in 1987.

In 1992, however, bus licensing was reintroduced for approved operators in the central area (see above). The busiest corridors are no longer contested by multiple operators, and traffic congestion is much reduced. Metro patronage recovered as it became more integrated with the new operators, and competes with bus on more favourable terms.

A third route, Line 5 (10.3 km, 12 stations), opened in March 1997, running from Baquedano on Line 1 to Americo Vespucio, following the alignment of the Avenida Vicuña Mackenna. Some 3 km is in tunnel, with the remainder at grade or elevated. A new fleet based on the Paris MP89 design has been delivered by GEC Alsthom, which also supplied the SACEM signalling and train control system for Line 5. The cars have aluminium bodyshells and three-phase drive. A further 42 cars were ordered in 1996 to raise capacity on existing lines.

In late 1996 a 2.8 km extension was approved, taking Line 5 from its Line 1 interchange at Baquedano to Santa Ana on Line 2, with three stations. This will provide relief for Line 1 over its busiest city-centre section.

Signalling on Lines 1 and 2 is being upgraded by CMW, reducing headway to 90 sec, and a further seven six-car trains for these lines were ordered from GEC Alsthom in February 1997.

Contracted bus

Current situation: The network of feeder buses established in 1987 has been expanded to 20 routes serving five stations. Service is provided under contract by 15 operators with a total fleet of some 500 buses.

Trolleybus

Current situation: The ETS trolleybus system, which was owned and run by the Valparaíso operator ETCE (qv), closed in 1994 due to financial difficulties. The system's precarious financial situation would have been transformed by construction of its proposed route serving the heavily trafficked Avenida Irarrázaval, but government approval for the scheme was denied, apparently due to lobbying by motor bus operators.

Later in the year it was reported that approval had been given for the new route, but by then ETS was no longer in a sufficiently strong financial position to be able to fund its construction without local government assistance, which was not forthcoming. The future of the system remains uncertain, but all the wiring is still in place, and ETS/ETCE hopes to resume service eventually. Meanwhile all the trolleybuses were transferred to ETCE's depot in Valparaíso in 1996.

Trolleybus

Number of routes: 1
Fleet: 33 trolleybuses

Shenfeng (1991)	8
Pullman (1952, rebodied 1991, ex-Valparaiso)	3
Pullman (1947/48, rebodied 1987/91, ex-Valparaiso)	15
FBW/SWS/MFO articulated (1959/64, ex-Zürich)	4
Berna/SWS/SAAS articulated (1965, ex-Genève)	3

Metrotren

Type of operation: Suburban heavy rail

Passenger journeys: (1995) 1.9 million

Current situation: The state railway subsidiary Via Sur operates 11 daily electric trains from Til Til in the north to Rancagua 80 km south. There is through ticketing at reduced rates to metro destinations.

Consideration is being given to extending Metrotren service to the suburb of Melipilla, which would require electrification of 27 route-km. Other possibilities include a 10 km route to Nuñoa, which might use second-hand emus from Spain, and lines to Til Til and Maipú.

UPDATED

Line 1 train at Universidad de Chile **1995**

Metrobus interchange at Cal y Canto station

SANTOS

Population: 600,000
Public transport: Bus services provided by municipally owned company with additional private operations. River ferries and private funicular. Suburban rail service

CSTC

Companhia Santista de Transportes Colectivos
Caixa Postal 1323, Av Rangel Pestana 100, 111000 Santos, Brazil
Telephone: +55 132 221901 Fax: +55 132 346439
Staff: 2,352

Current situation: The municipally owned company serves a population of some 240,000.
Developments: Four trolleybus routes were closed in 1993 due to competition from buses, and the remaining route (4.7 km) ceased operation in 1996.

Bus and trolleybus

Passenger journeys: (1991) Bus 75.4 million, trolleybus 8.4 million

Number of routes: Bus 40
Route length: Bus 961 km
Fleet: 244 buses

Mercedes (1975/79/80/81/83)	77
Mercedes (1986/87/88)	70
Others	97

Fare collection: Fixed conductor on board
Fare structure: Flat
Arrangements for elderly/disabled: Some buses have wheelchair lifts
Operating costs financed by: Fares 100%

Rubens Paiva terminal of CSTC

FEPASA

Ferrovia Paulista SA
Rua Maua 51, São Paulo 22724
Telephone: +55 11 223 7211 Fax: +55 11 220 9484

Suburban rail

Passenger journeys: (1991) 2.8 million

Current situation: FEPASA, the São Paulo state rail operator, inaugurated a suburban rail service in 1990 linking Ana Costa and Samarita (16 km), known as TIM (Trem Intra Metropolitano). Serving six stations, the diesel-hauled push-pull trainsets run over existing tracks.

Private bus

Passenger journeys: Approx 60 million (annual)

Fleet: 1,200 vehicles
Fare structure: Flat

Ferry

Current situation: Four publicly owned river ferries are operated.

TIM suburban train at Santos Ana Costa

SÃO PAULO

Population: 11 million, metropolitan area 17 million
Public transport: Bus services in the metropolitan area are run mostly by private operators. São Paulo city bus and trolleybus services are entirely provided by private companies through service contracts with São Paulo Transporte SA (SPTrans), the municipal transit agency which supervises operations and has developed specialised bus corridors along a few main arteries. The metro is operated by a company jointly owned by city, state and federal governments, with a major stake held by the state government, and is supervised by the State Municipal Transport Secretariat (SMT). SMT also supervises interurban metropolitan rail and bus services, provided respectively by the State Metropolitan Railways (CPTM) and Metropolitan Bus Transit Agency (EMTU). About 65 per cent of all daily trips in the metropolitan area are made by public transport

SMT

Secretaria Municipal de Transportes (SMT)
Municipal Transport Secretariat
Av Naçoes Unidas 7123, São Paulo 05477-000, Brazil
Telephone: + 55 11 814 7711 Fax: ext 130
Secretary: Carlos de Souza Toledo

Current Situation: SMT is responsible for city traffic and transport management. The transit department (DTP) deals with buses, taxis and related matters. São Paulo Transporte (SPTrans) acts on behalf of SMT/DTP with respect to bus transport activities and registration/inspection of taxis and paratransit vans.

SPTrans

São Paulo Transporte SA
Rua Treze de Maio 1376, São Paulo 01327-901, Brazil
Telephone: + 55 11 253 5566 Fax: + 55 11 35 5858
President: Francisco A N Christovam
Operations Director: Washington L E Corrêa

Current Situation: SPTrans, formerly CMTC (Companhia Municipal de Transporte Colectivos), was established in 1947 with a service contract to operate all the city's public transport, including buses and trams, which had been run by the foreign-owned São Paulo Light & Power Company. Lack of investment resulted in poor quality services and in the mid-1950s private operators began to appear, authorised by CMTC. All trams were replaced by trolleybuses by 1968.

By 1992, CMTC was operating only 25 per cent of services, with 31 private operators, licensed by the Municipal Transport Secretariat through CMTC, responsible for the rest. Under this arrangement, operators retained all income from fares, which resulted in maximisation of revenue, but at the expense of service quality. Flat fares made it possible for low-income families to relocate to the suburbs, whilst continuing to work in other parts of the city. Operators failed to take this population shift into account, while low levels of investment led to fleet shortages, poor availability and overcrowding. Even so, buses continued to handle three-quarters of all the city's public transport journeys.

In 1992, as original concessions expired, CMTC was once again designated exclusive operator, but with the power to contract out services which it did not wish to operate. In 1992, it was decided that all fare revenue would pass directly to CMTC, which remunerated contractors on the basis of kilometres run and fleet size. This was amended in 1993, when the number of passengers carried became the main element in the calculation.

In 1993/94, all services still being run by CMTC were transferred to private operators in order to raise efficiency and lower operating costs. This process was completed in December 1994, with all of CMTC's 2,700 buses and trolleybuses having been either scrapped or sold/leased to private operators. Staff numbers were cut from 25,000 to 2,000, those being off-loaded being mainly drivers, conductors or maintenance personnel. Most recently, in March 1995, the company's name was changed to São Paulo Transporte (SPTrans).

In 1996, 67 service contracts were being fulfilled by 48 private operators with staff totalling 54,000 and a total of 11,072 buses in fleets ranging from 30 to 400 buses.

Busways: Growing demand and increasing traffic congestion forced CMTC to look for alternatives to its mostly radial bus network. A trunk/feeder concept was adopted using bus-only corridors placed on central reservation. The Paes de Barros corridor commenced operation in 1975, featuring stops on offset islands located to the right of the bus flow in both directions. Bus convoying was adopted on the Nove de Julho and Celso Garcia routes to deal with the large numbers of public transport vehicles. This led to dramatic reductions in travel time, but the scheme proved difficult to operate on a permanent basis and eventually a Paes de Barros style busway was introduced. In 1991, the Vila Nova Cachoeirinho corridor began operation with trunk route buses running along busways on the left of each carriageway nearest to the median strip. Stops at raised islands allow level access to buses, thereby reducing dwell time and all vehicles are required to be fitted with extra doors on the left side. Such has been the success of this busway that it is to be the model for all future schemes.

Local feeder buses connect with the trunk routes at terminals. Trunk routes are served by larger vehicles, including trolleybuses, articulated buses or standard Padron commuter buses. In addition to these specialised corridors, part of the original radial bus network has been revamped to act as feeders, although others have survived to cater for specific flows.

Sixteen busways are in operation, totalling 182.6 km. Services are operated by 29 private companies with a combined fleet of 1,674 vehicles (1,226 articulated buses, 154 Padrons, 224 rigids, 28 articulated trolleybuses and 42 Padron trolleybuses). Daily patronage amounts to 3.2 million.

In total 18 corridors and 33 interchange terminals are planned. SPTrans recently flirted with the private sector on a possible joint venture to implement the remaining busways, but financial problems forced this idea to be abandoned. The city is therefore building more routes and has also asked companies currently providing services to upgrade their fleets for higher capacity running.

Trolleybus network: Although the trolleybus overhead, electrification systems and vehicles are owned by the municipality, services are provided by three private companies: Electrobus, Transbraçal and Viaçao Santo Amaro (ex-TCI). However, the operators are buying 37 new vehicles from Volvo, Marcopolo and Powertronics at a cost of R$9.8 million, but ownership of these will also revert to the municipality with the expiry of the operating concession in 2004.

Electrobus, which employs 1,450 staff and operates 10 routes, is based at the former CMTC Tatuapé garage, having taken over operation of a dilapidated fleet of 285 vehicles in April 1994. Of these, 44 had been cannibalised and the rest had serious structural, mechanical and electrical problems. As the average age of the fleet was 13 years, it was decided to undertake a major overhaul of all vehicles, including rebodying, to extend the life of the fleet by a further 10 years. The work, which was to be completed by February 1997, was funded by SPTrans, which is drawing up plans with the other two operators to undertake similar action on their fleets.

Developments: In 1995, a bus monitoring system was introduced using transponder/loop detector technology. Magnetic ticketing was due to be phased in starting in early 1997, with the entire fleet reverting to one-person operation. Studies are under way to implement an intermediate capacity system, with double-articulated trolleybuses running on segregated track using automatic guidance. The first phase should be in operation in 1997.

The change to front entry and driver inspection has reduced fraud and improved loading times

High-platform station on the Vila Nova Cachoeirinha busway, with five-door Scania bus

Trolleybuses carry about 15 per cent of all journeys

Steps are being taken to comply with a new law which states that by 2010 only electric and CNG-powered buses will be allowed to operate regular routes within city limits.

Paratransit services, with fleets of 9-16 vehicles are licensed by SPTrans to serve specific passengers flows, where existing long-distance services are inadequate. The role of these and other lesser modes is being analysed, within the scope of a broader study currently under way to design an information system to support SPTrans' management of the public transport network.

Bus and trolleybus

Passenger boardings: (1994) 1,800 million
Vehicle-km: (1994) 760 million

Number of routes: Bus 800, trolleybus 18
Route length: Bus 6,044 km, trolleybus 453 km
Fleet: 11,072 buses
In peak service: 10,029
Fleet: 480 trolleybuses

Scania articulated	1
Volvo articulated	1
Cames	117
Mafersa Padron	78
Scania Ciferal chopper-control	96
Scania Ciferal contactor-control	100
Scania Marcopolo chopper-control	87

In peak service: 275

Most intensive service: 2 min
One-person operation: None
Fare collection: Cash or prepurchase pass; discounted passes for students
Fare structure: Flat; elderly and disabled and some governmens employees travel free
Fare evasion control: Checks by driver; all routes operate front entry
Operational control: Route inspectors/automatic vehicle monitoring system
Arrangements for elderly/disabled: 200 routes have at least one lift-equipped bus; 70 lift-equipped vans operate demand-response service to eligible patrons
Bus priority: Reserved lanes for both trolleybuses and buses (see below); there are also other small lengths of busway and bus-only street and 500 km of bus-only lanes
Integration with other modes: Bus and trolleybus services integrated; 45% of routes feed metro or suburban rail stations
Operating costs financed by: (All city operations) Fares 85%, subsidy/grants 15%
New vehicles financed by: Government financial agencies/local financial institutions

Mercedes of Operator Viacão Gato Preto **1997**

Line 3 metro train at Ana Rosa

CPTM

Companhia Paulista de Trens Metropolitanos
Avenida Paulista 402, 01310-903 São Paulo
Telephone: +55 11 281 6000 Fax: +55 11 285 0323
President: J R Medeiros da Rosa
Operations & Maintenance: V M de Almeida Noronha
Engineering & Works Director: J Aurélio Brentani
Staff: 5,600

Type of operation: Suburban heavy rail

Passenger journeys: (1991) 320 million
(1994) 347 million
(1995) 770,000 daily

Current situation: CPTM was created in 1993 to bring the former CBTU and FEPASA suburban rail networks under common management with the metro; the suburban operations were taken over in 1994. Suburban services operate on two former CBTU routes out of Luz and Roosevelt stations (East system, 192 km, 163 stations, 1,600 mm gauge), and two former Fepasa routes from Julio Prestes station to Amador Bueno, with a branch from Osasco to Varginha (West system, 78 km, 35 stations, partly metre-gauge). The network is electrified at 3 kV DC. Trains run every 4-15 min at peak times.

Developments: Modernisation of the network has been under way since 1985, financed by the World Bank and the Brazilian National Development Bank. Work is currently in progress on the 83 km eastern and 108 km northeast/southeast (Jundiai—Paranapiacaba) lines, where the permanent way is being rehabilitated, catenary and power supply upgraded, and both CTC and ATC installed. A new fleet of 30 four-car trains was ordered in February 1997 from a consortium of GEC Alsthom, Adtranz and CAF.

Awaiting finance is the city-centre connection between the former Fepasa and CBTU lines to create a link that would relieve pressure on the metro's east-west route. Some 7.3 km of new track is required, and 19 km will be rehabilitated.

Still at the planning stage is an upgrading of services to the south of the city. In the initial phase, seven new stations would be built and 10 emus purchased. Later, a 9 km Campo Limpo—Santo Amaro link would be built. Track upgrading is also planned for the western line from Julio Prestes to Itapevi, along with overhaul of 106 emu cars.

Negotiations continue with the metro authority on the possible transfer of the latter's proposed eastern extension to CPTM (see below). Discussions have been in progress with Spain's national railway RENFE to purchase 50 second-hand Class 440 emus, which will be modernised before export.

Bus and metro integration in São Paulo

Rolling stock: 998 emu cars formed into 293 trains, of which 197 were available for service in 1996

Budd S-100 (1956)	M35 T46
GE S-400 (1962)	M39 T78
Mafersa S-400 (1976)	M56 T110
Sorefame S-160 (1979)	M40 T80
Cobrasma S-700 (1987)	M50 T50
Toshiba/Kawasaki (metre-gauge) (1958)	M30 T60
Cobrasma/BBC/MTE 5000 (1979)	M98 T196
Mafersa/Villares/Sorefame/ACEC 5500 (1979)	M10 T20

Metropolitano de São Paulo

Companhia do Metropolitano de São Paulo (CMSP)
Rua Augusta 1626, São Paulo 01304-902
Telephone: +55 11 283 7411 Fax: +55 11 283 5228
President: Paulo C Goldschmidt
Operations Director: P C Moreira da Silva
Planning Director: Caetano Jannini Netto

Current situation: As well as operating the metro, is responsible for four major bus terminals, operation of which is contracted out, and construction (but not operation) of feeder trolleybus routes.
Developments: With national and international funding sources exhausted, in late 1995 the authority sought financial assistance from the private contractors involved to enable metro construction to continue. Those investing would be repaid from future commercial income and ticket revenues (the metro now achieves an operating surplus). New trains are to be supplied on the same basis.

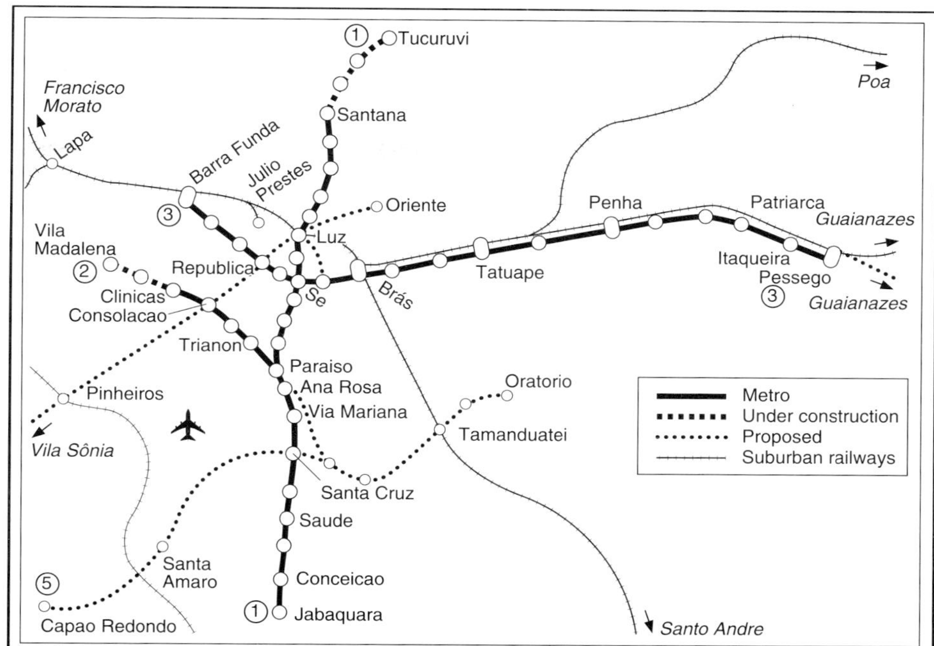

São Paulo metro

Metro

Staff: 8,500

Type of operation: Full metro, initial route opened 1974

Passenger journeys: (1993) 609 million
(1994) 623 million
(1995) 694 million

Route length: 43.6 km
in tunnel: 24.5 km
elevated: 5.5 km
Number of lines: 3
Number of stations: 41
in tunnel: 24
elevated: 7
Gauge: 1,600 mm
Track: 57 kg/m rail on continuous concrete beams in tunnels and on elevated sections; concrete sleepers on surface
Max gradient: 4%
Minimum curve radius: 300 m
Tunnel: Double-track cut-and-cover; single-track shield-driven bore
Electrification: 750 V DC, third rail

Service: Peak 1 min 38 s, off-peak 2 min 45 s
First/last train: 05.00/24.00

Fare structure: Flat, combined tickets available for through journeys by bus or suburban rail; 'Vale Transporte' passes; 6 months free travel for the unemployed
Integration with other modes: CMSP has taken a lead in integration through development of feeder suburban rail, bus and trolleybus services
Revenue control: Microprocessor-controlled electronic turnstiles
Signalling: ATS available, ATO throughout, being adapted to cut headway to 90 sec. All lines controlled from central control room at Paraíso.
Operating costs financed by: Fares 60%, other commercial sources 2.6%, government grants 37.4%

Rolling stock: 588 cars, formed into six-car trains

Mafersa Line 1 (1974)	M306
Mafersa/Cobrasma Line 2 (1982 onwards)	M276
GEC Alsthom/Adtranz Spain (1996)	M6

In peak service: 522
On order: 30 four-car trains from GEC Alsthom Transporte and Adtranz Spain

Developments: Fleet expansion, headway reduction and line extensions, designed to double the capacity of one of the most heavily utilised metros in the world, have been delayed by funding problems. Construction of the Santana—Tucuruvi (3.5 km, three stations) and Clinicas—Vila Madalena (2.9 km, two stations) extensions was expected to resume in 1996. Opening of these two short sections is expected to generate an additional 190,000 daily journeys. Private sector funding will be sought for completion of both.

The eastern extension from Pessego to Guaianazes (6 km, three stations) will not now be built as metro. The east-west line is already running well in excess of capacity and the extra traffic generated was thought likely to lead to saturation. CPTM will take over the project and build the line as a loop to shorten its own eastern route.

New metro construction proposals have been revised to give priority to areas poorly served by public transport. Top of the list, and scheduled to open in 2000, is Line 4 linking Luz with Vila Sônia in the southwest of the city. The initial section (9.1 km, 10 stations) will run from Paulista to Vila Sônia, serving en route a major interchange with CPTM suburban trains at Pinheiros. It is expected to attract 660,000 passengers daily. About half the US$1.46 billion cost will be financed by the World Bank (US$300 million) and BNDES (US$400 million), with the remainder coming from the private sector. Operation of the line would be let on a concession to the private companies involved, which would be required to complete the final section from Paulista to Luz by 2003.

This will be followed by the first portion of Line 5 — an isolated section from Santa Amaro to Capão Redondo (9.3 km, six stations).

Julio Prestes terminal

EMTU

Empresa Metropolitana de Transportes Urbana
194-196 Av Juruce, São Paulo 04080-010, SP
Telephone: +55 11 240 9208 Fax: +55 11 531 3844

Passenger journeys: 350,000 daily

Current situation: CMSP was authorised to build and operate a feeder trolleybus network outside the city's boundaries. EMTU later took over operations, but CMSP remains as the construction authority. Four routes in the southern suburbs were opened in 1988/90, known as the Medium Capacity Network. These total 37 km and run from Ferrazopolis and Piraporinha to Jabaquara metro station, Santo André station on the suburban rail system and the São Mateus terminal of the SPTrans trolleybus operation, and five other interchanges, on routes provided with segregated trolleybus lanes. The trolleybuses are in use operating alongside hired motor buses.
Developments: Operation and maintenance of EMTU's system was transferred to the private sector in 1992.

Other similar metro feeder routes were planned, but are now in doubt following withdrawal of government subsidies for electrically powered vehicles. An extension from Diadema to Brooklin on FEPASA's Jurubatuba line is the only one currently canvassed.

Fleet: 46 trolleybuses
Cobrasma/Tectronic (1986/90) 46

UPDATED

SAPPORO

Population: 1.7 million
Public transport: Bus, metro, and tramway operated by municipal authority. Suburban services provided by private bus companies and JR

Sapporo-shi Kotsu Kyoku

Sapporo City Transportation Bureau
Higashi 2-4-1 Oyachi, Atsubetsu-ku, Sapporo,
Hokkaido 004, Japan
Telephone: +81 11 896 2708 Fax: +81 11 896 2790
Managing Director: T Ikegami

Current situation: The three-line metro forms the nucleus of the city's transport system under the Long-Term Comprehensive Development Plan, with bus services seen increasingly as feeding the metro.

A Sound Management Plan was adopted in 1992 to improve the poor financial situation of the undertaking by such means as lower metro construction costs, staff reductions, fare increases and efforts to increase public transport use.

Bus

Staff: 1,447

Passenger journeys: (1991/92) 82 million
(1992/93) 80 million
(1993/94) 78 million
Vehicle-km: (1991/92) 19.6 million
(1992/93) 19 million
(1993/94) 18.3 million

Number of routes: 70
Route length: 409 km
Fleet: 555 vehicles, including Hino, Nissan, Mitsubishi-Fuso and Isuzu

One-person operation: All routes
Fare collection: Payment to farebox on exit, pass, stored-fare card
Fare structure: Zonal; metro transfer system; 'coupon tickets'; commuter passes; day tickets (metro/bus/tram); one-day Eco-Ticket gives reduced-rate travel on designated 'no car days' twice a month, when car drivers are encouraged to use public transport; stored-fare cards, 'With You Card' valid on metro/bus/tram, 'Common Card' valid on metro/tram/city bus/JR Bus/Chuo Bus
Fares collected on board: 62.9%
Operational control: Radio
Arrangements for elderly/disabled: Pass for free travel covered by subsidy; wheelchair accessible vehicles
Integration with other modes: Bus and metro systems closely integrated with many feeders and interchanges; transfer ticket system
Bus priority: 11 bus-only lanes (46.1 km); 5 bus priority lanes (13.2 km)
Operating costs financed by: Fares 80%, other commercial sources 0.7%, subsidy/grants 19.3%
Subsidy from: City
New vehicles financed by: Internal resources

Developments: Bus position indication system indicates time of arrival of next bus to passengers at stops. Hail-and-Ride introduced on one suburban route. New 'Factory Line' service connects industrial zone with metro stations. Latest vehicles feature air conditioning and lower floors.

Metro

Staff: 1,225

Type of operation: Full metro, rubber-tyred system, initial route opened 1971

Passenger journeys: (1991/92) 223 million
(1992/93) 219 million
(1993/94) 216 million
Car-km: (1991/92) 32.4 million
(1992/93) 31.8 million
(1993/94) 30.9 million

Route length: 45.2 km
in tunnel: 40.5 km
Number of lines: 3
Number of stations: 47
Gauge: Rubber-tyred trains on concrete guideway, Line 1 spacing 2,180 mm; Line 2, 2,150 mm
Track: Line 1 concrete slab track without sleepers, surface paved with epoxy-resin plastic; centre-guide steel

Series 7000 metro train on the Toho line 1995

Car 254 on Sapporo's remaining tram line 1997

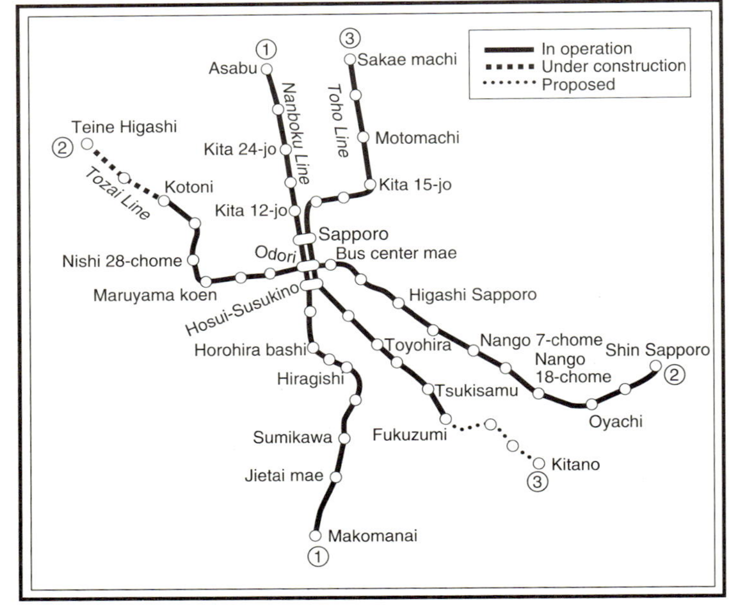

Sapporo's metro

I-beam. Line 2 similar but running track surface paved with steel plates; Line 3 track on concrete sleepers
Max gradient: 4.3%
Minimum curve radius: 200 m
Tunnel: Generally double-track, cut-and-cover; beneath the Toyohira river the section has been built by the caisson method. Elevated section has a circular aluminium shelter to prevent heavy snowfall affecting operations
Electrification: 750 V DC, third rail on Line 1; 1.5 kV DC, RS-AFB overhead conductor system on Lines 2 and 3

Service: Peak 3½-4 min, off-peak 6-7 min
First/last train: 06.15/23.30
Fare structure: 6 sections; AFC handles interchange between metro and bus and provides 25% discount on each fare; commuter passes; metro/bus/tram day tickets; one-day Eco-Tickets (see under bus); stored fare 'With You Card' valid on metro/bus/tram, and 'Common Card', valid additionally on JR Bus and Chuo Bus services
Revenue control: Central processor, automatic ticket vending and fare adjusting machines, coin collecting unit and automatic gates with stored-fare card readers; automatic commuter pass vendor at main stations
Arrangements for elderly/disabled: Lifts at 24 stations
Operating costs financed by: Fares 92%, other commercial sources 1%, subsidy/grants 7%
Signalling: Full ATC and CTC. Linked to the signalling is the Subway Total System, whose main subsystems comprise: optical total transmission line control; related operating control equipment; power control; automatic operations control; fire-control system; automatic inspection of rolling stock; ticket vending and inspection equipment; public address and surveillance. The system also allows automated driverless operation of empty trains over the 1.3 km link to Higashi depot

Rolling stock: 398 cars

Kawasaki 2000 Line 1	M128
Kawasaki 3000 Line 1	M40
Kawasaki 5000 Line 1 (1995)	M3 T3
Kawasaki 6000 Line 2	M72 T72
Kawasaki 7000 Line 3	M40 T40

On order: Six Series 5000 six-car trains

Developments: 5.5 km extension of Line 3 from Hosui-Susukino to Fukuzumi opened 1994. Construction started in 1994 of a 2.8 km extension of Line 2 from Kotoni to Teine Higashi for 1998 opening. Extension planned of Line 3 from Fukuzumi to Kitano (3.2 km).

Tramway
Staff: 135

Type of operation: Conventional tramway

Passenger journeys: (1991/92) 9.7 million
(1992/93) 9.5 million
(1993/94) 9.3 million
Car-km: (1993/94) 1.1 million

Number of routes: 1, retained as metro feeder
Route length: 8.4 km
Number of stops: 23
Gauge: 1,067 mm
Electrification: 600 V DC, overhead

Chuo Bus vehicles on Sapporo area services ***1995***

Service: 3-10 min
First/last car: 06.18/23.18
Fare collection: Farebox or prepurchase
Fare structure: Flat; tram/metro transfer tickets, day ticket (bus/metro/tram), one-day Eco-Ticket (see under bus); prepurchase coupon tickets, 1- and 3-monthly passes; stored-fare 'With You Card' valid on metro/bus/tram, and 'Common Card' valid additionally on JR Bus and Chuo Bus services

Rolling stock: 30 cars

Sapporo Sogo Tekko Kumiai (1958/61)	M18
Hitachi (1958)	M5
Nippon Sharyo (1961)	M1
Kawasaki (1985/87/88)	M6

Developments: Audio/visual 'tram approaching' indicators installed at nine stops. All passenger shelters are equipped with footway and roof heating to prevent snow accumulation.

JR Hokkaido
Hokkaido Railway Company
Hokkaido Ryokaku Tetsudo
Nishi 15-chome, Kita 11-jo, Chuo-ku, Sapporo 060
Telephone: +81 11 700 5717 Fax: +81 11 700 5719
Chair: Y Omori
President: S Sakamoto

Suburban/interurban rail
Passenger journeys: (1990/91) 49.5 million (Sapporo city)

Current situation: All-stations emu services operate Sapporo—Otaru (34 km) and Sapporo—Iwamizawa (40 km) on the Hakodate main line and Sapporo—Chitose airport (44 km) on the Chitose line. Some trains continue over longer distances. Local dmu service operates Sapporo—Daigaku-mae (30.5 km) on the Sassho line.

Bus
Current situation: JR buses run 44 routes serving the northwest and southeast suburbs in association with rail services, and as feeders to the metro. Transfers available to metro. Stored-fare 'Common Card' accepted on all routes in Sapporo.

Hokkaido Chuo Bus
Hokkaido Chuo Bus Company (Chuo Bus)
1-8-6 Shikinai, Otaru-shi, Hokkaido 047
Telephone: +81 134 24 1111

Current situation: Provides 61 suburban services in the Sapporo area, with transfer fare system to metro. Fleet of 965 buses and 161 coaches. Stored-fare 'Common Card' accepted on selected routes in Sapporo.

Jotetsu Bus
Jotetsu Bus Company
9-1-1 Toyahira-shijo, Toyohira-ku, Sapporo-shi 062
Telephone: +81 11 811 6141

Current situation: Provides six suburban services in the Sapporo area with 60 buses and 25 coaches. Jotetsu is a subsidiary of the Tokyu Corp which has extensive bus and rail interests in the Tokyo area.

UPDATED

SEATTLE
Population: City 531,000, King County area 1.6 million
Public transport: Bus, trolleybus and waterfront vintage tramway provided in metropolitan Seattle and King County by metropolitan agency responsible to county government. City operates monorail; state ferries. Other operators provide bus service in adjacent Snohomish and Pierce counties, which have joined with King County in forming a regional transit authority. Light rail and commuter rail proposed

RTA
Central Puget Sound Regional Transportation Authority
821 Second Avenue, MS 151, Seattle, WA 98104-1598, USA
Telephone: +1 206 684 6776 Fax: +1 206 684 1234
Email: tra@scn.org
Chair: Bruce Laing
Executive Director: Robert K White

Current situation: The RTA is a public agency created in 1993 to develop and operate a regional transport system in King, Pierce and Snohomish counties. It is governed by an 18-member board, of whom 17 are locally elected; the eighteenth member is the state transport department Secretary.
Developments: In 1994 the RTA adopted a 25-year regional transit master plan, which proposed construction of a 110 km light rail network, setting up of a 130 km commuter rail system over existing tracks, development of eight regional trunk bus corridors, and commitment to creating a co-ordinated fare structure accepted by all the region's operators. The cost of these proposals was $6.7 billion. See *JUTS 1995-96* for details.

The RTA presented the Phase I transit system and funding proposal to voters in March 1995, when it was rejected by a small margin. Subsequently, the RTA developed a reduced Phase I scheme as a 'starter system' and carried out much local consultation. A final revised proposal, costed at some $3.9 billion, was approved by voters in November 1996.

Under the plan, taxes will be raised over the coming 16 years to finance construction of a light rail line from Seattle to Seattle/Tacoma airport, develop a cross-city commuter rail line between South Tacoma and Everitt using existing rights-of-way, and introduce express bus routes.

A smartcard fare system is being developed to embrace all the area's operators.

Metro
King County Department of Transportation
Exchange Building, 821 Second Avenue, Seattle, WA 98104
Telephone: +1 206 684 1441
County Executive: Gary Locke
Director, Department of Transportation: Paul Toliver
General Manager, Transit: Rick Walsh
Staff: 3,717

SEMARANG

Population: 1 million
Public transport: Government-owned corporation provides part of public transport service, supplemented by independent minibuses and suburban buses

DAMRI

Djawatan Angkutan Motor Republik Indonesia
PO Box 76 Jatinegara, Jl Matraman Raya 25, Jakarta Timur, Indonesia
Telephone: +62 21 881131/881132
President: H Wirjatmo
Director of Operations: M Basoeki

Current situation: A fleet of Mercedes single-deck buses is operated on fixed-route urban services.

Private minibus/bus

Current situation: A large fleet of Daihatsu, Suzuki, Mitsubishi and Toyota Kijang 10-11 seaters supplements the services provided by DAMRI. Larger buses, with a seating capacity of between 20 and 30, provide suburban services radiating from the city-centre bus terminal.

Daihatsu Hijet mikrolet in Semarang urban service

SENDAI

Population: 970,000, metropolitan area 1.4 million
Public transport: Bus services provided by municipality and private company; metro; suburban rail

Sendai-shi Kotsu Kyoku

Sendai City Transport Bureau
1-4-15 Kimachidori, Aoba-ku, Sendai-shi, Miyagi-ken 980, Japan
Telephone: +81 22 224 5111 Fax: +81 22 224 5506

Bus

Staff: 1,179

Passenger journeys: (1993) 70.1 million
(1994) 67.5 million
(1995) 64.7 million
Vehicle-km: (1993) 24.2 million
(1994) 23.9 million
(1995) 24 million

Number of routes: 58
Route length: 661 km
Fleet: 678 vehicles, including Hino, Isuzu, Nissan Diesel and Mitsubishi Fuso
In peak service: 553
On order: 60 buses

Fare structure: Flat and distance-related, mixed system; multiride coupon tickets; wide range of passes including multimodal
Fare collection: Payment to farebox, prepurchase tickets and passes; prepaid card (bus, bus/metro)
One-person operation: All routes
Arrangements for elderly/disabled: Some wheelchair-accessible vehicles
Operating costs financed by: Fares 74.4%, other commercial sources 3.2%, subsidy 22.4%
Subsidy from: City

Wheelchair-accessible service of Sendai-shi Kotsu Kyoku **1996**

Isuzu midibus of Sendai-shi Kotsu Kyoku **1995**

Current situation: Metro feeder routes are organised around seven suburban bus/metro interchanges with through ticketing

Metro

Staff: 322

Type of operation: Full metro, initial route opened 1987

Passenger journeys: (1993/94) 58.4 million
(1994/95) 59.5 million
(1995/96) 61 million
Car-km: (1993/94) 6.8 million
(1994/95) 6.8 million
(1995/96) 6.8 million

Route length: 14.8 km
in tunnel: 11.8 km
Number of lines: 1
Number of stations: 17
Gauge: 1,067 mm
Max gradient: 3.5%
Minimum curve radius: 160 m
Electrification: 1.5 kV DC, overhead

Service: Peak 3.5 min, off-peak 7 min
Fare structure: Graduated; multiride tickets, bus/metro transfer tickets and passes, day tickets, 1- and 3-month student passes; 1-, 3- and 6-month commuter passes; prepaid cards
Fare collection: Full AFC
One-person operation: All trains
Signalling: Full ATO, ATC
Operating costs financed by: Fares 49.6%, other commercial sources 49.8%, subsidy/grants 0.6%
Subsidy from: National government 62.7%, city 37.3%

Rolling stock: 21 four-car trains
Kawasaki 1000 (1987 on) M42 T42
In peak service: 18 trains
On order: One four-car train

Current situation: Sendai's first metro route, the Nanboku line, links Izumi-Chuo in the north to Tomizawa in the south.

Miyagi Kotsu

Miyagi Kotsu Bus Co Ltd
3-33 Showa-machi, Sendai-shi 980, Japan
Telephone: +81 22 273 3071
Staff: 1,440

Passenger journeys: (1994) 39.5 million
Vehicle-km: (Annual) 28 million

Number of routes: 677
Route length: 5,278 km
Fleet: 624 buses including Isuzu, Mitsubishi, Hino and Nissan Diesel types; plus 149 coaches in charter division
Operating costs financed by: Fares 90%, subsidy/grants 10%
Subsidy from: National and local government

Current situation: Operates bus services throughout Miyagi Prefecture including Sendai city and suburbs. Miyagi Kotsu is part of the Meitetsu Group, which operates extensive bus and rail services in the Nagoya area.

Developments: Reorganisation of routes carried out on opening of metro, with bus/metro transfer tickets available on feeder buses. Route extensions to Sendai suburban housing developments planned.

JR East

East Japan Railway Company
Higashi Nihon Ryokaku Tetsudo
6-5 Marunouchi 1-chome, Chiyoda-ku, Tokyo 100
Telephone: +81 3 3215 9648 Fax: +81 3 3213 5291
Chair: S Yamanouchi
President: M Matsuda

Suburban/interurban rail

Passenger journeys: (1995/96) 57.4 million (Sendai city)

Current situation: Commuter emu services run on the Senseki line, Sendai—Takagimachi—Ishinomaki (50.3 km), and on the Senzan line, Sendai—Ayashi (15.2 km) with some trains continuing to Yamagata (62.8 km). Longer-distance all-stations local trains on Tohoku main line and Joban line serve some suburban stations in Sendai. Also infrequent local service Sendai—Rifu (12.2 km).

UPDATED

Metro train in Sendai's northern suburbs ***1995***

SEOUL

Population: 10.2 million; 13.5 million including satellite cities

Public transport: Bus services provided by 90 private groups or companies operating as co-operative under franchises issued by municipal transport board. Metro, with cross-city section shared with Korean National Railroad suburban services

Seoul Bus Transportation Cooperative

Seoul Bus Transportation Cooperative
Transport House, 4th Floor, PO Box 31400, 11-7 Sin-jeon dong, Gong dong gu, Seoul, Republic of Korea
Telephone: +82 2 415 4101
Managing Director: C G Li
Staff: (Central administration) 231

Current situation: Seoul's franchised bus operators work together under the Seoul Bus Transportation Cooperative, governed by an executive committee and with a substantial administration. Operations are grouped into city and express route groups, the city buses with conductors having high standee capacity, and the express buses, one-man operated, offering a premium seated service and hence known also as 'seat buses'.

In late 1993 plans were announced for many more express routes and introduction of a new distributor network of 'business class' buses running in the city centre.

Under powers delegated from the National Transport Ministry, Seoul metropolitan government is responsible for regulation and licensing of private bus operations and effectively issues franchises for mixed groups of services to individual companies. Previous city-owned bus operations were terminated after making losses and all bus services put in private hands. The transport ministry has overall control of fare levels. With very low car-ownership, buses account for about 60 per cent of the city's motorised public transport, but with development of the metro (now accounting for over 20 per cent and set to expand substantially) a significant reduction in bus use is planned. At the end of the 1980s, buses were carrying about 3,000 million passengers annually.

Operations are affected by a rapidly growing number of cars and a policy of decentralised city development into eight sub-centres. Severe traffic congestion has led to strict enforcement of regulations, and a tax is being considered on businesses that stimulate extra traffic, as well as possible implementation of a road pricing or toll system. Estimated bus share of trips by 2000 will be only 25 per cent, with the bus network seen as complementing the metro.

SMC bus in Seoul

Myong-dong station on metro Line 4 ***1995***

The readiness of new operators to replace any withdrawals ensures that there is no requirement for subsidy, and operators are assisted by allocation of a suitable 'mix' of operations. Regulations lay down detailed operating practices, including use of women conductors. Seat buses are licensed to provide express services over the same routes as conventional buses, at premium fares.

More than 28,000 taxis operate conventional taxi services, catering for about 15 per cent of demand.

Bus

Number of routes: 347 (city 264, express 83)
Route length: 3,620 km
Fleet: 8,500 buses

City service types	over 7,000
(mostly standard locally built 72-capacity)	
Express service types	1,329
(mostly 37-seater)	

One-person operation: City buses, none; seat buses, all services
Fare collection: Payment by cash or token to conductors/drivers
Fare structure: Flat, standard with metro; premium for seat buses; prepurchase discount tokens
Average peak-hour speed: 22.9 km/h
Operating costs financed by: Fares 100%

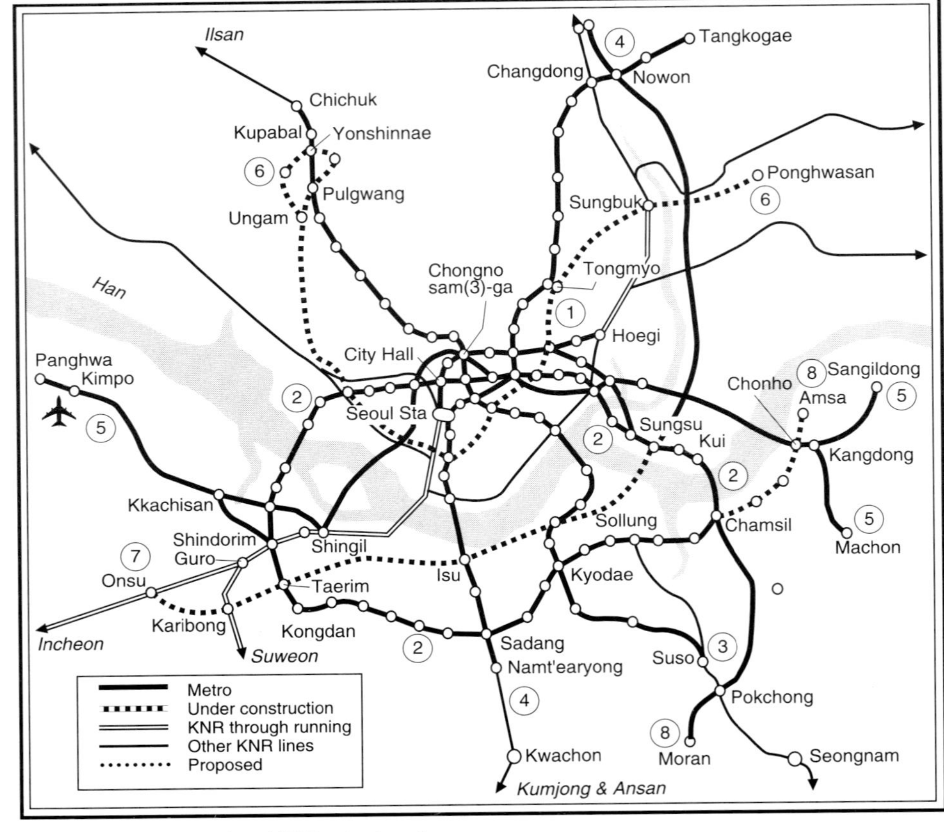

Seoul metro and associated KNR suburban lines

Seoul Metropolitan Subway

Seoul Metropolitan Subway Corporation
447-7 Bangbae-Dong, Socho-Ku, Seoul
Telephone: +82 2 520 5056 Fax: +82 2 582 9522
President: Jin-Hee Han
Director of Operations: Yong-Kyu Hong
Staff: 11,116

Type of operation: Full metro; first section opened 1974

Passenger journeys: (1993) 1,388 million
(1994)
(1995)

Route length: 131.6 km
Number of lines: 4
Number of stations: 114
Gauge: 1,435 mm
Track: 50 kg/m rail laid on timber sleepers and ballast; track rubber-padded for protection of city's historic East and South gates
Max gradient: 3.5%
Minimum curve radius: 400 m
Tunnel: Cut-and-cover; tunnels vibration-damped near East and South gates
Electrification: 1.5 kV DC, overhead (KNR suburban trains on Lines 1 and 4 dual-voltage, 25 kV 60 Hz and 1.5 kV DC)

Service: Peak 2½ min, off-peak 4-10 min
Integration with other modes: Trains from KNR Incheon and Suweon suburban lines operate through metro Line 1 to reach Sungbuk, while Line 4 metro trains run through to KNR's Ansan and Kwacheon lines
Revenue collection: Full AFC system at all metro stations and 51 KNR stations

Rolling stock: 1,602 cars

Hitachi (1974)	M40 T20
Daewoo (1977)	M24 T12
Daewoo (1980)	M32
Hyundai (1982)	M24
Hyundai (1983)	M100 T2
GEC (1984)	M268 T134
Hyundai (1988)	M64 T68
Daewoo (1990)	M138
(1991)	M210
(1992)	M144
(1993)	M322

On order: 268 cars for Line 5 from Hyundai

Seoul Metropolitan Rapid Transit

Seoul Metropolitan Rapid Transit Corporation

Developments: Construction of four new lines has been in progress since 1990. Severe traffic congestion led to a new metro Master Plan drawn up in 1988, and revised in 1993. Nine routes totalling 252 km were accorded priority for completion by 2000. This will more than double the size of the network, which will then be expected to cope with 50 per cent of daily public transport journeys. The new routes are being built and operated by the MRT Corporation.

Three of the lines are new cross-city links which are seen as vital if road traffic congestion is to be eased. In addition, new segregated tracks are to be built for the existing KNR cross-city service which at present shares tracks of metro Line 1.

With work on Lines 5, 6, 7 and 8 nearing completion, in March 1997 the Seoul Metropolitan Government approved the next phase of construction comprising Lines 9, 10, 11 and 12, plus an extension of Line 3. Totalling 120 km, the routes are expected to be completed by 2005.

KNR

Korean National Railroad
122, 2 ka Bongnae-dong, Chung-ku, Seoul 100162
Telephone: +82 2 392 1319 Fax: +82 2 392 0430

Type of operation: Suburban heavy rail

Passenger journeys: (1993) 571 million
(1994) 592 million
(1995) 654 million

Current situation: In addition to extensive services on six other suburban and cross-city routes, KNR operates a service of electric trains at 3.5-10 min intervals between Uijongbu and Cheongryangri to the northeast of Seoul, and Incheon, Suweon, Ansan and Bundang to the south-west. Total 171 route-km, 95 stations. These lines are electrified at 25 kV 60 Hz, but through trains operate over Lines 1 and 4 of the metro, so emus are dual-system 25 kV AC/1.5 kV DC. Operating costs are covered entirely by fares.

Developments: Through services from metro Line 4 to the Ansan and Kwacheon lines were inaugurated in mid-1994, and from Line 3 to Bundang at the end of 1994. A 20.1 km line linking Ilsan New Town with metro Line 3 at Chichuk was opened for service in December 1995.

Under construction for late 1997 opening is a 6.6 km extension from Suso on the Bundang line to Sollung on metro Line 2.

Rolling stock: 1,030 cars
On order: Total of 238 cars on order from Daewoo (42 cars) and Hyundai (196)

Hyundai bus in Seoul

SEVILLA

Population: 725,000
Public transport: Bus services provided by municipal authority with some suburban services by private firms; suburban trains run by state railway; metro or light rail under study

Tussam

Transportes Urbanos de Sevilla SAM (Tussam)
Diego de Riaño 2, Sevilla 41004, Spain
Telephone: + 34 54 420011 Fax: +34 54 418175
President: Mariano Palancar Penella
Director General: Miguel Bermejo Herrero
Staff: 1,099

Current situation: In 1985 the formerly separate bus and minibus operations were merged; minibuses were eliminated by 1991. The new route structure initially had a positive effect on patronage, though numbers began to decline again at the end of the 1980s. Subsequently the suburban services run by private firms were integrated into the fares system.

Bus

Passenger journeys: (1993) 83.2 million
(1994) 85.3 million
(1995) 88 million
Vehicle-km: (1993) 14.3 million
(1994) 14.1 million
(1995) 14 million

Number of routes: 35
Route length: 396 km
On priority right-of-way: 12.8 km
Fleet: 300 vehicles

Pegaso 6038	91
Renault PR100-2	122
Pegaso 5522	69
Pegaso 5317 midibus	18

In peak service: 260

Most intensive service: 4 min
One-person operation: All routes
Fare collection: Onboard ticket machines and magnetic validators
Fare structure: Flat; prepurchase 'bono-bus' multijourney magnetic tickets; magnetic monthly passes
Fares collected on board: 7.4%
Fare evasion control: Inspectors
Operational control: Central radio communication to all vehicles; automatic vehicle location
Arrangements for elderly/disabled: Free annual passes
Average distance between stops: 300 m
Average peak-hour speed: In mixed traffic, 11.1 km/h
Operating costs financed by: Fares 52%, other commercial sources 1.5%, subsidy/grants 46.5%
Subsidy from: National and municipal budgets

Renault PR100-2 on Tussam's outer-circle route **1996**

New vehicles financed by: Credits from commercial banks

Private bus

Passenger journeys: (1993) 6.1 million
(1994) 6.7 million
(1995) 6.3 million

Current situation: Five suburban routes are run by private firms, controlled by the municipal authority and with the same fare system as Tussam.

RENFE

Spanish National Railways (RENFE)
Avenida Ciudad de Barcelona 8, Madrid 28007
Telephone: +34 1 606 6401 Fax: +34 1 315 0384
Director: Rafael Rodriguez Rebollo
Staff: 141 (Sevilla area only)

Type of operation: Suburban heavy rail

Passenger journeys: (1993) 3.3 million
(1994) 3.9 million
(1995) 4.4 million

Current situation: Services operate on two routes extending to 134 km with 20 stations; a third route serving Cartuja island runs on special occasions.

Developments: Four suburban extensions are under study – west to El Alijarago, south to Dos Hermanos, north to Rinconda and east to Alcalá de Guadaira. The two existing routes are being upgraded.

Rolling stock: 17 Class 470 three-car emus

Light rail (proposed)

Current situation: Construction began in the 1970s of a three-line metro, but work was halted following the establishment of regional autonomy pending a thorough economic analysis. Some 5 km of tunnel had been completed, linking P Nueva in the city centre with La Plata in the southeast, as well as three unconnected station shells.

The Andalucian regional government had planned to start construction of a two-line light rail system in 1996, with finance from municipal, regional and central government sources, but a change in central government has led to budgetary restrictions.

Line 1 (11 km) would run north-south, while Line 2 is a 20 km east-west alignment. Some use may be made of the partially built metro tunnels to gain access to the city centre; 30 to 35 LRVs would be required.

UPDATED

SHANGHAI

Population: 7 million, metropolitan area 12.9 million
Public transport: Bus and trolleybus services provided by single municipally owned company. Cross-river ferry, but six bus routes and one trolleybus route run through the two under-river tunnels, and two bus routes also cross the new Huangpu bridge. Most movement is on foot or cycle. Metro; light rail planned

Shanghai Transit

Shanghai Transit
34 Yanan Dong Lu, Shanghai, People's Republic of China
Telephone: +86 21 321 1200
General Manager: Li Gansheng
Staff: 74,000

Passenger journeys: (1990) 5,437 million
Vehicle-km: (1990) 361.3 million

Operating costs financed by: Fares 100%

Current situation: Continued expansion of the very extensive and heavily used articulated trolleybus network is envisaged under Shanghai's current five-year plan. The articulated trolleybuses represent only about 15 per cent of the fleet, but carry about 30 per cent of the passengers.

Old Shanghai articulated trolleybus on Route 20 **1997**

There is serious overcrowding on both modes, which cater for some 15 million daily journeys. Traffic congestion is exacerbated by 6 million or so cycles. Despite constant route expansion and congestion relief measures, severe short-term capacity problems remain and a computerised urban traffic control system is being developed. The long-planned metro, the first short section of which is in operation, is seen as a means of relieving pressure on the busiest corridors.

Staggering of commuting hours has also been effective in reducing congestion, with some 684,000 employees working staggered shifts. As an inducement, ST offers chartered buses which may deviate from fixed routes.

The bus network serves urban areas and the suburbs well beyond the limits of trolleybus operation. Most of the fleet is articulated, but is to designs built for many years and is fitted mostly with petrol rather than diesel engines.

Developments: 1991 saw completion of a study by consultants Barton-Aschman Associates of improvements to ease the flow of traffic in the city's congested streets. Amongst the recommendations are one-way streets, rerouteing of certain bus and trolleybus services, creation of cycle-only streets, modifications to traffic regulations and improvements to traffic signals. Funded by the Japanese government and conducted under the guidance of the World Bank, the project was overseen by the City Planning & Design Institute.

Three trolleybus routes replaced by buses in 1994.

Bus

Passenger journeys: (1985) 4,008 million
(1990) 3,874 million

Number of routes: 368 (26 all-night)
Route length: 18,407 km
Fleet: 5,341 buses, more than 70% articulated, including:
2-axle: Shanghai SK640, SK640J
Articulated: Shanghai SK661, SK661F, SK661P, SK662, SK670
MAN diesel articulated 100
Some vehicles of older types still in use

Most intensive service: Less than 1 min on some routes at peak times
One-person operation: None
Fare collection: Payment to seated conductors, monthly passes
Fare structure: Stage
Average distance between stops: 798 m in urban area, 1,472 m in suburbs
Integration with other modes: Bus and trolleybus networks form integrated transport system

Current situation: To alleviate congestion during peak hours over 500 vehicles have been assigned to 23 bus routes for express journeys and short workings. Some 179 buses form a contingency fleet with radio communication to cope with unusual passenger flows and special mother-and-baby buses have been introduced on about 20 routes to ease the problems of nursing mothers in peak-hour conditions.

Developments: Diesel engines are being tested and a number of diesel buses are expected to be imported from Europe.

Automatic vehicle monitoring installed in a small fleet of buses as a pilot project.

Trolleybus

Passenger journeys: (1985) 1,002 million
(1990) 1,563 million

Number of routes: 22
Route length: 186 km
Fleet: 923 trolleybuses, all articulated with chopper control

Most intensive service: 1 min
One-person operation: None
Fare collection: Payment to seated conductors, monthly passes
Fare structure: Stage
Operational control: Emergency turning circles just outside city centre provided on trolleybus routes to allow vehicles to turn short if required. Parallel wiring or passing loops at a number of locations where routes share wiring
Average peak-hour speed: 17 km/h
Average distance between stops: 567 m, extended to over 1 km in central area during peak hours

Current situation: The network is currently operating near to capacity with traffic flows of 13,000 passengers/h on some sections, vehicles running at less than 1 min headways on some routes (requiring tight dispatching) and 178-passenger trolleybuses proving inadequate. The busiest trolleybus routes are supplemented by petrol bus shuttles over their peak sections. Technically the system is the most advanced in China.

Future plans: Two trolleybus routes are planned for the Pudong development area in the east of the city, linked to the main city network by the route opened through the cross-river tunnel in 1990.

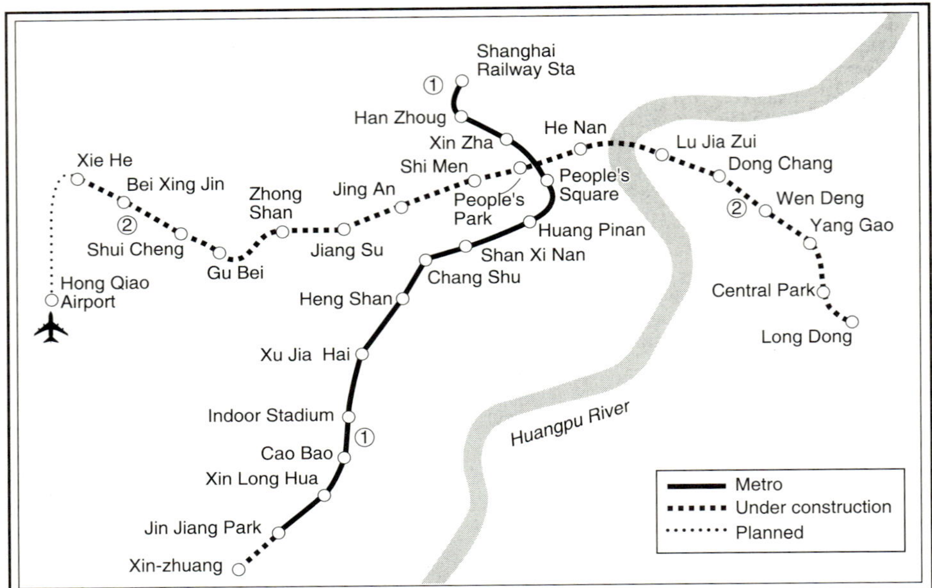

Shanghai metro

AEG (Adtranz) train on Line 1 ***1997***

Shanghai Metro

Shanghai Metro Corporation
12 Heng Shan Road, 200031 Shanghai
Telephone: +86 21 471 4457 Fax: +86 21 433 9598
General Manager: Shi Li-an
Staff: 1,498

Type of operation: Full metro, opened 1993

Passenger journeys: (1993, 9 months) 1.1 million
(1994, 9 months) 3.1 million

Route length: 16.1 km
in tunnel: 13.4 km
Number of lines: 1
Number of stations: 13
Gauge: 1,435 mm
Track: 60 kg/m rail; concrete sleepers in ballast on surface sections, concrete trackbed in tunnels
Max gradient: 3.2%
Minimum curve radius: 300 m
Electrification: 1.5 kV DC, overhead

Service: Peak 5-6 min, off-peak 8 min
First/last train: 05.00/23.00
One-person operation: None
Fare structure: Flat
Fare collection: Manual; AFC planned
Signalling: ATC, ATS and ATO
Surveillance: CCTV at stations

Rolling stock: 96 cars
AEG/Siemens (1992/93) M64 T32

Current situation: The 6.6 km southern portion of Line 1 opened in 1993 prior to inauguration of full public service in December 1994. Line 1 of the planned 176 km seven-line metro network links the city's two main rail terminals at Xin Ke Zhan in the north and Jin Jiang Park in the south. Extension 5 km southwards to Xin-zhuang under construction for late 1996 opening.

Since Shanghai's main traffic flows are primarily in the east-west direction, the first line has not had an immediate impact on the most seriously congested routes, though it serves major shopping areas and a sports stadium. Line 2 does run east-west, linking Jing-An Temple with Long-Dong Road (13.4 km, 10 stations); an extension to the airport is proposed.

Construction of Line 2 is expected to start in 1997 following award of a contract to the German Shanghai Metro Group joint venture of Adtranz and Siemens – the same group that equipped Line 1. Civil engineering work will be undertaken by local companies.

A further 35 six-car trains will be supplied for Line 2, which is scheduled to open in October 1999. These will be similar to the Line 1 cars, but will have AC traction motors, more powerful air conditioning and wider doors to assist in handling peak-hour loads of 60,000 passengers/h in each direction.

A network of six lines totalling some 200 km has been approved for construction by 2010. Amongst them, Line 3 would link He-nan Road with Zhong-yuan and there would be a northern extension of Line 1 to Ji-yuan Road.

Light rail/monorail (planned)

Current situation: Areas of lower population density are to be served by a six-line elevated light rail network approved in 1994 and extending to 118 km.

A contract for construction of Line 1 as a monorail was awarded in December 1995 to an Australian company Monotraction Pty Ltd. Linking Xin-zhuang with Min-hang, the 13 km line is expected to open in 1998.

UPDATED

SHEFFIELD

Population: City 528,000, county 1.3 million

Public transport: Bus services operated by private companies. Light rail system owned by Passenger Transport Executive and operated by a subsidiary company. The PTE, whose authority covers the surrounding urban areas of Doncaster, Rotherham, Barnsley and others, also contracts for provision of rail services

Easiaccess service of Mainline passes Supertram at Castle Square ***1997***

Mainline

Mainline Group Ltd
8 Riverside Court, Newhall Road, Sheffield S9 2TJ, England
Telephone: +44 114 256 7000 Fax: +44 114 243 1562
Managing Director: Peter Sephton
Operations Director: Ian Davies
Finance Director: Mike Pestereft
Engineering Director: Bernard Keane
Staff: 2,500

Current situation: The former bus operations of the PTE became a separate company in 1986, and were sold to an employee share ownership partnership in 1993. The PTE continues to own depots and infrastructure, but the company owns vehicles and ancillary services. Mainline agreed to sell a 20 per cent shareholding to Stagecoach, but the acquisition was rejected by the government in 1995 and the holding was transferred to the FirstBus group.

Developments: Single-deckers have been purchased to replace double-deck vehicles. Articulated buses are used on the busy shuttle route to the Meadowhall shopping centre. Early experiments with high-frequency minibus services have ceased, with new single-decks now carrying route branding.

A guided bus scheme is proposed for two major roads, and trials have taken place on a short test track at the Rotherham garage.

The low-cost subsidiary Sheaf Line, set up in 1989, was integrated into the main fleet in 1993. An 11 per cent interest was purchased in 1995 in local independent Northern Bus of Dinnington. The coach subsidiary Coachline was sold in 1996.

Bus

Passenger journeys: (1993/94) 100 million
(1994/95) 99.5 million
(1995/96) 99 million
Vehicle-km: (1993/94) 51 million
(1994/95) 52 million
(1995/96) 53 million

Number of routes: 300
Route length: 1,000 km
On priority right-of-way: 3 km

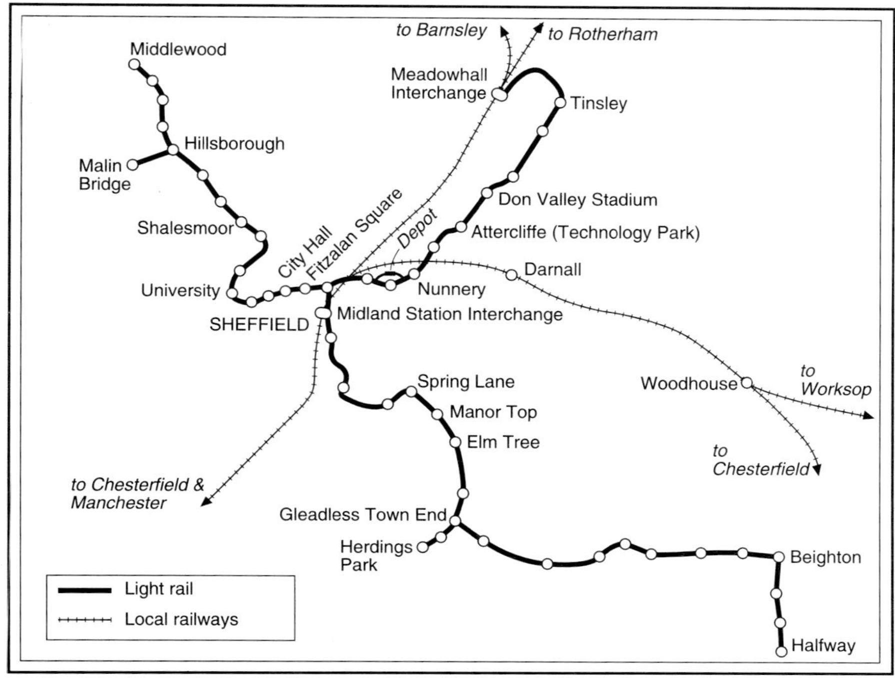

Sheffield's light rail routes

Fleet: 804 vehicles

Leyland double-deck	21
MCW double-deck	72
Dennis double-deck	312
Leyland single-deck	5
Volvo single-deck	225
Leyland-DAB articulated	13
Iveco minibus	1
Renault minibus	138
Freight Rover minibus	1
Others	16

In peak service: 686

Most intensive service: 5 min
One-person operation: 100%
Fare collection: Wayfarer equipment; passes
Fare structure: Stage; all system and area passes
Fare evasion control: Inspectors
Arrangements for elderly/disabled: SYPTE concessionary flat fare; services for the disabled in Sheffield and Doncaster with specially adapted vehicles; split-step entrances on latest buses; low-floor buses on 2 routes
Average distance between stops: 250 m
Average peak-hour speed: 16 km/h

Yorkshire Terrier

Yorkshire Terrier Ltd
Rother Valley Way, Holbrook Industrial Estate, Sheffield S19 5RW
Telephone: +44 114 247 0777 Fax: +44 114 248 9085
Managing Director: Bill Baldwin
Operations Director: Paul Beardsley
Staff: 170

Current situation: Established in 1988 when two routes were started with 14 single-decks, and services have since grown rapidly. The company is now a free-standing subsidiary of Yorkshire Traction.

Developments: The fleet of Leylands is being re-engined with the new Volvo 'green' engine. New Dennis Darts have been purchased.

Bus

Number of routes: 24
Fleet: 96 vehicles

Leyland National single-deck	64
Scania single-deck	6
Dennis Dart single-deck	16
Leyland and Scania coaches	10

Andrews Sheffield Omnibus

Andrews (Sheffield) Ltd
Green Lane Depot, Ecclesfield, Sheffield S30 3WY
Telephone: +44 114 246 5555 Fax: +44 114 257 0343
General Manager: Paul Payne
Staff: 140

Current situation: Established in 1986, Andrews (Sheffield) was bought by Yorkshire Traction in 1992. Sheffield Omnibus was acquired by YT in 1995 and operations were combined, trading as Andrews Shefffield Omnibus.

Bus

Number of routes: 11
Fleet: 74 vehicles

Leyland Olympian double-deck	5
Leyland Fleetline double-deck	20
Leyland National single-deck	29
Volvo B6R single-deck	15
Atlantean Sprint single-deck	2
Volvo B10B single-deck	3

Yorkshire Traction

Yorkshire Traction Co Ltd
Upper Sheffield Road, Barnsley S70 4PP
Telephone: +44 1226 202555 Fax: +44 1226 282313
Managing Director: Frank Carter
Operations Director: Michael Carter
Commercial Director: George Peach
Finance Director: John Meyers
Engineering Director: Norman Cook
Staff: 1,020

Current situation: A substantial part of the bus services in the South Yorkshire metropolitan area, serving Barnsley and surrounding area, is provided by YT, sold to its management in 1987. Operations lie almost wholly within the PTE area. Operations have expanded with purchase of Tom Jowitt Travel, Shearings and Globe of Barnsley, and the group has also acquired Lincolnshire Road Car, Strathtay Scottish of Dundee, Lincoln City Transport, Andrews, Sheffield Omnibus and South Riding.

Bus

Number of routes: 330
Fleet: 347 vehicles, comprising 80 double-deck, 140 single-deck, 93 minibus and 34 coaches

Other operators

Current situation: No other large operator lies within the Sheffield district, although East Midland of Chesterfield (350 vehicles) comes into the city. Local operators include Northern Bus Co and Thompson Travel.

South Yorkshire PTE

South Yorkshire Passenger Transport Executive
Exchange Street, Sheffield S2 5SZ, England
Telephone: +44 114 276 7575 Fax: +44 114 275 9908
Director General: Alex Ritchie
Director of Planning: Phil Haywood
Staff: 250

Current situation: Financial resources are raised by a levy on local authorities of Barnsley, Doncaster, Rotherham and Sheffield, which also receive some government revenue support grant for transport. The Passenger Transport Authority (PTA), which is a joint undertaking comprising 12 local authority representatives, is responsible for collecting the levy and determining policy. The PTE is the managing agency.

Concessionary fares for children, elderly and disabled people are funded by the PTE, which is also the administrative and marketing agency for a wide range of county-wide prepaid daily, weekly, monthly and annual travelcards and carnets on behalf of local bus and rail operators.

The PTE owns all bus infrastructure, and a major investment programme has provided multimodal interchanges in Sheffield, Meadowhall and Barnsley. It also contracts with Regional Railways Northeast to provide local rail services (see below). Travel information and a chain of travel information centres is also provided. A subsidiary company, South Yorkshire Supertram (see below), operates the light rail system which was completed in 1995.

Developments: Following completion of the light rail network in 1995, concern arose over poor patronage and consequent financial losses, amounting to some £9 million (including interest on debt) for the first nine months of operation. Intense bus competition has compounded difficulties with ticketing and marketing, as a result of which fares have been reduced and simplified. The four local authority owners called in consultants to advise on the problems. Sale of the network into the private sector is in progress, with the intention of repaying construction loans, but concern has been expressed that the sale price could be affected by the poor traffic figures, leaving the local authorities responsible for both the original loans and operating losses. At the end of 1996, discussions were being held with the government, and a buyer was expected to be announced in 1997.

Under Railplan 21, developed in conjunction with local district councils, further improvements in the local rail system are proposed.

The PTE has authority to build and operate trolleybus networks in Doncaster and Rotherham, but a dedicated pilot line constructed on private land near Doncaster was dismantled in 1993. A planned light rapid transit system for Doncaster is now likely to be based on Bombardier's GLT or guided trolleybus technology. The initial route would link the town centre with the Leisure Park.

Contracted rail

Operated by: Regional Railways Northeast Ltd
York YO1 1HT
Telephone: +44 1904 653022 Fax: +44 1904 523719
Managing Director: R Urie

Type of operation: Local rail

Passenger journeys: (1993) 6.5 million
(1994) 6.5 million
(1995)

Current situation: Operates several suburban/interurban services in the PTE area, of which seven routes from Sheffield are financially supported by the PTE. These are the Hallam lines (to Barnsley, Darton and Penistone, en route to Leeds and Huddersfield), the Don Valley line (to Rotherham, Doncaster and Thorne), the Kiveton line (to Kiveton Park, en route to Worksop), Sheffield to Leeds via the Dearne Valley route, and the South Yorkshire portion of the Doncaster to Leeds service. These total 189 km and serve 32 stations. Since 1992 the PTE has also made a financial contribution to maintain an hourly service between Doncaster and Scunthorpe. The PTE specifies fares and service levels on these routes.

Mainline Volvo articulated and Leyland National of Andrews in Waingate  **1997**

Yorkshire Terrier Dennis Dart with split-step entrance **1997**

Contracted bus

Current situation: Around 80 per cent of bus-km is provided by 30 operators competing in a free market. The PTE finances those socially valuable services not provided by the market, by specifying the remaining 20 per cent of bus-km and buying through competitive tendering.

Supertram

South Yorkshire Supertram Ltd
11A Arundel Gate, Sheffield S1 2PN
Telephone: +44 114 232 8282 Fax: +44 114 275 6145
Chief Executive: John Bygate
Operations Manager: G T Brown
Staff: 200

Type of operation: Light rail, opened 1994

Route length: 29 km
Number of lines: 3
Number of stops: 45
Gauge: 1,435 mm
Track: Part conventional ballasted, concrete slab on street sections
Max gradient: 10%
Minimum curve radius: 25 m
Electrification: 750 V DC, overhead

Service: Peak 10 min, off-peak 15 min
First/last car: 06.00/24.00
Fare structure: Stages
Fare collection: Cash to conductor; discounted carnets from sales outlets
Fare evasion control: Inspectors; penalty fare
Arrangements for elderly/disabled: Low-floor cars
Integration with other modes:
Signalling: Priority at road junctions

Rolling stock: 25 cars
Siemens-Duewag articulated (1993) M25
In peak service: 22

Developments: Though the operator refuses to divulge traffic figures, poor patronage continued to cause concern during 1996 (see above), when fares were reduced and marketing efforts stepped up, though there were signs of improvement at year-end. Conductors now travel on all cars, to strengthen revenue collection and in place of lineside ticket machines which were unreliable and subject to vandalism.

UPDATED

SHENYANG

Population: 2.9 million, in municipal area 5.5 million
Public transport: Services provided by Shenyang City Bus Company (bus) and the Shenyang City Electric Traction Company (trolleybus); light rail planned

Shenyang City Bus Company

Shenyang City Bus Company
No 19-2, Section 7, Daxi Road, Heping District, Shenyang, People's Republic of China
Telephone: +86 24 24716/27177
Staff: 3,726

Current situation: An expanding service network with six operational divisions covers city and suburbs. In central districts this is complementary to the trolleybus system (see below), but bus is the dominant mode in suburban areas and the network was carrying around 400 million passengers annually at the end of the 1980s.

The company also controls a bus assembly works, as well as a tyre recovery factory.

Bus

Number of routes: 54
Route length: (One way) 931.8 km
Fleet: 620 buses, including many articulated; most from own factory, some also from Wafangdian

Fare structure: Stage
Fare collection: Payment to seated conductors, monthly passes
Operating costs financed by: Fares 84%, other commercial sources 15.9%, subsidy 7.3%
Subsidy from: City government

SY561 trolleybuses in early morning service on Route 61

Shenyang City Electric Traction

Shenyang City Electric Traction Company
No 2, Section 5, Nanwu Road, Heping District, Shenyang
Telephone: +86 24 27780/27946
Staff: 3,512

Current situation: This is one of the largest trolleybus networks in China, carrying over 375 million passengers annually. Its vehicle needs are met entirely by a local factory. Many new trolleybuses have been placed in service, but some elderly rolling stock may still be in use. Several buses are also operated.

The company's own trolleybus factory introduced new vehicle types SY-D80C and SY-D90C in 1987.

Bus

Number of routes: 1
Route length: 14.4 km
Fleet: 42 buses

Trolleybus

Number of routes: 18
Route length: (One way) 177.9 km
Fleet: 487 trolleybuses (over 90% articulated), mainly Shenyang (articulated) but with some old Shanghai SK 663 (articulated) and SK 644

Fare collection: Payment to seated conductors, monthly passes
First/last trolleybus: 04.30/00.30
Operating costs financed by: Fares 91.2%, other commercial sources 8.8%, subsidy/grants 10.9%
Subsidy from: City government

Future plans: 34 km of new route being built as part of the 7th national five-year plan, with plans to increase the fleet and improve patronage. Three new depots and two additional substations will be needed and the fleet will be increased by 137 trolleybuses.

Light rail (planned)

Current situation: Local government approval was granted in 1992 for construction of a network of elevated light rail routes. In 1995 23 four-car trains were on order from GEC Alsthom Transporte, Spain.

UPDATED

SINGAPORE

Population: 2.9 million
Public transport: Bus services provided by privately owned companies working in consultation with the Land Transport Authority which issues licences. Additional privately operated 'Supplementary Public Transport Schemes' for peak-hour commuter services authorised, and 'Bus Plus' minibus services aimed at providing a high-quality alternative to the private car. All low-occupancy private vehicles entering the central business district during the day are required to display a special licence disc for which an additional fee is charged. Public buses are exempt. Included in the scheme is provision of cheap car parks at the periphery of the licensed area to encourage motorists to use buses or trains. Metro; local ferries; cable car; light rail planned.

Alexander Superbuses with SBS ***1996***

Land Transport Authority

Land Transport Authority
460 Alexandra Road, 28-00 PSA Building, Singapore 119963
Telephone: +65 375 7100 Fax: +65 375 7208

Current situation: The authority, created in 1995, is responsible for land transport policy and development. It is the owner and construction authority for the metro (see below).

Singapore Bus Service

Singapore Bus Service (1978) Limited
205 Braddell Road, Singapore 579701
Telephone: +65 284 8866 Fax: +65 287 0311
Chairman: Wong Hung Khim
Managing Director: Phua Tin How
Executive Vice President: Yik Ah Chui
Senior Vice President, Operations: Lim Gim Hong
Senior Vice President, Service Development: Woon Chio Chong
Staff: 7,483

Current situation: SBS has minimised the impact of the metro on its operations by extending service to developing new towns, and by rationalising services running parallel to MRT to serve other high-demand areas.
Developments: The joint service company Transit Link (set up by SBS, TIBS and MRT initially to facilitate through ticketing between the systems) is undertaking complete integration of the bus and metro networks. A major task has been restructuring and rationalisation of bus routes and services to complement the metro.

Singapore's first articulated bus joined the fleet in 1996 and has been on trial. Deliveries continued of 200 three-axle double-deck air conditioned Superbuses, as well as 150 single-deck.

Bus

Passenger journeys: (1993) 879 million
(1994) 906.3 million
(1995) 924.5 million
Vehicle-km: (1993) 229.7 million
(1994) 223.5 million
(1995) 227 million

Number of routes: 196
Route length: (One way) 2,556 km
On priority right-of-way: 86 km bus lanes

Fleet: 2,815 vehicles

Alexander 12 m Superbus (1994/95/96/97)	600
Volvo Superlong (1995/96)	315
Volvo articulated (1996)	150
Others	1,750

New vehicles required each year: 250
In peak service: 2,414

Most intensive service: 3-5 min
One-person operation: All services
Fare structure: Flat and graduated fares; concessionary period passes (validated by monthly stamps) available to schoolchildren, servicemen, students and shareholders
Fare collection: Flat and graduated fare services: fareboxes and automated driver-controlled microprocessor ticket-issuing equipment; onboard ticket machines accept stored-value tickets which offer rebates for transfers between trunk services, and between trunk service and MRT metro
Fare evasion control: Roving inspectors
Arrangements for elderly/disabled: Concession fare for over-60s; special seats
Average distance between stops: 400 m
Average peak-hour speed: In mixed traffic, 20 km/h
Bus priority: Restraint on cars entering central area through supplementary licence requirement with provision for park-and-ride; buses exempt from charge; 70 km of bus-only lanes operational 07.30-09.30 and 16.30-19.00 weekdays, 07.30-09.30 and 11.00-14.30 Saturdays
Integration with other modes: Fare system (including concessions) standardised between SBS and Tibs; transfer ticketing system with metro (see above)
Operating costs financed by: Fares 97%, other commercial sources 3%
New vehicles financed by: Commercial loans and internal funds

Tibs

Trans-Island Bus Services Ltd (Tibs)
A member of the TIBS Group of Companies
6 Ang Mo Kio Street 62, 569140 Singapore
Telephone: +65 482 3888 Fax: +65 482 3842
Chair: Lee Han Yang
Managing Director: Tan Hup Foi
General Manager: Teo Joo Huak
Staff: 1,339

Current situation: Tibs commenced operations in 1983 with a fleet of 37 buses on two routes. The company, a subsidiary of TIBS Holdings Ltd, operates in Yishun, Woodlands, Bukit Panjang, Sembawang and Punggol.

TIBS is a partner with Singapore MRT in Bus-Plus Services Pte Ltd (see below), which provides higher quality services at commuting times.

Developments: In conjunction with opening of the metro extension in February 1996, Tibs opened a new underground interchange at Woodlands station. The year also saw introduction of Singapore's first articulated buses, and a 'zero step, stepless aisle' bus.

Bus

Passenger boardings: (1993) 150 million
(1994) 152 million
(1995) 162 million
Vehicle-km: (1993) 38 million
(1994) 36 million
(1995) 41 million

Number of routes: 50
Route length: (one way) 774 km
Fleet: 597 vehicles

Nissan U31	103
Hino HT238K (1987/89)	35
Nissan Civilian (1989)	2
DAF SB220 low-floor (1990/92)	33
DAF SB220 low-floor (1995)	50

Passengers queue for circulator buses at Tibs' Woodlands regional interchange **1997**

Mercedes O405 of Tibs **1995**

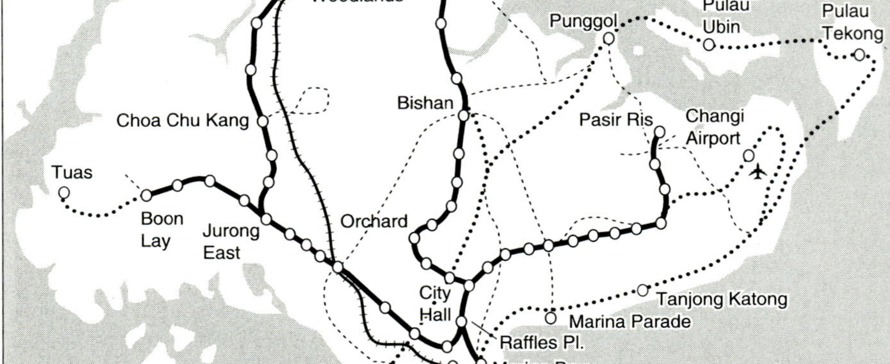

Singapore metro

Mercedes O405 low-floor (1994/95)	308
Mercedes O405 articulated (1996)	1
Scania L113 low-floor (1995)	50
Scania L113 no-step stepless-aisle (1996)	15

In peak service: 536

Fare collection: Cash payment to farebox; stored-value card to validator, valid also on metro
Fare structure: 0.8 km stages; premium for air conditioned buses
Arrangements for elderly/disabled: Reduced off-peak fares

Mercedes bus of independent operator on Route 15 in Scheme B

SSB

Singapore Shuttle Bus (Pte) Ltd
A member of the TIBS Group of Companies
Address and personnel as above
Staff: 72

Current situation: SSB, a wholly owned subsidiary of TIBS Holdings Ltd, started operations in 1975 to provide services from fringe car parks to the central business district under the City Shuttle scheme for dealing with peak-hour commuter flows when traffic restraint measures were introduced. Services were later extended to operate from housing estates and now run six days a week from 06.30 to 19.30.

Bus

Passenger boardings: (1993) 10.9 million
(1994) 10.1 million
(1995) 9.2 million
Vehicle-km: (1993) 4.2 million
(1994) 3.7 million
(1995) 3.7 million

Number of routes: 5
Route length: (one way) 116 km
Fleet: 74 buses

Hino RK176 (1985)	17
Nissan R87 (1985)	20
Nissan U31	36
Hino HT238K (1986)	1

In peak service: 70

Fare structure: 0.8 km stages; premium for air conditioned buses
Fare collection: Cash payment to farebox; stored value card to validator, also valid on metro
Arrangements for elderly/disabled: Reduced off-peak fares

Bus-Plus

Bus-Plus Services Pte Ltd
6 Ang Mo Kio Street 62, 569140 Singapore
Telephone: +65 484 0166/8566 Fax: +65 484 0129
Directors: Tan Hup Foi
Kwek Siew Jin
General Manager: Morris Piper
Staff: 60

Passenger boardings: (1994) 50,000
(1995) 260,000
Vehicle-km: (1994) 0.3 million
(1995) 1.5 million

Current situation: Bus-Plus, a joint venture between Singapore MRT Ltd and TIBS Holdings Ltd, started operations in 1994 with a fleet of 20 minibuses on two routes. It has since expanded to 45 vehicles on six routes. These link residential estates and the central business district during peak hours, providing a premium 'business class' service with higher comfort standards than conventional routes. The 14-seat minibuses have high-quality seats, electronic destination indicators and piped music.

As well as the standard fare collection system, passengers can also purchase monthly reservation tickets.

Fleet: 45 Toyota Coaster minibuses

MRT train at Woodlands

1997

Nissan U31 bus of SSB

Supplementary Public Transport Schemes

Current situation: In conjunction with rationalisation of conventional bus services and formation of SBS in 1973, the government sought other moves to increase public transport services and deal with increasing traffic congestion. Under Supplementary Public Transport Schemes A and B introduced in 1974, additional commuter services were authorised. These were described in *JUTS 1988*.

The two Supplementary Schemes carry about 150,000 passengers a day compared with the SBS and Tibs total of over 2 million.

SMRT

Singapore Mass Rapid Transit Ltd
251 North Bridge Road, Singapore 179102
Telephone: +65 339 4500 Fax: +65 334 0247
Chair: Goh Kim Loang
Managing Director: Kwek Siew Jin
Staff: 2,615

Current situation: SMRT operates and maintains the metro under licence from the Land Transport Authority. Its holding company, Temasek Holdings Pte Ltd, is majority shareholder for the time being. The intention is to allow SMRT to establish itself financially before its shares are offered for public subscription.

Metro

Type of operation: Full metro, initial route opened 1987

Passenger boardings: (1993) 243 million
(1994) 258.9 million
(1995) 278.1 million

Route length: 83 km
in tunnel: 19 km
Number of lines: 2
Number of stations: 48
underground: 15
elevated: 26
Gauge: 1,435 mm
Track: About 75% timber sleepers in ballast; concrete slab in tunnels; floating slab with rubber bearing pads near sensitive buildings
Electrification: 750 V DC, bottom-contact third rail

Service: Peak 3-4 min, off-peak 5-6 min
First/last train: 05.16/00.47
Fare structure: Graduated
Revenue control: Booking office and self-service ticket machines, automatic entry/exit barriers, all controlled by central computer; system uses magnetically encoded plastic tickets which can be reissued
Signalling: Full ATO, ATP and line supervision

Rolling stock: 85 six-car sets

Kawasaki (1986/87/89)	M264 T132
Siemens/SGP (1995)	M76 T38

In peak service: 61 sets

Developments: 16 km Woodlands extension opened in March 1996, linking the existing terminals at Choa Chu Kang and Yishun to form a loop.

Construction started in 1996 on the Northeast line (20 km, 18 stations) from World Trade Centre to Punggol. Also approved in November 1996 is a 6.4 km extension of the East line to serve Changi airport, scheduled to open in 2001.

Further construction is planned in the long term, under the Singapore Concept Plan which envisages new residential and commercial development on the islands of Pulau Ubin and Pulau Tekong. A major new circular route would serve the two islands and a West line extension to Tuas is also planned. In total, a further five metro routes are proposed for completion by 2010 under a huge public transport investment plan announced in January 1996.

Complementing the metro network will be several light rail lines designed as local feeders. Initially, two elevated automated people movers, each of about 10 km length, are planned to serve residential or commercial developments, one feeding Buona Vista metro station, the other serving Bukit Panjang from Choa Chu Kang station. Construction of the latter route (7.5 km, 13 stations, 18 cars) is in progress by a consortium of Adtranz, Keppel Integrated Engineering and Gammon.

A major programme of station improvements is in progress, including provision of covered walkways, cycle racks, paved footpaths, and car and taxi laybys. The intention is for many stations to become the focus of all local transport, providing easier interchange and seamless journeys. Also under way is an enhancement of the AFC system to accommodate stored-value cards.

Ferries

The Port of Singapore Authority
PSA Building, 460 Alexandra Road, Singapore 5011
Telephone: +65 274 7111 Fax: +65 274 4261

Current situation: A number of operators provide cross-harbour services to the Indonesian islands. In addition, local ferry operators, including the PSA, run ferries to several offshore islands for both industrial and leisure purposes. Some PSA ferries are also used for cross-harbour cruises. PSA ferry terminals handled some 4 million regional and domestic passengers in 1993. A PSA subsidiary also runs a cable car.

Local railway

Current situation: Malayan Railway (KTM) operates local trains from Singapore to Kulai in Malaysia using diesel railbuses.
Developments: KTM's line from Johor in Malaysia to Singapore is being electrified to provide a high-quality metro-style suburban service, scheduled to open in 1998. Also under construction is a 6 km branch from Senai to Sultan Ismail airport. A fleet of 21 emus is on order, similar to those operating in Kuala Lumpur.

UPDATED

SOFIA

Population: 1.1 million
Public transport: Bus, trolleybus and tramway services provided by separate undertakings, under overall control of municipal organisation; metro

GT

Gradski Transport-Sofia
Sofia, Bulgaria

Passenger journeys: (1990) 429 million

Current situation: Since the split-up of the former municipal operator SGT in 1991, the three modes have operated as separate businesses but are now overseen by GT.
Developments: A major study by consultants, commissioned by the European Bank for Reconstruction & Development, was under way in early 1994 to determine priorities for new investment in the city's public transport infrastructure.

Bus

Staff: 3,389

Current situation: There are four bus operating companies — Zemliane, Malashevtsi, Druzba and Republika — known as FAT 1, 2, 3 and 4, based on the four depots of the former operator SGT.

Passenger journeys: (1990) 135 million
(1994) 263 million
Vehicle-km: (1990) 58 million
(1994) 62.9 million

Number of routes: 96
Route length: 1,213 km
Fleet: 1,306 buses

Ikarus 280 articulated	648
Chavdar B14-20 articulated	15
Chavdar 11G5	411
Ikarus 260 and Chavdar 11M3/11M4	87
Mercedes-Benz Türk 0302T (1992)	25
Fiat 421AL ex-Torino	25
Mercedes O305 ex-Mainz	20
Mercedes O305G articulated ex-Mainz	70
MAN SG192 articulated (3 ex-Bremen)	5

In peak service: 715

One-person operation: All routes
Fare collection: Prepurchase with validation/cancellation machines on board, or payment to driver
Fare structure: Flat
Fare evasion control: Random inspection
Bus priority: 35 km of bus lanes
Average peak-hour speed: 17 km/h

Troleybusen Transport

Troleybusen Transport
Boulevard Kalitin 28, 1233 Sofia
Staff: 771

Trolleybus

Passenger journeys: (1990) 60 million
(1994) 34.4 million
Vehicle-km: 9.5 million
(1994) 8.9 million

Number of routes: 9
Route length: 90 km
Fleet: 218 trolleybuses

Ikarus-Ganz 280T articulated	148
DAC-Chavdar 317ETr articulated (stored)	4
Uritsky ZIU 682B	66

In peak service: 143

Trolleybus and tram share this subway in central Sofia ***1995***

Tramvaen Transport

Tramvaen Transport
Boulevard Knijaginija Marie Louise 193, 1233 Sofia
Telephone: +359 2 31251 Fax: +359 2 316184
Staff: 1,699**Type of operation:** Conventional tramway, initial route opened 1901

Passenger journeys: (1990) 234 million
(1994) 100 million
Car-km: (1990) 20.2 million
(1994) 15.1 million

Route length: 158 km
Number of lines: 16
Gauge: 1,009/1,435 mm (3 routes)
Electrification: 600 V DC, overhead

Fare structure: Flat
Fare collection: Prepurchase, validation and cancelling machines on board; also payment to driver; conductors reintroduced experimentally on 4 routes in 1993; roving inspectors
One-person operation: Except Routes 3, 5, 19 and 20
Operating costs financed by: Fares 15%, subsidy/grants 85%

Rolling stock: 420 cars; 1,009 mm gauge trams are equipped with post boxes

1,009 mm gauge	
Sofia 65 old 6-axle	M1
Sofia 70 old 8-axle	M84
Sofia 100 6-axle	M58
Bulgaria 1300 8-axle	M26
Sofia 100 6-axle	M56
Class 1000 6-axle	M4
MK88 6-axle prototype	M2
MK88 6-axle	M34
MK88 8-axle prototype (1991)	M1
ČKD Tatra T6A2	M40
1,435 mm gauge	
Class 1000 6-axle	M31
Sofia 100 6-axle conversion	M1
ČKD Tatra T6B5	M37
Duewag ex-Bonn	M36 T9

In peak service: 253

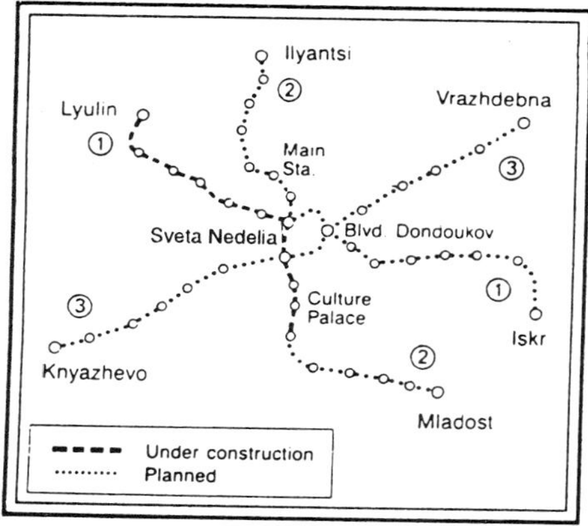

Sofia's planned metro system

Current situation: Conversion to 1,435 mm gauge is proceeding slowly; Line 20 serving the eastern suburbs was opened in 1987. Progress has been hampered by financial problems and political difficulties. The first route links Druzba with Gara Poduene, and was extended 1.3 km into the city centre at Teatr in 1992 where it runs on a new dual-gauge loop shared with metre-gauge lines 3 and 4.

Metre-gauge operations are concentrated mainly in the west of the city, where two new routes have been opened to serve housing developments. One of these, Route 21 running on Boulevard Aleksander Stambolijski to Lyulin 5, shares the tunnel built for the metro Line 1 to Lyulin (see below). The second (Route 22) serves Obelya 2. Construction of an extension to the Ovcha kupel 2 housing estate has been abandoned and the alignment used as a road.

Recent upgrading of 1,009 mm gauge Routes 2 (ex-14) and 19 includes provision for conversion to 1,435 mm gauge. A tunnel beneath Boulevard Dragan Tsankov is nearing completion, though it has yet to be decided if this will be used by an extension of the proposed 1,435 mm gauge Drvenitsa tram branch, or by the future metro line to Mladost.

Metro

Construction authority: Direction Metropoliten
Ul Kniaz Boris I 121, 1000 Sofia
General Manager: Stoyan Bratoev

Current situation: Progress has been slow and intermittent; work was accelerated in 1990 but was then stalled due to political difficulties. A 5 km section of Line 1 from Lyulin to Konstantin Velitschov was scheduled to open in late 1995, with an extension to the city centre at Sveta Nedelia Square (total length 7.7 km) following two years later.

Much of the alignment is completed, including a portion in the suburbs where a second tunnel has been constructed and is currently used by trams to reach Lyulin. When the metro opens, tram services will cease and the tunnel be given over to road traffic.

Part of Line 2 south from the city centre is also complete and awaiting track-laying.

The total planned network extends to 52 km with 48 stations, comprising Line 1 (18.3 km, 16 stations), Line 2 (18 km, 17 stations), and Line 3 (15.7 km, 15 stations). Gauge is 1,435 mm, electrification is 825 V DC third rail, and a fleet of 48 Russian-built cars has been delivered to the depot at Obelya.

UPDATED

SOUTHAMPTON

Population: 214,000
Public transport: Most city bus services provided by former municipally owned company with some areas served by private company. Cross-river ferry. Local rail services by BR

Plaxton-bodied Dennis Dart of Citybus on the Thornhill route ***1997***

Southampton CityBus

Southampton City Transport Co Ltd
226 Portswood Road, Southampton SO9 4XS, England
Telephone: +44 1703 553011 Fax: +44 1703 671448
Managing Director: Ian Phillips
Staff: 450

Current situation: Formerly owned by the city council, CityBus was established as a separate company in 1986. The new arrangements ended local co-ordination, and in 1987 competition began with a new company, Solent BlueLine, which later also took over the Southampton area operations of Hampshire Bus. CityBus was sold to its employees in 1993 and is held through an employee share ownership plan.
Developments: Hampshire County Council's real-time information system 'Romance' covers local routes. Recent deliveries have included large numbers of Dennis Dart midibuses. One is powered by CNG, and the newest have low floors for easy entry.

Bus

Passenger journeys: (1992/93) 16.9 million

Number of routes: 35
Route length: 488 km
On private right-of-way: 2 km
Fleet: 135 vehicles

Leyland Atlantean double-deck	60
Leyland Olympian double-deck	2
Dennis Dominator double-deck	1
Volvo B10B single-deck	2
Leyland Lynx single-deck	11
Dennis Dart single-deck	44
Leyland Atlantean single-deck	5
Ford Transit minibus	2
Red Ensign Coach unit	8

In peak service: 95

Most intensive service: 5 min
One-person operation: 100%
Fare collection: Cash payment to driver, prepurchase pass or ticket
Fare structure: Stage, with some zonal; tokens, monthly passes; day runabout tickets
Fares collected on board: 75%
Fare evasion control: Mobile inspectors; excess fares charged
Operational control: Route inspectors/mobile radio
Arrangements for elderly/disabled: Off-peak passes for pensioners, funded by city council; accessible network using specially equipped buses
Average peak-hour speed: In bus lanes, 25 km/h; in mixed traffic, 15 km/h
Bus priority: 24 individual schemes; 2 km of bus lanes and area co-ordinated traffic management favouring buses on one corridor
Integration with other modes: Services co-ordinated with local trains and ferries
Operating costs financed by: Fares 95%, other commercial sources 5%

Solent BlueLine

Musterphantom Ltd
169-170 High Street, Southampton SO1 0BY
Telephone: +44 1703 223224 Fax: +44 1703 339192
Managing Director: Stuart Linn

Current situation: Formed in 1987 as a venture to compete in Southampton by Southern Vectis, based on the Isle of Wight, operations began in competition with Southampton CityBus on four routes.

Bus

Number of routes: 18
Fleet: 107 vehicles

Bristol VR double-deck	34
Leyland Olympian double-deck	36
Volvo Olympian double-deck	4
Volvo B10B single-deck	4
Mercedes midibus	12
Iveco minibus	17

Other operators

Current situation: Marchwood Motorways operates 16 buses on contract to Solent BlueLine in its colours. Various other operators run longer-distance routes into the city.

South West Trains

South West Trains Ltd
(See main entry under London)

Current situation: Local electric trains, at least hourly, operate on two routes through the city, serving local stations and providing a link to Southampton airport at Eastleigh (7 km).
Developments: SWT, Railtrack and Hampshire County Council are studying proposals for several new stations to counter growing road traffic congestion, also for a service on the freight line to Hythe.

Waterfront Ferry

Current situation: A ferry (also leisure cruises) connects Southampton with Hythe, carrying about 0.4 million passengers annually.
Developments: White Horse Ferries purchased the route in 1994 after the previous operator went into liquidation. An operating subsidy is to be paid by Hampshire County Council for a five-year period.

UPDATED

SRINAGAR

Population: 616,000
Public transport: Bus services provided by state road transport corporation, The Kashmir Motor Drivers' Association and Western Bus Service; also private 'Matador', minibus and midibus operations

Jammu & Kashmir Road Transport

Jammu & Kashmir Road Transport Corporation
Maulana Azad Road, Srinagar 190001, India
Telephone: +91 194 475360 Fax: +91 194 452058
Managing Director: M M Afzal
Staff: 6,255

Current situation: RTC provides services both in Srinagar and elsewhere in the two states with a fleet of 729 buses which ran 12.8 million km in 1993/94. Its operation in Srinagar city is relatively small.

Bus (Srinagar operations)
Passenger journeys: (1988/89) 23.9 million
Vehicle-km: (1988/89) 36.6 million

Minibus
Current situation: Private minibus and Matador operations account for most urban journeys.

UPDATED

ST ETIENNE

Population: City 200,000, area served 315,000
Public transport: Bus, trolleybus and tramway services provided by franchised company for Siotas, a 'syndicat' grouping of 15 towns

STAS

Société des Transports Urbains de l'Agglomération Stéphanoise
Transpôle STAS, Les Grands Mâts, BP 55, 42272 Saint-Priest-en-Jarez cedex, France
Telephone: +33 4 77 92 82 00 Fax: +33 4 77 92 82 01
Director General: Bernard Simon
Operating Manager: Jacques Lagrange
Staff: 591

Passenger journeys: (All modes)
(1993) 47.4 million
(1994) 47 million
(1995) 45.5 million

Operating costs financed by: Fares 68%, subsidy/grants 32%
Subsidy from: Siotas
New vehicles financed by: Siotas

One-person operation: All routes
Fare structure: Flat; single tickets valid 1 h from cancellation; daily, weekly, weekend and monthly passes
Fare collection: Single tickets sold on bus and trolleybus; automatic machines at tram stops; 135 approved vendors; cancellers on board
Fare evasion control: Inspectors
Arrangements for elderly/disabled: Special services on demand; low-floor buses and trams; stops specially designed for ease of access

Current situation: STAS holds the franchise for operation of urban transport from the Syndicat Intercommunal pour l'Organisation des Transports de l'Agglomération Stéphanoise (Siotas), which is a grouping of St Etienne and 14 neighbouring towns. Eight routes are operated under contract by three operators.

The short tramway Route 4 carries 37 per cent of all STAS passenger-km, and is the only route to produce a financial surplus. Trolleybus Route 9 handles 10 per cent of passenger-km.

Developments: In 1993 STAS introduced magnetic ticketing throughout the network. Further tramway priority right-of-way was introduced during 1994, with all stops equipped with video to provide next-car information. Modernisation of the town centre interchange is in progress.

A new fleet of 60 trolleybuses is planned for commissioning in the late 1990s, of which 50 per cent would be articulated.

A second tram line is being studied, linking the SNCF station at Châteaucreux with Le Clapier.

GEC Alsthom/Vevey low-floor tram of STAS ***1996***

PCC tram and Route 1 trolleybus at Bellevue ***1996***

Bus and trolleybus
Vehicle-km: (1994) Bus 4.2 million, trolleybus 1.7 million
(1995) Bus 4.1 million, trolleybus 1.8 million

Number of routes: 24 bus, 7 trolleybus
Route length: 179 km
On private right-of-way: 10 km
Fleet: 130 buses

Renault PR100	23
Renault PR102	29
Renault PR312	40
Renault PR180 articulated	9
Mercedes O405GN articulated	20
CBM/Renault midibus	5
Peugeot J9 minibus	4

In peak service: 81
Average age of fleet: 7 years

Fleet: 66 trolleybuses

Renault ER100R	31
Renault ER100H	25
Renault PER180H articulated	10

In peak service: 50
Average age of fleet: 15 years

Contracted bus
Vehicle-km: (1994) 1.2 million
(1995) 1.2 million

Current situation: Eight routes totalling 81.6 km are operated under contract by three companies.

Tramway
Type of operation: Conventional tramway

Car-km: (1994) 1.5 million
(1995) 1.5 million

Route length: 9.3 km
Number of routes: 1
Number of stops: 26
Gauge: 1,000 mm
Electrification: 600 V DC, overhead

Service interval: Peak 2 min

Rolling stock: 40 tramcars

PCC standard	M20
PCC articulated	M5
GEC Alsthom articulated (1994)	M15

In peak service: 31 cars
On order: 20 cars from GEC Alsthom/Vevey Technologies for delivery starting in late 1997

UPDATED

ST LOUIS

Population: City 453,000, metropolitan area 2.1 million
Public transport: Bus and light rail service provided by regional authority serving St Louis and surrounding parts of Missouri and Illinois, controlled by representative board. Vanpool schemes

Bi-State Transit System

The Bi-State Development Agency
707 North First Street, St Louis, MO 63102, USA
Telephone: +1 314 982 1400 Fax: +1 314 982 1470
Chair: Robert J Furmanek
Executive Director:
Director of Communications: Linda Hancock
Staff: 1,900

Current situation: Bus and light rail service provision is the responsibility of the transport division of the Bi-State Development Agency. Created in 1949, the agency purchased and consolidated the region's 15 private bus operators in 1963. The service area covers St Louis and three county areas in each of Missouri and Illinois. Bi-State has responsibility for other transport and industrial development functions, and subsidises local bus operations (CitiLine) in St Clair County, Illinois. It also owns the St Louis Downtown Parks airport.

Fixed-route buses are supplemented by Call-a-Ride demand-responsive van operations serving both passengers with disabilities and residents in low-population density areas. The entire bus fleet should be fully accessible by 1997.

Developments: A 15-year public transport improvement plan was unveiled in 1992, with US$6.3 billion spending proposed on bus service upgrades, three new rail routes extending to 92 km and improved suburban bus service and paratransit. This was revised and presented as a 25-year programme 'MetroVision 2020' in 1995.

At the beginning of 1994, a state contribution towards operating deficits was agreed, and in August voters approved a ¼ per cent increase in sales tax to fund transit improvements. This tax was at first subject to periodic review, so prohibiting the undertaking from borrowing against future tax revenue, but in mid-1995 it was made permanent and thus gave Bi-State its first dedicated source of funding.

First project likely to benefit is the plan to introduce commuter rail service on two routes linking St Louis with Pacific and Crystal City, for which detailed planning started in 1995.

It is proposed to convert one-third of the bus fleet to CNG operation by 2000. A grant of $3.4 million to finance purchase of 13 CNG-powered buses was given in 1996.

A total of 75 buses operating seven routes were fitted with cycle racks during 1996 in a bike-and-ride programme. The chosen routes serve eight Metrolink stations where storage racks have been installed on account of heavy cycle traffic.

CNG-powered Flxible of Bi-State **1997**

Eastbound LRVs at Convention Center station **1996**

Bus

Passenger boardings: (1992/93) 37.7 million
(1993/94) 38 million
(1995/96) 37.4 million
Vehicle-km: (1992/93) 39.2 million
(1993/94) 39.3 million
(1995/96) 40.2 million

One-person operation: All routes
Fare collection: Exact fare to farebox; multitickets, passes
Fare structure: Flat; express supplement; transfer supplement; weekly passes; fares-free area in downtown
Fares collected on board: 100%
Fare evasion control: Undercover police surveillance system
Operational control: Route inspectors/mobile radio
Arrangements for elderly/disabled: Reduced fares and lift-equipped buses; 332,000 passengers carried in 1995/96 on Call-A-Ride demand-responsive services, partially contracted out to private operators
Integration with other modes: Extensive park-and-ride provision; carpooling scheme
Average distance between stops: 1 city block
Average peak-hour speed: In mixed traffic, 8.3 km/h
Operating costs financed by: Fares 22.6%, other commercial sources 5.1%, subsidy/grants 72.3%
Subsidy from: FTA and Illinois state grants; dedicated transport sales tax in St Louis city, St Louis County, Madison County and St Clair County
New vehicles financed by: FTA capital grants and local matching funds

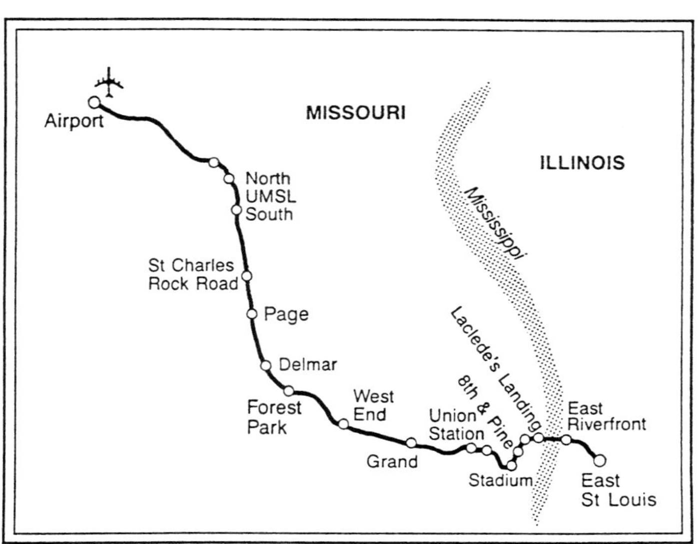

St Louis light rail

MetroLink

General Manager: Thomas Sehr

Type of operation: Light rail, initial route opened 1993

Passenger boardings: (1993/94) 7.6 million
(1994/95) 12 million
(1995/96) 12.9 million

Route length: 29 km
in tunnel: 1.8 km
Number of lines: 1
Number of stations: 18
Gauge: 1,435 mm
Track: 57 kg/m RE rail on timber sleepers, on concrete slab in tunnels
Electrification: 750 V DC, overhead

Number of routes: 124
Route length: (One-way) 3,631 km
On priority right-of-way: 8 km
Fleet: 688 vehicles

GMC T8H (1981)	153
GMC T6H (1981)	16
Neoplan articulated (1988)	40
Flxible 40 ft (1988/89/90/91)	246
Gillig Phantom (1992)	55
Flxible CNG-powered (1992)	2
Orion II (1993)	18
Goshen Sentry (1993)	13
Gillig Phantom (1995)	49
Eldorado Aerotech (1995)	48
Gillig Phantom (1996)	24
Neoplan AN440 articulated (1996)	24

In peak service: 507

Most intensive service: 3-15 min
Service: Peak 7½ min, off-peak 20 min
First/last car: 05.30/00.30

Fare structure: Flat
Fare collection: Prepurchase; proof-of-payment
Integration with other modes: Park-and-ride at 8 stations; 34 bus feeders have timed transfers
Arrangements for elderly/disabled: All stations accessible

Rolling stock: 31 cars
Siemens-Duewag SD400 (1992/93) M31
In peak service: 30
On order: A further six cars from Siemens for 1998 delivery

Current situation: Light rail line connects Lambert international airport (extension opened 1994) and East St Louis on an alignment mainly following disused rail rights-of-way. A short branch planned to serve the McDonnell Douglas aircraft works at Berkeley has been shelved.

Three further corridors are being studied as potential light rail routes. The priority route, for which the preliminary engineering was completed in September 1996, runs 39 km eastwards to Scott Joint-Use (Mid-America) airport in St Clair County, Illinois. In 1994, voters in St Clair approved a local tax increase to fund the initial phase to Belleville Area College (26 km, eight stations), and Federal funding of $236 million towards the $295 million cost was agreed in October 1996. Construction is scheduled to start in March 1998 for opening in September 2001.

To the west, St Charles County formed its own transit district in 1991, and is supporting proposed routes into the county. Other proposed extensions run into St Louis County, south to Oakville and southwest to Valley Park. Three of the four are included in the 15-year plan (see above).

UPDATED

STOCKHOLM

Population: City 704,000, Greater Stockholm county 1.7 million
Public transport: Bus, tramway and metro services provided under contract to company owned by Stockholm County Council and controlled by nominated board, with subsidiaries operating local rail and bus services, and also contracting bus service from private operators and suburban rail operations of Swedish State Railways (SJ). County-owned ferries

Ropsten metro/bus interchange with Scania CN113 of Swebus and Line 14 train  **1995**

Storstockholms Lokaltrafik

AB Storstockholms Lokaltrafik (SL)
Arenavägen 27, 120 80 Stockholm, Sweden
Telephone: +46 8 686 1000 Fax: +46 8 686 1503
General Manager: Leif Axén
Staff: 9,750

Passenger boardings: (All modes)
(1992) 539 million
(1993) 540 million
(1994) 546 million

Operating costs financed by: Fares 42%, other commercial sources 6%, subsidy/grants 56%
Subsidy from: County Council

Ethanol-powered city bus of SL Buss **1995**

Current situation: Greater Stockholm was one of the first West European cities to establish a fully integrated public transport system. The arrangements agreed in 1964 brought together bus, metro and tramway services operated in the 55 county municipalities by AB Stockholms Spårvägar (SS) (based on former tramway companies), Swedish State Railways (SJ), two municipal bus companies and 10 private operators. As a result of the agreement SS was reorganised as AB Storstockholms Lokaltrafik (SL) which began operations in 1967.

Through its subsidiaries, SL Tag AB and SL Lidingo, SL operates a narrow-gauge railway, a tramline over old rail tracks, and a rail line with metro cars converted to overhead pick-up. A fleet of SL-owned and contracted minibuses provides services for the disabled throughout the area.

A uniform fares system is based on a common distance-related tariff with the region divided into five zones. Fares are based on coupons offered at a one-third discount when purchased in strips of 20. Basic fare for one zone is two coupons with one per zone thereafter, up to a maximum of five coupons.

Municipal environmental regulations could force SL to abandon diesel-engined buses within 10 years, and various options for electric traction or gas-powered vehicles are being considered.

Developments: Management reorganisation in 1991 saw SL split into operating and planning divisions, the latter specifying service levels and contracting with the operators for provision of service. The bus, metro and local railways have been reorganised as subsidiaries, and the aim is for their operations to be put out to tender. The first package of bids in 1993 involved the three local railways, whose existing SL operators won the franchises. Tenders for operation of metro Line 3 and certain bus routes, sought in 1993, were won mainly by SL subsidiaries, as was that for metro Line 2 in late 1994.

Bus service is contracted mainly from two companies, SL Buss and Swebus, a Swedish State Railways subsidiary, which took over operations of five SL garages in 1993. AB Linjebuss became a contractor in a fresh round of tendering at the beginning of 1995.

Approval was given in 1991 for a package of public transport improvements over the period to 2005. Included were better quality service on the metro and construction of an orbital light rail line based on the existing short Line 12. This would help SL cater for the rapidly increasing number of non-radial and cross-city journeys. Other improvements now centre on a core network of clean-air buses running over reserved rights-of-way and with traffic light priority, which might subsequently be converted to trolleybus or light rail.

Road pricing is to be introduced in 1999, with the levy earmarked for construction of further sections of the city's ring road. The aim is to reduce by 25 per cent the number of cars entering the city centre. When this has been achieved, a programme of environmental improvements will be undertaken, including noise reduction measures.

SL Buss

Passenger boardings: (1992) 223 million
(1993) 226 million
(1994) 233 million
Vehicle-km: (1992) 85 million
(1993) 84 million
(1994) 85 million

Number of routes: 410
Route length: (One way) 7,500 km
Fleet: 1,907 vehicles, including those operated by Swebus

One-person operation: All routes
Fare collection: Prepurchase multitickets (coupons) or passes, or single coupons bought from driver
Fare structure: Zonal, based on coupon system with coupons sold separately or in booklets; monthly and annual season tickets for unlimited travel
Fares collected on board: 12%; 64% use monthly seasons, 24% prepaid discount tickets
Operational control: Route inspectors/mobile radio with centralised radio control
Average distance between stops: City area, 350 m; outer zones, 700 m
Average peak-hour speed: In mixed traffic, 20 km/h; in bus lanes, 30 km/h
Bus priority: System for bus priority by means of on-board traffic light control under test. Bus lanes provided and continuing programme for extensions; major traffic light priority scheme in city centre
Integration with other modes: All services and ticketing fully integrated; special bus services connect with Arlanda airport and ferries to Gotland and Finland
New vehicles financed by: County council loans

SL Tunnelbana

Type of operation: Full metro (T-Banan)

Passenger boardings: (1992) 247 million
(1993) 247 million
(1994) 244 million
Car-km: (1992) 77 million
(1993) 78 million
(1994) 80 million

Route length: 110 km
in tunnel: 64 km
Number of lines: 3 with branches
Number of stations: 100
in tunnel: 55
Gauge: 1,435 mm
Track: Flat-bottomed 50 kg/m rail
Max gradient: 4.8%
Minimum curve radius: 200 m
Tunnel: Concrete, rock and steel
Electrification: 650-750 V DC, third rail

Service: Peak 2-5 min, off-peak 3-5 min
First/last train: 05.00/02.00, 24 h service at weekends
Fare structure: As bus
Revenue control: Barriers in all ticket halls, automatic gates for monthly passes in most stations; spot checks
One-person operation: All trains
Signalling: Cab signalling with fixed lineside signals installed only at junctions; central control office linked to all trains by radio
Surveillance: CCTV at 31 stations for passenger/train control

Rolling stock: 870 cars

C2/C3	M37
ASJ/ASEA C4 (1960/67)	M200
ASJ/ASEA/Hägglunds	
C6 (1971/74)	M158
C7 (1973)	M8
ASEA/Hägglunds	
C8 (1974/75)	M44
C9 (1976/77)	M20
C12 (rebuilt 1977/82)	M165
C13 (rebuilt 1982/84)	M94
C14 (rebuilt 1986/90)	M126
C15 (1985/86)	M14
C14Z (1987/88)	M4

On order: A new fleet of 75 cars was ordered from ABB Transportation, Västerås, in early 1995, with an option to supply a further 125, designed to replace SL's oldest cars dating from the 1960s. Prototypes will be delivered for trials at the end of 1996

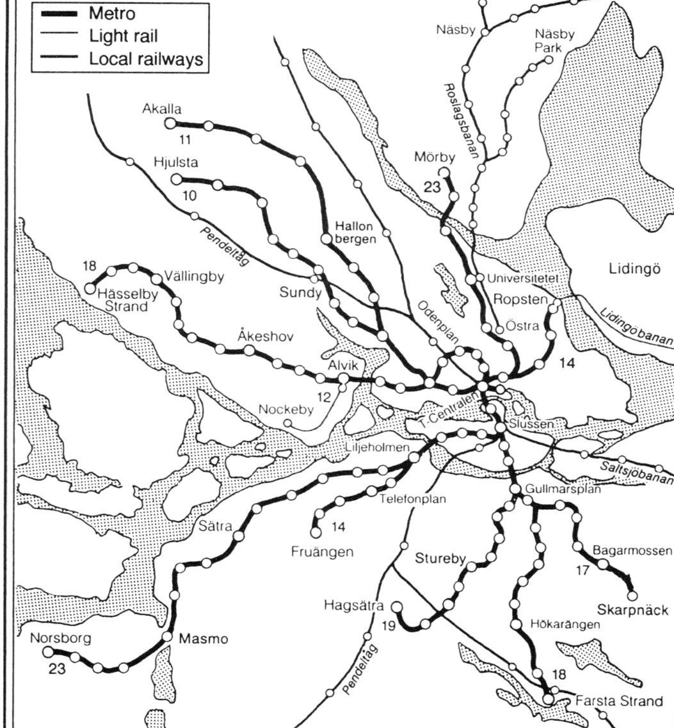

Stockholm's metro and local rail system

Tramway

Passenger boardings: (1993) 2 million
(1994) 2 million

Current situation: One former tram route remains, the 5.7 km Line 12 from Alvik to Nockeby. Following a decision to retain and upgrade the line, the rolling stock is being extensively rebuilt. There is also a short tourist tramway in the city centre.
Developments: An extension from Alvik to Gullmarsplan was approved in 1991 as the first stage of an orbital route for which 12 LRVs have been ordered. Opening is scheduled for 1999.

Rolling stock: 17 cars

Local railway

Passenger boardings: (1992) 12 million
(1993) 12 million
(1994) 13 million

Current situation: SL's three local railways are operated under contract by its subsidiaries SL Tag AB and SL Lidingo Trafik AB. They are the Roslagsbanan (65 km, 891 mm gauge, electrified 1.5 kV DC, 82 cars, 38 stations), the Saltsjöbanan (19 km, 1,435 mm gauge, electrified 750 kV DC, 28 cars, 18 stations) and the Lidingöbanan (9 km, 1,435 mm gauge, electrified 700 V DC), 20 cars.

The Roslagsbanan runs northwards from Stockholm Östra station to Kaårsta with branches to Näsby Park and Österskär. Daily journeys amount to about 22,000. Re-equipment with new rolling stock was completed in early 1995.

The Saltsjöbanan links Stockholm Slussen with Saltsjöbaden, with a branch to Solsidan. The line carries about 13,000 passengers daily. There are 18 stations.

The Lidingöbanan serves the island of Lidingö, with a bridge link to the metro at Ropsten. About 11,000 daily journeys.

Suburban railway

Operated under contract by: Swedish State Railways (SJ)

Type of operation: Suburban heavy rail

Passenger journeys: (1992) 54 million
(1993) 54 million
(1994) 54 million

Current situation: Services on four routes totalling 90 km with 47 stations provided under contract by SJ; 1,435 mm gauge; electrified 15 kV 16⅔ Hz. Trains run half-hourly, with extras during peak hours.

Under an agreement between SJ, the government and Stockholm county council, which runs until 2010, SL and the county council made a major financial commitment to raising capacity and improving standards on the lines into Stockholm Central station in works which were completed in 1992. Further double-tracking and other capacity improvements were approved in 1991 for the period through to 2005.

Rolling stock: 290 cars

Waxholms Ångfartygs

Waxholms Ångfartygs AB
PO Box 7422, 10391 Stockholm
Telephone: +46 8 614 6450 Fax: +46 8 611 8407
Managing Director: Leif Widmark
Staff: 25

Ferry

Passenger journeys: (1992) 3.6 million
(1993) 3.6 million
(1994) 3.9 million

Operating costs financed by: Fares 30%, other commercial sources 2%, county council subsidy 68%

Current situation: The 25 ships of WÅ, directly owned by Stockholm county council, form an integral part of the passenger services in the greater Stockholm area. There are 19 vessels operating in the sea inlets and to the islands of the archipelago, and six ply two routes in Stockholm harbour, Djurgården—Nybroplan and Slussen—Djurgården, at frequent intervals.

A-Train

A-Train AB
PO Box 935, 19586 Arlandstad
Telephone: +46 8 595 11440 Fax: +46 8 595 11450

Current situation: The Arlanda Link consortium is building a 22 km loop off the Stockholm—Uppsala main line to serve Arlanda international airport, for opening in 1999. The consortium has a 45-year concession to build the loop and operate a dedicated airport service.

UPDATED

STOKE-ON-TRENT

Population: Conurbation 340,000
Public transport: Bus services in 'Potteries' six-town conurbation mainly provided by private company. Local routes also operated by some private companies; local rail services

PMT

PMT Limited
Hobson Street, Burslem, Stoke-on-Trent ST6 2AQ, England
Telephone: +44 1782 524444 Fax: +44 1782 524499
Managing Director: Steven Ellis
Operations Director: Michael Frewer

Current situation: Until 1986 PMT was a subsidiary of state-owned National Bus but as part of the break up and sale of the group it was sold to its managers. In 1990, the company purchased Chester-based Crosville from Drawlane Holdings; the acquisition operates as a separate branded unit. PMT was purchased by Badgerline in 1994, and became a subsidiary of the FirstBus group in 1995. The company also trades as Red Rider in Merseyside and Pennine in Greater Manchester.

Plaxton-bodied Dennis Lance on PMT's Crewe-Hanley 'Silver Service' ***1997***

Bus

Number of routes: 153
Route length: 907 km
Fleet: 567 vehicles

Bristol/Leyland double-deck	127
Leyland National, Lynx, Optare Delta, Dart, Swift, Lance single-deck	114
Mercedes, Transit, Sherpa, Dodge, MCW, Optare minibus	321
Coaches	5

One-person operation: All routes
Fare collection: Payment to driver or passes
Fare structure: Distance-related and market-priced; passes
Average peak-hour speed: 18.7 km/h

Developments: PMT has installed a bus identification, communication and control system in its Stoke operating area, using satellite technology. The city's first permanent park-and-ride opened in Hanley in September 1996.

Other commercial operators

Current situation: Procters, Stevensons, Midland Red North, Moorland, Knotty Bus, Matthews Motors and Scraggs all operate in the area.

Central Trains

Central Trains Limited
PO Box 4323, Birmingham B1 1TH
Telephone: +44 121 643 4444 Fax: +44 121 654 4461
Managing Director: Mark Causebrook

Type of operation: Local rail

Current situation: Services provided about two-hourly to Stafford and peak-hours only to Manchester (both 25 kV AC), also to Crewe and Derby (diesel), serving local stations.

Light rail (proposed)

Current situation: The city council has authorised studies of proposed light rail systems both for the immediate Stoke area and for the conurbation.

UPDATED

ST PETERSBURG

Population: 3.2 million
Public transport: Bus, and trolleybus/tramway services operated by separate municipal undertakings. Metro. Suburban rail services

Upravlenie Automobil'novo Transporta

Upravlenie Automobil'novo Transporta
St Petersburg, Russia

Bus

Passenger journeys: Approx 225 million (annual)
Vehicle-km: Approx 60 million (annual)

Number of routes: 150
Route length: 1,100 km
Fleet: Approx 2,000 vehicles, comprising LAZ 699R, Liaz 677, Ikarus 280 articulated, Ikarus 250 and a few Ikarus 260, plus about 20 second-hand from France. The LAZ 699R and Ikarus 250s operate limited-stop express routes

One-person operation: All services
Fare collection: Prepurchase with validation/cancellation on board; payment to driver only on express routes, sometimes on exit
Fare structure: Flat, higher on express routes
Fare evasion control: Random inspection

Three-car set of LM68M trams at Ligovskiy Prospekt ***1996***

LenElektro Trans

LenElektro Trans
Ul ZodChego Rossi 1/3, St Petersburg 190011
Telephone: +7 812 311 3220

Trolleybus

Passenger journeys: Approx 500 million (annual)
Vehicle-km: 65 million (annual)

Double-coupled pair of ZIU9 trolleybuses on the Nevskiy Bridge ***1996***

Number of routes: 49
Route length: 550 km
Fleet: 1,050 vehicles
Uritsky ZIU9
Uritsky ZIU10

One-person operation: All services
Fare collection: Carnets of 10 tickets prepurchased or available from driver with validation/cancellation on board
Fare structure: Flat; monthly seasons
Fare evasion control: Random inspection
Average peak-hour speed: 16 km/h

Tramway

Type of operation: Conventional tramway

Route length: 678 km
Number of lines: 66
Number of stops: 1,215
Gauge: 1,524 mm

Fare structure: Flat
Fare collection: As trolleybus

Rolling stock: About 2,050 cars

LM68M	About M1,400
KTM5	M196
LVS86 articulated	About M450

Developments: Track has been removed from some streets in the city centre, and further restriction of tram routes in the centre is planned.

A major new depot under construction to house 300 trams, and there are plans for new central maintenance works to replace various sites around the city.

A prototype three-section articulated tramcar was tried out in 1994 prior to series production.

Petersburg Metro

Petersburg Metropoliten
Moskovskii Prospekt No 28, St Petersburg 198013
Telephone: +7 812 251 6668 Fax: +7 812 292 1441
Chief Executive: V A Garujgin
Chief Engineer: N I Firsov

Type of operation: Full metro, first line opened 1955

Passenger journeys: (1989) 850 million
(1993) 623 million

Route length: 91.7 km
Number of lines: 4
Number of stations: 54
Gauge: 1,524 mm
Max gradient: 4%
Minimum curve radius: 400 m
Electrification: 825 V DC, third rail

Service: Peak 1 min 35 s, off-peak 4 min
First/last train: 05.40/01.00
Fare structure: Flat
Revenue control: Prepurchase token to barrier; open access with photoelectric cell control
Stations: At many stations 'platforms' replaced by open halls with doors at either side, opened automatically to correspond with the train doors when the train has stopped. Platform doors close again before the train leaves
Signalling: Automatic train stop; radio-telephone communications with trains; ATO

Rolling stock: 1,300 cars, all motored, formed into five- and six-car sets
Mytischy D/E/EJ M1,300

Current situation: Further 14 km under construction, including northwest Line 4 extension with six stations.

RZD

Russian Railways (RZD), October Railway
Ostrovskogo pl 2, 191011 St Petersburg
Telephone: +7 812 168 6040 Fax: +7 812 311 8339

Type of operation: Suburban heavy rail

Current situation: Electrified (3 kV DC) commuter services operate on routes extending from the city's five terminals.

UPDATED

Pionerskaya metro station on Line 2 ***1996***

Suburban emu of the October Railway at Finlandskaya  ***1996***

St Petersburg's metro

STRASBOURG

Population: City 252,000, conurbation 450,000
Public transport: Bus and light rail services provided by franchised company CTS, owned mainly by the Communauté Urbaine de Strasbourg (52%) and Bas-Rhin département (26%), also operating regional routes. CTS is administered by a board which includes representatives from the city and CUS

CTS

Compagnie des Transports Strasbourgeois
14 rue de la Gare aux Marchandises, PO Box 51 R2, 67002 Strasbourg Cedex, France
Telephone: +33 3 88 77 70 11 Fax: +33 3 88 77 70 99
President: Roland Ries
Director General: Marc Le Tourneur
Operating Managers: J-P Basset
A Loos
Project Director, LRT: Alain Giesi
Project Manager, LRT: Georges Müller
Staff: 1,142

Passenger boardings: (both modes)
(1992) 42.7 million
(1993) 42.7 million
(1995) 54.1 million

Bus

Vehicle-km: (1992) 11.2 million
(1993) 11.6 million
(1995) 12.6 million

Number of routes: 25 urban, 10 interurban
Route length: Urban 288 km, interurban 316 km
On priority right-of-way: 5.8 km
Fleet: 363 vehicles, including 59 for interurban service

Urban fleet	
Renault SC10	125
Renault R312	69
Heuliez GX317	8
Van Hool 138	2
Mercedes/Heuliez articulated	50
Van Hool low-floor articulated	39
Renault S53	11
Interurban fleet	
Renault Tracer	9
Renault S53	44
Volvo/Heuliez	6

Average age of fleet: 6.7 years
In peak service: Urban 221

Most intensive service: 4 min
One-person operation: All routes
Fare structure: Urban, flat; interurban, zonal
Fare collection: 'Unipass' ticket from driver, valid up to 1 h, with free transfer, or prepurchase carnets with validation on board; daily, weekly and monthly passes; car or cycle parking plus return tram tickets issued at Etoile and Rotonde; Alsaplus pass for CTS/SNCF journeys
Arrangements for elderly/disabled: Special minibus services; reduced rate tickets and monthly passes for over-65s and invalids
Operating costs financed by: Fares 50%, other commercial sources 5%, subsidy/grants 46%
Subsidy from: 'Versement' from CUS (urban) and Bas Rhin Départment (interurban)

Developments: Bus routes unaffected by the tramway were restructured in 1993 with a 10 per cent increase in urban vehicle-km. Routes duplicating the tramway were revised in 1995.

Light rail

Type of operation: Light rail, initial route opened 1994

Passenger journeys: (1995) 63,000 daily
Car-km: (1995) 1.1 million

Route length: 9.8 km
Number of lines: 1
Number of stations: 18
Gauge: 1,345 mm
Electrification: 750 V DC, overhead

Strasbourg's 'Eurotram' ***1997***

Heuliez articulated on Route 6 in Graffstaden ***1996***

Service: Peak 3 min
First/last car: 04.30/00.30
Fare structure/collection: As bus
Integration with other modes: Several park-and-ride sites account for some 10% of daily journeys

Rolling stock: 26 cars
ABB (1993/94) M26
In peak service: 20
On order: Further 21 cars from Adtranz Derby, for delivery from April 1998; 11 are 33 m

Current situation: Full public service started on Line A in February 1995, when parallel bus routes were restructured to avoid duplication and act as feeders, principally at Baggersee and Rotonde. Traffic levels have surpassed all forecasts, running at between 60,000 and 65,000 passengers daily.

Strasbourg has enforced severe restrictions on car traffic; the city centre is pedestrianised and cars cannot drive from one side to the other. Their only access is to four 'loops' which extend to the edge of the central area.
Developments: Extension of Line A from Baggersee to Illkirch Graffstaden (2.8 km) is under construction for opening in May 1998. Work will start in 1997 on two east-west alignments. Line B will link Elsau with the city centre and Point Esplanade in the east, with Line C branching off at Republic to serve Foire Exposition and Hoenheim. Both should be in operation by 2000.

Increased frequency over the central section of Line A will be provided by Line D service between Rotonde and Etoile, terminating at Route de Polygone on a short branch which will be extended to Kehl in Germany sometime after 2000. It is also proposed to extend Line B to Neudorf and Neuhof, and to introduce tram service over some existing suburban rail alignments.

SNCF

French National Railways (SNCF), Strasbourg Region
3 boulevard du Président Wilson, 67803 Strasbourg
Telephone: +33 3 88 75 41 43

Current situation: Limited local services operate on five routes. The Alsace region has financed 200 km/h local services to Mulhouse using Corail stock and Sybic electric locomotives.

UPDATED

STUTTGART

Population: City 587,000, metropolitan area 2.3 million
Public transport: Bus, tramway/light rail, rack railway and funicular services provided by company with majority ownership by the city of Stuttgart, developing S-Bahn and associated feeder buses operated by German Railway (DB), other bus services by WEG/KVG and independent operators, all co-ordinated under Stuttgart Verkehrs- und Tarifverbund (VVS)

VVS

Verkehrs- und Tarifverbund Stuttgart GmbH (VVS)
Rotebühlstrasse 133, 70197 Stuttgart, Germany
Telephone: +49 711 66060 Fax: +49 711 6606 257
Directors: Dipl-Ing Wolfgang Wörner
Günter Mötsch
Reinhold Bauer

Current situation: Regional bus and rail developments, fares and services, publicity and planning in an area of 3,012 km² surrounding Stuttgart are co-ordinated by a Verkehrsverbund formed in 1978 by Stuttgarter Strassenbahnen and DB to provide finance for and co-ordination of the developing 10-line Stadtbahn and urban bus network operated by SSB and the six-line regional metro (S-Bahn) and associated feeder bus services operated by DB. The area includes the city of Stuttgart and 141 other towns and neighbourhoods, including Esslingen, Böblingen, Ludwigsburg and Waiblingen, with a total population of some 2.3 million. The only participants in VVS are SSB and DB, though some of the towns in the area have their own separate transport operations, now associated with VVS.

The Verkehrsverbund is controlled by a board of representatives of SSB, DB and local authorities, including the Baden-Württemberg Land government. Tariff standardisation applies to an inner area centred on Stuttgart comprising four zones.

Passenger boardings: (All modes)
(1993) 230 million
(1994) 280 million
(1995) 281 million

Fare structure: Zonal, single and multiride tickets; daily, weekly and monthly passes; annual subscription, discounted sales to employers who buy passes for all their staff; off-peak passes at reduced fares; first class available on S-Bahn; free transfers between modes and operators
Operating costs financed by: Fares 45%, subsidy/grants 55%
Subsidy from: Federal and state governments, city of Stuttgart, four surrounding counties

Buses of SSB

1995

SSB

Stuttgarter Strassenbahnen AG (SSB)
PO Box 801006, 70565 Stuttgart
Telephone: +49 711 78850 Fax: +49 711 7885 2891
Chair: Manfred Bonz
Managing Directors: Peter Höflinger
Reinhold Bauer
Staff: 2,822

Passenger journeys: (All modes)
(1993) 157.5 million
(1994) 164.5 million
(1995) 174.5 million

Operating costs financed by: Fares 43%, other commercial sources 13%, subsidy/grants 44%
Subsidy from: Local authority subsidy; federal and state grants for new investment

Current situation: SSB's majority shareholder is the city of Stuttgart. Operations extend outside the city to serve a total population of 900,000, with co-ordination on a regional level with DB under VVS.

Fare collection: Prepurchase from off-board ticket-issuing machines and ticket offices, or driver on buses only; cancellation/validation machines on board

Standard-gauge LRVs on mixed-gauge track at Bad Cannstatt

Fare structure: Zonal; single, day and multiride tickets, weekly, monthly and annual passes
Integration with other modes: Free transfer in VVS areas with tramway, S-Bahn and private rail and bus services

Bus

Vehicle-km: (1993) 14.1 million
(1994) 13.7 million
(1995) 14.1 million

Number of routes: 56
Route length: (One way) 423 km
On priority right-of-way: 12.2 km
Fleet: 266 vehicles, plus 73 hired

Mercedes O405 (1985/92)	72
Mercedes O305 (1981)	24
Mercedes O307 (1980/81)	8
Mercedes O405G articulated (1986/94)	111
Mercedes O305G articulated (1980/84)	25
Others	26

Average age of fleet: 7.1 years

Most intensive service: Peak 7½ min
One-person operation: All routes
Average distance between stops: 711 m
Average speed: 21.1 km/h

Developments: In accordance with the INVK (Integrated Local Transport Planning) strategy, bus services in parts of the city and region are to be restructured. Parallel with development of the LRT network, buses act mainly as feeders for the light rail and S-Bahn lines, and duplication of rail services is avoided.

Bus flow improvements in progress include provision of more bus lanes, projecting kerbs at stops, traffic signal priority and integration in computer-based monitoring. Special service of nine routes operates on Friday and Saturday nights.

Tramway/light rail

Type of operation: Conventional tramway being upgraded to 1,435 mm gauge Stadtbahn (LRT), with mixed 1,435/1,000 mm gauge operation on some sections

Car-km: (1993) LRV 7.6 million, tram 9.4 million
(1994) LRV 7.9 million, tram 8.3 million
(1995) LRV 8.5 million, tram 6.6 million

Route length: 108.9 km (LRT 84.2 km)
reserved track: 95.4 km
in tunnel: 18.5 km
Number of lines: LRT 9, tram 3
Number of stops: 176
Gauge: 1,000 mm and 1,435 mm
Max gradient: 7%, tramway 8.5%
Minimum curve radius: 50 m, tramway 25 m
Electrification: 750 V DC, overhead

Service: Peak 6-7½-10 min, off-peak 10-12 min
First/last car: 04.45/00.15
Arrangements for elderly/disabled: 101 of the 133 high-platform stations are accessible by ramp or lift

One-person operation: All routes
Operational control: Computer-based monitoring also provides passenger information

Rolling stock: 214 cars

Maschinenfabrik Esslingen GT4 (1961/64)	M100
Duewag DT8 LRV (1985/93/96)	M114
Works cars	M18
Electro-diesel locomotives	3

On order: 23 cars of a new DT8.10 design from Adtranz/Siemens for 1999 delivery, with an option for a further 27

Current situation: SSB has in progress a multistage conversion of tramway to light rail (Stadtbahn), along with conversion from metre to standard gauge now scheduled to be completed by 2005. Most of the route (87.5 per cent) is already segregated and there are 18.5 km of tunnel in the city centre; dual-gauge tracks have been laid on some routes.

Service on the three remaining metre-gauge lines is provided by 48 GT4 cars which have been refurbished internally. Route 13 is being converted to standard gauge for May 1998 completion, and is to be followed by much of Route 2.

Construction in progress of 9 km extension of U14 from Mühlhausen to Remseck-Neckargröningen for 1999 opening. Also U5 to be extended to Mühlhausen to give access to the new depot to be built at Remseck-Aldingen.

Rack railway/funicular

Current situation: A 2.2 km rack line on the Riggenbach-Lamelle system links Marienplatz with Degerloch, metre-gauge, 18 per cent maximum gradient, 680 V DC overhead, three cars. SSB also operates a 600 m funicular from Südheimer Platz to Waldfriedhof on a 27 per cent maximum gradient.

DB

Deutsche Bahn AG, Geschäftsbereich Nahverkehr
Regionalbereich Württemberg
Heilbronner Str 7, 70174 Stuttgart
Telephone: +49 711 2092 3330 Fax: +49 711 2092 3458
Manager: Wolfgang Seidemann

Regional metro

Type of operation: Regional metro (S-Bahn)

Passenger journeys: (1992) 74.8 million
(1993) 79.5 million
(1994) 82 million

Current situation: S-Bahn trains run over six routes with a total length of 174 km serving 69 stations, electrified 15 kV $16\frac{2}{3}$ Hz overhead. Peak-hour trains every 15 min, off-peak 30 min. Extension to Herrenberg and the airport opened 1993, being extended to Bernhausen. Suburban trains also run on non-S-Bahn routes. Operations co-ordinated under VVS.

Rolling stock: 122 ET 420 three-car trains

RBS

Regional Bus Stuttgart GmbH
PO Box 103940, 70034 Stuttgart
Telephone: +49 711 666070 Fax: +49 711 666 0799
Managing Directors: Peter Müller
Rudolf Schmidt

Current situation: Regional bus company owned by DB runs a network of 41 routes as feeders to the S-Bahn, carrying about 15 million passengers a year. Also provides services outside the VVS area.

Other operators

Current situation: Other bus services are provided by WEG Kraftverkehrsgesellschaft (KVG), and several independent operators within the framework of VVS.

UPDATED

SURABAYA

Population: 4 million
Public transport: Bus services operated by government-owned company and private operators of buses and minibuses, with substantial numbers of Bemo shared minibuses and Becak tricycle pedicabs. Ferries link Surabaya and Madura Island; metro planned

DAMRI

Djawatan Angkutan Motor Republik Indonesia
Proyek Biskota, Jl Jend Basoki Rakhmat 80, Surabaya, Java Timor, Indonesia
Telephone: +62 31 43920
Managing Director: Takrim Effendi
Staff: 1,200

Passenger journeys: (1989) 13 million
(1990) 12.8 million
(1991) 13 million

Bus

Current situation: The government-owned bus operations account for only a limited part of the public transport provision, with 10 routes, parts of which are contracted out to other operators. Separate flat fares for local and express services.
Fleet: 215 buses, mostly Mercedes OH306 and OH408 types, plus some Leyland Atlantean double-deck and Tata

Mercedes OH408 express bus of DAMRI in Surabaya city centre

Private bus/minibus

Supervised by: Urban Road Traffic Board
Jl Jend a Yani 268, Surabaya

Current situation: About 30 per cent of public transport journeys are accounted for by a fleet of some 3,200 Bemo 10-seater minibuses, mostly Mitsubishi L300 Colt and Daihatsu models, operating on 37 routes. An estimated 38,000 Becak tricycle pedicabs handle an even larger proportion. There are also a few independent operators of full-size buses, known as Bis Kota.

Metro (planned)

Current situation: A two-line metro is in design, with a 19 km north-south route likely to be built first. A consortium will take the project forward to the stage where a bidding process for a build-operate-transfer contract can be started. The three consortium members, who signed an agreement in October 1996, are the Indonesian railway operator Perumka, GEC Alsthom Transport and a local development and finance company.

Line 1 would run from the Tanjung Perak ferry terminal in the north to Purubaya bus station in the south, serving Perumka's main station and the city centre. In a later phase, Line 2 would link Laguna Indah in the east with residential developments at Kota Baru to the west. There would be interchange with Line 1 at New Kota.

UPDATED

SYDNEY

Population: 3.6 million
Public transport: Bus and ferry/catamaran services serving central urban area and Sydney harbour provided by State Transit Authority. The Department of Transport exercises overall responsibility for planning and co-ordination of all public transport including privately run bus, ferry, taxi and hire car services. State Rail Authority provides extensive suburban rail services over routes owned by the state Rail Access Corporation. Private bus operators serve suburban and outer areas. Monorail serves the Darling Harbour redevelopment; light rail under construction

State Transit

State Transit Authority of New South Wales
PO Box 1327, North Sydney, NSW 2059, Australia
Telephone: +61 2 9245 5777 Fax: +61 2 9245 5710
Chief Executive: John Stott
Staff: 4,100

Passenger journeys: (1993/94) 197.7 million
(1994/95) 194.9 million
(1995/96) 190.2 million

Current situation: State Transit's structure was reorganised at the start of 1993 to meet the government's requirement for a new and accountable business-like culture in the public sector, capable of meeting minimum service levels set by the Department of Transport. A smaller corporate head office now oversees eight major business units and three satellite depots, plus Sydney Ferries and a further business unit responsible for operations in Newcastle (180 km north). There are 25 operating contracts within ST's area.

The Sydney bus system serves a population of 1.7 million and covers an area of 645 km^2. Separate bus and ferry networks run in Newcastle. Details below refer only to Sydney.

Sydney Buses

(Sydney city and inner metropolitan area operations only)
General Manager, Sydney Buses: Guy Thurston
Staff: 3,225

Passenger journeys: (1993/94) 165 million
(1994/95) 168.1 million
(1995/96) 177.1 million
Vehicle-km: (1993/94) 60.5 million
(1994/95) 61.4 million
(1995/96) 65.7 million

Number of routes: 235
Route length: 946 km
Fleet: 1,366 vehicles

MAN SL202	50
Mercedes O305 Mk II to V	1,097
Mercedes O405 Mk VI (airport service)	18
Mercedes O305G articulated	30
Scania LII3RBL	50
Scania LII3CRB CNG-powered	100
Scania ultra-low-floor (1996)	16
Others	5

Average age of fleet: 10.9 years
On order: Balance of 300 Scania; 125 Volvo BI0L ultra-low floor, 30 MAN 11-220 HOCL/R NM 10.2 m ultra-low floor for delivery through to 1999

Most intensive service: 3 min
One-person operation: All routes
Fare collection: Payment to driver, or cancellation of prepurchase multitrip tickets or pass
Fare structure: Stage; multitrip tickets; quarterly and annual 'Travelpass' intermodal passes; off-bus multitrip tickets for use with onboard cancelling machines
Fares collected on board: 55%
Integration with other modes: Timed interchange with suburban rail services and ferries; intermodal 'Travelpass'; airport express bus
Bus priority: Peak-hour bus lanes and priority when joining traffic flow; priority traffic signals
Operational control: Route inspectors/mobile radio; two-way radio in all vehicles; central radio control room
Arrangements for elderly/disabled: Ultra-low-floor buses have ramp and space for two wheelchairs; half fare for elderly, with low-cost day tickets for unlimited bus/train/ferry travel after 09.00. Ministry of Transport subsidises taxi service for disabled; wheelchair users have specially modified vehicles, others use standard taxis and all pay half metered fare, state government subsidising remainder
Operating costs financed by: Fares 55%, other commercial sources 4.6%, subsidy/grants 40.4%
Subsidy from: State government contract payment
New vehicles financed by: Internal funds

Two generations of double-deck emu at Redfern

Nepean Nipper minibus of Westbus in suburban Penrith

Sydney Ferries

Staff: 408

Passenger journeys: (1993/94) 11 million
(1994/95) 11.9 million
(1995/96) 13.1 million

Number of routes: 11
Fleet: 27 vessels

Operating costs financed by: Fares 64%, other commercial sources 10%, subsidy/grants 26%

Current situation: Ferries provide an important link between Sydney Harbour residential suburbs and the major bus/rail interchange at Circular Quay. Extensive cruise services also operate.

Sydney Buses' latest delivery, Scania ultra-low-floor **1997**

Private bus

Represented by: Bus & Coach Association
27 Villiers Street, North Parramatta, NSW 2151
Telephone: +61 2 9630 8655 Fax: +61 2 9683 1465
President: S J J Bosnjak
Major operators in descending order of size are: Westbus, Busways (Rowe's), Metrolink (Oliveri), North & Western, Metrowest, Forest Coachlines, Shorelink, Punchbowl, West Bankstown, Bankstown-Strathfield Bus Line, Midshore, Canterbury Bus Line, Crossley Bus Line, Westaway, Neville's, Baxter's Holroyd, Harris Park Transport, Glenorie.

Current situation: Around 50 per cent of suburban services are operated by private firms with a fleet of 3,000 buses in the Sydney/Newcastle/Wollongong urban areas. Operators are given five-year performance-based contracts stipulating minimum service levels and standard fares.

CityRail

Division of the State Rail Authority of New South Wales
PO Box 349, Haymarket, Sydney 2000
Telephone: +61 2 9219 4331 Fax: +61 2 9219 1631
Group General Manager, CityRail: Richard Middleton

Type of operation: Suburban and interurban rail

Passenger journeys: (1993/94) 234.8 million
(1994/95) 249.6 million
(1995/96) 256.4 million

Current situation: CityRail operates an extensive suburban and interurban rail network totalling 1,700 km with 310 stations, mostly electrified 1.5 kV DC. The network extends well beyond the Sydney suburban area and includes intercity trains to Newcastle, Lithgow, Wollongong and the Southern Highlands. Statistics given here cover the entire network.

Fares cover 54 per cent of operating costs, other commercial sources 6 per cent, with the remainder being a state government payment to cover concession fares and for operating non-commercial services.

Developments: From July 1996, the New South Wales rail infrastructure was separated from day-to-day operations and vested in the new state-owned Rail Access Corporation. CityRail now pays annual access charges to operate its services.

With the entire new-generation Tangara fleet in service, refurbishment continues of earlier rolling stock. Some 120 suburban cars had been completed by mid-1996.

Construction is in progress of a direct underground link to the airport (10 km, four stations), for opening in 2000. This is a joint venture between the NSW government, Transfield Construction and project manager CRI Ltd, and is the first such scheme to allow private sector operation of a railway.

Also under construction is a 6 km loop and station to serve the 2000 Olympic stadium at Homebush Bay. This line should be open in early 1998.

Rolling stock: 1,454 emu cars and 36 diesel cars

Suburban double-deck	1,134
Intercity double-deck	240
Tangara outer-suburban (1994/95)	80
Endeavour diesel railcar	30
Class 629 diesel railcar	6

In peak service: 1,272 emu and 34 dmu cars

Sydney's Harbourlink monorail ***1995***

Sydney Monorail

TNT Transit Systems
220 Pyrmont Street, Darling Harbour, NSW 2000
Telephone: +61 2 9552 2288 Fax: +61 2 9660 0955
General Manager: R Ward
Deputy General Manager: Murray Harris
Marketing Manager: David Cox
Staff: 85

Type of operation: Straddle monorail, opened 1988

Current situation: A 3.6 km automated loop line with seven stations connects the city centre with Darling Harbour; electrified 500 V AC. Privately developed by TNT, the link is a fully commercial operation. Cars run every 4 min.

TNT has been contracted to operate the light rail line (see below), scheduled to open in mid-1997.

Rolling stock: 6 seven-car trainsets

Light rail

Under construction
Sydney Light Rail Company
Managing Director: Rob Schwarzer

Current situation: A 3.5 km light rail link from Central station to the Darling Harbour and City West (Ultimo) development areas is scheduled to open in mid-1997. TNT will operate the line under contract. Adtranz Australia has supplied seven Variotram LRVs for the initial service.

Developments: Two extensions have been proposed and are under consideration by the NSW government. These would extend the line to the central business district and westwards, adding a further 4.5 km of route and 15 cars.

UPDATED

SZCZECIN

Population: 413,000
Public transport: Bus and tramway services provided by municipal authority. Suburban rail services by State Railway (PKP)

MZK

Miějskie Zaklady Komunikacyjne (MZK)
ul Klonowicza 5, 71241 Szczecin, Poland
Telephone: +48 91 74411 Fax: +48 91 38993
Staff: 3,689

Passenger journeys: (All modes) (1990) 248.2 million

Operating costs financed by: Fares 37%, subsidy from city 73%

Current situation: In 1991 the former operating authority WPKM, which had provided public transport services in the cities of Szczecin, Stargard Szczecinski and Swinoujscie, was split into three organisations. The Szczecin operation came under the control of the local authority and took a new name. An annual grant towards operating costs comes from central government, allocated by the Administrator of the province of Szczecin.

Bus

Passenger journeys: (1990) 151.2 million
Vehicle-km: (1990) 23.9 million

Number of routes: 66
Route length: 719 km
Fleet: 440 vehicles

Jelcz PR110M	90
Jelcz M11	129
Ikarus 280 articulated	221

In peak service: 278

One-person operation: All routes
Fare collection: Prepurchase ticket or pass with validation and cancelling machines on board
Fare structure: Flat
Fare evasion control: Random inspectors
Average peak-hour speed: 19.6 km/h

Tramway

Type of operation: Conventional tramway with sections upgraded to light rail

Passenger journeys: (1990) 97 million
Car-km: (1990) 14.8 million

Route length: 110 km
Number of lines: 12
Gauge: 1,435 mm

Service: Peak 5 min; 24 h service
Fare structure: As bus
Average peak-hour speed: 14.6 km/h

Jelcz M11 of MZK in the city centre

Rolling stock: 353 cars

Konstal Chorzow	
N (1952-62)	M93
102N (1971/72)	M24
105N (1975/79)	M94
105Na (1981-90	M49
ND	T93

In peak service: 239

PKP

Polish State Railways (PKP)
ul Chalubinskiego 4, 00928 Warszawa

Type of operation: Suburban heavy rail

Current situation: Services on several lines in Szczecin urban area and on routes to Trzebiez Szczecinski (37 km), Kostrzyn (104 km) and Choszczno (75 km); irregular, but about hourly.

PKP suburban emu at Szczecin main station

TAIPEI

Population: City 2.5 million, metropolitan area 5 million
Public transport: Integrated bus services for designated urban area provided by City Bus Administration and nine private groups and companies regulated by Taipei City Government, which also licenses the single ferry operation. Suburban rail services provided by Taiwan Railway Administration being upgraded. Metro under construction; automated light metro

Taipei City Bus

Taipei City Bus Administration
5 Peiping East Road, Taipei City, Taiwan
Chief Administrator: Wua-Hsiung Lee
Staff: 3,087

Current situation: Publicly owned Taipei City Bus is responsible to the Reconstruction Bureau of Taipei Municipal Government which also regulates nine other private bus undertakings working in the United Operating System (see earlier editions of *JUTS* for history).

Taipei City Bus is the largest single operator, carrying about 1 million passengers daily. Three levels of service are offered: conventional and air conditioned buses, and minibuses.

Bus

Passenger journeys: (1992/93) 293.7 million
Vehicle-km: (1992/93) 50.8 million

Number of routes: Total 157; ordinary services 54, air conditioned 89, minibus 14
Route length: (One way) 1,520 km
Fleet: Total 1,356 buses; ordinary 238, air conditioned 1,075, minibuses 43; including locally bodied Hino, Isuzu, Volvo 6FA buses and Toyota and Mercedes (L508D) mini/midibus
In peak service: 1,216

Most intensive service: 3 min
Fare structure: 2 zones
Fare collection: Cash or prepurchase 10-zone tickets; additional tokens required for air conditioned services
Arrangements for elderly/disabled: Free with multi-journey tickets clipped by drivers; clippings counted for reimbursement of operator by government
Operating costs financed by: Fares 77.3%, other commercial sources 2.8%, subsidy/grants 17.7%, tax levy 1.8%
Subsidy from: Taipei Municipal Government (if received)

Private bus

Regulated by: DoT, Taipei City Government
17th Floor, No 222 Sec 5, Chung-hsiao E Road, Taipei
Director General of Transport: Robert S F Tang
Staff: 8,065

Current situation: Nine private companies participating in the United Operating System (see above): Hsin Hsin, Kuan Hua, Tayo, Ta Nan, Chi Nan, Taipei, Chung Shin, San Chung and Shoudu bus companies.

Fares and concessions are standardised between the independent operators and TCBA working within the UOS area, including prepurchase zone tickets and concessionary multijourney tickets. Most of the private operators run services from outside the city and in the outer suburbs as well as within the designated UOS area.

Another 10 long-distance bus operators carry some passengers within the Taipei metropolitan area.
Developments: Plans for ordering a new fleet of 636 buses in 1994 were abandoned after the city government refused to raise fares to the level requested by the operators.

Passenger journeys: (1990) 768 million
(1992) 768 million
Vehicle-km: (1990) 176 million
(1992) 183 million

Number of routes: 176
Route length: 3,852 km
Fleet: Total 3,422 (UOS commitment), including Isuzu, Hino, Mercedes, Mitsubishi, Renault, International, and Volvo. Fleets by operator are as follows (UOS only): Hsin Hsin (355), Kuan Hua (220), Tayo (375), Ta Nan (230), Chi Nan (84), Taipei (267), Chung Shin (205), San Chung (174), Shoudu (156).
In peak service: 2,080

One-person operation: All routes
Fare collection: Cash
Fare structure: 2 zones
Average peak-hour speed: 17 km/h
Operating costs financed by: Fares 100%

Ikarus 560 of TCBA

Ferry

Current situation: Tankang Shipping operates ferry service on the Tamshui river; four vessels ply a single route carrying about 100,000 passengers annually.

TRA

Taiwan Railway Administration
3 Peiping West Road, Taipei 10026
Telephone: +886 2 381 5226 Fax: +886 2 383 1367

Suburban rail

Type of operation: Suburban heavy rail

Passenger journeys: (Annual) 26 million

Current situation: TRA operates frequent local trains from Keelung through Taipei to Taoyuan and Hsinchu

Mitsubishi Fuso of Chung Shin Bus Co

(electrified 25 kV AC), using the city-centre tunnel opened in 1990, plus other suburban services.

Rolling stock: 12 four-car emus
Union Carriage (1990/91) M24 T24

TRTC

Taipei Rapid Transit Co Ltd
7 Pei Ping East Road, Taipei
Telephone: +886 2 396 2231 Fax: +886 2 395 6054
President: C W Chen

Current situation: TRTC was established in 1994 as operator of the metro. All construction is in the hands of DORTS (see below). Services on the initial 10.9 km portion of the Mucha line and on Line 1 were inaugurated in 1996. The Mucha line carried over 2 million passengers in its first year of operation.

Metro

Under construction

Department of Rapid Transit Systems, TMG (DORTS)
13/F 16 Nanking East Road, Taipei 10586
Telephone: +886 2 578 5678 Fax: +886 2 578 0999
Director General: L S Lin
Chief Engineer: Y C Chiang

Current situation: Construction started 1988 on the first segment of the Red Line 1 of planned 88 km five-line metro with 80 stations. The Red line extends 22.8 km northwards from the underground Taipei Main station of TRA (see above) in cut-and-cover (3 km) and elevated (11 km) before taking over the alignment of TRA's Tamshui line. The 1,435 mm gauge line has 750 V DC third-rail current collection. Originally scheduled to open in 1993, the initial section opened in 1996.

A total of 132 cars (22 six-car trains) for the Red line has been built in the USA by United Rail Car Partnership, a consortium of Nissho Iwai American Corp and Kawasaki Rolling Stock (USA). A further 216 cars to equip the Orange, Green and Blue lines are on order from a Siemens/SGP/Union Carriage consortium.

Other lines under construction are: a 10.3 km route from the city centre to Hsintien (Green line, opening 1997); the Nankang–Tucheng Blue line (23.9 km, opening 1998); and the 25.1 km Orange line from Kuting to Sanchung where it branches to serve Sanmin Road in Luchou and Hsinchuang. This is due to open in 2007.

The Mucha (Brown) line (24 km, 23 stations) has been equipped by Matra with VAL 256 automated medium-capacity rubber-tyred trains; construction has been managed by DORTS. This entirely elevated mini-metro runs to the east of Taipei city centre, linking Neihu in the north and serving new development areas. This was expected to be the first line to open, but commissioning was beset by problems and major remedial work has had to be carried out on the elevated structures. Trial running began in 1992, but public service on the 10.9 km section between Taipei Zoo and Sungshan airport was not inaugurated until March 1996.

A further six lines totalling 108 km are being evaluated, including an orbital route.

UPDATED

Taipei's metro routes

VAL 256 driverless train on the Mucha line ***1995***

Red line metro trials ***1996***

TAIYUAN

Population: 2 million
Public transport: Bus and trolleybus services provided by municipal agency, the former extending into the city's rural hinterland. Chinese Railways operates limited suburban rail services

Taiyuan City Transport Company

Taiyuan, People's Republic of China

Current situation: Trolleybuses are used on some of the principal arteries and, although the network has remained static for some years, the fleet has been extensively modernised with worn-out two-axle and articulated vehicles being replaced by new articulated. One route is physically separate from the rest of the system.

The bus fleet was also modernised during the 1980s. Several bus and trolleybus terminals are located around the main railway station and May 1st Square in the city centre.

Bus

Number of routes: Approx 30 (urban and suburban)
Fleet: Approx 250 buses (over 100 articulated), including Beijing BK670 and BK663 (articulated), Chongqing CQ662 (articulated), Hebei HB640 (two-axle) and others from factories at Beijing, Nanchang, Siping, Taiyuan and elsewhere
Recent deliveries: Beijing and Siping types

Fare collection: Payment of stage fares to seated conductors; monthly passes

Trolleybus

Number of routes: 5
Fleet: Approx 85 trolleybuses (all articulated), including Shanghai SK561G, Beijing BK562 and Taiyuan
Fare collection: As bus

TALLINN

Population: 442,000
Public transport: Bus, trolleybus and tramway services operated by separate municipal undertakings co-ordinated by the Department of Transport; suburban rail

Old Skoda 9Tr trolleybus and ex-Swedish Scania of Autobussikoondis ***1997***

Tallinn Tram & Trolleybus Co

Tallinna Trammi-ja Trollibussikoondis
Paldiski maantee 48A, 0006 Tallinn, Estonia
Telephone: +372 6 269100 Fax: +372 6 541125
Chief Engineer: Oskar Gustavson
Staff: 1,397

Current situation: The company is struggling to maintain service levels in the face of financial difficulties which prevent any major rehabilitation of rolling stock or infrastructure. In addition, while the city's population declines, the number of private cars has increased substantially.

Fare structure: Flat
Fare collection: On board or prepurchase and validation; 10, 20, 30 day and monthly passes
Arrangements for elderly/disabled: Reduced-rate passes; over-70s travel free
Operating costs financed by: Fares 29%, other commercial sources 10%, subsidy/grants 58%, deficit 3%

Trolleybus

Passenger journeys: (1991) 85.4 million
(1992) 88 million
(1994) 37.6 million

Route length: 79.5 km
Number of routes: 9
Fleet: 146 vehicles

Skoda 9Tr	17
Skoda 14Tr	98
Skoda 15Tr articulated	24
Ikarus 280T ex-Hoyerswerda	6
YuMZ-T1	1

In peak service: 101

Tramway

Type of operation: Conventional tramway

Passenger journeys: (1991) 100.3 million
(1992) 103.3 million
(1994) 42 million

Route length: 39 km
Number of routes: 4
Gauge: 1,067 mm

Rolling stock: 131 cars

ČKD Tatra T4 (1973/80)	M56
ČKD Tatra KT4 articulated (1981/91)	M75

In peak service: 68

Tatra T4s running Route 4 on Pärnu maantee ***1997***

Tallinn Bus Company

Tallinna Autobussikoondis AS
Kadaka tee 62A, 0026 Tallinn
Telephone: +372 6 509500 Fax: +372 6 509509
General Director: Mati Mägi
Technical Director: Hugo Linholm
Traffic Director: Tiit Orissaar
Business Development Manager: Koit Kaevats
Staff: 1,250

Current situation: In 1993 the former state-owned bus undertaking became a limited liability company owned by the Tallinn city government. Formerly an urban-only operation, the company began expansion into the suburbs in 1993, with three routes.

Bus

Passenger boardings: (1992) 138 million
(1993) 138.6 million
(1995) 87.1 million
Vehicle-km: (1992) 22.6 million
(1993) 24.5 million
(1995) 18.6 million

Number of routes: 48
Route length: 489 km
Fleet: 309 vehicles

Ikarus 260 (1982/89)	
Ikarus 280 (1981/88)	
Volvo/MAN/Scania/DAB-Leyland (1979/82)	20
Baltscan citybus (1995)	5

In peak service: 237
Average age of fleet: 10 years

Most intensive service: 6 min
One-person operation: 50% of routes
Fare structure: Common with other modes
Fare collection: Ticket vending machines on board
Average peak-hour speed: 17.5 km/h
Operating costs financed by: Fares: 44.6%, other commercial sources 2%, subsidy/grants 50%

Suburban rail

Current situation: Estonian Railways operates suburban services over 132 km of route, 1,520 mm gauge, electrified at 3 kV DC; zonal fares; fleet of Riga-built emus.

UPDATED

TAMPA

Population: 300,000, county area 800,000
Public transport: Bus and paratransit services provided by Regional Transit Authority controlled by representative board. Privately financed people mover; rail transit options studied

HART

Hillsborough Area Regional Transit Authority
4305 E 21st Avenue, Tampa, FL 33605, USA
Telephone: +1 813 623 5835 Fax: +1 813 664 1119
Chair: Enrique Woodruff
Executive Director: Sharon Dent
General Manager, Operations: Robert Potts
Staff: 409

Current situation: HART was established in 1980 with funding provided by an *ad valorem* tax. It expanded services rapidly to cater for major business and residential growth, together with shortages of parking and highway capacity for which public transport is seen as providing relief. It now operates throughout Hillsborough County and to a limited extent within Pinellas County across the bay. Developments have included establishment of express routes serving park-and-ride sites, and timed-transfer provided at five transit centres and in the downtown Marion Street transitway. Vanpools operate in Hillsborough and Pinellas counties; a replica tram service runs at mid-day linking downtown with historic Ybor City.

The privately funded Harbour Island People Mover links the city with an offshore commercial development (see below). HART has regulatory powers over the system, with an option to acquire and operate it after 15 years.

Developments: Recent ridership figures showed some growth after three years of decline, but the undertaking still faced the need to reduce costs and raise income. Examples of HART's marketing innovations include all-over advertisements on buses. Privatisation of services, which started in late 1995, has not been taken forward.

Studies have been undertaken of the feasibility of a midway stop on the people mover, and three major transit corridors have been reviewed to identify future mass transit needs. A 1.7 km downtown bus-only transit mall for Marion Street opened in 1989, with two terminals planned and projected use by 120 buses an hour during peak periods by 2005. Close by is an information centre where passengers can buy passes, store cycles and shower after making bike-on-bus trips.

There are also proposals for building a short city-centre tram route that would operate historic cars.

Bus

(Including contracted services)
Passenger boardings: (1992/93) 8.3 million
(1993/94) 9.4 million
(1994/95) 10.1 million
Vehicle-km: (1992/93) 9 million
(1993/94) 9.6 million
(1995/96) 10.6 million

Number of routes: 43
Route length: (One way) 1,281 km
Fleet: 173 vehicles

GMC (1982)	31
GMC (1985/86)	35
Flxible (1983/85/88/89)	89
Orion (1994)	3
Bluebird (1995)	5
Gillig (1996)	10

In peak service: 127

Fare collection: Payment to driver or prepurchase pass; exact fare only
Fare structure: Flat; higher rate for Express services; transfers valid 30 min; 20-journey Express and local passes; monthly passes
Arrangements for elderly/disabled: 76% of buses kneeling or lift-equipped working regular schedules; half fare
Bus priority: Marion Street downtown transitway extends 9 blocks
Integration with other modes: 28 park-and-ride lots in Hillsborough County, 1 in Pinellas County; cycle racks on all buses
Operating costs financed by: Fares 22.1%, other commercial sources 3.5%, subsidy/grants 25.1%, tax levy 49.3%
Subsidy from: Local 8.2% (from *ad valorem* tax), FTA 36.9%, State 54.9%

Rapid transit (proposed)

Current situation: Following rejection of light rail proposals on cost grounds, the currently preferred mode is commuter rail using existing rights-of-way. A 50 km route would run from Tampa to Lakeland, with four stations. The Tampa Bay Commuter Rail Authority has made feasibility and ridership studies, funded by a $0.5 million Federal grant.

People mover (proposed)

Current situation: Consultants have assessed a city-centre people mover network linked to the Harbour Island line.

Harbour Island People Mover

Type of operation: Cable-powered people mover

Current situation: A people mover link between central Tampa and a private residential development on Harbour Island opened in 1985; it carries about 0.3 million passengers a year. The 762 m Otis-designed 'horizontal elevator' is cable-powered and operates with two cars running on an elevated concrete guideway, each capable of carrying 100 standing passengers. Fares account for 50 per cent of operating costs, the remainder coming from the owner and from assessments on the property owners in the residential development.

The right-of-way was donated by the local authority, and in return Harbour Island will offer to sell the system to the Hillsborough Area Regional Transit Authority in 2000 for $1.

UPDATED

Harbour Island people mover

Buses of HART on the Marion Street transit parkway

TANGSHAN

Population: 1.3 million
Public transport: Bus services provided by municipal agency

Tangshan City Bus Company

Tangshan, People's Republic of China

Number of routes: Approx 15
Fleet: Approx 250 buses, many articulated, made by Changjiang, Hebei, Siping and Tianjin factories

Fare collection: Payment to seated conductors; monthly passes

Current situation: A brand-new city has been built adjacent to the old one which was almost totally destroyed by an earthquake in 1976 and only low-rise development has been permitted in the former city centre. Bus services have been adapted to meet the changed traffic patterns.

TASHKENT

Population: 2 million

Public transport: Bus and trolleybus/tramway services provided by municipal undertaking; metro. Following political changes, existing operators are likely to be replaced by a single city-wide authority

Toshshakhariu Lovchitrans

Toshshakhariu Lovchitrans
Ul Shirokaya 6, 700000 Tashkent, Uzbekistan

Current situation: The tramway system seems to be in decline; there have been several route closures in recent years as the trolleybus network has expanded, and routes suspended whilst metro Line 3 is under construction are unlikely to be resumed.

Bus

Number of routes: 45
Route length: 384 km
Fleet: Over 700 vehicles

Daewoo BS106	
Ikarus 260/280	
Daimler-Benz O405	185
Daimler-Benz O405G articulated	65

One-person operation: All routes
Fare collection: Payment to roving conductor or prepurchase pass
Fare structure: Flat
Average peak-hour speed: 17.6 km/h

Trolleybus

Number of routes: 19
Route length: 200 km
Fleet: Approx 425 vehicles, some ex-Riga

Uritsky ZIU682	About 300
Uritsky ZIU683 articulated	15
Skoda 14Tr	111

One-person operation: All routes
Fare collection: As bus
Fare structure: Flat
Average peak-hour speed: 15.2 km/h

Tramway

Type of operation: Conventional tramway

Route length: 228 km
Number of lines: 28
Gauge: 1,524 mm

Fare structure: Flat
Fare collection: As bus
One-person operation: All routes

Rolling stock: Approx 430 cars

Ust-Katav 71-605	About 290
Ust-Katav 71-608K	46
Ust-Katav 71-608KM	2
Riga RVZ6	20
ČKD Tatra T3	20
ČKD Tatra T6B5 (1994/95)	55

Daimler-Benz O405 city buses at May 1 **1997**

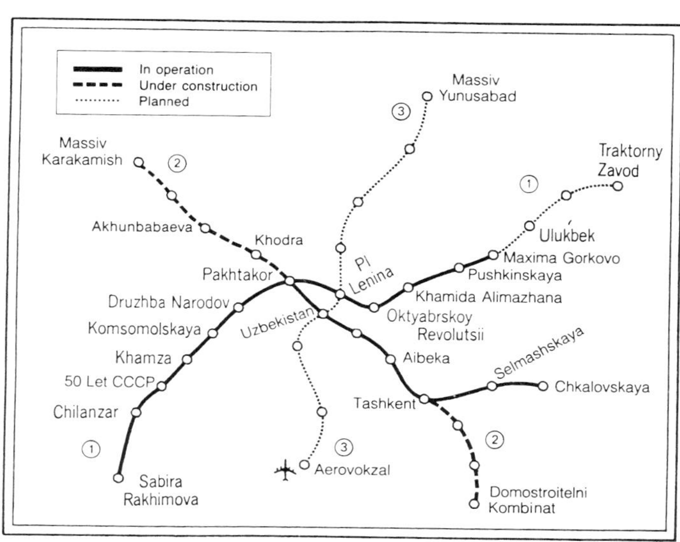

Tashkent metro

Tashkent Metro

Tashkent Metropolitena
Uzbekistan prospekt 92A, Tashkent 600015
Telephone: +7 371 323852
Chief Executive:
Shainoyat Rakhimovich Shaabdurakhimov
Chief Engineer: Khakim Gafurovich Gafurov

Type of operation: Full metro, first line opened 1977

Passenger journeys: (1993) 150 million

Route length: 30 km
Number of lines: 2
Number of stations: 26
Gauge: 1,524 mm
Max gradient: 4%
Minimum curve radius: 400 m
Electrification: 825 V DC, third rail

Service: Peak 2 min
First/last train: 06.00/01.00
Fare structure: Flat
Fare collection: Prepurchase plastic token to turnstile

Uzbek Railways' suburban train at Tashkent Voksal **1997**

Rolling stock: 146 cars, in four-car sets

Mytischy EJ-T	M146

Current situation: Line 3 under construction from Massiv Yunusabad to Uzbekistan, with partial opening scheduled for 1996. A southern extension of this line to the airport is planned.

Uzbek Railways (UTY)

Uzbekistan Temir Yollari

Suburban rail

Current situation: UTY runs suburban trains on several routes into Tashkent Voksal, electrified 3 kV DC.

UPDATED

TEL AVIV - JAFFA (YAFO)

Population: 350,000, conurbation 2 million
Public transport: Bus services provided by two co-operative groups. Suburban rail services; light rail proposed

DAN

DAN-Cooperative Society for Public Transport Ltd
39 Shaul Hamelech Blvd, PO Box 33038, Tel Aviv, Israel
Telephone: +972 3 693 3216 Fax: +972 3 693 3511
Staff: 3,220 (including 1,720 members)
Chair: Alex Abramovitz
Executive Traffic Director: Yoram Charabi
Staff: 3,500

Current situation: The DAN bus co-operative is the largest provider of bus services in Tel Aviv and its metropolitan area. Its operating territory covers the most densely populated areas, comprising the Tel Aviv metropolitan area and seven surrounding cities, with a population of 2 million, of which DAN services reach some 617,000. Of the DAN staff of 3,500 some 1,700 are member shareholders of the co-operative.

Intercity and tourist services are also operated, accounting for about 10 per cent of DAN activities and compensating for a decline in bus passengers evident over several years.

Developments: Automated ticketing system installed in 100 buses, being extended to the whole fleet; vehicle monitoring system under development.

Major bus terminal developed by DAN and EGGED opened 1993, designed to cater for 200,000 suburban and long-distance passengers daily.

MAN midibus in new DAN livery ***1995***

Bus

Passenger journeys: (1990/91) 223 million
(1992/93) 185 million
(1993/94) 189 million

Number of routes: 112
Route length: (One way) 2,820 km
Fleet: 1,460 vehicles

MAN SL 200	1,100
MAN articulated	230
Coaches	120
Minibuses	10

In peak service: 1,201
New vehicles required each year: 95
On order: 15 minibuses and 80 standard MAN buses per year

Most intensive service: 5 min
One-person operation: 100%
Fare collection: Payment to driver
Fare structure: Zonal
Average peak-hour speed: 17.3 km/h
Operating costs financed by: Fares 72%, government subsidy/grants 28%

EGGED

EGGED-Israel Transport Cooperative Society Ltd
Bet 'EGGED' Derech Petach-Tiqwa 142, Tel Aviv 64921
PO Box 33091, Tel Aviv 61330
Telephone: +972 3 432211 Fax: +972 3 696 5354
Chair: Shlomo Levin
Staff: 8,400 (national total)

Current situation: EGGED's Northern Region provides part of the Tel Aviv area bus services. It also runs services in most other parts of Israel, including city areas, and at regional and interurban level. The co-operative has about 5,800 members and some 3,200 additional hired staff. The total passenger carryings are about 1.5 million daily, with a 4,000 vehicle fleet operating more than 1,200 routes. The figures for Tel Aviv are approximations and reflect some regional as well as city services.

Bus

Passenger journeys: Approx 100 million (annual)
Vehicle-km: Approx 40 million (annual)

Number of routes: 25
Fleet: 400 buses, including Leyland and Mercedes

Most intensive service: 5-10 min
One-person operation: All routes
Fare collection: Tickets sold by driver from rack or prepurchased with cancellation by driver. Manual machines
Fare structure: Zonal
Fare evasion control: Inspectors
Average peak-hour speed: 17.2 km/h
Bus priority: 15.4 km of bus lanes in 7 sections in central area

TAMAR

Tel Aviv-Yafo Metropolitan Area Rapid Transit

Current situation: Formed in 1995, this organisation is responsible for developing plans for a rapid transit system for the region.

Following a consultant's report which recommended construction of a 50 km four-line light rail network as the basis for the city's public transport in the 21st century, the municipal authorities commissioned feasibility studies in 1995 from Parsons Brinckerhoff and Sofrétu in joint venture. TAMAR sought bids at the end of 1995 for a 30-year concession to design and build a 20 km light metro system at a cost of US$1 billion.

The two lines would comprise a loop linking IR's Central station with the city centre, university and coastal strip, with branches northeast to the Petah Tiqwa housing development, south to Bat Yam and Rishon le Zion, and to the central bus station. Some tunnelling would be required beneath city-centre streets. Trial bores for the tunnel sections were started in August 1996, and construction is expected to start by mid-1997 for opening in 2000.

Light rail is still envisaged as the mode for routes to Kiryat Ono and Tel-Hashomer.

Railway 2000

Israel Railways
PO Box 18085, Tel Aviv 61180
Director: Yitzahak Ben-Dov

Current situation: Cross-city service was inaugurated by Israel Railways in 1993 with completion of a 4.5 km double-track connection between IR's South and Central stations. Diesel-hauled suburban trains link Herzliyya in the north with Lod in the south. Two new stations on the cross-city line opened in late 1995.

Developments: Under IR's Railway 2000 plans, two new suburban lines are to be built, to Kfar-Sava and Ben Gurion international airport, the latter as the first stage of a new high-speed alignment between Tel Aviv and Jerusalem. The projects involve upgrading some 28 km of existing freight-only lines and 22 km new construction. A fleet of 100 emus would be required to provide a range of services capable of making an impact on the city's notorious traffic problems; electrification has been canvassed.

In May 1996, Railway 2000 was launched as a subsidiary of IR to carry the project forward. Funding has been approved for reconstruction of the first 4 km to Bnei Brak of the route to Kfar-Sava, along with some double tracking.

UPDATED

TIANJIN

Population: 5.4 million, municipal area 8 million
Public transport: Bus and trolleybus services operated by municipal companies and metro run by separate agency in limited operation. Urban development plans have favoured expansion of bus services and the trolleybus system is not to be extended. Metro of long-term future significance only

Tianjin City Transport

Tianjin City Transport Corporation
Tianjin, People's Republic of China

Tianjin City Transport Corporation buses

Bus
Number of routes: 59
Fleet: 1,400 buses, most locally built at Tianjin factory

Articulated	470
Double-deck ex-KMB Hong Kong	35

Fare collection: Fixed conductor
Fare structure: Flat

Tianjin City Trolleybus

Tianjin City Trolleybus Company
General Manager: Zhu Jian-Bin
Staff: 3,400

Current situation: Since 1980 route extensions have taken place and many new trolleybuses have been obtained from an associated vehicle manufacturing company, but contraction has taken place as the company expanded its bus operations. The seven routes operating in 1984 have been reduced to two.

Trolleybus and bus
Number of routes: 2
Route length: 81.5 km
Fleet: 300 trolleybuses and buses (over 100 articulated) including Tianjin and Shanghai types

Service interval: Every few minutes
One-person operation: None
Fare collection: Payment to seated conductors, monthly passes
Operating costs financed by: Fares 47%, other commercial sources 22%, subsidy/grants 31%
Subsidy from: Municipality

Tianjin Metro

Tianjin Metro Administration
97 Jie-Fang-Bei Road, He-ping, 300041 Tianjin
Telephone: +86 22 399815
General Manager: Liu Yuxi
Chief Engineer: Xu Geng-Tao

Type of operation: Full metro, initial route opened 1980

Passenger journeys: (1993) 15 million

Route length: 7.4 km
Number of lines: 1
Number of stations: 8
Gauge: 1,435 mm
Track: 50 kg/m rail laid on concrete sleepers
Max gradient: 3%
Minimum curve radius: 300 m
Tunnel: Cut-and-cover
Electrification: 750 V DC, third rail

Service: 15 min
First/last train: 06.00/22.00
Fare structure: Flat
Fare collection: Manual sale from booking offices
Integration with other modes: Because of limited rolling stock, passengers are not yet encouraged to use the metro instead of other public transport
Signalling: Automatic block

Rolling stock: 12 cars, former Beijing prototypes

Changchun BJ-111	M12

On order: A fleet of cars similar to those running in Beijing is to be built

Current situation: Limited public services are offered on the initial 5.2 km section opened in 1980 and 2.8 km extension to Xizhan (Tianjin West station) opened 1984. Trial public service will run until sufficient rolling stock is delivered. Northwards extension under construction, was scheduled to open 1989 but delayed. Now, a 10.8 km southern extension to Shuang Lin is under construction, funded by a US$112 million loan from the Australian government; opening scheduled for 1998.

Lines 2 and 3 planned, along with 44 km circular Line 4, as well as an outer circle light rail route which would feed buses running to the city centre.

Recently supplied Tianjin-built articulated trolleybuses

Metro train at Xin Hua terminus

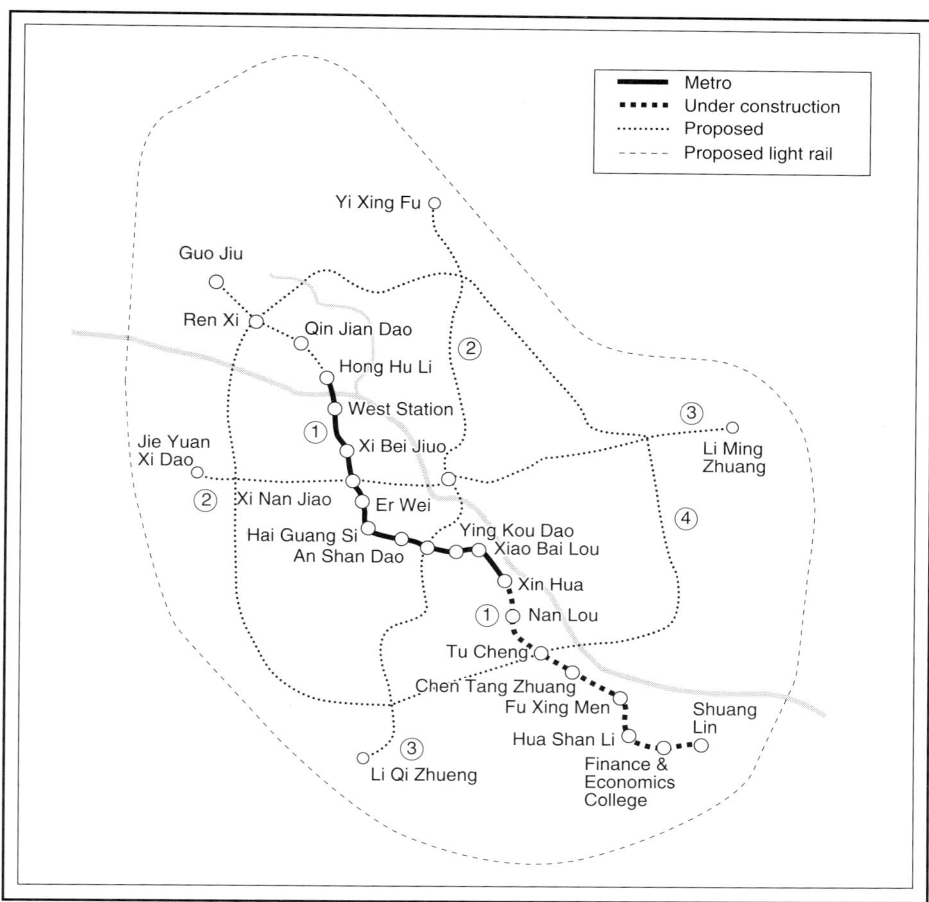

Tianjin metro

TIJUANA

Population: 1.5 million
Public transport: Extensive bus services provided by private operators; light rail planned

Bus

Main operators:
Auto Transportes Baja California Azul y Blanco J Magellanes
Linea Transportes Urbanos y Sub Urbanos de Baja California
Transportes Passajeros Urbanos y Sub Urbanos

Current situation: This fast-growing city across the Mexican border from San Diego is served exclusively by private operators. Because of the duty-free status of the area, equipment is usually US-built and ranges from second-hand transit buses to vans and schoolbus-derived types.

Mexicoach inaugurated an upmarket service from the US border at San Ysidro to downtown Tijuana in 1989, provoking violent protests from taxi drivers. In 1990 a further cross-border service was introduced jointly by Mexicoach and MTDB of San Diego, linking the light rail station at San Ysidro with central Tijuana.

Light rail (planned)

Current situation: The city authorities are studying light rail plans following studies made by Siemens for a route to the US border at San Ysidro, terminus of San Diego's light rail network. Contractors were expected to bid to build the initial line in late 1995, following agreement amongst a consortium of local businessmen to raise the necessary finance privately.

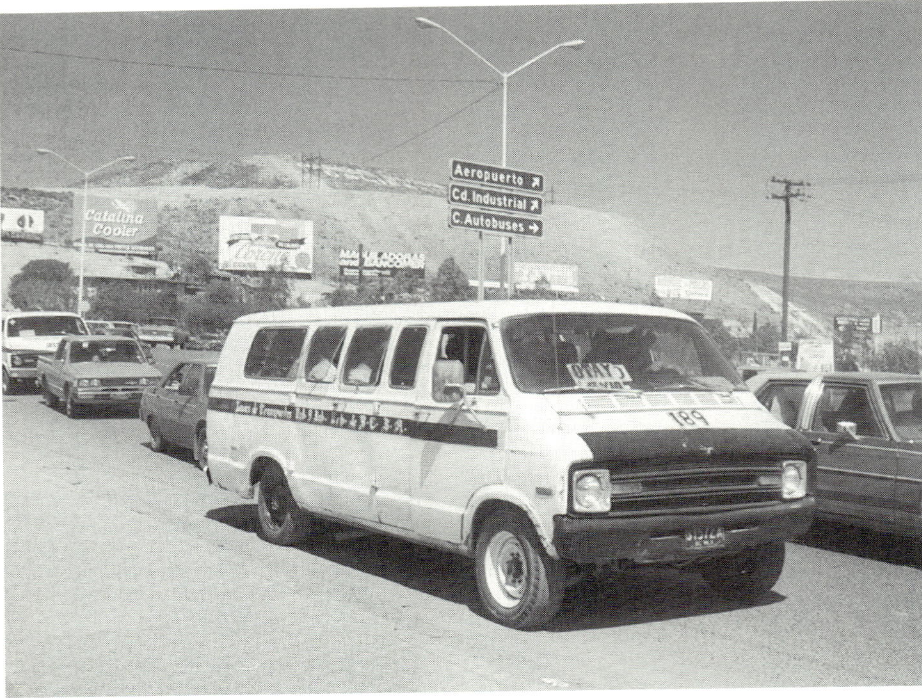

Van-type minibus of Linea Transportes Urbanos y Sub Urbanos de BC

Construction costs could be reduced by acquisition of up to 20 LRVs surplus from the San Diego fleet.

TIMIŞOARA

Population: 500,000
Public transport: Bus, trolleybus, tramway and some taxi services operated by municipal undertaking

RAT

Regie Autonomă de Transport Timişoara
Bdul Take Ionescu 56, Timişoara 1900, Romania
Telephone: +40 96 133240 Fax: +40 96 133354
General Manager: Tiberiu I Nerodea
Staff: 1,116

Passenger journeys: (All modes)
(1990) 48.8 million
(1991) 160 million
(1992) 199 million

Operating costs financed by: Fares 42%, subsidy/grants 58%

Current situation: The undertaking suffered considerable upheaval and loss of traffic during the political changes of 1989/90, though patronage has since recovered well. Reorganisation took place in 1991 under the new name RAT. The area of operation was reduced by splitting off outer-suburban and regional bus services to a separate company, with a loss of about 30 buses from the fleet. RAT also operates taxis, a fleet of small vans for local goods delivery, and a vessel carrying tourists on the River Bega.

Major works have continued to repair worn out and damaged tram tracks. Proximity to the Banat (Timiş) tramcar works has ensured good maintenance of the tram fleet, and both tram and trolleybus networks are in better condition than most other Romanian cities.

Bus and trolleybus

Passenger journeys: (1990) Bus 5.9 million, trolleybus 9.3 million
(1991) Bus 19.2 million, trolleybus 35.3 million
(1992) Bus 31 million, trolleybus 36.7 million
Vehicle-km: (1990) Bus 2.8 million, trolleybus 3.2 million
(1991) Bus 2.8 million, trolleybus 2.3 million
(1992) Bus 2.4 million, trolleybus 2.2 million

Number of routes: Bus 20, trolleybus 5
Route length: Bus 351 km, trolleybus 55.4 km
Fleet: 95 buses, mostly DAC and including 19 articulated, plus Van Hool/Fiat ex-Bruxelles
Fleet: 80 trolleybuses, including 3 Gräf & Stift and 9 Ikarus 280T ex-Eberswalde

Tram and trolleybus meet at Str Brediceanu  *1996*

CFR prototype railbus on local train *1996*

DAC 117E/217E articulated
Rocar 317E articulated — About 10
In peak service: 52 buses, 42 trolleybuses

Most intensive service: 10 min
Fare collection: Prepurchase, with validation/cancellation on board; some drivers sell tickets
Fare structure: Flat

Tramway

Passenger journeys: (1990) 31.6 million
(1991) 105.4 million
(1992) 131.4 million

Car-km: (1990) 8.9 million
(1991) 8.5 million
(1992) 9.4 million

Number of routes: 9
Route length: 90.9 km
Gauge: 1,435 mm

Rolling stock: 276 cars

Timiş	M134
Timiş trailers	T122
Hansa ex-Bremen (1963)	M20

In peak service: 120

Developments: Line 9 extension opened late 1992, Line 5 reconstruction completed early 1992. More tramcars are being supplied second-hand from Bremen, totalling 90 (M49, T41).

CFR

Cailor Ferate Romanie

Current situation: The state railway CFR operates suburban service over several routes.

UPDATED

TIRANA

Population: 250,000
Public transport: Until 1991, bus services provided by state-owned authority had a virtual monopoly of motorised passenger transport as there were no private cars and few other passenger-carrying vehicles such as taxis in Albania. Changed political circumstances have led to a rapid influx of privately owned vehicles, though most journeys are still made by cycle or on foot

Drejtoria Transport Tiranë

Ministry of Communications
Rruge Myslym Shyri 41, Tirana, Albania

Bus

Passenger journeys: Approx 30 million (annual)

Number of routes: 20
Route length: 175 km
Fleet: About 100 Saviem SC10, Mercedes-Benz O305 (some articulated) and MAN SG192 (articulated). Also Škoda buses rebodied by Shkodër (many articulated). A further 50 ex-Paris buses delivered 1991
Fare structure: Flat within city, outside distance-related; monthly passes
Fare collection: Tickets prepurchased from kiosks, cancelled on vehicle

Current situation: Since 1987 Albania has imported a large number of second-hand city buses from France and Germany which has enabled introduction of modern services with one-person operation and prepurchased tickets cancelled on board by machine. The French buses, all Saviem SC10s, are said to number 73 and previously ran in Lyon, Paris, Strasbourg, Nice and Clermont Ferrand. These generally work very frequent radial services from on-street terminals east and west of the central Skanderbeg Square, and east-west cross-city services.

Ex-Paris Saviem SC10 in Tirana

Standard and articulated Mercedes-Benz O305s from Lübeck and Pinneberg, and more recently articulated MAN SG192s from Mainz, Osnabrück and Bremerhaven, have also been acquired. The articulated buses work similar routes to the SC10s, while the rigid O305s work a north-south route whose northern terminus is Tirana railway station at a 5-min daytime service interval. A few Dutch-bodied O305s from Dordrecht are also used on the latter service.

All second-hand buses are still in the liveries of their former operators, though advertisements and insignia have been removed. These buses are generally about 15 years old. Other services are still worked by articulated buses which have Albanian Shkodër bodywork on what are thought to be old Škoda chassis, but trailers appear to be no longer in use. Most rigid buses in Tirana, apart from the Saviem and Mercedes-Benz, are believed to operate suburban and long-distance routes.

There appears now to be no reason why foreigners should not use local buses (see *JUTS 1990*), but destination displays are only infrequently present and route maps are not available. More recently, civil disorder has led to interruption of services.

TOKYO

Population: City (23 wards) 8.1 million, metropolitan area 11.8 million, conurbation 30 million (including Chiba, Kawasaki and Yokohama)
Public transport: Bus, tramway and metro services provided by municipal authority, with second metro system operated by rapid transit authority. Extensive suburban rail services operated by several private railways and JR, with through running to metro system from many lines; monorail and two automated guideway systems. Additional bus services by 12 independent operators licensed by Transport Ministry. Majority of travel is by rail modes with approx 75 per cent share of total passenger trips in the metropolitan area; suburban systems of JR and private railways account for about 25 per cent each, with the remainder by the metros.

Further major rail investment is planned under proposals put forward in 1985 by the Council for Transport Policy, affecting the metro, JR and private railways. Under the plans, some 530 km of route would be constructed within 50 km of central Tokyo by the year 2000 to serve expanding suburban areas and to disperse traffic and development from the congested central area to existing sub-centres at Shibuya, Shinjuku and Ikebukuro and new ones at Ueno-Asakusa, Kinshicho-Kameido and Ohsaki

'Green Arrows', Toei's upgraded New Urban bus Route 04 leaving Tokyo station

1997

Marunouchi lines); others 1.5 kV DC, overhead

sharing the Yurakucho line extension, diverging to reach

Tokyo commuter services. Additional tracks are

JR East's all double-deck Shonan Liner used on Tokaido line commuter services **1997**

proposed for the Chuo line between Mitaka and Tachikawa and freight lines are to be upgraded for passenger use.

In March 1996, the Saikyo line was extended 5 km over freight tracks from Shinjuku to Ebisu, site of a large-scale urban redevelopment project. The new line will relieve the parallel Yamanote line where loadings reach 245 per cent of capacity.

Longer trains are to be run at higher speeds and rolling stock capacity increased; Series 205 Yamanote line trains have one car with six doors per side and fold-away seats to increase peak capacity; Series 211 sets include double-deck cars, and 10-car Shonan Liner all double-deck emus operate commuter services on the Tokaido line.

The production Series 209 'disposable' commuter emus with a planned service life of 10 years, built at a cost of only 60 per cent of conventional units, entered service in 1993 on the Keihin-Tohoku inner-suburban service. In 1994, two prototype short-life E217 outer-suburban trains, each including two double-deck cars, entered service on the Yokosuka and Sobu lines. Double-deck Shinkansen trains have also been introduced to cater for increased long-distance commuting into Tokyo on the Joetsu and Tohoku lines.

Keihin Kyuko Dentetsu 'Keikyu'

Keihin Express Electric Railway
20-20 Takanawa 2-chome, Minato-ku, Tokyo 108
Telephone: +81 3 3280 9122 Fax: +81 3 3280 9193
President: K Hiramatsu

Interurban rail

Staff: 2,634

Passenger journeys: (1991/92) 445 million
(1992/93) 439 million
(1993/94) 438 million
Car-km: (1992/93) 89 million
(1993/94) 91 million

Current situation: More of a Yokohama commuting line, but runs through trains to central Tokyo (Shinagawa) and over Asakusa metro line and on to Keisei Railway tracks; 83.6 km, 1,435 mm gauge, electrified 1.5 kV DC.
Developments: The Kuko branch was extended in 1993 to a new interchange with the Tokyo monorail at Haneda in connection with expansion of Haneda airport; a through service operates to central Tokyo via the Asakusa line metro. A 3.2 km underground extension to the new airport terminal building is under construction, scheduled to open in 1998.

Rolling stock: 762 emu cars M652 T110

Bus

Staff: 1,792

Passenger journeys: (1992/93) 120.5 million
(1993/94) 117 million
Vehicle-km: (1992/93) 35.9 million
(1993/94) 37.6 million

Current situation: Keihin Kyuko also owns a fleet of 773 buses and 112 coaches; 349 routes are operated in southern Tokyo, Kawasaki, Yokohama and Kanagawa prefecture.

Keio Teito Dentetsu

Keio Teito Electric Railway
9-1, Sekido 1-chome, Tama City, Tokyo 206
Telephone: +81 423 373141
President: K Kuwayama

Interurban rail

Staff: 2,472

Passenger journeys: (1991/92) 586 million
(1992/93) 587 million
(1993/94) 588 million
Car-km: (1992/93) 98 million
(1993/94) 102 million

Route length: 84.8 km
Number of lines: 7
Operating costs financed by: Fares 88.7%, other commercial sources 11.3%

Current situation: Operates the main Keio line out of an underground terminal below the Keio department store at Shinjuku, with four branches totalling 72 km, 1,372 mm gauge, electrified 1.5 kV DC.

The 3.6 km underground Keio new line links the main line with the Toei Shinjuku line metro, enabling trains to run through to central Tokyo (Iwamoto-cho). Also 12.8 km 1,067 mm gauge Inokashira line, electrified 1.5 kV DC, runs from a terminal at Shibuya to Kichijoji.

In 1990/91 the Railway Division accounted for 59.8 per cent of the company's revenue, the Real Estate Division 20.3 per cent and the Bus Division 19.9 per cent.
Developments: Larger cars with five doors have been introduced to increase capacity; platforms have been lengthened to handle 10-car trains (Keio line) or large five-car trains (Inokashira line); track elevation is in progress to eliminate level crossings.

Rolling stock: 848 emu cars M515 T333
On order: 15 cars

Bus

Passenger journeys: (1993/94) 113 million
Vehicle-km: (1993/94) 34 million

Current situation: The Bus Division operates 244 local bus routes covering 4,032 km, carrying an average of 310,000 passengers a day. Fleet comprises 560 buses and 42 coaches, all air conditioned. Deliveries in 1995 included 42 Nissan Diesel one-step buses with wheelchair ramps.

Keisei Dentetsu

Keisei Electric Railway
10-3, Oshiage 1-chome, Sumida-ku, Tokyo 131
Telephone: +81 3 3621 2231

Interurban rail

Managing Director: H Hosokawa
Staff: 2,169

Passenger journeys: (1991/92) 276 million
(1992/93) 279 million
(1993/94) 281 million
Car-km: (1992/93) 76 million
(1993/94) 76 million

Current situation: Operates main line from Ueno station in Tokyo to Narita airport, and four branches totalling 91.6 km, 1,435 mm gauge, electrified 1.5 kV DC. Through running to Toei Asakusa metro line, the Hokuso Railway and the Chiba Express Railway.
Developments: A 2.1 km link to a new underground station beneath the terminal building at Narita international airport opened in 1991. The station is shared by JR trains. In 1992 the Chiba Express Railway, a Keisei subsidiary, opened the first 4 km of a proposed 15 km extension from Keisei-Chiba to Ama-ariki, and a further 6.7 km opened in 1995.

Rolling stock: 494 emu cars M432 T62

Bus

Managing Director: K Sato
Staff: 2,200

Passenger journeys: (Conurbation, including Chiba)
(1991/92) 138.8 million
(1992/93) 135.3 million
(1993/94) 136.5 million
Vehicle-km: (1992/93) 32.6 million

Current situation: Keisei's bus division runs 980 buses of which about 250 are operated on routes in Tokyo's north-eastern wards and the rest in adjoining Chiba prefecture. The fleet comprises Isuzu, Hino and Mitsubishi types; 50 coaches are also operated.

Hokuso Kaihatsu Tetsudo

Hokuso Development Railway
14-5, 2-chome, Narihira, Sumida-ku, Tokyo 103
Telephone: +81 3 3626 3310
President: K Sugiyama

Suburban rail

Passenger journeys: (1991/92) 16.5 million
(1992/93) 19.5 million
Car-km: (1992/93) 8.8 million

Current situation: This Keisei subsidiary was extended 11.7 km in 1991 to provide a new link between central Tokyo and Chiba New Town, scheduled to house 340,000 residents. The 19.8 km line, 1,435 mm gauge, electrified 1.5 kV DC, connects with the Keisei Railway at Takasago and with the 4 km Housing & Urban Development Railway, which serves Chiba New Town, at Komoro. A through running service is operated between Chiba New Town-Chuo and central Tokyo via the HUD railway, the Hokuso and Keisei railways, and the Toei Asakusa metro line.
Developments: An 8.5 km eastward extension beyond Chiba New Town-Chuo is under construction to serve new residential development areas.

Rolling stock: 7 eight-car emus M46 T10

Odakyu Dentetsu

Odakyu Electric Railway
8-3 Nishi-Shinjuku 1-chome, Shinjuku-ku, Tokyo 160
Telephone: +81 3 3349 2151 Fax: +81 3 3346 1899
President: T Takigami

Interurban rail

Staff: 3,285

Passenger journeys: (1990/91) 712 million
(1992/93) 711 million
(1993/94) 711 million
Car-km: (1992/93) 137 million
(1993/94) 140 million

Current situation: Operates main line from Tokyo Shinjuku to Odawara, with two branches, totalling 120.5 km, 1,067 mm gauge, electrified 1.5 kV DC. Some trains run through to Eidan's Chiyoda metro line and on to JR's Joban line, also onward from Odawara over mixed-gauge track on 1,435 mm gauge Hakone Tozan Railway to Hakone-Yumoto (6.1 km), and from Matsuda to Nomazu over JR's Gotemba line (50 km).
Developments: Measures to increase capacity include multiple double-tracking and works to allow 10-car express train operation.

Rolling stock: 1,055 emu cars M675 T380
In peak service: 969

Odakyu emu departing Shinjuku terminus in central Tokyo ***1997***

Odakyu Bus

Odakyu Bus
2-19-5 Senkawa-cho, Chofu-shi, Tokyo 182
Telephone: +81 3 5313 8211
President: K Kinoshita

Passenger journeys: (Conurbation including Kawasaki and Yokohama)
(1991/92) 78.5 million
(1992/93) 77.7 million
(1993/94) 76.3 million
Vehicle-km: (1992/93) 17.8 million

Current situation: A fleet of 396 buses and 65 coaches is operated by Odakyu Electric Railway's associate company Odakyu Bus, about 275 of them used on services in the Tokyo metropolitan area.

Seibu Tetsudo

Seibu Railway
1-11-1 Kusunokidai, Tokorozawa-shi, Saitama 359
Telephone: +81 429 26 2035 Fax: +81 429 26 2237
President: Y Tsutsumi

Suburban rail

Staff: 4,089

Passenger journeys: (1991/92) 674 million
(1992/93) 672 million
(1993/94) 667 million
Car-km: (1992/93) 139 million
(1993/94) 146 million

Current situation: Operates two busy suburban routes west from Ikebukuro and Shinjuku, with branches, totalling 172 km, 1,067 mm gauge, electrified 1.5 kV DC. These are particularly busy lines, with Ikebukuro terminal handling some 700 trains daily.

The Seibu Yurakucho line currently operates as a branch of the Eidan Yurakucho metro line, with all services provided by Eidan rolling stock. A 1.4 km extension of the line from Shin-sakuradai to Nerima on Seibu's Ikebukuro line opened in late 1994, but introduction of through running services is on hold pending completion of elevation and quadruple tracking of the Ikebukuro line.
Developments: To increase capacity and reduce overcrowding of peak trains from 200 to 150 per cent, Seibu plans to build an additional 13 km underground line beneath its existing Shinjuku line to speed up express trains running non-stop into Shinjuku terminal. Local trains would continue to serve stations on the existing line.

Rolling stock: 1,162 emu cars M744 T418
All air conditioned

ICTS

Type of operation: Intermediate capacity transit system, rubber-tyred guideway

Passenger journeys: (1991/92) 4,200 daily

Current situation: The 2.8 km Yamaguchi line rubber-tyred guideway, opened 1985, links two Seibu outer termini, Kyojomae and Yuenchi, about 25 km to the west of central Tokyo. Electrified at 750 V DC. Manual operation with driver on board.

Rolling stock: 12 cars in four-car sets
Niigata (1984/85) M12

Bus

Passenger journeys: (Conurbation)
(1990/91) 130.8 million
(1991/92) 138.8 million
(1992/93) 135.4 million

Current situation: Seibu's associated bus company owns a fleet of 709 buses and 98 coaches, about 400 of which are employed on services in the Tokyo metropolitan area, including Nissan/Fuji buses. The fleet includes lift-equipped vehicles.

Seibu Railway's Series 2000 trainset ***1997***

Tobu Tetsudo

Tobu Railway
1-2, 1-chome, Oshiage, Sumida-ku, Tokyo 131
Telephone: +81 3 3621 5057
President: K Nezu

Interurban rail

Staff: 7,193

Passenger journeys: (1992/93) 950 million
(1993/94) 950 million
(1994/95) 945 million
Car-km: (1992/93) 240 million
(1993/94) 244 million
(1994/95) 251 million

Current situation: Tokyo's largest interurban railway operates 13 lines totalling 464 km, 202 stations, 1,067 mm gauge, electrified 1.5 kV DC. Main lines link Asakusa and Ikebukuro with Nikko and Yorii. Some trains on the Isesaki and Tojo lines run through to central Tokyo over metro lines but, while commuting traffic is heavy, intercity and freight traffic dominate.

Rolling stock: 1,854 emu cars M1,035 T819

Bus

Staff: 3,031

Passenger journeys: (Conurbation)
(1990/91) 122.3 million
(1991/92) 125.9 million
(1992/93) 116.3 million

Current situation: Tobu Railway's bus operation has a fleet of 1,130 buses and 306 coaches, about 100 of which are used on Tokyo metropolitan area services. Recent deliveries include lift-equipped wheelchair-accessible vehicles.

Tokyo Kyuko Dentetsu 'Tokyu'

Tokyo Express Electric Railway
Tokyu Corporation
5-6, Nanpeidai-cho, Shibuya-ku, Tokyo 150
Telephone: +81 3 3477 6181 Fax: +81 3 3496 2965
President: S Shimizu

Current situation: In addition to important Tokyo-based rail and bus operations, the Tokyu Group has interests in other railways, bus companies and rolling stock manufacture (Tokyu Car).

Interurban rail

Staff: 3,221

and raise customer satisfaction. The length of priority right-of-way was almost doubled in 1995. Integration of fares with all operators has been adopted, with zonal fares now charged irrespective of mode.

Bus

Vehicle-km: (1993) 40.5 million
(1994) 41.6 million
(1995) 41 million

Number of routes: 68, plus some special routes
Route length: 774 km
On priority right-of-way: (Tram and bus) 62 km
Fleet: 1,006 vehicles

Iveco 471 Viberti (1985/88)	47
Iveco 580 TurboCity-S (1990)	30
Iveco 571 S-Euffeno (1988)	15
Bredabus 3001.12LL (1989)	20
Iveco 471 U-Euffeno (1985/88)	100
Iveco 480 TurboCity-U (1989/91)	118
Iveco 480 Viberti (1989/91)	152
Fiat 421 (1973/83)	302
Bredabus BB3001 08AC (1992)	5
Inbus AU280FT De Simon (1991)	30
Iveco 490 Altrobus dual-mode (1994)	2
Iveco 490 Viberti (1994)	45
Iveco 490 (1994)	19
Iveco 490E TurboCity UR-Green (1994)	100
Iveco 480 18.29 Viberti (1994)	21

In peak service: 790

Most intensive service: Peak 4-7 min, off-peak 6-13 min
One-person operation: All routes
Fare collection: Prepurchase passes and multitickets from automatic machines and shops
Fare structure: Flat within urban and suburban zones; tickets with time validity, passes and 10-journey multitickets (urban only); integrated 'Formula' weekly/ monthly passes allow all modes travel within specified zones
Fare evasion control: Roving inspectors
Average peak-hour speed: 17.8 km/h
Integration with other modes: Bus and tram services integrated and connect with rail stations and outer-suburban termini; fares integration between ATM, SATTI and FS started in 1996 (passes only)

Tramway/Light rail

Type of operation: Conventional tramway/light rail

Car-km: (1993) 9.8 million
(1994) 8.9 million
(1995) 9 million

Route length: 104.8 km, plus light rail 19.2 km
Number of lines: 9 tramway, 2 light rail
Gauge: 1,445 mm
Track: Part conventional sleepers on ballast
Max gradient: 5.8%
Minimum curve radius: 15 m
Electrification: 580 V DC, overhead

Service: Peak 4-7 min, off-peak 6-10 min
First/last car: 04.30/01.00
Fare structure: As bus
Fare collection: As bus
One-person operation: All cars
Signalling: Centralised control; priority at traffic lights in operation on Routes 3, 4, 9, 10, 16

Rolling stock: 299 cars

3100 (1949/58, rebuilt 1975/78)	M92
2800 (1958/60, rebuilt 1979/82)	M102
Fiat/Ansaldo/OMS 7000 LRV (1982/86)	M51
Fiat/Ansaldo/OMS 5000 LRV low-floor (1989/92)	M53
Restaurant tram (1958, rebuilt 1968)	M1

In peak service: 198

Iveco Turbocity on Via S Secondo ***1996***

Light metro (proposed)

Current situation: In 1991 the city council approved construction of a two-route automated light metro using VAL technology. In 1995, Phase I of Line 1 (Collegno—Torino Central FS station, 9.5 km, 15 stations) received preliminary approval for funding under Law 211.

Line 1 will run east-west from Campo Volo to Porta Nuova station in central Torino, and then turn south towards Nichelino. A second line, to be known as Line 4, runs north-south with a city-centre interchange with Line 1 and other rail services at Porta Nuova.

Trasporti Torinesi-SATTI

Consorzio Trasporti Torinesi/SpA Torinese Tranvie Intercomunali (TT/SATTI)
Address as ATM above
President: M Boidi
General Manager: Rodolfo Notaro
Staff: 1,190

Current situation: SATTI has responsibility for outer suburban and commuter bus services, serving Torino and the towns of Asti, Cuneo, Alessandria, Vercelli and the urban area of Ivrea, as well as two rail lines.

Passenger journeys: (All modes)
(1989) 16.9 million
(1991) 21.1 million

Operating costs financed by: Fares 22.7%, other commercial sources 5.5%, subsidy/grants 71.8%
Subsidy from: National government for rail services (45.6%), regional government for bus services (54.4%)

Bus

Passenger journeys: (1989) 13.1 million
(1991) 17.7 million
Vehicle-km: (1989) 8.2 million
(1991) 15.6 million

Number of routes: 89
Route length: (One way) 3,802 km
Fleet: 239 buses, plus 149 owned by ATM, mostly Fiat

Local railways

Passenger journeys: (1989) 3.7 million
(1991) 3.3 million

Current situation: SATTI operates local trains from Pont Canavese to Settimo (40 km, 1,435 mm gauge) and thence over FS tracks to Torino Porta Susa, and from Ceres to Dora (44 km, 1,435 mm gauge, electrified 3 kV DC over the 34 km between Germagnano and Dora).
Developments: The project to build an underground link to the FS station at Porta Nuova (see *JUTS 1994/95*) has been abandoned, but SATTI services will eventually be linked to the Passante (see below) for through running to Lingotto. The Ceres line is being modernised, with seven two-car low-floor emus on order, and a branch is planned to serve Caselle airport.

Rolling stock: 5 electric locomotives, 2 diesel locomotives, 197 diesel railcars, 4 two-car emus, 62 coaches

FS

Italian Railways (FS)
Piazza della Croce Rossa, Roma

Type of operation: Suburban heavy rail

Current situation: Frequent service provided on five routes, electrified 3 kV DC.
Developments: Construction continues of the first stage of the Passante cross-city line. A 6 km line with two stations, partly underground, will link Porta Susa with Lingotto, avoiding the main Porta Nuova terminus. Most suburban trains will be diverted over the new route when it is completed. An intermediate station will be built later at Zappata to allow interchange with the Torino—Bussoleno—Modane line.

In the long term, a second pair of tracks will be built alongside the Torino—Milano main line from Porta Susa to Stura, and SATTI trains will be extended from Dora to Porta Susa and beyond. Interchange is planned with pre-metro lines (see above) at several points.

UPDATED

TORONTO

Population: Conurbation 2.2 million
Public transport: Bus, metro, tramway and advanced light rail services provided by Transit Commission, responsible to Metropolitan Toronto Council. Metropolitan and Greater Toronto area bus and rail regional commuter services run by Government of Ontario (GO Transit)

TTC

Toronto Transit Commission
1900 Yonge Street, Toronto M4S 1Z2, Canada
Telephone: +1 416 393 4000 Fax: +1 416 488 6198
Chair: Paul Christie
Chief General Manager: David L Gunn
General Manager, Service Delivery: Gary Webster
General Manager, Engineering & Construction: Dennis Callan
General Manager, Executive & General Secretary: Vincent Rodo
General Manager, Administration: Juri Pill
Staff: 9,487

Passenger journeys: (1993) 395.5 million
(1994) 388 million
(1995) 388 million

Operating costs financed by: Fares 68%, subsidy/grants 32%
Subsidy from: Metropolitan Council and Province of Ontario

Current situation: Constituted in its present form in 1954, TTC serves the 630 km² Metropolitan Toronto area in co-ordination with a number of neighbouring systems including Markham Transit, Richmond Hill Transit, Vaughan Transit, Brampton Transit, Mississauga Transit, and the GO Transit commuter system (see below).
Developments: In 1993 the Ontario government announced its funding commitment to TTC's rapid transit expansion programme, and construction of two metro extensions was begun in 1994. These were the Eglinton Avenue West (4.7 km, five stations) and Sheppard Avenue East (6.4 km, five stations) sections. A year later, the newly elected Ontario government withdrew funding from the Eglinton project, which was abandoned. The future of the Sheppard line was also in doubt in 1996, but an August vote of the Metropolitan Council to shelve the project was reversed the following month. Construction continues, along with work on the Greenwood storage yard and maintenance depot, and the Harbourfront light rail line.

One reason for the cutbacks in metro construction was the deteriorating state of the existing infrastructure, and in particular the bus fleet which then averaged 13 years old and was in poor shape. The OBI/Ikarus articulateds introduced in 1987 are to be scrapped, and about one-third of the fleet is to be rehabilitated in a five-year programme. Delivery of 100 CNG-powered low-floor Orion Vs, the first new buses since 1991, was delayed in 1995 and did not enter service until 1996. It was also decided not to purchase new low-floor cars for the Harbourfront light rail line, the money saved being diverted to bus rehabilitation.

CNG-powered Orion V of TTC ***1995***

Bus

Passenger journeys: (1993)189.1 million
(1994) 191 million
(1995) 192.5 million

Vehicle-km: (1993) 99 million
(1994) 100.4 million
(1995) 100.9 million

Number of routes: 140
Route length: (One-way) 3,038 km
Fleet: 1,693 buses

GM 'New Look' T6H-53707N (1975-83)	569
GM/MCI Classic	84
Flyer various models (1977/81/85/86)	573
OBI Orion II (Wheel-Trans)	139
OBI/Ikarus OBI03-501 (1987)	60
OBI Orion V (1991/92)	106
OBI Orion V CNG-powered (1991)	25
OBI Orion V wheelchair lift (1996)	135
OBI Orion Vi low-floor (1995)	1
Overland Custom Coach ELF (Wheeltrans)	1

Average age of fleet: 9 years
In peak service: 1,357
On order: 100 low-floor CNG-powered buses from Ontario Bus Industries for delivery starting February 1997

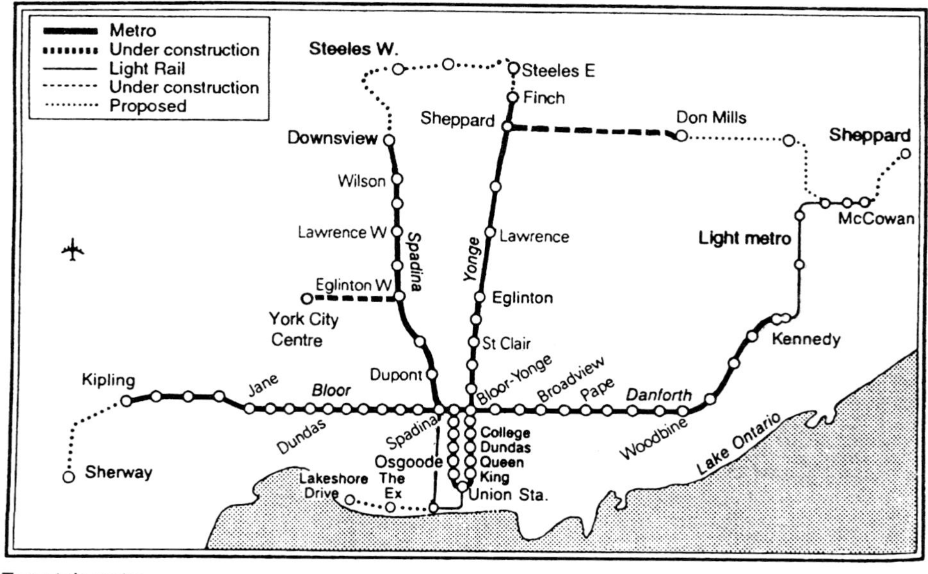

Toronto's metro

Most intensive service: 2-4 min
One-person operation: All routes
Fare collection: Pay-as-you-enter, exact fare or token to farebox; or prepurchase
Fare structure: Flat; free transfers; prepurchase multitickets and tokens; daily and monthly passes
Fare evasion control: Visual check by drivers, route supervisors and security staff
Integration with other modes: 229 timed connections at metro/ICTS stations during the morning peak; connections with GO Transit trains; numerous connections with other local transit authorities, without fare integration; 22 park-and-ride lots
Operational control: AVLC via computerised communications and information system, with control from seven divisions through onboard communications and data exchange system (TRUMP) fitted to all vehicles
Arrangements for elderly/disabled: Wheel-Trans door-to-door service uses 139 low-floor buses, plus 125 sedan/taxis and 25 wheelchair-accessible taxis operated by private contractors. Wheel-Trans staff handle reservations, despatching and scheduling; fares match regular TTC adult levels. Four community bus routes link seniors' centres, shopping areas, medical and community facilities. Pulse Bus provides same-day service for Wheel-Trans customers travelling within designated area
New vehicles financed by: Subsidy: Province 75%, Metropolitan Toronto 25%

Downsview metro station on the extension opened in March 1996 ***1997***

Metro

Type of operation: Full metro, first line opened 1954

Passenger journeys: (1993) 153 million
(1994) 151.2 million
(1995) 148.4 million
Car-km: (1993) 63.6 million
(1994) 63.8 million
(1995) 62.8 million

Route length: 56.4 km
Number of lines: 2
Number of stations: 61
Gauge: 1,495 mm

Track: 57.5 kg/m T-rail; open cut, conventional sleepers on ballast and concrete sleepers (on new sections) on ballast. Bored tunnel, rail laid on concrete bed; and rail laid on double concrete sleepers on resilient rubber pads
Tunnel: Cut-and-cover sections, steel-reinforced poured concrete box structures; bored tunnels, shield driven precast concrete or cast-iron linings
Electrification: 600 V DC, third rail

Service: Peak 2½ min, off-peak 4-7 min
First/last train: 05.47/01.34
Fare structure: Flat with free transfers to surface system
Revenue control: Conventional and wheelchair-accessible turnstiles; token and monthly pass activate turnstiles; high-gate turnstiles at automatic entry areas
Integration with other modes: Free transfer with surface systems at 36 stations; free paper transfer at 29 stations
Arrangements for elderly/disabled: Programme under way to improve access at 23 key stations (see below)
One-person operation: None
Signalling: Automatic block and interlocking signals and wayside signals
Centralised control: Centralised train despatch and control system; similar system installed on Scarborough ICTS line (see below)
Surveillance: Designated waiting areas at all stations consisting of well-lit location monitored by CCTV cameras and with voice intercom system

Rolling stock: 628 cars

MIW M1 (1962/63)	M36
Hawker Siddeley Canada H1 (1965/66)	M160
Hawker Siddeley Canada H2 (1971)	M76
Hawker Siddeley Canada H4 (1974/75)	M88
Hawker Siddeley Canada H5 (1976/79)	M136
UTDC/Can-Car Rail H6 (1986/89)	M126
Bombardier T1 (1995/96)	M6

In peak service: 492
On order: 210 cars on order from Bombardier; six-car prototype train delivered 1995, prior to series production between 1996 and 1999

Developments: 2.2 km extension of the Spadina line from Wilson to Sheppard Avenue (Downsview) opened March 1996.

Easier access to 23 major stations is being achieved by installation of lifts, and improved at all other stations by easier-to-use token machines, pictograms and seats at top and bottom of stairs. The T1 cars on order will have wheelchair access.

Tramway/light rail

Type of operation: Conventional tramway, light rail Harbourfront line

Passenger journeys: (1993) 46.1 million
(1994) 43.1 million
(1995) 44.7 million

GO train commuters at Clarkson on the Lakeshore West line ***1997***

Car-km: (1993) 11.5 million
(1994) 11.2 million
(1995) 11.1 million

Route length: 76 km
Number of lines: 10
Gauge: 1,495 mm
Track: 50 kg/m T-rail
Electrification: 580 V DC, overhead

Service: Peak 3-12 min, off-peak 5-16.5 min
Fare structure: As bus
Fare collection: As bus; proof-of-payment on Queen Street line
One-person operation: All cars

Rolling stock: 248 cars

UTDC/Swiss Industrial L1 (1977/78)	M6
UTDC/Hawker Siddeley Canada L2 (1979/81)	M190
UTDC/Can-Car Rail L3 (1987/89)	M52

In peak service: 178

Developments: A 3.6 km northwards extension of the Harbourfront line along Spadina Avenue, linking the central waterfront area with the Bloor—Danforth metro line at Spadina, is scheduled to open in mid-1997. This restores service closed in 1948 and 1960. The line terminates in an underground loop at Spadina metro station.

ALRT (Scarborough line)

Type of operation: Intermediate capacity advanced light metro transit system, opened 1985

Passenger journeys: (1993) 3.5 million
(1994) 3 million
(1995) 2.6 million
Car-km: (1993) 3.7 million
(1994) 3.6 million
(1995) 3.7 million

Route length: 6.5 km
elevated: 2.3 km
Number of routes: 1
Number of stations: 6
Gauge: 1,435 mm
Track: 115 lb/yd continuously welded T-rail fixed to concrete base with rubber insulation pads
Max gradient: 5.2%
Minimum curve radius: 35 m normal, 18 m minimum
Electrification: 600 V DC, ungrounded, collection from two power rails and reaction rail

Service: Peak 4 min, off-peak 8 min
Fare structure: Flat, free transfers
Revenue collection: Conventional and token and monthly pass-activated turnstiles; visual inspection
Integration with other modes: Fully integrated with rest of TTC system
One-person operation: None
Automatic control: Fully automatic with manual override, manual door operation
Signalling: Moving block; centralised control and dispatch

Rolling stock: 28 cars

UTDC/VentureTrans S1 (1984/85)	M28

In peak service: 24

Current situation: This fully automated system linking Scarborough with Kennedy metro station has cars powered by linear induction motors (LIMs) running on conventional steel-rail track. Proposed extension to Sheppard (3.2 km, three stations) is in abeyance.

New Flyer D40 on GO feeder service at York Region Terminal ***1996***

GO Transit

Government of Ontario Transit
20 Bay Street, Suite 600, Toronto M5J 3W3
Telephone: +1 416 869 3600 Fax: +1 416 869 3525
Chair: B R King (Acting)
Managing Director: R C Ducharme
Staff: 950

Current situation: GO Transit was established in 1967, funded by the Ontario provincial government, to provide services to attract commuter motorists off the highways and reduce the need for new road investment. A comprehensive rail and bus network has been built up serving a population of 4.5 million in an area up to 90 km from Toronto.

Since 1974 the operation has been run by the Toronto Area Transit Operating Authority, a provincial crown agency with representation from the regional municipalities served, including metropolitan Toronto. GO Transit sets service levels and fares and contracts train operations. CN and CP are the rail contractors. GO provides nearly 30,000 spaces for park-and-ride cars and manages several major bus terminals.

Developments: Wheelchair-accessible train service started in 1995, with 28 out of 49 stations now accessible, including Toronto Union.

Hamilton GO Centre opened April 1996, combining separate bus and rail stations into a single interchange located in the former Toronto, Hamilton & Buffalo station.

Passenger journeys: (Both modes)
(1993/94) 34.8 million
(1994/95) 33.8 million
(1995/96) 33.5 million

Operating costs financed by: Revenue (mostly fares) 65.3%

Suburban rail

Passenger journeys: (1993/94) 25.9 million
(1994/95) 25 million
(1995/96) 24.8 million

Current situation: Diesel-hauled suburban service operated under contract. Lakeshore route Oakville—Toronto—Pickering runs all day, with peak hour extension from Oakville to Hamilton and Pickering to Oshawa. Other routes to Stouffville, Richmond Hill, Milton, Bradford and Georgetown run peak hours only (one to four return journeys daily). Total 361 km, 1,435 mm gauge, zonal fares.

Rolling stock: 49 diesel locomotives, 331 double-deck coaches

Bus

Passenger journeys: (1993/94) 8.9 million
(1994/95) 8.8 million
(1995/96) 8.7 million

Route length: (One way) 1,264 km
Fleet: 179 buses

GMC (1974/77)	17
OBI Orion 01.508 (1985/87)	17
MCI MC9 (1981)	25
MCI 102A2 (1986/87/89/90)	69
New Flyer D40 (1991)	51

Current situation: Launched in 1970 as an extension of the Lakeshore rail route, the bus operation now provides service on five corridors, many feeding the rail lines.

UPDATED

TOULOUSE

Population: City 350,000, conurbation 650,000
Public transport: Urban and interurban bus services and metro organised in the conurbation and its environs by the Syndicat Mixte des Transports en Commun de l'Agglomération Toulousaine (SMTC), which comprises Toulouse, 52 surrounding towns and the département of Haute Garonne. SMTC grants concessions for bus and metro operations, and decides transport policy and fares levels. Limited suburban services provided by French National Railways (SNCF)

Metro/bus interchange at Basso-Cambo

Semvat

SA d'Economie Mixte des Transports Publics de Voyageurs de l'Agglomération Toulousaine (Semvat)
49 rue de Gironis, 31081 Toulouse Cedex, France
Telephone: + 33 5 62 11 26 11 Fax: +33 5 62 11 26 20
Director General: Francis Grass
Deputy Director General: Daniel Audibert
Staff: 1,550

Current situation: Semvat is the concessionaire appointed by SMTC to operate bus services in the city and conurbation. While the metro is operated under a concession by a separate company, MTD, both modes are marketed as a single network by Semvat.

Introduction of magnetic ticketing in 1992 led to a revised method of calculating journeys. Passengers had previously to cancel two tickets when changing vehicles; now transfers are free.

With opening of the first section of metro in 1993, bus services were completely revised to eliminate parallel routes. Five routes now run to metro interchanges and increased frequency has been provided on 16 routes. Within six months the metro had exceeded traffic forecasts for the second year of operation. In general, public transport usage has increased by 40 per cent since the metro opened.

Fare collection: Ticket sales by approved vendors on bus and from change-giving machines on metro stations; cancellers on board buses and in metro stations
Fare structure: Flat in each of 2 zones, inner covering Toulouse, Balma and Blagnac, and outer extending to 50 neighbouring towns; day, weekly and monthly passes; 10 and 12 journeys tickets
Fare evasion control: Penalty payment

Bus

Passenger journeys: (1993) 44.2 million
(1994) 28.4 million
(1995) 30 million
Vehicle-km: (1993) Urban 16.7 million, interurban 3.3 million
(1994) Urban 16 million, interurban 3.2 million
(1995)

Number of routes: Urban 53, interurban 22
Route length: Urban 607 km, interurban 1,363 km
On priority right-of-way: 9 km
Fleet: 561 vehicles

Saviem SC10	284
Heuliez 0305 articulated	10
Saviem S53/E7	80
Renault FRI	19
Heuliez GX107	123
Renault Tracer	27
Heuliez GX17	5
Others	13

Average age of fleet: 7.1 years
In peak service: Urban 345

Most intensive service: 3-4 min
One-person operation: All routes
Average distance between stops: 300-400 m
Average peak-hour speed: In mixed traffic, 8 km/h; in bus lanes (city-centre only), 14 km/h
Bus priority: Bus lanes, dedicated traffic signals, bus priority at intersections; 9 km reserved
Operational control: All buses have radios
Arrangements for elderly/disabled: 5 buses equipped for disabled riders; on-demand service in co-operation with city authorities and SETRAS (Service de Transport Spécialisé); free transer
Operating costs financed by: Urban — fares 47%, other commercial sources 3%, subsidy/grants 50%
Interurban — fares 74%, other commercial sources 3.5%, subsidy/grants 3.5%
Subsidy from: Employers' payroll tax (versement) 28%, local councils 22%; interurban, Haute Garonne département
New vehicles financed by: Loans and proceeds of employers' tax

Metro

Operated by: Métropole Transport Développement (MTD)
Staff: 120

Type of operation: Fully automated (unmanned) rubber-tyred metro, VAL system, opened 1993

Passenger journeys: (1993/94) 22.4 million
(1995) 21.5 million

Route length: 10 km
in tunnel: 9 km
Number of lines: 1
Number of stations: 15
Gauge: 2,060 mm between H-type guide bars
Electrification: 750 V DC, collection by shoes from guide bars

Service: Peak 1 min 40 sec
First/last train: 05.00/00.12
Integration with other modes: Feeder buses serve 5 stations

Rolling stock: 29 two-car trains

GEC Alsthom (1993)	M58

Developments: Approval of north-south Line B was confirmed in June 1996, though construction will not start until 2000. This 17 km line with 20 stations will link Les Minimes with Rangeuil university campus, providing interchange with Line A at Jean-Jaurès in the city centre. The route is not yet fully defined, and may include a loop near St Agne SNCF station to serve the Empalot district. Northwards extensions to Fondeyre and Borde-Rouge have also been agreed, as has a Line A extension eastwards to Gramont.

SNCF

French National Railways (SNCF), Toulouse Region
rue Marengo 9, 31079 Toulouse
Telephone: +33 5 61 10 11 10

Type of operation: Suburban heavy rail

Current situation: Limited suburban services provided on six routes into Toulouse Matabiau station, with seven stations within the city limits and a further eight in the conurbation area.
Developments: With opening of metro Line A, the suburban station at St Cyprien was renamed Arènes and Semvat tickets became valid over the SNCF line thence to Colomiers, which is knows as metro Line C. This portion of the Toulouse—Auch line, which is single-track and diesel-operated, is to be doubled to allow operation of a much-improved service.

UPDATED

TRIVANDRUM

Population: 825,000
Public transport: Bus services provided by state road transport corporation

Kerala State Road Transport

Kerala State Road Transport Corporation
Transport Bhawan, Fort Trivandrum 65023, India
Telephone: +91 471 462829 Fax: +91 471 462 2679
Managing Director: C K Appukutan Nair
Staff: (State-wide total) 25,960

Current situation: The State Road Transport Corporation provides services throughout most of Kerala State with a fleet of 3,482 buses. The Corporation as a whole carried some 929 million passengers in 1995/96.

Bus

(Trivandrum city operations)
Staff: 3,646

Passenger journeys: (1990/91) 163.3 million
(1991/92) 175 million
(1992/93) 182.3 million
Vehicle-km: (1990/91) 25 million
(1992/93) 26.8 million

Number of routes: 60
Route length: 650 km
Fleet: 471 buses

Ashok Leyland and Mercedes single-deck	469
Ashok Leyland double-deck	2

Most intensive service: 10 min
Fare collection: Roving conductors
Fare structure: Stage
Operating costs financed by: Fares 90%, subsidy/grants 10%

UPDATED

TUCUMÁN

Population: 503,000
Public transport: Bus services provided by private operators under contract to state and municipal authorities

Bus

Current situation: At the centre of this conurbation is the city of San Miguel de Tucumán, which with neighbouring towns of Yerba Buena, Banda del Rio Sali, Tafi Viejo and Lules has a population of some 700,000. Current bus provision dates from 1959 when private contractors were authorised to supplement operations of the ailing municipal undertaking.

San Miguel city is served by two distinct operations. One comprises 13 urban routes each run by a different operator under contract to the municipality; seven of these routes extend into the suburbs. The remaining area is covered by six companies authorised by the provincial authorities. The city council, traffic police and urban development authorities are also involved in decisions regarding route changes, fares and parking.

There is constant friction between the two groups, as the growing suburban operations compete increasingly (and illegally) with those restricted to the area within the city boundaries. Merger of the city services, forbidden under the 1959 legislation, has been authorised by the city council but not carried out, and there has also been no progress with a 1990 transport plan which proposed the reintroduction of trolleybuses, a suburban rail service and bus priority measures. Nevertheless, light rail proposals were being canvassed in 1995.

Severe recession and unemployment, coupled with increased car ownership, caused a 30 per cent decline in patronage in 1992/93 as well as encouraging growth in the number of taxis. These do not operate as shared taxis, but nevertheless tout illegally at bus stops. No new route has been introduced since 1986, though there have been some extensions of existing lines. A proposed orbital Route 19 was rejected by the mayor in 1995.

A 10.37 m version of El Detalle's OA101 on El Ranchilleño's suburban route to Lastenia ***1996***

Passenger journeys: (1994) Urban 100 million, suburban 50 million
Vehicle-km: (1994) Urban 37 million, suburban 18 million

Number of routes: Urban 13, suburban 23, plus many branches
Route length: Urban 313 km, suburban over 300 km
Fleet: 658 buses

Mercedes LO1114 (1980/88)	59
Mercedes OF1214/1315 (1987/1993)	325
Mercedes OH1314/1318/OHL1316 (1990/91/93/95)	154
El Detalle OA101 (1988/95)	120

Average age of fleet: 7.5 years
New vehicles required each year: 20% of fleet

Most intensive service: 3 min
One person operations: All routes
Fare collection: Token to driver on urban routes, cash to driver on suburban routes; conversion to electronic fareboxes in progress
Fare structure: Flat in urban area, sectional in suburbs; double fare on weekend nights
Operational control: Inspectors
Integration with other modes: None

TUNIS

Population: 1.4 million
Public transport: Bus services in Tunis and suburbs provided by central government corporation and some private operators. Light rail system run by another similar corporation, also responsible for suburban rail service. Both corporations directly responsible to Ministry of Transport & Communications. Other suburban rail services provided by national railway (SNCFT)

SNT

Société Nationale des Transports
PO Box 660, 1 avenue Habib Bourguiba, Tunis 1001, Tunisia
Telephone: +216 1 259422 Fax: +216 1 342727
President/Director General: M Moncer el Kafsi
Operating Manager: Ridha Essefi
Information & Publicity Manager: H Houa
Staff: 5,193

Current situation: In 1981 state-owned SNT was divided into three autonomous companies covering bus services in Tunis and its suburbs (SNT), the light rail system then under construction and the existing suburban rail line (SMLT — Société du Métro Léger de Tunis), and rural and interurban transport (SNTRI — Société de Transport Rural et Interurbain). Private operators were permitted from 1990.

Iveco AP160 on SNT's Route 10 at Place Barcelone station ***1996***

Developments: A credit from the Italian government financed purchase of 44 buses from local builder STIA; these were delivered in early 1995. Renovation of the Ali Belhouane bus terminal is in progress.

Amongst several service changes introduced in 1994, new urban Route 2 started operation in July as well as several new routes to tourist areas and beaches. Two routes were altered to serve light rail stations, and further changes were planned to accompany SMLT improvements in 1995.

Bus

Passenger boardings: (1991) 263 million
(1992) 280.6 million
(1993) 294 million
Vehicle-km: (1991) 46.7 million
(1992) 50 million
(1993) 51.7 million

Number of routes: 163
Route length: (One way) 2,597 km
On priority right-of-way: 10 km
Fleet: 855 vehicles

Fiat 418	505
Volvo B10M	74
Volvo articulated	3
Fiat 418 articulated	94
Ikarus IK280 articulated	36
Iveco AP160	45
STIA AP160 (1994/95)	44
Others	54

In peak service: 678

Most intensive service: 5 min
One-person operation: None
Fare collection: Season tickets, and onboard sales by seated conductor; some prepurchase, being extended
Fare structure: Stage; weekly and annual passes and season tickets; through ticketing to SMLT
Fares collected on board: 41%
Fare evasion control: Penalty payment
Average peak-hour speed: 10 km/h
Operating costs financed by: Fares 65.6%, other commercial sources 3.1%, subsidy/compensation 21.5%, deficit 9.8%
Subsidy from: Government; payments made to preserve financial equilibrium

Private operators

Current situation: The first privately operated bus services began in 1991. Amongst them is TCV which established a route from the city centre to La Marsa in direct competition with the TGM railway, which experienced a decline in first-class traffic in particular.

SMLT

Société du Métro Léger de Tunis (SMLT)
Incorporating Tunis-Goulette-Marsa Railway (TGM)
6 rue Khartoum, Tunis 1002
Telephone: +216 1 348555 Fax: +216 1 338100
Director General: Habib Allegue
Finance Director: H Zaatour
Infrastructure Director: B Hammami
Head of Information: R Kazdaghli
Staff: 1,470

Suburban railway (TGM)

Passenger journeys: (1993) 18.3 million
(1994) 18 million
(1995) 19.1 million

Current situation: 19.5 km suburban railway with 18 stations, 1,440 mm gauge, electrified 750 V DC overhead, linking Tunis, La Goulette and La Marsa; off-peak service of five trains/h.

Rolling stock: 36 cars
Duewag/MAN/Siemens (1977) M18 T18
On order: 18 two-car sets

Light rail

Type of operation: Light rail, initial route opened 1985

Passenger journeys: (1993) 71 million
(1994) 82 million
(1995) 88.3 million
Car-km: (Annual) 4.3 million

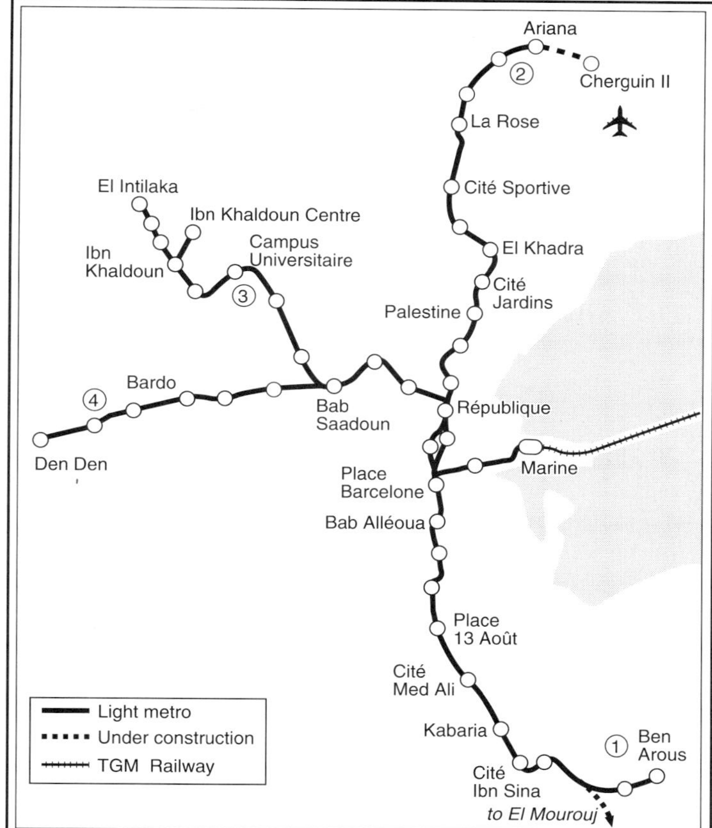

Tunis light rail

Line 3 LRV approaching Republique **1996**

TGM emu at La Goulette

Route length: 32 km
Number of lines: 5
Number of stations: 36
Gauge: 1,440 mm
Electrification: 750 V DC, overhead

Service: Peak 4 min, off-peak 12 min
Fare structure: 2 zones per route; through fares to bus

Rolling stock: 121 cars

Siemens-Duewag (1984/85)	M78
(1991/92)	M43

In peak service: 104 cars
On order: A further 14 sets from Siemens for 1997 delivery

Developments: Extension of Line 2 by 1.4 km under construction from Ariana to the Cherguin II industrial development. The alignment of the southwards extension from Ben Arous to the new town of El Mourouj has been revised. It will now be built as a branch of Line 1 running 6.5 km from Cité Ibn Sina. Construction was expected to start in 1995.

SNCFT

Société Nationale des Chemins de Fer Tunisiens
67 avenue Farhat Hached, Tunis
Telephone: +216 1 249999 Fax: +216 1 245044

Type of operation: Suburban heavy rail

Current situation: SNCFT operates suburban services on four routes totalling 142 km, carrying about 2 million passengers annually.
Developments: CTC introduced 1996 over the busiest section between Tunis Ville and Bordj Cedria (24 km), which carries about 200 trains a day.

Rolling stock: Diesel-hauled push-pull trainsets and dmus

UPDATED

UFA

Population: 1.1 million
Public transport: Bus and trolleybus/tramway services provided by separate municipal undertakings

Bus

Number of routes: 40, plus 15 express
Fleet: Includes Mercedes Türk O325, Chavdar articulated and Ikarus 260/280
Fare collection: Conductors

Tramvaino-Trolleibusnoe Upravlenie

Tramvaino-Trolleibusnoe Upravlenie
Revolutsionnaya ul 98, 400005 Ufa, Russia
Telephone: +7 3472 234403

Current situation: Both tram and trolleybus networks are in a poor state; half the fleet stands near-derelict in the depots and service is irregular with no effective scheduling. No fares are collected. Some large industrial concerns now operate their own buses to transport staff to and from work, thereby further undermining the network.

RVZ6 trams and a Mercedes Türk city bus on Oktyabrski prospekt ***1997***

Trolleybus

Number of routes: 17
Fleet: Approx 180 trolleybuses, ZIU9 and ZIU10

Tramway

Passenger journeys: (1989) 109 million
Number of routes: 16 operating out of 22
Route length: 156 km
Rolling stock: Approx 260 cars

ČKD Tatra T3 (1977/87)	About M100
RVZ6 (1980/87)	About M60
KTM5 (1992)	M15
KTM8 (1992/95)	M75
LM93 (1995/96)	About M10

NEW ENTRY

UJUNG PANDANG

Population: 709,000
Public transport: Government-owned transport corporation provides part of public transport services, supplemented by independent minibuses

DAMRI

Djawatan Angkutan Motor Republik Indonesia
Jalan G Latimojong 21, Ujung Pandang, Sulawesi Selatan, Indonesia
Telephone: +62 411 24226

Current situation: Public corporation operates several cross-city bus routes extending up to 20 km into suburban communities.

Fleet: Mercedes O306 and OH408 single-deck, Volvo double-deck
One-person operation: None
Fare collection: Conductor
Fare structure: Flat

Private bus

Current situation: A large fleet of 'Mikrolet' Daihatsu, Suzuki and Mitsubishi 10-seaters, radiating over several routes from the central market, supplements the government bus services. Most of these vehicles are one-man operated. Fares are usually 25 per cent (on longer routes 100 per cent) higher than those charged by government buses.

Mercedes OH408 bus of DAMRI, with 'Mikrolet' minibus

ULAN BATAAR

Population: 600,000
Public transport: Bus and trolleybus services provided by municipal undertaking responsible to Ministry of Transport

LIAZ 677 operating in Ulan Bataar

Municipal Motor Transport Committee

Municipal Workers' Council
Ulan Bataar, Mongolian People's Republic

Current situation: Services are provided by the local municipal committee under overall control of the Ministry of Transport & Communications. Figures for public transport in Mongolia's major urban centres indicate some 120 million passengers are carried annually.

Bus

Passenger journeys: Approx 35 million (annual)
Vehicle-km: Approx 5 million (annual)

Number of routes: 8
Fleet: Approx 150 buses, including LIAZ 677 and 697, Karosa SM, B731 and Paz 672
Fare collection: By conductress, seated at rear
Fare structure: Flat

Trolleybus

Current situation: Operation commenced in 1987 of an initial 13 km trolleybus route. Ultimately a 40 km system with 150 trolleybuses is planned.

Fleet: 36 trolleybuses

ZIU 682B	27
Trolza 52642	9

Karosa B731 followed by LIAZ 677 at central post office

UPDATED

UTRECHT

Population: 233,000
Public transport: Most bus services provided by municipal undertaking with some additional suburban routes operated by private regional bus companies; separate company responsible for operation of light rail line. Suburban/interurban services by Netherlands Railways (NS)

GVU

Gemeentelijk Vervoerbedrijf Utrecht (GVU)
PO Box 8222, 3503 RE Utrecht, Netherlands
Telephone: +31 30 236 3636 Fax: +31 30 231 6540
Chief Officer: J J P Kunst
Staff: 721

Current situation: GVU operates most urban and some suburban bus services in and around Utrecht. Other operators run interurban services into the city.

Bus

Passenger boardings: (1992) 34.6 million
(1993) 33.5 million
(1994) 35.5 million
Vehicle-km: (1992) 8.6 million
(1993) 8 million
(1994) 8 million

Number of routes: 19, plus 4 night
Route length: (One way) 223 km
On priority right-of-way: Approx 25 km
Fleet: 181 vehicles

DAF/Hainje standard	94
Volvo/Den Oudsten articulated	74
Hainje midibus	9
Fiat Ducato minibus	4

In peak service: 152
On order: 10 buses

Most intensive service: 3 min
One-person operation: All routes
Fare structure: Zonal; prepurchase nationally available 'Strippenkaart' tickets, also available on vehicle (see Amsterdam for details); passes; student ticket
Average distance between stops: 300-400 m
Average peak-hour speed: In mixed traffic, 16 km/h; in bus lanes, 25 km/h

Arrangements for elderly/disabled: Reduced fares
Integration with other modes: Services co-ordinated with those of neighbouring regional public transport authority and NS. National 'Strippenkaart' gives standard tram, bus and metro fares throughout the Netherlands
Operating costs financed by: Fares 29%, other commercial sources 5%, subsidy/grants 65% (surplus achieved in 1992)
Subsidy from: City council, drawing 100% government contribution

Sneltram

Midnet Groep NV, Sneltram Utrecht
Huis ter Heideweg 8, 3705 LZ Zeist
Telephone: +31 3404 26500 Fax: +31 3404 17947
Director: A F M Hilhorst

Current situation: The Sneltram light rail line was built by Netherlands Railways (NS) and at first operated by Westnederland, one of the government-owned regional bus undertakings. In 1991 Westnederland acquired the line and its equipment from NS.

Sneltram in Midnet livery at Zuilenstein **1996**

Developments: In a reorganisation of regional bus operations in 1994, the Sneltram came under the control of the new Midnet Groep which is a merger of parts of the former bus operators Centraal Nederland (CN) and Veluwse Autobus Diensten (VAD), and the most easterly part of Westnederland. Midnet also operates suburban and regional bus services.

Following elections in 1994, Utrecht's city council rescinded the earlier decision to build an extension from Moreelsepark to De Uithof, and a high-quality bus service is to be introduced instead. Nevertheless, a 2.5 km extension is being built to serve the Zenderpark housing development in IJsselstein, for 1998 opening. Midnet is developing an automatic vehicle location and control system for the Sneltram, which is also undergoing rehabilitation.

Studies are being made to assess whether the Sneltram can play a part in the Randstad 2000 scheme for S-Bahn style train service throughout the region.

Utrecht's Sneltram

Intelligent, sensitive, commanding: our brakes have leadership qualities

In the world's major cities, rail-bound commuter traffic is steadily gaining on private road transport. To progress into a passenger-friendly, economically and ecologically sustainable future, with mass transit systems based on light rail vehicles, low-floor streetcars and people movers, will call for exceptional performance in terms of both safety and reliability – not to mention comfort and fast passenger flow capabilities.

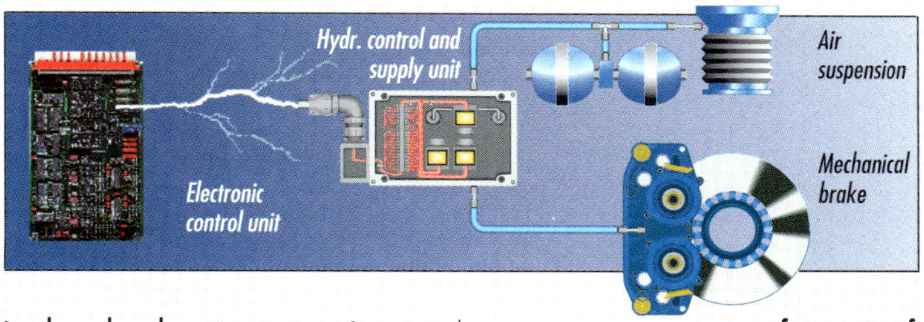

Knorr-Bremse systems engineering has already put mass transit firmly on the right track: Our microprocessor-controlled EHB electro-hydraulic braking system with integrated wheel slide protection and sensitive blending in line with prevailing load conditions, brings clear-cut advantages in its train. And with Knorr-Bremse hydro-pneumatic air suspension and kneeling systems installed, the vehicle needs only one operating medium, namely hydraulics. Enclosed in a compact design package, the result is a system that saves space and weight, enables the lowest floor levels to be realized and cuts both investment and operating costs.

Whatever the challenges facing light rail vehicles, Knorr-Bremse have the braking system to match, neatly packaged and future-proof – be it for ultra low floor streetcars or the new Copenhagen suburban units (a first in the heavy rail sector).

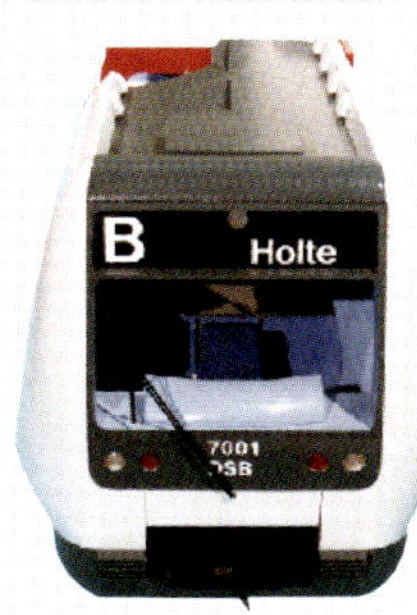

Copenhagen suburban unit

Knorr-Bremse: Braking with Tradition

KNORR-BREMSE
SYSTEMS FOR RAIL VEHICLES

KNORR-BREMSE SYSTEME FÜR SCHIENENFAHRZEUGE GMBH
Moosacher Straße 80 · D-80809 München · Germany
Telefon (089) 3547-0 · Telefax (089) 3547-2767

MANUFACTURERS

Rail Vehicles and Traction Equipment
Rail and Bus Components and Subassemblies
Electrification — Project Contractors and Equipment Suppliers
New Technology/Innovative Transit Systems
Buses — Chassis, Integrals and Bodies
Trolleybus Traction Equipment
Road Vehicle Chassis Components
Signalling, Communications and Traffic Control Equipment
Revenue Collection Equipment
Vehicle Maintenance Equipment and Services
Track Components and Maintenance Equipment

RAIL VEHICLES AND TRACTION EQUIPMENT

(*Manufacturer of traction equipment)

Company Listing by Country

ARGENTINA
Materfer

AUSTRALIA
Adtranz*
Clyde*
Goninan
Walkers

AUSTRIA
Adtranz
BWS
Elin*
SGP
Siemens

BELGIUM
BN Bombardier Eurorail
CMI

BRAZIL
Adtranz*
Gevisa*
Mafersa
Santa Matilde

CANADA
Bombardier

CHINA, PEOPLE'S REPUBLIC
CCC

CROATIA
Djuro Djaković

CZECH REPUBLIC
ČKD
MSV
Škoda

DENMARK
Adtranz

EGYPT
SEMAF

FINLAND
Adtranz*
Rautarüükki

FRANCE
ANF-Industrie
De Dietrich
GEC Alsthom*

GERMANY
Adtranz*
Duewag
DWA
Kiepe*
Linke-Hofmann-Busch
Siemens*
Talbot

HUNGARY
Ganz Ansaldo*
Ganz-Hunslet

INDIA
Bharat
Crompton Greaves
ICF

ITALY
Adtranz*
Ansaldo*
Breda
Costamasnaga
Fiat
Firema*
Sofer

JAPAN
Alna Koki
Hitachi
Kawasaki
Kinki Sharyo
Mitsubishi Electric*
Nippon Sharyo
Tokyu
Toshiba*

KOREA, REPUBLIC
Daewoo
Hanjin
Hyundai
Korea Shipbuilding & Engineering

LATVIA
RVR

MEXICO
Bombardier-Concarril

NETHERLANDS
Adtranz
Holec Ridderkerk*
Stork RMO

NORWAY
Adtranz*

POLAND
Konstal

PORTUGAL
Adtranz

ROMANIA
Astra

RUSSIA
Mytischi*
Ust-Katav

SOUTH AFRICA
Union Carriage

SPAIN
Adtranz*
CAF
GEC Alsthom Transporte

SWEDEN
Adtranz*

SWITZERLAND
Adtranz*
Alusuisse Road & Rail
Fiat-SIG
Schindler
SLM
'Vevey' Technologies

UK
Adtranz
Bombardier Prorail
Brush*
GEC Alsthom
GEC Alsthom Metro Cammell
Holec Ridderkerk UK
Railcare
RFS (E)

USA
Adtranz
AeroTrans
Amerail
Delaware Car
GE Transportation Systems*
Kawasaki Rail Car
Siemens Transportation Systems

Classified Listing

BODYSHELLS
Adtranz
AeroTrans
Alusuisse Road & Rail
Bombardier Prorail
BWS
DWA
Mafersa
SLM
Sofer
Stork RMO
Talbot
'Vevey' Technologies

BOGIES (see also Rail and Bus Components section)
Adtranz
ANF-Industrie
Duewag
DWA
Fiat
Fiat-SIG
Ganz-Hunslet
Nippon Sharyo
Santa Matilde
SEMAF
Siemens
Siemens Transportation Systems

COMMUTER/SUBURBAN CARS (unpowered)
Adtranz
Amerail
ANF-Industrie
BN
Bombardier
Bombardier-Concarril
Bombardier Eurorail
BWS
ČKD Praha
Daewoo
Delaware Car
DWA
Firema
Ganz-Hunslet
GEC Alsthom
Goninan
Hitachi
Holec Ridderkerk UK
Hyundai
Kawasaki
Kinki Sharyo
Linke-Hofmann-Busch
Nippon Sharyo
Siemens Transportation Systems
Talbot

COMPLETE ELECTRICAL TRACTION EQUIPMENT
Adtranz
Ansaldo
Bharat
Bombardier
Brush
Crompton Greaves
Elin
Fiat
Firema
Ganz Ansaldo

COMPLETE ELECTRICAL TRACTION EQUIPMENT *continued*
GEC Alsthom
GE Transportation Systems
Gevisa
Hitachi
Holec Ridderkerk
Kiepe
Mitsubishi
Siemens
Skoda
Toshiba

CONTRACT MAINTENANCE
Adtranz
ANF-Industrie
GEC Alsthom
Goninan
Materfer
Railcare
RFS (E)

DMU/DIESEL RAILCARS
Adtranz
ANF-Industrie
Bharat
Bombardier
Bombardier Eurorail
Bombardier Prorail
BWS
CAF
Clyde
Daewoo
De Dietrich
Duewag
Djuro Djaković
DWA
Ganz-Hunslet
GEC Alsthom
Goninan
Hanjin
Hitachi
Holec Ridderkerk
Holec Ridderkerk UK
Hyundai
ICF
Korea Shipbuilding & Engineering
Materfer
MSV
Nippon Sharyo
RVR
Siemens
Siemens Transportation Systems
Sofer
Talbot
Tokyu
Toshiba
Union Carriage

DOUBLE-DECK CARS
Adtranz
Amerail
ANF-Industrie
BN
Bombardier
Bombardier Eurorail
DWA
Firema
GEC Alsthom
Goninan
Hitachi
Kinki Sharyo
MSV
Schindler
Talbot

EMUS
Adtranz
Alna Koki
ANF-Industrie
Ansaldo
Astra
Bharat
BN
Bombardier
Bombardier Eurorail
BWS
CAF
CCC
Clyde
Daewoo
DWA
Ganz Ansaldo
Ganz-Hunslet
GEC Alsthom
Goninan
Hanjin
Hitachi
Holec Ridderkerk
Holec Ridderkerk UK
ICF
Kawasaki Rail Car
Kinki Sharyo
Linke-Hofmann-Busch
Materfer
MSV
Nippon Sharyo
RVR
Santa Matilde
Schindler
SEMAF
Siemens
Siemens SGP
Siemens Transportation Systems
Sofer
Stork RMO
Talbot
Tokyu
Toshiba
Union Carriage
'Vevey' Technologies
Walkers

LOW-FLOOR TRAMCARS/LRVs
Adtranz
ANF-Industrie
Astra
BN
Bombardier
Bombardier-Concarril
Bombardier Eurorail
BWS
Breda
CAF
ČKD Praha
De Dietrich
Duewag
Djuro Djaković
DWA
Elin
Fiat
Fiat-SIG
Firema
Ganz-Hunslet
GEC Alsthom
Hyundai
Kiepe
Linke-Hofmann-Busch
MSV
Schindler
SGP
Siemens
Siemens Transportation Systems
SLM
'Vevey' Technologies

METRO CARS
Adtranz
Alna Koki
Amerail
ANF-Industrie
Astra
Bharat
BN
Bombardier
Bombardier-Concarril
Bombardier Eurorail
Bombardier Prorail
BWS
Breda
CAF
CCC
ČKD Praha
Costamasnaga
Daewoo
Duewag
DWA
Fiat
Firema
Ganz Ansaldo
Ganz-Hunslet
GEC Alsthom
Hitachi
Holec Ridderkerk UK
Hyundai
ICF
Kawasaki
Kawasaki Rail Car
Kinki Sharyo
Korea Shipbuilding & Engineering
Linke-Hofmann-Busch
Mafersa
MSV
Mytischi
Nippon Sharyo
Rautaruukki
SEMAF
Siemens SGP
Skoda

REFURBISHMENT
Adtranz
Amerail
Bombardier Eurorail
Bombardier Prorail
Breda
ČKD Praha
Delaware Car
DWA
GEC Alsthom
Gevisa
Mafersa
Materfer
Railcare
Santa Matilde
Schindler
SEMAF

TRAMCARS/LRVs
Adtranz
Alna Koki
ANF-Industrie
Astra
BN
Bombardier
Bombardier-Concarril
Bombardier Eurorail
Breda
BWS
CCC
ČKD Praha
Costamasnaga
De Dietrich
Duewag
Djuro Djaković
DWA
Elin
Fiat
Fiat-SIG
Firema
Ganz Ansaldo
Ganz-Hunslet
GEC Alsthom
Holec Ridderkerk UK
Kinki Sharyo
Konstal
Linke-Hofmann-Busch
Mafersa
Materfer
Mitsubishi Electric
Nippon Sharyo
Railcare
Rautarüükki
RVR
Santa Matilde
Schindler
SEMAF
Siemens
Siemens SGP
Siemens Transportation Systems
Skoda
Stork RMO
Talbot
Toshiba
Union Carriage
Ust-Katav
Vevey
Walkers

Adtranz

ABB Daimler-Benz Transportation GmbH
Group Holding Headquarters and Group Corporate Center
PO Box 130127, 13601 Berlin, Germany
Telephone: +49 303 8320 Fax: +49 303 832 2000

Berlin office: Saatwinkler Damm 43, 13627 Berlin

Group Executive Committee
President and Chief Executive Officer (CEO): Kaare Vagner
Executive Vice President (EVP), Deputy CEO: Rolf Eckrodt

PAT and EVP, Business Segment A: Christer Bådholm
PAT and EVP, Business Segment B: Heinz F. Cronimund
PAT and EVP, Business Segment C: Rolf Eckrodt
PAT and EVP, Business Segment D: Chris Sheppard
EVP, Manufacturing & Technology: Joachim Gaissert
Chief Financial Officer and EVP: Ruben Ornstein
(PAT — Project Allocation Team Member) (Each EVP has specific regional and country, as well as product and/or service, responsibility, marked A, B, C, D below)

Region, country and service assignments
A — Asia Pacific, Australia, Baltic, Canada, Denmark, Finland, Israel, Norway, Sweden, Turkey, USA
B — Austria, Belgium, France, Greece, India, Italy, Netherlands, Pakistan, Portugal, Russian Federation and Associated States, Spain, Sri Lanka, Switzerland, North Africa
C — China, Germany, Middle East
D — Sub-Sahara Africa, Britain & Ireland, Eastern Europe, Latin America
MT — Manufacturing, supply management, research and development, engineering, systematics
CFO — Control, accounting, legal, tax, treasury, project finance

Senior Vice President (SVP), Advanced Technologies: Juergen Fleischer
SVP, Business Development & Acquisitions: Eberhard Beyer
PAT and SVP, Group Marketing: Dieter Klumpp
SVP, Human Resources: Ian Butler
SVP, Representation, Public Affairs: Klaus Milz
SVP, Corporate Communications: Peter Polzer
VP, Organisation and Strategy: Olof Persson

Corporate Centres
Belgium
Adtranz (Europe) Ltd, Group Corporate Center
Rue Froissart 123-133, 1040 Bruxelles
Telehone: +32 2 233 1161 Fax: +32 2 233 1162
Executive: Klaus Milz
Switzerland
ABB Daimler-Benz (Switzerland) Ltd
Affolternstrasse 44, 8050 Zurich
Telephone: +41 1 317 7398 Fax: + 411 317 7954
Executive: Heinz Cronimund

Adtranz emu on Shanghai metro Line 1 **1997**

Groups with worldwide responsibility for designated product-specific range
Germany
Total Rail Systems Group (TRS)
ABB Daimler-Benz Transportation GmbH
PO Box 130127, 13601 Berlin
Telephone: +49 303 832 1701 Fax +49 303 832 2004
Executive (acting): Christer Bådholm
Signal Group (SIG) (see Signalling & Communications)
ABB Daimler-Benz Transportation GmbH
PO Box 130127, 13601 Berlin
Telephone: +49 303 832 1721 Fax +49 303 832 2003
Executive: Lars Afzelius

Fixed Installations (Electrification) Group (FIX) Headquarters (see Electrification section)
ABB Daimler-Benz Transportation (Deutschland) GmbH
Mainzer Landstrasse 349-351, 60326 Frankfurt am Main
Telephone: +49 69 750 7551 Fax: +49 69 750 7584
Executive: Anders Larsson

Regional Transportation Companies, Regional and Branch Offices
RTC — Regional Transportation Company; BO — Branch Office; Regional Office, with its RM (Regional Manager), is the contact for countries where Adtranz has no own office. Regional offices are usually attached to an RTC or BO.

Albania: see Yugoslavia

Algeria: contact North Africa Region Office RM in Switzerland

Argentina (BO and Regional Office)
ABB Daimler-Benz Transportation (Argentina)
Av. del Libertator 2424, Piso 11a, RA 1425 Buenos Aires
Telephone: +541 808 8799 Fax: +541 808 8701 (808 8700 + extension 8488 for countries with tone-phone system, USA and Brazil)
Executive: Eugenio-Jorge Vago (also RM for Argentina and Chile)
RM, Latin America: Lutz Elsner (see Latin America)

Australia (RTC and Regional Office)
ABB Daimler-Benz Transportation (Australia) Pty Ltd
PO Box 1387, Milton, Qld 4034
Telephone: +61 73 858 2400 Fax: +61 73 367 2422
Executive: Lars Brodin (also RM for Australia, New Zealand, Oceania, Indonesia)
Other plants in Dandenong, (Vic), Maryborough (Qld), ABB Engineering Construction Pty, Ltd, Sydney (NSW)

Austria (RTC)
ABB Daimler-Benz Transportation Austria GmbH
PO Box 57, 2351 Wr. Neudorf
Telephone: +43 22 364 040 Fax: +43 22 364 1858
Executive: Manfred Fischer

Baltic States: see Sweden

Bangladesh: Contact South-West Asia Region Office in Switzerland

Belgium
For Belgium, France, Greece, Luxemburg, Mongolia, Netherlands, Russian Federation and Associated States (excluding Ukraine) — Group HQ, Berlin (qv)
Telephone +49 303 832 1501 Fax +49 303 832 2004
Regional Manager: Wolfgang Wegener

Bhutan: Contact South-West Asia Region Office, Switzerland

Bosnia/Herzegovina: see Yugoslavia

Brazil (RTC)
ABB Daimler-Benz Transportation (Brasil) Ltda
Av. dos Autonomistas 1496, 06020-902, 06020-902 Osaco-SP
Telephone: +55 11 704 8405 Fax: +55 11 702 9318
Executive: Albert Blum
RM, Latin America: Lutz Elsner (see Latin America)

Bulgaria (BO)
ABB Daimler-Benz Transportation (Bulgaria)
5 Triaditza Street, 1040 Sofia
Executive: Ivan Botev
Telephone: +359 2 980 7696 Fax: +359 2 981 4544
RM: John Kapala (see Poland)

Guangzhou metro train **1997**

Burma (Myanmar): see Malaysia

Cambodia: see Thailand

Canada: (BO)
ABB Daimler-Benz Transportation (Canada)
10300 Henri Bourassa, St Laurent, Quebec H4S 1Y4
Telephone +1 514 956 0691 Fax: +1 514 956 0424
Executive: Ray Kapila
RM: Ray Betler (see USA)

Chile: See RM, Argentina

China: (RTC)
ABB Daimler-Benz Transportation (China) Ltd
Beijing Liaison Office, (also Regional Office)
Unit 2501, Landmark Building, 8 North Dongsanhuan Bei Rd, Chaoyang District, Beijing 100004
Telephone: +86 106 506 6214 Fax: +86 106 506 6218/9
Executive: Wilhelm Buckwar (also RM for Hong Kong, China, Macao)

Changchun Adtranz Railway Company (Joint Venture)
5, Qingyin Road, Changchun, Jilin Province

ABB Daimler-Benz Transportation (China) Ltd
Shanghai Liaison Office
Room 1701, Hua Ting Guest House, 2525 Zhong Shan Xi Lu, Shanghai 200030
Telephone: +86 216 439 5005 Fax: +86 216 439 5011
Executive: Andrew Lezala
RM: Wilhelm Buckwar (see Beijing)

ABB Daimler-Benz Transportation (China) Ltd, Hongkong
Room 1301/2, Houston Centre, 63 Mody Rd, Tsimshatsui East, Kowloon, Honkong
Telephone: +85 22 368 0155 Fax: +85 22 369 1874
Executive: Cyril Moore
RM: Wilhelm Buckwar (see Beijing)
Other plant in Shenyang (see Signalling section)

Croatia: see Yugoslavia

Cyprus: see Belgium

Czech Republic: (BO)
ABB Daimler-Benz Transportation (Czech)
Sokolovska 73, 18600 Praha 8
Telephone: +420 22 180 8112/111 Fax: +420 22 180 8114
Executive: Josef Schorm
RM: John Kapala (see Poland)

Denmark: (RTC and Regional Office)
ABB Daimler-Benz Transportation (Denmark) a/s
Toldbodgade 39, 8900 Randers
Telephone: +458 642 5300 Fax: +458 641 5700
RM: Henrik Mortensen (for Israel)
Executive: Per Noerret
Other plant in Hvidovre (see Signalling section)

Adtranz ET474 emu **1997**

Egypt: (BO and Regional Office)
ABB Daimler-Benz Transportation (Egypt)
Commercial Center-Office No. 33, Nile Hilton Hotel, Tahrir Square, Cairo
Telephone: +202 579 0197/8 Fax: +202 579 0196
Executive and RM, Middle East: Rudi Stoecker

Ecuador: see Latin America

Finland: (RTC)
ABB Daimler-Benz Transportation (Finland) Oy
Atmitie 5c, 00370 Helsinki
Executive: Markku Tanttu
Telephone: +358 10 22 2060/10 2211
Fax: +358 10 22 2066
(The general Helsinki area code is now 9 but all Adtranz or ABB offices/companies in Finland are reached over their common individual code 10)

France: see Belgium

Germany: (RTC)
ABB Daimler-Benz Transportation (Deutschland) GmbH
Am Rathenau-Park, 6761 Hennigsdorf
German Adtranz company HQ
Telephone: +49 330 2890 Fax: +49 330 289 4050
Executive: Wolfgang Toelsner

ABB Daimler-Benz Transportation (Deutschland) GmbH
PO Box 100351, 6128 Mannheim
Business Area Systems and Components, Executive: Uwe Stohwasser
Telephone: +49 621 3810 Fax: +49 621 381 8788

ABB Daimler-Benz Transportation (Deutschland) GmbH
Frankenstrasse 140, 90461 Nürnberg
Business Area Mass Transit Executive: Werner Rauer
Telephone: +49 911 94560 Fax: +49 911 9456/1319
Other plants in Berlin, Braunschweig Kassel and Siegen

ABB Daimler-Benz Transportation (Deutschland) GmbH
Mainzer Landstr. 349-351, D-60326 Frankfurt am Main
Telephone: +49 69 750 70 Fax: +49 69 750 7316
Fixed Installations Executive: Anders Larsson

Ghana: see South Africa

Greece: see Belgium

Hungary: (RTC)
ABB Daimler-Benz Transportation (Hungary) Kft
PO Box 52, 1554 Budapest
Telephone: +361 270 5499 Fax: +361 270 5490
Executive: Matyas Racz
Holding company of MAV Dunakeszi Wagon Manufacturing and Repair Ltd
Allomaf Setany 19, 2120 Dunakeszi
Telephone +36 27 341 9517 Fax: +36 27 341 997
Executive: Lajos Varga
RM: John Kapala (see Poland)

India: (RTC)
ABB Daimler-Benz Transportation (India) Ltd
Guru Nanak Foundation Bldg, 15-16 Quatab Institutional Area, New Delhi 110 067
Telephone: +91 11 686 8019 Fax: +91 11 686 6553
Other plant in Baruda
Executive: Viren P Srivastava

Indonesia: (BO)
ABB Daimler-Benz Transportation (Indonesia)
Jl. Cikini Raya No. 69, Jakarta 10330
Telephone: +62 21 314 9115 Fax: +62 21 315 3963
Executive: Joachim Schulze-Warnecke
RM: Lars Brodin (see Australia)

Berlin S-Bahn BR481 emu **1997**

Ireland: (BO)
ABB Daimler-Benz Transportation (Ireland)
Belgard Rd, Tallaght, Dublin 42
Telephone: +353 1 405 7368 Fax: +353 405 7370
Executive: Colin Blackwood
RM: Stig Svard (see United Kingdom, Derby)

Israel: see Denmark

Italy: (RTC)
ABB Daimler-Benz Transportation (Italy) SpA
Centro Direzionale Milano, Oltre 2, Palazzo Cedri, V le Europa, 20090 Segrate MI
Telephone: +39 22 684 01 Fax: +39 22 684 0555
Executive: Norberto Achille
Other plant in Vado Ligure, Roma

Japan: (BO and Regional Office)
ABB Daimler-Benz Transportation (Japan)
Roppongi First Bldg, 1-9-9 Rop, Minato Ku, Tokyo 106
Telephone +81 35 562 0821 Fax: +81 35 562 0881
Executive: Gert Andersson (also RM for North East Asia-Pacific – Korea, Japan, Taiwan)

Korea: (RTC)
ABB Daimler-Benz Transportation (Korea) Ltd
143-42 Samsung-dong Kangnam-ku, Wonbang Bldg, 10th floor, 135-090 Seoul
Telephone: +82 2 569 1991 Fax: +82 508 2 4484
Executive: Gert Andersson

Laos: see Thailand

Latin America: Regional Office
ABB Daimler-Benz Transportation (Latin America)
762 South Military Trail, Deerfield Beach, FL 33445, USA
Telephone: +1 954 420 0302 Fax: +1 954 420 0798
RM, Latin America (Argentina, Brazil, Chile, Mexico, other Latin American countries): Lutz Elsner

Libya: see Switzerland (North Africa Regional Office)

Luxembourg: see Belgium

Macedonia: see Yugoslavia

Malaysia: (RTC)
ABB Daimler-Benz Transportation Malaysia SDN BHD
Suite 27-02, Menara Lion, 165 Jalan Ampang, 50450 Kuala Lumpur
Telephone: +603 262 7366 Fax: +603 262 7335
Executive: Rauno Boga (also RM for South East Asia-Pacific (Cambodia, Laos, Malaysia, Myanmar, Singapore, Thailand, Vietnam)

Malta: (RTC) – see Switzerland (North Africa Region Office)

Mauritania: see Switzerland (North Africa Region Office)

Mexico: BO
ABB Daimler-Benz Transportation (Mexico)
Rubén Dario 281, Piso 8, 11580 Mexico
Telephone: +525 282 2053 Fax: +525 280 2054
Executive: Guillermo Carrion

Middle East: see Egypt

Mongolia: see Russia

Morocco: see Switzerland (North Africa)

Netherlands: see Belgium

Nepal: see Switzerland (South-West Asia Region Office)

New Zealand: see Australia

Nigeria: see South Africa

Norway: (RTC)
ABB Daimler-Benz Transportation (Norway) AS
Stasjonsveien 1, 2011 Stroemmen
Telephone: +476 380 9600 Fax: +476 380 9601
Executive: Ornulf Myrvoll

Pakistan: see Switzerland (South West Asia RO)

Philippines: (RTC)
ABB Daimler-Benz Transportation (Philippines) Inc
14th floor, JMT Bldg, San Miguel Ave, 1655 Pasig Metro Manila
Telephone: +632 634 2167 Fax: +632 634 2168
Executive: Lino P Pangan
Regional Manager: Gert Andersson (see Japan)

Poland: (RTC and RO)
ABB Daimler-Benz Transportation (Poland) Ltd
ul. Bitwy Warszawskiej 1920 r. nr. 18, 02-366 Warszawa
Telephone: +48 22 658 1020 Fax: +48 22 608 0766
Executive: John Kapala [(also Regional Manager for Central Europe (Albania, Bulgaria, Romania, Hungary, Poland, Bosnia/Herzegovina, Croatia, Macedonia, Slovenia, Czech Republic and Slovakia)]
Other site: Lodz, Warszawa, Zory (see Signalling)

Portugal: (RTC)
ABB Daimler-Benz Transportation (Portugal) SA
Rua Vice-Almirante Azevedo Cout, PO Box 60005, P-2701 Amadora Codex.
Telephone: +351 1 496 9100 Fax: +351 1 499 1052
Executive: Manuel Norton
Other plant: Sines

Romania: (BO)
ABB Daimler-Benz Transportation (Romania)
16 I Cimpineau, 5th floor, 70100 Bucharest
Telephone: +401 330 049 Fax: +401 330 0690
Executive: Franz Weber
Regional Manager: John Kapala (see Poland)

Berlin standard-profile Class H emu **1997**

Jena's fully low-floor double-ended LRV **1997**

Russia: (BO and RO)
ABB Daimler-Benz Transportation (Russia)
Pokrovskij Boulevard, Korpus 3, 1st floor, 10100 Moscow
Telephone: +70 95 207 2959 Fax: +70 95 230 2313
Executive and Regional Manager for Russian Federation and Assoicated States and Mongolia: Franz Weber

Singapore: (RTC)
ABB Daimler-Benz Transportation (Singapore) Pty Ltd
2 Ayer Rajah Crescent, 4th floor, Singapore 139 935
Telephone: +65 773 8797 Fax: +65 775 1328
Executive: Stanley Low
Regional Manager: Rauno Boga (see Malaysia)

Slovakia: (BO)
ABB Daimler-Benz Transportation (Slovakia)
Nam SNP 15B, 81 106 Bratislava
Telephone: +421 732 3050 Fax: +421 732 6567
Executive: Rudolf Kvetan
Regional Manager: John Kapala (see Poland)

Slovenia: see Yugoslavia

Spain: (RTC)
ABB Daimler-Benz Transportation (España) SA
Complejo Triada—Torre A, planta 4 a, Avenida de Burgos 17, 28036 Madrid
Telephone: +341 383 6200 Fax: +341 383 6199
Executive: Jose Capparros
Other plants : Trapagaran 48510, Vizcaya; 28100 Alcobendas, Madrid (see Signalling and Electrification sections)

South Africa: (RTC and RO)
ABB Daimler-Benz Transportation South Africa (Pty) Ltd
PO Box 857, Johannesburg 2000
Telephone: +27 11 806 9111 Fax: +27 11 887 0565
Executive and Regional Manager for Sub-Sahara Africa: Gert Kruger

Sri Lanka: see Switzerland (South West Asia RO)

Adtranz fully low-floor double-ended LRV in Mainz **1997**

Fully low-floor GT8N LRV in Nürnberg **1997**

Adtranz lightweight RS1 diesel railcar **1997**

Ostra Ringväigen/Västerås 2, 72183
Telephone: +46 21 322000 Fax: +46 21 148271
Executive and Regional Manager for Nordic Countries and Turkey: Staffan Hakanson
Other plants in: Helsingborg, Kalmar, Surahammar, Hässleholm, Stockholm (see Signalling section)

Switzerland: (RTC and RO)
ABB Daimler-Benz Transportation (Switzerland) Ltd
PO Box 8384, 8050 Zurich
Executive: Beat M ller
Regional Manager, North Africa Region (Algeria, Libya, Malta, Mauritania, Morocco, Tunisia) and South West Asia Region (Bangladesh, Bhutan, Pakistan, Nepal, Sri Lanka): Werner Bohli
Telephone: +411 318 3333 Fax: +411 312 6159
Other plants in: Geneva, Turgi

Syria: see Egypt

Taiwan: (RTC)
ABB Daimler-Benz Transportation (Taiwan) Ltd
6th F 1, 8 Min-Chuan 2nd Rd, Kaohsiung
Telephone: +88 67 335 5931 Fax: +88 67 335 5934
Executive: Charles Chen
Regional Manager: Gert Andersson (see Japan)
Other plant: Taipei

Tanzania: see South Africa

Thailand: (RTC and RO)
ABB Daimler-Benz Transportation (Thailand) Ltd
Manorom Bldg, 12th floor, 10501 Bangkok
Telephone: +66 2 249 7272 Fax: +66 2 671 7597
Executive and Regional Manager for Laos and Cambodia: Somkiet Prathanee

Tunisia: see North Africa Region Office, Switzerland

Turkey: (BO)
ABB Daimler-Benz Transportation (Turkey)
Özden Konak Ishani, Kat 9, Kasap Sokak No. 2, 80280 Esentepe-Istanbul
Telephone: +90 212 275 2811 Fax: +90 212 275 2821

Executive: Ali Savci
Regional Manager: Staffan Hakanson (see Sweden)

Uganda: (BO)
ABB Daimler-Benz Transportation (Uganda)
PO Box 21821, Kampala
Telephone: +25 64 120 0419 Fax: +25 64 120 0419
Executive: Tom Barrow
Regional Manager: Gerrit Kruger (see South-Africa)

Ukraine
Daimler-Benz AG, General Agent for Ukraine, wul I Klimenko 5/2, 252680 Kiev 37
Telephone: +380 44 271 7842 Fax: +380 44 271 8555

United Kingdom: (RTC)
ABB Daimler-Benz Transportation (UK & Ireland) Ltd
Litchurch Lane, Derby DE24 8AD
Telephone: +44 133 234 4666 Fax: +44 133 226 6472
Executive and Regional Manager for UK and Ireland: Stig Svard

ABB Daimler-Benz Transportation (Rolling Stock) Ltd
Litchurch Lane, Derby DE 24 8AD.
Telephone: +44 133 234 4666 Fax: +44 133 226 6289

ABB Daimler-Benz Transportation (Customer support) Ltd
Litchurch Lane, Derby DE 24 8AD
Telephone: +44 133 234 4666 Fax: +44 133 225 1884
Executive: Stig Svard
Other plants: Crewe, Chart Leacon, Doncaster, Ilford, London, Manchester, Swindon

ABB Daimler-Benz Transportation (Total Rail Systems) Ltd
St Dunstan's Osmaston Rd, Derby DE 24 8B2
Executive: Keith Rands
Telephone: +44 133 226 6001 Fax: +44 133 225 1796
Other plants: Reading, Plymouth, Birmingham (see also Signalling section)

USA: (RTC and RO)
ABB Daimler-Benz Transportation (North America) Inc
1501 Lebanon Church Rd, Pittsburg, PA 15236-1491
Telephone: +1 412 655 7000 Fax: +1 412 655 5860
Executive and Regional Manager for US and Canada: Ray Betler
Other plants: Pittsburg, California; Elmira Heights, New York; West Miffin, Pennsylvania

Yugoslavia
General Agent for Yugoslavia, also Albania, Bosnia-Herzegovina and Croatia, Macedonia and Slovenia:
ABB Marketing (Eastern Europe) Ltd
Schaffhauserstrasse 418, 8050 Zurich, Switzerland
Telephone: +411 318 2970 Fax: +411 302 0452
Regional Manager: John Kapala (see Poland)

Artist's impression of Oslo airport shuttle **1997**

Lisboa metro ML90 trainset **1997**

Vietnam: (BO)
ABB Daimler-Benz Transportation (Vietnam)
HITC Building, 6th floor, Cau Giay Street, Tu Liem District, Hanoi
Telephone: +844 833 3826 Fax: +844 834 2037
Executive: Ernst Bening
Regional Manager: Rauno Boga (see Malaysia)

Adtranz, the world's largest rolling stock manufacturer, has undergone major changes as the two constituent parts of the company – the railway interests of ABB and Daimler-Benz respectively – have been welded together into one firm. Here we present the latest structure of the company.

Background

ABB (Asea Brown Boveri AG, Switzerland) and Daimler-Benz AG, Germany, merged their rail businesses in 1995 to form a new company. The 50:50 joint venture is called the Adtranz (ABB Daimler-Benz Transportation Systems) group and it has manufacturing subsidiaries (regional transport companies – RTCs) in 25 countries, branch offices (BOs) in 17 countries and several regional offices, in most countries attached to an RTC or a BO. Two further corporate centres are in Bruxelles and Zürich.

Adtranz acquired IVV (Ingenieur Gesellschaft für Verkehrs-Planung und Verkehrs-Sicherung GmbH), Braunschweig, in 1996. It was renamed ABB Daimler-Benz Transportation (Signal) GmbH.

At the end of 1996, Adtranz and Changchun Car Company, China (qv) signed a joint venture to produce rolling stock for urban transport applications. CCC is owned by the Chinese Railway Ministry and manufactures 1,200 passenger vehicles a year. From the beginning of 1997, a new company, the Changchun Adtranz Railway Company, was formed with 51 per cent of shares owned by Adtranz and 49 per cent owned by CCC. Planned production is 160 vehicles a year.

Portuguese manufacturer, Sorefame, was renamed Adtranz Portugal in 1996.

ABB Daimler-Benz Transportation (Hungary) KFT has been established in Budapest as a Regional Transportation Company and in 1996 acquired the Dunakeszi Vaggon Manufacturing and Repair workshop of MAV Hungary.

At the beginning of 1997 Adtranz acquired a 75 per cent share of Pafawag, Poland, which manufactures rolling stock, and it was renamed Adtranz Pafawag.

Products

Development, design, engineering, sales, production, installation, maintenance and after-sales service of rolling stock, systems, components and equipment for urban transport.

Electric and diesel traction vehicles for urban, suburban and regional transport; light rail vehicles; automated guided vehicles; special vehicles.

Maintenance, refurbishment and after-sales service for rolling stock.

SL Stockholm metro train **1997**

Metre-gauge Be4/4 motor car for GFM Switzerland **1997**

Contracts

Current and recent contracts include:

Australia – QR has taken delivery of a further 12 three-car trains for suburban services in Brisbane. Each three-car train has two power cars for operation at 25 kV and one driving trailer. The 12 stainless steel trainsets were built by Adtranz in Australia and Switzerland. Electrical equipment comprises GTO-equipped converters for three-phase drives and onboard auxiliary services.

A QR follow-up contract for an additional three four-car interurban emus with three-phase drive was completed in 1996.

A third series of six three-car interurban emus is being delivered during 1997.

Sydney Light Rail Ltd has awarded a contract for supply and installation of the Pyrmont Light Rail line. First rolling stock will be seven Variotram LRVs. These will enter service in 1997 between the Central railway station and a new area of Sydney, built on the Ultimo-Pyrmont peninsula. A later extension of the network and fleet has already been planned. The vehicles were being built by Adtranz in Australia, with propulsion equipment coming from Adtranz in Germany.

Belgium – SNCB is taking delivery of 240 Flexliner front modules for AM96 emus, from Adtranz in Denmark.

De Lijn has ordered 45 LRVs from a German consortium including Adtranz.

China – MTR Hong Kong's airport line was due to receive 23 trainsets from Adtranz/CAF in 1997.

Shanghai Metro Corporation (SMC) has agreed to the design, building and operation by an Adtranz-led consortium of Line 2 of the Shanghai metro. The contract includes 35 six-car trainsets, with the option of extending to eight cars during rush hours.

Guangzhou Metro Corporation has signed contracts with the German consortium Adtranz/Siemens for the construction of a metro system. Adtranz is supplying 120 metro cars with some components by Siemens, the first being handed over at the beginning of 1997. Final delivery is expected in 1999.

Czech Republic – Metro Praha has signed a contract with Adtranz and Siemens to supply electrical equipment for passenger cars.

Denmark – Four trainsets have been ordered for the København-Kastrup airport line, for delivery during 1998/9.

Thirteen L2D dmus ordered by six Danish private railways were due to be delivered in 1997. Derived from the IC3 dmu, the L2D consists of two cars and has a top speed of 140 km/h. The trailer car of the L2D set has a floor height of 600 mm and offers level boarding for passengers with prams, bicycles, heavy luggage or wheelchairs. Capacity is 129 seated and 60 standing. Up to five trains can be coupled in multiple.

Finland – Helsinki has ordered 20 Variotrams with an option for another 20. Delivery starts in 1998, with completion by 2000. Rautarüükki is responsible for building the bodyshells and for final assembly.

France – CTS Strasbourg has ordered 21 Eurotrams from Adtranz comprising 11 seven-module and 10 nine-module LRVs. They are being built by Adtranz in the UK and Italy, with final assembly in Lohr, France.

Six SBB Colibri shuttle trainsets are being modified by Adtranz to operate under different single-phase AC power supplies – along the Rhine from Frick to Basel under 15 kV lines, crossing into France and continuing under 25 kV lines to Mulhouse. The first set was due to enter service in 1997.

SNCF has taken delivery of three double power cars, with three-phase drive, for 800 V DC supply and rack-and-adhesion operation for the Swiss Martigny-Le Chatelard and French Vallorcine-Chamonix-Mont Blanc to St Gervais-Les Bains/Le Fayet route. MC Switzerland (see Switzerland) has taken delivery of two identical double power cars. All vehicles were built by 'Vevey' Technologies and Adtranz in Switzerland. They operate on third-rail current collection in France and overhead in Switzerland.

Germany – DB has contracts for 229 ET425 (196) and ET426 (43) S-Bahn trainsets with a consortium of Adtranz, Siemens and DWA for services around Frankfurt, München, Stuttgart, Dresden, Hannover, Leipzig and Mannheim.

DB's order for 110 three-phase drive Class ET423 emus for S-Bahn services in several cities is in advanced production. Each four-car set has two power cars. Deliveries start in 1998 and are expected to be completed in 2000. Each set has seats for 533, with a total capacity of 752.

Delivery of 45 three-phase driven DC-powered ET474 three-car trains for the Hamburg S-Bahn started at the end of 1996 and was expected to be completed by the end of 1997. An additional 58 ET474 three-car emus are being built for delivery in 1999.

DB has taken delivery of 10 production sets of the new-generation Class BR481 emus with three-phase drive for S-Bahn Berlin services. The initial order for 100 eight-car sets, being built by a consortium of Adtranz and DWA, has been increased by a further 400 sets for delivery through to 2005. The sets can be split into four- or two-car trains.

For BVG Berlin, a contract for 25 four-car Type HK small-profile metro trains with three-phase drive is in advanced production, with delivery starting in December 1998. Each four-car set seats 88 with 276 standing.

Out of a contract for 115 three-phase driven standard-profile Type H six-car emus (Underground 2000) Adtranz supplied two preproduction sets during 1996. Power is taken at 750 V from a third rail. The first delivery will be in 1998.

HHA Hamburg's third series of 20 Class DT4 four-car trains with mechanical parts from LHB is in production. Power is taken from a third rail at 750 V. Each formation has two sets of two cars with three bogies only – motor bogies at the outer ends and a common trailing bogie supporting inner ends of the two cars of a two-car set. These sets are permanently coupled to form four-car trains with a driving cab at outer ends. They have three-phase drive with water-cooled traction motors. Water heated by the motors is used to heat the passenger area.

Regio-Shuttle RS1 cars have been delivered to:

Württemberg Railway Company (WEG)

Schönbuch Railway (3 DT4 power cars and one driving trailer car).

Regental Railway, Bavaria (11 Type RS1 power cars).

Wieslauftal Railway (ZVVS) (one RS1 Regio-Shuttle diesel car delivered in 1996.

Rail-Charter GmbH Mannheim (30 RS1 Regio-Shuttle cars, delivered 1997) – 22 leased to the Hohenzollern Landesbahn (HzL), Hechingen, which now runs services for DB on the Tübingen–Sigmaringen line (DB continues to run intercity services over the line). Eight RS1 cars for services on the Kaiserstuhl Railway, Freiburg, are being leased to SWEG (Südwestdeutsche Verkehrs AG), Lahr, for the Kaiserstuhl Railway, Freiburg.

The Regio-Shuttle RS1 is a new design of lightweight diesel railcar with a 70 per cent low floor and two double doors. It has upholstered seats, space for wheelchairs, prams and bicycles. Each power car has room for 180 passengers (74 seated, 106 standing) and can operate either as a single unit or combined with a driving trailer car, or as traction vehicle for freight wagons. It is powered by two diesel engines, each rated at 228 kW.

More than 600 LRVs are in production and orders include:

Forty three-phase driven 100 per cent ultra-low-floor GT6M metre-gauge LRVs for BVG Berlin out of an order for 120. Deliveries were expected to be completed in 1997. An additional 60 vehicles have been ordered. BVG has also ordered one Variotram.

Bremen has taken delivery of 78 three-phase driven 100 per cent ultra-low-floor G8TN LRVs.

DVG Duisburg has received one Variotram.

OEG Mannheim received six 70 per cent ultra-low-floor Variotram LRVs during 1996.

Adtranz Class 365 Networker Express ***1997***

Augsburg received the last of 11 GTM6 LRVs during 1996.

München had received its 70 three-phase driven 100 per cent ultra-low-floor GT6N LRVs, by the end of 1996. An order for an additional 17 second-generation LRVs is in production.

All 14 GT8N LRVs for Nürnberg were delivered in 1996. An order for a second series of 26 of the same type is in production with delivery started in 1997 and completed by 1998.

VBK Karlsruhe received its third series of 12 three-phase driven 70 per cent low-floor GT8-100D/2SN dual-voltage 750 V DC/15 kV AC LRVs in 1997.

MVV Mannheim has received all of its 50 three-phase driven Duewag LRVs, with an option for an additional 10 cars. Electrical equipment is by Adtranz.

Electrical equipment is also installed in Duewag/DWA LRVs for DVB Dresden, EVAG Erfurt, LVB Leipzig and RSAG Rostock; in 16 chopper-controlled Duewag LRVs with standard floor height for SSB; 12 three-phase drive, dual-voltage GT8100D/2SN LRVs by Duewag, with an option for 10 more, for VBK Karlsruhe.

WSB Würzburg has ordered 20 three-phase driven Variotrams, to be produced jointly by Adtranz and LHB.

DB is also taking delivery of 50 Class 611 tilting dmus during 1997.

A second contract for 50 Class 612 tilting dmus is being delivered, with completion in 1999.

Three GTWm2/6 Class 596 dmus are operating on the DB Radolfszell-Stockach line. It is operated for DB by the Swiss private railway MThB (Mittel-Thurgau Bahn). The GTWm 2/6 consists of two low-floor driving cars and a central motor car. It can be supplied for various track gauges. It has been built by Adtranz with help from DWA, Stadler of Busnang, Switzerland, Alusuisse Road and Rail and SLM, Winterthur. The dmu is intended for non-electrified suburban, regional and secondary lines.

Hungary – Debrecen is equipping its tram fleet with chopper and microprocessor control by Adtranz.

Israel – The Ports & Railway Authority contract for seven Class C3D dmus is in production and includes supply of some components by suppliers in Israel. These are intended for commuter services around Haifa and Tel Aviv but will also operate on regional lines.

The C3D dmu is a commuter trainset belonging to the Flexliner family, which also includes the IC3D dmus and IR4E dmus of DSB Denmark.

Italy – The Genova-Casella Railway has ordered two E46A emus, with the motor and trailer bogies by Adtranz.

ATM Milano has ordered 20 single-ended Eurotram 100 per cent low-floor LRVs similar to those for Strasbourg, for delivery 1998 to 2001.

FS and FNME now have contracts in production for 82 double-deck emus built by an Italian consortium led by Breda and also including Ansaldo and Firema, for Milano cross-city services. Adtranz is providing the traction motors and some motor bogies, other electrical equipment and assembly. Each train seats 475, has three-phase drive and takes overhead power at 3 kV.

Satti (Ferrovie Torino-Ceres and Ferrovia Canavesana) has been taking delivery, since 1996, of seven low-floor two-car 3 kV Class Y0530 emus. Adtranz supplied the electrical equipment, with Fiat supplying mechanical components.

Ferrovia della Sardegna has ordered three low-floor, three-phase drive emus, in addition to two powered cars already received, with electrical equipment and motor bogies from Adtranz.

Torino-Ceres Railway has received four 3 kV emus. Adtranz supplied the complete electrical equipment, Fiat the bogies and mechanical equipment.

The Trento-Malè Railway has one further Type E86 emu on order in addition to four delivered in 1996. The emu has motor bogies by Adtranz.

Sardinian Railways has, since the end of 1996, been taking delivery of diesel electric Class ADe91 driving motor cars, each with two engines. Included in the order are five Class RPe902 trailer cars. They are operating on the 950 mm gauge lines in the Cagliari area.

Japan – Kumamoto is taking delivery of a three-phase driven 100 per cent ultra-low-floor LRV in 1997. Adtranz is supplying the traction systems, control and auxiliary systems, and bogies, in co-operation with Niigata, Japan.

Korea – SMG Seoul has received its order for 366 cars for the Seoul metro, of which 183 are powered. They are assembled by Hyundai Precision Industries, with propulsion systems by Adtranz. SMG exercised its option for 242 additional vehicles in 1994 and final delivery was in 1996.

Malaysia – Kuala Lumpur's STAR light rail transit system

BART emu refurbished by Adtranz ***1997***

Adtranz LRV in Izmir ***1997***

started operation on its first 9.5 km section in February 1996; the 34 LRVs were supplied by Adtranz. Construction of Phase 2 started in late 1996, and will include delivery of 56 LRVs by 1998.

Norway – NSB has ordered 16 emus for the new line between Oslo and its airport at Gardermoen, now in production. A development of the Swedish X2000 high-speed tilting train, these sets have a power rating of 2,645 kW, a maximum speed of 220 km/h and will consist of three cars with a total seating capacity of 184. Deliveries of first trains were expected by the end of 1997 and the contract schedule calls for completion by 1998. One of the trains is being equipped with an active tilting system to negotiate curves with higher speeds without interfering with passenger comfort. An option exists for adding this specification to the other 15 trainsets on order.

Philippines – LRTA Manila has awarded the contract for an extension of LRT Line 1 to a consortium led by Adtranz, Sweden, also including ABB Power Philippines and Marubeni Corporation. The existing two-car LRV sets are being enlarged to three-car sets and the 28 new airconditioned LRVs will operate in four-car sets, with project completion in 1998.

Portugal – Adtranz Portugal (formerly Sorefame) has supplied 10 four-car emus to CP Portugal in addition to 42 already supplied. A further seven two-car demus have been supplied to CP. Carris Lisboa has taken delivery of four LRVs and 38 ML980 metro trainsets.

Spain – CAF and ABB Daimler-Benz Transportation companies are involved in the following contracts with:
FGC Barcelona, which has received 16 four-car Class S/213 LRVs with three power cars plus one intermediate trailer. An additional 20 four-car trains are in production, with delivery starting in 1997.

RENFE, has increased its three-phase driven suburban UT447 fleet with a second series of 46 trains. Including the first series of 71 trains, this now brings the total fleet to 117 sets. RENFE is also taking delivery of 19 IR2D Flexliners for the Vigo–Santiago–La Coruña line in northern Spain.

CTB Bilbao, which in early 1996 received the last of 24 trainsets for the metro, is increasing its length from 26 to 40 km and will be ordering new trains. CAF of Spain produced the mechanical components of the power cars and Adtranz companies in Spain and Switzerland provided the electrical equipment.

Metro Madrid has specified Adtranz electrical equipment in a further 50 two-car sets. It has also ordered Adtranz traction equipment for 63 vehicles, with delivery between 1997 and 1998.

Sweden – Regional transport authorities Blekings Länstrafik and Kristianstad Långstraffik, Southern Sweden, took delivery of a Y2 Flexliner diesel trainset in 1997. Adtranz Denmark manufactured the trains while the plant in Sweden supplied the computer control system. The Y2 trains are similar to the Danish IC3 trains.

Regional operators, Kalmar Läns Trafik AB and AB Östgötatrafiken, took delivery of five Y2 Flexliner trainsets in 1996.

The SL Stockholm contract for 75 six-car articulated metro emus is at delivery stage. They are three-phase driven, with 2.5 times the passenger capacity of the present stock and will replace 200 of the oldest cars. The sets are designed for driverless operation and will be equipped with advanced passenger information systems.

Switzerland – Biel-Täuffelen-Ins Railway of the Oberaargau-Solothurn-Seeland Transport Group (OSST) and the Chemins de Fer Electrique Veveysans (CEV) of the Montreux-Oberland-Bernois (MOB) Railway Group are taking delivery of 11 GTW Be2/6 low-floor metre-gauge articulated LRVs, with final delivery in 1998. Seven, with an additional central spare module, will go to BTI.

The Mittel-Thurgau Bahn has ordered 10 GTW Be2/6 emus for the Radolfszell-Stockach line from Adtranz/ Stadler.

Rorschah-Heiden Railway (RHB) has ordered a BDeh3/6 low-floor rack railcar with electrical equipment by Adtranz, bogies by SLM and bodyshell from Stadler.

VBZ Zürich has ordered 17 low-floor five-section Cobra LRVs from a Swiss consortium comprising SWP, Adtranz and Fiat-SIG, with six being delivered by 1999. VBZ plans to have 74 in service by 2013.

Chemin de Fer des Montagnes Neuchâteloises, a metre-gauge regional railway in the Jura mountain area, ordered an additional BD4/4 1.5 kV DC power car by 'Vevey' Technologies and Adtranz in Switzerland.

SBB is taking delivery of 20 additional S-Bahn trains in production with a consortium which includes ABB Daimler-Benz Transportation, SLM, Fiat-SIG and Schindler. Each train consists of a three-phase drive locomotive, two double-deck intermediate passenger cars and one driving trailer.

Rhaetian Railway (RhB) is modernising its chopper-controlled Be4/4 emu motor cars and trailer cars with new power and control systems.

TSOL Lausanne has received five additional standard gauge chopper-controlled articulated LRVs, with mechanical parts from 'Vevey' Technologies and electrical equipment from ABB Daimler-Benz Transportation, Switzerland. All TSOL units have an auxiliary diesel engine to enable them to travel on SBB tracks. The first-series LRVs have been overhauled by 'Vevey' and Adtranz.

Chemin de Fer Fribourgois Gruyère-Fribourg Môat is taking delivery of two additional BDe4/4 metre-gauge motor cars, for passenger work and for hauling freight wagons. Power is taken at 800 V DC.

Turkey – The Izmir turnkey contract for a 9.2 km light rail line built by ABB Daimler-Benz Transportation (Sweden) is at delivery stage. Delivery of the 45 six-axle LRVs started in 1996 and was due to end mid-1997. First services were expected to be running in mid-1997.

United Kingdom – Chiltern Railways has ordered four three-car Class 166 dmus, and the contract includes maintenance of the existing fleet.

Connex South Eastern and West Anglia Great Northern have taken delivery of 164 cars formed into four-car Networker Express Class 365 sets for outer suburban services. These dual voltage cars (25 kV AC and 750 V DC) have a top speed of 160 km/h and a medium-density interior layout, designed to meet the needs of longer journeys to outer suburbs.

ABB Daimler-Benz Transportation, Customer Support Ltd, Derby, has carried out repair and refurbishing contracts on passenger cars, multiple units, metro trains and LRVs, including:
33 small-profile metro cars for Strathclyde PTE (Glasgow Underground Railway), all of which have now been delivered.

USA – ABB Daimler-Benz Transportation (USA) Inc is involved in contracts with:
MTA Maryland, for an additional 18 LRVs for the Baltimore light rail line, being delivered by AAI Corporation and Knorr Brake in 1997.
SEPTA, which is taking delivery of 222 stainless steel, heavy emu cars with three-phase drive. These provide motor car/driving trailer sets for the Market–Frankford line in Philadelphia. Delivery was due to start in 1997 with completion at the end of 1998.
BART San Francisco, which has a contract to refurbish 200 out of 439 cars for delivery between 1997 and 1999.

Developments

A new tilting system, neicontrol®, has been developed. It is electrically operated and inclination to a maximum of eight per cent is achieved through a servo system designed by Extel Systems Wedel (ESW). Tilt speed is limited to about 4°/s.

Adtranz Train Maintenance Services Division, Chart Leacon, England, was awarded an Investors in People award at the beginning of 1997.

UPDATED

AeroTrans

AeroTrans
2001 Salt Lake City, UT 84116, USA
Telephone: +1 801 322 3616 Fax: +1 801 322 3803
Marketing Director: Clarke B Lium

Products: People mover bodyshells – composite fibreglass bodywork; turnkey operations. Railway coaches – interior fittings, including doors, panels, toilets, floors and bulkheads for rapid transit cars.

Contracts: Nine two-car bodyshells have been delivered to Bombardier for service in Jacksonville, USA.

Other contracts include a six-vehicle Otis Elevator people mover for Getty Center, USA; four three-car vehicles for Senate Subway, Washington DC; six vehicles for people mover at Tampa Airport, USA.

UPDATED

AeroTrans car ***1995***

Bombardier Prorail

Bombardier Prorail Ltd
Horbury, Wakefield WF4 5QH, England
Telephone: +44 1924 271881 Fax: +44 1924 274650
A subsidiary of Bombardier Eurorail (qv)
Managing Director: Ralph W Bennett
Sales & Marketing Director: Colin S Walton
Engineering Director: Tony Brown
Financial Director: Keith R Brown
Operations Director: Anthony Booth

Products: Development, design, engineering, refurbishment, sales, service of rolling stock, including locomotives, emus, dmus, metro cars, bogies, light rail vehicles, GLT, freight wagons and general engineering.

Contracts: Refurbishment of 522 Piccadilly line cars for London Underground; refurbishment of Class 155 dmu fleet for West Yorkshire PTE under contract to Porterbrook Leasing; supply of works wagons for Ankara metro; and engineers' wagons for London Underground's Jubilee line extension project.

Supply of 24 LRVs for Tramlink Croydon, England. Bombardier Eurorail is a member of Tramtrack Croydon Ltd (TCL). TCL is financing, designing, constructing and will operate and maintain the line linking Croydon with Wimbledon, Beckenham, New Addington and Elmers End.

A contract for the refurbishment of 381 Mk II passenger coaches has been awarded by Eversholt Leasing, UK.

UPDATED

London Underground Piccadilly line car refurbished by Bombardier Prorail ***1997***

Breda

Breda Costruzioni Ferroviarie SpA
110B Via Ciliegiole, 51100 Pistoia, Italy
Telephone: +39 573 3701 Fax: +39 573 370292
Chairman: Dr Luigi Roth
Director General, Breda Group: Dr Ing Corrado Fici
Director General: Dr Ing Roberto Cai
Business Development Director: Dr Ing Claudio Mannucci
Mass Transit Business Development Director:
Dr Ing Claudio Fumigalli

USA subsidiary
Breda Transportation Inc
261 Madison Avenue, 28th Floor, New York, NY 10016-2303, USA
Telephone: +1 212 286 8000 Fax: +1 212 286 0700
Manager, Project Development: Lucia Di Meglio

Background: The company dates from 1886, when Ernesto Breda took over the steam locomotive manufacturer L'Elvetica. The group was reorganised in 1994, with management of the seven production activities being centralised in Breda Construzioni Ferroviarie.

Products: Metro cars and light rail vehicles, dual-mode buses, trolleybuses (qv).

Contracts: The first of 52 articulated LRVs for Muni San Francisco entered service in 1996. They have stainless steel bodywork, two motor bogies, inverter propulsion system, eight passenger doors, air conditioning and automatic couplers

An order was received in 1996 for construction jointly with Firema and Ansaldo (qv), of 19 three-section articulated cars for the automated mini-metro in København. Each car is 39 m in length, has 96 seats and space for 252 standing.

New metro cars and refurbished cars have been delivered to the Washington metro, USA; 30 cars for the Los Angeles metro with stainless steel bodies, plus option for a further 42; 32 cars for Lima metro, Peru; 60 cars for Napoli metro; 82 motor cars and 38 trailers for Roma metro.

MTA Los Angeles took delivery of 42 double-deck Metrolink cars in 1996-97.

Thirty-three single-ended articulated LRVs for Ankara have been built with two motor bogies, chopper control, eight doors and driver's cab.

A fleet of 60 double-deck emu power cars and 90 double-deck trailer cars is being delivered to FS Italy during 1997/98; seven diesel railcars were supplied to the Apulo-Lucane Railway in 1996.

UPDATED

Breda-built Muni LRV in San Francisco  ***1997***

Breda-built single-ended LRV for Ankara ***1997***

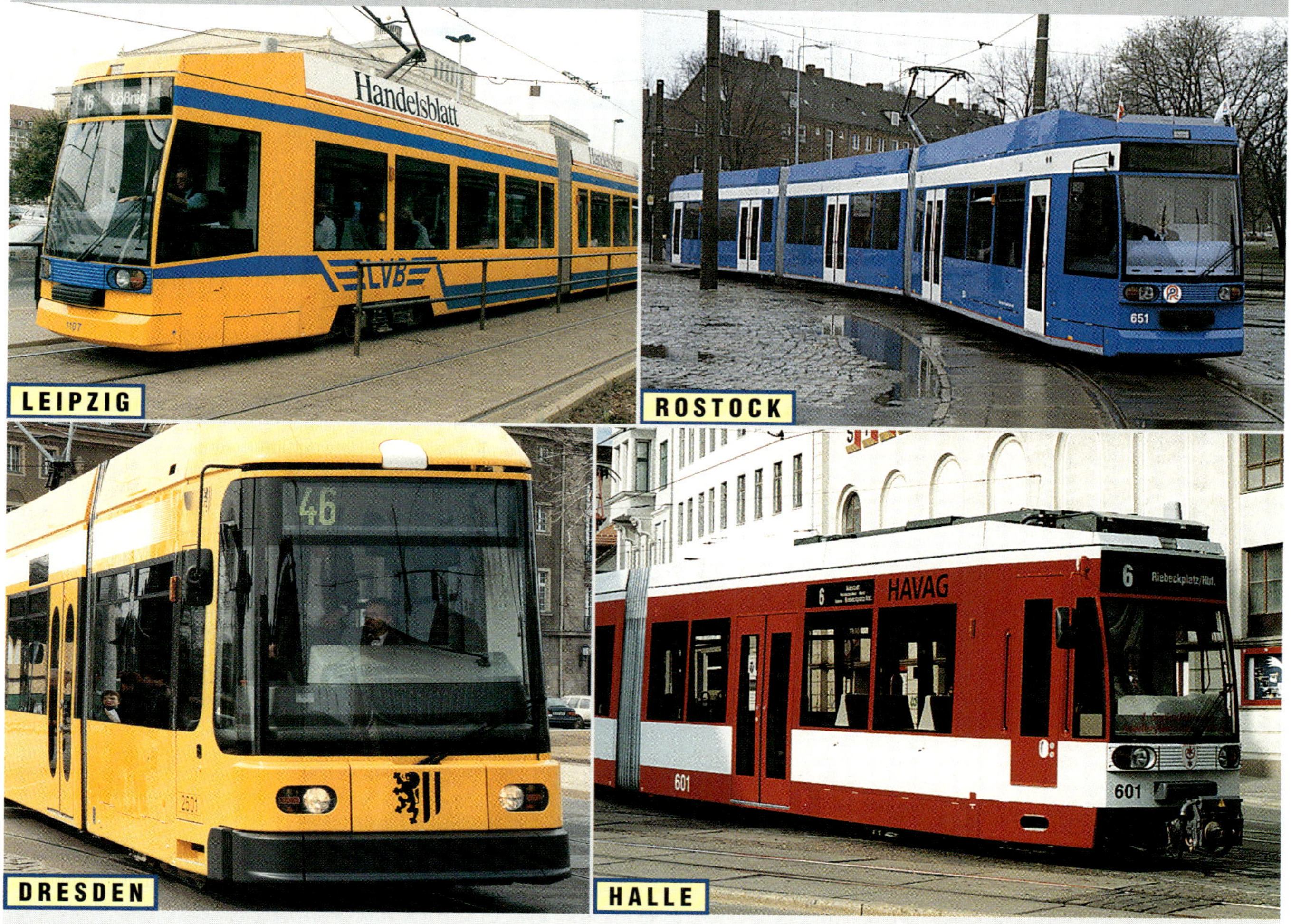

Brush

Brush Traction
A member of the FKI Group
PO Box 17, Loughborough LE11 1HS, England
Telephone: +44 1509 617000 Fax: +44 1509 617001
Director & General Manager: Alun L Williams
Sales Manager: Peter L Needham

Background: Brush Electrical Engineering was founded in 1889. Today the company is a major supplier of electric propulsion equipment and is able to undertake the refurbishment of complete vehicles or components.

Products: Complete AC and DC propulsion packages, including traction motors and control equipment, locomotive servicing and refurbishment.

Contracts: Brush has supplied traction equipment for London Docklands cars built in Belgium by BN. Also involved in supply of traction equipment based on GTO technology for London Underground's Central line cars, built by ABB Transportation.

Twenty-one battery-electric locomotives have recently been supplied to MTRC Hong Kong.

UPDATED

London Docklands light rail cars with Brush traction equipment

---

BWS

Bombardier-Wien Schienenfahrzeuge AG
Donaufelderstrasse 73-79, 1210 Wien, Austria
Telephone: +43 1 259 46100 Fax: +43 1 259 46107
Managing Director: Dr Hubert C Dlaska
Financial Director: Dipl-Bw Wilhelm J Borghans
Director, Operations: Dipl Ing Ernst Neckhfralm
Director, Engineering: Dr Michael Petz
Manager, Domestic Sales: Wilhelm Bachmayer

Background: The company is a subsidiary of Bombardier Eurorail and is derived from the former Lohner company which was founded in 1823. The present company dates from 1970 when it was acquired together with Rotax Werke GmbH by Bombardier, Canada. In 1991 it was incorporated into the Bombardier Eurorail group (qv).

Products: Light rail vehicles (standard and low-floor, 1,435 mm, metre and 900 mm gauge), diesel railcars, dual-voltage and hybrid-drive trains and rolling stock components.

Contracts: Include 68 partially low-floor metro cars (Type T) for Wien Transport for the U6 metro line; 80 low-floor K4000 LRVs for Köln, Germany, with Bombardier Eurorail as the contractor.

BWS is manufacturing the basic modules for 15 LRVs for Saarbrücken, Germany, which are then finally assembled at BN, Belgium (qv). Each LRV carries 243 with 96 seated and air conditioning is fitted in the intermediate car and in the driver's cab.

BWS dual-voltage Saarbrücken Supertram LRV ***1997***

Developments: In co-operation with BN, BWS is producing the Cityrunner low-floor LRV for standard or metre-gauge and able to negotiate curves of very small radius. The modular configuration consists of three or four running sections connected by bridge sections. It can run on railway and/or tramway tracks.

UPDATED

CAF

Construcciones y Auxiliar de Ferrocarriles SA
J M Iturrioz 26, 20200 Beasain-Guipúzcoa, Spain
Telephone: +34 43 880100 Fax: +34 43 881420
President: José María Baztarrica Garijo
Chairman & Chief Executive Officer:
José María Baztarrica Garijo
General Managing Directors: Alejandro Legarda
Andrés Arizcorreta

Products: Electric and diesel-electric multiple-units, metro cars, passenger coaches, light rail vehicles, all types of powered and trailing bogies.

Contracts: A further 46 Series 447 air conditioned three-car emus for RENFE suburban services are being supplied, in addition to the 71 already in service. Also being delivered are 16 dmus for RENFE regional services. These units have air conditioning and they are being assembled jointly by CAF and Adtranz, using Flex-Liner technology. A fleet of 16 Series 112 four-car emus have been supplied to FGC Barcelona with three-phase traction and aluminium bodies. CAF/Adtranz/GEC Alsthom are supplying 20 Series 213 three-car emus to

Hong Kong airport cars being assembled by CAF ***1997***

FGC Barcelona Spain. CAF is also building 37 LRVs for GVB Amsterdam. Each articulated car is 31 m long and seats 62 with 182 standing. They are for Amsterdam's Ring Sneltram line which partially opened in 1997. The complete line is due to open in 2002. Four S3 cars have pantograph and third-rail current collectors while 33 M4 cars are third rail only. Three-phase electrical equipment is being supplied by Holec Ridderkerk.

The rolling stock for MTRC Hong Kong's new airport railway is being built by CAF, comprising 11 high-specification seven-car sets for the Airport Express Line and 12 eight-car sets for the Lantau line. Both trains have air conditioned cars with aluminium bodies.

CAF has also built 14 four-car sets for London's Heathrow Express link, in association with Siemens Transportation Systems.

STC Mexico has ordered 78 FM95A motor cars, which will be supplied jointly by CAF and Bombardier.

An order has been placed by Metro de Madrid for 63 Series 2000 two-car emus. They will have air conditioning, CCTV, a central diagnostic system and new interior and exterior design.

CAF and GEC Alsthom are assembling 12 Series 2000 motor cars and five five-car Series 2100 sets for Barcelona Metro.

UPDATED

CCC

Changchun Car Company
5 Qingyin Road, Changchun, Jilin 130062, People's Republic of China
Telephone: +86 431 712934/702380
Fax: +86 431 293 8740
General Manager: Ma Shu-kun
Commercial Manager: Teng Mao-gen
Technical Director: Guang Ming-quan

Background: CCC is the largest Chinese manufacturer of passenger coaches and urban transit vehicles. It is owned by the Chinese Railway Ministry and employs 15,000. It produces 1,200 passenger coaches a year.

Products: Passenger coaches, metro cars.

Contracts: CCC supplied the rolling stock for the Beijing and Tianjin metros, and also exported a batch of cars for the Pyongyang metro, North Korea. The works is currently supplying further orders for Beijing, including a fleet of cars for Line 2 of the Tehran metro in 1996.

The latest metro design is the DK20 wide-body set, consisting of two driving motor cars and four non-driving trailer cars, for 750 V DC third-rail operation; each car is 19 m long, 3.51 m high and 2.8 m wide. Orders have been received from Tehran and Beijing.

CCC DK20 wide-body set **1995**

Developments: In 1997 Adtranz (qv) and Changchun established a joint venture for the production of urban transport rolling stock. It is called the Changchun Car Company and Adtranz owns 51 per cent with CCC owning the remaining 49 per cent. The company is focusing on local manufacturing, assembly and testing of metro cars, LRVs and multiple units as well as carbody shells. Annual production capacity is planned for 160 vehicles.

UPDATED

ČKD

ČKD Dopravní Systémy as
Ringhofferova 115/1, 15500 Praha 5, Czech Republic
Telephone: +420 2 6603 5664 Fax: +420 2 6603 7173
Managing Director: Josef Bouda
Technical Director: Jiří Němeček
Commercial department: Českomoravská 205, 19005 Praha 9
Telephone: +420 2 6603 8200 Fax: +420 2 6603 8801

Background: Founded in 1852 to build horse-drawn trams, production of rail vehicles began in Praha at the turn of the century. By 1980 up to 1,000 trams a year were being built. The name of the factory was changed to ČKD Tatra and in 1996 yet another name change took place when Transportation Systems Group was incorporated. It combines ČKD Tatra, ČKD Trakce and ČKD Lokomotiva.

Products: Tramcars and LRVs, bogies, traction motors, current collection equipment, general overhauls and refurbishment; consulting services.

RT6S low-floor tramcar **1997**

T3R tramcar **1997**

RT6N low-floor tramcar **1997**

Contracts
T3R tram: 110 to Praha, Ostrava, Brno, Izhevsk and other cities.
T6A2 tram: 20 to Szeged.
T6A5 tram: 120 to Ostrava, Brno, Praha and Bratislava.
T6B5 tram: 30 have been ordered by Tula, Odesa and Tashkent.
T7B5 tram: 20 have been ordered by Odesa.
KT4 tram: 20 have been ordered by Beograd.
RT6N: 35 of these low-floor articulated LRVs have been ordered by Praha, Brno, Poznan, Gdansk and other cities.
RT8M: 73 of these articulated LRVs have been ordered by Manila, Philippines.

Developments: An M1 metro car prototype has been constructed for Praha; aluminium alloy bodywork and framing is being developed; a high-speed tilting train is being developed in partnership with Fiat, Siemens and MSV.

UPDATED

Tatra T6A5 tramcar
1997

Clyde

Clyde Engineering Motive Power Division
Factory Street, Granville, PO Box 73, NSW 2142, Australia
Telephone: +61 29 637 8288 Fax: +61 29 897 2174
Group General Manager: J G Hanson
Manager, National & Export Sales: K C Thomson
Manager, Engineering Design & Development:
D E Butters

Background: Founded in 1893, the company is licensed to build General Motors EMD designs in Australia.

Products: Diesel and electric locomotives and multiple-units; traction motors; bogies; electronic control systems; speed control and monitoring units.

Contracts: Supplied traction motors and bogies for the New South Wales Tangara emu contract. Also built diesel-electric railcars for Adelaide suburban services.

CMI

Cockerill Mechanical Industries
1 avenue Greiner, 4100 Seraing, Belgium
Telephone: +32 4 330 2446 Fax: +32 4 330 2502
Managing Director: L Levaux
Sales Director: J F Levaux

Background: CMI became an independent subsidiary of Cockerill Sambre in 1982.

Products: Included in the company's range of shunting locomotives is a dual-mode (traction power or onboard battery) locomotive specially designed for maintenance and rescue work on metro and rapid transit lines.

UPDATED

Costamasnaga

Costamasnaga SpA
Piazza 4 Novembre, 22041 Como, Italy
Telephone: +39 31 869411 Fax: +39 31 855330
Managing Director: F Magni
Sales Manager: G Felten

Background: Costamasnaga started building rolling stock in 1924. The company traditionally concentrated on freight but since 1980 has been constructing passenger cars. Since 1989 its technical department has been designing new vehicles for urban transport.

Products: Metro car bodies, light rail vehicles, tramcars.

UPDATED

Crompton Greaves

Crompton Greaves Ltd
1 Dr V B Gandhi Marg, Bombay 400 023, India
Telephone: +91 22 202 8025

Rail Projects Division, Vandhna 11, Tolstoy Marg, New Delhi 110 001, India
Telephone: +91 11 331 5071/7075
Fax: +91 11 332 4360
Managing Director: K K Nohria
President, Industrial Systems: C P Dusad
Vice President, Rail Transportation: B Bannerjee
Deputy General Manager, Rail Transportation:
M P Singhal

Products: AC and DC traction motors; AC and DC auxiliary motors; brushless alternators; rail vehicles, thyristor electrical equipment, track maintenance vehicle.

Developments: Three-phase electric equipment for emus and locomotives has been developed.

UPDATED

Daewoo

Daewoo Heavy Industries Ltd
Rolling Stock Plant, 462-18, Sam-Dong, Euiwang-Shi, Kyunggi-Do, Republic of Korea
Telephone: +82 343 60 1114 Fax: +82 343 61 1913
Executive Managing Director: Joon-Koo Chung

Sales Office: Daewoo Centre Building 23rd Floor, 541, 5-Ga, Namdaemoon-Ro, Chung-Gu, Seoul, Republic of Korea
Telephone: +82 2 726 3177/9
Fax: +82 2 726 3186/756 2679
Sales Director: Soo-Hwan Kim

Daewoo-built emu delivered to Seoul for metro Lines 7 and 8
1997

Background: Founded in 1937, the present company dates from a 1973 decision to create a major South Korean rolling stock manufacturing industry. Daewoo has supplied over 15,000 rail vehicles to domestic and other customers.

Products: Locomotives, passenger coaches, diesel multiple-units, electric multiple-units and components.

Contracts: Include 200 emu cars for the Incheon Subway Authority; 226 emu cars for Seoul metro lines 7 and 8, delivered in 1996 (equipped with ATO/ATC, stainless steel bodyshells, mounted on bolsterless air sprung bogies, longitudinal seating for up to 54 in each car, with 106 standing); 344 cars for the Taiwan Railway Administration.

Developments: The 1992 prototype Maglev railcar for up to 40 passengers has been updated with the construction of two further Maglev cars carrying 120, due for completion in late 1998.

UPDATED

Daewoo-built emu delivered to Taiwan Railway Administration
1997

De Dietrich

De Dietrich Ferroviaire
PO Box 35, Reichshoffen 67891, Niederbronn, France
Telephone: +33 3 88 80 25 00 Fax: +33 3 88 80 25 12
Email: ddf@dx.net.fr
President: Michel Perricaudet
General Manager: Jean-Marie Bucher
Sales Manager: Daniel Sprauer

Products
TER: This is a railbus for suburban or regional lines for relatively short distances. It is of modular construction, seating up to 79, with 81 standing, and with a cab at each end. A two-car version has a maximum seating capacity of 160. A three-car option is available. The railbus has a top speed of 140 km/h.
TLP: This is a guided light transit vehicle running on flanged rubber tyres. The car has three sections and takes overhead power in the same way as a normal LRV; track gauge is 1,435 mm. The vehicle is 27 m long, with a floor height of 350 mm and capacity for up to 230 passengers. (See also TLP in New Technology section and Cogifer in Track Components section.)

De Dietrich TER diesel railbus ***1997***

Contracts: A consortium consisting of De Dietrich and LHB (qv) has been awarded a contract for 80 TER diesel railcars, ordered jointly by SNCF France and DB Germany, for delivery in 1998.

UPDATED

Delaware Car

Delaware Car Company
2nd and Lombard Streets, Wilmington, DE 19899, USA
Telephone: +1 302 655 6665 Fax: +1 302 655 7126
President: Harry E Hill
Chief Engineer: J Winter
Mechanical Superintendent: L J Reed
Vice President, General Manager: T J Crowley
Marketing & Special Projects Engineer: S F Rogowski
Manufacturing Manager: R A Fausnaugh

Background: Established in 1983.

Products: Refurbishment, repair and assembly of passenger rolling stock, including metro, suburban and commuter cars. Specialities include stainless steel parts fabrication and bogie repair and overhaul.

Contracts: Is carrying out structural repairs to 12 BART cars for Adtranz, in conjunction with the current refurbishment programme; structural repairs to a Blue Line articulated car for MTA Los Angeles; North Carolina DoT – refurbishment of five passenger cars and one lounge car to modern standards including a complete interior upgrade to ADA compliance, bogie rebuilding for high-speed operation, complete carbody restoration and addition of 480 V AC head end power supply; repair and refurbishment of the roofs of 50 Silver commuter cars for SEPTA Philadelphia; structural repairs to an aluminium-bodied car for Connecticut DoT.

UPDATED

SEPTA Broad Street metro car (left) and BART car under repair at Delaware Car

Djuro Djaković

Djuro Djaković
PO Box 105, Njegoševa 1, 55000 Slavonski Brod, Croatia
Telephone: +385 55 241926 Fax: +385 55 232007

Products: Diesel multiple-units and railcars; light rail vehicles and trams including eight-axle double-articulated LRV, with low-floor option.

Contracts: Four Series 9700 Djuro Djaković railcars have been rebuilt by a local bus manufacturer for the new light rail service linking Mirandela and Carvalhais, Portugal.

Articulated tram on trial with ZET Zagreb

Duewag

Duewag AG
PO Box 102153, 40012 Düsseldorf, Germany
Telephone: +49 211 98440 Fax: +49 211 984 4205
Board of Management: Josef Gerstner (Chair), Wirtsch, Bernd Schmidtchen
Director, Light Rail, Engineering: Karl Engemann
Director, Light Rail, Commercial: Klaush Alisch

PO Box 466, 47815 Krefeld
Telephone: +49 2151 4501 Fax: +49 2151 450214
Director, Main Line, Engineering: Werner Wabnitz
Director, Main Line, Commercial: Rudolf Mainka

Background: Major shareholder is Siemens Schienenfahrzeug. The company produces light rail rolling stock and associated products at the Düsseldorf works, and main line stock (including S-Bahn cars) at Krefeld.

Products: Cars for full metro and pre-metro systems; light rail vehicles with conventional and low floor; bogies; reinforced glassfibre components; interior fittings; advanced transport systems.

Contracts: Duewag is a member of the German Shanghai Metro Group responsible for equipping Line 1 of the Shanghai metro. The contract specified supply of 16 six-car trains.

Cities which have placed orders with Duewag include Köln, Bonn, Frankfurt, Düsseldorf, Duisburg, Dortmund, Essen, Kassel, Freiburg, Edmonton, Calgary, Pittsburgh, Sacramento, San Diego and Rotterdam. Recent contracts include supply of LRVs to Stuttgart, Köln, Bochum, Düsseldorf, Bonn, Karlsruhe and St Louis.

Duewag has supplied bogies for the Hong Kong Mass Transit Corporation and Kowloon-Canton Railway cars built by GEC Alsthom Metro Cammell; and more than 1,000 bogies for Singapore's Phase I and II metro cars.

Further low-floor cars have been ordered by Heidelberg, Bonn, Mannheim, Ludwigshafen, Erfurt, Leipzig, Dresden and Halle. Portland, Oregon, is the first US conurbation to run low-floor cars with AC drives.

Duewag supplied 20 centre sections to Dortmunder Stadwerke for lengthening of its Stadtbahn B80C LRVs, and 20 GT6-70D/N low- floor LRVs have been supplied to Karlsruhe.

Dürener Kreisbahn, Germany, has taken delivery of 16 diesel LRVs for its local services. A further 14 LRVs have been ordered by Tunis.

Duewag and Kiepe (qv) are constructing 59 low-floor trailers for Düsseldorf.

Developments: A low-floor diesel LRV has been developed for lightly used lines. It has four axles and is double-articulated; the low floor is between the two outer axles, the two axles over the centre section having smaller wheels. There is seating in the high-floor sections for around 30 and around 50 in the low-floor sections. It was designed as a result of studies by the German Association of Transport Operators (VoV).

The Combino ultra-low-floor tram was announced in 1996 and construction costs are reduced by 30 per cent through standardisation. Up to five body modules and off-the-shelf seating and door systems can be specified.

The floor height is 300 mm, and 1,000 mm or 1,435 mm gauge versions can be supplied.

RegioSprinter on the Dürener Kreisbahn ***1996***

UPDATED

DWA

Deutsche Waggonbau AG
Adlergestell 598, 12527 Berlin, Germany
Telephone: +49 30 67930 Fax: +49 30 6744560
Board Chairman: Peter Witt
Board Members, Marketing: Siegfried Möbius, T Walter Grawenhoff

Plants
Werk Ammendorf
Merseburger Strasse 377, 06132 Halle
Telephone: +49 345 4650 Fax: +49 345 7758431
Werk Bautzen
Fabrikstrasse 41, 02625 Bautzen
Telephone: +49 3591 3620 Fax: +49 3591 362881
Werk Görlitz GmbH
Brunnenstrasse 11, 02826 Görlitz
Telephone: +49 3581 330 Fax: +49 3581 405189
Werk Vetschau – bogies
Juri-Gagarin Strasse, 03226 Vetschau
Telephone: +49 354 33520 Fax: +49 354 332193

DWA double-deck driving trailer for DB ***1996***

Subsidiary companies
FAGA – electrical equipment for rail vehicles
Fahrzeugausrüstung Berlin GmbH
Andreasstrasse 71-73, 10243 Berlin
Telephone: +49 30 27440 Fax: +49 30 2792038
Managing Director: Jürgen Schmidt

IFS
Institut für Schienenfahrzeuge GmbH
Adlergestell 598, 12527 Berlin
Telephone: +49 30 679 32200 Fax: +49 30 679 32222
Managing Director: Prof Dr Uwe Ganzer

Background: DWA is the holding organisation and headquarters of four rolling stock assembly plants, two component manufacturers and a research institute for rail vehicles. In 1995, DWA was sold to US investment firm Advent International.

Products: Electric and diesel multiple-units, railcars, metro cars, LRVs, double-deck cars, powered and trailing bogies, bodyshells, overhaul of vehicles and refurbishment.

Contracts: Following orders placed in 1994/95, DB was to receive a further 121 double-deck driving trailer cars and 273 double-deck centre-entrance cars in 1996/98 with an option for a further 80 partly air conditioned cars. They have either low-floor (600 mm) or high-floor (1,150 mm) entrances.

Modernisation of 127 Tatra tramcars is being carried out for the Berlin undertaking during 1996/97.

A fleet of 13 NGT6 articulated low-floor light rail vehicles is being delivered to Rostock; 33 NGT8 LRVs are going to Leipzig; Dresden is taking 60 NGT6DD LRVs (option for 20); Erfurt is taking 5 NGTMGT6D cars; Halle is taking 35 NGTMGT6D LRVs. The NGT range has been built in co-operation with Duewag (qv) and Linke-Hofmann-Busch (qv) and the tramcars are being delivered through to 1998.

DB has ordered 100 ET481 emus for Berlin S-Bahn services, being built in co-operation with Adtranz; delivery started in 1996. An order exists for a further 400, and an option for 50, up to the year 2005.

Double-deck coaches have been supplied for service in several conurbations and regions in Germany. Each coach weighs 47 tonnes and is 26.8 m long. The composite version seats 42 first class and 81 second class. The second class cars seat 139.

Thuringia and Rhineland, Germany, have ordered three and two, respectively, diesel double-deck two-axle railbuses for use on lightly used lines. They are air conditioned and have a low-floor area and storage space for wheelchairs, cycles and prams. Each has two spiral stairways and seats 78, with 32 standing, is 16.3 m long and 4.63 m high.

Developments: In partnership with Adtranz and other companies, DWA has developed a diesel-electric railcar (GTW2/6) for lightly used lines. The double-articulated car has a low floor and an entrance 570 mm above rail level. A double-deck emu design seats from 181 (two-car version) to 532 (five-car).

DWA has also developed a diesel LRV (LVT/S) for lightly used lines. The two-axle car has a lightweight body in corrosion-resistant steel, a 600 mm wide entrance, 69 seats and a maximum speed of 100 km/h.

UPDATED

DWA LVT/S lightweight diesel railcar ***1997***

Berlin S-Bahn ET481/482 emu built by DWA ***1997***

Elin

Elin Energieanwendung GmbH
Penzinger Strasse 76, 1141 Wien, Austria
Telephone: +43 1 891000 Fax: +43 1 89100 178
Chair: Mag K Sernetz
Director of Transportation Technology: Ing P Rauter
Marketing Manager, Transportation Technology: Ing F Proksch

Subsidiary companies
Elin Motoren GmbH (EMG)
Elin Scilbahntechnik GmbH (EST)
Voith Elin Elektronik GmbH (VEE)

Products: Development, manufacture and installation of three-phase traction equipment for metros, trams, LRVs and battery-powered shunting locomotives, including water-cooled transistor (IGBT and GTO) traction inverters, microprocessor-based traction and vehicle control/monitoring systems, and water-cooled three-phase asynchronous traction motors.

IGBT traction inverter ***1996***

Elin water-cooled traction motor ***1996***

Contracts: Traction inverters with IGBT technology are being supplied to Škoda (qv).

Supply of three-phase water-cooled traction motors

and reduction gearboxes for Wien metro Line U3 trainsets; part of an order of 750 units.

Supply of high-voltage equipment, transformers and IGBT inverters for 15 dual-voltage LRVs for Saarbrüken, Germany.

Delivery of traction equipment for 150 ultra-low-floor trams for Wien, jointly developed by Elin, Siemens and SGP. The transportation technology division supplies the transistor inverters, traction motors and the microprocessor control/monitoring system for this project.

Developments: A family of water- and air-cooled IGBT inverters for urban transport and regional applications is being developed, with a rating of up to 2,000 kVA.

UPDATED

Fiat

Fiat Ferroviaria SpA
Piazza Galateri 4, 12038 Savigliano (CN), Italy
Telephone: +39 172 718333 Fax: +39 172 718306
Chair: M Pittaluga
Managing Director: G Cozza
Commercial Director: A Amoruso
Technical Director: G Gatti

Products: Suburban multiple-units, metro cars, light rail vehicles and tramcars; traction equipment for metro cars; bogies, transmissions and components.

Contracts: Supply of cars for Milano metro Line 3, and low-floor light rail vehicles for Trasporti Torinesi Torino. Also supply of bogies for Acotral Roma Line B cars, and supply of further cars for Milano metro Line 3.

Fiat railcar ***1997***

Fiat low-floor LRV ***1997***

Fourteen two-car emus are being delivered to Satti Torino during 1996/97.

UPDATED

Fiat-SIG

Fiat-SIG Schienenfahrzeuge AG
8212 Neuhausen Rhine Falls, Switzerland
Telephone: +41 52 674 7206 Fax: +41 52 674 6431
Managing Director: P Gsell
Sales Manager: Peter Huber
Public Relations Manager: Rolf Havenith

Products: Motor bogies, powered and trailing bogies.

Completely closed, airtight and noise-damping gangways. The gangways are suitable for rolling stock with screw, semi-permanent or automatic couplers.

Contracts: The first of eight low-floor middle sections with Fiat-SIG running gear was delivered to Cottbus, Germany, in 1996. Mülheim has ordered one low-floor middle section for testing.

Verkehrsbetriebe Zürich has ordered 17 Cobra trams.

An extra-wide sealed and airtight gangway for rail vehicles with large standing passenger volumes accommodates 8-10 people. The two halves can be joined manually from the outside. There are no steps or ramps. Orders for this gangway have come from RATP Paris, Roma metro and Taipei metro.

Developments: A new generation of running gear for urban transport applications has been developed.

A low-floor tram concept, the Cobra, developed together with Adtranz (qv) and Schindler (qv), has Fiat-SIG single-axle running gear. It is being built for operation on both 1,435 mm and metre-gauge track.

Running gear derived from the Cobra concept is used in the low-floor middle section of the KTNF6 tram for Cottbus, Germany.

UPDATED

SIG trailing bogie for Zürich S-Bahn trains

Fiat-SIG running gear for a Cobra tram for Zürich
1997

Firema

Firema Trasporti SpA
Viale Edison 110, 20099 Sesto, San Giovanni, Milano, Italy
Telephone: +39 2 249 4396 Fax: +39 2 262 5380
Chairman: Dr G Bono
Managing Director: Dr D Marchiorello
Export Manager: Dr M Fantini

Production plants
Officine Stanga Cittadella
OMS Works:
Corso Stati Uniti 3, 35100 Padova
Telephone: +39 49 899 6211 Fax: +39 49 899 6212
Citadella Works:
Via Rometta all'Olmo 5, 35013 Cittadella, Padova
Telephone: +39 49 597 1966 Fax: +39 49 940 0238

OCB Casaralta
Via Ferrarese 205, 40128 Bologna
Telephone: +39 51 358454 Fax: +39 51 363845

Fiore Officine Casertane
81020 S Nicola la Strada, Caserta
Telephone: +39 823 492920/493142
Fax: +39 823 466812/467691

Ercole Marelli Trazione
Viale Edison 110, 20099 Sesto S Giovanni, Milano
Telephone: +39 2 24941 Fax: +39 2 248 3508

Metalmeccanica Lucana
85050 Tito Scalo, Potenza
Telephone: +39 971 485088/485089
Fax: +39 971 485072

Retam Service:
Viale Edison 124, 20099 Sesto S Giovanni, Milano
Telephone: +39 2 249 4300 Fax: +39 2 249 4310

Other Firema Group companies
Firema Consortium
Firema Engineering Srl

Background: In 1994, the associated companies of the Firema Group were merged into one company, Firema Trasporti.

Products: Powered and trailing metro and suburban cars, light rail vehicles, double-deck cars; advanced guided transit systems.

Electro-mechanical and electronic traction equipment, chopper and inverter controlled, for locomotives, metro cars, tram and light rail vehicles, and trolleybuses; DC/DC and DC/AC static converters for auxiliary services; battery chargers; traction motors; onboard automation and supervision systems; substation equipment for AC and DC electrification.

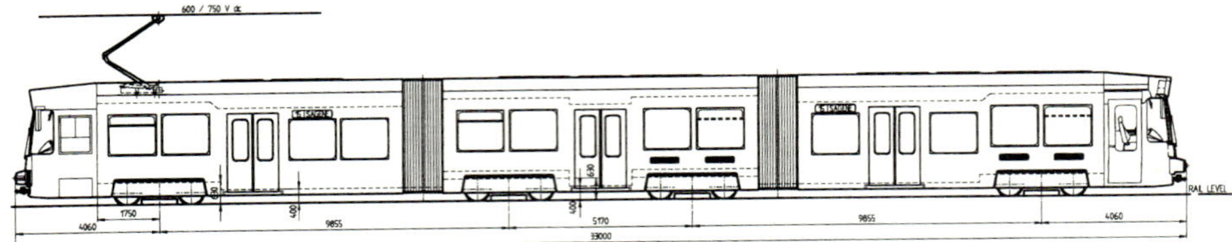

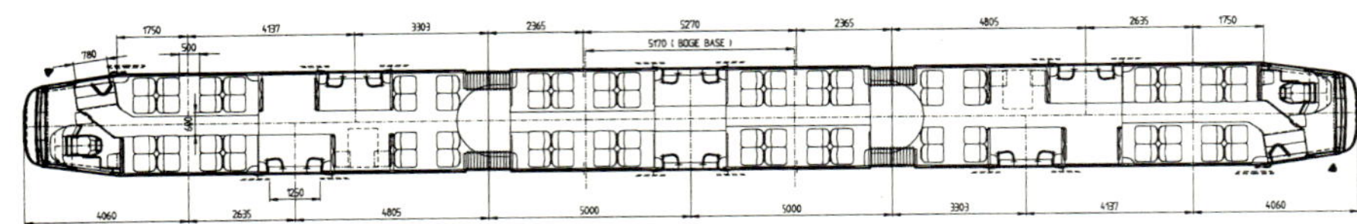

Oslo Sporveier LRV by Firema **1997**

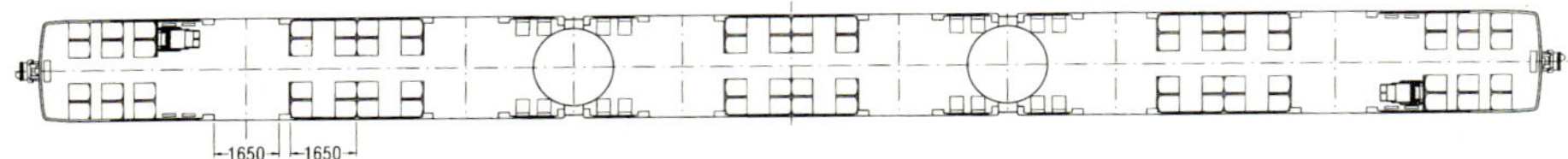

København Mini Metro cars by Firema **1997**

Contracts: Oslo Sporveier is taking delivery of 17 double-articulated low-floor LRVs with an option for 15 more. The electrical equipment is by Ansaldo Trasporti (qv).

Within the Mini Metro København turnkey project which has been assigned to Ansaldo Trasporti, Firema and Breda (qv) are supplying components for 19 vehicles.

Firema built 26 two-car LRVs for Manchester's Metrolink light rail system, 14 three-car sets for ATM Milano metro Line 3 and 8 three-car trains for Line 2. In addition, 24 low-floor trams have been delivered to ATM Torino.

Firema built 40 inverter-controlled motored cars for the Napoli metro, and 10 double-deck emus for FS and FNM Milano in consortium with other Italian companies.

Other work includes three orders for 3 kV DC trainsets — seven two-car sets for SEPSA Napoli, a further four two-car sets for Acotral's Roma—Viterbo line, and four double-articulated LRVs for the metre-gauge Trento-Malè Railway.

Firema is to be the supplier of the 16 LRVs required for Line 1 of the Midland Metro in Birmingham, England. Main contractor for the project is Ansaldo, which will supply DC chopper traction equipment with microprocessor control. The two-section articulated cars, designated Type T69, will have a low floor extending over about 60 per cent of their length, with a height at the boarding sills of 335 mm. There will be seating for 58 within a maximum capacity of 158, and space for two wheelchairs.

UPDATED

Ganz Ansaldo

Ganz Ansaldo Electric Ltd
PO Box 63, Lövöház u 39, 1024 Budapest, Hungary
Telephone: +36 1 175 3322 Fax: +36 1 156 2989
President: Dr János Barabás
Managing Director: Ing Giuseppe Fittavolini
Commercial Director: Dr M Sauli

Background: The company has developed from the electric traction division started by Ganz & Co in 1878. It was taken over by Ansaldo Trasporti (qv) in 1990.

Products: Tramcars and light rail vehicles, metro trains; electrical equipment for tramcars, LRVs, electric multiple-units and metro trains.

Contracts: An order for refurbishing 30 trams for BKV Budapest has been received. The trams will have new motor drives from Ansaldo Trasporti. The refurbishment includes a newly designed interior, new seating, improved lighting and air conditioning.

Ten articulated six-axle tramcars with chopper control and regenerative braking have gone into service with BKV Budapest.

UPDATED

Thyristor-controlled eight-axle tramcar in service with BKV Budapest

Ganz-Hunslet

Ganz-Hunslet Részvénytársaság
PO Box 29, 1430 Budapest, Hungary
Telephone: +36 1 210 1168/313 0887
Fax: +36 1 210 1175/1180
Sales Office: +36 1 210 1173
Chairman: Dr Gyula Várszegi
Executive Director: Stephen F Kostyal
Commercial Director: John A Kardos
Technical Director: Reinhard A Lemmerer
Works address: Budapest VIII, Vajda Péter ut 12

Background: Ganz-Hunslet is a shareholding company and has the goodwill and traditions of the Ganz (established 1844) and later Ganz-Mavag companies.

Products: Electric and diesel multiple-units, passenger coaches, metro cars, tramcars and LRVs, locomotives, bogies.

Contracts: A fleet of 40 unpowered commuter cars is in service with Hungarian State Railways (MAV) for locomotive-hauled or multiple-unit operation. An initial batch of power cars and driving trailers have GTO three-phase traction system supplied by ABB and entered service in 1996.

Following the successful trials of the prototype medium-floor-height (735 mm) articulated tramcar in Debrecen, the operator DKV exercised its option for a batch of 10 single-articulated units for 1996 delivery.

Ganz-Hunslet, together with Ganz Ansaldo, is refurbishing 30 Series 1300 articulated trams for BKV Budapest.

A fleet of 18 stainless steel three-car emus was delivered in 1994/95 to the Malayan Railway Administration (KTM) to operate on the newly electrified suburban lines in Kuala Lumpur. They were produced in partnership with Jenbacher Transportsysteme, a member of the JTS group.

Ganz-Hunslet is the supplier of bogies for the next batch of 22 KTM commuter emu sets being built by UCW, South Africa. An option exists for supply of bogies for a further 21 emus.

UPDATED

Ganz-Hunslet emu for Kuala Lumpur ***1995***

Ganz-Hunslet articulated tram in Debrecen ***1995***

GEC Alsthom

GEC Alsthom Transport Division
48 rue Albert Dhalenne, 93482 Saint-Ouen Cedex, Paris, France
Telephone: +33 1 41 66 90 00 Fax: +33 1 41 78 77 55
Managing Director: André Navarri
Deputy Managing Director: Michel Moreau
Web: http://www.gecalsthom.com

GEC Alsthom International
38 Avenue Kléber, 75795 Paris Cedex 16
Telephone: +33 1 47 55 20 00 Fax: +33 1 47 55 21 10/23 86

UK subsidiaries
GEC Alsthom Ltd
PO Box 70, Mill Road, Rugby CV21 1TB
Telephone: +44 1788 546600 Fax: +44 1788 546440

GEC Alsthom Infrastructure Group
PO Box 115, Rugby CV21 1ZN
Telephone: +44 1788 560630 Fax: +44 1788 552363/4

GEC Alsthom Traction Ltd
Channel Way, Preston PR1 8XL
Telephone: +44 1772 254777 Fax: +44 1772 553366
Contact: Terence Watson

GEC Alsthom Metro Cammell Ltd
PO Box 248, Birmingham B8 2YJ
Telephone: +44 121 328 5455 Fax: +44 121 695 3695
Contact: Peter Rigby

GEC Alsthom Transportation Projects Ltd
PO Box 131, Manchester M60 1AH
Telephone: +44 161 875 2358 Fax: +44 161 875 2131
Contact: Barry Howe

GEC Alsthom Railway Maintenance Services
PO Box 3799, Common Lane, Washwood Heath, Birmingham B8 2UG
Telephone: +44 121 695 3600 Fax: +44 121 695 3650

Background: GEC Alsthom was formed by the merger in 1989 of the Power Systems Division of GEC (of Great Britain) and Alsthom (France). The Division employs nearly 16,000 people in four European countries, and has sold equipment to more than 50 countries during the past 10 years. As a result of technology transfer agreements, vehicles to the company's designs have been manufactured in 20 countries. GEC Alsthom is jointly owned by General Electric Company, England and Alcatel Alsthom.

Linke-Hofmann-Busch (LHB qv) became a subsidiary company of GEC Alsthom in 1995.

A joint company, GEC Alsthom Faur Transport, was set up in 1995 following the acquisition of a majority shareholding by GEC Alsthom of the Romanian company, Faur. Faur builds rail vehicles in Romania and the joint company is refurbishing rolling stock. The GEC Alsthom Transport Division has traditionally been a manufacturer and supplier of rolling stock but has now extended its capabilities and facilities to include whole-life maintenance.

GEC Alsthom automated cars for Line D, Lyon metro
1996

has been received for Pusan metro from Hanjin Heavy Industries (qv). The order includes auxiliary converters and onboard information systems.

Mexico: An order from Bombardier Concarril and CAF has been received for 13 six-car trainsets for Mexico City Metro Line A. It is GEC Alsthom's first complete order for its new-generation ONIX traction system with AGATE electronic power control.

Spain: GEC Alsthom has won an order for the supply of 1,500 ONIX traction systems for trains on Line 2 of TMB Barcelona.

Sweden: GEC Alsthom is supplying seven four-car emus for the Arlanda Airport line which is expected to open in 1999.

United Kingdom: London Underground Ltd (LUL) has taken delivery of 106 six-car trainsets for the Northern line, on a lease/maintain basis. LUL is also taking delivery of 59 six-car trainsets for the new Jubilee line extension.

Developments: An agreement to acquire the Canadian company AMF from Canadian National Railways was announced in 1996. AMF specialised in maintenance and refurbishment of rolling stock, locomotives and coaches. Its subsidiary Geo Railmex, which specialises in diesel locomotive refurbishment, is operating in Mexico.

A co-operation agreement was signed in 1996 with Mitsubishi Electric (qv) concerning rail transport electrical equipment activities. The agreement covers joint development of systems and products, exchange of technology and mutual procurement of components.

GEC Alsthom has been selected by the European Union to lead a research and development programme to devise and develop a European Rail Traffic Management System.

Citadis is the name of a new modular tram for both standard and metre gauge. The ultra-low-floor Citadis has a floor height of 350 mm and bogies with single-wheel hub motors. The floor is raised over the more traditional bogies and the body construction is aluminium alloy panels on steel frames. The bogie design has been bought in from LHB (qv) and specifies GEC's ONIX asynchronous traction motor. Varying widths can be specified from 2.2 m upwards and the maximum length is 30 m (five sections).

An order for 28 has been received for Line 1 of Montpellier's future tram system. Each tram carries 271 and the fleet is scheduled for delivery in December 1998 for full service operation in 2000.

GEC Alsthom M12N Eole train ***1997***

An emu for British train operating companies has been unveiled. Named Juniper, the bodyshell is to the same design as Networker but slightly narrower to allow universal route availability. It can take power from third rail or overhead and has a top speed of 160 km/h. The four-car set consists of two driving motor and two trailer composite cars and seats 246 in 2+2 configuration. It will be built at GEC's Metro Cammell works, Birmingham. An order for eight Juniper sets (eight-car formation) has been received for the London Victoria–Gatwick Airport service.

UPDATED

GE Transportation Systems

GE Transportation Systems
2901 East Lake Road, Erie, PA 16531, USA
Telephone: +1 814 875 5385 Fax: +1 814 875 3154
General Manager, Transit Business Operations:
E H Orzetti
Manager, Transit Sales: D R Phelps
Marketing Specialist: B A Young

Products: Electro-mechanical and solid state DC cam and AC inverter propulsion systems; PWM rectifier AC/AC propulsion systems; phase controlled AC/DC propulsion systems; auxiliary systems including static converters and inverters.

Contracts: Include delivery of 80 carsets of auxiliary power equipment for BART San Francisco; 298 carsets of AC propulsion equipment for WMATA Washington cars; and 29 carsets of AC propulsion equipment for MUCTC Montreal; 77 AC powered carsets and auxiliary power equipment for Muni San Francisco; and 74 carsets, with AC power, for MTA Los Angeles.

UPDATED

Gevisa

Gevisa SA
Transit Area, Av Mofarrej, 592 CEP 05311-000, São Paulo SP, Brazil
Telephone: +55 11 261 4769
Fax: +55 11 260 0941/9605
Commercial Director: Ronald H Moriyama
Industrial Manager: João T Gemma
Commercial Manager: Carlos E Teixeira

Background: Villares, General Electric do Brasil and Safra Bank set up a joint venture in 1992 to take over the electric traction equipment business of Industrias Villares.

Products: Electric traction motors, auxiliary power and control equipment for metro cars, electric multiple-unit trains and light rail vehicles; motor generator sets for emus; rehabilitation of control equipment and traction motors.

Contracts: Include an order for the supply of 23 sets of traction equipment (camshaft control) for refurbishment of Series 101 cars for CPTM in São Paulo. The order also covered refurbishment of 92 traction motors.

Propulsion equipment (traction motors and camshaft control equipment) has been supplied for refurbishment of Series 200 emu cars for Flumitrens in Rio de Janeiro.

Goninan

A Goninan & Co Ltd
PO Box 3300, Hamilton, NSW 2303, Australia
Telephone: +61 49 235000 Fax: +61 49 695391
Chief Executive: J G Fitzgerald
Group General Manager, International: R M Hayes
Group General Manager, Service: W Princehorn
Group General Manager, Heavy Engineering: C Huggins
Group General Manager, Marketing: P Blanch
Group General Manager, Engineering & Sales:
Dr J C Brown
Financial Controller: M Parkinson

Background: Goninan's parent company is Howard Smith Ltd. Licences held: GE Transportation Systems (USA).

Products: Diesel and electric multiple-unit cars, including double-deck stock.

Tangara emu

Contracts: Goninan completed Australia's largest contract in 1995 when it delivered the 450th Tangara emu to NSW State Rail.

It has subcontracted Siemens Transportation Services for the refurbishment of electrical equipment of 102 class Z1 and Z2 trams, Melbourne.

Goninan MainTrain Auburn Service Centre is now responsible for the contract maintenance of the Sydney City Rail suburban emu fleet and State Rail Authority Freight Rail bogies.

A contract has been signed to provide 20 LRVs to the Kowloon-Canton Railway to expand its service to the Tuen Mun urban areas in Hong Kong's New Territories.

UPDATED

Hanjin

Hanjin Heavy Industries
118, 2-KA, Namdaemun-Ro, Chung-Ku, Seoul, Republic of Korea
Telephone: +82 2 728 5420/755 7485
Fax: +82 2 755 0928/756 5455
Senior Vice President, Plant and Rolling Stock: J C Mun
General Manager, Rolling Stock Sales: B C Choi
Assistant General Manager: M Y Jeong

Background: Hanjin has been building rolling stock since 1964.

Products: Railcars, dmus, diesel railcars, emus.

Contracts: Pusan Metro Line 2 is taking delivery of 336 cars, ready for opening in 1999. Taegu Subway Agency has ordered 216 cars for its metro, due to start operation in 1997. Electrical equipment is by GEC Alsthom.

Developments: A new assembly plant is being constructed is South Korea at Sang-Ju, Kyoung Sang Province. Production was due to start in 1997.

UPDATED

Hanjin Heavy Industries emu for Taegu Subway Agency
1997

Hitachi

Hitachi Ltd
6 Kanda Surugadai 4-chome, Chiyoda-ku, Tokyo 101, Japan
Telephone: +81 3 3258 1111 Fax: +81 3 3258 5212
General Manager, Sales: T Muraki
Department Manager, Sales: K Takagi

Main works
Kasado works: 794 Higashitoyoi, Kudamatsu City, Yamaguchi Pref 744
Mito works: 1070 Ichige, Hitachinaka-shi, Ibaraki Pref 312
Hitachi works: 1-1, 3-chome, Saiwai-cho, Hitachi City, Ibaraki Pref 317
Kokubu works: 1-1, 1-chome, Kokubu-cho, Hitachi City, Ibaraki Pref 316

Background: Principal subsidiary companies are Hitachi Cable, Hitachi Metals, Hitachi Chemical, Tokyo Monorail Co. Passenger rolling stock is manufactured at the Kasado works.

Products: Lightweight stainless steel emus, aluminium alloy emus, dmus, passenger coaches, monorail cars, traction substation equipment, electrical components for rolling stock, computerised traffic control systems, electrification control systems, automatic car diagnositics systems, station management systems.

AC propulsion system using GTO thyristor; automatic train operations. High-power IGBT-VVF inverter propulsion system with 2,000 V, 500 A IGBT-VVF inverter propulsion system.

Contracts: Include 360 commuter emus for Japan Railways Group members; 95 commuter emus for several Japanese private railways; 198 metro cars for the systems in Tokyo, Osaka and Nagoya; 120 stainless steel cars for Trensurb, Brazil; and 162 monorail cars.

Since 1993 Hitachi has received orders for 126 IGBT-VVF propulsion systems. Recent orders include IGBT-VVF inverters for West Japan Railway, Osaka Prefecture Urban Development, Teito Rapid Transit Authority, Keio Teito Electric Railway and Hokkaido Railway.

UPDATED

Hitachi Series 223-1000 high-power IGBT inverter-controlled emu for West Japan Railway  ***1996***

Hitachi Series 215 double-deck emu for East Japan Railway ***1996***

Holec Ridderkerk

Holec Machines en Apparaten BV
PO Box 4050, 2980 GB Ridderkerk, Netherlands
Telephone: +31 180 445 000 Fax: +31 180 445 443
Main works, Traction Division: 390 Ringdijk, Ridderkerk
Managing Director: E C Yntema
Marketing & Sales Director: Ir M M C Meinderd

Associated company
Holec Ridderkerk UK Ltd

Background: Holec Ridderkerk and Holec Ridderkerk UK Ltd are members of the Dutch Royal Begemann Group.

Products: Complete electrical installations for new or refurbished rolling stock and hybrid trolleybuses. These include traction drives, motors, auxiliary power supply and vehicle information systems. Also hub motors for low-floor trams, electronic bogie control, hybrid systems and people mover technology.

Model of NINA three-car emu for BLS Lötschbergbahn with Holec Ridderkerk electrical equipment ***1997***

Contracts: Amsterdam metro/LRV Ringlijn contract; refurbishment of Bucureşti LRVs; 36 metro cars for Rotterdam; 53 diesel-hydraulic suburban dmus for Netherlands Railways; eight suburban three-car NINA emus for BLS Lötschbergbahn; diesel-electric hybrid bus for Rotterdam; two trolleybuses for Arnhem.

UPDATED

Holec Ridderkerk UK Ltd

Holec Ridderkerk UK Ltd
Dogpool Lane, Stirchley, Birmingham B30 2XJ, England
Telephone: +44 121 471 1047 Fax: +44 121 414 1369
Managing Director: J J Ashley
Marketing & Sales Director: P C Johnson

Associated company
Holec Machines en Apparaten BV, Ridderkerk, Netherlands

Background: The company is part of the Dutch Royal Begemann Group.

Products: Design engineering, systems integration and project management of electric and diesel multiple-units, metro cars, and mass transit vehicles.

Engineering consultancy for all aspects of passenger rail vehicles, particularly relative to the UK and systems influenced by UK technology and standards.

Holec Class 323 suburban emu in Birmingham, UK ***1995***

Contracts: As HTPL from May 1989 to March 1994, the Birmingham staff were responsible for the marketing, design engineering and project management of eight Glasgow Underground trailer cars for Strathclyde Passenger Transport Executive, 43 three-car emus for British Rail (Class 323), and 18 three-car emus for the Malayan Railway Administration (KTM).

Currently, Holec Ridderkerk UK is carrying out the contract and warranty administration of the Class 323 units as well as a series of consultancy projects for various clients.

Developments: The Class 323, featuring a three-phase 25 kV 50 Hz AC regenerative traction package, was the first emu to gain acceptance in the UK from Railtrack's Electrical Engineering and Control Systems Safety Assessment Panel for nationwide operation on overhead electrified routes. The traction and control system has been supplied by Holec Machines and Apparaten BV of the Netherlands and does not require a separate interference current monitoring unit.

The traction and train subsystems have been configured to be compatible with lineside signalling telecommunications infrastructure. With no infrastructure changes necessary to these systems, the vehicles are non-route specific. Work has begun to gain comparable acceptance on the UK third rail 750 V DC system and for dual voltage operation.

UPDATED

Hyundai

Hyundai Precision & Ind Co Ltd
Rolling Stock Division
140-2, Gyedong, Chongro-ku, KPO Box 1677, Seoul, Republic of Korea
Telephone: +82 2 824 3786 Fax: +82 2 824 5475/5476
Works: 85 Daewon-dong, Changwon, Kyungnam
Telephone: +82 551 821341
President: Ki Chyul Yoo
Director, Sales & Marketing: Sang Kwal Nam
Senior Manager, Rolling Stock Exports: Y G Kim

Background: Manufacture of rolling stock started in 1970 with construction under licence of GM EMD diesel-electric locomotives and was later extended to railcars

Pusan metro stock

and passenger coaches. Annual capacity for metro car production totals 600 units.

Products: Locomotives, metro cars, light rail vehicles, diesel railcars, passenger coaches; magnetic levitation vehicle (see entry in New Technology/Innovative Transit Systems section).

Contracts: A fleet of 70 cars has been delivered to KNR for Seoul suburban services. Eight emu sets with stainless steel carbodies and VVVF control have been supplied for the Jabotabek suburban project in Jakarta. A further 30 passenger coaches were supplied to KTM Malaysia, as a follow-on order from the 80 delivered in 1993.

A fleet of 32 emus for the Taiwan Railway Administration has been built by Hyundai, GEC Alsthom and Union Carriage & Wagon (qv), while 22 three-car emus have been delivered to KTM.

VERIFIED

ICF

Indian Railways Integral Coach Factory
Perambur, Madras 600038, India
Telephone: +91 44 611091 Fax: +91 44 626 1829
General Manager: S N Mathur

Background: ICF was established in 1955 in collaboration with the Swiss Car & Elevator Manufacturing Co. The agreement ended in 1961, since when all products have been designed and engineered in-house. The company's annual capacity of emu cars is 210.

Products: Electric multiple-units, metro cars, diesel railcars.

Contracts: Include 144 cars for Calcutta metro, and 158 electric multiple-unit cars for Indian Railways AC and DC suburban services in various cities. Also supplied three battery/electric locomotives to haul maintenance trains on the Calcutta metro.

A prototype battery/electric car has been developed for maintenance and breakdown services on the Calcutta metro.

During 1995, ICF built 15 air conditioned coaches for DSVN Vietnam.

Calcutta metro train by ICF

Kawasaki

Kawasaki Heavy Industries Ltd
Rolling Stock Group
World Trade Center Building, 4-1 Hamamatsu-cho 2-chome, Minato-ku, Tokyo 105, Japan
Telephone: +81 3 3435 2589 Fax: +81 3 3435 2157
General Manager: S Shimoura
Sales Manager: K Yamauchi
Technical Director: T Fujinawa

Background: Kawasaki Heavy Industies was formed in 1969 by merger of Kawasaki Rolling Stock Manufacturing Co, Kawasaki Aircraft Co and Kawasaki Dockyard Co Ltd. In 1972, Kisha Seizo Kaisha Ltd was taken over and merged into Kawasaki Heavy Industries.

Products: Electric multiple-units and rapid transit coaches (including rubber-tyred).

Contracts: An order was received from NYCTA New York to supply a prototype ten-car set of new-generation metro stock for the IRT lines. These 15.5 m cars have three wide doors per side to aid rapid boarding, and are powered by three-phase AC traction motors.

Kawasaki led the consortium which built 66 trains for Singapore Mass Rapid Transit Corporation. Contracts in the domestic market include stainless steel and aluminium alloy commuter, long-distance and suburban electric cars for Japan Railways Group and private railways.

Is also supplying 50 cars to Maryland DoT/MARC and 114 double-deck cars to the Long Island Rail Road.

Kawasaki Rail Car

Kawasaki Rail Car Inc
One Larkin Plaza, Yonkers, NY 10701, USA
Telephone: +1 914 376 4700 Fax: +1 914 376 4779
President: Masashi Oka

Background: Established in 1985 as a US subsidiary of Kawasaki Heavy Industries Ltd.

Products: Electric multiple-units, rapid transit cars, passenger coaches.

Contracts: Include assembly of 50 double-deck cars for MTA Maryland, 114 double-deck cars for Long Island Rail Road, New York, and 17 double-deck cars for MBTA Boston. Delivery started in 1996 and is continuing through to 1998.

UPDATED

Kiepe

Kiepe Elektrik GmbH & Co KG
PO Box 130540, 40555 Düsseldorf, Germany
Telephone: +49 211 74971 Fax: +49 211 7497 300
Chairman: T Weber
General Manager, Marketing Sales: W Huober

Background: Kiepe was established in 1906. Formerly a subsidiary of ACEC, the company became part of GEC Alsthom in 1988 along with its Austrian subsidiary Kiepe Electric in Wien. In 1993 Kiepe became a subsidiary of AEG Rail Systems and in 1996, following the merger of AEG and ABB, Kiepe became a member of the Schaltbau Group, München when Adtranz sold AEG's stake in the company.

Kiepe-equipped dual-voltage LRV delivered to Saarbrücken
1997

Products: Traction control equipment for 600/750 V DC traction systems; three-phase AC and DC chopper power electronics for LRVs and trolleybuses, with regenerative braking in IGBT or GTO technology. Control electronics in microprocessor technology.

Contracts: Include equipment for 78 four-section low-floor trams for Bremen (1992/96), which includes three-phase PWM inverter drives, databus and onboard diagnostics systems. The same equipment has been delivered for 68 low-floor trams for Wien, 80 low-floor trams for Köln, and 43 low-floor trams for Düsseldorf. For Saarbrücken 15 dual-voltage LRVs are being supplied that can operate on 750 V DC in the city and on 15 kV AC 16⅔ Hz DB interurban lines.

Kiepe supplies components and subassemblies for most metro and LRV systems in Germany, and undertakes installation and wiring of electrical equipment in manufacturers' works.

UPDATED

Kinki Sharyo

The Kinki Sharyo Co Ltd
Subsidiary of the Kinki Nippon Railway
3-9-60, Inada-Shinmachi, Higashi-Osaka City 577, Japan
Telephone: +81 6 746 5240 Fax: +81 6 745 5135
President: Junro Ono
Executive Vice President: Shunji Matsumoto
Senior Managing Director: Teijiro Ito
Managing Director: Hirokazu Iyota
Director, Manufacturing: Hiroyuki Seki
Director, Sales: Yosuke Saida
General Manager, Rolling Stock Management: Shigehiro Ueda
Export General Manager: Atsushi Tokutake

Products: Electric multiple-unit stock for main line, commuter, rapid transit, metro and light rail systems, double-deck LRVs.

Contracts: Japanese orders include seven cars for JR East (Series 653 regional express cars); 20 Series 223 suburban trains, 45 Series 207, two Series 500 New-Type Shinkansen and nine Series 681 regional express cars for JR West; six Series 681 regional express cars for Hokuetsu; 108 Series 813 commuter cars for JR Kyushu; eight metro cars for the Asakusa Line, Tokyo Metropolitan Government; six metro cars for the Ginza line, Teito Rapid Transportation Bureau, Tokyo; 84 metro cars for the Tozai line, Kyoto Municipal Transportation Bureau; 8 Series 70 linear motor-powered cars for Osaka Municipal Transportation Bureau; 60 commuter cars for Kintetsu.

UPDATED

Kinki Sharyo Series 50 Kyoto metro Tozai line emu

1997

Kinki Sharyo Series 207 emu
1997

Konstal

Steel Construction Works Konstal
ul Katowicka 104, 41500 Chorzów, Poland
Telephone: +48 32 411051 Fax: +48 32 413397
Marketing & Sales Manager: Henryk Ciosiński

Products: Tramcars and light rail vehicles.

Contracts: Builds extensively for Polish and other East European tramways, and has supplied more than 2,000 of the Type 105N tramcar.

A new tramcar series, the 105Ne, 105Nf and 105Ng, is now in production.

Developments: At the end of 1996 GEC Alsthom signed an agreement to acquire a majority stake in Konstal.

UPDATED

Konstal tram in Warszawa
1997

Korea Shipbuilding & Engineering

Korea Shipbuilding & Engineering Corp
1-1 ka Jongro, Jongro-ku, Seoul, Republic of Korea
Telephone: +82 2 739 5577 Fax: +82 2 733 8113
Chair: Ryun Namkoong
President: Ho Namkoong
Managing Director: Jong-Chul Mun
Sales Director: Jun Kil Suh

Main works: Pusan

Products: Diesel and electric multiple-units.

Contracts: Supplied 12 trains for the Pusan metro.

Linke-Hofmann-Busch

Linke-Hofmann-Busch GmbH
PO Box 411160, 38239 Salzgitter, Germany
Telephone: +49 53 41 2105 Fax: +49 53 41 213943
General Management
Marketing: Thomas Dompke
Public Relations: Hans-Peter Kienhorn

Background: Established in 1839 as Gottfried Linke, the company merged with Gebruder Hofmann & Co in 1912 to form Linke-Hofmann Werke AG. In 1928 Busch Waggon & Maschinenfabriek joined the group, adding its name. In 1994 GEC Alsthom acquired 51 per cent of the shares of LHB. The controlling interest was acquired from Preussag AG, which retains a 49 per cent share in the company.

Products: Metro cars, low-floor LRVs and conventional tramway stock.

Contracts: Contracts include supply of 120 low-floor NGT8D LRVs for Magdeburger Verkehrstriebe, 30 low-floor LRV trailers for HEAG Verkehrsbetriebe, 20 low-floor LRVs of Type GTW for Würzburger Strassenbahn, 45 ET474 three-car emu trains for the Hamburg S-Bahn, and eight prototype S-Bane trains for København (with option for a further 112 sets).

The København trains, delivered during 1996, are to a novel design, with short wide carbodies mounted on steerable single-axle running gear; 8 out of 10 axles on an eight-car set are motored. Electric equipment is being supplied by Siemens. The bodyshell, 3.6 m wide at the waist, makes full use of the generous S-Bane loading gauge, allowing 3+3 seating and plenty of space to accommodate projected growth in patronage.

Low-floor SB9 trailer cars have been supplied to LEAG Verkehrs, Darmstadt.

Developments: Citadis is the name of a new tram intended to replace the standard low-floor LRV in use in Grenoble, Paris and other locations. The ultra-low-floor Citadis will have a floor height of 350 mm and will have bogies with single-wheel hub motors. The floor will be raised over the more traditional bogies and body construction is aluminium alloy panels on steel frames. Citadis is fitted with GEC's ONIX asynchronous traction motor. Varying widths can be specified from 2.2 m upwards and the maximum length is 30 m (five sections).

UPDATED

NGT8D low-floor LRV in Magdeburg ***1996***

København S-Bane rolling stock ***1997***

Mafersa

Mafersa SA
Avenida Raimundo Pereira de Magalhães 230, Vila Anastácio, São Paulo, SP 05092-901, Brazil
Telephone: +55 11 261 8911 Fax: +55 11 261 3764
President of the Board: José Gustavo de Carvalho

Main works
São Paulo, address as above
Caçapava, SP 12280-000, Rodovia Presidente Dutra, Km 128.6
Telephone: +55 122 521411 Fax: +55 122 521281
Contagem, MG 32341-490, Rua das Indústrias s/no, Parque São João
Telephone: +55 31 391 2411 Fax: +55 31 351 2881

Background: Founded in 1944, Mafersa is a major builder of railway rolling stock, buses and trolleybuses.

Products: Stainless and carbon steel cars for suburban, metro and long-distance services; light rail vehicles; car bodyshells; wheels and axles. Also undertakes refurbishing, replacement of main components and modernisation of passenger cars.

Contracts: A fleet of 89 cars has been supplied for Metrô do Distrito Federal, Brasilia. These are four-car chopper-controlled sets with all axles motored; crush capacity is 1,176 passengers.

In 1994 Mafersa signed a contract for refurbishment of 33 Series 101 commuter cars for CBTU, São Paulo, which was being carried out early in 1996.

Early in 1996, Mafersa signed a contract with CMRJ Rio de Janeiro for the refurbishment of 28 metro cars for Line 1 of the metro system. At the end of 1996, Mafersa signed a contract with CPTM São Paulo for the refurbishment of 18 Series 700 commuter cars, which is being carried out during the first half of 1997.

UPDATED

Cab end of Mafersa's Brasilia metro car

Railcare

Railcare Limited
3 Ibstock Road, Coventry CV6 6NL, England
Telephone: +44 1203 364897 Fax: +44 1203 644074
Managing Director: Barry Turnbull
Business Development Director: Paul Robinson
Engineering Director: Dave Furlong
Finance Director: Eric McDonnell
Human Resources Director: Clive Jelley

Subsidiary companies
Railcare Wolverton
Stratford Road, Wolverton MK10 5NT
Telephone: +44 1908 221177 Fax: +44 1908 224414
General Manager: Jim Macfadyen

Railcare Springburn
79 Charles Street, Glasgow G21 2PS
Telephone: +44 141 335 2782 Fax: +44 141 335 2152
General Manager: Quentin Reynolds

Railcare Coventry, address as for Railcare Ltd
General Manager: Tim Humphrey

Background: Railcare Ltd, a joint venture of Babcock International and Siemens, was formed in 1995 to purchase heavy maintenance facilities from British Rail. Railcare acquired the former BR works at Wolverton and Glasgow in 1995. Tickford Rail, the interior design and supply business, is part of the Railcare Group.

Products: Rolling stock refurbishment and maintenance; equipment overhaul; interior design and supply.

Contracts: Include heavy maintenance for rolling stock leasing companies and supply of seating for the Jubilee line. Also undertaking refurbishment of 101 trains of London Underground stock. In total 753 cars from the Victoria, Northern and Bakerloo lines are undergoing an extensive refit after stripping down to bare bodyshell. Work carried out by Tickford Rail (qv). Railcare has refurbished Class 319 emus for Connex South Central's London to Brighton service. The work includes fitting two-each-side Chapman seats, carpets and a lounge area.

London Underground Victoria line train refurbished by Railcare **1996**

UPDATED

Rautarüükki

Rautarüükki Oy
PO Box 217, 90101 Oulu, Finland
Telephone: +358 81 327500 Fax: +358 81 327178
Works: 88200 Otanmaki
93400 Taivalkoski
Managing Director: Matti Haapakangas
Marketing Director: Aki Kaumanen

Background: Valmet Corporation and Rautarüükki Oy have merged their rolling stock manufacturing businesses forming Oy Transtech Ltd, which was established in 1991. Oy Transtech was merged back into parent company Rautauruüki at the beginning of 1996.

Products: Electric trainsets, metro cars, tramcars, passenger coaches, diesel locomotives.

Contracts: 42 double-deck aluminium-bodied passenger coaches have been supplied to Finnish State Railways. Rautarüükki is building the bodyshells and carrying out final assembly of 20 Adtranz Variotrams for HKL Helsinki. Delivery starts 1998, with completion by 2000.

Oy Transtech's metro trainset for Helsinki

UPDATED

RFS(E)

RFS(E) Ltd
PO Box 400, Hexthorpe Road, Doncaster DN1 1SL, England
Telephone: +44 1302 790037
Fax: +44 1302 790058
Commercial Director: John Meehan
Fleetcare Director: Martin Pridmore
Operations Director: Mick Bostock
Finance Director: Robert Johnson

Background: Formed from the privatisation of British Rail Engineering Ltd's Doncaster works in 1987, RFS(E) was bought out by its management in 1994.

Products: Manufacture, overhaul, repair and conversion of rolling stock, locomotives and ancillary equipment; operational maintenance.

Contracts: In conjunction with Doncaster Rail Maintenance Ltd, RFS(E) has refurbished Class 156 dmus for Porterbrook Leasing, UK. RFS(E) repainted the units and carried out roof repairs.

RFS(E) is refurbishing 87 six-car trains for the Piccadilly line, London Underground. Work started in 1995 and is expected to last till 1999.

UPDATED

Class 156 railcar refurbished at RFS(E) **1997**

RVR

Riga Carriage Building Works
201 Brivibas Street, Riga 226098, Latvia
Telephone: +371 2 275327 Fax: +371 2 555219
President: J Anderson

Products: Electric and diesel multiple-units for suburban traffic; tram and light rail cars; traction motors, braking systems, wheelsets.

Contracts: Include supply of suburban and main line coaches for Bulgaria, former Yugoslav countries and Cuba. Has built emus and dmus for suburban operations in many Russian cities, and continues to supply several of the Russian railway networks.

Delivery of suburban emus to JZ Yugoslavia has recommenced.

Developments: RVR has produced its TR2 six-axle prototype. Two examples on trial in Riga. All axles are motored and the tram has a high floor.

VERIFIED

RVR's standard ER29 emu

Santa Matilde

Companhia Industrial Santa Matilde
Av Koeler 260, 25 638 Petrópolis, Rio de Janeiro, Brazil
Telephone: +55 242 438656 Fax: +55 242 422165
Works: Tres Rios, Rio de Janeiro
President: H J P Duarte da Fonseca
Vice Presidents: A L P Duarte da Fonseca
S Torres Meurer

Background: Founded in 1916 as a mining enterprise, Santa Matilde started repair of rolling stock in 1926 and entered the manufacturing business in 1946. It holds licences from MAN (now Adtranz), Germany, for construction of electric multiple-units and LRVs.

Products: Electric multiple-units, passenger coaches, including stainless steel construction; light rail vehicles; bogies.

Recife emu by Santa Matilde

Schindler

Schindler Waggon AG
4133 Pratteln, Switzerland
Telephone: +41 61 825 9111 Fax: +41 61 825 9205
General Manager: Pierino Piffaretti
Manager, Development Production: Hans R Käser
Export Manager: Reinhard Christeller

Background: Founded in 1945 by the Schindler Elevator Co, the company specialises in carbody construction. LRVs are made at the Pratteln works, while production of carbodies in composite materials is at Schindler's other works in Altenrhein.

Products: Low-floor LRVs, tramcars, suburban single- and double-deck emus; refurbishment of vehicles; components for interior fittings; general engineering.

Contracts: Verkehrsbetriebe Zürich has ordered 17 Cobra trams. Available in metre or 1,435 mm gauge, the Cobra LRV has a full-length continuous low floor, and is based on modular construction of lightweight fibre-reinforced materials. Extra-wide doors allow easy access without steps, and floor height is only 300 mm above rail level.

Schindler supplied 70 new-technology centre-section light rail cars made from fibre-composite materials to CVG Cottbus, Germany, in 1995.

Deliveries have included supplies of double-deck coaches and driving trailers for the Zürich S-Bahn; type Be 4/4 low-floor centre sections for BLT Basel; metre-gauge LRVs for Zürich's Forchbahn; type Be 4/6 (Tram 2000) articulated vehicles and powered trailer cars for VBZ Zürich; type Be 4/6 articulated tramcars for BVB Basel; type De 4/4 750 mm gauge LRVs for the Waldenburgerbahn; and low-floor metre-gauge LRVs and intermediate coaches of aluminium alloy construction for Swiss private railways RBS, WSB and BD.

Schindler low-floor LRV for Swiss private railways

SBB Switzerland took delivery in 1996/97 of 58 bilevel intercity push-pull trainsets. Each set consists of a driving trailer and six vehicles. The corridor is at first floor level.

UPDATED

SEMAF

Société Générale Egyptienne de
Matériel des Chemins de Fer
Ein Helwan, Cairo, Egypt
Telephone: +20 2 782358/782177 Fax: +20 2 788413
Chairman: Eng T El-Maghraby
Technical Director: Eng A Rahik
Commercial Manager: A Farid
Works Manager, Coach & Metro: Dr Eng L Melek
Works Manager, Wagons & Bogies: Eng El-Sherbini

Products: Passenger cars, railcars, light rail vehicles, tramcars.

Contracts: Include trams for Cairo, Helwan, Heliopolis and Alexandria. Current production totals more than 100 tramcars per year.

SEMAF has assembled 72 cars for Line 2 of the Cairo metro, under a contract awarded jointly with Kinki Sharyo. An initial batch of 18 cars was supplied complete from Japan. It has also assembled a further 12 tramcars for Alexandria from parts supplied by Kinki Sharyo.

SEMAF's light rail cars and tramcars have electrical equipment, traction motors, pantographs, wheelsets and axleboxes imported from Japan under an agreement signed in 1979 with Mitsubishi Corporation.

Cairo metro emu **1997**

Siemens

Siemens AG
Transportation Systems Group (VT)
Mass Transit Rolling Stock Division (VT5)
PO Box 3240, 91050 Erlangen, Germany
Telephone: +49 9131 725176 Fax: +49 9131 720505
Divisional Executive Management
Technical: R Kehl
Commercial: T Rackow

UK Representative: Siemens Transportation Systems Ltd
Siemens House, Windmill Road, Sunbury-on-Thames
TW16 7HS
Telephone: +44 1932 752973 Fax: +44 1932 752979

USA Representative: Siemens Transportation Systems (qv)

Background: In 1995, Siemens Duewag Corporation in the USA was renamed the Mass Transit Division of Siemens Transportation Systems.

Products: Rolling stock for urban and suburban guided public transport.

Siemens has developed complete LRVs with a floor height down to 150 mm above rail level. They have three-phase AC drives and microcomputer controls. Siemens is also involved in development of ultra-light emus and metro cars. A twin-engined lightweight diesel railcar has been designed for regional operators in Germany.

Contracts: A fleet of 14 Class 332 25 kV four-car emus are being delivered for the Heathrow Express Project, England. ATP and AWS is fitted and other communications facilities include a fault-logging computer, track-to-train and in-train communication, train data recorder and cab secure radio. The seating is 2+2 with tip-up seats in the vestibules. Air conditioning is fitted and there is a public telephone. The luggage stacks and seating are located such that passengers can view their luggage. Wheelchair accommodation is provided and there is a dedicated secure luggage area for checked-in baggage.

Siemens' Mass Transit Rolling Stock Division (VT5) has developed from a supplier of electrical equipment to a supplier of complete vehicles. It has delivered vehicles for urban transport systems of which about half were for the European market, including Sheffield, UK, with the remainder to the USA, Canada, Mexico, Colombia, Tunisia and other countries.

Major contracts have been awarded in Asia (Singapore and Taipei metros) and USA (Los Angeles light rail and Portland low-floor LRVs).

Contracts for construction of a metro for the city of Ghangzhou in southeast China have been signed by the Ghangzhou Metro Corporation and a consortium consisting of the Transportation Systems Group of Siemens AG and Adtranz, under the leadership of Siemens. Line 1 is 18.5 km in length, will have 16 stations and runs mostly underground on an east-west axis. It is expected to open in 1999.

A consortium led by the Transportation Systems Group of Siemens has signed a contract with the municipal authorities in Bursa, Turkey, to build a light metro system on a turnkey basis. Siemens' share of the DM500 million order is more than DM250 million, with consortium members Ansaldo Trasporti receiving DM80 million and Turkish firm Guris receiving DM150 million for the civil works portion of the agreement.

Class 332 Heathrow Express emu **1997**

SGP's Singapore metro train with Siemens propulsion technology **1995**

Siemens LRV of South Yorkshire Supertram **1997**

Other major turnkey projects include the joint project for Puerto Rico metro and with Adtranz for BERTS Bangkok.

Ten three-section low-floor LRVs have been delivered to Carris, Lisboa, for operation on the Lina de Bélem line. Each car carries 210, with 65 seated.

Indian Railways Rail Coach Factory, Kapurthala, has signed an agreement with Siemens to build LRVs for Indian cities on a technology transfer basis. Electric traction equipment is being supplied by Siemens.

A further 14 LRVs for Tunis were being delivered early in 1997.

Developments: The Combino ultra-low-floor tram was announced in 1996, offering construction costs reduced by 30 per cent through standardisation. Up to five body modules and off-the-shelf seating and door systems can be specified. The first order for Combino came in December 1996, when ViP Potsdam ordered 48 cars.

A RegioSprinter entered trial service in Calgary, Canada, in 1996, and was judged a success.

The VT1 division now handles signalling, safety and control systems for main line customers. It used to handle rail signalling and safety systems, with VT2 handling control systems. VT2 now handles the same as VT1 but for mass transit customers. VT3 becomes Rail Electrification division, purely for rail. A management buyout took the non-rail power distribution sector to an independent organisation - Power Transmission and Distribution Group.

UPDATED

Siemens SGP

Siemens SGP Verkehrstechnik GmbH
Brehmsstrasse 16, 1110 Wien, Austria
Telephone: +43 1 740690 Fax: +43 1 707 51690
Managing Director: Ing Günter Janak, Mag Manfred Dönz
Sales Director for Austria, Slovenia, Croatia and Slovakia: Ing Franz Kasparek (Siemens AG, Austria)
Sales Director Worldwide: Rainer Kehl (Siemens AG, Erlangen)
Main works: Wien; Graz

Background: Siemens took a 74 per cent shareholding in SGP in 1993.

Products: Metro cars, light rail vehicles, ultra-low-floor tramcars.

Contracts: Between 1989 and 1991 Siemens SGP delivered 45 two-car sets for the Wien metro system. A further 42 two-car sets were delivered between 1992 and January 1995. Two prototypes of the ultra-low-floor tramcar for Wien were delivered in 1995. Called the ULF197, it has 51 seats and has a floor height of 197 mm. It is 23.6 m long and is powered by vertically mounted AC motors with Sibas microprocessor-based control technology.

The first series of ULF197 cars was to be delivered to WienerLinien in 1997.

Siemens SGP is supplying 216 carbody shells and 432 bogies for Taipei metro cars, 21 twin railcar sets for the Wien metro and the running units for 105 metro cars for BTS Bangkok, Thailand, with delivery expected 1998.

De Lijn, Belgium, ordered 45 low-floor trams in 1996 for delivery over five years starting in 1998. Each metre-gauge car carries 67 seated and 183 standing; 31 are going to Antwerpen and 14 to Gent.

Siemens SGP is building 240 double-deck suburban cars for local services in the Wien district. Designed by OBB, each seats 114, with a higher density on the lower deck for short-distance passengers and a lower density on the upper deck for longer journeys.

The formation of each push-pull trainset is five non-driving trailers and one driving trailer.

UPDATED

Siemens SGP ultra-low-floor tram in Wien

1997

Siemens SGP double-deck car ***1997***

Siemens Transportation Systems

Siemens Transportation Systems Inc
Head Office, 186 Wood Avenue South, Iselin, NJ 08830, USA
Telephone: +1 908 205 2200 Fax: +1 908 603 7379
President & Chief Executive Officer: J Morrison
Vice President & General Manager: G Ernst
Vice President & Chief Financial Officer: G Donahue

Mass Transit Division
7464 French Road, Sacramento, CA 95828
Telephone: +1 916 688 5014 Fax: +1 916 689 3513

Siemens SD100 six-axle LRV in Denver
1996

Siemens low-floor LRV prototype for Portland, USA ***1996***

Products: Light rail vehicles, commuter cars, bogies, propulsion systems, diesel and electric multiple units, AC traction motors and components. (see also Electrification section)

Contracts: Siemens has over 300 LRVs in operation throughout North America, including Sacramento, San Diego, Pittsburgh, St Louis, Denver and Portland, USA, and in Edmonton and Calgary in Canada. Siemens Transportation Systems was also awarded the contract to supply 52 LRVs to MTA Los Angeles for the Green Line.

Additional vehicles are in course of delivery to San Diego, and 23 LRVs are being built for Salt Lake City. Siemens is also supplying 64 heavy-rail vehicles for the San Juan Tren Urbano turnkey rail project. Siemens is consortium leader for this project and is providing project management, rails and power system for the 17.2 km routes and communications/train-control systems, in addition to the vehicles.

Siemens Regiosprinter on trials in Calgary ***1997***

The company was recently awarded the contract to supply 23 LRVs to Tri-Met Portland to supplement an existing fleet of 39.

Developments: Siemens and Amtrak West USA jointly launched a demonstration tour of the Siemens Regiosprinter diesel railbus at the end of 1996.

UPDATED

Škoda

Škoda Dopravni Technika sro
Škoda Transportation Systems
Tylova 57, 31600 Plzeň, Czech Republic
Telephone: +42 19 773 5002 Fax: +42 19 773 9059
Managing Director: Milan Kalina
Marketing & Sales Director: František Podzemskv
Technical Director: Petr Heller

Background: Škoda was founded in 1919 for the manufacture of electric locomotives and has now moved into production of LRV and metro cars, and associated traction equipment.

Products: Development and manufacture of rolling stock; electric locomotives; metro/commuter cars; LRV manufacture and refurbishment; electric traction drives and components; turnkey projects including vehicles and electrification.

Contracts: Refurbishment of trams has been carried out for Plzeň and Liberec. The work included upgrading of the interior, fitting of IGBT drives and bogie rebuilding.

Praha metro cars are being reconstructed and refurbished. The work includes installation of IGBT drive and a communications system. Škoda has also fitted new cabs and modified bogies.

Developments: A light electric locomotive has been introduced, suitable for urban use. It has asynchronous motors and GTO thyristor drive.

An ultra-low-floor tramcar with 350 mm floor height and asynchronous drive is being constructed.

Double-deck commuter cars are being built in association with MSV Studénka.

UPDATED

Tramcar refurbished by Škoda ***1996***

Škoda low-floor LRV design ***1997***

Praha metro car refurbished by Škoda ***1997***

SLM

SLM
(Swiss Locomotive and Machine Works Ltd)
8401 Winterthur, Switzerland
Telephone: +41 52 264 1010 Fax: +41 52 213 8765
Chairman: U Scherrer
President: R Kummrow
Vice President, Engineering: St Amacker
Vice President, Sales: P E Graf
Vice President: E Just
Vice President, Commercial: M Tritschler

Background: SLM is a member of the Sulzer Corporation.

Products: Steerable traction and non-powered bogies for LRVs; complete vehicles for adhesion and rack railways; low-floor LRV for regional traffic.

Contracts: Supplied 13 sets of frameless traction units (one per set) and trailer bogies (two per set) for 11 low-floor articulated railcars for the Biel-Täuffelen-Ins-Bahn and for the Chemin de fer Electriques Veveysans, both metre-gauge railways in Switzerland. One set (standard-gauge) has been developed for a diesel-electric low-floor articulated railcar.

Twenty-four traction and trailer bogies have been supplied to the metre-gauge rack railway operators in France.

Developments: A low-floor LRV for regional traffic, the Futuro, is available.

Lightweight frameless traction units and trailer bogies both featuring radial self-steering wheelsets for low-floor articulated railcars have been developed.

UPDATED

SLM Futuro regional LRV ***1997***

Sofer

Sofer Officine Ferroviarie SpA
Via Miliscola 37, 80078 Pozzuoli, Napoli, Italy
Telephone: +39 81 526 2522 Fax: +39 81 526 2288
General Manager: Dott Ing Fausto Cutuli

Products: Diesel and electric railcars, multiple-unit trainsets, passenger coaches; powered bogies.

Contracts: Amongst recent contracts was supply of motor bogies for the Breda-built cars ordered by Washington metro, and for Los Angeles.

Articulated train for the Circumvesuviana Railway

Stork RMO

Stork RMO BV
PO Box 1250, 1000 BG Amsterdam, Netherlands
Telephone: +31 20 523 3700 Fax: +31 20 622 0617
Managing Director: Ing J A Pijnappels
Project Co-ordinator: Ir J A Verwer
Chief Engineer: Prof Ir C P Keizer

Products: Powered and trailer bogies for trains, metro cars and LRVs; automatic retractable interconnecting gangways for trainsets; radial powered and trailer bogies; overhaul of bogies and components.

Contracts: Stork RMO flexible bogies are used for the newest trainsets on Netherlands Railways including the SM90 double-deck emu. Powered bogies have been supplied for LRVs in Amsterdam, Rotterdam, and Den Haag. Stork is also building the bogies for the Bombardier Eurorail cars that will run on the new Rotterdam metro.

Stork is building the bogies for GEC Alsthom TGV trainsets.

UPDATED

Stork RMO bogie ***1995***

Talbot

Waggonfabrik Talbot GmbH & Co KG
Jülicher Strasse 213-237, 52070 Aachen, Germany
Telephone: +49 241 18210
Fax: +49 241 1821 214
Managing Director: Stefan Stiefel
Directors of Marketing & Sales: Dieter Havenith; Hugo Lemmer
Director, Passenger Rail Products: Dr Georg Hauschild
Director, Bogies: Jürgen Jakob

Background: Talbot is a subsidiary of Bombardier Eurorail.

Products: Electric and diesel multiple-units, including bi-level cars; bogies.

Contracts: Recent contracts include 120 three-car Talent dmus for DB Germany. Diesel-hydraulic transmission is fitted to 75 and the remaining 45 have diesel-electric transmission.

Other contracts include 53 single-deck two-car dmus for NS Netherlands; eight single-deck three-car emus for BLS Switzerland.

Developments: Development of the Talent family of dmus is taking place and new bi-level coaching stock is being developed.

Tilting technology has been installed in a VT614 emu for DB.

UPDATED

Talbot Talent low-floor dmu prototype ***1997***

Tokyu

Tokyu Car Corporation
3-1 Ohkawa, Kanazawa-ku, Yokohama 236, Japan (head office and Yokohama plant)
Telephone: +81 45 785 3009 Fax: +81 45 785 6550
Sales office: 7-2, Yaesu 2-chome, Chuo-ku, Tokyo 104
Telephone: +81 3 3272 8091 Fax: +81 3 3272 3656
Omiya plant: 610-1, Kushibiki-cho 2-chome, Omiya, Saitama-prefecture 331
Hanyu plant: 705-23, Komatsudai 2-chome, Hanyu, Saitama-prefecture 348
Osaka plant: 200, Otoriminami-machi 3-cho, Sakai, Osaka 593
President: Takahisa Tozawa
Vice Presidents: Tetsuo Noguchi, Katsuyoshi Koizumi

Background: Formed in 1948 from the Yokohama works of the Tokyu Corporation, the company built the first all-stainless steel cars in Japan in 1962 following a technical agreement with Budd (USA). Tokyu absorbed the Teikoku Car & Manufacturing Co of Osaka in 1968 to become one of Japan's biggest rolling stock suppliers for domestic railways and those in other countries. Annual capacity is more than 700 emu cars and passenger coaches.

Products: Electric and diesel railcars, passenger cars.

Contracts

The East Japan Railway has taken delivery of Series E501 emus with lightweight stainless steel bodywork. Each unit consists of 10 cars, with four motored, or 15, with six motored. Power supply is AC or DC and the unit is fitted with VVVF inverter control. The electrically operated passenger doors are fitted with anti-obstruction devices.

Keio Teito Electric Railway has ordered the Series 1000 for commuter services on the Inogashira Line in Tokyo. Construction is in lightweight stainless steel and VVVF inverter control is fitted. Each unit consists of five cars, two being motored.

Tokyu Series 1000 emu on Keio Teito Electric railway ***1997***

UPDATED

Toshiba

Toshiba Corporation
Railway Projects Department
1-1 Shibaura 1-chome, Minato-ku, Tokyo 105-01, Japan
Telephone: +81 3 3457 4924 Fax: +81 3 5444 9422
President: Taizo Nishimuro
General Manager: Shigenori Yamakawa
Senior Manager, Railway Projects Dept: Shunji Uchino

Products: Electric traction equipment, auxiliary power supply; train control/monitoring equipment for emus and LRVs; electric and diesel locomotives.

Contracts: KNR Korea has ordered 60 sets of traction equipment for its No 1 line in addition to 330 carsets, supplied also by Toshiba.

A further 220 carsets have been received by KNR for its Kwa-chon and No 1 lines serving suburban regions of Seoul.

The National Authority for Tunnels, Egypt, took delivery of 750 V DC third rail and AC drive systems for 135 carsets on Cairo metro Line 2 between 1993 and 1996. Rheostatic control systems for 90 electric carsets powered by 1,600 V DC overhead have been supplied to Egyptian National Railway.

An order for Series 500 VVVF inverter-controlled traction equipment for nine Shinkansen trainsets (144 cars) has been received from JR West, Japan.

UPDATED

Union Carriage

Union Carriage & Wagon Co (Pty) Ltd
PO Box 335, Nigel 1490, South Africa
Telephone: +27 11 739 2411 Fax: +27 11 739 5156
Works: Marievale Road, Vorsterkroon, Nigel 1490
Chief Executive: R Bingham
Commercial Executive: A M Clegg
Marketing Executive: Z Maqetuka

Products: Electric multiple-units, diesel multiple-units, railcars, passenger coaches, electric and diesel locomotives. Holds licences from Duewag (LRVs) and Adtranz (emus and bogies).

Contracts: 216 metro cars for Taipei metro; 64 push-pull locomotives for Taiwan Railway Administration; 66 emu cars for KTM, Malaysia.

Four-car emu for Taipei's cross-city line

Ust-Katav

Ust-Katav Tramway Works
456040 Ust-Katav, Russia
Telephone: +7 351 67 26541 Fax: +7 351 67 25548
General Director: Yuri Kirilitchev

Background: Ust-Katav was formerly the S M Kirov Works.

Products: Tramcars and light rail vehicles.

Contracts: Has supplied tramcars to the systems in many cities of the former USSR. Among recent orders were KTM-8 cars for Moskva (70), Barnaul (10) and Chelyabinsk.

Ust-Katav has abandoned manufacture of the former Kirov standard 71-605 (KTM-5M3) design which has been in production since the mid-1960s. In its place comes a new range of standard LRVs designed to replace traditional Tatra and Riga-built cars for which spare parts are now unobtainable in Russia. The first design is the KTM-11, a two-car double-ended development of the KTM-8. A prototype has been on trial on the underground rapid tramway in Volgograd since 1991, and six sets were supplied to Krivoi Rog in 1992.

Current production is almost entirely the 71-608KM type, Moskva being almost the only customer.

Ust-Katav KTM 71-608KM tramcar **1996**

'Vevey' Technologies

'Vevey' Technologies SA Villeneuve
PO Box 32, 1844 Villeneuve, Switzerland
Telephone: +41 21 967 0505 Fax: +41 21 967 0500
Director: H Vorburger
Technical Manager: F Dalliard
Marketing & Sales Manager: F Canetti

Background: Founded in the 1860s, the former ACMV (Ateliers de Constructions Mécaniques de Vevey) became 'Vevey' Technologies in 1993. It is a member of the Dutch Royal Begemann Group.

Products: Electric multiple-units, light rail vehicles, low-floor tramcars, powered and trailing bogies, automated light vehicles.

Contracts: 46 low-floor articulated trams are in service in Genève, as well as 12 new-generation low-floor cars in Bern. A batch of 15 similar cars for STAS St Etienne was built in conjunction with GEC Alsthom, and 12 light rail vehicles were supplied for TSOL in Lausanne. A further five cars were built for TSOL in 1994.

Vevey also built the bodies and mechanical parts for a non-urban version of the low-floor LRV ordered by the

Low-floor car in St Etienne **1996**

'Vevey' Technologies Lille VAL cars under construction **1997**

Swiss/Italian Centovalli Railway (FART/SSIF). In total 12 cars were built; electrical equipment was by ABB (now Adtranz).

MC Switzerland has taken delivery of three two-car rack and adhesion trainsets with electrical equipment by Adtranz (qv). CFM Neuchâteloises, Switzerland, has ordered a motor car from Vevey with electrical equipment by Adtranz.

Vevey is building 34 two-car sets of VAL 208 cars for the Lille metro Line 2 extension to Roubaix and Tourcoing.

Eight low-floor lightweight trainsets with electric traction have been ordered for the Bern—Lötschberg—Simplon Railway. They are built by a consortium of Vevey, Talbot and Holec, with traction equipment from Adtranz.

The units are called NINA (NIederflurNAverkehr) and 80 per cent of the floor is 550 mm above rail. Each NINA unit carries 130 seated second-class passengers, 16 seated first-class and 132 standing passengers. Delivery is expected in 1998/99.

Developments: Urbos is the name of a new integral low-floor no-step design of four-axle three-section vehicle. The first and second sections each have one axle and the third has two. The vehicle is designed to keep costs down, with several variants available. There are three modules — the wheelset, side window, and door; the wheels are self-steering. The three-section vehicle seats around 50.

UPDATED

Walkers

Walkers Limited
23 Bowen Street, Maryborough, Queensland 4650, Australia
Telephone: +61 71 218100 Fax: +61 71 224400
General Manager: R Hardy
Marketing Manager: J Prickett
Manager, Engineering & Services: R Bailey
Commercial Manager: G Nelson

Background: Founded in 1864, Walkers opened its Maryborough works in 1868. Electric multiple-units are produced in association with Adtranz. Walkers is a subsidiary company of Evans Deakin Industries, Brisbane.

Products: Complete cars for suburban, rapid transit and interurban operations, and light rail vehicles.

Contracts: Walkers delivered 20 emu cars for the Brisbane—Rockhampton intercity service. It also supplied 46 two-car emu sets to Westrail for Perth suburban services, and has built a further 12 three-car emus for Queensland Railways.

Walkers built 34 articulated LRVs for the Kuala Lumpur STAR light rail system, with traction equipment supplied by main contractor AEG. A further 56 cars were ordered in 1995 to operate Phase II of the system and expand capacity.

Thirty-six three-car emu sets were delivered to Queensland Railways during 1995/96.

Developments: In a joint venture with Adtranz Australia, Walkers is building five two-car emus for Westrail Perth. They will be similar in design to previous emus.

UPDATED

Walkers emus for Brisbane (left) and Perth

accessibility

Widespread distribution network

The SAB WABCO Group has established a strong presence in most major railway markets in the world. We are present in all important expanding markets and have recently established our own organisations in China, India and Korea. With around 2,500 skilled employees strategically located in 25 industrial centres across the world, we are ideally placed to satisfy the local requirements of rail and tramway systems in all quarters of the globe.

This widespread distribution of technical and human resources ensures that expert personnel are close at hand for consultation and assistance as well as being familiar with local conditions.

Our systems and components can be found on high-speed trains, tilting trains, metros, locomotives, multiple unit trains, light rail vehicles, automatic light vehicles, and freight cars all over the world.

The new SAB WABCO Group

On January 1st, 1997, the railway operations of the Swedish Cardo Group and the German Thyssen Industrie AG were united into one multi-national company called SAB WABCO.

SAB WABCO operates under the following well-known trade names: SAB WABCO, BSI, Tebel Technologies, Davies & Metcalfe and Gutehoffnungshütte Radsatz. The combined programme embraces a complete range of brake products and systems, couplings, wheelsets, wheels, automatic doors and electronic control systems for the railway industry.

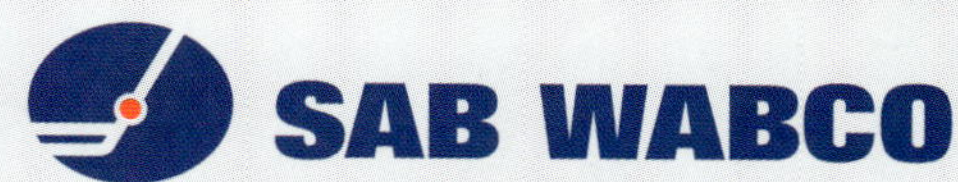

Headquarters: Cardo BSI Rail AB,
P.O. Box 193, SE- 201 21 Malmö, Sweden.
Tel: +46 40 35 04 60, Fax: +46 40 30 38 03

A company in the Cardo BSI Rail Group

Hepworth Rail
Holdsworth
Hydrovane
Hygate
Invertec
Knorr-Bremse Systems
KV
Lab Craft
MAC
Metalastik
MTB
Oleo
Percy Lane
Powernetics
Proximeter
Raychem
Robert Wagner
Rose Bearings
Sabre
SMC
Stone International
Stone UK
Tecalemit
Thomas Electronics
Thorn Transport Lighting
Time 24
Timken
Transintech
Transmatic
Triplex
Twiflex
Webasto
Westinghouse Brakes
Williamson
Woodhead

USA
Air-O-Matic
American Seating
Bostrom
Braun
Carrier Transicold
Coach and Car
Crow River
Dellner Couplers
Deutsch Relays
EG & G Rotron
Electric Fan Engineering
Ferraz
Firestone
Johnson Matthey
Knorr-Brake
Lift-U
Microphor
Motor Coils
Nelson
New York Air Brake
Power Parts
Ricon
Q'Straint
Specialty Bulb
Sportworks
Startmaster
Stewart & Stevenson
Stone Safety
Stone Safety Service
Texstar
Thermo King
Timken
Transmatic
Transpec
Unicel
Vapor
Veam
WABCO

Classified Listing

AXLEBOXES/BEARINGS
FAG
Lucchini
Metalastik
Rose Bearings
SKF
Timken

BOGIES
Adtranz
GMT
Knorr-Bremse
SLM
Sumitomo

BODYSHELL CONSTRUCTION
Cromweld
Hübner

BRAKES AND BRAKE COMPONENTS
Bergische Stahl-Industrie
Bharat
Bowmonk
Bremskerl
Davies & Metcalfe
Don
Dorbyl
European Friction Industries
Freudenberg
Hanning & Kahl
Hydrovane
Knorr-Bremse
Lucchini
Mannesman
Métal Déployé
MZT Hepos
New York Air Brake
Oerlikon-Knorr
POLI
SAB WABCO
Sabre
Sumitomo
Time 24
Twiflex
Veam
WABCO
Westinghouse Brakes

CLIMATE CONTROL/HEATING
Adtranz
Airscrew Howden
Autoclima
Carrier Transicold
Clayton
Coachair
Dorbyl
EBAC
EG & G Rotron
Electric Fan Engineering
Faiveley Transport
HFG
Konvekta
Luwa
MAC
Mobitec
SAB WABCO
Sigma
SMC
Startmaster
Stone Ibérica
Stone International
Stone Safety
Stone UK
SÜTRAK
Temoinsa
Thermo King
Toshiba
Vapor
Veam
Webasto

COUPLERS AND ASSOCIATED EQUIPMENT
Bergische Stahl-Industrie
Davies & Metcalfe
Dellner Couplers
Dorbyl
Jarret
New York Air Brake
Oleo
SAB WABCO
Scharfenberg
Sécheron
Sumitomo
Twiflex
WABCO

DOORS AND DOOR EQUIPMENT
Alna Koki
Berensden Pimatic
Bode
Craig & Derricott
Deans Powered Doors
EAO
Faiveley Transport
HP
Hydrovane
IFE
Kiepe
Knorr-Bremse
KV
London Mat Industries
SAB WABCO
Sguinzi Pietro
SMC
Tamware
Transintech
Vapor
Westinghouse Brakes

INTERIORS
Engineering Development Unit
MTB
Robert Wagner
Ruspa
Temoinsa
Transintech
Unicel
VAW

LIGHTING AND ASSOCIATED EQUIPMENT
Adtranz
Atlas International
Cleff
Invertec
Lab Craft
Percy Lane
Ruspa
SAB WABCO
SBF
Specialty Bulb
Stone Ibérica
Stone International
Stone UK
Teknoware
Thorn Transport Lighting
Transmatic
Transtechnik
Veam

LIVERY
The Halo Company
Williamson

PANTOGRAPH/THIRD RAIL CURRENT COLLECTORS
Faiveley Transport
Ferraz
Knorr-Bremse
SAB WABCO
Sécheron
WABCO

REFURBISHMENT
Adtranz
Airex
Coach and Car
Engineering Development Unit
Lydney
Temoinsa
Texstar
Transintech
Vapor
Voith
WABCO

RESTRAINT/SAFETY SYSTEMS
Air Vehicles
CSPL
Q'Straint
Ricon
Sportworks
Stewart & Stevenson

SEATING
Air Vehicles
American Seating
Bostrom
British Furtex Fabrics
Chapman Seating
Chardon
Coach and Car
Deans Powered Doors
Dorbyl
Emsta
FAINSA
FISA
Holdsworth
Kiel
MTB Equipment
Rica Seats
Ruspa
Transintech
VBK
Vogelsitze

SUSPENSION/RUNNING GEAR/LUBRICATION SYSTEMS
Disc-Lock Europe
FAG
Firestone
Fuchs
GMT
Hydrovane
IBG Monforts
Klübner
Knorr-Bremse
Koni
KV
Mediter
Metalastik
Nuti
SAB WABCO
Tecalemit
Timken
WECO
Woodhead

TESTING EQUIPMENT/DATA RECORDERS
Bowmonk
Deuta Werke
Engineering Development Unit
Ferranti
Knorr-Bremse
Powernetics

TOILET EQUIPMENT
EVAC
Faiveley Transport
Microphor
Temoinsa

TRACTION MOTORS AND EQUIPMENT
Adtranz
Crompton Greaves
Eaton
Energy Controls
FAG
Fels
Ferraz
GEC Alsthom
GEC Plessey Semiconductors
Mitsubishi Electric
Motor Coils
Parizzi
Sécheron
SEPSA
Startmaster
Tibram

TRANSMISSIONS AND ELECTRICAL EQUIPMENT
Adtranz
David Brown
Deutsch Relays
Freudenberg
Ganz-David Brown
GEC Alsthom
Hygate
Johnson Matthey
Kiepe
LPA Industries
Métal Déployé
Power Parts
Powernetics
Raychem
SEPSA
Thomas Electronics
Time 24
Timken
Voith
ZF Hurth
ZF Padova

VIGILANCE SYSTEMS
Davies & Metcalfe
Proximeter

WHEELCHAIR EQUIPMENT
American Seating
Braun
Crow River
Lift-U
Q'Straint
Stewart & Stevenson

WHEELSETS
Dorbyl
GMT
Lucchini
Roues et Trains Montes
Sumitomo
ZDB

WINDOWS/GLAZING
Alna Koki
Cleff
Hepworth Rail
Isoclima
Nelson
Percy Lane
Sguinzi Pietro
Socar
Transpec
Triplex

Adtranz

ABB Daimler-Benz Transportation GmbH
PO Box 130127, 13601 Berlin, Germany
Telephone: +49 30 38320 Fax: +49 30 3832 2000
(See main entry under Rail Vehicles and Traction Equipment)

Products: Development, engineering, design, production, supply, installation, refurbishment, support services for systems, subassemblies and components on rail vehicles. The product range comprises train communication and control and fault diagnosis, traction power converters, onboard power supply, auxiliaries, climate control HVAC (heating, ventilation, air conditioning) systems.

Product range includes propulsion systems, bogies, vehicle bodyshells and onboard power supply systems.

Adtranz has established System Lead Centres (SLC) which manage, worldwide, all design and production activities for the abovementioned systems, subassemblies and components.

SLC Propulsion delivers complete drive packages including traction motors, drive systems amd power converters, nowadays mostly for three-phase traction applications, but still also for conventional DC traction drives with chopper control. In the high-power range, advanced, compact, high-efficiency power conversion equipment with GTO technology is supplied for locomotives.

IGBT technology is applied in the medium power range for heavy mass transit and regional multiple-unit traction vehicles, and in the low-power range for LRVs.

SLC TCC (traction communication and control) delivers complete electronic control systems. The microprocessor-based MITRAC® TCC system operates in all Adtranz vehicles for control and supervision of train, motive power, drive control and diagnosis.

SLC Bogies provides products and technology for all bogie types. Heavy bogies (Fexifloat) for locomotives, bogies for multiple units, metro cars, LRVs and other rail applications. Focus is on design and production, technology development and technology transfer to partner companies.

SLV Vehicle Bodyshells provides design for all types of application, fabricated from carbon steel, stainless steel or aluminium as well as from composite materials.

Onboard power supply systems are available for vehicle types, in the power output range from 15 to 250 kVA. From 1985 to the end of 1996 over 3,000 vehicles, including motor cars and LRVs for regional or urban transport services, have been equipped with Adtranz onboard converters. Most of these vehicles have been produced by Adtranz companies but also by other manufacturers.

Adtranz onboard converters have been specified on over 4,600 vehicles.

UPDATED

Air Vehicles

Air Vehicles
Three Gates Road, Cowes PO31 7UT, England
Telephone: +44 1983 293194 Fax: +44 1983 291987
Managing Director: Charles Eden
Technical Director: Stuart Edwards

Products: Design, development and manufacture of lightweight transport seating systems with emphasis on safe passenger restraint in the event of a collision.

NEW ENTRY

Airex Composites

Airex AG
9320 Arbon, Switzerland
Telephone: +41 71 477746 Fax: +41 71 462385
General Manager: Georg Reif
Marketing Manager: Thibault de Kalbermatten
Associated company: Alusuisse Road & Rail (see Rail Vehicles and Buses sections)

Products: Large composites mouldings for rail vehicles and buses; complete structures such as driver's cabs with Airex rigid foam core; aluminium-faced foam sandwich composite.

Contracts: Include driver's cab in phenolic resin composite for Berlin metro cars built by Adtranz.

Air-O-Matic

Air-O-Matic Power Steering
6501 Barberton Avenue, Cleveland, OH 44102, USA
Telephone: +1 216 281 7810 Fax: +1 216 281 1132
President: Theodore J Berger
Chief Financial Officer: T John Berger
Vice President, Marketing: Christopher Berger

Parent company: Maradyne Inc

Products: Power steering for buses and trolleybuses.

Airscrew Howden

Airscrew Howden Limited
111 Windmill Road, Sunbury TW16 7EF, England
Telephone: +44 1932 765822 Fax: +44 1932 761098
Head of Sales, Fans & Motors: Gwyn Jones

Products: Fans and other components for heating and ventilation.

VERIFIED

Alcad

Alcad Ltd
Castle Works, Station Road, Hampton TW12 2BY, England
Telephone: +44 181 941 8996 Fax: +44 181 941 9012
General Manager: P J Lines

Products: Nickel cadmium batteries.

Contracts: Contracts include 212 XMR Ni/Cd batteries for emergency auxiliary power on new cars for London Underground's Northern line; traction power XHR Ni/Cd batteries for maintenance locomotives on the Taipei metro in Taiwan.

Alna Koki

Alna Koki
4-5, Higashi Naniwa-cho, 1-chome, Amagasaki 660, Japan
Telephone: +81 6 401 7281 Fax: +81 6 401 6168
President: Masatoyo Uji
Managing Director, Sales & Production:
Yoshonobu Sugomoto
Engineering Director: Shigeo Ueki

Subsidiary company: Nippon Fukuso Glass Co

Products: Aluminium window sashes for rail vehicles and buses; honeycomb-sandwich construction doors and panels for rail vehicles and buses.

American Seating

American Seating Company
Transportation Products Group
401 American Seating Center, Grand Rapids, MI 49504, USA
Telephone: +1 616 732 6406 Fax: +1 616 732 6491
President, Transportation Products: Dave McLaughlin
Director of Administration, Transportation Products Group: Dick Grinage

Products: Passenger and driver seating for bus and rail vehicles; wheelchair restraint systems.

Ansaldo

Ansaldo Trasporti
425 Via Argine, 80147 Napoli, Italy
(See main entry under Rail Vehicles and Traction Equipment)

Products: Chopper and inverter electronic drives for rail vehicles and trolleybuses; AC and DC traction motors; power supply equipment for onboard auxiliary services.

VERIFIED

Atlas International

Atlas International
Merrington Lane, Spennymoor DL16 7UR, England
Telephone: +44 191 301 3115 Fax: +44 191 301 3110
Logistics Manager: T Burton

Products: Inverters and lighting components for buses and rail vehicles.

NEW ENTRY

Autoclima

Autoclima SpA
Via Rondò Bernardo 11/3, 10040 Beinasco, Italy
Telephone: +39 11 358 0876
Fax: +39 11 358 2388/3583527
Managing Director: Giorgio Moffa
General Manager: Giovanni Mosso
Sales Manager: Mirella Serra

Products: Air conditioning equipment, roof-mounted or in-vehicle.

Contracts: Driver air conditioning equipment has been installed in buses of ATAF Firenze. Air conditioning/heating units have been installed in ONCF Morocco cars.

Developments: An air conditioning unit for the driving area of service buses has been introduced.

UPDATED

Berensden Pimatic

Berensden PMC Oy
PO Box 21, 32701 Hutittinen, Finland
Telephone: +358 2 566721 Fax: +358 2 568501
Director: Tuomo Väänänen
Export Manager: Paul Nikku
Product Manager: Markku Rekioja
A member of Berensden PMC Group

Products: Automatic door systems; pressure-sealed gangway doors; interior doors; fire barrier doors; electro-pneumatic and electric-powered door gear for rail vehicles.

UPDATED

Bergische Stahl-Industrie

BSI-Verkehrstechnik
Papenberger Strasse 38, 42859 Remscheid, Germany
Telephone: +49 2191 150 Fax: +49 2191 152215
Sales Manager: O Berghaus
Technical Director: W Wiebelhaus

Parent company: Thyssen Guss AG

Products: Complete brake systems and equipment for mass transit vehicles; automatic couplers.

Developments: Thyssen Guss has restructured the company and the gearbox section has been sold to Voith Turbo GmbH (qv).

UPDATED

Bharat

Bharat Brakes and Valves Ltd
22 Gobra Road, Calcutta 700014, India
Telephone: +91 33 244 3854/1756/0857/0858
Fax: +91 33 244 0855
Deputy Manager, Modernisation & Product Development: S Sen Gupta

Products: Air brake system components; slack adjusters; distributor valves; air exhausters; air compressors.

NEW ENTRY

Bode

Gebrüder Bode & Co GmbH
Ochshäuser Strasse 14, 34123 Kassel, Germany
Telephone: +49 561 50090 Fax: +49 561 55956
Commercial Director: Rainer Wicke
Technical Director: Siegfried Heinrich
Export Manager: Horst-Dieter Bernhardt
Sales Manager: Jürgen Holz

Products: Sliding doors; plug doors (inswing/outswing, pressure-sealed); pneumatic/electric door drives; ramp systems; step systems; door controls.

Contracts: Main supplier to Mercedes-Benz, MAN, Neoplan and other European bus builders as well as Duewag, LHB, MBB and other European railway car manufacturers.

UPDATED

Bostrom

H O Bostrom
818 Progress Avenue, Waukesha, WI 53186, USA
Telephone: +1 414 542 0222 Fax: +1 414 542 3784
Presidents: John Bostrom, Kurt Bostrom
Sales & Marketing: Dave Parks

Products: Driver seating systems.

NEW ENTRY

Bowmonk

Bowmonk Limited
Diamond Road, St Faith's Industrial Estate, Norwich NR6 6AW, England
Telephone: +44 1603 485153 Fax: +44 1603 418150
General Manager: Y Hatcher
Managing Director: Roy J Street

Products: Decelerometers for road vehicle brake testing; recalibration service. European agent for fuel tank water eliminators manufactured by American Transportation Technology Corp.

The Mk VI portable electronic brake tester is self-contained and no extra wheels or sensors need to be fitted to the vehicle under test. It has a built-in printer and can store the results of up to 50 brake tests.

UPDATED

Braun

The Braun Corporation
PO Box 310, 1014 S Monticello, Winamac, IN 46996, USA
Telephone: +1 219 946 6153 Fax: +1 219 946 4670

Products: Range of mobility products; wheelchair lifts; driving aids.

Bremskerl

Bremskerl (UK) Ltd
Unit 2, Stable Yard, Windsor Bridge Road, Bath BA2 3AY, England
Telephone: +44 1225 442895 Fax: +44 1225 442896
General Manager, UK: C Prior

German company:
Bremskerl-Reibbelagwerke, Emmerling & Co
PO Box 1860, 31658 Nienburg/Weser
Telephone: +49 5025 880 Fax: +49 5025 8810
Managing Director: H Emmerling
Sales Director: R Wolf

Products: Asbestos-free organic disc brake pads and tread brake blocks.

Contracts: Pads and blocks are in operation on many European railway systems and LRT systems; also in USA.

British Furtex Fabrics

British Furtex Fabrics
Luddenfoot Mills, Luddenfoot, Halifax HX2 6AQ, England
Telephone: +44 1422 882161 Fax: +44 1422 882516
Chief Designer: Anthony L Priestly

Products: Upholstery velvets and moquettes for the coach and bus industry.

NEW ENTRY

Carrier Transicold

Carrier Transicold Division, Carrier Corporation
PO Box 4805, Carrier Parkway, Building TR20, Syracuse, NY 13221, USA
Telephone: +1 315 432 7132 Fax: +1 315 432 7218
President: Randall Hogan
General Manager, USA and Canada: Michael Kays
Vice President, ETO: Lucien Lafond
General Manager, Latin America: Hector Quezads
Vice President, Asia/Pacific: Thomas Malone

Products: Air conditioning and heating systems for rail and bus applications, roof-mounted, rear-mounted or in-vehicle; air conditioners for small vehicles; components including compressors, evaporator and heater coils, open drive and semi-hermetic compressors.

Contracts: Joint ventures for air conditioners have been announced in China, India and Brazil.

Chapman Seating

Chapman Seating Ltd
79 Miles Road, Mitcham CR4 3YL, England
Telephone: +44 181 640 6011 Fax +44 181 640 1050
Sales Manager: M Newbold

Products: Driver's, passenger and specialised seating.

NEW ENTRY

Chardon

Chardon
6 rue de Champagnole, PO Box 1, 38370 Les Roches de Condrieu, France
Telephone: +33 4 74 56 40 70 Fax: +33 4 74 56 90 88

Products: Seating for buses and coaches, including sleeper seats.

Clayton

Clayton
Hunter Terrace, Fletchworth Gate, Burnsall Road, Coventry CV5 6SP, England
Telephone: +44 1203 691916 Fax: +44 1203 691969

Products: Underseat, saloon, convector and blown heaters and accessories; demisters and climate control systems for road and rail vehicles.

UPDATED

Cleff

Cleff Fahrzeugteile GmbH
PO Box 260180, 42243 Wuppertal, Germany
Telephone: +49 202 647990 Fax: +49 202 6479988

Products: Ventilation and lighting systems for buses and coaches; windows for rail vehicles.

Coach and Car

Coach and Car Equipment Corp
1951 Arthur Avenue, Elk Grove Village, IL 60007, USA
Telephone: +1 847 437 5760 Fax: +1 847 437 9656
President: Gene Germaine
Director, Sales & Marketing: Mark Maloney

Products: Seating for bus and rail vehicles.

Contracts: Supplied over 3,000 carsets of seats to Adtranz, Bombardier, Kawasaki, Siemens-Duewag and Amtrak for various new and refurbished cars.

UPDATED

Coachair

Coachair Manufacturing Australia Pty Ltd
PO Box 60, Archerfield, Queensland 4108, Australia
Telephone: +61 7 277 8411 Fax: +61 7 277 3026

Products: Air conditioning equipment for rail vehicles and buses.

Craig & Derricott

Craig & Derricott Ltd
Hall Lane, Walsall Wood, Walsall WS9 9DP, England
Telephone: +44 1543 375541 Fax: +44 1543 452610
Managing Director: Rod Pettit
Rolling Stock Co-ordinator: Lionel Collins
Field Sales Manager: Mike Ingram
Marketing Manager: Richard Kennedy

Products: Switchgear and control panels, rotary switches and isolators, rotary switches with driver key and other interfaces, passenger alarm switches, mushroom-headed push-buttons, limit and reed switches.

Contracts: Switching components and control panels have been supplied to GEC Alsthom Metro Cammell for the Jubilee and Northern line cars for London Underground; to ABB Transportation (now Adtranz) for use on British Rail Classes 465, 323 and 165 multiple-units; for the Bakerloo, Northern, Piccadilly and Central line cars of London Underground; Docklands Light Railway cars; LRVs for Manchester Metrolink and Strasbourg.

Crompton Greaves

Crompton Greaves Limited
Rail Projects Division
Vandhna, 11 Tolstoy Marg, New Delhi 110001, India
Telephone: +91 11 331 5071/7075
Fax: +91 11 332 4360
Managing Director: K K Nohria
Vice President, Rail Transportation Systems: B Banerjee
Deputy General Manager, Rail Transportation: M P Singhal

Products: Traction transformers, SF6 gas interrupters and circuit breakers, DC traction motors, AC and DC auxiliary motors, brushless alternators for coaches, static converters/inverters.

UPDATED

Cromweld

Cromweld Steels Ltd
The Old Vicarage, Tittensor, Stoke-on-Trent ST12 9HY, England
Telephone: +44 1782 374139 Fax: +44 1782 373388

USA subsidiary
Reliance Metalcenter, 3855 Silica Drive, Colorado Springs, CO 80910, USA
Telephone: +1 719 390 4911 Fax: +1 719 390 4817
Product Manager: Jack Northart

Products: Corrosion-resistant bus framework; 3CR12 is a ferritic stainless steel, available in tube, sheet and plate.

UPDATED

Crow River

Crow River Industries Inc
14800 28th Avenue North, Minneapolis, MN 55447, USA
Telephone: +1 612 559 1680 Fax: +1 612 557 8310
President: James B Hickey Jr
Vice President, Sales & Marketing: Jerry K Sirjord
Chief Finance Officer: William Milne

Products: Wheelchair lifts and associated equipment.

Developments: An electric vairable-speed lift has been developed that fits most full-sized vans.

UPDATED

CSPL

Carstyle Safety Products Ltd
34 Gratton Road, Queens Park, Bedford MK40 4EF, England
Telephone: +44 1234 352243 Fax: +44 1234 354298
Managing Director: David Lamb
Technical & Sales Manager: Carey Lamb

Products: Seat belts for buses and coaches, made to British Standard specification.

David Brown

David Brown Rail Equipment Ltd
Park Road, Huddersfield HD4 5DD, England
Telephone: +44 1484 422180 Fax: +44 1484 435292
Managing Director: J A Vigor
Director & General Manager: N Crossley
Project Manager: N Antrobus
Part of the David Brown Group

Subsidiary company
Hygate Transmissions (qv)

Products: Design and manufacture of gears, gearboxes and associated parts for light rail, multiple-units and main line locomotives.

UPDATED

Davies & Metcalfe

Davies & Metcalfe plc
Injector Works, Romiley, Stockport SK6 3AE, England
Telephone: +44 161 430 4272 Fax: +44 161 494 2828
Managing Director: K W Pennington
Technical Manager: M J Leigh
Commercial Manager: M I Taylor
Sales Manager: J O Boyle

Subsidiary companies
Davies & Metcalfe (Repairs & Overhauls Division) Ltd, Leek, England
Davies & Metcalfe Engineering Ltd, Sydney, Australia
Davies & Metcalfe (India) Pvt Ltd, New Delhi, India

Associated company
Bergische-Stahl Industrie, 42859 Remscheid, Germany

Products: Electronic, pneumatic and electropneumatic brake control systems; air compressors; air dryers; electronic overspeed protection equipment; automatic couplers; wheel and axle-mounted disc brakes and pads; brake rigging regulators; brake cylinders; track brakes; tread brake units; wheelslip detection and correction equipment; final drive units; vigilance systems; point setting mechanism.

Contracts: A contract was awarded by Adtranz for supply of brake control equipment for the Class 325 emu trains for the Royal Mail. Davies & Metcalfe supplied EPB/1 brake control equipment and Metcalfe/Mannesmann wheel slip/slide protection equipment in 1995.

Brake control equipment has been supplied to De Dietrich for 28 coaches for Irish Rail and to Tokyu Car for 17 dmus, also for Irish Rail.

Deans Powered Doors

Deans Powered Doors Ltd
PO Box 8, Grovehill, Beverley HU17 0JL, England
Telephone: +44 1482 868111 Fax: +44 1482 881890
Managing Director: Peter Cawood
Sales & Marketing Manager: Malcolm Phillips

Products: Powered doors and door operating mechanisms; seating, bodyside lights; luggage racks; seat frames; hot-bonded door production process to give strong, lightweight door leaves.

Dellner Couplers

Dellner Couplers AB
Vikavagen 144, 79195 Falun, Sweden
Telephone: +46 23 765400 Fax: +46 23 765410
Email: info@dellner.se

Dellner Couplers Inc
8334 Arrowridge Boulevard, Charlotte, NC 28273, USA
Telephone: +1 704 527 2121 Fax: +1 704 527 2125

Dellner Kupplungen GmbH
Stahlstrasse 4a, 42281 Wuppertal, Germany
Telephone: +49 202 504026 Fax: +49 202 506021

Dellner Couplers UK
2 Birchway, Gayton L60 3SX, England
Telephone: +44 151 342 3852 Fax: +44 151 342 7040
Marketing Director: A P Pastouna

Products: Automatic couplers.

Contracts: Equipment for Ankara metro cars, Boston Red line cars, and light rail vehicles in Philadelphia, San Francisco, Boston, Baltimore and Napoli. New retracting coupler for Mannheim; double-deck trains for FS, Italy; suburban trains for Praha; people mover couplers for Vancouver and Kuala Lumpur. In addition, over 35 regenerative systems supplied, along with multiplexing equipment.

Deuta Werke

Deutsche Tachometerwerke GmbH
PO Box 200260, 51432 Bergische Gladbach, Germany
Telephone: +49 220 29580 Fax: +49 220 2958 145

Products: Incident recorder with recoverable memory module, ability to record speed and time, evaluation software and speed-dependent contacts.

Electrical and electronic tachometers, switching devices and recorders, clocks and other on-train instrumentation. SIFA deadman's handle safety system; counters; electronic data storage.

Contracts: Has supplied electronic data storage units to the German Railway (DB) and Danish State Railways (DSB).

VERIFIED

Deutsch Relays

Deutsch Relays Inc
65 Daly Road, East Northport, NY 11731, USA
Telephone: +1 516 499 6000 Fax: +1 516 499 6086
President: Jean-Marie Painvin
Vice President, Operations: Tom Sadusky
Director of Marketing: James Bedell

UK company
Deutsch Ltd
Birches Industrial Estate, East Grinstead RH19 1RW
Telephone: +44 1342 410033 Fax +44 1342 410005
Managing Director: D J Burt

French subsidiary
Relais Electroniques Deutsch
St Jean de la Rue, France

Products: Hermetically sealed relays for reliable operation under severe environmental conditions. Mating relay sockets or bases as well as other mounting systems. PCB and racking assembly design and production.

Contracts: Components have been supplied to Adtranz for cars operated by SEPTA, Philadelphia.

UPDATED

Disc-Lock Europe

Disc-Lock Europe Ltd
PO Box 134, Sittingbourne ME9 8BZ, England
Telephone: +44 1795 844332 Fax: +44 1795 843986
Sales Executive: Scott Hope

Products: Safety wheel nuts.

NEW ENTRY

Don

BBA Friction Ltd
PO Box 18, Hunsworth Lane, Cleckheaton BD19 3UJ, England
Telephone: +44 1274 854000 Fax: +44 1274 854057
Business Manager, Railway Product Group: Steve Morris
Senior Technical Engineer: John Brightmore
Aftermarket Director: Graham Ranger

Products: Composition brake blocks and disc pads for mass transit rail applications; drum and disc brake linings for buses.

Contracts: Customers include London Underground and bus companies in UK and Europe.

Developments: A new range of disc pads for buses and coaches has been announced.

UPDATED

Dorbyl

Dorbyl Rail Transport Products Ltd
PO Box 229, Boksburg 1460, South Africa
Telephone: +27 11 914 1400 Fax: +27 11 914 3885
Managing Director, Dorbyl Transport Products: Rob Duff

Products: Seating; air conditioning equipment; fuel and brake pipes; pressings and mouldings, interlocking couplers.

Subsidiary companies
Dorbyl Beperk
113 Kotzenberg Street, Rosslyn 0200, South Africa
Telephone: +27 12 541 3348/3352
Fax: +27 12 541 3528

Products: Friction material.

Metpro America Inc
548 Sunrise Highway, West Babylon, New York 11704
Telephone: +1 516 661 8004 Fax: +1 516 661 8820
Marketing Executive: William Pellegrino

Products: Composition brake blocks.

SWASAP
PO Box 366, Germiston 1400, South Africa
Telephone: +27 11 825 3110 Fax: +27 11 873 1825

Products: Rail vehicle axles and wheelsets.

Contracts: Brake blocks have been supplied to Spoornet, South Africa, and other South African rail operators.

NEW ENTRY

EAO

Electro-Apparatebau Olten AG
Tannwaldstrasse 88, 4601 Olten, Switzerland
Telephone: +41 62 286 9111 Fax: +41 62 286 2162
Marketing Directorr: Christian Galli
Export Manager: Ron Haverman
Export Sales Manager: Beat Lienhard
Subsidiary companies in England, Germany, Hong Kong, Japan, Netherlands, Sweden and USA

Products: Driver control panel components, push buttons, indicators, buzzers, rotary switches, external door push buttons, static convertors.

UPDATED

Eaton

Cutler-Hammer
Power Controls Division
Peacock Way, Melton Constable NR24 2BZ, England
Telephone: +44 1263 860581 Fax: +44 1263 861417
Technical Manager: John Everitt
Resistor Business Manager: Malcolm Fisher
Parent company: Westinghouse & Cutler-Hammer Products, Ottery St Mary EX11 1AG

Products: Power resistors for transport applications, including naturally cooled roof or under-car-mounted resistors, designed to meet the load requirements of each vehicle. Infra-red temperature monitoring and protection system offering remote indication and status.

EBAC

EBAC Ltd
St Helen Industrial Estate, Bishop Auckland DL14 9AL, England
Telephone: +44 1388 605061 Fax: +44 1388 609845
Managing Director: J M Elliott
Sales Director: Graham Higgs

Products: Design and manufacture of heating, ventilation and air conditioning units and systems; heat pump systems; microprocessor control and diagnostic systems for HVAC; repair, overhaul and maintenance of HVAC and associated products; R134a conversions of air conditioning and refrigeration systems; dehumidifiers for storage and other applications; space heaters. HVAC systems now use 'ozone friendly' R134a, and existing units can be converted to this standard.

Contracts: Cab air conditioning and ventilation for London Underground's Jubilee line trains; HVAC systems for DB VT611 stock.

EG & G Rotron

EG & G Rotron
9 Hasbrouck Lane, Woodstock, NY 12498, USA
Telephone: +1 914 679 1542 Fax: +1 914 679 1878

Subsidiary company
EG & G Rotron UK
Coronation Road, High Wycombe HP12 3TP, England
Telephone: +44 1494 451661 Fax: +44 1494 452425

Products: Air conditioning equipment; condenser and evaporator motors; blowers; water circulating pumps.

NEW ENTRY

Thomas Electronics

Thomas Electronics
Congleton CW12 1DT, England
Telephone: +44 1260 298527/298528
Fax: +44 1260 298529
Managing Director: Simon Bernard

Products: Engine protection systems; flasher units; battery chargers; inverters; audible warnings; tyre pressure monitoring systems; vehicle security.

Thorn Transport Lighting

Thorn Transport Lighting Ltd
Transport Lighting Division
Elstree Way, Borehamwood WD6 1HZ, England
Telephone: +44 181 967 6336 Fax: +44 181 967 6337
General Manager: Bob Richardson

Products: Light fittings, inverters and lighting components for buses and rail vehicles.

UPDATED

Tibram

Tibram AG
Aarestrasse 29, 3661 Uetendorf, Switzerland
Telephone: +41 33 345 1057 Fax: +41 33 345 5957

Products: Earthing brushes for locomotives, LRVs and emus, rated at 750-1000 A; insulators; brush holders; air exchangers; parts for axle housings.

UPDATED

Time 24

Time 24 Ltd
Unit 69, Victoria Road, Burgess Hill RH15 9TR, England
Telephone: +44 1444 257655 Fax: +44 1444 259000
Sales Manager: Chris Young
Quality Assurance Manager: Robert Thomas
Production Director: Mark Willifer
Director: David Shore

Products: Traction and brake controllers; cable assemblies, harnesses and looms.

Contracts: Panel wiring for London Underground Northern line trains; brake controllers for Swedish operators.

UPDATED

Timken

The Timken Company
Canton, OH 44706, USA

British Timken Division of The Timken Company
Duston, Northampton NN5 6UL, England
Telephone: +44 1604 752311 Fax: +44 1604 586635
Managing Director, British Timken: I W Tucker
General Manager, Rail: D N Valentine
Telephone: +44 1604 586665 Fax: +44 1604 586615

Products: Tapered roller bearings; AP and SP tapered roller bearing cartridge units; complete axleboxes and motor suspension units. Timken supplies tapered roller bearings and ancillary equipment including transmissions, axleboxes, traction motor suspension units and other equipment such as cooling fans and screw compressors. Also used extensively in bus transmission and axle applications.

Developments: A joint venture has been set up with the Shandong Yantai Bearing Factory in the People's Republic of China, known as the Yantai Timken Co Ltd.

UPDATED

Toshiba

Toshiba Corporation
Railway Projects Department
Toshiba Building, 1-Shibaura 1-chome, Minato-ku, Tokyo 100-01, Japan
Telephone: +81 3 3457 4924 Fax: +81 3 5444 9422
(See main entry under Rail Vehicles and Traction Equipment)

Products: Heating, ventilation and air conditioning equipment; AC and DC electrification equipment.

UPDATED

Transintech

Transintech Ltd
PO Box 21, Derby Carriage Works, Litchurch Lane, Derby DE24 8AP, England
Telephone: +44 1332 257500 Fax: +44 1332 371950
Commercial Director: Andrew Burrows

Background: Transintech began as an independent company in 1995 following the purchase of the former Interiors Division of Adtranz (qv) by a management buy-in team in association with Mac Composites, Loxko plc and Kobe Steel.

Products: Complete interiors; refurbishment; seating; doors; GRP cab fronts; complete cab modules; wiring looms; electrical control and switch panels.

Contracts: Include complete interiors of saloon and cab for Adtranz Strasbourg Eurotram; refurbishment of London Underground's Metropolitan line A stock; Jubilee line car interiors.

Transmatic

Transmatic Inc
6145 Delfield Industrial Drive, Waterford, MI 48329, USA
Telephone: +1 810 623 2500 Fax: +1 810 623 2839
President: O K Dealey Jr
Vice President, Sales & Marketing: M T Hoffman
Vice President, Environmental Systems:
D Scott McConnell

UK subsidiary
Transmatic Europe Ltd
B3 Hortonwood 10, Telford TF1 4ES, England
Telephone: +44 1952 608383 Fax: +44 1952 677693
Managing Director: Terry Calnon

Products: Interior lighting and advertising coving for buses and urban transit vehicles; multipurpose lighting/air conditioning duct modules; surface-mounted fluorescent lighting; destination sign lighting; interior cleaning systems for buses and rail vehicles.

Contracts: Systems have been supplied to major operators in USA, including Los Angeles, New York and Chicago. Also to Adelaide and Hobart, Australia; Wellington, New Zealand; Kowloon Motor Bus and Citybus, Hong Kong; Kuala Lumpur; Göteborg, Sweden; Edinburgh and Belfast, UK.

Developments: The L20 modular lighting/ducting system has been developed for low-floor vehicles.

UPDATED

Transpec

Transpec
575 Robbins Drive, Troy, MI 48083-4554, USA
Telephone: +1 810 588 8720 Fax: +1 810 588 1588
President: Ronald C Lamparter
General Manager: James A Haigh
Director of Sales: Michael Martinez
International Sales: Robert A Peticca

Products: Combination roof ventilator and emergency exits for buses and rail vehicles.

VERIFIED

Transtechnik

Transtechnik GmbH
Ohmstrasse 1-3, 83607 Holzkirchen, Germany
Telephone: +49 8024 9900 Fax: +49 8024 990300
Email: info@transtechnik.com
Web: www.transtechnik.com
Chair: Wilhelm Sterff
Managing Director: Robert Sterff
Manager, Marketing Communications:
Tom Weber-Reichardt
Sales: Andreas Baerend
Technical & Engineering: Helmut Eisinger

International Marketing Office:
Transtechnik PSI
Chiltern House, High Street, Chalfont St Giles HP8 4QH, England
Telephone: +44 1494 871544 Fax: +44 1494 873118
Marketing Manager: Ian Lavis

Products: Auxiliary power converters for all rail vehicle and trolleybus onboard services and special power electronic applications.

Contracts: Converters have been supplied for the P2000 LRVs in Los Angeles. They have an AC output of 66 kVA and a DC output of 12 kW.

UPDATED

Triplex

Triplex Safety Glass Co Ltd
Triplex House, Eckersall Road, Kings Norton, Birmingham B38 8SR, England
Telephone: +44 121 433 3344 Fax: +44 121 433 3541
Managing Director: Brian J McGinty
Customer Development Director: Mike A Fallon
General Manager, Sales: Garry Sweeny

Assembly plant: Knowsley Road, Eccleston, St Helens WA10 4QB

Products: Toughened and laminated glass for transit vehicles.

Twiflex

Twiflex Limited
104 The Green, Twickenham TW2 5AQ, England
Telephone: +44 181 894 1161 Fax: +44 181 894 6056
Managing Director: J T Starbuck
Sales Director: A S Hughes

Parent company: Tomkins plc

Products: 'Layrub' flexible couplings and shafts; 'Laylink' flexible couplings and shafts; 'Twiflex' disc brake systems, automatic clutch couplings and flexiclutch couplings.

Unicel

Unicel Corporation Transportation
Composites Division
1520 Industrial Avenue, Escondido, CA 92029, USA
Telephone: +1 619 741 3912 Fax: +1 619 741 8832
Vice President: Michael Henderson
Sales Manager: Thomas F Ryan

Products: Lightweight composites and honeycomb panels for passenger car interiors.

Contracts: Include customers from Europe, Japan, South Korea and USA.

Vapor

Vapor
6420 West Howard Street, Niles, IL 60714, USA
Telephone: +1 847 967 8300 Fax: +1 847 965 9870
President & General Manager: D M Kerr
Senior Vice President: J A Machesney
Vice President, Sales & Marketing: K N Nippes
A Mark IV Industries company

Associated company
Vapor Canada Inc
10655 Henri Bourassa West, St Laurent, PQ H4S 1A1, Canada

Products: Automatic door control systems and accessories; environmental controls; relays, contactors.

Contracts: Include door equipment for the 680 cars built by ABB Transportation for London Underground's Central line, plus equipment for Northern line cars being built by GEC Alsthom (qv); supplying Kawasaki (qv) with equipment for Maryland DoT/MARC III (50 sets) and Long Island Rail Road (114 sets).

Also supplying Amerail with equipment for the Metra Highliner emu refurbishment programme (140 sets), Metra gallery cars (173 sets), Caltrans cars (88 sets) and BART San Francisco cars (80 sets); equipment to Breda for Muni San Francisco LRVs (44 sets) and Los Angeles Red line cars (42 sets); equipment for 30 carsets supplied for Siemens LRVs for Portland.

VERIFIED

VAW aluminium

VAW aluminium AG
Georg-von-Boeselager Str 25, 53117 Bonn, Germany
Telephone: +49 228 55202 Fax: +49 228 552 2268
Chair: Jochen Schirner
Board Members: Dr Karl Heinz Dörner
Manfred Eicker, Jürgen Hermans, Karl D Wobbe

UK subsidiary
VAW West Yorkshire Foundries Ltd
PO Box 159, Clarence Road, Leeds LS1 1QX, England
Telephone: +44 113 283 1042 Fax: +44 113 242 2429

Products: Metal production and fabrication including rolling and converting of aluminium; aluminium engine castings; flexible packaging; extruded products.

UPDATED

VBK

Vestfold Bil & Karosseri AS
PO Box 98, 3191 Horten, Norway
Telephone: +47 3307 3700 Fax: +47 3307 3725
General Manager: Olav Fossgard
Seating Department Manager: Jo Laaveg
Marketing Co-ordinator, Seating: Kristin Helgesen

Products: Seating for rolling stock; interior equipment, including luggage racks, crew compartment, luggage module.

Veam

Veam, Division of Litton Systems Inc
100 New Wood Road, Watertown, CT 06795, USA
Telephone: +1 203 274 9681 Fax: +1 203 274 4963
President: Constance Zagar

Products: Electrical, optical and pneumatic connectors for trainline, brake systems, air conditioning, speed sensing, communications, lighting, automatic coupling and traction motor applications.

VERIFIED

Vogelsitze

Vogelsitze
Kleinsteinbacher Strasse 44, 76228 Karlsruhe, Germany
Telephone: +49 721 47020 Fax: +49 721 4702 170

Subsidiary company
Vis-Vogel Interieur Schienenfahrzeuge
Eisenbahnstr 3, 06132 Halle/Ammendorf, Germany

Products: Seating.

VERIFIED

Voith

Voith Turbo GmbH & Co KG
Railway Components and Systems Division
PO Box 1930, 89509 Heidenheim, Germany
Telephone: +49 7321 370 Fax: +49 7321 377000
Chairman of Rail Products: Dr Ing Hermann Bruns
General Manager, Turbo Transmissions:
Dipl Ing Karl Dahler
General Manager, Axles Drives: Dr Ing Klaus Brosius

Subsidiary companies
Japan, South Korea, Hong Kong, Australia and major European countries

Products: Turbo transmissions for rail vehicles, axle drives, cooling units, cardan shafts; torsional vibration dampers.

Components for light rail vehicles and tramways: axle drives (bevel gearboxes and spur gearboxes); Voith Hydrolock limited-slip differentials.

Hydrolock: this is a hydrostatic limited-slip for modern single-wheel drives. It consists of an enclosed planetary gearbox driven by a spur or bevel gear stage, which allows independent rolling of the wheels without alteration of existing low-floor concepts in LRVs or trams. The drive is via only one motor. Hydrolock has the characteristics of a single-wheel motor drive, but with the advantages of a rigid wheelset. It is offered as an alternative to more complex separately controlled electric motors.

Contracts: Hydrolock limited-slip differential has been developed for LRVs in Stuttgart and 14 are being supplied.

UPDATED

WABCO

Westinghouse Air Brake Company
Passenger Transit Division
PO Box 11, Spartanburg, SC 29304-0011, USA
Telephone: +1 867 433 5900 Fax: +1 867 433 0176

Products: Brake systems for rolling stock; couplers; electronic control equipment; current collection systems, pantographs and overhead electrification equipment.

Is North American licensee for BSI products, including gear units, track and disc brakes.

UPDATED

Webasto

Webasto Thermosystems (UK) Ltd
White Rose Way, Doncaster Carr, Doncaster DN14 5JH, England
Telephone: +44 1302 322232 Fax: +44 1302 322231
Commercial Director: Roger Edwards

Products: Air conditioning, heaters; independent combustion heaters for engine pre-heating and passenger saloon heaters.

UPDATED

Westinghouse Brakes

Westinghouse Brakes Limited
PO Box 74, Foundry Lane, Chippenham SN15 1HY, England
Telephone: +44 1249 442000 Fax: +44 1249 655040
Managing Director: J A Cotton
Sales & Marketing Director: J E Clark
Engineering Director: W B S Johnston
Sales & Marketing Manager: C Blake
Commercial Manager & Senior Projects Manager: P R Johnson
Aftersales Business Division Manager: T Park

A member of the BTR Rail Group and a subsidiary of Westinghouse Brake and Signal Holdings Ltd

Products: Brake systems — air and vacuum brake equipment, electropneumatic brake equipment with digital (Westcode) or analogue control for metro and commuter passenger vehicles. Equipment includes rotary and reciprocating air compressors, air dryers, brake and traction controllers, brake actuation equipment and wheelslip control equipment.

Platform screen door systems; aftersales service including overhaul, repair and long-term maintenance.

Contracts: Brakes and detrainment doors supplied for London Underground Jubilee line cars; brakes and detrainment doors for Northern line cars; brakes for Heathrow Express emus; brakes for Hong Kong Lantau line emus; platform screen doors for Jubilee line and for Kuala Lumpur LRT Phase II.

UPDATED

Williamson

T & R Williamson Ltd
36 Stonebridgegate, Ripon HG4 1TP, England
Telephone: +44 1765 607711 Fax: +44 1765 607908
Managing Director: Abubakar A Sheibani
General Manager: R J Herod
Technical Service Manager: N Kershaw

Products: Specialist livery and protective coatings for all types of urban transport vehicles, including anti-graffiti and fire-retardant finishes.

Woodhead

Woodhead Shock-Absorbers
Church Street, Ossett WF5 9DL, England
Telephone: +44 1924 273521 Fax: +44 1924 276167
Chairman: S Beyazit
Sales Manager: A C Kart

Products: Twin-tube hydraulic dampers for LRVs and metro cars; door closing gear dampers.

Contracts: Adtranz, for Eurotram; Greater Manchester Metrolink LRVs; London Underground Ltd; supply of dampers for BX1-Series bogies for UK second-generation emu/dmu stock.

UPDATED

ŽDB

ŽDB AS
Wheelsets Division
Bezručova 300, 73593 Bohumín, Czech Republic
Telephone: +420 69 608 3328/2610
Fax: +420 69 608 2805
President & General Manager: Tomšej Jakub
Managing Director, Wheelset Division: Balcárek Vilem
Marketing Manager: Dipl Ing Eduard Kalisch

Products: Wheelsets, with and without disc brakes, monobloc technology, axles and tyres for LRVs.

Contracts: Wheelsets have been supplied to light railways and railways in Germany, Austria, Russia, Slovakia, Italy, Norway, Sweden, Egypt, Korea and USA.

UPDATED

ZF Hurth

ZF Hurth Bahntechnik GmbH
Adelheidstr 40, 88046 Freidrichschafen, Germany
Telephone: +49 7541 30601 Fax: +49 7541 306400

Products: Helical, hypoid and bevel gear axle drive units for fully or partially suspended drives; input couplings, axle gearboxes and flexible axle couplings for LRVs, multiple-unit trains and locomotives; transmissions for diesel railcars; special transmissions (including planetary wheel hub drives) for low-floor vehicles; custom-designed gears.

UPDATED

ZF Padova

ZF Padova SpA
Via Penghe 48, 35030 Caselle di Selvazzano Dentro, Padova, Italy
Telephone: +39 49 829 9311 Fax: +39 49 829 9550
Managing Director: Francesco Petilli

Background: ZF Padova was formerly Meccanica Padana Monteverde (MPM).

Products: Drive axles for rail vehicles (including rubber-tyre), special drive units. Computer programs (including FEA) for calculation and design of drive units to customers' specifications. Trials can be carried out on recirculating power test rigs which automatically simulate the actual duty cycles of the vehicle involved.

ELECTRIFICATION — PROJECT CONTRACTORS AND EQUIPMENT SUPPLIERS

Company Listing by Country

AUSTRALIA
Adtranz

AUSTRIA
Adtranz

BELGIUM
GEC Alsthom ACEC Transport

CANADA
Carbone of America
Cegelec BG Automatec

FINLAND
Adtranz
Electric Rails

FRANCE
Carrier Kheops
Cegelec
Faiveley Transport
Jacques Galland
Lerc
Spie Enertrans

GERMANY
Adtranz
Elpro
Siemens

HUNGARY
Ganz Ansaldo

INDIA
Crompton Greaves

ITALY
Adtranz
Ansaldo
Firema
Parizzi
Pfisterer

JAPAN
Fuji Electric
Hitachi
Mitsubishi Electric
Toshiba

NORWAY
Adtranz

POLAND
Elektrim

PORTUGAL
Adtranz

SPAIN
Adtranz
Sainco

SWEDEN
Adtranz

SWITZERLAND
Adtranz
Arthur Flury
Furrer + Frey
Kummler & Matter
Melcher
Premel
Sécheron
Sefag

UK
Adtranz
Balfour Beatty
Brecknell, Willis
Cegelec Projects
Clough Smith
GEC Alsthom Transportation Projects
James Scott
Pirelli
PMES
RMC
Transmitton
Whipp & Bourne

USA
Adtranz
Delta Star
Electro Wire
Siemens Transportation Systems
TransTech

Classified Listing

CIRCUIT BREAKERS
Ansaldo
Crompton Greaves
Elektrim
Firema
Fuji Electric
Gardy
GEC Alsthom ACEC Transport
Mitsubishi Electric
Sécheron
Siemens
Toshiba
Whipp & Bourne

COMPLETE SYSTEMS — OVERHEAD
Adtranz
Ansaldo
Balfour Beatty
Delta Star
Electric Rails
Elektrim
Elpro
Firema
Furrer + Frey
Ganz Ansaldo
James Scott
Kummler & Matter
Pirelli
Siemens
Siemens Transportation Systems
Spie Enertrans

COMPLETE SYSTEMS — THIRD RAIL
Adtranz
Brecknell, Willis
Delta Star
Firema
Siemens

CURRENT COLLECTORS — OVERHEAD/PANTOGRAPH
Brecknell, Willis
Carbone of America
Faiveley Transport

CURRENT COLLECTORS — THIRD RAIL
Brecknell, Willis
Faiveley Transport
TransTech

FITTINGS FOR OVERHEAD, INCLUDING INSULATORS AND POLES
Adtranz
Arthur Flury
Brecknell, Willis
Delta Star
Faiveley Transport
Jacques Galland
Lerc
Pfisterer
Premel
Sefag

INSPECTION EQUIPMENT
Furrer + Frey

POWER SUPPLY & CONTROL
Adtranz
Balfour Beatty
Carrier Kheops
Cegelec
Cegelec Projects
Electric Rails
Elektrim
Elpro
Fuji
Ganz Ansaldo
GEC Alsthom
Melcher
Mitsubishi
PMES
RMC
Sainco
Siemens
Transmitton

SUBSTATIONS
Adtranz
Ansaldo
Cegelec
Cegelec BG Automatic
Electric Rails
Elektrim
Elpro
Firema
Fuji Electric
Hitachi
Mitsubishi
PMES
SAE (India)
Sainco
Sécheron
Siemens
Siemens Transportation Systems
Toshiba

TROLLEYBUS ELECTRIFICATION EQUIPMENT
(See also Trolleybus Traction Equipment)
Adtranz
Arthur Flury
Clough Smith
Elpro
Furrer + Frey
Kummler & Matter
Pfisterer
Pirelli
Siemens
Spie Enertrans

WIRE (OVERHEAD)/CABLE
Electro Wire
Elektrim
Elpro
Pirelli
Siemens

GEC Alsthom ACEC Transport

GEC Alsthom ACEC Transport SA
PO Box 4211, 6000 Charleroi, Belgium
Telephone: +32 71 445411 Fax: +32 71 445775

Products: Ultra-fast DC circuit breaker.

VERIFIED

GEC Alsthom

GEC Alsthom Transportation Projects
PO Box 134, Manchester M60 1AH, England
Telephone: +44 161 872 2431 Fax: +44 161 875 2131
(See main entry under Rail Vehicles and Traction Equipment)

Products: Composite main line, suburban and rapid transit electrification schemes, including project management, provision and installation of complete systems and equipment; provision of electric rolling stock and propulsion equipment.

Developments: GT Railway Maintenance Ltd, a joint venture between GEC Alsthom and Tarmac Construction has acquired the Central Infrastructure Maintenance Company (CIMCo) from British Rail. CIMCo is responsible for maintenance of Railtrack's signalling and electrification equipment in the Midlands, East Anglia, mid-Wales and the West Coast route between London and Carlisle.

UPDATED

Hitachi

Hitachi Ltd
6 Kanda Surugadai 4-chome, Chiyoda-ku, Tokyo 101, Japan
Telephone: +81 3 3258 1111 Fax: +81 3 3258 5212
(See main entry under Rail Vehicles and Traction Equipment)

Products: Substation equipment for AC and DC electrification projects; diode and thyristor rectifiers; power regenerative inverters; transformers; AC and DC switchgear; control and protection devices; computerised systems — substation supervisory remote-control systems, automatic car diagnosis system, station management system, security system.

Jacques Galland

Jacques Galland SA
20 rue de l'Insurrection Parisienne, 94600 Choisy-le-Roi, France
Telephone: +33 1 46 80 25 72 Fax: +33 1 46 80 83 42
Manager: Denis Galland
Technical Manager: Philippe D'Huy

Products: Lightweight section insulators; catenary materials for wide range of applications including tramways.

Contracts: Catenary equipment has been supplied to tramways and metros in Lille, Grenoble, Lyon, and Paris (St Denis—Bobigny).

UPDATED

James Scott

James Scott Ltd
80-110 Finnieston Street, Glasgow G3 8LA, Scotland
Telephone: +44 141 221 3866 Fax: +44 141 226 3068
Sales & Marketing Director: Mick Beck

Products: Complete catenary systems for light rail and other rail installations.

Contracts: Complete replacement overhead system for Fleetwood—Blackpool tramway, England.

Kummler & Matter

Kummler & Matter AG
Hohlstrasse 176, 8026 Zürich, Switzerland
Telephone: +41 1 247 4747 Fax: +41 1 291 0262
President & Chief Executive Officer: Dr H Meier
Vice President & Division Manager: Daniel Steiner
Export Sales Manager: Rodolfo Middelmann
Head of Trolleybus & Light Rail Engineering Department: Willy-Urs Brassel

Associated companies
Kummler & Matter (Holland)
Kummler & Matter Trolvill (Hungary)
Licensee: L B Foster Co, Doraville, GA, USA

Products: Overhead catenary for rail and trolleybus installations; lightweight trolleybus power collection system.

Contracts: Include installations in Switzerland, France, USA and Italy.

UPDATED

Lerc

Lerc SA
Chemin des Hamaïdes, PO Box 119, 59732 Saint Amand les Eaux Cedex, France
Telephone: +33 3 27 22 85 50 Fax: +33 3 27 22 85 55
Export Manager: F Romet

Products: A range of insulators with silicon shed shells for railway, tramway and metro lines.

Melcher

Melcher AG
Ackerstrasse 56, 8610 Uster, Switzerland
Telephone: +41 1 944 8111 Fax: +41 1 940 9858
Email: info@melcher-power.com
Web: http://www.melcher-power.com
President: Thomas Seiler
Product Manager: Claude Abächerli

Products: DC-DC converters, inverters, battery chargers — 64 product families with output power in a range of 1 to 1,000 W. All Melcher power products are ISO 9001 certified. Miniature-size switching regulator.

Contracts: Customers include GEC Alsthom, Siemens, Adtranz, GM and many transport undertakings.

Developments: In 1996 Electrowatt AG sold the Melcher Group to Melcher management and to SBC Equity Partners, a subsidiary of Swiss Bank corporation.

UPDATED

Mitsubishi Electric

Mitsubishi Electric Corporation
2-3, Marunouchi 2-chome, Chiyoda-ku, Tokyo 100, Japan
Telephone: +81 3 3218 3429 Fax: +81 3 3218 2895
(See main entry under Rail Vehicles and Traction Equipment)

Products: Traction substation equipment, rectifiers, transformers, air conditioning equipment, high-speed circuit breakers, centralised supervisory control of power supply systems.

Pfisterer

Pfisterer Srl
Via A Pacinotti 31, 20094 Corsico, Italy
Telephone: +39 2 4510 0213 Fax: +39 2 447 9008
Managing Director: Dr Ing Osvaldo Nannini
Export Manager: Dr Ing Paolo Zorzan

Products: Silicon rubber composite insulators for overhead electrification systems; clamps, voltage detectors, earthing devices; all suitable for trolleybus, tramway, metro and main line rail systems.

Contracts: Has supplied arm insulator silicon rubber and tension insulators to Belgian National Railways (SNCB). Other equipment supplied in recent years to the Nord Milano Railway (FNME), ATM Milano tramway and Torino's trolleybus network, as well as to Italian Railways (FS) for various main line projects.

Pirelli

Pirelli Construction Co Ltd
PO Box 6, Leigh Road, Eastleigh SO50 5YE, England
Telephone: +44 1703 295400 Fax: +44 1703 295111
Managing Director: J A L Lewis
Business Director, Utilities: R J W Barrett
Chief Engineer: S Ford

Products: Design, provision and installation of overhead electrification equipment for tramway, light rail and trolleybus networks; all types of power, signalling and communication cables; civil and electrical engineering.

Power and telecommunications cables, including track feeder cables. The company has introduced low-smoke zero halogen (LSOH) cables for power, signalling and communications purposes. They are for metro systems and were developed in conjunction with London Transport.

Contracts: Supplied equipment for the Leeds local railways electrification, UK, for which 120 track-km of overhead was installed.

Installation of power supplies for London Underground's Jubilee line extension project.

UPDATED

PMES

Power Magnetics & Electronic Systems Ltd
Armitage Road, Rugeley WS15 1DR, England
Telephone: +44 1889 585151 Fax: +44 1889 577324
Managing Director: J C Sheldon
Sales & Marketing Executive: C C T Millard
Sales Manager: T W Boston
Business Manager: A S Clark

Background: Was formerly Thorn Automation, which had been supplying transformer/rectifier systems for 40 years.

Products: Transformers, rectifiers and associated substation equipment for main line and light rail electrification; turnkey contracts for complete DC substation supply including AC and DC switchgear, TRUs and circuit works.

Contracts: Provision of 19 transformer rectifiers for London Underground Northern line renewal programme; turnkey contract from Railtrack, UK, to extend the Chester to Hooton electrification; turnkey project to update Docklands Light Railway DC power system, including depot, control and seven substations; contract for Japanese client for nine transformer rectifiers for a Southeast Asian application.

UPDATED

Premel

Premel SA
Via del Carmagnola 16, 6517 Arbedo, Switzerland
Telephone: +41 92 293261 Fax: +41 92 277789
Director: Ing Reto Bolgiani
Distributor: ETA Service SA, Residenza 51, 6528 Camorino, Switzerland
Telephone: +41 91 829 3261 Fax: +41 91 829 1369

Products: Electromechanical compensating tensioner for overhead lines.

Contracts: With Swiss Federal Railways, for St Gotthard and Simplon tunnels.

UPDATED

RMC

RMC Concrete Products Ltd
St Helen Auckland, Bishop Auckland, DL14 9AJ, England
Telephone: +44 1388 603961 Fax: +44 1388 450056
Sales Manager: James Tristram

Products: Cable trough system for power and telecommunications protection which includes Imperial Units, cabinet bases, T-pieces, taper units and a standard range of troughs and the Lidloc anti-vandal locking lid system.

Contracts: UK clients include Railtrack and the Department of Transport.

NEW ENTRY

Sainco

Sainco
Los Vascos 17, 28040 Madrid, Spain
Telephone: +34 1 554 5800 Fax: +34 1 535 2285
Sales Manager: José Martínez-Joranco

Products: Advanced remote-control systems for traction power supply electrical substations.

Sécheron

Sécheron Ltd
Avenue de Sécheron 14, 1211 Genève, Switzerland
Telephone: +41 22 739 4111 Fax: +41 22 738 7305
General Manager: Claude Chabanel
Group Sales Manager: Ivano Caffari
Sales Manager: Jimmy Cuche

Subsidiary companies
Autometers Sécheron, Noida, New Delhi, India
CKD Sécheron spol sro, Praha, Czech Republic
Pixy AG, Baden, Switzerland
Sécheron Hasler Praha spol sro, Czech Republic
Shanghai Sécheron Electrical Apparatus Co Ltd, Shanghai, People's Republic of China
Škoda Sécheron spol sro, Blovice, Czech Republic

See also Rail and Bus Components and Signalling, Communications and Traffic Control Equipment sections

Products: Complete DC substations, including stationary and portable equipment; solid-state rectifier and inverter equipment; DC switchgear equipped with high-speed circuit breakers; on-load switches, isolators; harmonic filters; control and monitoring equipment; electronic protection relays; cast-resin or oil-immersed transformers; medium-voltage switchgear; microprocessor-based remote-control and protection systems. Also project co-ordination, network calculations, computer simulations and energy recovery.

Contracts: Include supply of DC switchgear for Lines 6, 7 and 8 of Seoul metro as well as line 1 of Incheon metro and Line 2 of Pusan metro.

UPDATED

Sefag

Sefag AG
Werkstrasse 7, 6102 Malters, Switzerland
Telephone: +41 41 497 1991 Fax: +41 41 497 2269
Managing Director: K O Papailiou
Technical Director: W Fluri
Sales Director: W Bachmann
Works Director: W Wipfli

Products: Silcosil insulators with silicon sheds as suspension, dead-end and post insulators, and as special insulators for tunnels and high-speed rail.

Contracts: Supplied to Swiss Federal Railways, Austrian Federal Railways, Bern-Lötschberg-Simplon Railway and other railways in Switzerland; also to railways in other countries.

UPDATED

Siemens

Siemens Aktiengesellschaft
Transportation Systems Group (VT)

Transmission Lines & Catenaries Division (VT3)
PO Box 3240, Werner-von-Siemens Strasse 67, 91050 Erlangen, Germany
Telephone: +49 9131 22457 Fax: +49 9131 727969
Division Executive Management
Technical: H Habekmann
Commercial: L Zagel

Catenaries Mass Transit Systems Subdivision (VT32)
Subdivision Executive Management: J Wolf

Products: Catenaries for mass transit, urban and suburban lines; third-rail supply and installation for metros; project engineering, materials supply and erection, as well as training, commissioning and maintenance; supply of components for contact line systems.

Contracts: More than 20,000 track-km of contact line systems (AC and DC) have been supplied and installed in Germany and worldwide, including Portland, San Jose, Dublin, Guadalajara, Tunis light rail, Rotterdam, MTRC Hong Kong, Konya (Turkey), Monterrey, Guangzhou, Ankara and Wien.

Traction Power Supplies Subdivision (VT34)
Subdivision Executive Management: W Kuttner

Products: Traction power supply equipment, DC for urban transport and AC for main line systems, comprising substations including mobile units, AC high/medium voltage switchgear, transformers, rectifiers, static and rotating convertors; DC switchgear including high-speed DC circuit breakers, protection and control equipment, power cables.

Contracts: Worldwide contracts include metro systems in Taipei, Shanghai, Budapest, Stockholm, Barcelona, Shanghai; light rail systems in Los Angeles, Denver and Portland; railway customers include DB, RENFE, SNCB, ÖBB, and Railways of the People's Republic of China. Siemens is supplying traction power supply equipment for the Bangkok elevated road and train system. It is also consortium leader for the project which includes supply of metro cars by Adtranz and track by Balfour Beatty.

Turnkey Systems Division (VT4)
PO Box 3240, Werner-von-Siemens Strasse 67, 91050 Erlangen
Telephone: +49 9131 727419 Fax: +49 9131 721807
Division Executive Management
Technical: F Hasselbacher
Commercial: K Neubeck

Products: Manufacture and supply of equipment with full turnkey project capability worldwide, comprising planning, design and construction of both electrical and civil works, project management, installation and commissioning; training of operational and maintenance staff; after-sales service; financing.

Contracts: Recent turnkey contracts have been for light rail systems in Tunis, Medellin, Konya and Ankara (Turkey) and Guadalajara; and for metro systems in Shanghai and Athens.

UPDATED

Siemens Transportation Systems

Siemens Transportation Systems Inc
Headquarters and Mainline Infrastructure Division, 186 Wood Avenue South, Iselin, NJ 08830 USA
Telephone: +1 908 205 2210 Fax: +1 908 603 7379
President & Chief Executive Officer: J Morrison

Traction Electrification Division
300 Oswego Pointe Drive, Suite 106, Lake Oswego, OR 97034
Telephone: +1 503 699 0071 Fax: +1 503 699 0076

Products: Components for complete traction power substations for AC and DC urban transport rail systems, including catenary equipment, components and static convertors.

Contracts: Tri-Met Portland awarded two contracts to Siemens Transportation Systems for the 29 km Westside light rail extension. Siemens is also providing the substations and catenaries for Amtrak's northeast corridor electrification.

UPDATED

Spie Enertrans

Spie Enertrans
Parc Saint-Christophe, Pôle Edison, 10 avenue de l'Enterprise, 95861 Cergy-Pointoise, France
Telephone: +33 1 34 22 50 00 Fax: +33 1 34 22 62 50

Products: Complete overhead wiring systems.

Contracts: Systems have been installed in Bobigny, Grenoble, Lille and Rouen.

NEW ENTRY

Toshiba

Toshiba Corporation
Railway Projects Department
Toshiba Building, 1-Shibaura 1-chome, Minato-ku, Tokyo 105-01, Japan
Telephone: +81 3 3457 4924 Fax: +81 3 5444 9422

Products: Substation equipment for AC and DC electrification; transformers, rectifiers, circuit breakers, GIS, SVC and arresters. Remote-control and supervisory systems.

UPDATED

Transmitton

Transmitton Limited
Smisby Road, Ashby-de-la-Zouch LE65 2UG, England
Telephone: +44 1530 415941 Fax: +44 1530 414224
Managing Director: David Moore
Sales & Marketing Director: Philip Stockdale
Engineering Director: David Cubitt
Finance Director: Guy Bryant

Products: Supervisory control and data acquisition (SCADA) systems for power supply applications; central master control systems for signalling, passenger information and CCTV installations; data logging, point-to-point and inter-trip telemetry systems.

Contracts: Has supplied power supply control systems to Railtrack South West, London Underground and Sheffield Supertram.

UPDATED

TransTech

TransTech of SC
196 Old Augusta Road, Piedmont, SC 29673, USA
Telephone: +1 864 299 3870 Fax: +1 864 277 7100
President: R J Grattan
Commercial Director: G C Nesta
Technical Director: K Rieder

Products: Traction motor components, brush holders, connectors, control components; licensee for Stemmann (Germany) and Brecknell, Willis (UK) pantographs and components; slip springs, festoon systems, electrical distributors; Ringsdorff carbon collector shoes; Klein sanding systems. Pantograph refurbishment; current collectors, ground brush assemblies, conductor rail. Composite stainless steel/aluminium conductor rail.

Contracts: Recent contracts include supply of pantographs to Kinki Sharyo for DART Dallas LRVs, to Siemens-Duewag for Los Angeles Green line LRVs and Portland LRVs, to Adtranz for New Jersey Transit ALP-44 locomotives and to Breda for LRVs for Muni San Francisco.

Also supplied equipment to Sumitomo/Nippon Sharyo for Los Angeles LRVs; to Adtranz for MTA Baltimore cars; and to Siemens-Duewag for St Louis LRVs.

Whipp & Bourne

Whipp & Bourne
A Division of FKI Engineering plc
Switchgear Works, Castleton, Rochdale OL11 2SS, England
Telephone: +44 1706 32051 Fax: +44 1706 345896
Managing Director: B Bullock
Engineering Director: S E Lane
Service Director: M E Leach
Sales & Marketing Director: L C Toma
Marketing Manager: P R Thompson

Products: Switchgear for electrical distribution in railway electrification projects and other industries, including high-speed DC circuit breakers for rating up to 12,000 A, 3,000 V DC, and 255 kA, semi-high-speed DC circuit breakers with ratings up to 3150 A, 1000 V and 80 kA short circuit; a range of microprocessor-based protection relays designed for the protection of DC traction systems; medium voltage metal-clad vacuum switchgear for ratings up to 3,150 A 15 kV short circuit, rating up to 50 kA; seismic tested medium voltage switchgear is also available; microprocessor-controlled Auto Recloser, with ratings up to 630 A, 27 kV short circuit, rated up to 12 kA.

Contracts: Contracts include provision of DC switchgear for further extensions to Line 4 of the Seoul metro and DC switchgear for Railtrack and London Underground.

UPDATED

NEW TECHNOLOGY/INNOVATIVE TRANSIT SYSTEMS

Company Listing by Country

BELGIUM
GLT

CANADA
ART
M-VI Monorail System
UM III
WEDway

FRANCE
Poma 2000
SK
TLP
Translohr
VAL

GERMANY
SIPEM

ITALY
Leitner

JAPAN
Hitachi
Newtran
Portliner
VONA (Vehicle Of New Age)

KOREA, REPUBLIC
HML

NETHERLANDS
Advanced Netherlands Transport

SWITZERLAND
Intamin
Von Roll Tramways

UK
PPM Light Tram

USA
Adtranz
Aerobus
Aeromovel
Futrex
Otis Monorail
Poma-Otis Shuttle
Raytheon
TGT
Unimobil Transporter

Classified Listing

AIR-POWERED SYSTEMS
Aeromovel

CABLE-POWERED SYSTEMS
Leitner
Poma-Otis Shuttle
Poma 2000
SK System
Von Roll Tramways

LINEAR MOTOR PROPULSION
ART
HML
Newtran
Poma-Otis Shuttle
TGT
WEDway

MONORAILS
Adtranz
ART
Futrex
Hitachi
Intamin
M-VI Monorail System
Otis Monorail
TGT
UM III

ROAD COMPATIBLE SYSTEMS
Advanced Netherlands Transport
GLT
PPM Light Tram
TLP
Translohr

RUBBER-TYRED SYSTEMS
Adtranz
Advanced Netherlands Transport
GLT
Intamin
Newtran
Otis Monorail
Poma-Otis Shuttle
Poma 2000
Portliner
Raytheon
SIPEM
TLP
Translohr
UM III
Unimobil Transporter
VAL
Vona

SUSPENDED SYSTEMS
Aerobus
Intamin
SIPEM
TGT
Von Roll Tramways

New technology/innovative systems in urban transit

Systems operating in a full urban environment

Name/location	Date opened	Supplier	Route length *km*	Stations	Cars	Daily journeys	Train operation	Remarks
Portliner Kobe, Japan	1981	Kawasaki/ Kobe Steel	6.4	9	72	50,000	Automatic no crew	Elevated; branch planned
Newtram Osaka, Japan	1981	Niigata/Vought	6.6	8	68	63,000	Automatic crew carried	Elevated
VONA Yukarigaoka, Japan	1982	Nippon/Sharyo	3.6	6	9	5,000	Manual crew carried	Straddle monorail, one-way loop
New Shuttle Ina, Japan	1983	Niigata/Vought	12.7	13	40	15,000	Manual crew carried	Elevated
Kokura Monorail Kitakyushu, Japan	1985	Hitachi/Kawasaki	8.4	12	72	11,000	Manual crew carried	Elevated monorail
ART Scarborough, Canada	1985	ART	7.2	6	22	72,000	Automatic crew carried	Mostly elevated; linear motor propulsion; extension planned
Metromover Miami, USA	1985	Westinghouse	3	10	12	12,000	Automatic no crew	Elevated people mover loop; 2 branches open 1994
SkyTrain Vancouver, Canada	1986	ART	21.4	15	114	120,000	Automatic no crew	Mostly elevated; linear motor propulsion; extensions opened 1990 and 1994
Docklands LRT London, England	1987	GEC	12	16	80		Automatic crew carried	Mostly elevated; short bored tunnel section; extended 1992 and 1993
DPM Detroit, USA	1987	ART	4.6	13	13	7,000	Automatic	Elevated loop; linear motor propulsion
Yamanote line Chiba, Japan	1988		15.3	18	88	13,000	Automatic	Suspended monorail
Poma 2000 Laon, France	1989	Poma	1.6	3	3	4,000	Automatic no crew	Cable-hauled rubber-tyred system, on alignment of former tram route
Kanazawa seaside Yokohama, Japan	1989	Mitsubishi/ Niigata	11	14	90	30,000	Manual crew carried	Rubber-tyred guideway system, designed to Japanese government-approved standards
Rokko Island Kobe, Japan	1989	Kawasaki	4.5	16	36	11,000	Automatic no crew	Kobe's second people mover serves a new artificial island; guideway a variant of Portliner
Osaka metro line 7 Osaka, Japan	1990		5.2	5	52		Manual crew carried	Small profile cars powered by linear motor
VONA Nagoya	1991	Nippon/Sharyo	7.4	7	56		Automatic crew carried	4 km extension planned
VAL Lille, France	1983	Matra	13.5	18	76	190,000	Automatic no crew	Partially elevated, cut-and-cover, and bored tunnel; Line 2 opened 1989, extended 1995
Lyon Line D, France	1991	GEC Alsthom/ Matra	12	13	76	145,000	Automatic no crew	
Tama, Japan	1992		5					
Toulouse, France	1993	Matra	10	15	50	150,000	Automatic no crew	Lines 2 and 3 planned
Tokyo, Teleport City, Japan	1993		12					
Taipei, Taiwan	1996	Matra	12	20	102		Automatic no crew	Elevated
NTS Hiroshima, Japan	1994	Niigata	18.4	21	132	75,000	Automated, rubber tyres	
Tokyo Bay Area, Japan	1995	Niigata					Automated, rubber tyres	
Park Shuttle Rotterdam, Netherlands	1997	Advanced Netherlands Transport	1.4	2	3	200 passengers per hour	Automatic	Rubber tyres
Otis Monorail by Severn-Lamb Bandar Sunway, Malaysia	1997	Otis Elevator	4 km				Automatic	Monorail

Adtranz

ABB Daimler-Benz Transportation GmbH
PO Box 130127, 13601 Berlin, Germany
Telephone: +49 30 38320 Fax: +49 30 3832 2000
(See main entry under Rail Vehicles and Traction Equipment)

Types of system: Monorail and automated guided transit system (AGT).

Description
Monorail: Electrically powered straddle monorail with rubber-tyred cars, in trains up to 10, running on box-section elevated guideway. Rubber-tyred wheels bearing on the surface of the guideway provide drive from 40 kW traction motors, with auxiliary wheels below the surface providing both lateral and vertical guidance. The drive wheels have steel rims for support in the event of reduced or lost tyre pressure. Control systems are available ranging from simple manual driving to fully automated operation. In full ATO mode, headways of 90 sec are possible, and maximum capacity is 6,000 passengers/h. Top speed of 45 km/h.

The guideway is a prefabricated welded box-section girder supported on columns at roughly 30 m intervals; minimum curve radius is 20 m and maximum gradient 6 per cent. Pairs of conductor rails mounted on each side of the girder carry traction power and control circuits. The guideway can be heated for locations where ice may form. Switching is by a pair of guideway sections which slide into place for one or other route.

AGT: Rubber-tyred cars run on a dedicated concrete guideway, with lateral guidance provided by further tyres bearing on central guideway I-beam. All axles driven by 75 kW motors. Microprocessor-based control system provides full ATO, ATP and ATS. Vehicle capacities are 45 (C-45) or 100 (C-100) passengers.

Development
Monorail: The first urban transit application was the 3.4 km Darling Harbour TNT Harbour-Link in Sydney (qv), which entered public service in 1988. Other recent installations are at Merry Hill shopping centre, Birmingham UK, at the Expo 92 site in Sevilla, Spain, and the Jurong Bird Park, Singapore. The airport monorail at Newark New Jersey is now running. The 3 km line links the central terminal area with four terminals. A fleet of 10 six-car trains is running on a dual-track system.
AGT: A development of the system first applied in 1971 at Tampa international airport, AGT has since been installed or is under construction at a further 15 locations. The Miami Metromover, opened in 1985, was the first US urban people mover system. Other systems are installed at the new Greater Pittsburgh and Denver international airports.

There are three AGT systems in the UK, two at London Gatwick Airport and one at London Stansted Airport.

An Adtranz AGT system has been installed in Changi Airport, Singapore, linking the two terminals. The system extends to 1.3 km and carries up to 9,000 passengers per hour.

Frankfurt airport is getting 10 new AGT vehicles for its people mover system.

Leonardo da Vinci airport Roma has ordered an AGT system, being supplied by Adtranz USA, to connect its main terminal (station E) to D satellite terminal. The contract includes four CX100 cars, power distribution, guideways, communications equipment and maintenance. Two-car trains will run on the elevated guideway scheduled to open in 1999.

Kuala Lumpur has ordered a CX100 AGT car for the airport line from Adtranz Malaysia. It opens in 1998 and when completed will have two two-car trains serving satellite buildings.

Adtranz USA is supplying 18 CX100 cars for the Bukit Panjang AGT system in Singapore. The 7.5 km system has 13 stations and opens in 1998.

UPDATED

Merry Hill monorail, West Midlands, UK ***1995***

Adtranz AGT cars at Singapore's Changi Airport ***1996***

Computer impression of Bukit Panjang AGT CX100 train ***1997***

ANT

Advanced Netherlands Transport
Carosserie Akkermans, Po Box 60, 4750 AB Oud-Gastel, Netherlands
Telephone: +31 10 447 8727 Fax: +31 165 511 931
Directors: O Pruis, N de Ronde Bresser

Type of system: Park Shuttle electronically guided people mover

Description: Rubber-tyred automatic vehicle, seating six with two standing and a maximum speed of 30 km/h. It is computer-controlled and guidance is by wires sunk into the roadway. There is no mechanical guidance. It can run on public roads, with laser beams detecting obstacles.

Park Shuttle car by ANT Netherlands ***1997***

Development: Park Shuttle was developed on behalf of the Dutch government with the participation of bus company ZWN Openbaar Vervoer as the operator, Frog Navigation Systems, which supplied the technology, and local authority Capelle a/d IJssel – Bedrijvenpark Rivium. The vehicle was built by Carosserie Akkermans. Test operation was to start in 1997 between Kralingse Zoom metro station, in the eastern suburbs of Rotterdam, and the Rivium Business Park, 1.2 km away, with three vehicles. Travel time is put at three to four minutes and the capacity is 200 passengers an hour in each direction.

NEW ENTRY

Aerobus

Aerobus International Inc
811 Rusk, Suite 1750, Houston, TX 77002-2814, USA
Telephone: +1 713 222 6655 Fax: +1 713 222 7,501
President: Hunter L Martin Jr

Type of system: Suspended cable guideway.

Background: Originally developed in Switzerland and Canada, the patents and technology are owned by Aerobus International. The design was inspired by the SLRT (Suspended Light Railway Technology) competition in which Aerobus was one of three finalists. Engineering and manufacturing expertise is assembled from both Switzerland and USA.

Description: Electrically powered vehicles operate on suspended cable guideway on light, cable-supported, tracks, up to 8 per cent gradients and with speeds of up to 80 km/h. A family of articulated vehicles is available from 2 to 8 modules with a maximum vehicle capacity of 333. Spans of 200-300 m are normal, with up to 600 m possible for river crossings or to pass over major obstacles.

Aerobus vehicle on suspended cable guideway
1996

Aeromovel

Aeromovel USA Inc
Suite 330, 39899 Balentine Drive, Newark, CA 94560, USA
Telephone: +1 510 353 1128 Fax: +1 510 657 6218
President & Chief Executive Officer: Ervon R Koenig

Type of system: Air-propelled automated guideway transport system.

Description: A lightweight high-capacity car runs on steel wheels on steel rail track mounted on the top surface of an elevated hollow concrete box girder. It has no electric motor or magnet and uses air propulsion, much in the same way as a sailing ship. A pylon projects from the bottom of the car bogie into the hollow beam, where it forms a flat plate entirely occupying the cross-section of the beam. Stationary centrifugal air blowers generate an air flow in the beam, causing the plate, and hence the vehicle, to be propelled.

A 1.1 km demonstration track has been in operation in Porto Alegre, Brazil (see Porto Alegre entry).

A 3.2 km route at the Taman Mini-Indonesia theme park in Jakarta, Indonesia, opened in 1989.

Aeromovel installation in Brazil ***1996***

ART

Bombardier Inc
Transportation Systems Division
PO Box 220, Station A, Kingston, Ontario K7M 6R2, Canada
Telephone: +1 613 384 3100 Fax: +1 613 384 5240
(See main entry for Bombardier under Rail Vehicles and Traction Equipment)

Type of system: Advanced Rapid Transit system (ART), also known as SkyTrain in Vancouver, powered by linear induction motors (LIM), with steerable-axle bogies, and moving block ATC; traction power at 600-750 V DC from side contact rail.

Also intermediate-capacity people mover systems – UM III monorail and linear-induction powered WEDway people mover (qv).

Description: ART is a driverless, medium to high capacity, rapid transit system. The principal features of ART are LIM power and steerable suspension which provide high-quality ride under variable climatic conditions. The moving block ATC allows a flexible response to sudden changes in passenger demand.

Bombardier reports very little noise, vibration or electromagnetic interference with the ART system. The LIM has no moving parts and there is no gearbox noise. LIMs in service have averaged 4 million km between defects. The compact size of the LIM reduces the size and weight of the cars, so that they are some 25 per cent lighter than conventional rotary-motor vehicles. The low floor allows operation in 4.3 m diameter tunnels, offering capital savings, and cars can operate normally on 6 per cent gradients. The combination of LIM power and moving block ATC allows 60 sec headways.

Development: The Vancouver SkyTrain, opened in 1986, is cited as the longest automated rapid transit system in the world at 28.9 km and serves 20 stations. The fleet is 150 and ridership is 20 million passengers a year.

The 7.1 km Scarborough line in Toronto opened in 1985 and a third system, the Detroit Downtown People Mover, opened in 1987. The latter is a 4.7 km single-track

Vancouver's SkyTrain ART system ***1996***

loop with 12 cars and carries upwards of 57,000 people a day.

A wider second-generation car, the ART Mk II, has larger wheels and is 16.7 m long. It increases passenger carrying capacity of the ART System by 50 per cent.

Kuala Lumpur LRT System Two: Renong Berhad, Kuala Lumpur, has selected Bombardier to supply an automated rapid transit system linking Kuala Lumpur's western and eastern suburbs with the centre. Projek Usahasma Transit Ringan Automatik Sdn Bhd (PUTRA) is the owner/operator of the system.

Bombardier is building 70 ART Mk II vehicles for the line powered by linear induction motors, onboard and wayside ATC and communication systems, the linear motor reaction rail, special tools, test and maintenance equipment, systems integration engineering, testing and commissioning, operations and maintenance training as well as O&M advisory support during revenue service.

The mostly elevated 29 km dual-lane guideway system has 24 stations and is scheduled to open in 1998, the year of the Commonwealth Games. At first the system will have a capacity of 10,000 passengers/h per direction but it is designed to accommodate 30,000/h.

The Mk II cars have larger wheels than the Mk I cars and increase the carrying capacity of the ART system by 50 per cent.

UPDATED

Kuala Lumpur ART Mk II unit ***1997***

Futrex

Futrex Inc
1905 Pittsburgh Avenue, Charleston, SC 29405, USA
Telephone: +1 803 853 3207 Fax: +1 803 853 3212
President & Chief Executive Officer: Byron Waldman
Vice President, Planning & Development:
Thomas R Waldron
Engineer: Lawrence K Edwards

Type of system: System 21 is the name given by Futrex to its side-suspended low-cost monorail.

Description: Cars travel in either direction on a triangular monobeam allowing two-way traffic. Each car carries 24 seated and 28 standing. In most installations, System 21 will operate in two- or four-car trains.

Development: A System 21 line has been proposed for Myrtle Beach, Southern California.

NEW ENTRY

Model of Futrex System 21 cars at station ***1997***

GLT

Bombardier Eurorail — Division BN
Avenue Louise 65, 1050 Bruxelles, Belgium
Telephone: +32 2 535 5511 Fax: +32 2 539 2815
Vice President, Marketing: Berend K van Dijk
Vice President, Technology: Constant Peten
Director, Urban Productline: Francis Ancelet

Type of system: Guided or unguided bi-mode rubber-tyred electric vehicle.

Description: GLT (Guided Light Transit) has been developed by BN as a low-cost mass transit system with the advantages of electric propulsion. Operation of the rubber-tyred vehicles can be unguided on ordinary roads or guided by means of a central rail mounted on a guideway little wider than the vehicle body. Propulsion is by electric motors with current collected at 750 V DC by pantograph from an overhead line, or alternatively produced on board by a diesel generator.

A full-scale trial of GLT has been in operation since 1988 at Rochefort in Belgium. Demonstrations have also taken place in the Netherlands, UK, and France.

In 1990 an agreement was concluded with Spie-Batignolles, which is now responsible for infrastructure work.

Development: A new full-length low-floor version has been designed for the city of Caen, France. The first of the 20 vehicles was expected to be delivered in 1998, though a further study is being carried out by Caen into the merits of the GLT system compared with other light transit systems.

UPDATED

GLT vehicle in Caen, France ***1997***

Hitachi

Hitachi Ltd
Transportation and Building Systems Dept (XL)
6, Kanda Surugadai 4-chome, Chiyoda-ku, Tokyo 101-10, Japan
Telephone: +81 3 3258 1111
Fax: +81 3 3258 5211/5216
General Manager, Sales: T Muraki
Department Manager, Sales: K Takagi

Products: Monorail cars. Turnkey monorail systems.

Series 1000 straddle monorail cars at Tokyo airport
1996

HML

Hyundai Precision & Ind Co Ltd
Rolling Stock Division
140-2, Gyedong, Chongro-ku, KPO Box 1677, Seoul, Republic of Korea
Telephone: +82 2 824 3786 Fax: +82 2 824 5475/5476
(See main entry under Rail Vehicles and Traction Equipment)

Type of system: Magnetically levitated vehicles powered by linear induction motor run on elevated guideway; current collected from side-mounted bars at 600 V DC.

Description: Lightweight aluminium vehicles seating 40 and mounted on three independent air-sprung 'bogies' run on an elevated guideway. Levitation is achieved by means of attraction; electromagnets in the bogies attract steel rails mounted underneath the guideway. A 12 mm air gap is maintained. The 24 magnets are arranged in a staggered formation within the bogies so that the attraction also provides guidance. Propulsion is by single-sided linear induction motor, with traction control by VVVF inverter. Operation control is by radio communication link from a central command.

In the HML03 version, the car is 17.6 m long and 3 m wide. It has operated at 50 km/h though its maximum design speed is put at 150 km/h.

HML03 in service at the Taejon Expo in 1993

Intamin

Intamin AG
Verenastrasse 37, 8832 Wollerau, Switzerland
Telephone: +41 1 786 9111 Fax: +41 1 785 0202
Vice President: Roy Vocking
Monorail Project Engineer: Franz Zürcher

Type of system: Straddle and suspended monorails, people movers, electric rubber-tyred vehicles; complete systems. The P60/60 Monorail has a speed of 50 to 80 km/h; the P24 monorail carries up to 18,000 passengers/h.

Contracts: A fully automatic system was installed serving a shopping centre in Rio de Janeiro, Brazil in 1995; a system with eight automatic guided trains was installed in Gelsenkirchen, Germany, in 1996; a line with air conditioned trains was installed in Bangkok, Thailand, in 1995; a straddle monorail 'Panorama railway' was installed at the 1993 IGA international horticulture exhibition site in Stuttgart and a People Porter system at Expo 93 in South Korea.

A fully automatic system was installed at Shenzhen, China, in 1993.

UPDATED

'Panorama railway' monorail

Leitner

Leitner SpA
People Transportation System Division, Via Galvani 33, 39100 Bolzano, Italy
Telephone: +39 471 545555 Fax: +39 471 545566
President: Kurt Leitner
General Manager: Enzo Urbani
Marketing Manager: Franco Dal Pos
Sales Manager: Ermenegildo Zordan
R&D Manager: Giuseppe Conte

Type of system: Cableway systems, gondola lifts, chair lifts, ski lifts.

Description: Rope-hauled vehicle on fixed track, up to 4 km long. Longer systems use sections in sequence. The system can carry up to 5,000 passengers/h, with an incline of up to 15 per cent and curves with a minimum radius of 30 m. Each car carries from 20 to 80 and runs at about 30 km/h with one minute intervals between trains.

Leitner city transport system car at Sterzing, Italy ***1997***

Development: 1996: Inclined lift, La Villa, Italy. 1995: funicular train, carrying 450, in Napoli, Italy; inclined lift, Cogolo, Italy.1993: gondola 12-seat lift at Expo 93, Seoul, South Korea. 1992: gondola lift (12 seat) in Taomina, Italy; gondola lift at Expo 92, Sevilla.

Leitner city transport system car on turntable ***1997***

Several projects are in design stage in Italy (16), Switzerland (3), UK (2), Brazil (2) and other countries (6).

A lift system has been developed for stations on elevated tracks.

UPDATED

M-VI Monorail System

Bombardier Inc
Transportation Systems Division
PO Box 220, Station A, Kingston, Ontario K7M 6R2, Canada
Telephone: +1 613 364 3100 Fax: +1 613 389 5240
(See main entry for Bombardier under Rail Vehicles and Traction Equipment)

Type of system: Automatic straddle-type monorail for operation in variable climates.

Description: This is the urban transport version of the Mark VI Monorail delivered to Walt Disney World Resort, Orlando, Florida. Three-car trainsets carry between 5,000 and 20,000 passengers/h. Pneumatic tyres at the car ends support and propel the vehicle, driven by AC motors. Lateral guidance is by upper and lower side tyres.

Development: The M-VI Monorail is similar to the Mark VI Monorail except that it has an increased interior height, AC propulsion, wider doors and a more conventional seating configuration.

NEW ENTRY

M-VI Monorail system ***1997***

Newtran (NTS)

Niigata Engineering Co Ltd
Engineering and Construction Division, 9-3 Kamatahon-cho 1-chome, Ohta-ku, Tokyo 144, Japan
Telephone: +81 3 3739 8931 Fax: +81 3 3737 1985
Manager, International Sales Dept: Hideki Mori
Associate Director, Engineering Division: Hiromi Soma
Sales Manager: S Ohno

Type of system: Automated rubber-tyred light transit on concrete guideway with lateral guidance by wheels; switching achieved by a simple blade device. Traction power at 750 V DC or 600 V AC three-phase is collected from a third rail.

Description: As built in Osaka in 1981, and known as Newtram, two-axle rubber-tyred cars with capacity for 75 passengers are propelled by a single 90 kW motor driving one axle, with thyristor conversion of AC traction power to variable-voltage DC.

The line is entirely elevated and links the metro terminal at Suminoekoen with the Port Town area of reclaimed land for housing and industry. It extends to 6.6 km, with eight stations, and is equipped with ATO and ATP. Scheduled operating speed is 28 km/h, with a maximum of 60 km/h.

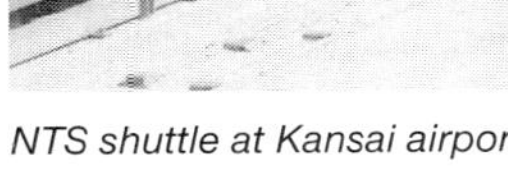

NTS shuttle at Kansai airport ***1996***

NTS train on the Yurikome line, Tokyo waterfront ***1997***

Development: Other applications are as New Shuttle in Saitama, Seibu Railway's Yamaguchi line and the Kanazawa Seaside line in Yokohama. An 18.4 km route was installed in Hiroshima (opened 1994), where it is known as Astram, running to the Asian Games site. Another is in the Tokyo Bay area. Called the Yurikome line, it runs in the Tokyo waterfront area, and started revenue operation in November 1995. The 12 km line runs from Shinbashi, through Shiuodome, to the Ariake area. It has 12 stations and six-car trains.

A further NTS was installed at Kansai International airport, Osaka, which opened in 1994. There are two lines, with a total track length of 2.4 km, three stations per line. Four three-car sets operate on each line.

UPDATED

Otis Monorail by Severn-Lamb

Otis Elevator Company
Otis Transit Systems Inc
4 Farm Springs, Farmington, CT 06032, USA
Telephone: +1 860 676 5318 Fax: +1 860 676 6687
President: David Perl

Type of system: Automated or manually controlled people mover in straddle monorail configuration.

Description: Lightweight electrically powered monorail cars have a monocoque composite construction. On-board AC motors drive through pneumatic rubber tyres which incorporate run-flat rims. Service braking is regenerative and fail-safe motor brakes are provided for emergency use.

Lateral guidance is by urethane-tyred wheels bearing on the monobeam sidewalls. The monobeam can be made of steel or concrete, to suit prevailing weather conditions.

The cars have automatic plug-type sliding doors on both sides. Air conditioning, public address and passenger displays are optional. In automatic operation, dispatching is by dual-redundant programmable logic controllers in scheduled or on-demand mode. Four car versions carry from 54 to 120 passengers at speeds of up to 48 km/h.

Development: Monorail installations by Severn-Lamb, England, in Blackpool and Gateshead, in Floriade den Haag-Zoetermeer, Holland, and in Genting Highlands, Malaysia, led to the development of the Otis Monorail. An Otis monorail development facility and 300 m test track was built in 1995 in Stratford-upon-Avon, England.

Otis Monorail by Severn-Lamb **1996**

A 4 km loop has been built at Bandar Sunway, Malaysia. A 15 km extension is planned.

UPDATED

Poma-Otis Shuttle

Otis Elevator Company
Otis Transit Systems Inc
4 Farm Springs, Farmington, CT 06032, USA
Telephone: +1 860 676 5318 Fax: +1 860 676 6687
President: David Perl

Type of system: Automated people movers, cable driven, with the option of air-cushion suspension and linear induction motor drive.

Description: The Poma-Otis Shuttle 1 system uses the proven technology of lifts (elevators) to propel lightweight vehicles over an inexpensive steel guideway. The vehicle is propelled by a wayside-mounted lift drive machine via a steel drive cable.

Poma-Otis Shuttle II has cable propulsion and the vehicles have Hovair air-cushion suspension.

Poma-Otis Shuttle III has Hovair air-cushion suspension and linear induction motor propulsion. These self-propelled vehicles are capable of complex guideway alignments and unlimited travel distance.

All Poma-Otis shuttle products have rubber-tyred lateral guidance and regenerative service braking. Fail-safe emergency braking systems are also provided. The vehicles have monocoque composite construction and include automatic sliding doors on both sides. Air conditioning, public address and passenger information displays are optional. Scheduled or on-demand mode dispatching is controlled by dual redundant programmable logic controllers. Four vehicle sizes carry 40 to 140 passengers at speeds of up to 48 km/h.

Development: The first installation opened at Duke University, North Carolina, in 1981 used linear-motor propulsion, and the Poma-Otis Shuttle was developed from this. Shuttle installations include a 1.3 km underground system at Serfaus, Austria, and a 760 m elevated line at Tampa, Florida; both link amenities with parking garages. A 10,000 passenger/h system entered service in 1993 at Narita airport, Tokyo, and an installation at Cincinnati/Northern Kentucky international airport opened in 1994.

Poma-Otis Shuttle at Harbour Island, Tampa, Florida **1995**

Other contracts include a parking connection line at the J Paul Getty Center in Los Angeles, USA and a transit connection in Boston, USA.

UPDATED

Poma 2000

Poma Systèmes de Transport Urbain
109 rue Aristide Bergès, PO Box 47, 38340 Voreppe, France
Telephone: +33 4 76 28 70 00 Fax: +33 4 76 28 71 91

Type of system: Cable-hauled rubber-tyred cars on concrete guideway, lateral guidance by four horizontal rubber tyres per axle.

Description: Unpowered rubber-tyred cars are hauled by cable mounted in the centre of a concrete or steel guideway 3.1 m wide. Each cable loop is driven by a 120 kW separately excited DC motor, and normally requires an auxiliary cable for acceleration and deceleration purposes. In the Laon system (see below), only a single cable is used, with changeover from one cable to the next taking place at each station. Maximum speed is 45 km/h; the Laon cars carry between 40 and 60 passengers.

Development: The Poma 2000 system was developed from Poma's range of cable car and ski lift systems for ski resorts. At Laon in France (population 40,000), where a low-density means of transit was required to link upper and lower parts of the town, a simple single-cable version was installed in 1989.

A 737 m Poma 2000 system is being installed by Sasib between Cascina Gobba on Milano metro Line 2 and the San Raffaele hospital. It was expected to open in 1997.

Poma 2000 in urban setting at Laon

Portliner

Kawasaki Heavy Industries Ltd
World Trade Centre Building, 4-1, Hamamatsu-cho 2-chome, Minato-ku, Tokyo 105, Japan
Telephone: +81 3 3435 2588 Fax: +81 3 3435 2157

Type of system: Automated rubber-tyred light metro on steel/concrete guideway, lateral guidance by wheels bearing on guidebars, traction power at 600 V AC three-phase.

Description: Two-axle rubber-tyred cars normally have all axles driven by 90 kW DC motors. Maximum gradient is 5 per cent and minimum curve radius 30 m. Full ATO and ATP systems are fitted for driverless operation.

KCV (Kawasaki Computer-controlled Vehicle) system, under development since 1970 and tested on a 1.3 km track in 1974, was used for a link to the reclaimed Port Island industrial area. The 6.4 km Portliner route has nine stations.

A second route of 4.5 km opened in 1989 to serve Rokko Island, a new residential and industrial development.

Portliner on Rokko Island, Kobe

PPM Light Tram

Parry People Movers Ltd
Overend Road, Cradley Heath B64 7DD, England
Telephone: +44 1384 569171 Fax: +44 1384 5637753
Managing Director: John Parry
Marketing Director: Mark Parry

Type of system: Light tramway running on narrow-gauge track, powered by flywheel energy storage system recharged periodically from concealed conductor rail.

Description: Lightweight four-wheel vehicles 6 m long and seating 20 to 27 (plus standing passengers) have a single axle driven from a flywheel energy storage system charged by an electric motor and regenerative braking. Current is collected at 70 V DC when the vehicle is at rest at terminals or stops, or periodically while in motion, from discontinuous lengths of conductor rail. On level track the vehicle can run for 4 to 5 km before recharging is necessary. Maximum speed is put at 50 km/h.

Permanent way, usually metre gauge but regaugeable from 610 mm to 1,435 mm, is laid from prefabricated sections. The narrow gauge helps minimise construction and civil engineering work; minimum curve radius is 15 m, but 9 m is possible at low speed. On reserved track, standard rail and sleepers can be used; for on-street running a twin rail section with a bitumen infill provides the standard tramway flangeway. At stops, the top-contact conductor rail is concealed beneath a concrete kerb.

PPM Light Tram on temporary track in Barking, UK

Development: A prototype test track in a 0.3 km loop opened at Himley Park, West Midlands, UK, in 1992, with Railways Inspectorate approval to carry fare-paying passengers. Some 10,000 were carried in the first 12 months of operation.

Several local authorities have proposed the installation of light tramways, using the PPM system. These include Swansea and Weymouth in the UK, and Wellington, New Zealand. Two vehicles have been ordered by a leasing company.

In Weymouth test running commenced over on-street tracks linking Weymouth rail station with the quayside in 1996 and fare-paying operation was due to start in 1997.

A new two-axle LRV, the Urban Shuttle Light Tram, seats 16 with 14 standing. The single-ended version can carry up to 35 passengers. It runs on 1,435 mm gauge, is 7.3 m long, 2.4 m wide, 2.5 m high and has a floor height of 400 mm.

Llandudno, UK: A planning application to construct a metre-gauge tramway has been submitted for operation to start in 1998. Parry is supplying seven single-ended flywheel-powered trams and each will seat 20 with 15 standing, with two doors for entry and exit. They will run on Parry's patented track with lightweight rails and tie-rods that are inserted into the bitumen road surface without substantial reconstruction. Access to pipes and other services under the road can be achieved more easily than with conventional track systems.

UPDATED

PPM 'Heritage' style trams demonstrated at Swansea **1995**

Raytheon

Raytheon Electronic Systems
1001 Boston Post Road, Marlborough, MA 01752-3789, USA
Telephone: +1 508 490 2448 Fax: +1 508 490 3944

Type of system: Personal rapid transit.

Description: Each car on the PRT2000™ system carries up to four and is wheelchair accessible. It is powered by dual 600 V AC induction motors and runs on rubber tyres. Capacity is 10,000 passengers/h per direction with a platform capacity of 3,000 passengers/h. Vehicle speed is up to 48 km/h. The guideway is an open structure with a centre walking surface. Full AVP, AVO and AVS (automatic vehicle supervision) is specified.

Development: A line has been planned for Rosemont, Chicago, adjacent to O'Hare International Airport. It is expected to open in 1999.

NEW ENTRY

Raytheon PR2000 system car at station **1997**

SK

Soulé ST
Transportation Systems Dept
97 Rue Saint Lazare, 75008 Paris, France
Telephone: +33 1 53 20 45 00 20 Fax: +33 1 53 20 07 40/45 07
General Manager: André Pascal
Sales & Marketing Director: Daniel Sam-Giao

Soulé ST is part of RATP Paris

Type of system: Automated semi-continuous cable-hauled people mover.

Description: The SK System has been developed for short-distance applications from 200 m to 5 km. Cars are hauled along a fixed track by cable, with a minimum headway of 20 sec; capacity of each vehicle is 29 passengers.

At stations, deceleration mechanisms slow the cars to 1 km/h to allow passengers to board and alight, also making it possible for wheelchair users to board. Turntables at each terminal allow the vehicles to change track and direction in a limited space. SK is designed as an alternative to moving walkways or shuttle buses and can carry up to 6,000 passengers/h in each direction.

Development: The first SK system began operation at the Villepinte exhibition centre near Roissy-Charles de Gaulle airport, Paris, where the 310 m track has transported over 14 million passengers since commissioning in 1986. Other installations in Vancouver (150 m, 1986) and Yokohama (650 m, 1989) were followed by a new generation of SK systems at Paris Noisy-le-Grand (520 m, commissioned in 1992) and at Charles de Gaulle airport. Two lines (3.5 km and 850 m, eight stations) link three terminal buildings with railway stations at CDG airport. Construction started in 1995, with commissioning expected in 1997.

UPDATED

The SK 6000 prototype for Charles de Gaulle airport **1995**

The SK installation at Noisy-le-Grand, Paris **1995**

SIPEM

Siemens Aktiengesellschaft
Transportation Systems Group (VT)
PO Box 65, Elsens Strasse 87-96, 12414 Berlin, Germany
Telephone: +49 30 6174 1620 Fax: +49 30 6174 1632
Division Executive Management
Technical: T Brodocz
Commercial: W Burkhardt
UK Representative: Siemens Transportation Systems Ltd, Sopers Lane, Poole BH17 7ER
Telephone: +44 1202 782000 Fax: +44 1202 782311

Type of system: Automatic suspended people mover with rotary motor propulsion, traction power at 380 V AC 50 Hz collected from four-pole conductor rail inside the guideway.

Description: The Siemens People Mover (SIPEM) cabins are suspended from an elevated guideway, the bogies running within the beam on solid rubber tyres; rubber rollers provide lateral guidance. Maximum speed is 60 km/h with a minimum headway of 60 sec. Automatic coupling of cabins permits adaption to changes in ridership, with a maximum of 8,000 passengers/h in one direction. On-demand or scheduled automatic operation is possible; vehicles are driverless and stations do not require staff. Large networks can be built quickly with minimum environmental disturbance using prefabricated guideway columns and beams.

A three-level automatic supervision, process control and protection system monitors and controls all vehicle movements from an operations control centre.

Development: Test tracks to prove the propulsion and guideway switching mechanism were built in the early 1970s, and in 1979 a 1.4 km full-scale demonstration track was built at Erlangen. This system is known as H-Bahn. Its first application was a 1.1 km line connecting the two campuses of the University of Dortmund, Germany (see Dortmund entry), opened in 1984. The line was subsequently extended into an urban area beyond the University limits, using the new SIPEM technology based on experience with H-Bahn. From the start, the Dortmund H-Bahn was given an unrestricted operating licence in accordance with BOStrab regulations and the Public Transportation Act.

Siemens People Mover (SIPEM) and track at Dortmund

TGT

Titan Global Technologies Ltd
PO Box 617, 85 Chestnut Ridge Road, Montvale, NJ 07656-0617, USA
Telephone: +1 201 930 0300 Fax: +1 201 307 0649
Chairman & Chief Executive Officer:
Robert James Frankel
Vice Presidents: Solomon Kramer, Saul Heifetz
Vice President, Finance, & Treasurer: Stanley Schleger

Type of system: Automated linear motor powered suspended monorail.

Description: Astroglide: automated cars seating 50-100 passengers are suspended from a single or double track structural steel guideway with automatic switching and bypass tracks for flexible operation. Propulsion is by linear induction motor with maximum speed put at 120 km/h. Cars can be operated singly or as trains computer-coupled using the automatic demand-responsive control system at 20-40 sec headways.

There are two variants — PRT, carrying 6-10 passengers at up to 25 km/h, and Jetrail, carrying 35-50 at up to 56 km/h.

Development: TGT's predecessor, Titan PRT, installed Astroglide systems in US airport and pleasure ground locations, including Love Field airport, Dallas, Los Angeles County Fair Ground at Pomona, California, and the Miami Seaquarium. An installation is also being developed for the Compaq Computer Corporation campus at Houston, Texas.

UPDATED

Astroglide car at Miami Seaquarium

Arrow vehicles at LA County Fairplex, Pomona

TLP

De Dietrich Ferroviaire
PO Box 35, Reichshoffen, 67891 Niederbronn, France
Telephone: +33 3 88 80 25 00 Fax: +33 3 88 80 25 12
President: Michel Perricaudet
General Manager: Jean-Marie Bucher
Sales Manager: Daniel Sprauer

Type of system: Guided rubber-tyred light transit.

Description: Guided light transit vehicle running on flanged rubber tyres. The vehicle has three sections and takes overhead power in the same way as a conventional light rail vehicle. The car is 27 m long with a low floor; it carries up to 230 passengers. Existing bus depots can be used for maintenance, cleaning and garaging.

Vehicle and infrastructure are marketed in association with Cogifer.

UPDATED

Front view of De Dietrich/Cogifer TLP LRV

1996

Translohr

Lohr Industrie
29 rue du 14-Juillet, 67980 Hangenbieten, France
Telephone: +33 3 88 38 98 00 Fax: +33 3 88 96 06 36

Type of system: Rubber-tyred guided light rail vehicle, for road or rail use.

Description: Translohr is designed as an intermediate city system and is based on a central rail with guidance provided by two wheels that clamp on to it. The vehicle has a low floor, 180 mm, with stepless boarding. Batteries supply power for off-wire operation.

UM III Monorail System

Bombardier Inc
Transportation Systems Division
PO Box 220, Station A, Kingston, Ontario K7M 6R2, Canada
Telephone: +1 613 364 3100 Fax: +1 613 384 5240
(See main entry for Bombardier under Rail Vehicles and Traction Equipment)

Type of system: Automated electrically powered straddle monorail capable of operation in sub-tropical temperatures or severe ice and snow.

Description: The system can be configured to operate with single vehicles or trains up to 10 cars. The cars run on dual pneumatic tyres, with lateral guidance being provided by side tyres perpendicular to the guidebeam sides. Each car seats 8 with standing room for up to 27. The cars are accessible to mobility-impaired passengers.

The system is designed to carry between 500 and 10,000 passengers/h in elevated, at-grade or underground applications. The cars travel at 32 km/h and can negotiate gradients of up to 10 per cent.

Development: Hillsborough County Aviation Authority in Tampa, Florida, selected the UM III system to link Tampa international airport's new long-term vehicle park with the main terminal. It opened in 1991 and now operates a 24 h service in continuous or demand-responsive mode on headways of 90 sec.

UM III monorail in Tampa, Florida ***1995***

A second deployment of the UM III Monorail is at Jacksonville, Florida. Jacksonville Transportation Authority has selected UM III to replace its former downtown people mover system. Revenue operation is expected to start in 1998.

UPDATED

Unimobil Transporter

Universal Mobility Inc
2040 East 4800 South Street, Salt Lake City, UT 84117, USA
Telephone: +1 801 278 4421
President: R Clay Groesbeck

Type of system: People mover shuttle straddling steel guideway, lateral guidance by wheels bearing on sidewalls.

Description: Two-axle rubber-tyred cars run singly or in trains on an elevated steel box-construction guideway, each axle powered by a 56 kW motor. Lateral guidance is provided by four guide wheels per axle which bear against the vertical sidewall of the guideway. Car capacity is 40 passengers, and top speed is put at 42 km/h.

Unimobil I

VAL

Matra Transport International
PO Box 531, 92542 Montrouge Cedex, France
Telephone: +33 1 49 65 75 00 Fax: +33 1 49 65 70 93

Background: Since 1996 Matra Transport International has been a joint venture between Lagardere and Siemens.

Type of System: Fully automated guideway transit system.

Description: Lightweight two-car sets run on a guideway with primary suspension by rubber tyres. Further pairs of horizontal tyres bear on H-type guidebars to provide lateral guidance. All axles are powered by 150 kW motors with current collected at 750 V DC from the guidebars.

VAL 206 has a capacity for 160 to 208 passengers. VAL 208 cars carry 140 to 240 passengers and VAL 258 cars carry 85 to 140 passengers.

VAL is a fixed-block system in which trains are detected by an ultrasonic sensor. As the train proceeds through the section, signals are emitted inductively from the train to a continuous cable laid in the track. The signalling logic detects the train's signal until it is verified to have left the section by the ultrasonic detector.

VAL control centre ***1997***

Prototype VAL 208 ***1997***

Two further inductive cables are used to control train speed. These have transpositions arranged so as to induce running at normal speed or to initiate braking.

In the event of out-of-course running a computer at the operations centre automatically speeds up or slows down the trains to restore normal timetable running.

VAL can cope with unscheduled demand by inserting additional trains into the network as required by remote command from the control centre.

Operating experience since 1983 on Line 1 in Lille, where headways are now 60 sec, shows VAL achieving 99.8 per cent availability and the high quality of service produced considerably increased ridership and revenues.

Development: The VAL system in Lille has 62 stations and is 50 km in length. Other VAL systems are operating in Rennes and Toulouse. In Toulouse, which opened in 1993, ridership has increased by more than 40 per cent during the first two years of service. In 1991 a VAL system opened between Antony and Paris-Orly Airport. Called OrlyVAL, it links the airport with the RATP metro.

In the USA a VAL system entered service at Chicago's O'Hare airport in 1992 and operates 24 hours a day.

The Mucha line opened in Taipei in 1996 and has carried two million passengers in the first year of operations.

UPDATED

Von Roll Tramways

Von Roll Tramways Ltd
Fabrikstrasse 2, 3001 Bern, Switzerland
Telephone: +41 31 308 5444 Fax: +41 31 308 5498
International Marketing Manager: Remy Supersaxo

Subsidiary company
Von Roll Tramways Inc
753 West Main Street, PO Box 869, Watertown, NY 13601, USA
Telephone: +1 315 788 1280 Fax: +1 315 788 1321

Type of system: Reversible aerial cableways, gondola ropeways, funicular railways.

Description: Reversible aerial cableway: two pylons on each cabin, suspended from a carriage which runs on one- or two-track cables between terminals. The carriages are connected to the haulage cable, which forms an endless loop. Thus, if one cabin is moving up, the other moves down. Cabin capacities range from 20 to 200 and speeds of up to 12 m/sec are possible. The cableway typically traverses long spans, 2,000 m or more, with tall towers linking them and the drive system in one of the terminals. Straight alignments only.

Development: For more than 100 years Von Roll has designed and made cableway systems, with 1,500 installations worldwide. They are designed for crossing existing infrastructure, railways, buildings, expanses of water or rough terrain.

The latest developments are fully automated installations specially adapted for mass transport. This includes the 3-S System, for flows of more than 6,000 passengers/h, or a fully-automated funicular with several stations on the line, each vehicle carrying 400 or more.

Systems in operation include: Roosevelt Island aerial tramway, New York; Singapore cable car; Haifa Carmelit underground funicular; Lyon St Just underground funicular; Yokohama Fair passenger gondola railway; Hakone Gora–Sounzan funicular, Japan; Télécabine d'Oran, Algeria; and Hong Kong Peak Tram funicular.

UPDATED

Von Roll cable car, Singapore ***1997***

Von Roll Haifa Carmelit Funicular, Israel ***1996***

VONA

Nippon Sharyo Ltd
1-1 Sanbonmatsu-cho, Atsuta-ku, Nagoya 456-91, Japan
Overseas contact 36-2 Nihombashi-Hakozaki-cho, Chuo-ku, Tokyo 103, Japan
Telephone: +81 3 3668 3330 Fax: +81 3 3669 0239

Type of system: Automated guideway transit system.

Development: VONA (Vehicle Of New Age) service inaugurated over 3.6 km in Yukarigaoka, near Tokyo, in 1982. In Tokadai new town near Nagoya a 7.4 km loop line with seven stations opened in 1991; 56 cars.

VONA train of Tokadai Transit Company, Nagoya ***1995***

WEDway PeopleMover System

Bombardier Inc
Transportation Systems Division
PO Box 220, Station A, Kingston, Ontario K7M 6R2, Canada
Telephone: +1 613 364 3100 Fax: +1 613 389 5240
(See main entry for Bombardier under Rail Vehicles and Traction Equipment)

Type of system: Automated linear induction motor-propelled people mover.

Description: Propelled by linear induction motors (LIM) embedded in the track, lightweight cars can operate singly or coupled together. A typical three-car formation carries 18 passengers seated and up to 42 standing. The operating speed is around 23 km/h.

Development: The WEDway PeopleMover technology was first developed by Walt Disney Company, with the first installation at Walt Disney World Resort, Orlando. A second installation was opened in 1981 at Houston international airport, and extended in 1990 to 3.2 km.

In 1994, the WEDway PeopleMover became the fourth technology since 1909 to link the US Capitol Building with nearby Senate buildings and the first to operate as an automated driverless transit system. The Senate Subway runs four automated three-car trains in tunnel between the Capitol Building and nearby Senate offices in both pinched-loop and shuttle modes, with online switching and short headways. Peak-hour capacity is 1,400 passengers/h per direction. The Transportation Systems Division's US subsidiary, TGI, contracted for the design, manufacture, procurement, integration, testing and commissioning on a turnkey basis.

Senate Subway, Washington, WEDway PeopleMover ***1997***

UPDATED

BUSES — CHASSIS, INTEGRALS AND BODIES

Company Listing by Country

* Supplier of trolleybus bodywork and battery electric vehicles
C Supplier of chassis
I Supplier of integrals
B Supplier of bodywork

ALBANIA
Shkodër (CIB)

ARGENTINA
El Detalle (B)
Materfer (B)
Mercedes-Benz Argentina (C)

AUSTRALIA
Ansair (B)
Austral Denning (IB)
Custom Coaches (B)
Mercedes-Benz Australia (C)
MotorCoach (IB)
PMC Adelaide (B)
Porter (B)
Volgren (B)

AUSTRIA
Kutsenits (B)
OeAF*
Steyr (I)

BELGIUM
Jonckheere (CIB)
Van Hool (IB)*

BELARUS
Neoplan (I)

BRAZIL
Caio (B)*
Ciferal (B)
Cobrasma (B)*
Ford (Brasil)
Mafersa (I)*
Marcopolo (B)*
Mercedes-Benz do Brasil (CI)
Nielson (B)
Scania Brazil (CI)
Thamco (B)
Volkswagen do Brasil (C)
Volvo do Brasil (C)

BULGARIA
Chavdar (IB)*

CANADA
MCI (I)
New Flyer (I)*
NovaBUS (I)
Orion (I)*
Prévost (I)
Thomas (CIB)

CHINA, PEOPLE'S REPUBLIC
Beijing (I)*
CFAC (I)
Qinling (C)
Shanghai (CI)*
Shenyang (I)*

CROATIA
TAZ (B)

CUBA
Girón (C)

CZECH REPUBLIC
Avia (C)
Karosa (I)*
Škoda (I)*

DENMARK
Aabenraa (B)
DAB (IB)

ECUADOR
Thomas (I)

EGYPT
El Nasr (IB)
Ghabbour (B)

FINLAND
CARRUS Ajokki (B)
CARRUS Delta (B)
CARRUS Wiima (B)
Kiitokori Oy (B)
Lahti (B)

FRANCE
Citroën (CI)
Durisotti (B)
Gruau (B)
Heuliez (I)
Peugeot (CI)
Ponticelli (C)*
Renault (CI)*

GERMANY
Contrac (B)*
Ernst Auwärter (IB)
Ford (Germany) (I)
Göppel (B)
Kowex (B)
MAN (I)*
Mercedes-Benz (CI)*
Neoplan (IB)
Setra
Volkswagen (CI)

GHANA
Neoplan-Ghana (IB)

GREECE
Biamax
ELBO (CB)
Saracakis (B)

HUNGARY
Csepel (C)
Ikarus (IB)*
Rába (C)

INDIA
Ashok (CI)
Bharat (I)*
Tata (C)

INDONESIA
Mercedes-Benz Indonesia (CI)
New Armarda (B)

IRAN
Shahab (B)

IRAQ
Salah-al-Din (IB)

IRELAND
Asco (B)
Ewo (B)

ISRAEL
Haargaz (B)
Merkavim (B)

ITALY
Autodromo (B)*
BredaMenarinibus (I)*
Cacciamali (B)
De Simon (B)
Iveco (CI)*
Mauri (IB)*
Menarini (IB)*
Sitcar (B)
Socimi (I)*
Tomassini (B)

JAPAN
Daihatsu (C)
Fuji (B)
Hino (IB)
Isuzu (CIB)
Kawajyu (B)
Kitamura (B)
Mazda (I)
Mitsubishi (CI)
Nissan Diesel (CI)
Nissan Motor (CI)
NSK-Coach (B)
Toyota (CI)

KENYA
Banbros (B)
Labh Singh Harnam Singh (B)

KOREA, DEMOCRATIC PEOPLE'S REPUBLIC
SYNRI (I)*

KOREA, REPUBLIC
Daewoo (IB)
Hyundai (CI)

LATVIA
RAF (I)

MACEDONIA
Sanos (B)

MEXICO
Capre (B)
Dina (C)
MASA (IB)
Mercedes-Benz Mexico (CI)
Thomas Built Buses de Mexico (IB)

MOROCCO
Berliet Maroc (I)

NETHERLANDS
Berkhof (BI)*
Bova (I)
BUSiness (B)
DAF Bus (C)
Den Oudsten (IB)*
Kusters (B)
Q-Bus (B)
Smit (B)
Spijkstaal (B)*

NIGERIA
Mercedes-Benz Nigeria (C)

NORWAY
Arna (B)

PERU
Camena (I)
Volvo del Peru (C)

PHILIPPINES
Del Monte (B)

POLAND
Autosan (IB)
Jelcz (I)*

PORTUGAL
Caetano (IB)*
Camo (B)

ROMANIA
Rocar (IB)*

RUSSIA
AMO-ZIL (IB)
LIAZ (I)
PAZ (I)
Trolza (I)*

SERBIA
FAP-Famos (CIB)*
Ikarbus (IB)*

SINGAPORE
Alexander (Far East) (B)

SLOVENIA
Autoradgona (B)

SOUTH AFRICA
Busaf (B)
ERF (C)
Minibus (B)
TFM (B)

SPAIN
Castrosua (B)
Hispano (B)*
Irizar (B)
Nissan Motor Iberica (C)
Pegaso (CI)
Unicar (B)

SRI LANKA
Dimo

SWEDEN
Helmark (B)
Säffle (B)
Scania (CI)
Volvo (C)*

SWITZERLAND
Alusuisse Road & Rail (B)
Hess (B)*
NAW (C)*

THAILAND
Isuzu Motors (C)

TUNISIA
STIA (B)

TURKEY
BMC Sanayi (B)
MANAS (I)
Mercedes-Benz Türk (IB)

UKRAINE
LAZ (I)*

UK
Alexander (B)*
Autobus Classique (B)
Buscraft
Deansgate (B)
Dennis (C)
Duple (Metsec) (B)
East Lancs (B)
ERF (C)
Ford (UK) (CI)
FTL Omni (I)*
Jubilee (B)
LDV (CI)
Marshall (IB)
Mellor (B)
Northern Counties (B)
Olympus (B)
Optare (IB)*
Plaxton (IB)
Robin Hood (B)
Talbot (I)
UVG (B)
Volvo Bus (C)
Whitacres (B)
Wright (B)

USA
AAI (B)*
AmTran (B)
Blue Bird (CB)
Boyertown Logan (B)
Cable Car (B)
Carpenter (B)
Champion (B)
Chance (I)
Diamond (B)
Eagle (I)
El Dorado National (I)*
Freightliner (C)
Gillig (I)
Goshen (B)
MCI (I)*
Metrotrans (B)
NABI (IB)
Navistar (CB)
Neoplan USA (I)
NovaBUS (I)
Orion (I)
Spartan (C)
Specialty Vehicles (B)*
Thomas (CIB)
Turtle Top (B)
US Electricar (I)*
Wide One (B)
World Trans (B)

VIETNAM
Daewoo (IB)

ZIMBABWE
AVM (CB)

Classified Listing

AIR CONDITIONING AVAILABLE
AAI
Alexander
Alexander (Far East)
Autosan
Carpenter
Champion
Chance
Dina
Duple (Metsec)
Eagle
FAP-Famos
Gillig
Goshen
Haargaz
KMC
MCI
Mercedes-Benz
Merkavim
Metrotrans
Minibus
MotorCoach Australia
NABI
Neoplan
New Flyer
Orion
Plaxton
PMC Australia
Robin Hood
Setra
Thomas
Toyota
Turtle Top
Van Hool
Volvo

ALUMINIUM CONSTRUCTION
Alexander
Alexander (Far East)
Alusuisse Road & Rail
BredaMenarinibus
Caetano
CFAC
Ciferal
Contrac
DAB
Duple (Metsec)
East Lancs
Hess
Lahti
Marcopolo
Mauri
Mercedes-Benz
Metrotrans
Nielson
Northern Counties
Optare
Plaxton
Renault
Säffle
Scania
Volgren
Wright

ARTICULATED VEHICLES
Aabenraa
Alexander
Ansair
Arna
Ashok
Beijing
Berkhof
BredaMenarinibus
Busaf
Caetano
Caio
Camo
CARRUS Oy
Castrosua
Chance
Chavdar
Ciferal
Csepel
DAB
DAF Bus
De Simon
ERF
FAP-Famos
Fuji
Girón
Haargaz
Hess
Heuliez
Hispano
Ikarbus
Ikarus
Iveco
Jelcz
Karosa
LAZ
LIAZ
Mafersa
MAN
MANAS
Marcopolo
Mauri
Mercedes-Benz
Mercedes-Benz do Brasil
Merkavim
NAW
Neoplan
Neoplan USA
New Flyer
North American Bus Industries (IB)
NovaBUS
OeAF
Orion
Pegaso
Porter
Prévost
Renault
Rocar
Säffle
Sanos
Saracakis
Scania
Scania Brazil
Setra
Shanghai
Shenyang
Shkodër
Škoda
Steyr
Thamco
Trolza

ARTICULATED VEHICLES *continued*

Unicar
Van Hool
Volgren
Volvo
Volvo Bus
Volvo do Brasil

BATTERY ELECTRIC

Autodromo
Bharat
Cobus
Daihatsu
El Dorado National
Ford
FTL Omni
Gillig
Hino
Iveco
Mercedes-Benz
Neoplan
New Flyer
Optare
Orion
Ponticelli
Škoda
Specialty Vehicles
Spijkstaal
Trolza
US Electricar
Van Hool
Volvo

BODYWORK/CHASSIS SUITABLE FOR GUIDED BUS OPERATION ON FIXED TRACK

Alexander
Dennis
MAN
Mercedes-Benz
Optare
Plaxton
Renault
Scania
Volvo Bus
Volvo do Brasil

CKD (COMPLETELY KNOCKED DOWN) KITS

Alexander
AVM
Berliet Maroc
Dina
Duple (Metsec)
Hispano
Ikarus
Isuzu
Iveco
Mercedes-Benz
Neoplan-Ghana
Optare
Steyr
Unicar
Volvo

CNG (COMPRESSED NATURAL GAS) POWER OPTION

Berkhof
Blue Bird
Boyertown Logan
Carpenter
Dennis
El Detalle
El Dorado National
Iveco
MAN
Mercedes-Benz
Mercedes-Benz do Brasil
Neoplan
New Flyer
NovaBUS
Optare
Orion
Renault
Scania
Van Hool
Volvo

DOUBLE-DECK VEHICLES

Alexander
Alexander (Far East)
Ashok
Berkhof
Busaf
Caetano
DAF Bus
Dennis
Duple (Metsec)
East Lancs
ERF
Jonckheere
MAN
Marcopolo
Mercedes-Benz
Mitsubishi
Neoplan
Neoplan-Ghana
Neoplan USA
Northern Counties
OeAF
Optare
Scania
Smit
Van Hool
Volvo
Volvo Bus

MEET EMISSION REGULATIONS (EURO-2)

Berkhof
BredaMenarinibus
DAB
DAF Bus
Dennis
Den Oudsten
ELBO
Ernst Auwärter
Heuliez
Ikarus
Iveco
MAN
Marshalls
Mercedes-Benz
Neoplan
NovaBUS
Optare
Renault
Scania
Setra
Škoda
Toyota
Van Hool
Volvo
Volvo Bus

FRONT ENGINE POWERED VEHICLES

Ashok
AVM
Blue Bird
Buscraft
BUSiness
Camena
Carpenter
Daewoo
DAF Bus
Dimo
El Dorado National
ERF
Ford
Freightliner
Hino
Hyundai
Isuzu
Iveco
Labh Singh
LDV
LIAZ
MAN
Mercedes-Benz
Mercedes-Benz Argentina
Mercedes-Benz do Brasil
Mercedes-Benz Indonesia
Mitsubishi
Navistar
Neoplan-Ghana
Nissan Diesel
Nissan Motor
Nissan Motor Iberica
Orion
PAZ
RAF
Renault
Robin Hood
Säffle
Scania
Scania Brazil
Spartan
Tata
Toluca
Toyota
Turtle Top
Volkswagen
Volkswagen do Brasil
Volvo

LNG (LIQUEFIED NATURAL GAS) and LPG (LIQUEFIED PETROLEUM GAS) POWER OPTIONS

DAF Bus
Gardner
Gillig
Ikarus
NABI
Neoplan
New Flyer
Volvo Bus

LOW-FLOOR CHASSIS/BODYWORK

Alexander
Banbros
Berkhof
BredaMenarinibus
Cacciamali
CARRUS Oy
Castrosua
CFAC
Champion
Chance
Contrac
DAB
Dennis
Den Oudsten
De Simon
ELBO
El Dorado National
Ernst Auwärter
FTL Omni
Gillig
Göppel
Hess
Heuliez
Hino
Hispano
Ikarus
Iveco
Jelcz
Jonckheere
Kawajyu
Kitamura
Lahti
MAN
Marshall
Mauri
Mercedes-Benz
Mitsubishi
NAW
Neoplan
Neoplan-Ghana
Neoplan USA
New Flyer
Nissan Diesel
NovaBUS
OeAF
Optare
Orion
Plaxton
PMC Adelaide
Porter
Renault
Scania
Scania Brazil
Setra
Sitcar
Škoda
Steyr
Talbot
UVG
Van Hool
Volvo
Volvo Bus
Wright

REFURBISHMENT/REMANUFACTURING

Marshall
Robin Hood

ROAD TRAINS/REPLICA VEHICLES
Boyertown Logan
Cable Car
Chance

SCHOOL BUSES
Alexander
AmTran
Ansair
Blue Bird
Caio
Capre
Carpenter
Champion
Custom
Gruau
Heuliez
Iveco
Jubilee
MAN
Marcopolo
Navistar
PMC Adelaide
Porter
Thamco
Thomas
Toyota
Volgren
Volkswagen

THREE-AXLE RIGID VEHICLES
Alexander
Alexander (Far East)
AMO-ZIL
Ansair
Berkhof
Bova
Caetano
Camo
DAF Bus
Dennis
Diamond
ERF
FAP-Famos
FTL Omni
Hino
MCI
Mercedes-Benz
Minibus
Neoplan
Neoplan-Ghana
Nielson
Prévost
Rába
Säffle
Scania Brazil
Setra
Škoda
Volvo
Volvo Bus
Volvo do Brasil

TROLLEYBUS MANUFACTURERS
AAI
Beijing
BredaMenarinibus
Caio
FAP-Famos
Hess
Hispano
Ikarbus
Ikarus
Iveco
Jelcz
Mafersa
MAN
Marcopolo
MASA
Mauri
Mercedes-Benz
NAW
Neoplan
New Flyer
OeAF
Renault
Rocar
Sanos
Shanghai
Shenyang
Škoda
SYNRI
Trolza
Van Hool
Volvo

Aabenraa

Aabenraa Karrosseri vej A/S
Dronning Margrethes 75, 6200 Aabenraa, Denmark
Telephone: +45 74 62 12 14 Fax: +45 74 62 09 31
Managing Director: Stefan Guttmann

Background: In 1994, Aabenraa was acquired by Volvo (qv). It was formerly owned by Kässbohrer, now Setra (qv).

Products: Bus bodies, including articulated.

Range: Single-, two- and three-door city bus bodies are produced, mainly in 9, 10.85 and 12 m lengths, seating up to 55, and an 18 m articulated seating 75 or carrying 57 seated and 87 standees. They are built using the Säffle System 2000 construction method.

Contracts: Main supply is to the Danish market, with some exports to other Nordic countries.

Developments: A new low-floor bus has been built, with three doors, on a Volvo chassis. It is accessible for users of prams and wheelchairs.

UPDATED

Aabenraa low-floor bus on Volvo chassis ***1997***

AAI

AAI Transportation Systems
PO Box 126, Hunt Valley, MD 21030-0126, USA
Telephone: +1 410 628 3477 Fax: +1 410 628 8799
Vice President, Transportation Systems: Jackson R Bell
Marketing Consultant: Robert Pully

Subsidiary company
Electric Transit Inc
PO Box 509, Hunt Valley, MD 21030-0509
Telephone: +1 410 628 8416 Fax: +1 410 628 8799
Co-Presidents: Ladislav Tetal/Richard R Erkeneff

Background: AAI has been in existence for 45 years and is establishing itself in the public transport market, both road and rail. A new company, ETI, has been set up in partnership with AAI and Škoda (qv), to produce trolleybuses which are the first to be built in the USA for more than 40 years.

The AAI trolleybus is based on the Škoda 14Tr design ***1997***

Products

Trolleybus: This was unveiled in 1996 as a pre-production trolleybus for Miami Valley Regional Transit Authority, Dayton, Ohio.

Electric Transit Inc is constructing the bodyshells and installing the electrical system. Škoda is supplying the chassis, body frame, electrical gear. The trolleybus is based on the Škoda 14Tr design. The vehicles for Dayton are 2.6 m wide. The prototypes are 2.44 m wide. The wheelchair lift on the production model is at front of bus (on the prototype model the lift was at back). There are seats for 41.

Contracts: Three prototypes have been in service in Dayton; a further 57 are under construction.

Boston has indicated an interest in buying an articulated version of the trolleybus.

NEW ENTRY

AAI trolleybus in service with Miami Valley RTA, Dayton ***1997***

Alexander

Walter Alexander Ltd
91 Glasgow Road, Falkirk FK1 4JB, Scotland
Telephone: +44 1324 621672 Fax: +44 1324 632469
Chairman: Terry Whitmore
Chief Executive: Bill Cameron
Commercial Director: Anthony Pursey
Manufacturing Director: Gordon MacLennan
Human Resources Director: Ray Cramb
A member of the Mayflower Corporation plc

Belfast plant: Hydepark Industrial Estate, Mallusk, Belfast BT36 8RP, Northern Ireland
Telephone: +44 1232 342006 Fax: +44 1232 342678
Managing Director: Mike Ford-Hutchinson

Hong Kong office: Walter Alexander Hong Kong Ltd
16-B Queen's Centre, 16/Floor, 58-64 Queen's Road East, Wanchai, Hong Kong
Telephone: +852 2866 8136 Fax: +852 2865 6078
Managing Director: Nigel McGaughey

Walter Alexander (Far East) Pte Ltd, Singapore (qv)

Background: Alexander is part of the Mayflower Corporation plc. Mayflower acquired the company in 1995.

Products: Aluminium bus bodies, single- and double-deck, mini, midi and articulated, body kits.

Alexander ALX200 low-floor body with Stagecoach, Swindon ***1997***

Range

The range uses Alexander aluminium alloy extrusions. All bodies offer features to assist the partially disabled and optional features include double glazing (bonded or gasket), air conditioning and coach interiors on some bodies.

Export: All models are available for export either completely built up (CBU) or in kit form for local assembly. The construction system allows for a degree of local material content to further enhance the attraction of local assembly.

Minibus

Sprint: Seating 25-33, 7-8.4 m, principally offered on Mercedes-Benz Vario chassis cowls. Welfare and school versions available.

Midibus

Dash: Low-step 250 mm high, 1,200 mm wide doorway, luggage space and non-slip flooring on Volvo B6 (qv) and Dennis Dart (qv) chassis.

Single-deck

Strider: City bus body, with provision for guided busway operation, on Scania N113 or L113, Volvo B10B, Mercedes-Benz O405 and Dennis Lance chassis; length 11.5-11.8 m, seating 48-51 with 25 standing.

Strider Artic: 17.6 m long, on Mercedes O405G chassis, seating 60 with 60 standing.

Setanta: City bus body, seating up to 53 with 28 standing and 11.7 m long, with luggage pen, sloping step-free gangway, gasket-glazed square tinted windows, bus stopping sign and sliding anti-vandal screen, plus security cameras. It is mainly offered on the DAF SB220 chassis, for the Irish market only.

PS-type: Urban bus body, seating up to 49, 11.5 m long, only on Volvo B10M chassis.

Q-type: 12 m long, for mounting on Volvo B10M chassis. It seats up to 55 with 24 standing, for Irish markets.

Ultra: Single-deck ultra-low-floor bus body, built at the Belfast plant using the Säffle System 2000 construction. It seats up to 45 and is 12 m long. It has a Volvo B10L underframe and is built using System 2000 aluminium alloy construction. Designed for city work, a CNG version is available.

Double-deck

Royale: This seats 76-81 and is 9.6-10.3 m long, 4.4 m high (with a 4.2 m low height option) on Volvo Olympian and Scania N113 chassis.

Royale/R Type: This is for export, seating up to 110 and up to 12 m long, principally on Volvo Olympian three-axle chassis, with optional air conditioning and coach interior.

Contracts: Kowloon Motor Bus Hong Kong is taking delivery, beginning 1997, of 185 12 m Dennis Trident ultra-low-floor chassis, bodied by Alexander. KMB has ordered 340 three-axle Olympians with Alexander bodywork, supplied in kit form.

Translink Belfast has ordered 60 Alexander Ultras with double glazing and anti-bandit laminated windscreens.

Stagecoach Holdings ordered 660 bodies for 1996 delivery; 200 double-deckers were supplied to Singapore Bus Service in 1996. Stagecoach has ordered a further 310 bodies for 1997/98.

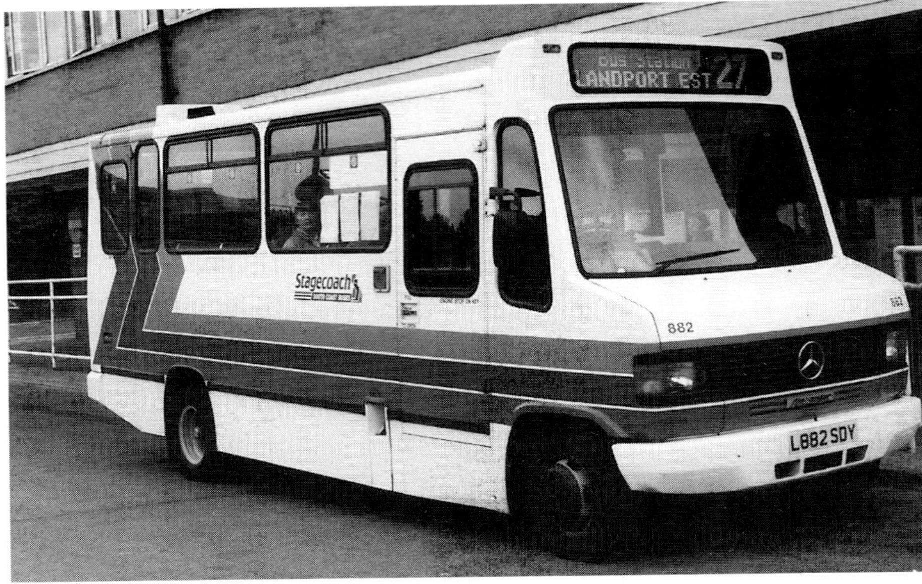

Alexander Sprint body on Mercedes-Benz 709D in Lewes **1997**

Alexander Ultra body on Volvo B10L with Timeline Travel, Bury **1997**

Developments: The ALX range of single- and double-deck low-floor bodywork uses a new glazing system, with windows bolted into the structure to give the look of bonded windows with the advantages of easy replacement. The range features the same front end styling with round headlamps. A minibus, body the ALX100, is designed for the Mercedes-Benz Vario 810D or 814D chassis. The ALX200 midibus body is available on the Dennis Dart SLF and Volvo B6LE chassis in 9.5 m, 10.2 m and 10.6 m lengths. The ALX300 is 12 m for mounting on the Volvo B10BLE or similar chassis. The ALX400 is a 10.5 m low-floor double-deck body. A three-axle version, the ALX500, is for the 12 m Dennis Trident or equivalent Volvo chassis.

A southern parts centre with additional mobile technical support has been set up in Billericay, southeast England.

UPDATED

Alexander Dash midibus on Dennis Dart chassis **1997**

Alexander Royale double-deck body on Yorkshire Coastliner service **1997**

Alexander (Far East)

Walter Alexander (Far East) Pte Ltd
7500A Beach Road 14-322, The Plaza, Singapore 0719
Telephone: +65 296 5896 Fax: +65 296 6642
Managing Director: Kenneth Ho

Products: Single- and double-deck bus bodies

Range: Specialises in design and supply of aluminium body kits tailored for the Far East market. The kits are mainly acquired from the parent company but many parts are procured locally. The vehicles are derivatives of the established R series double-deck and Alexander (qv) single-deck buses including the new Strider (qv).

The company can either assemble the kits or supervise assembly within specific territories and also provides an after-sales service for the region.

Contracts: 500 double-deck two- and three-axle air conditioned bus bodies have been delivered to Singapore Bus Service.

Developments: A new company, Dragon Pioneer, has been formed bentween Alexander and KMB Hong Kong to build city buses.

UPDATED

Alexander (Far East) R Type Royale body in Singapore
1996

Alusuisse Road & Rail

Alusuisse Road & Rail Ltd
Buckhauserstrasse 11, 8048 Zürich, Switzerland
Telephone: +41 1 497 4422 Fax: +41 1 497 4585
Managing Director: Jürg Zehnder
Marketing & Sales: Giorgio Tognon
(See also entry under Rail Vehicles and Traction Equipment)

Background: A subsidiary of Alusuisse-Lonza Holding Ltd which has plants in Switzerland, Germany, France, Italy, UK, Czech Republic, Australia and USA. Alusuisse Road & Rail is the engineering, marketing and sales organisation representing all Group companies on the rolling stock and bus market.

Products: Design, stress calculation, static strain gauge testing and fatigue testing of bus bodies; supply of easy-to-assemble aluminium components for bus bodies such as aluminium and composite structures which can be bolted, screwed or bonded, for the manufacture of low-floor buses, articulated vehicles, double-deck buses and coaches.

Contracts: Major bus builders use Alusuisse Road & Rail technology for bus manufacture.

UPDATED

Scania Omnicity manufactured using Alusuisse Road & Rail technology ***1997***

AMO-ZIL

AMO-ZIL
23 Avtozavodskaja ul, 109280 Moskva, Russia
Telephone: +7 095 275 3328 Fax: +7 095 274 0078
President: V T Sajkin
Deputy Director: N Ignatov
Foreign Trade Firm: Zil-export

Background: ZIL is one of Russia's largest truck manufacturers though it is perhaps best known in western countries for its seven-seater limousines. A new company, Novotruck, was set up in 1992/93, to build heavy trucks. It is a partnership between AMO-ZIL and the US firms Paccar and Caterpillar.

Products: Truck-derived chassis suitable for bus bodywork.

ZIL offers the Perkins 145T diesel engine (qv) in its 131D all-wheel drive three-axle truck.

ZIL components are used in the Ikarus 545 midibus.

An AMO-ZIL B44210 tractor unit is used as part of the Trolza (qv) 6020 high-capacity articulated unit, carrying 100 on urban and suburban routes.

Developments: Bus production has started in Uzbekistan by Chasautozil, a joint venture between Usautotrans (the state transport company), the Choresm automobile plant and ZIL. In 1996 the city of Moskva bought a 30 per cent stake in ZIL.

UPDATED

AmTran

AmTran Corporation
PO Box 6000, Conway, AR 72033, USA
Telephone: +1 501 327 7761 Fax: +1 501 450 9640
Vice President, Sales and Marketing: Ron Johnson

Products: School bus bodies

Range
AmTran RE: Powered by a rear-mounted International T444E diesel engine, seating up to 56 and up to 12 m long. The body has a flat windscreen and extra safety features. It is mounted on an International chassis.

UPDATED

AmTran charter bus of Laidlaw Orlando
1997

Ansair

Ansair
A division of Ansett Transport Industries (Operations) Ltd, which is itself half-owned by TNT Group Ltd
Garden Drive, Tullamarine, Victoria 3043, Australia
Telephone: +61 3 962 33333 Fax: +61 3 962 32887
Lot 7, Patriarch Drive, Kingston, Tasmania 7050
Telephone: +61 02 295700 Fax: +61 02 292781
General Manager: Barrie Martin
Marketing & Sales Manager: Ian McCrohon

Products: Bus and coach bodies, including articulated.

Range: Urban transit buses, school buses and long-distance coaches. Chassis on which Ansair products are built include MAN SL202, 16.292 and 10.180; Mercedes-Benz LO812 mini, OH1418, 1625 and O303; Renault PR100 and PR180 articulated; Scania K, L and N113; Volvo B10M plus Isuzu LT111P and UD RB30P.

Ansair also manufactures seating for buses, trains, trams, ferries and aircraft.

Orana: Streamlined bus body for urban use. Available in three-axle (14.5 m) or two-axle (12.2 m) configurations and can be mounted on mid- and rear-engine chassis with rail, lattice, space or no-step frames.

Production: Maximum annual capacity is 200. A new plant was established at Tamworth, NSW in 1995.

Ansair Orana transit bus ***1995***

Contracts: The Tamworth facility built 300 units for the State Transit Authority of NSW. Included in this contract were Orana transit buses, which have also been ordered by the Metropolitan Transport Trust of Tasmania.

Developments: A 91-seat (3+2) bus body on the MAN 22.240 bus chassis has been introduced.

UPDATED

Arna

Arna Busser AS
5262 Indre Arna, Bergen, Norway
Telephone: +47 55 249900 Fax: +47 55 249999
General Manager: Hans Peter Mittet

Products: Bus and coach bodies, including articulated.

Range: Two-door bodies on Scania, Volvo, DAF, MAN and Mercedes-Benz chassis. Also midibus bodies.

Production: Maximum annual output of 200 depending on type. Production in 1995 was 130.

Developments: A new coach body, the Comet, was introduced in 1995. It has bonded glazed windows and twin doors. A new city bus is being introduced in 1997.

UPDATED

Arna Comet body on Volvo chassis
1997

Asco

Asco Coachwork
Blessington, Co Wicklow, Ireland
Telephone: +353 45 865305 Fax: +353 45 865305

Background: In 1993, the company changed its name from Wicklow to Asco Coachwork.

Products: Minibus, midibus and midicoach bodies

Range
Asco: Minibus bodywork on Peugeot Boxer, Fiat Ducato, Citroën Relay/Jumper and Mercedes-Benz 609, 709, 811 and 814 chassis and van conversions.

Also on LDV 400 and Mercedes-Benz 408 – both to 16-seat public service vehicle specification. A luggage compartment is available for the conversion based on the Mercedes-Benz 408.

UPDATED

Asco minibus conversion on Mercedes O609D van
1995

Ashok

Ashok Leyland Limited
19 Rajaji Salai, Madras 600001, India
Telephone: +91 44 589141 Telex: 041 8271
Chair & Managing Director: R J Shahaney

Main works
Ennore, Madras 600057
Sipcot Industrial Complex, Hosur 635126, Tamil Nadu
MIDC Industrial Area, Gadegaon, Bhandara 441904, Maharashtra
Matsya Industrial Area, Alwar 301030, Rajasthan

Background: Ashok Motors was established in 1948 to assemble Austin cars and in 1950 acquired sole rights for assembly and distribution of Leyland commercial vehicles. Capacity was raised to 15,000 by 1982 and 37,000 per year in 1990, involving setting up three new plants on green field sites. Associated companies are Ennore Foundries Ltd and Lanka Ashok Leyland Limited, Sri Lanka (assembly operation). Ashok Leyland is jointly owned by Land Rover Leyland Industrial Holdings Ltd, which in turn is jointly owned by the Hindiza Group and Iveco. Iveco has a 37.5 per cent share.

Products: Bus chassis including double-deck and prototype integral and articulated; engines.

Range
Viking: City bus seating up to 61, in left-hand drive and right-hand drive versions.
Titan: Double-deck bus with front engine (AL400 series), carrying 78, 43 seated on the upper deck, 25 on the lower. RHD only.
Integral: 52-seat service bus.
B16 Articulated: 15.3 m long, carrying 150, 82 seated. RHD only.
Chital: Short wheelbase minibus, seating 27, 7.13 m long and with Iveco 8040.05 engine driving through a five-speed synchromesh gearbox. LHD/RHD.
Cheeta: This is a single-deck service bus seating 57.

Ashok is building 27- and 59-seater city and intercity buses, powered by Iveco engines. Included is India's first CNG-powered city bus, a prototype of which entered service with BEST Bombay in January 1997.

Production: In 1995 this was around 11,400.

UPDATED

Articulated bus from Ashok Leyland

Ashok-Leyland CNG-powered bus with BEST Bombay
1997

Austral Denning

Austral Denning
PO Box 422, Zillmere, Queensland 4014, Australia
Telephone: +61 7 3265 0555 Fax: +61 7 3265 6399
General Manager: Glen Bailey
National Sales and Marketing Manager: Tim Robertson
Engineering Manager: John Hatchman

Background: Austral Denning is a division of JRA Ltd, Australia.

Products: Austral and Denning bus and coach bodies.

Range
Highlander: Luxury coach, three-axle integral or body, 12.2 m, 12.5 m, 14.5 m lengths.
Aspire: Luxury coach, two-axle integral or body, 12.32 m long.

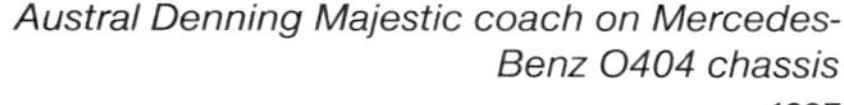

Austral Denning Majestic coach on Mercedes-Benz O404 chassis
1997

Austral Starliner: Bus or coach body to fit most European makes of chassis. The all-steel body has a jig-built tubular frame and composite side panels with overall length to suit seating or chassis requirements. Suitable for city bus, urban and day charter coach operations.
Metroliner: This is a city bus body chassis with a rear engine and low floor.
Majestic: Three-axle luxury coach.

Developments: A buyer was being sought in 1996 for JRA Ltd, which operates the trading businesses of PMC, Austral Denning and Hino Bus Australia.

UPDATED

Austral Denning Starliner multipurpose bus
1997

Autobus Classique

Autobus Classique
Unit 5, Hellaby Lane Business Park, Rotherham S66 8HN, England
Telephone: +44 1709 700220 Fax:+44 1709 701530
Sales Director: Alann White
Sales Manager: John Senior
Financial Director: Michael Wrightson

Range: Small buses and coaches, both conversions and purpose-built bodies, in the 12 to 33 seat range.
Classique: This is a bus or coach body seating between 12 and 24 on Mercedes-Benz 308D, 609D, 410D or 711D chassis.
Nouvelle: This is based on 811D and 814D chassis cowls and is 8.4 m long. It has direct-glazed windows and coach-style rear end. It has an Iveco-Ford windscreen and seats up to 33. Because the chassis is under 7.5 tonnes in weight, the vehicle is allowed in the outside lane on UK motorways and is exempt from speed limiter regulations.

Contracts: Eight Nouvelle bodies on Mercedes 814D chassis have been supplied to UK operator Speedlink with a further eight on 811D chassis going to Bebbs of Llantwit Fardre, Wales.

Production: For 1997 this was expected to be more than 100.

Autobus Classique ***1997***

Developments: In 1996 the company was acquired by Optare (qv). The Nouvelle II was launched in 1996 with a restyled front end and interior styling, based on the Mercedes-Benz upgraded 814D Vario chassis.

UPDATED

Autodromo

Carrozzeria Autodromo Modena Soc
Via Malavolti 18, 41100 Modena, Italy
Telephone: +39 59 250360 Fax +39 59 250088

Products: Bus and coach bodywork

Range
Bassoto: Carries up to 109 (25 seated, 84 standing) and integral construction. It is powered by the MAN D0826-LUH12 engine.

Other products include the *Pollicino* minibus on Iveco Daily chassis carrying up to 35 passengers with facilities for the disabled.

UPDATED

Autodromo Bassotto three-door bus
1997

Autoradgona

Autoradgona Gornja Radgona n sol o
Proizvodno Transportno Podjetje
Ljutomerska 26, 69250 Gornja Radgona, Slovenia
Telephone: +386 9 74007/74511/74941
Foreign Trade Manager: Ivan Zvegla

Background: The firm is a member of the Integral group which is also involved in urban and freight transport, coach operations, tourism and catering. It was acquired by TAM (qv) in 1992.

Products: Minibus bodies

Autosan

Autosan SA
cka Fabryka Autobusów
ul Lipińskiego 109, 38500 Sanok, Poland
Telephone: +48 137 50282/50426
Fax: +48 137 50430/50400/50429/50195
Managing Director: Andrzej Krzanowski
Marketing Director: Roman Majewski
Technical Manager: Marek Zmarz

Background: Previously known as Sanocka Fabryka Autobusów (SFA Sanok), Autosan is one of two major bus manufacturing companies in Poland. Output comprises city and interurban buses, touring coaches, trucks, vans, trailers and semi-trailers. SZC (Sobieslaw Zasada Centrum) bought 51 per cent of Autosan and 51 per cent of Jelcz in 1994.

Products: Buses and coaches

Range

H10: This is 11.2 m long and has an unladen weight of 10.5 tonnes. It carries 77 and has two or three doors, air-operated by the driver. It is powered by a rear-mounted longitudinal six-cylinder 148 kW engine.

Autosan H10-11.12N bus for wheelchair passengers

An interurban version, the H10-10 is 10.38 m long with a 5 m wheelbase and unladen weight of 9.4 tonnes, designed to carry 43 seated, powered by a 6CT107/A1 six-cylinder engine providing 125 kW.

H10-11: Two versions of the H10, for carrying wheelchair passengers, one carrying 11 wheelchairs plus 5 seated and the other for 2 wheelchairs plus 33 seats. Both vehicles have wheelchair lifts.

The H10-12 is a touring coach, 11.86 m long.

H6: Small city bus with 18 seats plus 14 standing, based on the Star 732 running units, although the design of the H6 body allows the use of chassis units from other firms.

Developments: A new 10 m dual-purpose body, the Lider, has up to three doors and carries 70. It has Mercedes-Benz running units.

Autosan and Jelcz (qv) are now part of the Zasada Group, though firms will continue to trade separately. The Zasada dealer is also the Mercedes-Benz dealer for Poland and Mercedes-Benz engines are increasingly being used by both manufacturers.

Jelcz also assembles bodywork for the O405 and the local content is about 20 per cent.

Autosan is still building the H9 41-seat intercity bus but now mainly for the export market. A new range of 10 m city buses has been launched with two or three doors. A Mercedes-Benz OM366A engine drives through either a manual or Allison automatic gearbox and air or leaf suspension can be specified.

UPDATED

Autosan H10-11 bus

Avia

Avia s p
Beranových 140, 19900 Praha 9 – Letňany, Czech Republic
Telephone: +420 2 859 0505 Fax: +420 2 859 0428
General Director: Kit-Su Ching

Background: A controlling interest in Avia was obtained by Daewoo (qv) and Steyr (qv) in 1996.

Products: Light truck chassis suitable for bus bodywork, up to 6 tonnes.

Range

A21.1 FC: This boxvan body is 5 m long and 2 m wide. It is powered by the Avia 712.18.1 engine, rated at 61 kW. The metal body is to a Renault specification and can be supplied as a minibus.

The AG2/AG3 3.61 D407 has a turbocharged diesel engine, five-speed box, power-assisted steering and air-over-hydraulic brakes. It has a gross vehicle weight of 2.28 tonnes.

Contracts: Deliveries of chassis suitable for bus bodywork to Bulgaria and the former Yugoslavia have ceased and vehicles are now built just for the Czech market.

VERIFIED

Avia A21 minibus

AVM

W Dahmer & Co (Pvt) Ltd
PO Box 2085, Harare, Zimbabwe
Telephone: +263 4 486774 Fax: +263 4 486512
A subsidiary of the Lonrho Group
Managing Director: M Lurie
General Manager: C Forman
General Manager, Marketing & Sales: I Teasdale

Background: AVM builds the majority of buses in Zimbabwe and buses have about 60 per cent local content. Associated companies are Truck Bodies Engineering, Ace Engineering and Italian Coachbuilders.

Products: Bus chassis and bodywork

AVM CD1576 intercity bus with wider body

1995

Range

CD782: A 12.5 m 75-seat front-engined bus model is produced for the Zimbabwe market. The chassis is of bolted construction to facilitate assembly and servicing and allow supply in CKD form for export. DAF engines and ZF constant mesh transmissions are used. The buses are built in both forward entrance, one-person-operated urban, and conductor-carrying rural versions, the former able to carry 25 standees and the latter with roof luggage rack. Bodywork as well as chassis is supplied. The chassis has a 6.42 m wheelbase and gross unladen weight of 7,000 kg. Alternative driveline configurations can be supplied.

CD768: An 11 m 65-seat bus model, the CD768, meeting local length restrictions in neighbouring countries, is offered for export. This also uses a front-mounted DAF engine.

CD1576: This has an identical power train to the CD782 but with a wider body, better ventilation and more effective insulation. It is offered as an intercity bus.

Production: Totals about 30 buses and 30 trucks per month.

Banbros

Banbros Ltd
PO Box 76511, Nairobi, Kenya
Telephone: +254 2 541011/558836 Fax: +254 2 540274
Managing Director: M S Bansal
General Manager: K Raj

Subsidiary company
Sarwan Singh Bansal Ltd
PO Box 72777, Nairobi

Products: Bus and coach bodywork, including city buses, express buses and coaches.

Contracts: Buses have been supplied to Akamba Bus Service, Kenya Army and Coast Line Safaris.

UPDATED

Banbros bus body
1997

Beijing

Beijing Motor & Public Transportation Corporation
44 Nanlishi Lu, Beijing, People's Republic of China

Background: Operator of extensive bus and trolleybus services in Beijing, a division of the company builds its own standard and articulated vehicles, and also supplies a number of other cities. Beijing designs are also built in other parts of China.

Products: Buses and trolleybuses

Range

BD 562 trolleybus: The current BD 562 appears in two variants, with chopper control and conventional electrical equipment, and in standard two-axle and articulated lengths.

Contracts: As well as supplying the Beijing operation, trolleybuses have been delivered to other cities including Harbin and Taiyuan.

BD 562 articulated trolleybus

Berkhof

Berkhof Heerenveen BV
PO Box 118, 8440 AC Heerenveen, Netherlands
Telephone: +31 513 618500 Fax: +31 513 629789
Managing Director: K van Beijmerwerdt
Commercial Director: S G Bruggeling
Commercial Director: P Donck
Manager, Purchase Department: H de Lang
Parent company: Berkhof Valkenswaard, Netherlands

Subsidiary companies
Carosserie Kusters Venlo, Netherlands (qv)
Denolf & Depla, Belgium
Jonckheere Bus & Coach, Belgium

Marketed in the UK by AVE Berkhof, Market Street, Bracknell RG12 1JB
Telephone: +44 1344 861787 Fax: +44 1344 860780

Berkhof Premier ultra-low-floor 18 m articulated bus
1997

Berkhof Midi 2000SL **1997**

Berkhof Premier 12 m bus with rear balcony for TRCB France **1997**

Berkhof 2000NLF 12 m bus on Dennis Lance SLF chassis **1997**

Background: The Berkhof Group comprises six companies in the Netherlands and Belgium.

Products: Integral buses and bus bodies, including low-floor, articulated and midibuses, manufactured in stainless steel. Roof, front and rear panelled in glass fibre reinforced plastic and side panels also in grp.

Range
Midi Junior: Available on MAN, Volvo or Dennis chassis, total length 9 m, width 2.3 m. There are 38 seats.
Midi 2000SL: Available on MAN, Volvo or Dennis chassis, total length 9 m, width 2.3 m. There are 38 seats. It has a different roof from the Junior.
Standard 2000NL: This is available on DAF, Dennis, MAN, and Volvo chassis, in lengths from 9 to 15 m and 18 m articulated (NLG).
2000NLF: This is a low-floor body available on DAF, Dennis and Volvo chassis, in lengths from 8 to 15 m and 18 m articulated.
2000NLE: This is a low-floor midibus body available on the Dennis SLF chassis. It is a basic bus designed to keep maintenance costs down.
Premier: This is an integral low-floor bus and is available from a midi up to 15 m in length. An 18 m articulated version and a 24 m double articulated version is available. The body frame is of Cromweld 3CR12 stainless steel. It has a mid-mounted engine.
Premier SB250: This has the same specification as the Premier, but with a rear engine.
Excellence: This is an interurban and touring coach available on chassis including the DAF SBR3015 and Volvo B12.

Production: Annual output is 900 buses and coaches, and 600 minibuses.

Contracts: Netherlands orders include Premier SB250 buses for use in Dordrecht, articulated buses for Rotterdam and 2000NLE low-floor buses for the Amsterdam area. 2000NL articulated and 12 m rigid versions have been delivered for use in Luxembourg and Midi 2000SL, 2000NL 12 m and 2000NLG articulated 18 m buses are going to Switzerland.

160 buses on DAF TB2175 chassis and with Berkhof bodies have been delivered to Ethiopia.

Five ultra-low-floor bodies on Dennis Lance SLF chassis have been delivered to Stagecoach Ribble, Manchester, England.

Berkhof Excellence 500GL interurban coach **1997**

Berkhof Premier 12 m bus built for operation in Turkey **1997**

Developments: An ultra-low-floor bus, the Premier SB250, has been introduced with stainless steel framing and a rear engine.

A joint venture to build buses has been set up with DAF Bus (qv) and RATB, Bucureşti.

UPDATED

Berliet Maroc

Berliet Maroc
PO Box 2624, Ain Sebaa, Casablanca, Morocco
Telephone: +212 2 733290/732107
Fax: +212 2 733240/731042

Director General: Omar Amraoui
Associated with Renault VI

Background: Assembly operations for vehicles supplied CKD by Renault Véhicules Industriels. The company is part-owned by Renault VI and partly by local private interests including investment companies and private insurance companies.

Products: Bus chassis

Bharat

Bharat Heavy Electricals Ltd (BHEL)
Transportation Business Department
Lodhi Road, New Delhi 110003, India
Telephone: +91 755 469 9375/461 6756/6544
Fax: +91 755 462 9423/461 7749/0779

General Manager, Transportation: R P Raghuwanshi
Additional General Manager: S P Bindra

Products: BHEL is a large electrical equipment manufacturer supplying the power plant and transport industries (see Bharat entry in Rail Vehicles). Its Electric Vehicle Division has developed battery-powered buses.

Range
Electravan: This is an 18-seat minibus having a maximum speed of 45 km/h and a cruising speed of 40 km/h. It has a range of 70 km on the level and has a 96 V 300 A/h lead acid battery assembly.

The Electravan has a separately excited 30 kW DC motor (20 hp).

Electrabus: This carries 40, 30 seated. It has a cruising speed of 40 km/h and a range of 75 km. It has a 300 A/h 160 V lead acid battery pack and a 28 kW DC series-wound motor.

Production: 300 vehicles annually.

Contracts: Vehicles have being supplied for service in the ancient caves in the Ajanta region. More than 100 Electravans are in operation with Delhi Energy Development Agency.

BHEL Electrabus

Blue Bird

Blue Bird Corporation
PO Box 937, Fort Valley, GA 31030, USA
Telephone: +1 912 757 7100
Fax: +1 912 474 9138
President and Chief Executive Officer: Paul Glaske
Vice President, Sales: Richard Maddox
Director, International Operations: Mark Welden
Overseas associates: Canadian Blue Bird, Brantford, Ontario
Assembly operations in Monterey, Mexico, Venezuela and Saudi Arabia
UK Agent: Coach Europe, Jet House, Station Road, Ratby LE6 0JN
Telephone: +44 116 238 7741 Fax: +44 116 238 7128

Background: A management-led buyout was completed in 1992.

Products: Buses and minibuses; bus bodywork (including kits for overseas assembly).

Range
Q-bus: This is for airport and city shuttle work and has a coach-type interior. It is powered by a rear-mounted Cummins 6BTA 5.9 litre diesel engine driving through an Allison AT545 transmission.
CS Bus: Available as either forward or rear engine option, diesel or CNG. For light transit, commuter or activity vehicle operations, in lengths from 7.3 m to 11.8 m.

Blue Bird 8.8 m Q-Bus of Shamrock, Pontypridd ***1997***

Contracts: The CS is being imported to the UK. It is 11.3 m long, with a rear engine, and primarily for school transport.

Blue Bird CS Bus with front-mounted engine ***1997***

Developments: The *TranShuttle* bus has been introduced, with flat floor and front-mounted engine. A low-floor version of the Q-Bus has been developed. An electric-powered version is under development.

UPDATED

BMC Sanayi

BMC Sanayi ve Ticaret AS
Kemalpasa Caddesi 32, 25060, Izmir, Turkey
Telephone: +90 232 4791870 Fax: +90 232 4790848/4791288
Chairman: M Emin Karamehmet
Vice Chairman and Managing Director:
Mehmet Demirpence
Deputy General Manager, Sales & Marketing:
Turgut Cankiliç
Board Members: A Samsa Karamebmet, Neslisan Yilmaz, F Şadi Gücüm, Osman Berkmen, Burhan Karaçam, Ismail Sezer Bilgili, Cemil Köksal, Kemal Ünlü, Mehmet Gür

UK office
Havenfields, Aylesbury Road, Great Missenden HP16 9LS
Telephone: +44 1494 890888 Fax: +44 1494 890884

Background: BMC was established in 1964 for the manufacture of tractors, trucks, buses and vans under licence from the former British Motor Corporation. It is now part of the Cukurova Group, Turkey, and has a licence agreement with Volvo Corporation.

Products: Bus bodies.

Range
220-17B3: Three-door bus seating 36 passengers with 54 standing.
220-17B2: Two-door bus, seating 43 passengers with 47 standing.
110-08: Two-door dual-purpose vehicle. Touring coach specification available.

BMC Sanayi 220-17B3 bus ***1997***

3.0MDM: Minibus, seating 14 plus driver.
3.0GDM: Midibus, seating 17 plus driver.

Production: Up to 500 buses and 1,000 midibuses a year are built.

Contracts: Bus chassis have been delivered to Nigeria and Ghana. Complete buses have been delivered to Russia.

NEW ENTRY

BOVA

BOVA BV Autobusfabriek
PO Box 5, 5550 AA Valkenswaard, Netherlands
Telephone: +31 40 208 4611 Fax: +31 40 204 2045
Managing Director: M Hendrikse

Background: Bova first started building coaches in 1931. In 1969 it built its first integral coach and in 1983 announced the Futura, with its distinctive styling.

Products: Integral interurban, express and touring coaches.

Range
Futura: Available in two heights and five lengths. Powered by DAF or MAN engines.
Futura FL: Dual-purpose vehicle for interurban and express work, 12 m and 15 m lengths. Powered by DAF or MAN engines.
Futura FH: Luxury coach, 10 m, 12 m, 13 m, 14 m and 15 m options. Powered by DAF or MAN engines.

Production: Sales increased fourfold in the past three years to reach more than 50 vehicles in 1996, with further growth expected for 1997. Distribution in the UK is by Optare (qv) and Moseley.

UPDATED

Bova Futura FHD coach of Yorkshire Travel, Dewsbury ***1997***

Boyertown Logan

Boyertown Logan Body Works
PO Box 230, Booneville, AR 72927, USA
Telephone: +1 501 675 3220 Fax: +1 501 675 3350
In US only: 800 876 5539
President: William R Placek
Vice President, Sales: Thomas E McKean

Background: Boyertown Logan Body Works acquired the assets of Boyertown Body Works (started in 1872) and Logan County Body Works in 1992.

Products: Rubber-tyred replica vintage trolley/tram vehicles.

BredaMenarinibus

BredaMenarinibus SpA
Via San Donato 190, 40127 Bologna, Italy
Telephone: +39 51 637 2111 Fax: +39 51 510353

Parent company
Breda Costruzioni Ferroviarie SpA
Via Ciliegiole 110/b, 51100 Pistoia, Italy
Telephone: +39 573 3701 Fax: +39 573 370292
Chairman: Dr Luigi Roth
General Director, Breda Group: Dr Ing Corrado Fici
Business Development Director: Dr Ing Claudio Mannucci
Mass Transit Business Development Director:
Dr Ing Claudio Fumagalli

US subsidiary
BTI Breda Transportation Inc
261 Madison Avenue, New York, NY, 10016-2303, USA
Telephone: +1 212 286 8000 Fax: +1 212 286 0700

Background: BredaMenarinibus was created by Breda Costruzioni Ferroviarie following acquisition of the bus builder Menarini. Breda has plants in Bologna, Pistoia and Roma for manufacture of buses and trolleybuses for city, intercity and tourist operations.

Products: City buses, coaches and trolleybuses.

Range: Five body lengths from 7 to 18 m, for city and interurban use.
BMB 230: A low-floor bus for Italian town use.

Production: Annual capacity is 800 to 1,000.

Contracts: 333 articulated buses are being supplied to Firenze, Bologna, Genova and Roma.

SEMITAG Grenoble has taken delivery of a 6M230CU bus; a CNG-powered bus has been supplied to Firenze; 27 trolleybuses with inverter-controlled propulsion and auxiliary diesel power unit for Cremorna, Bari and Genova. Several batches of similar vehicles have been built for other towns in Italy.

Developments: BredaMenarinibus and Breda Costruzioni Ferroviarie are developing a new low-floor articulated trolleybus with an auxiliary power unit.

UPDATED

BredaMenarinibus low-floor articulated city bus ***1996***

BredaMenarinibus low-floor BMB 230 city bus ***1995***

Busaf

Dorbyl Transport Products
Bus Division (Busaf)
PO Box 4008, Korsten, Port Elizabeth 6014, South Africa
Telephone: +27 41 412665 Fax: +27 41 412665 ext 205
Executive Director: Rob Duff
Dorbyl Chief Executive: W W Cooper
Chairman: Dr J H Loor
Directors: J Malherbe, W E Bührmann, J B Magwaza, G R Pardoe

Dorbyl Transport Products
PO Box 229, Boksburg 1460, South Africa
Telephone: +27 11 914 1400 Fax: +27 11 914 3885
Managing Director: Rob Duff

Background: Established in 1945 by Metro Cammell, England, the majority shareholding was bought in 1967 by Dorman Long (South Africa), which became Dorbyl when it merged with Van der Byl Engineering in 1973. It became Busaf in 1978.

Products: Single- and double-deck bus and coach bodywork, including articulated and minibuses.

Articulated bus based on MAN 16.220 chassis

Range: The double-deck model carries up to 99, and can be to coach or bus specification.

The semi-trailer, developed by Busaf at its Letaba works, carries 119, 89 seated, and can be based on ERF or MAN chassis.

The articulated unit is based on the MAN 16220 forward control chassis.

Contracts: The bus division of Dorbyl had a successful year with buses and coaches being supplied to South Africa, Zimbabwe and Zambia. Johannesburg City Council took delivery of 100 buses in 1996.

Developments: Parent company, Dorbyl Transport Products, took a 70 per cent interest in ERF South Africa (qv) in 1996.

UPDATED

Buscraft

Buscraft Ltd
Unit 4D, Odyssey Centre, Corporation Road, Birkenhead L41 1HY, England
Telephone: +44 151 666 2224 Fax: +44 151 666 1119
Managing Director: Jan Bredenkamp
Marketing Director: Barry Johns

Products: Small buses and coaches.

Range

Impala: Based on Mercedes-Benz 814 chassis cowl with rear air suspension, seating 35.

NEW ENTRY

Buscraft Impala coach body on Mercedes-Benz 814 chassis

1997

BUSiness

BUSiness BV
PO Box 410, 5500 AK Veldhoven, Netherlands
Telephone: +31 40 554433 Fax: +31 40 554411
Director: O E P Veldhuizen
Works address: De Run 4425, 5503 LS Veldhoven

Products: 12-seat minibus (13 standing) based on Peugeot Boxer chassis cowl. Also conversions on Mercedes, Ford, Iveco, Fiat and Citroën base vehicles.

The BUSiness 2002 body can be mounted on Citroën, Peugeot or Fiat chassis. It carries up to 25 and has a flat floor 320 mm above the road surface. The vehicle can kneel a further 50 mm.

Contracts: Buses have been supplied to Groningen, Maastricht, Rotterdam, Basel, Schaffhausen and Genève.

UPDATED

BUSiness 1001 minibus conversion

1996

Cable Car

Cable Car Concepts Inc
Dept B, PO Box 6500, Deltona, FL 32728, USA
Telephone: +1 407 860 0333 Fax: +1 407 574 3600
President: R B McFadden

Products: Mini trackless trolleys (replica tramcars), seating 21 to 32 and trolley trams (mini road trains) carrying up to 97.

VERIFIED

Cacciamali

Carrozerie Cacciamali
Via VI Novembre, 25030 Mairano, Italy
Telephone: +39 30 975361 Fax: +39 30 975226

Products: Buses up to 10 m, on Iveco Daily, A-series and other Iveco chassis.

The Cacciamali TCM890 low-floor midibus is available in left- or right-hand-drive form. It is mounted on an Iveco 59.12 or Mercedes-Benz 814D chassis and was imported into the UK by Robin Hood Vehicle Industries, under the Ibis name.

Contracts: A Cacciamali 16-seat Tamar-bodied minibus has been delivered to Pink Elephant Parking, Heathrow Airport, London; three Ibis coaches have been delivered to R&I Coaches, London, UK.

Developments: A city bus with an Iveco engine has been announced.

UPDATED

Caetano

Salvador Caetano Indústrias Metalúrgicas e Veículos de Transporte SARL
Estrada Nacional 222, Km 1, Oliveira do Douro, Apartado 51, 4401 Vila Nova de Gaia Codex, Portugal
Telephone: +351 2 782 0753/1904/1604
Fax: +351 2 782 5876
President: Salvador Caetano
Managing Director: J L Abreu Teixeira
Commercial Director: Manuel Amaral

UK subsidiary
Salvador Caetano (UK) Ltd
Mill Lane, Heather, Coalville LE67 2QE
Telephone: +44 1530 263333 Fax: +44 1530 263379
Managing Director: Mike Stannard
Sales Director: Derek Wakefield
Executive Marketing Director: Alan Page

Background: Established in 1946, Salvador Caetano has developed new construction methods based on technological agreements with other builders and assembly arrangements. Toyota vehicles, including the Coaster midibus, are assembled at Ovar, Portugal, and the company is now 27 per cent owned by Toyota through two equity stakes, and itself owns a Toyota dealership.

Caetano midibus body on MAN 10150 chassis with Carris, Lisboa ***1997***

Products: Buses and trolleybuses including articulated; bus and coach bodywork.

Range
Algarve: This is a luxury coach body available on many chassis, seating from 33 to 55, and as a standard high or super-high deck.
Integral city bus: Whilst Caetano can offer integrally built city buses, requirements from the Portuguese market for diesel buses have largely been for body-on-chassis construction.
Porto Star: 71-seat double-deck bodywork on MAN three-axle running units rated at 367 bhp (274 kW).
Trolleybus: Integral trolleybuses, both standard and articulated.
Optimo III: 24-seat body on the purpose-built Toyota chassis. It was improved in 1990, with a more streamlined front and better seating. In 1992, a new engine, the Toyota HZT 6-cylinder turbocharged engine, was included in the specification, developing 97 kW (172 hp). It can now seat up to 25, with a luxury version seating 21.

Contracts: Bus bodies have been exported to Peru and other countries in joint deals with Pegaso, and also jointly with Fiat. Caetano has assembled Duple (Metsec) (qv) kits on Dennis Dragon chassis for Hong Kong. It has also assembled Cobus airside buses, using Alusuisse construction.

Developments: The Optimo IV replaces the Optimo III. As before it has a Toyota chassis with bodywork by Caetano, but has a Toyota four-cylinder engine meeting Euro-2 regulations.

UPDATED

Caio

Companhia Americana Industrial de Onibus
Rodovia Marechal Rondon, km 252, Zona Industriel, CEP 18603-970, Botucatu, São Paulo, Brazil
Telephone: +55 149 213311 Fax: +55 149 213329
Chairman of the Board of Directors:
José Gildo Vendramini
Superintendent Director: Cláudio Regina
Industrial Director: José Massa Neto
Technical Director: José Rogério Cardarelli
Commercial Director: José Gildo Vendramini
Non-executive President: Ruggero Cardarelli

Subsidiary company
Cia Americana Industrial de Onibus do Norte, Jabotão

Background: CAIO has a 15 per cent holding in Mercedes-Benz Omnibuses Mexico SA.

Caio body on Scania do Brasil L113CL city bus chassis

Products: Bus, trolleybus and minibus bodies, including articulated.

Range: City bus bodies are produced to the government standard 'Padron' design with wide entrance and exit, flat floor and good visibility. The company has developed trolleybuses for the Brazilian market, and offers a body design suited for trolleybus equipment. It is 18.15 m long and bodywork is based on a Volvo Brasil B58 chassis (qv) with electrical equipment by Villares. The three-door body contains seats for 54 and standing room for 126.
Vitoria: This has one, two or three doors and is up to 12.1 m long. It seats up to 43 on either upholstered or fibreglass seats. It is based on Scania, Mercedes-Benz, Ford B-1618 chassis or Volvo B58 chassis. An articulated version on a Volvo B58 or Scania S-113 chassis seats 61. Intercity and express versions are available.
Vitoria articulated: This is an urban bus chassis, 18.12 m long, on Volvo B58E chassis.
Mobile: This is a minibus based on a normal control Ford chassis.
Taguá: This is based on a normal control Mercedes truck chassis and is for school use. It has two doors.
Cardina V: This is a midi coach, on Mercedes-Benz or Volkswagen chassis, seating up to 35.

VERIFIED

Camena

Inversiones Commerciales Camena SA
Avenida Industrial No 400, Lima, Peru
Telephone: +51 14 522712 Fax: +51 14 640850
Executive President: Carlos Olguin
Finance & Administrative Manager: Luis Perez Bisrror

Products: Bus bodywork

Range: Bodies are mounted on Volvo and Mitsubishi chassis.
Junior Bus: This mounted on either a Mitsubishi Canter or Camena chassis and seats up to 29. It is 7.08 m long and 2.2 m wide.
Senior: The Senior 1 is an interurban body on a Mitsubishi Fuso front-engined chassis and is 10.5 m long and 2.6 m wide. It seats up to 41.

The Senior 2 is a touring coach on a Volvo B7 chassis and is 11.9 m long and 2.5 m wide. It seats up to 48.
Master: This is a touring coach on a Volvo B10M mid-engined chassis and is 13.5 m long and 2.6 m wide. It seats 58.

Camena Junior Bus on Mitsubishi chassis

Camena Senior 1 bus on Mitsubishi chassis

Camena Master Bus on Volvo chassis

Camo

Camo-Indústria de Autocarros SA
Apartado 8, Canelas, 4405 Valadares, Vila Nova de Gaia, Porto, Portugal
Telephone: +351 2 711 4778/4803/4951
Fax: +351 2 711 4951
General Manager: Manuel Leão E Seabra

Background: A subsidiary of Auto-Sueca set up with Volvo interests to mount bodies on Volvo chassis assembled locally.

Products: Bus and coach bodies. The latest vehicle is the U90 articulated bus, on Volvo B10MA three-axle chassis.

UPDATED

Camo body on Volvo B7R chassis
1997

Capre

Carrocerias Preconstruidas SA
Fulton No 8, Tlalnepantla, Edo de Mexico CP 54030, Mexico
Telephone: +52 565 6600/3022 Fax: +52 565 3304
General Director: J I Amaya
Planning Director: Mario Mugica
Commercial Director: Alfredo Notni
Technical Director: Ricardo Pous
Design Engineering Director: Julian Espino

Background: Capre was set up in 1954 in San Bartolo Naucalpan to make buses.

Products: Bus and minibus bodies

Range: Includes the CD and Boxer, both with Mercedes-Benz engines, batches of which were delivered in 1991 to Mexico City operator Ruta 100. Conventional bus bodies on Dina/Navistar, Mercedes-Benz, Chrysler and Ford chassis are produced.

Developments: Capre now owns Hispano (qv) and production is carried out jointly though the different model ranges have been retained. A new factory was opened in 1995 at Cartuja, Zaragoza.

UPDATED

Capre CD bus on Ramirez chassis with Mercedes-Benz engine

Carpenter

Carpenter Manufacturing Inc
1100 Industries Road, Richmond, IN 47374, USA
Telephone: +1 317 965 4000 Fax: +1 317 965 4125
President: Timothy Durham

Background: Carpenter acquired bus body builder Crown Coach Inc, USA, in 1994.

Products: Bus and minibus bodies

Range: Bodies up to 55-passenger capacity are mounted on Chevrolet, Ford, GM and Navistar truck chassis.
Classic: This offers a choice of seating capacity for 20 to 52, and is suitable for mounting on front-engined Ford, Chevrolet, GMC or Navistar truck-derived chassis with petrol or diesel engines. It comes in 23 body lengths, from 4.8 m to 10.1 m.
Classmate: This is a mid-sized bus on the Chevrolet Chevvy Van chassis cowl and seats up to 16 and features a 2.3 m wide interior and interior headroom of 1.9 m or 2 m.

Carpenter Counselor body

Cadet: This has a wider body that comes in four lengths designed to seat 12 to 27. It is available on Chevrolet or GMC P-series chassis with petrol or diesel engines. To ease access, the Cadet has a low entrance step and wide opening doorway. The 2.3 m wide body narrows to 2.1 m at the front to reduce wind resistance.
Counselor: This can be forward control or rear-engined. It seats up to 60 and can be powered by Cummins, Caterpillar, Hercules CNG, or Detroit Diesel methanol engines.
Coach: This carries up to 90 and is to a Crown Coach design.

All buses come in both school bus and transit configurations with air conditioning, destination display, farebox, power doors and wheelchair lift options.

Production: Carpenter bodies are in widespread use as school buses in the USA and Latin America. Production runs at up to 32 per day.

Developments: The Crown and Coastline are on rear-engine chassis and seat between 28 and 55.

UPDATED

Carpenter Classic body on Navistar International chassis
1997

CARRUS Oy

CARRUS Oy
Fabianinkatu 9, 00100 Helsinki, Finland
Telephone: +358 9 825841 Fax: +358 9 821414
Managing Director: Harry Ström
Customer Liaison: Esko Mustonen

Products: Bus and coach bodies and special vehicles. Annual production is around 550 bus bodies and 150 special vehicles. There are about 850 employees. Carrus Oy has three production units for bus bodies and two subsidiaries, which make midibuses and special vehicles.

All bus and coach bodies are built on the Carrus Stainless principle, with stainless steel for load-bearing structures — framework and side panelling.

CARRUS Oy Ajokki
PO Box 15, 33721 Tampere, Finland
Telephone: +358 3 277111 Fax: +358 3 277 1277

Products: Intercity bus bodies, tourist coaches on Volvo, Scania and Mercedes-Benz chassis.

Developments: Vector and Regal new tourist coach bodies.

CARRUS Oy Delta
PO Box 23, 21421 Lieto, Finland
Telephone: +358 2 871711 Fax: +358 2 871002

Products: Luxury tourist coach bodies on Scania, Volvo and Mercedes-Benz chassis.

Developments: A new range, Star, with three models, 302, 502 and 602, has been introduced.

CARRUS Oy Wiima
PO Box 23, 01531 Vantaa, Finland
Telephone: +358 9 825841 Fax: +358 9 821414

Products: City and intercity bus bodies

Range: Bodies with welded steel tube framework are offered on various makes of chassis including articulated. The City-204 series covers low-floor and articulated buses, which are built to withstand the hard northern road and climate conditions. The vehicles have double-glazed side and rear windows, fresh-air defrosters and front heating units for the driver. There is also roof channel ventilation with heating radiators and recirculating heaters for the passenger saloon.

The City-204 bodies can have two or three single/double doors and varying seating layouts.

Production: Annual capacity is over 200 bodies.

Contracts: City-204 buses have been supplied to a number of Scandinavian operators, on Volvo and Scania chassis.

Developments: A low-floor articulated version of the 204 was introduced in 1996. Carrus and Volvo are setting up a joint venture to build city buses in Poland using the Carrus stainless steel system. It is based in Wrocław next to the Volvo truck plant.

Kiitokori Oy
PO Box 22, 47401 Kausala, Finland
Telephone: +358 5 744701 Fax: +358 5 744 7111

Products: Mini and other small buses, airport buses

UPDATED

Carrus City U low-floor bus body on Volvo B10 L chassis ***1996***

Chavdar

Chavdar United Bus Works
Botevgrad, 2140 Bulgaria
Telephone: +359 997 131 2444
Fax: +359 997 131 2145

Exports: Balkancarimpex
Boul Kliment Ohridski 48, 1040 Sofia
Telephone: +359 2 65501/753301/778201
Fax: +359 2 771301
Director General: Alexander Tsokev
Advertising Manager: Mrs R Nikolova

Products: Buses. Engines. Chavdar bus production is exported under the 'Balkancar' name. Also builds trolleybuses.

Range
B13-20: The 11 m 11G6 city bus features modern square styling and integral welded steel construction. Designed to carry up to 96 (72 standing), there are forward-facing single seats for 24.

The Rába engine is installed underfloor between the axles. Transmission is by a manual four-stage ZF gearbox. There is independent front suspension and a 5.65 m wheelbase. Unladen weight is 9,300 kg and maximum laden weight 16,000 kg, while maximum speed is 69 km/h.
B14-20: Articulated version of B13-20.

Chavdar also offers interurban and luxury coaches in limited numbers.

UPDATED

Chavdar B14-20 articulated bus in Ufa, Russia
1996

Ciferal

Ciferal, Comércio e Industria S/A
Rua Pastor Manoel Avelino de Souza 2064, 25250-000 Xerém, Duque de Caxias, RJ, Brazil
Telephone: +55 21 779 1011 Fax: +55 21 779 1032
Export Division, Telephone: +55 21 779 1724
President: Lelis Marcos Teixeira
Commercial Director: Fernando Magalhães
Export Manager, South America & Caribbean:
Antonio Carlos Vinhas
Export Manager, MERCOSUL Middle East:
Rafael Adauto da Costa

Background: The company expanded in 1992 to a new 300,000 m³ plant 50 km from its previous 40,000 m³ location in Rio de Janeiro. It now employs 1,600.

Products: Bus bodies

Range: Aluminium-structured bus bodies for urban and suburban use. Short- and long-distance coaches built on Mercedes, Scania and Volvo chassis produced in Brazil. Also minibuses and airport buses.
Mikron: This is a minibus body, carrying up to 27, on Mercedes-Benz LO812 or 708, Ford and VW chassis. Two doors can be fitted.
Highway: 13.2 m long, 3.6 m high, for 50 passengers, built of aluminium and fibreglass, on Scania, Mercedes and Volvo chassis.
Articulated Urban: This is 18.2 m long, on Scania or Volvo chassis.
GLS: This is an urban bus on Mercedes, Scania, Volvo, Ford and VW chassis.

Ciferal bi-articulated three-section bus on Volvo chassis ***1995***

Production: 2,113 bodies were produced during 1994, 2,078 being for the home market.

Citroën

SA Automobiles Citroën
62 Boulevard Victor-Hugo, 92208 Neuilly-sur-Seine Cedex, France
Telephone: +33 1 45 78 61 61 Fax: +33 1 47 48 51 09

Products: Minibuses and chassis

Range: The front-wheel-drive Jumper van (named Relay in UK) is available with a choice of three diesel engines of 71, 86 and 103hp (53, 64 and 77 kW). Payloads range from 1,165 kg to 1,605 kg.

The current Jumper (Relay) was launched in 1994 and is available with a choice of three wheelbases and roof heights. The body design, on which minibus conversions

Citroën Jumper with Q-Bus JumBus conversion
1997

can be carried out, offers very wide full height side or rear doors. Internally the Relay offers a low loading height and wider than normal interior width combined with excellent

Citroën Jumpy Combi ***1996***

headroom. A 17 seat school bus is offered by Advanced Vehicles, Clay Cross, England, based on the Relay.

The Citroën models are powered by a choice of PSA 1.9 litre or 2.5 litre diesel engines, naturally aspirated or turbocharged.

There are 12- and 15-seat minibus variants available in the UK, converted by Autotrim, Halifax or Advanced Vehicles and available through the Citroën dealer network. They have three-point seatbelts and high-back seats can be specified.

Developments: A new small 1.9 litre diesel or turbo diesel passenger carrier, the Jumpy Combi (called the Dispatch in the UK) seats up to 9 and is 4.4 m long. Twin side load doors are standard and this compact vehicle is expected to become popular for wheelchair-accessible taxi/small bus operations.

A 17-seat minibus specially adapted for schools has seat belts, mobile phone and free signwriting.

UPDATED

Contrac

Contrac GmbH
Max-Planck-Ring 43, 65205 Wiesbaden, Germany
Telephone: +49 6122 95530 Fax: +49 6122 51461
Managing Directors: Jürgen Kamps, Lothar Elbel

Subsidiary companies
Contrac Beijing, China
Contrac International (GB) Ltd

Products: Low-floor small buses and airport buses. Mechanical subassemblies are by NAW (qv) and bodywork is by Caetano (qv).

Range
Cobus 1000: This is a low-floor diesel airport bus, 6.535 m long and with an entrance height of 240 mm, when kneeling. The width is 1.94 m. There are no steps inside. Air conditioning can be fitted.

Cobus 3000: Low-floor airport bus, 14 m long, with six doors and 3 m wide. The entrance height, when kneeling, is 270 mm and it carries 140. It is of aluminium alloy construction.

UPDATED

Csepel

Csepel Autógyár FA
PO Box 38, 2311 Szigetszentmiklós, Hungary
Telephone: +36 24 366871 Fax: +36 24 367310
Director: Antal Varga

Background: The main customer traditionally was Ikarus until the Russian market collapsed and Ikarus made its own underframes. Only gearboxes and steering, both under ZF licences, were sourced from Csepel which faced financial difficulties until bought out in July 1996 by Hungarian-American investor Dr Szalay. Csepel has links with Cummins (qv).

Products: Bus chassis, including articulated. Trucks (8 to 10 tonnes).

Range
844: This is rear-engined and is 12 m long. It is available as a city bus or as a long-distance model. Power is from a Cummins C 8.3 l engine, and suspension is air over-leaf.

The 844.16M city bus version is powered by a rear-mounted Cummins 6BTA, driving through an Allison automatic gearbox. The 844.16G is powered by a Cummins 6CTA engine. The bus chassis can be fitted with two-, three- or four-door bodywork.

856: This is powered by a Cummins L10 engine and is similar to the 844 chassis.

888.02: This is an articulated bus chassis, 17.5 m long, powered by a rear-mounted Cummins 8CTA driving through a ZF 4HP transmission with hydraulic retarder.

613.02B: This is a midibus type, 7.2 m long, in coach or city bus specification. The chassis is rear engined, with a Cummins 4BTAA-3.9 engine driving through a Voith Midimat transmission. The floor height of the bus version is 535 mm; that of the coach version is 695 mm.

Production: Between 150 and 200 bus chassis are produced each year.

Developments: The possibility of low-cost bus chassis for the UK is being looked at, in association with Auwärter. The present low-floor range includes the 613.04 7.7 m and 633 8.7 m chassis with the options of Cummins, Mercedes-Benz and MAN engines.

A minicoach chassis, the 613, has been exhibited in Australia.

UPDATED

Csepel bus chassis with Ikarus body

1996

Csepel 844 chassis with Ikarus body

1997

Custom Coaches

Custom Coaches Sales Pty Ltd
PO Box 3, 34 Marian Street, Guildford, NSW 2161, Australia
Telephone: +61 2 9632 0221 Fax: +61 2 9632 1653
NSW Sales Division: 31-39 Sturt Street, Smithfield, NSW 2161
Telephone: +61 2 9892 1966 Fax: +61 2 9632 7448
Managing Director: J Violet
Director: G Violet
General Manager: B Reardon
Sales Manager: N Stott
Other Sales Divisions at Preston, Victoria and Arundel, Queensland
Minibus assembly plant: Gold Coast, Queensland

Custom Coaches Mini Series II body on Mercedes 814 chassis **1997**

Custom Coaches Series 400 coach on Mercedes O404 chassis **1997**

Products: Bus and coach bodies

Range
Mini: This is based on the Mercedes-Benz 812 chassis and seats around 30.
210 series: This is a two-door bus body, seating around 60, mounted on a Volvo B10M chassis.
288 series: For city bus work, with galvanised steel framework, twin-door option and deep windscreen. Can be mounted on various chassis including Volvo B10M and B10B.
310 series: For school/charter operations. It is a front entrance dual-purpose body, and can be mounted on a Mercedes-Benz chassis.
315 series: This is a single-entrance city bus body on a Mercedes chassis.
325 series: This is a bus body, with two doors, seating around 60. It can be mounted in an Isuzu chassis.
Series 400: The first vehicles to be bodied at the new Gold Coast plant have been 44-seat coaches to a design known as Series 400. They are on Mercedes-Benz O404 chassis.

UPDATED

DAB

DAB A/S
Kejlstrupvej 71, 8600 Silkeborg, Denmark
Telephone: +45 86 823300 Fax: +45 86 815654
Managing Director: Paul Arne Jensen

Background: Dansk Automobil Byggeri (DAB) was established in 1912. The company started by building bodywork on imported chassis. During the post-war period, DAB was taken over by industrialist Henry Pedersen, but the majority shareholding belonged to Leyland, UK, until 1987, when the management bought out from the Rover Group. From 1990 it was a member of the United Bus Group, which took a 70 per cent controlling interest in the company in 1993. Following the demise of United Bus, DAB traded independently, having been bought out by its directors.

In 1994 it was acquired by Scania (qv), following a long period of co-operation, including bodying Scania chassis and after-sales responsibility for Scania vehicles in Denmark. DAB continues with its present range and in the long term the product ranges of DAB and Scania will be co-ordinated and replaced with a jointly developed range.

DAB Series 11 Service Bus with hydrostatic drive **1996**

Products: Buses, chassis and bodywork, including articulated.

Range
City bus (including articulated): Integral city and interurban buses to a standard mid-underfloor-engined design in lengths from 9.5 to 18 m articulated, using primarily DAF running units in locally produced underframes, characterised by members drilled to remove excess weight from unstressed sections. Bodywork is based on light alloy profiles of system M5438, supplied by Alusuisse-Lonza, and similar bodywork is also offered for mounting separately on other chassis. The latest integral buses use the DAF LT turbocharged engine providing up to 286 bhp at 2,200 rev/min. They feature skirting radiator heating systems, DAF axles and air suspension.

Separate bodywork is also available, based on light alloy profiles supplied by Alusuisse on a welded structure with glassfibre front and rear ends.
Service bus: This is based on the earlier Travolator model and has a floor height of 230 mm, with a boarding height of 80 mm. There are no steps and fittings are provided for wheelchairs. The wheels are at the extreme corners of the vehicle and power comes from a DAF 6.2 litre turbocharged engine (156 kW), with the option of either petrol, LPG or diesel engines up to 170 kW. The final drive is through a hydrostatic transmission, with a motor in each wheel hub. The vehicle can carry up to 50 or up to eight wheelchair passengers. It is 8.6 m long, 2.5 m wide and 2.8 m high.
Citybus 1200: An aluminium body on the low-floor Alliance City underframe, built by former United Bus subsidiary Den Oudsten. It is for the Scandinavian market. It has a low floor and is powered by a DAF RS1200L engine, driving through a ZF 4 HP500 gearbox, with retarder. It is 12 m long and has a floor height of 230 mm.

Production: About 250 vehicles per year.

Contracts: 51 LPG-powered vehicles with 12 m DAF Bus underframes have been ordered by DSB København. Each low-floor bus carries 100 passengers, 39 seated.

UPDATED

Daewoo

Daewoo Motor Co Ltd
199, Changchon-dong, Puk-gu, Inchon, Republic of Korea
Telephone: +82 32 520 2114 Fax: +82 32 524 4362
Managing Director: Jae Ho Kim
Seoul office: Daewoo Center, 541 Namdaemunno 5-ga, Chung-gu, Seoul
Telephone: +82 2 776 4031/4035 Fax: +82 2 754 0669

Products: Buses

Range: Includes 12 m front-engine versions that have been delivered to Bangkok, with locally produced Thai bodywork, supplies totalling 300 in 1991 and 200 in 1992.

Voith D851.2 transmissions have been fitted to prototypes.

Daewoo has taken a 60 per cent share in a venture to build buses in Vietnam.

Production: In 1995 was around 4,500 buses.

Developments: Steyr-Daimler Puch has been acquired by Daewoo. Collaboration had already existed on the production of light monobloc diesel engines. They are being built by Russian manufacturer, GAZ.

A 61 per cent share in the Polish commerical vehicle manufacturer, FS, was acquired in 1995. Daewoo bought 65 per cent of Steyr-Daimler-Puch in October 1995. A controlling interest in Avia (qv) has been obtained by Daewoo.

UPDATED

Daewoo bus in Seoul

DAF Bus

DAF Bus International
PO Box 7122, 5605 JC Eindhoven, Netherlands
Telephone: +31 40 250 0500 Fax: +31 40 257 0904
Managing Director: Michael Van Rossem
Technical Director: Louis Spaninks

DAF Bus International products are sold in the UK through:
Hughes DAF, Lodge Garage, Whitehall Road, West Gomersal BD19 4BJ, England
Telephone: +44 1274 681144 Fax: +44 1274 651198

Background: In 1989, DAF NV transferred its bus and coach underframe manufacture and development to a new company DAF Bus. DAF Bus International is now owned by a Dutch consortium, with a minority stake held by DAF Trucks (19 per cent). The minority stake was acquired by US truck manufacturer Paccar in 1996. The main partners are the VDL Group of specialised companies in the metal and plastics industries, with a 51 per cent shareholding, and De Rooy Transport, a parts distribution and transport company, with 30 per cent.

DAF International BV is the Netherlands importer for DAB (qv).

Products: Bus and coach underframes, including articulated; steering and drive units, including engines and axles.

Range: Chassis are manufactured with front- mid- and rear-mounted engines. DAF makes engines in variants for urban, interurban bus, and tourist coach operations. All engines now meet Euro-1 exhaust emissions standards with Euro-2 available on all models.

SB220: This city and interurban bus underframe is powered by a horizontally mounted 8.65 litre ATI Euro-2 engine, driving through a ZF or Voith automatic gearbox, with integral retarder. Air suspension is standard, as is encapsulation of the engine and gearbox to reduce noise and vibration. The SB220 features a kneeling facility which enables it to be lowered by 100 mm. The SB220 is also available as a pusher articulated underframe and as a dual-purpose chassis, the SB225.

A low-floor version of the SB220, the SB220 Low Floor can take bodywork with a floor height of 320 mm. It has a new front axle module and can be powered by the 8.65 litre LPG engine.

A version powered by liquefied petroleum gas (LPG) has multipoint LPG injection. DAF reports that this offers extra benefits when compared with the present generation of LPG engines.

The DAF LT160 LPG engine was announced in 1995 and has timed multipoint liquid LPG injection, designed to improve reliability. A three-way catalytic converter cuts nitrogen dioxide emissions to 0.7 g/kWh, which is below the proposed Euro-3 standard. It produces 50 per cent less noise than a diesel engine. Costs are cited at 7 per cent lower than those for a diesel engine.

DB250: This chassis has been developed for double-deck city bus bodywork and has a 200 kW 8.65 RS DAF-ATI engine. It is transversely mounted at the rear and drives through a ZF or Voith gearbox.

SB2750: This is for semi-coach or express operation and features a rear-mounted vertical 8.65 litre engine developing 22 kW (302 hp) and has air suspension.

SB3000 range: This is a rear-engined underframe for semi-integral bodywork. It is air suspended and various engine options are available, up to the 315 kW (430 hp) Euro-2 engine. This range of chassis is available with either an AVS electropneumatic eight-speed manual synchromesh gearbox or a five-speed automatic ZF5 HP600 gearbox, both of which have retarders. AVS preselect gearshift can be specified.

SBR3000 WS: This is a three-axle version of the SB3000 and is suitable for double-deck coaches. The new SBR3015 WS has a steered third axle to improve manoeuvrability and is designed for buses and coaches up to 15 m long. For tough operating conditions in export markets, DAF Bus International offers two heavy-duty models which can be supplied either partly built or in completely knocked down form for local assembly.

TB2100: A rugged front-engined chassis for export markets, with conventional leaf springing. The chassis uses the vertical DAF 8.25 litre engine developing 170 kW/230 hp.

Bus powered by DAF LT160 LPG engine ***1996***

DAF Bus SB250 with Northern Counties Palatine II body with Harris Bus, Lakeside ***1997***

SB2100: This is similar to the TB2100 chassis, but with a rear-mounted ATI engine developing 200 kW (272 hp).

An electronic diagnostic tool, Pitcat, locates defects quickly. It uses a chip that maintains the information of each particular vehicle make, allowing quick diagnoses.

Production: The UK market accounts for 25 per cent of coach production and 32 per cent of bus production. Current capacity is around 1,000 units a year.

Contracts: Chassis are supplied to operators in Europe, the Far East and Africa.

Developments: A precision gearshift mechanism has been announced which needs less effort and eliminates cable play.

An ultra-low-floor Northern Counties Paladin body on DAF Bus SB220 chassis with LPG-fuelled engine has gone on trial in the UK. It is powered by the specially designed DAF GG 8.65 litre engine. The extra cost per vehicle is estimated at £20,000.

DAF Bus SBR3015 chassis ***1996***

A joint venture to build buses has been set up between DAF Bus, Berkhof (qv) and RATB Bucureşti.

A modular coach underframe, the SB4000, was introduced at the end of 1996.

UPDATED

Daihatsu

Daihatsu Motor Co Ltd
1-1, Daihatsu-cho, Ikeda-shi, Osaka 563, Japan
Telephone: +81 727 54 3047   Fax: +81 727 53 6880

Daihatsu UK Ltd
Poulton Close, Dover CT17 OHP
Telephone: +44 1304 213030   Fax: +44 1304 213525
Managing Director: Tony Darwall-Smith

Hijet production for Europe: Piaggio
Piaggio Veicoli Europei
Italy viale, R Piaggio 23, 56025 Pontedera
Telephone: +39 587 272548   Fax: +39 587 290906
Piaggio assembles the Daihatsu Hijet for the European market and, except for the UK, it is known as the Porter. In the UK, the name remains as the Daihatsu Hijet.

Products: Buses and minibuses

Range: Light truck designs are adapted for use as buses and midibuses.

Delta: Available either as a chassis cab or a van conversion.

The V119B-U 26-seater bus is 6.18 m long. It is powered by a 3.6 litre diesel engine.

Hijet: This is powered by the three-cylinder Otto 993 cc 29 kW engine. The standard version seats six. Since 1992 there has been an agreement with Italian manufacturer Piaggio to build vans and pick-ups based on the Hijet microvan.

The Daihatsu microvan range was reintroduced into the UK at the end of 1993. The engine meets Euro-1 exhaust emission standards. An electric 8.7 kW (12 hp) version is available; it has not yet been offered as a passenger carrier, though conversion is possible. The batteries take up half the load space and a 65 km range is stated, with a maximum speed of 65 km/h.

Daihatsu/Porter: The Daihatsu Hijet microbus has been launched in Britain under the MPV name (MultiPurpose Vehicle) and has sun roofs for both the passenger saloon and driving cabin. It seats six and is powered by a 993 cc three-cylinder engine. All seats have three-point safety belts. The Hijet is now built at the Piaggio factory in Pisa, Italy.

Daihatsu Hijet microbus **1996**

The Hijet has the option of a diesel 1,221 cc four-cylinder direct injection engine driving through a five-speed gearbox.

Contracts: Daihatsu minibuses are exported to the Middle East, Asia, South America and Africa.

VERIFIED

Del Monte

Del Monte Motor Works
283 Del Monte Avenue, Quezon City, Philippines
Telephone: +63 2 361 4279/4186   Fax +63 2 362 4689
President: Narciso O Morales
Executive Vice President & Assistant General Manager: Florentino L Angulo
Technical Director: Rolando Mariano

Products: Bus bodies

Range: A major supplier of bus bodywork to private operators in the Philippines and to government-owned corporations. Bus bodies are mounted on chassis from Hino, Isuzu, Fuso, Mitsubishi, Nissan, MAN, Mercedes-Benz, Fiat, Iveco, Volvo, DAF, Ashok Leyland, GMC, Ford, Hyundai and Ssangyong (Korea).

Dennis

Dennis Specialist Vehicles
Dennis Way, Guildford GU1 1AF, England
Telephone: +44 1483 571271   Fax: +44 1483 301697
Managing Director: J Smith
Bus Sales Director: R Heard
Parent company: Trinity Holdings plc. See also Duple (Metsec)

Associated companies
UMW Dennis, Malaysia
Dennis Eagle, Warwick, UK

Products: Single- and double-deck bus and coach chassis.

Range

Dart: This midibus chassis has a capacity of 39 seated and 15 standing. It is available in 8.5 m, 9 m and 9.8 m lengths and is 2.3 m wide. It has a Cummins B-series 5.9 litre engine coupled to the Allison AT545 four-speed automatic transmission. The chassis has an Eaton rear axle, GKN front axle and full air brakes with automatic adjusters.

Lance: This high-capacity single-deck bus chassis is powered by an in-line rear-mounted Cummins C8.3 engine, coupled to a ZF 4HP500 automatic gearbox with integral hydraulic retarder. Air suspension is standard and three lengths are available, 10.5 m, 11 m and 11.5 m. Up to 77 can be carried, 51 seated. Single or twin doors can be fitted.

Super Dart SLF: This is an ultra-low-floor version of the Dart. It is 10.6 m long and has a revised front-end layout that allows a wide gangway on bodied vehicles. Up to 43 seated and 20 standing can be carried. A left-hand-drive version is available. The Dart SLF is also available in 9.2 and 9.8 m lengths.

The largest 10.6 m Dart carries up to 46 – about the same as a so-called full-sized 12 m ultra-low-floor bus but some 20 per cent cheaper.

Emphasis is placed on affordability of the Dart SLF. The chassis is self-supporting for ease of bodybuilding and Dennis has taken care to reduce intrusion of the wheel arches by specifying small wheels.

While the Dart SLF is likely to be more popular in the UK than the larger Lance SLF, this heavier chassis carries a high number of standees – up to 100. It can be plated outside UK as an 18 tonne bus. With the 70 kg per passenger rule the Lance SLF can carry more than 100 standing.

Bodywork for the Dart SLF is being offered by Berkhof, Holland, Volgren, Australia, and DesignLine, New

Dennis Lance with Plaxton Verde body **1997**

Dennis Dart SLF with Northern Counties bodywork **1997**

Zealand. In the UK bodybuilders include East Lancs, Plaxton, Wrights, UVG, Alexander and Marshall. Sales and service centres for the Dart SLF have been established in Guildford, Durham, the Lancashire region and Bristol.

A gas-powered version of the Dart SLF is available.

Lance SLF: This is on ultra-low-floor chassis, with a wide flush door mounting. There is provision for a centre door wheelchair ramp. It has a floor height of 320 mm, 240 mm kneeling. It is powered by a Cummins C-series 8.3 litre engine driving through a ZF 4HP500 automatic gearbox with integral retarder; it has independent ZF front suspension, incorporating disc brakes. It is available in left-hand-drive form and is being marketed in the Netherlands.

Javelin: This is a coach chassis with mid-mounted engine in a variable-length chassis, designed to maximise luggage space. This is the company's first all-welded chassis. A bus version is available, with the same mid-mounted C8.3 Cummins engine, driving through a ZF S6-90 six-speed manual or ZF 4HP500 automatic gearbox. The chassis is for 8.5, 10, 11 and 12 m body lengths.

Dragon/Condor: These are three-axle export double-deck versions of the Dominator bus chassis, where high payloads are required.

Guided buses

Dennis Dart midibuses with Plaxton Pointer bodies have been running since 1995 on a guided busway in Ipswich, UK, equipped with guide wheels. There is a station with raised platforms halfway along the guideway, serving the local shopping and community centre with next-bus-due indicator. The busway was developed by Suffolk County Council and local bus company Eastern Counties, and was supervised by Maunsell Transport Planning (qv).

Contracts: The 1,000th Dart SLF chassis was produced in 1997; the number included 31 for British Bus subsidiary London & Country.

Dennis reports around 5,000 standard/SLF Darts are in service with more than 200 operators in Britain as well as in Australia, Holland, Hong Kong, Macao and Malaysia. The total UK market share of the Dennis Dart is put at 55 to 60 per cent.

The first export Dart SLFs have been delivered to Croydon, Australia, Ritchies Transport, New Zealand, KMB, Hong Kong and to Holland.

The Sri Lanka market has now improved, following a change of government, and the factory has reopened. Because Dennis subsidiary Duple (Metsec) (qv) is using aluminium alloy construction for its bodybuilding in Sri Lanka, operators have appreciated the low maintenance costs and more orders are expected.

By the end of 1996, Dennis had taken orders for 700 Dart SLFs. It now has 55 to 65 per cent of the UK midibus ultra-low-floor market. Orders have come from First Bus, Cowie, Stagecoach, London, Brighton, Plymouth and Southampton as well as from smaller independents, and orders are now mainly for the SLF version of the Dart.

Transmac Macao has taken delivery of 10 Dennis Darts with air conditioned Plaxton Pointer bodies, for a new route to the airport.

A total of 421 double-deck chassis, low-floor Tridents and three-axle Dragons, are being supplied to operators in Hong Kong.

Dennis Arrow with Northern Counties body in London ***1997***

Dennis Dart SLF with Plaxton bodywork at special bus platform, Plymouth, England ***1997***

Production: 1,177 buses and coaches were registered in 1996, the best year ever recorded by Dennis, representing an increase of 34 per cent in sales over 1994.

Developments: The *Trident* is a double-deck low-floor three-axle bus chassis with an in-line Euro-2 Cummins M11 engine, driving through a ZF five-speed automatic transmission. It replaces the Dragon and the chassis frame is all-welded and a gently sloping ramp leads up to the flat floor area in front of the rear axle. Kowloon Motor Bus has ordered 200 12 m versions of the Trident, bodied by Alexander (qv).

The *Arrow* is a double-deck version of the Lance and can take bodywork up to 10.5 m long and the chassis layout allows 82 forward-facing seats.

Production of the Dominator double-deck chassis ceased in 1996 and Dennis is now offering the lighter Arrow double-deck chassis with Euro-2 Cummins C-series engine. The Dominator-derived Dragon three-axle chassis continues in production.

A CNG-powered bus, based on the Plaxton Pointer midibus body and Dennis Dart chassis, has been produced. Power for the new bus comes from a Cummins B-series engine developed to run on CNG.

There are 16 CNG Darts with Southampton Citybus, England.

A three-axle version of the Javelin has been built for the New Zealand market. It is 12.6 m long and is plated at 21 tonnes.

UPDATED

Den Oudsten

Den Oudsten Bussen BV
PO Box 26, 3440 AA Woerden, Netherlands
Telephone: +31 3480 12345 Fax: +31 3480 19242
Managing Director: P Petermeijer
Technical Manager: A Pleiger
Commercial Manager: M P Baris
Other Den Oudsten Group members:
Den Oudsten Specials BV, Montfoort, Netherlands
New Flyer Industries Ltd, Winnipeg, Canada
New Flyer of America (ND) Inc, Grand Forks, ND, USA

Background: Den Oudsten was founded in 1926. Woerden, a Dutch body builder, joined Den Oudsten and is now a wholly owned subsidiary. Den Oudsten was a member of the United Bus Group until the Group applied for financial protection. Den Oudsten's assets were bought by the Den Oudsten Group, the former owner of the company, and the company was renamed Den Oudsten Bussen.

Products: Alliance city buses, including the new Alliance B90 with ultra-low floor.

Production: 220 buses (integral and on chassis) were built in 1994, of which 45 per cent were exported.

Contracts: include delivery of 75 Alliance-based buses to Palestine.

UPDATED

Den Oudsten Alliance city bus ***1997***

De Simon

De Simon srl
Zona Industriale Rivoli, 33010 Osoppo, Italy
Telephone: +39 432 986001 Fax: +39 432 986267
Chair: Alvio de Simon
General Manager: Giovanni de Simon

Background: The Stanga-Cittadella Group, which is prominent in the rail rolling stock sector, and Friulia, a regional holding company, are in partnership with De Simon.

De Simon was formerly a member of the Inbus consortium and now continues as an independent producer of bodywork for a range of city buses to Italian specifications.

In 1994, De Simon signed an agreement with Van Hool for production and sale of a range of city buses in Italy.

Products: Low-floor city bus bodies, midibuses, touring coaches.

De Simon Intercity IL/TL260.3 two-door dual-purpose bus ***1997***

Range

Starline: UM (urban) and IM (interurban) midibuses, based on MAN 11.220 and 11.230 chassis, with Euro-2 engines and with two-door bodywork to carry a total of 50 (IM) or 70 (UM). Floor height is 350 mm for the city version and 650 mm for the interurban version.

Both vehicles are 9 m long, 2.3 m wide and 2.9 m high. They have stainless steel bodywork.

De Simon/Van Hool A300 and AG300: Available as city or interurban buses. The A300 has 110 or 90 passenger capacity options and is 10.8 m or 12 m long. The articulated version, the AG3500 can carry either 130 or 150 and is 18 m long. MAN Euro-2 engine can be specified. Bodywork is in stainless steel.

Starbus LL30-GV30: Dual-purpose vehicle with Scania running units (with engines meeting Euro-2 exhaust emission standards), seating 51 to 55 (49 with toilet). There is the option of 10.7 m or 12 m lengths, and two heights can be specified, 3.28 m or 3.6 m, with three floor heights. The bodywork is stainless steel.

AU AS AI 280FT: This is an articulated vehicle with up to four doors, produced in city, urban or intercity configurations. It is now available with MAN (qv) chassis.

Contracts: 12 Van Hool De Simon buses have been delivered to cities in Italy — three A300 to ATR Forli, two AG300 to ACT Bolzano, three AG300 to ATC Bologna, four A300 to ATVO S Doná, with an option for 27.

Thirty-five Pinifarina Starbus intercity buses have been delivered to ACTT Taranto, TRAIN Siena, Dupraz Bus Genève, ETAC Benevento, AMAF Fano, COPIT Pistoia, Riviera Trasporti Imperia, ASP Asti, AIM Vicenza and Gestione Governativa della Circumvesuviana di Napoli.

Twenty Starline UM35 buses have been delivered to ACT Bolzano, Fogliati Alba, ASDM Brescia, ACTT Treviso, ASPES Pesaro, ATVO S Dona and Cortina d'Ampezzo.

Thirteen Starline IM55 buses have been ordered by Riviera Trasporti Imperia and SPT Como.

Developments: A new interurban bus, the IL/TL260.3, is available in 9 m, 12 m and 18 m articulated versions. Bus, dual-purpose or full touring coach specifications are available.

UPDATED

Diamond

Diamond Coach Corporation
PO Box 489, 2300 West Fourth Street, Oswego, KS 67356, USA
Telephone: +1 316 795 2191 Fax: +1 316 795 4816
President: Richard Seybolt
National Sales Manager: Bob Love

Products: Midibus bodies

Range

VIP: Carries between 17 and 25 on single and twin rear axle chassis (normal control). Wheelchair lift can be fitted. The VIP body series is built to 2.44 m width. Ford chassis with petrol engines are used, though there is an International Harvester diesel option. Body structure is a lightweight combination of fibreglass and honeycomb techniques. Many seating plans can be provided for 14 to 25, with up to three wheelchairs.

DC: Forward control with door behind front axle, seating between 18 and 35, powered by a Cummins 5.9 litre 6BT diesel engine driving through an Allison AT545 4-speed automatic gearbox.

UPDATED

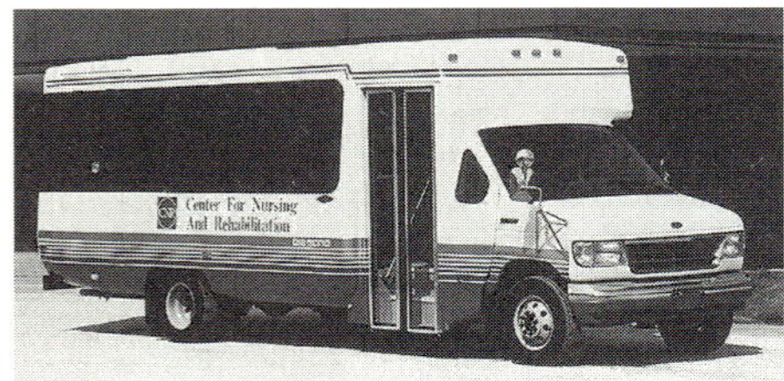

Diamond VIP body ***1995***

Diamond DC coach ***1997***

Dimo

Dimo Auto Assembly Ltd
65 Jetawana Road, Colombo 14, Sri Lanka
Telephone: +94 1 449797 Fax: +94 1 449080
Chief Executive Officer: Ranjith Pandithage
Finance Director: Sarath Clement Ganegoda
General Manager, Vehicle Division:
Arura Gahanath Pandithage
Manager, Automobile Service Dept:
Devaka S Amarasuriya
Parent company: Diesel & Motor Engineering Co Ltd

Background: The parent company, Diesel & Motor Engineering Company, was founded in 1939. Bus body production started in 1991 and is carried out by Dimo associate Dimo Auto Assembly Ltd (DAAL). It is the only assembly line in Sri Lanka and uses around 55 per cent of locally manufactured components. Assembly is carried out in co-operation with Mercedes-Benz.

Products: Bus bodies on Mercedes-Benz and Tata chassis.

Range
City Bus: This was introduced in 1992 and can be mounted on the Mercedes-Benz OF113 and Tata LPO1313 chassis. The roll-cage, roof and sides are made from galvanised steel. The front and rear cowls are of glass-reinforced plastic.
Luxury Coach: This was introduced in 1993 and is on the Mercedes-Benz OH1622 chassis. Reclining seats, kitchen, toilet and television can be fitted.

Dimo city bus on Mercedes-Benz chassis for Sri Lanka ***1995***

Production: 50 bodies a month can be produced.

Contracts: Include 1,000 bus bodies for the government of Sri Lanka.

Dina

Diesel Autobuses SA de CV
Margaritas 433, de Guadeloupe, Chimalistac, 01050 DF, Mexico
Telephone: +52 915 325 0927/525 627 0206
Fax: +52 915 679 6997/525 722 7162
Chairman: Rafael Gómez Flores
Chief Operating Officer: Jim Bernacchi
Chief Financial Officer: José Luis Olvera
Executive Vice President, Sales & Marketing:
Francois Bouffard

Works addresses
Domicilio Conocido, Corredor Industrial, S/N CD Fray Bernadino de Sahagun 43990
Telephone: +52 596 30500/32900 Fax: +52 596 33941
Poniente 134 No 680 Col, Industrial Vallejo, Mexico 02300 DF

Subsidiary companies
Motor Coach Industries International Inc
Dina Autobuses SA de CV
An associate of General Motors (49% stake)
USA subsidiary: Dina Transportation
16800 Greenspoint Park Drive, Suite
155-S, Houston, TX 77060
Telephone: +1 713 876 3802 Fax: +1 713 876 3113
President: Gisel Bieling

Background: The government-owned Diesel Nacional, established in 1957, is the largest commercial vehicle producer in Mexico. Dina also controls the Mexican Perkins engine plant and these engines are used in a number of the Dina models.

In 1994, the Dina Group acquired MCI, USA/Canada (qv).

Products: Buses and coaches

Range
Citus: Urban and city bus, launched in 1994, is available in four lengths, 9, 10, 11 and 12 m. It has a Navistar NGD T444E engine and Allison automatic transmission can be specified.

Dina Viaggio intercity coach ***1997***

Viaggio: The Viaggio 850 is an intercity coach with spring or air suspension. The Viaggio 1000 has two axles and is for touring work.

MCI and Dina coaches in 12 m, 13 m and 13.7 m lengths for interurban, suburban and touring markets.

UPDATED

Duple (Metsec)

Duple (Metsec) Ltd
Garratts Lane, Cradley Heath, Warley B64 5RE, England
Telephone: +44 121 559 0888 Fax: +44 121 559 0333
Managing Director: Tom McCloy
Sales Director: Scott Hamilton

Background: Duple (Metsec) is a Trinity Holdings company, which also includes Dennis Specialist Vehicles (qv).

Products: Design and supply of CKD bus and coach body kits for assembly outside the UK. Single- and double-deck bodies can be in either galvanised steel or aluminium alloy. All are designed to suit major chassis types.

Duple (Metsec) air conditioned bus on Dennis Dragon chassis with KMB in Hong Kong ***1997***

EL2000: This is a single-deck bus body with a choice of three designs. It has been supplied on Volvo, Dennis and Scania chassis, as well as rebodying on Leyland Leopard, Leyland Tiger, Volvo B58 and Volvo B10M chassis. The body seats between 46 and 62 with 24 standing on a level floor. The aluminium-framed bodywork has glass fibre mouldings on the lower panels and stainless steel wheel arches. The windscreens are rubber glazed. The front and rear sections are grp moulded.

Production: In 1996 150 vehicles were produced.

Contracts: With UK operators Bournemouth Transport, Rossendale Transport and City of Nottingham Transport.

Nineteen Spryte bodies on Dennis Dart SLF chassis have been delivered to British Bus subsidiary London & Country. A Mayne & Son, Manchester, England, has taken delivery of four Scania N113DRB chassis with East Lancs double-deck bodywork. They have coach seating.

Ten Cityzens have been delivered to Brighton & Hove, England, for its Unibus 25 route serving Sussex University. Each carries 90, including 12 standing.

Developments: A new double-deck body, the Premyer, is steel-framed and can be mounted on Volvo B10M and Olympian chassis.

UPDATED

ELBO

Hellenic Vehicle Industry SA
Industrial Area Sindos, 54110 Thessaloniki, Greece
Telephone: +30 31 798 502 Fax: +30 31 798426
Sales Manager: H Valetopoulos

Background: ELBO was founded in 1972 as Steyr Hellas SR to make trucks and tractors. In 1986 it became the Hellenic Vehicle Industry. Its plant now covers an area of 270,000 m². The workforce is 850.

Products: Buses, particulate filters, trucks, military vehicles

Range

A100: Urban/city bus on a DAF SB220LT chassis with a Euro-2 engine driving through a Voith Diwa 8-63 transmission. It seats 29 with 71 standing and is 11.6 m long. The floor height is 700 mm and air suspension is fitted.

A low-floor version of the A100 has a floor height of 630 mm and is on a Scania L113 chassis, with a Scania DSC1124 Euro-2 engine driving through a ZF 5HP600 automatic transmission.

Europe: This is on an ELBO 800 chassis and is powered by a Cummins 6CTAA 8.3-275 engine driving through a ZF CS6-90 gearbox. It has air suspension and seats around 32 with about 60 standing. It has three doors.

C93-405N: This has a Mercedes-Benz O405N low-floor chassis with no steps at the front. The floor height at the two front doors is 370 mm and at the third door, behind the axle, it is 580 mm. It seats 37 with around 50 standing.

U-90: This is on a Mercedes-Benz O405 chassis and has three double doors, seating 21 with around 70 standing in the high-capacity version. Other seating arrangements can be specified.

Mini A-50: This is on an ELBO 600 chassis and is powered by a MAN D0824 engine driving through a Voith Midimat B auto transmission with hydraulic retarder. Various seating arrangements can be supplied.

Contracts: 40 buses have been supplied to Bucureşti, 15 to Singapore and 45 to Thessaloniki.

UPDATED

ELBO urban bus A100 on DAF chassis **1996**

ELBO A100 low-floor bus on Scania chassis **1997**

El Detalle

El Detalle
Argentina
Brazil assembly plant: El Detalle do Brazil, Automotores Ltda, Estrada Cavalhada 900, CEP 94190-230, Parque do Anjos, Gravatai, RS
Telephone: +55 51 488 1339/2344
Fax: +54 51 345 1766
President: Juan Carlos Surdo

Products: Bus chassis for urban, suburban and highway buses

Range: The OA-101 is a two-door vehicle with engine ratings of 143, 157 and 298 kW (192, 210 and 400 hp), 4,200-5,700 kg and wheelbase of 4.6, 5.17, 6.17 and 7.1 m.

OA-101/2/4: Chassis from 9.8 m to 13.5 m, powered by Deutz 913 Series engines, with ZF steering, Eaton or Allison transmissions, Rockwell-Braseixos front axles, Eaton rear axles and air suspension. CNG option being tested.

Contracts: El Detalle has 22 per cent of the national Brazilian market.

El Dorado National

El Dorado National Co
304 Avenue B, Salina, KS 67401, USA
Telephone: +1 913 827 1033 Fax: +1 913 827 0965

13900 Sycamore Way, Chino, CA 91710, USA
Telephone: +1 909 591 9557 Fax: +1 909 591 5285
President: Andy Imanse
Senior Vice President: Sheldon Walle
Director of Transit Sales: Gentry C Shaw
Parent company: Thor Industries

Background: El Dorado National was established in 1991 following the merging of El Dorado Bus and National Coach Corporation. El Dorado Bus started building buses in 1979 and National had been building since 1975. El Dorado Bus was acquired by Thor Industries, manufacturer of recreational vehicles, in 1988.

Products: Small and mid-size buses

Range

Aerotech: This is on the Ford E-350 chassis and seats up to 29. Wheelchairs can be carried and perimeter seating fitted.

Aero-XT: Built on the Chevrolet GP cutaway chassis, this model can carry up to 29 without a third axle.

Escort RE: Rear engine mid-size bus, seating up to 33, 8.76 m or 11.3 m long. It can be supplied with one or two doors and perimeter seating can be fitted. It can be powered by CNG, diesel or propane engines, driving through an Allison automatic gearbox. Leaf springs or air suspension can be specified. A CNG version is available.

Escort RE-A: This version is designed for the tour and charter markets and has air suspension. It seats up to 41.

RE-29-E: This is an electric bus, called the Zero Emission Bus. It is 8.76 m long. It has a top speed of 77 km/h and a range of 112 km. The batteries have a storage capacity of

80 kWh at a voltage of 320. Four modules consisting of 40 individual cells of 250 AH are connected in series. Each module has a rating of 80 V. The electrical system is 12 V with negative ground. It has two GMHE Power Control Systems AC electric motors and an AC inverter. Regenerative braking is possible and a propane-powered generator is provided to supplement the main batteries while the bus is in operation. A wheelchair lift and perimeter seating can be fitted. It was designed jointly with Hughes Power Control Systems (qv) and APS Systems.

Transmark-RE: This is a rear-engine coach seating up to 33 and can be adapted to carry disabled people.

MST: This is the Mid-Sized Transit on an Oshkosh front-engine bus chassis or on a Chevrolet chassis, seating up to 31.

Escort FE: This is designed to combine the comforts of a car with the reliability of a bus, bridging the gap between van conversions and coaches. It carries from 12 to 27 and is based on the Chevrolet P-30 chassis.

Aerolite: This is the smallest of the El Dorado family and is built on the single rear wheel Ford E350 chassis cowl (cutaway) and does not require a commercial driver's licence. It seats up to 14.

ELF: This is a no-step low-floor vehicle, based on the Ford E350 cab and controls. It seats up to 21 and there are positions for eight wheelchairs.

The *Li'l Elf* is a smaller version, also based on the Ford E350 cab and controls, seating up to 17 or carrying five wheelchairs. It also has a no-step low floor.

Developments: A low-floor version of the RE is available.

UPDATED

El Dorado National low-floor bus ***1997***

El Dorado MST bus ***1996***

El Dorado Transmark RE of Le Bus ***1997***

El Nasr

El Nasr Automotive Manufacturing Co
Information Centre, Eng. Kamel El-Shabrawy, Wadi Hof, Helwan, Cairo, Egypt
Telephone: +20 2 369 1901/2608 Fax: +20 2 369 2612/5425
Chair: Eng Said El-Naggar
Commercial Director: Eng Hamed Bassiouny
Technical Director: Eng Farouk Mohamadee

Products: Buses, minibuses, microbuses and coaches, including bodywork.

Range

Nasr 935: This is a luxury touring coach, powered by rear-mounted Iveco 8210.02 diesel engine driving through a ZF S680 manual six-speed gearbox. It seats 55 plus driver and courier. A rear door is provided on the same side as the front door.

Nasr 935 coach

Nasr 924: This is an interurban coach, powered by a Nasr F6L 614 diesel, driving through a ZF S5-35/2 five-speed manual gearbox.

Nasr 941: A new minibus with an Iveco 8040 diesel engine and seats 29. It is 7.2 m long and 2.26 m wide. The gross vehicle weight is 7,160 kg. The rear luggage compartment has a capacity of 1 m^3. Leaf springing is standard.

Contracts: Cairo Transport Authority has taken delivery of 35 Nasr 935 coaches; Masryat has taken 200 Nasr 924/965 interurban buses; 50 high-deck coaches have been delivered to Ahmos to Trade.

UPDATED

Nasr 941 minibus ***1995***

ERF

ERF Limited
Sun Works, Sandbach CW11 9DN, England
Telephone: +44 1270 763223 Fax: +44 1270 766068
Managing Director: J W Bryant
Export Sales: C J Waggott

ERF South Africa (Pty) Ltd
PO Box 3944, 5 Clarke Street North, Alrode 1451, Alberton, Transvaal, South Africa
Telephone: +27 11 864 2640 Fax: +27 11 864 7131

Products: Bus chassis

Range: Though the UK parent company is primarily a truck builder, ERF in 1979 introduced a straight-framed bolted construction single-deck bus chassis with front-mounted engine. Since then mid- and front-engine units have been developed including a three-axle double-deck chassis.

Trailblazer (forward-engine): Intended for the rugged and arduous operating conditions found in southern Africa, the front-engine chassis with bolted ladder frame is available in wheelbases to suit 11 to 12.5 m maximum legal capacity single-deck bodies. There is a choice of the ADE 407 (Mercedes-derived) naturally aspirated engine coupled with Rockwell S160E rear axle or ADE 354T (Perkins six-cylinder 354T) turbocharged unit coupled with Rockwell R140 rear axle. The Gardner 6LXB is available for other markets. Drive is through a fluid flywheel to a mid-mounted ZF six-speed manual or four- or five-speed semi-automatic transmission to South African built Self Changing Gears or ZF or Voith fully automatic design. ZF8066 hydraulic power steering is fitted with ERF's 'Rough Terrain' steering linkage, together with large bore heavy-duty telescopic shock-absorbers at the front and rear, and extra long front and rear springs. ERF's leaf-air 'Velvet-Ride' suspension is also available.

Super Trailblazer (mid-engine): A version of the Trailblazer is available with the ADE 407H horizontal engine in mid-mounted position and Rockwell S160E rear axle. The same transmission choices as the forward-engine version are offered.

Trailblazer RE (rear-engine): A rear-engine version of the Trailblazer has been developed for luxury coach applications. The ADE 407T 280 bhp turbocharged engine is used, with the S160E rear axle and Voith fully automatic or ZF manual transmission.

Trailblazer 'Jumbo': A Trailblazer 'Jumbo' articulated 20 m bus chassis has also been developed to a legal load capacity of 185 passengers, with 86 seated. It is built to order with either the front or mid-engine standard Trailblazer front section with trailing rear axle.

A 12 m Trailblazer chassis has been developed for use in African countries. It is powered by a front-mounted Gardner 6LXB 10.45 litre unit with fully automatic ZF HP500 gearbox and Velvet-Ride air suspension.

Gardner-engined ERF Trailblazer and trailer in Malawi

ERF Trailblazer with Kenya Bus at Nairobi bus station **1997**

Developments: Canadian truck manufacturer Western Star, Canada, bought ERF in 1996. It also owns Orion Bus Industries (qv).

Dorbyl Transport Products, South Africa (see Busaf), took a 70 per cent interest in ERF South Africa in 1996. ERF South Africa is based in Alberton and supplies buses and trucks to South Africa and neighbouring territories.

UPDATED

Ernst Auwärter

Ernst Auwärter Karosserie- und Fahrzeug-bau KG
Industriegebiet Kringstrasse 2, 71144 Steinenbronn, Germany
Telephone: +49 7157 4081 Fax: +49 7157 9390
Managing Director: Ernst Auwärter
Marketing Director: Ingeborg Bahn
Technical Director: Jürgen Schöllhammer

Products: Mini and midibus bodies, also full-sized coach bodywork.

Range: Primarily a luxury touring coach body builder, Ernst Auwärter also produces a number of small bus and coach bodies on chassis from Mercedes and Volkswagen.

Teamstar City: 7.37 m city midibus on the Mercedes 811D and 814 chassis carries up to 40 (20 standing).

The Teamstar City model is available with a low floor, rear platform and kneeling capability, suitable for up to 20 seated, and three wheelchairs plus 15-20 standing.

Clubstar City: 7.6 m city bus on the 0814/33 and 0814/37 carries up to 57 (27 seated and 30 standing) and the Clubstar 1117/49 carries 60.

EA also offers wheelchair lift-equipped versions of both its minibuses and full-sized coaches.

The Clubstar MAN Midi is on the new MAN M230 chassis with a 169 kW rear engine and air suspension, the 8.7 m version carrying 34 seated and 20 standing.

The Economy Mercedes O614 is converted to a small 7.1 m city bus, carrying up to 40 (20 seated).

EA Teamstar with low-floor rear platform **1997**

EA Panorama VW LT46 minibus **1997**

EA Microstar Multimax three-axle minibus on Volkswagen T4 chassis **1995**

Microstar: The Microstar 12-seat minibus, based on the Volkswagen Caravelle, has 1.3 m wide doors and a step floor height of 320 mm.
Microstar Multimax: A twin-axle version, based on the Volkswagen T4 and seating 13 with 10 standing. It has a low floor with no steps. The boarding step height is 320 mm.
Eurostar SHD: This is based on the Mercedes-Benz O404 and is EA's first full-size coach. It is 3.75 m high.
Sunny Sprinter 412: This is based on the Mercedes-Benz Sprinter and seats 20. There is capacity for four wheelchairs. It has a large windscreen and electric-powered door. It is 6.5 m long.

EA Microstar on Volkswagen T4 chassis **1995**

Production: 190 vehicles annually.

Developments: A new version of the Teamstar, the 814/42, is based on the Mercedes-Benz 814 Vario chassis and has a low-floor rear platform.

Another new model, the Panorama VW LT46 is on a LT46 chassis and seats up to 19.

UPDATED

Ewo

Ewo Coach Builders
Derrybeg Industrial Estate, Gweedore, Co Donegal, Ireland
Telephone: +353 75 31528 Fax: +353 75 31930

Products: Bus bodies.

NEW ENTRY

FAP-Famos

SP FAP Famos FFB-Komerc SA Beograd
PO Box 68, Francuska 61-65, 11001 Beograd, Serbia
Telephone: +381 11 182182 Fax: +381 11 636961
President: Peter Drobnjak
General Manager: K Kijak
Sales Manager: Z Lucic

Factories
Chassis components and truck production: FAP, Priboj
Engines, gearboxes, clutches: FAMOS, Sarajevo
Buses and bus bodies: FAS 'Il Oktomvri', Skopje

Background: Links with Daimler-Benz have led to a number of Mercedes coach models being licence-built and German technology being adopted in other types produced. The main FFB bus and coach production plant is that of Fabrika ZA Autobusi in Skopje, Macedonia (FAS), where integral vehicles are assembled from Mercedes and FAP-Famos running units under the Sanos name.

Products: Buses and coaches, including articulated buses and trolleybuses. Bus and coach bodywork. CKD kits.

Range
Sanos S115: The FAP-Sanos S115 12 m integral bus for urban operations with pressed plywood seating for 25; total capacity is 115. Provision is made for a seated conductor at the rear. Wheelbase is 6.15 m with air suspension.

Power is from a mid-mounted horizontal Mercedes diesel engine.
S200ZG: The 18 m articulated version of the S115 has an underfloor engine in the front section and has total capacity for 156. Unladen weight is 13,000 kg.
S213GNR/V0: Urban rear engine bus, integral body construction; length 11.57 m ; 100 passengers (39 seated).
D4420G: Urban bus, frame construction, 11.3 m long, carrying 26 seated, 74 standing. Powered by Famos 2F 216B engine, mounted at the front.
C515: Integral bus, 12 m long, for interurban and long-distance tourist work. Powered by Mercedes-Benz OM 442 engine driving through ZF S690 gearbox. Touring coach specification available, as is ABS braking.
S511: 9.3 m bus, integral, for interurban and tourist work. Powered by MB OM441 engine, rear-mounted driving through Famos or ZF gearbox. Konvekta or Sutrak air conditioning and touring coach specification available.
S415/413: The S415/413 integral bus range is designed for less arduous duties, but includes urban and suburban variants.

This type is also available as a suburban (carrying 90) or interurban bus (carrying 53).

The S415 is 11.98 m long, with a capacity for 35 seated and 69 standing, and the S413 is 11.03 m, seating 31 with 68 standees.
S200TR trolleybus: 18 m three-axle articulated trolleybus.
S315: This is based on the Mercedes O303, having mainly locally built Daimler-Benz engines and driving through a ZF S690 gearbox. An automatic option is available, as are air conditioning, toilet and catering facilities.

Developments: A joint venture between FAP and Sanos (qv) has resulted in the S522 Hobo, a double-deck coach with 76 seats. It is powered by a MAN 2866 engine driving through a ZF S6-150 gearbox.

UPDATED

FAP-Famos S213 urban bus

FAP-Famos S200ZG articulated bus

FAP-Sanos S115 integral city bus

Under technical agreements the Hess body construction techniques have been adopted by a number of builders, including Volgren in Australia, Designline in New Zealand and Caetano in Portugal. Licence agreements are also in operation in China, Indonesia, Singapore, Malaysia, USA, Africa and Morocco.

Developments: A low-floor trolleybus with Hess Co-Bolt body and Siemens electrical traction on a NAW chassis has been announced.

UPDATED

Hess interurban 9.3 m bus with under-floor and rear luggage compartments
1997

Heuliez

SA Heuliez-Bus
PO Box 27, 79700 Rorthais, France
Telephone: +33 5 49 81 07 07 Fax: +33 5 49 81 09 91
Chair & Managing Director: Christian Cheron
Commercial Manager: Roger Cesbron

Background: Heuliez was once 100 per cent owned by the Henri Heuliez Group but since 1994 Volvo Bus Corporation and Renault VI have each owned 37.5 per cent. It is associated with the Volvo group.

Products: Integral buses and coaches, including articulated, bus and coach bodies and spare parts. Specialist developments.

Range

Compacbus GX77H: Launched on the French market in 1989, this midibus has been developed in co-operation with RTM Marseille and with the assistance of Sofrétu.

It has an overall width of 2.2 m and is 8.9 m long, yet carries up to 75 pasengers. The Renault MIPS 06.02.12 diesel engine drives through an Allison AT 545 automatic gearbox.

GX107: Brought into production in 1985 after seven years' development as the GX97, the GX107 is the standard version of the Heuliez GX series of integral buses based on Renault running units. Built with self-supporting structure and modern aerodynamic styling it has a rear-mounted Renault MIPS 06.20.45 six-cylinder turbo-charged engine producing 137 kW (186 hp) at 1,900 rev/min or alternatively rated at 152 kW (206 hp), coupled with the fully automatic ZF 4HP 500 or Voith D 851 transmission.

GX187 articulated: Complementing the new-generation standard city bus is the GX187 articulated bus. It is 17.86 m long and comes in a variety of formats with maximum capacity of 170. Standard power plant is the Renault MIPS 06.20.45 turbocharged engine rated at 186 kW (253 hp) at 2,100 rev/min, coupled with the ZF fully automatic integral retarder-equipped 4HP 500, 5HP 500 or Voith 864 gearbox.

GX217: Built on Volvo B10L underframe.

GX317: Low-floor integral bus using Renault VI running units, developed by Renault and Heuliez, based on the Renault 312 chassis. It is 12 m long, has three doors and is powered by a transverse rear engine. The floor height is 320 mm (240 mm when kneeling). It carries 116, 22 seated. An articulated version is planned. Heuliez is also building on Volvo B10M and B10B chassis.

GX417: This is built on the Volvo B10LA underframe.

GX27/37H: For use as a dual-purpose interurban or school bus, Heuliez has developed its GX27/37H mid-sized vehicle seating either 34 adults or 53 children. The vehicle, with a Renault engine, features the Heuliez patented drawbridge-type emergency rear door slide and roof escape vents. Air suspension is offered.

Interbus GX87: Since 1992, French legislation has allowed operation of articulated coaches, and the new GX87 articulated coach is 18 m long and seats 81, in both suburban and interurban forms. It is on a Volvo B10M articulated chassis, with a floor height of 920 mm. It is powered by a Volvo THD 102 KB engine, driving through a Volvo G7 gearbox.

Interbus GX57: This is a 12 m standard vehicle on a Volvo B10B chassis. Its 285 hp engine is at the rear, and it seats from 55 to 59, with a 6 m³ luggage compartment. It has air suspension.

Access: This is an ultra-low-floor bus available in both articulated and rigid form. The articulated version seats 39 with around 130 standing. It has a maximum length of 17.97 m.

Production: Maximum annual output is around 600. Spare parts are supplied for both the standard and articulated buses.

UPDATED

Volvo B10L articulated bus with Heuliez GX417 bodywork ***1996***

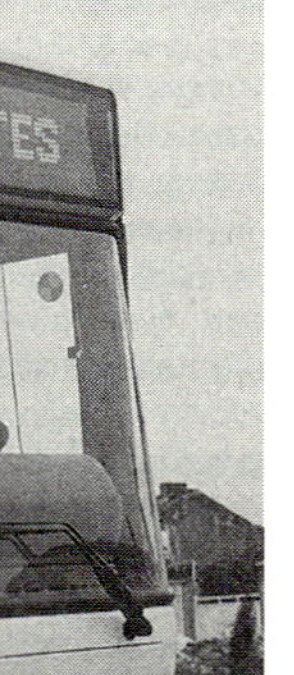

Heuliez no-step low-floor body on Renault chassis ***1995***

Hino

Hino Motors Ltd
7-17 Nihonbashi 1-chome, Chuo-ku, Tokyo 103, Japan
Telephone: +81 3 3272 1891 Fax: +81 3 3272 4822
Deputy General Manager, Public Relations: Toru Matsui

Background: Hino Motors is the commercial vehicle specialist associate of the Toyota Group. Hino has its own bodybuilding subsidiary, Hino Auto Body Ltd, Yokohama.

Products: Complete buses and bus bodies

Range
Blue Ribbon HU/HT: Hino's largest city bus is the Blue Ribbon HT/HU which features a low-floor option and comes in 10.28, 10.68 and 11.15 m lengths, the two smaller versions using the rear-mounted M10U 172 kW (230 hp) engine, and the larger model the K13U 201 kW unit. Capacities are 82 to 95 passengers. Bodywork is available from Hino Auto Body or other builders.
Blue Ribbon RK: The 9.5 m RK has the J08C(J-II) 160 kW (215 hp) engine mounted at the rear.
Rainbow RR/RJ: The Hino Rainbow city integral bus design has now been replaced by the Blue Ribbon series of city buses, but the Rainbow chassis continues to be offered for smaller coach applications. The RR-1JJ has a 4.49 m wheelbase, overall length of 8.99 m and width of 2.3 m, with power from the Hino J08C(J-II) 160 kW (215 hp) six-cylinder 7.96 litre engine common to the RJ series. Capacity is 61 with a GVW of 10,045 kg. Various styles of internal layout are available. The smaller Rainbow model RJ-1JJ has a 4.49 m wheelbase, and overall length of 8.99 m.
Liésse RX: 6.99 m bus or coach. The RX4JF has a rear-mounted engines rated at 108 or 130 kW (145 or 115 hp).

Production: Annual bus output is around 6,500 units, mainly heavyweight full-sized vehicles.

UPDATED

Hino Blue Ribbon city bus ***1996***

Hispano

Hispano Carrocera SA
Carretera de Castellón, Km 230.5, Camino del Canal s/n, 50720 La Cartuja, Zaragoza, Spain
Telephone: +34 76 720500 Fax: +34 76 720507/8
Vice President: Gerado Mugica Jiminénez de la Cuesta
Sales Manager: Javier Garcıa Domingo

Background: The company was created in 1984 and in 1993 moved to a new plant some 112,000 m² in size. Early in 1994 Hispano Carrocera was bought out by Capre SA, Mexico (qv).

Products: Bus, trolleybus and coach bodies

Range: Bus bodies are produced with two doors, three doors (one or two leaf), 8 to 12 m, and in articulated 18 m versions. Bus bodies for low-floor chassis are produced.
Vita: This is a touring coach seating up to 47 with centre toilet and luggage stowage under the floor, conforming to EC roll-over regulations. A version for express work is available.
Vitamin: A smaller version of the Gillig Phantom bus Vita, this is for midibus work. It is 7 to 9 m long.

Contracts: Apart from the Spanish market, buses have been delivered to operators in Ecuador, the United Kingdom, Singapore, Romania and South Africa.
Hispano has signed a technology transfer contract with an operator in the People's Republic of China.

Developments: Hispano buses have been approved for sale on the French market. Protoype buses for Hong Kong and Singapore (18 m articulated bus) have been delivered.

UPDATED

Hispano articulated low-floor bus on Renault chassis ***1997***

Hispano Vita coach on Mercedes chassis ***1997***

Hispano articulated trolleybus on Mercedes chassis ***1997***

Hyundai

Hyundai Motor Co
140-2 Ke-Dong, Jongro-ku, PO Box 3490, Seoul, Republic of Korea
Telephone: +82 2 744 0211/0311 Fax: +82 2 741 0470
General Manager: D Y Cho
Main works: 700 Yang Chung-Dong, Jung-Ku, Ulsan

Products: Buses and coaches

Range
FB500: A front-engined bus designed for ease of handling in urban traffic but also available for interurban coach operations. Uses the D6BR six-cylinder, 182 hp engine. Up to 44 seats, 10.17 m long.
RB520: A rear-engined bus or coach; 10.45 m long and able to seat up to 46; D6BR engine.
RB600: Also rear-engined, the RB600 is 11.4 m long; designed to seat 45 on longer journeys. Uses the D6AU 215 hp engine.
Aero/Aero E: Long-distance coach models with rear-mounted D6AU in the Aero-Economy (Aero E) 11.4 m model and the more powerful D8AY eight-cylinder 305 hp engine in the Aero 11.9 m coach, the most luxurious in the range.
H100: chassis cab and panel van, with a low price and the chassis of tubular cross-beam construction. The GVW is 2.8 tonnes.

Hyundai city bus in Chelyabinsk ***1997***

Production: HMC supplies more than half South Korean domestic demand for buses and coaches. Production in 1995 was around 4,800.

UPDATED

Ikarbus

Ikarbus AD Belgrade-Zemun
Auto-Put 24, 11080 Zemun, Serbia
Telephone: +38 11 609822/600671
Fax: +38 11 600453
President: Stanislav Glumac
Marketing Director: Dario Ćurić

Background: Formerly Ikarus of Zemun (not related to the Hungarian bus manufacturer Ikarus), Ikarbus is now a joint stock company, part of the FAP-Famos group.

Products: Urban and suburban buses, including articulated; trolleybuses and intercity buses. Bus bodywork.

Range
IK-101: This is a three-door city bus, 11.69 m long and 2.45 m wide, carrying up to 110. It has a MAN D2866UM engine, driving through a Famos (ZF) 6MS80 manual gearbox. There is an option of Mercedes OM447H engine and Voith D851 transmission. It has air suspension.
IK-102: Similar to the IK-101, but with Rába D2356M6U engine.
IK-201: Articulated city bus with up to four double doors, length 16.76 m, width 2.45 m, carrying up to 160. Engine and gearbox options as above (MAN/Mercedes, Famos/Voith).
IK-202: Articulated, similar to the IK-201, but with Rába D2356M6U engine and Famos gearbox.
IK-103: This is 11.86 m long and 2.45 m wide, carrying up to 110, with a large wrap-round windscreen. It is powered by a choice of MAN D2866UH, Mercedes-Benz OM447H or MAN D0826LUH engines driving through Famos, Voith or MAN gearboxes.
IK-103P: This is a suburban/intercity version of the IK-103 with up to two single doors and carrying up to 85.
IK-201L: Articulated city bus, 16.94 m long and 2.45 m wide, carrying up to 160. It has up to four doors and a choice of MAN D2866 or Mercedes-Benz OM447H engines, driving through Famos, Voith or ZF gearboxes.
IK-301 Interurban: This was introduced in 1994. It is 11.86 m long and 2.5 m wide, carrying up to 53. It has a MAN D2866TUH, MAN D2866UH or Mercedes-Benz OM447H engine, driving through a Famos (ZF) 6MS80 gearbox. It has air suspension.

Ikarbus IK-201L

Production: The Ikarbus bus and specialist vehicle factory has a capacity of 1,000 vehicles a year. About half its volume is accounted for by its city bus building programme.

Developments: Newly introduced is the IK106, a low-floor three-door bus, to carry 105 passengers. The floor is flat, with a step above the rear axle. It is powered by a Mercedes-Benz engine driving through a Voith transmission.

UPDATED

Ikarus

Ikarus Vehicle Manufacturing Company Ltd
Margit utca 114, 1165 Budapest, Hungary
Telephone: +36 1 252 9666 Fax: +36 1 163 7066
Managing Director: Zoltan Vadnai
Commercial Director: Joszef Brumbauer
Plants: Budapest and Székesfehérvár

Associated company
Ikarus EAG
PO Box 98, 1631 Budapest

UK distributor: Hughes DAF, Lodge Garage, Whitehall Road West, Cleckheaton BD19 4BJ
Telephone: +44 1274 681144 Fax: +44 1274 651198

USA distributor: North American Bus Industries (NABI) (qv)

Background: Ikarus Body & Coach Building Works was established in 1949 and enjoyed a practically unlimited market in the Comecon common market of Soviet satellite states. Ikarus Rt was established as a joint stock limited liability company in 1991. ATEX, a Russian-controlled investment firm, took a 31.7 per cent share in Ikarus, now renamed Ikarus Vehicle Manufacturing Company Ltd. Until recently, engines and running gear were made and assembled at the Rába factory, Hungary (qv), with gearbox, steering and floor frame being assembled at the Csepel Truck Manufacturing Factory (as it was known in the 1960s). It is now Csepel Automotive (qv).

By the 1980s, production was a steady 12,000 to 13,000 buses a year. Following the collapse of Comecon in 1991/92, production fell from 12,450 in 1988 (of which the former Soviet Union accounted for 7,721) to 3,582 in 1992. In 1995 it was 1,142, the largest customers being

Ikarus 405 midibus with Voith Midimat transmission ***1996***

Ikarus articulated 417 low-floor bus ***1996***

Ikarus two-door 400 body in UK ***1996***

Ikarus 415 city buses on DAF chassis at Leeds airport ***1997***

members of the Commonwealth of Independent States, including Russia. To counteract this, Ikarus has diversified into special bus production, tools and spare part manufacture for the automotive industry. Staff has been reduced to 2,600.

Ikarus has now split into two companies, Ikarus EAG (Special Coach Factory) being responsible solely for coaches and with separate shareholdings of 68 per cent by Ikarus and 32 per cent by Bayal, Turkey.

Products: Buses, coaches, minibuses, trolleybuses, railbuses, CKD kits.

Range

200 series: This bus was developed at the end of the 1960s, with 200,000 being sold by 1993. It is 9.5, 11 or 12 m long. The articulated version is 16.5 m or 18 m long.

300 series: This is a luxury touring coach, either integral or body-on-chassis.

400 series: This is a city or urban bus for the UK market, 11.5 m rigid or 18 m articulated, with a rear under-floor engine. It uses the DAF SB220 chassis, left-hand drive.

405: This is a 7.3 m midibus for city work, powered by a Perkins Phaser engine, driving through a Voith Midimat gearbox.

Trolleybuses: Trolleybus versions of the 200 and 400 series are produced. A dual-mode bus, the 435TD has a diesel engine as well as electric propulsion.

411: This is a low-floor bus, with a floor height of 320 to 350 mm.

Production: Around half of the annual production of 3,200 goes to Russian and Ukraine.

Contracts: 17 low-floor pusher articulated buses have been delivered to Wuppertal, Germany.

The Indonesian government is taking 400 articulated buses, with final assembly being carried out locally.

Ikarus won the World Bank funded contract to supply 168 CKD versions of 283 articulated buses to Kurgan, Siberia. BKV Budapest bought 90 405 midibuses in 1995.

Developments: An ultra-low-floor articulated bus, the 417, was announced in 1995; it is 17.97 m long, 2.5 m wide and 2.805 m high. The total weight is 26.5 tonnes and it can carry 53 seated with 103 standing. The floor is flat throughout and the step height at all doors is 330 mm. There are no steps inside the vehicle.

It is powered by a Cummins C83-290 11 turbocharged engine, driving through a ZF 4HP590 gearbox. The articulation is by Hübner and the coachwork is in steel with anti-corrosion protection. A Webasto heater is provided and there are four roof vents/emergency exits. A Bode wheelchair lift can be fitted.

UPDATED

Irizar

Irizar
20 216 Ormaiztegui, Guipuzcoa, Spain
Telephone: +34 43 881900 Fax: +34 43 889101
Part of Caja Laboral Popular co-operative group
Managing Director: Koldo Saratxaga

UK distributor: Scania Bus & Coach UK Ltd
Claylands Avenue, Worksop S81 7DJ
Telephone: +44 1909 500822 Fax: +44 1909 500165
Managing Director: Don MacIntosh

Products: Coach bodies.

Range

Century 1235: 12 m body with 3.5 m height, seating around 49, with washroom and air conditioning.

Century 1237: 12 m body with 3.7 m height, seating up to 57.

Intercentury: 12 m long, 3.2 m high, for intercity work, seating up to 57. It is on a MAN chassis is for dual-purpose work.

Production: Annual capacity is 800.

Irizar Century body on Scania K113 three-axle chassis belonging to Applebys ***1997***

As well as the Spanish market, Irizar has representation in France, Holland, Belgium, Ireland, Spain and Scandinavia. Exports accounted for 50 per cent of production in 1995/96.

Four Scania K113TRB three-axle coaches with Irizar Century bodywork have been sold to Supreme Holidays, Hadleigh, UK.

In total 650 vehicles were produced in 1995, a 38 per cent increase in sales.

Developments: A prototype 15 m three-axle coach on Scania chassis has been developed and is the first of its kind for the Spanish market.

UPDATED

Isuzu

Isuzu Motors Limited
6-26-1 Minami-oi, Shinagawa-ku, Tokyo 140, Japan
Telephone: +81 3 5471 1111 Fax: +81 3 5471 1090
President: Kazuhira Seki

Subsidiaries
In addition to those listed below there are also subsidiaries in the Philippines, China, Egypt and Turkey

Isuzu Motors America Inc
46401 Commerce Centre Drive, Plymouth Township, MI 48170, USA
Telephone: +1 313 455 7595
American Isuzu Motors Inc
13181 Crossroads Parkway North, 4th Floor, City of Industry, CA 91746-0480, USA
Telephone: +1 213 699 0500
Isuzu Motors Co (Thailand) Ltd
38 Poochao Saming Road, Samrong-Tai, Phra Pradeng, Samutprakan 10130, Thailand
Telephone: +66 394 2541 Fax: +66 394 2552
Tri Petch Isuzu Sales Co Ltd
1705 Phaholyothin Road, Lardyao, Chatuchak District, Bangkok 10900, Thailand
Telephone: +66 2 513 0101 Fax: +66 2 513 2981

Products: Light and heavy-duty trucks and buses. Engines, transmissions and other major chassis components are built.

Range: Complete buses and chassis are offered in a variety of configurations and lengths ranging from 7 m to 12 m and seating 29 to 54. Isuzu-built diesel engines are fitted.

Standard Isuzu buses have traditionally been designed for rugged operating conditions with a heavy-duty ladder-type frame, though more sophisticated integral city buses are now in production.

MR series: Front engine and two variants, weighing up to 7.2 and 8.5 tonnes. Choice of 6BD1 six-cylinder 5.79 litre engine or 6BG1 six-cylinder 6.5 litre engines. Seating up to 33.

Isuzu SHD Super Cruiser ***1996***

MT series: Front engine. Two versions, weighing 12.5 or 13.5 tonnes. Engine options as for MR series. Seating up to 46.

LT series: Available with new 6HH1 six-cylinder 8.2 litre engine in two gross vehicle weights, 13.5 and 14.5 tonnes. Seating capacity is up to 50.

CJR/CQR/CHR series: The CJR bus has a separate chassis suited to a variety of bodywork for interurban and tourist use. It is powered by the 6QA1/6RA1/6RB1 engine and is for bodywork seating up to 54.

SHD (LV) Super Cruiser: Available as an interurban coach or luxury version, the integral coach is powered by a rear-mounted 10PE1 380 kW diesel engine. Anti-lock braking is provided; length is 11.97 m.

An emissions control system is based on a sensor which stops the engine when it idles. When the accelerator is depressed, the engine automatically starts up. Isuzu reports a 10 per cent reduction in nitrogen oxide emissions.

A permanent magnet retarder has been produced for Isuzu buses.

Production: Isuzu has an annual output exceeding 2,000 vehicles.

Contracts: About half the annual bus production is exported. Markets supplied include the Far East, Middle East and the Pacific region, with new markets developing in South America through CKD assembly operations in Colombia, Ecuador and Venezuela. CKD kits of the integral buses in the range are supplied both direct and for assembly through the worldwide manufacturing operations of General Motors, and versions with chassis are built clear of protuberances for ease of installation of bodies locally.

Developments: A one-step low-floor city bus prototype has been delivered to Osaka City Bus for evaluation. The vehicle has a floor height of 550 mm.

UPDATED

Iveco

Iveco SpA Bus Division
Via Puglia 35, 10156 Torino, Italy
Telephone: +39 11 6872111 Fax: +39 11 273 4759
General Manager: E Valente
Commercial Manager: V Lasalvia
Engineering Manager: M Boccenti

UK subsidiary
Iveco Bus
Iveco Ford House, Station Road, Watford WD1 1SR
Telephone: +44 1923 246400 Fax: +44 1923 226346
Manager: Harry Chambers

Background: Iveco was formed in 1975 after an agreement between Fiat SpA of Torino (with which three vehicle manufacturers — OM, Lancia Veicoli Speciali and Unic of France — had already joined forces) and Klöckner-Humboldt-Deutz of Köln (through Magirus-Deutz) to merge their vehicle manufacturing operations. Subsequently KHD pulled out of the joint venture and now the Iveco shareholding interest fully belongs to Fiat SpA.

In 1986 Iveco and Ford of Britain entered into a joint venture, Iveco Ford Truck Ltd to market in the UK the Cargo range and the complementary Iveco range of vehicles.

In 1989 Iveco acquired the complete share capital of Orlandi, the oldest bodybuilder in Italy, and the complete share capital of Sicca, specialised producer of chassis for buses and coaches.

In 1991 Iveco acquired 60 per cent share capital of the Spanish Enasa-Pegaso Group and in 1994 bought the remaining 40 per cent thus consolidating its industrial presence in the major European countries.

Iveco TurboCity-U articulated bus ***1996***

In addition to its 21 plants and 13 research centres in Italy, France, Germany, UK and Spain, Iveco has 23 industrial collaborations, 14 licensees with shareholding interests and nine licensees without shareholding interests outside Europe. Iveco International Operations works through its subsidiaries and industrial manufacturing/assembly activities of buses and chassis in China, Egypt, Ethiopia, India (Iveco owns 37.5 per cent of Ashok Leyland (qv)), Iran, Kenya, Libya, Tunisia, Turkey, Venezuela and Vietnam. This activity is based on supply of components and CKD sets from Iveco.

Products: Complete buses and coaches, chassis, chassis for articulated buses and trolleybuses, CKD kits. Low emission vehicles, zero emission vehicles (electric).

City range

DownTown: This is a low-floor urban bus 7 m long with front engine and a floor height of 330 mm (no step apart from initial step from road). It seats 9 with 33 standing and has two doors.

The engine, complying with Euro-2, has a power of 76 kW (102 bhp); there is automatic transmission, independent suspension at front, single wheels at the rear, disc brakes and a wheelchair lift can be fitted.

CityClass: This has an ultra-low floor and is of integral construction. It is 10.7 m or 12 m long and carries up to 113. There are 21 standard versions with two, three or four doors in city and urban configuration. There are no steps at any door and the floor height is 330 mm (340 mm at the back). A kneeling mechanism lowers this to 250 mm.

It is powered by the 8360.41 turbocharged after-cooled Iveco water-cooled Euro-2 engine with either 164 kW or 210 kW output.

The wheelbase is 5.11 m or 6.15 m and the width is 2.5 m.

TurboCity 490E: This semi-integral welded steel rear-engined city bus is offered in 10.7 m, 12 m and 18 m (articulated) lengths carrying 105, 115 and 165 passengers respectively with a high proportion of standees. Power for both variants, the 490E.10.22 and 490E.12.22, is the same, coming from a 164 kW (220 hp) 8460.21 turbocharged Iveco Fiat water-cooled Euro-2 engine. The engine for the articulated version, the 490E.18.29, is the 8460.41, turbocharged and after-cooled, 214 kW (290 hp).

Iveco TurboCity-U 490 CNG **1996**

Wheelbases are 5.11 m, 6.15 m and 5.3 + 6.63 m. The interior body floor height is 550 mm with two steps. The front section of the articulated version has a floor height of 330 mm with no step (apart from the one from the road). Seats are cantilevered from the body sides. Maximum gross vehicle weight is 19,000 kg. There are three- or four-doorway options on the 12 m bus and a three-doorway specification on the 10.7 m version. Four doors can be specified for the 18 m version.

TurboCity-S Green 590: These suburban buses, known as the 590E.10.22, 590E.12.22 and 590E.18.29, come in 10.7 m, 12 m and 18 m two- or three-door versions, with a capacity for 93, 105 (42 seated and 63 standees) and 124 passengers and with the same power plant as the city buses. The interior body floor height is 550 mm with two steps.

Trolleybus Chassis: Chassis lengths of 10, 12 and 18 m (articulated) are available. Electrical equipment, motor and final drive are not fitted.

Rear engine chassis range

EuroRider: This is a multipurpose chassis 12 m long with a rear engine; chassis height is 700 mm. The engine is the Iveco 8460.41, complying with Euro-2. It has a mechanical or automatic gearbox. It is available with air suspension for a normal body or for a high-deck body. It has disc brakes at the front and drum at the rear. ABS braking is fitted.

The EuroRider chassis is available in the UK for interurban bus or luxury coach bodies. Beulas (Spain) bodywork is offered for the coach version. The floor height is 650 mm at the entrance and complies with DPTAC-2 regulations. The rear-mounted engine complies with Euro-2 regulations. A Telma retarder is fitted and ZF power steering is standard. A network of 16 specialist dealers has been appointed for the EuroRider range.

EuroMidi: This is derived from the EuroCargo truck chassis and seats around 33. It is powered by a six-cylinder turbocharged engine driving through a six-speed transmission.

AP 160: This is for export markets where rugged and less sophisticated bus chassis are required. It weighs 18 tonnes gross and comes in 11.3 and 12 m lengths for city and intercity service, equipped with a rear-mounted 8460.41 Euro-1 six-cylinder engine producing from 194 kW (260 hp) to 216 kW (290 hp). The chassis are designed for high ground clearance and have reinforced

Iveco CityClass with four doors **1996**

Iveco Altrobus hybrid bus **1996**

Iveco EuroMidi chassis with Indcar body **1996**

Karosa

Karosa State Corporation
PO Box 3, 56603 Vysoké Mýto, Czech Republic
Telephone: +420 468 21260/21252/21288
Fax: +420 468 21386/21339
Exports: Motokov
Na Strži 63, 14062 Praha 4
Main works: Vysoké Mýto, Brandýs n O, Slatiňany, Hořice, Jaroměř, Polička
Managing Director: Stanislav Jankåu

Background: Karosa and Renault VI have established a joint venture. The new company is called Karosa SA and Renault has a 34 per cent share, later to be raised to 52 per cent. Renault engines and gearboxes meeting Euro-1 and now Euro-2 emission regulations will be integrated into the Karosa range and new bus designs derived from those of Renault will be developed.

The European Bank for Reconstruction & Development has provided financial support in the form of an eight-year loan, for Karosa to modernise its product line so that it can compete fairly on the European market.

Karosa B931 bus **1996**

Products: Single-deck buses, including articulated, and coaches.

Range: 730-Series vehicles designed for interurban (C734) and for urban transport (city buses B731, B732).
B731, B732: These are urban buses designed to carry up to 63 standing and 31 seated. The turbocharged ML636 diesel engine produces 152.4 kW at 2,000 rev/min, and the Praga 2 M70 automatic transmission (B731) or Praga 5 P80 manual five-speed gearbox (B732) is installed behind the rear driven axle. The front wheels have independent suspension.
C734: For interurban use, powered by the ML636 engine, rated at 152 kW and driving through the Praga 5 P80 manual five-speed gearbox. There are similar dual-purpose and express coach variants known as the LC735 and LC736 respectively, powered by the ML637 turbocharged engine.
B741: This is an articulated urban/interurban bus with seats for 60 and space for 70 standees within the overall length of 17.36 m.
*B931:*This is a city bus, produced jointly with Renault VI. It is powered by the Renault MIHR 062045B/3 152 kW engine driving through a ZF 4HP500 automatic gearbox . It is 11.35 m long and seats 32 with 63 standing. The floor height is 890 mm.
LC757: The HD12 variant of this design is a touring coach with toilet and washroom, seating up to 46 in one or two-door layout. It is 11.9 m long and is powered by a Cummins LTAA 10-325 turbocharged engine.

Production: 441 buses were delivered in 1995.

Contracts: 200 Karosa B731 buses are being supplied to Office des Chemins de Fer et des Transports en Commun for use in the greater Beirut area. They have Renault VI running units.

Developments: Karosa and Renault VI have produced the Recreo, based on Karosa bodywork with Renault running units, for the expanding French school bus market.

UPDATED

Kawajyu

Kawajyu Auto Body Ltd
Kagamihara, Gifu, Japan

Products: Bus and coach bodies

Range: Kawajyu is the main builder of bus and coach bodywork for Isuzu chassis.

Kitamura

Kitamura Manufacturing Co Ltd
401 Dekijima, Niigata-shi 950, Japan
Telephone: +81 252 839131 Fax: +81 252 846224
Commercial Director: Sadao Ikarashi

Other plants: Tokyo, Osaka, Nagoya, Sendai, Kanazawa, Sapporo

Products: Bus and coach bodies; specialist and minibus conversions.

Range: Kitamura is one of the two main independent bodybuilders in Japan. Predominantly standard city bus bodies and minibus conversions on Isuzu chassis are produced.

Kowex

Kowex Fahrzeugtechnic GmbH, Industriegebiet, 74232 Abstatt, Germany
Germany
Telephone: +49 7062 5490 Fax: +49 7062 954929

Background: Kowex has re-entered the bus market after some years' absence.

Products: Buses and midibuses

Range: The Regio SL is a midibus with 14 seats and room for 25 standing. It is based ont the Mercedes-Benz 814D and there are six different versions on offer.

A dual-purpose bus is available.

NEW ENTRY

Kusters

Carosserie Kusters Venlo BV
PO Box 38, 5900 AA Venlo, Netherlands
Telephone: +31 77 517045 Fax: +31 77 517048
A member of the Berkhof group

Background: Kusters has been in coachbuilding since 1920 and is now a member of the Berkhof group.

Products: Mini and midibus bodies on Mercedes 611D and 614D chassis, seating up to 25.

Range
Speeder: This a midibus body on the Mercedes-Benz 814 chassis and seats 25 in bus or coach configurations.
Mid-City: With a 350 mm floor height and double doors this midibus is also available with a CNG drive.

Kusters Speeder midibus on Mercedes-Benz Sprinter chassis
1996

Kutsenits

Kutsenits International
Siget 39-41 Industriegebiet, 7053 Hornstein, Austria
Telephone: +43 2689 22160 Fax: +43 2689 221610

Products: Small buses

Range
City: These midibuses have a feature window at the front and the bodies are mounted on Volkswagen chassis.

Contracts: 20- and 37-seat buses are being supplied on Volkswagen Transporter and L80 chassis through the Volkswagen dealer network in Germany.

UPDATED

Kutsenits City midibus body

Labh Singh Harnam Singh

Labh Singh Harnam Singh Ltd
PO Box 45569, Athi River Road Industrial Area, off Addis Ababa Road, Nairobi, Kenya
Telephone: +254 2 540636/7 Fax: +254 2 541879
Managing Director: Gurmej S Sokhi

Products: Bus and coach bodywork

Range: City bus bodies can be supplied on DAF front-engined chassis, seating around 30 with room for about 30 standing. The front door is behind the front axle, and the rear door is behind the rear axle. Bodies can also be supplied on ERF chassis.

Smaller bus bodies are supplied on Isuzu chassis, seating around 30, depending on specification, and bodies can also be supplied on truck chassis.

Contracts: 50 12 m bodies on ERF Trailblazer chassis have being supplied to Stagecoach International subsidiary, Kenya Bus. Each body seats 52 with 52 standing. Ten 11 m bodies on ERF chassis were delivered to Kenya Bus during 1995, each body seating 45 with 53 standing.

UPDATED

Labh Singh 12 m body on ERF Trailblazer of Kenya Bus **1997**

Lahti

Lahden Autokori Oy
15540 Villähde, Finland
Telephone: +358 3 887100 Fax: +358 3 887 1200
Managing Director: Juhani Saario

Products: Bus bodies and coaches.

Range: Lightweight aluminium bodies. A basic design is built, with various options of roof height up to 3.75 m and interior formats to suit city, suburban, long-distance bus, and luxury touring roles. The city variant, the Lahti 402 low-floor, is available on most two-axle chassis up to 13 m and three-axle chassis up to 14.5 m.

Contracts: 20 Lahti 402 buses on Scania N113 chassis have been delivered to København. Exports have been made to Scandinavian, Baltic and Central European countries.

Developments: In 1996 Lahti launched the Falcon 540 tourist coach which is built in aluminium alloy and complies with EC R66 roll-over regulations.

UPDATED

Lahti 402 ultra-low-floor bus on Scania N113 chassis **1997**

Lahti 402 ultra-low-floor bus on three-axle Scania L113 chassis **1997**

LAZ

Lvovskyi Automobusnyi Zavod
Stryiska Str 45, Lvov, 290618 Ukraine
Telephone: +380 0322 636055 Fax: +380 0322 636075
President: Stepan Davydiak
Financial Director: Vasyl Trach
Accountant: Nadiya Kolos
Technical Director: Yevstachi Kostiv
Director, Foreign Trade: Roman Popovych

Products: Buses and trolleybuses

Range
LAZ 52523: This has a six-cylinder Renault engine, meeting Euro-1 regulations, and carries up to 120.
LAZ 52522: 11 m trolleybus, seating 26 and carrying 108; two doors and two axles.
LAZ 4202: This is a 9.7 m medium-capacity bus powered

by the KAMAZ-740 V8 engine which produces 132 kW (180 hp) at 2,600 rev/min.

697R/699R: Buses 9.19 m and 10.54 m long; introduced in 1956 but updated successively.

697R buses are still being built; the 697 is the short version for city service while the 699R is the longer intercity semi-coach.

LAZ 5208: Coach, with Renault Euro-1 engine, air conditioning, Blaupunkt audio/video, ABS brakes and high floor.

LAZ 6205: This articulated bus has a Renault Euro-1 engine and carries up to 200.

Contracts: LAZ has supplied four 52522 trolleybuses to Ashgabat, Turkmenistan.

Developments: A joint venture between Usautotrans, Uzbekistan's state transport company, and LAZ has been set up to build 700 and 1,000 buses annually. An 11.2 m city bus has been submitted for type approval in Germany.

UPDATED

LAZ 52523 bus in Omsk ***1997***

LDV

LDV
Common Lane, Washwood Heath, Birmingham B8 2UP, England
Telephone: +44 121 322 2000 Fax: +44 121 322 3296/4852
Marketing & Commercial Director: David Gardner
Executive Directors: Clive Griffiths, Ken Ogilvie

Background: LDV makes light commercial vehicles of between 2 and 4.2 tonnes GVW.

Following the collapse of DAF NV, Leyland DAF Vans went into receivership, but production has carried on as normal. A management buyout was made in 1993.

Products: Light vans, minibuses, crew buses and chassis cowls.

Range: LDV markets two body widths of van, with many options available. There are two basic ranges, Pilot and Convoy, which replace the 200 and 400 Series vans. The drive train remains the same and all the changes are within the bodyshells. A 13-seat Convoy minibus replaces the 12-seat 200 Series. A 17-seat version on the long-wheelbase Convoy has also been announced.

The Pilot is powered by a 2 litre petrol engine, or a 2 litre direct injection diesel engine, driving through a five-speed gearbox. The Convoy is powered by a choice of two petrol and two diesel engines. The 2 and 3.5 litre V8 petrol engines run on unleaded fuel, with the choice of 2.5 litre naturally aspirated and turbocharged diesels. The manual gearbox has five speeds.

An assembly plant has been opened in South Africa and annual production is expected to be 400.

UPDATED

LDV postbus in service with Royal Mail ***1997***

LIAZ

Likino Autobusnij Zavod
1 Kalinin Str, Likino-Dulevo, 142670 Moskva region, Russia
Exports:A/O LIAZ
Telephone: +7 096 413 8200 Fax: +7 096 412 0711
General Manager: G A Tarulenkov
Director, Foreign Trade: V Kostin

Background: LIAZ started bus manufacture in 1960 with the ZIL 158W, which was developed from the 158 made by ZIL (qv) at the Lichacov works in Moskva. The mainstay of the LIAZ works was the popular 677 petrol-engined city bus, though the main model now is now the 5256. The company is now quoted on the Praha Stock Exchange.

Products: Buses

Range

5256 city bus: This has three doors, seating 16, 28 or 36, and is 11.98 m long, 2.5 m wide and 3 m high. Total passenger capacity is 117 to 120. The kerb weight is 9.6 tonnes and GVW is 17.6 to 17.8 tonnes. It has three high-power heaters for work in cold climates; four fans and three roof-hatch vents provide ventilation. A glass partition is available to separate the driver's area from the rest of the bus. An interlock mechanism prevents the bus doors being closed when the engine is at any speed other than idle.

LIAZ-6220: This is an articulated version of the 5256, with four doors.

Contracts: LIAZ has concentrated almost entirely on meeting domestic demand.

UPDATED

LIAZ-5256 city bus with driver's partition

LIAZ-6220 articulated bus

Mafersa

Mafersa SA
Av Raimundo Pereira de Magalhães, 230 Vila Anastácio, São Paulo, SP 05092-901, Brazil
Telephone: +55 11 261 8911 Fax: +55 11 261 3764
President of the Board: José Gustavo de Carvalho

Background: Better known as a builder of rail rolling stock, Mafersa has developed bus and trolleybus production. See main entry under Rail Vehicles.

Products: Integral buses, chassis (rigid and articulated) and trolleybuses.

Range
M210: Available as a 12 m two-axle 86-capacity vehicle. The Cummins 6CTA 8.3 218 hp engine is used with ZF S6-90 gearbox, with Mafersa front axle and a Rockwell rear axle.
Ligeirinho M240: This is an integral 12 m two-axle urban bus with a Cummins 6CTA 8.3 240 hp engine driving through an Allison MTB-647 gearbox.
Chassis: Two-axle 11.85 m, 2.46 m or 2.56 m wide with air suspension, for types M210 and M240 buses.

Articulated version with three axles, 17.98 m long and with air suspension. Anti-jack-knife SOT/TOS system fitted.
Trolleybus: 12 m integral trolleybus, two axles, air suspension, with chopper control, carrying up to 91.

M240 urban bus for high platform loading at a station in Curitiba ***1995***

Production: 97 integral buses and five chassis were produced in 1995.

MAN

MAN Nutzfahrzeuge AG
A subsidiary company of MAN AG
PO Box 500620, 80976 München, Germany
Telephone: +49 89 158001 Fax: +49 89 150 3972
Chairman: Klaus Schubert
Commercial Director: Dr Günther Dietz
Chief of Bus Section: Boudewijn Heilijgers
Export Manager, Buses: Manfred Mechnich

Main bus production plant: Salzgitter

Overseas bus manufacture and assembly companies
Australia: MAN Automotive Pty Ltd
South Africa: MAN Automotive (Pty) Ltd
Turkey: MANAS (qv)
UK office: MAN Truck & Bus Ltd, Frankland Road, Swindon SN5 8YU
Telephone: +44 1793 490231 Fax: +44 1793 485260
Bus & Special Projects Manager: Richard Noy
PSV Service Manager: Chris Wood

Background: MAN is a specialist producer of commercial vehicles, engines, axles and other components. It acquired Büssing in 1971. MAN created a separate bus section in 1984, based at Salzgitter. Overseas manufacturing associates operate in Austria (where OeAF/Gräf & Stift (qv) specialises in trolleybuses) and Turkey (MANAS, qv), and there are additional assembly operations in South Africa and Australia.

Small city buses are built in arrangement with Göppel of Augsburg, which mounts the bodywork.

All the buses manufactured as complete vehicles for the West European market are offered by MAN as underframes for assembly overseas.

Products: Integral coaches and buses including double-deck and articulated. Bus chassis. Trolleybuses and guided buses.

Range: Includes complete standard city, suburban/interurban, and touring buses and coaches and double-deck and articulated buses. There are also separate chassis on which a variety of bodywork can be built locally overseas.

Complete buses
NL202: This has a boarding height of 315 mm at the forward door. It is powered by a turbocharged and charge-cooled D08 engine mounted on the off-side to make room for a third door. A choice of Voith-Renk and ZF automatic gearboxes is available. From the front door the floor is ramped to the centre platform and door, where there is space for a wheelchair; an optional kneeling facility is provided.
NL222FR: This is the Euro-2 equivalent of the previous NL203FR chassis.
SG242/292 articulated: In 16.5 and 17.4 m lengths with the rear-mounted underfloor 177 kW or 213 kW engine, and choice of steered or unsteered trailing axle. Maximum capacity is 50 plus 124 standees.
NG272: Articulated low-floor bus, 17.9 m long, with two or three doors, and developed from the NL202. Powered by a turbocharged intercooled MAN D0826LUH (200 kW) engine.
ND202: A double-deck bus has been developed with an ultra-low floor and three doors. It is built on the MAN running units by Adtranz (qv). It has a wheelchair lift at the front and a ramp at the central entrance. The lower deck has seats for 25, with 23 standing. The upper deck seats 46. Bolted aluminium alloy is used for the body frame and panelling. It is powered by a 6.9 litre D0826 Euro-2 engine driving through a Voith automatic transmission. It is 11.735 m long, 2.48 m wide, 4.12 m high and the floor height is 370 mm; headroom downstairs is 2 m, upstairs it is 1.685 m. The gross vehicle weight is 18 tonnes.
NL202DE: MAN and Voith are working with Rockwell and Siemens on an electric drive. A prototype was produced in 1997.

MAN NÜ263 low-floor interurban bus ***1997***

Trolleybus
Trolleybus: Designated SL-T, this is available in standard (11.55 m) or articulated (16.5 m) lengths, and has a 600 V motor. Production is the responsibility of the subsidiary OeAF/Gräf & Stift (qv).

Chassis
11.220: 11 m powered by a MAN Euro-2 engine.
16.240 FOC chassis: The MAN 16.240 FOC front-engined chassis is available for export in various wheelbases to accommodate left- or right-hand drive bodywork from 11 to 12 m. The 16.240 has been used as the basis of a simple articulated bus by MAN's South African subsidiary. Power is from 147 kW to 177 kW engines.
16.240/16.290 HOC chassis: A rugged rear-engined chassis rated up to 18.2 tonnes, the 16.240/16.290 HOC comes in lengths suitable for 11 or 12 m bodywork with left- or right-hand drive, and the D2866 213 kW or 177 kW engine is installed. Air suspension is optional.
16.360 HOCL chassis: This has air suspension, a very low floor frame between the axles, and has a GVW of 18.2 tonnes. It takes 12 m bodies and is powered by a MAN turbocharged intercooled D2866LOH (265 kW) engine.
8.150/9.150/8.170/9.170 FOC: These front-engined

medium-size 8 or 9 tonne models are the responsibility of both MAN and its partner Volkswagen and come with a 110 kW or 125 kW turbocharged engine and will take 6-8 m bodywork with optional air suspension on the rear axle. They are suited for both left- and right-hand drive.

Coaches
FRH402 Lion's Star: This integral coach is powered by a rear-mounted 420 hp six-cylinder turbocharged engine driving through a ZF 85 180 eight-speed transmission. It has a flat floor.
Lion's Coach RH353 and RH313: Derivatives of the MAN Lion's Star.

Contracts: 15 buses on 11.220 chassis have been delivered to MTL London, with Marshall Midi bodies. A further nine were delivered at the end of 1996.

In total 65 low-floor articulated vehicles have been ordered for Köln, Germany. BVG Berlin has ordered 86 ND202 double-deck buses. MAN is supplying 250 city buses to Kazakhstan, building them at its Ankara, Turkey, plant.

Production: Production in 1995 was 3,100.

MAN Lion's Coach RH353 built in Turkey **1997**

Developments: FRH402 Lion's Star: this high-deck touring coach now has a Euro-2 engine, redesigned running gear, more rigid chassis and disc brakes on all wheels.

Two vehicles were introduced in 1996. The ÜL313/353 coach from the Lion's family is for scheduled runs over longer distances, while for shorter distances the NÜ263/313 is a low-floor bus carrying more passengers.

Newly introduced is the RH353 Lion's Coach Highliner. With a height of 3.7 m the vehicle carries up to 51 passengers. The coach is manufactured by MANAS, MAN's Turkish subsidiary.

The MAN coach bodies satisfy the requirements of roll-over directive ECE R66. In addition, all newly developed buses and coaches are equipped with the new Lucas disc brakes on both axles. Parts prone to corrosion, such as front and rear claddings and wheel arches, are made of synthetic material; the luggage compartment flaps are aluminium pressings.

Low-floor buses are fitted with new engine types. The NL222, NL262 and NL312 variants have the EDC-controlled D08 six-cylinder engine with ratings of 220 hp and 260 hp and a 10 litre in-line five-cylinder 310 hp engine.

The articulated versions – the MAN NG262 and NG312 – are fitted with 10 litre engines.

The NL222, NL262 and NL312 have been specified with new engines as follows:
NL222: Turbocharged and intercooled six-cylinder engine with a piston displacement of 6.9 litres and an output of 162 kW/220 hp at 2,400 rpm. Maximum torque: 850 Nm from 1,300 to 1,500 rpm.
NL262: Turbocharged and intercooled six-cylinder engine with a piston displacement of 6.9 litres and an output of 191 kW/260 hp at 2,300 rpm. Maximum torque: 1,000 Nm from 1,350 to 1,700 rpm.
NL312: Turbocharged and intercooled five-cylinder in-line engine with a piston displacement of 10 litres and an output of 228 kW/310 hp at 2,000 rpm. Maximum torque: 1,250 Nm from 1,000 to 1,500 rpm.
NL232 CNG: six-cylinder engine with a piston displacement of 12 litres and an output of 170 kW/230 hp at 2,200 rpm. Maximum torque: 830 Nm at 1,000 rpm.

Articulated buses
NG262: With turbocharged and intercooled five-cylinder in-line engine with a piston displacement of 10 litres and an output of 191 kW/260 hp at 2,000 rpm. Maximum torque: 1,050 Nm from 1,000 to 1,500 rpm.
NG312: Turbocharged and intercooled five-cylinder in-line engine with a piston displacement of 10 litres and an output of 228 kW/310 hp at 2,000 rpm. Maximum torque: 1,250 Nm from 1,000 to 1,500 rpm.

The 230 hp CNG engine is available for NG vehicles too.

Buses with the 10 litre engines have a lateral radiator which reduces the number of passenger seats in the rearmost row to three seats.
263/313 low-floor intercity: This is designed for urban and interurban transport with large numbers of passengers. The entry height is 320 mm at the front and 340 mm at the centre doors. It accommodates 94 passengers (48 seats and standing room for 44 to 46 persons). Luggage racks are provided inside and the bus is available with two or three doors of various widths. The central door is relocated towards the rear just in front of the rear axle to speed passengers flow.

It is the first vehicle from MAN's low-floor programme to appear in the latest design with ellipsoid headlights and a deep, single-piece windscreen. The driver's instrument panel contains only that instrumentation that is necessary – only the speedometer and one display providing information on all other functions and operating values. Defects are indicated by means of yellow check lamps as an additional warning, while red lights signal an alarm. The saloon interior is provided with two roof hatches which double as emergency exits. Two roof-mounted

MAN ÜL313 interurban bus **1997**

MAN 11.190 of Thamesdown Transport with Marshall bodywork **1997**

blowers and hopper-windows provide ventilation. The saloon heater is relocated to the engine compartment. An option is the roof-mounted City Cooler airconditioner from Webasto.

Three Euro-2 engine options, horizontally mounted at the vehicle rear, are available. The first is the economical in-line six-cylinder engine with a power output of 191 kW/260 hp. For powerful acceleration two five-cylinder engines are available rated at 191 kW (260 hp) and 228 kW (310 hp). The top speed of the NÜ263/313 is 100 km/h.

A CNG-powered in-line six-cylinder engine is available.

Gearboxes include the three-speed Voith D851.3/D863.3, the four-speed Voith D854.3/D864.3, the four-speed Renk D874, the five-speed ZF 5 HP500 and the six-speed manual unit, the ZF S6-85.

The front and rear axles are newly developed. Optionally available is the electronically controlled air suspension (ECAS) with six bellows to minimise the air requirement on the front and rear axles. To reduce body roll, a stabiliser can be additionally installed on the front axle on request.

Compressed-air disc brakes from Lucas are fitted.

ÜL313/353: This is the bus version of the RN313/353 single-decker touring coach. It is for school bus, short excursions and interurban work. A 1,300 mm double-width central door is fitted.

It has 49 to 55 seats and standing room for up to 40. The two twin seats opposite the centre door can be lifted to provide room for a pram or a wheelchair or for extra passengers. The interior side walls are covered with washable needle fleece and the centre aisle is flat. A luggage compartment with a capacity of up to 6 m^3 is provided and can be loaded from both sides. In winter, sports equipment can be accommodated in the rear.

Power is provided from a six-cylinder in-line engine rated at 228 kW (310 hp) or 257 kW (350 hp), driving through a ZF S6-85 or HP590 gearbox.

Compressed-air disc brakes on both axles are fitted to all vehicles from the Lion's family. A wear-free third brake may be selected from various retarder systems. ABS is a standard feature on all MAN buses/coaches.

RN 313/353 Lion's Comfort: This is a single-decker 12 m dual-purpose coach for luxury coach and intercity work. It has wide outward-opening doors at the front and also at the centre or rear. A toilet, kitchen and air conditioning system are available.

It is powered by a Euro-2 in-line six-cylinder engine driving through either a ZF S6-85 six-speed gearbox or ZF S6-1600 version.

In a joint collaboration with Siemens and Voith, MAN is producing diesel electric buses for 1997 delivery.

Developments: A MAN NL223 12 m bus for Erlangen, Germany, has been converted to run on electric power using hydrogen-supplied fuel cells. The project is joint funded by the Bavarian Ministry of Trade, MAN, Siemens and Linde (supplier of gas cylinders and hydrogen).

UPDATED

MANAS

MAN Kamyon ve Otobüs Sanayi AS
Esenboğa Havaalani Yolu 22 km, 06105 Ankara, Turkey
Telephone: +90 312 398 0220/0275
Fax: +90 312 398 0340
Marketing & Sales Director: Eke Kumbaracibasi
Export Manager: Ali Özbey

Background: MANAS is 80 per cent owned by MAN AG, Germany, and 20 per cent by others.

Products: Articulated and rigid city buses.

Range: Buses which are modified MAN designs are offered for the Turkish market and abroad, assembled from parts supplied from Germany.

SL232: This is powered by a rear-mounted MAN D0826LOH diesel rated at 169 kW (230 hp). It meets Euro-1 standards and drives through a manual gearbox, with the option of an automatic transmission. It is 11.75 m long.

SG272: This is an articulated city bus powered by the MAN D2865LUH diesel six-cylinder rear-mounted engine producing 198 kW (270 hp). It meets Euro-1 standards. The bus is 17.91 m long.

S2000 Lion's Coach: This is a luxury coach, built at the MANAS plant for the European market.

Production: 440 to 540 buses a year are produced.

Contracts: The main market is operators in Turkey, but buses are also supplied to the Russian Federation and Associated States and the Middle East. In addition, five SL222 city buses with Euro-2 engines have been delivered to Croatia, 35 have gone to Slovenia and four have gone to Germany.

In 1996 MANAS completed a contract, following a World Bank loan, for the supply of 240 SL232 city buses to the Ministry of Transport, Kazakhstan.

Another contract has been completed for the city of Pavlodar, Kazakhstan, for the supply of a further 33 SL232 buses.

Forty S2000 Lion's Coaches have been ordered by German operators.

UPDATED

MANAS articulated bus ***1995***

MANAS SL232 bus delivered to Almaty in 1996 ***1997***

MANAS SG272 articulated bus ***1997***

Marcopolo

Marcopolo SA
RS 230 - Bairro Anna Rech, 95060-650 Caixas do Sul, RS, Brazil
Telephone: +55 54 222 4422 Fax: +55 54 222 4911

Subsidiaries
Marcopolo Trading SA
Address as above
Marcopolo Indústria de Carrocerias SA, Estrada de Eiras, Coimbra, Portugal
Telephone: +351 39 431856 Fax: +351 39 439174

Products: Bus, coach and trolleybus bodies, including articulated, double articulated and minibuses.

Range: City, interurban and touring coach designs.
Torino: This is a series of urban bus designs, suited to locally built Mercedes, Scania and Volvo chassis. City, intercity, articulated, three-section articulated and trolleybus versions are available.

A three-section articulated bus based on the Torino design is in service in Curitiba, Brazil. It is 25 m long. The new model is intended for light rail-style rapid transit in big cities, with high-platform loading and operating from metro-style stations. It is on a Volvo B58 chassis.

Body structure is of galvanised steel tube with exterior panelling in aluminium. Two double-piece doors are provided. The Padron design has 34 seats and standing capacity of 60. Articulated versions of the standard city bus are also built.
Micro Senior: This is for city, school and touring use and seats up to 26 in its suburban version.
Allegro, Viaggio, Paradiso: These are intercity and touring coaches. The Paradiso is a high-deck coach. The Allegro and Viaggio are available also on VW and Ford chassis.
Generation V: This is a new generation of intercity buses, available in standard height (GV850), standard-plus height (GV1000), mid-level (GV1150), high-deck (GV1450), low driver (Paradiso GV1450) and double-deck (GV1800).

Production: In 1994, 3,828 bodies were produced, with 1,225 going for export. Total production for 1996 was around 8,000.

Contracts: 50 bodies on Scania chassis have been delivered to Stagecoach Portugal.

CKD and ready-built versions are exported to South, Central and North America, Africa, Asia and Europe. They are on Mercedes-Benz, Scania, Volvo, Volkswagen and Dina chassis.

Developments: The Marcopolo coach body on the Dennis Javelin was revamped in 1996 with an additional step, new Fainsa seats and a new forced-air ventilation system.

UPDATED

Marcopolo Torino GV city bus body on Volvo B58 chassis ***1995***

Marcopolo Torino GV body on Mercedes-Benz chassis ***1995***

Marcopolo Viaggio body on Dina chassis ***1997***

Marshall

Marshall SPV
Airport Works, Newmarket Road, Cambridge CB5 8RX, England
Telephone: +44 1223 373737/373480
Fax: +44 1223 373713
Managing Directors: Alan Lines
Marketing & Communications Manager:
Terence Scown-Geary
Bus Operations Director: Mike Winter

Background: Marshall re-entered the bus and coach market after a gap of some 10 years and bought the designs for mini and midibuses from Carlyle Group UK, which ceased building buses in 1991.

Marshall acquired the bus and truck product designs from AWD which ceased trading in 1992. AWD had, in turn, inherited the design drawings from Bedford. Marshall constructs and markets the Marshall Bedford Truck range, some of which have been converted for basic passenger-carrying use.

Products: Bus and minibus bodywork; complete buses.

Range: Minibus and midibus bodies based on Cromweld 3CR12 stainless steel frames.
Minibus: This is 8.5 m long and is a low-floor minibus with a 320 mm entrance, kneeling to 250 mm and a step-free flat floor up to the rear axle, over which are two 200 mm steps. It is 2.37 m wide and meets UK DPTAC regulations for disabled people. It has an unladen weight of 5.236 tonnes. It is powered by a 3.9 litre Cummins 4BT

Marshall City midibus on MAN 11.220 chassis
1997

four-cylinder compact engine driving through an Allison AT542 four-speed automatic transmission. A Perkins engine can be substituted for the Cummins option. It has 24 V electrics and an I-beam GKN S46L front axle.

The body frame is stainless steel and the panelling is in aluminium alloy. It has gasket glazing. The vehicle seats 29 with 14 standing. A wheelchair ramp can be fitted and there are optional child seats. An overhead blown heating and ventilation system is fitted.

Capital: This is an ultra-low-floor midibus, 8.5 m to 10.8 m in length and seating up to 43. It has kneeling air suspension, overhead heating and ventilation and drum brakes. It can be mounted on the Dennis Dart SLF chassis. Step height is 325 mm, with no further steps up to the rear axle, allowing the use of wheelchairs and prams.

City: Midibus, 10m or 10.6 m, seating 38 or 43 with up to 15 standing; split-step entrance, air suspension, convection floor heating, drum brakes, luggage pen. Based on the MAN 11.220 and 13.220 chassis.

C37: Midibus based on the Dennis Dart chassis in 8.5 m, 9 m and 10 m lengths, seating up to 43 with 17 standing. A split-step entrance can be specified.

C34: Midibus based on the Volvo B6 chassis in 8.5 m, 9 m and 10 m lengths, seating up to 43 with 17 standing. A split-step entrance can be specified.

C31: Minibus based on the Iveco 59.12 seating 27 with 10 standing; luggage pen; floor height of 650 mm with first step height of 250 mm.

A welfare version of the C31 is available.

C19: Minibus mounted on the Mercedes-Benz 709D chassis cowl and seating 29 with 6 standing.

C16: Minibus mounted on the Mercedes-Benz 811D chassis cowl and seating 33 with 12 standing.

Contracts: 15 buses on 11.220 chassis have been delivered to MTL London, with Marshall Midi bodies. A further nine were delivered at the end of 1996.

Other customers include London General and West Midlands Travel.

Ultra-low-floor integral Marshall Minibus
1997

Marshall Maxibus on Iveco chassis
1997

A double-decker Metrobus refurbishment programme for West Midlands Travel, England, has completed 300 buses so far. The programme will last till April 2000.

Developments: The *Maxibus* has been introduced, based on the Dennis Lance, Volvo B10B, B10M or Iveco EuroRider chassis.

An 11.8 m low-floor bus based on the NL222FR chassis has been announced by Marshall and MAN (qv). It has an engine meeting Euro-2 regulations.

UPDATED

MASA

Mexicana de Autobuses SA de CV
Lago, Guadaloupe 289, Fracc Industrial Cartagena, 54900 Tultitlan, Edo de Mexico, Mexico
Telephone: +52 91 20522 Fax: +52 91 20892

Background: MASA was created in 1959 from the acquisition of Sociedad Mexicana de Credito Industrial (SOMEX). The present operation was set up at Tultitlan in 1972 and expanded in 1980 but the company ceased trading in the mid-1980s. MASA was sold to private investors in 1988 and has since been restructured.

Products: Bus and trolleybus bodywork, integral buses.

Range: MX80/90/100 integral urban transit buses with lengths of 9.7, 10.2 and 11.2 m respectively. All models have Detroit Diesel engines. The smaller types have Spicer manual transmissions while the MX100 has an Allison automatic transmission. Eaton and Dirona axles are fitted.

The Premier and Premier Elite highway buses and FL1537 are also offered.

Production: Some 80 per cent of the urban and city buses in Mexico and half of the country's present fleet of coaches have been produced by MASA.

Developments: A new range of city buses has been developed in a joint venture between Nielson and MASA:

U9: 33-seat.
U12: 90-passenger.
U18: articulated bus carrying165, 33 seated.
Spectrum: 33-seat urban bus.
Genesis: city/urban bus.
Coaches: Strada, Busscar and Premier.

UPDATED

Materfer

Materfer SA
J B Alberdi 1061 Casteros, Buenos Aires, Argentina
Telephone: +54 1 750 7854 Fax: +54 1 750 1475
Chair: Dr Guillermo Scarsogio
General Manager: Enzo Filipelli
Commercial Director: Antonio Matlana

Background: Established in 1950 as Fiat-Materfer, the company became known as Materfer SA in 1983. It produces light rail vehicles, electric and diesel multiple-units, and expanded into medium- and long-distance bus and coach production in 1994. (See main entry under Rail Vehicles and Traction Equipment.)

Products: Medium- and long-distance buses and coaches

Mauri

Mauri & C sas
Via Togliatti, 20033 Desio, Milano, Italy
Telephone: +39 2 362 626247 Fax: +39 2 362 629189
General Manager: Ambrogio Mauri
Technical Officer: Umberto Mauri

Background: Traditionally a bus bodybuilder, Mauri also bodied trams for Milano in the early 1970s, and trolleybuses in the late 1970s.

Products: Standard and articulated buses and trolleybuses; bus bodywork.

Mauri 18PT30 articulated bus

Mazda

Mazda Motor Corporation
PO Box 18, Hiroshima 730 91, Japan
Telephone: +81 82 282 1111 Fax: +81 82 287 5237

Products: Midi/minibuses

Range: The E2000/2200 seats up to 8. The 2000 is petrol-driven, while the 2200 has a diesel engine. The standard version comes with sliding doors on both sides and a rear tailgate.

It is distributed by Nissan Motor (qv) under the Vanette name.

In Britain, the Mazda E2200 and E2000 Autotrekker minibus model is produced by Autocheck Conversions and seats up to 12; it has a high roof and option of a high specification including coach seats and individual reading lights.

Mazda E2200 diesel-powered minibus
1996

MCI

Motor Coach Industries Ltd
10 East Golf Road, Des Plaines, IL 60016-2291, USA
Telephone: +1 847 299 9900 Fax: +1 847 299 0375
Chairman: Rafael Gómez Flores
Chief Operating Officer: Jim Bernacchi
Chief Financial Officer: José Luis Olvera
Executive Vice President, Sales & Marketing:
Francois Bouffard

Manufacturing plant: 552 West Stutsman, Pembina, ND 58271, USA
Telephone: +1 701 825 6234 Fax: +1 701 825 6394

Canadian subsidiary
1149 St Matthews Avenue, Winnipeg R3G 0JB
Telephone: +1 204 786 3301 Fax: +1 204 888 6369
Executive Vice President and General Manager:
R J Munro

Hausman Bus Sales Inc
10 East Golf Road, Des Plaines, IL 60016-2291, USA
Telephone: +1 847 299 9900 Fax: +1 847 299 0375
Vice President, Central Region: Patricia Ziska
Vice President, Western Region: Dean Carson
Vice President, Eastern Region: Dan Marazzo

Background: MCI has manufacturing facilities in Winnipeg, Manitoba and Pembina, and is owned by Dina Autobuses Inc (qv). In 1987 Greyhound acquired, through MCI, the General Motors' North American transit bus manufacturing interests, including GMC's RTS advanced design bus built at Pontiac, for integration with TMC production at the Roswell, New Mexico, site. MCI announced in 1993 that it was leaving the transit bus business and TMC was put up for sale. The GM Canada plant at St Eustache, Quebec, was bought out by the NovaBUS Corporation and trades separately under the NovaBUS name (qv).

In 1994, Dina acquired MCI International and its subsidiaries, including MCI, Hausman Bus Sales, Universal Coach Parts, MCI Financial Services and Custom Coach Corporation. Custom Coach was sold in 1996.

Products: MCI motor coaches for intercity, suburban, charter and commuter routes.

Range: MCI and Dina coaches in 12 m (40 ft), 13 m (43 ft) and 13.7 m (45 ft) lengths for interurban, suburban and touring markets. Four models are produced.

102EL3, 102DL3, 102D3 and MC12: The 102EL3 and 102DL3 are flagship models, 13.7 m long and featuring integral construction with a welded semi-monocoque frame.

The 102D3 and MC12 are 12 m in length. Extensive use of stainless steel below the floor is intended to achieve durability and corrosion resistance. Air conditioning, heating and air suspension are standard. Amenities include reclining seats, enclosed parcel racks and passenger control panels with individual lights and power air outlets. Seating arrangements can vary from 29 to 57.

Standard power train is Detroit Diesel but Cummins and Caterpillar engines can be specified.

Production: Up to seven coaches a day from the Winnipeg and Pembina plants.

Developments: Dina (qv) and MCI are jointly marketing the MCI range and the new Dina Viaggio 1000 coach.

UPDATED

MCI 102DL3 commuter coach with wheelchair lift
1997

MCI 102B3 of Canadian Greyhound Bus
1997

Mellor

Mellor Coachcraft
Miall Street, Rochdale OL11 1HY, England
Telephone: +44 1706 860610 Fax: +44 1706 860402
Managing Director: S L Procter
Production Director: G K Hudson
Sales Manager: P Winrow

Background: Formerly a subsidiary of the Plaxton Group (qv), Mellor is now a division of Woodhall Nicholson Ltd.

Products: Minibus van conversions; coachbuilt buses. Wheelchair facilities are provided.

Range: Minibuses from 8 to 16 seats and midibuses from 17 to 33 seats on all popular makes of vans and chassis cowls.

Mellor dual-door body on Iveco electric chassis ***1995***

Duet: This is a two-door body on an Iveco 59/12 4.5 m wheelbase chassis. It was developed for UK operator, Thames Transit, for service in Oxford. It seats 26 with 12 standing and facilities are provided for disabled and elderly people including a bus stopping sign, special seat between the two doors, tactile information plates and yellow handrails. Destination displays are at the front, side and rear. The framing is Cromweld stainless steel.

VERIFIED

Mellor two-door body on Iveco of Thames Transit, Oxford ***1997***

Mercedes-Benz

Mercedes-Benz AG
EvoBus GmbH
Hanns-Martin-Schleyer-Strasse, 68301 Mannheim, Germany
Telephone: +49 621 7400 Fax: +49 621 743 2937
Sales Manager: Martin Feller
Domestic Sales: H Heckt
Export Sales: H Smits

UK subsidiary
Mercedes-Benz (UK) Ltd
Mercedes-Benz Centre, Tongwell, Milton Keynes MK15 8BA
Telephone: +44 1908 668899 Fax: +44 1908 664351
Bus and Coach Consultant: I Soden

Mercedes O405N bus ***1996***

Background: Mercedes-Benz is one of the world's largest bus manufacturers with an annual production in Germany of around 3,500 units and a worldwide bus and minibus output of approximately 29,000 units a year. MB vehicles appear with the badge Mercedes-Benz.

Besides its operations in Germany, Mercedes-Benz maintains a variety of overseas subsidiaries or associates worldwide. The bus division relies on domestic production plants in Mannheim, Wörth (chassis only) and Düsseldorf, as well as manufacturing subsidiaries in Argentina, Brazil, Mexico, South Africa, Iran (Khodro), Ludwigsfelde and Turkey (Mercedes-Benz Türk (qv)).

In 1996 Mercedes-Benz negotiated an agreement with Yangzhou Motor Coach Corporation, China, to build 7,000 buses and coaches a year at a new plant in Jangsu Province.

Buses and coaches are assembled in at least 25 countries, including Australia, Indonesia, and Spain. In addition, Mercedes-Benz was strongly involved in development of the Indian Tata bus manufacturing operation. Mercedes-Benz has taken the lead in development of the O-Bahn guided bus.

Products: Complete integral buses and coaches and chassis, including articulated chassis on integral and ladder frame basis, and articulated trolleybuses. The products are built in more than 200 versions.

Mercedes builds only low-emission vehicles (LEVs). The emission figures for LEV engines are reduced by one half and they meet current EU guidelines. LEV engines have a specification including quieter engine running and high tractive power-to-weight ratio. LEV engines meet Euro-2 regulations.

Mercedes 814D Speedy minibus ***1996***

Mercedes-Benz Traveliner 12 minibus ***1996***

Range

City and intercity buses

In co-operation with the German Association of Public Transport Authorities (VDV), Mercedes-Benz developed a city bus range, the O305, which was introduced in 1969. A second generation of city buses, the O405, replaced this product in 1984. The O405, like its predecessor, was standardised with the requirements and experience of public transport companies in mind. Mercedes-Benz alone has produced more than 20,000 of the O305 and O405 units.

Reflecting changing demand in Europe, a lower floor height, from 760 mm to 370 mm, was introduced for both rigid and articulated buses.

Sprinter battery-electric powered minibus **1996**

O405 Cityranger guided bus on Yorkshire Rider test track in Leeds, UK

O405: This is 11.8 m long and is powered by a six-cylinder in-line OM447hLA engine, developing up to 157 kW. Also available are the OM447hLA (184 kW) and the OM447hLA (220 kW). It carries 98 (44 seated) or 106 with 38 seated.

The O405 chassis, in both rigid and articulated form, is marketed in the UK in right-hand-drive form, as the Cityranger. It is bodied by Wright (qv).

O405N: Ultra-low-floor vehicle with a floor height of 370 mm. There are no longer raised platforms in the front section. The horizontal engine moved to the rear off-side corner. Three engine power outputs are available, 157 kW, 184 kW and 220 kW.

A midibus version is available, 10.4 m long.

O405G: This is the articulated version of the O405 and is 17.8 m long. It is powered by an OM447hLA (184 kW) engine. In addition, an intercooled OM447hLA is available for the O405G. The O405G is a pusher-type configuration, power being supplied to the rear trailer axle. Anti-jacknife equipment is fitted. It can carry 154 with 60 seated, or 165 (53 seated).

O405GN: This is a low-floor version of the O405G. The floor height is 370 mm and it is a pusher-type configuration. It carries 163 with 51 seated or 162 (47 seated). It can be equipped with an OM447hLA (184 kW) or OM447hLA (220 kW) engine.

O405NÜL: Interurban low-floor version with a floor height of 370 mm. It has coach seating and luggage racks. Engine power options are 184 kW and 220 kW.

O407: This is an interurban version of the O405. Luggage racks are standard, in addition to coach seating and luggage lockers. It seats 53 with 43 standing, or 49 seated with 50 standing. It can be equipped with two engine types – the OM447hLA (184 kW) or the intercooled OM447hLA.

O550: This looks much more like a coach but is intended for dual-purpose work – regular service operations and excursions. All seats are on the same level, luggage racks and lockers are provided and it can carry 53 seated, 43 standing or 49 seated (50 standing). Engine power options are 184 kW and 220 kW.

The O405, O405G and O407 models are also available as chassis for bodying by outside contractors.

Mercedes-Benz O404 coach **1997**

Guided buses and trolleybuses

O-Bahn: This system consists of buses operating on their own right-of-way, at ground level, in tunnel, or elevated.

The O405 chassis is being marketed in the UK with provision for fitting guide wheels for busway use. This reflects the interest taken in the UK in guided bus operation as an economic alternative to light rail to combat growing traffic congestion.

Hybrid vehicles: Buses are driven by electric motor or diesel, allowing them to leave the overhead wires.

CNG: The low-floor service buses O405N, O405GN and O405NÜ are powered by a compressed natural gas (CNG) system. The engine develops 175 kW (238 hp).

O405T/O405GTD: These are articulated trolleybus versions of the O405G and the O405GT, and were developed with Swiss manufacturer FBW.

O405GNTD: This is the articulated trolleybus version of the O405GN. It is a hybrid vehicle with an OM447hLA Euro-2 engine and is driven by four electric hub motors.

Wright-bodied bus with Mercedes-Benz O405 chassis **1997**

Minibuses

Sprinter 208D, 212D, 214, 308D, 312D, 408D, 412D, 414: minibuses with a GVW up to 3.5 tonnes and seating up to 13. They are powered by either diesel or petrol engines, delivering 58 kW, 70 kW or 77 kW.

Sprinter 410D: 4.6 tonne GVW van for minibus conversion, powered by Mercedes-Benz five-cylinder 63 kW (OM364), 79 kW (OM364A) and 102 kW (OM364LA) diesel engines. It seats up to 15.

Traveliner: This is the name of the complete minibus marketed in the UK. It seats up to 17 and is based on the Sprinter. It is available in normal and high-roof configurations.

308E: This is an electric drive version of the Sprinter.

609D/611D/614D Vario: The 609D is a 5.6 tonne GVW van for minibus conversion, powered by M-B four-cylinder 66 kW engine, to seat up to 20 with 6 standing. The 611D and 614D are uprated versions of the 609D.

709D Vario: 6.6 tonne GVW chassis cowl for small bus bodies, to seat up to 25 with 8 standing. Powered by M-B four-cylinder 66 kW diesel engine. Air suspension is available.

711D: 6.4 tonne GVW chassis with 86 kW diesel engine, for bodywork to take up to 25 seats. Van version available at 5.9 tonnes.

811D Vario: 7.2 tonne GVW chassis cowl for small bus body, seating up to 33 in bus specification. Powered by M-B four-cylinder 85 kW diesel engine with option of G41/

D100A automatic gearbox. Coach specification available.
814D Vario: 7.2 tonne GVW chassis cowl for small bus body, seating up to 33, now available in coach specification. Powered by four-cylinder turbocharged, intercooled 100 kW diesel engine.
814D Vario Bus: This is based on the 814D and is offered in several European countries as a midicoach, seating up to 22, and can be fitted with air conditioning.

Chassis
OF Series: These chassis have front-mounted engines. They are designed for gross vehicle weights from 11 to 16 tonnes and strong U-section side members with riveted cross members help absorb undulations on poor road surfaces.
O Series: Leaf-sprung and air-sprung chassis, with rear-mounted engines, designed to provide the basis of sturdy buses for use in export conditions. They can be supplied in right- and left-hand drive versions, for local bodying. The range is designated according to engine output, overall length and carrying capacity. Though built to ladder frame design, they can be supplied with outriggers to accommodate bodybuilders' needs. The chassis is available in a wheelbase of 5.7 m and passenger doors can be fitted in front of or behind the front axle. Entrance height is 800 mm and body lengths can be 11 or 12 m.

Power units of 250 kW (340 hp) or 280 kW (381 hp) are available and GVW up to 17.6 tonnes can be specified, as can ABS braking.

Coaches
O404: Mercedes-Benz started production of this coach in 1990, with production of the O303 ending in 1992. It comes in three versions: the RH, raised floor; RHD, high deck; SHD, super high deck.

Coaches have contoured side panelling; pressed metal replaces most of the steel framework and this keeps the weight down. Long-term protection against corrosion is helped by cataphoretic dip priming. There is a choice of three engines, from 213 kW (290 hp) to 280 kW (381 hp). The O404 is available in 10, 11 and 12 m lengths. Also available as chassis in three different lengths and heights from 9.2 m to 15 m. Disc brakes are provided on front and rear axles.
O350 Tourismo: This is an intercity coach and is produced by Mercedes-Benz Türk (qv). The engine power is 280 kW.

Contracts: Avtrokon, a major bus manufacturing group in Russia, is still building the original Mercedes-Benz O303 coach under licence and an agreement with EvoBus has extended this to the O405 and O405G articulated bus.

Developments: Mercedes-Benz merged with Daimler-Benz in 1997. The 23 business units of the existing Daimler-Benz group have been assigned to the divisions of passenger cars, commercial vehicles, aerospace and the services, plus the rail and microelectric businesses. The new group is headed by Dr Jurgen Schrempp, former chairman of Daimler-Benz.

Optare Prisma on Mercedes-Benz O405 chassis ***1997***

A new small bus chassis, the Vario O810D, features air suspension on both front and rear axles. It is powered by the new 4.25 litre OM904LA engine and can be specified with manual or automatic gearbox. Disc brakes are fitted all round.

HY-PASSE project: A hydrogen-powered bus is being tested in 1997.

A fuel-cell-powered Mercedes-Benz van is being tested under a project named neCAR. The fuel cell works on the principle of hydrogen combining with oxygen to generate electricity.

Two low-floor interurban buses have been unveiled. The O505 is a 12 m dual-purpose bus with front disc brakes and powered by a Mercedes-Benz diesel engine. The O405 now has revised suspension, driver warning system and intelligent cruise control. It has disc brakes all round and seats 53. A diesel-electric hybrid 709D has gone into service in Portsmouth, with FirstBus subsidiary, Provincial. The original engine and transmission is retained. Added to it is a belt-drive electric motor, powered by lead acid batteries. The project has been funded by EC-based ENTRANCE and the vehicle was designed by Hybrid Vehicles. In diesel mode, the electric motor acts as a generator to recharge the batteries.

From 1997 the O405N is being supplied to the UK as a complete running frame. All panelling, glazing, painting and trimming is carried out by UVG (qv).

A wire guidance system for buses allows vehicles to have the same limited clearances as LRVs without the need for rail infrastructure. Called Inductive Track Guidance it uses two wires buried around 30 mm deep and 300 mm apart in the roadway and energised with a low voltage from substations at 2 km intervals. The bus is fitted with a guidance computer and transponder and can negotiate curves and points. A safety override allows manual control when necessary. The computer system was developed by Daimler-Benz and can be fitted to rigid and articulated Mercedes-Benz chassis. The wire guidance system was developed by Cegelec AEG (see Signalling, Communications and Traffic Control Equipment). Roadworks are far less with this system, which can be installed with a standard slot-cutting tool.

A joint venture, Yaxing-Benz, has been set up by Daimler-Benz and the People's Republic of China, for the production of chassis and vehicles. The joint venture is shared with Yangzhou Motor Coach and forms the biggest coach and bus builder in China, producing 7,000 complete vehicles and 5,000 chassis a year.

UPDATED

Mercedes-Benz Argentina

Mercedes-Benz Argentina SA
A subsidiary of Daimler-Benz AG
PO Box 3890, Av del Libertador 2424, 1425 Buenos Aires, Argentina
Telephone: +54 1 801 7061/8 Telex: 0121335
Main production plant: Ruta Nacional No 3 km 435, 1759 Gonzalez Catan

Products: Buses and bus chassis; purpose-built and truck-derived bus and minibus designs.

Range
OHL1316: Midibus with rear engine.
OH1420; OH1522; OH1526; OHL1419: City bus chassis with rear engine and automatic gearbox.
OF1215: 8.8 m chassis for urban bus work, to carry 26, with a two-door body.
OF1315/1318/1320: 9.5 to 10 m chassis for urban bus work, for bodywork with 29 seats and two doors.
OH/L1316: 9.61 and 10.18 m chassis for urban bus work, to carry 27 to 30 seated, with a two-door body.
OH1316G: 9.61 and 10.18 m chassis as for OH1316, but with Mercedes M366G CNG engine.
OH/L1419: 11 m chassis to carry 34 seated, with a two-door body.

Contracts: Has 66 per cent of the market for buses and coaches in Argentina.

Mercedes-Benz Australia

Mercedes-Benz (Australia) Pty Ltd
A subsidiary of Daimler-Benz AG
PO Box 4214, Mulgrave North, Victoria 3170, Australia
Telephone: +61 3 9566 9266
Fax: +61 3 9561 7088/9566 9147
Senior Executive, Special Product Group: Ian G Boyle

Products: Bus and coach chassis

Range: Chassis are imported from Mercedes-Benz Germany and Mercedes-Benz Brazil, and include the 811, LO814 midibus up to the O404 three-axle coach.

Chassis are either fully built up or assembled from CKD kits. Bus and coach bodies are provided by local operators.

UPDATED

Mercedes-Benz Australia bus with OH1418 chassis ***1996***

Mercedes-Benz Australia midibus ***1996***

CNG MetroRiders are in service with UK operators Cambus and Reading Buses.

Developments: A new venture in Sri Lanka has been announced in which Optare provides transferable technology to create a new bus design for the demanding conditions there. Optare is providing technical support in developing a bus manufacturing operation near Colombo capable of building 500 vehicles a year. Optare is one of three shareholders in the new company formed to build buses, Ceymo Automobile (Pvt) Ltd. Optare's partners are Ceylinco (an insurance company), and Itochu Group (a Japanese trading house).

The new bus, called *ColomboRider* has a Chinese-built chassis from Chaoyong Diesel, Yangzhou. The steel-framed two-door 10 m body carries 60 and combines features from the Optare MetroRider and Delta bodies. Production was expected to start in 1997.

The *MetroRider 4* has been introduced, featuring a Euro-2 engine and compliance with UK DPTAC regulations for mobility-impaired people; 40 have been ordered by North East Bus. There are two lengths, 7.7 m, with 25 seats and 8.4 m, with 31 seats. There is space for 10 standing. A Cummins 6B turbocharged engine drives through an Allison AT545 automatic transmission. There are Fastflow doorway options for simultaneous boarding and alighting for speeding up services on high-density operations.

In 1996, Optare acquired Autobus Classique (qv), Rotherham, England.

A One-Stop-Shop service has been started to combine under one roof vehicle purchase, finance, specification, development, manufacture and after-sales support.

The Mercedes-Benz link has been extended with vehicle financing available through the Optare/Mercedes-Benz Bus Plan.

A new business division of the Optare Group, Optare CoachSales, has been established following the acquisition of the Bova UK importership by Bova BV (qv). CoachSales is concentrating on expanding its direct sales of Bova coaches in both the bus and coach sectors of the UK industry.

Optare ColomboRider bus **1997**

UPDATED

Orion

Orion Bus Industries Inc
5395 Maingate Drive, Mississauga L4W 1G6, Canada
Telephone: +1 905 625 9510 Fax: +1 905 625 5218
President: D K Sheardown
Chief Operating Officer: Kelly Kennedy

American subsidiary
Base Road, RD-1, Oriskany, NY 13424, USA
Telephone: +1 315 768 8101 Fax: +1 315 768 7790

Background: A wholly owned manufacturing subsidiary of Ontario Bus Industries Inc (OBI), the New York manufacturing base was established in 1982 for assembly of Orion buses. In 1995, Western Star Truck Holdings of Kelowna, British Columbia, acquired OBI from the Government of Ontario, renaming it Orion Bus Industries.

Products: Single-deck complete buses, specialist vehicles and tractor-trailer vehicles.

Range
Orion V: An integral heavy-duty vehicle in 9.1 m, 10.6 m and 12.2 m lengths tailored to transit bus, coach or airport shuttle requirements; width is 2.4 or 2.6 m.

The Orion transit bus versions for urban and suburban duties can seat up to 47 plus 34 standees. Axles are from Rockwell and basic power plant is the Detroit Diesel 6V 92TA DDEC 189 kW (253 hp) engine with Allison HT747 four-speed automatic transmission. Optional engines include the Detroit Diesel series 50 and Cummins L10 and C series. Optional transmissions are available from ZF and Voith. Front suspension kneeling and wheelchair lift can be incorporated and air conditioning can be specified.

CNG-powered 9.1 m Orion V of LYNX Orlando **1997**

Orion CNG: A version of Orion V, powered by CNG.
Orion II: A small heavy-duty low-profile front-wheel-drive bus in 6.4 m and 7.6 m lengths and 2.4 m wide. It features a detachable 'power train module' with the engine, transmission, cooling system, front-wheel-drive assembly, suspension and steering all removable as a unit from the main body structure. The wheel bearings and brake system components on all four axles are interchangeable. The design is intended for full transit operations with easy access for disabled and wheelchair passengers by electric ramps. Engine options include the Harvester 7.3 litre providing 126 kW (170 hp) by Navistar or a petrol engine with fuel injection and a catalytic converter. Transmission is the Allison Automatic AT545.

Floor height throughout the passenger compartment is 305 mm. The front suspension kneeling feature is standard, with the floor height at the front reduced to 203 mm. An optional rear kneeling capability lowers the rear door to within 101 mm of the ground. Integral swing-out ramps are provided for both doors.

The 6.4 m version of the Orion II is designed to carry up to 18 ordinary seated passengers or 7 wheelchairs, and the 7.6 m version will take 24 or 9 wheelchairs.

Orion Peoplemover: A tractor-trailer bus combination. The drive engine is a propane-powered Ford V8 producing 142 kW (190 hp) at 4,000 rev/min. Two auxiliary propane-powered, four-cylinder Ford engines,

12.2 m single-door Orion V of LYNX Orlando on suburban express **1997**

6.4 m Orion II showing low flat floor **1997**

one in each vehicle, are provided to operate the air conditioning.

The floors are carpeted, 78 upholstered seats are provided and large wrap-round windows allow unobstructed vision for up to 150 passengers. CCTV permits the driver to monitor the interior of the trailer. The tractor can be easily uncoupled from the trailer and operated independently, as in a city transit operation. While designated for transit operations, this vehicle is particularly promoted for use as an airport shuttle and other non-transit applications.

Orion VI: It has a step height of 353 mm and a very low floor with no steps from front to rear. An integral front ramp helps boarding by wheelchair passengers. It is diesel-powered. An electric version is powered by motors on the rear wheels.

Carbon fibre tanks carry CNG for the Orion VI low-floor bus. Called EDO LiteRiders, they are designed for roof mounting.

Production: Expected to be 1,000 buses in 1996.

Contracts: Include 13 CNG buses for Pierce Transit, Tacoma, 146 low-floor buses for Milwaukee County Transit System, 212 buses for WMATA Washington, 47 Orion VIs for CDTA Albany, 85 buses for RTA New Orleans, 400 CNG Orion VI buses for TTC Toronto and 178, mainly CNG, buses for New York City DoT.

UPDATED

Propane-powered Orion Peoplemover on Niagara Parks service ***1997***

PAZ

Pavlovo Autobusnij Zavid
Pavlovsk, Russia
Exports: c/o Avtoexport
14 Volkhonka, 119902 Moskva
Telephone: +7 095 202 8535/8337
Telex: 411135/4111253

Avtokron President: Boris Kaminsky

Background: PAZ is part of the Avtokron bus manufacturing group, Golizynow, Moskva, the country's largest bus manufacturer. Avtokron builds Mercedes vehicles under licence to EvoBus (see Setra).

Bus production started in 1950.

Products: Buses

Range

PAZ-672V: The 7.15 m PAZ-672V 3.6 m wheelbase bus is 2.44 m wide and suited for narrow city streets and mountain roads. Observation windows are fitted in the roof to suit the vehicle for tourist use. The bus can carry up to 46 with 24 seated, and has a V-8 four-stroke front-mounted petrol engine giving 115 hp (85 kW) with a mechanical four-speed gearbox.

Production: Together with other Avtokron subsidiaries, this is around 2,500 vehicles a year.

Contracts: PAZ minibuses are extensively used throughout the former Soviet Union for both urban bus and other collective transport duties. Examples are also operating in Habana, Cuba.

PAZ-672V bus

Pegaso

Iveco Pegaso
Bus Division
Avda de Aragón 402, 28022 Madrid, Spain
Telephone: +34 1 750 1000 Fax: +34 1 747 8085
President: Juan Molina Vivas
Director, Buses: Luis Martínez Lorenzo
Technical Director: Federico Lobo Sanchéz
Sales Manager, Agencies: Jacinto Casajuana Monell
Sales Manager, Direct: Alberto Romero Benito

Production plants: Valladolid, Venezuela (vans) and Barcelona (buses)

Subsidiaries in: Chile, Belgium, France
Subsidiary company: Seddon Atkinson, Great Britain

Background: The Pegaso range of buses and trucks was the responsibility of the ENASA holding company, in which Iveco had a 60 per cent share until 1994. It is now wholly owned by Iveco.

Products: Complete buses and coaches, including articulated. Bus and coach bodywork. Engines, transmissions and axles.

Range

100 minibus series: The 100.40 is 5.3 m long and has 14 seats, while the 100.56 has 21 seats and is 6.2 m long.

5522: This is a version of the TurboCity built in Barcelona for the Spanish market.

Production: 203 buses were built in 1994 compared with 443 the previous year. Iveco-Pegaso has around 30 per cent of the Spanish market.

Peugeot

Automobiles Peugeot
PO Box 0116, 75 avenue de la Grande Armée, 75761 Paris Cedex 16, France
Telephone: +33 1 40 66 55 11 Fax: +33 1 45 62 70 20
Subsidiary company: Peugeot Talbot (UK) (see Talbot)

Background: In 1980 Peugeot acquired Chrysler's European interests including the Dodge and Karrier commercial vehicle ranges, and though in 1981 these passed to Renault Véhicules Industriels (qv), the Peugeot car-related manufacturing activities still embrace some light and medium van output forming the basis of minibuses.

Products: Mini and midibus chassis, engines and gearboxes.

Range: Chassis and chassis cabs from the Peugeot range of vans and light trucks, suitable as the basis of mini and midibuses with specialist bodywork, are produced by Durisotti amongst others.

SEVEL (Société Européenne des Véhicules Légères), which builds the Ducato for Peugeot, builds also for Peugeot. The vans are marketed by Peugeot as the Boxer and by Citroën as the Relay.

Peugeot Boxer minibus
1996

Plaxton

Plaxton Coach & Bus
Subsidiary of Henlys plc
Eastfield, Scarborough YO11 3BY, England
Telephone: +44 1723 581500 Fax: +44 1723 581328
Managing Director: Neil Berresford
Sales and Marketing Director: David Quainton

Background: Plaxton parent company, Henlys, acquired UK bodybuilder Northern Counties in 1995.

In a joint venture between Henlys UK and Volvo, Prévost (qv) was acquired in 1996 to enable Plaxton to penetrate the North American market.

Products: Coach and bus bodies

Range

Pointer: Built on an aluminium frame and magnagrip riveted, the Pointer is available on chassis including the Dennis Dart, in the 8.5 to 10 m range.

Seating capacities vary from 35 to 43. Features for disabled (DPTAC in UK) include a 240 mm first entrance step and 1.280 m front door aperture.

Dennis Dart midibuses with Plaxton Pointer bodies are running on a guided busway in Ipswich, UK, equipped with guide wheels. The busway is part of a rapid transit-style route that links the railway station, town centre, a large housing development and an out-of-town shopping centre. The Pointer bodywork has semi-coach seating, 'bus stopping' signs and a low floor; it seats 34 with 15 standing.

A low-floor version of the Pointer is on the Dennis Dart SLF or Volvo B6LE chassis and has a floor that kneels to 250 mm from ground level. The normal height is 320 mm. Body width has been increased to 2.4 m, allowing full-width 900 mm seats. Minimum gangway width between front wheel arches is 800 mm. Maximum seating capacity is 44 with space for 19 standing.

Verde: This is avaliable on Volvo or Scania chassis and seats around 50.

Beaver: Bodywork is provided on Mercedes or Iveco Ford 49.10 chassis cowls. That on the Mercedes 709D has 25 seats with room for 8 standing. Bodywork on the Mercedes 811D 4.25 m chassis cowl has seats for 25 also, while on the 4.8 m version there are 33 seats. There are more than 1,500 Beavers in service.

Premiere and *Excalibur:* These coach bodies have been designed to meet ECE R66 roll-over requirements.

The seating has been designed to meet ECE R80, ensuring passenger safety by setting standards of energy absorption. Inertia-reel seat belts and anchorages, where fitted, meet the loading requirements set by ECE R14.

Plaxton Pointer low-floor bus on Shrewsbury park-and-ride ***1997***

Premiere and Excalibur are offered with a range of specifications and can be mounted on many chassis.

Prestige: The steel-framed Prestige is offered as a 3.5 m or 3.7 m high body. The first 3.7 m high versions have been built on Volvo B12R chassis for sale in France. They are designated 350 and are designed specifically for the French market.

Tinted double glazing, pleated curtains and microprocessor-controlled heating are fitted and a Webasto oil-fired heater is available as an option. The

Plaxton Pointer body on Dennis Dart with CNG engine ***1996***

Plaxton Pointer low-floor bus on high-quality route in Brighton, UK ***1997***

standard specification includes 49 reclining seats with inertia-reel seat belts, adjustable footrests and fold-down tables.

Interurban: This is based on the Premiere and comes with fixed seats as standard and a partition around the driving compartment which incorporates space for ticket-issuing equipment. A destination display is provided behind the three-piece windscreen. The body is for medium-distance travel.

An articulated version, based on the Volvo B10M chassis is available, seating 71.

Production: In 1996, 1,730 bus and coach bodies were produced, including 603 Pointers.

Contracts: Deliveries include 11 Beavers for Derby City Transport, 11 Beavers for Rhondda Buses, South Wales, 11 Beavers for Provincial Portsmouth/Gosport, 20 Interurbans for Scottish express services, 18 Pointers for Docklands Transit, London, 35 for Metroline London, 15 low-floor Pointers for Brighton Buses for a special low-floor route, 12 for London & Country, 4 for Midland Red North's Shrewsbury park-and-ride service, 16 for Barton Buses in the Nottingham area, 14, each fitted with an extra baby seat, for Western National, England, 13 Pointers for SMT Edinburgh and 10 articulated Interurbans for Stagecoach Holdings.

Developments: A new Beaver body on the new air-suspension Mercedes-Benz Vario O810D chassis has been styled by Ogle and built at Plaxton's Small Bus division at Anston, England. The standard door aperture is 930 mm with an optional 1,290 mm width. The first entrance step has been reduced to 200 mm from the ground and the interior height is increased by 50 mm.

The Pointer body has been restyled, with new front and rear styling.

UPDATED

Plaxton Beaver body on Mercedes-Benz Vario chassis ***1997***

Plaxton Interurban articulated coach on Stagecoach high-capacity route ***1997***

PMC Adelaide

PMC Adelaide
A division of JRA Limited
365 Bilsen Road, Geeburg, Queensland 4012, Australia
Telephone: +61 8 47 2544 Fax: +61 8 341 2970
General Manager: Ray Spiller
Deputy General Manager: John Berkinshaw
Contracts Manager: Neil Wheatley
National Sales & Marketing Manager: Graham Weekley

Works address: 7 Brandwood Street, Royal Park, South Australia 5014, Australia

Background: PMC Adelaide is one of three bus building companies in Australia previously controlled through the holding company JRA. It is primarily a bodybuilder and assembler of imported chassis from Hino, Japan.

Products: Buses, and bus and coach bodywork.

Range

PMC 160: This bus body has bonded waist panels and seats up to 53. It can be mounted on all recognised bus chassis and can be configured as a low-floor city bus, school bus, day charter coach or touring coach.

PMC Commuter: This is an economy version of the PMC 160 and has a flat windscreen, one-piece fibreglass roof and direct-glazed bonded side windows.

Apollo: This is a body for fitting on to two- or three-axle chassis and is fitted out to luxury standards.

Cub: This is a medium-duty bus for smaller tour and commuter operations, seating 24 to 43. Hopper or top-slide windows are fitted and the windscreen is four-piece. Air conditioning can be fitted, as can a walk-in Airporter luggage compartment. It can be fitted out as a school bus, two-door service bus or as a hotel courtesy vehicle.

Apollo: Touring coach on Volvo and other two- or three-axle chassis, with air conditioning.

PMC Cub bus body ***1996***

PMC Commuter bus ***1996***

PMC 160 interurban bus ***1996***

Contracts: Supply of city bus bodywork to local government transit authority TransAdelaide on MAN Australia running units — 307 units with ultra-low-floor, ramps and wheelchair and handicap facilities. Delivery is one per week.

Developments: A new Cadet midibus chassis has been unveiled.

UPDATED

PMC 160 ultra-low-floor city bus with wheelchair ramp
1996

Ponticelli

Ponticelli Frères
Zone Industrielle, 77220 Gretz-Armainvilliers, France
Telephone: +33 1 64 42 14 00 Fax: +33 1 64 07 19 04

Products: Bus chassis

Range
PR200: Ladder-frame chassis for 9 m overall length bodywork.
PR230: Ladder-frame chassis, 9.25 m to 11.8 m long for maximum GVW of 17 tonnes.
Electric Bus: 6.72 m long, 8.4 tonnes GVW with maximum load of 3.4 tonnes front and 5.4 tonnes rear. Leroy Somer PMV160R 400 V electric motor.

UPDATED

Ponticelli Electric Bus with Gruau body
1996

Porter

Howard Porter (1936) Pty Ltd
PO Box 76, Hamilton Hill, WA 6163, Australia
Telephone: +61 9 337 3533 Fax: +61 9 331 2931
Executive Director: Thomas G Porter
Managing Director: Colin R Stewart

Products: Bus and coach bodywork, including articulated.

Range
Commuter: 42-seat/25-standee low-floor city bus and articulated versions. Wide entrance door, rear exit door, low floor and step height. An articulated bus, based on Mercedes 405 running units, is available.
Tourist tram: This replica vehicle on a Mitsubishi chassis has wooden seats, drop sash windows, clerestory roof and an open doorway.
Aurora: 33-seat high-specification touring coach with modern styling, powered by rear-mounted V8 diesel.

Bodies have been mounted on chassis from Mercedes, Isuzu, Leyland, DAF, Scania, Renault, MAN, Volvo, Hino and Mitsubishi, as well as custom-built models.

Commuter articulated bus on Mercedes O305 chassis for Transperth

Prévost

Prévost Car Inc
35 Gagnon Boulevard, Sainte-Claire G0R 2V0, Canada
Telephone: +1 418 883 3391 Fax: +1 418 883 4157
President: André Normand
Vice President, Sales: François Bouffard

Background: In a joint venture between Henlys UK and Volvo, Prévost was acquired in 1996 to enable Henlys and Volvo subsidiary company, Plaxton, to penetrate the North American market.

Prior to the takeover, Prévost was state owned, by the Province of Quebec.

Products: Coaches, including articulated.

Range: Includes the Mirage XL on a three-axle underframe and the H5-60, a five-axle 18 m articulated coach. A 12 m version of the articulated coach is the H3-40. Running gear is mainly Detroit Diesel engines with Allison automatic transmission.

The H3-45 was introduced in 1995. It has three axles, accommodates up to 58 passengers and is 13.7 m in length.

Prévost H5-60 articulated coach operated by Mid-American

Prévost is offering Volvo driveline components and the tri-axle Volvo B12 chassis, with a Plaxton body, is being sold in North America.

VERIFIED

Q-Bus

Q-Bus BV
Cartesiusweg 90, 3534 BD Utrecht, Netherlands
Telephone: +31 30 447799 Fax: +31 30 447788

Products: Minibuses

Range: Van conversions and coachbuilt minibuses are constructed on Ford Transit, Mercedes-Benz, Iveco TurboDaily, Peugeot Boxer and Citröen Jumper base vehicles.

NEW ENTRY

Q-Bus conversion on Peugeot Boxer 350LH
1997

Qinling

Qinling Automotive
1 Xiexing Road, Zhongliangshan, Jiulongpo District, Chongqing, People's Republic of China
Telephone/Fax: +86 811 66 4125
Manager: Wu Yun

Background: Qinling was set up with backing from Isuzu (15 per cent), Chongqing Automotive Industrial Co (75 per cent) and United Capitals Co (10 per cent) in 1985.

Products: Manufacture of light-duty trucks and buses

Rába

Rába
PO Box 50, 9002 Gyór, Hungary
Telephone: +36 96 412111/414111
Fax: +36 96 414 3111

Products: Chassis for buses and coaches.

Range
B147.00: High-floor bus chassis for body to maximum weight of 18.1 tonnes and powered by Rába D2156.HM6 naturally aspirated 10 litre diesel engine driving through a six-speed S6-90U manual gearbox; leaf springs.
B147.10: As for B147.00 but with parabolic leaf springs and D2156.MT6 turbocharged engine.
B147.60/B188.60: Bus chassis with air suspension. Powered by D2156.HM6 engine driving through the S6-90 gearbox. The B188.60 is powered by the MT6 turbocharged version.

A three-axle coach chassis has been developed.

Rába chassis with Ikarus 395 coach bodies in Budapest ***1996***

Rába three-axle chassis with Ikarus coach body
1996

RAF

RAF Latvija
18 Aviacijas Street, 3001 Jelgava, Latvia
Telephone: +371 27191/41519 Fax: +371 29224

Products: Minibuses

Background: Formerly at Riga, RAF started producing buses in 1954.

Range
RAF 22038-02: This is a van-derived minibus seating 12. It has a length of 5.07 m and is 1.94 m wide. The headroom is 1.4 m and the overall height is 2.07 m. The gross vehicle weight is 2.74 tonnes. It has a four-stroke front-mounted 100 hp (73.5 kW) petrol engine and drives through a four-speed synchromesh gearbox. It has independent front suspension and leaf springs. A luxury version with additional trim and other extras is available.

UPDATED

RAF minibus
1997

Renault

Renault VI
40 rue Pasteur, PO Box 302, 92156 Suresnes Cedex, France
Telephone: +33 1 40 99 71 11 Fax: +33 1 40 99 75 88
Director General: Shémaya Levy
Secretary General: Marc Randon
Commercial Director: Pierre Colmant
Manufacturing plants: Annonay and Vénissieux

Overseas bus manufacturing subsidiaries and associates: Algeria, Côte d'Ivoire, Morocco, Senegal, Spain, Tunisia, UK (see below)
Assembly operations: Morocco, Bolivia, Australia, Indonesia

Robin Hood

Robin Hood Vehicle Industries Ltd
Unit 4, Barton Park Industrial Estate, Chickenhall Lane, Eastleigh SO50 6RR, England
Telephone: +44 1703 613374 Fax: +44 1703 613391
Managing Director: Robbie Hood
Overseas Sales Department Director: Maurice Anelli
Sales Manager: Dave Bishop

Products: Minibus bodies; refurbishment.

Range
RH2000: Midicoach with an innovative lift-up front for easy maintenance.

Developments: Robin Hood was bought out by Buddens Coaches of Romsey early in 1997.

UPDATED

Robin Hood Cacciamali Midi coaches ***1996***

Rocar

SC Rocar SA
3–5 Ostrov Street, Bucureşti 5, Romania
Telephone: +40 1 337 3054/2860 Fax: +40 1 337 2862
General Manager: Dan Vuerich
Sales & Marketing Manager: Emilian Vladuca
Head of Export/Import Department: Dan Mánescu

Background: Rocar SA, established in 1956, and De Simon srl, Osoppo, Italy (qv), agreed in 1993 on incorporation of a new Italian-Romanian joint venture, Rocar De Simon, to market buses; 55 per cent of the capital shares are owned by the Italian group; marketing and after-sales service is by both companies.

De Simon bus models are made under licence in the Rocar plants in Bucureşti and marketed under the Rocar De Simon name. Former DAC, Roman and Rocar Romanian-designed buses are all now produced under the Rocar name.

Products: Buses, trolleybuses, minibuses

Rocar Range
Trolleybuses
E212: Two-axle bus 11.57 m long and 3.7 m high including electrical gear. It has a kerb weight of 11,100 kg and seats 22 with 73 standing. It has three doors. The TN76 traction motor is mounted between the axles and is air cooled. It is rated at 125 kW. Air suspension is fitted.
E217: Articulated version of 212E.
E312: As for 212 series but with chopper control.
Diesel bus range
U112/U117: Underfloor engine, two-axle and articulated city buses
T111: Interurban rear-engine bus based on MAN licence, now modernised in appearance.

Rocar De Simon Range
T207: Minibus with front engine.
Starbus UL70: This is a city bus 12 m long.
Starbus IL70: Similar to the UL70, but for intercity work. Also 12 m long.
Starbus US70: Articulated version of the UL70, 18 m long.
Starbus Pininfarina GV: A high-floor touring coach, 12 m long.

Contracts: The main markets are Romania, Syria, Bulgaria, Uruguay, Argentina, Colombia, Russia, Ukraine (trolleybuses), Albania (city buses), Egypt (minibuses) and Hungary.

Developments: A new range of city buses with MAN and Rába engines is available. Urban versions have Renault and Mercedes engines.

UPDATED

Rocar Starbus UL70 12 m city bus ***1997***

Rocar E312 trolleybus ***1997***

Säffle

Säffle Karosseri AB
A wholly owned subsidiary of Volvo Bus Corporation, Sweden
PO Box 59, 66100 Säffle, Sweden
Telephone: +46 533 12580 Fax: +46 533 15645

Products: Bus bodies, including articulated.

Range: Bodies are offered only on Volvo-built chassis primarily for the Nordic market. Both structure and panelling are made of aluminium, with front and rear end in glass-reinforced plastic. City bus, dual-purpose, touring coach and express bus bodies are mounted on Volvo

B10M, B10MA articulated, B10B, B10L, B10LA and B10M three-axle chassis (14.5 m, three/two-door), B9M, B10B (rear-engined, city bus).

System 2000: Bus models, rigid and articulated, for urban and interurban use. The rigid vehicle is on a Volvo B10M chassis and seats 50 with 21 standing. It is 13 m long and 2.58 m wide.

The articulated version is on a Volvo B10M articulated chassis and is 18 m long, 2.58 m wide. It seats 66 with 50 standing.

The Säffle System 2000 is being built by Aabenraa in Denmark and under licence by Walter Alexander Belfast and Xian Silver Bus Corporation, China.

UPDATED

Säffle-bodied Volvo B10L articulated bus
1996

Salah-Al-Din

Salah-Al-Din
Iskhandariya, Iraq

Products: Commercial vehicles including truck-derived minibuses. Substantial numbers of vehicles to designs originated by Renault have been assembled in Iraq under the name Salah-Al-Din. Designs include light trucks and vans converted locally for bus use.

Sanos

Fabrika Za Avtobusi 'Il Oktomvri'
U1 516 br 10, 91000 Skopje, Macedonia
Telephone: +389 91 38815 Telex: 51148
Associated with FAP-Famos

Products: Bus and coach bodies including articulated and trolleybuses.

Range: The factory, known as FAS, is part of the commercial vehicle manufacturing combine based on FAP-Famos (qv). Production of bodywork on FAP-Famos chassis and completion of integral vehicles takes place under the Sanos name. Amongst vehicles produced are coaches based on Mercedes-licensed designs, standard and articulated, integral and chassised buses, and most recently a prototype articulated trolleybus based on Škoda electric equipment in a FAP-Famos chassis.

Contracts: 10 TMZ-Sanos buses have been delivered to Yaroslavl, Russia.

UPDATED

Sanos bodywork on FAP-Famos S115 city bus

Saracakis

Saracakis Brothers SA
PO Box 1200, 71 Leoforos Athinon, GR101, Base 73, Athens, Greece
Telephone: +30 1 346 5321 Fax: +30 1 346 7329

Background: The firm is the exclusive agent of Volvo in Greece.

Products: Bus bodies, including articulated.

Contracts: Saracakis bodied and supplied 72 Volvo B10M articulated buses to the Urban Transport Organisation of Thessaloniki (OASTH); 12 are two-axle and the rest articulated. The vehicles were delivered during 1993 and complement the OASTH fleet of nearly 500.

Developments: A new city bus body was launched in 1996.

UPDATED

Saracakis-bodied Volvo of East Crete Bus Services at Iraklion
1997

Scania

Scania Buses & Coaches
641 81 Katrineholm, Sweden
Telephone: +46 150 58500 Fax: +46 150 53230
Managing Director: Arne Karlsson
Financial Director: Håkan Frisk
Export Director: Rolf Teljeby
Technical Director: Per Hallberg
Public Relations Officer: Gunnar Boman

Scania HQ
151 87 Södertälje
Telephone: +46 8 5538 1000 Fax: +46 8 5538 5559

Bus manufacturing subsidiaries
Scania do Brasil SA, São Paulo (qv)
DAB a/s, Denmark
Scania Kapena, Poland

Scania Bus and Coach (UK) Ltd, Tongwell, Milton Keynes MK15 8HB
Telephone: +44 1908 210210 Fax: +44 1908 210186
Managing Director: Don McIntosh
National Bus Sales Manager: Peter Crawford
Scania Vehicle Management Ltd
Managing Director: Gordon Waldron
For England, Wales and Northern Ireland, coach sales are through:
Scania Bus & Coach Ltd
Claylands Avenue, Worksop S81 7DJ
Telephone: +44 1909 500822 Fax: +44 1909 500165
Managing Director: Don MacIntosh

Scania OmniCity ultra-low-floor bus **1997**

Background: Scania is one of the world's leading manufacturers of trucks and buses for heavy transport, and also of industrial and marine engines. It has 21,000 employees and has been in existence for more than 100 years.

The Danish bus builder DAB (qv) was acquired by Scania in 1994. DAB will continue production of its current range.

In France there is a partnership between Scania and Irizar (qv) and Scania-France now represents Irizar.

Scania started a joint venture with the Polish company Kapena, Slupsk, for the assembly of trucks and buses in Poland. The first Polish-built MaxCi rolled out in 1994. The new company is known as Scania Kapena SA. The start-up workforce was around 50.

Scania started a Russian joint venture in 1995. The company is called Russcan.

Scania become a stand-alone company in 1996 following the break-up of SAAB Scania Holdings and is wholly owned by Investor AB, a Swedish public investment company.

Scania Vehicle Management Ltd was launched in 1996, for contract hire, rental and support.

Products: Rear-engined bus chassis made up of units designed either for use in integral construction, or with chassis frames for conventional bodyworking, as single- or double-deck and articulated vehicles. Conventional front-engined chassis. Bodywork for integral models. Kits. DAB compact city bus (qv).

Range
Chassis
Rear-engined chassis with transverse or longitudinal power plants, and front-engined chassis.

Rear-engined chassis are primarily designed for integral bodywork. Chassis with longitudinal engines are designated K93 and K113 (and K113T with trailing axle bogie), whilst that with transverse rear engine is designated N113.

The power train on Scania chassis is by the DSC range of engines. Compressed natural gas (CNG) and ethanol versions are available. The engines are fitted with EDC (Electronic Diesel Control) and meet Euro-2 emission regulations.

There is a choice of G777 five-speed manual, G801 eight-speed manual and GR801 gearboxes with CS and CAG options. With CS (Comfort Shift), the gear change movement is transmitted through an electric/pneumatic link. The gear is only engaged when the clutch pedal is depressed.

With CAG (Computer-Aided Gear changing) a microprocessor suggests the appropriate gear, which is engaged when the clutch is depressed. The G801R has Scania's integral hydraulic retarder. Automatic gearboxes supplied are by Voith (qv).

A hybrid bus, based on DAB technology, is powered by electricity with a diesel alternative. Final drive is by three-phase asynchronous motors.

N113 range
The N113 range of chassis is made up of a front section comprising the front axle, front suspension and driver controls, and a rear section with engine, transmission and rear-axle assembly. Power comes from the range of Scania's 11 litre units, with power outputs varying from 164 to 239 kW (220 to 320 hp). Scania's DSC 1124 engine meets Euro-2 emission regulations. Boarding heights are low – around 200 mm with kneeling function.

N113DR and N113A: These are produced for double-deck and articulated buses respectively.

N113 ALB: This is a pusher articulated bus chassis.

CN113 MaxCi: Around 65 per cent of the floor is flat with no steps and the rear raised section slopes gently to the rear. The bodywork has three doors, two with no steps and the rear one, behind the rear axle, with two steps. The windows are direct glazed.

A version of the CN113 MaxCi has been developed for the UK market. It has an entrance/exit step height of 320 mm (reducing to 230 mm with kneeling), with a gangway floor height of 350 mm over two-thirds of the vehicle length.

Note: The C prefix denotes that the bodywork is by Scania.

L113 range
The L113 chassis for suburban buses has a rear engine that is inclined to allow a longer and lower floor. The chassis can be adapted to lengths between 11 and 13 m. It is powered by the Scania DS11 34 engine, driving through a choice of three gearboxes, including computer-aided, fully automatic and manual.

The L113 CLL has a low floor up to the rear axle.

FlexCi: An ultra-low-floor bus chassis having no step at the front. It is based on the L chassis range and has a floor height of 350 mm at the front. An interurban version has a floor height of 650 mm. Engines from 164 to 238 kW are available (220 to 320 hp). The engine unit is inclined and in line, keeping down capital costs. As a city bus, the

Scania Axcess-ultralow bus operated by Bullocks, Cheadle, UK **1996**

Scania OmniCity articulated ultra-low-floor bus **1997**

chassis can carry up to 120. As an interurban model, it carries around 60. A choice of straight or angled entrance is available. One, two or three doors can be fitted, with sloping, stepped, medium height or low-floor options. Minimum step height is 320 mm from the ground.

Axcess-ultralow: This is for the UK market and offers a step height of 320 mm, which can be further lowered to 200 mm when kneeling. In standard layout, the vehicle has 47 seats. The drive train is that of the L113CRL, with a Scania 11 litre engine and ZF 4HP500 automatic gearbox mounted in line with the chassis. The use of a drop-beam front axle has allowed Wright (qv) to build a body with a low step-free entrance suitable for wheeled shopping trolleys, pushchairs and wheelchairs.

Front engine

Two types of front-engine chassis are available, F93H and F113H, both heavy-duty designs for city and transit routes primarily in third-world markets. They are largely based on truck components to facilitate service and spares back-up, and have 9 or 11 litre engines.

Front-engine chassis are fitted with conventional leaf springs.

All vehicles have direct-acting air brakes with separate circuits for front and rear which conform to EC specifications. The air-operated parking brake acts on the rear wheels and is controlled by a lever on the instrument panel. ABS is available as an option. Easy-action hydraulic power-steering with automatic self-centring is fitted.

Scania N113CRL with Wright Pathfinder body operated by Lowland Bus, Scotland ***1996***

Coach and express bus chassis

K93 CLB: This has a 9 litre engine. It can also have an 11 litre engine (*K113*) and automatic transmission.

K113 TLA: This is fitted with a twin rear axle and independent front wheel suspension, intended principally for double-deck and high-floor touring coaches. It has a floor height of 465 mm.

A right-hand-drive version, the K113 TRA, is available in the UK.

K113 CLA: This has an independent front wheel suspension to improve road handling. Three engine options are available, one with electronic diesel control, and the gearbox is Scania's seven-speed GR801 with Comfort Shift or Computer-Aided Gear changing. It has ABS braking.

K113TRB: This has three axles and was introduced in 1995. It is being sold in the UK.

Scania L113 chassis with single-deck Wright body in Birmingham ***1997***

Mayne of Manchester Scania N113 with East Lancs Cityzen double-deck body ***1997***

Factory-built buses

OmniCity: This ultra-low-floor bus has been developed with innovative styling and bodywork of aluminium alloy. It has a transverse Euro-2 engine inclined at 60° which allows four seats above the engine compartment. It is powered by a 9 litre engine driving through an automatic transmission. The engine is inclined, allowing a double door to be provided behind the rear axle. The centre aisle is 120 mm wider than normal and 880 mm wide at the front for ease and speed of access. The step height at the front is 320 mm (90 mm lower when kneeling) and there are no steps inside the vehicle. The bodywork is Alusuisse bolted aluminium alloy.

An articulated version is available.

Production of other vehicles currently consists of the CN113 city and transit bus on the N113 chassis, available in two versions: a standard model and a city low-floor model. The Scania CN113 is designed for one-person operation on very busy local routes. It has a transverse rear-mounted engine contained in a soundproof compartment. The standard version seats up to 50, and both models are available with three doors and a variety of door configurations.

The CN113A pusher articulated 18 m bus on the N113A chassis is also produced.

CL113: This is an interurban bus based on the L113 chassis, 13 m long and 2.6 m wide, seating 54, with 7 m^3 luggage space extending across the width of the bus.

All factory-built Scania buses have integral bodywork. Strong impact protection from floor to window level is fitted to both sides of the vehicle and covered with stainless steel sheet. Thick steel plates provide extra protection in front of and alongside the driver's position.

All rear-engine chassis are equipped with full air suspension front and rear which actively suppresses roll. Constant boarding height is maintained by level valves regardless of load. Kneeling is also available.

Production: Order bookings in South America declined by about 24 per cent. The total market in western Europe, measured as the number of buses and coaches for more than 30 passengers, increased by 4.7 per cent to 16,385 buses. Scania increased its market share from 8.8 per cent to 9.9 per cent. Spain was Scania's largest European market. In Portugal, Scania doubled its sales and became the market leader. In the UK, Scania received its largest-ever single order, totalling 144 city and intercity buses. In 1996 Brazil was, again, Scania's largest bus market, despite a decline by 11 per cent to approximately 15,000 buses.

Shanghai SK562GP articulated trolleybus ***1996***

Contracts: Maynes, Manchester, England, has taken delivery of four Scania N113DRB chassis with East Lancs

Guided buses
Scania has supplied Yorkshire Rider with N113CRLs with

Smit

Smit Carrosseriefabriek BV
PO Box 19, 8501 BA Joure, Netherlands
Telephone: +31 5138 12610 Fax: +31 5138 17434

Background: In February 1996 DAF Bus bought 56 per cent of the shares of Smit, Berkhof obtained 14 per cent and a private investor obtained 30 per cent.

Products: Mostly coaches are built, though there are suburban/commuter versions.

Range
Orion: Luxury coach body in high-floor and twin rear axle versions.
Economy: For interurban work and similar duties, this seats 52 with 26 standing. It is 12 m long and 3.2 m high, and has two-door bodywork.
Interliner: This seats 50 to 54 with up to 28 standing and is 3.45 m high.
Jupiter: This is the double-deck version of the Orion and carries up to 78.

Smit also builds city bus and shuttle bus bodies.

Smit Orion Jupiter double-deck coach **1997**

Contracts: Smit manufactures 22 per cent of the total number of Dutch coaches and exports to Belgium, Germany, Africa and Scandinavia.

Developments: DAF Bus International took over Smit in 1996.

UPDATED

Spartan

Spartan Motors Inc
PO Box 440, 1000 Reynolds Road, Charlotte, MI 48813, USA
Telephone: +1 517 543 6400 Fax: +1 517 543 7728
President: John Sztykiel
International Sales Director: David Gruber
International Sales Manager: Edward Hendler

Products: Custom designed and built chassis for buses, fire appliances, coaches, motor homes and specialist applications.

Range: Front- and rear-engined ladder-frame chassis in various formats. The chassis are available in various lengths with a range of GVWs and feature air brakes, leaf spring or air suspension and diesel or natural gas power; automatic transmissions.

Spartan is the owner of a manufacturing facility in Mexico to make bus chassis for the Latin American market.

In 1995 Spartan entered into an agreement to produce chassis for Carpenter Manufacturing, USA.

The Spartan single-deck chassis is being imported from the USA for bodying by East Lancs (qv). It is powered by a rear-mounted Cummins B-series engine driving through an Allison MTB643 gearbox. Suspension is full air and the brakes are S-cam drum.

Developments: Spartan is offering a low-floor chassis.

UPDATED

Spartan single-deck chassis with East Lancs body with Yorkshire Traction **1997**

Specialty Vehicles

Specialty Vehicles Manufacturing Corp
16371 Gothard Street, Suite C, Huntington Beach, CA 92647-3652 USA
Telephone: +1 714 848 8455 Fax: +1 714 848 2114
President: Nancy Munoz
Marketing & Sales Manager: Jacqueline Vargas

Products: People movers, replica trolleys, road trains and buses.

Range
There are four product lines, producing road trains (trams in USA), replica trolleys, buses and minibuses.
4000 series: This consists of a 7 m power car and 7.3 m trailer, carrying 18 and 28 passengers.
5000 series: A mid-sized vehicle available in lengths from 7 to 9.1 m with several floor plans. The exterior is all glass-fibre with the sides laminated to a steel framework.
Old Time trolleys: This is a series of replica vehicles designed to look like trams. The standard version of the 3000 series seats 31 and is powered by a Cummins B-series 5.9 litre engine.

Specialty Vehicles replica trolley car **1996**

Specialty Vehicles electric bus

Electric versions are available of both buses and reproduction trolleys.

Contracts: Road trains have been shipped to Singapore zoo and nine large Old Time trolleys have been supplied to South Korea.

Hino and Specialty Vehicles have entered into an agreement to supply chassis to the USA for Barth RSV to build replica Old Time trolley bodies. The complete vehicles are for sale in Japan and Eastern Asia.

Developments: The Party Trolley is based on a classic pub, with bar, lounge tables, sink, refrigerator, air conditioning and television.

UPDATED

Spijkstaal

Spijkstaal Elektro BV
PO Box 9, 3200 AA Spijkenisse, Netherlands
Telephone: +31 101 612266 Fax: +31 101 623958
Managing Director: Ing W Heijboer
Works address: Zilstraat 9, 3201 CX Spijkenisse

Products: Electric vehicles

Range

Ecobus: This seats 32 passengers. It has a range of 70 km and a battery change takes 3 min. It is 6.7 m long, 2 m wide and 2.6 m high. Empty weight, including batteries, is 4.3 tonnes and the floor height is 340 mm. The motor is rated at 25 kW at 96 V. The battery pack is 96 V, 376 Ah.
Caravelle: This is a microbus version, based on a Volkswagen van, seating 8, and has nickel-cadmium batteries, a 60 kW motor and a top speed of 100 km/h. Battery recharging takes one hour.

A diesel-electric hybrid ultra-lightweight bus is being built for service in Rotterdam by a consortium of Fokker, Special Products, Holec Ridderkerk and Spijkstaal.

UPDATED

Spijkstaal low-floor electric Ecobus **1996**

Steyr

Steyr Bus GmbH
PO Box 377, 1111 Wien, Austria
Telephone: +43 1 764511 Fax: +43 1 763124
Managing Director: Anders Galfvensjö
Directors of Marketing & Sales: Hans Schmid
Harald Rumpel

Background: Parent company is Volvo Bus Corporation, Sweden, which bought 75 per cent in 1990. A 61 per cent share in the Polish commercial vehicle manufacturer FS was acquired in 1995.

A controlling interest in Avia (qv) was acquired in 1996 by Daewoo (qv) and Steyr-Daimler-Puch, which is a separate company, and Daewoo bought 65 per cent of Steyr-Daimler-Puch in October 1995.

Products: Bus bodies based on Volvo chassis and minibuses of own design.

Range

SS11 Transitbus: This city bus is on the Volvo B10B rear-engined chassis. Power is from the Volvo THD102KD, THD102KF, THD103KF, THD103KB or THD103KD diesel engines, encapsulated, and driving through ZF 4HP 500/590 or ZF 5HP 500/590 automatic gearboxes, each with integral retarder. It can also be mounted on the Volvo B10L low-floor no-step chassis.

The body is integral, 11.7 m long, and is of welded steel. There are three doors on the standard version. There are seats for 36 and standing room for 56.
SL12: Intercity bus on Volvo B10B rear-engine chassis. It has the Volvo EGS (electropneumatic Easy Gear Shift) G7 box. The body is of similar construction to the SS11.
SG18MU articulated: An articulated version of the Transitbus on the Volvo B10M mid-engine chassis. The SG18MU, which has a length of 18 m and a width of 2.5 m, has seats for 48 and maximum standing room for 106.
Steyr City-bus: The smaller City-bus is aimed at the market for small buses for park-and-ride and dial-a-bus systems, special transport for the disabled and city-centre operations. It has a platform height of 300 mm, no steps or raised platforms and an internal height of more than 2 m. It has 15 seats and room for 15 standing. Wheelbase is 3.3 m, wheel track 1.72 m and overall length 5.8 m. Turning circle is 14 m.

Contracts: Steyr buses have been sold in recent years to Germany (30 to Berlin, on B10L, in 1997), Switzerland and France as well as in Austria, where Steyr holds a market share of about 25 per cent. CKD kits have been exported to Jelcz, Poland.

Developments: In 1995, the sales and marketing side of OeAF/Gräf & Stift was merged with that of Steyr in a new company, OeAF & Steyr Nutzfahrzeuge OHG (qv), which is now the major supplier of buses over 10 tonnes in Austria.

UPDATED

Steyr City-bus on Volvo B10L ultra-low-floor chassis  **1996**

Steyr City-bus minibus with flat floor **1995**

B10M articulated: The articulated bus chassis based on

World Trans

World Trans Inc
PO Box 2946, Hutchison, KS 67504-2946, USA
Telephone: +1 316 283 9500 Fax: +1 316 283 5252
President: Phil Roberts
Sales Manager: Carol M Walle

Background: World Trans was formerly Collins.

Products: Mini and midibus bodies and specialist conversions.

Range
Civitran: This is based on the Ford E350 9.5 tonne van chassis cowl. It carries up to 16, or seven plus two wheelchairs. The vehicle is 5.7 m long and 1.9 m wide.
Diplomat: This 7.32 m bus carries up to 25 and can have a wheelchair lift.
3000 Series: A rear-engined shuttlebus with a Cummins 6BT5.9 litre engine. The specification allows dual doors with the option of a mid-mounted door on the offside or nearside. It seats between 18 and 20.

UPDATED

Wright

Robert Wright & Son (Coachworks) Ltd
Galgorm Industrial Estate, Fenaghy Road, Ballymena BT42 1PY, Northern Ireland
Telephone: +44 1266 41212/1246 233962
Fax: +44 1266 49703
Chairman: C T Hurst
Chief Executive: William T Wright
Assistant Managing Director: Jeff Wright
Sales Director: Jack Kernohan
UK Sales Manager: Charles Moseby
Design Director: Trevor Erskine
Materials Director: Ian Kerr
Aftersales Manager: George Richards

Products: Bus bodies

Range: All bus bodies are constructed on chassis, using the Alusuisse system. The framework is jig-built. There are variants for disabled passengers and a choice of lifts.
Nim-Bus: This is a small intercity bus on Mercedes-Benz 709D or 811D chassis, seating 29 or 33.
Endurance: This city bus body has a dual door layout and seats for 51 with up to 25 standing. Mounted on Scania N113 or Volvo B10B chassis.
Pathfinder 320: This is a very low-floor city bus body on the Scania N113CRL chassis or Dennis Lance SLF chassis. There is no step between the front entrance and forward of the rear axle. It seats up to 35 in dual-door configuration and 40 with a single door. Up to 32 standing can be carried. The floor height is 320 mm and the floor is level. It has a curved windscreen in up to three sections and the side windows can be gasket glazed or directly bonded. It is to full UK requirements for disabled people.
Axcess-ultralow: Introduced in 1995 with Alusuisse construction and the Scania L113CRL chassis. It is 12 m long and seats 49. The floor is flat up to the rear axle. The entrance step height is 320 mm and can be lowered to 200 mm.
Crusader: Ultra-low-floor midibus body on the Dennis Dart SLF or Volvo B6LE midibus chassis. It is of bolted aluminium construction for structural integrity and ease of repair. It is available on chassis from 9.4 m to 10.8 m with seating capacities up to 51. A two-door version is available. The step-free entrance is 1.3 m wide and the ride height is 320 mm with a kneeling option to 235 mm. Glazing is rubber gasket.

Wright Crusader ultra-low-floor midibus body on Dennis Dart SLF chassis ***1997***

Wright Axcess-ultralow bus on Scania L113 chassis on Edinburgh—Hawick service, Scotland ***1997***

Contracts: FirstBus, UK, is taking 145 Scania Axcess-ultralow buses with bodywork by Wrights over a two-year period starting April 1997. A further 102 will be bodied by Wrights, on Volvo chassis. 38 Crusader midibuses have been delivered to FirstBus subsidiaries, UK. Travel West Midlands, Birmingham, has taken delivery of 50 Crusaders on Volvo B6LE chassis. Travel West Midlands has taken delivery of 65 Liberator bodies on B10B chassis with an option for a further 150 on B10L chassis. Bus Eirann is taking nine Endurance bodies on Volvo B10B chassis and a Liberator on B10L chassis. Action Bus Canberra has ordered 25 Crusaders on Dennis Dart SLF chassis.

Developments: A 12 m bus on the Volvo B10L chassis, the *Liberator* is an ultra-low-floor body seating 47 with around 20 standing. It has an entrance height of 320 mm, which kneels to 230 mm. There are no steps along the floor as far as the back two rows of seats. It ramps gently over the rear axle. The Liberator carries 70, with 46 seated.

Scania distributor Scantruck has formed an agreement with Wrights to become parts and service distributor for the South East of England.

UPDATED

Wright Liberator ultra-low-floor bus body on Volvo B10L chassis in Manchester ***1997***

Wright Nim-Bus on Mercedes-Benz 811D chassis with Trent Motor Traction, England ***1996***

TROLLEYBUS TRACTION EQUIPMENT

Company Listing by Country

CZECH REPUBLIC
Škoda

GERMANY
Kiepe
Siemens

HUNGARY
Ganz Ansaldo

ITALY
Ansaldo
Breda
Firema

JAPAN
Mitsubishi
Toshiba

ROMANIA
UMEB

RUSSIA
Dynamo

UK
Brush
Eaton

USA
Adtranz
Electric Transit
GE Transportation Systems
GM Hughes

Classified Listing

AC PROPULSION
Adtranz
Brush
GE Transportation Systems
Kiepe
Mitsubishi

ARTICULATED
Adtranz
Breda
Ganz Ansaldo
Siemens

CHOPPER CONTROL
Breda
Firema
Ganz Ansaldo
Kiepe
Škoda
Toshiba

HYBRID – DUAL MODE
Adtranz
Breda
Siemens

LOW-FLOOR
Breda
Ganz Ansaldo
Siemens
Škoda

THYRISTOR CONTROL
Dynamo
Škoda
Toshiba

Adtranz

ABB Daimler-Benz Transportation GmbH
USA subsidiary
ABB Daimler-Benz Transportation (USA) Inc
1501 Lebanon Church Road, Pittsburgh, PA 15236-1491, USA
Telephone: +1 412 655 5335 Fax: +1 412 655 5860
President: Ray Betler
Vice President, Marketing: Kenneth Fraelich
(See main entry under Rail Vehicles and Traction Equipment)

Products: AC and DC electric propulsion equipment and control systems; refurbishment and support services.

Contracts: 236 sets of AC propulsion equipment have been supplied for Breda dual-mode articulated trolleybuses for Seattle, the largest AC powered fleet in North America. Some 88 sets of AC inverter propulsion equipment and 132 AC auxiliary inverters supplied for Taipei metro cars.

Other contracts, in association with other companies, include 20 articulated trolleybuses for ATC Bologna, eight for TEP Parma. Deliveries include the first five of a larger order for articulated trolleybuses for ATC Milano.

UPDATED

Seattle Metro trolleybus with Adtranz equipment ***1997***

Ansaldo

Ansaldo Trasporti SpA
Head Office: 425 Via Argine, 80147 Napoli, Italy
Works: Via Nuova delle Brecce 260, 80147 Napoli, Italy
Telephone: +39 81 565 0111
Fax: +39 81 565 0698/0699
Chairman: Bruno Musso
Vice Chairman & Managing Director: Luciano Cravarolo
Company General Manager: Decio Lordi
Deputy General Manager, Technology Development: Carlo Rizzi
Deputy General Manager, Business Development: Gabriele Testa
Director, Vehicles & Power Supply Business Unit: Luciano Cravarolo (acting)
Director, Strategy & International Marketing: Silvano Brandi
Director, Signalling & Automation: Walter Alessandrini
Director, Turnkey Systems: Claudio Artusi
(See main entry under Rail Vehicles and Traction Equipment)

Products: Trolleybus traction units as part of complete transport system supply — propulsion equipment, motors, electronics converters and controls, chopper and inverter electronic drives, electrification equipment and power supply installations.

Contracts: In 1995 Genova Transport Authority awarded Ansaldo a contract for 20 trolleybuses with IGBT inverter drive.

UPDATED

Breda

Breda Costruzioni Ferroviarie SpA
Via Ciliegiole, 51100 Pistoia, Italy
Telephone: +39 573 3701 Fax: +39 573 370292
Chairman: Dr Luigi Roth
General Director, Breda Group: Dr Ing Corrado Fici
General Director, Breda: Dr Ing Roberto Cai
Business Development Director: Dr Ing Claudio Mannucci
Mass Transit Business Development Director:
Dr Ing Claudio Fumagalli

USA subsidiary
BTI Breda Transportation Inc
261 Madison Avenue, New York, NY 10016-2303, USA
Telephone: +1 212 286 8000 Fax: +1 212 286 0700

Background: BredaMenarinibus was created by Breda Costruzioni Ferroviarie following acquisition of the bus builder Menarini. Breda has plants in Bologna, Pistoia and Roma for manufacture of buses and trolleybuses for city, intercity and tourist operations.

Breda trolleybus ***1997***

Products: Trolleybuses, dual-mode buses and coaches.

Range: Nine body lengths from 7 to 18 m, seating 12 to 63, for use in city centres and for interurban work.

Breda has developed a low-floor bus (the MBb230) for Italian town use.

Production: Annual capacity is 800 to 1,000.

Contracts: 33 articulated dual-mode trolleybuses have being supplied to Milano and 14 have been ordered by Riviera Trasporti, San Remo. The trolleybuses have chopper-controlled power supply and an auxiliary system for emergency operation. Further batches of similar vehicles have been built for other Italian cities.

UPDATED

Brush

Brush Traction Ltd
PO Box 17, Loughborough LE11 1HS, England
Telephone: +44 1509 617000 Fax: +44 1509 617001

Products: Complete AC and DC propulsion packages, including traction motors and control equipment.

Dynamo

Dynamo Electrical Works
Moskva, Russia
Exports through:
V/O Sovelectro, 1/2 kor 1, ul Sadovaya-Spasskaya, 107078 Moskva, Russia
Telephone: +7 095 208 2837 Telex: 411003 SOEL

Products: Electric motors

Range: Supplier of 550-600 V series wound DK-210 electric motors with bias winding for installation in trolleybuses produced by Trolza (qv).

Eaton Ltd

Cutler-Hammer
Power Controls Division
Peacock Way, Melton Constable NR24 2BZ, England
Telephone: +44 1263 860581 Fax: +44 1263 861417
(See main entry under Rail and Bus Components)

Products: Major supplier of forced-air-cooled dynamic braking resistors, or naturally cooled resistors for roof or under-car application.

Electric Transit

Electric Transit Inc
4027 Colonel Glenn Highway, Suite 407, Dayton, OH 45431, USA
Telephone: +1 513 427 5486 Fax: +1 513 427 1069
General Manager: Leo J Holihan

Background: ETI is jointly owned by AAI Corporation and Škoda (see Bus Manufacturers section).

Products: Traction equipment; electric transit vehicles.

Contracts: Construction of 57 two-axle trolleybuses for Miami Valley RTA Dayton based on Škoda (qv) propulsion systems. A further order has been announced for the supply of trolleybuses for Muni San Francisco.

UPDATED

ETI/AAI trolleybus for Miami Valley RTA
1997

Firema Trasporti SpA

Ercole Marelli Trazione Unit
Via Boschetti 6, 20121 Milano, Italy

Commercial office & works: Viale Edison 110, 20099 Sesto San Giovanni, Milano, Italy
Telephone: +39 2 24941 Fax: +39 2 248 3508
(See main entry under Rail Vehicles and Traction Equipment)

Products: Trolleybus traction equipment.

UPDATED

Ganz Ansaldo

Ganz Ansaldo Electric Ltd
Lövöház utca 39, 1024 Budapest, Hungary
Telephone: +36 1 175 3322 Fax: +36 1 156 2989
(See main entry under Rail Vehicles and Traction Equipment)

Products: Electrical traction equipment.

VERIFIED

Ganz-equipped Ikarus low-floor trolleybus

GE Transportation Systems

GE Transportation Systems
2901 East Lake Road, Erie, PA 16531, USA
Telephone: +1 814 875 5385 Fax: +1 814 875 3154
General Manager, Transit & OHV: Ed Orzetti
Manager, Transit Sales: Dave Phelps

Products: Electro-mechanical and solid state DC cam and AC inverter propulsion systems; phase-controlled AC/DC propulsion systems; auxiliary systems, including static converters and inverters.

Developments: A new venture, GE-Harris Railway Electronics, has been created by GE Transportation Systems Division and Harris Corporation, to manufacture and market electronic systems for transport authorities.

UPDATED

GM Hughes

GM Hughes Power Control Systems
3050 West Lomita Boulevard, PO Box 2923, Bldg 237, M/S 1455, Torrance, CA 90509-2923, USA
Telephone: +1 310 517 5717 Fax: +1 310 517 5727
Marketing Manager: Fred Silver

Products: Power electronics and AC induction motors for heavy vehicle drive systems and auxiliary systems such as air conditioning, power steering, DC to DC converters and battery charging. Power ratings vary from 1 to 240 kW.

Product trade marks are Dolphin Drive Systems and MagneCharge Systems.

Kiepe

Kiepe Elektrik GmbH & Co KG
PO Box 130540, 40555 Düsseldorf, Germany
Telephone: +49 211 74971 Fax: +49 211 7497 300
Chairman: T Weber
General Manager, Marketing & Sales: W Huober

Background: Kiepe acquired the trolleybus activities of Adtranz (qv) in 1995. See also main entry under Rail Vehicles and Traction Equipment.

Products: Complete electrical and electronic equipment for trolleybuses rated 600/750 V DC.

Range: Three-phase AC (direct pulse inverter) and DC chopper power electronics controlled by microprocessor technology, with regenerative braking, built-in diagnosis interface, and roll-back inhibitors. Contactor bank or rotating pedal controllers give switched resistor control.

Contracts: Currently supplying three-phase equipment for: Arnhem, Netherlands; Bologna and Parma, Italy; Bern, Biel and Zürich, Switzerland; Salzburg, Austria.

UPDATED

Artist's impression of Kiepe-equipped trolleybus in Bologna
1996

Mitsubishi

Mitsubishi Electric Corporation
2-2-3 Marunouchi Chiyoda-ku, Tokyo, Japan
Telephone: +81 3 3218 3429
Fax: +81 3 3218 3594
President: Takashi Kitoaka

Products: Electrical equipment for rail and road vehicles.

Contracts: 200 sets of VVVF inverters are being supplied to STE Mexico City for trolleybuses.

NEW ENTRY

Siemens

Siemens Aktiengesellschaft
Transportation Systems Group (VT)
Mass Transit Rolling Stock Division (VT5)
PO Box 3240, 91050 Erlangen, Germany
Telephone: +49 9131 70 Fax: +49 9131 72 6933
(See main entry under Rail Vehicles and Traction Equipment)
UK representative: Siemens Transportation Systems, Siemens House, Windmill Road, Sunbury on Thames TW16 7HS
Telephone: +44 1932 752973 Fax: +44 1932 752979

Products: Propulsion and auxiliary equipment for trolleybuses and battery-operated buses; dual-mode propulsion systems.

Contracts: Electrical equipment has been supplied for two-axle and articulated trolleybuses for several operators worldwide, including Genève, Switzerland.

Developments: A new trolleybus propulsion system has been developed by Siemens that brings down the total cost of a complete trolleybus to little more than 20 per cent above the cost of a conventional diesel bus.

The unit is called ELFA — Electric Low-Floor Axle — and is drop-centre allowing a low floor. Two small lightweight traction motors are fitted in the drop section, driving through a reduction gear train.

The motor is rated at 105 kW, and is supplied with alternating current by two inverters. Each motor weighs 85 kg and is 425 mm in length, with a cross section of 245 mm by 245 mm. Each inverter weighs 17 kg to 30 kg depending on specification and is around 500 mm long with a cross section of about 200 mm by 153 mm. The width between the reduction units is 1,100 mm, allowing a gangway over the drop centre.

The motor and inverter are mass-produced for machine tools, industrial robots and battery vehicles so there are no development costs.

Siemens has been talking to a body builder in the UK with a view to producing a complete trolleybus. It will be offered in diesel-electric, battery only, trolleybus or hybrid diesel/trolleybus configurations.

UPDATED

NAW/Hess articulated low-floor trolleybus with Siemens propulsion equipment in Genève ***1996***

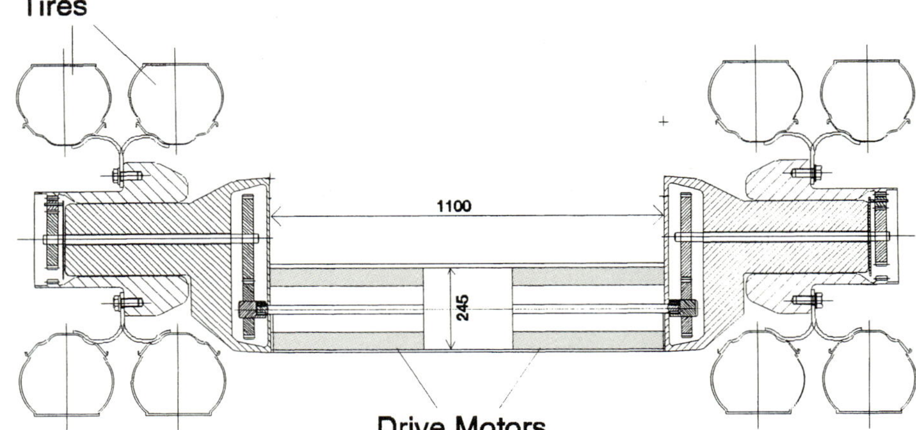

Siemens ELFA — electric low-floor axle for city buses ***1997***

Škoda

Škoda Ostrov Company Ltd
Dolní Žďár 43, 36329 Ostrov, Czech Republic
Telephone: +420 164 2960/69 Fax: +420 164 2764
General Manager: Jiří Juránek
Vice President, Commercial: Jan Hrubec

Products: Trolleybuses, complete trolleybus systems, electrical units, including motors and solid-state control and power systems. (For complete trolleybuses see Buses section.)

Converters with IGBT modules are supplied for trolleybuses and trams.

Range: The 14Tr, which is typical of the Škoda range of trolleybuses, has thyristor control for starting and braking. Stepless electric drive control is designed to achieve smooth accelerating and braking from 60 km/h to 10 km/h, with a complete halt by use of the air brake.

The series wound four-pole traction motor is self-ventilated. It is rated at 100 kW (continuous), with a current start limitation of 260 or 320 A, according to type of use, at a nominal 1,540 rev/min. It incorporates both chopper control for acceleration and resistor braking by thyristor control. Required voltage is 600 V or 700 V DC (+20 per cent or −33 per cent). The continuous-rated output is 100 kW or 120 kW, with a current of 182 A at 1,540 rev/min or 175 A at 1,500 rev/min.

22Tr: A new no-step articulated low-floor trolleybus 17.8 m long and 2.5 m wide. The three-axle bus carries 140 with 40 seated. The floor height is 360 mm, 560 mm at the back. There is an auxiliary 160 V accumulator drive.

21Tr: Rigid version of 22Tr.

UPDATED

Škoda Ostrov low-floor trolleybus
1995

Toshiba

Toshiba Corporation
Railway Projects Department
1-1, Shibaura 1-chome, Minato-ku, Tokyo 105-01, Japan
Telephone: +81 3 3457 4924 Fax: +81 3 5444 9422
President: T Nishimuro

Products: Electrical traction equipment for trolleybuses and electric battery buses.

Range: Has produced large varieties of electric and diesel-electric power systems for locomotives, railcars and trolleybuses. A fleet of 15 trolleybuses supplied for operation at the Kurobe Dam by the Kansai Electric Power Co Ltd has Toshiba traction equipment with a one-hour rated output of 120 kW and maximum speed of 70 km/h.

In 1996 a fleet of eight similar trolleybuses was supplied to Kurobe Kanko Co Ltd for operation in the Tateyama Tunnel.

A prototype BT 900 series battery bus was operated in 1989 by the Nagoya City Transportation Authority, based on a Hino vehicle. It has seating capacity for 26, continuous rated output of 60 kW and a maximum speed of 60 km/h. Running distance without recharge is 170 km. A thyristor chopper control system with regenerative braking is incorporated. Battery voltage is 384 V DC.

UPDATED

Toshiba-powered trolleybus on the Kurobe Dam route

UMEB

UMEB-SA
4 gen Vasile Milea Street, Bucureşti, Romania
Telephone: +40 1 631 6500/5220/3151
Fax: +40 1 312 3928
General Manager: Giurgiu Constantin
Marketing Manager: Constantinoiu Nicolae

Background: In 1993 the company changed its name from Maşini to UMEB-SA, a joint stock company.

Products: Trolleybus electrical equipment — motors and auxiliary equipment.

ROAD VEHICLE CHASSIS COMPONENTS

Company Listing by Country

CANADA
Ballard

FRANCE
Peugeot Citroën Motors
Renault VI
Telma

GERMANY
MAN
Mercedes-Benz
Renk
Voith
ZF

HUNGARY
Rába

ITALY
Iveco

JAPAN
Hino
Isuzu

SOUTH AFRICA
Atlantis

SWEDEN
Scania

UK
Cummins (UK)
Dana
Eaton
Gardner
Hoesch Woodhead
Holset
Perkins
Spicer Europe
ZF Great Britain

USA
Allison Transmission
Caterpillar
Cummins
Detroit Diesel Corporation
Hercules
Rockwell
ZF Industries

Classified Listing

ABS BRAKING SYSTEMS
Dana
Rockwell
Telma

CATALYTIC CONVERTERS
Detroit Diesel

CNG/LNG POWERED ENGINES
Ballard
Caterpillar
Cummins
Cummins (UK)
Detroit Diesel
Hercules
Perkins

ENGINES MEETING EURO-1 and EURO-2 REGULATIONS
Ballard
Cummins (UK)
Gardner
Mercedes-Benz
Perkins
Rába
Renault VI
Scania

ETHANOL/METHANOL POWERED ENGINES
Ballard
Detroit Diesel

LUBRICATION SYSTEMS
Telma

MICROPROCESSOR/COMPUTER/ELECTRONIC CONTROL
Allison Transmission
Caterpillar
Cummins (UK)
Detroit Diesel
Eaton
Iveco
Renk
Rockwell
Scania
Spicer Europe
Telma
Voith
ZF

POWER TAKE-OFF UNITS
Dana
Gardner
Spicer Europe
ZF

RETARDERS
Allison
Hino
Scania
Telma
Voith
ZF

SUSPENSION SYSTEMS
Hoesch Woodhead
Peugeot Citroën Motors
ZF

TRANSMISSIONS
Allison Transmission
Dana
Eaton
Peugeot Citroën Motors
Renk
Rockwell
Scania
Spicer Europe
Voith
ZF

Allison Transmission

Allison Transmission
4700 West 100th Street, Indianapolis, IN 46222, USA
Telephone: +1 317 242 5000 Fax: +1 317 242 3626
President: John F Smith
Director of Engineering: Harvey Won
Senior Marketing Specialist: Greg Sickmeier
OEM Account Manager: Earl Schroeder
General Sales Manager Worldwide: Lawrence Dewey
Managing Director Allison Transmission Europe: Michael Headley

Products: Automatic transmissions

Range: 10 transmission models are available for bus and coach applications. Within each model number, the second numeral (3 or 4) indicates the number of forward gear ranges. Both B and R indicate the availability of a retarder.

The range includes AT 542/545 and HT 740/746/747 four-speed transmissions.

B300/400/500: World Transmission series, six-speed with or without hydraulic retarder.

VR 731RH: This is for right-hand rotation engines.

The Allison six-speed overdrive allows the use of deeper axle ratios, allowing the use of smaller engines.

The World Transmission B500 bus series offers a hydraulic torque converter with lock-up clutch and integral torsional vibration damper, planetary gear package, pressure-balanced rotating clutches and electronic controls. A lock-up clutch in the torque converter allows bypassing of the hydraulic stage of power conversion, providing a direct mechanical link between the engine and transmission at sustained speeds. In any range, there is never any interruption of power to the wheels.

The microprocessor in the World Transmission electronics set up monitors each shift, adjusting the rate of fill or exhaust from a clutch during the shift to provide a smooth ride.

The computer can stop shifts into gear if the vehicle doors are open or if a wheelchair lift is operating. In addition, the microprocessor provides diagnostic information for use in troubleshooting.

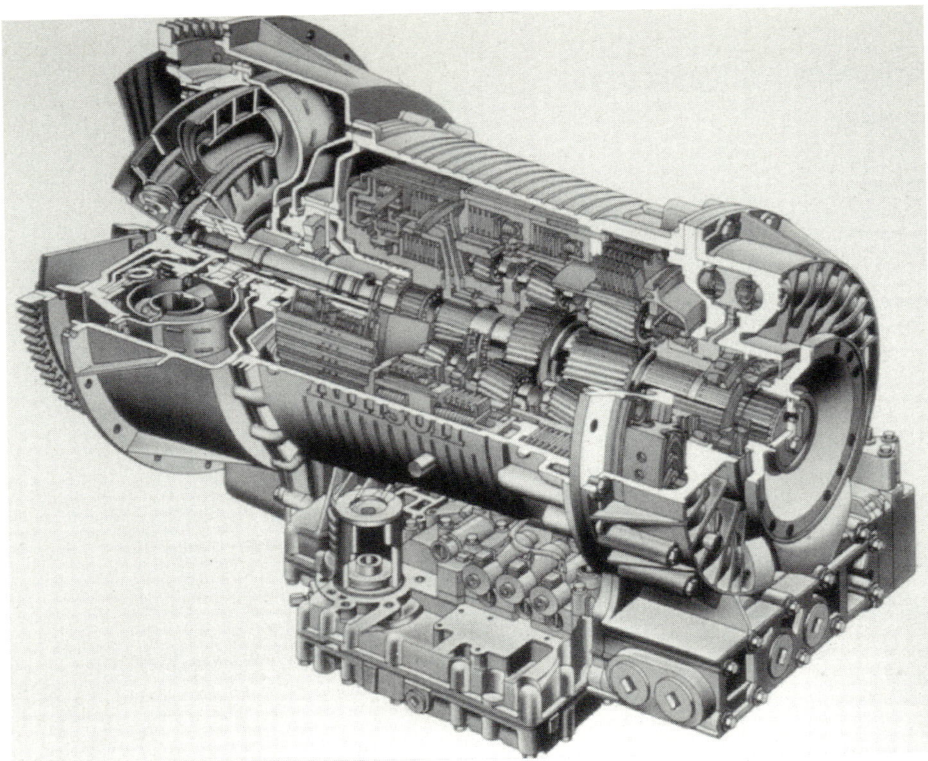

Allison B500R automatic transmission with retarder showing torque converter (left) and retarder (right) ***1997***

The retarder control can be either a hand lever, foot pedal or automatically applied. When a separate control is used, the electronic controls can allow the driver to modulate the retarder's braking force. The automatic application, either when the accelerator is released or when the brake pedal is initially depressed, provides the greatest brake life savings for the vehicle.

Developments: The MT/MT643 transmission is rated at up to 156 kW and is suitable for urban transport operation.

UPDATED

Atlantis

Atlantis Diesel Engines (Pty) Ltd (ADE)
PO Box 1222, William Gourlay Street, Atlantis Industria, Cape Town 8000, South Africa
Telephone: +27 21 226 38911 Fax: +27 21 226 38219
Managing Director: Fritz Körte
Technical Director: Ron Shires

Background: ADE was established by the South African Industrial Development Corporation. The company is licensed to produce Perkins and Mercedes-Benz diesel engines. ADE started production in 1981 and since then more than 180,000 engines have been built. ADE is now supplying the South African market with most of its bus and truck engines. The company offers a product support network.

Products: Diesel engines 24 to 735 kW and components.

Range: ADE offers for bus and coach applications five- and six-cylinder in-line engines in vertical and horizontal configurations and larger V8 and V10 units. These models are also available in turbocharged and intercooled and compensated formats. Special bus ratings are offered at 1,900 rev/min with low idle speeds of 500 rev/min. These ratings were developed to give urban bus operators optimum fuel efficiency in stop-start applications. Repower conversion kits are available to allow bus operators to upgrade existing vehicles with ADE engines.

Ballard

Ballard Power Systems
107-980 West 1st Street, North Vancouver BC, Canada V7P 3N4
Telephone: +1 604 986 9367 Fax: +1 604 986 3262
Marketing Director: Paul Lancaster

Products: Zero emission engines, based on fuel cell technology, able to run on natural gas, methanol or hydrogen.

Contracts: As part of Ballard's test programme, six New Flyer D40LF low-floor buses with the prototype fuel cell system have entered service, three with CTA Chicago and three with BC Transit, Vancouver. An agreement was signed in 1996 for three buses powered by fuel cells to enter service with BC Transit.

An order has been received from Daimler-Benz to supply fuel cells to develop a fuel cell-powered vehicle.

NEW ENTRY

New Flyer D40LF low-floor bus with prototype Ballard fuel cell system at Los Angeles Union station ***1997***

Caterpillar

Caterpillar Inc, Engine Division
PO Box 610, Mossville, IL 61552-0610, USA
Telephone: +1 309 675 1000 Fax: +1 309 578 6466
Chair: D V Fites
Vice President: R L Thompson
Sales Managers, OEM: T J Gove, J J Parker
Overseas subsidiaries: Brazil (São Paulo and Brasilia), Americas (Peoria, IL), Australia, Singapore, Japan (with Mitsubishi), Switzerland

Background: A joint venture company, Caterpillar Shanghai Diesel Engine Works, has been set up in Shanghai, China, to make diesel engines.

Products: Diesel and natural gas engines.

Range

3116: This engine is rated from 127 kW to 205 kW (170 bhp to 275 bhp). It is a 6.6 litre 2,600 rev/min four-cycle six-cylinder in-line unit and is available for smaller bus city/shuttle applications.
3176: Electronically controlled, from 205 kW to 261 kW (275 to 350 bhp), 10.3 litre, 2,000 rev/min four-cycle six-cylinder in-line unit, for larger buses such as the Ikarus USA city bus.
3306/3406: The six-cylinder 3306 10.5 litre unit and the 14.6 litre 3406 engine are offered worldwide.
G3306: This is a natural gas engine and is offered in CNG, LNG and LPG (HD-5) configurations, rated at 187 kW (250 hp) at 2,100 rev/min. First applications are to city buses. Other natural gas engines are being developed.

Caterpillar 3176 electronically controlled engine

Cummins

Cummins Engine Co Inc
PO Box 3005, Columbus, IN 47201, USA
Telephone: +1 812 377 5000 Fax: +1 812 377 3082
Executive Vice President: C Roberto Cordaro
Chairman and Chief Executive Officer:
James A Henderson
Vice President, Bus Business: James J Farrar
Director, Worldwide Bus Business: Clark K Ahrens
Sales Manager: Gary R Farrell

Products: Diesel and natural gas engines ranging in power from 119 to 336 kW (160 to 450 hp).

Range

B5.9: This 5.9 litre engine has a rating from 160 to 230 hp (119 to 172 kW). The same displacement natural gas engine, lean burn, has a 195 hp (145 kW) rating.
C8.3: This 8.3 litre engine is rated from 225 to 325 hp (168 to 242 kW). The C8.3 natural gas engine has been in production since January 1996 and has 250 to 270 hp (187 to 201 kW) ratings.
L10: The L10 10 litre natural gas engine has a rating of 280 to 300 hp (209 to 224 kW).
M10: This has urban bus ratings of 280 hp (209 kW) and 330 hp (246 kW), and coach ratings of up to 450 hp (336 kW).

Developments: Cummins has developed joint ventures with Scania, Komatsu (Japan), Telco (Tata, India), Wartsila of Finland and China National Heavy-Duty Truck Corp. Its first joint venture was with Kirloskar of India around 1965.

A joint venture with Iveco was announced in 1996; called EEA (European Engine Alliance), it will design and manufacture a new series of diesel engines.

UPDATED

Cummins C8.3 diesel engine ***1995***

Cummins (UK)

Cummins Engine Co Ltd
Yarm Road, Darlington DL1 4PW, UK
Telephone: +44 1325 460606 Fax: +44 1325 359380
Automotive Sales Director: P Burningham
Technical Director: Colin Brown
Information: Paul Carter/Neil Harrison
A subsidiary of Cummins Engine Company Inc Group (USA)
Production plants: Shotts, Scotland; Darlington, England
Reconditioning plant: Diesel ReCon, Cumbernauld, Scotland

Products: Diesel engines

Range: Cummins manufactures a wide range of engines in the UK for European passenger applications, covering the 100-330 bhp (76-246 kW) power sector and certified to Euro-2 emission standards.

B series: The 5.9 litre six-cylinder B series engine has become Europe's most widely specified proprietary engine in the light and middleweight chassis range. The B series is available in Dennis and Optare passenger vehicles.

The B series is produced in naturally aspirated, turbocharged and turbo/aftercooled formats, covering the 100-180 bhp (76-134 kW) sector.
C series: The 8.3 litre six-cylinder C series is available in power ratings covering the 150-265 bhp (112-198 kW) sector. Though a larger design, the C series uses the same advanced engineering techniques as the B. Its NOx emission level is 9 g, well below the 14.4 g standard set by the EC. It is the power unit in both the Dennis Lance city bus chassis and Dennis Javelin coach (qv).
M series: A new range of Euro-2 engines builds on the reputation of the L10. M series models are light and compact in relation to their size and are suitable for use in double-deck buses and touring coaches. Reliability and durability have been increased through features such as steel-crowned articulated pistons. Service intervals between major overhauls have been increased to one million kilometres. The Cummins CELECT electronically managed fuel system is a standard feature on all M series engines.
CNG/LNG: In 1991 Cummins introduced its first-generation L10 Cummins for LNG or CNG and is used for buses and other vehicles in urban transport situations. It is also offering natural gas versions of the six litre B series engines. The CNG engines meet Euro-3 regulations. The diesel B series engine, which powers the UK Dennis Dart range, now meets Euro-2 standards. A CNG-powered bus, based on the Plaxton Pointer midibus body and Dennis Dart chassis, has been produced. Power for the new bus comes from a Cummins B series engine developed to run on CNG.

Cummins M11 engine ***1996***

Cummins B series natural gas engine ***1996***

Dennis Dart bus with Plaxton body, powered by CNG conversion on Cummins B series engine ***1997***

A remanufacturing service is offered by Diesel ReCon UK, a subsidiary of Cummins Engine Co. Instead of replacing a whole engine, operators can specify a short engine. This is a remanufactured unit which comprises the heart of the engine but minus application-specific components including fuel pump, turbocharger, compressor, manifold and plumbing arrangements. It is available for B, C and L10 series.

Developments: Cummins has developed joint ventures with Scania, Komatsu (Japan), Telco (Tata, India), Wartsila of Finland and China National Heavy-Duty Truck Corp. Its first joint venture was with Kirloskar of India around 1965.

A joint venture with Iveco was announced in 1996; called EEA (European Engine Alliance) it will design and manufacture a new series of diesel engines.

UPDATED

Dana

Dana Spicer Europe Ltd
Birch Road, Witton, Birmingham B6 7JR, England
Telephone: +44 121 344 4477 Fax: +44 121 344 4003
A subsidiary of Dana Corporation

Products: Axles, including rigid drive, steer drive and dead steer types for light and heavy commercial trucks, four-wheel drive utility, buses and off-highway applications. Other products include brakes, ball joints, differentials and auxiliary gearboxes, overdrive units and drop forgings for automotive engineering.

Range: For buses and coaches, a rear axle is available for vehicles up to 10 tonnes GVW. The Kirkstall division makes front and rear axles for buses and coaches between 10 and 24 tonnes GVW.

UPDATED

DDC

Detroit Diesel Corporation (DDC)
13400 Outer Drive, West Detroit, MI 48239-4001, USA
Telephone: +1 313 592 5292/5112
Fax: +1 313 592 7066/7288
Email: pscully11@aol.com
President: Ludvik Koci
Chairman: Roger Penske
Vice President, Bus & Coach Sales: Patrick J Scully

Products: Diesel, methanol and natural gas engines, for coach and bus.

Range

Series 50: This has a DDEC computerised fuel management system and is based on the four-cylinder 8.46 litre air-to-air intercooled design. Up to 315 bhp (235 kW).

Series 50G: A CNG (natural gas) engine, derived from the Series 50, up to 275 bhp (205 kW).

Series 40: Six-cylinder four-stroke, up to 330 hp (246 kW).

Series 30G: alternative fuelled, six-cylinder, four-stroke, up to 210 bhp (157 kW), for lighter-duty applications.

VERIFIED

Eaton

Eaton Limited
Eaton House, Staines Road, Hounslow TW4 5DX, England
Telephone: +44 181 569 5996 Fax: +44 181 572 7002
Vice President, Truck Components, Europe: A E Best
Marketing Director, Truck Components, Europe: H Klein
Main works: UK, France, Spain
Parent company: Eaton Corporation

Products: Truck driveline components

Range: The main range of gearboxes is also known as Eaton Fuller and is for both bus and truck applications.

The Eaton gearbox line includes the advanced Twin Splitter transmission and the semi-automated SAMT unit. The Twin Splitter is a twin countershaft, splitter gearbox with 12 forward speeds. It offers up to 800,000 km durability, up to 1,815 Nm torque capability and reduced driver effort. Twin Splitter control is by means of a four-position H gate with a splitter switch offering three positions. Splitter operation can be preselected, without necessarily using the clutch.

The Eaton semi-automated derivative of the Twin Splitter is the SAMT gearbox. This unit is programmed to suit the vehicle duty application. Clutch control is only required for starting and stopping. An electronic gear selector control provides shift actuation.

Eaton SAMT gearbox

A range of five-, six- and nine-speed medium-duty synchromesh transmissions is available, catering for torques up to 1,100 Nm.

Gardner

L Gardner & Sons Ltd
Barton Hall, Hardy Street, Patricroft, Eccles, Manchester M30 7WA, England
Telephone: +44 161 789 2201 Fax: +44 161 787 7549
Managing Director: Stan Lawrenson
Engineering Director: Alan Hilton
Sales & Marketing Director: Gareth Williams

Background: The company was started by Lawrence Gardner in 1868 and began production of engines in 1891. It pioneered diesel engine development from 1918 onwards and the first diesel engine was installed on a bus in Britain in 1931.
The company is now fully accredited to the BS5750 and ISO 9000 standards.

Products: Diesel engines for buses, coaches, trucks, marine and other applications.

Range: Engines from 21 kW (28 bhp) to 313 kW (420 bhp). With the exception of the 2LW engines, all models are in-line six-cylinder units, available in either vertical or horizontal form, with engine capacities including 10.45, 12.7 and 15.5 litre.
LG1200 Euro-2: This meets Euro-2 legislation without the need for electronics. It is available in four ratings — 164, 187, 208 and 224 kW (220, 250, 280 and 300 bhp).

It has a modification to the fuel injection equipment to retain the flat torque curve characteristics. The piston compression ratio is increased from 15:1 to 16:1, reducing NOx levels and improving cold-starting white smoke emissions and part-load hydrocarbon emissions.

Air-to-air charge cooling improves both NOx and smoke particulate emissions. Reduced injection hole sizes reduce smoke and its contribution to particulate emissions, while maintaining low NOx levels. The turbocharger has been changed to increase airflow, particularly at low engine speed, to improve smoke levels and driveability.

The piston cooling jets have been removed and the valve guides have been modified to reduce the oil flow between guide and valve. The injection pump timing is retarded to control NOx emissions and reduce combustion noise.

Remanufactured engines
The Gardner remanufactured engine range was introduced in 1988, followed in 1991 by the Green environmentally friendly versions.

Integral to the success of this range are features including green or standard specification, three-year warranty, low revving and fuel efficiency.

Contracts: Gardner engines are available in bus and coach chassis supplied by a number of UK manufacturers including Volvo and Dennis Specialist Vehicles. The LG1200 series is in service in London, Manchester and Hong Kong, and Dennis is offering the LG1200 in its standard specification.

In Hong Kong, Gardner continues to have a strong presence with some 4,000 buses operated by China Motor Bus, Citybus and Kowloon Motor Bus. In addition, mainland China is becoming an important market.

Africa is a popular market for Gardner-engined buses with engines supplied to Malawi, Kenya and South Africa, on both ERF and Dennis chassis.

The latest order for Gardner engines has come from Stagecoach, UK, for remanufactured Leyland engines.

A joint venture company has been set up with Goodview Bus Manufacturing, Guangzhou, China, to make and sell single- and double-deck buses. The bus will have a Gardner 6LXB engine, driving through a Voith automatic transmission. Orders have been secured from 12 Chinese cities for the single-deck version.

UPDATED

Gardner remanufactured vertical engine ***1996***

Gardner LG1200 engine which meets Euro-2 regulations ***1996***

Hercules

Hercules Engine Company
101 Eleventh Street SE, Canton, Ohio 44707-3802, USA
Telephone: +1 216 438 1038 Fax: +1 216 438 1313
Chair: C M Harmon Jr
President: G R Smith
Vice President, Sales: M C Ervin

Background: Once a supplier of diesel and petrol engines for military purposes, Hercules has now developed a range of CNG-powered engines for transport applications, prompted by requirements of the US Clean Air and Energy Policy acts. It continues to build conventional engines.

Products: Diesel and natural gas powered vehicle engines.

Hino

Hino Motors Ltd
7-17 Nihonbashi 1-chome, Chuo-ku, Tokyo 103, Japan
Telephone: +81 3 3272 1891 Fax: +81 3 3272 4822

Products: Diesel engines, 108-321 kW (145-430 bhp).

Range: A feature of Hino diesels is HMMS (Hino Micro-Mixing System). This relies on a high degree of micro-swirl turbulence to mix fuel and inlet air. This mixing improves combustion efficiency and reduces fuel consumption.

The Hino automotive diesel engine line-up includes four- and six-cylinder models in the 5.3-13.27 litre swept volume range and a large 20.78 litre V8.

A diesel engine has been developed that stores kinetic energy when the vehicle is braked, using a hybrid inverter controlled motor and retarder. It uses an alternating current motor inside the engine's flywheel housing as a retarder, and to generate electricity for auxiliary uses. It can also be used to start the engine, providing extra power when moving off.

UPDATED

Hoesch Woodhead

Hoesch Woodhead Ltd
177 Kirkstall Road, Leeds LS4 2AQ, England
Telephone: +44 113 244 1202 Fax: +44 113 242 0387
Chief Executive: R L Spencer

Background: Is a subsidiary of Krupp Hoesch Automotive, Bochum, Germany.

Products: Vehicle suspension systems

Range: Divisions of Hoesch Woodhead manufacture leaf springs, coil springs, parabolic springs, torsion and anti-roll bars.

SIGNALLING, COMMUNICATIONS AND TRAFFIC CONTROL EQUIPMENT

Company Listing by Country

AUSTRALIA
Philips Traffic & Engineering Systems
Teknis

BELGIUM
GEC Alsthom ACEC Transport
SAIT-Devlonics

CANADA
IRD Teleride Sage
Mark IV
Primetech
Wardrop

CHINA, PEOPLE'S REPUBLIC
Casco Signal

DENMARK
Dedicom
Focon

FRANCE
Alcatel Alsthom
Cegelec CGA
CS-Transport
Fels
GEC Alsthom Transport
Gorgy Timing
Lumiplan
Matra Transport
MDO
Mors
Silec
SLE
Steria
SYSECA

GERMANY
Adtranz
Alcatel SEL
Bosch
Cegelec AEG
Hanning & Kahl
Krauss-Maffei
Krueger
Lumino
Meister Electronic
Siemens
Trion
Wandel & Goltermann

HUNGARY
Ganz Ansaldo

INDIA
Crompton Greaves

IRELAND
Data Display

ISRAEL
Ofek

ITALY
Aesys
Ansaldo
Firema
Italtel Telesis
Sasib Railway
Solari
Telecom Sud

JAPAN
Habuka
Hitachi
KE
Mitsubishi Electric
Nippon Signal

NETHERLANDS
Algemene Sein Industrie
Etrometa
Fokker Space
Nederland Haarlem
Peek
Simac

SPAIN
Sainco
SEPSA

SWEDEN
ATSS
Mobitec
PS Presentation System
Thoreb

SWITZERLAND
Ascom Radiocom
EBO
Fahel
FP Displays
HPW
Moser-Baer
Omega Electronics
Sécheron
Siemens Schweiz

UK
BAeSEMA
Bosch
Cegelec AEG
DAC
Data Display (UK)
EEV
Ferranti
GEC Alsthom
GEC-Marconi Aerospace
GEC-Marconi Defence Systems
Hanover Displays
Hoskyns
Howells
IGG
Jasmin Simtec
Mirror Technology
Poletech
Racal Acoustics
Raychem
Redifon MEL
RSL
Sema
Siemens Traffic Controls
Siemens Transportation Systems
Techspan
Time 24
Transmitton
Vaughan Harmon Systems
Vultron
WCL
Westinghouse Signals

USA
Advanced Surveillance Technologies
American Loop
Amtech
Andrew
Doron
EMX International
Globe
GRS
Harmon
Loronix
Midwest Electronic Industries
Motorola
Nu-Metrics
Oval Window Audio
Quantum Sky
Rockwell
Siemens Transportation Systems
Talking Signs
Telephonics
Transit Control Systems
Union Switch & Signal
Vapor

Classified Listing

ATC
Adtranz
CS Transport
Firema Trasporti
GEC Alsthom
Matra Transport
Sasib Railway
Siemens
Siemens Schweiz
Union Switch & Signal
Westinghouse Signals

ATO
Adtranz
Firema Trasporti
GEC Alsthom
Sasib Railway
Siemens
Westinghouse Signals

ATP
Adtranz
ATSS
Firema Trasporti
GEC Alsthom
Sasib Railway
SEPSA
Siemens
Westinghouse Signals

CLOCKS
EEV
Gorgy Timing
Moser-Baer
Solari

CTC
Adtranz
Alcatel
Algemene Sein Industrie
Casco Signal
CS-Transport
Firema Trasporti
GEC Alsthom
Howells
Sainco
Sasib Railway
Siemens Schweiz
Teknis
Thoreb
Wardrop
Westinghouse Signals

GLOBAL POSITIONING SYSTEMS (GPS)
GRS
Hanover Displays
Italtel Telesis
Jasmin Simtech
Meister Electronic
Quantum Sky
Racal
Rockwell
Simac

PUBLIC ADDRESS
Adtranz
Alcatel Alsthom
American Loop
DAC
Fahel
Firema Trasporti
Focon
Italtel Telesis
Jasmin Simtec
Meister Electronic
Midwest Electronic
Moser-Baer
Oval Window Audio
SEPSA
Silec
Talking Signs
Telephonics
Thoreb
Transmitton
Wandel & Goltermann
WCL

RADIO COMMUNICATIONS SYSTEMS
Adtranz
Alcatel Alsthom
Amtech
Andrew
Ascom Radiocom
Bosch
Cegelec CGA
DAC
Dedicom
GEC-Marconi
Harmon
Italtel Telesis
Jasmin Simtech
KE
Motorola
Nu-Metrics
Primetech
Redifon MEL
SAIT-Devlonics
Siemens
Siemens Transportation Systems
Simac
Telephonics
Transmitton
Vaughan Systems
WCL
Westinghouse Signals

RADIO CONTROL
Adtranz
DSC Communications
GEC Alsthom
Motorola

SURVEILLANCE
Advanced Surveillance
Italtel Telesis
Loronix
Mirror Technology
Primetech
Rockwell
Steria
Telephonics

SIMULATION SYSTEMS
Adtranz
Doron
Fokker Space
Hoskyns
Krauss-Maffei

TRAFFIC CONTROL
Adtranz
Ansaldo
BAeSEMA
Bosch
Cegelec AEG
Cegelec CGA
CS-Transport
Dedicom
EMX International
Fahel
Ganz Ansaldo
GEC Alsthom
Hanning & Kahl
Hanover Displays
Harmon
Hitachi
HPW
IRD Teleride Sage
Italtel Telesis
Moser-Baer
Nederland Haarlem
Nippon Signal
Nu-Metrics
Ofek
Peek
Philips Traffic & Engineering Systems
Poletech
Rockwell
Sainco
SAIT-Devlonics
Sema
Siemens Traffic Controls
SLE
Solari
Steria
SYSECA
Vapor
Vaughan Harmon Systems
Westinghouse Signals

VIGILANCE
Italtel Telesis
Loronix
Westinghouse Signals

VISUAL DISPLAYS
Adtranz
Aesys
Cegelec CGA
DAC
Data Display
EEV
Focon
FP Displays
Globe
Gorgy Timing
Habuka
Hanover Displays
Harmon
IGG
Jasmin Simtech
Krueger
Lumino
Lumiplan
Mark IV
MDO
Meister Electronic
Mobitec
Mors
Omega
PS Presentation System
Racal Acoustics
Redifon MEL
RSL
Sécheron
SEPSA
SLE
Solari
SYSECA
Techspan
Thoreb
Transmitton
Trion
Vultron

Adtranz

ABB Daimler-Benz Transportation GmbH
PO Box 130127, 13601 Berlin, Germany
Telephone: +49 303 832 1721 Fax: +49 303 832 2003
Executive: Lars Afzelius
(See main entry under Rail Vehicles and Traction Equipment)

China: Adtranz Signal Ltd, 16 Bei 3-Zhong Lu, Tiexi District, 110025 Shenyang
Telephone: +86 24 564 2805 Fax: +86 24 564 2808
Executive: Raymond Black

Denmark: ABB Daimler-Benz Transportation (Signal) AS, PO Box 1509, 2650 Hvidovre
Telephone: +45 36 390100 Fax +45 31 495750
Executive: Jrgen Green-Pedersen

Germany: ABB Daimler-Benz Transportation (Signal) Germany GmbH, Wolfenbutteler Strasse 86/ Obergstrasse 5, 38012 Braunschweig
Breite Strasse 26-46, 38016 Braunschweig, Germany
Telephone: +49 531 2240 Fax: +49 531 224 1065
Executive: Karl Ulrich Dobler

Italy: ABB Daimler-Benz Transportation (Signalling Division), Via Campo Romano 59, 00173 Roma
Telephone: +39 67 25721 Fax: +39 67 267 1072
Executive: Franco Pietrini

Poland: Adtranz Zwus Signal SpZ, UL Modelarska 12, 40142, Katowice
Telephone: +48 32 104 2250 Fax: +48 32 104 2244
Executive: Henryk Hytry
ABB Daimler-Benz Transportation Rail Engineering Ltd, UL Hoza 63/65, 00681 Warszawa
Telephone: +48 22 629 8403 Fax: +48 22 2447

Spain: ABB Daimler-Benz Transportation Sẽnal SA, Valportillo Segunda 5-7, 28100 Alcobendas (Madrid)
Telephone: +34 1 581 9393 Fax: +34 1 581 0750
Executive: Ismael Olea

Sweden: ABB Daimler-Benz Transportation (Signal) AB, PO Box 42505, 12616 Stockholm
Telephone: +46 8 681 5000 Fax +46 8 681 5100
Executive: Hans-Olof Hofverberg

UK: Adtranz, Signal House, Letcombe Street, Reading RG8 1AX
Telephone: +44 118 953 8231 Fax: +44 118 953 8239
Executive: Ray Haines
ABB Daimler-Benz Transportation (Signal) Ltd, Estover Close, Plymouth PL6 7PU
Telephone: +44 1752 732525 Fax: +44 1752 731643
ABB Daimler-Benz Transportation (Signal) Ltd
10 Holliday Street, Birmingham B1 1TP
Telephone: +44 121 654 4228 Fax: +44 121 654 4677
Executive: Trevor Lamper

Products: Advanced traffic management systems and CTC: computerised interlocking; ATC, ATP, and ATO radio signalling; rolling stock information systems; point machines; level crossing protection systems; barriers; track circuits and detectors; passenger information and ticketing systems.

Development and production of decentralised electronic control system; computer-supported network structure; route and journey planning; computer-supported journey; vehicle deployment and roster planning for public transport in towns and regional areas; computer-supported staff deployment system for transport and service companies. Drive simulation systems.

Contracts
Brazil: Trensurb (Empresa de Trens Urbanos) de Porto Alegre in southern Brazil has awarded to Adtranz Brazil the contract for the 6.5 km extension of a metro line between Sapucaia and Sao Leopoldo districts.
Germany: A central control for the traffic management system has been installed for the people mover at Frankfurt airport.
Norway: A traffic management system for Oslo Central and adjoining stations has been installed.
Philippines: A complete signalling system, including traffic control, ATP and wayside equipment for its Manila LRT Line 3 is being installed. Completion is at the end of 1998.
South Korea: Electronic interlocking, ATP, ATO, track circuits and colourlight signals for Pusan metro Line 2. ATO for Seoul metro Lines 5, 7 and 8. Metro Seoul took delivery of a drive simulator in 1996, supplied by Adtranz Austria.
Spain: Turnkey signalling contract for the new Metro de Bilbao network, which has 30 stations. It has also been equipped with a combination of systems and service from Adtranz signalling group companies and suppliers from Spain, Sweden and the UK. Metro Madrid Line 10 received three Ebilock950 electronic interlocks, including double-carrier ATP adaptation, eight stations, 65 signals, 100 track circuits and 16 points over the 9 km line.
Sweden: Radio signalling system for the Västervik–Linköping line.
All signalling for the Mälarbanan line and Stockholm's Arlanda Airport link.
Rolling stock information system for Malmbanan. Electronic interlockings (23) for SJ. SL Stockholm received an electronic interlocking system for the Roslagsbanan. The system controls 6 km of track with 110 signals and 42 turn-outs, including four stations.
Turkey: All signalling for light rail system in Izmir.
UK: Resignalling of the North London and Woking–Surbiton lines, both for Railtrack.

UPDATED

Advanced Surveillance Technologies

Advanced Surveillance Technologies Inc
High Tech Video Systems, 1271 N Plano Road, Richardson, TX 75081, USA
Telephone: +1 214 669 39999 Fax: +1 214 669 1199
Vice President, Operations: Bob Cooper

Products: Multicamera video monitoring systems on bus or LRV. Systems with two, three or four industrial security cameras with advanced digital multiplexers and time-lapse VCRs for mounting in vehicle. Designed for continuous use with recording on to single tape.

Aesys

Aesys
Via Artigiani 41, 24060 Brusaporto, Italy
Telephone: +39 35 683000 Fax: +39 35 680030
General Manager: Dr Marcello Biava
Assistant to General Manager: Giuseppe Biava

Products: Electronic bus destination signs; new stop announcements; information displays at bus stops; fuel delivery control systems; vehicle control systems; LED bus destination signs.

Contracts: Bus destination equipment has been delivered to AMT Genova and Tram Rimini (also next stop announcements, fuel delivery systems and vehicle control systems).

NEW ENTRY

Alcatel Alsthom

Alcatel Alsthom
33 Rue Emeriau, 75725 Paris, France
Fax: +33 1 45 77 88 61

SEL Division
Alcatel Canada Inc
1235 Ormont Drive, Weston, Ontario M9L 2W6, Canada
Telephone; +1 416 742 3900 Fax: +1 416 742 1136
Marketing Manager: Mark Halinaty

Products: Voice, data and video communication networks, based on any transmission system, including SDH and Sonet technology.

Contracts: Include traffic management system in London; emergency call networks in Ghangzhou, China.

GEC Alsthom Transporte, an Alcatel Alsthom subsidiary, is supplying signalling, telecommunications and fire safety equipment for the Shenyang metro. Delivery is due be completed in 1998.

UPDATED

Alcatel SEL

Alcatel SEL AG
Transport Automation, Lorenzstrasse 10, 70435 Stuttgart, Germany
Telephone: +49 711 821 43795 Fax: +49 711 821 46813
General Manager: Friedrich Smaxwil
Marketing Director: Horst Vogel
Public Relations Director: Dr Theo Wichers

Products: Turnkey signalling systems for tramways, light rail, metros, people movers and heavy rail; SEL designs, manufactures and installs all major components; CTC, SELCOM™ remote-control systems; INTERSIG® microprocessor-based interlocking systems; SELTRAC™ automatic train control; IDTS® inductive data transmission systems; SELTRAIN advanced train control; MULTILOG™ solid state event recorder; LDCS™ low-density control systems; axle counters; automatic train stops; point machines and decentralised LRT control logic for automatic routing; pre-emptive signalling and level crossing control.

UPDATED

Algemene Sein Industrie

Algemene Sein Industrie BV
Moeder Teresalaan 100, 3527 WB Utrecht, Netherlands
Telephone: +31 30 292 9611 Fax: +31 30 294 7621
General Manager: R O van Manen
Sales & Marketing Manager: H J van Adrichem

A company in the Sasib Railway Group

Products: Specialists in turnkey projects for signalling and telecommunications schemes; complete signalling and control equipment, and associated components; automatic train control; computer-controlled CTC and NX interlocking; track circuit equipment; coded track signal control; level crossing warning equipment; cab signals/ speed control; automatic vehicle identification equipment.

Signalling projects can be undertaken on a consortium basis.

UPDATED

American Loop

American Loop Systems Inc
29 Silver Hill Road, Suite 100, Milford, MS 01757, USA
Tel: +1 508 634 0200 Fax: +1 617 666 5228
Project Co-ordinator: Robert A Gilmore

Products: MobiLoop hearing assistance system for buses and rail vehicles to provide accessibility for people who are hard of hearing.

Amtech

Amtech Corporation
17304 Preston Road, E100 Dallas, TX 75252-5613, USA
Telephone: +1 214 733 6059 Fax: +1 214 733 6619
President & Chief Executive Officer:
G Russell Mortenson

Products: Radio communications systems; hardware and software; radio frequency identification (RFID) technology for trucks, rail vehicles and other transport equipment.

VERIFIED

Andrew

Andrew Corporation
10901 Roosevelt Boulevard, Suite C 1200, St Petersburg, USA
Telephone: +1 813 577 3611 Fax: +1 813 577 7873
Sales Manager: Scot Thompson

UK office: Ilex Building, Mulberry Business Park, Fishponds Road, Wokingham RG11 2GY
Telephone: +44 1734 776886 Fax: +44 1734 794005
Manager: Simon Lawrence

Products: Antenna systems, monitoring systems, GPS location systems; automated voice announcement system.

NEW ENTRY

Ansaldo

Ansaldo Trasporti SpA
425 Via Argine, 80147 Napoli, Italy
Telephone: +39 81 565 0111
Fax: +39 81 565 0698/0699
Chairman: Bruno Musso
Director, Signalling & Automation: Walter Alessandrini
Director, Turnkey Systems: Claudio Artusi
(See main entry under Rail Vehicles and Traction Equipment)

Products: Power signalling apparatus; electronic relay interlocking; electronic track circuiting and continuous cab signalling; microcomputer-based automatic train operation equipment; centralised traffic control; train describer and automatic line supervision systems; level crossing automation and traffic control systems. Ansaldo also provides computer design for signalling and electrification systems with advanced technology.

Contracts: Include a centralised traffic control system for SNCFT Tunisia between Tunis and Bordj Cedria; supply of automatic train control and ticket barrier equipment for the Tehran metro.

UPDATED

Ascom Radiocom

Ascom Radiocom AG
Belpstrasse 37, 3000 Berne 14, Switzerland
Telephone: +41 31 999 1111 Fax: +41 31 999 2700
General Manager, Railway Division: Patrick Richard
Product Line Manager: Ahmet Yücel-Schäfer
Parent company: Robert Bosch GmbH
PO Box 106050, 70049 Stuttgart
Telephone: +49 711 8110 Fax: +49 711 811 6630

Associated company
Ascom Systec AG
Freiburgstrasse 581, 3172 Niederwangen, Germany
Telephone: +49 31 980 7111 Fax: +49 31 980 7159
Area Sales Manager: Laurence Hug

Products: Mobile radio communications, including radio transceivers, trunked radios and base stations (see Bosch). Bosch has been involved in pioneer work on the digital PMR standard and the DISCO SR 440 has a digital/analogue dual function system with encryption.

UPDATED

ATSS

AT Signal System AB
A subsidiary of Ansaldo Trasporti SpA
PO Box 8142, 16308 Spånga, Sweden
Telephone: +46 8 621 9500 Fax: +46 8 621 1424
Managing Director: Roberto Bauducco

Products: ATP systems, traffic control centres and general signalling equipment.

Contracts: ATP systems have been supplied to operators in Sweden, Norway, Italy, Austria, Malaysia and USA.

NEW ENTRY

BAeSEMA

BAeSEMA Ltd
Apex Tower, 7 High Street, New Malden KT3 4LH, England
Telephone: +44 181 942 9661 Fax: +44 181 942 9771
Director, Transportation Systems Group: Steve Howes
Marketing Manager, Rail Systems: Brian Easteal

1 Atlantic Quay, Broomielaw, Glasgow G2 8JE, Scotland
Telephone: +44 141 204 2737 Fax: +44 141 221 6435
Marketing Manager, Road & Rail Systems: John Glen

Parent company: British Aerospace plc and Sema Group plc (qv)
Offices in France, Sweden, Italy, Netherlands, Singapore, Belgium, Germany, Spain, Hohg Kong, Malaysia.

Products: Design and supply of road traffic management systems; systems engineering including definition, feasibility studies and project definition; system supply to include integration, project engineering, design and development support; contract R&D; independent validation and verification; engineering services to include safety assessment, ARM, simulation, ergonomics, human factors.

Contracts: Clients include Highways Agency, UK; Birmingham City Council (supply of MATTISSE—Midlands Advanced Transport Telematics Information System for Strategies in Europe); design and supply of a level crossing monitoring system for Railtrack; software design support to London Underground's Jubilee line extension project; software consultancy for the Channel Tunnel control and communications system.

UPDATED

Bosch

Robert Bosch GmbH
Zitadellenweg 34, 13578 Berlin, Germany
Telephone: +49 711 8110 Fax: +49 711 811 6630

UK subsidiary
Bosch Telecom Ltd
PO Box 98, Broadwater Park, North Orbital Road, Denham UB9 5HJ
Telephone: +44 1895 834466 Fax: +44 1895 838548

Products: Mobile radio communications, including radio transceivers, trunked radios and base stations (see Ascom); satellite systems; security techniques; traffic control techniques.

Bosch has been involved in pioneer work on the digital PMR standard and the DISCO SR 440 has a digital/analogue dual function system with encryption.

Ascom Radiocom range of trunked radios in the VHF and UHF bands; Dikos 210 digital communications system; Flexplex XMP1 combined PCM transmission and cross-connect system; intercom systems for platform and trackside operations.

Casco Signal

Casco Signal Ltd
1150 Qiu jiang Lu, Shanghai 200071, People's Republic of China
Telephone: +86 21 663 7080 Fax: +86 21 663 9223
President: Lu Delian

Products: Microcomputer based CTC; DSS (dispatcher supervision system); marshalling yard control systems.

Contracts: Include the Shanghai Metro, JingJiu line and Hong Hai Railroad.

NEW ENTRY

Cegelec AEG

Cegelec AEG Automation Systems
Eskdale Road, Winnersh, Wokingham RG41 5PF, England
Telephone: +44 1734 698330 Fax: +44 1734 699607

Germany Office
Cegelec AEG Anlagen-und-Automatisierungstechnik GmbH
Geamatics Haus, Lyoner Strasse 9, 60528 Frankfurt
Telephone: +49 696 6490 Fax: +49 696 649 3000

Background: Cegelec acquired a 100 per cent interest in AEG Anlagen-und-Automatisierungstechnik GmbH in 1995 and is now part of the Alcatel Alsthom group.

Product: A wire guidance system for buses allows vehicles to have the same limited clearances as LRVs without the need for rail infrastructure. Called Inductive Track Guidance it uses two wires buried around 30 mm deep and 300 mm apart in the roadway and are energised with a low voltage from substations at 2 km intervals. The bus is fitted with a guidance computer and transponder and can negotiate curves and points. A safety override allows manual control when necessary. The computer system was developed by Daimler-Benz and can be fitted to rigid and articulated Mercedes-Benz chassis. The wire guidance system was developed by Cegelec AEG. Roadworks are far less with this system, which can be installed with a standard slot-cutting tool.

A test facility was established during 1996 at Newcastle upon Tyne with the possibility of opening a wire-guided route serving the Newcastle Quayside redevelopment area. An Optare-bodied Mercedes-Benz O405 bus was converted for the test (see Mercedes-Benz, Buses section).

The former AEG designed and constructed the wire-guidance system in the service tunnel of Eurotunnel.

NEW ENTRY

Cegelec CGA

Cegelec CGA
CGA de Cegelec Division
PO Box 57, 91229 Brétigny/Orge Cedex, France
Telephone: +33 1 69 88 52 00 Fax: +33 1 69 88 58 50
Commercial Director: Renaud Da
General Manager, UK Transport Systems Division: Tim Cavanagh

Subsidiaries
CFEE, France (parking revenue collection)
Alta Technology Inc, USA
CGA Italia SpA, Italy
Cegelec ATA de Venezuela
Offices in Taiwan, South Korea and Egypt

Products: Automatic vehicle monitoring systems for bus, trolleybus and tram/light rail; traffic light pre-emption; vehicle location; onboard and at-stop passenger information displays, scheduling and statistics; voice and data radio transmission.

Contracts: Include supply of automatic vehicle monitoring systems to Nantes, Rouen, Strasbourg, Marseille, Reims, Lausanne, Barcelona, Bilbao, Valencia, Cagliari, Ulm and Mexico City.

UPDATED

Crompton Greaves

Crompton Greaves Ltd
Rail Projects Division
Vandhna, 11 Tolstoy Marg, 110 001 New Delhi, India
Telephone: +91 11 331 5071/7075
Fax: +91 11 332 4360
Managing Director: K K Nohria
President, Industrial Systems: C P Dusad
Vice President, Rail Transportation: B Banerjee
Deputy General Manager, Rail Transportation: M P Singhal

Products: Signalling relays, point machines, axle counters, mosaic control and indication panels; route relay interlocking, solid state signalling; signal multiplexers.

UPDATED

CS-Transport

CS-Transport
4 Avenue du Canada, PO Box 243, Les Utis, 91944 Courtaboeuf, France
Telephone: +33 1 69 29 65 65 Fax: +33 1 69 29 07 07
Chief Executive Officer: G Dubot
Executive Vice President, Operations: B Gantois
Executive Vice President, Marketing & Sales: J M Aubriot
Executive Technical Director: A Roche

Subsidiary companies: Signaltechnik, Koblenz, Germany (100%); Ecosen, Caracas, Venezuela (48%); ACELEC, France (50%)

Products: Control systems for urban and suburban railways.

CTC systems; ATC; SACEM and SESAM and ATO systems; vital relays; hot axlebox and wheel detectors; odometer; electric point machines; electronic treadles; level crossing systems.

DAC

DAC Limited
Shobnall Street, Burton on Trent DE14 2HD, England
Telephone: +44 1283 500500 Fax: +44 1283 500400
Managing Director: G Hopkin
Financial Director: T Balmer
Marketing Director: A J Gleave
Operations Director, Energy: P Cooper
Operations Director, Telecom & Transport: R V Midgley

Products: Weather and vandal-resistant telephones for rail and road applications including simple analogue, cellular and intelligent systems. Onboard train (metro, light and heavy rail) passenger communications.

Supplies distributed industrial PA and radio systems for road and rail builders, suitable for tunnelling applications; has supplied equipment for London's Jubilee line extension and the Channel Tunnel. Self-monitoring and reporting telephone (SMART) for its range of weather and vandal-resistant analogue telephones; simple diagnostics for onboard train communication systems.

Contracts: Held with Midland Metro for public address and crew communications systems; Heathrow Express onboard passenger communications; vandal and weatherproof telephones for Railtrack and London Underground; European Overnight Service onboard passenger communications.

UPDATED

Data Display

Data Display Co Ltd
Deerpark Industrial Estate, Ennistymon, Co. Clare, Ireland
Telephone: +353 65 71242 Fax: +353 65 71311

Subsidiary company
Data Display UK Ltd
408 Montrose Avenue, Slough Trading Estate, Slough SL1 4TP, England
Telephone: +44 1753 694255 Fax: +44 1753 694220
Sales Director: Paul Neville
Sales: Lorraine Case
Marketing Manager: Suzanne Fagan

Products: Electronic passenger information display systems using LED systems.

Contracts: Held with St Petersburg railways; SNCF; Lisboa metro; Irish Rail (Heuston station). A contract was awarded in 1996 to supply BR Business Systems with passenger information displays for the launch of the company's new Train Positioning & Tracking by Satellite (TPT) system. The TPT system was developed by Racal-BRT (qv) in association with BR Business Systems.

Developments: The StarCom desktop display, using vacuum fluorescent technology has been introduced for check-in desks, bus stops, town centres and similar locations.

UPDATED

Dedicom

Sasib Railway Dedicom A/S
Priorparken 530, 2605 Brøndby, Denmark
Telephone: +45 4343 8400 Fax: +45 4343 8401
Managing Director: Reiner van Manen
Sales & Marketing Manager: Ole Vinther

Products: Design, supply and installation of communications networks for rail and road systems, including train radio equipment, signalling systems, optical fibre systems, block section systems, axle counters and SCADA systems for remote monitoring.

Contracts: Include supply of optical fibre cable, telecommunication systems, interlocking equipment, SCADA equipment and signalling systems to DSB, Denmark; signalling and telecommunications systems to Indian Railways; telecommunications equipment to railways in China; train radio systems to KTM Malaysia.

Doron

Doron Precision Systems Inc
PO Box 400, Binghamton, NY 13902-0400, USA
Telephone: +1 607 772 0478 Fax: +1 607 772 6760

Vice President & Chief Executive Officer: Karl J Hirshman

Products: Bus driver simulation systems; interactive L300VMT-Bus simulator.

UPDATED

EBO

EBO AG
Zürichstrasse 103, 8134 Adliswil, Switzerland
Telephone: +41 1 487 2211 Fax: +41 1 487 2277

Products: Cable management systems; halogen-free cable trays and ground ducts in grp; pultruded profiles for ladders, grates and guard rails.

Contracts: Supplied equipment to railway stations at Lyon and Roissy, France; trays for passenger coaches in various countries; ground ducts for Swedish and Norwegian railways.

VERIFIED

EEV

EEV Limited
Waterhouse Lane, Chelmsford CM1 2QU, England
Telephone: +44 1245 493493 Fax: +44 1245 492492
Managing Director: J C Spinks
Sales Manager: J C Staples

Products: LCD information displays for fixed and on-board applications; platform signs and destination equipment.

Customised display boards for passenger information applications including bus stop, bus terminals and airports.

Contracts: Front of train destination boards for Class 465 Networker emus; platform clocks for British railway stations and London Underground, UK.

Etrometa

Etrometa BV
PO Box 132, Kerkewal 49, 8400 AC Gorredijk, Netherlands
Telephone: +31 5133 3435 Fax: +31 5133 3112
Managing Director: John B Leenhouts
Technical Manager: P F Smits

Products: Operating information systems, including passenger counting and revenue data collection; sensitive steps and infra-red detection for passenger counting; remote-sensing kneel protection for buses with kneeling capability. TRANSMIS modular vehicle electronics system for data collection.

Fahel

Fahel AG
Kirchbergstrasse 201, 3400 Burgdorf, Switzerland
Telephone: +41 34 422 2252 Fax: +41 34 422 6740
Project Leader: Theodor Balmer

Products: Passenger information and traffic control systems.

NEW ENTRY

Fels

Fels SA
2 rue J M Jacquard, 67400 Illkirch Graffenstaden, France
Telephone: +33 3 88 67 10 60 Fax: +33 3 88 67 04 10

Products: Electrical contacts; special connectors.

Contracts: Supplier of electrical contact equipment to SNCF and RATP; supply of contact equipment to GEC Alsthom.

Ferranti

Ferranti Technologies Ltd
Cairo Mill, Waterhead, Oldham OL4 3JA, England
Telephone: +44 161 624 0281 Fax: +44 161 624 5244
Managing Director: T R Tuckley
Commercial Director: P Davies
Finance Director: F Brinksman
Operations Director: D J Platt
Sales & Marketing: Andrew Beesley

Products: Non-contact distance/velocity measurement for traction braking, signalling; auxiliary power conversion for ancillary systems; NAMAS accredited environmental testing; stabilisation technology for tilt control.

Developments: Non-contact distance/velocity measurement device (DVMD).

UPDATED

Firema Trasporti SpA

Ercole Marelli Trazione Unit
Viale Edison 110, 20099 Sesto San Giovanni, Milano, Italy
Telephone: +39 2 24941 Fax: +39 2 248 3508
(See main entry under Rail Vehicles and Traction Equipment)

Products: Complete signalling systems for tramway, light rail and metros; electronic remote-control and CTC systems; ATC, ATP, ATO and ATS; onboard computer; automatic voice announcement of next stop, public address for buses and trains.

UPDATED

Focon

Focon Electronic Systems A/S
PO Box 269, Damvang, 6400 Sønderborg, Denmark
Telephone: +45 74 429899 Fax: +45 72 429697
Managing Director: Jens Osterlund
Sales Manager: Niels-Henrik Hansen

Products: Audio-visual and communication systems for onboard applications, passenger entertainment systems, public address, alarm, crew communications and talk-back systems, automatic seat reservation systems.

Fokker Space

Fokker Space BV
PO Box 32070, 2303 DB Leiden, Netherlands
Telephone: +31 71 52 45 000
Fax: +31 71 52 45 999
Email: info@fokkerspace.nl
Product Manager, Civil Simulators: Jos A Hoogstraten

Associated company
Fokker Special Products BV
PO Box 59, 7900 AB Hoogeveen, Netherlands
Telephone: +31 528 285258/285147
Fax: +31 528 285007
Sales Manager, Non-Aerospace Programs: Louw H Schots

Products: Driver simulation systems. Includes a low-priced video system, combined with computer-generated images, available as full in-cab simulation system and also as software for computer.

The system is customised for each operator, who produces a video tape of the line for which training is required. This can then be added to with signals, traffic, emergency incidents and similar problems that the driver will be expected to deal with.

An addition to the simulation system is a train commissioning/decommissioning training programme in which the driver is trained to carry out the necessary procedures and then tested on them.

NEW ENTRY

FP Displays

FP Displays AG
PO Box 823, Zürich, Switzerland
Telephone: +41 1 810 6858 Fax: +41 1 810 8136

Products: Dot matrix displays

Range: Visilight dot matrix liquid crystal messages in both graphics or text, scrolled or flashed.

VERIFIED

Ganz Ansaldo

Ganz Ansaldo Electric Ltd
Lövöház u 39, 1024 Budapest, Hungary
Telephone: +36 1 175 3322 Fax: +36 1 156 2989
President: Dr G Kara
General Manager: S Smirne
Commercial Director: Dr M Sauli

Products: Signalling and interlocking equipment; level crossing controls; colourlight signals; central traffic control system for metro and suburban lines; complete turnkey systems.

VERIFIED

GEC Alsthom Transport

GEC Alsthom Transport, Signalling Group
Headquarters: 33 rue des Bateliers, PO Box 165, 93404 Saint-Ouen Cedex, France
Telephone: +33 1 40 10 63 35 Fax: +33 1 40 10 61 00
Managing Director: J Larroumets

GEC Alsthom Signalling France
Address as above
Managing Director: P Garelli
Commercial Director: T Smagghe
Public Relations Manager: P Dubreuil

GEC Alsthom Signalling Ltd
Borehamwood Industrial Park, Rowley Lane, Borehamwood WD6 5PZ, England
Telephone: +44 181 953 9922 Fax: +44 181 207 5905
Managing Director: J Penney
Marketing Manager: R Penny

GEC Alsthom ACEC Transport
PO Box 4211, 6000 Charleroi, Belgium
Telephone: +32 71 445411 Fax: +32 71 445775
Managing Director: C Jacquet
Commercial Director: D Hausman

Products: Complete range of signalling systems for main line and urban transport networks, from conception through design and installation to full life support. Solid-state interlocking, ATC, ATP, ATO and ATS, CTC; passenger information systems, automatic graph systems, radio centralised traffic control, train management systems, computer-aided maintenance systems; safety plug-in relays; automatic level crossing barriers; control panels and illuminated diagrams; electric point machines, microwave communications; colourlight signals; jointed and jointless track circuits; fail-safe data communications; axle counters; wheel detectors; fault-free software.

Contracts: Automatic train control system for MRTC Hong Kong metro, using SACEM, on three lines; SACEM signalling system for the rail link with the new Hong Kong airport; supply of solid state interlocking system for Belgian National Railways; modernisation of signalling equipment for the Tanggerang line of Jabotabek, Jakarta, Indonesia, including supply of solid state interlocking system and SIGVIEW train control system for urban use.

SACEM system on Lines 1, 2 and 5 of Santiago metro, Chile.

GEC Alsthom Canada has signed an agreement with Télécité to market its passenger information systems worldwide.

Signalling equipment for the 14 km STAR light metro, Kuala Lumpur, is being delivered during 1997/98. The equipment is being supplied by GEC Alsthom ACEC, Belgium. It will incorporate the company's train management system, TAMSY, which has also been supplied for the Bruxelles metro and includes an automatic speed control facility.

An order from Metrovias Argentina to upgrade the Buenos Aires metro signalling system has been received. CMW Equipamentos is supplying onboard signalling systems for 79 trains and a complete ATC system covering 53 stations on Lines B, C, D and E.

Developments: GEC Alsthom has acquired a 60 per cent shareholding in the Brazilian company CMW Equipamentos SA.

A standardised trackside/train data transmission system is being developed in which a single beacon transmits and receives safety-related information. A research programme to investigate compatibility of existing onboard and trackside equipment by different rail networks is being set up.

GT Railway Maintenance Ltd, a joint venture between GEC Alsthom and Tarmac Construction, has acquired the Central Infrastructure Maintenance Company (CIMCo) from British Rail. CIMCo is responsible for maintenance of Railtrack's signalling and electrification equipment in the Midlands, East Anglia, mid-Wales and the West Coast route between London and Carlisle.

An agreement to sell, distribute and install products of Canadian company Télécité in Europe, Asia, South America, Africa and Australia has been signed. Télécité specialises in the design and manufacture of LED rail passenger information systems, including train instrumentation, control and passenger information.

UPDATED

GEC-Marconi Aerospace

GEC-Marconi Aerospace
Abbey Works, Titchfield, Fareham PO14 4QA, England
Telephone: +44 1329 853000 Fax: +44 1329 853797

Products: Monitoring and diagnostic system for permanent way machinery.

Contracts: A train monitoring system is being installed on London Underground Jubilee line extension rolling stock.

UPDATED

GEC-Marconi Radar and Defence Systems

GEC-Marconi Radar and Defence Systems
Electronic Systems Division
Browns Lane, The Airport, Portsmouth PO3 5PQ, England
Telephone: +44 1705 664966 Fax: +44 1705 672934
Divisional Director: Don Pardoe
Marketing Manager: David J Abbott

Products: Vehicle data logging system; design and manufacture of 'black box' accident data recorders, maintenance data recorders, data replay using state-of-the-art analysis software. The technology is being applied to development of similar products for road vehicles.

Contracts: Supplied vehicle data logging system for the Manchester Metrolink tram system.

Globe

Globe Transportation Graphics
875 Hollins Street, Baltimore, MD 21201, USA
Telephone: +1 410 685 6750 Fax: +1 410 752 8828
Graphic Services Coordinator: Jill A Shaffer

Products: Interior and exterior signs, graphics and passenger displays.

Contracts: Signs have been supplied to MTA Baltimore, Amtrak, MTDB San Diego and WMATA Washington DC.

NEW ENTRY

Gorgy Timing

Gorgy Timing
8 Av Pierre de Coubertin, ZI Percevaliere 7402, 38174 Seyssinet, France
Telephone: +33 4 76 70 19 60 Fax: +33 4 76 49 06 21

Products: Radiosynchronised clocks; time centres; electronic message displays.

UPDATED

GRS

General Railway Signal Corporation
PO Box 20600, Rochester, NY 14602-0600, USA
Telephone: +1 716 783 2000 Fax: +1 716 783 2276
President: Mario Maestroni
Vice President, International Operations: George F Street
Vice President, US Domestic Sales: Daniel Donatello
Director, Corporate Marketing: Zal Shahbaz

Products: Design and manufacture of all types of control products and systems for urban transport operations. GRS provides modern signal and automatic train control systems for light and heavy rail systems, commuter rail, high-speed rail and driverless automated guideway transit.

The range includes a growing family of microprocessor-based products for wayside and onboard subsystems, communications subsystems and central supervisory control.

Control systems include: VPI®; Micro Cabmatic®; and TMS™ Transportation Management System, which provides train control, operations reporting and SCADA in one package using industry standards, including UNIX, C and X Windows.

GRS microprocessor-based systems incorporate Numerically Integrated Safety Assurance Logic (NISAL) which provides fail-safe operations without redundant hardware.

Contracts: GRS has installed signal and control systems in Madrid, Barcelona, London, the Netherlands, Shanghai, South Korea, Taipei and many US cities. Recent projects include control systems for Toronto, BART San Francisco, Shanghai and Taipei Red line metros.

Developments: Atlas® ATC system, a radio communications-based flexible block control system, designed for improved performance and low-life costs; AURORA®, a LED level crossing signal light; Cybertrax® data radio, for code line replacement, level crossing monitoring and a communication link to AEI equipment.

UPDATED

Habuka

Habuka Ltd
3-23-8 Sengoku, Bunkyo-ku, Tokyo, Japan
Telephone: +81 3 3941 4325 Fax: +81 3 3945 9802
Managing Director: Takashi Habuka

Products: Destination indicators (blinds, magnetic and LED type); roller blinds (manual and motorised).

Contracts: 40 sets of front and side destination indicators have been delivered to Mongolian State Bus.

Developments: LED displays for Chinese and Arabic characters have been developed.

UPDATED

Hanning & Kahl

Hanning & Kahl GmbH & Co
PO Box 1342, 33806 Oerlinghausen, Germany
Telephone: +49 5202 707600 Fax: +49 5202 707629
General Manager: Eckart Dümmer
Sales Director: Wolfgang Helas
Technical Director: Dr Carsten Kipp

Products: Point controls with electronic interlocking; HFP track circuit and HFK mass detector; depot switch control systems; signalling control systems; vehicle position reporting system.

Contracts: Has supplied extensively to European tram and light rail networks, including HTM Den Haag, WVB Wien, TPG Genève, GS Göteborg, GVB Graz, ATM Torino, Manchester Metrolink and Sheffield Supertram, and also to KCR Hong Kong.

UPDATED

Hanover Displays

Hanover Displays Limited
Hanover House, Daveys Lane, Lewes BN7 2BQ, England
Telephone: +44 1273 477528 Fax: +44 1273 483186
Managing Director: D G Williams
Sales & Service Manager: A Williams
Technical Director: W Goodchild

Subsidiary
Hanover Sarl
Bureau 124, Tertia 3000, rue Henri Matisse, 59300 Aulnoye-les-Valenciennes, France

Products: Electronic information display systems using electromagnetic flip-dot and LED technologies for use in vehicles and fixed installations including bus stops and stations. The systems provide large memory capacity with simple reprogramming facilities for route network updating. An autonomous driver's controller is provided, but the signs can also be slaved to onboard electronic equipment such as ticket machines.

Automatic vehicle location system HYLOC uses GPS satellite transmission coupled with door-opening and wheel-rotation data to give accurate vehicle location. This information can be used to activate onboard signs, speech and ticketing equipment, for traffic light priority, and to provide bus-stop information. No street-based installation is required.

Contracts: Held with Evobus, MAN and Bombardier.

Developments: A flexible version of the company's flip-dot sign specifically for new rail vehicles with steeply inclined curved screens has been introduced. The new sign bends to the shape of the screen and fixes against it without the need for a second window. This approach ensures the best possible visibility which would otherwise be compromised by new shapes of rail vehicles.

UPDATED

Harmon

Harmon Industries
1300 Jefferson Court, Blue Springs, MO 64015, USA
Telephone: +1 816 229 3345 +1 816 229 0556
President & Chief Executive Officer: Björn E Olsson

Executive Vice President, Finance: Charles M Foudree
Executive Vice President, Marketing, Sales & Support: Gary E Ryker
Director, International Marketing & Sales: Timothy D Finet

Other locations outside the USA
Harmon Industries, Chemin de Gap 1-3, 1006 Lausanne, Switzerland

Harmon Industries, 16 Milebush, Leighton Buzzard LU7 7UB, England

Vaughan Harmon Systems Ltd, The Maltings, Hoe Lane, Ware SG12 9LR, England
Telephone: +44 1920 462282 Fax: +1920 460702
Managing Director: Andrew St Johnston

Henkes Harmon Ind Pty Ltd, 14 Summit Court, Mooroolbark, Victoria 3138, Australia

Vale Harmon Enterprises, 2700 Brabant Marineau, Saint Laurent, Canada H4S IL1

Products: Signal and train control products including crossing warning systems, radio communications, train inspection systems, peripheral test equipment and services; contract engineering, signal installation and material management; train describers; centralised traffic control systems; passenger information systems.

Contracts: Projects in Chicago, New York, Philadelphia, Los Angeles, Denver, San Diego, Michigan, New Jersey, San Francisco, St Louis, Washington, Montréal, Australia and the People's Republic of China.

Developments: Incremental train control system demonstration, communications-based train control systems; advanced microprocessor technologies.

A hot box detection system has been developed jointly by Vaughan Harmon and Tony Chapman Electronics, England.

UPDATED

Hitachi

Hitachi Ltd
6 Kanda Surugadai 4-chome, Chiyoda-ku, Tokyo 101, Japan
Telephone: +81 3 3258 1111 Fax: +81 3 3258 5212
(See main entry under Rail Vehicles and Traction Equipment)

Products: Traffic control systems, automatic train operation and automatic train protection equipment; autonomous train integration networks; onboard train information systems, including fault isolation.

Developments: Railway system modulator, named New JUMPS, which improves the performance of ATP or ATO and connects main subsystems.

Hoskyns

Hoskyns Group plc
Hoskyns House, 130 Shaftesbury Avenue, London W1V 8HH, England
Telephone: +44 171 434 2171 Fax: +44 171 437 6223

Products: Computer services and information technology including computer-based driver training system using text, graphics, photos and video sequences to simulate operating conditions.

Contracts: A training system has been installed for Eurostar drivers on the Paris–London route.

Howells

Howells Railway Products Ltd
Longley Lane, Sharston Industrial Estate, Wythenshawe, Manchester M22 4SS, England
Telephone: +44 161 945 5567 Fax: +44 161 945 5597
Sales Engineer: Alan Cooper

Products: AWS electroindicators; impedance bonds; lineside disconnection box; terminal blocks; signal passed at danger indicators

Contracts: Customers include Adtranz, Amtrak, Railtrack, Daewoo, GEC Alsthom Signalling, Northern Ireland Railways and SNCF.

NEW ENTRY

HPW

Häni-Prolectron AG
Industriestr, 9552 Bronschhofen, Switzerland
Telephone: +41 71 913 7373 Fax: +41 71 913 7374

Products: VICOS-LIO AVM automatic vehicle location and control systems; IBIS onboard passenger information systems; IRIS infra-red transmission systems; IFES, DIES, REDI and ISAS planning and statistics programs; PACOS passenger information systems; traffic light priority systems; ballasts for fluorescent lamps; AC/DC, DC/DC charging units/converters; door closing/opening systems.

UPDATED

IGG

IGG Data Display
IGG House, Martin Road, Havant PO9 5TL, England
Telephone: +44 1705 450400 Fax: +44 1705 473446
Managing Director: Dennis Lockwood
Sales Manager: Brian Lowing
Director: Paul Neville

Background: IGG was acquired by Data Display (qv) in 1996.

Products: LED, LCD and lamp display systems for passenger information, platform and on-train (also buses, trams); platform station entrance, ticket hall and line interchange displays in three-colour LCD technology. Bus stop displays in ultra-bright LED. Front of train displays in ultra-bright yellow LCDs.

Contracts: Include supply of platform display systems for London Underground's Jubilee line extension; and for the Strasbourg tramway.

UPDATED

IRD Teleride Sage

IRD Teleride Sage
Suite 500, 156 Front Street W, Toronto, Ontario M5J 2L6, Canada
Telephone: +1 416 596 1940 Fax: +1 416 595 5653
Chairman: Dr Josef Kates
Director of Sales & Marketing, Canada: Andy Hay

UK subsidiary
Teleride Sage Ltd
30 Gaolgate Street, Stafford ST16 2NT, England
Telephone: +44 1785 224424 Fax: +44 1785 225552

Products: Driver management, bidding and dispatch system combined with a computer-aided dispatch and automated vehicle location system. Computer systems for scheduling, traffic management, mobile communications, control engineering, public information and marketing, fleet maintenance/materials.

Contracts: Include supply of a computer-aided dispatch system to Portland, Oregon, and installing an operator management and timekeeping system for Toronto Transit Commission. Enhanced PC versions of an automated telephone information system and information operator system are being installed in Philadelphia and Seattle, respectively. Supply of a driver management and timekeeping system for Seattle Metro, USA.

UPDATED

Italtel Telesis

Italtel Telesis SpA
Piazzale Zavattari 12, 20149 Milano, Italy
Telephone: +39 2 4388 2014 Fax: +39 2 4388 2920
Managing Director & Chief Executive Officer: Alberto Nicoletti Altimari
Marketing & Sales Director: Gian Primo Monaci
Technical Director: Vittorio Formenti

Background: Italtel Telesis is controlled by Italtel, a Stet and Siemens company. The company also has an automatic fare collection subsidiary (see Revenue Collection section).

Products: Information technology systems for traffic and transport; urban traffic control systems; GPS and radio-based automatic vehicle monitoring (AVM) systems; passenger information systems; communication networks for mass transport systems; security systems for rail stations.

Contracts: AVM and passenger information systems have been installed for ATM Torino, ATAF Firenze, AMT Catania and ACTP Sassari; 144 centralised signal controllers have gone to Bologna.

NEW ENTRY

Jasmin Simtec

Jasmin Simtec
Sellers Wood Drive, Bulwell, Nottingham NG6 8UX, England
Telephone: +44 115 927 3741 Fax: +44 115 927 8614
Email: jasmin@jasmin uk.demon.co.uk.
Sales Director: Phil Dennis
Business Development Director: John Michaelis

Products: Passenger information systems; train monitoring and control systems; onboard passenger entertainment/information systems; geographic positioning systems; train/crew communication systems.

The technology is suitable for rail or bus applications.

Contracts: An integrated passenger and crew communication system is being fitted to new rolling stock for the Northern line of London Underground; other passenger information systems are being supplied to LUL Piccadilly line, Irish Rail, M40 Trains, UK, and MTRC Hong Kong.

CCTV systems are being supplied to MTRC Hong Kong, M40 Trains and LUL Piccadilly line.

Developments: An enhanced graphical user interface for application in complex control environments enables common interface to multiple systems.

UPDATED

KE

Kokusai Electric Ltd
Information Systems Division, P'S Higashi-Nakano, Nakano-ku, Tokyo 164, Japan
Telephone: +81 3 3365 9173 Fax: +81 3 3365 9179

Subsidiary company
Kokusai Electric Europe GmbH
Gruitener Strasse 3, 40699 Erkrath, Germany
Telephone: +49 2104 43058 Fax: +49 2104 47802

London office
9 Ryan Drive, Great West Road, Brentford TW8 9ER, England
Telephone: +44 181 568 0066 Fax: +44 181 568 7858

Products: Train radio communication systems

Contracts: Kokusai is supplying a train radio system for Seoul Subway Line 2.

NEW ENTRY

Krauss-Maffei

Krauss-Maffei AG
Krauss-Maffei Strasse 2, 80997 München, Germany
Telephone: +49 89 8899 2491 Fax: +49 89 8899 3043
Sales Director: O Bungers

Products: Driver training simulators

Contracts: Simulators have been supplied to Deutsche Bahn AG, Swiss Federal Railways, Stadwerke München, Stuttgarter Strassenbahnen AG, Metropolitano de Lisboa EP, S-Bahn Berlin GmbH.

UPDATED

Krueger

Krueger Apparatebau GmbH & Co KG
PO Box 1328, 22860 Schenefeld, Germany
Telephone: +49 40 830390 Fax: +49 40 830 39115
Managing Director: Dr Ing Frank-Michael Schneider

Products: Vehicle and station information systems, including automatic controlled roller blinds, dot matrix route number and destination signs; liquid crystal and LED signs and boards, keyboards, onboard computers; public announcement systems for vehicles and stations.

UPDATED

Loronix

Loronix Information Systems
820 Airport Road, Durango, CO 81301, USA
Telephone: +1 970 259 6161 Fax: +1 970 385 4886
Email: keven@loronix.com
President, Chief Executive Officer & Director: M Dean Gilliam
Chief Technical Officer: Peter A Jankowski
Marketing Manager: Keven Ellison

Products: CCTV recording and storage system for buses and rail vehicles.

NEW ENTRY

Lumino

Lumino Licht Elektronic GmbH
Oppumer Strasse 81, 47799 Krefeld, Germany
Telephone: +49 2151 81960 Fax: +49 2151 819659

Products: Destination indicators for bus stations and railway platforms; information displays; bus to terminal communications systems.

Lumiplan

Lumiplan Technologies de Communication
344 Boulevard Marcel Paul, PO Box 4006, 44806 Saint Herblain, France
Telephone: +33 2 40 92 15 43 Fax: +33 2 40 92 14 26

Products: Dot matrix passenger information systems.

Contracts: Systems have been installed for Semitan Nantes; Centro Birmingham; and Merseytravel Liverpool.

Mark IV Industries

Mark IV Industries Inc
F-P Electronics Division
6030 Ambler Drive, Mississauga L4W 2P1, Canada
Telephone: +1 905 624 3020 Fax: +1 905 625 6197
Sales Manager: Geoff Jones

Head Office: Mark IV Industries Ltd, One Town Centre, PO Box 810, 501 John James Audubon Parkway, Amherst, NY 14228, USA

Products: Electronic display components and systems for outdoor applications; passenger information displays for public transport applications; variable message signs for highway applications.

Matra Transport

SA Matra Transport
PO Box 531, 48-56 rue Barbès, 92542 Montrouge Cedex, France
Telephone: +33 1 49 75 70 00 Fax: +33 1 49 65 70 93
Chief Executive Officer: Frederic d'Allest
General Manager: Bernard Sillion
Vice President, Engineering: Daniel Bourasseau
Vice President, Sales: Antoine Massabki
Vice President, Marketing & Communications: Philippe Dalmas

Products: SACEM, Antares and PA135N — automatic train control systems; MAGGALY and Meteor — full automation systems; SCADA — supervisory control and data acquisition system.

Contracts: On RER Line A in Paris, installation of SACEM has cut headway from 2½ to 2 min and increased passenger capacity by 25 per cent. SNCF RER Line C is being equipped with the new digital ATC system Antares. Additionally, Matra equipment has been installed on nearly all Paris metro lines, and in Caracas, Mexico City and Lyon. The MAGGALY system was commissioned on Line 4 of the Lyon metro in 1992.

Meteor has been developed for the new Paris metro line of the same name. It allows operation of trains both with and without drivers.

VERIFIED

MDO

MDO France Mobiler
27 rue de l'Égalité, 28190 Courville sur Eure, France
Telephone: +33 2 37 23 85 00 Fax: +33 2 37 23 36 10
Director General: Pascal Lacosta

Products: Visual displays for bus stops.

NEW ENTRY

Meister Electronic

Meister Electronic GmbH
37 Kölner Strasse, 51149 Köln (Porz), Germany
Telephone: +49 2203 170120 Fax: +49 2203 170130
General Manager: Fritz Meister
Product Manager: Wolfgang Seifert

Products: Passenger information systems including public address, display systems, global positioning systems.

Vehicle positioning system using passive transponders and inductive data transmission (VPS).

Infrared driver control system of train doors.

Contracts: Include passenger information systems for Amsterdam metro, display systems for BGV Berlin, VPS systems for HAVAG Halle and GPS systems for HLB Frankfurt.

Developments: GPS has been introduced for ticket machine pricing communication.

UPDATED

Midwest Electronic Industries

Midwest Electronic Industries Inc
4945 W Belmont Avenue, Chicago, IL 60641, USA
Telephone: +1 708 593 8855 Fax: +1 708 593 8909
Engineering Sales Manager: L Chefalo

Products: Integrated passenger information systems for bus and rail applications, including VITAL information system and Mobilpage public address system.

Mirror Technology

Craswell Scientific Limited
Unit 4, Redwood House, Orchard Trading Estate, Toddington GL54 5EB, England
Telephone: +44 1242 621534 Fax: +44 1242 621529
Directors: G T Poyner; R M J Chambers

Products: Platform mirrors for surveillance in driver-only operation for light rail and main line systems.

Contracts: Suppliers of original and maintenance exchange mirrors to South Eastern Trains; Metrolink, Manchester; Sheffield Supertram; and Docklands Light Rail, London.

Suppliers of original and maintenance exchange mirrors for WAGN, GNER and GE railways, UK.

UPDATED

Mitsubishi Electric

Mitsubishi Electric Corporation
2-3 Marunouchi 2-chome, Chiyoda-ku, Tokyo 100, Japan
Telephone: +81 3 3218 3430 Fax: +81 3 3218 2895

Products: Automatic train protection and automatic train operation equipment; train information systems; onboard fault monitoring equipment. (See main entry under Rail Vehicles and Traction Equipment.)

VERIFIED

Mobitec

Mobitec AB
Bultgatan 40, 44240 Kungälv, Sweden
Telephone: +46 303 94000 Fax: +46 303 92175
General Manager: Bengt Bodin
Subsidiary company: Mobitec-Sütrak AB

Products: Electronic destination display equipment, including full matrix displays; seven-segment and roller blind displays; real-time display system for terminals and stops; automatic voice announcement of next stop; internal next-stop signs.

Mors

Mors SA
Centre Affaires Paris Nord, Tour Continental, PO Box 200, 93153 Blanc Mesnil, France
Telephone: +33 1 49 39 32 32 Fax: +33 1 48 65 33 58
Division Manager, Railways: Bernard Delors

Products: Trainborne electromechanical relays, passenger information systems, radio location and communications.

Moser-Baer

Moser-Baer AG
Champs-Montants 12A, 2074 Marin, Switzerland
Telephone: +41 32 753 8302/8304
Fax: +41 32 753 8615
Managing Director: Urs Moser
Sales Manager: Moritz Flury
Assistant: Birgitta Flodin

Products: Self-setting and radio-controlled timekeeping equipment and master clocks; secondary clock systems, analogue or digital, for indoor or outdoor use; public address systems; interfaces for time and data recording by computers, ticket printers, traffic control processors and recording equipment.

Contracts: Moser-Baer clock systems are widely used, with around 200 installations on national railways and metros.

Developments: LED clocks for indoor use; computer interfaces for time-transmission.

UPDATED

Motorola

Motorola Inc
1301 East Algonquin Road, Schaumburg, IL 60196-1065, USA
Telephone: +1 708 576 5766 Fax: +1 708 576 0078

Land Mobile Products Sector, Radio Network Solutions Group
Europe, Africa, Mideast Division
Motorola Ltd, Jays Close, Viables Industrial Estate, Basingstoke RG22 4PD, England
Telephone: +44 1256 58211/484505
Fax: +44 1256 469838
Land Mobile Products Sector LMPS consists of five groups.

Products: Communications systems, radio control and paging equipment and computer-aided dispatching.

Land Mobile Products Sector (LMPS) manufactures analogue and digital two-way voice and data radio products and systems for conventional, shared and private applications worldwide.

RNSG designs, manufactures and distributes analogue and digital two-way voice and data radio systems.

Nederland Haarlem

Nederland Haarlem
Traffic Control, Parking & Industrial Systems
PO Box 665, Oudeweg 115, 2003 RR Haarlem, Netherlands
Telephone: +31 23 518 9191 Fax: +31 23 532 4303
Managing Director: C S Lutgendorff
Sales Manager: J A Baan

Products: Traffic control systems; lane indication systems; queue and speed detection; black ice warning systems; tunnel control.

TravelMan® information systems; illuminated signs; traffic signals; dot-matrix signs; lighting poles.

Contracts: Work has been carried out in Austria, Belgium, England, Germany, Norway, Poland and Switzerland.

UPDATED

Nippon Signal

Nippon Signal Co Ltd
3-1 Marunouchi 3-chome, Chiyoda-ku, Tokyo, Japan
Telephone: +81 3 3287 4604 Fax: +81 3 3287 4649
President: O Miyaji

Products: Centralised traffic control, electronic interlocking equipment, electronic block systems, transponder automatic train control and protection, relay interlocking, automatic block signalling, level crossing signals and automatic gates, overlay track circuits, remote-control equipment, programmed route control equipment, inductive wireless remote-control equipment, electric point machines, traffic control systems, relays for signalling, integrated traffic control system by computer, passenger information systems.

Nu-Metrics

Nu-Metrics
University Drive, PO Box 518, Uniontown, PA 15401, USA
Telephone: +1 412 438 8750 Fax: +1 412 438 8769
President: Dr Harry R Sampey
Vice President, Operations: Greg Friend
Vice President, Marketing: Barbara A Kovell
Customer Sales: Sandy Paul

Products: Distance measuring equipment; vehicle magnetic imaging (VMI); VMI traffic counters, classifiers; wireless systems; communications software; data management software.

Ofek

Ofek Technologies Ltd
PO Box 4530, Jerusalem, Israel
Telephone: +972 2 561 9631 Fax: +972 2 561 9756

Products: Sysal automatic road vehicle location system.

Contracts: Is currently installing a system in Beer-Sheva, Israel. Has installed equipment in Amiens and Thionville, France.

Developments: Joint marketing initiative in North America with Israel Aircraft Industries (IAI).

UPDATED

Omega Electronics

Omega Electronics SA
PO Box 6, rue des Prés 149, 2500 Bienne 4, Switzerland
Telephone: +41 32 343 3777 Fax: +41 32 343 3800
Managing Director: W Salathé

Products: Passenger information systems. LCD display with white characters on a blue background; also three-colour LED display for general use.

UPDATED

Oval Window Audio

Oval Window Audio
33 Wildflower Court, Nederland, CO 80466, USA
Telephone: +1 303 447 3607 Fax: +1 303 447 3607
Director of Research & Development: Norman Lederman

Products: Mobiloop hearing assistance system for buses and rail vehicles.

NEW ENTRY

Peek

Peek Traffic
PO Box 987, 1200 AZ Hilversum, Netherlands
Telephone: +31 35 891769 Fax: +31 35 891760
Managing Director: Albert Ruimschotel

Products: VETAG (vehicle identification system); VECOM (vehicle communication), a two-way high-speed data communication system between vehicle and trackside; Transmation (Transport Automation), complete management information gathering and processing network.

Bus Tracker system for location of buses, improved fleet usage, improved management and better control.

Contracts: Automatic point switching systems have been provided for light rail networks, with in some cases automatic vehicle monitoring as well, in Den Haag, Amsterdam, Utrecht, Rotterdam, Wien, Graz, Torino, Genève, Philadelphia, Calgary, Boston, San Jose, San Francisco, Portland and San Diego; also in Denver, Roma, and 14 cities in eastern Germany.

Metro and commuter rail systems equipped include Den Haag (semi-metro), Bruxelles, Tyne & Wear, Chicago's Skokie Swift line and London Underground. Also involved in bus priority projects in 80 towns in the Netherlands, in Grenoble, Le Mans and Stockholm; and automatic control and management systems for compact bus/tram stations in Amsterdam, Lyon, Eindhoven and Zaandam.

Amsterdam's Amstelveen hybrid metro/tramway line is equipped with onboard timetable adherence system to ensure scheduled arrivals at critical traffic intersections. VECOM controls passenger information displays at stops and on board.

Philips Traffic & Engineering Systems

Philips Traffic & Engineering Systems
2 Greenhills Avenue, Moorebank, NSW, Australia
Telephone: +61 2 9600 5500 Fax: +61 2 9601 7665
Marketing Manager: Stephen McClymont
Sales Manager: Mario Battaglia

A division of Philips Electronics Australia Ltd

Products: Road traffic control systems, traffic lanterns, intelligent multi-channel vehicle detectors; data communication equipment; lamp monitoring systems; area traffic control monitoring systems (SCATS, BLISS); dial-up systems (DUST); vehicle identification systems; video detection; congestion and incident management; toll collection systems; remote emission sensing (SMOG DOG).

Contracts: Installations have been set up in Australia, New Zealand, Brunei, China, Hong Kong, Ireland, Malaysia, Singapore, Netherlands, Thailand, India and the Middle East. Recent projects include SCATS installations in Tianjin and Shanghai.

UPDATED

Poletech

Poletech Systems Ltd
Bowbridge Road, Newark NG24 4EQ, England
Telephone: +44 1636 611426 Fax: +44 1636 612121
Chairman: James R Lee
Managing Director: Dr A J Lawrenson

Products: Poletech pole mounting system allowing quick replacement of pole; Flatpak cable access boxes.

Contracts: Supply of traffic signal bases to London Traffic Control Signal Unit.

Developments: A new product, Flatpak, was introduced in 1996. It is a cable and access box made of polyethylene which folds flat for transporting.

Poletech Systems received UK ISO 9001 quality standard accreditation in 1996.

UPDATED

Primetech

Primetech Electronics Inc
275 Kesmark Street, Dollard des Ormeaux, Quebec H9B 3J1, Canada
Telephone: +1 514 421 0023 Fax: +1 514 421 1241
Director of Marketing: Barry Simcoe

Products: Trainline multiplexing and radio-linked transmission; train monitoring systems; event logging; computerised diagnostics and maintenance; intelligent surveillance.

VERIFIED

PS Presentation System

PS Presentation System AB
PO Box 654, 58107 Linköping, Sweden
Telephone: +46 13 111225 Fax: +46 13 130747
Main Works: Hamngatan 9, Linköping
Managing Director: Mikael Hult
System Sales: Thomas Hult

Products: Passenger information public monitor presentation systems; TV monitors display information in colour. System also available with LCD, LED and electromagnetic flip-dot displays.

Quantum Sky

Quantum Sky Inc
108W Chicago Blvd, Tecumseh, MI 49286, USA
Telephone: +1 517 424 8000 Fax: +1 517 424 8300
Web: http://www.qsky.com
Chief Operating Officer: Dr S George Schiro

Products: DataGuide™ GPS-based stop announcement system, precise to 1 cm; GPS vehicle location.

NEW ENTRY

Racal Acoustics

Racal Acoustics Ltd
Waverley Industrial Park, Hailsham Drive, Harrow HA1 4TR, England
Telephone: +44 181 427 7727 Fax: +44 181 427 0350
Managing Director: D L McDonald
Sales & Marketing Director: A Dent

Associated company
Racal-BRT

Products: Signboard system of modular liquid crystal display information boards; complete information systems, including control and software.

Modular Signset systems providing customised information displays with fast delivery times. PC-based single or multistation information display systems designed for regional and light rail lines. VMA (variable message advisor) sign system for providing messages at ticket offices and on platforms.

Weatherproof and vandal-resistant telephones; emergency/trackside telephones; commercial headsets.

Contracts: A 16-channel high-capacity Rapidax Ranger with remote diagnostic software has been supplied to Slovenian Railways.

Voice recorders have been supplied to London Underground and MTRC Hong Kong.

Systems in use at London Paddington, King's Cross, Victoria and Charing Cross stations, at Reading and Ayr, and in the Manchester area. Systems also supplied to Italian Railways (FS).

Developments: A Train Positioning and Tracking by Satellite (TPT) system. The TPT system was developed by Racal-BRT in association with BR Business Systems.

UPDATED

Raychem

Raychem Limited
Faraday Road, Dorcan, Swindon SN3 5HH, England
Telephone: +44 1793 528171 Fax: +44 1793 572516
Managing Director: Nicholas Godden
European Electronics Division Manager: Charles J Abbe
Communications Manager: Franc Murphy

Products: Low-fire-hazard cable and harness components; multiplex databus systems; permanent identification systems; interconnection devices; freeze protection of contact rails, points and crossings, brake and diesel fuel lines; temperature and condensation control; HV and LV cable accessories.

Computerised marking with TMS System 90 equipment reduces time and effort spent on electrical installations for locomotives.

Redifon MEL

Redifon MEL Limited
Newton Road, Crawley RH10 2TU, England
Telephone: +44 1293 518855 Fax: +44 1293 561096
Transport Sales Manager: S J Chilver

Products: Inductive loop track-to-train data transmission system, available in both one-way and two-way variants. This system can be used for correct side door and selective door opening. Current and next station on-train information can also be provided. Applications requiring in-cab signalling and platform edge door control and synchronisation, can also be satisfied with these equipments. High-availability radio-based data transmission system for use in signalling applications.

Voice compression systems.

Public address matrix controller for multiple input sources using both analogue and digital prerecorded and real-time voice announcements.

Real-time bus passenger information systems.

Inductive loop Warning System for trackside maintenance staff, developed jointly with British Rail.

Contracts: Provision of track-to-train transmission systems for both the Jubilee line extension and Northern line projects of London Underground. Is also supplying a voice processing system for use on the Jubilee line extension, and a public address matrix system controller.

Supply of a platform screen door synchronisation system for LRT II, Kuala Lumpur.

Rockwell

Rockwell International Corp
Collins Avionics and Communications Division
350 Collins Road, NE, Cedar Rapids, IA 52498, USA
Telephone: +1 319 395 5100 Fax: +1 319 295 4777
Email: cacd@cacd.rockwell.com
Web: www.cacd.rockwell.com
Director: Gregory W Tomsic

Products: Electronic systems for surveillance and control of vehicles in traffic; advanced traffic management systems; passenger information systems.

UPDATED

RSL

Regional Services Ltd
Unit 3, Fullwood Close, Aldermans Green Industrial Estate, Coventry CV2 2SS, England
Telephone: +44 1203 618189 Fax: +44 1203 622246

Products: Video display units consisting of monitors, line receivers and digital video converters.

NEW ENTRY

Sainco

Sainco Trafico
Albarracín 21, 28037 Madrid, Spain
Telephone: +34 1 304 4266 Fax: +34 1 327 0217
General Manager: Joaquin Corodado
Marketing Manager: I del Barrio
Activity Manager: Martinez Jorcano

Products: CTC; advanced remote-control systems for traction power substations; communication systems.

Contracts: Include communications systems, CTC and signalling systems for Ferrocarriles Nacionales de Mexico.

UPDATED

SAIT-Devlonics

SAIT-Devlonics
Member of the SAIT-RadioHolland Group
Chaussée de Ruisbroek 66, 1180 Bruxelles, Belgium
Telephone: +32 2 370 5478 Fax: +32 2 376 6873
Manager: R Landrie

Products: Radiotelephony and data transmission systems; remote control of road/trackside equipment; centralised traffic management systems; passenger information systems; radio control system developed for use in tunnels; modems, X25, ISDN.

Sasib Railway

Sasib Railway SpA
Via di Corticella 87-89, 40128 Bologna, Italy
Telephone: +39 51 4191 111 Fax: +39 51 529 594
CEO and Managing Director: Giuseppe Bonfigli

A company within the Sasib Railway Business Area

Signalling Division (address as above)
General Manager: Stefanino Amaroli
Sales Manager, Italy: Augusto Cei
Technical Manager: Rolando Bassignani

Telecommunications Division
Via Dell'Elettronica 17/19, 37139 Basson Verona, Italy
Telephone: +39 45 851 0522 Fax: +39 45 851 0530
General Manager: Paride Pezzi

Export Division (address as for head office)
General Manager, Export Division: Emilio Gallocchio
Sales Manager, Export Division: P E Prina Mello
Technical Manager, Export Division: Adriano Ghetti

Other locations
Sasib Railway Ibérica SA
c/Estudiantes 5, 28040 Madrid, Spain
Telephone: +34 1 535 2500 Fax: +34 1 554 9953
General Manager: Antonio Pujol
Sales Manager: M Tolmos

Scitel Telematics Ltd
Lehel út 3/b 1 Floor, 1062 Budapest, Hungary
Telephone: +36 1 1401 516 Fax: +36 1 1401 735
General Manager: Tamas Györkönyi

Sasib Hellas SA
53 Solomou Street, 10432 Athens, Greece
Telephone: +30 1 523 8625 Fax: +30 1 523 8647
General Manager: John Korialos

Casco Signal Ltd (qv)
Algemene Sein Industrie bv (qv)
General Railway Signal Corporation (GRS) (qv)

Products
Signalling: Design, supply, installation and commissioning of signalling, telecommunications and electrification systems.

Electronic and relay-based route control interlocking systems; steady and coded-current automatic block; continuous and intermittent cab signalling and speed control; CTC and train describer systems; ATP, ATO and ATS; electromechanical and electronic equipment for signalling installations such as track circuits; DC and AC safety relays; level crossing protection; mosaic-type control panels.

Telecommunications: computerised workstations; telephone operator installations; internal and portable telephones; single line control systems; CTC; passenger information systems; track-to-train and train-to-train communications via cellular and private UHF radio networks; fibre optics.

Contracts: Upgrading the Millennium line of the Budapest metro, including provision of CTC, SDH digital transmission system, CCTV, SCADA, fire alarm, help points and a passenger information system.

Upgrading of CTC for Line A Roma metro.

Developments: Sasib Railway has formed a consortium with Fiat, called Italrail, for light rail turnkey projects.

UPDATED

Sécheron

Sécheron Ltd
14 Avenue de Sécheron, 1211 Genève, Switzerland
Telephone: +41 22 739 4111 Fax: +41 22 738 7305
Chief Executive Officer: Claude Chabanel
Executive Vice President, Marketing & Sales: Paul Bieri
Sales Manager: Jimmy Cuche
Marketing Manager: René Jenni

Subsidiary companies
Autometers Sécheron, Noida, New Delhi, India
ČKD Sécheron spol sro, Praha, Czech Republic
Pixy AG, Baden, Switzerland
Sécheron Hasler Praha spol sro, Czech Republic
Shanghai Sécheron Electrical Apparatus Co Ltd, Shanghai, People's Republic of China
Škoda Sécheron spol sro, Blovice, Czech Republic
See also Electrification and Rail and Bus Components sections

Products: Microprocessor-controlled on-train monitoring and recording systems, optical pulse generators for axlebox or gearbox mounting; modular cab display systems for ATC/ATP applications; compact liquid crystal displays (LCD), high-performance LCDs based on PC systems.

Contracts: Include supply of modular cab display systems for UT446 motive power for RENFE, Spain, optical pulse generators for the SACEM equipment of Santiago metro and for MTRC Hong Kong.

NEW ENTRY

Sema

Sema Group Systems Ltd
Rail Control Systems
Lindsay House, 149 Farringdon Road, London EC1R 3AD, England
Telephone: +44 171 830 4333 Fax: +44 171 278 0574
Business Manager: W Parkman

Parent company Sema Group plc and British Aerospace plc own BAeSEMA (qv)

Products: Design and supply of computer systems; electronic signalling; passenger information; ticketing software; traffic management planning; management information systems; transport consultancy.

VERIFIED

SEPSA

Sistemas Electrónicos de Potencia SA
Polig Indust La Estación, C/ Albatross 7 y 9, 28320 Pinto Madrid, Spain
Telephone: +34 1 691 5261 Fax: +34 1 691 3977
President: Nicolas Fuster
General Manager: Felix Ramos
Commercial Director: Antonio Sosa
Technical Director: Carlos de la Viesca

Products: Public address systems; automatic station announcer; internal and external displays (LED or dot-matrix); monitoring/control systems for auxiliary and traction equipment; crash event recorders; ATP systems.

Contracts: Include supply of equipment to MTRC Hong Kong, STC Mexico, Metrorrey Monterrey and to undertakings in Barcelona, Madrid, Valencia and Bilbao.

UPDATED

Siemens

Siemens AG Transportation Systems Group
Mass Transit Signalling and Control Systems
Ackerstrasse 22, 36126 Braunschweig, Germany
Telephone: +49 531 226 2230 Fax: +49 531 226 4249
Executive Management Division
Technical: Dr Friedrich Hagemeyer
Commercial: Michael Duttenhofer

Products: Microcomputer and relay interlocking; block systems; intermittent and continuous ATC (ATP and ATO); coded audio-frequency jointless track circuits; axle counters; speed check systems; inductive control of points and signals from rail vehicles; point machines; signals. Fail-safe microcomputer system based on Intel microprocessors in 16 bit technology.

High-performance intermittent ATC with continuous monitoring and protection, as part of the ZUB 100 family. This offers the capability of continuous ATC, with track-to-train transmission, as recommended by ORE and used in the LZB system. Modular continuous ATC as an upgrade of the LZB 500 and 700 systems is compatible with these and offers improved performance.

The FTGS jointless track circuit has been upgraded for continuous data transmission capability in ATC applications. Microcomputer-based single and multiple axle-counting systems. Complete signalling projects.

VICOS OC (Vehicle and Infrastructure Control and Operating System—Operation management system for Commuter/underground) control systems family for operations control of urban railways and undergrounds; supervision and control of interlocking; train tracking; automatic train routing; timetable management; automatic train spacing and train dispatching.

Telecommunications for urban transport applications.

Contracts: Contracts have been received for the Stockholm Lidingöbanan, Zürich S-Bahn and also for undertakings in München, Berlin, Athens, Guangzhou, Puerto Rico, Nürnberg and Wien.

Malaysian Railways has signed a contract for a joint venture in Kuala Lumpur.

Developments: SICAS (Siemens Computer-Aided Signalling) interlocking.

UPDATED

Siemens Schweiz

Transportation Systems Department
Industriestrasse 42, 8304 Wallisellen, Switzerland
Telephone: +41 1 832 3232 Fax: +41 1 832 3600
Managing Director: J Leimgruber
Export Director: G Wahl

Products: Complete signalling systems; geographical and packaged circuit interlockings; CTC, ATC; video information systems; signals and point machines; automatic train control systems; automatic train routeing; signalling systems; track circuits.

UPDATED

Siemens Traffic Controls

Siemens Traffic Controls Ltd
Sopers Lane, Poole BH17 7ER, England
Telephone: +44 1202 782431 Fax: +44 1202 782435
General Manager: David Carter
Marketing Manager: Ian Day

Products: Road traffic controllers (junction and pedestrian); urban traffic control systems (fixed time and adaptive—SCOOT), control office equipment, data transmission and field equipment; motorway control and communications systems; variable image processing systems for traffic monitoring, incident detection and enforcement (ARTEMIS).

Contracts: SCOOT systems have been installed in the UK, North and South America, China, Middle East and South East Asia. Major supplier of variable traffic signs to UK Department of Transport Highways Agency. ARTEMIS image processing systems in UK.

Siemens Transportation Systems Inc

Siemens Transportation Systems Inc
Headquarters and Mainline Infrastructure Division, 186 Wood Avenue South, Iselin, NJ 08830, USA
Telephone: +1 908 205 2200 Fax: +1 908 603 7379
President & Chief Executive Officer: J Morrison

Products: Signalling, safety and management control systems for mass transport systems and main line railways.

UPDATED

Siemens Transportation Systems Ltd

Siemens Transportation Systems Ltd
Sopers Lane, Poole BH17 7ER, England
Telephone: +44 1202 782067 Fax: +44 1202 782838
General Manager: P C Lavars
Business Sales Manager: A J Rose

Products: Radio systems are offered covering requirements from cab secure radio for driver-only train operation to relatively simple systems for lightly utliised light rail or bus systems; short-range digital radio links for transmission of large volumes of data at high speeds are available in the GHz frequency bands; train management systems, controlling functions and integrated with passenger information and communication; light rail control and communication systems; automatic and centralised passenger information systems; product and system maintenance.

VERIFIED

Silec

Société Industrielle de Liaisons Electriques
61 rue Salvador Allende, 92002 Nanterre, France
Telephone: +33 1 46 69 22 00 Fax: +33 1 46 69 22 98
Chair: H Vicat
Managing Director: J P Malaquin

Products: Computerised onboard audio information system for transit vehicles, announces the name of the next stop in advance of arrival.

Bus fleet management system; train detectors; track-to-train transmission.

Simac

Simac Techniek NV
PO Box 340, 5500 AH Veldhoven, Netherlands
Telephone: +31 40 258 2944 Fax: +31 40 258 2707
Managing Director: Bert Duursma

Subsidiary company
Simac Technig Ltd
Leyland DAF Buildings, Eastern Bypass, Thame OX9 3FB, England

Products: Fleet management and vehicle location using Inmarsat-C GPS (global positioning system); fuel management; cellular radio, all making use of LOGIQ onboard computer systems.

SLE

SLE
A Mark IV Industries Company
avenue Emmanuel Pontremoli, Nice La Plaine 1, Building F4, 06200 Nice, France
Telephone: +33 4 93 71 77 72 Fax: +33 4 93 71 77 70
Managing Director: Gilbert Melano
Export Manager: Didier Moraldo
Project Managers: Eric Marquet, Eric Laurence

Products: Onboard and stationary passenger information systems; Videobus bus stop and Infobus onboard information display; Busmatic automatic traffic light priority system; computer-aided dispatching; automatic vehicle location and monitoring.

AIDA is an improved fleet management and passenger information system comprising vehicle location, computerised dispatching, and video/audio passenger information.

Contracts: Has supplied systems to transport undertakings in Helsinki, Nice, Orvieto and Terni (Italy). The Countdown bus-stop passenger information system demonstrated on London Transport's bus route 18 was supplied by SLE and has been expanded to 350 sites. Other passenger information systems are in operation in Chambery and Cannes, France; Cayenne, French Guyana; and Monaco.

Solari

Solari Di Udine SpA
29 Via Gino Pieri, 33100 Udine, Italy
Telephpne: +39 432 4971 Fax: +39 432 480160
President: Massimo Paniccia
Sales Manager, Systems: Marco Zoratti
Sales Manager, Products: Roberto Fidel

Products: Information display and traffic control systems; clock systems; attendance recording systems; access control; data collection systems.

UPDATED

Steria

Steria Group
12 rue Paul Dautier, 78142 Vélizy PO Box 57, France
Telephone: +33 1 34 88 60 00 Fax: +33 1 34 88 62 62
President: Michel Gautier
Executive Vice Presidents: Jean-Claude Narconti
Eric Hayat
Sales Manager: Eric Hayat

Products: Traffic regulation and monitoring systems, road pricing and supervisory systems, railway supervisory and monitoring systems; passenger information systems, data processing, management control, training simulators and programmes, computer-aided diagnosis, traffic simulation; ticketing systems.

UPDATED

SYSECA

SYSECA
Member of Thomson-CSF Company
97 avenue Pierre Brossolette, 92120 Montrouge, France
Telephone: +33 1 41 48 00 00 Fax: +33 1 41 48 13 13
Manager of Transport Department: L Narcisse
Marketing & Sales Manager, Transport:
E Colin de Verdiere

UK Office
Syseca Ltd, Southmoor House, Southmoor Road, Wythenshawe, Manchester M23 9SY
Telephone: +44 161 946 1001 Fax: +44 161 946 7000

Products: Centralised control systems for metro, light rail and heavy rail applications, including traffic supervision, and regulation and public information display systems; SCADA systems; computer-aided operating systems for bus networks.

Contracts: Systems in use in: Atlanta, Baltimore, Bilbao, Caracas, Hong Kong, Lille, Los Angeles, Marseille, Mexico City, Montreal, New York, Paris, Rio de Janeiro, São Paulo, Singapore, Taipei, and Washington. Bus systems are in use in 10 French cities.

UPDATED

Talking Signs

Talking Signs Inc
812 North Boulevard, Baton Rouge, LA 70802, USA
Telephone: +1 504 344 2812 Fax: +1 504 344 2811
President: C Ward Bond
Vice President, Operations: David Steed

Products: Infra-red remote sign technology for labelling and location for visually impaired people. For use on buses to identify approaching stops, bus stops and for use in stations.

Contracts: Signs have been installed for WMATA Washington, BART San Francisco, and Capital Metro, Austin, TX.

Techspan

Techspan Systems plc
Church Lane, Chalfont St Peter SL9 9RF, England
Telephone: +44 1753 889911 Fax: +44 1753 887496
Managing Director: Edward Terris
Finance Manager: Richard Nolan
Sales Executive: Russell Hartwell
Sales Manager: John Wintle
Part of the SES group of companies

Products: Electronic passenger information systems using LCD, LED and dot-matrix techniques; video monitor systems; design, development, manufacture, installation and maintenance complete package; variable message signs; fixed text message signs for urban traffic control systems; modular LCD boards designed for use in direct sunlight; recorded announcement systems.

Contracts: Turnkey contracts for design, supply, installation and maintenance of passenger information systems for international rail terminals at Waterloo, London and Ashford, England.

Teknis

Teknis Electronics Pty Ltd
Angas Mews, 75A Angas Street, Adelaide, SA 5000, Australia
Telephone: +61 8 223 5411 Fax: +61 8 223 5499
Managing Director: J M Smith
Technical Director: K Bladon

Products: Electronic control systems, communications technology, SCADA systems, level crossing control, warning system for track workers.

Electronic Flagman, work gang protection system; Safecross, level crossing warning device; DDU, train drivers display for in-cab signalling and train orders; WIM (wheel impact monitoring) used for detecting and identifying wheel flats or damaged wheels causing impact on track structure; Telemetry, for CTC and microwave systems.

Telecom Sud

Telecom Sud srl
Via Delle Monachelle 70, 00040 Pomezia, Italy
Telephone: +39 691 22526 Fax: +39 691 23081
President: Dr Ing Stefano Bosmani

Products: Computer-controlled radio communication systems

NEW ENTRY

Telephonics

Telephonics Corporation
815 Broad Hollow Road, Farmingdale, NY 11735, USA
Telephone: +1 516 755 7000 Fax: +1 516 549 6018
Manager, Business Development: Norbert Trokki

Products: Integrated digital communications systems for rail vehicles, encompassing public address, passenger/crew intercom, automated announcements, radio communications, event recording, passenger entertainment, and CCTV surveillance.

VERIFIED

Thoreb

Thoreb AB
Gruvgatan 37, 42130 Västra Frölanda, Sweden
Telephone: +46 31 496910 Fax: +46 31 473985
Managing Director: Thore Brynielsson
Marketing Manager: Magnus Johansson

Products: Automatic vehicle location, passenger counting, data communication, passenger information displays and communication systems for public transport vehicles.

Transit Control Systems

Transit Control Systems
2641 Walnut Avenue, Tustin, CA 92680, USA
Telephone: +1 714 669 9940 Fax: +1 714 669 0460
President: Peter J Anello
Vice President, Marketing & Contracts: J C Collins
Chief Engineer: J Kiel

Products: Operator's command and control consoles, head-end control logic, monitoring and communication equipment, and air conditioning systems with microprocessor controls for rapid transit vehicles; manual controllers, microprocessor controls and diagnostic equipment.

Contracts: Supply of control panels for Dayton Trolleybus, USA; supply of operator's consoles, controls and communications and diagnostic monitoring equipment for BART San Francisco, Los Angeles Red line, and Muni San Francisco; also air conditioning equipment with microprocessor controls for MBTA Boston Red line cars.

VERIFIED

Transmitton

Transmitton Limited
Smisby Road, Ashby-de-la-Zouch LE6 5UG, England
Telephone: +44 1530 415941 Fax: +44 1530 414224
Managing Director: David Moore
Sales & Marketing Director: Philip Stockdale
Engineering Director: David Cubitt
Finance Director: Guy Bryant

Products: Supervisory control and data acquisition (SCADA) systems for power supply applications; central master control systems for signalling, passenger information and CCTV installations; data logging, point-to-point and inter-trip telemetry systems.

Contracts: Has supplied power supply control systems to Railtrack South West, London Underground and Sheffield Supertram.

Trion

Trion Präzisionselektronic GmbH & Co
Voltastrasse 5, 13355 Berlin, Germany
Telephone: +49 30 463 5037 Fax: +49 30 464 3710
Managing Director: Sami Tabbara
Marketing Manager: Manfred Hildebrandt

Products: In-cab computerised diagnostic display units for LRVs and metro cars. Passenger information systems for ticket machines.

Contracts: Latest contracts include supply of equipment for Berlin and Stockholm metros; people mover systems in Norway; S-Bahn, Berlin; trams in Berlin, Mainz, Halle, Zwickau, Jena, Cherzow, USA and Japan.

NEW ENTRY

Union Switch & Signal

Union Switch & Signal Inc
1901 Main Street, Columbia, SC 29201, USA
Telephone: +1 803 929 1200 Fax: +1 803 929 6965
President & Chief Executive Officer: W Alessandrini
Vice President, Planning & Communications: A Florence
Vice President, Customer Satisfaction: J Pickering
Part of the Ansaldo group

Wayside Control Products Division
PO Box 539, 645 Russell Street, Batesburg, SC 29006
Telephone: +1 803 532 4432 Fax: +1 803 532 2940
Vice President, Wayside Control Products Division: K Riddet

Transportation Control Systems Division/Vehicle Control Systems Division
1000 Technology Drive, Pittsburgh, PA 15219-3120
Telephone: +1 412 688 2400 Fax: +1 412 688 2399
Vice President, Transportation Control Systems Division: M Pracht
Vice President, Vehicle Control Systems Division: T Giras

Products: Computerised dispatching and operations control centres; communications-based control systems; wayside control systems; onboard control. Dispatching and operations control centres feature open-system architecture, centralised or distributed processing configurations, and digital data communications between the centre and the field. Wayside systems include vital logic control, ranging from vital relays to the Microlok® vital microprocessor-based control system; AF-900 digital FSK track circuit for urban transport ATC applications; electric and electropneumatic points machines; searchlight and colourlight signals. Microcab® onboard control system for a range of applications from basic cab signalling to full onboard ATC.

Contracts: Currently working on equipment for the MBTA operations control centre, Boston; Seoul metro Lines 7 and 8.

UPDATED

Vapor

Mark IV Industries Company
6420 West Howard Street, Niles, IL 60714, USA
Telephone: +1 847 967 8300 Fax: +1 847 965 9864
Vice President, Sales & Marketing: K N Nippes

Associated companies
Vapor Canada Inc
10655 Henri Bourassa West, St Laurent, Quebec H4S 1A1, Canada
President: D M Kerr
Telephone: +1 514 335 4200 Fax: +1 514 335 4321
Executive Vice President, Sales & Marketing: M Hardt
Sales Manager: P Buckley

Vapor International Holland BV
Atoomweg 496, 3542 AB Utrecht, Netherlands

Vapor UK
28 Springdale Court, Mickleover, Derby DE3 5SW, England

Products: Vapor represents Peek Traffic BV of Hilversum, Netherlands, in the sale and support of vehicle identification systems for bus and rail applications in North America. Included are vehicle identification systems, vehicle-to-wayside communications, intelligent vehicle systems, schedule adherence, passenger counting, automatic vehicle location and next-bus signs at bus stops.

Contracts: Vapor VETAG vehicle identification systems are in service on SEPTA Philadelphia, Boston's Green line, the Portland, Calgary, Denver, Santa Clara and San Diego light rail systems, Chicago's Skokie Swift line, and San Francisco Muni cable car and light rail network.

VETAG installations have been installed on the Dallas light rail and the Northern Indiana Commuter Transportation district's South Shore line.

VERIFIED

Vaughan Harmon Systems

Vaughan Harmon Systems Limited
The Maltings, Hoe Lane, Ware SG12 9LR, England
Telephone: +44 1920 462282 Fax: +44 1920 460702
Managing Director: A St Johnston

Backgrounds: Vaughan Systems was acquired by Harmon (qv) in 1996 and has become Vaughan Harmon Systems.

Products: Information and control systems for main line and for urban transport systems, including network timetabling, train reporting, staff and management information, large and small train describers, signalling control centres, and passenger information systems.

Train describers and signal control systems are available with colour or monochrome VDU maps, main panel LED displays and facilities for train reporting and enquiry. The Vaughan Small Train Describer is available for low-cost small installations, typically 50 berths with either digital or serial interfaces to the interlocking. Automatic code insertion and route setting facilities are available from stored timetable or that received via a network from a central facility.

Train reporting systems are of two types, those providing automatic train reporting with enquiry facilities, or automatic reporting by exception. The latter uses the timetable as the basis on which the exception reports are prepared.

Area timetable systems have been installed connected to networks. These enable timetables to be made available to all the components forming part of the transport control and information system. These include automatic train reporting by exception, automatic code insertion, passenger information systems, local and area staff information systems.

Modular signalling control system capable of expansion into a fully integrated railway control system including traction power, telecommunications and track-to-train radio.

UPDATED

Vultron

Vultron International Ltd
City Park Industrial Estate, Gelderd Road, Leeds LS12 6DR, England
Telephone: +44 113 263 0323 Fax: +44 113 279 4127
Managing Director: J H Moorhouse
Sales Director: Howard Pearcy

USA office
2600 Bond Street, Rochester Hills, MI 48309
Telephone: +1 810 853 2200 Fax: +1 810 853 7571
Vice President, Sales: Leon Leigh

Products: Electronic destination sign systems in liquid crystal display or electronic magnetic dots; passenger information systems; multicolour dot system and liquid crystal display in upper and lower case characters. Range of signs complying with UK DPTAC requirements for disabled people.

Contracts: A Digi-dot display has been installed at Bristol Parkway offering text on six lines of 30 characters.

Supplied equipment for British stations and trains, including Classes 158, 321, 320, 442 and 165; major supplier of bus destination equipments.

VERIFIED

Wandel & Goltermann

Wandel & Goltermann Kommuni-kationstechnik GmbH
PO Box 1361, 72796 Eningen u A, Germany
Telephone: +49 7121 9860 Fax: +49 7121 986100
Managing Director: Fariborz Khavand
Director, Public Transportation Systems:
Karl-Heinz Bahnmüller
Director, Public Safety Systems: Alex Treffers

Products: Onboard computers, next-stop displays, digital announcement equipment, public address systems with integrated passenger alarm intercom for buses and trains.

Contracts: Include supply of equipment for Netherlands Railways, Berlin S-Bahn and München transport; also for low-floor trams in Düsseldorf and München.

Wardrop

Wardrop Engineering Inc
Suite 600, 6725 Airport Road, Mississauga, Ontario, Canada L4V 1V2
Telephone: +1 905 673 3788 Fax: +1 905 673 8007
CEO and General Manager: Ernie Card
Principal Manager, Software: Henry A Martin
Project Manager: Steven Gallant

Products: PC-based CTC and passenger counting systems (see Revenue Collection Equipment section)

Contracts: Supply of CTC for the extension of TTC Toronto's Spadina line.

NEW ENTRY

WCL

Westinghouse Cubic Ltd
177 Nutfield Road, Merstham RH1 3HH, England
Telephone: +44 1737 644921 Fax: +44 1737 643693
Managing Director: John Lincoln
General Manager: Steve Harris
Operations Director: Nigel Bryant
Director, Strategic Operations: Peter Ellwood

Subsidiary company
WCL Derwent House, Kendal Avenue, Park Royal, London W3 0XA
Telephone: +44 181 992 8070 Fax +44 181 992 8072

Products: CCTV, public address, passenger information, passenger assistance and radio systems.

Contracts: Equipment has been supplied for London Underground's Jubilee line extension and for LU tunnel lighting and power installations.

Westinghouse Signals

Westinghouse Signals Limited
A member of the BTR Rail Group
PO Box 79, Pew Hill, Chippenham SN15 1JD, England
Telephone: +44 1249 441441 Fax: +44 1249 652322
Managing Director: J D Mills
Contracts Director: C M W Harding
Product Group Director: D Pickering
Technical Director: P Cross
Marketing Manager: G B Nelson

Associated companies
Westinghouse Brake and Signal Co (Australia) Ltd
Dimetronic SA (Spain)
Safetran Systems Corporation (USA)

Products: Signals, point machines, track circuits (jointless and jointed), safety relays, electronic interlockings and safety processors, control panels and VDU displays, workstations, data transmission systems; automatic train control (ATC) incorporating automatic train protection (ATP), automatic train operation (ATO), and automatic train supervision (ATS); relay interlocking; solid state interlocking (SSI); train-to-signalbox radio, centralised traffic control (CTC), electronic control centres; passenger information systems; train describers and traction power telecontrol; train management systems.

Westrace is a second-generation safety processor developed by Westinghouse Signals and its three associated signalling companies to satisfy a range of safety applications which range from simple wayside interlockings to complete CTC. The equipment can provide trainborne safety processing for ATP systems, can be configured as a solid state highway crossing controller, or can simply provide safe data transmission.

The control and monitoring system (CMS) for train management provides: communication between intelligent subsystems (brakes, traction etc); transmission of information between train subsystems and the operator; access to built-in diagnostic data of intelligent subsystems; transmission of information to trackside; diagnosis and recording of train faults; implementation of trainwide control functions; and integration of non-intelligent subsystems via intelligent I/O interface modules. The maintenance support system (MSS) complements CMS, providing depot-based facilities which receive downloaded data from the CMS, gathering use and trend data for planned and preventative maintenance, thereby achieving higher fleet utilisation.

Westronic System Two is a modular microprocessor-based data handling and transmission system that can be configured to suit an expanding range of railway applications, including CTC, train description, passenger information, traction power telecontrol, station plant supervision, panel processing and supervision of train radio systems.

Contracts: Signalling and train control systems were supplied to Oslo Sporveier during 1995 and 1996, including automatic train control and centralised traffic control with automatic route setting. The Westrace microprocessor-controlled safety-critical train control system is be used to allow remote monitoring.

Westrace transmission-based signalling and safety processing system is being installed on London Underground's Jubilee line.

VERIFIED

AES PRODATA

World Leaders in Automated Fare Collection

Specialising in the design, manufacture and project management of Automated Fare Collection (AFC) products and systems.

All modes of public transport

- Rail
- Tram
- Bus
- Ferry

All types of ticket technology including

- Magnetic Stripe
- Contact Smart Card
- Contactless Smart Card
- Hybrid Smart Card

Installations worldwide including cities in:

Argentina, Australia, Austria, Belgium, Brazil, Canada, Denmark, Egypt, France, Hong Kong, Mexico, Norway, Sweden, Tunisia, Turkey and the United Kingdom

Offices Worldwide

- **Australia** - Perth, Melbourne, Sydney, Brisbane
- **Belgium** - Zaventem
- **Brazil** - São Paolo
- **Canada** - Mississauga
- **France** - Besançon
- **Hong Kong**
- **Sweden** - Stockholm-Globen
- **United Kingdom** - Bolton

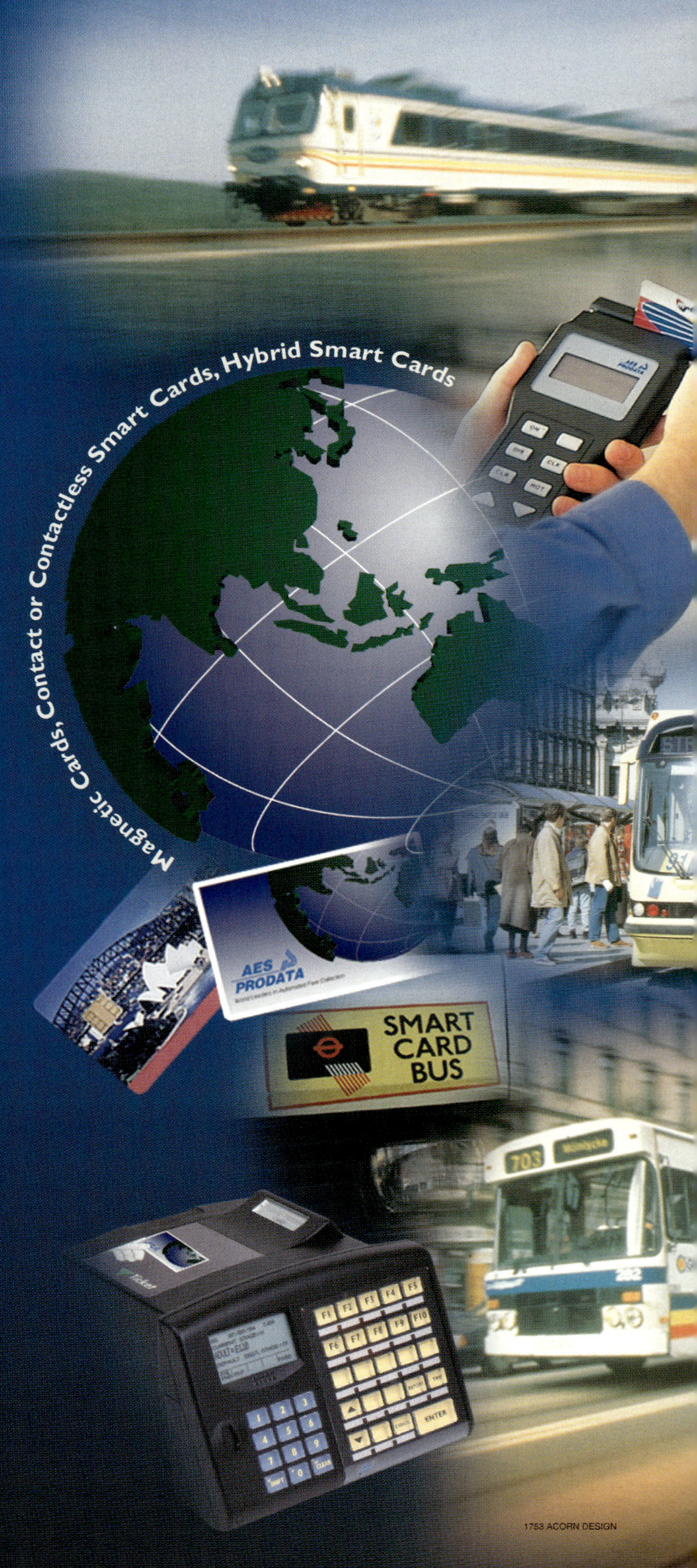

AES PRODATA

AES Prodata (Europe)
Leuvensesteenweg 540, B2
1930 Zaventem, Belgium
Telephone: + 32 2 722 8911
Facsimile: + 32 2 720 8794

AES Prodata Holdings
247-249 Balcatta Road
Balcatta, WA 6021, Australia
Telephone: +61 8 9273 1100
Facsimile: +61 8 9344 3686

AES Prodata (Canada)
Unit 18, 151 Brunel Road
Mississauga, ONT L4Z IX3, Canada
Telephone: +1 905 890 2794
Facsimile: +1 905 890 4590

1753 ACORN DESIGN

REVENUE COLLECTION EQUIPMENT

Company Listing by Country

AUSTRALIA
Abberfield Technology
AES Prodata

BELGIUM
AES Prodata
Automatic Systems

CANADA
Cegelec
Microtronix
Wardrop

CROATIA
SKALA

DENMARK
Scanpoint

FINLAND
Buscom

FRANCE
Ascom Monétel
Cegelec CGA
Dassault
Schlumberger
Steria

GERMANY
Adtranz
ELGEBA
Fleischhauer-Gizeh
Höft & Wessel
Klüssendorf
Krauth
Scheidt & Bachmann
Siemens Transportation Systems

ITALY
EIS Elettronica
Firema Trasporti
Italtel Telesis
Italdis
Mael
Mecstar
Mobile Data Processing
Tecnotel
Tecnotour-Eltec
Telesistemi

JAPAN
Nippon Signal
OMRON
Sanyo Electric
Toshiba

SWEDEN
Cambist

SWITZERLAND
Ascom
Fahel
Mars Electronics
Sadamel

UK
Booth
Burall Infocard
Magnordata
Metric Group
Newbury Data
Scan Coin
Thorn
Time 24
Transmo
Wayfarer
WCL

USA
Agent
BZA
Cubic
Denominator
Diamond
GFI Genfare
Globe
Main
Mars Electronics
Rand McNally
Roger Williams Mint
Standard Change-Makers

Classified Listing

ACCESS CONTROL
AES Prodata
Ascom Monétel
Automatic Systems
Cegelec
Cegelec CGA
Dassault
Firema Trasporti
Italdis
Scheidt & Bachmann
Telesistemi
Toshiba
Wardrop
Wayfarer
WCL

BOOKING OFFICE MACHINES
CHANGE MACHINES
Abberfield Technology
Adtranz
AES Prodata
Agent
Ascom Monétel
Cambist
GFI Genfare
Nippon Signal
Sanyo Electric
Scan Coin
Scheidt & Bachmann
Standard Change-Makers
Tecnotour-Eltec
Telesistemi
Toshiba
Wayfarer
WCL

COMPLETE AFC SYSTEMS
AES Prodata
Ascom
Ascom Monétel
Cubic
Dassault
Firema Trasporti
Klussendorf
OMRON
Tecnotel
Tecnotour-Eltec
Telesistemi
Thorn
Transmo
Wayfarer
WCL

FAREBOXES
AES Prodata
Cubic
Diamond
GFI Genfare
Main

ONBOARD MACHINES
AES Prodata
Ascom Monétel
Cegelec CGA
Mael
Mobile Data Processing
Newbury Data
Sadamel
Scanpoint
Scheidt & Bachmann
SKALA
Tecnotel
Tecnotour-Eltec
Wayfarer

PORTABLE
AES Prodata
BZA
Diamond
Mael
Metric Group
Newbury Data
Sadamel
Scanpoint
Thorn
Wayfarer

SMARTCARD SYSTEMS
Adtranz
AES Prodata
Ascom Monétel
Buscom
BZA
Cubic
Dassault
ELGEBA
GFI Genfare
Höft & Wessel
Klüssendorf
Krauth
Metric Group
OMRON
Scanpoint
Scheidt & Bachmann
Schlumberger
Siemens Transportation Systems
Transmo
Wayfarer
WCL

STAND-ALONE MACHINES
AES Prodata
Agent
Ascom Monétel
Italtel Telesis
Metric Group
Wayfarer

TICKET/TOKEN/CARD SUPPLIER
Booth
Burall Infocard
Buscom
Fleischhauer-Gizeh
Globe
Magnordata
Mecstar
Rand McNally
Roger Williams Mint
Scanpoint
Steria
Time 24
Transmo

VALIDATORS/CANCELLERS/COUNTERS
Abberfield Technology
Adtranz
AES Prodata
Ascom
Ascom Monétel
Cegelec
Cegelec CGA
Denominator
GFI Genfare
Italtel Telesis
Mars Electronics
Microtronix
OMRON
Scanpoint
SKALA
Tecnotour-Eltec
Telesistemi
Thorn
Toshiba
Wayfarer

Abberfield Technology

Abberfield Technology Pty Ltd
32 Cross Street, Brookvale, NSW 2100, Australia
Telephone: +61 2 9939 2844 Fax: +61 2 9938 3462
Managing Director: John M Colyer

UK office: Abberfield (Europe) Ltd, 4 Andover Street, Sheffield S3 9EG, UK
Telephone: +44 114 272 7108 Fax: +44 114 272 7108
UK Manager: Dennis Sutherland

Products: Ticket vending machines and ticket validators; ticketing systems for all modes of transport. Note and coin-to-coin change machines.

Contracts: Provision of ticket vending and validating machines for Sheffield Supertram, England. Also ticket validating, change machines and turnstile controls for the Oasis Monorail, Gold Coast, Queensland.

UPDATED

Adtranz

ABB Daimler-Benz Transportation GmbH
PO Box 13127, 13601 Berlin, Germany
Telephone: +49 303 8320 Fax: +49 303 832 2000
(See main entry under Rail Vehicles and Traction Equipment)

Products: Ticket printers, systems for issuing tickets and producing accounting sales data, electronic payment and smartcards, automatic ticket vending machines, ticket cancellers.

Range: Microprocessor-controlled electronic print and record units (AFR200) for stationary and mobile operations. The AFAB system for issuing tickets and accounting sales data, comprising electronic print and record units, memory modules and depot units. The automatic ticket vending machine AFA400 is designed for installation on vehicles or at stations; it is microprocessor-based and can take paper currency as well as five types of coins. A recycling unit can pay out change. Microprocessor-controlled cancellers assembled from modular components. The machines offer remote control of up to 20 cancellers by time division multiplex via two or four control wires or an IBIS-bus.

Developments: The ACT 400 is a new smartcard terminal, designed for contact or proximity cards. ANDY is a new handheld ticket printer for paper tickets with an option for electronic payment with smartcards.

UPDATED

AES Prodata

AES Prodata Holdings
247-249 Balcatta Road, Balcatta, WA 6021 Australia
Telephone: +61 8 9273 1100 Fax: +61 8 9344 3686
Chief Executive Officer: P J Fogarty
Managing Director: Chris Ring
General Manager: Stephen Waterhouse
Marketing Manager: John Farrer

AES Prodata (Europe)
Leuvensesteenweg 540, bus 2, 1930 Zaventem, Belgium
Telephone: +32 2 722 8911 Fax: +32 2 720 8794
Chief Executive Officer: Franky Carbonez
Vice President: Walter Raffo
General Manager, Marketing: Torben Nielsen

Principal subsidiaries
AES Prodata Brazil
AES Prodata Hong Kong
AES Prodata France
AES Prodata Scandinavia
AES Prodata UK

Background: AES Prodata is the fare collection subsidiary of ERG. It has experience in the design, manufacture and project management of AFC systems. The company offers a turnkey approach to the supply and installation of components for a complete AFC system.

Products: Fare collection systems based on magnetic tickets, contact and contactless smartcards and hybrid smartcards; for bus, tram, ferry, rail and light rail.

Range: Includes advanced on-board ticket issuing, card validation and inspection; ticket vending machines, point-of-sale terminals; on-station equipment such as barriers and validators; hardware and software for data communication, storage and handling; depot station and central clearing house computer systems.
Latest products include: the P2000, a portable ticket issuer/verifier used by SNCB; the TP4000, a driver console combining contactless smartcard technology with a paper ticket printer; and the V3000, the first validator capable of reading hybrid smartcards.

Contracts: Major installations include Ankara, Hong Kong, Melbourne, Taipei, as well as a number of urban and regional systems in Brazil, France, the Canary Islands and Romania.

AES Prodata the leader of a consortium consisting of Bull and Resarail 2000, a subsidiary of the French railways SNCF, won a contract to provide the city of Valenciennes, France, with a multimodal transport system. This will be the first system utilising a hybrid card; a card capable of acting as both a contactless and a contact smartcard. The hybrid card will be used in the network of buses in Valenciennes and in regional trains. The cards will also be capable of use in parking and suburban buses. The project was scheduled to go into commercial operation in June 1997.

AES Prodata has won a contract to provide the Moskva metro with a new AFC system. Approximately 1,600 of the existing turnstiles will be equipped with a gate adaption kit based on magnetic and smartcard technology. The contract also includes the development of gate reader data collection software, the supply of on-station computers and software for issuing and personalising contactless smartcards. Implementation was due to start in September 1997.

The State Transit Authority of New South Wales awarded AES Prodata a contract to supply the Sydney Ferries with a new-generation fare collection system. The system will comprise ticket vending machines with touchscreens and state-of-the-art gate technology based on magnetic tickets. It can be upgraded to smartcard technology as and when necessary. The project is scheduled to go into commercial operation in the first half of 1998.

UPDATED

Agent

Agent Systems Inc
2015 Midway Road, Suite 111, Dallas, TX 75006, USA
Telephone: +1 214 774 0400 Fax: +1 214 392 7301
President: Brian G Walters
Marketing Manager: Bruce W Davies

Products: Automatic fare collection systems.

Range: Computer control systems for fare collection; debit/credit card-only ticket vending machines; represents Scheidt & Bachmann (qv) in North American market for ticket vending machines and fare gate products.

Contracts: Fare collection systems have been provided to Long Island Rail Road, Metro-North Railroad, New Jersey, MTA Maryland, BART San Francisco and North Diego County Transit Development Board.

NEW ENTRY

Ascom

Ascom Autelca SA AG
Vendomation Division
Worbstrasse 201, 3073 Gümligen-Berne, Switzerland
Telephone: +41 31 999 6111 Fax: +41 31 999 6405

A shock discovery for the Transit Industry. Everyone's needs are different.

Too many transit systems are designed along precisely the same lines.

Not with THORN. Our Automatic Fare Collection Systems use proven technology to meet any Transit Authority's requirements:

- different payment methods
- complete range of products (from Ticket Vending Machines to Automatic control Gates)
- Central computer hardware and software systems, as stand alone or fully integrated

The reason for this is simple. We believe in working much closer with our customers as a team, which gives us a responsiveness and flexibility that's second to none.

You can judge our success by the number and quality of installations we've worked on worldwide, and their reliability.

They're not mass transit systems. They're systems that answer the needs of the individual.

Thorn
Transit Systems
International

THORN Transit Systems International
Wookey Hole Road, Wells, Somerset BA5 1AA, England
Tel: +44 (0)1749 670222 Fax: +44 (0)1749 679363

SBS

Spray Booth Systems Inc
PO Box 15070, 5124 Kaltenbrun, Fort Worth, TX 76119, USA
Telephone: +1 817 793 7727 Fax: +1 817 483 4625

Products: Spray painting booths, vehicle washing systems.

SEFAC

Société d'Estampage et de Forge Ardennes Champagne
1 rue Andre Compain, 08800 Montherme, France
Telephone: +33 3 24 53 01 82 Fax: +33 3 24 53 20 23/24
Managing Director: F Finet
Railway Marketing Manager: Vincent Jolliot
Railway Engineering Manager: E Letellier

Head office:110 rue de la République, PO Box 15, 45201 Le Chambon-Feugerolles
Telephone: +33 1 77 40 18 18 Fax: +33 1 77 89 17 45

Subsidiary companies
SEFAC Lift & Equipment Corporation
7175 Oakland Mills Road, Columbia, MD 21046, USA
Telephone: +1 410 964 0806 Fax: +1 410 964 0877
Manager: Richard Kergen

SEFAC SA
Camino de Rejas, Nave 10, 28820 Coslada, Spain
Telephone: +34 1 672 3612 Fax: +34 1 672 3396
Manager: R Serrano

Products: Mobile lifts, jacks, bogie lifts, cleaning systems, depot/garage equipment for railways, metro, LRT and bus applications; dust removal systems.

Contracts: Recent contracts include equipment for SNCF Noisy Le Sec, MTRC Hong Kong (Lantau Airport) and National Authority for Tunnels, Cairo.

UPDATED

Simmons

Simmons Machine Tool Corp
1700 N Broadway, Albany, NY 12204, USA
Telephone: +1 518 462 5431 Fax: +1 518 462 0371
President: T H Smith
Vice President, Sales & Service: D W Davis

Products: Wheelshop equipment; underfloor profiling machines.

Smith Bros & Webb

Smith Bros & Webb Limited
Britannia House, Arden Forest Industrial Estate, Alcester B49 6EX, England
Telephone: +44 1789 400096 Fax: +44 1789 400231
Managing Director: K H Harrison

Products: Automatic washers for rail and road vehicles; Streamline Major automatic high-throughput commercial vehicle washing machine.

Contracts: Recent contracts include cleaning systems for Cowie Group bus companies in Britain and drive-through train washers in Sydney, Colombo, Izmir, Cairo, Porto and Lisboa, Portugal and London Underground.

Bus wash systems have gone to UK operators Midland Red North, Stafford; Greater Manchester Buses (5); South London Buses and Yorkshire Rider.

UPDATED

Somers

Somers Vehicle Lifts Ltd
15 Forge Trading Estate, Mucklow Hill, Halesowen B62 8TR, England
Telephone: +44 121 501 1077 Fax: +44 121 501 1458
Divisional Manager, Mobile Lifts: Alister Collings
Marketing: Tim Jackson

Products: Mobile road and rail vehicle lifts, scissors lifts and support stands.

Developments: A new range of lightweight mobile vehicle lifts is designed for minibuses and other smaller vehicles.

UPDATED

SSI

SSI Corporation
255 Fire Tower Drive, Tonawanda, NY 14150, USA
Telephone: +1 905 795 9274 Fax: +1 905 795 1350
President: Seymour Techner

Products: Modular train and bus washing systems; vehicle interior vacuum cleaning systems; dryers.

Contracts: Has supplied equipment to Amtrak, Boston; WMATA Washington; TriMet Portland; DART Dallas; Connecticut Department of Transport: Singapore MRT.

VERIFIED

Technorizon

Technorizon Systems (UK) Ltd
54 Angel Hill, Sutton SM1 3EW, England
Telephone: +44 181 641 2229 Fax: +44 181 644 1151
Chairman: Des Cockerill

Products: Vehicle washing systems.

NEW ENTRY

Valematic

Valematic
Elles House, 4B Invincible Road, Farnborough GU14 7QU, England
Telephone: +44 1252 362800 Fax: +44 1252 373695
Managing Director, Operations: Graham Round

Products: Trident, Brushwash® and Jetwash® cleaning systems for buses and coaches. Equipment is supplied with water reclamation facilities.

Whiting

Whiting Corporation
15700 Lathrop Avenue, Harvey, IL 60426-5198, USA
Telephone: +1 810 263 1940 Fax: +1 708 210 5030
Director of International Marketing: C J Skorpinski
Manager, Product Systems: Marvin M Milligan
Region Sales Managers: Greg Ciecierski
R L Garavaglia (Telephone: +1 810 263 1940)
Ken Lankey (Telephone: +1 864 627 3767)

Products: Drop tables, locomotive and car body supports, turntable equipment, transfer tables, portable electric jacks and overhead bridge cranes.

Contracts: Recent contracts include equipment for Amtrak, Metra Chicago, Union Pacific, Burlington Northern, WMATA Washington and SEPTA Philadelphia.

UPDATED

Wilcomatic

Wilcomatic Ltd
Commercial Division, 123 Beddington Lane, Croydon CR9 4NX, England
Telephone: +44 181 684 9900 Fax: +44 181 684 0489
Sales Manager: Paul Goluwski

Background: Wilcomatic has been supplying vehicle wash equipment since 1966 and is a subsidiary of European Motor Holdings plc.

Products: Vehicle washing equipment (drive-through two- and four-brush machines); under-chassis washers; own range of washing chemicals.

NEW ENTRY

Windhoff

Windhoff AG
PO Box 1963, 48409 Rheine, Germany
Telephone: +49 5971 580 Fax: +49 5971 58209
President: Dr Bernd Windhoff
Managing Director: Dipl-Ing Heinz Lörfing
Export Manager: Dipl-Ing Helmut Pühs

Products: Heavy-duty lighting installation for vehicle servicing; lifting jacks; bogie exchange installations; axle and bogie lifts; traversers; turntables; multipurpose track maintenance machines; overhead line inspection and maintenance vehicles; special rail cranes; crib ballast removers; underground vehicles; catenary inspection vehicles.

Contracts: Windhoff's contracts have included supply of equipment for the Singapore metro, Australian National, New South Wales Railways, Indonesian State Railways, SNCZ Zaire, Ugandan Railways Corporation, Indian Railways, German Railway, Tunisian National Railways, Luxembourg Railways, and Netherlands Railways.

While Speno looks after your rails, urban life goes happily on.

The Speno HRR 12M brings to urban transport the rail grinding technology developed by Speno for the world's leading railways. It has been designed to rectify and completely reprofile Vignole and grooved rails, either on standard gauge (1435 mm) or on metric gauge (1000 mm) tracks.

Grinding without restriction in urban areas is made possible by these HRR 12M features:

- A powerful dust collection system;
- Metal shields confining the grinding sparks under the frame;
- Reduced noise level during grinding.

The hi-rail concept will reduce mobilization time and costs, giving our customers an optimum flexibility when planning grinding campaigns. The Speno HRR 12M can be on-tracked and off-tracked without external assistance. On track it can reach the work site running light at 40 km/h. Even a 20 m radius curve or a 70‰ gradient won't stop the HRR 12M.

While the Speno HRR 12M looks after your rails almost unnoticed, urban life goes happily on.

HAR 8

SPENO INTERNATIONAL S.A.
26, Parc Château-Banquet, C.P.16, CH-1202 Geneva, Switzerland
Tel.: +41 22 906 46 00 Fax: +41 22 906 46 01

Abloy

Abloy
2-3 Hatters Lane, Croxley Business Park, Watford WD1 8YY, England
Telephone: +44 1923 255066 Fax: +44 1923 210641
Director: Julie Day

Products: Locking systems for track installations and other applications.

Contracts: SJ Sweden has been supplied with 60,000 padlocks, 20,000 industrial cam locks and Abloy's Great Grand Master Key System based on its Disklock Pro.

Padlocks have also been supplied to Railtrack, UK.

NEW ENTRY

ALH Systems

ALH Systems Ltd
Station Road, Westbury BA13 4TN, England
Telephone: +44 1373 858234 Fax: +44 1373 858235
Managing Director: Robin E M Thomas
Production Director: John R G Clark
Sales Director: B Stell
Finance Director: T M A Collins

Products: Resilient fixing of rail systems; Series Six, a polyurethane-based material, developed by ALH originally as a gas pipe encapsulant system, has seen extensive use during the past 10 years. Light rail embedment.

LR55 advanced shallow-depth track system for LRVs, developed jointly by Edgar Allen Engineering, ALH Systems and Tarmac Precast Concrete Ltd. The inventor and patent holder is Prof Lewis Lesley.

A section of track embedded with Series Six has undergone tests with South Yorkshire Supertram, Sheffield, UK.

VERIFED

Aqua

Aqua Signal & Telegraphic Systems
Belmont House, Garnett Place, Skelmersdale WN8 9UP, England
Telephone: +44 1695 51933 Fax: +44 1695 51891

Products: Railway drainage systems.

NEW ENTRY

Balfour Beatty

Balfour Beatty Railway Engineering Ltd
Osmaston Street, Sandiacre NG10 5AN, England
Telephone: +44 115 921 8218 Fax: +44 115 921 8219
Managing Director: Bob Somerville
General Manager Designate: Keith Churn
UK Client Account Manager: Gary Elliott
Marketing Director: Phil Bean
Sales & Marketing Administrator: Katherine Marriott

Part of BICC Group

Parent Company: Balfour Beatty Ltd, One Angel Square, Torrens Street, London EC1V 1SX
Telephone: +44 171 216 6800 Fax: +44 171 216 6950

Products: Design, manufacture, installation and maintenance of complete track and traction power installations; switches, swing-nose crossings and complete turnouts; fabricated and cast baseplates and other components. Supply of spheroidal graphite and grey iron castings; lever boxes; fabricated crossings; shallow-depth switches; friction buffer stops; high-speed points.

Contracts: Major contracts have included track for the Channel Tunnel terminal at Folkestone; the Tuen Mun light rail in Hong Kong; the Lantau and Airport railway, Hong Kong; Tsing Ma Bridge; the Beckton extension of London's Docklands Light Railway; Manchester Metrolink and Sheffield Supertram; Singapore MRT's Woodlands extension, the Ankara metro, London Underground's Central line point and crossing renewals, and for track renewal and maintenance on British Rail's (now Railtrack) Chiltern line. This was the first BR track maintenance contract to be awarded to the private sector.

Also, construction of tunnel and trackwork for Jubilee line, London Underground, between Green Park and Waterloo.

Major orders received for supply of turnouts to Hong Kong, USA, and London Underground. A contract was issued in 1996 by PATH New York for tunnel network junction renewals at Hoboken and Grove Street, New Jersey, and 33rd Street, Manhattan. From 1996, Balfour Beatty has been responsible for the construction of trackwork for the Lantau Airport Railway and has supplied to Amtrak for its North East Corridor.

Developments: A gantry mill machine has been installed. Designed and built by Forest Liné, Albert, France, it can accommodate 38 m rails and is capable of machining operations throughout the entire length of rail, including web drilling. Twin 50 kW vertical cutting heads are serviced by ten-position auto-tool changers for the vertical heads, and five-position auto-tool changers for the horizontal drilling attachments. It is controlled by a Siemens 840C computer serviced by CAD/CAM programming. Completely finished machined rails are unloaded from the machine automatically.

UPDATED

Bance

R Bance & Co Ltd
Cockcrow Hill House, St Mary's Road, Surbiton KT 65HE, England
Telephone: +44 181 398 7141 Fax: +44 181 398 4765
Managing Director: R Bance

Products: Portable track maintenance plant; impact wrench and auger; rechargeable work lamps; single rail Super-Skate trolley; track level gauges; rail disc cutters; Alumi-Cart two-person portable rail inspection vehicle and trailer; mobile ultrasonic rail flaw detector; tapered rail joint shims; rail contact and fastening clamps; electronic measuring.

UPDATED

British Steel

British Steel Track Products
Moss Bay, Derwent Howe, Workington CA14 5AE, England
Telephone: +44 1900 64321 Fax: +44 1900 64800
Managing Director: A V L Williams
Works Manager: K Hill
Commercial Manager: S W Askew
Parent company: British Steel plc

Products: Heavy and light rails, conductor rail, bridge and crane rail, fishplates, baseplates, steel sleepers and special turnout rails.

Also in-line rail heat treatment unit in full production, producing 'Hi-Life' rail. Further work is in hand to develop a 'designer' rail, and different rail sections and grades to broaden the market base. Certain new asymmetrical sections in production for switch and crossing work.

Contracts: BS Track Products has produced a batch of 220 m long factory-welded rail for the Heathrow Express line, England. Also contracts in Canada, Benin, India and Egypt.

Developments: BS Track Products and Royal Volker Stevin have formed a jointly owned company GrantRail Ltd (see separate entry). It has been formed from the tracklaying division of British Steel subsidiary Grant Lyon Eagre Ltd (see separate entry), and Royal Volker Stevin's railway engineering company Railbouw (UK) Ltd.

UPDATED

BWG

Butzbacher Weichenbau GmbH
PO Box 305, 35503 Butzbach, Germany
Telephone: +49 6033 892119 Fax: +49 6033 892123
General Manager: E Bittel
Director, Marketing & Engineering: H Höne
Engineering Manager: E Nuding
Sales Manager: N J Krenytzky

Works: 101 Wetzlarer Stasse, 35510 Butzbach

Products: Points and crossings; semi-welded frogs; asymmetric switch rails; fire-pearlitic hardening; kinematic gauge optimisation (KGO); vulcanised baseplates, inside stock rail fastening system; integrated sleepers; vibration-dampened rail systems.

Contracts: Supply of UIC60 trackwork components to DORTS, Metro Taipei, Taiwan; to DB S-Bahn, Frankfurt.

CAN Geotechnical

CAN Geotechnical Ltd
Smeckley Wood Close, Chesterfield Trading Estate, Chesterfield S41 9PZ, England
Telephone: +44 1246 261111 Fax: +44 1246 261626
Director: John Batty

Products: CAN-Span work platform for bridge underdeck inspection without recourse to a track possession.

NEW ENTRY

Cembre

Cembre SpA
Via Serenissima 9, 25135 Brescia, Italy
Telephone: +39 30 36921 Fax: +39 30 336 5766

UK office
Cembre Ltd, Fairview Industrial Estate, Kingsbury Road, Curdworth, Sutton Coldfield B76 9EE
Telephone: +44 1675 470440 Fax: +44 1675 470220

Products: Petrol-powered and electric portable rail drill.

NEW ENTRY

C F & I Steel

C F & I Steel
PO Box 1830, Pueblo, CO 81002, USA
Telephone: +1 719 561 6000 Fax: +1 719 561 7256
Vice President & General Manager: James W Colzani
Vice President, Commercial: R L Head

Products: Rail

Contracts: Southern California Regional Railroad Authority (Los Angeles Metrolink).

Chipman Rail

Chipman Rail plc
The Goods Yard, Horsham RH12 2NR, England
Telephone: +44 1403 260341 Fax: +44 1403 264799
Managing Director: Brian Ollier

Background: The company was formerly a division of Nomix-Chipman Ltd but was demerged to form a separate company in 1996.

Products: Spraying equipment and high-pressure leaf jetting and traction gel application equipment; weed chemicals and equipment; drain clearing.

Contracts: Has secured a three-year leaf clearance programme from Britain's Railtrack South. The contract, which is the first of its type awarded to a private concern, is based on Chipman Rail's use of high-pressure water jet engineering and sandite gel formulation technology. The project follows development of a dedicated leaf jetting train. The train comprises a leaf blasting coach, four water tank wagons and two locomotives and is employed over much of Railtrack South's permanent way which is affected by leaf falls each autumn.

The leaf clearance unit travels at a constant speed of 32 km/h. Its leading water jet softens up the leaves, which are then broken up and removed by the second jet. The sandite – a sand/gel composite – is then applied, and the resulting residues jet washed off. The process ensures effective track adhesion for train wheels even in difficult weather conditions.

UPDATED

Clouth

Clouth Gummiwerke AG
Conveyor Belt Division, Environmental Technology
Niehler Strasse 102-116, 50733 Köln, Germany
Telephone: +49 221 7773 624 Fax: +49 221 7773 700
Members of the Board: Norbert Martin,
Dr Ullrich Masberg
Manager, Marketing & Sales: Michael Kottmann
Research & Development Managers: Alexander Repczuk
Dr Wilhelm Engst

Australia and Asia representative
Delkor Pty Ltd, PO Box 176, St Peters, NSW 2044
Telephone: +61 2 9550 5111 Fax: +61 2 9550 5625

UK representative
Delkor, Winterfield Road, Paulton BS18 5RF
Telephone: +44 1761 417079 Fax: +44 1761 414435

Products: Sub-ballast mats for vibration control; protective mats (Clouth-ASM®) for waterproof coatings of bridges and structures; rolling-rubber-springs (Clouth Rollfeder®) for primary and secondary suspension for rail vehicles; resilient track fastenings; elastomeric bridge bearings; mass-spring systems; Clouth Oil-Ex® elastomeric mat to absorb liquid hydrocarbons, such as oil, lubricants of low viscosity, motor fuels and organic solvents.

Contracts: A one-and-a-half year contract has been awarded for supply of sub-ballast mats for MBTA Boston, USA. Clouth, with its licensee Delkor Pty, Australia, is supplying resilient Clouth-Alternative 1 rail fasteners for the Check Lap Kok–Tsing-Ma Bridge on MTRC Hong Kong's Airport line, from 1995 to 1997. The two companies have also supplied 9,200 Köln Egg direct fixing fasteners for reconstruction of the Sydney Harbour bridge, Australia.

Developments: A new high-resilience rail fastener for vibration control is the Clouth Rail Pad or Clouth-CRP®. It complements the existing range of resilient rail fasteners and is moderately priced. It is based on a floating support of the ribplate which holds the rail and its fastening elements. With the Clouth-CRP® the ribplate is bedded on a resilient rubber pad. Heat-treated bolts anchor this fastener to the base and coil springs prevent the fastener from lifting off.

UPDATED

Cogifer

Compagnie Générale d'Installations Ferroviaires
40 quai de l'Ecluse, 78290 Croissy sur Seine, France
Telephone: +33 1 34 80 45 00 Fax: +33 1 34 80 03 08
President: Régis Bello
President, Cogifer TP: Henri Dehé
President, Cogifer Industries: C Schwartz
President, Cogifer Sicatelec: J L Wagner
Marketing Manager: Alain Montgaudon

Subsidiaries
Cogifer TP (railway and public installations)
Cogifer Industries (points and crossings)
Cogifer Sicatelec (signalling and catenary)

Products: Supply, installation and maintenance of track, points and crossings for metro, tramway and light rail systems; electric switching and detecting equipment.

Contracts: Has supplied track and components to more than 20 light rail networks including Strasbourg and Rouen, France; Cairo Metro, Egypt; Santiago Metro and Mexico City Metro.

UPDATED

Costain Dow Mac

Costain Dow Mac
Tallington, Stamford PE9 4RL, England
Telephone: +44 1778 311444 Fax: +44 1778 311395
Managing Director: M M Minassian
Technical Director: H P J Taylor
Divisional Commercial Manager: P R Adams
Parent company: Tarmac Precast Concrete

Products: Prestressed concrete sleepers; Bomac level crossings; switch and crossing bearers; tunnel linings; tunnel track solutions; arch bridge units; prestressed concrete bridge beams; full design service. Crossing bearers and tunnel track systems, with particular emphasis on noise and vibration reduction and street track systems.

Contracts: Supplying sleepers and other precast concrete products to Britain's Railtrack, London Underground, UK Department of Transport and local authorities.

Developments: In 1996 Tarmac Precast Concrete took over Costain Dow Mac.

UPDATED

Cowans Sheldon

Clayton Equipment Clarke Chapman Ltd
Hatton, Derby DE65 5EB, England
Telephone: +44 1283 812382 Fax: +44 1283 814772
Product Sales Manager: P Fraser
Parent company: Rolls Royce Power Engineering Ltd

Products: Diesel-hydraulic rail-mounted cranes for general and wrecking duties, also diesel-mechanical and diesel-electric range; rail handling vehicles for continuously welded rail; twin and single line tracklaying machines; rail side-loading cranes; ballast regulating machines; ballast cleaning machines; lightweight hydraulic rerailing equipment.

Multitasking railway cranes; track maintenance equipment.

CXT

CXT Incorporated
PO Box 14918, Spokane, WA 99214, USA
Telephone: +1 509 924 6300 Fax: +1 509 927 0299
Email: CXT@IEWAY.com
President & Chief Executive Officer: John G White
Vice President & Chief Financial Officer: Russ Skrypchuk
Vice President & General Manager, Tie Division:
Derek Firth

Works: 2420 N Sullivan Road, Spokane, WA 99216

Products: Prestressed concrete sleepers for track and turnouts; prefabricated buildings and precast concrete retaining walls.

CXT has developed design capabilities for turnouts; for track with a facility for gauge widening; for tangent sleeper development and for standard track sleepers.

Contracts: Concrete sleepers supplied to the Calgary LRT, MTA Baltimore, Vancouver, MBTA Boston, Denver, Portland and Southern California Regional Rail Authority, as well as many freight railways.

UPDATED

Edgar Allen

Edgar Allen Engineering Limited
PO Box 42, Shepcote Lane, Sheffield S9 1QW, England
Telephone: +44 114 244 6621 Fax: +44 114 242 6826
Managing Director: S R Adams
Sales Director: J E Steele
Financial Director: J Canterill
Technical Manager: T Grindle
Sales Manager: R Dibbo
Production Services Manager: D Turner
Quality Manager: D Pennock

Parent company: ANI Aurora plc, Aurora House, Meadowhall Road, Sheffield S9 1JD

Products: Design and manufacture of standard and specialist trackwork for main line, light rail and tram systems.

LR55 advanced shallow-depth track system for LRVs, developed jointly by Edgar Allen Engineering, ALH Systems and Tarmac Precast Concrete Ltd. The inventor and patent holder is Prof Lewis Lesley.

Developments: Cast titan steel was developed in conjunction with British Rail and has proved to be a comparable alternative to austenitic manganese steel in both main line rail and light rail applications. It is suitable for welding into CWR track.

UPDATED

Edilon

Edilon BV
PO Box 1000, 2003 RZ Haarlem, Netherlands
Telephone: +31 2353 19519 Fax: +31 2331 10751
Managing Director: R Vogelaar
Technical Director: A Aalberts

Works: Nijverheidsweg 23, 2031 CN, Haarlem
Subsidiary company: Edilon Corkelast SA, Spain

Products: Resilient track fastening and support systems; embedded rail system using Edilon Corkelast compound; adhesives.

Contracts: Have been held with Valencia Tramway, South Yorkshire Supertram and Madrid metro.

Elektro-Thermit

Elektro-Thermit GmbH
PO Box 101043, 45010 Essen, Germany
Telephone: +49 201 173 2373 Fax: +49 201 173 1994
Directors: J-H Wirtz
G J Mulder
Parent company: Th Goldschmidt AG, Essen

Products: Thermit rail welding portions, casting moulds, welding equipment, rail grinders and hydraulic trimmers, insulated rail joints. Carries out electric build-up welding of rails and crossings, build-up and reprofiling of rails with side-wear, both grooved and flat-bottom section. Also improvement of rail properties by submerged arc welding: anti-corrugation welding, system RIFLEX; anti-wear welding, system ETEKA 5; anti-noise welding. Joint-welding of head-hardened rails; head-hardening of rail for in situ insulating joints.

Contracts: Rail welding contracts with many state railways and major European urban transit systems.

VERIFIED

Eliatis

Eliatis sarl
Pré-Boissieux, 38430 Moirans, France
Telephone: +33 4 76 35 64 55 Fax: +33 4 76 35 64 53
Managing Directors: Jean Luc Perrin, Olivier Gallifet

Products: Aspirail road-rail unit for vacuum cleaning roadway and tram rails, including leaf removal. Can be fitted on to existing vehicles. Speed of operation is 25 km/h. Optional Total Road-Rail system for use on all surfaces including asphalt, ballast, sand and grass.

Contracts: Aspirail is in use on the Grenoble, Nantes and Strasbourg tramways, France.

VERIFIED

EWEM

EWEM AG
Thundorferstrasse 58, 8500 Frauenfeld, Switzerland
Telephone: +41 52 375 2000 Fax: +41 52 375 2011
Director: A A G van Hees
Production sites: in Brazil, Indonesia, Thailand

Products: DE/Deenik elastic rail fastenings, fishplates, pads, insulators, baseplates, shoulders.

UPDATED

Fassetta

Fassette mécanique
Avenue Gabriel Péri, 13400 Aubagne, France
Telephone: +33 4 42 03 11 54 Fax: +33 4 42 84 08 31
Managing Director: F Fassetta

Products: Gantries for switch and track laying rail positioning machines; machines for stressing operations; standard and special lorries; rail drills; abrasive rail saws; sleeper drills; rail derusting and grinding equipment; timber sleeper manufacture and machining plants.

UPDATED

First Engineering

First Engineering 7th Floor, Buchanan House, 58 Port Dundas Road, Glasgow G4 0HG, UK
Telephone: +44 141 335 3005 Fax: +44 141 335 3006
General Manager, Construction Division: John Laidlaw
Engineering Director: Peter Ramsey

Background: The company was formed in 1996 as a result of a successful management/employee buy-out of the former Scottish Infrastructure Maintenance Company of British Rail.

Products: Project management for infrastructure management, construction/projects and facilities management.

Contracts: Main client is Railtrack Scotland, for which First Engineering provides infrastructure maintenance services.

NEW ENTRY

Gamble

Gamble
Nowhurst Lane, Broadbridge Heath, Horsham RH12 3PL, England
Telephone: +44 1403 210121 Fax: +44 1403 263689

Products: Road-rail equipment including ballast broom attachment for lines with third rail, crane with various attachments including dipper arms, tool hangers, notched bucket and concrete breaker; road-rail access platform.

NEW ENTRY

Getzner Chemie

Getzner Chemie GesmbH
PO Box 159, Herrenau 5, 6700 Bludenz-Buers, Austria
Telephone: +43 5552 63310 Fax: +43 5552 66864
Managing Director: R Pfefferkorn
Sales Director: P Burtscher

Associated company: Getzner Werkstoffe GmbH, Nördliche Münchner Strasse 27a, 82031 Grünwald, Germany

Products: Sylomer® and Sylodyn® elastomers for track construction; ballast mats for metro, light rail and main line track; elastic bearings for track slabs; resilient baseplate pads and resilient rail pads; level crossing infill; elastic box profiles for grooved rail.

UPDATED

Grant Lyon Eagre

Grant Lyon Eagre Limited
Hebden Road, Scunthorpe DN15 8XX, England
Telephone: +44 1724 862131 Fax: +44 1724 295243
Chairman: A V L Williams
General Manager: Dr T J Bessell
Works Manager: S Flower
Parent company: British Steel plc

Products: Design and manufacture of switches, crossings and special track components including expansion switches, buffer stops and insulated joints for urban rail systems. Prefabrication and installation of track layouts and junctions.

Contracts: Recent contracts include supply of switches and crossings to the London Docklands Light Railway, London Underground, STAR Kuala Lumpur, Railtrack UK and Tranzrail New Zealand.

UPDATED

GrantRail

GrantRail Ltd
Scotter Road, Scunthorpe DN15 8EF, England
Telephone: +44 1724 295200 Fax: +44 1724 295220
Email: 101775,332@Compuserve,Com
Trackwork Manager: Ray Rogers
Marketing & Business Development: Graeme Ferguson

Background: British Steel and Royal Volker Stevin formed GrantRail as a jointly owned company. It has been formed from the tracklaying division of British Steel subsidiary, Grant Lyon Eagre Ltd (qv), and Royal Volker Stevin's railway engineering company Railbouw (UK) Ltd.

Products: Construction, renewal and maintenance of LRT, metro, underground and heavy rail systems.

Complete systems are offered for LRT projects, covering planning, supply of rail and installation.

Contracts: Major customers are Railtrack UK, London Underground and Midland Metro.

NEW ENTRY

Hanning & Kahl

Hanning & Kahl GmbH & Co
PO Box 1342, 33806 Oerlinghausen, Germany
Telephone: +49 5202 707600 Fax: +49 5202 707629
General Manager: Eckart Dümmer
Sales Director: Wolfgang Helas
Technical Director: Dr Carsten Kipp

Products: Points mechanisms for all gauges and types of rail with magnetic, motor or electrohydraulic drive; manual point setting mechanisms; point mechanism for grooved rail.

UPDATED

Holland

Holland Company
1020 Washington Avenue, Chicago Heights, IL 60411, USA
Telephone: +1 708 756 0650 Fax: +1 708 756 2641
President: Philip C Moeller
Vice President, Sales: L F Okrat
International Sales Manager: Eugene Parker

Products: Hollube wear eliminators; air hose supports; side frame keys; flash-butt rail welding equipment; rail pullers; base grinders; rail hydro-stressers. Sale and contracting of electric flash-butt welding equipment; rail/road mobile welders; portable welding plant and related equipment. Super-Puller for in-track closure and repair welding, which, in addition to aligning the weld, prevents the flash-butt weld from distortion by track forces during the cooling cycle, and allows the operator to adjust the neutral laying temperature of the rail. Also new K-355H welder head, designed for lower maintenance.

The MobileWelder is a road-rail unit which makes high-quality depot flash-butt welds in-track.

Track analysis using Holland's TrackStar® testing vehicle.

UPDATED

Insul 8

Insul 8 Corporation
10102 F Street, Omaha, NE 68127-1181, USA
Telephone: +1 402 339 9300 Fax: +1 402 339 9627
President: Don Brockley
Project Manager: Richard Prell

Other offices in Canada, Australia and Manchester, England.

Background: Insul 8 is part of the Delachaux Group, Gennevilliers, France.

Products: Conductor rail systems for all transit applications. Specialises in conductor rail with stainless steel on aluminium extrusion.

Contracts: Include BART San Francisco; BC Transit, Canada; Newark Redevelopment; Jacksonville and Kuala Lumpur, Malaysia.

UPDATED

Interep

Interep SA
Rue de L'Industrie, 43110 Aurec/Loire, France
Telephone: +33 4 77 35 20 21 Fax: +33 4 77 35 26 17
Managing Director: Daniel Boffy
Sales & Marketing Manager: Philippe Charbonnier
Research & Development Manager:
Jean-Philippe Montagnon

Products: Microcellular rubber foams to reduce vibrations, for use as a ballast mat or under the sleeper for conventional ballasted tracks (marketed under the name Caoutchouc Mousse); also pad under block or baseplate for non-ballasted tracks.

Contracts: Microcellular rubber pads for non-ballasted tracks have been supplied to Bilbao, Spain, RATP Paris (Eole and Meteor) and Athens, Greece.

Developments: A microcellular rubber mat with advanced damping properties, Type 43-45, is suitable for metro systems. An in-house dynamic test machine for controls and simulation has been developed.

UPDATED

IPA

Industria Prefabbricati e Affini
Strada Provinciale per Trescore, 24050 Calcinate, Italy
Telephone: +39 35 442 3077 Fax: +39 35 442 3205
Manager: Enzo De Biasio

Products: Concrete sleepers, complete slab track system, noise barriers, prefabricated bridge and building components.

Jafco

Jafco Tool's Ltd
Queen Street, Darlaston, Wednesbury WS10 8XA, England
Telephone: +44 121 526 6363 Fax: +44 121 526 4173
Managing Director: Jane Anthill

Products: Track maintenance hand tools for use on electrified and non-electrified rails; track gauges; train uncoupling bars.

Contracts: Customers include Railtrack UK and London Underground.

NEW ENTRY

John Kelly (Lasers)

John Kelly (Lasers) Ltd
Broombank Road, Chesterfield S41 9QJ, England
Telephone: +44 1246 261616 Fax: +44 1246 261673

Products: Laser machine control for ballast cleaners, tampers, dynamic track stabilisers and crawler tilt dozers.

NEW ENTRY

Kaufmann

A Kaufmann AG
Railway Technics
Pilatusstrasse 2, 6300 Zug, Switzerland
Telephone: +41 41 711 6700 Fax: +41 41 855 1704
Manager: Alois Kaufmann-Von Dach

Products: Contact clamps, electrodes, earthing equipment, fastenings and other track accessories and components.

KLDLABS

KLDLABS Inc
300 Broadway, Huntington Station, NY 11746, USA
Telephone: +1 516 549 4222 Fax: +1 516 351 7190
President: Steven A Magnus

Products: Orian rail inspection, measurement and analysis systems.

NEW ENTRY

Kloos Railway Systems

Kloos Railway Systems BV
PO Box 3, 2690 AA Kinderdijk, Netherlands
Telephone: +31 78 691 4000 Fax: +31 78 691 4542
Managing Director: J van Houwelingen

Works: West-Kinderdijk 24, 2953 XW Alblasserdam, Netherlands

Products: Design, development and construction of standard and custom-built materials for main line, metro and light rail systems; complete turnouts, crossings, expansion joints; specialised constructions.

Contracts: Turnouts and other equipment have been supplied to Angola, Brazil, Colombia, Egypt, Germany, Ghana, Greece, Hong Kong, Indonesia, Iran, Netherlands, Portugal, Sudan and Turkey.

UPDATED

Lindapter

Lindapter International
Lindsay House, Brackenbeck Road, Bradford BD7 2NF, England
Telephone: +44 1274 521444 Fax: +44 1274 521130
Email: lindapter@dial.pipex.can
Managing Director: G R Browning
Sales Office Manager: Steve Christie
Export Sales Manager: Malcolm Eastwood
Technical Support Manager: M Knight
Product Manager: N A Tilsley

Products: Holdfast adjustable rail clips: the Soft clip holds rails in precise alignment while the hard clip prevents vertical rail movement. A Spring clip also caters for rail wave while holding the rail down. A Type BR clip suits flat-bottom or bridge rails up to an 8° slope. The Temporary Support System supports and insulates running rails while essential repair work is being carried out.

Contracts: Include Roma metro; East Coast electrification, UK; London Underground Jubilee line.

UPDATED

Le Matériel de Voie

Le Matériel de Voie SA
4 place de la Pyramide, Cedex 33, 92070 Paris La Défense, France
Telephone: +33 1 49 00 66 55 Fax: +33 1 49 00 56 66
Administrative Manager: Gérard Glas

Products: Rail, baseplates, grooved rail, materials for narrow-gauge track.

Matisa

Matisa Matériel Industriel SA
PO Box 58, 1023 Crissier, Switzerland
Telephone: +41 21 631 2111 Fax: +41 21 631 2168
General Manager: R von Schack
Sales Director: Y Caffari
Technical Director: J Ganz
Subsidiaries: Paris (Sens), Roma, Madrid, Donaueschingen, Tokyo
Works: Arc-en-Ciel 2, 1023 Crissier

Products: Track construction, monitoring and maintenance machinery.

Developments: M2000 multipurpose self-propelled track measuring vehicle for recording track geometry, rail profile, corrugation, catenary position and other parameters; real-time data analysis.

UPDATED

Mourgeon Industrie

Mourgeon Industrie et Engineering SA
15 rue Gay Lussac, Zone Industrielle, 94438 Chennevières S/M, France
Telephone: +33 1 45 94 20 20 Fax: +33 1 45 94 46 08

Products: Tamping equipment; road-rail hydraulic excavator accessories; sleeper bale for handling up to 11 sleepers at a time; tamping attachment with which track is tamped, lined and levelled without use of tamping machine.

VERIFIED

Newag

Newag GmbH & Co KG
Ripshorster Strasse Tor 73, 46117 Oberhausen, Germany
Telephone: +49 208 865 0322 Fax: +49 208 865 0320
Managing Director: C Kohl
Technical Director: W Kern
Sales Director: G Halfmann

Products: Track maintenance machines and equipment; tracklaying trains; catenary maintenance vehicles and equipment.

Ortec

Ortec GmbH
Mühlenweg 25, 51588 Nümbrecht, Germany
Telephone: +49 2293 91040 Fax: +49 2293 910431
Managing Director: Hermann J Ortwein

Products: Light rail installations, including resilient fixings/embedding, fastenings, rail coating material to reduce wheel noise and wear on bends; track landscaping with special plants between rails to reduce noise.

NEW ENTRY

Pandrol

Pandrol Rail Fastenings Ltd
63 Station Road, Addlestone KT15 2AR, England
Telephone: +44 1932 834500 Fax: +44 1932 850858
Managing Director: G M Lodge
Marketing Director: J Beal-Preston

Products: Design and manufacture of track fastening systems and associated installation equipment; resilient rail pads; Vortok Coils (qv).

Developments: Work continues in the field of dynamic behaviour of track to understand fully the influence upon the total track structure of each of its components. Particular reference is being made to the generation of noise and vibration. The company has developed a range of new fastenings for specific applications including the Pandrol Fastclip®, a low-maintenance captive switch-on/switch-off rail fastening system.

UPDATED

Pandrol Jackson

Pandrol Jackson Inc
200 South Jackson Road, Ludington, MI 49431, USA
Telephone: +1 616 843 3431 Fax: +1 616 843 4830
President & Chief Executive Officer: A Zaydel
Executive Vice President, Chief Financial Officer & Administration: R J Orrow
Senior Vice President, Engineering & Manufacturing: A Zaydel
Senior Vice President, Contracted Services/Marketing & International Sales: F Brady
Vice President, North American Sales & Marketing: P Brown
Vice President, Engineering/Manufacturing, Rail Flaw Detection: M Havira
Vice President, Engineering/Manufacturing, Stone-blower: B Bradshaw
Vice President, Parts, Service & Mexico Sales: J Reilly

Vice President, Manufacturing: R Nash
Works:
Pandrol Jackson Ultrasonic Manufacture, 28 Eagle Road, Danbury, CT 06810, USA
Telephone: +1 203 778 6811 Fax: +1 203 778 8670
Pandrol Jackson Contract Services, 309 Clark Street, E Syracuse, NY 13057, USA
Telephone: +1 315 437 2547 Fax: +1 315 463 0180

Products: Design and manufacture of track maintenance machines, including production grinders, points and crossing grinders, tamping machines and sleeper changers; ultrasonic equipment, including rail flaw detection cars; contract services for measurement of rail corrugation, and for main line production and points and crossings grinding.

Developments: Systems are being developed to measure accurately rail profiles in situ to provide data for planning rail maintenance. Rail flaw detection systems are under development to measure rail flaws automatically. A new system for track levelling by stone blowing is being developed in the United States under contract to Railtrack UK.

UPDATED

Partner Jonsered

Partner Jonsered Power Products UK
Oldends Lane, Stonehouse GL10 3SY, England
Telephone: +44 1453 820305/306
Fax: +44 1453 971577
Marketing Manager: Shirley Pitts

Products: Hand-held power tools for rail maintenance/installation.

NEW ENTRY

Percevaut

Percevaut
14 avenue de la Plage, 94340 Joinville-le-Pont, Paris, France
Telephone: +33 1 43 97 62 80 Fax: +33 1 48 89 14 26

Products: Tunnel fan jets; exhaust gas scrubber; rail cleaner vehicle.

NEW ENTRY

Permaquip

Permaquip
Giltway, Giltbrook, Nottingham NG16 2GQ, England
Telephone: +44 115 938 7000 Fax: +44 115 938 7001
UK Sales Manager: Alan Leyland

Products: Tools and equipment for maintenance and construction of track; 47 kg expandable trolley system.

UPDATED

Phoenix

Phoenix AG
PO Box 900854, 21048 Hamburg, Germany
Telephone: +49 40 76671 Fax: +49 40 7667 2211
President: Konrad Ellegast
Vice Presidents: Dr B Meister; H J Zwarg
Sales Manager: J Eggers

UK subsidiary
Phoenix (GB) Ltd
Timothy's Bridge Road, Stratford-upon-Avon CV37 9NQ, England
Telephone: +44 1789 205090 Fax: +44 1789 298638

Products: Range of elastomeric products for tracklaying; rail fastenings, sub-ballast matting, rail seatings, noise absorbers, grooved rail and flangeway sealing sections.

UPDATED

Plasser & Theurer

Plasser & Theurer, Export von Bahnbaumaschinen
Johannesgasse 3, 1010 Wien, Austria
Telephone: +43 1 515 720 Fax: +43 1 513 1801
Main works: Pummererstrasse 5, 4021 Linz/Donau
Subsidiaries: Worldwide including Australia, Brazil, Canada, Denmark, France, Germany, Hong Kong, India, Italy, Japan, South Africa, Spain, UK, USA

UK subsidiary
Plasser & Theurer International Sales (UK) Ltd
St Andrews House, St Mary's Walk, Maidenhead SL6 1QZ
Telephone: +44 1628 788648 Fax: +44 1628 770428

Products: Tracklaying and maintenance machinery; levelling, lifting, lining and tamping machines; ballast distributing, profiling and cleaning machines; rail rectification, grinding and welding machines; vacuum scraper excavators; catenary maintenance and inspection cars; track geometry measuring cars.

UPDATED

Rail Products & Fabrications

Rail Products & Fabrications
3422 1st Avenue South, Seattle, WA 98134, USA
Telephone: +1 206 622 0125 Fax: +1 206 621 9626
Email: railprod@aol.com

Products: Rail, points and crossings, special trackwork components.

Contracts: Include supply of equipment to MTDB San Diego, Muni San Francisco, Tri-Met Portland and the SEPTA Philadelphia Railworks programme.

UPDATED

Railtest

Railtest
PO Box 243, Derby DE24 8ZZ, England
Telephone: +44 1332 262626
Fax: +44 1332 264608
Sales & Marketing Director: Barry Winchurch

Products: Acceptance testing of rail vehicles and components including on-track plant; evaluation and commissioning of new and modified traction rolling stock; independent infrastructure assessment service, covering track geometry; structure gauging, ultrasonic rail inspection, overhead line and track inspection.

Rail Operations section provides operation and management of the Old Dalby Test Track and Development Centre, with four tunnels, 3 km of overhead catenary and a variety of track types, gradients and canted curves.

UPDATED

Rawie

A Rawie GmbH
PO Box 3529, 49025 Osnabrück, Germany
Telephone: +49 541 912070 Fax: +49 541 912 0736

Products: Friction buffer stops.

Relayfast

Relayfast
8th Floor, Buchanan House, 58 Port Dundas Road, Glasgow G4 0HG, Scotland
Telephone: +44 141 335 2668 Fax: +44 141 335 3468
Business Development Director: Hugh Harvie
Marketing Manager: Rosalyn Dunn

Subsidiary company
Western Track Renewals Co Ltd

Products: Track renewals, LRT installations; track maintenance; on-track machine maintenance; on-track machine hire.

NEW ENTRY

RMC

RMC Concrete Products Ltd
St Helen Auckland, Bishop Auckland DL14 9AJ, England
Telephone: +1388 603961 Fax: +1388 450056
Works: Aston Church Road, Saltley, Birmingham B8 1QF
Telephone: +44 121 327 0844 Fax: +44 121 327 7545
Operations Manager: Nick Gainsford
Sales Manager: James Tristram

Products: Pretensioned concrete sleepers and associated track materials for third rail electrification, main line track, twin-block for main line track.

Contracts: Half of the annual requirement of concrete sleepers by Railtrack is supplied by RMC Concrete.

UPDATED

Robel

Robel GmbH & Co
PO Box 750770, 81337 München, Germany
Telephone: +49 89 742 1440 Fax: +49 89 724 2186
Managing Director: B Ströbl

Products: Track maintenance machinery and equipment; power wrenches; drilling machines; rail grinding machines; rail loading and transporting units; rail lifting equipment; track lifting and slewing machines; powered gangers' trolleys and trailers; small transport trolleys; road-rail excavators and switch laying units.

VERIFIED

Rotamag

Rotamag
Rail Division
PO Box 206, Sheffield S9 5YX, England
Telephone: +44 114 291 1020 Fax: +44 114 261 8186
Managing Director: Mike Bryan
Director: Vic Archer
Divisional Manager: David Flint

Products: Rail drilling and cutting systems; lighting systems; oil pollution control; mobile boring machine; rail cutters.

Contracts: Railtrack; London Underground; Glasgow Underground.

Developments: A 48 V battery-powered rail drill is now available.

UPDATED

Sateba

Sateba
262 boulevard Saint-Germain, 75007 Paris, France
Telephone: +33 1 40 62 26 00 Fax: +33 1 40 62 26 01
Chief Executive Manager: Claude Cazenave
Deputy General Manager: D Valles

Products: Design and manufacture of Vagneux system of concrete sleepers, and prestressed concrete sleepers for turnouts; design and commissioning of sleeper manufacturing plants. Also technical studies, assistance and staff training.

Contracts: Has designed and supplied concrete sleepers for metros in Paris, Cairo and Seoul, and for light rail systems in Grenoble, Rouen, Nantes, Lille and Strasbourg.

UPDATED

Schwihag

Schwihag Gesellschaft für Eisenbahnoberbau mbH
Lebernstrasse 3, 8274 Tägerwilen, Switzerland
Telephone: +41 71 669 2230 Fax: +41 71 669 2231
Managing Director, Technical: Dipl-Ing Armin Heim
Managing Director, Commercial:
Dipl-Betriebswirt Karl-Heinz Schwiede

Products: Rail anchoring systems for pointwork, point operating systems, permanent way equipment including chair plates and check rail plates.

Contracts: Held with MTRC Hong Kong; SNCF France, DB Germany.

Scotland TRC

Scotland Track Renewals Company
8th Floor, Buchanan House, 58 Fort Dundas Road, Glasgow G4 0HG, Scotland
Telephone: +44 141 335 2422 Fax: +44 141 335 3468
Business Development Manager: Keith Gourlay

Products: Existing track renewal, light rail installations, maintenance, on-track machine hire/maintenance.

NEW ENTRY

Semperit

Semperit Technische Produkte GmbH
Triester Bundesstrasse 26, 2632 Wimpassing, Austria
Telephone: +43 2630 310 458 Fax: +43 2630 310 488
Sales Manager, Railtracks: Peter Horn

Products: Rubber damping mats

NEW ENTRY

Sika

Sika Ltd
Watchmead, Welwyn Garden City AL7 1BQ, England
Telephone: +44 1707 394444 Fax: +44 1707 329129
Managing Director: B Baggersgaard
Marketing Manager: M Moore

Products: Rail fixing systems; adhesive sealants; high-performance adhesives.

UPDATED

Skelton

H J Skelton & Co Ltd
9 The Broadway, Thatcham RG19 3JA, England
Telephone: +44 1635 865256 Fax: +44 1635 865710
Director: Jeremy Smith

Products: Points, crossings; rails (flat-bottomed and grooved); Vossloh rail fastenings; insulated rail joints; sliding friction buffer stops; crane rails and turnouts; high-speed buffer stops, to stop trains at 56 km/h; special trackwork.

Developments: Buffer stops to suit low-floor LRVs and a redesigned element to provide an improved braking capacity.

UPDATED

Skelton

H J Skelton (Canada) Ltd
165 Oxford Street E, London, Ontario N6A 1T4, Canada
Telephone: +1 519 679 9180 Fax: +1 519 679 0193
General Manager: Peter Fraser
Sales Director: Geoffrey Richey

Products: Supplier of a wide variety of track components, special trackwork, sliding rail expansion joints, switch machines, sliding rail buffer stops, Icosit polyurethane/cork grout for undersealing grooved rail and injected pads for direct fixation. Specialises in LRT in-street applications, also railway rail (both T and grooved), crane rails and turnouts. High-speed buffer stops/bumping posts, to stop trains at up to 56 km/h.

Contracts: Five-year supply contract for TTC Toronto for all-manganese frogs, crossings and points for tram tracks; special trackwork for Calgary LRT; removable crossovers for Muni San Francisco; sliding friction buffer stops by Rawie for San Diego, Toronto, Kuala Lumpur, Baltimore, Portland, Connecticut State Pier; Icosit polyurethane grout for Tri-Met Portland, PA Transit Pittsburgh, Denver LRT and Toronto; Vossloh screw spikes for CN Rail.

UPDATED

SPEFAKA

Spezialfahrzeugaufbau und Kabeltechnik GmbH
Verlängerte Apoldaer Strasse 18, 06116 Halle, Germany
Telephone: +49 345 560 2265/2265
Fax: +49 345 5608161
General Manager: G Hofmann

Products: Road-rail vehicles from 3 to 25 tonnes for installation and maintenance of catenary infrastructures for urban and interurban railway; railcars (light, medium and heavy) with hydrostatic drive, adjustable for varying track gauges; hydraulic platforms; rail cleaners; high-pressure cleaning apparatus; ballast cleaning; re-railing equipment; road-rail trailers with cable and wire drums/reels or as motive power.

Contracts: Supply of equipment and vehicles to Siemens, Adtranz, Kummler + Matter and city transport systems in Bruxelles, Bratislava, Berlin, Köln, Chemnitz and Halle.

Developments: Include a concrete mixer and pile driver for pole foundations and specialised vehicles for maintenance of rail and trackbed in one operation.

UPDATED

Speno

Speno International SA
PO Box 16, 26 Parc Château-Banquet, 1211 Genève 21, Switzerland
Telephone: +41 22 906 4600 Fax: +41 22 906 4601
Managing Director: J J Méroz
Deputy General Manager: Jim Cooper
Sales Director: D Arvet-Thouvet
Technical Director: J P Jaeggi
Works: Via Banchina Darsena, Porto Marghera, Italy
Subsidiaries: Nippon Speno KK, Tokyo; Speno Rail Maintenance (Australia) Pty Ltd, Belmont, Western Australia

Products: In-track rail grinders, ultrasonic rail flaw detection vehicles, rail longitudinal and cross-profile measuring systems.

The RR8M machine is a compact grinder incorporating features only found in heavy-duty machines – dust collection, accurate tilting of the grinding process and computer storage of grinding patterns. The HRR12M has a rapid on/off track capability which can operate on both Vignole and grooved rail to standard and metre gauges.

Contracts: Service and supply contracts with major urban, state and mining railways.

UPDATED

Spie Batignolles

Spie Batignolles
Departement Voies Ferrees, Parc Saint Christophe, 95861 Cergy Pontoise, France
Telephone: +33 1 34 22 50 02 Fax: +33 1 34 22 62 80

Products: Underground track installation; LRT installations; workshop installations.

NEW ENTRY

Stedef

Railway Division of Allevard Industries
320 Bureaux de la Colline, 92213 Saint-Cloud Cedex, France
Telephone: +33 1 41 12 33 00 Fax: +33 1 49 11 07 22
Managing Director: D Françon
General Manager: Jean-Paul Dervaux
Area Manager, America: P Y Cathou
Area Manager, Europe & Africa: J J Roger
Area Manager, Asia: S Edenwald

Products: Ballastless track system (VSB patented), rail fastening systems. VSB Stedef system, consisting of sleepers made of two concrete blocks with a steel tie-bar, double elastic rail fastenings with high-tensile steel blades, and grooved elastomer pads, laid directly onto a concrete slab.

Contracts: Recent installation contracts from Australia, Brazil, Denmark, France, Great Britain, Italy, Spain, Switzerland, USA and Venezuela.

Tensol Rail

Tensol Rail SA
Bureau de vente, Case Postale, 3001 Bern, Switzerland
Telephone: +41 31 308 5359 Fax: +41 31 302 5504
Marketing Director: Theo Geissbühler
Part of the Von Roll Group

Products: Rack and other rail installations.

NEW ENTRY

Tiefenbach

Tiefenbach GmbH
Nierenhofer Strasse 68, 45257 Essen, Germany
Telephone: +49 201 48630 Fax: +49 201 4863158
Technical Field Service Manager: Achim Weirather

Products: Microcomputer-controlled electrically operated point motors; level crossing systems; cable haulage systems.

NEW ENTRY

Tiflex

Tiflex Limited
Member of the James Walker Group
Hipley Street, Old Woking GU22 9LL, England
Telephone: +44 1483 757757
Fax: +44 1483 755374/757715
Managing Director: Malcolm P Fleming
Director & Trackelast Product Manager: Hugh M Kenyon
Director: Hugh T Rogers
Trackelast Product Engineer: S C Barlow
Works: Treburgie Water, Liskeard PL14 4NB

Products: Trackelast resilient track support materials for all types of permanent way construction to protect track structure from impact loads; rail pads; baseplate pads and continuous rail support pads and, for reducing ground-borne vibration, Trackelast under-sleeper pads, ballast mats and low-stiffness baseplate pads. New polymer applications for track construction.

Contracts: Trackelast resilient track support materials have been used extensively on the Hong Kong Mass Transit, Tuen Mun tramway, Rotterdam, Madrid, Barcelona, Milano, London and Paris metros, and the London Docklands Light Railway; also tramways in Den Haag, Göteborg and Utrecht, and on British suburban lines. Rail pads have been supplied for London Underground's Jubilee line extension; track support bearings have been supplied for the Tsing Ma bridge, Hong Kong.

UPDATED

TSO

Travaux du Sud-Ouest SA
Chemin du Corps de Garde, PO Box 8, 77501 Chelles Cedex, France
Telephone: +33 1 64 72 72 00 Fax: +33 1 64 26 30 23
President: Emmanuèle Perron
Export Manager: Claude Petit

Products: Turnout-laying cranes and equipment; track construction and maintenance for main line and metro systems; ballast mats for ballasted track in tunnel; aluminothermic and flash-butt welding.

Contracts: Recent work includes supply and installation of trackwork on the Tamsui line of the Taipei metro; ballastless tracklaying in the Channel Tunnel; tracklaying on the TGV Nord and TGV Rhône-Alpes high-speed lines.

UPDATED

VAE

VAE Aktiengesellschaft
Rotenturmstrasse 5-9, 1010 Wien, Austria
Telephone: +43 1 531180 Fax: +43 1 531 18222
President: Edmund Auli
Works: Alpinestrasse 1, 8350 Zeltweg
Subsidiary companies: In Australia, Canada, USA, Hungary, Spain, UK, Latvia and Lithuania.

Products: Turnouts and crossings, frogs and switches, ballastless track system with plastic sleepers, fastening materials, turnout monitoring system VAE Roadmaster 2000, hot-box detectors.

VERIFIED

Van Welzenes

Van Welzenes Spoorbouw BV
PO Box 834, Kilkade 53, 3300 AV Dordrecht, Netherlands
Telephone: +31 78 179200 Fax: +31 78 185722

Products: Track components and tracklaying equipment; tracklaying and maintenance service.

Vortok

Vortok International
63 Station Road, Addlestone KT15 2AR, England
Telephone: +44 1932 828812 Fax: +44 1932 828691
Managing Director: J R Byles
Technical Director: R F Morton
Works: 6-7 Haxter Close, Belliver Industrial Estate, Roborough, Plymouth PL6 7DD

Subsidiary: Multiclip Company Ltd

Products: Components for the repair and rehabilitation of timber sleepers. These include Vortok Coil for loose screws, spikes and additives for wood preservation.

Contracts: Supplier to most European railway companies.

UPDATED

Vossloh Rail Systems

Vossloh Rail Systems GmbH
PO Box 1860, 58778 Werdohl, Germany
Telephone: +49 2392 520 Fax: +49 2392 52375
Managing Directors: Ulrich Rieger
Sales Manager: F G Heisler
Regional Sales Manager: J Spors (Overseas Business Office, Düsseldorf)
Works: Vosslohstrasse 4, 58791 Werdohl

Products: Elastic rail fastening systems for concrete, wooden and steel sleepers on ballasted and slab tracks, direct-fixing fasteners, sleeper anchors, systems for sleeper rehabilitation, systems for noise reduction and vibration damping, rail web cushioning.

Contracts: Has supplied equipment for the Ankara Ankaray light rail scheme, phases I and II of the Istanbul metro, and the Taipei, Cairo, Barcelona and Medellin metros, as well as rail fastenings for Kuala Lumpur's STAR light rail transit.

UPDATED

WALO

Walo Bertshinger AG
Road Construction Department, PO Box 7534, 8023 Zürich, Switzerland
Telephone: +41 1 745 2311 Fax: +41 1 740 3140
Director: Sandro Contratto

Product: Trackbed construction using precast concrete.

NEW ENTRY

Western-Cullen-Hayes

Western-Cullen-Hayes Inc
2700 West 36th Place, Chicago, IL 60632-1617, USA
Telephone: +1 773 254 9600 Fax: +1 773 254 1110
Web: www.wch.com
President: R L McDaniel
Vice President, Marketing: George S Sokulski
Customer Services Manager: William M Crain

Products: Safety signals and accessories, gate arms, level crossing warning systems, flashing light signals, switch lamps and targets, bumping posts and accessories, wheel stops, switch point machines, chocks, switch point guards, track drills, rail benders, rail tongs, journal and hydraulic jacks, derails and accessories, rerailers, dragging equipment detectors, and other custom-built equipment.

UPDATED

CONSULTANCY AND CONTRACTING SERVICES

AUSTRALIA
Kuttner, Collins Group
Rust PPK Consultants Pty Ltd
TMG International Pty Ltd

BELGIUM
IDPO
OGM
SEMA Group Belgium
Stratec
Transurb Consult

CANADA
Giro Inc
Laidlaw Transit Inc
Toronto Transit Consultants Ltd
Transurb Inc

FRANCE
EcoPlan International
Semaly
SMM Société du Métro de Marseille
Sofrétu-Systra-Sofrerail
Sogelerg Ingénierie snc

GERMANY
DE-Consult
Dorsch Consult Ingenieurgesellschaft mbH
ETC Transport Consultants GmbH
FFG Fahrzeugwerkstätten Falkenried GmbH
Haas Consult
ICB
Jürgen Rauch
Rail Consult
Socialdata
TransTec
TTK
VCK

GREECE
Doxiadis Associates

HONG KONG
MVA Asia

HUNGARY
Uvaterv Engineering Consultants Ltd

INDIA
Bharat Heavy Electricals Ltd
NATPAC
Pallavan Transport Consultancy Services Ltd
RITES

IRELAND
CIE Consult

ITALY
Ansaldo Trasporti SpA
Centro Studi Traffico
Italferr-SIS TAV SpA
MM

JAPAN
Japan Railway Technical Service (JARTS)
Pacific Consultants

NETHERLANDS
Goudappel Coffeng
Hague Consulting Group
NEA Transport Research and Training

NORWAY
Norconsult AS

SWEDEN
SwedeRail

SWITZERLAND
Electrowatt Engineering Ltd
ENOTRAC AG

THAILAND
Electrowatt Engineering Asia Ltd

UK
Accent Marketing & Research Ltd
Advanced Railway Research Centre
Ove Arup & Partners
W S Atkins Consultants Ltd
BAeSEMA
Balfour Beatty
BDC
Bovis Construction Group
BR Buisness Systems
BR Research
Carr Agnabrell Associates
Colin Buchanan and Partners
Cre'active Design
Davis Associates
DBS Consultancy
DCA Design International Ltd
Design Research Unit
Design Triangle
DHV Economics
Marcial Echenique & Partners
Economic Studies Group
The Engineering Link
W A Fairhurst & Partners
GEC Alsthom Transportation Projects Ltd
Sir Alexander Gibb & Partners Ltd
Halcrow Fox
Halcrow Transmark
Sir William Halcrow & Partners Ltd
Charles Haswell & Partners Ltd
Hoskyns Group
IBIS
John Brown Engineers & Constructors Ltd
Keith Haynes Associates
Laser Rail
Listavia International Consultants Ltd
Maunsell Parsons Brinckerhoff Ltd
Merz and McLellan Limited
Metro Consulting Ltd
Mott MacDonald
Mouchel
The MVA Consultancy
NEL
New Markets Ltd
Ogle Design Ltd
Oscar Faber
Owen Williams Consulting Engineers
Peter Davidson Consultancy
RailData
The Railway Consultancy
Railway Technology Strategy Centre
Ross Silcock Ltd
Rust Kennedy & Donkin Ltd
Scott Wilson Mainline
Southdown Environmental Consultants
Southern Vectis plc
Steer Davies Gleave
TAS Partnership
TecnEcon Ltd
Thorburn Colquhoun
Tilney Lumsden Shane Ltd
Transcorp
Transplan
Transport Resources International
Transport Design Consortium
Travers Morgan International Ltd
Robert L Trillo
Urban Initiatives
Vectra

USA
Ammann & Whitney
ATC/Vancom Inc
ATE Management & Service Co Inc
Michael Baker Jr Inc
Barton-Aschman Associates, Inc
Bechtel Corporation
BERGER/ABAM Engineers
The Louis Berger Group
Booz, Allen & Hamilton
Cambridge Systematics, Inc
CAM Industries Inc
Charles River Associates Incorporated
Corradino Group
Daniel, Mann, Johnson & Mendenhall
DAVE Transportation Services Inc
De Leuw, Cather & Co
Duchscherer Oberst Design, PC
Thomas K Dyer Inc
Dynamics Research Corporation
Edwards & Kelcey Inc
Fluor Daniel Inc
GRA Inc
Delon Hampton & Associates
Harris
Harza Engineering Co
Hatch Mott MacDonald
HDR Engineering Inc
ICF Kaiser Engineers, Inc
Ilium Associates Inc
Jakes Associates, Inc
JD Franz Research
JHK & Associates
KPMG Peat Marwick
Lea + Elliott
J W Leas & Associates
Arthur D Little/Cambridge Consultants Ltd
LS Transit Systems Inc
LTK Engineering Services
Multisystems Inc
Parsons Brinckerhoff Inc
Raytheon Company
Rummel, Klepper & Kahl
Strategies Unlimited
STV Group Inc
Sundberg-Ferar Inc
Systan, Inc
TAMS Consultants, Inc
Transmetrics Inc
The Urban Analysis Group Inc
Harry Weese Associates
Wilbur Smith Associates

Capability: CIE Consult draws on the expertise of CIE group companies Iarnrod Eireann (the Irish state rail network), Bus Atha Cliath (the Dublin city bus operator), and Bus Eireann (operator of all other bus services) to provide consultancy services in all aspects of public transport management, particularly restructuring and commercial orientation operations and staff training; civil and mechanical engineering; signalling and telecommunications.

Projects: Recent work includes a study of urban transport in the Czech Republic and Uzbekistan, a transport sector reform programme in Hungary and consulting assistance for the preparation of the proposed urban transport project in Ukraine. A study was also undertaken in Belarus.

Other projects include:

Urban transport and road freight transport components of the World Bank's transport rehabilitation project for Mongolia.

Latvia: master plan project for the reorganisation and development of the public road passenger transport system.

Estonia: Tapa-Petseri operations renewal project, Estonian Railways.

Lithuania: transition management support project for Lithuanian Railways.

Poland: provision of marketing training programme for Polish State Railways.

Pakistan: consulting assistance to the Private Power and Infrastructure Board.

Mozambique: consulting assistance for the rehabilitation of the Dondo—Muanza line.

UPDATED

The Corradino Group

200 South 5th Street, Suite 300N, Louisville, KY 40202, USA
Telephone: +1 502 587 7221 Fax: +1 502 587 2636
Managing Principal: Joseph C Corradino
Established: 1971

Capability: Civil engineering, design and construction management; systems and management planning; transport and environmental engineering; land use and urban design; urban planning, environmental assessment and transport modelling.

Cre'active Design

St Johns Innovation Centre, Cowley Road, Cambridge CB4 4WS, England
Telephone: +44 1223 421141 Fax: +44 1223 421036
Executives: Neil Bates, Tony Hume

Capability: Designers, rolling stock engineers and ergonomists providing planning and development skills from feasibility studies through to implementation, in industrial design, ergonomics, three-dimensional computer simulation, rolling stock design, tender specification and project management. Services include concept studies, design schemes, production of specifications and finalised design details, computer simulations, full-size mock-ups, prototypes and user trials.

Daniel, Mann, Johnson & Mendenhall

3250 Wilshire Boulevard, Los Angeles, CA 90010, USA
Telephone: +1 213 381 3663 Fax: +1 213 380 5126
Director of Transport: Gerald W Seelman
Established: 1946
Staff: 1,200

Capability: Planning, design, engineering and construction management services for all facets of transport. In urban transport, activities range from feasibility studies to design and project management.

Projects: The company has led a joint venture since 1967 in planning, design and construction management of the Baltimore metro.

In joint venture, DMJM is responsible for design and engineering management of the Los Angeles Red line metro, Blue line light rail and Green line light rail.

DMJM, in a joint venture, provides construction management and general engineering services for the Alameda Corridor Transportation Authority project to improve rail and road routes from the ports of Los Angeles and Long Beach to downtown Los Angeles. The 34 km route is expected to be completed in 2001.

As principal consultant, DMJM was responsible for all facilities on the SkyTrain system in Vancouver.

VERIFIED

DAVE Transportation Services Inc

26111 Antonio Parkway, Rancho Santa Margarita, CA 92688, USA
Telephone: +1 714 888 3283 Fax: +1 714 888 8990
President: James L Pierson
Vice President & Chief Financial Officer: C Marty Powell
Vice President, Strategic Development: Thomas J Higgins
Vice President, Corporate Development: Timothy B Colins
Vice President, Administration: Laverne David
Vice President, Financial Planning: John K Miller
Vice President, Operations, Eastern Division: Mark D Wells
Vice President, Operations, Western Division: John R Helm
Established: 1969
Staff: 3,000

Capability: Contract management and operations of fixed-route, shuttle and demand-responsive services. Maintenance training and consulting including bus route inspections. Transport management and paratransit brokerage programme administration. Transport planning and consulting.

Projects: Includes ADA planning and service implementation studies, development of policy and procedures manuals, and transport operational analyses.

UPDATED

Davis Associates

Davis Associates Ltd
Wyllyotts Close, Potters Bar EN6 2HN, England
Telephone: +44 1707 663665 Fax: +44 1707 663668
Directors: Gary Davis, Karen Davis
Senior Ergonomics Consultant: Andrew Baker

Capability: Ergonomics, human factors and systems analysis for urban transport systems.

Risk reduction through ergonomics auditing, specification and design of driving cabs, passenger saloons, station facilities, CCTV and information displays, human-computer interaction and control centres.

Areas of expertise include: analysis of user requirements, design for the mobility and sensorially impaired, boarding and alighting behavioural research, handrails, seating, luggage provision, mock-up user trials, video analysis, information design and signage, human computer interaction (HCI) evaluation, usability evaluation, job design, and health and safety.

Projects: Include cab ergonomics audits and research for British Railways Board; Docklands Light Railway B90 vehicle ergonomics; Docklands P stock safety audit for Mott MacDonald; ergonomics assessment of prototype secondary door locks, BR InterCity; IC3 passenger seat ergonomics for Danish State Railways; Kowloon-Canton Railway cab refurbishment ergonomics for Jones Garrard; KCR through-train ergonomics for Transcorp; Manchester Metrolink cab ergonomics for GEC Alsthom; passenger seat ergonomics for RENFE; MTR emu cab and saloon modernisation for Jones Garrard.

London Underground Ltd D78 stock refurbishment for Jones Garrard; control room desks for Northern line and Victoria line, LUL; control room ergonomics design and specification for KCR; Mornington Crescent station focal point/ticket office, London Underground; centralised control centre console for Mail Rail; Tuen Mun light rail operations control centre, for KCR and Siemens Plessey Controls; Jubilee line service control centre, Alcatel Canada; Seven Sisters station control point for Mowlem Facilities Management; Fulham Broadway station control room for Maurice Baguley & Partners; Strathclyde control room upgrade for Adtranz.

Enhanced one-person operation mirror and monitors, London Underground; Nottingham LRT design strategy (ergonomics) for Cre'active Design; ticket issue machine user interface for Westinghouse Cubic.

UPDATED

DBS Consultancy

2-10 Carbrook Hall Road, Sheffield S9 2DB, England
Telephone: +44 114 273 6227 Fax: +44 114 273 6182
Director: A J Wood
Contact: S Bagshaw

Capability: Design of viaducts and bridges in city centres; LRT/highways/traffic swept path alignment, horizontal/vertical alignment, integration of tracks into highway environment, co-ordination of statutory works and supervision of civil engineering works; architecture; quantity surveying; drainage engineering; project management.

Projects: Supertram, Sheffield: preliminary design of swept path alignment; junctions; CAD design of route; traffic/LRT signals operation, including priority; signing; carriageway marking; six-span viaduct construction; gateway bow-arch bridge to the city — design and construction; consultancy and advisory roles in relation to various other LRT proposals in the UK.

UPDATED

DCA Design International Ltd

19 Church Street, Warwick CV34 4AB, England
Telephone: +44 1926 499461 Fax: +44 1926 401134
Managing Director: Michael Groves
Established: 1958
Staff: 40

Capability: Design consultancy specialising in visual and ergonomic design, and component engineering. Services include exterior styling, interior design, engineering and electronic design, graphic design, model and full-size mock-up making, human factors, production drawing, three-dimensional computer modelling, visualisation and animation, and market research; ISO 9001.

Projects: Responsible for the visual design of London Underground's 1990 Central line stock, and for design of the Tangara double-deck trains in New South Wales. Visual and ergonomic aspects of the proposed Class 341 CrossRail and Class 371 Thameslink 2000 trains have also been undertaken, including full-size mock-ups; also for new buses in London.

Other projects include ticket systems and hardware, telecommunications and business equipment, vending machines, driver and passenger seat design, emergency passenger evacuation tests, composite structural research; and fire, smoke and toxicity material research and application, corporate identity, bus and coach projects and rail vehicle refurbishment.

UPDATED

DE-Consult

Deutsche Eisenbahn-Consulting GmbH
A subsidiary of German Railway (DB) and Deutsche Bank AG
Mittelstrasse 5/5a, 12529 Schönefeld bei Berlin, Germany
Telephone: +49 30 63430 Fax: +49 30 6343 1010
Oskar-Sommer-Strasse 15, 60596 Frankfurt am Main
Telephone: +49 69 63190 Fax: +49 69 6319 295
Board of Managing Directors
Chair: Dr Hermann Lenke
Dipl-Ing Gerhard F Scheller
Dipl-Kfm Thomas Nedtwig
Established: 1966
Staff: 1,600

Capability: Range of advisory services from project identification, planning and evaluation, preliminary and detailed design to supervision of construction; permanent way, rolling stock and workshops, signalling and telecommunications; management consulting, operations planning, transport economics and marketing, manpower development and training.

Installation and operation of Transrapid and automated people movers.

Projects: Malaysia: express rail link to Kuala Lumpur International Airport.
Netherlands: Amsterdam metro.
Thailand: Bangkok mass transit system.
India: consultancy for passenger train workshop facilities.

Also reconstruction and renovation of the Berlin urban railway city circle; reconstruction of 12 km of elevated S-Bahn in the centre of Berlin; Berlin north-south tunnel railway link; transport facilities in the centre of Berlin; Hanau—Offenbach urban railway; Hamburg city to airport line; City of Karlsruhe and region; dual system urban railway; light rail/main line, common use of infrastructure; extension of the city line to the World Expo 2000 site, Hannover; urban railway from Rostock to Warnemünde; Dresden—Pirna urban railway; Leipzig urban railway; Athens metro; Medellin metro; Shanghai metro.

UPDATED

De Leuw, Cather & Co

1133 15th Street, NW Washington, DC 20005, USA
Telephone: +1 202 775 3300 Fax: +1 202 775 3422
President: Robert S O'Neil
A subsidiary of The Parsons Corporation

Associated companies
Steinman Boynton Gronquist & Birdstall
Barton-Aschman Associates Inc

Capability: Feasibility studies, engineering, design, procurement, construction, construction management and complete programme management of mass transit projects.

Projects: Washington DC: since 1966 has been general engineering consultant to Metrorail.
Kuala Lumpur, Malaysia: consulting engineer for LRT project.
Portugal: design of modification to suspension bridge to carry both road and rail.
London, UK: project representative for Department of Transport for development of Channel Tunnel Rail Link.
Manila, Philippines: managing partner of a joint venture for expansion of LRT system, including an additional line with 11 stations.
Bangkok, Thailand: preliminary design consultant for 20 km underground metro system with 20 stations.
New York, USA: structural investigation programme for whole transport system, employing electronic data collection to develop an asset management data base for the underground railway system.
Los Angeles: construction management of the initial Red line metro system.
Boston, USA: prime consultant for design of a modernised operations control centre for LRT and metro systems.
Newark International Airport, USA: construction management of ground access monorail linking urban rail network and Amtrak service.

UPDATED

Design Research Unit

The Old School, Exton Street, London SE1 8UE, England
Telephone: +44 171 633 9711 Fax: +44 171 261 0333
Email: dru@hk.super.net
Directors: Ian Liddell, Maurice Green, Chris Ellingham
Established: 1943
Staff: 30

Capability: Station planning (architectural landscape design), graphic design and building condition surveys.

Projects: Architectural and planning work has been undertaken for many transport authorities including London Underground's Jubilee line extension, East London and Metropolitan lines; Centro in Birmingham, St Vincent Street station; for London Docklands Light Railway Bank and West India Quay stations; and numerous planning studies, as well as graphic design at Canary Wharf. DRU has also audited designs for London's CrossRail and the Chelsea—Hackney line for the DoT.

Worldwide experience has included 25 metro stations, a control centre and depots in Hong Kong, and designs for Baghdad, Taipei, Singapore and Athens; detail design for København mini metro and general architectural services in Toronto and Kuala Lumpur.

UPDATED

Design Triangle

The Maltings, Burwell, Cambridge CB5 0HB, England
Telephone: +44 1638 743070 Fax: +44 1638 743493
Partners: Siep Wijsenbeek, Andrew Crawshaw, Andrew Clark

Associated companies
Hippo Design, Montreal, Canada
Peter Bayly, Melbourne, Australia

Capability: Specialist design service for the transport industry: design combined with ergonomics and engineering for operators and manufacturers of public transport and specialist vehicles; industrial design for manufacturers of transport-related products; design management consultancy for operators.

Projects: Include the design of the Heathrow Express rolling stock for BAA; design of the cabs and exterior of the trains for the Hong Kong airport rail link; LRV exterior and interior design and saloon ergonomics for Manchester Metrolink; Northern line design concepts for London Underground; interior and exterior design for London Docklands Light Railway Beckton extension; and design management of various projects for British train operating companies, including new uniforms.

STIB Bruxelles is operating the Tram 2000 vehicles, for which Design Triangle designed the exterior and interior.

DHV Economics

Priory House, 45-51 High Street, Reigate RH12 9RU, England
Telephone: +44 1737 240101 Fax: +44 1737 221502

Capability: Consultancy in market research, economic analysis and public transport planning.

Projects: With its Portuguese subsidiary FBO, has carried out market research, demand forecasting and revenue appraisal studies to evaluate private sector DBOT bids for the new railway across the Tagus bridge in Lisboa.

In 1995 DHV analysed the results of a survey by Regional Railways North East, UK, on customer attitudes to Class 156 train refurbishment.

Dorsch Consult Ingenieurgesellschaft mbH

PO Box 210243, 80672 München, Germany
Telephone: +49 89 57970 Fax: +49 89 570 4867
President: Dipl-Ing Helmut Dorsch
Transport Division Manager: Dipl-Ing Peter Herrmann

Capability: Transport master plans, analyses and forecasts, traffic management, traffic infrastructure studies, institution building, company organisation studies, research activities.

VERIFIED

Doxiadis Associates

487 Messogion Avenue, Agia Paraskevi, 15343 Athens, Greece
Telephone: +30 1 601 6860 Fax: +30 1 601 6875
Vice President, Transportation:
Anastassios C Antonopoulos
Established: 1951
Staff: Transportation division 45

Capability: Transport planning and engineering design, traffic management, analysis and design, urban planning, project management, highway engineering, construction supervision and maintenance. Also participates in study teams for preparation of comprehensive development, regional and urban plans.

Projects:
Jordan: review of issues faced by road transport including improvement of bus services in greater Amman by introducing new routes, reviewing taxation and licensing arrangements, fares and possible privatisation. Also development of options to facilitate trade with particular reference to freight movements.

UPDATED

Duchscherer Oberst Design, PC

737 Delaware Avenue, Buffalo, NY 14209-2298, USA
Telephone: +1 716 882 0100 Fax: +1 716 873 2760
President: David C Duchscherer
Marketing Manager: Rae L Duchscherer
Established: 1951
Staff: 47

Capability: Architectural, civil and structural engineering services; experienced in planning, design and construction of bus maintenance, garaging and administration facilities, multimodal facilities, rapid transit stations and interchanges, bridges and highways.

Projects: Project locations include Lansing, MI, Ashville and Greensboro, NC, Buffalo, NY, Hempstead, NY, Providence, RI, Rochester, NY and Knoxville, TN. Projects vary from multimodal transport stations to bus maintenance and storage facilities.

The firm worked with the State of Connecticut on the Tri-State bus maintenance facility study which included investigation into reducing dead mileage, recommendations on repair procedures and intervals for optimal bus life, as well as specification of space requirements for servicing and stores.

Thomas K Dyer Inc

1762 Massachusetts Avenue, Lexington, MA 02173, USA
Telephone: +1 617 862 2075 Fax: +1 617 861 7766
President: Charles L O'Reilly Jr
Vice Presidents: Glenn E Hartsoe
David C Wuestmann
Robert E Sutton

HDR Engineering Inc

8404 Indian Hills Drive, Omaha, NE 68114-4049, USA
Telephone: +1 800 366 4411 Fax: +1 402 399 1238
National Director, Transportation: James Shuttle
Established: 1939

Capability: Professional services for design of roads, bridges, airports, railways and urban transit systems; also carries out planning and design, inspection and project management.

Hoskyns Group plc

Hoskyns House, 77-79 Cross Street, Sale M33 1HF, England
London office: Hoskyns House, 130 Shaftesbury Avenue, London W1V 8HH
Telephone: +44 171 434 2171 Fax: +44 171 437 6233
Director, Transport Sector: Mike Fill
Product Manager: Martyn Lewis

Capability: Supplier of computer services, offering a wide range of solutions and expertise to transport operators; incident reporting systems, privatisation advice, technical architecture reviews, education and training.

IBIS

IBIS Transport Consultants Ltd
12 High Street, Chalfont St Giles HP8 4QA, England
Telephone: +44 1494 876058 Fax: +44 1494 875629
Managing Director: I M D Barrett

Capability: Offers consultancy and contract management services in urban, interurban and rural bus operation to public transport undertakings, government organisations, planning authorities and aid agencies. Its specialist team can provide practical technical and managerial assistance in all aspects of bus operation, from initial appraisal and feasibility studies through to project implementation and continuing management advice.

Projects
Pakistan: feasibility study for joint venture investment in urban passenger transport.
Mongolia: operations and maintenance input for restructuring of an urban bus company, including preparation of business plan.
Tanzania: restructuring a bus company for privatisation.
Barbados: engineering and maintenance analysis for the national bus company.
Kenya: provision of contract management to two urban bus companies.
Zimbabwe: planning and advisory services to national bus group management.
Sri Lanka: technical input to a bus rehabilitation project.

Work has also been undertaken in Fiji, Hong Kong, Hungary, Latvia, Nigeria, Saudi Arabia, Uganda and Vietnam as well as in the UK.

UPDATED

ICB

Ingenieur-Consult Verkehrstechnik GmbH
Rudower Chaussee 4, Haus 8, 12489 Berlin, Germany
Telephone: +49 30 670 5990 Fax: +49 30 670 59911
Email: icb-gmbh.berlin@t-online.de
Managers: Dipl Ing Rainer Patzig, Dipl Ing Thomas Just
Hamburg office: Teilfeld 5, 20459 Hamburg
Telephone: +49 30 374 9340 Fax: +49 30 374 2623

Capability: Railway and transport engineering including planning and implementation of railway projects; taking over building supervision from railway organisations; tender preparation; traffic development planning; project co-ordination.

Projects: Include work in Germany, Russia and Malaysia.

NEW ENTRY

ICF Kaiser Engineers, Inc

9300 Lee Highway, Fairfax, VA 22031-1207, USA
Telephone: +1 703 934 3600 Fax: +1 703 934 9740
Chief Executive: James O Edwards
President, Engineering & Construction Group: Alvin S Rapp
Executive Vice President: George F Brown
Senior Vice President, Transportation, West Coast: James Ellis
Established: 1914
Staff: 7,500
Other offices: Taipei, Lisboa, Mexico City, Paris, Manila

Capability: Mass transit and rail feasibility studies, development, design, engineering, project management and construction services.

The company also provides specialised services in the areas of safety and system assurance, automated guideway transit, buses, LRT, metros, underground structures ventilation analysis, systems engineering and integration, quality assurance, security planning for mass transit, as well as a range of environmental services from assessments to full corrective actions.

Projects: USA mass transit schemes in Baltimore, Boston, Miami, Chicago, Los Angeles, Seattle, Portland, Sacramento, Dallas, Jacksonville, New Jersey, Cleveland and St Louis. International projects in Taipei, Manila, Lisboa, London, Panama, Colombia and Mexico.

UPDATED

IDPO

Industrial Design Planning Office, Philippe Neerman & Co NV SA
Beverlaai 73, 8500 Kortrijk, Belgium
Telephone: +32 56 225660 Fax: +32 56 228584

Capability: Design of rolling stock; network system design.

Contracts: Customers include, Matra, RATP, De Dietrich, SGP and Faiveley.

Ilium Associates Inc

600 108th Avenue NE, Suite 660, Bellevue, WA 98004, USA
Telephone: +1 206 646 6525 Fax: +1 206 646 6522
President: Carolyn Perez Andersen
Vice President: Robert M Prowda
Established: 1972

Capability: Consumer research and analysis; preparation of marketing strategies and plans; graphic design of signage systems; corporate identities, including vehicle graphics and uniforms; brochures, posters and map design.

Projects:
Dallas: recently completed signage information systems for LRT.
Eugene, OR: recently completed signage information systems at rail stations.
Olympia, Washington: recently completed signage information systems at rail stations.
Washington State: signage system for ferry system including vessels and terminals.
Hartford, New Haven, Stamford: completed strategic marketing plan for transport undertakings.
Metrolink Los Angeles: operation of customer service centre.
San Diego: consumer research on user acceptance.
Easy Streets, CTTransit Connecticut and RTA Riverside CA: new vehicle designs.

UPDATED

Italferr-SIS TAV SpA

Via Marsala 53, 00185 Roma, Italy
Telephone: +39 6 49751 Fax: +39 6 49752360
Chairman: Emilio Maraini
Vice Chairman & Managing Director: Bruno Cimino
Managing Director: Carlo Ianniello
General Managers: Giovanni Marengo, Alessandro Rizzardi
Commercial Director: Gaetano Piepoli
Established: 1984

Capability: The consultancy subsidiary of Italian Railways (FS) offers expertise in metro and other guided transit systems, as well as high-speed and conventional main line railways.

Projects: Is responsible for revamping the urban nodes of Torino, Milano, Genova, Venezia, Bologna, Roma, Palermo, Bari and Napoli in conjunction with the development of the Italian high-speed rail system.

Other projects include a feasibility study for an integrated transit system in Roma; study and design or a rapid transit system connecting Rimini with San Marino; feasibility study, design and assistance during construction of the Lima metro; detailed design of the Saronno–Malpensa airport section of FNME Milano; study for a mass transit system for San Salvador.

UPDATED

Jakes Associates, Inc

1735 North First Street, Suite 302A, San Jose, CA 95112, USA
Telephone: +1 408 453 7201 Fax: +1 408 453 5813
Email: JAI9330@aol.com
President: Andrew S Jakes
Project Development Director: David Mori
Technical Director: Edward H Lechner

Capability: Consulting in transport technologies, including rail, automated guideway transit and bus systems; procurement and project management; specification development and design review; feasibility and engineering studies; maintenance analyses; business development services.

Projects:
Las Vegas: development of the monorail system.
Washington: personal rapid transit system for Seatac City.
Big Bear, CA: mountain railway.
Sacramento, CA: strategic plan for city-ride bus system.

UPDATED

Japan Railway Technical Service (JARTS)

TSK Building, 8-13 Hongo 4-chome, Bunkyo-ku, Tokyo 100, Japan
Telephone: +81 3 5684 3171/3179
Fax: +81 3 5684 3170
President: Hiroshi Okada
Executive Vice Presidents: Sadaaki Kuroda
Naofumi Takashige
Established: 1965
Staff: 82

Capability: Studies, surveys, design, planning specifications, preparation of contract documents, and project control and supervision of railway, metro, monorail and advanced guided transit; construction of new lines; modernisation and improvement of track; electrification; dieselisation; modernisation of rolling stock; installation of ATC, CTC, seat reservation systems, vending machines and automatic departure indicators.

Projects: JARTS contributed to the project management in the Jakarta metropolitan area under a Master Plan for the Jabotabek system, and has made studies for electrification of trunk lines in Myanmar. Provided advice on the new West Beijing station, China; feasibility studies for transport in Shanghai, and commuter rail service between Tientsin and Tangku. Feasibility study of the rapid transit project in Chongging.

J D Franz Research

1804 Tribute Road, Suite K, Sacramento, CA 95815-4313, USA
Telephone: +1 916 646 5595 Fax: +1 916 646 4839
President: Jennifer D Franz

Capability: Consultancy in public opinion, public policy and market research.

Projects: Has worked for Sacramento Regional Transit on light rail ridership and promotion. For Systen Inc, surveyed HOV lane commuters for the Metropolitan Transportation Commission.

A system of maps designed to pinpoint passenger origins and destinations has been developed.

VERIFIED

JHK & Associates

A SAIC company
1900 North Beauregard St, Suite 300, Alexandria, VA 22311, USA
Telephone: +1 703 820 5455 Fax: +1 703 820 7970
Chief Executive Officer: Jack L Kay
Established: 1971
Staff: 300

Capability: Systems engineering, traffic engineering, and transit planning; traffic control systems; traffic design; transport research; modelling; parking; roadway lighting; environmental analysis.

John Brown Engineers & Constructors Ltd

20 Eastbourne Terrace, London W2 6LE, UK
Telephone: +44 171 262 8080 Fax: +44 171 402 0702
Associate Director, Transportation: Michael Nay
Offices: Bangalore, Bombay, Brisbane, Essen, Houston, Johannesburg, Maastrict, Melbourne, Montreuil, Perth, Sydney, Vancouver and Zoetermeer

Capability: Feasibility studies; procurement; project finance; railway safety analysis; railway infrastructure.

Jürgen Rauch

Helene-Weber-Allee 15, 80637 München, Germany
Telephone: +49 89 157 6866 Fax: +49 89 157 2473
Managing Director: Dr Ing Jürgen Rauch

Capability: Design of rail, light rail and bus stations, integration of stations into urban environment. Consulting and planning for station costings, structures and materials. Planning of station passenger guide systems, lighting and automatic train systems.

Projects: Recent work has been carried out in south and east Germany and in northern Spain.

UPDATED

Keith Haynes Associates

9 Summerfields, Hunsbury Hill, Northampton NN4 9YN, England
Telephone: +44 1604 767136 Fax: +44 1604 767136
Director: Keith Haynes

Capability: Training and development.

Projects: Transit Ambassador nine-module program for improving customer relations, being implemented for the Canadian Urban Transit Association.

KPMG Peat Marwick LLP

2001 M Street NW, Washington, DC 20036-3310, USA
Telephone: +1 703 442 0030 Fax: +1 703 556 0195
Practice Director for Transportation Consulting Services: Raymond H Ellis
Marketing Director: Amy Orringer
UK office: 5th Floor, 1 Puddle Dock, London EC4V 3PD
Telephone: +44 171 311 1000 Fax: +44 171 311 3311
Principal: Colin M Sharman
Established: 1896
Staff: 73,000 in 1,100 offices in 142 countries

Capability: Financial planning and management; public/private partnerships; project planning; ridership traffic and revenue forecasting; information techology; human resources.

Projects: Clients include MTA New York City Transit, MTA Long Island Rail Road, MTA Metro North Railroad, Port Authority of New York & New Jersey, RTA Chicago, CTA Chicago, MBTA Boston, New Jersey Transit, SEPTA Philadelphia, LAMTA Los Angeles, WMATA Washington, MTA Houston, METRO Seattle, DART Dallas, RTD Denver, GCRTA Cleveland, MDTA Miami, LYNX Orlando, Tri-Met Portland, City and County of Honolulu, COTA Columbus, SMART Detroit, TARC Louisville, TRT Norfolk.

Other clients include the FTA and FHWA of the US Department of Administration, Amtrak's strategic business units, Northeast Corridor, Amtrak West and the departments of transportation of more than 40 states.

UPDATED

Kuttner, Collins Group

8 West Street, North Sydney, NSW 2060, Australia
Telephone: +61 2 9929 7411 Fax: +61 2 9959 5153

Capability: Mechanical, electrical and civil engineering consultancy, including railway and rapid transit project design and feasibility studies.

Laidlaw Transit Ltd

Markham, Ontario L3P 1M4, Canada
Telephone; +1 905 294 5104 Fax: +1 905 294 6377
Senior Vice President: Glenn Needler

Capability: Contract management, operations and maintenance services for transit authorities, often using its own vehicles.

Laser Rail

Jessop House, 39 Smedley Street East, Matlock DE4 3FQ, England
Telephone: +44 1629 760750 Fax: +44 1629 760751
Managing Director: David Johnson
Director: Alison B Johnson

Capability: Structure gauging software, track design analysis, track gauging training/certification.

NEW ENTRY

Lea + Elliott

1009 West Randol Mill, Arlington, TX 76012, USA
Telephone: +1 817 261 1446 Fax: +1 817 861 3296
Principal: Wolfgang Bamberg
Established: 1979
Staff: 43

Capability: Specialises in planning, engineering and procurement of people mover and other innovative systems, technology and equipment covering technical and economic feasibility; preliminary engineering; specification development; bid evaluation; project management; and operations and maintenance. Experienced in turnkey and public/private co-ventures.

Projects
Automated guideway transit, USA: planning, engineering and implementation activities in Miami, Detroit, Newark-Elizabeth, Las Colinas, Honolulu, Jacksonville, US Senate Subway and Norwalk—El Segundo; and at about a dozen airports including Ben Gurion, Israel.

Houston technology assessment; independent safety audits of Los Angeles Green line and San Francisco Muni LRT systems; FTA rail modernisation and standardisation study; BART San Francisco and SEPTA Philadelphia project management/oversight.

VERIFIED

J W Leas & Associates

1084 E Lancaster Avenue, Rosemont, PA 19010, USA
Telephone: +1 610 525 1952 Fax: +1 610 527 9136
President: J Wesley Leas
Vice President: Alan J Cruickshank

Capability: Fare structure projections and collection system analyses for transit networks, including integrated bus/rail operations; fare collection; equipment and fare media specifications; alternatives evaluation; test monitoring; revenue control procedures and performance auditing.

Listavia International Consultants Ltd

13 Woodmancourt, Godalming GU7 2BT, England
Telephone: +44 1483 428932 Fax: +44 1483 428932
Principals: Warren S Lister, G T Lister
Established: 1970

Capability: Feasibility studies, route surveys, tender evaluation, contract administration, detailed design of innovative city and airport transport systems.

Projects: Involvement in the Channel Tunnel service tunnel transport system, the Southampton Transit proposal and several airport transit projects. Appointed project leader to Guildford Rapid Transit Ltd since 1990.

VERIFIED

Arthur D Little/Cambridge Consultants Ltd

Acorn Park, Cambridge, MA 02140-2390, USA
Telephone: +1 617 498 5828 Fax: +1 617 498 7173
Director of Transportation Practice: Todd Burger

UK offices:
Science Park, Milton Road, Cambridge CB4 4DW, England
Telephone: +44 1223 420024 Fax: +44 1223 420021
Manager, Railway Transportation Safety Group: Roger Hill
Manager, Technology Consulting, Product & System Development: Frank Morris

Berkeley Square House, Berkeley Square, London W1X 6EY, England
Telephone: +44 171 409 2277 Fax: +44 171 491 8983
Manager, Transportation Management Consulting: David Brown

Offices in: Amsterdam, Berlin, Bogota, Bruxelles, Buenos Aires, Caracas, Göteborg, Houston, Los Angeles, Madrid, Mexico, Milano, Monterey, Moskva, München, New York, Paris, Philadelphia, Praha, Riyadh, San Francisco, Santa

Barbara, São Paulo, Singapore, Stockholm, Sydney, Taipei, Tokyo, Toronto, Washington, Wien, Wiesbaden, Zürich

Capability: Includes financial planning and management; operations management; risk assessment and safety management; organisation management; technology, product and system assessment. Broad development capability from instrumentation to communications and control systems, including automatic fare collection, information, security and maintenance support systems. Project planning, evaluation and project management.

Projects: Include preparation of safety cases; risk analysis; reliability assessment; introduction of safety management systems; security assessment; audit of signalling hardware and software; development of maintenance support systems; development of communications systems; design of control centres; market assessment for a signalling product.

UPDATED

LS Transit Systems Inc

1515 Broad Street, Bloomfield, NJ 07003, USA
Telephone: +1 201 893 6000 Fax: +1 201 893 3131
President: Albrecht P Engel
Vice Presidents: S Feinsod, D Fordham
Assistant Vice President, Marketing:
Judith Jones-Grinvalds

Capability: Includes project management, operations analysis and simulation, design, engineering and construction management for track, signals, communications, traction power, vehicles, stations, vehicle maintenance and yards; bus transport systems; commuter, high-speed, metro and light rail systems; automated people movers.

UPDATED

LTK Engineering Services

Member of the Klauder Group
Two Valley Square, Suite 300, 512 Township Line Road, Blue Bell, PA 19422, USA
Telephone: +1 215 542 0700 Fax: +1 215 542 7676
President: George N Dorshimer
Director, Business Development: David H Oglevee
Established: 1921
Staff: 110

Capability: Engineering, management and planning services for transport projects, particularly advice on equipment purchase and follow-on engineering services.

Projects: Include:
MBTA Boston: engineering services for development of a 100-vehicle LRV order, and for procurement of 75 to 125 low-floor LRVs. Providing vehicle follow-on engineering services for procurement of 86 metro cars.
Los Angeles: assisted in purchase of the 54 LRVs for the Long Beach light rail line and for procurement of cars for the Green line. Also managed purchase of 94 bi-level cars and 23 diesel locomotives for start-up of the Metrolink commuter service in 1992.
Portland: for Tri-Met provided systems engineering for vehicles, workshops, signalling, communications and fare collection.
Metro-North: work with MN and the Connecticut DoT on procurement of M6 cars.
Shanghai: provided technical assistance during a series of vehicle design conferences with the German consortium undertaking manufacture of cars for the Shanghai metro.
Washington: LTK assisted WMATA with its Rohr and Breda car orders, providing technical services, inspection and acceptance testing.
SEPTA: as part of SEPTA's modernisation programme, LTK is providing comprehensive study and design facilities for upgrading of the Regional Rail Division's power supply system.

Maunsell Parsons Brinckerhoff Ltd (MPB)

Downsview House, 141 Station Road East, Oxted RH8 0QE, England
Telephone: +44 1883 730157 Fax: +44 1883 722914
Managing Director: Robert Chaning Pearce
Directors: P J Jarvis, P Nagle, D T Palmer, A R Umney
UK offices: Manchester, Birmingham, Cardiff, Norwich, Glasgow

Subsidiary company
Merz and McLellan (qv)

Associate companies
Maunsell Transport Planning Ltd
Address as above
Telephone: +44 1883 732211 Fax: +44 1883 730146
Director: John Harbridge
St James's House, 7 Charlotte Street, Manchester M1 4DZ, England
Telephone: +44 161 236 0766 Fax: +44 161 236 0694
Director: Neil Collie

Capability: Bus transport and traffic control systems; planning, design and implementation of public transport systems, particularly rail systems; comprehensive services include planning, civil and structural engineering, architectural planning and design; mechanical and electrical services; tunnel and station ventilation; signalling and control systems; primary and traction power supplies, rolling stock; interference studies.

Projects
Merseyside, UK: contract management and site supervision for bus shelter erection in association with bus shelter manufacturer Neuhaus.
London Underground's Northern line: is undertaking numerical modelling of the track alignment and tunnel shape of the 80 km of tunnel and 45 km of surface lines.
Jubilee line, London: detail design of tunnel and station ventilation system and independent design check of station services.
Jubilee line extension, London: detail design of Westminster and Waterloo stations and running tunnels.
East London line: detail planning and design of stations and trackwork.
Croxley rail link: planning and engineering design for Transport & Works Act application.
Docklands Light Railway, London: detail design of Beckton extension.
Central line, London: specialist advisers on signalling to London Underground.
Croydon Tramlink: route surveys and preliminary design of trackwork and civil/structural works.
London Heathrow Express: trackwork design.
Quality Bus: these seminars run by Maunsell demonstrate a package of high-quality bus improvement measures to deliver an achievable solution to the urban transport problem. Included is the Kesgrave Bus Demonstration Project, Ipswich, where a guided bus system has been installed that has resulted in a 50 per cent increase in ridership, of which some 25 per cent has come from previous car drivers.

UPDATED

Merz and McLellan Limited

Amber Court, William Armstrong Drive, Newcastle Business Park, Newcastle upon Tyne NE4 7YQ, England
Telephone: +44 191 226 1899 Fax: +44 191 226 1104
Head of Transportation Projects: Les J Brunton
A subsidiary company of Maunsell Parsons Brinckerhoff (qv)
Offices in: Australia, India, Indonesia, Chile, Hong Kong, Nigeria, Qatar, Sudan, Singapore, Switzerland, United Arab Emirates, Zimbabwe
Associates and agencies in: Argentina, Brazil, Canada, Chile, Czech Republic, Ethiopia, Iran, Jordan, Kuwait, Mexico, Peru, Saudi Arabia, Uruguay, USA, Venezuela, Vietnam
Established: 1899
Staff: 425

Background: Merz and McLellan merged with Maunsell Parsons Brinckerhoff Inc (qv) in 1995.

Capability: System and engineering feasibility studies and specification of passenger vehicles, traction and control equipment, power supply and distribution (including overhead line), signalling, communications and SCADA systems, and fare collection equipment. Engineering and design of electrical and mechanical fixed ancillary systems, such as environmental control and building services in passenger, office and maintenance facilities, and auxiliary equipment including tunnel ventilation and pumping systems.

Projects
London: projects include London Underground East London line study (E&M works); also project management services for the Waterloo & City line upgrading; carried out Docklands Light Railway obstacle detection study.
Newcastle-upon-Tyne, UK: power study for Tyne & Wear metro.
Blackpool, UK: engineers and advisers to Blackpool Borough Council on the promenade and tramway electrical infrastructure project.

Metro Consulting Ltd

11 Carteret Street, London SW1H 9DL, England
Telephone: +44 171 222 2526 Fax: +44 171 222 2527
Managing Director: W A E Bray
Development Director: Ron Taylor
General Manager, Sales & Marketing: Harvey Robinson

Capability: Management services, railway engineering, safety assessment, asset management and information, graphic design, including training, signalling communications, station control and infrastructure management.

Projects: Include management assignments for London Underground, Railtrack and in Hong Kong.

NEW ENTRY

MM

MM Strutture ed Infrastrutture del Territorio SpA
Via del Vecchio Politecnico 8, 20121 Milano, Italy
Telephone: +39 2 77471 Fax: +39 2 780033
General Manager: Adolfo Colombo
Technical Director: Bruno Cavagna
Legal Affairs & Corporate Director: Mario Martino
Manager of Marketing & Commercial/Public Relations: Marco Broglia
Deputy Technical Director: Felice Gaddi
Project Management Director: Guiseppe Siciliano
Manager of General Activities: Salvatore Crapanzano

Capability: Design of rail-based mass transit systems, including light rail, urban and regional planning; traffic surveys; feasibility studies; parking space and architectural planning; urban environment appraisal; geotechnical and topographical surveys; modelling; programme planning and management; procurement and tender advice; construction supervision.

Projects: MM was set up in 1955 to design and build the Milano metro. MM is also designing light rail lines to complement the light rail network.
Napoli metro: design and project management has been carried out, including installation of equipment for Line 1 (16 km, 10 stations).
Torino metro Line 1: advised on light rapid transit schemes including design of civil engineering works.
Milano—Malpensa line: supply of construction management services.
Alexandria, Egypt: study of transport systems.
Santo Domingo, Dominican Republic: reorganisation and development of city and surrounding area.

Mott MacDonald

St Anne House, 20-26 Wellesley Road, Croydon CR9 2UL, England
Telephone: +44 181 686 5041 Fax: +44 181 681 5706
Senior Directors: R Beresford CBE, T J Thirlwall, P M Chesworth, R B Fox, D Gadd, G Lowe
Company Secretary: P C Gregory
Offices in: Australia, Bangladesh, Belarus, Bulgaria, Cambodia, China, Bahrain, Czech Republic, Egypt, Ethiopia, Germany, Ghana, Gibraltar, Hong Kong, India, Indonesia, Ireland, Jamaica, Japan, Korea, Lesotho, Libya, Malaysia, Mozambique, Nepal, New Zealand, Nigeria, Oman, Pakistan, Philippines, Portugal, Qatar, Saudi Arabia, Singapore, Spain, Sri Lanka, Taiwan, Tanzania, Thailand, Trinidad, Uganda, United Arab Emirates, USA
Established: 1902

Capability: Planning, design and implementation of urban public transport systems; comprehensive service in transport planning, civil and structural engineering, and mechanical and electrical engineering; traffic engineering and highway planning; tunnel and station ventilation; train control, signalling and communications; studies of electromagnetic compatibility and safety from traction interference; rolling stock and traction power supply performance; rolling stock procurement advice.

Projects
London Docklands Light Railway: safety studies; rolling stock door modifications; power supply assessments; independent technical audit of signalling upgrade and resignalling.
London Underground: management of safety of congestion; ventilation and smoke control studies; signalling procurement specification for Central line; Morden station remodelling, new track layout, study of existing formation and drainage, detailed structural survey; Jubilee line extension settlement studies, design of new London Bridge station, monitoring of Westminster station complex.
Croydon Tramlink enabling works, UK: design support to Railtrack; assistance with specifications; outline designs and tender documentation.
Ivanhoe line: Mott MacDonald has been commissioned for Phase 2 of the Ivanhoe line, restoring passenger service between Leicester and Burton-on-Trent.
Other projects
Bangkok Metro: joint venture with De Leuw Cather and Thai companies.
Channel Tunnel Rail Link: in a joint venture with Ralph M Parsons and Sir Alexander Gibb, Mott MacDonald is the Secretary of State's Project Representative.
Taipei Metro: joint venture with China Engineering Consultants to supply technical support for signalling, power supplies, safety and reliability.
Liverpool: feasibility study for conversion of Wapping and Waterloo disused rail tunnels for use as road.
Hollywood, USA: management of construction of the Los Angeles Metro Red line extension.
Birkenhead, UK: feasibility study into extension of heritage tramway into a loop.

UPDATED

Mouchel

West Hall, Parvis Road, West Byfleet KT14 6EZ, England
Telephone: +44 1932 341155 Fax: +44 1932 340673
Chairman: Colin Coulson
Managing Director: John Murray
Directors, Transportation: James Measures, Bill Wyley

Capability: Expertise in transport planning and civil engineering, demand forecasting, economic assessment of projects, development impact studies, civil and structural engineering, communications and signalling design, project management and environmental consultancy.

Projects
Brighton, UK: public transport modelling in centre.
London: rail interchange feasibility study and economic assessment, London Docklands. Temporary station feasibility study, Docklands Light Railway. Uxbridge bus priority study for London Borough of Hillingdon.
London Underground: Southwark station, Jubilee line extension; advance works for Canary Wharf station, Jubilee line extension.
Weymouth, UK: heritage tramway study.
Gloucester/Cheltenham, UK: LRT studies and patronage forecast.
Guildford, UK: bus station remodelling.
Other projects: rail patronage forecast, Gwent County Council, Wales; rail corridor revitalisation, Dyfed and West Glamorgan, Wales; ferry service studies, UK and internationally.

Multisystems Inc

10 Fawcett Street, Cambridge, MA 02138, USA
Telephone: +1 617 864 5810 Fax: +1 617 864 3521
President: John P Attanucci
Vice President: Keith W Forstall, Korla Karash

Subsidiary companies
Access Transportation Services Inc, Pittsburgh
Transportation Management Services Inc, Alexandria, VA
Established: 1966
Staff: 325

Capability: Management consulting and software products firm founded by faculty members of the Department of Civil Engineering of Massachusetts Institute of Technology. Through its Planning & Policy Analysis Group the firm consults in the areas of transport information systems and management. Services include management and operations analysis, transit and paratransit planning, fare policy analysis, transport modelling and forecasting, market research and evaluation, and design of management information systems. Management and brokerage of paratransit systems is undertaken through a subsidiary, Transportation Management Services Inc. The Information Technology Group provides software systems for paratransit scheduling, fleet maintenance and parts inventory, Geographic Information Systems (GIS), ridership data collection and analysis, service planning, customer information and bid processing, dispatch control and timekeeping.

UPDATED

The MVA Consultancy

MVA House, Victoria Way, Woking GU21 1DD, England
Telephone: +44 1483 728051 Fax: +44 1483 755207
Email: consultancy@mva.co.uk
Web: http//www.mva-group.com
Chair: Martin G Richards
Managing Director: Michael Roberts
Directors: David Ashley, Denvil Coombe, Geoff Copley, Andrew Last, Prof Tony May, Hugh Munro, Hugh Neffendorf, John Wicks
Divisional Directors: Mike Brewer, Martin Dix, Peter Hague, Bil Harrison, Clive Gilliam, Eileen Hill, Steve Lowe, Mike Slinn, Andrew Skinner, Steve Williamson
Established: 1968
Staff: 380

Associated companies
MVA Systematica
MVA Asia (qv)

Capability: Consultancy covering planning, operation, management and marketing of transport systems and related facilities across all modes. Scope includes policy and planning studies; demand forecasting; mathematical modelling and statistics; market research and marketing; public consultation; economic and financial studies; traffic management and control; traffic impact analysis; transport telematics; parking; computer-aided route and service planning; fares systems and fare collection; computer-assisted vehicle and crew scheduling; computing and economics.

Improvement of information systems for passenger services.

TRIPS, MVA's suite of programs for highway and public transport planning, is in use worldwide by national, regional and local governments, consultants, research institutes and universities. MVA is also international marketing agent for the UK DoT's traffic engineering software Transyt, Trafficq, Contram, Oscady, Arcady and Picady.

Projects: Has undertaken integrated transport studies in Bradford, Birmingham, Bristol, Edinburgh, Leicestershire, London, Luton/Dunstable and Merseyside, UK, and also in Paris and São Paulo. These involved development of an appraisal framework and generation of economic, financial and travel demand forecasts across all modes.

Several UK local authorities have used MVA to advise on the traffic impact of large development proposals. The firm has prepared plans for traffic management and calming, road safety and bus priority projects, is advising on car parking in Singapore, Beirut and Bologna, and is also involved in several telematics schemes on behalf of the EC.

Also advises local authorities, rail companies and bidders for train operating unit franchises on rail development issues covering new infrastructure. Revenue impacts, advice on Section 56 funding, social cost-benefit and franchise bid support. Has also worked with BAA to provide passenger and revenue forecasts for Heathrow Express.

For the UK DoT, MVA managed the London Congestion Charging Research programme.

MVA is conducting a continuous study for the London boroughs and London Transport to measure the volume and value of concessionary fares, and has measured the generative effect of concessionary fares for several UK conurbations.

Other projects have included light rail planning studies in Manchester, Sheffield, Croydon, Edinburgh, London, Cardiff, Roma, Amsterdam and Tel Aviv.

UPDATED

MVA Asia

3rd Floor, East Town Building, 41 Lockhart Road, Wanchai, Hong Kong
Telephone: +852 2529 7037 Fax: +852 2527 8490
Managing Director: Fred N Brown
Directors: Martin Richards, Mick Roberts, Hugh Neffendort, Terry Bowker

Associated companies
The MVA Consultancy (qv)
MVA Systematica
Established: 1978 as part of The MVA Consultancy, 1989 as MVA Asia
Staff: 70

Capability: Consultancy services in the fields of transport, traffic and planning studies for road, rail, ferry and air travel; economic and financial appraisal; demand forecasting; highway planning and appraisal; project development and management. The firm has a strong social and market research capability, including marketing consultancy and public consultation studies. Offers computer-aided route and service planning, vehicle and crew scheduling, and advises on fare collection systems. Other services include traffic engineering, design and implementation; traffic surveillance and control.

MVA Asia, supported by MVA Systematica, distributes and supports Trips and MicroTrips, a comprehensive and portable transport planning suite installed at over 300 locations worldwide. MVA is also international marketing agent for the UK DoT software traffic engineering programs Transyt, Trafficq and Contram. MVA has exclusive rights in the UK and Hong Kong for the VIPS computer-aided public transport planning package.

Projects
Asia: involved in a number of rail projects for governments and the private sector throughout Asia.
Hong Kong: MVA is responsible for the transport planning and design aspects of the Kowloon Sky Rail, a privately funded proposed downtown distributor.

MVA is responsible for ground transport access planning for the new Hong Kong international airport, including a dedicated rail service and domestic mass transit links. Also developed measures for improving transport access to the existing airport.

Other projects include work on train control technology for Railtrack UK and a study on technologies for moving people in urban areas, prepared for the Department of Transport, UK.

NEW ENTRY

Raytheon Company

1001 Boston Post Road, Marlboro, MA 01752, USA
Telephone: +1 508 490 2448 Fax: +1 508 490 3944
President & Chief Executive Officer: Benjamin D Redd
Vice President, Programme Manager, Rail:
John C Johnston

Capability: Engineering, design and construction services with special capabilities in signalling, communications and rail traction power. Services include planning, engineering design and construction for electrification, signalling, train control, communications, vehicle procurement and inspection, and operational control. The Transportation Infrastructure Group is responsible for all projects in railway and rail urban transport and in electrical power transmission and distribution.

Projects: Subsidiary company, Raytheon Engineers & Constructors, Kinkisharyo USA and Itochu Rail Car have formed a new company, the Twenty-First Rail Corporation, to design, build and operate the New Jersey LRT system.

Provision of construction management for rehabilitation of catenary on the New Haven line, and for electrification of CTA Chicago's Midway airport extension.

Communications: designed public address, telephone, radio, fibre optics, security, CCTV and SCADA systems for the Washington metro, Pittsburgh light rail rehabilitation, St Louis Metro Link and other projects. Provided engineering and design services for upgrading of communications of NYCTA's Fourth Avenue metro line.

UPDATED

RITES

Rail India Technical & Economic Services Ltd
A Government of India enterprise
New Delhi House, 27 Barakhamba Road, New Delhi 110001, India
Telephone: +91 11 331 5692/4264
Fax: +91 11 331 5286
Managing Director: B Singal
Group General Manager, Urban Transport:
A K Chakravarty
Established: 1974
Staff: 2,000

Capability: Traffic surveys, urban transport planning, feasibility studies, tender designs, construction and contract management, project monitoring, modelling of transport demand, traffic engineering; system design; computer applications, traffic management proposals; bus system rationalisation.

Projects: Current work includes project report for multimodal rapid transit system for Delhi; feasibility studies for circular rail line extension to Calcutta metro; Bandra—Kurla rail link for Bombay urban rail system; Kanpur—Lucknow mass transit system study; mass transit study for Simla and Pune; policies for urban areas in various cities; urban transport project in Gantok (Sikkim); integrated urban development studies for Kanpur, Varanasi and Naamchi.

UPDATED

Ross Silcock Ltd

Old Brewery Court, 156 Sandyford Road, Newcastle upon Tyne NE2 1XG, England
Telephone: +44 191 261 8101 Fax: +44 191 261 8340
Managing Director: David Silcock
Principals: Mike Goodge, Alan Ross, John Barrell, Chris Robson

Capability: Traffic and road safety engineering, traffic calming, safety audits, traffic and development impact studies, public transport studies, professional development and training, monitoring and evaluation.

Projects
Newcastle upon Tyne, UK: five road safety schemes for South Tyneside Metropolitan Borough Council.
London, England: evaluation of impact of western extension of Docklands Light Railway; evaluation of public transport options to major road investment for Department of Transport; advice on safety policy for National Express, UK.
Egypt: public transport studies.
Peru: road safety study.
St Andrews, Kirkcaldy and Levenmouth, Scotland: cycling study, begun in 1995 for Fife Regional Council for implementation of urban cycle route networks.

A three-year study of pedestrian behaviour and exposure to risk was started in 1996, with video cameras collecting data in situations known to lead to road accidents. The aims are to quantify risk in different circumstances, establish requirements for longer term monitoring and provide guidance on traffic management and efforts to modify pedestrian behaviour.

Was appointed in 1996 to carry out a Regional Technical Assistance Project (RETA) for the Asian Development Bank. The project is to review road safety trends and characteristics. Road safety and traffic engineering advice is being given to Vientiane, Laos.

UPDATED

Rummel, Klepper & Kahl

81 Mosher Street, Baltimore, MD 21217, USA
Telephone: +1 410 728 2900 Fax: +1 410 728 2992
Partners responsible for transit: William K Hellmann
David W Wallace
Established: 1923
Staff: 260

Capability: Civil engineering, including transport, and highway engineering. In rail transit provides preliminary engineering for line and station location, access and parking and complete final design services.

Projects: Has been involved in major projects on sections of both the Washington and Baltimore metros.

Rust Kennedy & Donkin Ltd

A Rust Limited Company
Westbrook Mills, Godalming GU7 2AZ, England
Telephone: +44 1483 425900 Fax: +44 1483 425136
Managing Director: John R Springate
Business Development Director: Roland R Vye
Division Director: Bob A Gray
Operations Director: Toby G Mustard
Offices in 13 countries
Predecessors established: 1862
Parent company: Rust Limited

Associate companies
Rust PPK Pty, Australia
Business Sector Manager, Transport: Piers Brogan
Rust Consulting Limited, England
Business Development Manager: Doug Willis

Capability: Planning, engineering and project and programme management for heavy and light rail systems, conventional and guided busways, general highway and traffic, airports and port facilities and bridges.

Services cover feasibility studies, economic assessment and patronage forecasts, urban planning and development, system design and specification, route selection and alignment design, parliamentary submissions, grant applications, engineering and advice on organisation, operation and maintenance, safety and training consultancy.

Projects
Hong Kong: installation supervision of automatic train protection and bidirectional operation for KCR, and project management of all aspects of construction of the regional links extension of the Tuen Mun light rail.
Bangkok MRT: specification and tender evaluation for the elevated metro being developed by the Tanayong Corp.
Philippines: feasibility studies and design/construction management for the Manila LRT project (jointly with Electrowatt, Switzerland). Metropolitan Cebu traffic engineering and management project.
Bangladesh: Greater Dhaka Metropolitan Area Integrated Transportation Study (UNDP).
Heathrow Express, London: advisors to BAA on operations and safety, and E&M advisor in respect of the extension to Terminal 5.
South Yorkshire Supertram, Sheffield, UK: engineering project management for the complete system; specification for infrastructure and rolling stock and assessment of tenders, and construction supervision.
Docklands Light Railway, London: feasibility studies and design work including alignment of initial system, ongoing operations advice including study of the Lewisham extension.
Midland Metro, Birmingham, UK: engineering advisor to the Ansaldo/Laing consortium, selected for the DBOM concession.
London Underground: refurbishment of power supplies and elimination of all non-traction DC supplies on Central line.
Croydon Tramlink, London, UK: Preparation of estimates of capital, operating and other costs.
West European Railway Market Study: responsible for the study to identify likely main line and mass transit railway investment in the 16 main west European countries outside the UK and to identify opportunities for UK railway equipment suppliers.
Other projects: complete railway and management restructuring studies in Bulgaria, Pakistan, Lithuania, Slovenia, Algeria, Nigeria and Russia. Traffic control and surveillance systems in Australia, Philippines, Hong Kong and China.

UPDATED

Rust PPK Consultants Pty Ltd

PPK House, 9 Blaxland Road, Rhodes, Concord West, NSW 2138, Australia
Telephone: +61 2 9743 0333 Fax: +61 2 9736 1568
Email: rustsys@ozemail.com.on
Chief Executive Officer: Denis White
Manager, Transport: Piers Brogan
Director, International Business: Bob Hogarth

In 1996 Rust PPK acquired/merged with TEC Consulting Pty Ltd, a public transport planning and traffic engineering consultancy.

Capability: Planning, engineering, and project management for heavy and light rail systems, integrated bus rapid transit (guided and unguided busways), public transport policy and transport interchange design, general highway and traffic modelling, airports and port facilities and bridges.

Licence held for TRANPLAN, from Urban Analysis Group to sell in most of southeast Asia and the Pacific. Also from T-Mode Corporation for exclusive distribution rights for T-Mode 12 in Australia and New Zealand.

Projects
Sydney: Rust PPK is involved in a bus rapid transit concept for the Olympic Games in 2000.
Dhaka, Bangladesh: urban transport project, Phase 1.
Liverpool: strategic public transport and interchange development study.
P R China: Shenyang traffic and transport design project; Liaoning Province urban traffic and transport project.
England: Penryn/Falmouth traffic study.
Ghana: urban transport project.
Tanzania: Tanzania roads feasibility study.
Indonesia: Sumatra East coast roads feasibility study.
Malaysia: Kota Kinabalu traffic and transport study.
Pakistan: Lahore ring road feasibility study and design.
Philippines: technical assistance to physical planning (TAPP project).

UPDATED

Scott Wilson Mainline

Western House, 1 Holbrook Way, Swindon SN1 1BY, England
Telephone: +44 1793 515742 Fax: +44 1793 515846
Part of the Scott Wilson Kirkpatrick group
Staff: 150

Capability: Transport and environmental planning; environmental studies; land surveying; national, regional and urban transport studies; public transport studies, bus systems and priorities, light and heavy rail systems; intermodal interchanges, urban traffic control, informatics, traffic management, economic and financial studies; traffic calming and development advice; feasibility studies; design; preparation of contract documents; supervision of construction; maintenance management and project management services of highways, bridges, tunnels, railways.

Projects
London: Heathrow Express line from London to Heathrow Airport.
Nottingham: strategic transport study for the greater Nottingham area examined the economic, planning and transport trends, and recommended bus, LRT and rail solutions, and improvements to the road network.
Johannesburg, South Africa: provided technical and economic audit and review of the proposed light rail network.

UPDATED

SEMA Group Belgium

Rue de Stalle 96, 1180 Bruxelles, Belgium
Telephone: +32 2 333 5511 Fax: +32 2 333 5522
President: Michel Theys
Other offices: France, UK, Spain, Netherlands, Germany, Singapore, Switzerland, Sweden
Established: 1960 as Sobemap SA

Capability: Strategic planning for public and private transport systems; network reorganisation; feasibility studies; traffic management; administrative restructuring; application of new technology; computer modelling; surveys; environmental studies; land use and town planning; marketing studies.

Projects
Bruxelles: marketing and image study carried out for STIB; also a regional development plan for the city, including transport and housing behavioural surveys and a socio-cultural analysis; study of tariff structure of STIB.
Bangkok: feasibility study and establishment of master plan for bus terminals, under aegis of Transurb Consult.
Lagos: assessment of the public transport system, also with Transurb Consult.

Semaly SA

25 Cours Emile Zola, 69625 Villeurbanne, France
Telephone: +33 4 78 94 86 00 Fax: +33 4 78 89 68 57
Manager: Hervé Chaine
Established: 1981

Capability: Semaly undertakes financial and economic studies, feasibility studies, preliminary and detail design work, construction management, operational management and training.

Projects
France: in 1996, Semaly was awarded the contract for the engineering of the LRT system in Clermont Ferrand; work continues on the design of the LRT system for Montpellier and on the second line of the Strasbourg LRT system.
Firenze, Italy: feasibility studies and preliminary engineering for LRT system.
Dublin, Ireland: Semaly is project manager for the LRT system.
Genève LRT; Athens, Cairo, Kuala Lumpur; LRT systems of Porto and Lisboa.

UPDATED

SMM Société du Métro de Marseille

44 avenue Alexandre Dumas, 13272 Marseille cedex 8, France
Telephone: +33 4 91 23 25 25 Fax: +33 4 91 23 25 00
General Manager: Michel Croc
Deputy General Manager: Jacques Tribout
Technical Director: Guy Lavergne

Capability: SMM is the public company which designs the metro and light rail systems in Marseille. It can offer project engineering capability in transport and communications; design and operation of advanced transit systems; infrastructure design; network reconfiguration studies; design and construction management.

Socialdata

Institut für Verkehrs- und Infrastrukturforschung GmbH
Postfach 701629, 81375 München, Germany
Telephone: +49 89 71081 Fax: +49 89 716420
Managing Director: Werner Brög
Established: 1979 (predecessors 1972)
Staff: 28

Capability: Preparation of information and options for marketing and planning; surveys, forecasting and modelling for public and private transport use; cycle, pedestrian and parking studies; urban and interurban transport; price effect and tariff modelling; study of the effect of new technology and energy restrictions.

VERIFIED

Sofrétu-Systra-Sofrerail

5 avenue du Coq, 75009 Paris, France
Telephone: +33 1 40 16 6100 Fax: +33 1 40 16 6104
Chief Executive Officer: Pierre Louis Rochet
Executive Vice President, Business Development: Maurice Simony
Technical Executive Vice President: Gérard Mermillod
Vice President, Finance and Legal Affairs: Christian Bret
Vice President, Engineering and Human Resources: Serge Dassonville

Subsidiaries
Ingerail, France; Kuo-Tung-Lien-Ho, Taiwan; SFCM, China; TPP, France; SOTEC Ingéniere, France.
Systra Group affiliated companies
Canarail, Canada; Systra USA (LSTS-RTS)
MVA Group Ltd, UK, France, Hong Kong, Malaysia; Situs (Italy).

Capability: The company was set up at the end of 1995 with the merger of Sofrétu and Sofrerail, engineering subsidiaries of the Paris Transport Authority (RATP) and French National Railways (SNCF) respectively, through Groupe Systra, its holding company. It offers urban and regional transport consultancy services ranging from project identification to operation and maintenance.

Capability covers technical, economic and financial feasibility studies; transport planning, traffic flow estimates, selection of systems, layout of networks, financial planning for investment; basic and detailed design, including functional and technical specifications; assistance in construction, including preparation of bidding documents, analysis of tenders, drawing-up contracts, civil works supervision and quality control; acceptance tests in commissioning; staff recruitment, training, drawing-up of operating rules; also offers assistance to operators in administrative, technical and financial organisation, improvements in operating and maintenance methods, modernisation of fleet and equipment, and staff training.

Projects
Orléans, France: is leader of the joint venture Systra/Setec for the construction of the first line of the LRT system.
Mexico: technical assistance in the construction of metro Line B.
Santiago de Chile: design and supervision of construction works of metro Line 5.
P R China: engineering for the construction of a tunnel on Guangzhou metro.
Hong Kong: assistance for the implementation of the new SACEM signalling system on MTR.

UPDATED

Sogelerg Ingénierie snc

25 Rue du Pont des Halles, Chevilly-Larue, 94666 Rungis, France
Telephone: +33 1 45 60 12 34 Fax: +33 1 46 86 09 86
Chairman & Chief Executive Officer: L J Companyo
Chief Executive Officer: J Gaillard
Deputy General Manager: Denis Laroche
Vice President, Transport: Michel Gourdon
Vice President, International Business Development: Didier Benouville

Capability: Feasibility studies, planning, engineering, basic and detailed design, procurement and construction management, programme management of urban transport systems.

Projects
Lyon metro: preliminary and basic design; detailed design of civil work; project management.
Orly Airport VAL: detailed design of trackway.
Toulouse VAL: participation in basic design and construction supervision.
Bordeaux VAL: participation in design work.
Strasbourg LRT: project management consulting services.
Caen guided bus: complete technical design (layout, electric and mechanical equipment, rolling stock) and project management consulting services.
West Paris suburban zone: combined underground motorway-mass transit system; preliminary design of transit system.
Karachi, Pakistan: mass transit corridor 2, basic design (civil work and electromechanical systems).
Greater Cairo Regional Metro: basic and detailed design, project management and commissioning of Line 1 and Line 2; Ramses administration and control centre; Tura workshops; technical assistance for maintenance, with French consortium Interinfra.
Athens metro: basic and detailed design (including civil works, electromechanical equipment, rolling stock); engineering management, project management and commissioning of Line 1 and Line 3, with a Franco-German consortium Interinfra-Siemens.

Other services include urban and transport studies in Bordeaux, Nice, Versailles, Le Mans, Nancy, France; Merida, Venezuela; Guadalajara, Monterrey and Mexico City, Mexico.

UPDATED

Southdowns Environmental Consultants

Suite A3, 16 Station St, Lewes, East Sussex BN7 2DB, England
Telephone: +44 1273 488186 Fax: +44 1273 488187
Email: secl@tcp.co.uk
Web: http://www.tcp.co.uk/secl
Director: Patrick Williams

Capability: Assessment of environmental noise and vibrational impacts from railways. Mitigation of constructional and operational impacts. Technical support for liaison and consultation with public, local and other government bodies.

Projects: With national and international railways.

NEW ENTRY

Southern Vectis plc

Nelson Road, Newport PO30 1RD, England
Telephone: +44 1983 522456 Fax: +44 1983 524961
Managing Director: Stuart Linn

Capability: Drawing on the company's experience in bus and coach operation, the consultancy section offers expertise in commercial, management, marketing and ticketing aspects of bus and tramway operation, including network design/assessment and commercial franchising.

Projects: Recent work includes an innovative venture with a Polish local authority that has led to the development of a highly successful local bus system.

The recently developed Great Britain Bus Timetable gives countrywide interurban and rural bus information for the first time in 60 years. The TBC Hotline is a user-pays enquiry service giving information on British train, bus and express coach services.

UPDATED

Steer Davies Gleave

32 Upper Ground, London SE1 9PD, England
Telephone: +44 171 919 8500 Fax: +44 171 827 9850
Managing Director: James Steer
Directors: Peter Twelftree, Charles Russell, Luis Willumsen, Brian Martin
Company Secretary: Don Nutt
Press & General Enquiries: Miranda Turner
Other offices: Leeds, Brighton, Dublin
Established: 1978

Capability: Transport planning and policy; demand modelling and forecasting; business strategy and marketing; feasibility, design and implementation; private and corporate finance; market research; traffic management and parking; environmental assessment; policy research; public consultation and training. Experience covers bus, light rail, metro, people mover, suburban rail, taxi, community transport and waterbus/ferry modes.

Projects: Responsible for major transport studies in Dublin, Roma, Portsmouth/Gosport, Leeds, Santiago, Puerto Rico and London.

Seven-year contract to advise East Sussex County Council on public transport issues including the procurement and monitoring of public transport services throughout the county.

Bus priority studies in Merseyside, northwest London and Roma using in-house CAD design scheme.

Responsible for LRT, guided bus, metro and suburban rail studies in Portsmouth, Manchester, Merseyside, Leeds and Dublin. Lead consultant for Leeds Supertram, and has examined feasibility of the Sunderland extension of the Tyne & Wear metro over main line tracks.

Arlanda, Sweden: business plan and advice for the Arlanda Link consortium.

UK: private sector procurement and funding projects for Docklands Light Rail extension, Lewisham, Merseyside Rapid Transit and South Hampshire LRT.

UPDATED

Stratec SA

Boulevard Reyers 156, 1040 Bruxelles, Belgium
Telephone: +32 2 735 0995 Fax: +32 2 735 4917
Email: stratec@infoboard.BE
Managing Director: Hugues Duchateau
Directors: Françoise Boon, Luc Dens, Claude Rochez, Rodolphe de Borchgrave, Alain Counet
Commercial Manager: Hugues Duchateau
Founded: 1984
Staff: 20

Capability: Transport planning and engineering; regional and urban development planning; environmental management; public service management; business strategy; travel demand management programmes.

Projects: Development of transport plan for Liège; environmental impact study for the Regional Development Plan on the Walloon Region and Bruxelles-Capital Region; budget control study for STIB Bruxelles; HieLoW computer program to help modelling of discrete choice behaviours, mainly for forecasting demand for public/private transport or park-and-ride.

NEW ENTRY

Strategies Unlimited

201 San Antonio Circle, Suite 205, Mountain View CA 94040, USA
Telephone: +1 415 941 3438 Fax: +1 415 941 5120
Email: strtultd@ix.netcom.com
Principal: George Bechtel

Capability: ITS systems, such as route guidance, collision warning, vehicle location and information provision.

Projects: A study on collision warning for vehicles including buses has been carried out. The collision warning system has been installed on the Greyhound, USA, fleet of 7,500 buses.

UPDATED

STV Group Inc

205 West Welsh Drive, Douglassville, PA 19518, USA
Telephone: +1 610 385 8200 Fax: +1 610 385 8501
Chairman & Chief Executive Officer: Michael Haratunian
President & Chief Operating Officer:
Dominick M Servedio

Subsidiary
STV Incorporated; STV Environmental; STV Construction Services; STV International; STV Architects; STV/Silver & Ziskind
Offices in: Izmir, Lahore, Manila, Jakarta, Phnom Penh, Freetown and across USA
Established: 1968
Staff: 25 locations

Capability: Engineering, architectural, planning, environmental and construction management services. The group is involved in planning and design of urban transport systems.

Projects: Programme and construction management in joint venture for the St Louis MetroLink LRT extension, USA.

Construction management in joint venture for Blue line Pasadena extension for Los Angeles County MTA; modernisation of CTA Chicago's Skokie shops; consulting services for procurement of Long Island Rail Road's 114 cars and 23 AC-powered locomotives.

Engineering services for bridges, stations, utilities and track on NJ Transit Hudson—Bergen LRT system.

Maintenance shops, trackwork, bridges and construction services for Amtrak Northeast corridor and Florida Overland Express high-speed rail systems.

UPDATED

Sundberg-Ferar Inc

4359 Pineview Drive, Walled Lake, MI 48390, USA
Telephone: +1 810 360 3800 Fax: +1 810 360 6900
President: Curtis J Bailey
Vice Presidents: Gerald L Blake, Jeff DeBoer, Mark Bonner
Established: 1934

Capability: Industrial design firm specialising in light rail, metro and commuter cars.

Projects: Exterior design for new-generation underground car, MTA New York; has made designs for BART San Francisco; WMATA Washington; New Haven commuter area; Chicago commuter area; LIRR (double-deck commuter car); Baltimore metro; Rio de Janeiro metro, Brazil; MARTA Atlanta; Miami metro and Los Angeles; and recently completed a design for the DART system for Dallas. Redesigned metro car interiors for BART San Francisco.

Computer visualisation of new double-deck passenger car for Long Island Rail Road.

UPDATED

SwedeRail

Klarabergsviadukten 78, 10550 Stockholm, Sweden
Telephone: +46 8 762 3781 Fax: +46 8 106243
President: Bernt Andersson
Senior Vice President: Bo Marklund
Vice President: Sunit Ray
Managers: Robert Hallenborg, Björn Andersson, Jan Gullbrandsen

Capability: The transport consultancy of Swedish State Railways offers technical and management services from initial planning through to project implementation; feasibility studies; design, supervision, maintenance and operation; environment preservation; economics and business management; personnel training.

UPDATED

Systan, Inc

343 Second Street, Los Altos, CA 94022, USA
Telephone: +1 415 941 3311 Fax: +1 415 949 3395
Managing Director: Roy E Lave
Established: 1966

Capability: Systems analysis and policy research; experienced in transit and paratransit system planning and evaluation, impact and services assessment, microcomputer applications, economic and financial feasibility studies, market surveys and system modelling.

TAMS Consultants, Inc

The TAMS Building, 655 Third Avenue, New York, NY 10017, USA
Telephone: +1 212 867 1777 Fax: +1 212 697 6354
President: Dana E Low
Managers responsible for transit: Patrick J McAward Jr, Frank A Baragona, Kenneth F Standig
Established: 1942
Staff: 420 in 19 offices (USA and international)

Capability: Architectural and engineering planning and design for railway, bus and rail transit facilities, including stations, tunnels, structures, maintenance shops and related facilities.

Projects: Include design of passenger stations, tunnels, underground structures, cut-and-cover sections, elevated structures and vehicle maintenance facilities. Recent projects include engineering and architectural designs for improvements to New York Penn Station for Amtrak and Long Island Rail Road; engineering design for restoration of Washington Union station; rehabilitation of Union Station, New Haven; rehabilitation of East New York Bus Garage; expansion of Jamaica Yard workshops and storage areas for NYCTA; modifications to the PATH station at Pavonia; rehabilitation of eight stations for Metro-North; planning and design for restoration of Hoboken, terminal passenger facilities; designs to incorporate provision for access by the disabled to 14 NJT stations and six commuter rail stations for Connecticut DoT and Metro-North.

TAS Partnership

Britannic House, 1a Chapel Street, Preston PR1 8BU, England
Telephone: +44 1772 204988 Fax: +44 1772 562070
Partner: Peter Huntley

Capability: Passenger transport research; funding mechanisms; scheme maps/diagrams; publishing advice and support.

TecnEcon Ltd

Glen House, 125 Old Brompton Road, London SW7 3RP, England
Telephone: +44 171 373 7755 Fax: +44 171 370 3328
Managing Director: Jeff Ody
Commercial Director: Alan Power
Director, Transport Policy & Research: Philip Bates
International Transport Planning: Stephen Rutherford
Transport Planning Services UK: Eddie Strankalis
Public Transport: Hermann Maier
Traffic & Parking Studies, South-East: David Warriner
Northern Regional Director: Dr Stephen Pells
Associate, Light Rail Projects: Peter Gross
Established: 1985
Middle East Regional Office:
PO Box 52750, Dubai, United Arab Emirates

Capability: Multimodal urban transport planning specialists in modelling and operational studies, economic and financial appraisal; market research into public transport attitudes and product development in relation to real-time passenger information systems; technical assistance and policy advice to international lending agencies, governments and transport operators. Advice on public transport franchising and private finance for transport infrastructure projects.

Projects
Traffic Director for London: monitoring of the Priority Red Route network using vehicle real-time monitoring equipment and Wayfarer bus ticket information.
London Docklands: demand modelling for metro system extensions.
London Transport: assistance with intermediate modes, Thameslink 2000 and Channel Tunnel Rail Link impact studies; train service modelling to test upgrades for metro lines.
London Underground: pedestrian modelling for major stations on Victoria and Central lines.
Newcastle upon Tyne, UK: price elasticity of travel demand study.
Sheffield, UK: bus shelter design and bus station layout design.
Greater Manchester PTE: central area bus study.
West Yorkshire PTE: transport demand study.
Hereford & Worcester: new station study.
Warwickshire county council: rail corridor study.
Malaysia: bus lane design, Kuala Lumpur.
P R China: Beijing metro financial viability and private finance study for Line 3.
Russia: St Petersburg transport strategy study.

Travel information, economic evaluation, vehicle monitoring, traffic control, public transport operation, booking systems for intermodal transport and fleet management consultancy services are available, in partnership with Ian Catling Consultancy.

UPDATED

Thorburn Colquhoun

Transportation Division, Frogmore Hall, Watton at Stone, Hertford SG14 3RU, England
Telephone: +44 1920 830011 Fax: +44 1920 830911
Director: C J Darling
Associate Directors: A Wakeman, K Holloway, S C P Fulcher, B H Lee
Offices in: Ireland, Angola, Guinea, Ghana, Kuwait, Russia, Zambia, Cyprus, Poland
Established: 1994 (as Thorburn Colquhoun)
Staff: 437

Capability: Consultancy services in transport policy, planning, economics, engineering, operations, management, training and research. Thorburn Colquhoun Transportation provides transport services for the whole company.

Work includes bus and rail system planning, minibus and paratransit studies, service costing, policy studies and information systems. Also highway appraisal, transport facilities design, transport planning, economics, bus priority, parking and urban traffic control.

Projects: Traffic management studies, review of rapid transit options, parking and urban traffic control, bus priority systems, bus planning studies and public transport/pedestrianisation schemes in Dublin, London, Manchester and other cities.

Urban transport projects in Spain, Papua New Guinea. Railway traffic costing in Indonesia and regional planning studies in Botswana, Malawi, Portugal, Tanzania, Uganda and Zimbabwe.
London, UK: journey time survey for City of London and Department of Transport.
Bexley, England: bus priority studies.
London Borough of Kingston: route studies.

Regional traffic studies for Department of Transport, UK, including Eastern Region traffic model and South Midlands DFBO model.

UPDATED

Tilney Lumsden Shane Ltd

5 Heathmans Road, London SW6 4TJ, England
Telephone: +44 171 731 6946 Fax: +44 171 736 3356
Director: Marvin Shane

Capability: Creative design and management consultancy in environmental and interior design for vehicles and buildings.

Projects: Ticket offices and retail outlets for British Rail and InterCity; restaurants for British Airways and London Transport; interactive information units for British Airports Authority; refurbishment of Routemaster buses for London Buses companies; buffet and bar car for Eurostar train; interior concept and design for Channel Tunnel overnight Hotel Train; Eurostar control room and departure lounge.

UPDATED

TMG International Pty Ltd

Level 14, 55 Clarence Street, Sydney, NSW 2000, Australia
Telephone: +61 2 9262 4111 Fax: +61 2 9262 4110
Directors: David Hyland, Dale Coleman, Alex Wardrop, Keith Walker, Paul Anderson, Michael Hamlyn, Richard Power, Lloyd Silver, Warwick Talbot
Offices: Adelaide, Brisbane, Hong Kong, Sydney, Taipei, Tel Aviv, Kuala Lumpur, Jamaica, Philadelphia
UK office: 42 Shad Thames, London SE1 2YD
Telephone: +44 171 403 1928 Fax: +44 171 403 4564
Email Compuserv: 100537,2174
Directors: Peter Coysten, Ian Hodgson

Capability: Railway and public transport policy, planning, engineering and operations consultancy; offers transport planning, economic feasibility studies, project management, project planning, railway engineering and public transport operations analysis.

Expertise in track maintenance, signalling and communications, and undertakes analyses including development of train performance and signalling system simulation, timetable development and feasibility testing, and train and motive power scheduling models.

Toronto Transit Consultants Ltd

A subsidiary of the Toronto Transit Commission
1835 Yonge Street, Suite 300, Toronto M4S 1X8, Canada
Telephone: +1 416 393 3925 Fax: +1 416 484 6826
President: Kenneth G Knight
Established: 1981

Capability: Planning and operations; feasibility studies for urban rail lines; training; signalling cost estimates for LRT systems.

Transcorp

1a Lonsdale Square, Islington, London N1 1EN, England
Telephone: +44 171 466 4433 Fax: +44 171 700 0597
Email: tcorp@fmgroup.co.uk
Principals: Peter Trickett, David Cowler

Capability: Feasibility and concept studies, exterior design, interior design, corporate design, computer simulation, tender assessment, product specification.

Projects: Clients include British Airports Authority, Chiltern Railways, Ganz-Hunslet, Greater Nottingham Rapid Transit, Holec, Kinki Sharyo, London Underground, Greater Manchester Metro and SNCF.

NEW ENTRY

Transmetrics Inc

4010 Moorpark Avenue, Suite 112, San Jose, CA 95117, USA
Telephone: +1 408 984 7794 Fax: +1 408 244 8250
President: Jack Ybarra
Vice President: Denis Pu
Vice President: Frank Addiego

Capability: Consultants in engineering, planning and construction management of railways, highways and airports.

TransPlan

Transport & Planning Research Network
45 Beatrice Road, Thorpe Hamlet, Norwich NR1 4BB, England
Telephone: +44 1603 667314 Fax: +44 1603 667314
Director: Chris Wood

Capability: Environmental transport and planning consultancy specialising in sustainability.

Projects: Include: development of a regional LRT proposal for East Anglian Light Rail Transit Association for Norwich area; research towards good practice in the integration of public transport and cycling, especially; research into the development of car-free housing.

UPDATED

Transport Design Consortium

5 Heathmans Road, London SW6 4TJ, England
Telephone: +44 171 731 8190 Fax: +44 171 736 3356
Directors: Michael Rodber, Marvin Shane, Roger Jones, Michael Denny

Capability: Consultancy in styling, engineering, environmental, graphic, industrial and interior design; corporate identity, project management and design management.

Projects
London Underground: designed the refurbishing of London Underground's Victoria, Northern, Piccadilly and Bakerloo line trains. Produced interior design guidelines for all concerned with design and implementation of LU train interiors. Also carried out feasibility study for introduction of platform edge door screens as part of the Central line modernisation scheme.
General: with Adtranz devised a blueprint for the metro car of the future, using a concept model to demonstrate the future direction required for public transport to compete successfully with the private car. The concept explores the advantages of lightweight aluminium bodies and articulation bogies, so that several cars can be treated as one long vehicle, allowing a radical rethink of internal space.
Hong Kong: interior design of Airport Express and suburban trains for the rail link to the new Hong Kong airport.

VERIFIED

Transport Resources International

The Old Granary, Main Street, Ashby St Ledgers, Rugby CV23 8UN, England
Telephone: +44 1788 89139 Fax: +44 1788 891459
Partners: Janet Jack, Doug Jack
Established 1986

Capability: Market and product research and strategies; company acquisition and disposal; confidential commercial projects; bus fleet evaluations; UK/EC legislation and their effect on the bus industry; legal/ commercial terms, documents and agreements; press and public relations; market analysis and statistical data; market databases, regularly updated; product liability legislation and its implications.

Projects: Regular clients include internationally known commercial vehicle manufacturers, bodybuilders and component suppliers.

NEW ENTRY

TransTeC

Transport und Technologie Consult Hannover GmbH
Lister Strasse 15, 30163 Hannover, Germany
Telephone: +49 511 965330 Fax: +49 511 965 3399
Email: transtec@ttchan.de
Managing Directors: Bernd Kosiek, Hans-Heinrich Tonne, Ulrich Lüdtke

Associated companies
TransTeC Bauplanungs-und Management-gesellschaft Hannover mbH
Mo Trans Mobility and Transport Technology EEIG, TRUST Transmodel User Support Team EEIG
Established: 1986
Staff: 140

Capability: Bus and light rail planning, construction, operating and training, engineering and project management for electrical infrastructure, data processing and information management, staff training.

Implementation and support of edp systems for network and service planning; vehicle scheduling and duty rostering.

As a subsidiary of ÜSTRA, Hannover, TransTec is able to draw on operating experience.

Projects: Engineering of Hannover LRT infrastructure; tunnel and surface lines, stations and stops, electrical infrastructure, depots and workshops, road reconstruction, traffic diversions and site management; completion of Garbsen extension in 1996.

Engineering services for LRT systems in Manchester (Metrolink Phase II) and Croydon, London. Tender evaluation for København mini metro.

Low-cost modernisation programme for small tram system in Halberstadt, Germany. Feasibility study of tramway underpass at Rostock railway station. Transport network for Magdeburg.

EPON vehicle scheduling/duty rostering system for Amsterdam, Netherlands and PTT Switzerland. VIP transport planning system for Dresden, Germany and other cities.

In 1997 is working on the extension of Hannover LRT to the Expo 2000 World Exhibition grounds and inner-city tunnel link; light rail depot conversion from railway workshops, Hannover, traffic management system for Expo 2000; implementation of smartcard system, Ravensburg.

UPDATED

Transurb Consult

Rue Ravenstein 60, Bte 18, 1000 Bruxelles, Belgium
Telephone: +32 2 548 5311 Fax: +32 2 513 9419
Chief Executive: Erik Vandenbroele
Established: 1973
Subsidiaries: TUC Rail and Technirail Belgium, Comazar, Zaire, Transurb Argentina, Transurb Gabon, Transurb Malaysia

Capability: Draws on the operating, engineering and planning skills of Belgium's public transport operators. It offers planning, feasibility and preliminary design studies, and detailed engineering and construction management of projects as well as operational advice, management training and technical assistance in day-to-day operations of all modes of mass transport.

Privatisation and restructuring of mass transport networks, ranging from advice to shareholding.

Transurb Inc

85 Saint Catherine St West, Montreal H2X 3P4, Canada
Telephone: +1 514 871 0178 Fax: +1 514 397 9750
President: Pierre Asselin
Vice President, Transportation: Dennis Thibault

Capability: Undertakes services from initial studies to project management, including demand and traffic surveys, geological inspection, civil engineering design, railway design, procurement and construction management.

Transurb has recently completed the feasibility study of high-speed rail services serving Quebec, for the Governments of Ontario and Quebec.

UPDATED

Travers Morgan International Ltd

Mead House, Cantelupe Road, East Grinstead RH19 3DG, England
Telephone: +44 1342 327161 Fax: +44 1342 315927
Director, Railways Transit: Roger D Sawyers
Key consultants in urban transport: C J Holland, A D Foster, S A Rafferty, G Currie, K R Johnson, P J Whatmough, P F Amos, I P Wallis, R G Bullock, P S Prince, P Wiltshire
Established: 1929
Staff: 1,000

Capability: Feasibility studies, economic modelling and evaluation, transport planning, railway and rapid transit engineering, project management and procurement. Light rail system specification, power supply, civil engineering, alignment, environmental impact, swept path analysis.

Robert L Trillo

The Homestead, Broadlands, Brockenhurst SO42 7SX, England
Telephone: +44 1590 622220 Fax: +44 1590 622220
Principal: Eur Ing Robert L Trillo

Capability: Consultancy and design work on all forms of waterborne transport, including hovercraft: investment feasibility studies and project appraisal for development financing; market studies for new forms of marine craft, with special emphasis on environmentally acceptable high-speed craft for urban transport; conceptual and preliminary design of craft.

TTK

Transport Technologie-Consult Karlsruhe GmbH
Gerwigstrasse 53, 76131 Karlsruhe, Germany
Telephone: +49 721 625 030 Fax: +49 721 625 0333
Director: Dr Ing Udo Sparmann
TTK is a subsidiary of the Albtal-Vekehrs-Gesellschaft mbH (AVG) and the PTV group.

Capability: Planning of railway and tramway infrastructure, feasibility studies, operational concepts, commercial analysis, research, rolling stock development.

Projects: Include feasibility studies in Hamm, Hagen, Krefeld, Salzburg, Ljubljana and Oslo. Operational concept study in Kiel and planning of infrastructure in Heilbronn.

NEW ENTRY

The Urban Analysis Group Inc

50 Oak Court, Suite 110, Danville, CA 94526-4048, USA
Telephone: +1 510 838 1363 Fax: +1 510 838 1372

Capability: Offers URBAN/SYS, a comprehensive integrated set of urban planning and related software tools including the following:
TRANPLAN: a set of integrated programs for the transport planning process. It encompasses the four-step travel demand model of trip generation, trip distribution, modal choice and trip assignment for both highway and public transport systems. The public transport software uses coding and analysis techniques similar to the US DoT's Urban Transport Planning System (UTPS).
NIS (Network Information System): this is a flexible, interactive, graphics editor for displaying and maintaining spatial data, including highway and transit network descriptions, and area (polygon) boundary and attribute data. Networks and related attributes can be graphically displayed using colours, patterns, annotation and bandwidths. Networks can be interactively updated.
TPMENU (TranPlan MENU): this is a menu shell that combines TRANPLAN functions, NIS and supplementary software. The menu system can be modified, modelling procedures updated and new programs incorporated by editing text configuration files.
DBC (DataBase Capable): this offers a simple means of combining URBAN/SYS travel demand forecasting software with other software applications, including air emission models and GISs, by accessing a shared database. The DBC environment extends the capabilities of URBAN/SYS and provides access to supplemental data for URBAN/SYS processing.

Projects: URBAN/SYS is in use with several public agencies. The DoT, Florida, selected TRANPLAN and NIS as the basis for the application of FSUTMS (Florida Standard Urban Transportation Model Structure). The states of Georgia, Illinois, Indiana, Louisiana, Michigan, Minnesota, Mississippi, Oklahoma, Nevada, North Dakota, Texas and Wisconsin have each produced a state-wide licence which includes all public agencies within their respective states. The capabilities of URBAN/SYS, combined with the availability of source code, hardware portability, software enhancements and the quality of technical support, have led to the selection of URBAN/SYS software by more than 700 consultants, public agencies and academic institutions in 20 countries.

UPDATED

Urban Initiatives

35 Heddon Street, London W1R 7LL, England
Telephone: +44 171 287 3644 Fax: +44 171 287 9489
Partners: C Whife, K Campbell
Associates: J E Lloyd, J Dryden, J Caulton
Founded: 1989

Capability: Planning and design consultancy specialising in urban planning and design; transport planning and traffic engineering; infrastructure planning and environmental assessment; development planning and economics.

Projects: Include
London Underground: validation of station planning guidelines; appraisal of station designs for Crossrail and East London line, and development of central London station strategy for proposed Chelsea—Hackney line.
Railtrack: development opportunities and pedestrian links around London Bridge station; development of scheme options for bus interchange at Cardiff station.
Centro, Birmingham: preparation of design guidelines for Line 2 of the LRT system.

LT Planning: creation of database on trip information for London rail network.
Westminster City Council: feasibility studies for LRT line between Waterloo and Kings Cross, and advisors on rail planning and traffic impacts.
London Rail Development Unit: analysis of trip data for appraisal of new schemes.
Greater Manchester PTE: proposals for regeneration of Piccadilly station and surrounding area.
Vauxhall Interchange Study for Vauxhall Regeneration Company, looking at improvement options for the underground and rail stations situated in a major traffic gyratory scheme.

UPDATED

Uvaterv Engineering Consultants Ltd

PO Box 453/421, 1537 Budapest 114, Hungary
Telephone: +36 1 156 9000 Fax: +36 1 156 7002
General Director: Gyula Bretz
Director, Highways, Railways & Airport Design: Dr L Karsay
Director, Bridges, Structures & Mechanical Engineering: Dr Tibor Sigray
Director, Buildings & Underground Railways: G Soós
Established: 1948

Capability: Engineering and general consultancy services for rail, metro and road systems; network planning, architectural design, structural and electrical engineering, signalling systems, traffic management.

Projects: Includes advice to the Budapest metro and studies for the Tripoli rapid transit project.

VERIFIED

VCK

Verkehrs-Consult Karlsruhe GmbH
Tullastrasse 71, 76131 Karlsruhe, Germany
Telephone: +49 721 962310 Fax: +49 721 96231 11
Director: Dipl Ing Dieter Ludwig

Capability: Implementation of LRT systems; LRT conferences.

Projects: Include: public transport model for Heilbronn, 1992; Regional LRT system for Ulm, 1993; LRT feasibility studies for Rostock (1993), Osnabrück (1994), Graz (1994), Aachen (1994), Saar (1996), Wörth (1996) and Wiesbaden (1994).

Vectra

Europa House, 310 Europa Boulevard, Westbrook, Warrington WA5 5YQ, England
Telephone: +44 1925 444648 Fax: +44 1925 444701
Principal: Stefano Scannali
A wholly owned subsidiary of Amey plc
Offices in: Aberdeen, Scotland; Bristol, England; Leiden, Netherlands; Kuala Lumpur, Malaysia

Capability: Engineering mechanics and design, safety and reliability.

Projects: Clients include GEC Alsthom and London Underground.

NEW ENTRY

Harry Weese Associates

10 West Hubbard Street, Chicago, IL 60610, USA
Telephone: +1 312 467 7030 Fax: +1 312 467 7051
Principals: John Corley, David Munson
Established: 1947
Staff: 45

Capability: Architectural consultant to urban transport authorities, offering specific services for station and facilities design, multimodal facilities design, landscaping and urban design.

Projects
Washington DC: work has included design of 86 stations on the Washington metro.
Chicago: loop station renovation and Midway airport station design; Northwestern terminal station reconstruction.
Hamilton: commuter station design.
Toronto: consultant to the TTC's rail expansion programme and section design architect for York city centre station.
Other projects in USA: design of 20 Miami metro stations, 10 Los Angeles Red line stations, and 14 Buffalo LRT stations.

The company was architect for rehabilitation of Washington Union station, and was part of the team that produced the master plan for redevelopment of New York's Grand Central terminal.

VERIFIED

Wilbur Smith Associates

PO Box 92, 1301 Gervais Street, NationsBank Tower, Columbia, SC 29201, USA
Telephone: +1 803 758 4500 Fax: +1 803 251 2064
Chair & President: Robert A Hubbard
Senior Vice President, International: J W Bonniville
Senior Vice President, Transport Planning & Economics: R V Zuelsdorf
Vice Presidents: G Schneider, Stephen W Schar, William T Stone
Offices in: Bangkok, Hong Kong, London, Singapore and other cities worldwide
Established: 1952
Staff: 650 in 30 offices

Capability: Transport planning, engineering and economic consultancy services including multimodal system planning, and planning and design of light rail, heavy rail and people mover systems, as well as bus transit operations analysis, including HOV and park-and-ride. Services include urban transport modelling, ridership forecasts, feasibility studies, alternative alignment studies, traffic and environmental impact analysis, traffic control, preliminary engineering, final design plans and contract documents, field supervision and construction engineering and inspection. Services also include industrial design, signage and graphics, and related visual communications systems, and interior space planning.

Projects
San Diego: WSA was selected for a congestion pricing demonstration project in 1996, involving a demonstration programme on an existing high-occupancy vehicle (HOV) lane.
USA: the Tampa Bay commuter rail feasibility study; BART Oakland Airport connecting link, California; Eureka rail corridor feasibility, Phase II study; Denver air train study; Bayshore corridor system planning, California; Florida rail system plan; Washington state rail study.
Thailand: high-speed train study.
Hong Kong: Ma On Shan railway study.
Jamaica: road-based projects transport sector study.
Malaysia: project management for elevated personal rapid transit system to serve central Kuala Lumpur and a proposed major linear city.
Singapore: Sentosa transport plan.
Bangkok Transit Master Plan; BART Access Strategy Study; Richmond, Virginia, multimodal terminal study; Chicago personal rapid transit ridership study; rail consolidation studies, CA.

UPDATED

Index

C

D

E

F

L

M

N

O

P

Q

R

S

Printed and bound in Great Britain by Butler & Tanner Ltd, Frome and London